KV-026-959

Fifth Edition volumes:

1 (2008), 2 (2017), 3 (2011), 4 (2011), 5 (2013), 6 (2011), 7 (2015), 8 (2015), 9 (2017), 10 (2017), 11 (2015), 12 (2015), 12A (2015), 13 (2017), 14 (2016), 15 (2016), 15A (2016), 16 (2017), 17 (2017), 18 (2009), 19 (2011), 20 (2014), 21 (2016), 22 (2012), 23 (2016), 24 (2010), 25 (2016), 26 (2016), 27 (2015), 28 (2015), 29 (2014), 30 (2012), 31 (2012), 32 (2012), 33 (2013), 34 (2011), 35 (2015), 36 (2015), 37 (2013), 38 (2013), 38A (2013), 39 (2014), 40 (2014), 41 (2014), 41A (2014), 42 (2011), 43 (2011), 44 (2011), 45 (2010), 46 (2010), 47 (2014), 47A (2014), 48 (2015), 49 (2015), 50 (2016), 50A (2016), 51 (2013), 52 (2014), 53 (2014), 54 (2017), 54A (2017), 55 (2012), 56 (2017), 57 (2012), 58 (2014), 58A (2014), 59 (2014), 59A (2014), 60 (2011), 61 (2010), 62 (2016), 63 (2016), 64 (2016), 65 (2015), 66 (2015), 67 (2016), 68 (2016), 69 (2009), 70 (2012), 71 (2013), 72 (2015), 73 (2015), 74 (2011), 75 (2013), 76 (2013), 77 (2016), 78 (2010), 79 (2014), 80 (2013), 81 (2010), 82 (2010), 83 (2010), 84 (2013), 84A (2013), 85 (2012), 86 (2013), 87 (2017), 88 (2012), 88A (2013), 89 (2011), 90 (2011), 91 (2012), 92 (2015), 93 (2017), 94 (2017), 95 (2017), 96 (2012), 97 (2015), 97A (2014), 98 (2013), 99 (2012), 100 (2009), 101 (2009), 102 (2016), 103 (2016), 104 (2014)

Consolidated Index and Tables:

2017 Consolidated Index (A–E), 2017 Consolidated Index (F–O), 2017 Consolidated Index (P–Z), 2018 Consolidated Table of Statutes, 2018 Consolidated Table of Statutory Instruments, 2017 Consolidated Table of Cases (A–G), 2017 Consolidated Table of Cases (H–Q), 2017 Consolidated Table of Cases (R–Z, ECJ Cases)

Updating and ancillary materials:

2017 annual Cumulative Supplement; monthly Noter-up; annual Abridgments 1974–2016

September 2017

HALSBURY'S
Laws of England

Volume 94

2017

 LexisNexis®

Members of the LexisNexis Group worldwide

United Kingdom	RELX (UK) Ltd, trading as LexisNexis, 1–3 Strand, London WC2N 5JR and 9–10 St Andrew Square, Edinburgh EH2 2AF
Australia	Reed International Books Australia Pty Ltd trading as LexisNexis, Chatswood, New South Wales
Austria	LexisNexis Verlag ARD Orac GmbH & Co KG, Vienna
Benelux	LexisNexis Benelux, Amsterdam
Canada	LexisNexis Canada, Markham, Ontario
China	LexisNexis China, Beijing and Shanghai
France	LexisNexis SA, Paris
Germany	LexisNexis GmbH, Dusseldorf
Hong Kong	LexisNexis Hong Kong, Hong Kong
India	LexisNexis India, New Delhi
Italy	Giuffrè Editore, Milan
Japan	LexisNexis Japan, Tokyo
Malaysia	Malayan Law Journal Sdn Bhd, Kuala Lumpur
New Zealand	LexisNexis New Zealand Ltd, Wellington
Singapore	LexisNexis Singapore, Singapore
South Africa	LexisNexis, Durban
USA	LexisNexis, Dayton, Ohio

FIRST EDITION	*Published in 31 volumes between 1907 and 1917*
SECOND EDITION	*Published in 37 volumes between 1931 and 1942*
THIRD EDITION	*Published in 43 volumes between 1952 and 1964*
FOURTH EDITION	*Published in 56 volumes between 1973 and 1987, with reissues between 1988 and 2008*
FIFTH EDITION	*Published between 2008 and 2014, with reissues from 2014*

ISBN 978-1-4743-0603-4

9 781474 306034

ISBN for the set: 9781405734394

ISBN for this volume: 9781474306034

Typeset by LexisNexis
Printed and bound by CPI Group (UK) Ltd, Croydon, CR0 4YY

Visit LexisNexis at www.lexisnexis.co.uk

HALSBURY ADVISORY BOARD

Editor of this Volume
SIMON CADDE, LLB

Managing Editor
HELEN HALVEY, LLB

SHIPPING AND MARITIME LAW

Consultant Editor

ANDREW TETTENBORN, LLB (Cantab),
Professor of Commercial Law,
Institute of International Shipping and Trade Law,
Swansea University;
Barrister (non-practising)

The law stated in this volume is in general that in force on 1 September 2017, although subsequent changes have been included wherever possible.

Any future updating material will be found in the Noter-up and annual Cumulative Supplement to Halsbury's Laws of England.

TABLE OF CONTENTS

		PAGE
How to use Halsbury's Laws of England		xi
References and Abbreviations		xiii
Table of Statutes		xix
Table of Statutory Instruments		xxv
Table of Procedure		xxxvii
Table of European Union Legislation		xxxix
Table of Conventions etc		xli
Table of Cases		xlv

Volume 93

Table of Contents		1
1.	Introduction	11
2.	Admiralty Jurisdiction of the High Court	81
3.	Merchant Ships	203
4.	Hovercraft	305
5.	Masters and Crews	333
6.	Pilotage and Towage	467
Index		489

Volume 94

Table of Contents		1
7.	Safety and Security at Sea	11
8.	Collisions	119
9.	Accident Investigations and Inquiries	205
10.	Salvage and Wreck	233
11.	Liens on Ships, Freight and Cargo	309
12.	Limitation of Liability of Shipowners etc	325
13.	Lighthouse Authorities	347
14.	Offences and Legal Proceedings	367
Index		465

HOW TO USE HALSBURY'S LAWS OF ENGLAND

Volumes

Each text volume of Halsbury's Laws of England contains the law on the titles contained in it as at a date stated at the front of the volume (the operative date).

Information contained in Halsbury's Laws of England may be accessed in several ways.

First, by using the tables of contents.

Each volume contains both a general Table of Contents, and a specific Table of Contents for each title contained in it. From these tables you will be directed to the relevant part of the work.

Readers should note that the current arrangement of titles can be found in the Noter-up.

Secondly, by using tables of statutes, statutory instruments, cases or other materials.

If you know the name of the Act, statutory instrument or case with which your research is concerned, you should consult the Consolidated Tables of statutes, cases and so on (published as separate volumes) which will direct you to the relevant volume and paragraph.

(Each individual text volume also includes tables of those materials used as authority in that volume.)

Thirdly, by using the indexes.

If you are uncertain of the general subject area of your research, you should go to the Consolidated Index (published as separate volumes) for reference to the relevant volume(s) and paragraph(s).

(Each individual text volume also includes an index to the material contained therein.)

Updating publications

The text volumes of Halsbury's Laws should be used in conjunction with the annual Cumulative Supplement and the monthly Noter-up.

The annual Cumulative Supplement

The Supplement gives details of all changes between the operative date of the text volume and the operative date of the Supplement. It is arranged in the same volume, title and paragraph order as the text volumes. Developments affecting particular points of law are noted to the relevant paragraph(s) of the text volumes.

For narrative treatment of material noted in the Cumulative Supplement, go to the Annual Abridgment volume for the relevant year.

Destination Tables

In certain titles in the annual *Cumulative Supplement*, reference is made to Destination Tables showing the destination of consolidated legislation. Those Destination Tables are to be found either at the end of the titles within the annual *Cumulative Supplement*, or in a separate *Destination Tables* booklet provided from time to time with the *Cumulative Supplement*.

The Noter-up

The Noter-up is issued monthly and notes changes since the publication of the annual Cumulative Supplement. Also arranged in the same volume, title and paragraph order as the text volumes, the Noter-up follows the style of the Cumulative Supplement.

For narrative treatment of material noted in the Noter-up, go to the Annual Abridgment volume for the relevant year.

REFERENCES AND ABBREVIATIONS

ACT	Australian Capital Territory
A-G	Attorney General
Admin	Administrative Court
Admlty	Admiralty Court
Adv-Gen	Advocate General
affd	affirmed
affg	affirming
Alta	Alberta
App	Appendix
art	article
Aust	Australia
B	Baron
BC	British Columbia
C	Command Paper (of a series published before 1900)
c	chapter number of an Act
CA	Court of Appeal
CAC	Central Arbitration Committee
CA in Ch	Court of Appeal in Chancery
CB	Chief Baron
CCA	Court of Criminal Appeal
CCR	County Court Rules 1981 (as subsequently amended)
CCR	Court for Crown Cases Reserved
CJEU	Court of Justice of the European Union
C-MAC	Courts-Martial Appeal Court
CO	Crown Office
COD	Crown Office Digest
CPR	Civil Procedure Rules
Can	Canada
Cd	Command Paper (of the series published 1900–18)
Cf	compare
Ch	Chancery Division
ch	chapter
cl	clause
Cm	Command Paper (of the series published 1986 to date)
Cmd	Command Paper (of the series published 1919–56)
Cmnd	Command Paper (of the series published 1956–86)
Comm	Commercial Court

Comr	Commissioner
Court Forms (2nd Edn)	Atkin's Encyclopaedia of Court Forms in Civil Proceedings, 2nd Edn. See note 2 post.
CrimPR	Criminal Procedure Rules
DC	Divisional Court
DPP	Director of Public Prosecutions
EAT	Employment Appeal Tribunal
EC	European Community
ECJ	Court of Justice of the European Community (before the Treaty of Lisbon (OJ C306, 17.12.2007, p 1) came into force on 1 December 2009); European Court of Justice (after the Treaty of Lisbon (OJ C306, 17.12.2007, p 1) came into force on 1 December 2009)
EComHR	European Commission of Human Rights
ECSC	European Coal and Steel Community
ECtHR Rules of Court	Rules of Court of the European Court of Human Rights
EEC	European Economic Community
EFTA	European Free Trade Association
EGC	European General Court
EWCA Civ	Official neutral citation for judgments of the Court of Appeal (Civil Division)
EWCA Crim	Official neutral citation for judgments of the Court of Appeal (Criminal Division)
EWHC	Official neutral citation for judgments of the High Court
Edn	Edition
Euratom	European Atomic Energy Community
EU	European Union
Ex Ch	Court of Exchequer Chamber
ex p	ex parte
Fam	Family Division
Fed	Federal
Forms & Precedents (5th Edn)	Encyclopaedia of Forms and Precedents other than Court Forms, 5th Edn. See note 2 post
GLC	Greater London Council
HC	High Court
HC	House of Commons
HK	Hong Kong
HL	House of Lords
HMRC	Her Majesty's Revenue and Customs
IAT	Immigration Appeal Tribunal
ILM	International Legal Materials

INLR	Immigration and Nationality Law Reports
IRC	Inland Revenue Commissioners
Ind	India
Int Rels	International Relations
Ir	Ireland
J	Justice
JA	Judge of Appeal
Kan	Kansas
LA	Lord Advocate
LC	Lord Chancellor
LCC	London County Council
LCJ	Lord Chief Justice
LJ	Lord Justice of Appeal
LoN	League of Nations
MR	Master of the Rolls
Man	Manitoba
n.	note
NB	New Brunswick
NI	Northern Ireland
NS	Nova Scotia
NSW	New South Wales
NY	New York
NZ	New Zealand
OHIM	Office for Harmonisation in the Internal Market
OJ	The Official Journal of the European Union published by the Publications Office of the European Union
Ont	Ontario
P.	President
PC	Judicial Committee of the Privy Council
PEI	Prince Edward Island
Pat	Patents Court
q.	question
QB	Queen's Bench Division
QBD	Queen's Bench Division of the High Court
Qld	Queensland
Que	Quebec
r	rule
RDC	Rural District Council
RPC	Restrictive Practices Court
RSC	Rules of the Supreme Court 1965 (as subsequently amended)
reg	regulation
Res	Resolution

revsd............................	reversed
Rly.............................	Railway
s................................	section
SA.............................	South Africa
S Aust	South Australia
SC.............................	Supreme Court
SI..............................	Statutory Instruments published by authority
SR & O.......................	Statutory Rules and Orders published by authority
SR & O Rev 1904	Revised Edition comprising all Public and General Statutory Rules and Orders in force on 31 December 1903
SR & O Rev 1948	Revised Edition comprising all Public and General Statutory Rules and Orders and Statutory Instruments in force on 31 December 1948
SRNI	Statutory Rules of Northern Ireland
STI............................	Simon's Tax Intelligence (1973–1995); Simon's Weekly Tax Intelligence (1996-current)
Sask...........................	Saskatchewan
Sch............................	Schedule
Sess	Session
Sing...........................	Singapore
TCC	Technology and Construction Court
TS.............................	Treaty Series
Tanz	Tanzania
Tas............................	Tasmania
UDC..........................	Urban District Council
UKHL	Official neutral citation for judgments of the House of Lords
UKPC.........................	Official neutral citation for judgments of the Privy Council
UN............................	United Nations
V-C	Vice-Chancellor
Vict	Victoria
W Aust........................	Western Australia
Zimb	Zimbabwe

NOTE 1. A general list of the abbreviations of law reports and other sources used in this work can be found at the beginning of the Consolidated Table of Cases.

NOTE 2. Where references are made to other publications, the volume number precedes and the page number follows the name of the publication; eg the reference '12 Forms & Precedents (5th Edn) 44' refers to volume 12 of the Encyclopaedia of Forms and Precedents, page 44.

NOTE 3. An English statute is cited by short title or, where there is no short title, by regnal year and chapter number together with the name by which it is commonly known or a description of its subject matter and date. In the case of a foreign statute, the mode of citation generally follows the style of citation in use in the country concerned with the addition, where necessary, of the name of the country in parentheses.

NOTE 4. A statutory instrument is cited by short title, if any, followed by the year and number, or, if unnumbered, the date.

TABLE OF STATUTES

PARA

A

Aviation and Maritime Security Act 1990
s 9 1147
10 1148
11 1149
12 1150
13 1151
14 1152
(3) 1054, 1055
15 1153
16 1154
18 1155
51 (1) 1156

B

British Nationality Act 1948
s 33 (1) 389

C

Cinque Ports Act 1821
s 1, 2 211
4 .... 210, 212
5A 211
18 .... 210, 211
Civil Jurisdiction and Judgments Act 1982
s 26 86
Coastguard Act 1925
s 1 (1) 58
Crown Proceedings Act 1947
s 29 964
(1), (2) 179
Customs and Excise Management Act 1979
s 81 25

F

Foreign Enlistment Act 1870
s 19 138

H

Hovercraft Act 1968
s 1 382
2 383
3 384
4 (1)–(3) 381
6 385

L

Local Government Act 1972
s 254 (1) 210
(2)(i) 210
271 (3) 210
Local Government Finance Act 1988
Sch 5 para 12 1046

PARA

M

Magistrates' Courts Act 1980
s 3A 1053–1055
Merchant Shipping Act 1995
s 1 (1), (2) 230
2 (1)–(4) 231
3 1062
4 1063
5 (1), (2) 232
6 (1), (2) 233
7 (1)–(5) 235
8 (1)–(7) 254
9 (1)–(6) 245
(7) 245, 1064
(8), (9) 245
10 (1), (2) 247
11 249
12 (1)–(5) 250
13 302
14 1065
15 1066
16 (1) 252, 306
(2)–(5) 252
(6) 237
17 357
18 (1)–(5) 246
19 (1)–(6) 248
20 253
21 (1)–(3) 251
23 (2) 245
24 (1)–(3) 423
25 457
(5) 458
(7) 458
(8) 1073
26 458
27, 28 468
29 469
30 484
31 485
(6) 1075
32 473
33 486
34 474
35 475
36 476
37 477
38 (1) 487
(2), (3) 470
(4) 487
39 479
40 481
41 480
42 603
43 490
44 500
(4) 1077
45 501
46 502
47 503
(5) 1078
48 505
50 (1) 503

xix

PARA

Merchant Shipping Act 1995—*continued*

s 50 (2)	1081
51	506
(1), (2)	1082
52	1083
53	496
54	503
(1), (2)	1084
55 (5)	449
57	1104
58	1102
59	1103
60	539
61	524
62	508
63	530
64	537
65	525, 531
66	1085
67	508
68	536
70	1187
71	1188
72	1189
73	548
(8)	549, 550
74	549
75	550
76	44
77 (1)	551
(2)–(5)	552
(6)	1086
78	553
79	559
(4)	1078
80 (1)–(3)	551
(4)	1094
81	447
(2)	1101
84 (1)	457, 501
(2)	1073
(3)	468, 548
(4)	548
(5)	458
85	602
(2)	626
86	602
87	645
88 (1), (2)	601
(4)	601
91 (5)–(7)	635
92 (1), (2)	727
(4)	1135
93	446
94	1140
95	1141
96	1142
97	1143
98	1144
99	1145
100	1146
100A	673
100B (1)–(4)	674
(6), (7)	1130
100F	658
100G (1)–(4)	659
(5)	659, 1127
(6)	658, 659
101	1136

PARA

Merchant Shipping Act 1995—*continued*

s 102	444
103	1137
(2)	1054
104	1138
105	445
106	1139
107 (1), (2)	643
(3)	1123
108	644
108A	675
109	457
110	488
111	473
112	489
(5)	1075
113	474
114	470
116	503
(1), (2)	1081
118	1108
119 (2), (3)	539
120	423
121 (1)–(4)	607
(5)	607, 1111
122	608
123	609
124	609
(2)	1112
(4), (5)	1112
(7)	1112
125 (1)	610
(2)	1113
(3)	610
126 (1)	611
(2)	1114
(3)	611
127	503
185 (1), (2)	992
(2A)–(2E)	992
(4), (5)	992
186 (1)–(5)	1009
187	771
(1), (2)	1010
(3)	777, 778, 1010–1012
(4)–(6)	1010
(7)	777, 1010, 1011
188	777
(1)–(4)	1011
189	778
(1)–(4)	1012
190 (1)–(6)	1013
191 (1)–(6)	1014
(8), (9)	1014
192 (1), (2)	1015
192A	1016
193 (1), (2)	1018
(4)–(6)	1018
194	1021
195	1023
196	1024
197	1025
197A	1026
198	1027
199	1028
200	1022
201	1030
203	1031
204	1032

PARA

Merchant Shipping Act 1995—*continued*

s 205 1033
206 1034
207 1035
208 1036
209 1037
210 1038
211 1039
212 1040
213 1041
214 1042
215, 216 1043
217 1044
218 1045
219 1183
220 1184
221 1046
222 1047
222A 1029
224 (2)–(6) 851
225 887
226 919
227 920
228 902
229 903
230 854
   (7) 118
231 (1)–(4) 936
232 (1)–(3) 936
   (4) 1157
233 (1), (1A) 936
   (2) 1158
234 (1)–(6) 946
   (7) 1159
235 (1)–(3) 958
236 (1) 935
   (2), (3) 1160
237 (1) 947
   (2), (3) 1161
238 937
239 949
240 956
241 950
242 951
243 (1) 952, 956
   (2) 952
   (3)–(6) 956
244 (1), (2) 949
245 1162
246 1163
247 940
248, 249 929
250, 251 936
252 (1) 939, 945
   (2)(a) 945
      (b) 939
      (c), (d) 957
   (3) 939
   (4)–(9) 957
   (10) 939
253 (1) 945, 957, 1048
   (2)–(4) 957, 1048
254 939
   (1), (2) 1048
255 (2) 923
255A (1)(a) 926
     (2) 926
255B (1)–(8) 934
255C 939

PARA

Merchant Shipping Act 1995—*continued*

s 255D (1)–(5) 942
255E (1)–(5) 943
255F (1)–(3) 944
    (5), (6) 944
255G, 255H 953
255I 939, 944
255J (1)–(4) 931
   (6) 931
   (7) 931, 955
255K (2) 933
255L 933
255M (1) 931
    (2), (3) 931, 933
    (4), (5) 933
255N, 255O 932
255P (1)–(7) 955
255Q 930
255R (6) 927
   (7) 926
255S (1), (2) 928
   (3)–(5) 933
   (6) 930
   (7) 953
255T 953
255U 926
256 46
257 47
   (3), (4) 1175
258 (5) 1176
259 49
260 49
   (1) 1177
261 51
262 52
263 53
264 54
265 55
266 1178
267 (1), (2) 815
   (3)–(6) 816
   (7)–(10) 815
268 (1)(a) 830
   (2), (3) 830
   (5) 830
   (6) 1085
   (7), (8) 830
   (9)(a) 830
   (10) 830
269 (1)(b) 844
   (2)(a) 844
   (3)–(5) 844
   (7) 844
270 831
271 (1)–(6) 846
272 847
273 848
274 1049
275 1050
277 1051
279 1052
280 1053
281 1054
282 1055
283 1056
284, 285 1190
286 1057
287 1058
288 1059

PARA

Merchant Shipping Act 1995—*continued*
s 289 (1), (2) 1060
    (3) 1059
290 1061
291 74
    (4) 247
    (6) 237
292 (1), (2) 37
294 38
295 62
296 61
297 59
298 41
299 41
    (6) 1179
300 40
    (7) 1182
301 39
302 63
304 65
305 64
306 39
306A 39
307 17
308 19
309 20
310 .... 21, 382
313 (3) 230
313A 18
314 210
    (3) 16, 539, 852, 1039
    (4) 254
315 (1)–(5) 16
Sch 1 para 1 237
           2–6 306
           7 318
           8 321
           9 333
           10 328
           11 323
           12 324
           13 335
           14 . 306, 318, 323, 324, 335
   2 601
   3A para 1–3 675
         4 676
         5 675
         6–9 1131
         10–13 675
         14–16 677
         17–23 675
         24 677
   7 Pt II para 1 .... 993, 994
         2 993
         3 (1), (2) 994
         4 (1)–(3) 995
         5 (1)–(3) 998
         6 (1), (2) 999
         7 (1), (2) 1000
         8 (1) 1003
           (3) 1003
         9 1004
         10 1005
         11 1003
         12 993
         13 .... 176, 992
   8 para 4A 1045
   11 Pt II para 2 851
           3 1135

PARA

Merchant Shipping Act 1995—*continued*
   Sch 11 Pt II para 3 (2) 858
             4 880
             5 864
             6, 7 852
   11ZA 926
   11A para 1 66
          2 67
          3 68
          4 69
          5 70
          6 71
          7 72
          9 73
          12 68
         14–16 66
   14 para 1 (1)–(3) 16
          2 245
         3, 4 503
         5 (1), (2) 539
         6 (1), (2) 1104
         9 (1)–(4) 1018
           (5) 1039
         11 .... 210, 852

Merchant Shipping and Maritime Security Act 1997
s 24 (1), (2) 959
    (3) 963
    (5) 963
    (6)(a) 961
    (7) 959
    (8) 963
26 1186
Sch 5 1186

N

Naval Prize Act 1864
s 46 5

O

Offences against the Person Act 1861
s 17 1164
37 1165

P

Pilotage Act 1987
s 1 (1)–(3) 575
  (4), (4A) 575
  (5)–(11) 575
2 576
3 577
  (8) 1168
4 578
6 579
7 580
8 581
8A, 8B 581
9 582
10 583
11 584
12 585
13 586
14 587
15 588

PARA

Pilotage Act 1987—*continued*
s 15 (2)–(5)	1169
16	589
17 (1)	590
(2)–(4)	1170
(5)	590, 1170
(6)	1170
(7), (8)	590
18 (1), (2)	591
(3), (4)	1171
19 (1)	592
(2)	1172
20 (1)	593
(2)	1173
21	1174
22	594
23	595
31 (2)	576
32 (3)	578, 580, 581
Sch A1	577
1 para 3	580
4	578
5	581
6	595

Piracy Act 1850
s 5	139

Prevention of Oil Pollution Act 1971
s 31	382

Protection of Wrecks Act 1973
s 1 (3)	1166
(5), (6)	1166
2 (1)	948
(3)	1166
3 (2)	948
(3), (4)	1166

Public Service Pensions Act 2013
s 31	1018–1020
Sch 8 para 1–4	1019
10 para 4	1020
8	1019
13	1018

R

Railways and Transport Safety Act 2003
s 78, 79	1105
80	1106
81 (2)	1105
82	1105, 1106
83	1105
84–86	1107
88 (5)	1107
(6)	1105
89 (2)(a), (b)	1105
(c)	1107
(d)–(h)	1105
(5)	1105
90 (1), (2)	1105
(3)	1107

PARA

Railways and Transport Safety Act 2003—*continued*
s 90 (4)	1105
91 (1)	1105
112	22

S

Senior Courts Act 1981
s 20 (1)(a)	104, 106, 109–113, 125–127, 132–135, 139
(b)	91, 180, 194
(c), (d)	85
(2)(a)	104
(b)	106
(c)	109
(d), (e)	110
(f)	112
(g), (h)	111
(j)	113
(k), (l)	125
(m), (n)	126
(o)	127
(p)	127, 132
(q)	133
(r)	134
(s)	135, 139
(3)(a)	85
(b)	180
(c)	194
(4)	106
(6)	113
(7)	86
21 (1)	94
(2)–(5)	93
(7), (8)	93
22	94
23	86
24 (2)	85
46A (1)	1053
62 (2)	85
150 (1)	216
(2)	217
153 (2)	85

Serious Crime Act 2007
Sch 6 Pt 1 para 18	1149

Shipping and Trading Interests (Protection) Act 1995
s 1, 2	75
3 (1)–(3)	75
(4)–(7)	1180
4	76
6	1181
7 (1)	1180, 1181
(2)	1181
9 (2)	1180, 1181
(3)	75

TABLE OF STATUTORY INSTRUMENTS

PARA

A

Admiralty Jurisdiction (Bermuda)
Order 1974, SI 1974/2148 217
Admiralty Jurisdiction (British Indian
Ocean Territory) Order 1984, SI
1984/540 217
Admiralty Jurisdiction (Cayman
Islands) Order 1964, SI 1964/922
.... 217
Admiralty Jurisdiction (Falkland
Islands) Order 1966, SI 1966/686
.... 217
Admiralty Jurisdiction (Gibraltar)
Order 1987, SI 1987/1263 .... 16, 217
Admiralty Jurisdiction (Guernsey)
Order 1993, SI 1993/2664 216
Admiralty Jurisdiction (Montserrat)
Order 1968, SI 1968/1647 217
Admiralty Jurisdiction (St Helena and
its Dependencies) Order 1969, SI
1969/858 217
Admiralty Jurisdiction (Turks and
Caicos Islands) Order 1965, SI
1965/1529 217
Admiralty Jurisdiction (Virgin Islands)
Order in Council 1961, SI
1961/2033 217
Aviation Security and Piracy (Overseas
Territories) Order 2000, SI
2000/3059 .... 1156, 1186

F

Fishing Vessels (Code of Practice for
the Safety of Small Fishing
Vessels) Regulations 2001, SI
2001/9 .... 607, 608
Fishing Vessels (EC Directive on
Harmonised Safety Regime)
Regulations 1999, SI 1999/2998
.... 607, 608
Fishing Vessels (Life-Saving
Appliances) (Guernsey) Order
1990, SI 1990/2147 16
Fishing Vessels (Safety of 15–24 Metre
Vessels) Regulations 2002, SI
2002/2201 .... 607, 608
Fishing Vessels (Safety Provisions)
(Amendment) Rules 1998, SI
1998/928 17
Fishing Vessels (Safety Provisions)
(Guernsey) Order 1990, SI
1990/2148 16
Fishing Vessels (Safety Provisions)
Rules 1975, SI 1975/330 .... 607, 608
r 126B 609

PARA

Fishing Vessels (Safety Provisions) Rules
1975, SI 1975/330—*continued*
Sch 1 609
Fishing Vessels (Working Time: Sea-
fishermen) Regulations 2004, SI
2004/1713
reg 5 .... 515, 516
6 515
7 516
8 519
9 516
10 .... 515, 516, 519
11, 12 516
13 (1) 515, 516
(2)–(6) 515
14 515
15 519
16, 17 518
18 (1) 515, 516, 519
(2) 515, 519
(3) 515
19, 19A 516
20 517
Sch 1 515

G

General Lighthouse Authorities
(Beacons: Automatic Identification
System) Order 2006, SI
2006/1977 1018
General Lighthouse Authorities
(Beacons: Hyperbolic Systems)
Order 1986, SI 1986/2285 1018
General Lighthouse Authorities
(Beacons: Hyperbolic Systems)
Order 1991, SI 1991/347 1018
General Lighthouse Authorities
(Beacons: Maritime Differential
Correction Systems) Order 1997,
SI 1997/3016 1018

H

Hovercraft (Application of
Enactments) Order 1972, SI
1972/971 382
art 3 (1) 923
4 964
8 (1) 923
Sch 1 Pt A 964
Hovercraft (Application of
Enactments) Order 1989, SI
1989/1350 382
Hovercraft (Births, Deaths and
Missing Persons) Regulations
1972, SI 1972/1513
reg 3 418
4 419

PARA

Hovercraft (Births, Deaths and Missing
   Persons) Regulations 1972, SI
   1972/1513—*continued*
   reg 5, 6 420
       8 421
       9 422
       Appendix A, B 418
               C–E 419
Hovercraft (Civil Liability) Order
   1986, SI 1986/1305 386
   art 7 152
Hovercraft (Fees) Regulations 1997, SI
   1997/320 417
Hovercraft (General) Order 1972, SI
   1972/674
   art 2 387
       4 390
       5 391
         (5)–(8) 392
         (9)–(12) 393
       6 394
       7 395
       7A 396
       8 397
       11 398
       13, 14 400
       15 401
       16 400
       17 399
       17A 402
       18 403
       19 404
       20 405
       21 406
       22 408
       23 407
       24 409
       25 412
       26 410
       27 411
       28 413
       29 414
       30 410
       31 415
       32 416
       33 (1)–(5) 1072
       34 388
       35 417
       36 389
   Schedule Pt A, B 1072

I

International Maritime Organisation
   (Immunities and Privileges) Order
   2002, SI 2002/1826 12
International Sea-Bed Authority
   (Immunities and Privileges) Order
   2000, SI 2000/1815 11
International Tribunal for the Law of
   the Sea (Immunities and
   Privileges) Order 2005, SI
   2005/2047 10

PARA

M

Maritime Security (Jersey) Order
   2014, SI 2014/4265 1156
Merchant Shipping (Accident
   Reporting and Investigation)
   Regulations 2012, SI 2012/1743
   reg 3 (1)(a) 816, 817
         (b) 816, 818
         (c) 816, 819
         (d) 816, 820
       (2) 816
       4 (1)–(3) 821
       5 822
       6 823
       7 824
       8 (2) 824
         (3) 825
         (4)–(8) 824
         (9), (10) 825
       9 824
       10 (1)–(9) 827
       11 (2)–(6) 825
         (8) 824
         (9)–(12) 825
         (13) 826
       12 (1)–(9) 826
       13 825
       14, 15 828
       16 829
       17 (1) 828
         (2) 829
         (3) 828, 829
       18 823
       19 (1) 823
         (2) 827
         (3) 825, 828
       20 816
Merchant Shipping Act 1970 (Cayman
   Islands) Order 1988, SI 1988/246
   16
Merchant Shipping Act 1970
   (Guernsey) Order 1981, SI
   1981/1809 16
Merchant Shipping Act 1970
   (Overseas Territories) Order
   1988, SI 1988/1086 16
Merchant Shipping Act 1970
   (Unregistered Fishing Vessels)
   Regulations 1991, SI 1991/1365
   17
Merchant Shipping Act 1970
   (Unregistered Ships) Regulations
   1991, SI 1991/1366 17
Merchant Shipping Act 1974 (Cayman
   Islands) Order 1988, SI 1988/789
   16
Merchant Shipping Act 1979 (Belize)
   Order 1980, SI 1980/1509 16
Merchant Shipping Act 1979 (British
   Virgin Islands) Order 1980, SI
   1980/1511 16
Merchant Shipping Act 1979 (Cayman
   Islands) Order 1980, SI
   1980/1512 .... 16, 627

PARA

Merchant Shipping Act 1979 (Cayman Islands) Order 1988, SI 1988/790 16

Merchant Shipping Act 1979 (Falkland Islands) Order 1980, SI 1980/1513 16

Merchant Shipping Act 1979 (Guernsey) Order 1980, SI 1980/569 16

Merchant Shipping Act 1979 (Guernsey) Order 1981, SI 1981/1810 16

Merchant Shipping Act 1979 (Guernsey) Order 1988, SI 1988/1851 16

Merchant Shipping Act 1979 (Isle of Man) Order 1980, SI 1980/1526 16

Merchant Shipping Act 1979 (Isle of Man) Order 1984, SI 1984/1161 16

Merchant Shipping Act 1979 (Montserrat) Order 1980, SI 1980/1515 16

Merchant Shipping Act 1979 (Overseas Territories) Order 1989, SI 1989/2400 16

Merchant Shipping Act 1979 (Pitcairn) Order 1980, SI 1980/1516 16

Merchant Shipping Act 1979 (Saint Helena) Order 1980, SI 1980/1517 16

Merchant Shipping Act 1979 (Sovereign Base Areas) 1980, SI 1980/1518 16

Merchant Shipping Act 1979 (Turks and Caicos Islands) Order 1980, SI 1980/1519 16

Merchant Shipping Act 1988 (Cayman Islands) Order 1988, SI 1988/1841 16

Merchant Shipping Act 1988 (Guernsey) Order 1991, SI 1991/2875 16

Merchant Shipping Act 1988 (Isle of Man) Order 1989, SI 1989/679 16

Merchant Shipping Act 1988 (Unregistered Ships) Regulations 1991, SI 1991/1367 17

Merchant Shipping Acts 1983 and 1984 (Isle of Man) Order 1984, SI 1984/1985 16

Merchant Shipping (Additional Safety Measures for Bulk Carriers) Regulations 1999, SI 1999/1644 602

Merchant Shipping and Fishing Vessels (Control of Noise at Work) Regulations 2007, SI 2007/3075 628

Merchant Shipping and Fishing Vessels (Control of Vibration at Work) Regulations 2007, SI 2007/3077 629

Merchant Shipping and Fishing Vessels (Health and Safety at Work) (Artificial Optical Radiation) Regulations 2010, SI 2010/2987 631

Merchant Shipping and Fishing Vessels (Health and Safety at Work) (Asbestos) Regulations 2010, SI 2010/2984 631

Merchant Shipping and Fishing Vessels (Health and Safety at Work) (Biological Agents) Regulations 2010, SI 2010/323 631

Merchant Shipping and Fishing Vessels (Health and Safety at Work) (Carcinogens and Mutagens) Regulations 2007, SI 2007/3100 631

Merchant Shipping and Fishing Vessels (Health and Safety at Work) (Chemical Agents) Regulations 2010, SI 2010/330 631

Merchant Shipping and Fishing Vessels (Health and Safety at Work) (Electromagnetic Fields) Regulations 2016, SI 2016/1026 631

Merchant Shipping and Fishing Vessels (Health and Safety at Work) (Employment of Young Persons) Regulations 1998, SI 1998/2411

  reg 3–9 450
    10–12 1080
    13–16 450
  Schedule 450

Merchant Shipping and Fishing Vessels (Health and Safety at Work) Regulations 1997, SI 1997/2962

  626
  reg 24 1115

Merchant Shipping and Fishing Vessels (Lifting Operations and Lifting Equipment) Regulations 2006, SI 2006/2184 638

Merchant Shipping and Fishing Vessels (Manual Handling Operations) Regulations 1998, SI 1998/2857

  626
  reg 7 1115

Merchant Shipping and Fishing Vessels (Medical Stores) Regulations 1995, SI 1995/1802

  reg 3, 4 498
    6–11 498

Merchant Shipping and Fishing Vessels (Personal Protective Equipment) Regulations 1999, SI 1999/2205

  632
  reg 11–17 1079

PARA

Merchant Shipping and Fishing Vessels
(Provision and Use of Work
Equipment) Regulations 2006, SI
2006/2183 638

Merchant Shipping and Fishing Vessels
(Safety Signs and Signals)
Regulations 2001, SI 2001/3444
reg 3–6 626
7 1115
Schedule 626

Merchant Shipping (Anti-Fouling
Systems) Regulations 2009, SI
2009/2796 14

Merchant Shipping (Boatmasters'
Qualifications, Crew and Hours
of Work) Regulations 2015, SI
2015/410 63
reg 5 502
Pt 2 (reg 6–36) 503
3 (reg 37–41) 503
4 (reg 42–44) 503
5 (reg 45–49) 503
6 (reg 50–53) 503
7 (reg 54) 503

Merchant Shipping (Bridge Visibility)
(Small Passenger Ships)
Regulations 2005, SI 2005/2286
.... 602

Merchant Shipping (Cargo Ship
Construction) Regulations 1997,
SI 1997/1509 602

Merchant Shipping (Carriage of
Cargoes) Regulations 1999, SI
1999/336
reg 3 649
4 (1)–(5) 649
(6), (7) 649, 1126
5 (1)–(4) 650
(5) 1126
6 (1), (2) 651
(3) 1126
7 (1) 652
(2) 1126
8 (1) 653
(2) 1126
9 (1)–(5) 655
(6), (7) 1126
10 (1)–(8) 656
(9) 656, 1126
11 (1)–(4) 657
(5) 657, 1126
(6) 657
12–14 1126
15 654

Merchant Shipping (Carriage of
Packaged Irradiated Nuclear Fuel
etc) (INF Code) Regulations
2000, SI 2000/3216
reg 3–5 647
6, 7 1125

Merchant Shipping (Categorisation of
Registries of Relevant British
Possessions) Order 2003, SI
2003/1248 246

PARA

Merchant Shipping (Categorisation of
Waters) Regulations 1992, SI
1992/2356
reg 3 605

Merchant Shipping (Certificates of
Competency as AB) (Barbados)
Order 1957, SI 1957/1371 503

Merchant Shipping (Certificates of
Competency as AB) (Canada)
Order 1959, SI 1959/2213 500

Merchant Shipping (Certificates of
Competency as AB) (Ghana)
Order 1963, SI 1963/1316 503

Merchant Shipping (Certificates of
Competency as AB) (Gilbert and
Ellice Islands Colony) Order
1972, SI 1972/1105 503

Merchant Shipping (Certificates of
Competency as AB) (Isle of Man)
Order 1986, SI 1986/2220 503

Merchant Shipping (Certificates of
Competency as AB) (Malta)
Order 1975, SI 1975/1045 503

Merchant Shipping (Certificates of
Competency as AB) (Mauritius)
Order 1960, SI 1960/1662 503

Merchant Shipping (Certificates of
Competency as AB) (New
Zealand) Order 1956, SI
1956/1895 503

Merchant Shipping (Certificates of
Competency as AB) (Nigeria)
Order 1964, SI 1964/700 503

Merchant Shipping (Certificates of
Competency as AB) (Trinidad and
Tobago) Order 1960, SI
1960/1663 503

Merchant Shipping (Certification of
Deck Officers and Marine
Engineer Officers) (Guernsey)
Order 1988, SI 1988/1991 16

Merchant Shipping (Compulsory
Insurance: Ships Receiving Trans-
shipped Fish) Regulations 1998,
SI 1998/209 1016
reg 8, 9 1127

Merchant Shipping (Confirmation of
Legislation and Repeals) (Jersey)
Order 2004, SI 2004/1284 16

Merchant Shipping (Counting and
Registration of Persons on Board
Passenger Ships) Regulations
1999, SI 1999/1869
reg 4–7 640
8 641
9 642
10 640
11 (1), (2) 1121
12 (1), (2) 1121

Merchant Shipping (Crew
Accommodation) (Fishing Vessels)
(Amendment) Regulations 1998,
SI 1998/929 17

PARA

Merchant Shipping (Crew
Accommodation) Regulations
1997, SI 1997/1508
reg 3 (1), (2) 490
    4–35 490
    36 (2) 490
    37 490
    38, 39 1076
Schedule 490
Merchant Shipping (Crew Agreements,
Lists of Crew and Discharge of
Seamen) Regulations 1991, SI
1991/2144
reg 3 (1) 460
    (2) 423
    4 458
    5 459
    6 460
    7 461
    8 462
    9 463
    10 (1) 460, 462
    (2) 461–463
    11 .... 553, 554
    12 553
    14 554
    15–17 555
    18 556
    19 553
    20 557
    21 558
    22 .... 1087, 1089
    (1) 1090
    (2) 1088
    (3) 1088, 1090
    25 468
    26 468
    (1)–(4) 1074
Merchant Shipping (Dangerous Goods
and Marine Pollutants)
Regulations 1997, SI 1997/2367
reg 4–8 646
    9 1125
    10–22 646
    23–25 1125
Merchant Shipping (Disqualification of
Holder of Seaman's Certificates)
Regulations 1997, SI 1997/346
.... 509
Merchant Shipping (Distress Signals
and Prevention of Collisions)
(Guernsey) Order 1986, SI
1986/1163 16
Merchant Shipping (Distress Signals
and Prevention of Collisions)
(Guernsey) Order 1989, SI
1989/2410 16
Merchant Shipping (Distress Signals
and Prevention of Collisions)
Regulations 1996, SI 1996/75
reg 1 (4) 701
    2 690
    3 726
    4, 5 690
    6, 7 1134

PARA

Merchant Shipping (Diving Safety)
Regulations 2002, SI 2002/1587
.... 601
Merchant Shipping (Domestic
Passenger Ships) (Safety
Management Code) Regulations
2001, SI 2001/3209 627
reg 10 1119
Merchant Shipping (Emergency
Equipment Lockers for Ro/Ro
Passenger Ships) Regulations
1988, SI 1988/2272 602
Merchant Shipping (Emergency
Information for Passengers)
Regulations 1990, SI 1990/660
.... 639
Merchant Shipping (Entry into
Dangerous Spaces) Regulations
1988, SI 1988/1638 626
Merchant Shipping (EPIRB
Registration) Regulations 2000, SI
2000/1850 726
Merchant Shipping (Falkland Islands
Colours) Order 1998, SI
1998/3147 231
Merchant Shipping (Fees) Regulations
2006, SI 2006/2055 63
reg 3 505
Sch 1 Pt 15 505
Merchant Shipping (Fees) Regulations
2015, SI 2015/315 63
Merchant Shipping (Fire Protection:
Large Ships) Regulations 1998, SI
1998/1012 633
Merchant Shipping (Fire Protection:
Small Ships) Regulations 1998, SI
1998/1011 633
Merchant Shipping (Flag State
Directive) Regulations 2011, SI
2011/2667 14
Merchant Shipping (Formal
Investigations) Rules 1985, SI
1985/1001
r 2 (2) 833
    4 (1) 831
    4A 832
    5, 6 833
    7 (1), (2) 834
    (3) 835
    (4), (5) 836
    (6) 837
    8 837
    9 838
    10 839
    11 840
    12 841
    13 842
    14 843
    15 845
Schedule 831
Merchant Shipping (Gas Carriers)
Regulations 1994, SI 1994/2464
.... 602
Merchant Shipping (Gibraltar
Colours) Order 1996, SI
1996/281 231

PARA

Merchant Shipping (High Speed Craft)
  Regulations 2004, SI 2004/302
  602
  reg 3 (2) 617
      4 618
      5 619
      6 620
      7A 621
      8 623
      9 624
      10 1110
      11 625
Merchant Shipping (Hours of Work)
  Regulations 2002, SI 2002/2125
  reg 3 423
      4 511
      5 (1), (2) 511
        (3) 639
        (4), (5) 511
      6–9 511
      12, 12A 512
      13 511
      14–19 514
      20 (1)(a) 511, 512
         (b), (c) 511
         (d) 511, 512
         (2) 511
         (4) 512
         (5) 511
      22, 22A 512
      23 513
  Sch 1 511
Merchant Shipping (Increased
  Penalties) Regulations 1979, SI
  1979/1519 248
Merchant Shipping (International
  Safety Management (ISM) Code)
  Regulations 2014, SI 2014/1512
  14
  reg 15, 16 1118
Merchant Shipping (Liability and
  Compensation for Oil Pollution
  Damage) (Transitional Provisions)
  (Overseas Territories) Order
  1997, SI 1997/2578 16
Merchant Shipping (Liability of
  Shipowners and Others)
  (Calculation of Tonnage) Order
  1986, SI 1986/1040 998
Merchant Shipping (Liability of
  Shipowners and Others) (New
  Rate of Interest) Order 2004, SI
  2004/931 1003
Merchant Shipping (Life-Saving
  Appliances For Passenger Ships
  Of Classes III To VI(A))
  Regulations 1999, SI 1999/2723
  639
Merchant Shipping (Life-Saving
  Appliances For Ships Other Than
  Ships Of Classes III To VI(A))
  Regulations 1999, SI 1999/2721
  639
Merchant Shipping (Light Dues)
  Regulations 1997, SI 1997/562
  1033

PARA

Merchant Shipping (Limitation of
  Liability for Maritime Claims)
  (Overseas Territories) Order
  1997, SI 1997/2579 16
Merchant Shipping (Load Line)
  Regulations 1998, SI 1998/2241
  reg 4 660
      5 661
      6 662
      7 663
      8 664
      9 665
      10 667
      11 668
      12 (1)–(3) 661
      13 669
      14 666
      25–31 663
      32, 33 671
      34 672
      35 1128
      36 1129
      37 1128
Merchant Shipping (Load Lines
  Certificates) (Various Countries)
  Order 1968, SI 1968/1110 16
Merchant Shipping (Maintenance of
  Seamen's Dependants) Regulations
  1972, SI 1972/1635 481
Merchant Shipping (Mandatory
  Surveys for Ro-Ro Ferry and
  High Speed Passenger Craft)
  Regulations 2001, SI 2001/152
  606
Merchant Shipping (Marine
  Equipment) Regulations 2016, SI
  2016/1025 638
Merchant Shipping (Maritime Labour
  Convention) (Medical
  Certification) Regulations 2010,
  SI 2010/737
  reg 3 423
      5 (1)(a) 464
        (2), (3) 464
      6 (1)–(6) 464
      7 (1)–(5) 464
      8–11 464
      12 (1)–(4) 465
      13 (1)–(4) 466
      14 (1)–(8) 467
      15 (1), (2) 499
      16, 17 464
      18 (1) 464
         (2) 464, 499
         (3) 466
         (4), (5) 464
      19, 20 464
Merchant Shipping (Maritime Labour
  Convention) (Minimum
  Requirements for Seafarers etc)
  Regulations 2014, SI 2014/1613
  14
  reg 3 423
      4–7 448
      8 456
      9 452
      10 (1)–(3) 451

PARA

Merchant Shipping (Maritime Labour
Convention) (Minimum Requirements for
Seafarers etc) Regulations 2014, SI
2014/1613—*continued*

reg 10 (4)–(7)	453
11	455
12–14	454
15	452
16	482
18	482
19 (2)	540
20, 21	540
22	541
23	542
24	543
25–28	540
29 (1)–(3)	490
(4)–(7)	491
30 (1)–(4)	490
31, 32	490
33 (1)–(3)	490
(4), (5)	491
34	492
35, 36	493
37	495
38–40	494
41	492
43	497
44–46	496
48	545
49	544
50	546
51	546, 547
53	545
54 (1), (2)	48
(3), (4)	49
(5)	51
55	48
56, 57	50
58 (1), (2)	50
(4), (5)	50
59 (1)	448, 452–454, 456, 491–494, 496, 497, 540–543
(2)(a)	451, 453
(b)	454
(c)	452
(d)	493
(e), (f)	496
(3)(a), (b)	454
(c)	543
(d), (e)	540
(f)	491
(h)	493
(i)	492
(4)(a)	483
(b)	482
(c)	543
(d), (e)	491
(5)(a)–(e)	490
(f)	495
(g)	492
(h)	544
60	448, 451–454, 456, 482, 483, 540–544
Sch 1	451
2	454

PARA

Merchant Shipping (Maritime Labour Convention) (Survey and Certification) Regulations 2013, SI 2013/1785	604
Merchant Shipping (Metrication) (Isle of Man) Order 1984, SI 1984/1164	16
Merchant Shipping (Minimum Standards of Safety Communications) Regulations 1997, SI 1997/529	639
Merchant Shipping (Ministry of Defence Commercially Managed Ships) Order 1992, SI 1992/1293	19
Merchant Shipping (Ministry of Defence Ships) Order 1989, SI 1989/1991	19
Merchant Shipping (Ministry of Defence Yachts) Order 1992, SI 1992/1294	19
Merchant Shipping (Ministry of Technology Ships) Order 1966, SI 1966/269	19
Merchant Shipping (Modification of Enactments) (Bareboat Charter Ships) Order 1994, SI 1994/774	230
art 1 (2)	458
2, 3	255
Merchant Shipping (Monitoring, Reporting and Verification of Carbon Dioxide Emissions) and the Port State Control (Amendment) Regulations 2017, SI 2017/825	678
Merchant Shipping (Musters, Training and Decision Support Systems) Regulations 1999, SI 1999/2722	639
Merchant Shipping (Officer Nationality) Regulations 1995, SI 1995/1427	507
Merchant Shipping (Official Log Books) Regulations 1981, SI 1981/569	552
Merchant Shipping (Oil Pollution) Act 1971 (Guernsey) Order 1981, SI 1981/244	16
Merchant Shipping (Oil Pollution and General Provisions) (Guernsey) Order 1998, SI 1998/260	16
Merchant Shipping (Oil Pollution and General Provisions) (Isle of Man) Order 2004, SI 2004/3041	16
Merchant Shipping (Oil Pollution) (Anguilla) Order 1997, SI 1997/2580	16
Merchant Shipping (Oil Pollution) (Belize) Order 1975, SI 1975/2164	16
Merchant Shipping (Oil Pollution) (British Antarctic Territory) Order 1997, SI 1997/2582	16

PARA

Merchant Shipping (Oil Pollution)
(British Indian Ocean Territory)
Order 1997, SI 1997/2583 16

Merchant Shipping (Oil Pollution)
(Cayman Islands) Order 1998, SI
1998/1261 16

Merchant Shipping (Oil Pollution)
(Falkland Islands) Order 1997, SI
1997/2584 16

Merchant Shipping (Oil Pollution)
(Gibraltar) Order 2004, SI
2004/3042 16

Merchant Shipping (Oil Pollution)
(Gilbert Islands) Order 1975, SI
1975/2168 16

Merchant Shipping (Oil Pollution)
(Jersey) Order 1997, SI
1997/2598 16

Merchant Shipping (Oil Pollution)
(Montserrat) Order 1998, SI
1998/1262 16

Merchant Shipping (Oil Pollution)
(Pitcairn) (Amendment) Order
1998, SI 1998/1067 16

Merchant Shipping (Oil Pollution)
(Pitcairn) Order 1997, SI
1997/2585 16

Merchant Shipping (Oil Pollution)
(Saint Helena) Order 1998, SI
1998/1263 16

Merchant Shipping (Oil Pollution)
(Seychelles) Order 1975, SI
1975/2172 16

Merchant Shipping (Oil Pollution)
(Solomon Islands) Order 1975, SI
1975/2173 16

Merchant Shipping (Oil Pollution)
(South Georgia and the South
Sandwich Islands) Order 1997, SI
1997/2588 16

Merchant Shipping (Oil Pollution)
(Sovereign Base Areas)
(Amendment) Order 1998, SI
1998/1068 16

Merchant Shipping (Oil Pollution)
(Sovereign Base Areas) Order
1997, SI 1997/2587 16

Merchant Shipping (Oil Pollution)
(Turks and Caicos Islands) Order
1997, SI 1997/2589 16

Merchant Shipping (Oil Pollution)
(Tuvalu) Order 1975, SI
1975/2174 16

Merchant Shipping (Oil Pollution)
(Virgin Islands) Order 1997, SI
1997/2590 16

Merchant Shipping (Passenger Ship
Construction: Ships of Classes I,
II and II(A)) Regulations 1998, SI
1998/2514
Pt II (reg 6–19) 602
III (reg 20–26) 637
IV (reg 27–36) 637
V (reg 37–47) 602
VI (reg 48–51) 602

PARA

Merchant Shipping (Passenger Ship
Construction: Ships of Classes I, II and
II(A)) Regulations 1998, SI 1998/2514—
continued
Pt VII (reg 52–61) 602
VIII (reg 62–78) 602
IX (reg 79–84) 602
X (reg 85–89) 602

Merchant Shipping (Passenger Ship
Construction: Ships of Classes III
to VI(A)) Regulations 1998, SI
1998/2515
Pt III (reg 15–20) 637
IV (reg 21–29) 637

Merchant Shipping (Passenger Ships
on Domestic Voyages)
Regulations 2000, SI 2000/2687
.... 605

Merchant Shipping (Passenger Ships)
(Safety Code for UK Categorised
Waters) Regulations 2010, SI
2010/680 604

Merchant Shipping (Port State
Control) Regulations 2011, SI
2011/2601
reg 2 (3) 678
3 (1), (2) 678
(4) 679
4 (1)–(3) 679
5 (1)–(4) 679
6 (1)–(6) 679
7, 8 679
9 (1)–(11) 680
(12) 678
(13) 679
(14) 680
10–13 681
14 (1) 680
(2) 681
(3), (4) 680
15, 16 680
17 681
18 680
19 682
20 679
21 683
22 679
23 (1) 680
(2)(a) 681
(b), (c) 680
(3), (4) 679
(5) 682
(6) 679, 682
24 680
25 679

Merchant Shipping (Prevention of
Pollution) (Drilling Rigs and
Other Platforms) Order 2005, SI
2005/74 .... 22, 229

Merchant Shipping (Prevention of
Pollution: Substances Other than
Oil) (Intervention) Order 1997, SI
1997/1869 675

Merchant Shipping (Provisions and
Water) Regulations 1989, SI
1989/102 492

PARA

Merchant Shipping (Radio
Installations) Regulations 1998, SI
1998/2070 636

Merchant Shipping (Registration, etc)
Act 1993 (Commencement No 1
and Transitional Provisions)
Order 1993, SI 1993/3137
art 3 (1) 254

Merchant Shipping (Registration of
Colonial Government Ships)
Order 1963, SI 1963/1631 19

Merchant Shipping (Registration of
Federation of Nigeria
Government Ships) Order 1957,
SI 1957/861 19

Merchant Shipping (Registration of
New Zealand Government Ships)
Order 1946, SR & O 1946/1086
.... 19

Merchant Shipping (Registration of
Queensland Government Ships)
Order 1968, SI 1968/1092 19

Merchant Shipping (Registration of
Scottish Fishery Cruisers,
Research Ships etc) Order 1960,
SI 1960/2217 19

Merchant Shipping (Registration of
Ships) (Highlands and Islands
Shipping Services) Order 1961, SI
1961/1514 19

Merchant Shipping (Registration of
Ships) Regulations 1993, SI
1993/3138
reg 2 (1)–(6) 255
3, 4 256
5 255
6 257
7 (1) 258, 259
(2) 258
8 (1)–(5) 259
9 259
10 260
11 261
12, 13 262
14 263
15 264
16 265
17 266
18 (1) 267
19 268
20 269
21 270
22 272
23 271
24 273
25–27 274
28 275
29 276
29A 275, 313, 314
29A (3) 1067
29B 275, 313, 314
30 (1) 277
(2) 278
(3), (4) 277
31 279
32 .... 280, 281
33 (2) 286

PARA

Merchant Shipping (Registration of Ships)
Regulations 1993, SI 1993/3138—
continued
reg 34 287
35 288
36 289
37 .... 298, 299
38 303
39 296
40 297
41 304
42 305
43 307
44 308
45 309
46 310
47 311
48 312
49 313
(3) 1068
50 313
(4) 1068
51 314
(5) 1068
52 315
53 316
54, 55 .... 315, 316
56 317
57 319
58 320
59 322
60 325
61 326
62 335
63 336
64 337
65, 66 338
67, 68 339
70 340
71 341
72 342
72A 343
73 358
74 359
75 .... 358, 359
77 360
78 361
79 362
80 363
81 363
82 364
83 365
84 366
(3) 1068
86 367
87 368
88 344
89 345
90 346
91 347
92 348
(e) 353
93 349
94 350
95 351
96 352
97 353
98 354
99 355

PARA

Merchant Shipping (Registration of Ships)
    Regulations 1993, SI 1993/3138—
    continued
    reg 100 356
        101, 102 .... 317, 368
        103 369
        104 370
        105 371
        106 372
        107 379
        108 373
        109 374
            (2) 1071
        110 375
        111 376
        112 377
        113 378
        113A 380
        114 (1) 1070
            (2) 1069
            (4) 375, 1071
            (5), (6) 1070
            (7) 1067, 1068, 1070, 1071
            (8) 1070
            (9) 1068
        122 279
    Sch 1 278
        2 279
        3 para 1, 2 281
            3 282
            4 283
            5 284
            6 285
            7 281
        4 para 1 290
            2 291
            3 292
            4 293
            5 294
            6 295
        5 para 1 299
            2 300
            3 301

Merchant Shipping (Registration of
    Sierra Leone Government Ships)
    Order 1951, SI 1951/143 19

Merchant Shipping (Registration of
    South Australian Government
    Ships) Order 1971, SI 1971/872
    19

Merchant Shipping (Registration of
    Submersible Craft) Regulations
    1976, SI 1976/940 601

Merchant Shipping (Registration of
    Western Australia Government
    Ships) Order 1964, SI 1964/270
    19

Merchant Shipping (Repatriation)
    Regulations 1979, SI 1979/97
    reg 2–10 548
        12–17 548

Merchant Shipping (Reporting
    Requirements for Ships Carrying
    Dangerous or Polluting Goods)
    Regulations 1995, SI 1995/2498
    reg 3 648
        5 (1), (2) 648

PARA

Merchant Shipping (Reporting Requirements
    for Ships Carrying Dangerous or
    Polluting Goods) Regulations 1995, SI
    1995/2498—*continued*
    reg 9–11 648
        15–18 1125
        19 648

Merchant Shipping (Returns of Births
    and Deaths) Regulations 1979, SI
    1979/1577
    reg 2–10 644
        12 644
        13 1124
    Sch 1–3 644

Merchant Shipping (Revocation)
    (Bermuda) Order 2002, SI
    2002/3147 16

Merchant Shipping (Ro-Ro Passenger
    Ships) (Stability) Regulations
    2004, SI 2004/2884 602

Merchant Shipping Safety Convention
    (Guernsey) No 1 Order 1935, SR
    & O 1935/562 16

Merchant Shipping Safety Convention
    (Guernsey) No 2 Order 1935, SR
    & O 1935/563 16

Merchant Shipping (Safety
    Convention) (Guernsey) Order
    1990, SI 1990/2150 16

Merchant Shipping Safety Convention
    (Isle of Man) Order 1934, SR &
    O 1934/1414 16

Merchant Shipping Safety Convention
    (Singapore) No 1 Order 1953, SI
    1953/1218 16

Merchant Shipping Safety Convention
    (Singapore) No 2 Order 1953, SI
    1953/1219 16

Merchant Shipping Safety Convention
    (Straits Settlements) No 2 Order
    1935, SR & O 1935/716 16

Merchant Shipping (Safety of
    Navigation) Regulations 2002, SI
    2002/1473
    reg 4–9 643
        10, 11 1120
    Sch 3 643
        4 1120

Merchant Shipping (Salvage
    Convention) (Overseas Territories)
    Order 1997, SI 1997/2586 16

Merchant Shipping (Seamen's
    Allotments) Regulations 1972, SI
    1972/1698 476

Merchant Shipping (Seamen's
    Documents) Regulations 1987, SI
    1987/408
    reg 2–4 559
        5, 6 560
        7, 8 561
        10 562
            (2) 1091
        11 563
            (2) 1092
        12 564

PARA

Merchant Shipping (Seamen's Documents)
Regulations 1987, SI 1987/408—
continued

reg 12 (2) 1093
    13, 14 561
    15, 16 565
    17 565
      (2) 1095
    18–21 566
    22 (1) 567
      (2) 1096
      (3) 567
    23 (1) 568
      (2) 1097
    24 569
    25 570
    26 (1) 570
      (2) 1098
    27 (1), (2) 571
      (3) 1099
    28 (1) 572
      (2) 1100
    29 573
    30 .... 1091–1093, 1095–1100
Sch 3 566
   4 565

Merchant Shipping (Seamen's Wages
and Accounts) Regulations 1972,
SI 1972/1700

reg 4–8 473

Merchant Shipping (Seamen's Wages)
(Contributions) Regulations 1972,
SI 1972/1699 474

Merchant Shipping (Section 52
Inquiries) Rules 1982, SI
1982/1752

r 4 525
  5 526
  6 527
  7 528
  8 529
  9 538

Merchant Shipping (Section 63
Inquiries) Rules 1997, SI
1997/347

r 3 .... 531, 538
  4 531
  5 532
  6 533
  7 534
  8 535

Merchant Shipping (Ship Inspection
and Survey Organisations)
(Revocation) Regulations 2011, SI
2011/3056 14

Merchant Shipping (Standards of
Training, Certification and
Watchkeeping) Regulations 2015,
SI 2015/782

reg 4–44 503
    45–50 504
    51, 52 503
    53 504
    54 .... 503, 504
    55 (1) 503
      (2), (3) 503, 504
      (4) 503

PARA

Merchant Shipping (Standards of Training,
Certification and Watchkeeping)
Regulations 2015, SI 2015/782—
continued

reg 55 (5) 504
      (6), (7) 503, 504

Merchant Shipping (Submersible Craft
Construction and Survey)
Regulations 1981, SI 1981/1098
             601

Merchant Shipping (Submersible Craft
Operations) Regulations 1987, SI
1987/311 601

Merchant Shipping (Survey and
Certification) Regulations 2015,
SI 2015/508 604

Merchant Shipping (Technical
Requirements for Inland
Waterway Vessels) Regulations
2010, SI 2010/1075 .... 14, 604

Merchant Shipping (Tonnage)
(Overseas Territories) Order
1988, SI 1988/1085 16

Merchant Shipping (Tonnage)
Regulations 1997, SI 1997/1510
             248

Merchant Shipping (United Kingdom
Wreck Convention Area) Order
2015, SI 2015/172 927

Merchant Shipping (Vessel Traffic
Monitoring and Reporting
Requirements) Regulations 2004,
SI 2004/2110 648

Merchant Shipping (Vessels in
Commercial Use for Sport or
Pleasure) Regulations 1998, SI
1998/2771

reg 3 612
    4 613
    5 614
    6, 7 615
    8 1109
    9 616
Sch 1 613
   2 614

Merchant Shipping (Working Time:
Inland Waterways) Regulations
2003, SI 2003/3049

reg 3 423
    5, 6 520
    7 523
    8 521
    9 .... 520, 523
    10–12 521
    13 520
    14 (a)–(c) 520
      (d) 520, 521
    15 520
    16 523
    17 (1) 520, 521, 523
      (2) 520
    18, 18A 521
    19 522
Sch 1 520

PARA

O

Oil in Navigable Waters (Guernsey)
   Order 1966, SI 1966/393 16
Oil in Navigable Waters (Isle of Man)
   Order 1966, SI 1966/394 16
Order in Council dated 9 February
   1920 (Registration of Ministry of
   Agriculture and Fisheries Vessels),
   SR & O 1920/260 19
Order in Council dated 14 July 1921
   (Registration of Board of Trade
   Vessels), SR & O 1921/1211 19
Order in Council dated 8 December
   1924 (Registration of Australian
   Government Vessels), SR & O
   1924/1391 19
Order in Council dated 10 August
   1926 (Registration of Straits
   Settlements Vessels), SR & O
   1926/1036 19
Order in Council dated 5 November
   1929 (Registration of Vessels in
   the Service of the Indian
   Government), SR & O 1929/986
   19
Order in Council dated 15 May 1930
   (Registration of Northern Ireland
   Government Vessels), SR & O
   1930/336 19
Overseas Territories (Change of
   Name) (No 8) Order 2011, SI
   2011/2981 16

P

Pensions Increase (Commissioners of
   Irish Lights) Regulations 2014, SI
   2014/563 1020
Pilotage Act 1987 (Pilots' National
   Pension Fund) Order 1987, SI
   1987/2139 578
Pollution Prevention and Control
   (Fees) (Miscellaneous
   Amendments and Other
   Provisions) Regulations 2015, SI
   2015/1431 63
Port Security Regulations 2009, SI
   2009/2048 14
Prevention of Oil Pollution Act 1971
   (Overseas Territories) Order
   1982, SI 1982/1668 16
Protection of Wrecks (RMS Titanic)
   Order 2003, SI 2003/2496
   art 1 (2) 959
       3 959
       4 (1) 962
         (2) 960
       5 (1)–(3) 960
         (4)(a) 961
         (5) 960
       6 (1) 962
         (2), (3) 961
       7 (1), (2) 961

PARA

Protection of Wrecks (RMS Titanic) Order
   2003, SI 2003/2496—*continued*
   art 8 (1)–(4) 961
       9 (1)–(4) 961
       10 963
   Schedule 96

R

Railways and Transport Safety Act
   2003 (Commencement No 2)
   Order 2004, SI 2004/827
   art 3 (c) 1106
Registration of Government Ships
   (British Antarctic Territory) Order
   1963, SI 1963/1494 19

S

Ship and Port Facility (Security)
   Regulations 2004, SI 2004/1495
   reg 2 (2), (3) 684
       3 684
       4 (1), (2) 684
       6 (1)–(4) 685
         (5), (6) 1132
       7 (1), (2) 685
       8 (1)–(7) 688
         (8), (9) 1132
       9 688
       10, 11 1133
       12 1132
       13, 14 689
       15 1132
       16 689
       17 686
       18 (2) 686
       19 687
       20 .... 688, 689
   Schedule 684
Statistical Returns (Carriage of Goods
   and Passengers by Sea)
   Regulations 1997, SI 1997/2330
   reg 3 42
       4 1122
   Schedule 42
Statutory Harbour Undertakings
   (Pilotage Accounts) Regulations
   1988, SI 1988/2216 587

W

Wireless Telegraphy (Channel Islands)
   Order 1969, SI 1969/1369 16
Wireless Telegraphy (Isle of Man)
   Order 1969, SI 1969/1371 16

TABLE OF PROCEDURE

Civil Procedure

Civil Procedure Rules 1998, SI 1998/3132 (CPR)

PARA

CPR
r 61.1 (1) 91
    (2)(g) 166
      (h) 174
    (3) 91
    (4) 140
  61.2 (1)–(3) 91
  61.3 (1)–(3) 158, 160
    (4) 168
    (5) 160
    (6) 168
  61.4 (1) 180–183, 185
    (2), (3) 181
    (4) 180
    (5) 182
    (6) 183
    (7), (8) 181
    (9) 185
    (10)–(12) 203
  61.5 (1)–(6) 161
    (7), (8) 162
    (9) 164
  61.7 (1)–(4) 166
    (5) 167
  61.8 (1) 163, 164
    (2), (3) 174
    (4) 175
    (5), (6) 174
    (7) 169
    (8)–(10) 173
  61.9 (1) 190
    (2) 192
    (3)–(5) 190, 192
    (6) 191
  61.10 (1)–(5) 178
  61.11 (1) 196, 198, 200
    (2), (3) 196
    (4)–(8) 197
    (9)–(12) 198
    (13), (14) 199
    (15) 201
    (16), (17) 200
    (18)–(22) 196
  61.13 205

Practice Directions relating to Civil Procedure

PARA

Practice Direction PD 23A: Applications
  para 1 45
Practice Direction PD 61: Admiralty Claims
  para 1.1 91
  2.1–2.3 158
  3 158
  3.4, 3.5 168

PARA

3.6 160
  (1) 163
3.7, 3.8 160
3.9 169
3.10 168
3.11 .... 160, 168
3.12 160
4.1 .... 182, 183
4.2 (1) 183
4.3, 4.4 182
4.5 181
5.1 (1) 161
5.2 161
5.3 (2)–(4) 161
5.4 161
5.5 (1), (2) 163
5.6 .... 164, 173
5.7 173
6.1–6.4 166
7.1–7.3 174
7.4, 7.5 175
8.1 .... 190, 192
9.1–9.8 178
10.1 (1), (2) 196
10.2–10.4 197
10.5–10.8 198
10.9, 10.10 196
10.11 (1), (2) 196
10.12 196
10.13 (1), (2) 196
10.14 .... 199, 201
10.15, 10.16 201
10.17 .... 200, 201
10.18 196
12.1 .... 186–188, 192
12.2 .... 186, 193
12.3–12.5 187
12.6 189
13.1 143
13.2 144
13.3 145
14 162
14.1, 14.2 175

TABLE OF EUROPEAN UNION LEGISLATION

Secondary Legislation

Decisions

PARA

Council Decision (EC) 77/587 (OJ L239, 17.9.77, p 23)
.... 14
Council Decision (EC) 2004/246 (OJ L78, 16.3.2004, p 22)
.... 14

Directives

PARA

Council Directive (EC) 79/115 (OJ L33, 08.02.1979, p 32)
.... 14, 596
Council Directive (EC) 92/29 (OJ L113, 30.4.92, p 19) 14
Council Directive (EC) 96/40 (OJ L196, 7.8.96, p 8) 14
Council Directive (EC) 1999/35 (OJ L138, 1.6.1999, p 1)
.... 14, 603, 625, 694
Council Directive (EC) 1999/63 (OJ L167, 2.7.1999, p 33)
.... 14
Council Directive (EC) 2009/15 (OJ L131, 28.05.09, p 47)
.... 14
Council Directive (EC) 2009/42 (OJ L141, 6.6.2009, p 29
.... 42
European Parliament and Council Directive (EC) 1999/95 (OJ L14, 20.01.2000, p 29)
.... 14
European Parliament and Council Directive (EC) 2002/59 (OJ L208, 05.08.2002, p 10)
.... 14
European Parliament and Council Directive (EC) 2003/88 (OJ L299, 18.11.2003, p 9)
.... 14
European Parliament and Council Directive (EC) 2005/65 (OJ L310, 25.11.2005, p 28)
.... 14
European Parliament and Council Directive (EC) 2006/87 (OJ L389, 30.12.2006, p 1)
.... 14
European Parliament and Council Directive (EC) 2008/13 (OJ L76, 19.3.2008, p 41)
.... 14
European Parliament and Council Directive (EC) 2008/106 (OJ L323, 3.12.2008, p 33)
.... 14
European Parliament and Council Directive (EC) 2009/16 (OJ L131, 28.5.2009, p 57)
.... 14, 678
European Parliament and Council Directive (EC) 2009/18 (OJ L131, 28.5.2009, p 114)
.... 14
European Parliament and Council Directive (EC) 2009/20 (OJ L131, 28.5.2009, p 128)
.... 14
European Parliament and Council Directive (EC) 2009/21 (OJ L131, 28.5.2009, p 132)
.... 14
European Parliament and Council Directive (EU) 2014/90 (OJ L257, 28.2.2014, p 146)
.... 14

Regulations

PARA

Council Regulation (EC) 954/79 (OJ L121, 17.5.79, p 1)
.... 78
Council Regulation (EC) 3051/95 (OJ L320, 30.12.1995, p 14)
.... 632

PARA

Council Regulation (EC) 1419/2006 (OJ L269, 28.9.2006, p 1)
.... 14

European Parliament and Council Regulation (EC) 1406/2002 (OJ L208, 5.8.2002, p 1
.... 14

European Parliament and Council Regulation (EC) 2099/2002 (OJ L324, 29.11.2002, p 1)
.... 14

European Parliament and Council Regulation (EC) 782/2003 (OJ L115, 9.5.2003, p 1)
.... 14

European Parliament and Council Regulation (EC) 725/2004 (OJ L129, 29.4.2004, p 6)
.... 14, 684

European Parliament and Council Regulation (EC) 789/2004 (OJ L138, 30.4.2004, p 19)
.... 14

European Parliament and Council Regulation (EC) 336/2006 (OJ L64, 4.3.2006, p 1)
.... 14, 627

European Parliament and Council Regulation (EC) 1490/2007 (OJ L332, 18.12.2007, p 1)
.... 14

European Parliament and Council Regulation (EC) 530/2012 (OJ L172, 30.6.2012, p 3)
.... 14

Parliament and Council Regulation (EU) 2015/757 (OJ L123, 19.5.2015, p 55)
.... 678

Recommendations

PARA

Council Recommendation (EC) 78/584 (OJ L194, 19.7.78, p 17)
.... 14

Council Recommendation (EC) 79/114 (OJ L33, 8.2.79, p 31)
.... 14

Council Recommendation (EC) 80/907 (OJ L259, 2.10.80, p 29)
.... 14

Council Recommendation (EC) 83/419 (OJ L237, 26.8.83, p 34)
.... 14

TABLE OF TREATIES AND CONVENTIONS, ETC

PARA

Agreement between the United Kingdom, the United States of America, Canada and the Republic of France, concerning the Shipwrecked Vessel RMS Titanic (Cm 5798) 959

Agreement relating to the Implementation of Part XI of the United Nations Convention on the Law of the Sea of 10 December 1982 (New York, 28 July 1994; Misc 44 (1994); Cmnd 2705) 9

Convention for the Establishment of the Inter-Governmental Maritime Consultative Organisation (1958) (TS 54 (1958); Cmnd 589) 12

Convention on a Code of Conduct for Liner Conferences (Geneva, 6 April 1974) 78

Convention on Fishing and Conservation of the Living Resources of the High Seas (Geneva, 29 April to 31 October 1958; TS 39 (1966); Cmnd 3028) 8

Convention on Limitation of Liability for Maritime Claims (London, 1 to 19 November 1976; TS 13 (1990); Cm 955)
art 1 (1)–(7) 993
2 (1), (2) 994
3 995
4 996
5 997
6 (1), (2) 998
(4) 998
7 (1), (2) 999
8 1000
9 (1), (2) 1001
10 (1)–(3) 1002
11 (1)–(3) 1003
12 (1)–(4) 1004
13 (1)–(3) 1005
14 1006
15 1007
18 (1) 1008

Convention on the Continental Shelf (Geneva, 29 April to 31 October 1958; TS 39 (1964); Cmnd 2422) 8

Convention on the High Seas (Geneva, 29 April 1958; TS 5 (1963); Cmnd 1929) 8

Convention on the Territorial Sea and the Contiguous Zone (Geneva, 29 April 1958; TS 3 (1965); Cmnd 2511) 8

International Convention for the Unification of Certain Rules of Law respecting Collisions (Brussels, 23 September 1910; TS 4 (1913); Cd 6677)
art 4 775

International Convention on Salvage 1989 (London, 28 April 1989; Cm 1526)
art 1 (a)–(c) 850
(d), (e) 853
(f), (g) 851
2 852
3–5 851
6, 7 853
8 856
9 957
10 958
11 859
12 863
13 878
14 879
16 864
17 868
18, 19 865
20 915
21 916
22 917

	PARA
23	918
24	886
25, 26	921
27	922
28–34	851

International Convention on the Removal of Wrecks (Nairobi, 18 May 2007; Cm 8243)

art 1.1	927
1.2–1.4	923
1.5, 1.6	925
1.7	942
1.8	930
1.9	934
1.10	925
1.11	926
2.1–2.3	926
2.4	926, 927
2.5	941
3.1–3.5	927
4.1–4.3	928
4.4 (a)(i)	926
(ii)	941–944
(iii)	927
(b)	943
5	934
6	925
7, 8	938
9.1	941
9.2, 9.3	942
9.4	943
9.5	942, 943
9.6–9.8	944
9.9	942
9.10	943, 944
9.11	941, 944
10, 11	953
12.1–12.8	930
12.11	930, 954
12.12	931
12.13, 12.14	930
13	953
14–21	926

International Regulations for Preventing Collisions at Sea (London, 20 October 1972; TS 77 (1977); Cmnd 6962)

r 1 (a)–(e)	691
2	693
3 (a)	691
(b)	701
(c)	699
(d), (e)	691
(f)	708
(g)	701
(h)	708
(i)	701
(j)	699, 714
(k)	702
(l)	709
(m)	691
4	695–699, 701
5	695
6	696
7	697
8	698
9	699
10	701
11	702, 705–708
12	702
13	703
14	704
15	705

	PARA
16	706
17	707
18	708
19	709
20	710
21	711
(f)	712
22	711
23	712
24 (a)–(c)	713
(e)–(h)	714
25	715
26	716
27	717
28	718
29	719
30	720
31	721
32 (a)	722
(b)	723
33	722
34	723
35	724
36	725
37	726
Annex I	710
II	716
III	722
IV	726

Maritime Labour Convention 2006 (Cm 7049)

reg 1.2	464
1.3	503
1.4	456
2.1	451
2.2	482
2.3	511
2.4	451
2.5	540
2.6	545
2.7	504
2.8	502
3.2	492
4.1	492
4.2	546
4.3, 4.4	503
4.5	451
5.1	604

Protocol on the Privileges and Immunities of the International Seabed Authority (Kingston, 27 March 1998; TS 25 (2004); Cm 6260) 11

United Nations Convention on the Law of the Sea (Montego Bay, 10 December 1982 to 9 December 1984; TS 3 Misc 11 (1983); Cmnd 8941) 9

art 101–103	1186

TABLE OF CASES

PARA

A

A Turtle Offshore SA v Superior Trading Inc [2008] EWHC 3034 (Admlty), [2009] 2 All ER (Comm) 624, [2009] 1 Lloyd's Rep 177, [2008] All ER (D) 147 (Dec) 600

Abidin Daver, The [1984] AC 398, [1984] 1 All ER 470, [1984] 2 WLR 196, [1984] 1 Lloyd's Rep 339, 128 Sol Jo 99, HL 100–101

Abodi Mendi, The [1939] P 178, 108 LJP 60, 83 Sol Jo 275, 55 TLR 451, 63 Ll LR 100, sub nom Spanish Republican Government v Abodi Mendi [1939] 1 All ER 701, CA 164

Aboukir, The (1905) 21 TLR 200, P, D and Admlty 871

Acanthus, The [1902] P 17, 71 LJP 14, 9 Asp MLC 276, 85 LT 696, 18 TLR 160, P, D and Admlty 801

Accomac, The [1891] P 349, 7 Asp MLC 153, 66 LT 335, 7 TLR 649, CA 900

Ace Insurance SA-NV v Zurich Insurance Co [2001] EWCA Civ 173, [2001] 1 All ER (Comm) 802, [2001] 1 Lloyd's Rep 618, (2001) Times, 27 February, [2001] All ER (D) 21 (Feb) 100

Acrux, The. See Cassa Nazionale Della Previdenza Marinara v Proceeds of Sale of Italian SS Acrux (Banca Di Sicilia Intervening), The Acrux

Activ, The (1901) 17 TLR 351, P, D and Admlty 808
Ada, The (1873) 2 Asp MLC 4, 28 LT 825, PC 705
Adalia, The (1870) 3 Mar LC 345, 22 LT 74 733

Adelphi Hotel (Brighton) Ltd, Re, District Bank Ltd v Adelphi Hotel (Brighton) Ltd [1953] 2 All ER 498, [1953] 1 WLR 955, 97 Sol Jo 489 330

Admiral Codrington v Canadian Raider (1921) 9 Ll L Rep 477, P, D and Admlty 700

Admiralty (HMS P31) v Bretagne (1921) 7 Ll L Rep 127, P, D and Admlty 762

Admiralty Comrs v Josefina Thorden (Owners), The Josefina Thorden [1945] 1 All ER 344, 61 TLR 222, sub nom United Kingdom Lord High Admiral v M/V Josefina Thorden (Owners) and Cargo 172 LT 186 914

Admiralty Comrs v North of Scotland and Orkney and Shetland Steam Navigation Co Ltd. See Boy Andrew (Owners) v St Rognvald (Owners)

Admiralty Comrs v SS Amerika. See Amerika, The
Admiralty Comrs v SS Ausonia (Owners) (1920) 2 Ll L Rep 123, HL 758

Admiralty Comrs v SS Chekiang [1926] AC 637, 95 LJP 119, [1926] All ER Rep 114, sub nom The Chekiang 17 Asp MLC 74, 32 Com Cas 91, 135 LT 450, 42 TLR 634, HL 801–803, 806

Admiralty Comrs v SS Susquehanna [1926] AC 655, 95 LJP 128, 17 Asp MLC 81, 33 Com Cas 1, [1926] All ER Rep 124, 135 LT 456, 42 TLR 639, HL 806

Admiralty Comrs v SS Valeria (Owners) [1922] 2 AC 242, 92 LJKB 42, 16 Asp MLC 25, [1922] All ER Rep 463, 128 LT 97, HL 804

Admiralty Comrs v SS Volute (Owners) [1922] 1 AC 129, 91 LJP 38, 15 Asp MLC 530, [1921] All ER Rep 193, [1922] All ER Rep 193, 66 Sol Jo 156, 126 LT 425, 38 TLR 225, HL 768, 770

Admiralty Comrs v Susan V Luckenbach SS (Owners). See Susan V Luckenbach, SS (Owners) v Admiralty Comrs, The Susan V Luckenbach

Admiralty Comrs v Valverda (Owners) [1938] AC 173, [1938] 1 All ER 162, 107 LJKB 99, 19 Asp MLC 146, 43 Com Cas 139, 82 Sol Jo 153, 158 LT 281, 54 TLR 305, HL 883

Admiralty, The v Aberdeen Steam Trawling and Fishing Co Ltd (1910) 47 SLR 509, 1910 SC 553, Ct of Sess 800
Adriatic, The (1875) 3 Asp MLC 16, 33 LT 102 727
Adriatic, The (1915) 85 LJP 12, sub nom Wellington, The 32 TLR 49, P, D and Admlty 600

Adriatic, The, and The Wellington (1914) 30 TLR 699, P, D and Admlty 784

PARA

Aegean Sea Traders Corpn v Repsol Petroleo SA, The Aegean Sea [1998] 2 Lloyd's Rep 39,
 [1998] Lexis Citation 4119, [1998] All ER (D) 135 994
Aeneas, The [1935] P 128, 52 Ll L Rep 59, 104 LJP 74, 18 Asp MLC 571, 154 LT 246, P,
 D and Admlty 694
Aeolus, The (1873) LR 4 A & E 29, 42 LJ Adm 14, 1 Asp MLC 516, 21 WR 704, 28 LT
 41, HC 869
Africa Occidental, The [1951] 2 Lloyd's Rep 107, P, D and Admlty
 873
Africa, The (1854) 1 Ecc & Ad 299, 164 ER 173, 8 LT 582
 .... 865, 884–885
African Steamship Co v Swanzy and Kennedy (1856) 2 K & J 660, 25 LJ Ch 870, 4 WR
 692, 69 ER 947, 27 LTOS 248 148
Africano, The [1894] P 141, 63 LJP 125, 7 Asp MLC 427, 6 R 767, 42 WR 413, 70 LT
 250, P, D and Admlty 178, 190, 978, 983
Afrika, The (1880) 5 PD 192, 49 LJP 63, 4 Asp MLC 266, 42 LT 403, P, D and Admlty
 904
Afrika, The (1937) 57 Ll L Rep 215, PC 707
Afromar Inc v Greek Atlantic Cod Fishing Co, The Penelope II [1979] 2 Lloyd's Rep 42;
 affd [1980] 2 Lloyd's Rep 17, 124 Sol Jo 46, CA 196
Agamemnon, The (1883) 5 Asp MLC 92, 48 LT 880, P, D and Admlty
 865
Agincourt, The (1877) 2 PD 239, 47 LJP 37, P, D and Admlty
 240
Aglaia, The (1888) 13 PD 160, 57 LJP 106, 6 Asp MLC 337, 37 WR 255, 59 LT 528, 4
 TLR 691, DC 861–862, 869
Agra and Elizabeth Jenkins, The (1867) LR 1 PC 501, 4 Moo PCCNS 435, 36 LJ Adm 16,
 2 Mar LC 532, 16 WR 735, 16 ER 382, 16 LT 755, PC
 769
Aguadillana, The (1889) 6 Asp MLC 390, 60 LT 897, P, D and Admlty
 .... 749, 752
Ahmed v Governing Body of the University of Oxford [2002] EWCA Civ 1907, [2003] 1
 All ER 915, [2003] 1 WLR 995, [2003] ICR 733, [2003] 10 LS Gaz R 27, (2003)
 Times, 17 January, [2002] All ER (D) 356 (Dec) 205
Aid, The (1822) 1 Hag Adm 83, 166 ER 30 .... 120, 864
Aid, The (1881) 6 PD 84, 50 LJP 40, 4 Asp MLC 432, 29 WR 614, 44 LT 843, CA
 758
Aiden Shipping Co Ltd v Interbulk Ltd, The Vimeira (No 2) [1986] AC 965, [1986] 2 All
 ER 409, [1986] 2 WLR 1051, [1986] 2 Lloyd's Rep 117, 130 Sol Jo 429, [1986] LS
 Gaz R 1895, [1986] NLJ Rep 514, HL 148, 204
Aizkarai Mendi, The [1938] P 263, [1938] 3 All ER 483, 107 LJP 141, 19 Asp MLC 228,
 159 LT 490, 54 TLR 1022, P, D and Admlty 147, 149
Akerblom v Price (1881) 7 QBD 129, 50 LJQB 629, 4 Asp MLC 441, 29 WR 797, 44 LT
 837, CA 861, 869, 871, 883–884
Al Tabith and Alanfushi, The [1995] 2 Lloyd's Rep 336, CA
 .... 153, 1013
Alabano, The [1892] P 419, 7 Asp MLC 347, CA 788
Albano, SS v Allan Line Steamship Co Ltd [1907] AC 193, 76 LJPC 33, 10 Asp MLC 365,
 96 LT 335, 23 TLR 344, PC 705
Albany, The, and The Marie Josaine [1983] 2 Lloyd's Rep 195
 .... 153, 1013
Albert Crosby, The (1870) LR 3 A & E 37, 18 WR 410, HC
 432
Albert Edward, The (1875) 44 LJ Adm 49, 24 WR 179, DC
 765
Albion, The, France, Fenwick and Tyne and Wear Co Ltd v Swan, Hunter and Wigham
 Richardson Ltd [1953] 2 All ER 679, sub nom Swan, Hunter and Wigham Richardson
 Ltd v France, Fenwick Tyne and Wear Co Ltd, The Albion [1953] 1 WLR 1026,
 [1953] 2 Lloyd's Rep 82, 97 Sol Jo 524, CA 600
Albion, The. See Stone (Thomas) Shipping Ltd v Admiralty, The Albion
Albionic, The [1941] P 99, 70 Ll L Rep 257, 57 TLR 662, P, D and Admlty; affd [1942] P
 81, 72 Ll L Rep 91, 111 LJP 52, 167 LT 148, 58 TLR 154, CA
 .... 510, 869
Aldora, The, Tyne Tugs Ltd v M/V Aldora [1975] QB 748, [1975] 2 All ER 69, [1975] 2
 WLR 791, [1975] 1 Lloyd's Rep 617, 119 Sol Jo 253 .... 115, 886

PARA

Aldrich v Simmons (1816) 1 Stark 214, 171 ER 451, NP
.... 781

Alexander v Simms (1854) 5 De GM & G 57, 23 LJ Ch 721, 2 Eq Rep 861, 2 WR 329, 43
ER 791 332

Alexander, The (1812) 1 Dods 278, 165 ER 1310, HC 93, 425, 435, 968

Alexander, The (1842) 1 Wm Rob 346, 6 Jur 241, 166 ER 602, 7 LT 340, 1 Notes of
Cases 380 432

Alexandra (Newport and South Wales) Docks and Rly Co (Lady Tredegar) v Cape Colony
(1920) 4 Ll L Rep 116, P, D and Admlty 783

Alfred, The (1850) 3 Wm Rob 232, 14 Jur 155, 166 ER 949, 7 Notes of Cases 352
.... 801

Alfred, The. See Wellfield (Owners) v Adamson and Short, The Alfred

Alice, The and The Princess Alice (1868) LR 2 PC 245, 5 Moo PCCNS 333, 38 LJ Adm 5,
3 Mar LC 180, 17 WR 209, 19 LT 678, PC 758

Alida Gorthon, The [1956] 1 Lloyd's Rep 567, CA 222

Aline, The (1839) 1 Wm Rob 111, 166 ER 514 .... 976–977, 980, 984

Allan The v The Flora (1866) 2 Mar LC 386 744

Allen v Quebec Warehouse Co (1886) 12 App Cas 101, 56 LJPC 6, 56 LT 30, PC
.... 735

Alletta, The [1974] 1 Lloyd's Rep 40 208

Ally, The [1952] 2 Lloyd's Rep 427, P, D and Admlty 974, 990

Alma Shipping Corpn v Union of India, The Astraea [1971] 2 Lloyd's Rep 494
.... 133

Alma, The [1903] P 55, 72 LJP 21, 9 Asp MLC 375, 51 WR 415, 88 LT 64, 19 TLR 149,
P, D and Admlty 202

Almizar, The [1970] 1 Lloyd's Rep 67, CA; on appeal [1971] 2 Lloyd's Rep 290, HL
.... 220, 222

Alnwick, The. See Robinson v Alnwick (Owners), The Alnwick

Alston (RL), The (1882) 8 PD 5, CA 740

Altair, The [1897] P 105, 66 LJP 42, 8 Asp MLC 224, 45 WR 622, 76 LT 263, 13 TLR
286, P, D and Admlty 598, 742, 865, 884

Aluflet SA v Vinave Empresa de Navegaçao Maritima LDA, The Faial [2000] 1 Lloyd's Rep
473 93

Ambatielos, The Cephalonia [1923] P 68, 14 Ll L Rep 2, 92 LJP 45, 16 Asp MLC 120,
128 LT 699, 39 TLR 183, sub nom Ambatielos, The [1923] All ER Rep 303, P, D and
Admlty 125, 970

Amelia, The (1873) 2 Asp MLC 96, 21 WR 707, 29 LT 118
.... 789

American Farmer, The (1947) 80 Ll L Rep 672, P, D and Admlty
.... 114, 118, 855, 911, 924

American Hoesch Inc and Riblet Products Inc v SS Aubade etc and Maritime Commercial
Corpn Inc [1971] 2 Lloyd's Rep 423 156

Amerika, The [1914] P 167, 83 LJP 157, 12 Asp MLC 536, 58 Sol Jo 654, 111 LT 623, 30
TLR 569, CA; affd sub nom Admiralty Comrs v SS Amerika [1917] AC 38, 86 LJP 58,
13 Asp MLC 558, [1916–17] All ER Rep 177, 61 Sol Jo 158, 116 LT 34, 33 TLR
135, HL 149, 221, 807

Amerique, The (1874) LR 6 PC 468, 2 Asp MLC 460, 31 LT 854, PC
.... 891–892, 900

Amgulf Polymers & Chemicals Ltd v The Owners and/or Demise Charterers of MV
Athinoula [2001] 2 All ER (Comm) 821, [2000] Lexis Citation 4652, [2000] All ER
(D) 2310 204

Andalina, The (1886) 12 PD 1, 6 Asp MLC 62, 35 WR 336, 56 LT 171, P, D and Admlty
.... 982

Anders Knape, The (1879) 4 PD 213, 48 LJP 53, 4 Asp MLC 142, 40 LT 684, P, D and
Admlty 855

Anderson v Butler's Wharf Co Ltd (1879) 48 LJ Ch 824
.... 332

Anderson v Hoen, The Flying Fish (1865) Brown & Lush 436, 3 Moo PCCNS 77, 34
LJPM & A 113, 2 Mar LC 221, 167 ER 434, 16 ER 29, 12 LT 619, PC
.... 149, 221, 798

Anderson v Ocean Steamship Co (1884) 10 App Cas 107, 54 LJQB 192, 5 Asp MLC 401,
33 WR 433, [1881–5] All ER Rep 663, 52 LT 441, HL 133, 885

Anderson v Pitcher (1800) 2 Bos & P 164, 126 ER 1216
.... 5

PARA

Andoni, The [1918] P 14, 87 LJP 28, 14 Asp MLC 326, 119 LT 154, P, D and Admlty
.... 574

Andrea Ursula, The. See Medway Drydock and Engineering Co Ltd v MV Andrea Ursula,
    The Andrea Ursula

Andros Springs (Owners) v Owners of World Beauty, The World Beauty [1970] P 144,
    [1969] 3 WLR 110, sub nom The World Beauty, Owners of Steam Tanker Andros
    Springs v Owners of Steam Tanker World Beauty [1969] 3 All ER 158, [1969] 1
    Lloyd's Rep 350, 113 Sol Jo 363, CA 805

Aneroid, The (1877) 2 PD 189, 47 LJP 15, 3 Asp MLC 418, 36 LT 448, P, D and Admlty
.... 973

Angel Bell, The. See Iraqi Ministry of Defence v Arcepey Shipping Co SA (Gillespie Bros
    intervening), The Angel Bell

Anglo-Algerian Steamship Co Ltd v Houlder Line Ltd [1908] 1 KB 659, 77 LJKB 187, 11
    Asp MLC 45, 13 Com Cas 187, 98 LT 440, 24 TLR 235
.... 793

Anglo-Indian, The (1875) 3 Asp MLC 1, 33 LT 233, sub nom Anglo-Indian (Owners) v
    Prust, The Anglo-Indian and The Excel 23 WR 882, PC
.... 739

Anglo-Newfoundland Development Co Ltd v Pacific Steam Navigation Co [1924] AC 406,
    93 LJPC 182, 16 Asp MLC 385, 131 LT 258, HL 770

Anglo-Saxon Petroleum Co Ltd v Damant [1947] KB 794, [1947] 2 All ER 465, 80 Ll L
    Rep 459, [1948] LJR 153, CA 893

Ann, The v The Batavier. See Batavier, The
Anna and Bertha, The (1891) 7 Asp MLC 31, 64 LT 332, P, D and Admlty
.... 165

Anna H, The [1994] 1 Lloyd's Rep 287; affd [1995] 1 Lloyd's Rep 11, (1994) Times, 5
    August, CA 96–97

Anna Helena, The (1883) 5 Asp MLC 142, 49 LT 204, P, D and Admlty
.... 886, 891, 909

Anna Salen, The [1954] 1 Lloyd's Rep 475, P, D and Admlty
.... 694, 700

Anna, The (1876) 1 PD 253, 46 LJP 15, 3 Asp MLC 237, 34 LT 895, CA
.... 432

Anna, The. See Port Caledonia, The and The Anna
Annandale, The (1877) 2 PD 218, 47 LJP 3, 3 Asp MLC 489, 26 WR 38, 37 LT 139, CA
.... 136

Annapolis, The (1861) Lush 355, 1 Mar LC 127, 167 ER 150, 5 LT 37, PC
.... 871

Anne, The (1860) 12 Ir Jur 360 736

Anneliese, The, ship Arietta S Livanos (Owners) v ship Anneliese (Owners) [1970] 2 All ER
    29n, [1970] 1 Lloyd's Rep 355, 114 Sol Jo 262 .... 220, 771

Annette, The [1919] P 105, 88 LJP 107, 35 TLR 288, P, D and Admlty
.... 3, 86, 240

Annette, The (1873) LR 4 A & E 9, 42 LJ Adm 13, 1 Asp MLC 577, 21 WR 552, 28 LT
    372, HC 212

Annie Hay, The. See Coldwell-Horsfall v West Country Yacht Charters Ltd, The Annie Hay
Annie, The [1909] P 176, 78 LJP 81, 11 Asp MLC 213, 100 LT 415, 25 TLR 416, P, D
    and Admlty 112, 744

Annie, The (1886) 12 PD 50, 56 LJP 70, 6 Asp MLC 117, 35 WR 366, 56 LT 500, P, D
    and Admlty 968

Annot Lyle, The (1886) 11 PD 114, 55 LJP 62, 6 Asp MLC 50, 34 WR 647, 55 LT 576,
    CA 734, 738

Anon. See Constancia, La
Anselma De Larrinaga, The (1913) 29 TLR 587, P, D and Admlty
.... 804

Antares II, The and The Victory [1996] 2 Lloyd's Rep 482
.... 220

Antilope, The (1873) LR 4 A & E 33, 42 LJ Adm 42, 1 Asp MLC 513, 21 WR 464, 28 LT
    74, HC 887

Antonis P Lemos, The. See Samick Lines Co Ltd v Antonis P Lemos (Owners)
Apollinaris Co v Nord Deutsche Insurance Co [1904] 1 KB 252, 73 LJKB 62, 9 Asp MLC
    526, 9 Com Cas 91, 52 WR 174, 89 LT 670, 20 TLR 79
.... 437

Apollo, The (1824) 1 Hag Adm 306, 166 ER 109 240

PARA

Apollon, The, British Transport Docks Board v Apollon (Owners) [1971] 2 All ER 1223,
    [1971] 1 Lloyd's Rep 476, 115 Sol Jo 325, P, D and Admlty
    600
Appleton v Lord Braybrook (1817) 2 Stark 6, 6 M & S 34, 105 ER 1155, 171 ER 554
    430
Apsleyhall, The (1924) 19 Ll L Rep 227, CA 149
Aquila, The (1798) 1 Ch Rob 37, 165 ER 87 .... 872, 924
Arabert, The [1959] 1 Lloyd's Rep 63, CA 770
Aralia, The. See Flower and Everett Ltd v Thomas W Hughan & Co, The Aralia
Aratra Potato Co Ltd v Egyptian Navigation Co, The El Amria [1981] 2 Lloyd's Rep 119,
    [1981] Com LR 136, CA 100, 102
Archer, HMS [1919] P 1, 88 LJP 3, 35 TLR 80, P, D and Admlty
    .... 152–153, 786, 1013
Argentino, The (1888) 13 PD 191, 58 LJP 1, 6 Asp MLC 348, 37 WR 210, 59 LT 914,
    CA; affd sub nom Gracie (Owners) v Argentino (Owners), The Argentino (1889) 14
    App Cas 519, 59 LJP 17, 6 Asp MLC 433, 61 LT 706, HL
    804
Argo, The v The Helen and George. See Helen and George, The
Argo, The (1859) Sw 462, 166 ER 1217 759
Argo, The (1900) 9 Asp MLC 74, 82 LT 602, CA 769
Argon II, HMS Trawler v Porthcawl (Owners) (1920) 2 Ll L Rep 370, P, D and Admlty
    736
Argonaftis, The [1989] 2 Lloyd's Rep 487 .... 143, 800
Argonaut, The (1883) unreported, CA 890
Argus v Volga (1922) 11 Ll L Rep 102, P, D and Admlty
    735
Aria Inc v Credit Agricole Corporate and Investment Bank [2014] EWHC 872 (Comm),
    [2014] All ER (D) 244 (Mar) 90
Armstrong v Gaselee (1889) 22 QBD 250, 58 LJQB 149, 6 Asp MLC 353, 37 WR 462, 59
    LT 891, 5 TLR 182 184
Arno, The (1895) 8 Asp MLC 5, 72 LT 621, 11 TLR 453, CA
    890
Arnold v Cowie, The Glenduror (1871) LR 3 PC 589, 8 Moo PCCNS 22, 1 Asp MLC 31,
    17 ER 221, 24 LT 499, PC 900
Arraiz, The (1924) 16 Asp MLC 451, 132 LT 715, 40 TLR 867, CA
    .... 153, 1013
Artemisia (Owners) v Douglas (Owners) [1927] AC 164n, HL
    .... 205, 758
Arthur v Barton (1840) 9 LJ Ex 187, 6 M & W 138, 151 ER 355, 7 LT 224, Exch Ct
    432
Arthur Gordon, The (1861) Lush 270, 1 Mar LC 88, 9 WR 582, 167 ER 121, 4 LT 563,
    PC 739
Arthur, The (1862) 1 Mar LC 228, 6 LT 556 883
Aruba, The (1930) 37 Ll L Rep 225, CA 741
Arum, The [1921] P 12, 90 LJP 166, 37 TLR 38, P, D and Admlty
    204
Ashton, The [1905] P 21, 74 LJP 28, 10 Asp MLC 88, 53 WR 639, 92 LT 811, 21 TLR
    126, P, D and Admlty 700, 705
Assaye, The [1905] P 289, 74 LJP 145, 10 Asp MLC 183, 54 WR 203, 94 LT 102, 21 TLR
    677, P, D and Admlty 700
Assistance v Lagarto (1923) 17 Ll L Rep 264, P, D and Admlty
    783
Associated Herring Merchants v Reitsma 1958 SLT 57 156
Associated Portland Cement Manufacturers (1910) Ltd v Ashton [1915] 2 KB 1, 84 LJKB
    519, 13 Asp MLC 40, 20 Com Cas 165, 112 LT 486, CA
    .... 242, 782
Association and The Romney, The. See Morris v Lyonesse Salvage Co Ltd, The Association
    and The Romney
Assunta, The [1902] P 150, 71 LJP 75, 9 Asp MLC 302, 50 WR 544, 86 LT 660, 18 TLR
    570, P, D and Admlty 159
Assyrian, The (1890) 6 Asp MLC 525, 63 LT 91, CA 220
Astraea, The. See Alma Shipping Corpn v Union of India, The Astraea
Astrakhan, The [1910] P 172, 79 LJP 78, 11 Asp MLC 390, 102 LT 539, 26 TLR 329, P,
    D and Admlty 806

PARA

Astro Valiente Compania Naviera SA v Pakistan Ministry of Food and Agriculture (No 2),
    The Emmanuel Colocotronis (No 2) [1982] 1 All ER 823, [1982] 1 WLR 1096, [1982]
    1 Lloyd's Rep 286, 126 Sol Jo 343 103
Athamas, The (1917) 14 Asp MLC 276, 119 LT 117, P, D and Admlty
    .... 891, 909
Athenic, The (1932) 42 Ll L Rep 7, [1932] WN 10, 48 TLR 158, P, D and Admlty
    169
Athens Sky Cia Naviera SA v Port Service Corpn Ltd, The Tribels [1985] 1 Lloyd's Rep
    128 172
Atlantic Star, The, Motor Vessel Atlantic Star (Owners) v Motor Vessel Bona Spes (Owners)
    [1973] QB 364, [1972] 3 All ER 705, [1972] 3 WLR 746, [1972] 2 Lloyd's Rep 446,
    116 Sol Jo 821; on appeal [1974] AC 436, [1973] 2 All ER 175, [1973] 2 WLR 795,
    [1973] 2 Lloyd's Rep 197, 117 Sol Jo 371, HL 86, 100–101
Atlas, The (1827) 2 Hag Adm 48, 166 ER 162 .... 80, 134
Atlas, The (1862) Lush 518, 31 LJPM & A 210, 8 Jur NS 753, 1 Mar LC 235, 10 WR
    850, 167 ER 235, 6 LT 737, sub nom Hewett v Aylen, The Atlas 15 Moo PCC 329,
    15 ER 519, PC 863, 894
Atle Marine v The Skylark (Owners), The Skylark [1965] P 474, [1965] 3 All ER 380,
    [1965] 3 WLR 759, [1965] 2 Lloyd's Rep 250, 109 Sol Jo 793, P, D and Admlty
    135
Attila, The (1879) 5 QLR 340 744
A-G v Anglo-American Oil Co Ltd, The F J Wolfe. See F J Wolfe, The
A-G v Fargrove Steam Navigation Co Ltd (1906) 23 TLR 230
    478
A-G v Norstedt (1816) 3 Price 97, (1716) 146 ER 203 .... 977, 979
Attrill v Dresdner Kleinwort Ltd [2012] EWHC 1189 (QB), [2012] IRLR 553, [2012] 21
    LS Gaz R 18, [2012] NLJR 714, [2012] All ER (D) 97 (May); affd sub nom Attrill v
    Dresdner Kleinwort Ltd [2013] EWCA Civ 394, [2013] 3 All ER 607, [2013] IRLR
    548, [2013] ICR D30, [2013] All ER (D) 217 (Apr) 471
Atwood v Sellar & Co (1879) 4 QBD 342, 27 WR 726, sub nom Attwood v Sellar 48
    LJQB 465, 4 Asp MLC 153, 41 LT 83; affd sub nom Atwood v Sellar (1880) 5 QBD
    286, 4 Asp MLC 283, 28 WR 604, 42 LT 644, sub nom Attwood v Sellar 49 LJQB
    515, CA 436
Audley v Duff (1800) 2 Bos & P 111, 126 ER 1185 5
August 8, The [1983] 2 AC 450, [1983] 2 WLR 419, [1983] 1 Lloyd's Rep 351, 127 Sol Jo
    68, PC 92
August Korff, The [1903] P 166, 72 LJP 53, 9 Asp MLC 428, 89 LT 194, P, D and Admlty
    .... 863, 865
Auguste Legembre, The [1902] P 123, 71 LJP 53, 9 Asp MLC 279, 50 WR 622, 86 LT
    358, 18 TLR 373, P, D and Admlty 866, 873
Aurora, The (1861) Lush 327, 167 ER 145 710
Austen v Pearl Motor Yachts Ltd [2014] EWHC 3544 (Comm), [2014] All ER (D) 04
    (Nov) 32
Austin Friars Steam Shipping Co v Strack [1905] 2 KB 315, 74 LJKB 683, 10 Asp MLC
    70, 53 WR 661, 49 Sol Jo 537, 93 LT 169, 21 TLR 556, DC; on appeal [1906] 2 KB
    499, 70 JP 528, 75 LJKB 658, 94 LT 875, 22 TLR 701, CA
    .... 487, 510
Austin Friars Steamship Co Ltd v Spillers & Bakers Ltd [1915] 1 KB 833, 84 LJKB 544, 20
    Com Cas 100, 59 Sol Jo 205, 31 TLR 147; affd [1915] 3 KB 586, 84 LJKB 1958, 13
    Asp MLC 162, 20 Com Cas 342, 113 LT 805, 31 TLR 535, CA
    431
Australasian Steam Navigation Co v Morse (1872) LR 4 PC 222, 8 Moo PCCNS 482, 1
    Asp MLC 407, 20 WR 728, 17 ER 393, 27 LT 357 443
Australia (SS) (Owners) v SS Nautilus (Cargo Owners), The Australia [1927] AC 145, 25 Ll
    L Rep 141, 95 LJP 145, 17 Asp MLC 86, 32 Com Cas 82, [1926] All ER Rep 461,
    135 LT 576, 42 TLR 614, HL 205, 220, 758
Australia, The [1894] P 239. See Englishman, The and The Australia
Australia, The [1927] AC 145. See Australia (SS) (Owners) v SS Nautilus (Cargo Owners),
    The Australia
Australia, The (1859) 13 Moo PCC 132, Sw 480, 7 WR 718, 166 ER 1226, PC
    440–441
Australian Commercial Research and Development Ltd v ANZ McCaughan Merchant Bank
    Ltd [1989] 3 All ER 65 101
Australian Direct Steam Navigation Co, Re (1875) LR 20 Eq 325, 44 LJ Ch 676, Ct of Ch
    987

PARA

Australian Steam Navigation Co v Smith & Sons (1889) 14 App Cas 318, 61 LT 134, PC
.... 700

Australmead, The [1924] P 36, 93 LJP 15, 16 Asp MLC 247, 130 LT 288, 40 TLR 71, P,
D and Admlty 751

Aventicum, The [1978] 1 Lloyd's Rep 184 .... 93, 478

B

Baarn, The [1933] P 251, 46 Ll L Rep 63, 102 LJP 120, 18 Asp MLC 434, 150 LT 50, 49
TLR 554, CA 207

Babbs v Press [1971] 3 All ER 654, [1971] 1 WLR 1739, [1971] 2 Lloyd's Rep 383, 135 JP
604, 115 Sol Jo 723, DC 223, 1170

Babcock Fitzroy Ltd v The Ship M/V Southern Pasifika [2012] NZHC 1254, [2012] 2
Lloyd's Rep 423 .... 974, 984, 987

Bahamas Oil Refining Co v Kristiansands Tankrederie A/S and Shell International Marine
Ltd, The Polyduke [1978] 1 Lloyd's Rep 211 432

Bahamas Oil Refining Company International Ltd v Owners of the Cape Bari
Tankschiffahrts GMBH & Co KG (Bahamas) [2016] UKPC 20, 166 NLJ 7710, [2016]
4 LRC 530, [2016] All ER (D) 125 (Jul) 195, 993, 995

Bahia, The (1864) Brown & Lush 292, 11 Jur NS 90, 2 Mar LC 174, 5 New Rep 221, 167
ER 368, 12 LT 145 436

Bain Clarkson Ltd v Owners of Sea Friends [1991] 2 Lloyd's Rep 322, (1991) Times, 18
April, CA 111, 132

Baker v Buckle (1822) 7 Moore CP 349 330

Baku Standard, SS (Master and Owners) v SS Angèle (Master and Owners) [1901] AC 549,
70 LJPC 98, 9 Asp MLC 197, 84 LT 788, 17 TLR 584, PC
.... 814, 899

Balaena v Cairngarth (1921) 6 Ll L Rep 354, P, D and Admlty
.... 754

Balcombe, The [1926] P 82, 95 LJP 51, 17 Asp MLC 33, 134 LT 766, 42 TLR 312, P, D
and Admlty 184

Baltyk, The [1948] P 1, [1947] 2 All ER 560, 80 Ll L Rep 668, P, D and Admlty
.... 600

Banco, The, Monte Ulia (Owners) v Banco (Owners) [1971] P 137, [1971] 1 All ER 524,
[1971] 2 WLR 335, [1971] 1 Lloyd's Rep 49, CA 7, 83, 86, 92–93, 158, 160, 162

Banda and Kirwee Booty (1866) LR 1 A & E 109, 35 LJ Adm 17, 12 Jur NS 819, HC
.... 867

Bangor Castle, The (1896) 8 Asp MLC 156, 74 LT 768, P, D and Admlty
.... 321, 981

Bank of America National Trust and Savings Association v Epidavros Gulf Shipping Co SA,
The Cape Sounion [1990] 2 Lloyd's Rep 329 970

Bank of Tokyo-Mitsubishi UFJ Ltd v Owners of the MV Sanko Mineral, The Sanko
Mineral [2014] EWHC 3927 (Admlty), [2015] 2 All ER (Comm) 979, [2015] 1 Lloyd's
Rep 247, [2014] All ER (D) 14 (Dec) 90, 93, 964

Bankers Trust International v Todd Shipyards Corpn, The Halcyon Isle [1981] AC 221,
[1980] 3 All ER 197, [1980] 3 WLR 400, [1980] 2 Lloyd's Rep 325, 124 Sol Jo 479,
PC 976, 983, 986

Banner v Berridge (1881) 18 Ch D 254, 50 LJ Ch 630, 4 Asp MLC 420, 29 WR 844, 44
LT 680 321

Banshee, The (1887) 6 Asp MLC 130, 56 LT 725, CA 220

Banshee, The (1887) 6 Asp MLC 221, 57 LT 841, CA 703

Barclay & Co Ltd v Poole [1907] 2 Ch 284, 76 LJ Ch 488, 10 Asp MLC 574, 97 LT 632
.... 321

Barefoot, The (1850) 14 Jur 841, 6 LT 371 .... 911, 913

Barge T-429, The [1957] 1 Lloyd's Rep 135 .... 746, 757

Barker v Highley (1863) 15 CBNS 27, 32 LJCP 270, 10 Jur NS 391, 1 Mar LC 383, 2
New Rep 489, 11 WR 968, 143 ER 692, 9 LT 228 238

Barnes v The Charterers of the Motor Vessel (The Snow Bunting) [2012] 2 Lloyd's Rep
647, [2012] Lexis Citation 129 .... 86, 690

Baron Vernon SS v SS Metagama 1927 SC 498, 1927 SLT 349, Ct of Sess; affd (1928) 29
Ll L Rep 253, 1928 SC (HL) 21, HL 796, 798

Barras v Aberdeen Steam Trawling and Fishing Co Ltd [1933] AC 402, 102 LJPC 33, 18
Asp MLC 384, 38 Com Cas 279, [1933] All ER Rep 52, 77 Sol Jo 215, 149 LT 169,
49 TLR 391, HL 487

PARA

Bartlett v Admiralty, The Vadne [1959] 2 Lloyd's Rep 480, P, D and Admlty
.... 153, 1013
Batavier III, The (1925) 23 Ll L Rep 21, [1925] WN 244, 16 Asp MLC 563, [1925] All ER
Rep 656, 70 Sol Jo 75, 134 LT 155, 42 TLR 8, P, D and Admlty
.... 771
Batavier, The (1845) 2 Wm Rob 407, 10 Jur 19, 166 ER 808, 6 LTOS 258, 4 Notes of
Cases 356 736
Batavier, The (1853) 1 Ecc & Ad 169, 164 ER 98 861
Batavier, The (1854) 1 Ecc & Ad 378, 164 ER 218, sub nom The Ann v The Batavier 6 LT
581; affd sub nom Netherlands Steam Boat Co v Styles, The Batavier (1854) 9 Moo
PCC 286, 14 ER 305, 28 LTOS 129, PC 110, 739, 741
Battersea, The (1912) Shipping Gazette, 14 February 749
Baumwoll Manufactur von Carl Scheibler v Furness [1893] AC 8, 62 LJQB 201, 7 Asp
MLC 263, 1 R 59, 68 LT 1, 9 TLR 71, [1891–4] All ER Rep Ext 1710, HL
.... 242, 782
Baxter v Blanchard. See Blanshard, Re
Bazias 3 and Bazias 4, The [1993] QB 673, [1993] 2 All ER 964, [1993] 2 WLR 854,
[1993] 1 Lloyd's Rep 101 175
Beal v Marchais, The Bougainville and The James C Stevenson (1873) LR 5 PC 316, 2 Asp
MLC 1, 21 WR 653, 28 LT 822, PC 708
Beale & Thompson (1803) 127 ER 221, 3 Bros & P 405
.... 869
Beauchamp v Marquis of Huntley (1822) Jac 546, 37 ER 956, Ct of Ch
.... 101
Beaverford, The (Owners) v The Kafiristan (Owners) [1938] AC 136, 43 Com Cas 21, 53
TLR 1010, sub nom The Kafiristan [1937] 3 All ER 747, 58 Ll L Rep 317, 106 LJP
91, 19 Asp MLC 139, 81 Sol Jo 844, 157 LT 439, HL 858, 865, 868
Beaverford, The, Owners of Dumb Barge Sunweld v Canadian Pacific Rly Co [1960] 3 All
ER 612, [1961] 1 WLR 793, [1960] 2 Lloyd's Rep 216, P, D and Admlty
.... 184
Beckford v Kemble (1822) 1 Sim & St 7, 57 ER 3 101
Bedeburn, The [1914] P 146, 83 LJP 109, 12 Asp MLC 530, 111 LT 464, 30 TLR 513, P,
D and Admlty 869
Beechwood Birmingham Ltd v Hoyer Group UK Ltd [2010] EWCA Civ 647, [2011] QB
357, [2010] 3 WLR 1677, [2011] 1 All ER (Comm) 460, [2010] Bus LR 1562, [2010]
RTR 33, [2010] All ER (D) 52 (Jun) 805–806
Behnke v Bede Shipping Co Ltd [1927] 1 KB 649, 96 LJKB 325, 17 Asp MLC 222, 32
Com Cas 134, [1927] All ER Rep 689, 71 Sol Jo 105, 136 LT 667, 43 TLR 170
.... 236
Beldon v Campbell (1851) 20 LJ Ex 342, 6 Exch 886, 155 ER 805, 17 LTOS 257
.... 885
Belfast Harbour Comrs v Lawther and Marine Investment Society, The Edward Cardwell
(1865) 12 LT 677, 17 I Ch R 54 332
Belgia, The (1941) 71 Ll L Rep 21, P, D and Admlty 855
Belgic, The (1875) 2 PD 57n, 3 Asp MLC 348, 35 LT 929, CA; affd (1876) 2 PD 59n, CA
.... 785
Bellanoch, The [1907] P 170, 76 LJP 83, CA; affd sub nom Canning (Owners) v Bellanoch
(Owners), The Bellanoch [1907] AC 269, 76 LJP 160, 97 LT 153, HL
.... 707, 720
Bellcairn, The (1886) 5 Asp MLC 582, 54 LT 544, P, D and Admlty
.... 238
Bellerophon, HMS (1874) 44 LJ Adm 7, 3 Asp MLC 58, 33 LT 412; affd (1875) 33 LT
412, PC 741, 745, 786
Benares, The (1850) 14 Jur 581, 5 LT 185, 7 Notes of Cases Supp 1
.... 125, 976, 982
Benlarig, The (1888) 14 PD 3, 58 LJP 24, 6 Asp MLC 360, 60 LT 238, P, D and Admlty
.... 863
Benson v Chapman (1849) 2 HL Cas 696, 8 CB 950, 13 Jur 696, 137 ER 781, 9 ER 1256,
HL 436
Benwell Tower, The (1895) 8 Asp MLC 13, 72 LT 664, P, D and Admlty
.... 321, 327, 330, 332, 334
Berdan v Greenwood (1880) 20 Ch D 764n, 46 LT 524n, CA
.... 204
Bergen, The [1997] 1 Lloyd's Rep 380 96–97
Bernard, The [1905] WN 73, CA 204

PARA

Bernina (2), The (1887) 12 PD 58, 56 LJP 17, 6 Asp MLC 75, 35 WR 314, 56 LT 258, CA; affd sub nom Mills v Armstrong, The Bernina (1888) 13 App Cas 1, 52 JP 212, 57 LJP 65, 6 Asp MLC 257, 36 WR 870, [1886–90] All ER Rep 823, 58 LT 423, 4 TLR 360, HL 767, 770, 792

Bernina, The (1886) 11 PD 31, 6 Asp MLC 65, 55 LT 781, P, D and Admlty 800

Berny, The [1979] QB 80, [1978] 1 All ER 1065, [1978] 2 WLR 387, [1977] 2 Lloyd's Rep 533, 121 Sol Jo 707 158

Bertie, The (1886) 6 Asp MLC 26, 55 LT 520, 2 TLR 690, P, D and Admlty 969

Berwickshire, The [1950] P 204, [1950] 1 All ER 699, 83 Ll L Rep 376, 94 Sol Jo 227, 66 (pt 1) TLR 568, P, D and Admlty 147, 809

Beryl, The (1884) 9 PD 137, 53 LJP 75, 5 Asp MLC 321, 33 WR 191, 51 LT 554, CA 205, 697, 758

Bethania, The (1 November 1910, unreported) 739

Betsey Caines, The (1826) 2 Hag Adm 28, 166 ER 154 .... 430, 814

Betsey, The (1813) 1 Dods 289, 165 ER 1314, HC 980

Betsey, The (1843) 2 Wm Rob 167, 7 Jur 755, 166 ER 717, 1 LTOS 410, 2 Notes of Cases 409 884

Beucker v Aberdeen Steam Trawling and Fishing Co Ltd (1910) 47 SLR 513, 1910 SC 655, Ct of Sess 800

Beulah, The (1842) 1 Wm Rob 477, 7 Jur 207, 166 ER 650, 3 LT 182, 2 Notes of Cases 61 .... 904, 906

Beynon v Godden (1878) LR 3 Ex D 263, 4 Asp MLC 10, 26 WR 672, 39 LT 82, CA 330

Bharatkhand, The [1952] 1 Lloyd's Rep 470, P, D and Admlty 793, 795

Bibby v Boissevain, The Egyptian (1863) 1 Moo PCCNS 373, 9 Jur NS 1159, 1 Mar LC 358, 15 ER 742, 8 LT 776, PC 734

Bien, The [1911] P 40, 80 LJP 59, 11 Asp MLC 558, 104 LT 42, 27 TLR 9, P, D and Admlty 765

Bilbao, The (1860) Lush 149, 1 Mar LC 5, 167 ER 72, 3 LT 338 785

Bineta, The, Dalby v Others claiming to be Owners of M/Y Bineta [1966] 3 All ER 1007n, [1967] 1 WLR 121, [1966] 2 Lloyd's Rep 419, 110 Sol Jo 788, P, D and Admlty 236

Biola, The (1876) 3 Asp MLC 125, 3 Char Pr Cas 178, 24 WR 524, 34 LT 185, P, D and Admlty 204

Bird v Gibb, The De Bay (1883) 8 App Cas 559, 52 LJPC 57, 5 Asp MLC 156, 49 LT 414, PC 899–900

Birkenhead, The (1848) 3 Wm Rob 75, 166 ER 891, 6 Notes of Cases 365 786

Birkett v Hayes [1982] 2 All ER 710, [1982] 1 WLR 816, 126 Sol Jo 399 147

Birkley v Presgrave (1801) 1 East 220, 102 ER 86 133

Birnam Wood, The [1907] P 1, 76 LJP 1, 10 Asp MLC 325, 51 Sol Jo 51, 96 LT 140, 23 TLR 58, CA 985

Birnam, The (1907) 76 LJP 28, 10 Asp MLC 462, 96 LT 792, P, D and Admlty 906

Bishop v Cunard White Star Co Ltd, The Queen Mary [1950] P 240, [1950] 2 All ER 22, 94 Sol Jo 305, 66 (pt 1) TLR 828, 83 Lloyd L R 415, P, D and Admlty 149

Bitinia, The [1912] P 186, 82 LJP 5, 12 Asp MLC 237, 107 LT 208, 28 TLR 497, P, D and Admlty; affd (1912) 82 LJP 8, 29 TLR 99, CA 691

Black v Lord Braybrook (1817) 2 Stark 7, 6 M & S 39, 105 ER 1157, 171 ER 555 430

Black v Williams [1895] 1 Ch 408, 64 LJ Ch 137, 2 Mans 86, 13 R 211, 43 WR 346, 11 TLR 77 .... 321, 334

Black Prince, The (1862) Lush 568, 1 Mar LC 251, 167 ER 258 805

Blackcock, The. See Morgengry, The and The Blackcock

Blaikie v Stembridge (1860) 6 CBNS 894, 6 Jur NS 825, 8 WR 239, 141 ER 703, sub nom Blakie v Stembridge 29 LJCP 212, 2 LT 570 781

Blanche, The (1887) 6 Asp MLC 272, 58 LT 592, P, D and Admlty 328, 330

PARA

Bland v Ross, The Julia (1860) Lush 224, 14 Moo PCC 210, 15 ER 284, PC
.... 598, 783

Blanshard, Re (1823) 2 B & C 244, 107 ER 374, sub nom Baxter v Blanchard 3 Dow &
Ry KB 177 104

Blazer, The (6 February 1911, unreported) 330

Blenden Hall, The (1814) 1 Dods 414, 165 ER 1361, HC
.... 891, 910

Blenheim (Owners) v Impetus (Owners), The Impetus [1959] P 111, [1959] 2 All ER 354,
[1959] 2 WLR 820, [1959] 1 Lloyd's Rep 269, 103 Sol Jo 453, P, D and Admlty
.... 600

Blenheim, The (1846) 2 Wm Rob 421, 10 Jur 79, 166 ER 814, 4 Notes of Cases 393
.... 731

Blenheim, The (1854) 1 Ecc & Ad 285, 164 ER 165 798

Blessing, The (1878) 3 PD 35, 3 Asp MLC 561, 26 WR 404, 38 LT 259, P, D and Admlty
.... 424

Blidensal, The [1923] P 26, 92 LJP 30, 39 TLR 86, P, D and Admlty
.... 204, 735

Bligh, Harbottle & Co, the Owners of the Cargo on board the Fusilier v Richard Simpson
and Others, Owners of the Aid, Northumberland, Champion, and Lotus (1865) Brown
& Lush 341, 3 Moo PCCNS 51, 167 ER 391 .... 120, 864, 874, 896, 969

Blow Boat, The [1912] P 217, 82 LJP 24, P, D and Admlty
.... 229

Blue Bell, The [1895] P 242, 64 LJP 71, 7 Asp MLC 601, 11 R 790, 72 LT 540, DC
.... 699, 753

Blue Nile Shipping Co Ltd v Iguana Shipping and Finance Inc [2004] EWHC 1506
(Admlty), [2004] 2 Lloyd's Rep 469, [2004] All ER (D) 305 (Jun)
.... 993–994

Blue Sky One Ltd v Mahan Air [2010] EWHC 631 (Comm), [2010] NLJR 843, [2010] All
ER (D) 02 (Jun) 318

Blyth Shipbuilding and Dry Docks Co Ltd, Re, Forster v Blyth Shipbuilding and Dry Docks
Co Ltd [1926] Ch 494, 95 LJ Ch 350, [1926] All ER Rep 373, 134 LT 634, CA
.... 236

Board of Trade v Baxter, The Scarsdale. See Scarsdale, The

Bodlewell, The [1907] P 286, 70 LJP 61, 10 Asp MLC 479, 96 LT 854, 23 TLR 356, P, D
and Admlty 806

Boiler ex Elephant, The (1891) 64 LT 543, CA 886, 924

Bold Buccleugh, The (1853) Pritchard's Admiralty Digest (3rd Edn) 221
.... 739

Bold Buccleugh, The. See Harmer v Bell, The Bold Buccleugh

Bolina, The (1844) 3 Notes of Cases 208 757

Bomarsund, The (1860) Lush 77, 167 ER 41 862

Bonifaz, The [1967] 1 Lloyd's Rep 321, P, D and Admlty
.... 204

Bonita, The (1861) 1 Lush 252, 30 LJPM & A 145, 1 Mar LC 145, 5 LT 141
.... 441

Bonnie Kate, The (1887) 6 Asp MLC 149, 57 LT 203, P, D and Admlty
.... 239

Bonvilston, The (1914) 30 TLR 311, P, D and Admlty 429

Borre, The [1921] P 390, 7 Ll L Rep 117, 91 LJP 1, 15 Asp MLC 334, 55 Sol Jo 715, 125
LT 576, 37 TLR 668, P, D and Admlty 165

Borussia, The (1856) Sw 94, 4 WR 502, 166 ER 1037, 27 LTOS 72
.... 732

Bostonian (Owners, Master and Crew) v Gregerso (Owners), The Gregerso [1973] QB 274,
[1971] 2 WLR 955, [1971] 1 Lloyd's Rep 220, 115 Sol Jo 74, sub nom The Gregerso,
motor tug Bostonian (Owners) v motor ship Gregerso (Owners) [1971] 1 All ER 961,
P, D and Admlty 872

Bosworth (No 2), The, Steam Trawler Wolverhampton Wanderers (Owners) v Motor Vessel
Bosworth (Owners), her cargo and freight [1960] 1 All ER 729, [1961] 1 WLR 319,
[1960] 1 Lloyd's Rep 163, 105 Sol Jo 149, CA 120, 204, 864

Bosworth (No 3), The. See Grand Union (Shipping) Ltd v London SS Owners' Mutual
Insurance Association Ltd, The Bosworth (No 3)

Bosworth, The, Steam Trawler Wolverhampton Wanderers (Owners) v Motor Vessel
Bosworth (Owners), her Cargo and Freight [1960] 1 All ER 146, [1961] 1 WLR 312,
[1959] 2 Lloyd's Rep 537, 105 Sol Jo 159, P, D and Admlty
.... 909

                                                                            PARA
Bothnia, The (1860) Lush 52, 29 LJPM & A 65, 167 ER 28, 2 LT 160
.... 736
Boucau, The [1909] P 163, 78 LJP 87, 11 Asp MLC 240, 100 LT 617, 25 TLR 265, P, D
   and Admlty 789
Bougainville and The James C Stevenson, The. See Beal v Marchais, The Bougainville and
   The James C Stevenson
Bouygues Offshore SA v Caspian Shipping Co [1998] 2 Lloyd's Rep 461, (1998) Times, 7
   August, CA 176, 196, 1003
Bouygues Offshore SA v Caspian Shipping Co (No 3) [1998] 2 Lloyd's Rep 461, CA
.... 176, 196
Bouygues Offshore SA v Caspian Shipping Co (No 4) [1998] 2 Lloyd's Rep 461, CA
.... 176, 196
Bouygues Offshore SA v Caspian Shipping Co (No 5) [1998] 2 Lloyd's Rep 461, CA
.... 176, 196
Bow Spring v Manzanillo II [2004] EWCA Civ 1007, [2004] 4 All ER 899n, [2005] 1
   WLR 144, [2005] 1 All ER (Comm) 53n, [2005] 1 Lloyd's Rep 1, (2004) Times, 19
   August, [2004] All ER (D) 522 (Jul) 205, 766
Bowbelle, The [1990] 3 All ER 476, [1990] 1 WLR 1330, [1990] 1 Lloyd's Rep 532,
   (1990) Times, 21 March 176
Bowcher v Noidstrom (1809) 1 Taunt 568, 127 ER 954
.... 781
Bowen v Fox (1829) 10 B & C 41, 8 LJOSMC 68, L & Welsb 50, 5 Man & Ry KB 4, 109
   ER 366 425
Boy Andrew (Owners) v St Rognvald (Owners) [1948] AC 140, [1948] LJR 768, sub nom
   Admiralty Comrs v North of Scotland and Orkney and Shetland Steam Navigation Co
   Ltd [1947] 2 All ER 350, sub nom The St Rognvald 80 Ll L Rep 559, HL
.... 769
Boynton, The (1898) 14 TLR 173, P, D and Admlty 705
Brabo, The. See Tyne Improvement Comrs v Armement Anversois SA, The Brabo
Bradley v H Newsom Sons & Co [1919] AC 16, 88 LJKB 35, 14 Asp MLC 340, 24 Com
   Cas 1, [1918–19] All ER Rep 625, 119 LT 239, 34 TLR 613, HL
.... 890, 924
Branksome Hall, The (1934) 48 Ll L Rep 43, DC 789
Branston, The (1826) 2 Hag Adm 3n 870
Bremen, The (1906) 10 Asp MLC 229, 94 LT 380, P, D and Admlty
.... 899
Breydon Merchant, The [1992] 1 Lloyd's Rep 373, [1991] Lexis Citation 2283
.... 995–996
Bridge Oil Ltd v Owners and/or Demise Charterers of the Ship Giuseppe di Vittorio (1997)
   Times, 10 November, [1997] Lexis Citation 4276, [1997] All ER (D) 39, CA
.... 90, 126
Briggs v Merchant Traders' Ship Loan and Insurance Association (1849) 13 QB 167, 18
   LJQB 178, 13 Jur 787, 116 ER 1227, 13 LTOS 68 875
Briggs v Wilkinson (1827) 7 B & C 30, 5 LJOSKB 349, 9 Dow & Ry KB 871, 108 ER 636
.... 330
Bristol and West Building Society v Evans Bullock (5 February 1996, unreported)
.... 203
Britain, The (1839) 1 Wm Rob 40, 166 ER 489, 7 LT 224
.... 885
British Airways Board v Laker Airways Ltd [1985] AC 58, [1984] 3 All ER 39, [1984] 3
   WLR 413, 128 Sol Jo 531, [1984] LS Gaz R 2849, 134 NLJ 746, HL
.... 101
British Aviator, The [1965] 1 Lloyd's Rep 271, sub nom Crystal Jewel (Owners) v British
   Aviator (Owners) 109 Sol Jo 215, CA 220, 222, 694
British Commerce, The (1884) 9 PD 128, 53 LJP 72, 5 Asp MLC 335, 33 WR 200, 51 LT
   604, P, D and Admlty 799, 814
British Fame (Owners) v Macgregor (Owners), The Macgregor [1943] AC 197, [1943] 1
   All ER 33, 74 Ll L Rep 82, 112 LJP 6, 86 Sol Jo 367, 168 LT 193, 59 TLR 61, HL
.... 220, 771
British Holly, The (1924) 20 Ll L Rep 237, P, D and Admlty
.... 735
British Patrol, The [1968] 1 Lloyd's Rep 117, CA 204, 222
British Trade, The [1924] P 104, 18 Ll L Rep 65, 93 LJP 33, 16 Asp MLC 296, [1924] All
   ER Rep 519, 130 LT 827, 40 TLR 292, P, D and Admlty
.... 127, 970

PARA

Broadmayne, The [1916] P 64, 85 LJP 153, 13 Asp MLC 356, 60 Sol Jo 367, 114 LT 891,
    32 TLR 304, CA 92, 969
Brodie v Howard (1855) 17 CB 109, 25 LJCP 57, 1 Jur NS 1209, 4 WR 44, 139 ER 1010,
    26 LTOS 91 244
Bromsgrove, The [1912] P 182, 82 LJP 2, 12 Asp MLC 196, 106 LT 815, P, D and Admlty
    753
Brond v Broomhall [1906] 1 KB 571, 75 LJKB 548 105
Brooklyn City, The (1885) 2 Pritchard's Admiralty Digest (3rd Edn) 2371
    700
Brouard v Dumaresque (1841) 3 Moo PCC 457, 13 ER 186, PC
    333
Brown v Mallett (1848) 5 CB 599, 17 LJCP 227, 12 Jur 204, 136 ER 1013, 11 LTOS 64
    945
Brown v Stapyleton (1827) 4 Bing 119, 5 LJOSCP 121, 12 Moore CP 334, 130 ER 713
    860
Brown v Tanner (1868) LR 3 Ch App 597, 37 LJ Ch 923, 3 Mar LC 94, 16 WR 882, 18
    LT 624, CA in Ch 332
Brown v Thornton (1837) 6 Ad & El 185, 6 LJKB 82, 1 Jur 198, 1 Nev & PKB 339, Will
    Woll & Dav 11, 112 ER 70, [1835–42] All ER Rep 298
    430
Bruckenholme, The v HMS Supply. See HMS Supply
Bruxellesville, The [1908] P 312, 77 LJP 156, 11 Asp MLC 24, 98 LT 251, 24 TLR 223, P,
    D and Admlty 798
Bryce v Canadian Pacific Rly Co (1908) 8 WLR 230, 13 BCR 446
    700
Buckhurst, The (1881) 6 PD 152, 51 LJP 10, 4 Asp MLC 484, 30 WR 232, 46 LT 108, P,
    D and Admlty 710, 720
Buffalo, The and Other Barges (1937) 58 Ll L Rep 302, P, D and Admlty
    891
Bulgaria, The [1964] 2 Lloyd's Rep 524, P, D and Admlty
    172
Bulk Atalanta (Owners of the Ship) v Forest Pioneer (Owners of the Ship) [2007] EWHC
    84 (Comm) 709
Bure, The (1850) 14 Jur 1123, 16 LTOS 285 164
Burgon v Sharpe (1810) 2 Camp 529, 170 ER 1241, NP
    428
Burn v Herlofson and Siemensen, The Faust (1887) 6 Asp MLC 126, 56 LT 722, 3 TLR
    382, CA 332
Burnock, The (1914) 12 Asp MLC 490, 110 LT 778, 30 TLR 274, P, D and Admlty
    909
Burns v Nowell (1880) 5 QBD 444, 44 JP 828, 49 LJQB 468, 4 Asp MLC 323, 29 WR 39,
    43 LT 342, CA 235
Burns, The [1907] P 137, 5 LGR 676, 71 JP 193, 76 LJP 41, 10 Asp MLC 424, 51 Sol Jo
    276, 96 LT 684, 23 TLR 323, CA 92
Burton v English (1883) 12 QBD 218, 53 LJQB 133, 5 Asp MLC 187, 32 WR 655, 49 LT
    768, CA 437
Burton v Pinkerton (1867) LR 2 Exch 340, 31 JP 615, 36 LJ Ex 137, 2 Mar LC 494, 547,
    15 WR 1139, 16 LT 419, 17 LT 15, Exch Ct 510
Bushby v Munday (1821) 5 Madd 297, 56 ER 908, [1814–23] All ER Rep 304
    101
Buteshire, The [1909] P 170, 78 LJP 108, 11 Asp MLC 278, 100 LT 1005
    189
Bywell Castle, The (1879) 4 PD 219, 4 Asp MLC 207, 28 WR 293, [1874–80] All ER Rep
    819, 41 LT 747, CA 761–762, 770
Byzantion, The (1922) 12 Ll L Rep 9, 16 Asp MLC 19, 127 LT 756, 38 TLR 744
    169

C

CDE SA v Sure Wind Marine Ltd (The SB Seaguard and the Odyssee) [2015] EWCA Civ
    1035, [2016] 1 All ER (Comm) 843, [2016] 1 Lloyd's Rep 125, 165 NLJ 7674, [2015]
    All ER (D) 146 (Oct) 92, 152–153, 1013
CMA CGM SA v Classica Shipping Co Ltd [2004] EWCA Civ 114, [2004] 1 All ER
    (Comm) 865, [2004] 1 Lloyd's Rep 460, [2004] 11 LS Gaz R 36, (2004) Times, 27
    February, [2004] All ER (D) 192 (Feb) 993

PARA

C M Palmer, The (1873) 2 Asp MLC 94, 21 WR 702, 29 LT 120, PC
.... 710, 733, 762
C S Butler, The (1874) LR 4 A & E 178, 43 LJ Adm 17, 2 Asp MLC 237, 22 WR 759, 30
LT 475 .... 117, 893, 895
C S Butler, The (1874) LR 4 A & E 238, 2 Asp MLC 408, 23 WR 113, 31 LT 549, HC
.... 229
Cadeby, The [1909] P 257, 78 LJP 85, 11 Asp MLC 285, 101 LT 48, 25 TLR 630, P, D
and Admlty 757
Cadiz, The (1876) 3 Asp MLC 332, 35 LT 602, P, D and Admlty
.... 855
Cairnbahn, The [1914] P 25, 83 LJP 11, 12 Asp MLC 455, 110 LT 230, 30 TLR 82, CA
.... 775, 778, 784
Cairnbahn, The (No 2) [1913] WN 165, 29 TLR 559, P, D and Admlty; on appeal (1914)
30 TLR 309, CA 778
Cairo, The (1874) LR 4 A & E 184, 43 LJ Adm 33, 2 Asp MLC 257, 22 WR 742, 30 LT
535, HC 121, 855
Cairo, The. See Watson and Parker v Gregory, The Cairo
Calcutta, The (Owners) v Emma, The (Owners), The Calcutta (1869) 3 Mar LC 336, 21
LT 768, PC 789
Calderon, The (1912) Times, 26 March 757, 788
Caledonia, The (1869) LR 4 A & E 11, 42 LJ Adm 13n, 17 WR 626, 28 LT 372n, HC
.... 212
Caliph, The [1912] P 213, 82 LJP 27, 12 Asp MLC 244, 107 LT 274, 28 TLR 597, P, D
and Admlty 1013
Calliope, The [1970] P 172, [1970] 1 All ER 624, [1970] 2 WLR 991, [1970] 1 Lloyd's
Rep 84, 113 Sol Jo 996, P, D and Admlty 143, 771
Calvin Austin, SS v Lovitt (1905) 35 SCR 616, Can SC 700
Calypso, The (1828) 2 Hag Adm 209, 166 ER 221 855
Calyx, The (1910) 27 TLR 166, P, D and Admlty 861–862
Cambo Shipping Co Ltd v Dampskibsselskabet Magnus (1920) 57 SLR 59, 1920 SC 26, Ct
of Sess 205
Cambria, The (1848) 2 Pritchard's Admiralty Digest (3rd Edn) 1822
.... 911
Cambrian, The (1897) 8 Asp MLC 263, 76 LT 504, P, D and Admlty
.... 863
Cambric, The [1912] WN 272, 29 TLR 69, P, D and Admlty; affd [1913] WN 313, CA
.... 153, 1013
Cambridge, The (1829) 2 Hag Adm 243, 166 ER 233 510
Camellia, The (1883) 9 PD 27, 53 LJP 12, 5 Asp MLC 197, 32 WR 495, 50 LT 126, P, D
and Admlty 863
Camilla, The (1858) Sw 312, 6 WR 840, 166 ER 1152, 31 LTOS 282
.... 424, 472
Cammell v Sewell (1860) 5 H & N 728, 29 LJ Ex 350, 6 Jur NS 918, 8 WR 639, 157 ER
1371, 2 LT 799, Ex Ch 443
Campbell (Donald) & Co Ltd v Pollak [1927] AC 732, 96 LJKB 1093, 1132, [1927] All
ER Rep 1, 71 Sol Jo 450, 803, 137 LT 656, 43 TLR 495, 787, HL
.... 222
Campell v Bordieu (1747) 2 Stra 1265 5
Canadian American Shipping Co v SS Woron. See Woron, The
Canadian Pacific Rly Co v SS Storstad [1920] AC 397, 89 LJPC 52, 14 Asp MLC 530, 122
LT 440, 36 TLR 114, PC 207
Candlewood Navigation Corpn Ltd v Mitsui OSK Lines Ltd, The Mineral Transporter, The
Ibaraki Maru [1986] AC 1, [1985] 2 All ER 935, [1985] 3 WLR 381, [1985] 2 Lloyd's
Rep 303, 129 Sol Jo 506, PC 790
Cannan v Meaburn (1823) 1 Bing 243, 1 LJOSCP 84, 8 Moore CP 127, 130 ER 98
.... 443
Canning (Owners) v Bellanoch (Owners), The Bellanoch. See Bellanoch, The
Canova, The (1866) LR 1 A & E 54, 12 Jur NS 528, HC
.... 871, 884
Cap Bon, The [1967] 1 Lloyd's Rep 543, P, D and Admlty
.... 172
Cap Palos, The [1921] P 458, 91 LJP 11, 15 Asp MLC 403, [1921] All ER Rep 249, 126
LT 82, 37 TLR 921, CA 600
Cape Packet, The (1848) 3 Wm Rob 122, 166 ER 909, 8 LT 582, 6 Notes of Cases 565
.... 895

PARA

Cape Sounion, The. See Bank of America National Trust and Savings Association v
  Epidavros Gulf Shipping Co SA, The Cape Sounion
Capella, The [1892] P 70, 7 Asp MLC 158, 66 LT 388, P, D and Admlty
  .... 204, 894, 911, 913
Capella, The (Cargo Ex) (1867) LR 1 A & E 356, 2 Mar LC 552, [1861–73] All ER Rep
  433, 16 LT 800 865
Capitan San Luis, The [1994] QB 465, [1994] 1 All ER 1016, [1994] 2 WLR 299, [1993]
  2 Lloyd's Rep 573 .... 190, 204
Carbonnade, The (Owners) v Ruta, The (Owners) [2001] 1 All ER 450, [2000] 1 All ER
  (Comm) 847, [2000] 1 Lloyd's Rep 359, [2000] ICR 1024, [2000] 12 LS Gaz R 39,
  (2000) Times, 21 March, [2000] Lexis Citation 1471, [2000] All ER (D) 169, sub nom
  The Ruta [2000] 1 WLR 2068 .... 127, 977, 982
Card v Hope (1824) 2 B & C 661, 2 LJOS 96, 4 Dow & Ry KB 164, 107 ER 529
  238
Cardiff Hall, The [1918] P 56, 87 LJP 113, 14 Asp MLC 328, 119 LT 156, P, D and
  Admlty 204, 789
Carlotta, The [1899] P 223, 68 LJP 87, 8 Asp MLC 544, 47 WR 702, 80 LT 664, 15 TLR
  362, P, D and Admlty 691
Carlston, The [1926] P 82, 95 LJP 51, 17 Asp MLC 33, 134 LT 766, 42 TLR 312, P, D
  and Admlty 184
Carlton, The [1931] P 186, 100 LJP 100, 18 Asp MLC 240, 145 LT 423, 47 TLR 517, P,
  D and Admlty 600
Carmichael v Brodie, The Sir Ralph Abercrombie (1867) LR 1 PC 454, 4 Moo PCCNS
  374, 16 ER 358, PC 896–897
Carolina, The (1875) 3 Asp MLC 141, 34 LT 399, P, D and Admlty
  470
Caroline, The (1861) Lush 334, 1 Mar LC 145, 167 ER 149, 5 LT 89
  .... 863, 865
Carolus, The (1837) 3 Hag Adm 343n 762
Carrie, The [1917] P 224, 86 LJP 178, 14 Asp MLC 321, 119 LT 128, 33 TLR 573, P, D
  and Admlty 118, 855, 868, 891, 924
Carrier Dove, The (1863) Brown & Lush 113, 2 Moo PCCNS 260, 1 Mar LC 341, 167
  ER 321, 8 LT 402, PC 732
Carron Iron Co v Maclaren (1855) 5 HL Cas 416, 24 LJ Ch 620, 3 WR 597, 10 ER 961,
  26 LTOS 42 101
Carron, The (1853) 1 Ecc & Ad 91, 164 ER 53, sub nom The Pursuit v The Carrou 7 LT
  441 758
Carse v North British Steam Packet Co (1895) 22 R 475, 32 SLR 418, 2 SLT 577
  770
Carslogie Steamship Co Ltd v Royal Norwegian Government [1952] AC 292, [1952] 1 All
  ER 20, [1951] 2 Lloyd's Rep 441, 95 Sol Jo 801, [1951] 2 TLR 1099, HL
  801–802
Cary v White (1710) 2 Eq Cas Abr 722, 2 ER 708, 5 Bro Parl Cas 325, HL
  432
Cassa Nazionale Della Previdenza Marinara v Proceeds of Sale of Italian SS Acrux (Banca
  Di Sicilia Intervening), The Acrux [1965] P 391, [1965] 2 All ER 323, [1965] 3 WLR
  80, [1965] 1 Lloyd's Rep 565, 109 Sol Jo 231, P, D and Admlty
  .... 93, 109, 130, 966, 970
Cassiopeia, The (1879) 4 PD 188, 48 LJP 39, 4 Asp MLC 148, 27 WR 703, 40 LT 869,
  CA 160
Castanho v Brown and Root (UK) Ltd [1981] AC 557, [1981] 1 All ER 143, [1980] 3
  WLR 991, [1981] 1 Lloyd's Rep 113, 124 Sol Jo 884, HL
  101
Castor, The [1932] P 142, 101 LJP 88, 18 Asp MLC 312, [1932] All ER Rep 839, 147 LT
  359, 48 TLR 604, P, D and Admlty 177, 888
Castrique v Behrens (1861) 3 E & E 709, 30 LJQB 163, 7 Jur NS 1028, 1 Mar LC 45, 121
  ER 608, 4 LT 52, [1861–73] All ER Rep Ext 1616 321
Castrique v Imrie (1870) LR 4 HL 414, 39 LJCP 350, 3 Mar LC 454, 19 WR 1, [1861–73]
  All ER Rep 508, 23 LT 48, HL 965, 991
Cathcart, The (1867) LR 1 A & E 314, 2 Mar LC 500, 16 LT 211, HC
  330
Catherine, The v The Clarence. See Clarence, The
Catherine, The (1847) 3 Wm Rob 1, 11 Jur 739, 166 ER 863, 10 LTOS 35, 5 Notes of
  Cases 398 988

PARA

Cato v Irving (1852) 5 De G & Sm 210, 21 LJ Ch 675, 16 Jur 161, 64 ER 1084, 18 LTOS
  345 .... 321, 332
Cato, The (1866) 35 LJ Adm 116 884
Cato, The (1930) 37 Ll L Rep 33, P, D and Admlty 899
Catur Samdura, The [2010] SGHC 18, [2010] 1 Lloyd's Rep 305
  .... 93, 111
Cavendish, The. See Oceangas (Gibraltar) Ltd v Port of London Authority, The Cavendish
Cawdor, The (1898) 8 Asp MLC 475, 79 LT 357, P, D and Admlty
  240
Cayo Bonito, The [1904] P 310, 73 LJP 93, 9 Asp MLC 603, 91 LT 102, 20 TLR 576, P,
  D and Admlty 855, 873
Cayzer Irvine & Co v Carron Co (1884) 9 App Cas 873, 54 LJP 18, 5 Asp MLC 371, 33
  WR 281, 52 LT 361, HL 694, 763–764, 767–768, 770
Cedric, The [1920] P 193, 89 LJP 228, 15 Asp MLC 285, 125 LT 120, 36 TLR 443, P, D
  and Admlty 778
Cella, The (1888) 13 PD 82, 57 LJP 55, 6 Asp MLC 293, 36 WR 540, 59 LT 125, CA
  .... 126, 966, 973, 983, 989
Celtic King, The [1894] P 175, 63 LJP 37, 7 Asp MLC 440, 6 R 754, 70 LT 562, 10 TLR
  222, P, D and Admlty 105, 330–331
Celtic, The. See Ellerman Lines Ltd v Murray
Ceramic, The (Owners) v The Testbank (Owners). See Testbank, The
Ceres, The (1857) Sw 250, 166 ER 1121 734
Ceylon Coaling Co v Goodrich. See Elmville, The
Ceylon, The [1920] P 187, 89 LJP 173, 15 Asp MLC 100, 123 LT 681, 36 TLR 419, P, D
  and Admlty 691
Champion, The [1934] P 1, 47 Ll L Rep 40, 103 LJP 9, 18 Asp MLC 453, 150 LT 318, 50
  TLR 39, DC 110, 229
Champion, The (1863) Brown & Lush 69, 1 Mar LC 340, 167 ER 303, 8 LT 401
  .... 911, 913
Champion, The. See Socrates, The and The Champion
Chandler v Grieves (1792) 2 Hy Bl 606n 487
Chaparral, The. See Unterweser Reederei GmbH v Zapata Off-Shore Co, The Chaparral
Chappell v Bray (1860) 6 H & N 145, 30 LJ Ex 24, 9 WR 17, 158 ER 60, 3 LT 278, Exch
  Ct 244
Charger, The, British Transport Docks Board v Owners of Proceeds of Sale of Steam Ships
  or Vessels Charger, Probe, Vigia, Dideki, Surveyor, Constellation, Errol and Regency
  [1966] 3 All ER 117, [1968] 1 WLR 1707, [1966] 1 Lloyd's Rep 670, 110 Sol Jo 444,
  112 Sol Jo 879, P, D and Admlty 975, 982
Charkieh, The (1873) LR 4 A & E 120, 42 LJ Adm 70, 2 Asp MLC 121, 22 WR 63, 29
  LT 404, HC 3
Charles Amelia, The (1868) LR 2 A & E 330, 38 LJ Adm 17, 3 Mar LC 203, 17 WR 624,
  19 LT 429, HC 991
Charles Jackson, The (1885) 5 Asp MLC 399, 52 LT 631, P, D and Admlty
  238
Charles le Borgne, The [1920] P 15 note 1 802
Charles Napier, The (1880) 5 PD 73, 49 LJP 23, 4 Asp MLC 231, 28 WR 718, 42 LT 167,
  CA 429
Charles, The (1872) LR 3 A & E 536, 1 Asp MLC 596, 21 WR 13, 26 LT 594, HC
  906
Charlotta, The (1831) 2 Hag Adm 361, 166 ER 275 .... 872, 910
Charlotte Wylie, The (1846) 2 Wm Rob 495, 166 ER 842, 8 LT 153, 5 Notes of Cases 4
  .... 888, 969
Charlotte, The [1920] P 78, 2 Ll L Rep 570, 89 LJP 62, 15 Asp MLC 98, 64 Sol Jo 276,
  123 LT 685, 36 TLR 204, P, D and Admlty 172
Charlotte, The (1848) 3 Wm Rob 68, 12 Jur 567, 166 ER 888, 11 LTOS 473, 6 Notes of
  Cases 279 .... 861, 867, 881, 885
Chartered Mercantile Bank of India, London and China v Netherlands India Steam
  Navigation Co Ltd (1883) 10 QBD 521, 47 JP 260, 52 LJQB 220, 5 Asp MLC 65, 31
  WR 445, 48 LT 546, CA 2–3, 82, 86, 770
Chasteauneuf v Capeyron (1882) 7 App Cas 127, 51 LJPC 37, 4 Asp MLC 489, 46 LT 65,
  PC 236
Chateaubriand, The [1916] WN 105, 85 LJP 152, P, D and Admlty
  874

PARA

Cheapside, The [1904] P 339, 73 LJP 117, 9 Asp MLC 595, 53 WR 120, 91 LT 83, 20
  TLR 655, CA 189
Cheerful, The (1885) 11 PD 3, 55 LJP 5, 5 Asp MLC 525, 34 WR 307, 54 LT 56, P, D and
  Admlty 863
Chekiang, The. See Admiralty Comrs v SS Chekiang
Chem Orchid, The [2015] SGHC 50, [2015] 2 Lloyd's Rep 666
  93
Chetah (Owners) v Annie Grant (Owners), The Chetah (1868) LR 2 PC 205, 5 Moo
  PCCNS 278, 38 LJ Adm 1, 3 Mar LC 177, 17 WR 233, 19 LT 621, PC
  900
Chieftain, The (1863) Brown & Lush 104, 32 LJPM & A 106, 9 Jur NS 388, 1 Mar LC
  327, 2 New Rep 528, 11 WR 537, 167 ER 316, 8 LT 120
  .... 172, 331
Chimbusco Pan Nation Petro-Chemical Co Ltd v The Owners and/or Demise Charterers of
  the Ship or Vessel Decurion [2013] 2 Lloyd's Rep 407, HK CA
  93
China-Pacific SA v Food Corpn of India, The Winson [1979] 2 All ER 35, [1979] 1 Lloyd's
  Rep 167; on appeal [1981] QB 403, [1980] 3 All ER 556, [1980] 3 WLR 891, [1980]
  2 Lloyd's Rep 213, 124 Sol Jo 614; revsd [1982] AC 939, [1981] 3 All ER 688, [1981]
  3 WLR 860, [1982] 1 Lloyd's Rep 117, 125 Sol Jo 808, HL
  885
Chioggia, The [1898] P 1, 66 LJP 174, 8 Asp MLC 352, 46 WR 253, 77 LT 472, 14 TLR
  27, P, D and Admlty 169
Chittagong, SS (Owners) v SS Kostroma (Owners) [1901] AC 597, 70 LJPC 121, 85 LT
  430, sub nom Chittagong, The, Kostroma (Owners) v Chittagong (Owners) 9 Asp
  MLC 252, PC 751
Choko Star, The. See Industrie Chimiche Italia Centrale and Cerealfin SA v Alexander G
  Tsavliris & Sons Maritime Co, Panchristo Shipping Co SA and Bula Shipping Corpn,
  The Choko Star
Chr Knudsen, The [1932] P 153, 43 Ll L Rep 423, 101 LJP 72, 18 Asp MLC 347, [1932]
  All ER Rep 326, 148 LT 60, 48 TLR 619, P, D and Admlty
  110
Christiana, The (1849) 7 Notes of Cases 2; affd sub nom Hammond v Rogers and Rodd,
  The Christiana (1850) 7 Moo PCC 160, 13 ER 841, 7 LT 648, 7 Notes of Cases Supp
  xli, PC 735
Christiansborg, The (1885) 10 PD 141, 54 LJP 84, 5 Asp MLC 491, 53 LT 612, 1 TLR
  634, CA 171
Christina, The (1848) 3 Wm Rob 27, 166 ER 872; affd sub nom Petley v Catto, The
  Christina (1848) 6 Moo PCC 371, 13 ER 726, 6 Notes of Cases 361, PC
  .... 599, 742
Christy v Row (1808) 1 Taunt 300, 127 ER 849, [1803–13] All ER Rep 740
  889
Churchward v Palmer, The Vivid. See Vivid, The
Cil v Owners of the Turiddu (First National Bank of Maryland intervening) [1999] 2 All
  ER (Comm) 161, [1999] Lexis Citation 2196, [1999] All ER (D) 696
  478
Cinque Ports (Lord Warden) v R (1831) 2 Hag Adm 438, 2 State Tr NS App 1014, 166 ER
  304 .... 139, 210
Cito, The (1881) 7 PD 5, 51 LJP 1, 4 Asp MLC 468, 30 WR 836, 45 LT 663, CA
  890
Citos, The (1925) 22 Ll L Rep 275 872
City of Antwerp and The Friedrich, The. See Inman v Reck, The City of Antwerp and The
  Friedrich
City of Berlin, The [1908] P 110, 77 LJP 76, 11 Asp MLC 4, 98 LT 298, CA
  .... 205, 758
City of Brooklyn, The (1876) 1 PD 276, 3 Asp MLC 230, 24 WR 1056, 34 LT 932, CA
  739
City of Buenos Ayres, The (1871) 1 Asp MLC 169, 25 LT 672
  802
City of Calcutta, The (1898) 8 Asp MLC 442, 79 LT 517, 15 TLR 108, CA
  .... 883, 885
City of Cambridge, The (1873) LR 4 A & E 161, HC; affd sub nom Wood v Smith, The
  City of Cambridge (1874) LR 5 PC 451, 43 LJ Adm 11, 2 Asp MLC 239, 22 WR 578,
  30 LT 439, PC 735

PARA

City of Chester, The (1884) 9 PD 182, 53 LJP 90, 5 Asp MLC 311, 33 WR 104, 51 LT
485, CA 863, 881, 886, 892, 896–897
City of Lincoln, The (1889) 15 PD 15, 59 LJP 1, 6 Asp MLC 475, 38 WR 345, [1886–90]
All ER Rep 272, 62 LT 49, CA 763, 798
City of London, The (1857) Sw 245, 166 ER 1119, 30 LTOS 236
.... 710
City of Manchester, The (1880) 5 PD 221, 49 LJP 81, 4 Asp MLC 261, 42 LT 521, CA
.... 222
City of Mecca, The (1879) 5 PD 28, 4 Asp MLC 187, P, D and Admlty; revsd (1881) 6 PD
106, 50 LJP 53, 4 Asp MLC 412, 44 LT 750, CA 965
City of Newcastle, The (1894) 7 Asp MLC 546, 71 LT 848, P, D and Admlty
.... 855
City of Peking, The v Compagnie des Messageries Maritimes, The City of Peking (1888) 14
App Cas 40, 58 LJPC 64, 6 Asp MLC 396, 61 LT 136, PC
.... 733, 747, 789
City of Peking, The v Compagnie des Messageries Maritimes, The City of Peking (1890) 15
App Cas 438, 59 LJPC 88, 6 Asp MLC 572, 39 WR 177, 63 LT 722, PC
.... 805
Clan Colquhoun, The [1936] P 153, 54 Ll L Rep 221, 105 LJP 65, 19 Asp MLC 11, 155
LT 231, 52 TLR 349, sub nom Port of London Authority v SS Clan Colquhoun
(Owners) [1936] 1 All ER 429, P, D and Admlty 600
Clan Grant, The (1887) 12 PD 139, 56 LJP 62, 6 Asp MLC 144, 35 WR 670, 57 LT 124,
P, D and Admlty 125
Clan Steam Trawling Co v Aberdeen Steam Trawling and Fishing Co (1908) 45 SLR 462,
1908 SC 651, 15 SLT 897, Ct of Sess 865, 868
Clan Sutherland, The [1918] P 332, 88 LJP 26, P, D and Admlty
.... 894–895, 906
Clara Camus, The (1925) 23 Ll L Rep 181, 16 Asp MLC 570, 134 LT 50, CA; revsd
(1926) 26 Ll L Rep 39, 17 Asp MLC 171, 136 LT 291, HL
.... 220, 771
Clara, The (1880) 12 Otto 200 736
Clarence, The (1850) 3 Wm Rob 283, 14 Jur 557, 166 ER 968, 7 Notes of Cases 579, sub
nom Catherine, The v The Clarence 5 LT 121 .... 793, 803
Clarence, The (1854) 1 Ecc & Ad 206, 164 ER 119 758
Clarisse, The. See Gann v Brun, The Clarisse
Clark (Inspector of Taxes) v Perks [2001] EWCA Civ 1228, [2001] 2 Lloyd's Rep 431,
[2001] STC 1254, 74 TC 187, [2002] ICR 302, [2001] 31 LS Gaz R 32, (2001) Times,
2 October, 145 Sol Jo LB 214, [2001] All ER (D) 397 (Jul)
.... 229
Claudio, The (1924) 18 Ll L Rep 442, P, D and Admlty
.... 739
Cleadon, The. See Stevens v Gourley, The Cleadon
Cleary v McAndrew (Cargo ex), The Galam. See Galam, The (Cargo ex)
Clieveden, The. See Diana, SS v SS Clieveden, The Clieveden
Club Cruise Entertainment and Travelling Services Europe BV and Department for
Transport [2008] EWHC 2794 (Comm), [2009] 1 All ER (Comm) 955, [2009] 1
Lloyd's Rep 201, [2008] All ER (D) 172 (Nov) 26, 1140, 1142–1143
Clutha Boat 147, The [1909] P 36, 78 LJP 41, 11 Asp MLC 199, 100 LT 198, P, D and
Admlty 699, 753, 769
Clutha, The (1876) 45 LJP 108, 3 Asp MLC 225, 35 LT 36, P, D and Admlty
.... 189
Clutterbuck v Coffin (1842) Car & M 273, 1 Dowl NS 479, 11 LJCP 65, 6 Jur 131, 3
Man & G 842, 4 Scott NR 509, 133 ER 1379 471
Clydach, The (1884) 5 Asp MLC 336, 51 LT 668, P, D and Admlty
.... 700
Clyde Navigation Co v Barclay (1876) 1 App Cas 790, 3 Asp MLC 390, 36 LT 379, HL
.... 739, 759
Clyde Navigation Trustees v Bowring SS (1929) 34 Ll L Rep 319, 1929 SC 715, Ct of Sess
.... 806
Clyde Navigation Trustees v Wilhelmsen (1915) 52 SLR 304, 1915 SC 392, 1915 SLT 141,
Ct of Sess 700
Clyde, The (1856) Sw 23, 166 ER 998, 5 LT 121, 240 .... 793, 796
Clydesdale Bank Ltd v Walker and Bain 1926 SC 72, Ct of Sess
.... 321, 331

                                                                        PARA
Cobequid Marine Insurance Co v Barteaux (1875) LR 6 PC 319, 2 Asp MLC 536, 23 WR
    892, 32 LT 510, PC 438–439
Coch v Allcock (1888) 21 QBD 178, 57 LJQB 489, 36 WR 747, 4 TLR 630, CA
    204
Cockatrice, The [1908] P 182, 77 LJP 74, 11 Asp MLC 50, 98 LT 728, 24 TLR 339, P, D
    and Admlty 716
Cohen v Rothfield [1919] 1 KB 410, 88 LJKB 468, [1918–19] All ER Rep 260, 63 Sol Jo
    192, 120 LT 434, CA 101
Colchester Corpn v Brooke (1845) 7 QB 339, 10 JP 217, 15 LJQB 59, 9 Jur 1090, 115 ER
    518, 5 LTOS 192 765
Coldwell-Horsfall v West Country Yacht Charters Ltd, The Annie Hay [1968] P 341,
    [1968] 1 All ER 657, [1968] 2 WLR 353, [1968] 1 Lloyd's Rep 141, 112 Sol Jo 131,
    P, D and Admlty 86
Collier, The (1866) LR 1 A & E 83, 12 Jur NS 789, 2 Mar LC 473, 16 LT 155, HC
    .... 865, 867
Collins v Lamport (1864) 4 De GJ & Sm 500, 34 LJ Ch 196, 11 Jur NS 1, 2 Mar LC 153,
    5 New Rep 177, 13 WR 283, 46 ER 1012, 11 LT 497 328–331
Collins v Simpson Steamship Co (1907) 24 TLR 178, CA
    .... 487, 510
Colorado, The [1923] P 102, 92 LJP 100, 16 Asp MLC 145, [1923] All ER Rep 531, 67
    Sol Jo 383, 128 LT 759, 39 TLR 216, CA 321, 983, 986
Columbia, The (1838) 3 Hag Adm 428, 166 ER 464 855
Columbus, The (1848) Pritchard's Admiralty Digest (3rd Edn) 239
    741
Columbus, The (1849) 3 Wm Rob 158, 13 Jur 285, 166 ER 922, 6 Notes of Cases 671
    .... 796, 798
Comet, Lightship (Owners) v The WH No 1 (Owners), The WH No 1 and The Knight
    Errant [1911] AC 30, 80 LJP 22, 11 Asp MLC 497, 103 LT 677, HL
    .... 742, 784
Comitas, The (1934) 49 Ll L Rep 43, P, D and Admlty 899
Commune de Mesquer v Total France SA: C-188/07 [2008] ECR I-4501, [2009] All ER
    (EC) 525, [2008] 3 CMLR 445, [2008] 2 Lloyd's Rep 672, [2009] PTSR 588, [2008]
    All ER (D) 308 (Jun), ECJ 14
Compagnie des Forges et Acieries de la Marine et d'Homecourt v Gibson & Co (1920) 57
    SLR 260, 1920 SC 247, 1920 SLT 168, Ct of Sess 707
Compania Colombiana De Seguros v Pacific Steam Navigation Co [1965] 1 QB 101,
    [1964] 1 All ER 216, [1964] 2 WLR 484, [1963] 2 Lloyd's Rep 479, 108 Sol Jo 75
    156
Compania Naviera Bachi v Henry Hosegood & Co Ltd [1938] 2 All ER 189, 60 Ll L Rep
    236, 19 Asp MLC 186, 82 Sol Jo 316, 158 LT 356 1185
Compania Naviera Vascongado v SS Cristina [1938] AC 485, [1938] 1 All ER 719, 107
    LJP 1, 19 Asp MLC 159, 82 Sol Jo 253, 159 LT 394, 54 TLR 512, HL
    86
Compania Naviera Vasconzada v Churchill and Sim [1906] 1 KB 237, 75 LJKB 94, 10 Asp
    MLC 177, 11 Com Cas 49, 54 WR 406, 50 Sol Jo 76, 94 LT 59, 22 TLR 85
    431
Comtesse de Fregeville, The (1861) Lush 329, 1 Mar LC 106, 167 ER 146, 4 LT 713
    432
Conoco Britannia, The [1972] 2 QB 543, [1972] 2 All ER 238, [1972] 2 WLR 1352,
    [1972] 1 Lloyd's Rep 342, 116 Sol Jo 221 .... 92, 111, 190
Consett, The (1880) 5 PD 77, 4 Asp MLC 230, 28 WR 622, 42 LT 33, CA
    148
Constable's (Sir Henry) Case (1600) 5 Co Rep 106a, 77 ER 218, [1558–1774] All ER Rep
    505, Stuart Moore's Law of Foreshore & Seashore 233 .... 122, 139, 923
Constancia, La (1846) 2 Wm Rob 460, 10 Jur 845, 166 ER 829, 4 Notes of Cases 512,
    sub nom Anon 7 LTOS 451 .... 125, 970
Constancia, The (1866) 15 WR 183 .... 980, 985
Constitution, The (1879) 4 PD 39, 48 LJP 13, 4 Asp MLC 79, 27 WR 739, 40 LT 219, P,
    D and Admlty 964, 969
Contest v Age (1923) 17 Ll L Rep 172, P, D and Admlty
    783
Contest and Bantam Cock, Steam Tugs (Owners, Masters and Crews) v SS Ovre (Owners)
    and SS Conde de Zubiria, her Cargo and Freight (1920) 2 Ll L Rep 21, P, D and
    Admlty 855

PARA

Cook v Dredging and Construction Co Ltd [1958] 1 Lloyd's Rep 334
.... 229

Coombes v Mansfield (1855) 3 Drew 193, 24 LJ Ch 513, 3 Eq Rep 566, 1 Jur NS 270, 3
WR 345, 61 ER 877, 25 LTOS 29 321

Coral Isis, The [1986] 1 Lloyd's Rep 413 101

Corbett v Pearce [1904] 2 KB 422, 68 JP 387, 73 LJKB 885, 90 LT 781, 20 TLR 473, DC
.... 229

Corchester, The [1957] P 84, [1956] 3 All ER 878, [1956] 3 WLR 1090, [1956] 2 Lloyd's
Rep 595, 100 Sol Jo 928, DC 224

Corcrest, The (1946) 80 Ll L Rep 78, P, D and Admlty 873

Corennie, The [1894] P 338n, P, D and Admlty 700

Corinthian, The [1909] P 260, 78 LJP 121, 11 Asp MLC 208, 53 Sol Jo 650, 101 LT 265,
25 TLR 693, CA 700

Coriolanus, The (1890) 15 PD 103, 59 LJP 59, 6 Asp MLC 514, 62 LT 844, P, D and
Admlty 867

Cornelia Henrietta, The (1866) LR 1 A & E 51, 12 Jur NS 396, 14 WR 502, HC
.... 330, 988

Cornish Rose, The [1936] P 174, [1936] 2 All ER 805, 55 Ll L Rep 237, 105 LJP 114, 52
TLR 648, P, D and Admlty 189

Coromandel, The (1857) Sw 205, 166 ER 1097, 8 LT 441, 6 LT 371
.... 924

Corps v Paddle Steamer Queen of the South (Owners), The Queen of the South [1968] P
449, [1968] 1 All ER 1163, [1968] 2 WLR 973, [1968] 1 Lloyd's Rep 182, 112 Sol Jo
270, P, D and Admlty 85, 110–111, 126, 164, 169, 173, 178, 975

Corstar (Owners) v Eurymedon (Owners), The Eurymedon. See Eurymedon, The

Cory & Son Ltd v France, Fenwick & Co Ltd [1911] 1 KB 114, 80 LJKB 341, 11 Asp
MLC 499, 55 Sol Jo 10, 103 LT 649, 27 TLR 18, [1908–10] All ER Rep Ext 1081,
CA 755

Cory Bros & Co v Stewart (1886) 2 TLR 508, CA 330–331

Cosmopolitan, The (1848) 6 Notes of Cases, Supp xvii, xx–xxvii
.... 924

Cossman v British America Assurance Co (1887) 13 App Cas 160, 57 LJPC 17, 6 Asp
MLC 233, [1886–90] All ER Rep 957, 58 LT 122, 4 TLR 65, PC
.... 911, 913, 924

Cossman v West; (1887) 13 App Cas 160, 57 LJPC 17, 6 Asp MLC 233, [1886–90] All ER
Rep 957, 58 LT 122, 4 TLR 65, PC 911, 913, 924

Countess of Harcourt, The (1824) 1 Hag Adm 248, 95975
.... 510

Cox v Ergo Versicherung AG [2014] UKSC 22, [2014] AC 1379, [2014] 2 All ER 926,
[2014] 2 WLR 948, [2014] RTR 280, (2014) Times, 14 April, [2014] All ER (D) 16
(Apr) 82

Cox v May (1815) 4 M & S 152, 105 ER 791 875

Craftsman, The [1906] P 153, 75 LJP 87, 10 Asp MLC 274, 95 LT 157, P, D and Admlty
.... 807

Craigellachie, The [1909] P 1, 77 LJP 145, 11 Asp MLC 103, 99 LT 252, P, D and Admlty
.... 739

Craighall, The [1910] P 207, 79 LJP 73, 11 Asp MLC 419, 103 LT 236, CA
.... 182

Crathie, The [1897] P 178, 66 LJP 93, 8 Asp MLC 256, 45 WR 631, 76 LT 534, 13 TLR
334, P, D and Admlty 809

Creen v Wright (1876) 1 CPD 591, 3 Asp MLC 254, [1874–80] All ER Rep 747, 35 LT
339, CPD 424, 472

Creteforest, The [1920] P 111, 2 Ll L Rep 319, 365, 89 LJP 136, 15 Asp MLC 48, 123 LT
591, 36 TLR 367, P, D and Admlty 204

Crimdon, The [1900] P 171, 69 LJP 103, 9 Asp MLC 104, 48 WR 623, 82 LT 660, 16
TLR 403, P, D and Admlty 167

Crispin, The (1929) 35 Ll L Rep 197, CA 147

Crooks v Allan (1879) 5 QBD 38, 49 LJQB 201, 4 Asp MLC 216, 28 WR 304, 41 LT 800
.... 133

Crouan v Stanier [1904] 1 KB 87, 73 LJKB 102, 9 Com Cas 27, 52 WR 75, 47 Sol Jo 728,
19 TLR 664 868

Crown Estate Comrs v Roberts [2008] EWHC 1302 (Ch), [2008] 4 All ER 828, [2008] 2 P
& CR 255, [2008] 2 EGLR 165, [2008] All ER (D) 175 (Jun)
.... 923, 950

PARA

Croxteth Hall, The Celtic. See Ellerman Lines Ltd v Murray
Cruiser, The v The Taquary (1913) 50 SLR 839, 1913 SC 1107, 1913 2 SLT 135, Ct of
  Sess 900
Crus V, The (1862) Lush 583 884–885
Crusader, The [1907] P 15, 76 LJP 19, 10 Asp MLC 353, 96 LT 126, P, D and Admlty; on
  appeal [1907] P 196, 76 LJP 102, 10 Asp MLC 442, 97 LT 20, 23 TLR 382, CA
  .... 870, 884
Crystal Jewel (Owners) v British Aviator (Owners). See British Aviator, The
Cuba, The v McMillan (1896) 26 SCR 651 700
Cuba, The (1860) Lush 14, 6 Jur NS 152, 167 ER 8, 8 LT 335
  886
Cumberland, The (1836) Stuart Vice-Admiralty Court Cases Lower Canada 75
  734
Cumbrian, The (1887) 6 Asp MLC 151, 57 LT 205, P, D and Admlty
  .... 876, 883, 969
Cunard White Star Line Ltd v Admiralty Comrs, The Queen Mary (1949) 82 Ll L Rep 303,
  [1949] WN 75, 93 Sol Jo 236, HL 769
Currie v M'Knight [1897] AC 97, 66 LJPC 19, 8 Asp MLC 193, 75 LT 457, 13 TLR 53,
  HL 82–83, 92–93, 964, 967
Cynthia, The (1852) 16 Jur 748, 3 LT 682, 6 LT 165, 20 LTOS 54
  425
Cythera, The. See Societe Maritme Caledonienne v The Cythera and Her Cargo

D

DSV Silo-und Verwaltungsgesellschaft mbH v Sennar (Owners), The Sennar [1985] 2 All
  ER 104, [1985] 1 WLR 490, [1985] 1 Lloyd's Rep 521, 129 Sol Jo 248, [1985] LS
  Gaz R 1863, [1985] NLJ Rep 316, HL 102
Daien Maru No 18, The [1986] 1 Lloyd's Rep 387, Sing CA
  208
Daioz, The (1877) 47 LJP 1, 3 Asp MLC 477, 37 LT 137, CA
  .... 204, 222
Dalmare SpA v Union Maritime Ltd, The Union Power [2012] EWHC 3537 (Comm),
  [2013] 2 All ER 870, [2013] 2 All ER (Comm) 70, [2013] Bus LR 810, [2012] All ER
  (D) 129 (Dec) 32
Dalton v Denton (1857) 1 CBNS 672, 5 WR 203, 140 ER 277, 6 LT 228
  .... 735, 770
Dalyell v Tyrer (1858) EB & E 899, 28 LJQB 52, 5 Jur NS 335, 6 WR 684, 120 ER 744,
  31 LTOS 214 782
Daniel M, The [1940] P 159. See Gusty, The and The Daniel M
Daniel M, The [1967] 2 Lloyd's Rep 498. See Scarcity, The and The Daniel M
Dantzic Packet, The (1837) 3 Hag Adm 383 .... 896, 911
Dapueto v James Wyllie & Co, The Pieve Superiore (1874) LR 5 PC 482, 43 LJ Adm 20, 2
  Asp MLC 319, 22 WR 777, 30 LT 887, PC 111, 973
Darby v Baines (1851) 9 Hare 369, 21 LJ Ch 801, 68 ER 550
  238
Daressa, The [1971] 1 Lloyd's Rep 60, P, D and Admlty
  802
Dart, The (1899) 8 Asp MLC 481, 80 LT 23, P, D and Admlty
  863
Davys v Richardson (1888) 21 QBD 202, 57 LJQB 409, 36 WR 728, 59 LT 765, 4 TLR
  608, CA 189
Dawkins v Simonetti (1880) 50 LJP 30, 29 WR 228, 44 LT 266, CA
  101
De Bay, The. See Bird v Gibb, The De Bay
De Garey v Clagget (1795) 2 Park's Marine Insurances (8th Edn) 708
  5
De Mattos v Gibson (1858) 4 De G & J 276, 28 LJ Ch 165, 5 Jur NS 347, 7 WR 152, 45
  ER 108, [1843–60] All ER Rep 803, 32 LTOS 268, CA in Ch; on appeal (1859) 4 De
  G & J 284, 28 LJ Ch 498, 5 Jur NS 555, 7 WR 514, 45 ER 108, 33 LTOS 193, CA in
  Ch 330–331
De Wolf v Pitcairn (1869) 17 WR 914 321
Dean v Richards, The Europa (1863) Brown & Lush 89, 2 Moo PCCNS 1, 15 ER 803,
  167 ER 313, PC 968

PARA

Dee Conservancy Board v McConnell [1928] 2 KB 159, 26 LGR 204, 92 JP 54, 97 LJKB
    487, 17 Asp MLC 433, [1928] All ER Rep 554, 138 LT 656, CA
    787
D'Eguino v Bewicke (1795) 126 ER 697, 2 Hy Bl 551 5
Deichland, The [1990] 1 QB 361, [1989] 2 All ER 1066, [1989] 3 WLR 478, [1989] 2
    Lloyd's Rep 113, 133 Sol Jo 596, (1989) Times, 27 April
    .... 92, 96–97, 190
Delantera Amadora SA v Bristol Channel Shiprepairers Ltd and Swansea Dry Dock Co,
    The Katingaki [1976] 2 Lloyd's Rep 372 974
Demosthenes, The (1926) 26 Ll L Rep 99, P, D and Admlty
    855
Denise (The) (Owners) v The Denise (Charterers). See Vessel SA v CP Ships (UK) Ltd
Despatch, The (1860) Lush 98, 14 Moo PCC 83, 167 ER 51, 3 LT 219, PC
    736
Despina R, The. See Eleftherotria (Owners) v Despina R (Owners), The Despina R
Det Forenede Dampskibs Selskab v Barry Rly Co (1919) 1 Ll L Rep 658
    600
Deval Denizeilik VE Ticaret AS v Oceantrade Corp [2007] EWHC 2372 (Comm), [2008] 1
    All ER (Comm) 673, [2008] 1 Lloyd's Rep 450, [2007] ArbLR 50, [2007] All ER (D)
    272 (Oct) 964
Devonshire (Owners) v Barge Leslie (Owners). See Seacombe, The
Devonshire, The [1912] P 21, 81 LJP 36, 12 Asp MLC 137, 56 Sol Jo 140, 106 LT 241, 28
    TLR 107, CA; affd sub nom Devonshire (Owners) v Barge Leslie (Owners) [1912] AC
    610, 12 Asp MLC 210, 107 LT 179, 28 TLR 551, sub nom The Devonshire 81 LJP
    94, 57 Sol Jo 10, HL 183
Devonshire, The [1952] 2 Lloyd's Rep 95. See Mortiboys v Skinner, The Devonshire
Devonshire, The 81 LJP 94. See Seacombe, The
Devonshire, The and St Winifred [1913] P 13, 82 LJP 61, 12 Asp MLC 314, 108 LT 427,
    29 TLR 86, P, D and Admlty 600
Dewell v Moxon (1808) 1 Taunt 391, 127 ER 885 431
Diana, SS v SS Clieveden, The Clieveden [1894] AC 625, 64 LJPC 22, 6 R 515, 10 TLR
    589, PC 700
Diana, The (1874) 2 Asp MLC 366, 31 LT 203 814
Dickinson v Kitchen (1858) 8 E & B 789, 120 ER 293, sub nom Kitchen v Irvine 28 LJQB
    46, 5 Jur NS 118 .... 321, 328, 330, 333
Dictator, The [1892] P 304, 61 LJP 73, 7 Asp MLC 251, 67 LT 563, P, D and Admlty
    .... 83, 92, 811
Dictator, The [1892] P 64, 61 LJP 72, 7 Asp MLC 175, [1891–4] All ER Rep 360, 67 LT
    863, P, D and Admlty 160
Diplock v Blackburn (1811) 3 Camp 43, 170 ER 1300 429
Dirphys (Owners) v Soya (Owners), The Soya. See Soya, The
Disperser, The [1920] P 228, 89 LJP 257, 15 Asp MLC 112, 123 LT 683, 36 TLR 578, P,
    D and Admlty 152–153, 199, 1013
Dixon v Sadler (1839) 9 LJ Ex 48, 5 M & W 405, 151 ER 172, Exch Ct; affd sub nom
    Sadler v Dixon (1841) 11 LJ Ex 435, 8 M & W 895, 151 ER 1303, Ex Ch
    603
Djerada, The [1976] 2 Lloyd's Rep 40, CA 771
Dobson v Wilson (1813) 3 Camp 480, 170 ER 1453, NP
    133
Doeg v Trist (1897) 2 Com Cas 153, 13 TLR 320 238
Dolabella, The (1944) 77 Ll L Rep 292, P, D and Admlty
    204
Domby, The (1941) 69 Ll L Rep 161, P, D and Admlty 871
Domett v Young (1842) Car & M 465, 174 ER 591, NP
    439
Domira, The (1913) 29 TLR 557, P, D and Admlty; affd (1914) 30 TLR 521, CA
    118
Don Ricardo, The (1880) 5 PD 121, 49 LJP 28, 4 Asp MLC 225, 28 WR 431, 42 LT 32, P,
    D and Admlty 174
Donkin v Hastie (1897) 61 JP 568 510
Dora, The [1919] P 105, 88 LJP 107, 35 TLR 288, P, D and Admlty
    .... 3, 86, 240
Dormont v Furness Rly Co (1883) 11 QBD 496, 47 JP 711, 52 LJQB 331, 5 Asp MLC
    127, 49 LT 134 945
Dorothy Foster, The (1805) 6 Ch Rob 88, 165 ER 860 889

PARA

Douglas, The (1882) 7 PD 151, 51 LJP 89, 5 Asp MLC 15, 47 LT 502, CA
.... 763, 787, 945

Doward v Lindsay, The William Lindsay (1873) LR 5 PC 338, 2 Asp MLC 118, 22 WR 6,
29 LT 355, PC 733, 735, 760, 789

Dowell v General Steam Navigation Co (1855) 5 E & B 195, 26 LJQB 59, 1 Jur NS 800, 3
WR 492, 119 ER 454, 3 CLR 1221, 25 LTOS 158 770

Dowthorpe, The (1843) 2 Wm Rob 73, 7 Jur 609, 166 ER 682, 3 LT 341, 2 Notes of
Cases 264, HC 321, 970

Doyle v Dallas (1831) 1 Mood & R 48, 174 ER 17 438

Dredger No 9 (Owners) v Wheatear (1920) 3 Ll L Rep 229, P, D and Admlty
.... 700

Dresser UK Ltd v Falcongate Freight Management Ltd, The Duke of Yare [1992] QB 502,
[1992] 2 All ER 450, [1992] 2 WLR 319, [1991] 2 Lloyd's Rep 557, (1991) Times, 8
August, 135 Sol Jo LB 126 .... 99, 154, 918

Droege v Suart, The Karnak. See Karnak, The
Drury and Hudson, Re, ex p Leslie (1833) 3 LJ Bcy 4 244

Dry Bulk Handy Holding Inc v Fayette International Holdings Ltd [2013] EWCA Civ 184,
[2013] 1 WLR 3440, [2013] 2 All ER (Comm) 295, [2013] 2 Lloyd's Rep 38, [2013]
All ER (D) 137 (Mar) 964

Duc d'Aumale (No 2), The [1904] P 60, 73 LJP 8, 9 Asp MLC 502, 52 WR 319, [1900–3]
All ER Rep 510, 89 LT 486, 20 TLR 14, P, D and Admlty
.... 865

Duchesse de Brabant, The (1857) Sw 264, 6 WR 329, 166 ER 1129, 30 LTOS 282
.... 172

Duke of Buccleuch, The (1889) 15 PD 86, 36 Sol Jo 394, 62 LT 94, 6 TLR 99, CA
.... 205

Duke of Cornwall, The (1862) Pritchard's Admiralty Dig (3rd edn) 226
.... 741

Duke of Manchester, The. See Shersby v Hibbert, The Duke of Manchester
Duke of Sussex, The (1841) 1 Wm Rob 270, 166 ER 573, 5 LT 558, 1 Notes of Cases 161
.... 742

Duke of Yare, The. See Dresser UK Ltd v Falcongate Freight Management Ltd, The Duke
of Yare

Duna, The (1860) 12 Ir Jur 384 736
Duna, The (1861) 1 Mar LC 159 977
Dunbeth, The [1897] P 133, 66 LJP 66, 8 Asp MLC 284, 76 LT 658, P, D and Admlty
.... 437

Dundee (1821) Times, 5 December 758
Dundee, The (1823) 1 Hag Adm 109, 166 ER 39 .... 760, 793, 968
Dunelm, The (1884) 9 PD 164, 53 LJP 81, 5 Asp MLC 304, 32 WR 970, 51 LT 214, CA
.... 692, 720

Dunn v Bucknall Bros [1902] 2 KB 614, 71 LJKB 963, 9 Asp MLC 336, 8 Com Cas 33, 51
WR 100, [1900–3] All ER Rep 131, 87 LT 497, 18 TLR 807, CA
.... 808

Dunottar Castle, The [1902] WN 70, P, D and Admlty 867
Dunstanborough, The [1892] P 363n, P, D and Admlty 733, 746, 756, 769
Dupleix, The [1912] P 8, 81 LJP 9, 12 Asp MLC 122, 106 LT 347, 27 TLR 577, P, D and
Admlty 92, 208, 811

Duranty v Hart, The Hamburg (Cargo Ex) (1864) Brown & Lush 253, 2 Moo PCCNS
289, 33 LJPM & A 116, 10 Jur NS 600, 2 Mar LC 1, 12 WR 628, 167 ER 362, 10
LT 206 436

D'Vora, The, Socony Bunker Oil Co Ltd v SS D'Vora of Haifa (Owners) [1952] 2 All ER
1127, [1952] 2 Lloyd's Rep 404, 97 Sol Jo 11, sub nom Secony Bunker Oil Co Ltd v
SS D'Vora (Owners), The D'Vora [1953] 1 WLR 34, P, D and Admlty
.... 126

Dwina, The [1892] P 58, 61 LJP 71, 7 Asp MLC 173, 66 LT 862, P, D and Admlty
.... 143, 204, 893, 895

E

EK, The [1966] 1 Lloyd's Rep 440, P, D and Admlty 204
EU, The (1853) 1 Ecc & Ad 63 .... 863, 910
Earl of Eglinton, The (1855) Sw 7, 166 ER 989, 8 LT 178
.... 892

PARA

Earl Spencer, The (1875) LR 4 A & E 431, 2 Asp MLC 523, 23 WR 661, 32 LT 370, P, D
and Admlty; affd (1875) 3 Asp MLC 4, 33 LT 235, PC 739
Earle v Rowcroft (1805) 8 East 126, 103 ER 292, [1803–13] All ER Rep 166
.... 428, 1185
Earle's Shipbuilding and Engineering Co Ltd v Aktieselskabet D/S Gefion and Forth
Shipbuilding and Engineering Co Ltd (1922) 10 Ll L Rep 305, CA
.... 974
East India Co v Ekines (1718) 2 Bro Parl Cas 382, 1 ER 1011
.... 438
Eastern Belle, The (1875) 3 Asp MLC 19, 33 LT 214 321
Eastern Monarch, The (1860) Lush 81, 167 ER 43, 8 LT 441
.... 855
Ebor Jewel, The (1949) 83 Ll L Rep 64, P, D and Admlty
.... 899
Eclipse, The (1862) Lush 410, 31 LJPM & A 201, 8 Jur NS 315, 1 Mar LC 192, 10 WR
431, 15 ER 493, 6 LT 6, sub nom Hamburgh American Steam Navigation Co v North
of Scotland Banking Co, The Eclipse and The Saxonia 15 Moo PCC 262, PC
.... 710
Edenmore, The [1893] P 79, 7 Asp MLC 334, 1 R 574, 41 WR 654, 69 LT 230, P, D and
Admlty 881, 883, 897, 899
Edina, The (1855) 4 WR 91 979
Edison Mariner, The [1955] 1 Lloyd's Rep 235, P, D and Admlty
.... 700
Edison, The. See Liesbosch, Dredger (Owners) v SS Edison (Owners)
Edmund Handcock (1929) Ltd v Furness-Houlder Argentine Lines Ltd, The Princesa. See
Princesa, The
Edward Cardwell, The. See Belfast Harbour Comrs v Lawther and Marine Investment
Society, The Edward Cardwell
Edwards v Havill (1853) 14 CB 107, 23 LJCP 8, 17 Jur 1103, 2 WR 12, 139 ER 45, 2
CLR 1343, 22 LTOS 87 432
Edwards v Quickenden and Forester [1939] P 261, 63 Ll L Rep 189, 108 LJP 128, 83 Sol
Jo 134, 55 TLR 583, P, D and Admlty 110, 229
Edwin, The (1864) Brown & Lush 281, 33 LJPM & A 197, 2 Mar LC 36, 2 New Rep
382, 12 WR 992, 167 ER 365, 10 LT 658 970
Effort, The (1834) 3 Hag Adm 165, 166 ER 367 891
Effort, The (1847) 5 Notes of Cases 279 755
Effra, The. See Yvonne, The and The Effra
Efthimis, The. See Hawke Bay Shipping Co Ltd v The First National Bank of Chicago, The
Efthimis, Pavlina, Titika P and Juvena
Eglantine, Credo and Inez, The [1990] 2 Lloyd's Rep 390, CA
.... 771, 774
Egyptian, The (1864) 2 Mar LC 56, 10 LT 910 794–795
Egyptian, The. See Bibby v Boissevain, The Egyptian
Egyptienne, The (1825) 1 Hag Adm 346n 240
El Amria, The. See Aratra Potato Co Ltd v Egyptian Navigation Co, The El Amria
El Argentino [1909] P 236, 78 LJP 102, 11 Asp MLC 280, 101 LT 80, 25 TLR 518, P, D
and Admlty 331–332
El Oso, The (1925) 21 Ll L Rep 340, 16 Asp MLC 530, 133 LT 269, P, D and Admlty
.... 183–184
El Uruguayo (1928) 30 Ll L Rep 118, P, D and Admlty 204
Eland, The, The Eland and The Monte Urquiola [1969] 2 Lloyd's Rep 328, P, D and
Admlty 204
Elderslie Steamship Co v Borthwick [1905] AC 93, 74 LJKB 338, 10 Asp MLC 24, 10
Com Cas 109, 53 WR 401, 92 LT 274, 21 TLR 277, HL
.... 600
Eleanor, The v The Alma (1865) 2 Mar LC 240, Holt Adm 259
.... 744
Eleanor, The (1805) 6 Ch Rob 39, 165 ER 842 80
Eleftheria (Owners of Cargo lately laden on board ship or vessel) v Eleftheria, The
(Owners), The Eleftheria [1970] P 94, [1969] 2 All ER 641, [1969] 2 WLR 1073,
[1969] 1 Lloyd's Rep 237, 113 Sol Jo 407, P, D and Admlty
.... 102
Eleftherotria (Owners) v Despina R (Owners), The Despina R [1979] AC 685, [1979] 1 All
ER 421, [1978] 3 WLR 804, [1979] 1 Lloyd's Rep 1, 122 Sol Jo 758, HL
.... 207, 800

PARA

Eleonore, The (1863) Brown & Lush 185, 33 LJPM & A 19, 1 Mar LC 400, 3 New Rep
  95, 12 WR 218, 167 ER 328, 9 LT 397 143
Elin, The (1882) 8 PD 39, 5 Asp MLC 120, P, D and Admlty; on appeal (1883) 8 PD 129,
  52 LJP 55, 5 Asp MLC 120, 31 WR 736, 49 LT 87, CA
  .... 975–977, 979, 981–982
Elise, The [1899] WN 54 911
Elise, The (1859) Sw 436, 166 ER 1203 885
Eliza, The (1823) 1 Hag Adm 182, 166 ER 65 510
Eliza, The (1833) 3 Hag Adm 87, 166 ER 338 980
Eliza, The (1862) Lush 536, 1 Mar LC 251, 167 ER 242, 7 LT 257
  855
Elizabeth and Jane, The (1841) 1 Wm Rob 278, 166 ER 576, 1 Notes of Cases 177
  240
Elizabeth, The (1870) 3 Mar LC 345, 22 LT 74 .... 733, 762
Elkhound, The (1931) 39 Ll L Rep 15, P, D and Admlty
  855
Ella Constance, The (1864) 33 LJPM & A 189 861
Ella, The [1915] P 111, 84 LJKB 97, 30 TLR 566, P, D and Admlty
  110
Ellerman Lines Ltd v Murray [1931] AC 126, 36 Com Cas 159, [1930] All ER Rep 503,
  sub nom The Croxteth Hall, The Celtic 100 LJP 25, 18 Asp MLC 184, 144 LT 441,
  47 TLR 147, HL 487
Elliott Steam Tug Co Ltd v Admiralty Comrs [1921] 1 AC 137, 89 LJKB 977, 15 Asp
  MLC 81, 64 Sol Jo 634, 123 LT 754, HL 867
Ellora, The (1862) Lush 550, 167 ER 249 855
Elmville, The [1904] P 319, 9 Asp MLC 606, 91 LT 151, sub nom Ceylon Coaling Co v
  Goodrich 73 LJP 104, P, D and Admlty 429
Elmville, The (No 2) [1904] P 422, 73 LJP 120, 10 Asp MLC 23, 53 WR 287, 91 LT 330,
  20 TLR 783, P, D and Admlty 971
Elpis, The (1872) LR 4 A & E 1, 42 LJ Adm 43, 1 Asp MLC 472, 21 WR 576, 27 LT 664,
  HC 983
Elswick Park, The [1904] P 76, 72 LJP 79, 9 Asp MLC 481, 89 LT 217, P, D and Admlty
  862
Elton, The [1891] P 265, 60 LJP 69, 7 Asp MLC 66, 39 WR 703, 65 LT 232, 7 TLR 434,
  P, D and Admlty 204, 866, 876, 914
Emanuel v Soltykoff (1892) 8 TLR 331, CA 204
Emerald, The, The Greta Holme [1896] P 192, 65 LJP 69, 8 Asp MLC 138, 74 LT 645,
  CA; revsd sub nom No 7 Steam Sand Pump Dredger (Owners) v Greta Holme
  (Owners), The Greta Holme [1897] AC 596, 66 LJP 166, 8 Asp MLC 317, [1895–9]
  All ER Rep 127, 77 LT 231, 13 TLR 552, HL 798, 806
Emilie Galline, The [1903] P 106, 72 LJP 39, 9 Asp MLC 401, 88 LT 743, P, D and
  Admlty 813, 855, 866, 871
Emilie Millon, The [1905] 2 KB 817, 75 LJKB 31, 10 Asp MLC 162, 93 LT 692, CA
  .... 178, 975, 982
Emily Charlotte v Newona (1920) 4 Ll L Rep 156, P, D and Admlty
  600
Emlyn, The [1918] P 67, 87 LJP 62, 14 Asp MLC 329, 119 LT 156, P, D and Admlty
  5
Emmanuel Colocotronis (No 2), The. See Astro Valiente Compania Naviera SA v Pakistan
  Ministry of Food and Agriculture (No 2), The Emmanuel Colocotronis (No 2)
Emmy Haase, The (1884) 9 PD 81, 53 LJP 43, 5 Asp MLC 216, 32 WR 880, 50 LT 372,
  P, D and Admlty 727, 762
Emperor, The and The Lady of the Lake (1865) 3 Mar LC App 50, Holt Adm 37, PC
  710
Empress Eugenie, The (1860) Lush 138, 167 ER 66 .... 143, 798
Empress of Britain, The (1913) 29 TLR 423, P, D and Admlty
  796
Empusa, The (1879) 5 PD 6, 48 LJP 36, 4 Asp MLC 185, 28 WR 263, 41 LT 383, P, D
  and Admlty 148
Enchantress, The (1860) Lush 93, 30 LJPM & A 15, 167 ER 49, 2 LT 574
  .... 119, 904–905
Endeavour, The (1890) 6 Asp MLC 511, 62 LT 840, P, D and Admlty
  800
Energy, The (1870) LR 3 A & E 48, 39 LJ Adm 25, 3 Mar LC 503, 18 WR 1009, 23 LT
  601, HC 599, 742

                                                                                          PARA
England, The (1886) 12 PD 32, 56 LJP 115, 6 Asp MLC 140, 35 WR 367, 56 LT 896, P,
    D and Admlty 240
Englishman, The and The Australia [1894] P 239, 63 LJP 133, 7 Asp MLC 603, 6 R 743,
    43 WR 62, 70 LT 846, P, D and Admlty 774, 784
Enterprises of Panama Inc, SS, Liverpool (Owners) v Ousel (Owners), The Liverpool (No 2)
    [1963] P 64, [1960] 3 All ER 307, [1960] 3 WLR 597, [1960] 2 Lloyd's Rep 66, 104
    Sol Jo 824, CA 798
Erato, The (1888) 13 PD 163, 57 LJP 107, 6 Asp MLC 334, 59 LT 840, P, D and Admlty
    .... 855, 886, 892
Erna, The (1927) 27 Ll L Rep 170, P, D and Admlty 183
Esk, The (1869) LR 2 A & E 350, 38 LJ Adm 33, 3 Mar LC 242, 17 WR 1064, 20 LT
    587, HC 720
Esk, The, and The Niord (1870) LR 3 PC 436, 7 Moo PCCNS 276, 1 Asp MLC 1, 24 LT
    167, PC 705
Espanoleto, The [1920] P 223, 90 LJP 32, 15 Asp MLC 287, 125 LT 121, 36 TLR 554, P,
    D and Admlty 152, 1013
Esrom, The and The Hopper Wills No 66 [1914] WN 81, P, D and Admlty
    204
Essarts v Whinney (1903) 9 Asp MLC 363, 88 LT 191, 19 TLR 235, CA
    332
Esso Bernicia, The. See Esso Petroleum Co Ltd v Hall Russell & Co Ltd and Shetland
    Islands Council, The Esso Bernicia
Esso Malaysia, The, Cox v The Esso Malaysia (Owners) [1975] QB 198, [1974] 2 All ER
    705, [1974] 3 WLR 341, [1974] 2 Lloyd's Rep 143, 118 Sol Jo 681
    792
Esso Petroleum Co Ltd v Hall Russell & Co Ltd and Shetland Islands Council, The Esso
    Bernicia [1989] AC 643, [1989] 1 All ER 37, [1988] 3 WLR 730, [1989] 1 Lloyd's
    Rep 8, 132 Sol Jo 1459, HL 578, 589
Esso Petroleum Co Ltd v Southport Corpn. See Southport Corpn v Esso Petroleum Co Ltd
Ettrick, The. See Prehn v Bailey, The Ettrick
Eugene, The (1834) 3 Hag Adm 166, 166 ER 364 910
Eugenie, The (1844) 3 Notes of Cases 430 861
Europa, The (1850) 14 Jur 627; on appeal (1851) Pritchard's Admiralty Digest (3rd Edn)
    223 .... 739–740, 788
Europa, The. See Dean v Richards, The Europa
European and Australian Royal Mail Co Ltd v Peninsular and Oriental Steam Navigation
    Co (1866) 12 Jur NS 909, 2 Mar LC 351, 14 WR 843, 14 LT 704
    229
European and Australian Royal Mail Co Ltd v Royal Mail Steam Packet Co (1858) 4 K &
    J 676, 5 Jur NS 310, 70 ER 281 333
European Commission v Hellenic Republic: C-45/07 [2009] ECR I-701, [2009] 2 CMLR
    995, [2009] 1 Lloyd's Rep 425, ECJ 12
European Gateway, The [1987] QB 206, [1986] 3 WLR 756, [1986] 2 Lloyd's Rep 265,
    130 Sol Jo 748, [1986] LS Gaz R 3253, sub nom The Speedlink Vanguard and The
    European Gateway [1986] 3 All ER 554 828
European, The (1885) 10 PD 99, 54 LJP 61, 5 Asp MLC 417, 33 WR 937, 52 LT 868, P,
    D and Admlty 757
Eurymedon, The [1938] P 41, 59 Ll L Rep 214, 107 LJP 81, 19 Asp MLC 170, 82 Sol Jo
    52, 158 LT 445, 54 TLR 272, sub nom Corstar (Owners) v Eurymedon (Owners), The
    Eurymedon [1938] 1 All ER 122, CA 736, 752, 769–770
Eurymedon, The (1942) 73 Ll L Rep 217, HL 220
Euxine, The (1871) LR 4 PC 8, 8 Moo PCCNS 189, 41 LJ Adm 17, 40, 1 Asp MLC 155,
    20 WR 561, 17 ER 283, 25 LT 516, PC 159
Eva v Knuthenborg (1921) 9 Ll L Rep 494, P, D and Admlty
    789
Eva, The [1921] P 454, 8 Ll L Rep 268, 315, 91 LJP 17, 15 Asp MLC 424, 126 LT 223,
    37 TLR 920, P, D and Admlty 169, 981, 983
Evangelismos, The (1858) 12 Moo PCC 352, Sw 378, 166 ER 1174, PC
    235
Ever Success, The [1999] 1 Lloyd's Rep 824, [1998] All ER (D) 73
    .... 127, 970
Everard v Kendall (1870) LR 5 CP 428, 39 LJCP 234, 3 Mar LC 391, 18 WR 892, 22 LT
    408 .... 110, 229, 690
Evje, The [1960] 2 Lloyd's Rep 221, P, D and Admlty 694

PARA

Evpo Agnic, The [1988] 3 All ER 810, [1988] 1 WLR 1090, [1988] 2 Lloyd's Rep 411,
132 Sol Jo 1299, (1988) Times, 21 July 93, 158, 161
Ewell Grove, The (1835) 3 Hag Adm 209 886
Excelsior, The (1868) LR 2 A & E 268, 37 LJ Adm 54, 3 Mar LC 151, 19 LT 87, HC
.... 732, 735, 755, 759, 765, 785
Exeter, The (1799) 1 Ch Rob 173, 165 ER 139 .... 976, 980
Expert, The (1877) 3 Asp MLC 381, 36 LT 258, P, D and Admlty
.... 148
Ezardian, The [1911] P 92, 80 LJP 81, 11 Asp MLC 602, 104 LT 400, P, D and Admlty
.... 748

F

F D Lambert, The [1917] P 232n, 14 Asp MLC 278, 119 LT 119, P, D and Admlty
.... 118, 855, 868
F J Wolfe, The [1946] P 91, 79 Ll L Rep 111, 115 LJP 54, 90 Sol Jo 187, 174 LT 245, 62
TLR 118, sub nom A-G v Anglo-American Oil Co Ltd, The F J Wolfe [1946] 1 All ER
359, CA 5
Faedrelandet, The [1895] P 205, 64 LJP 122, 8 Asp MLC 1, 72 LT 650, CA
.... 710, 720
Fagernes, The [1927] P 311, 96 LJP 183, 17 Asp MLC 326, 71 Sol Jo 634, 138 LT 30, 43
TLR 746, CA 121
Fagerstrand, The (1929) 33 Ll L Rep 67, P, D and Admlty
.... 762
Fairlie, The (1868) 37 LJ Adm 66 333
Fairplay XIV, The [1939] P 57, 62 Ll L Rep 108, 108 LJP 65, 55 TLR 80, P, D and Admlty
.... 152, 189, 1013
Fairport (No 3), The [1966] 2 Lloyd's Rep 253, P, D and Admlty
.... 130
Fairport (No 4), The, Vogiatzis v Owners of SS Fairport (Moschakis intervening) [1967] 2
All ER 914n, [1967] 1 WLR 964, [1967] 1 Lloyd's Rep 602, 111 Sol Jo 584, P, D and
Admlty 171, 178
Fairport (No 5), The [1967] 2 Lloyd's Rep 162, P, D and Admlty
.... 126
Fairport, The [1912] P 168, 81 LJP 108, 12 Asp MLC 165, 106 LT 382, P, D and Admlty
.... 899
Fairport, The (1882) 8 PD 48, 52 LJP 21, 5 Asp MLC 62, 31 WR 616, 48 LT 536, P, D
and Admlty 970, 991
Fairport, The (1884) 10 PD 13, 54 LJP 3, 5 Asp MLC 348, 32 WR 448, 52 LT 62, P, D
and Admlty 130, 333
Fairport, The. See Vogiatzis v SS Fairport, The Fairport
Falcke v Scottish Imperial Insurance Co (1886) 34 Ch D 234, 56 LJ Ch 707, 35 WR 143,
56 LT 220, 3 TLR 141, CA 866, 969
Falcon, The [1981] 1 Lloyd's Rep 13 .... 162, 164, 175, 178
Falkland, The (1863) Brown & Lush 204, 9 Jur NS 1113, 1 Mar LC 367, 167 ER 337, 9
LT 1, sub nom Grindley v Stevens, The Falkland and The Navigator 1 Moo PCCNS
379, PC 744
Fanchon, The (1880) 5 PD 173, 50 LJP 4, 4 Asp MLC 272, 29 WR 399, 42 LT 483, P, D
and Admlty 329
Fancy, The [1917] P 13, 86 LJP 38, 13 Asp MLC 603, 116 LT 224, 33 TLR 153, P, D and
Admlty 707
Fanny M Carvill (Owners) v Peru (Owners), The Fanny M Carvill (1875) 13 App Cas
455n, 2 Asp MLC 565, 24 WR 62, 32 LT 646, 44 LJ Admin 34, PC
.... 769
Fanny, The (1883) 5 Asp MLC 75, 48 LT 771, CA 428
Farnley Hall, The (1881) 4 Asp MLC 499, 46 LT 216, CA
.... 897
Father Thames, The [1979] 2 Lloyd's Rep 364 .... 92, 782, 964
Faust, The. See Burn v Herlofson and Siemensen, The Faust
Favorite, The (1844) 2 Wm Rob 255, 166 ER 751, 2 LTOS 405
.... 855, 870
Favourite, The (1799) 2 Ch Rob 232, 165 ER 299 425
Fehmarn, The [1958] 1 All ER 333, [1958] 1 WLR 159, [1957] 2 Lloyd's Rep 551, 102 Sol
Jo 123, CA 111

PARA

Feliza, The Whitwell v Perren. See Whitwell v Perrin

Fenham, SS (Owners) v Wake and Wake, The Fenham (1870) LR 3 PC 212, 6 Moo PCCNS
    501, 3 Mar LC 484, 16 ER 815, 23 LT 329, [1861–73] All ER Rep Ext 1687, PC
    694

Fenham, The. See Fenham, SS (Owners) v Wake and Wake, The Fenham

Fenix, The v The Mobile. See Mobile, The

Fenton v City of Dublin Steam Packet Co (1838) 8 Ad & El 835, 8 LJQB 28, 2 Jur 1087,
    1 Per & Dav 103, 1 Will Woll & H 628, 112 ER 1054 782

Fenton v J Thorley & Co Ltd [1903] AC 443, 72 LJKB 787, 52 WR 81, 5 WCC 1, 89 LT
    314, 19 TLR 684, [1900–3] All ER Rep Ext 1161, HL 1187

Ferdinand Retzlaff, The [1972] 2 Lloyd's Rep 120 .... 204, 801–803

Ferguson, ex p (1871) LR 6 QB 280, 35 JP 468, 40 LJQB 105, 1 Asp MLC 8, 19 WR 746,
    24 LT 96 229

Feronia, The v The Northampton. See Northampton, The

Feronia, The (1868) LR 2 A & E 65, 37 LJ Adm 60, 3 Mar LC 54, 16 WR 585, 17 LT
    619, HC 321, 981

Ferret, The. See Phillips v Highland Rly Co, The Ferret

Festive Holidays Ltd v demise charterers of the Ocean Glory. See The Ocean Glory

Fina Canada, The [1962] 2 Lloyd's Rep 445, CA 220, 222, 758

Firethorn, The (1948) 81 Ll L Rep 178, P, D and Admlty
    852

Fish & Fish Ltd v Sea Shepherd UK [2011] CSOH 122, 2012 SLT 156, 2011 Scot (D) 17/8,
    OH 110

Fisher v CHT Ltd [1965] 2 All ER 601, [1965] 1 WLR 1093, 109 Sol Jo 612
    204

Fiumana, The (1931) 39 Ll L Rep 32, P, D and Admlty 700

Five Steel Barges (1890) 15 PD 142, 6 Asp MLC 580, 63 LT 499, sub nom Steel Barges 59
    LJP 77, 39 WR 127, P, D and Admlty 84, 116, 866, 871, 874, 914

Flecha, The (1854) 1 Ecc & Ad 438, 164 ER 252, 3 LT 58
    432

Fleece, The (1850) 3 Wm Rob 278, 166 ER 966, 7 Notes of Cases 534
    .... 874, 888, 910–911

Fletcher v Braddick (1806) 2 Bos & PNR 182, 127 ER 593
    429

Fletcher and Campbell v City Marine Finance Ltd [1968] 2 Lloyd's Rep 520
    327

Flora, The (1866) LR 1 A & E 45, 35 LJ Adm 15, 2 Mar LC 325, 14 LT 192
    811

Flore, The (1929) 34 Ll L Rep 172, P, D and Admlty 855

Florence, The (1852) 16 Jur 572, 19 LTOS 304 .... 510, 869

Flower and Everett Ltd v Thomas W Hughan & Co, The Aralia (1949) 82 Ll L Rep 884, P,
    D and Admlty 757

Flying Fish, The. See Anderson v Hoen, The Flying Fish

Flying Serpent, The, The Niobe. See Niobe, The

Forfarshire, The [1908] P 339, 78 LJP 44, 11 Asp MLC 158, 99 LT 587, P, D and Admlty
    600

Forman & Co Pty Ltd v The Liddesdale [1900] AC 190, 69 LJPC 44, 9 Asp MLC 45, 82
    LT 331, PC 428

Fornjot, The (1907) 24 TLR 26, P, D and Admlty 160

Fortunity, The, Motor Cruiser Four of Hearts (Owners) v Fortunity (Owners) [1960] 2 All
    ER 64, [1961] 1 WLR 351, [1960] 1 Lloyd's Rep 252, 105 Sol Jo 159, P, D and
    Admlty 796

Fowles v Eastern and Australian Steamship Co Ltd [1916] 2 AC 556, 13 Asp MLC 447,
    115 LT 354, 32 TLR 663, [1916–17] All ER Rep Ext 1370, PC
    576

Frances (Ketch) (Owners) v Highland Loch (Owners), The Highland Loch [1912] AC 312,
    81 LJP 30, 12 Asp MLC 106, 49 SLR 691, 106 LT 81, 28 TLR 213, HL
    .... 731, 763

Frankfort, The [1910] P 50, 79 LJP 49, 11 Asp MLC 326, 101 LT 664, CA
    .... 749, 769

Frankland, The [1901] P 161, 70 LJP 42, 9 Asp MLC 196, 84 LT 395, 17 TLR 419, P, D
    and Admlty 775

Franklin v Hosier (1821) 4 B & Ald 341, 4 B & Ald 342, 106 ER 962
    974

PARA

Frans Maas Logistics (UK) Ltd v CDR Trucking BV [1999] 1 All ER (Comm) 737, [1999]
    2 Lloyd's Rep 179, [1999] Lexis Citation 2550, [1999] All ER (D) 322
    99
Fraser v Equatorial Shipping Co Ltd and Equatorial Lines Ltd, The Ijaola [1979] 1 Lloyd's
    Rep 103 974
Fraser and Weller v Oceanic Steam Navigation Co (No 2). See Olympic, The
Fraser and White Ltd v Vernon [1951] 2 Lloyd's Rep 175
    597
Frazer v Cuthbertson (1880) 6 QBD 93, 50 LJQB 277, 29 WR 396
    .... 238, 244, 780
Frazer v Hatton (1857) 22 JP 114, 2 CBNS 512, 26 LJCP 226, 3 Jur NS 694, 5 WR 632,
    140 ER 516, 30 LTOS 165 471
Freeman v East India Co (1822) 5 B & Ald 617, 1 Dow & Ry KB 234, 106 ER 1316
    443
Freightline One, The [1986] 1 Lloyd's Rep 266 .... 173, 178
Fremantle, The [1954] 2 Lloyd's Rep 20, P, D and Admlty
    143
Friedeberg, The (1885) 10 PD 112, 54 LJP 75, 5 Asp MLC 426, 33 WR 687, 52 LT 837,
    CA 148
Friesland, The [1904] P 345, 73 LJP 121, 10 Asp MLC 9, 91 LT 324, 20 TLR 699, P, D
    and Admlty 885
Frisia, The [1960] 1 Lloyd's Rep 90, CA 886, 900
Fritz Thyssen, The. See Mitera Marigo (M/V) (Owners) v M/V Fritz Thyssen (Owners), The
    Fritz Thyssen
Front Ace, The (Owners) v Ship Vicky 1, The (Owners) [2008] EWCA Civ 101, [2008] 2
    All ER (Comm) 42, [2008] 2 Lloyd's Rep 45, [2008] All ER (D) 377 (Feb)
    804
Frosta, The [1973] 2 Lloyd's Rep 348 703
Fulham, The [1898] P 206, 67 LJP 78, 8 Asp MLC 425, 47 WR 62, 79 LT 127, 14 TLR
    507, P, D and Admlty; on appeal [1899] P 251, 68 LJP 75, 8 Asp MLC 559, 47 WR
    598, 43 Sol Jo 568, 81 LT 19, 15 TLR 404, CA . 121, 123, 919, 936, 947, 949, 1161–1163
Funabashi, The, Sycamore Steamship Co Ltd v Owners of SS White Mountain [1972] 2 All
    ER 181, [1972] 1 WLR 666, 116 Sol Jo 120 147
Fusilier, The (1865) Brown & Lush 341 at 350, PC 896

                                                    G

Gaetano and Maria, The (1882) 7 PD 137, 51 LJP 67, 4 Asp MLC 535, 30 WR 766, 46
    LT 835, CA 2, 443
Galam, The (Cargo ex) (1863) Brown & Lush 167, 33 LJPM & A 97, sub nom Cleary v
    McAndrew (Cargo ex), The Galam 2 Moo PCCNS 216, 10 Jur NS 477, 1 Mar LC
    408, 3 New Rep 254, 12 WR 495, 15 ER 883, 9 LT 550, PC
    .... 889, 977, 979
Galatea, The (1858) 4 Jur NS 1064, Sw 349, 7 WR 21, 166 ER 1162, 32 LTOS 49
    871
Gananoque, The (1862) Lush 448, 167 ER 199 .... 424, 472
Ganges, The (1869) LR 2 A & E 370, 38 LJ Adm 61, 3 Mar LC 342, 22 LT 72, HC
    904
Gann v Brun, The Clarisse (1856) 12 Moo PCC 340, Sw 129, 14 ER 940, 166 ER 1056, 8
    LT 178, 582, PC 213, 900, 909–910
Gannet (Owners) v Algoa (Owners), The Gannet [1900] AC 234, 69 LJP 49, 9 Asp MLC
    43, 82 LT 329, HL 205, 220, 758
Gardner v Cazenove (1856) 1 H & N 423, 26 LJ Ex 17, 5 WR 195, 156 ER 1267, 172 ER
    175, 7 LT 339, Exch Ct 332
Garnum v Bennet (1728) 1 Barn KB 96, 2 Stra 816, 94 ER 67
    429
Gartland Steamship Co and Lablanc v R [1960] 1 Lloyd's Rep 388, Can SC
    .... 690, 771
Garvin v Bibby, The Florence Nightingale and The Maeander (1863) Brown & Lush 29, 1
    Moo PCCNS 63, 9 Jur NS 475, 1 Mar LC 301, 11 WR 542, 15 ER 627, 8 LT 34, PC
    700
Gas Float Whitton No 2, The [1896] P 42, 65 LJP 17, 8 Asp MLC 110, 44 WR 263, 73
    LT 698, CA; affd sub nom Wells v Gas Float Whitton No 2 (Owners), The Gas Float
    Whitton No 2 [1897] AC 337, 66 LJP 99, 8 Asp MLC 272, 76 LT 663, 13 TLR 422,
    HL 2, 82, 115, 139, 229, 850, 860, 923, 964, 969

PARA

Gatoil International Inc v Arkwright-Boston Manufacturers Mutual Insurance Co, The
Sandrina [1985] AC 255, [1985] 1 All ER 129, [1985] 2 WLR 74, [1985] 1 Lloyd's
Rep 181, 128 Sol Jo 870, 1985 SLT 68, HL 93, 111, 851, 926

Gaul, The (Department of the Environment, Transport and the Regions Marine Accident
Investigation Branch, Marine Accident Report 4/99, Report on the Underwater Survey
of the Stern Trawler GAUL H.243 and the supporting Model Experiments, August
1998–January 1999) unreported 223

Gaupen, The (1925) 22 Ll L Rep 57, [1925] WN 138, P, D and Admlty
.... 974, 990

Gay Tucan, The, Slater (Owner of Ship Gay Tucan) v Appleby (Trustee of Ship Gay Tucan)
[1968] 3 All ER 819, [1969] 1 WLR 163, [1968] 2 Lloyd's Rep 245, 113 Sol Jo 104,
P, D and Admlty 175, 177

Gazelle, The (1842) 1 Wm Rob 471, 7 Jur 497, 166 ER 648, 2 Notes of Cases 39
.... 205, 758

Gazelle, The (1844) 2 Wm Rob 279, 8 Jur 428, 166 ER 759, 3 Notes of Cases 75
.... 794, 804

Geestland, The [1980] 1 Lloyd's Rep 628 875

Gemma, The [1899] P 285, 68 LJP 110, 8 Asp MLC 585, [1895–9] All ER Rep 596, 81 LT
379, 15 TLR 529, CA 92, 208, 811

General Steam Navigation Co v Hedley, The Velocity (1869) LR 3 PC 44, 6 Moo PCCNS
263, 39 LJ Adm 20, 3 Mar LC 308, 18 WR 264, 16 ER 725, 21 LT 686, PC
.... 705

Generous, The (1868) LR 2 A & E 57, 37 LJ Adm 37, 3 Mar LC 40, 16 WR 519, 17 LT
552, HC 884

Georg, The [1894] P 330, 7 Asp MLC 476, 71 LT 22, P, D and Admlty
.... 177, 206, 882, 887, 976

George and Richard, The (1871) LR 3 A & E 466, 1 Asp MLC 50, 20 WR 245, 24 LT
717, HC 798

George Dean, The (1857) Sw 290, 6 WR 263, 166 ER 1143, 30 LTOS 220
.... 116, 887, 889, 906

George Gordon, The (1884) 9 PD 46, 53 LJP 28, 5 Asp MLC 216, 32 WR 596, 50 LT
371, P, D and Admlty 172

George Home, The (1825) 1 Hag Adm 370 510

George Roper, The (1883) 8 PD 119, 52 LJP 69, 5 Asp MLC 134, 31 WR 953, 49 LT 185,
P, D and Admlty 731

George, The (1845) 2 Wm Rob 386, 9 Jur 670, 166 ER 800, 4 Notes of Cases 161
.... 739

Gerda Toft, The [1953] 2 Lloyd's Rep 249, P, D and Admlty
.... 739

Germania, The [1904] P 131, 73 LJP 59, 9 Asp MLC 538, 90 LT 296, P, D and Admlty
.... 887

Gertor, The (1894) 7 Asp MLC 472, 70 LT 703, P, D and Admlty
.... 738, 763, 793

Gertrud, The (1927) 29 Ll L Rep 5, [1927] WN 265, 17 Asp MLC 343, 138 LT 239, 44
TLR 1, P, D and Admlty 165

Gertrude, The (1861) 30 LJPM & A 130 924

Gertrude, The (1888) 13 PD 105, 6 Asp MLC 315, 36 WR 616, 59 LT 251, 4 TLR 431,
CA 143

Giacinto Motta, The [1977] 2 Lloyd's Rep 221 776

Gilbert v Trinity House Corpn (1886) 17 QBD 795, 56 LJQB 85, 35 WR 30, 2 TLR 708,
DC 945

Gilbert Rowe, The. See Rowan Companies Inc and Rowan Drilling UK Ltd v Lanbert
Eggink Offshore Transport Consultants Vof Kirkstead Ltd and JCE Shipping Ltd, The
Gilbert Rowe

Gipsey King, The (1847) 2 Wm Rob 537, 11 Jur 357, 166 ER 858, 9 LTOS 131, 5 Notes
of Cases 282 .... 599, 735

Gipsy Queen, The [1895] P 176, 7 Asp MLC 586, 11 R 766, 43 WR 359, 39 Sol Jo 344,
72 LT 454, 11 TLR 296, CA 905–906

Girolamo, The (1834) 3 Hag Adm 169, 166 ER 368 736

Glannibanta, The (1876) 1 PD 283, 24 WR 1033, sub nom The Transit 3 Asp MLC 233, 2
Char Pr Cas 18, 34 LT 934, CA 220, 739, 758

Glascow Packet (or The Glasgow Packet) (1844) 2 Wm Rob 306, 8 Jur 674, 166 ER 770,
3 LTOS 263, 3 Notes of Cases 107 .... 911, 913

Glasgow, The (otherwise The Ya Macraw) (1856) 2 Jur NS 1147, Sw 145, 5 WR 10, 166
ER 1065, 28 LTOS 13 439

PARA

Glatton, HMS [1923] P 215, 16 Ll L Rep 273, 93 LJP 12, 39 TLR 690, P, D and Admlty
.... 234

Glaucus and City of Florence [1948] P 95, 81 Ll L Rep 131, 64 TLR 124, P, D and Admlty
.... 5

Glen Line Ltd v W J Guy & Sons, The Glenaffric [1948] P 159, [1948] LJR 1128, 92 Sol
Jo 111, sub nom W J Guy & Son v Glen Line Ltd [1948] 1 All ER 245, CA
.... 600

Glencore Grain Ltd v Agros Trading Co Ltd [1999] 2 All ER (Comm) 288, [1999] 2
Lloyd's Rep 410, [1999] 31 LS Gaz R 42, (1999) Times, 12 July, [1999] Lexis Citation
2202, [1999] All ER (D) 715 103

Glenduror, The. See Arnold v Cowie, The Glenduror

Glenfinlas, The [1918] P 363n, 14 Asp MLC 594n, [1918–19] All ER Rep 365n, 122 LT
655n 802

Glenfruin, The (1885) 10 PD 103, 54 LJP 49, 5 Asp MLC 413, 33 WR 826, [1881–5] All
ER Rep 461, 52 LT 769, P, D and Admlty 865

Glengariff, The [1905] P 106, 75 LJP 90, 10 Asp MLC 103, 53 WR 537, 93 LT 281, 21
TLR 299, P, D and Admlty 700

Glengarry, The (1874) 2 PD 235n, 43 LJ Adm 37, 2 Asp MLC 230, 23 WR 110, 30 LT
341 731

Glengyle, The [1898] P 97, 67 LJP 48, 8 Asp MLC 341, 46 WR 308, 42 Sol Jo 289, 78 LT
139, 14 TLR 231, CA; on appeal sub nom Glengyle, The (Owners), Her Cargo and
Freight v Neptune Salvage Co Ltd (Owners of The Hermes and Newa), The Glengyle
[1898] AC 519, 67 LJP 87, 8 Asp MLC 436, 78 LT 801, 14 TLR 522, HL
.... 881, 892, 900

Glenluce, The (1930) 170 LT Jo 399, P, D and Admlty 431

Glenmorven, The [1913] P 141, 82 LJP 113, 29 TLR 412, P, D and Admlty
.... 125, 871

Glider Standard Austria SH 1964, Re [1965] P 463, [1965] 2 All ER 1022, [1965] 3 WLR
568, [1965] 2 Lloyd's Rep 189, 109 Sol Jo 649, P, D and Admlty
.... 86, 104

Global Mariner v Atlantic Crusader [2005] EWHC 380 (Admlty), [2005] 2 All ER (Comm)
389, [2005] 1 Lloyd's Rep 699, [2005] NLJR 594, [2005] All ER (D) 21 (Apr)
.... 205

Globe, The (1848) 6 Notes of Cases 275 741

Glory, The (1849) 13 Jur 991, 166 ER 932 894

Glynn v Margetson & Co [1893] AC 351, 62 LJQB 466, 7 Asp MLC 366, 1 R 193,
[1891–4] All ER Rep 693, 69 LT 1, 9 TLR 437, HL 437

Glynoeron, The (1905) 21 TLR 648, P, D and Admlty 935, 1160

Gniezno, The. See Popi (Motor Vessel) (Owners) v SS Gniezno (Owners), The Gniezno

Godiva, The (1886) 11 PD 20, 55 LJP 13, 5 Asp MLC 524, 34 WR 551, 54 LT 55, P, D
and Admlty 183

Gold Shipping Navigation Co SA v Lulu Maritime Ltd [2009] EWHC 1365 (Admlty),
[2010] 2 All ER (Comm) 64, [2009] 2 Lloyd's Rep 484, [2009] All ER (D) 181 (Jun)
.... 152–153, 1013

Golden Trader, The [1975] QB 348, [1974] 2 All ER 686, [1974] 3 WLR 16, [1974] 1
Lloyd's Rep 378, 118 Sol Jo 441 175

Golondrina, The (1867) LR 1 A & E 334, HC 906

Good Herald, The [1987] 1 Lloyd's Rep 236 .... 95, 160

Gordon v Hare (1823) 1 LJOSKB 70 .... 429, 432

Gordon v Morley (1747) 2 Stra 1265, 93 ER 1171 5

Goring, The [1988] AC 831, [1988] 1 All ER 641, [1988] 2 WLR 460, [1988] 1 Lloyd's
Rep 397, 132 Sol Jo 334, [1988] 14 LS Gaz R 50, [1988] NLJR 61, (1988) Times, 26
February, HL 80, 115, 850–851, 863

Gorliz, The (1917) 14 Asp MLC 282, 119 LT 123, P, D and Admlty
.... 118

Gorm, The [1961] 1 Lloyd's Rep 196, P, D and Admlty 739

Goulandris Bros Ltd v B Goldman & Sons Ltd [1958] 1 QB 74, [1957] 3 All ER 100,
[1957] 2 WLR 596, [1957] 2 Lloyd's Rep 207, 101 Sol Jo 762
.... 133, 156

Goulandris, The [1927] P 182, 96 LJP 85, 17 Asp MLC 209, [1927] All ER Rep 592, 137
LT 90, 43 TLR 308, P, D and Admlty 883, 969, 991

Governor Raffles, The (1815) 2 Dods 14, 165 ER 1400, HC
.... 869

Graces, The (1844) 2 Wm Rob 294, 8 Jur 501, 166 ER 765, 3 LTOS 320
.... 883

PARA

Gracie (Owners) v Argentino (Owners), The Argentino. See Argentino, The

Graingers, No 4, The, British Oil and Cake Mills Ltd v John H Whitaker (Tankers) Ltd [1964] 3 All ER 705, [1964] 1 WLR 1474, [1964] 2 Lloyd's Rep 415, 108 Sol Jo 920, P, D and Admlty 183–184

Grand Union (Shipping) Ltd v London SS Owners' Mutual Insurance Association Ltd, The Bosworth (No 3) [1962] 1 Lloyd's Rep 483, 106 Sol Jo 689 .... 120, 864

Grant v Norway (1851) 10 CB 665, 20 LJCP 93, 15 Jur 296, 138 ER 263, 16 LTOS 504 .... 427–428, 431–432

Gratitudine, The (1801) 3 Ch Rob 240, 165 ER 450, [1775–1802] All ER Rep 283 .... 134, 435, 437

Great Eastern Steamship Co, Re, William's Claim (1885) 5 Asp MLC 511, 53 LT 594, [1881–5] All ER Rep Ext 1213 .... 243, 457

Great Eastern, The (1864) Brown & Lush 287. See Great Ship Co v Sharples, The Great Eastern

Great Eastern, The (1867) LR 1 A & E 384, 36 LJ Adm 15, 2 Mar LC 553, 17 LT 228, HC 130, 424, 970

Great Eastern, The (1868) LR 2 A & E 88, 3 Mar LC 58, 17 LT 667, HC 427

Great Pacific, The. See Stephens v Broomfield, The Great Pacific

Great Ship Co v Sharples, The Great Eastern (1864) Brown & Lush 287, 3 Moo PCCNS 31, 2 Mar LC 97, Holt Adm 167, 16 ER 12, 167 ER 368, 11 LT 5, PC 707, 740

Great Western Rly Co v Royal Norwegian Government [1945] 1 All ER 324, 78 Ll L Rep 152, 114 LJKB 337, 172 LT 228, 61 TLR 236 600

Green v Briggs (1848) 6 Hare 395, 17 LJ Ch 323, 12 Jur 326, 67 ER 1219, 11 LTOS 412 .... 238–239, 244

Green v Royal Exchange Assurance Co (1815) 6 Taunt 68, 1 Marsh 447, 128 ER 958 439

Gregerso, motor tug Bostonian, The (Owners) v motor ship Gregerso (Owners). See Bostonian (Owners, Master and Crew) v Gregerso (Owners), The Gregerso

Gregerso, The. See Bostonian (Owners, Master and Crew) v Gregerso (Owners), The Gregerso

Gregos, The [1985] 2 Lloyd's Rep 347 974

Grein v Imperial Airways Ltd [1937] 1 KB 50, [1936] 2 All ER 1258, 106 LJKB 49, 42 Com Cas 10, 80 Sol Jo 735, 155 LT 380, 52 TLR 681, CA 112

Greta Holme, The. See Emerald, The, The Greta Holme

Grill v General Iron Screw Collier Co (1866) LR 1 CP 600, 35 LJCP 321, Har & Ruth 654, 12 Jur NS 727, 2 Mar LC 362, 14 WR 893, 14 LT 711; affd (1868) LR 3 CP 476, 37 LJCP 205, 3 Mar LC 77, 16 WR 796, 18 LT 485, Ex Ch 760

Grindley v Stevens, The Falkland and The Navigator. See Falkland, The

Grovehurst, The [1910] P 316, 79 LJP 124, 11 Asp MLC 440, 103 LT 239, CA 739

Guernsey Coast, The (1950) 83 Ll L Rep 483, P, D and Admlty 855, 873

Guildford. See Temple Bar, The (Owners) v Guildford (Owners), The Guildford

Guinness (Arthur), Son & Co (Dublin) Ltd v The Freshfield (Owners), The Lady Gwendolen [1965] P 294, [1965] 2 All ER 283, [1965] 3 WLR 91, [1965] 1 Lloyd's Rep 335, 109 Sol Jo 336, CA 694

Guiseppe di Vittorio, The [1998] 1 Lloyd's Rep 136, CA 93

Gulf Azov Shipping Co Ltd v Chief Humphrey Irikefe Idisi [2001] EWCA Civ 505, [2001] 2 All ER (Comm) 673, [2001] 1 Lloyd's Rep 727, [2001] All ER (D) 100 (Mar) 167

Gulf of Suez, The [1921] P 318, 90 LJP 321, 15 Asp MLC 328, 125 LT 653, 37 TLR 704, CA 705

Gulf Venture, The [1986] 1 Lloyd's Rep 130n; affd [1986] 2 Lloyd's Rep 129, CA 190

Gumm v Tyrie (1865) 6 B & S 298, 34 LJQB 124, 5 New Rep 413, 13 WR 436, 122 ER 1206, Ex Ch 331

Gunn v Roberts (1874) LR 9 CP 331, 43 LJCP 233, 2 Asp MLC 250, 22 WR 652, 30 LT 424 432

PARA

Gustaf, The (1862) Lush 506, 31 LJPM & A 207, 1 Mar LC 230, 167 ER 230, 6 LT 660
.... 981–982, 984, 987, 990

Gustafsberg, The [1905] P 10, 74 LJP 42, 10 Asp MLC 61, 53 WR 350, 92 LT 630, 21
TLR 79, P, D and Admlty 700

Gusty, The and The Daniel M [1940] P 159, 67 Ll L Rep 104, 109 LJP 71, 19 Asp MLC
366, 84 Sol Jo 454, 164 LT 271, 56 TLR 785, P, D and Admlty
.... 763

H

HMS Daffodil, The. See Hermione, The

HMS Hawke, The. See Olympic, The and HMS Hawke

HMS Supply (1865) 2 Mar LC 262, 12 LT 799, sub nom Bruckenholme, The v HMS
Supply Holt Adm 189 2

HMS Thetis, The (1833) 3 Hag Adm 14 867,881

HMS Topaze (1864) 2 Mar LC 38, 12 WR 923, 10 LT 659, sub nom Promise, The v HMS
Topaze Holt Adm 165 2

H M Hayes, The (1861) Lush 355, 1 Mar LC 127, 5 LT 37, PC
.... 742

Haabet, The [1899] P 295, 68 LJP 121, 8 Asp MLC 605, 48 WR 223, 81 LT 463, 15 TLR
548, P, D and Admlty 134

Halcyon Isle, The. See Bankers Trust International v Todd Shipyards Corpn, The Halcyon
Isle

Halcyon Skies, The [1977] QB 14, [1976] 1 All ER 856, [1976] 2 WLR 514, [1976] 1
Lloyd's Rep 461, 120 Sol Jo 27 .... 127, 130, 478

Halcyon the Great, The [1975] 1 All ER 882, [1975] 1 WLR 515, [1975] 1 CMLR 267,
[1975] 1 Lloyd's Rep 518, 119 Sol Jo 10 178

Halkett, ex p. See Mavor, Re, ex p Halkett

Halki Shipping Corpn v Sopex Oils Ltd [1998] 2 All ER 23, [1998] 1 WLR 726, [1998] 1
Lloyd's Rep 465, [1998] NPC 4, (1998) Times, 19 January, 142 Sol Jo LB 44, [1997]
All ER (D) 130 103

Hall v Jupe (1880) 49 LJQB 721, 4 Asp MLC 328, 43 LT 411, CPD
.... 438

Halley, The. See Liverpool, Brazil and River Plate Steam Navigation Co Ltd v Benham, The
Halley

Halsey v Albertuszen, The Jonge Andries. See Jonge Andries, The

Hamburg (Cargo Ex), The. See Duranty v Hart, The Hamburg (Cargo Ex)

Hamburg Star, The [1994] 1 Lloyd's Rep 399 111

Hamburgh American Steam Navigation Co v North of Scotland Banking Co, The Eclipse
and The Saxonia. See Eclipse, The

Hamburgh American Steam Navigation Co v North of Scotland Banking Co, The Eclipse
and The Saxonia. See Saxonia, The

Hamilton v Baker, The Sara (1889) 14 App Cas 209, 58 LJP 57, 6 Asp MLC 413, 38 WR
129, 61 LT 26, 5 TLR 507, [1886–90] All ER Rep Ext 1348, HL
.... 127, 964

Hammond v Rogers and Rodd, The Christiana. See Christiana, The

Hamtun, The (owners) v The St John (owners) [1999] 1 All ER (Comm) 587, [1999] 1
Lloyd's Rep 883, [1999] Lexis Citation 2538, [1999] All ER (D) 249
.... 862

Handytankers KS v Owners and/or demise charterers of the ship or vessell M/V Alas [2014]
HKCFI 1281, [2015] 1 Lloyd's Rep 211, HK HC 93

Hanna, The (1877) 3 Asp MLC 505, 37 LT 364, P, D and Admlty
.... 177

Hannibal, The and The Queen. See Queen, The

Hans Hoth, The [1953] 1 All ER 218, [1952] 2 Lloyd's Rep 341, P, D and Admlty
.... 429

Hansa, The (1887) 6 Asp MLC 268, 58 LT 530, P, D and Admlty
.... 798

Hansen v Dunn (1906) 11 Com Cas 100, 22 TLR 458 436

Hanson v Royden (1867) LR 3 CP 47, 37 LJCP 66, 3 Mar LC 8, 16 WR 205, 17 LT 214
.... 471

Happy Return, The (1828) 2 Hag Adm 198, 166 ER 217
.... 870

PARA

Harkaway, The [1928] P 199, 31 Ll L Rep 190, 97 LJP 113, 17 Asp MLC 503, 139 LT
615, 44 TLR 649, P, D and Admlty 736, 752
Harley v Harley (1860) 11 I Ch R 451 236
Harlow, The [1922] P 175, 91 LJP 119, 15 Asp MLC 498, 126 LT 763, 38 TLR 375,
[1922] All ER Rep Ext 849, P, D and Admlty 229
Harmer v Bell, The Bold Buccleugh (1852) 7 Moo PCC 267, 13 ER 884, [1843–60] All ER
Rep 125, 19 LTOS 235, PC 83, 93, 110, 964, 967–968, 977, 987, 991
Harmonides, The [1903] P 1, 72 LJP 9, 9 Asp MLC 354, 51 WR 303, 87 LT 448, 19 TLR
37, P, D and Admlty 797
Harmonie, The (1841) 1 Wm Rob 178, 166 ER 539, 8 LT 121
.... 987
Harmonie, The (1841) 1 Wm Rob 179, 166 ER 540 164
Harmony v Faraday (1920) 5 Ll L Rep 177, P, D and Admlty
.... 783
Harmony v Northborough (1923) 15 Ll L Rep 119, P, D and Admlty
.... 783
Harms Bergung, Transport & Heavylift GmbH & Co KG v Harms Offshore AHT 'Uranus'
GmbH & Co KG [2015] EWHC 1269 (Admlty), [2015] 2 All ER (Comm) 953, [2015]
2 Lloyd's Rep 175, [2015] All ER (D) 72 (May) 104, 106
Harper (H G) & Co v J Bland & Co Ltd (1914) 84 LJKB 738, 13 Asp MLC 49, 20 Com
Cas 143, 112 LT 724, 31 TLR 116 431
Harriet, The (1868) 3 Mar LC 138, 18 LT 804 321
Harrington v Halkeld (1778) 2 Park's Marine Insurances (8th Edn) 639
.... 5
Harrington, The (1888) 13 PD 48, 57 LJP 45, 6 Asp MLC 282, 59 LT 72, P, D and
Admlty 798
Harriot, The (1842) 1 Wm Rob 439, 166 ER 636, 6 LT 194, 8 LT 581, 1 Notes of Cases
613 865
Harris v Anderson (1863) 14 CBNS 499, 143 ER 541 742
Harris v Carter (1854) 3 E & B 559, 23 LJQB 295, 18 Jur 1014, 2 WR 409, 118 ER
1251, 2 CLR 1582, 23 LTOS 66 471
Harris v Watson (1791) Peake 72, 170 ER 94, [1775–1802] All ER Rep 493
.... 471
Harrison v Dodd (1914) 78 JP 206, 12 Asp MLC 503, 111 LT 47, 30 TLR 376, DC
.... 471
Harrison v Gurney (1821) 2 Jac & W 563, 37 ER 743, Ct of Ch
.... 101
Harrods (Buenos Aires) Ltd, Re [1992] Ch 72, [1991] 4 All ER 334, [1991] 3 WLR 397,
[1991] BCLC 666, [1991] BCC 249, 135 Sol Jo 184, (1991) Times, 25 March
.... 100
Hartfort v Jones (1698) 1 Ld Raym 393, 2 Salk 654, 91 ER 1161
.... 913
Hartlepool, The (1950) 84 Ll L Rep 145, P, D and Admlty
.... 171
Hartley v Ponsonby (1857) 7 E & B 872, 26 LJQB 322, 3 Jur NS 746, 5 WR 659, 119 ER
1471, 29 LTOS 195 471
Harvest Home, The [1905] P 177, 74 LJP 65, 10 Asp MLC 118, 93 LT 395, CA
.... 727, 739, 774, 865
Harvest, The (1886) 11 PD 90, 6 Asp MLC 5, 55 LT 202, CA
.... 700
Hassan v Trader Navigation Co Ltd [1965] 2 Lloyd's Rep 378, Mayor's and City of
London's Ct 469
Hassel, The [1962] 2 Lloyd's Rep 139, P, D and Admlty
.... 802
Hattersley & Sons Ltd v George Hodgson Ltd (1905) 22 RPC 229, 21 TLR 178, CA
.... 220
Hatton v Akt Durban Hausen (1919) 56 SLR 100, 1919 SC 154, Ct of Sess
.... 204
Haughland, SS v SS Karamea. See Karamea, The
Havana, The. See Richelieu and Ontario Navigation Co v Taylor, The Havana
Haversham Grange, The [1905] P 307, 74 LJP 115, 10 Asp MLC 156, 53 WR 675, 93 LT
733, 21 TLR 628, CA 801–802
Haviland Routh & Co v Thomson (1864) 37 Sc Jur 147, 3 M 313
.... 333

PARA

Hawke Bay Shipping Co Ltd v The First National Bank of Chicago, The Efthimis, Pavlina,
    Titika P and Juvena [1986] 1 Lloyd's Rep 244, [1984] Lexis Citation 1450; affd [1986]
    1 Lloyd's Rep 244, CA 100–101
Hawkins v Twizell (1856) 5 E & B 883, 25 LJQB 160, 2 Jur NS 302, 119 ER 709, sub
    nom Hawkins v Furzill 4 WR 242, 26 LTOS 235 970
Hay v Le Neve (1824) 2 Sh Sc App 395 .... 767, 770
Hayman v Molton (1803) 5 Esp 65, 170 ER 739, NP 440
Hayter v Nelson and Home Insurance Co [1990] 2 Lloyd's Rep 265
    103
Hazelmere, The [1911] P 69, 80 LJP 25, 11 Asp MLC 536, 103 LT 890, CA
    .... 705, 754
Heather Bell, The [1901] P 272, 70 LJP 57, 9 Asp MLC 206, 49 WR 577, 84 LT 794, 17
    TLR 541, CA 329–330
Hebe, The (1844) 2 Wm Rob 246, 166 ER 747, 2 LTOS 404
    869
Hebe, The (1847) 2 Wm Rob 530, 166 ER 855, 5 LT 121, 5 Notes of Cases 176
    804
Hebe, The. See Singapore, The and The Hebe
Hebridean Coast, The. See Lord Citrine, The (Owners) v Hebridean Coast (Owners), The
    Hebridean Coast
Hector, The (1883) 8 PD 218, 52 LJP 47, 51, 5 Asp MLC 101, 31 WR 881, 48 LT 890,
    CA 222, 739
Hedley v Pinkey & Sons Steamship Co [1892] 1 QB 58, 56 JP 308, 61 LJQB 179, 7 Asp
    MLC 135, 40 WR 113, 66 LT 71, CA; on appeal [1894] AC 222, 63 LJQB 419, 7 Asp
    MLC 483, 6 R 106, 42 WR 497, 70 LT 630, 10 TLR 347, HL
    .... 427, 603
Heilmann v Falkenstein (1917) 33 TLR 383 101
Heinrich, The (1872) LR 3 A & E 505, 41 LJ Adm 68, 1 Asp MLC 260, 20 WR 759, 26
    LT 372, HC 981, 985
Helen and George, The (1858) Sw 368, 166 ER 1170, sub nom The Argo v The Helen and
    George 8 LT 335 883–884
Helen R Cooper, The (1871) LR 3 A & E 339, 40 LJ Adm 46, HC
    204
Helene Roth, The [1980] QB 273, [1980] 1 All ER 1078, [1980] 2 WLR 549, [1980] 1
    Lloyd's Rep 477, 124 Sol Jo 25 .... 93, 158, 160
Helenus and Motagua, The [1982] 2 Lloyd's Rep 261 881
Helgoland, The (1859) 5 Jur NS 1179, Sw 491, 166 ER 1228, sub nom The Heligoland 4
    LT 28, 92 980
Helios, Akt v Ekman & Co [1897] 2 QB 83, 66 LJQB 538, 8 Asp MLC 244, 2 Com Cas
    163, 76 LT 537, CA 746
Helme v Smith (1831) 7 Bing 709, 131 ER 274 244
Helvetia, The (1894) 8 Asp MLC 264n, P, D and Admlty
    863
Henrietta, The (1837) 3 Hag Adm 345n 204
Henry Morton, The (1874) 2 Asp MLC 466, 31 LT 859, PC
    754
Henry, The v The Vivid. See Vivid, The
Henry, The (1810) Edw 192, 2 Eng Pr Cas 32, 165 ER 1079, HC
    855
Henry, The (1851) 15 Jur 183, 16 LTOS 553 884–885
Heranger, SS (Owners) v SS Diamond (Owners) [1939] AC 94, 62 Ll L Rep 204, 108 LJP
    12, 19 Asp MLC 250, 83 Sol Jo 151, 160 LT 241, 55 TLR 318, HL
    .... 694, 729
Herceg Novi (owners) v Ming Galaxy (owners) [1998] 4 All ER 238, [1998] 2 Lloyd's Rep
    454, (1998) Times, 30 July, [1998] Lexis Citation 2815, [1998] All ER (D) 348
    .... 100, 1007
Hercules, The (1819) 2 Dods 353, 1 Hag Adm 143, 165 ER 1511, HC
    80
Hercules, The (1885) 11 PD 10, 5 Asp MLC 545, 34 WR 400, 54 LT 273, P, D and
    Admlty 178
Hereward, The [1895] P 284, 64 LJP 87, 8 Asp MLC 22, 11 R 798, 44 WR 288, 72 LT
    903, P, D and Admlty 107, 241
Hermione, The [1922] P 162, 91 LJP 136, 15 Asp MLC 493, [1922] All ER Rep 570, 126
    LT 701, sub nom HMS Daffodil 38 TLR 381, P, D and Admlty
    884

PARA

Hero (Owners) v Admiralty Comrs [1912] AC 300, 81 LJP 26, 12 Asp MLC 108, 56 Sol
     Jo 269, 106 LT 82, 28 TLR 216, HL 768, 770, 786
Heron II, The. See Koufos v C Czarnikow Ltd, The Heron II
Herzogin Marie, The (1861) Lush 292, 1 Mar LC 144, 167 ER 126, 5 LT 88
     478
Hesselmoor, The and The Sergeant [1951] 1 Lloyd's Rep 146, P, D and Admlty
     .... 153, 1013
Hestia, The [1895] P 193, 64 LJP 82, 7 Asp MLC 599, 11 R 808, 43 WR 668, 72 LT 364,
     P, D and Admlty 863, 866, 883–884
Hewett v Aylen, The Atlas. See Atlas, The
Hibbert v Pigou (1783) 3 Doug KB 224, 99 ER 624 5
Hibbs v Ross (1866) LR 1 QB 534, 30 JP 613, 7 B & S 655, 35 LJQB 193, 12 Jur NS
     812, 2 Mar LC 397, 14 WR 914, 15 LT 67 780
Hibernia, The (1874) 2 Asp MLC 454, 24 WR 60, 31 LT 805, PC
     .... 710, 739
Hicks v Walker (1856) 20 JP 517, 4 WR 511, 27 LTOS 83
     471
Higham v Stena Sealink Ltd [1996] 3 All ER 660, [1996] 1 WLR 1107, [1996] 2 Lloyd's
     Rep 26, [1996] PIQR P 351, (1996) Times, 26 February
     152
Highland Loch, The. See Frances (Ketch) (Owners) v Highland Loch (Owners), The
     Highland Loch
Highlander, The (1843) 2 Wm Rob 109, 166 ER 696, 2 Notes of Cases 316
     330
Hingston (or Kingston) v Wendt (1876) 1 QBD 367, 45 LJQB 440, 3 Asp MLC 126, 24
     WR 604, 34 LT 181, DC 876
Hirondelle, The (1905) 22 TLR 146, CA 759
Hispanica de Petroleos SA and Cia Iberica Refinadera de Petroleos SA v Vencedora
     Oceanica Navegacion SA, The Kapetan Marcos NL [1986] 1 Lloyd's Rep 211; affd
     [1986] 1 Lloyd's Rep 211, [1984] Lexis Citation 1654, CA
     156
Hjemmett, The (1880) 5 PD 227, 49 LJP 66, 4 Asp MLC 274, 42 LT 514, P, D and Admlty
     597
Hobbs, Savill & Co Ltd v The Vasilia (Owners), Albaran Bay Corpn [1972] 1 Lloyd's Rep
     51 178
Hodgkinson v Fernie (1857) 2 CBNS 415, 26 LJCP 217, 3 Jur NS 818, 140 ER 479
     782
Hoegh Silvercrest, The [1962] 1 Lloyd's Rep 9, P, D and Admlty
     110
Hoek van Holland Maatschappij v Clyde Shipping Co (1902) 40 SLR 194, 5 F 227, 10 SLT
     612, Ct of Sess 762
Hogstad v Coombe Dingle (1921) 8 Ll L Rep 153, P, D and Admlty
     751
Hohenzollern, The [1906] P 339, 76 LJP 17, 10 Asp MLC 296, 95 LT 585, 22 TLR 778, P,
     D and Admlty 177, 888
Holderness v Shackels (1828) 8 B & C 612, Dan & Ll 203, 7 LJOSKB 80, 3 Man & Ry
     KB 25, 108 ER 1170, [1824–34] All ER Rep 339 244
Hollandia, The [1983] 1 AC 565, [1982] 3 All ER 1141, [1982] 3 WLR 1111, 126 Sol Jo
     819, sub nom Morviken, The [1983] 1 Lloyd's Rep 1, [1983] Com LR 44, HL
     .... 103, 851, 992
Holman v Peruvian Nitrate Co (1878) 5 R 657, 15 SLR 349
     428
Holman & Sons Ltd v Merchants' Marine Insurance Co Ltd [1919] 1 KB 383, 88 LJKB
     435, 14 Asp MLC 433, 24 Com Cas 102, 120 LT 478, 35 TLR 138
     874
Homburg Houtimport BV v Agrosin Private Ltd, The Starsin [2003] UKHL 12, [2004] 1
     AC 715, [2003] 2 All ER 785, [2003] 2 WLR 711, [2003] 1 All ER (Comm) 625,
     [2003] 1 Lloyd's Rep 571, [2003] 19 LS Gaz R 31, (2003) Times, 17 March, [2003]
     All ER (D) 192 (Mar) 242
Homer, The [1973] 1 Lloyd's Rep 501, CA 705
Hong v A and R Brown Ltd [1948] 1 KB 515, [1948] 1 All ER 185, [1948] LJR 1816, 92
     Sol Jo 124, 64 TLR 132, CA 204
Honor, The, Cargo ex (1866) LR 1 A & E 87, 35 LJ Adm 113, 12 Jur NS 773, 2 Mar LC
     445, 15 WR 10, 15 LT 677, HC 870
Honshu Gloria, The [1986] 2 Lloyd's Rep 63 178

PARA

Hontestroom, SS v SS Sagaporack 1927] AC 37, 25 Ll L Rep 377, 95 LJP 153, 17 Asp
MLC 123, 136 LT 33, 42 TLR 741, [1927] All ER Rep Ext 831, HL
.... 220
Hook v Cunard Steamship Co Ltd [1953] 1 All ER 1021, [1953] 1 WLR 682, [1953] 1
Lloyd's Rep 413, 117 JP 226, 97 Sol Jo 335 445
Hooper v Gumm (1862) 2 John & H 602, 10 WR 644, 70 ER 1199, 6 LT 891
.... 321
Hooper v Lusby (1814) 4 Camp 66, 171 ER 22, NP 239, 244
Hope, The v The Lady Anne. See Lady Anne, The
Hope, The (1838) 3 Hag Adm 423 906–907
Hope, The (1843) 2 Wm Rob 8, 166 ER 659, 4 LT 774
.... 750
Hope, The (1873) 1 Asp MLC 563, 28 LT 287 .... 976, 980–981
Hopkins v M'Bride (1901) 50 WR 255, 46 Sol Jo 52, 18 TLR 53, DC
.... 471
Hopper v Burness (1876) 1 CPD 137, 45 LJQB 377, 3 Asp MLC 149, 24 WR 612, 34 LT
528, CPD 443, 889
Hopper Wills No 66, The. See Esrom, The and The Hopper Wills No 66
Horlock v Beal [1916] 1 AC 486, 85 LJKB 602, 13 Asp MLC 250, 21 Com Cas 201,
[1916–17] All ER Rep 81, 60 Sol Jo 236, 114 LT 193, 32 TLR 251, HL
.... 487
Horlock, The (1877) 2 PD 243, 47 LJP 5, 2 Asp MLC 41, 36 LT 622, P, D and Admlty
.... 105, 108
Hornet, The [1892] P 361, 7 Asp MLC 262, 1 R 549, 68 LT 236, DC
.... 746, 770
Hough v P & O Containers Ltd (Blohm and Voss Holding AG third parties) [1999] QB
834, [1998] 2 All ER 978, [1998] 3 WLR 851, [1998] 2 Lloyd's Rep 318, [1998] 17
LS Gaz R 32, (1998) Times, 6 April, 142 Sol Jo LB 127, [1998] All ER (D) 109
.... 102
Howard v Tucker (1831) 1 B & Ad 712, 9 LJOS 108, 109 ER 951
.... 431
Hoyanger, The (1946) 79 Ll L Rep 284, P, D and Admlty
.... 204
Hudson and Humphrey v Barge Swiftsure (Owners), The Swiftsure (1900) 9 Asp MLC 65,
82 LT 389, 16 TLR 275, P, D and Admlty 328
Hudson Bay, The [1957] 2 Lloyd's Rep 506, P, D and Admlty
.... 203–204
Humber Boat Works Ltd v Owners of MV 'selby Paradigm' [2004] EWHC 1804 (Admlty),
[2004] 2 Lloyd's Rep 714, [2004] NLJR 1362, [2004] All ER (D) 71 (Aug)
.... 190
Humbergate, The [1952] 1 Lloyd's Rep 168, P, D and Admlty
.... 691
Hunter v Parker (1840) 10 LJ Ex 281, 7 M & W 322, 151 ER 789, 9 LT 53, Exch Ct
.... 438, 441
Hunter v Prinsep (1808) 10 East 378, 103 ER 818, [1803–13] All ER Rep 446
.... 440, 889
Huntley v Sanderson and Wilkinson (1833) 1 Cr & M 467, 2 LJ Ex 204, 3 Tyr 469, 149
ER 483, Ex Ch 433
Huntsman, The [1894] P 214, 7 Asp MLC 431, 6 R 698, 70 LT 386, P, D and Admlty
.... 238
Huntsman, The (1911) 11 Asp MLC 606, 104 LT 464, P, D and Admlty
.... 707
Hurst, The [1952] 1 Lloyd's Rep 96, P, D and Admlty 769
Hutchison v Clydeport Operations Ltd 1998 SC 336, 1998 SLT 765, Ct of Sess
.... 577
Hutton v Ras Steam Shipping Co Ltd [1907] 1 KB 834, 76 LJKB 562, 10 Asp MLC 386,
12 Com Cas 231, 51 Sol Jo 247, 96 LT 515, 23 TLR 295, CA
.... 130
Hyman v Helm (1883) 24 Ch D 531, 32 WR 258, 49 LT 376, CA
.... 101

PARA

I

ICL Shipping Ltd v Chin Tai Steel Enterprise Co Ltd, The ICL Vikraman [2003] EWHC
2320 (Comm), [2004] 1 WLR 2254, [2004] 1 All ER (Comm) 246, [2004] 1 Lloyd's
Rep 21, [2003] ArbLR 26, [2003] All ER (D) 193 (Oct) 197, 1003, 1005
I Congreso del Partido [1978] QB 500, [1978] 1 All ER 1169, [1977] 3 WLR 778, [1977]
1 Lloyd's Rep 536, 121 Sol Jo 743; affd [1981] 1 All ER 1092, [1980] 1 Lloyd's Rep
23, 123 Sol Jo 689; revsd sub nom Playa Larga, The (Owners of Cargo lately laden on
board) v I Congreso del Partido (Owners), Marble Islands, The (Owners of Cargo
lately laden on board) v I Congreso del Partido (Owners), I Congreso del Partido
[1983] 1 AC 244, [1981] 2 All ER 1064, [1981] 3 WLR 328, [1981] 2 Lloyd's Rep
367, 125 Sol Jo 529, HL 93, 810
Ibis VI, The [1921] P 255, 90 LJP 289, 15 Asp MLC 237, 65 Sol Jo 514, 125 LT 378, 37
TLR 557, 6 Ll LR 545, CA 204
Ida, The v The Wasa of Nicolaistadt (1866) 15 LT 103 744
Ida, The (1860) Lush 6, 167 ER 3, 1 LT 417 92
Ida, The (1886) 6 Asp MLC 21, 55 LT 59, P, D and Admlty
.... 238
Idas, The (1863) 167 ER 300 241
Ijaola, The. See Fraser v Equatorial Shipping Co Ltd and Equatorial Lines Ltd, The Ijaola
Ikala, The. See Strathfillan, SS (Owners) v SS Ikala (Owners), The Ikala
Ile de Ceylan, The [1922] P 256, 91 LJP 222, 16 Asp MLC 23, [1922] All ER Rep 264,
128 LT 154, 38 TLR 835, P, D and Admlty 964, 981
Ilo, The [1982] 1 Lloyd's Rep 39 .... 855, 869, 881
Ilos, The (1856) Sw 100, 166 ER 1040 790
Immacolata Concezione, The (1882) 8 PD 34, 4 Asp MLC 593, 31 WR 644, 47 LT 388, P,
D and Admlty 169
Immacolata Concezione, The (1883) 9 PD 37, 52 LJP 19, 5 Asp MLC 208, 32 WR 705, 50
LT 539, P, D and Admlty 981–982, 984, 987, 990
Imperial Royal Privileged Danubian Steam Navigation Co v Greek and Oriental Steam
Navigation Co, The Smyrna (1864) 2 Moo PCCNS 435, 15 ER 965, 11 LT 74
.... 691, 748
Impetus, The. See Blenheim (Owners) v Impetus (Owners), The Impetus
Impex Transport A/S v AG Thames Holdings Ltd [1982] 1 All ER 897, [1981] 1 WLR
1547, [1981] 2 Lloyd's Rep 566, 125 Sol Jo 777 189
Inchmaree, The [1899] P 111, 68 LJP 30, 8 Asp MLC 486, 80 LT 201, P, D and Admlty
.... 855
Independence, The (1861) Lush 270, 1 Mar LC 88, 9 WR 582, 4 LT 563, sub nom
Maddox v Fisher, The Independence 14 Moo PCC 103, 15 ER 245, PC
.... 739, 762
Independence, The. See Independence, The
Indian Chief, The (1888) 14 PD 24, 58 LJP 25, 6 Asp MLC 362, 60 LT 240, P, D and
Admlty 720, 749
Indian Endurance (No 2), The, Republic of India v India Steamship Co Ltd [1998] AC 878,
[1997] 4 All ER 380, [1997] 3 WLR 818, [1998] 1 Lloyd's Rep 1, [1997] 43 LS Gaz R
29, [1997] NLJR 1581, (1997) Times, 23 October, [1997] Lexis Citation 4217, 141
Sol Jo LB 230, [1997] All ER (D) 21, HL 92, 96–97, 156
Indian, The v The Jessie (1865) 2 Mar LC 217, 12 LT 586
.... 735
Indian, The. See Indian, The v The Jessie
Indomitable, The (1859) 5 Jur NS 632, Sw 446, 166 ER 1208, 33 LTOS 127
.... 134
Indus, The [1957] 1 Lloyd's Rep 335, P, D and Admlty 694
Indus, The (1886) 12 PD 46, 56 LJP 88, 6 Asp MLC 105, 35 WR 490, 56 LT 376, 3 TLR
213, CA 789
Industrie Chimiche Italia Centrale and Cerealfin SA v Alexander G Tsavliris & Sons
Maritime Co, Panchristo Shipping Co SA and Bula Shipping Corpn, The Choko Star
[1990] 1 Lloyd's Rep 516, (1990) Times, 24 March, CA
.... 853
Industrie, The (1871) LR 3 A & E 303, 40 LJ Adm 26, 1 Asp MLC 17, 19 WR 728, 24 LT
446, HC 110, 753, 766
Industry, The (1835) 3 Hag Adm 203, 166 ER 381 881
Inflexible, HMS (1857) Sw 200, 5 WR 517, 166 ER 1094, 28 LTOS 374
.... 799, 802, 814

PARA

Inman v Reck, The City of Antwerp and The Friedrich (1868) LR 2 PC 25, 5 Moo PCCNS
 33, 37 LJ Adm 25, 16 ER 427, PC 761
Inna, The [1938] P 148, 60 Ll L Rep 414, 107 LJP 110, 19 Asp MLC 203, 159 LT 439, 54
 TLR 744, P, D and Admlty 884, 976–977, 979
Innisfail, The (1876) 3 Asp MLC 337, 35 LT 819, P, D and Admlty
 734
Innisfallen, The (1866) LR 1 A & E 72, 35 LJ Adm 110, 12 Jur NS 653, 2 Mar LC 470,
 16 LT 71, HC 240, 330
International Transportation Service Inc v Owners of the Ship 'Convenience Container'
 [2006] HKCFI 465, [2006] 2 Lloyd's Rep 556, HK CFI 90
Iona, The (1867) LR 1 PC 426, 4 Moo PCCNS 336, 16 LT 158, sub nom London and
 Edinburgh Shipping Co v Eaton, The Iona 2 Mar LC 479, PC
 739
Ionian Bank Ltd v Couvreur [1969] 2 All ER 651, [1969] 1 WLR 781, 113 Sol Jo 107
 101
Iraqi Ministry of Defence v Arcepey Shipping Co SA (Gillespie Bros intervening), The Angel
 Bell [1981] QB 65, [1980] 1 All ER 480, [1980] 2 WLR 488, [1980] 1 Lloyd's Rep
 632, 124 Sol Jo 148 318
Ireland v Thomson (1847) 4 CB 149, 17 LJCP 241, 136 ER 460
 441
Irina Zharkikh and Ksenia Zharkikh, The [2001] 2 Lloyd's Rep 319
 93
Iron Duke, The (1845) 2 Wm Rob 377, 9 Jur 476, 166 ER 797, 4 Notes of Cases 94; affd
 sub nom Williams v Chapman (1846) 4 Notes of Cases 585, PC
 739
Iron-Master, The (1859) Sw 441, 166 ER 1206 797
Isca, The (1886) 12 PD 34, 56 LJP 47, 6 Asp MLC 63, 35 WR 382, 55 LT 779, P, D and
 Admlty 599, 742
Isis, The (1883) 8 PD 227, 53 LJP 14, 5 Asp MLC 155, 32 WR 171, 49 LT 444, P, D and
 Admlty 189
Islamic Republic of Iran Shipping Lines v Steamship Mutual Underwriting Association
 (Bermuda) Ltd [2010] EWHC 2661 (Comm), [2011] 2 All ER (Comm) 609, [2011] 1
 Lloyd's Rep 195, [2010] All ER (D) 261 (Oct) 32
Island and Barge Ltd v SS Makedonia (Owners), The Makedonia [1958] 1 QB 365,
 [1958] 1 All ER 236, [1958] 2 WLR 256, [1957] 2 Lloyd's Rep 575, 36 ATC 376,
 [1958] TR 63, 102 Sol Jo 124 886
Isle of Cyprus, The (1890) 15 PD 134, 59 LJP 90, 6 Asp MLC 534, 38 WR 719, 63 LT
 352, P, D and Admlty 204
Italian State Rlys v Minnehaha (1921) 6 Ll L Rep 12, CA
 800

J

Jackson v Vernon (1789) 126 ER 69, 1 Hy Bl 114 330
Jacob, The (1802) 4 Ch Rob 245, 165 ER 600 .... 435, 991
Jacob, The (1860) 12 Ir Jur 379 735
Jade, The, The Eschersheim, Erkowit (Owners) v Salus (formerly Rotesand) (Owners),
 Erkowit (Cargo Owners) v Eschersheim (Owners) [1976] 1 All ER 920, [1976] 1 WLR
 430, [1976] 2 Lloyd's Rep 1, 120 Sol Jo 315, HL 97, 110–111
Jalakrishna, The [1983] 2 Lloyd's Rep 628 100
Jalamatsya, The [1987] 2 Lloyd's Rep 164 161
James and Ann, The. See Oxford, The v The James and Ann
James Armstrong, The (1875) LR 4 A & E 380, 3 Asp MLC 46, 33 LT 390
 .... 177, 206, 882, 889, 899, 904
James Seddon, The (1866) LR 1 A & E 62, 35 LJ Adm 117, 12 Jur NS 609, 2 Mar LC
 443, 14 WR 973, 15 LT 636, HC 433
James W Elwell, The [1921] P 351, 8 Ll L Rep 115, 90 LJP 132, 355, 15 Asp MLC 418,
 125 LT 796, 37 TLR 178, 835, P, D and Admlty .. 126, 134, 163, 964, 966, 973, 978, 981,
                                                                                      983, 987
James Watt, The (1844) 2 Wm Rob 270, 8 Jur 320, 166 ER 756, 3 LTOS 5, 3 Notes of
 Cases 36 762
James Westoll, The [1923] P 94n, 16 Asp MLC 453n, 132 LT 717n, CA
 .... 153, 1013
James, The (1856) 10 Moo PCC 162, Sw 55, 4 WR 353, 166 ER 1016, 27 LTOS 1, PC
 744

PARA

Jane and Matilda, The (1823) 1 Hag Adm 187, 166 ER 67
.... 457
Jane Bacon, The (1878) 27 WR 35, CA 599, 739, 742
Jane, The (1831) 2 Hag Adm 338 905
Janet Court, The [1897] P 59, 66 LJP 34, 8 Asp MLC 223, 76 LT 172, P, D and Admlty
.... 855, 891
Janet Wilson, The (1857) Sw 261, 6 WR 329, 166 ER 1127, 30 LTOS 22
.... 980, 982
Jangmi, The (known as Grigorpan) [1988] 2 Lloyd's Rep 462, (1988) Times, 3 June; affd
[1989] 2 Lloyd's Rep 1, CA 158
Japp v Campbell (1887) 57 LJQB 79, 4 TLR 53 .... 321, 330
Jarlinn, The, J R Rix & Sons Ltd v Owners of SS or Motor Vessel Jarlinn [1965] 3 All ER
36, [1965] 1 WLR 1098, [1965] 2 Lloyd's Rep 191, 109 Sol Jo 497, P, D and Admlty
.... 162, 164
Jarvis Brake, The [1976] 2 All ER 886, [1976] 2 Lloyd's Rep 320, 120 Sol Jo 351
.... 164
Jassy, The [1906] P 270, 75 LJP 93, 10 Asp MLC 278, 95 LT 363, P, D and Admlty
.... 86, 967
Jefferies v Legendra (1691) 3 Lev 320, 4 Mod Rep 58, 2 Salk 443, 1 Show 320, Holt KB
465, 83 ER 709, 90 ER 1156, 89 ER 599, 90 ER 730, Carth 216
.... 5
Jefford v Gee [1970] 2 QB 130, [1970] 1 All ER 1202, [1970] 2 WLR 702, [1970] 1
Lloyd's Rep 107, 114 Sol Jo 206 147
Jenny Lind, The (1872) LR 3 A & E 529, 41 LJ Adm 63, 1 Asp MLC 294, 20 WR 895, 26
LT 591, HC 981, 983
Jersey Jurats, Re (1866) LR 1 PC 94, 3 Moo PCCNS 456, 16 ER 173, PC
.... 216
Jersey, The [1942] P 119, 111 LJP 72, 86 Sol Jo 313, 167 LT 337, 58 TLR 346, P, D and
Admlty 787
Jessie, The and The Zaanland [1917] P 138, 86 LJP 108, 14 Asp MLC 139, 117 LT 342,
33 TLR 367, P, D and Admlty 733, 762–763
Joannis Vatis (No 2), The [1922] P 213, 10 Ll L Rep 756, 91 LJP 196, 16 Asp MLC 13,
127 LT 494, 38 TLR 566, P, D and Admlty 92, 147, 172, 201, 809, 811, 991
Joannis Vatis, The [1922] P 92, 9 Ll L Rep 456, 91 LJP 182, 15 Asp MLC 506, 126 LT
718, CA 207, 790
Jogoo, The [1981] 3 All ER 634, [1981] 1 WLR 1376, [1981] 1 Lloyd's Rep 513, 125 Sol
Jo 790 .... 173, 178
Johan and Siegmund, The (1810) Edw 241 240
Johannes, The (1860) 1 Lush 182, 30 LJPM & A 91, 1 Mar LC 24, 167 ER 87, 3 LT 757
.... 120–121, 864
John and Jane, The (1802) 4 Ch Rob 216, 165 ER 590 924
John Boyne, The (1877) 3 Asp MLC 341, 25 WR 756, 36 LT 29, P, D and Admlty
.... 184
John Buddle, The (1847) 5 Notes of Cases 387 736
John Harley, The v The William Tell (1865) 2 Mar LC 290, 13 LT 413
.... 757
Johnny Two, The [1992] 2 Lloyd's Rep 257 162
Johnson v Black, The Two Ellens (1872) LR 4 PC 161, 8 Moo PCCNS 398, 41 LJ Adm 33,
1 Asp MLC 208, 20 WR 592, 17 ER 361, 26 LT 1 .... 126, 169, 321, 983, 991
Johnson v Royal Mail Steam Packet Co (1867) LR 3 CP 38, 37 LJCP 33, 3 Mar LC 21, 17
LT 445 330–331
Johnson v Shippen (1703) 2 Ld Raym 982, 92 ER 154, sub nom Johnson v Shippin 11
Mod Rep 30, sub nom Jonson v Shepney 6 Mod Rep 79, sub nom Johnson v Shippin
1 Salk 35, 91 ER 37, sub nom Jonson v Shepney 87 ER 836, sub nom Johnson v
Shepney Holt KB 48, 90 ER 925 435
Jonathan Goodhue, The (1859) Sw 524, 166 ER 1246, 3 LT 825
.... 980–982
Jones, ex p (1816) 4 M & S 450, 105 ER 900 244
Jones v Geddes (1846) 1 Ph 724, 14 Sim 606, 41 ER 808, 60 ER 493, Ct of Ch
.... 101
Jonge Andries, The (1857) Sw 226, 166 ER 1108; affd sub nom Halsey v Albertuszen, The
Jonge Andries (1857) 11 Moo PCC 313, Sw 303, 6 WR 198, 14 ER 714, 166 ER
1148, 30 LTOS 251, PC 869, 884
Jonge Bastiaan, The (1804) 5 Ch Rob 322, 165 ER 791
.... 863, 874

PARA

Jonson v Shepney. See Johnson v Shippen
Jorgensen v Neptune Steam Fishing Co Ltd (1902) 39 SLR 765, 1902 4 F 992, 10 SLT 206
.... 121
Josefina Thorden, The. See Admiralty Comrs v Josefina Thorden (Owners), The Josefina
	Thorden
Joseph Harvey, The (1799) 1 Ch Rob 306 869
Joyce v Capel (1838) 8 C & P 370, 173 ER 536 780
Julia, The. See Bland v Ross, The Julia
Julindur, The (1853) 1 Ecc & Ad 71, 164 ER 42, 11 LT 113
.... 331
Juno, The (1894) 7 Asp MLC 506, 11 R 679, 71 LT 341, P, D and Admlty
.... 739, 749
Jupiter (No 2), The [1925] P 69, 21 Ll L Rep 116, 94 LJP 59, 16 Asp MLC 491, [1925]
	All ER Rep 203, 133 LT 85, CA 104
Jupiter (No 3), The [1927] P 122, 96 LJP 62, P, D and Admlty; affd [1927] P 250, 97 LJP
	33, 17 Asp MLC 250, [1927] All ER Rep 237, 137 LT 333, 43 TLR 741, CA
.... 240

K

KBS, The (1928) 166 LT Jo 52 204
Kaffir Prince, The [1917] P 26, 31 TLR 296, P, D and Admlty
.... 888
Kafiristan, The [1937] 1 All ER 40, CA 865
Kafiristan, The [1937] 3 All ER 747, HL 858
Kafiristan, The. See Beaverford, The (Owners) v The Kafiristan (Owners)
Kafue, The [1920] P 15 note 2 802
Kairos Shipping Ltd v Enka & Co LLC [2014] EWCA Civ 217, [2014] 1 WLR 3883,
	[2014] 1 All ER (Comm) 909, [2014] 1 Lloyd's Rep 586, [2014] All ER (D) 59 (Mar)
.... 196, 996, 1003
Kaiser Wilhelm der Grosse, The [1907] P 259, 76 LJP 138, 10 Asp MLC 504, 51 Sol Jo
	498, 97 LT 366, 23 TLR 554, CA 700, 705
Kaiser Wilhelm II, The (1915) 85 LJP 26, 31 TLR 615, CA
.... 740, 756, 771
Kaleten, The (1914) 30 TLR 572, P, D and Admlty 161, 163, 811, 968
Kamal XXVI (owners and/or demise charterers) v Ariela (owners) [2009] EWHC 177
	(Comm), [2009] All ER (D) 90 (Feb) 800
Kanawha, The (1913) 12 Asp MLC 317, 108 LT 433, P, D and Admlty
.... 189
Kangaroo, The [1918] P 327, 88 LJP 5, P, D and Admlty
.... 855, 863, 866, 868
Kapetan Marcos NL, The. See Hispanica de Petroleos SA and Cia Iberica Refinadera de
	Petroleos SA v Vencedora Oceanica Navegacion SA, The Kapetan Marcos NL
Kapitan Shvetsov, The [1998] 1 Lloyd's Rep 199, CA 100
Karamea, The [1921] P 76, 90 LJP 81, 15 Asp MLC 318, 124 LT 653, 37 TLR 174, CA;
	affd sub nom Haughland, SS v SS Karamea [1922] 1 AC 68, 91 LJP 22, 15 Asp MLC
	430, 38 TLR 161, HL 220, 694, 705, 707, 771
Karnak, The (1868) LR 2 A & E 289, 37 LJ Adm 41, 3 Mar LC 103, 17 WR 56, 18 LT
	661; varied sub nom Droege v Suart, The Karnak (1869) LR 2 PC 505, 6 Moo
	PCCNS 136, 38 LJ Adm 57, 3 Mar LC 276, 17 WR 1028, 16 ER 677, 21 LT 159
.... 134, 443
Kashmir, The [1923] P 85, 92 LJP 113, 16 Asp MLC 81, 128 LT 681, 39 TLR 197, CA
.... 153, 1013
Katcher, The [1969] P 65, [1968] 3 All ER 344, [1969] 2 WLR 395, [1968] 1 Lloyd's Rep
	232, 112 Sol Jo 136, P, D and Admlty 153, 189, 1013
Kate B Jones, The [1892] P 366, 7 Asp MLC 332, 69 LT 197, P, D and Admlty
.... 870, 881
Kate, The [1899] P 165, 68 LJP 41, 8 Asp MLC 539, 47 WR 669, 80 LT 423, 15 TLR
	309, P, D and Admlty 796, 809
Kate, The (1936) 54 Ll L Rep 120, P, D and Admlty 770
Kathleen, The (1874) LR 4 A & E 269, 43 LJ Adm 39, 2 Asp MLC 367, 23 WR 350, 31
	LT 204, HC 178, 890
Katingaki, The. See Delantera Amadora SA v Bristol Channel Shiprepairers Ltd and
	Swansea Dry Dock Co, The Katingaki
Keay v Fenwick (1876) 1 CPD 745, CA 244

PARA

Keith v Burrows (1877) 2 App Cas 636, 46 LJQB 801, 3 Asp MLC 481, 25 WR 831, 37
LT 291, HL 328, 330–332
Kennedy v Earl of Cassilis (1818) 2 Swan 313, 36 ER 635
.... 101
Kennersley Castle, The (1833) 3 Hag Adm 1, 166 ER 308
.... 425, 435
Kenora, The [1921] P 90, 90 LJP 181, 37 TLR 263, P, D and Admlty
.... 894
Kent, The (1862) Lush 495, 167 ER 225 240
Kepler, The (1875) 2 PD 40 732
Kerly, Son and Verden, Re [1901] 1 Ch 467, 70 LJ Ch 189, 49 WR 199, 211, [1900–3] All
ER Rep 858, 45 Sol Jo 120, 206, 83 LT 524, 699, 17 TLR 123, 189, CA
.... 165
Keroula, The (1886) 11 PD 92, 55 LJP 45, 6 Asp MLC 23, 35 WR 60, 55 LT 61, P, D and
Admlty 240
Kestrel, The (1866) LR 1 A & E 78, 12 Jur NS 713, 2 Mar LC 472, 16 LT 72, HC
.... 330
Khanna v Lovell White Durrant (a firm) [1994] 4 All ER 267, [1995] 1 WLR 121, [1994]
45 LS Gaz R 37, (1994) Times, 19 July 204
Khedive, The. See Stoomvart Maatschappy Nederland v Peninsular and Oriental Steam
Navigation Co, The Khedive
Kidston v M'Arthur and Clyde Navigation Trustees (1878) 5 R 936, 15 SLR 631
.... 945
Killeena, The (1881) 6 PD 193, 51 LJP 11, 4 Asp MLC 472, 30 WR 339, 45 LT 621, P, D
and Admlty 863
Kilmaho, The (1900) 16 TLR 155, CA 885
Kingalock, The (1854) 1 Ecc & Ad 263, 18 Jur 409, 164 ER 153, 8 LT 334
.... 871, 884
Kingston-by-Sea, The (1849) 3 Wm Rob 152, 166 ER 920, 9 LT 811, 10 LT 242, 6 Notes
of Cases 651 744
Kingsway, The [1918] P 344, 87 LJP 162, 14 Asp MLC 590, [1918–19] All ER Rep 360,
122 LT 651, CA 799–800, 802
Kirby v Scindia (Owners), The Scindia (1866) LR 1 PC 241, 257, 4 Moo PCCNS 84, 106,
16 ER 248, PC 220, 912
Kirby Hall, The (1883) 8 PD 71, 52 LJ Adm 31, 5 Asp MLC 90, 31 WR 658, 48 LT 797,
P, D and Admlty 205
Kitano Maru, SS (Owners) v SS Otranto (Owners), The Otranto. See Otranto, The
Kitchen v Irvine. See Dickinson v Kitchen
Kite, The [1933] P 154, 46 Ll L Rep 83, 102 LJP 101, 18 Asp MLC 413, [1933] All ER
Rep 234, 149 LT 498, 49 TLR 525, P, D and Admlty 600, 757
Kjobenhavn, The (1874) 2 Asp MLC 213, 30 LT 136, PC
.... 710, 752, 789
Kleinwort Benson Ltd v Sherkate Sahami Sakht, The Myrto (No 2) [1984] 2 Lloyd's Rep
341, [1984] Lexis Citation 1462 .... 173, 178
Knapp v Port of London Authority and Cory Bros Shipping Ltd (third party) [1977] 1
Lloyd's Rep 662 600
Knaresbro, The (1900) [1907] P 38n 700
Knarwater, The (1894) 63 LJP 65, 6 R 784, CA 743
Knight v Faith (1850) 15 QB 649, 19 LJQB 509, 14 Jur 1114, 117 ER 605, 15 LTOS 277
.... 438
Kolpino, The (1904) 73 LJP 29, P, D and Admlty 884
Kong Magnus, The [1891] P 223, 6 Asp MLC 583, 63 LT 715, P, D and Admlty
.... 147, 796, 809, 991
Koningin Juliana, The. See Thuroklint (Owners) v Koningin Juliana (Owners), The
Koningin Juliana
Konstantinidis v World Tankers Corpn, The World Harmony [1967] P 341, [1965] 2 WLR
1275, sub nom The World Harmony, Konstantinidis v World Tankers Corpn Inc
[1965] 2 All ER 139, [1965] 1 Lloyd's Rep 244, P, D and Admlty
.... 94, 810
Koufos v C Czarnikow Ltd, The Heron II [1969] 1 AC 350, [1967] 3 All ER 686, [1967] 3
WLR 1491, [1967] 2 Lloyd's Rep 457, 111 Sol Jo 848, HL
.... 808
Koursk, The [1924] P 140, 93 LJP 72, 16 Asp MLC 374, [1924] All ER Rep 168, 68 Sol
Jo 842, 131 LT 700, 40 TLR 399, CA 775

PARA

Kronprinz Olav, The [1921] P 52, 5 Ll L Rep 203, 90 LJP 398, 15 Asp MLC 312, 125 LT
684, CA 199
Krypton, The and other Barges [1954] 2 Lloyd's Rep 451, P, D and Admlty
.... 891
Krysia Maritime Inc v Intership Ltd [2008] EWHC 1523 (Admlty), [2008] 2 Lloyd's Rep
570, (2008) Times, 20 October, [2008] All ER (D) 08 (Jul)
.... 770
Krysia Maritime Inc v Intership Ltd, The Krysia and Europa [2008] EWHC 1880 (Admlty),
[2009] 1 All ER (Comm) 292, [2008] 2 Lloyd's Rep 707, [2008] NLJR 1148, (2008)
Times, 20 October, [2008] All ER (D) 12 (Aug) 771
Kumanovo, The (Owners) v Massira, The (Owners) [1998] 2 Lloyd's Rep 301, [1998] All
ER (D) 14 .... 149, 807
Kurt Arlt, The, SS or M/V Petrel (Owners) v SS or M/V Kurt Arlt (Owners) [1962] 2 All
ER 27, [1962] 1 Lloyd's Rep 31, sub nom Petrel (Owners) v Kurt Arlt (Owners), The
Kurt Arlt [1962] 1 WLR 439, 106 Sol Jo 392, P, D and Admlty
.... 694
Kwang Tung (Owner) v Ngapoota (Owners), The Ngapoota [1897] AC 391, 66 LJPC 88,
13 TLR 420, PC 762
Kwasind, The (1915) 84 LJP 102, CA 112

L

LD Commodities Rice Merchandising LLC and another v Owners and/or Demise
Charterers of the Vessel Styliani Z [2015] EWHC 3060 (Admlty), [2016] 1 Lloyd's Rep
395, [2015] All ER (D) 260 (Oct) 92
La Plata, The (1857) Sw 220, 166 ER 1105; revsd (1857) Sw 298, 166 ER 1147, 30 LTOS
214, PC 700
Lack v Seward (1829) 4 C & P 106, 172 ER 628 .... 735, 746
Lady Anne, The (1850) 15 Jur 18, 7 Notes of Cases 364, sub nom The Hope v The Lady
Anne 5 LT 241 744
Lady Belle, The [1933] P 275, 46 Ll L Rep 342, 102 LJP 134, 18 Asp MLC 451, [1933]
All ER Rep 881, 150 LT 117, 49 TLR 595, P, D and Admlty
.... 183
Lady Duncannon (Owners) v Eisenach (Owners) [1936] 1 All ER 855, 19 Asp MLC 28,
155 LT 442, P, D and Admlty 888
Lady Emerald, The (1932) 44 Ll L Rep 176, P, D and Admlty
.... 793
Lady Gwendolen, The. See Guinness (Arthur), Son & Co (Dublin) Ltd v The Freshfield
(Owners), The Lady Gwendolen
Lady Katherine Barham, The (1861) Lush 404 919
Lady of the Lake, The (1870) LR 3 A & E 29, 39 LJ Adm 40, 3 Mar LC 317, 18 WR 528,
21 LT 683, HC 106, 241
Lady Worsley, The (1855) 2 Ecc & Ad 253, 164 ER 417
.... 913
Laertes, The (Cargo Ex) (1887) 12 PD 187, 56 LJP 108, 6 Asp MLC 174, 36 WR 111, 57
LT 502, P, D and Admlty 865
Laing (Sir James) & Sons Ltd v Barclay, Curle & Co Ltd [1908] AC 35, 77 LJPC 33, 10
Asp MLC 583, 97 LT 816, HL 236
Laird v Brownlie, The Ulster (1862) Lush 424, 1 Moo PCCNS 31, 8 Jur NS 1067, 1 Mar
LC 234, 10 WR 794, 15 ER 614, PC 744, 754
Lake Farragut, The [1921] P 305, 90 LJP 369, P, D and Admlty
.... 699, 753
Laming & Co v Seater (1889) 16 R 828, 26 SLR 500 330
Lamington v Wentworth (1922) 12 Ll L Rep 203, 259, P, D and Admlty
.... 788
Lancashire, The (1874) LR 4 A & E 198, 2 Asp MLC 202, 29 LT 927, HC
.... 752
Lancaster, The (1883) 9 PD 14, 5 Asp MLC 174, 32 WR 608, 49 LT 705, CA
.... 900
Larchbank (Owners) v British Petrol (Owners), The Larchbank [1943] AC 299, 74 Ll L
Rep 135, 112 LJP 10, 86 Sol Jo 391, 168 LT 161, 59 TLR 116, HL
.... 5
Largo Law, The (1920) 15 Asp MLC 104, 123 LT 560, P, D and Admlty
.... 153, 1013

                                                                                              PARA
Larnax, The (1873) 2 Asp MLC 94, 21 WR 702, 29 LT 120, PC
.... 710, 733
Lash Atlantico, The [1987] 2 Lloyd's Rep 114, CA 207
Lavington International Ltd v The Nore Challenger and The Nore Commander (Bareboat
   Charterers) [2001] 2 All ER (Comm) 667, [2001] 2 Lloyd's Rep 103, [2001] Lexis
   Citation 1389, [2001] All ER (D) 142 (Apr) 126
Law Guarantee and Trust Society v Russian Bank for Foreign Trade [1905] 1 KB 815, 74
   LJKB 577, 10 Asp MLC 41, 10 Com Cas 159, 92 LT 435, 21 TLR 383, CA
.... 329–331
Lawson v Dumlin (1850) 9 CB 54, 19 LJCP 139, 137 ER 811, 14 LTOS 350
.... 779
Layard v Esperance (Owners) and Sobieski (Owners). See Sobieski, The
Le Jonet, The (1872) LR 3 A & E 556, 41 LJ Adm 95, 1 Asp MLC 438, 21 WR 83, 27 LT
   387, HC 855, 869, 899
Leda, The (1856) 2 Jur NS 119, Sw 40, 4 WR 322, 166 ER 1007
.... 121
Leduc & Co v Ward (1888) 20 QBD 475, 57 LJQB 379, 6 Asp MLC 290, 36 WR 537,
   [1886–90] All ER Rep 266, 58 LT 908, 4 TLR 313, CA
.... 437
Legatus, The (1856) Sw 168, 5 WR 154, 166 ER 1077, 5 LT 121
.... 799, 814
Lemington, The (1874) 2 Asp MLC 475, 23 WR 421, 32 LT 69
.... 92, 782, 967
Leo, The (1862) Lush 444, 31 LJPM & A 78, 1 Mar LC 200, 167 ER 198, 6 LT 58
.... 968
Leoborg, The [1962] 2 Lloyd's Rep 146, 106 Sol Jo 592, P, D and Admlty
.... 125
Leoborg, The (No 2) [1963] 2 Lloyd's Rep 268, P, D and Admlty
.... 178
Leoborg, The (No 2) [1964] 1 Lloyd's Rep 380, P, D and Admlty
.... 127
Leon Blum, The [1915] P 290, 13 Asp MLC 273, 31 TLR 582, CA
.... 597–598, 865, 871, 885, 904
Leon XIII, The, Wardrop v The Leon XIII (1883) 8 PD 121, 52 LJP 58, 5 Asp MLC 73, 31
   WR 882, 47 LT 659, CA 128, 478
Leonidas, The (1841) 1 SVAR 226 744
Lepanto, The [1892] P 122, 7 Asp MLC 192, 66 LT 623, P, D and Admlty
.... 863, 881, 924
Lethulier's Case (1690) 2 Salk 443, 91 ER 384 5
Levante, The (1927) 28 Ll L Rep 42, P, D and Admlty 204
Leverington, The (1886) 11 PD 117, 55 LJP 78, 6 Asp MLC 7, 55 LT 386, CA
.... 700
Libra, The (1881) 6 PD 139, 4 Asp MLC 439, 45 LT 161, CA
.... 692
Lidskjalf, The (1856) Sw 117, 166 ER 1050, 3 LT 448 735
Liesbosch, Dredger (Owners) v SS Edison (Owners) [1933] AC 449, 102 LJP 73, 77 Sol Jo
   176, sub nom The Edison 45 Ll L Rep 123, 18 Asp MLC 380, 38 Com Cas 267,
   [1933] All ER Rep 144, 149 LT 49, 49 TLR 289, HL 793, 796–797
Liffey, The (1887) 6 Asp MLC 255, 58 LT 351, P, D and Admlty
.... 866, 935, 1160
Lighter (No 3), The (1902) 18 TLR 322, PC 714
Ligo, The (1831) 2 Hag Adm 356, 166 ER 273 757
Lillois, The [1955] 1 Lloyd's Rep 383, P, D and Admlty
.... 751
Lilly v Ewer (1779) 1 Doug KB 72, 99 ER 50 5
Limerick, The (1876) 1 PD 411, 3 Asp MLC 206, 34 LT 708, CA
.... 321
Linda Flor, The (1857) 4 Jur NS 172, Sw 309, 6 WR 197, 166 ER 1150, 30 LTOS 234
.... 169, 976–977, 981–982
Linda, The [1988] 1 Lloyd's Rep 175 .... 92, 99
Linda, The (1857) 4 Jur NS 146, Sw 306, 6 WR 196, 166 ER 1149, 30 LTOS 234
.... 798, 814
Lindenhall, The [1945] P 8, 78 Ll L Rep 215, 114 LJP 67, 172 LT 229, 61 TLR 284, CA
.... 600
Lindsay v Gibbs (1859) 3 De G & J 690, 28 LJ Ch 692, 5 Jur NS 376, 7 WR 320, 44 ER
   1435, 33 LTOS 20 239

PARA

Lindsay v Leathley (1863) 3 F & F 902, 2 Mar LC 121, 176 ER 410, 11 LT 194, NP 438
Lipson v Harrison (1853) 2 WR 10, 22 LTOS 83 866
Lista, The (1946) 79 Ll L Rep 401, P, D and Admlty 116
Liston v Carpathian (Owners) [1915] 2 KB 42, 84 LJKB 1135, 13 Asp MLC 70, 20 Com Cas 224, 112 LT 994, 31 TLR 226 .... 431, 471, 510
Litherland, Re, ex p Howden (1842) 2 Mont D & De G 574, 11 LJ Bcy 19 331
Little Joe, The (1860) Lush 88, 6 Jur NS 783, 167 ER 46, 2 LT 473 .... 204, 855
Lively, The (1848) 3 Wm Rob 64, 166 ER 887, 6 Notes of Cases 206 870
Liverpool (No 2), The. See Enterprises of Panama Inc, SS, Liverpool (Owners) v Ousel (Owners), The Liverpool (No 2)
Liverpool Bank v Foggo. See Simpson v Fogo
Liverpool Marine Credit Co v Hunter (1868) LR 3 Ch App 479, 37 LJ Ch 386, 3 Mar LC 128, 16 WR 1090, 18 LT 749, CA in Ch 321
Liverpool Marine Credit Co v Wilson (1872) LR 7 Ch App 507, 41 LJ Ch 798, 1 Asp MLC 323, 20 WR 665, 26 LT 717, CA in Ch 321, 332, 334
Liverpool, Brazil and River Plate Steam Navigation Co Ltd v Benham, The Halley (1868) LR 2 PC 193, 5 Moo PCCNS 262, 37 LJ Adm 33, 3 Mar LC 131, 16 WR 998, 16 ER 514, 18 LT 879 967
Liverpool, The [1893] P 154, 7 Asp MLC 340, 1 R 601, 68 LT 719, P, D and Admlty 871
Liviett, The (1883) 8 PD 24, 52 LJP 81, 5 Asp MLC 151, 49 LT 411, P, D and Admlty 891
Livietta, The (1883) 8 PD 209, 52 LJP 81, 5 Asp MLC 132, 49 LT 411, P, D and Admlty 985, 988
Llandovery Castle, The [1920] P 119, 2 Ll L Rep 273, 89 LJP 141, 15 Asp MLC 152, 124 LT 383, P, D and Admlty 152, 1013
Llanelly, The [1914] P 40, 83 LJP 37, 12 Asp MLC 485, 110 LT 269, 30 TLR 154, DC 705
Llanover, The [1947] P 80, 80 Ll L Rep 433, [1948] LJR 108, 177 LT 591, 63 TLR 468, P, D and Admlty 796
Llanover, The (1944) 77 Ll L Rep 198, P, D and Admlty 204
Llanover, The (1946) 79 Ll L Rep 159, P, D and Admlty 757, 788
Lloyd v General Iron Screw Collier Co (1864) 3 H & C 284, 33 LJ Ex 269, 10 Jur NS 661, 2 Mar LC 32, 4 New Rep 298, 12 WR 882, 159 ER 539, 10 LT 586, Exch Ct 770
Lloyd v Guibert (1865) LR 1 QB 115, 6 B & S 100, 35 LJQB 74, 2 Mar LC 283, 122 ER 1134, 13 LT 602, Ex Ch 443
Lloyd v Sheen (1905) 10 Asp MLC 75, 93 LT 174, DC 487, 510
Lloyd Pacifico, The [1995] 1 Lloyd's Rep 54 .... 111, 132
Loch Tulla, The (1950) 84 Ll L Rep 62, P, D and Admlty 863
Lochlibo, The (1850) 3 Wm Rob 310, 14 Jur 792, 166 ER 978; on appeal sub nom Pollok v M'Alpin, The Lochlibo (1851) 7 Moo PCC 427, 13 ER 945, PC 736, 788
Lockwoods, The (1845) 9 Jur 1017 893
Lomonosoff, The [1921] P 97, 90 LJP 141, 37 TLR 151, P, D and Admlty 855, 861, 868
London v Exeter City and Sea Serpent (1922) 12 Ll L Rep 423, P, D and Admlty 757
London and Edinburgh Shipping Co v Eaton, The Iona. See Iona, The
London Corpn, The [1935] P 70, 51 Ll L Rep 68, 104 LJP 20, 18 Asp MLC 535, [1935] All ER Rep 393, 79 Sol Jo 86, 152 LT 487, 51 TLR 224, CA 800
London Merchant, The (1837) 3 Hag Adm 394, 166 ER 451 .... 872, 881
London Steamship Owners' Insurance Co v Grampian Steamship Co (1890) 24 QBD 663, 59 LJQB 549, 6 Asp MLC 506, 38 WR 651, 62 LT 784, 6 TLR 288, CA 772
London, HMS [1914] P 72, 83 LJP 74, 12 Asp MLC 405, 109 LT 960, 30 TLR 196, P, D and Admlty 793, 802

PARA

London, The. See Morgan v Sim, The London

Londonderry (Owners) v Dolbadarn Castle (Owners) (1845) 4 Note of Cases Supplement
xxxi 739

Longford, The (1881) 6 PD 60, 50 LJP 28, 4 Asp MLC 385, 29 WR 491, 44 LT 254, P, D
and Admlty 116, 204, 874

Longford, The (1889) 14 PD 34, 58 LJP 33, 6 Asp MLC 371, 37 WR 372, 60 LT 373, 5
TLR 256, [1886–90] All ER Rep Ext 1433, CA 92

Lord v Pacific Steam Navigation Co Ltd, The Oropesa [1943] P 32, [1943] 1 All ER 211,
112 LJP 91, 168 LT 364, 59 TLR 103, CA 763

Lord Bangor, The [1896] P 28, 65 LJP 6, 8 Asp MLC 217, 11 R 822, 73 LT 414, P, D and
Admlty 743

Lord Citrine, The (Owners) v Hebridean Coast (Owners), The Hebridean Coast [1961] AC
545, [1961] 1 All ER 82, [1961] 2 WLR 48, [1960] 2 Lloyd's Rep 423, 105 Sol Jo 37,
HL 803–806

Lord Strathcona (No 2), The [1926] P 18, 23 Ll L Rep 225, 95 LJP 168, 17 Asp MLC 24,
134 LT 511, P, D and Admlty 169

Lord Strathcona, The [1925] P 143, 22 Ll L Rep 368, 95 LJP 5, 16 Asp MLC 536, 69 Sol
Jo 762, 133 LT 765, 41 TLR 638, P, D and Admlty 169, 329–331

Lorentzen (as Director of Shipping and Curator of Royal Norwegian Government) v The
Alcoa Rambler (Alcoa SS Co Inc, Owners) [1949] AC 236, PC
.... 705

Louis Sheid, The [1958] 1 Lloyd's Rep 606, P, D and Admlty
.... 757, 759, 788

Louisa, The [1906] P 145, 75 LJP 76, 10 Asp MLC 256, 94 LT 558, P, D and Admlty
.... 886

Louisa, The (1843) 2 Wm Rob 22, 166 ER 664, 2 Notes of Cases 149
.... 904

Louisa, The (1848) 3 Wm Rob 99, 12 Jur 946, 166 ER 900, 8 LT 440, 6 Notes of Cases
531 988

Louise, The (1901) 18 TLR 19, DC 780

Love v Baker (1665) 1 Cas in Ch 67, Nels 103, 21 ER 801, 22 ER 698, sub nom Lowe v
Baker Freem Ch 125, 22 ER 1101 101

Love Bird, The (1881) 6 PD 80, 4 Asp MLC 427, 44 LT 650, P, D and Admlty
.... 759

Lowe v Baker. See Love v Baker

Lowther Castle, The (1825) 1 Hag Adm 384, 166 ER 137
.... 510

Lu Shan, The [1991] 2 Lloyd's Rep 386, [1991] Lexis Citation 1464
.... 153, 1013

Lucile Bloomfield, The [1967] 2 Lloyd's Rep 308, P, D and Admlty
.... 143

Lucile Bloomfield, The, Motor Vessel Ronda (Owners) v SS Lucile Bloomfield (Owners)
[1966] 3 All ER 294n, [1966] 1 WLR 1525, [1966] 2 Lloyd's Rep 239, P, D and
Admlty; on appeal [1967] 2 All ER 633n, [1967] 1 WLR 697n, [1967] 1 Lloyd's Rep
341 .... 204, 222, 771

Luhesand, The [1955] 2 Lloyd's Rep 203, P, D and Admlty
.... 204

Luimneach, The (1936) 54 Ll L Rep 5, CA 806

Luna, The [1920] P 22, 89 LJP 109, 15 Asp MLC 152, 124 LT 382, 36 TLR 112, P, D and
Admlty 600

Lusitania, The. See Pierce v Bemis, The Lusitania

Luxford v Large (1832) 5 C & P 421 741
Luxford v Large (1833) 5 C & P 421, 172 ER 1036 110
Lycaon, The (1949) 82 Ll L Rep 691, P, D and Admlty 899
Lyn, The (1883) Pritchard's Admiralty Digest (3rd Edn) 291
.... 735
Lyrma (No 2), The [1978] 2 Lloyd's Rep 30 979

M

MIOM 1 Ltd v Sea Echo ENE [2010] EWHC 3180 (Admlty), [2010] All ER (D) 113 (Dec)
.... 771

MSC Mediterranean Shipping Co SA v Delumar BVBA [2000] 2 All ER (Comm) 458,
[2000] 2 Lloyd's Rep 399, [2000] Lexis Citation 3520, [2000] All ER (D) 988
.... 996

PARA

MSC Mediterranean Shipping Co SA v The Tychy (owners) [1999] 1 All ER (Comm) 819,
    [1999] 2 Lloyd's Rep 11, (1999) Times, 30 April, [1999] Lexis Citation 2410, 143 Sol
    Jo LB 122 93
MV Eleftheria v MV Hakki Deval [2006] EWHC 2809 (Admlty), [2006] All ER (D) 96
    (Nov) 693
M/V Derbyshire, Re (1999) Times, 28 October 844
Maasdam, The (1893) 7 Asp MLC 400, 6 R 716, 69 LT 659, 10 TLR 31, P, D and Admlty
    911
Mac, The (1882) 7 PD 126, 51 LJP 81, 4 Asp MLC 555, 46 LT 907, CA
    229
McDougall v Aeromarine of Emsworth Ltd [1958] 3 All ER 431, [1958] 1 WLR 1126,
    [1958] 2 Lloyd's Rep 345, 102 Sol Jo 860 236
Macgregor Laird, The [1867] WN 308 884–885
Macgregor Laird, The [1953] 2 Lloyd's Rep 259, P, D and Admlty
    .... 204, 872
Macgregor, The. See British Fame (Owners) v Macgregor (Owners), The Macgregor
McHenry v Lewis (1882) 22 Ch D 397, 52 LJ Ch 325, 31 WR 305, 47 LT 549, CA
    101
Maciej Rataj, The [1992] 2 Lloyd's Rep 552, CA; on appeal sub nom Maciej Rataj, The,
    Tatry (cargo owners) v Maciej Rataj: C-406/92 [1999] QB 515, [1994] ECR I-5439,
    [1999] 2 WLR 181, [1995] All ER (EC) 229, [1995] 1 Lloyd's Rep 302, (1994) Times,
    28 December, [1995] IL Pr 81, ECJ 92, 95–96, 99
MacIver v J & A Gardner Ltd 2001 SLT 585, OH 626
Mackenzie v Pooley (1856) 25 LJ Ex 124, 11 Exch 638, 4 WR 262, 156 ER 986, 26 LTOS
    223 434
Mackintosh v Mitcheson (1849) 18 LJ Ex 385, 4 Exch 175, 154 ER 1171, 13 LTOS 344
    432
McLean and Hope v Fleming (1871) LR 6 QB 558n, LR 2 Sc & Div 128, 1 Asp MLC 160,
    25 LT 317, HL 427
McLellan v Gumm (1867) LR 2 Ch App 282 327
Macleod, The (1880) 5 PD 254, 50 LJP 6, 29 WR 340, P, D and Admlty
    130
M'Manus v Crickett (1800) 1 East 106, 102 ER 43 781
Macroom, The (1927) 28 Ll L Rep 34, 17 Asp MLC 288, 71 Sol Jo 472, 137 LT 418, P, D
    and Admlty 183
MacShannon v Rockware Glass Ltd [1978] AC 795, [1978] 1 All ER 625, [1978] 2 WLR
    362, 122 Sol Jo 81, HL 100
Maddox v Fisher, The Independence. See Independence, The
Madonna D'Idra, The (1811) 1 Dods 37, 165 ER 1224, HC
    .... 970, 980, 982
Madras, The [1898] P 90, 67 LJP 53, 8 Asp MLC 397, 78 LT 325, P, D and Admlty
    .... 598, 855
Maeburn v Leckie (1822) cited in Abbott's Law of Merchant Ships and Seaman (14th Edn)
    15 438
Maersk Nimrod, The. See Petrofina SA v AOT Ltd, The Maersk Nimrod
Magalhaens v Busher (1814) 4 Camp 54, 171 ER 18, NP
    5
Magdalen, The (1861) 31 LJPM & A 22, 1 Mar LC 189, 5 LT 807
    .... 893–894, 911
Maggie Armstrong, The v The Blue Bell (1865) 2 Mar LC 318, 14 LT 340
    735
Magna Charta, The (1871) 1 Asp MLC 153, 25 LT 512, PC
    205
Maid of Kent, The (1881) 6 PD 178, 50 LJP 71, 4 Asp MLC 476, 29 WR 897, 45 LT 718,
    P, D and Admlty 79, 143
Makedonia, The. See Island Tug and Barge Ltd v SS Makedonia (Owners), The Makedonia
Malcomson v General Steam Navigation Co, The Ranger and The Cologne (1872) LR 4 PC
    519, 9 Moo PCCNS 352, 1 Asp MLC 484, 21 WR 273, 17 ER 546, 27 LT 769, PC
    705
Mali Ivo, The (1869) LR 2 A & E 356, 38 LJ Adm 34, 3 Mar LC 244, 20 LT 681, HC
    .... 3, 86
Manchester Regiment, The [1938] P 117, 60 Ll L Rep 279, 107 LJP 63, 19 Asp MLC 189,
    159 LT 227, 54 TLR 710, P, D and Admlty 703, 707, 739

PARA

Manchester Trust Ltd v Furness, Withy & Co Ltd [1895] 2 QB 539, 8 Asp MLC 57, 1
Com Cas 39, 14 R 739, 44 WR 178, 73 LT 110, sub nom Manchester Trust Ltd v
Turner, Withy & Co Ltd 64 LJQB 766, 11 TLR 530, CA
.... 242, 428
Manley v Kyles (1923) 16 Ll L Rep 272, P, D and Admlty
.... 735
Manning v Gist (1782) 3 Doug KB 74, 99 ER 545 5
Manor, The [1907] P 339, 77 LJP 10, 10 Asp MLC 446, 96 LT 871, CA
.... 329–330
Mardina Merchant, The [1974] 3 All ER 749, [1975] 1 WLR 147, [1974] 2 Lloyd's Rep
424, 119 Sol Jo 63 .... 158, 169, 173
Marechal Suchet, The [1896] P 233, 65 LJP 94, 8 Asp MLC 158, 45 WR 141, 74 LT 789,
12 TLR 510, P, D and Admlty 159
Maréchal Suchet, The [1911] P 1, 80 LJP 51, 11 Asp MLC 553, 103 LT 848, 26 TLR 660,
P, D and Admlty 597–598, 783, 871
Margaret Mitchell, The (1858) 4 Jur NS 1193, Sw 382, 166 ER 1174, 7 LT 803
.... 439–441
Margaret, The v The Tuscar (1866) Holt Adm 14, 15 LT 86
.... 741
Margaret, The (1881) 6 PD 76, 50 LJP 67, 4 Asp MLC 375, 29 WR 533, 44 LT 291, CA
.... 733, 756, 769–770
Margery, The [1902] P 157, 71 LJP 83, 9 Asp MLC 304, 50 WR 654, 86 LT 863, DC
.... 885
Margolle v Delta Maritime Co Ltd [2002] EWHC 2452 (Admlty), [2003] 1 All ER (Comm)
102, [2003] 1 Lloyd's Rep 203, [2002] All ER (D) 418 (Nov)
.... 996
Marguerite Molinos, The [1903] P 160, 72 LJP 56, 9 Asp MLC 424, 89 LT 192, P, D and
Admlty 855, 873
Maria Jane, The (1850) 14 Jur 857, 8 LT 582 .... 865, 867
Maria, The (1809) Edw 175, 165 ER 1073, HC 910
Maridive VII v Key Singapore, The Key Singapore [2004] EWHC 2227 (Comm), [2005] 1
All ER (Comm) 99, [2005] 1 Lloyd's Rep 91, [2004] All ER (D) 225 (Oct)
.... 599, 742, 865, 895
Marie, The (1882) 7 PD 203, 5 Asp MLC 27, 47 LT 737, P, D and Admlty
.... 894
Marigola, The (1929) 34 Ll L Rep 217, P, D and Admlty
.... 798
Marine Craft Constructors Ltd v Erland Blomqvist (Engineers) Ltd [1953] 1 Lloyd's Rep
514 .... 110, 229
Marinegra, The [1959] 2 Lloyd's Rep 65, CA; affd [1960] 2 Lloyd's Rep 1, HL
.... 758
Marion, The (1884) 10 PD 4, 54 LJP 8, 5 Asp MLC 339, 33 WR 432, 51 LT 906, P, D
and Admlty 107, 241
Mariposa, The [1896] P 273, 65 LJP 104, 8 Asp MLC 159, 45 WR 191, 75 LT 54, 12
TLR 518, P, D and Admlty 885
Maritime Trader, The [1981] 2 Lloyd's Rep 153, [1981] Com LR 27
.... 93
Mark Lane, The (1890) 15 PD 135, 6 Asp MLC 540, 39 WR 47, 63 LT 468, P, D and
Admlty 884
Markland, The (1871) LR 3 A & E 340, 1 Asp MLC 44, 24 LT 596, HC
.... 171
Marlborough Hill, The v Cowan & Sons [1921] 1 AC 444, 5 Ll L Rep 362, 90 LJPC 87,
15 Asp MLC 163, 26 Com Cas 121, 124 LT 645, 37 TLR 190, PC
.... 159
Marlborough, The (1943) 76 Ll L Rep 102, Ct of Sess 873
Marmion, The (1913) 29 TLR 646, P, D and Admlty 742
Marpesia, The (1872) LR 4 PC 212, 8 Moo PCCNS 468, 1 Asp MLC 261, 17 ER 387, 26
LT 333, PC 744, 788–789
Marpessa, The [1891] P 403, 61 LJP 9, 7 Asp MLC 155, 40 WR 239, [1891–4] All ER
Rep 187, 66 LT 356, P, D and Admlty 807
Marquis of Huntly, The (1835) 3 Hag Adm 246 886
Marriott v Anchor Reversionary Co Ltd (1861) 3 De GF & J 177, 30 LJ Ch 571, 7 Jur NS
713, 1 Mar LC 91, 9 WR 726, 45 ER 846, 4 LT 590 333
Mars, The and other Barges (1948) 81 Ll L Rep 452, P, D and Admlty
.... 872
Martha, The (1859) Sw 489, 166 ER 1226 894

PARA

Martin v Temperley (1843) 4 QB 298, 7 JP 145, 12 LJQB 129, 3 Gal & Dav 497, 7 Jur
150, 114 ER 912, 11 LT 159 780
Martin Luther, The (1857) Sw 287, 166 ER 1141 .... 897, 906
Mary Ann, The (1823) 1 Hag Adm 158 908
Mary Ann, The (1846) 10 Jur 253, 4 Notes of Cases 376
.... 435
Mary Ann, The (1865) LR 1 A & E 8, 35 LJ Adm 6, 12 Jur NS 31, 2 Mar LC 294, 14
WR 136, 13 LT 384, HC 321, 968–969
Mary Pleasants, The (1857) Sw 224, 166 ER 1107 .... 116, 876
Mary Stewart, The (1844) 2 Wm Rob 244, 166 ER 746, 2 LTOS 375
.... 757
Mary Tug Co v British Indian Steam Navigation Co, The Meanatchy [1897] AC 351, LR
24Ind App 129, 1 CWN 329, 66 LJPC 92, ILR 24 Calc 627, PC
.... 734–735, 762
Mary, The (1843) 1 Wm Rob 448 862
Mary, The (1879) 5 PD 14, 48 LJP 66, 4 Asp MLC 183, 28 WR 95, 41 LT 351, P, D and
Admlty 742
Massachusetts, The (1842) 1 Wm Rob 371, 166 ER 612, 4 LT 839
.... 759
Mathesis, The (1844) 2 Wm Rob 286, 8 Jur 582, 166 ER 762, 3 Notes of Cases 133
.... 164
Mathilda, The (1883) 5 Asp MLC 75, 48 LT 771, CA 428
Maude, The (1876) 3 Asp MLC 338, 36 LT 26, P, D and Admlty
.... 911
Mavor, Re, ex p Halkett (1814) 2 Rose 194, sub nom Halkett, ex p 3 Ves & B 135, 35 ER
430 435
Mawan (now named) Mara, The [1988] 2 Lloyd's Rep 459
.... 158, 169
Maxima, The (1878) 4 Asp MLC 21, 39 LT 112, P, D and Admlty
.... 330
Meanatchy, The. See Mary Tug Co v British Indian Steam Navigation Co, The Meanatchy
Meandros, The [1925] P 61, 94 LJP 37, 16 Asp MLC 476, 132 LT 750, 41 TLR 236, P, D
and Admlty 874, 964, 969
Mecca, The [1895] P 95, 64 LJP 40, 7 Asp MLC 529, 11 R 742, 43 WR 209, 39 Sol Jo
132, 71 LT 711, 11 TLR 139, CA 432
Mediana, The [1899] P 127, 8 Asp MLC 493, 80 LT 173, CA; on appeal sub nom
Mediana (Owners) v Comet (Owners, Master and Crew of the Lightship), The
Mediana [1900] AC 113, 69 LJP 35, 9 Asp MLC 41, 48 WR 398, [1900–3] All ER
Rep 126, 44 Sol Jo 259, 82 LT 95, 16 TLR 194, HL 793, 806
Medina, The (1876) 1 PD 272, P, D and Admlty; affd (1876) 2 PD 5, 3 Asp MLC 305, 25
WR 156, 35 LT 779, CA 143, 883–884
Medway Drydock and Engineering Co Ltd v MV Andrea Ursula, The Andrea Ursula
[1973] QB 265, [1971] 1 All ER 821, [1971] 2 WLR 681, [1971] 1 Lloyd's Rep 145,
115 Sol Jo 32, P, D and Admlty 86, 92–93, 810
Medway Oil and Storage Co Ltd v Continental Contractors Ltd [1929] AC 88, 98 LJKB
148, [1928] All ER Rep 330, 140 LT 98, 45 TLR 20, HL
.... 222
Meggie, The (1866) LR 1 A & E 77, HC 241
Meiklereid v West (1876) 1 QBD 428, 40 JP 708, 45 LJMC 91, 3 Asp MLC 129, 24 WR
703, 34 LT 353 243
Mekhanik Evgrafov and Ivan Derbenev, The (No 2) [1988] 1 Lloyd's Rep 330
.... 189, 196
Melanie (Owners) v San Onofre (Owners) [1925] AC 246, 20 Ll L Rep 288, 94 LJP 17, 16
Asp MLC 479, 132 LT 567, 41 TLR 206, HL 863, 868, 886
Melanie (Owners) SS v SS San Onofre (Owners) [1927] AC 162n, 63 Sol Jo 552, 35 TLR
507, HL 205, 220, 758
Mellona, The (1847) 3 Wm Rob 7, 11 Jur 783, 166 ER 865, 9 LTOS 474, 5 Notes of
Cases 450, HC 739, 798
Mellona, The (1848) 3 Wm Rob 16, 12 Jur 271, 11 LTOS 182, 6 Notes of Cases 62
.... 968
Melpomene, The (1873) LR 4 A & E 129, 42 LJ Adm 45, 1 Asp MLC 515, 21 WR 956,
28 LT 76, HC 863
Memnon v Paulsboro (1920) 5 Ll L Rep 250, CA 770
Mendip Range (Owners) v Radcliffe [1921] 1 AC 556, 90 LJP 209, 15 Asp MLC 242,
[1921] All ER Rep 224, 124 LT 706, 37 TLR 474, HL 707, 717

PARA

Menetone v Gibbons (1789) 3 Term Rep 267, 100 ER 568
.... 435
Mentor, The (1799) 1 Ch Rob 179, 1 Eng Pr Cas 96, 165 ER 141
.... 786
Merak, The (Owners of Cargo on Board) v The Merak (Owners), The Merak [1965] P
  223, [1965] 1 All ER 230, [1965] 2 WLR 250, [1964] 2 Lloyd's Rep 527, 108 Sol Jo
  1012, CA 103, 156
Mercator, The (1910) 26 TLR 450, P, D and Admlty 886
Mercedes de Larrinaga, The [1904] P 215, 73 LJP 65, 9 Asp MLC 571, 90 LT 520, 20
  TLR 375, P, D and Admlty 204
Merchant Prince, The [1892] P 179, 7 Asp MLC 208, [1891–4] All ER Rep 396, 67 LT
  251, 8 TLR 430, CA 737, 757, 788
Merchant Prince, The (1885) 10 PD 139, 54 LJP 79, 5 Asp MLC 520, 34 WR 231, 53 LT
  914, P, D and Admlty 710
Merchant Shipping Acts 1894 to 1906, Re, Appeal by Dunn, Second Officer of SS City of
  Lincoln (1947) 80 Ll L Rep 692, DC 224
Merdeka, The [1982] 1 Lloyd's Rep 401 164
Meredith, The (1885) 10 PD 69, sub nom White v Ditchfield, The Meredith 5 Asp MLC
  400, 52 LT 520, P, D and Admlty 238
Merle, The (1874) 2 Asp MLC 402, 31 LT 447 967
Merrimac, The (1868) 18 LT 92 870
Mersey Docks and Harbour Board v Hay, SS The Countess [1923] AC 345, 92 LJP 65, 16
  Asp MLC 161, 67 Sol Jo 481, 129 LT 325, 39 TLR 302, HL
  .... 201, 973, 975, 982, 984
Mersey Docks and Harbour Board v Marpessa (Owners) [1907] AC 241, 76 LJP 128, 10
  Asp MLC 464, [1904–7] All ER Rep 855, 51 Sol Jo 530, 97 LT 1, 23 TLR 572, HL
  806
Mersey Docks and Harbour Board v Turner, The Zeta [1893] AC 468, 57 JP 660, 63 LJP
  17, 7 Asp MLC 369, 1 R 307, 69 LT 630, 9 TLR 624, HL
  .... 3, 80, 86, 110, 765, 967
Mersey Docks and Harbour Board and Admiralty Comrs, Re [1920] 3 KB 223, 90 LJKB
  148, sub nom Mersey Docks and Harbour Board v Admiralty Comrs 15 Asp MLC 24,
  123 LT 462, 36 TLR 547, DC 804
Mersey Docks and Harbour Board Trustees v Gibbs (1866) LR 1 HL 93, 30 JP 467, 11 HL
  Cas 686, 35 LJ Ex 225, 12 Jur NS 571, 2 Mar LC 353, 14 WR 872, 11 ER 1500,
  [1861–73] All ER Rep 397, 14 LT 677, HL 945
Messageries Imperiales Co v Baines (1863) 1 Mar LC 285, 11 WR 322, 7 LT 763
  427
Metall Market OOO v Vitorio Shipping Co Ltd, The Lehmann Timber [2013] EWCA Civ
  650, [2014] QB 760, [2014] 2 WLR 979, [2013] 2 All ER (Comm) 585, [2013] 2
  Lloyd's Rep 541, [2013] All ER (D) 59 (Jun) 974, 990–991
Metcalfe v Britannia Ironworks Co (1877) 2 QBD 423, 46 LJQB 443, 3 Asp MLC 407, 25
  WR 720, 36 LT 451, CA 889
Meteor, The v The Sylph. See Sylph, The
Metvale Ltd v Monsanto International Sarl [2008] EWHC 3002 (Admlty), [2009] 1 All ER
  (Comm) 1158, [2009] 1 Lloyd's Rep 246, [2008] All ER (D) 83 (Dec)
  .... 993, 1003
Mikado, The. See NCNB Texas National Bank v Evensong Co Ltd, The Mikado
Milan, The (1861) Lush 388, 31 LJPM & A 105, 1 Mar LC 185, 167 ER 167, 5 LT 590
  740
Milanese, The (1881) 45 LT 151, Pritchard's Admiralty Digest (3rd Edn) 222, HL
  739
Milburn & Co v Jamaica Fruit Importing and Trading Co of London [1900] 2 QB 540, 69
  LJQB 860, 9 Asp MLC 122, 5 Com Cas 346, 83 LT 321, 16 TLR 515, CA
  133
Miller & Co v Potter, Wilson & Co (1875) 3 R 105, 13 SLR 70
  435
Millicent, The [1891] WN 162, P, D and Admlty 136
Mills v Armstrong, The Bernina. See Bernina (2), The
Millwall, The [1905] P 155, [1904–7] All ER Rep Ext 1387, sub nom Page v Darling and
  Gaselee, The Millwall 74 LJP 61, 82, 10 Asp MLC 113, 53 WR 471, 93 LT 426, 429,
  21 TLR 346, CA 600
Mimosa, The [1944] WN 74, P, D and Admlty 771

PARA

Mineral Dampier, The (Owners) v Hanjin Madras, The (Owners)[2001] EWCA Civ 1278, [2001] 2 All ER (Comm) 805, [2001] 2 Lloyd's Rep 419, [2001] All ER (D) 457 (Jul) 707

Minerva, The [1933] P 224, 46 Ll L Rep 212, 102 LJP 129, 18 Asp MLC 426, [1933] All ER Rep 870, 149 LT 567, 49 TLR 563, P, D and Admlty 110

Minerva, The (1825) 1 Hag Adm 347, 166 ER 123 510

Ministry of Trade of the Republic of Iraq v Tsavliris Salvage (International) Ltd [2008] EWHC 612 (Comm), [2008] 2 All ER (Comm) 805, [2008] 2 Lloyd's Rep 90, [2008] All ER (D) 14 (Apr) 851–853, 919

Minna Craig Steamship Co v Chartered Mercantile Bank of India, London and China [1897] 1 QB 460, 66 LJQB 339, 8 Asp MLC 241, 2 Com Cas 110, 45 WR 338, 41 Sol Jo 310, 76 LT 310, 13 TLR 241, CA 965

Minna, The (1868) LR 2 A & E 97, HC 759, 790

Minneapolis, The [1902] P 30, 71 LJP 28, 9 Asp MLC 270, 86 LT 263, P, D and Admlty 867, 906–907

Minnehaha, The (1861) Lush 335, 167 ER 149, [1861–73] All ER Rep 346, sub nom Ward v M'Corkill, The Minnehaha 15 Moo PCC 133, 7 Jur NS 1257, 1 Mar LC 111, 9 WR 925, 4 LT 810, sub nom The Storm King and The United Kingdom (Owners) v The Minnehaha (Owners) 30 LJPM & A 211, PC 597–598, 871, 900

Minnetonka, The [1904] P 202, 73 LJP 62, 9 Asp MLC 544, 52 WR 672, 90 LT 354, P, D and Admlty; revsd [1905] P 206, 74 LJP 97, 10 Asp MLC 142, 53 WR 521, [1904–7] All ER Rep 873, 93 LT 581, 21 TLR 407, CA 150, 808

Minnie, The [1894] P 336, 7 Asp MLC 521, 11 R 705, 71 LT 715, CA 700

Miraflores (Owners) v George Livanos (Owners) [1967] 1 AC 826, [1967] 1 All ER 672, [1967] 2 WLR 806, [1967] 1 Lloyd's Rep 191, 111 Sol Jo 211, HL 110, 204, 220, 771, 774, 778

Miranda, The (1872) LR 3 A & E 561, 41 LJ Adm 82, 1 Asp MLC 440, 21 WR 84, 27 LT 389, HC 865

Mitchell v Darthez (1836) 2 Bing NC 555, 5 LJCP 154, 1 Hodg 418, 2 Scott 771, 132 ER 217 889

Mitcheson v Oliver (1855) 5 E & B 419, 25 LJQB 39, 1 Jur NS 900, 119 ER 537, 3 CLR 1104, 25 LTOS 258, Ex Ch 432

Mitera Marigo (M/V) (Owners) v M/V Fritz Thyssen (Owners), The Fritz Thyssen [1968] P 255, [1967] 1 All ER 628, [1967] 2 WLR 919, [1967] 1 Lloyd's Rep 104, 111 Sol Jo 353, P, D and Admlty; affd [1968] P 261n, [1967] 3 All ER 117n, [1967] 3 WLR 990, [1967] 2 Lloyd's Rep 199, CA 795, 798

Mobile, The (1856) Sw 69, 166 ER 1024, sub nom The Fenix v The Mobile 7 LT 258; on appeal sub nom Mobile, The (1856) 10 Moo PCC 467, Sw 127, 4 WR 708, 166 ER 1055, 28 LTOS 129, PC 744

Modica, The [1926] P 72, 24 Ll L Rep 155, 95 LJP 100, 17 Asp MLC 30, 135 LT 61, P, D and Admlty 204

Molière, The [1925] P 27, 94 LJP 28, 16 Asp MLC 470, 132 LT 733, 41 TLR 154, P, D and Admlty 112, 778, 800

Monarch, The (1839) 1 Wm Rob 21, 166 ER 481 206

Monarch, The (1886) 12 PD 5, 56 LJP 114, 6 Asp MLC 90, 35 WR 292, 56 LT 204, P, D and Admlty 869

Monica S, The [1968] P 741, [1967] 3 All ER 740, [1968] 2 WLR 431, [1967] 2 Lloyd's Rep 113, 112 Sol Jo 131, P, D and Admlty 83, 93, 160

Monica, The [1912] P 147, 81 LJP 92, 12 Asp MLC 164, 106 LT 349, 28 TLR 154, P, D and Admlty 183

Monkseaton, The (1889) 14 PD 51, 58 LJP 52, 6 Asp MLC 383, 37 WR 523, 60 LT 662, CA 204

Mons, The [1932] P 109, 43 Ll L Rep 151, 101 LJP 67, 18 Asp MLC 311, 147 LT 260, 48 TLR 555, P, D and Admlty 981–982

Montague v Babbs [1972] 1 All ER 240, [1972] 1 WLR 176, [1972] 1 Lloyd's Rep 65, 136 JP 144, 116 Sol Jo 95, DC 1170

Monte Rosa, The [1893] P 23, 62 LJP 20, 7 Asp MLC 326, 1 R 557, 41 WR 304, 68 LT 299, P, D and Admlty 733, 756, 769–770

Moore v City of Malines (Owners) and Purvis Shipping Co Ltd (1947) 81 Ll L Rep 96, P, D and Admlty 427, 471

PARA

Morgan v Castlegate Steamship Co, The Castlegate [1893] AC 38, 62 LJPC 17, 7 Asp
MLC 284, 1 R 97, 41 WR 349, 68 LT 99, 9 TLR 139, HL
.... 92, 127, 131, 433, 756, 966–968, 970–971

Morgan v Sim, The London (1857) 11 Moo PCC 307, 14 ER 712, sub nom The City of
London, Morgan v Sim Sw 300, 30 LTOS 236, PC 757

Morgengry, The and The Blackcock [1900] P 1, 69 LJP 1, 8 Asp MLC 591, 48 WR 121,
81 LT 417, 16 TLR 14, CA 774

Morris v Lyonesse Salvage Co Ltd, The Association and The Romney [1970] 2 Lloyd's Rep
59, P, D and Admlty 122, 139

Morris v Robinson (1824) 3 B & C 196, 5 Dow & Ry KB 34, 107 ER 706, [1824–34] All
ER Rep 347 .... 440, 443

Morrison Steamship Co Ltd v SS Greystoke Castle (Owners of Cargo lately laden on)
[1947] AC 265, [1946] 2 All ER 696, [1947] LJR 297, 176 LT 66, 63 TLR 11, HL
.... 133, 807–808

Mortiboys v Skinner, The Devonshire [1952] 2 Lloyd's Rep 95, P, D and Admlty
.... 143

Morviken, The. See Hollandia, The
Moschanthy, The [1971] 1 Lloyd's Rep 37, P, D and Admlty
.... 111

Moss (James) & Co v African Steamship Co, The Calabar (1868) LR 2 PC 238, 5 Moo
PCCNS 291, 3 Mar LC 195, 16 ER 525, 19 LT 768, PC
.... 739

Mouna, The [1991] 2 Lloyd's Rep 221, (1991) Times, 7 May, [1990] Lexis Citation 1822,
CA 153, 1013

Mount Vernon, The (1891) 7 Asp MLC 32, 64 LT 148, P, D and Admlty
.... 238

Mourne, The [1901] P 68, 70 LJP 7, 9 Asp MLC 155, 83 LT 748, 17 TLR 194, P, D and
Admlty 754

Mud Hopper No 4, The (1879) 4 Asp MLC 103, 40 LT 462, P, D and Admlty
.... 814, 899

Mudlark, The [1911] P 116, 80 LJP 117, 27 TLR 385, P, D and Admlty
.... 229

Mulbera, The [1937] P 82, 57 Ll L Rep 31, 106 LJP 57, 19 Asp MLC 103, 156 LT 348,
53 TLR 314, P, D and Admlty 757

Mulliner v Florence (1878) 3 QBD 484, 42 JP 293, 47 LJQB 700, 26 WR 385, 38 LT 167,
CA 990

Mungana, The. See Nestor, SS (Owners) v SS Mungana (Owners), The Mungana
Murphy v Palgreave (1869) 21 LT 209 741

Myrto (No 2), The. See Kleinwort Benson Ltd v Sherkate Sahami Sakht, The Myrto (No 2)
Myrto, The [1977] 2 Lloyd's Rep 243; revsd [1978] 1 Lloyd's Rep 11, CA
.... 178, 330

Mystery, The [1902] P 115, 71 LJP 39, 9 Asp MLC 281, 50 WR 414, 86 LT 359, DC
.... 204, 785

N

NCNB Texas National Bank v Evensong Co Ltd, The Mikado [1992] 1 Lloyd's Rep 163
.... 108

NR Gosfabrick, The (1858) 4 Jur NS 742, Sw 344, 6 WR 871, 166 ER 1160, 31 LTOS
345 432

NV Bureau Wijsmuller v The Tojo Maru (Owners, Cargo and Freight) [1968] 2 Lloyd's
Rep 436, CA 91

Nador, The [1909] P 300, 78 LJP 106, 11 Asp MLC 283, 100 LT 1007, P, D and Admlty
.... 789

Nagasaki Spirit, The. See Semco Salvage & Marine Pte Ltd v Lancer Navigation Co Ltd,
The Nagasaki Spirit

Napier Star, The [1933] P 136, 45 Ll L Rep 139, 102 LJP 57, 18 Asp MLC 400, [1933] All
ER Rep 886, 149 LT 359, 49 TLR 342, P, D and Admlty
.... 147, 800, 809

Napier Star, The [1939] P 330, 64 Ll L Rep 197, 108 LJP 159, 19 Asp MLC 302, 161 LT
285, 55 TLR 879, P, D and Admlty 771, 778

Nasmyth, The (1885) 10 PD 41, 54 LJP 63, 5 Asp MLC 364, 33 WR 736, 52 LT 392, P, D
and Admlty 885

PARA

Nassau, The [1965] 1 Lloyd's Rep 236, P, D and Admlty
.... 147
Nautical Challenge Ltd v Evergreen Marine (UK) Ltd [2017] EWHC 453 (Admlty)
.... 700, 705
Nautik, The [1895] P 121, 64 LJP 61, 7 Asp MLC 591, 11 R 716, 43 WR 703, 72 LT 21,
    P, D and Admlty 97, 160
Nazym Khikmet, The [1996] 2 Lloyd's Rep 362, CA 93, 158
Nedenes, The (1924) 20 Ll L Rep 327, 41 TLR 243, P, D and Admlty
.... 201
Nedenes, The (1925) 23 Ll L Rep 57, P, D and Admlty 153, 1013
Nelly Schneider, The (1878) 3 PD 152, 4 Asp MLC 54, 27 WR 308, 39 LT 360, P, D and
    Admlty 107, 241
Nelson Line (Liverpool) Ltd v James Nelson & Sons Ltd [1908] AC 16, 77 LJKB 82, 10
    Asp MLC 581, 13 Com Cas 104, 52 Sol Jo 170, 97 LT 812, 24 TLR 114, HL
.... 600
Neptune the Second, The (1814) 1 Dods 467, 165 ER 1380, HC
.... 734
Neptune, The (1824) 1 Hag Adm 227, 166 ER 81 .... 478, 510, 868, 968, 970
Neptune, The (1842) 1 Wm Rob 297, 8 LT 582 912
Neste Chemicals SA v DK Line SA and Tokumaru Kaiun KK, The Sargasso [1994] 3 All
    ER 180, [1994] 2 Lloyd's Rep 6, (1994) Times, 4 April 99
Nestor, SS (Owners) v SS Mungana (Owners), The Mungana [1936] 3 All ER 670, P, D and
    Admlty 905
Netherlands Steam Boat Co v Styles, The Batavier. See Batavier, The
Nevada, The (1872) 27 LT 720 739
New v Burns (1894) 64 LJQB 104, 14 R 339, 43 WR 182, 39 Sol Jo 58, 71 LT 681, 11
    TLR 53, CA 204
New Australia, The [1958] 2 Lloyd's Rep 35, P, D and Admlty
.... 906
New Draper, The (1802) 4 Ch Rob 287, 165 ER 615 .... 104, 240
New Pelton, The [1891] P 258, 60 LJP 78, 7 Asp MLC 81, 65 LT 494, P, D and Admlty
.... 758
Newbattle, The (1885) 10 PD 33, 54 LJP 16, 5 Asp MLC 356, 33 WR 318, 52 LT 15, CA
.... 189
Newman v Walters (1804) 3 Bos & P 612, 127 ER 330
.... 855, 866, 869–870, 907
Ngapoota, The. See Kwang Tung (Owner) v Ngapoota (Owners), The Ngapoota
Niceto de Larrinaga, The, Navarro (Widow) (Administratrix of the estate of Navarro) v
    Larrinaga Steamship Co Ltd [1966] P 80, [1965] 2 All ER 930, [1965] 3 WLR 573,
    [1965] 2 Lloyd's Rep 134, 109 Sol Jo 633, P, D and Admlty 152, 1013
Nicholson, Re, ex p Harrison (1814) 2 Rose 76 244
Nicholson v Chapman (1793) 126 ER 536, [1775–1802] All ER Rep 67, 2 Hy Bl 254
.... 923
Nicholson v Leith Salvagae and Towage Co Ltd (1923) 60 SLR 278, 1923 SC 409, 1923
    SLT 229, Ct of Sess 904
Nicholson v Mounsey and Symes (1812) 15 East 384, 104 ER 890
.... 779
Nicol v Hennessy (1896) 1 Com Cas 410, 44 WR 584, 40 Sol Jo 601, 12 TLR 485
.... 238
Nicolaas Witzen, The (1837) 3 Hag Adm 369 909
Nicolaou v Minister of War Transport [1944] 2 All ER 322, 171 LT 159, 60 TLR 524
.... 4
Nicolaou Georgios, The [1952] 2 Lloyd's Rep 215, P, D and Admlty
.... 143, 903
Nicolina, The (1843) 2 Wm Rob 175, 166 ER 720, sub nom R v The Nicolene 1 LTOS
    411 905
Nina, The (1867) LR 2 PC 38, 5 Moo PCCNS 51, 37 LJ Adm 17, 3 Mar LC 47, 17 LT
    585 .... 128, 478
Niobe, The (1888) 13 PD 55, 6 Asp MLC 300, 59 LT 257, sub nom Flying Serpent, The,
    The Niobe 57 LJP 33, 36 WR 812, P, D and Admlty 599, 742, 784
No 7 Steam Sand Pump Dredger (Owners) v Greta Holme (Owners), The Greta Holme. See
    Emerald, The, The Greta Holme
Nor, The (1874) 2 Asp MLC 264, 30 LT 576, PC 762
Nora, The [1956] 1 Lloyd's Rep 617, P, D and Admlty 694

                                                                                    PARA
Nord Sea and Freccia del Nord, The [1989] 1 Lloyd's Rep 388
.... 99, 158, 160
Norden, The (1853) 1 Ecc & Ad 185, 164 ER 107, 8 LT 335
.... 867
Nordglimt, The [1988] QB 183, [1988] 2 All ER 531, [1988] 2 WLR 338, [1987] 2 Lloyd's
    Rep 470, 132 Sol Jo 263, [1988] 11 LS Gaz R 44 .... 92, 96–97, 156, 161, 175
Nordlake (Owners and/or demise charterers of the vessel) v Sea Eagle (Owners of the
    vessel) now named MV Elbella [2015] EWHC 3605 (Admlty), [2016] 2 All ER
    (Comm) 449, [2016] 1 Lloyd's Rep 656, [2016] All ER (D) 95 (Jan)
.... 699, 770–771, 774
Norma, The (1860) Lush 124, 1 Mar LC 7, 167 ER 58, 3 LT 340
.... 116
Norma, The (1876) 3 Asp MLC 272, 35 LT 418, PC 707
Normandie (Owners of Norwegian SS) v Pekin (Owners of British SS), The Pekin [1897]
    AC 532, 66 LJPC 97, 8 Asp MLC 367, 77 LT 443, 13 TLR 487, PC
.... 705
Normandy, The [1904] P 187, 73 LJP 55, 9 Asp MLC 568, 52 WR 634, 90 LT 351, 20
    TLR 239, DC 690
Normandy, The (1900) 16 TLR 567, P, D and Admlty 807
Norseman, The. See Rederi AS Norseman and Rederi AS Norse Lady v British Transport
    Commission, The Norseman
North German Lloyd Steamship Co v Elder, The Schwalbe, (1861) Lush 239, 14 Moo PCC
    241, 1 Mar LC 42, 15 ER 295, 4 LT 160, PC 741
Northampton, The (1853) 1 Ecc & Ad 152, 164 ER 89, sub nom Feronia, The v The
    Northampton 7 LT 258 734
Northcote v Henrich Björn (Owners), The Henrich Björn (1886) 11 App Cas 270, 55 LJP
    80, 6 Asp MLC 1, 55 LT 66, 2 TLR 498, HL 125–126, 966, 983
Northumbria, The (1869) LR 3 A & E 6, 39 LJ Adm 3, 3 Mar LC 314, 18 WR 188, 21
    LT 681, HC 796, 809
Norwalk Victory, The (1949) 82 Ll L Rep 539, P, D and Admlty
.... 172
Norwhale, The, John Franetovich & Co v Ministry of Defence [1975] QB 589, [1975] 2
    All ER 501, [1975] 2 WLR 829, [1975] 1 Lloyd's Rep 610, 119 Sol Jo 319
.... 152, 1013
Notara v Henderson (1872) LR 7 QB 225, 41 LJQB 158, 1 Asp MLC 278, 20 WR 443, 26
    LT 442, Ex Ch 437
Notting Hill, The (1884) 9 PD 105, 53 LJP 56, 5 Asp MLC 241, 32 WR 764, 51 LT 66,
    CA 808
Nourse v Liverpool Sailing Ship Owners' Mutual Protection and Indemnity Association
    [1896] 2 QB 16, 65 LJQB 507, 8 Asp MLC 144, 1 Com Cas 388, 44 WR 500, 74 LT
    543, 12 TLR 406, CA 120, 864
Nowy Sacz, The [1979] QB 236, [1978] 2 All ER 297, [1977] 3 WLR 979, [1977] 2
    Lloyd's Rep 91, 121 Sol Jo 828 .... 703, 707
Nymph, The (1856) Sw 86, 166 ER 1033 .... 127, 964, 969–970, 972

                                           O

OLL Ltd v Secretary of State for Transport [1997] 3 All ER 897, [1997] NLJR 1099
.... 58
Oakfield, The (1886) 11 PD 34, 55 LJP 11, 5 Asp MLC 575, 34 WR 687, 54 LT 578, P, D
    and Admlty 204
Oakley v Speedy (1879) 4 Asp MLC 134, 40 LT 881 781
Ocean Crown v Five Oceans Salvage Consultants Ltd [2009] EWHC 3040 (Admlty),
    [2010] 2 All ER (Comm) 931, [2010] 1 Lloyd's Rep 468, [2009] All ER (D) 296 (Nov)
.... 878
Ocean Glory, The [2002] 1 Lloyd's Rep 679, sub nom Festive Holidays Ltd v demise
    charterers of the Ocean Glory [2001] All ER (D) 344 (Nov)
.... 204
Ocean Hound, The (1950) 84 Ll L Rep 5, P, D and Admlty
.... 873
Ocean Iron Steamship Insurance Association Ltd v Leslie (1888) 22 QBD 722n, 6 Asp
    MLC 226, 57 LT 722 .... 238, 244
Oceaneering International AG (The Sarah), Re [2010] CSOH 161, [2011] 1 Lloyd's Rep
    546, OH 126

PARA

Oceangas (Gibraltar) Ltd v Port of London Authority, The Cavendish [1993] 2 Lloyd's Rep
  292, [1993] 31 LS Gaz R 40, (1993) Times, 24 May, 137 Sol Jo LB 159
  .... 576, 578, 589
Oceanic Crest Shipping Co v Pilbara Harbour Services Pty Ltd (1986) 160 CLR 626, Aust
  HC 578
Oceano, The (1878) 3 PD 60, CA 705
Octavie, The (1863) Brown & Lush 215, 33 LJPM & A 115, 1 Mar LC 420, 3 New Rep
  252, 167 ER 341, 9 LT 695 .... 128, 478
Ogle v Wrangham (1790) cited in Abbott's Law of Merchant Ships and Seaman (14th Edn)
  130 244
Okehampton, The [1913] P 173, 83 LJP 5, 12 Asp MLC 428, 18 Com Cas 320, 110 LT
  130, 29 TLR 731, CA 790
Oldekerk, The [1974] 1 Lloyd's Rep 95 .... 751, 754
Olsen and Ugelstad v G T Gray & Co (1921) 9 Ll L Rep 565
  974
Olympic, The [1913] P 92, 82 LJP 41, 12 Asp MLC 318, [1911–13] All ER Rep 469, 108
  LT 592, 29 TLR 335, sub nom Fraser and Weller v Oceanic Steam Navigation Co (No
  2) 57 Sol Jo 388, CA 487
Olympic, The and HMS Hawke [1913] P 214, 83 LJP 113, 29 TLR 441, CA; on appeal
  sub nom Olympic (Owners) v Blunt, Olympic (Owners) v Admiralty Comrs, The
  Olympic [1915] AC 385, 84 LJP 49, 12 Asp MLC 580, 112 LT 49, 31 TLR 54, HL
  .... 705, 758
O'Neil v Armstrong Mitchell & Co [1895] 2 QB 418, 65 LJQB 7, 8 Asp MLC 63, 14 R
  703, [1895–9] All ER Rep 1073, 73 LT 178, 11 TLR 548, CA
  510
Ophelia, The [1914] P 46, 83 LJP 65, 12 Asp MLC 434, 110 LT 329, 30 TLR 61, CA
  204
Oporto, The [1897] P 249, 66 LJP 49, 13 TLR 254, CA
  700
Optima, The (1905) 74 LJP 94, 10 Asp MLC 147, 93 LT 638, P, D and Admlty
  .... 160, 964
Opy v Adison (1693) 12 Mod Rep 38, 88 ER 1149, sub nom Opy v Child 1 Salk 31, 91
  ER 33 80
Orangemoor, The (1915) 31 TLR 190, P, D and Admlty
  177
Orbona, The (1853) 1 Ecc & Ad 161, 164 ER 93, 8 LT 582
  913
Orchis, The (1890) 15 PD 38, 59 LJP 31, 6 Asp MLC 501, 38 WR 472, 62 LT 407, 6 TLR
  197, CA 330
Orduna (Owners) v Shipping Controller [1921] 1 AC 250, 90 LJP 67, HL
  .... 705, 707
Orelia, The (1833) 3 Hag Adm 75, 166 ER 334 987
Orient, The. See Yeo and Yeo v Tatem and Dwerryhouse Braginton, The Orient
Orienta, The [1895] P 49, 64 LJP 32, 7 Asp MLC 529, 11 R 687, 39 Sol Jo 165, 71 LT
  711, 11 TLR 116, CA 131, 169, 433, 971
Oropesa, The. See Lord v Pacific Steam Navigation Co Ltd, The Oropesa
Orpheus, The (1871) LR 3 A & E 308, 40 LJ Adm 24, 3 Mar LC 531, 23 LT 855, HC
  811
Orr-Lewis v Orr-Lewis [1949] P 347, [1949] 1 All ER 504, [1949] LJR 682, 65 TLR 269,
  P, D and Admlty 101
Osprey, The [1967] 1 Lloyd's Rep 76, P, D and Admlty 204
Otranto, The [1930] P 110, 36 Ll L Rep 25, 99 LJP 82, 142 LT 544, CA; revsd sub nom
  Kitano Maru, SS (Owners) v SS Otranto (Owners), The Otranto [1931] AC 194, 38 Ll
  L Rep 204, 100 LJP 11, 18 Asp MLC 193, [1930] All ER Rep 665, 144 LT 251, 47
  TLR 163, HL 220, 707, 771
Otter, The (1874) LR 4 A & E 203, 2 Asp MLC 208, 22 WR 557, 30 LT 43, HC
  757
Overseas Tankship (UK) Ltd v Miller Steamship Co Pty, The Wagon Mound (No 2) [1967]
  1 AC 617, [1966] 2 All ER 709, [1966] 3 WLR 498, [1966] 1 Lloyd's Rep 657, 110
  Sol Jo 447, [1967] ALR 97, [1966] 1 NSWR 411, PC 793
Overseas Tankship (UK) Ltd v Morts Dock and Engineering Co Ltd, The Wagon Mound
  [1961] AC 388, [1961] 1 All ER 404, [1961] 2 WLR 126, [1961] 1 Lloyd's Rep 1, 105
  Sol Jo 85, [1961] ALR 569, PC 756, 793

PARA

Overseas Union Insurance Ltd v New Hampshire Insurance Co: C-351/89 [1992] 1 QB
     434, [1992] 2 All ER 138, [1991] ECR I-3317, [1992] 2 WLR 586, [1992] 1 Lloyd's
     Rep 204, (1991) Times, 20 August, ECJ 99
Ovingdean Grange, The [1902] P 208, 71 LJP 105, 9 Asp MLC 295, 87 LT 15, CA
     770
Owen Wallis, The (1874) LR 4 A & E 175, 43 LJ Adm 36, 2 Asp MLC 206, 22 WR 695,
     30 LT 41, HC 746
Oxford, The v The James and Ann (1922) 10 Ll L Rep 119, P, D and Admlty
     765

P

PK Airfinance US Inc v Blue Sky Two Ltd [2010] EWHC 631 (Comm), [2010] NLJR 843,
     [2010] All ER (D) 02 (Jun) 318
PLM 8, The [1920] P 236, 90 LJP 45, 15 Asp MLC 51, 123 LT 560, 36 TLR 552, P, D
     and Admlty 153, 1013
Pacific, The [1898] P 170, 67 LJP 65, 8 Asp MLC 422, 46 WR 686, 79 LT 125, P, D and
     Admlty 121
Pacific, The (1864) Brown & Lush 243, 33 LJPM & A 120, 10 Jur NS 1110, 2 Mar LC
     21, 3 New Rep 709, 167 ER 356, 10 LT 541 321
Pacific, The (1884) 9 PD 124, 53 LJP 67, 5 Asp MLC 263, 33 WR 124, 51 LT 127, P, D
     and Admlty 741
Pactolus, The (1856) Sw 173, 5 WR 167, 166 ER 1079, 28 LTOS 220
     800
Page v Darling and Gaselee, The Millwall. See Millwall, The
Palace Shipping Co Ltd v Caine [1907] AC 386, 76 LJKB 1079, 10 Asp MLC 529, 13
     Com Cas 51, 51 Sol Jo 716, 97 LT 587, 23 TLR 731, HL
     510
Palatine, The (1872) 1 Asp MLC 468, 27 LT 631 744
Palembang, The [1929] P 246, 98 LJP 129, 18 Asp MLC 45, 141 LT 399, 45 TLR 495, P,
     D and Admlty 720
Palmer v Rouse (1858) 22 JP 773, 3 H & N 505, 27 LJ Ex 437, 6 WR 674, 157 ER 569,
     31 LTOS 220, Exch Ct 860, 923
Paludina, The. See Singleton Abbey (SS) (Owners) v SS Paludina (Owners), The Paludina
Panda, The (1842) 1 Wm Rob 423, 166 ER 631, 1 Notes of Cases 603
     139
Pansy v Inchbrayock (1921) 6 Ll L Rep 150, P, D and Admlty
     741
Pantanassa, The, Norsk Bjergningskompagni AS v Pantanassa (Owners) [1970] P 187,
     [1970] 1 All ER 848, [1970] 2 WLR 981, [1970] 1 Lloyd's Rep 153, P, D and Admlty
     116
Panthea, The (1871) 1 Asp MLC 133, 25 LT 389 981
Panther and The Ericbank, The. See Trishna (Owners, Master and Crew) v Panther and
     Ericbank (Owners), The Panther and The Ericbank
Panther, The and The Ericbank, Steam Barge Trishna (Owners) v Motor Tug Panther
     (Owners). See Trishna (Owners, Master and Crew) v Panther and Ericbank (Owners),
     The Panther and The Ericbank
Papayanni v Hocquard, The True Blue (1866) LR 1 PC 250, 4 Moo PCCNS 96, 16 ER
     252, PC 891
Parlement Belge, The (1880) 5 PD 197, 4 Asp MLC 234, 28 WR 642, [1874–80] All ER
     Rep 104, 42 LT 273, CA 3, 86, 92, 964, 967, 969
Parr v Applebee (1855) 7 De GM & G 585, 24 LJ Ch 767, 3 WR 645, 44 ER 228, 26
     LTOS 45 321
Partafelagid Farmur v Grangemouth and Forth Towing Co [1953] 2 Lloyd's Rep 699, Ct of
     Sess 600
Patriotto, The v The Rival (1860) 2 LT 301 735
Paul, The (1866) LR 1 A & E 57, 35 LJ Adm 16, 2 Mar LC 325, 14 LT 192, HC
     177
Pauline Constance Eleonore (Owners, etc) v Hamburgh American Steam Packet Co, The
     Germania (Owners), The Germania (1869) 3 Mar LC 269, 21 LT 44, PC
     739
Pauline, The (1845) 2 Wm Rob 358, 9 Jur 286, 166 ER 790, 6 LT 558, 3 Notes of Cases
     616 923

PARA

Peace, The (1856) Sw 115, 4 WR 635, 166 ER 1048, 27 LTOS 255
.... 888

Pearson v Göschen (1864) 17 CBNS 352, 33 LJCP 265, 10 Jur NS 903, 2 Mar LC 68, 4
New Rep 404, 12 WR 1116, 144 ER 142, 10 LT 758 431

Peerless, The (1860) Lush 30, 29 LJPM & A 49, 167 ER 16, 2 LT 25; affd sub nom Prouse
v European and American Steam Shipping Co, The Peerless (1860) Lush 103, 10 Moo
PCC 484, 30 LJPM & A 89, 15 ER 182, 3 LT 125, PC 733, 735, 789

Pekin, The. See Normandie (Owners of Norwegian SS) v Pekin (Owners of British SS), The
Pekin

Pelopidas (owners) v TRSL Concord (owners) [1999] 2 All ER (Comm) 737, [1999] 2
Lloyd's Rep 675, [1999] Lexis Citation 3645, [1999] All ER (D) 1074
.... 699

Penelope II, The. See Afromar Inc v Greek Atlantic Cod Fishing Co, The Penelope II

Peninsular and Oriental Steam Navigation Co v R [1901] 2 KB 686, 70 LJKB 845, 9 Asp
MLC 228, 85 LT 71, 17 TLR 610 457

Pennsylvania, The (1874) 2 Asp MLC 378   740

Penny v Wimbledon UDC and Iles [1899] 2 QB 72, 64 JP 406, 68 LJQB 704, 47 WR 565,
[1895–9] All ER Rep 204, 43 Sol Jo 476, 80 LT 615, 15 TLR 348, CA
.... 787

Pensher, The (1857) Sw 211, 166 ER 1100, 29 LTOS 12
.... 798–799

Pepper (Inspector of Taxes) v Hart [1993] AC 593, [1993] 1 All ER 42, [1992] 3 WLR
1032, [1992] STC 898, 65 TC 421, [1993] IRLR 33, [1993] ICR 291, [1993] NLJR
17, [1993] RVR 127, (1992) Times, 30 November, HL 851, 926

Pepperell, The (1855) Sw 12, 166 ER 992 741

Peracomo Inc v Telus Communications Co, The Realice 2014 SCC 29, [2014] 2 Lloyd's
Rep 315, Can SC 996

Percy, The (1837) 3 Hag & Adm 402, 166 ER 454, 3 LT 825
                       321

Perfective, The (1949) 82 Ll L Rep 873, P, D and Admlty
.... 899

Perla, The (1857) Sw 230, 166 ER 1111, 8 LT 612 .... 893, 895, 907

Perla, The (1858) 4 Jur NS 741, Sw 353, 166 ER 1164, 7 LT 397
                       432

Persia, The [1902] WN 210, P, D and Admlty 906

Peruvian Guano Co v Bockwoldt (1883) 23 Ch D 225, 52 LJ Ch 714, 5 Asp MLC 29, 31
WR 851, [1881–5] All ER Rep 715, 48 LT 7, CA 101

Peter Benoit, The (1915) 84 LJP 87, 31 TLR 227, CA; affd (1915) 85 LJP 12, 13 Asp MLC
203, 60 Sol Jo 88, 114 LT 147, 32 TLR 124, HL 771

Peter Pan v Mendocino (1921) 6 Ll L Rep 519, P, D and Admlty
.... 707

Petley v Catto, The Christina. See Christina, The

Petone, The [1917] P 198, 86 LJP 164, 14 Asp MLC 283, 119 LT 124, 33 TLR 554, P, D
and Admlty 127, 988, 991

Petrel (Owners) v Kurt Arlt (Owners), The Kurt Arlt. See Kurt Arlt, The, SS or M/V Petrel
(Owners) v SS or M/V Kurt Arlt (Owners)

Petrel, The [1893] P 320, 62 LJP 92, 7 Asp MLC 434, 1 R 651, 70 LT 417, 9 TLR 566, P,
D and Admlty 776

Petrofina SA v AOT Ltd, The Maersk Nimrod [1992] QB 571, [1991] 3 All ER 161,
[1992] 2 WLR 266, [1991] 1 Lloyd's Rep 269 .... 93, 111

Phantom, The (1866) LR 1 A & E 58, 12 Jur NS 529, 2 Mar LC 442, 14 WR 774, 15 LT
596, HC 861, 884

Philadelphia, The [1917] P 101, 86 LJP 112, 14 Asp MLC 68, 116 LT 794, CA
.... 796

Philippine Admiral, The, Philippine Admiral (Owners) v Wallem Shipping (Hong Kong) Ltd
[1977] AC 373, [1976] 1 All ER 78, [1976] 2 WLR 214, [1976] 1 Lloyd's Rep 234,
119 Sol Jo 865, PC 86

Phillips v Baillie (1784) 3 Doug KB 374, 99 ER 703 5

Phillips v Highland Rly Co, The Ferret (1883) 8 App Cas 329, 52 LJPC 51, 5 Asp MLC
94, 31 WR 869, 48 LT 915, PC 970

Philotaxe, The (1877) 3 Asp MLC 512, 37 LT 540, P, D and Admlty
.... 734

Pickernell v Jauberry (1862) 3 F & F 217, 176 ER 98, NP
.... 431

Pickwick, The (1852) 16 Jur 669 .... 910–911, 924

                                                                                              PARA
Picton, The [1910] P 46, 79 LJP 53, 11 Asp MLC 358, 101 LT 917, P, D and Admlty
.... 716, 741
Pierce v Bemis, The Lusitania [1986] QB 384, [1986] 1 All ER 1011, [1986] 2 WLR 501,
   [1986] 1 Lloyd's Rep 132, 130 Sol Jo 202, [1986] LS Gaz R 705
.... 119, 122, 139
Pieve Superiore, The. See Dapueto v James Wyllie & Co, The Pieve Superiore
Pilot, The v The Theodore. See Theodore, The
Pinna, The (1912) Times, 29 November 868
Pinnas, The (1888) 6 Asp MLC 313, 59 LT 526, P, D and Admlty
.... 894, 899
Pioneer Container, The [1989] HKLR 465 156
Pirie & Co v Middle Dock Co (1881) 4 Asp MLC 388, 44 LT 426
.... 133
Pladda, The (1876) 2 PD 34, 46 LJP 61, P, D and Admlty
.... 732, 735, 788–789
Plato, The v The Perseverance (1865) Holt Adm 262 744
Playa Larga, The (Owners of Cargo lately laden on board) v I Congreso del Partido
   (Owners), Marble Islands, The (Owners of Cargo lately laden on board) v I Congreso
   del Partido (Owners), I Congreso del Partido. See I Congreso del Partido
Po, The [1991] 2 Lloyd's Rep 206, CA 97
Point Anne Quarries Ltd v The M F Whalen (1922) 13 Ll L Rep 40, 39 TLR 37, [1923] 1
   DLR 45, PC 597, 783
Point Breeze, The [1928] P 135, 30 Ll L Rep 229, 97 LJP 88, 17 Asp MLC 462, 139 LT
   48, 44 TLR 390, P, D and Admlty 172, 991
Polemis and Furness Withy & Co, Re [1921] 3 KB 560, 90 LJKB 1353, 15 Asp MLC 398,
   27 Com Cas 25, [1921] All ER Rep 40, 126 LT 154, 37 TLR 940, CA
.... 793
Polestar Maritime Ltd v YHM Shipping Co Ltd (The Rewa) [2012] EWCA Civ 153, [2012]
   2 All ER (Comm) 447, [2012] 1 Lloyd's Rep 510, [2012] All ER (D) 158 (Feb)
.... 32
Pollok v M'Alpin, The Lochlibo. See Lochlibo, The
Polo II, The [1977] 2 Lloyd's Rep 115 172
Polpen Shipping Co Ltd v Commercial Union Assurance Co Ltd [1943] KB 161, [1943] 1
   All ER 162, 74 Ll L Rep 157, 112 LJKB 198, 87 Sol Jo 129, 168 LT 143, 59 TLR 106
.... 86, 229
Polyduke, The. See Bahamas Oil Refining Co v Kristiansands Tankrederie A/S and Shell
   International Marine Ltd, The Polyduke
Polynésien, The [1910] P 28, 79 LJP 45, 11 Asp MLC 354, 101 LT 749, P, D and Admlty
.... 747, 789
Polzeath, The [1916] P 117, P, D and Admlty; affd [1916] P 241, 85 LJP 241, 13 Asp MLC
   595, 116 LT 370, 32 TLR 647, CA 235
Pongola, The (1895) 8 Asp MLC 89, 73 LT 512, P, D and Admlty
.... 244
Pontida, The (1884) 9 PD 177, 53 LJP 78, 5 Asp MLC 330, 33 WR 38, 51 LT 849, CA
.... 432
Popi (Motor Vessel) (Owners) v SS Gniezno (Owners), The Gniezno [1968] P 418, [1967] 2
   All ER 738, [1967] 3 WLR 705, [1967] 1 Lloyd's Rep 441, 111 Sol Jo 543, P, D and
   Admlty 152, 169 189, 1013
Port Caledonia, The and The Anna [1903] P 184, 72 LJP 60, 9 Asp MLC 479, 52 WR
   223, 89 LT 216, P, D and Admlty 813, 855, 866, 884
Port Chalmers v Kerry Range (1921) 9 Ll L Rep 137, P, D and Admlty
.... 741
Port Hunter, The [1910] P 343, 80 LJP 1, 11 Asp MLC 492, 103 LT 550, 26 TLR 610, CA
.... 900
Port of London Authority v SS Clan Colquhoun (Owners). See Clan Colquhoun, The
Port Victor, The, Cargo ex [1901] P 243, 70 LJP 52, 9 Asp MLC 182, 49 WR 578, 84 LT
   677, 17 TLR 538, CA 84, 116, 866, 874, 914
Port Victoria, The [1902] P 25, 71 LJP 36, 9 Asp MLC 314, 50 WR 383, 86 LT 804, 18
   TLR 165, P, D and Admlty 763, 766
Portarlington (Lord) v Soulby (1834) 3 My & K 104, 40 ER 40, [1824–34] All ER Rep
   610 101
Porter v George Robb & Sons Ltd 1961 SLT (Sh Ct) 14, Sh Ct
.... 800
Porto Alexandre, The [1920] P 30, 1 Ll L Rep 191, 89 LJP 97, 15 Asp MLC 1, [1918–19]
   All ER Rep 615, 122 LT 661, 36 TLR 66, CA 86

PARA

Portreath, The [1923] P 155, 92 LJP 116, 16 Asp MLC 227, [1923] All ER Rep 601, 129
    LT 475, 39 TLR 356, P, D and Admlty 869
Post Office v Estuary Radio Ltd [1968] 2 QB 740, [1967] 3 All ER 663, [1967] 1 WLR
    1396, [1967] 2 Lloyd's Rep 299, 111 Sol Jo 636, CA 86
Power Curber International Ltd v National Bank of Kuwait SAK [1981] 3 All ER 607,
    [1981] 1 WLR 1233, [1981] 2 Lloyd's Rep 394, [1981] Com LR 224, 125 Sol Jo 585
    100
Powstaniec Wielkopolski, The [1989] QB 279, [1989] 1 All ER 198, [1988] 3 WLR 723,
    [1989] 1 Lloyd's Rep 58, 132 Sol Jo 1458, (1988) Times, 14 July
    115
Prehn v Bailey, The Ettrick (1881) 6 PD 127, 4 Asp MLC 465, 45 LT 399, CA
    875
President van Buren, The (1924) 16 Asp MLC 444, [1924] All ER Rep 334, 132 LT 253, P,
    D and Admlty 600
Preston Corpn v Biornstad, The Ratata. See Ratata, The
Preveze, The [1973] 1 Lloyd's Rep 202 152
Pride of Canada, The (1863) Brown & Lush 208, 1 Mar LC 406, 3 New Rep 93, 167 ER
    338, 9 LT 546 904
Pride of Wales and The Annie Lisle, Re Mortgagees of (1867) 2 Mar LC 458, 15 WR 381,
    15 LT 606 334
Prince George, The (1837) 3 Hag Adm 376, 166 ER 445
    .... 321, 982
Prince Leopold de Belgique, The [1909] P 103, 78 LJP 57, 11 Asp MLC 203, 100 LT 201,
    25 TLR 183, P, D and Admlty 700, 705
Prince of Saxe Coburg, The. See Soares v Rahn, The Prince of Saxe Coburg
Prince of Wales, The (1848) 12 Jur 163, 6 Notes of Cases 39
    855
Princesa, The [1946] P 79, 77 Ll L Rep 478, 115 LJP 62, 173 LT 294, 61 TLR 537, sub
    nom Edmund Handcock (1929) Ltd v Furness-Houlder Argentine Lines Ltd, The
    Princesa [1945] 2 All ER 429n, CA 597
Princess Alice, The (1849) 3 Wm Rob 138, 166 ER 914, 6 Notes of Cases 584
    125
Princess Alice, The. See Alice, The and The Princess Alice
Princess Helena, The (1861) Lush 190, 30 LJPM & A 137, 1 Mar LC 108, 167 ER 91, 4
    LT 869 149
Princess Royal, The (1870) LR 3 A & E 41, 39 LJ Adm 43, 22 LT 39, HC
    875
Princess, The [1929] P 287, 98 LJP 158, 18 Asp MLC 56, 142 LT 94, 45 TLR 627, P, D
    and Admlty 757
Princess, The (1885) 5 Asp MLC 451, 52 LT 932, DC 800
Princesse Marie José, The (1913) 12 Asp MLC 360, 109 LT 326, 29 TLR 678, P, D and
    Admlty 172
Princeton, The (1878) 3 PD 90, 47 LJ Adm 33, 3 Asp MLC 562, 38 LT 260, P, D and
    Admlty 734
Prins Bernhard, The, Rolimpex Centrala Handlu Zagranicznego v Owners of Motorship or
    Vessel Prins Bernhard [1964] P 117, [1963] 3 All ER 735, [1963] 3 WLR 1043, [1963]
    2 Lloyd's Rep 236, 107 Sol Jo 812, P, D and Admlty 160, 163
Prinses Juliana, The [1936] P 139, [1936] 1 All ER 685, 54 Ll L Rep 234, 105 LJP 58, 18
    Asp MLC 614, 155 LT 261, 52 TLR 296, P, D and Admlty
    .... 429, 700, 748
Prinz Heinrich, The (1888) 13 PD 31, 57 LJP 17, 6 Asp MLC 273, 36 WR 511, 58 LT
    593, P, D and Admlty 876, 883, 914, 969
Priscilla, The (1870) LR 3 A & E 125, 3 Mar LC 503, 23 LT 566, HC
    744
Promise, The v HMS Topaze. See HMS Topaze
Prouse v European and American Steam Shipping Co, The Peerless. See Peerless, The
Providence, The (1825) 1 Hag Adm 391, 166 ER 139 .... 425, 471
Puffin, The (1925) 21 Ll L Rep 10, P, D and Admlty 740
Pugh v Henville [1957] 2 Lloyd's Rep 261, DC 471
Pulkovo and Oden, The [1989] 1 Lloyd's Rep 280 204
Punta Lara, The (1910) 26 TLR 268, P, D and Admlty 906–907
Purcell Bros Ltd v Owners, Charterers and All Persons Claiming to be Interested in the
    Motor Vessel Star Viking [2015] NIQB 70 178

PARA

Purissma Concepcion, The (1849) 3 Wm Rob 181, 13 Jur 545, 967, 166 ER 930, 8 LT
178, 7 Notes of Cases 150 .... 870, 872, 883
Pursuit, The v The Carrou. See Carron, The
Putbus, The [1969] P 136, [1969] 2 All ER 676, [1969] 2 WLR 1241, [1969] 1 Lloyd's
Rep 253, 113 Sol Jo 223 176
Pyman SS Co v Admiralty Comrs [1919] 1 KB 49, 88 LJKB 277, 14 Asp MLC 364, 119
LT 735, 35 TLR 79, CA 874
Pyrennee, The (1863) Brown & Lush 189, 3 New Rep 250, 167 ER 330
.... 969

Q

Queen (No 2), The (1869) 19 LT 706 982
Queen Elizabeth, The (1949) 82 Ll L Rep 803, 93 Sol Jo 425, P, D and Admlty
.... 855, 892
Queen Mary, The. See Bishop v Cunard White Star Co Ltd, The Queen Mary
Queen Mary, The. See Cunard White Star Line Ltd v Admiralty Comrs, The Queen Mary
Queen of the Orwell, The (1863) 1 Mar LC 300, 11 WR 499, 7 LT 839
.... 727
Queen of the South, The. See Corps v Paddle Steamer Queen of the South (Owners), The
Queen of the South
Queen Victoria, The (1891) 7 Asp MLC 9, 64 LT 520, CA
.... 734, 753
Queen, The (1867) LR 2 A & E 53, 37 LJ Adm 12, HC; affd sub nom Hannibal, The and
The Queen [1925] AC 262, PC 868
Quickstep, The (1890) 15 PD 196, 59 LJP 65, 6 Asp MLC 603, 63 LT 713, 6 TLR 476,
DC 204, 784
Quinn (or Quin) v Burch Bros (Builders) Ltd [1966] 2 QB 370, [1966] 2 All ER 283,
[1966] 2 WLR 1017, 110 Sol Jo 214, CA 112

R

R v Carrick District Council, ex p Prankerd, The Winnie Rigg [1999] QB 1119, [1999] 2
WLR 489, [1998] 2 Lloyd's Rep 675, [1998] 33 LS Gaz R 34, (1998) Times, 1
September, [1998] Lexis Citation 2850, 142 Sol Jo LB 228, [1998] All ER (D) 373
.... 173
R v City of London Court Judge and Payne [1892] 1 QB 273, 61 LJQB 337, 7 Asp MLC
140, 40 WR 215, 36 Sol Jo 138, 66 LT 135, 8 TLR 191, CA
.... 80, 84
R v City of London Court Judge and SS Michigan (Owners) (1890) 25 QBD 339, 59 LJQB
427, 6 Asp MLC 547, 38 WR 638, 63 LT 492 457
R v Collector of Customs, Liverpool (1813) 2 M & S 223
.... 244
R v Ewen (1856) 2 Jur NS 454 136
R v Forty-nine Casks of Brandy (1836) 3 Hag Adm 257, 166 ER 401
.... 122, 139, 924
R v Goodwin [2005] All ER (D) 286 (Dec) 1102
R v Goodwin [2005] EWCA Crim 3184, [2006] 2 All ER 519, [2006] 1 WLR 546, [2006]
2 All ER (Comm) 281, [2006] 1 Cr App Rep 354, [2006] 1 Lloyd's Rep 432, (2006)
Times, 4 January, [2005] All ER (D) 111 (Dec) 229, 1102
R v Keyn (1876) LR 2 Ex D 63, 2 QBD 90, 41 JP 517, 46 LJMC 17, 13 Cox CC 403,
CCR 3, 80
R v Lynch and Jones [1898] 1 QB 61, 67 LJQB 59, 8 Asp MLC 363, 18 Cox CC 677, 46
WR 205, 42 Sol Jo 83, 77 LT 568, 14 TLR 78, CCR 457
R v Morris [1972] 1 All ER 384, [1972] 1 WLR 228, [1972] RTR 201, 56 Cr App Rep
175, 136 JP 194, 116 Sol Jo 17 1187
R v Property Derelict (1825) 1 Hag Adm 383, 166 ER 136
.... 122, 139, 924
R v Scriveners' Co (1830) 10 B & C 511, 8 LJOSKB 199, 5 Man & Ry KB 543, 109 ER
540 430
R v Southport Corpn and Morris. See Southport Corpn v Morriss
R v The Nicolene. See Nicolina, The
R v Two Casks of Tallow (1837) 3 Hag Adm 294, 166 ER 414, 6 LT 558
.... 122

PARA

R (Adolph Woermann) v Hessa (1922) 10 Ll L Rep 734, CA
.... 789

R (on the application of International Association of Independent Tanker Owners
    (Intertanko) v Secretary of State for Transport: C-308/06 [2008] ECR I-4057, [2008] 3
    CMLR 203, [2008] 2 Lloyd's Rep 260, [2008] All ER (D) 04 (Jun), ECJ
.... 14
Racer, The (1874) 2 Asp MLC 317, 30 LT 904 862
Racine, The [1906] P 273, 75 LJP 83, 10 Asp MLC 300, 95 LT 597, 22 TLR 575, CA
.... 796

Radiant, The. See Yuille v B and B Fisheries (Leigh) Ltd and Bates, The Radiant
Radnorshire, The (1880) 5 PD 172, 49 LJP 48, 4 Asp MLC 338, 29 WR 476, 43 LT 319,
    P, D and Admlty 204
Raft of Timber, The (1844) 2 Wm Rob 251, 8 Jur 154, 166 ER 749, 3 LT 58
.... 80, 115, 860
Raisby, The (1885) 10 PD 114, 54 LJP 65, 5 Asp MLC 473, 33 WR 938, 53 LT 56, P, D
    and Admlty 876, 969
Raithwaite Hall, The (1874) 2 Asp MLC 210, 30 LT 233
.... 694
Ralph Creyke, The (1886) 6 Asp MLC 19, 55 LT 155, P, D and Admlty
.... 746, 749–750
Rambler, The v The Kotka [1917] 2 IR 406, CA 891, 897, 900
Rambler, The (1906) 10 Asp MLC 350 763
Ramsden, The [1943] P 46, 75 Ll L Rep 86, 112 LJP 49, 168 LT 284, 59 TLR 175, P, D
    and Admlty 600
Ran, The, The Graygarth [1922] P 80, 91 LJP 113, 15 Asp MLC 517, 66 Sol Jo 182, 126
    LT 675, 38 TLR 208, [1921] All ER Rep Ext 774, CA 784
Ranger and The Cologne, The. See Malcomson v General Steam Navigation Co, The
    Ranger and The Cologne
Ranza, The (1898) 79 LJP 21n, P, D and Admlty 707
Rasche, The (1873) LR 4 A & E 127, 42 LJ Adm 71, 22 WR 240, HC
.... 886, 906
Ratata, The [1897] P 118, 66 LJP 39, 8 Asp MLC 236, 76 LT 224, CA; affd sub nom
    Preston Corpn v Biornstad, The Ratata [1898] AC 513, 8 Asp MLC 427, 47 WR 156,
    78 LT 797, 14 TLR 500, HL 218, 597–598, 783
Rathbone Bros & Co v D MacIver Sons & Co [1903] 2 KB 378, 72 LJKB 703, 9 Asp
    MLC 467, 8 Com Cas 303, 52 WR 68, 47 Sol Jo 653, 89 LT 378, 19 TLR 590, CA
.... 600
Ravenna, The [1918] P 297, 87 LJP 215, CA 700
Rebecca, The (1804) 5 Ch Rob 102, 165 ER 712 .... 988, 991
Red Cross, The (1907) 10 Asp MLC 521, 97 LT 610, P, D and Admlty
.... 700, 705
Rederi AS Norseman and Rederi AS Norse Lady v British Transport Commission, The
    Norseman [1957] P 224, [1957] 2 All ER 660, [1957] 3 WLR 263, [1957] 1 Lloyd's
    Rep 503, 36 ATC 173, [1957] TR 193, 101 Sol Jo 556, P, D and Admlty
.... 809
Refrigerant, The [1925] P 130, 95 LJP 11, 16 Asp MLC 559, 134 LT 26, P, D and Admlty
.... 597, 600
Regalia, The (1884) 5 Asp MLC 338, 51 LT 904, P, D and Admlty
.... 240
Regina Del Mare, The (1864) Brown & Lush 315, 167 ER 381
.... 169
Re-hearing of the formal Investigation into the loss of the MV Derbyshire [2003] 1 All ER
    (Comm) 784, [2002] All ER (D) 24 (Oct) 223, 844
Reid v Darby (1808) 10 East 143, 103 ER 730 440
Reiher, The (1881) 4 Asp MLC 478, 45 LT 767, P, D and Admlty
.... 739
Reiter Petroleum Inc v The Ship 'sam Hawk' [2016] FCAFC 26, [2016] 2 Lloyd's Rep 639
.... 976, 986
Reliance, The (1833) 3 Hag Adm 66, 166 ER 331 435
Rellim, The (1922) 39 TLR 41, P, D and Admlty 974
Rena K, The [1979] QB 377, [1979] 1 All ER 397, [1978] 3 WLR 431, [1978] 1 Lloyd's
    Rep 545, 122 Sol Jo 315 .... 103, 175
Rene, The (1922) 16 Asp MLC 24, 128 LT 96, 38 TLR 790, P, D and Admlty
.... 983
Rene, The (Owners) v The Alenquer (Owners) [1955] 1 WLR 263, [1955] 1 Lloyd's Rep
    101, 99 Sol Jo 186, P, D and Admlty 117, 863, 893

PARA

Reney v Kirkcudbright Magistrates [1892] AC 264, 61 LJPC 23, 7 Asp MLC 221, 67 LT 474, HL 755, 785

Renpor, The (1883) 8 PD 115, 52 LJP 49, 5 Asp MLC 98, 31 WR 640, 48 LT 887, CA 120, 866, 885, 914

Repetto v Millar's Karri and Jarrah Forests Ltd [1901] 2 KB 306, 70 LJKB 561, 9 Asp MLC 215, 6 Com Cas 129, 49 WR 526, 84 LT 836, 17 TLR 421 431

Repulse, The (1845) 2 Wm Rob 396, 9 Jur 738, 166 ER 804, 7 LT 225, 4 Notes of Cases 166 884

Rewia, The [1991] 2 Lloyd's Rep 325, (1991) Financial Times, 12 July, CA 431

Reynolds v Jex (1865) 7 B & S 86, 34 LJQB 251, 6 New Rep 291, 13 WR 968 431

Rhadamanthe, The (1813) 1 Dods 201, 165 ER 1283, HC 134, 976, 980

Rhondda, The. See Scicluna v Stevenson, The Rhondda
Rialto, The [1891] P 175, 60 LJP 71, 7 Asp MLC 35, 64 LT 540, P, D and Admlty 204, 884

Rich v Coe (1777) 2 Cowp 636, 98 ER 1281 429

Richelieu and Ontario Navigation Co v Taylor, The Havana [1910] AC 170, 79 LJPC 65, 11 Asp MLC 315, 101 LT 501, PC 754

Richelieu and Ontario Navigation Co (Owners of SS Canada) v SS Cape Breton (Owners) [1907] AC 112, 76 LJPC 14, 95 LT 896, 23 TLR 185, PC 217

Richmond Shipping Ltd v Vestland D/S and A/S, The Vestland [1980] 2 Lloyd's Rep 171 973

Richmond, The (1902) 19 TLR 29, DC 600

Riga, The (1872) LR 3 A & E 516, 41 LJ Adm 39, 1 Asp MLC 246, 20 WR 927, 26 LT 202, HC 126, 169, 432, 983

Rijnstroom, The [1899] WN 33, 8 Asp MLC 538, 80 LT 422, P, D and Admlty 148

Rilland, The [1979] 1 Lloyd's Rep 455 .... 878, 881, 886

Ring, The [1931] P 58, 100 LJP 118, 18 Asp MLC 238, 145 LT 166, 47 TLR 384, P, D and Admlty 165

Rinquist v Ditchell (1799) 2 Camp 555n, sub nom Runquist v Ditchell 3 Esp 64, 170 ER 539 5

Rio Verde, SS (Owners) v SS Abaris (Owners) and Lieutenant Taylor, RNVR, Steam Tug Great Emperor (1920) 2 Ll L Rep 411, P, D and Admlty 743

Ripon City, The [1897] P 226, 66 LJP 110, 8 Asp MLC 304, [1895–9] All ER Rep 487, 77 LT 98, 13 TLR 378, P, D and Admlty .. 83, 92–93, 110, 131, 134, 321, 433, 964, 966–967, 971

Ripon City, The [1898] P 78, 67 LJP 30, 8 Asp MLC 391, 46 WR 586, 78 LT 296, 14 TLR 219, P, D and Admlty 330

Risoluto, The (1883) 8 PD 109, 52 LJP 46, 5 Asp MLC 93, 31 WR 657, 48 LT 909, P, D and Admlty 804

Ritchie v Couper (1860) 28 Beav 344, 54 ER 398 238

River Lagan, The (1888) 57 LJP 28, 6 Asp MLC 281, 58 LT 773, P, D and Admlty 204

River Rima, The [1987] 3 All ER 1, [1987] 2 Lloyd's Rep 106, 131 Sol Jo 887, [1987] LS Gaz R 1967, (1987) Times, 4 May; affd [1988] 2 All ER 641, [1988] 1 WLR 758, [1988] 2 Lloyd's Rep 193, 132 Sol Jo 968, [1988] 28 LS Gaz R 46, HL 126, 983

River Wear Comrs v Adamson (1877) 2 App Cas 743, 42 JP 244, 47 LJQB 193, 3 Asp MLC 521, 26 WR 217, [1874–80] All ER Rep 1, 37 LT 543, HL 780

Riverman, The [1928] P 33, 97 LJP 39, 17 Asp MLC 344, 138 LT 303, 44 TLR 140, P, D and Admlty 600, 784

Roanoke, The [1908] P 231, 77 LJP 115, 11 Asp MLC 253, 52 Sol Jo 426, 99 LT 78, 24 TLR 526, CA 707

Rob Roy, The (1849) 3 Wm Rob 190, 166 ER 934, 7 Notes of Cases 280 710

Robert Dickinson, The (1884) 10 PD 15, 54 LJP 5, 5 Asp MLC 341, 33 WR 400, 52 LT 55, P, D and Admlty 240

PARA

Robert Dixon, The (1879) 5 PD 54, 4 Asp MLC 246, 28 WR 716, 42 LT 344, CA
.... 597–599, 742, 783
Robert Ingham, The (1861) Lush 327 710
Robert Koeppen, The [1926] P 81n, 24 Ll L Rep 289, P, D and Admlty
.... 204
Roberta, The [1938] P 1, 58 Ll L Rep 374, 107 LJP 40, 82 Sol Jo 193, 158 LT 391, 53
   TLR 1048, CA 172
Robertson v Amazon Tug and Lighterage Co (1881) 7 QBD 598, 51 LJQB 68, 4 Asp MLC
   496, 30 WR 308, 46 LT 146, [1881–51] All ER Rep Ext 1714, CA
   .... 597, 783
Robertson v Caruthers (1819) 2 Stark 571, 171 ER 739, NP
.... 438
Robertson v Portpatrick and Wigtownshire Joint Committee (1919) 56 SLR 173, 1919 SC
   293, 1918 2 SLT 56, Ct of Sess 755
Robinson v Alnwick (Owners), The Alnwick [1965] P 357, [1965] 2 All ER 569, [1965] 3
   WLR 118, [1965] 1 Lloyd's Rep 320, 109 Sol Jo 230, CA
   .... 152–153, 1013
Robson v Sykes [1938] 2 All ER 612, 61 Ll L Rep 16, 82 Sol Jo 493, 54 TLR 727, DC
.... 510
Rockabill, The [1937] P 93, [1937] 1 All ER 191, 56 Ll L Rep 149, 106 LJP 107, 19 Asp
   MLC 76, 156 LT 296, CA 755, 771, 785
Rodocanachi v Milburn (1886) 18 QBD 67, 56 LJQB 202, 6 Asp MLC 100, 35 WR 241,
   56 LT 594, 3 TLR 115, CA 808
Roebuck, The (1874) 2 Asp MLC 387, 31 LT 274 428
Roecliff, The (1869) LR 2 A & E 363, 38 LJ Adm 56, 3 Mar LC 243, 17 WR 745, 20 LT
   586, HC 811, 968
Rogers v Hoyle [2014] EWCA Civ 257, [2015] QB 265, [2014] 3 All ER 550, [2014] 3
   WLR 148, [2014] All ER (D) 131 (Mar) 828
Romance, The [1901] P 15, 70 LJP 1, 9 Asp MLC 149, 83 LT 488, P, D and Admlty
   .... 713–714, 720
Romney Marsh (Lords Bailiff-Jurats) v Trinity House Corpn (1870) LR 5 Exch 204, 39 LJ
   Ex 163, 3 Mar LC 398, 18 WR 869, 22 LT 446, Exch Ct; affd (1872) LR 7 Exch 247,
   41 LJ Ex 106, 20 WR 952, Ex Ch 763
Rona, The (1873) 2 Asp MLC 182, 29 LT 781, PC 740
Rory, The (1882) 7 PD 117, 51 LJP 73, 4 Asp MLC 534, 46 LT 757, CA
.... 189
Rosalie, The (1853) 1 Ecc & Ad 188, 18 Jur 337, 164 ER 109
.... 893
Rosalie, The (1880) 5 PD 245, 50 LJP 3, 4 Asp MLC 384, 44 LT 32, P, D and Admlty
.... 769
Rosalind, The (1920) 5 Ll L Rep 139, 175, 211, 90 LJP 126, 37 TLR 116, P, D and
   Admlty 790, 796
Rosario, The (1876) 2 PD 41, 46 LJP 52, 3 Asp MLC 334, 35 LT 816, P, D and Admlty
.... 904
Rose of England, The (1888) 6 Asp MLC 304, 59 LT 262, DC
.... 746
Rose, The (1843) 2 Wm Rob 1, 7 Jur 381, 166 ER 656, 2 Notes of Cases 101
.... 741
Rose, The (1873) LR 4 A & E 6, 42 LJ Adm 11, 1 Asp MLC 567, 21 WR 511, 28 LT 291,
   HC 105
Rosehaugh, The (1854) 1 Ecc & Ad 267, 164 ER 155 869
Rosetta, The (1888) 6 Asp MLC 310, 59 LT 342, P, D and Admlty
.... 789
Ross v Walker (1765) 2 Wils 264, 95 ER 801 970
Ross v Woodford [1894] 1 Ch 38, 63 LJ Ch 191, 8 R 20, 42 WR 188, 38 Sol Jo 42, 70 LT
   22 204
Rowan Companies Inc and Rowan Drilling UK Ltd v Lanbert Eggink Offshore Transport
   Consultants Vof Kirkstead Ltd and JCE Shipping Ltd, The Gilbert Rowe [1997] 2
   Lloyd's Rep 218 149
Royal Arch, The (1857) Sw 269, 6 WR 191, 166 ER 1131, 30 LTOS 198
   .... 321, 969, 980, 991
Royal Eagle, The (1950) 84 Ll L Rep 543, P, D and Admlty
.... 110
Royal Fusilier, The (1926) 25 Ll L Rep 566, P, D and Admlty
.... 801

                                                                                          PARA
Royal Sovereign, The (1950) 84 Ll L Rep 549, P, D and Admlty
.... 110
Royal Wells, The [1985] QB 86, [1984] 3 All ER 193, [1984] 3 WLR 698, [1984] 2
    Lloyd's Rep 255, 128 Sol Jo 498, [1984] LS Gaz R 2362
.... 178, 981–982
Royalist, The (1863) Brown & Lush 46, 32 LJPM & A 105, 9 Jur NS 852, 167 ER 291
.... 424
Ruabon Steamship Co v London Assurance [1900] AC 6, 69 LJQB 86, 9 Asp MLC 2, 5
    Com Cas 71, 48 WR 225, [1895–9] All ER Rep 677, 44 Sol Jo 116, 81 LT 585, 16
    TLR 90, HL 801
Ruben Martinez Villena, The [1987] 2 Lloyd's Rep 621 190
Ruby Queen, The (1861) Lush 266, 167 ER 119 .... 92, 735, 967
Runquist v Ditchell. See Rinquist v Ditchell
Rusden v Pope (1868) LR 3 Exch 269, 37 LJ Ex 137, 3 Mar LC 91, 16 WR 1122, 18 LT
    651, Exch Ct 330, 332
Russland, The [1924] P 55, 17 Ll L Rep 306, 93 LJP 18, 16 Asp MLC 288, 68 Sol Jo 324,
    130 LT 763, 40 TLR 232, P, D and Admlty 172, 979, 983–984
Rutberg v Williams [1962] 1 QB 12, [1961] 2 All ER 649, [1961] 2 WLR 958, [1961] 1
    Lloyd's Rep 580, 125 JP 468, 10 Sol Jo 444, DC 223

                                              S

SC Rolinay Sea Star Srl v Owners and/or demise charterers of the Bumbesti, The Bumbesti
    [2000] QB 559, [2000] 2 WLR 533, [1999] 2 All ER (Comm) 187, [1999] 2 Lloyd's
    Rep 481, [2000] 2 All ER 692, (1999) Times, 12 July, [1999] Lexis Citation 3438,
    [1999] All ER (D) 691 .... 93, 111
SS Alcantra (Owners) v Sailing Ship Tovarisch (Owners), The Tovarisch. See Tovarisch, The
SS Celia (Owners) v SS Volturno (Owners) [1921] 2 AC 544, 90 LJP 385, 15 Asp MLC
    374, 27 Com Cas 46, [1921] All ER Rep 173, [1921] All ER Rep 110, 126 LT 1, 37
    TLR 969, HL 207
Sabina, The (1842) 7 Jur 182 .... 979, 982
Sadler v Dixon. See Dixon v Sadler
Saint Angus, The [1938] P 225, 61 Ll L Rep 186, 107 LJP 135, 19 Asp MLC 221, 159 LT
    464, 54 TLR 947, P, D and Admlty 739
St Anna, The [1983] 2 All ER 691, [1983] 1 WLR 895, [1983] 1 Lloyd's Rep 637, 127 Sol
    Jo 344 93
St Aubin, The [1907] P 60, 76 LJP 25, 10 Asp MLC 298, 95 LT 586, P, D and Admlty
.... 746
St Audries, The (1886) 5 Asp MLC 552, 54 LT 278, P, D and Admlty
.... 705
St Blane, The [1974] 1 Lloyd's Rep 557 .... 117, 895
St Chad (No 2), The [1962] 2 Lloyd's Rep 347, P, D and Admlty
.... 143
St Chad, The. See Saul v St Andrews Steam Fishing Co Ltd, The St Chad
St Charles, The (1927) 29 Ll L Rep 312, 17 Asp MLC 399, 138 LT 456, CA
.... 149, 806
St Elefterio, The, Schwarz & Co (Grain) Ltd v St Elefterio ex Arion (Owners) [1957] P
    179, [1957] 2 All ER 374, [1957] 2 WLR 935, [1957] 1 Lloyd's Rep 283, 101 Sol Jo
    410, P, D and Admlty 93, 111
St George, The [1926] P 217, 95 LJP 181, 17 Asp MLC 164, [1926] All ER Rep 553, 136
    LT 252, 42 TLR 766, P, D and Admlty 134
St Lawrence, The (1880) 5 PD 250, 49 LJP 82, P, D and Admlty
.... 125, 330, 432
St Melante, The (1947) 80 Ll L Rep 588, P, D and Admlty
.... 899
St Merriel, The. See Smith's Dock Co Ltd v The St Merriel (Owners), The St Merriel
St Olaf, The (1877) 2 PD 113, 46 LJP 74, 3 Asp MLC 341, 36 LT 30, P, D and Admlty
.... 105
St Rognvald, The. See Boy Andrew (Owners) v St Rognvald (Owners)
St Winifred, The. See Devonshire, The and St Winifred
Salabangka, The [1943] P 13, 74 Ll L Rep 47, 112 LJP 22, 168 LT 240, 59 TLR 38, P, D
    and Admlty 204
Salacia, The (1829) 2 Hag Adm 262, 166 ER 240 899

PARA

Salacia, The (1862) Lush 545, 32 LJPM & A 41, 9 Jur NS 27, 1 Mar LC 261, 11 WR 189,
  167 ER 246, 7 LT 440 980–981
Salomon v Customs and Excise Comrs [1967] 2 QB 116, [1966] 3 All ER 871, [1966] 3
  WLR 1223, [1966] 2 Lloyd's Rep 460, 110 Sol Jo 833 86
Saltburn, The (1894) 7 Asp MLC 474, 6 R 702, 71 LT 19, P, D and Admlty
  904
Salvador, The (1909) 26 TLR 149, P, D and Admlty 597
Samauri, The (1945) 78 Ll L Rep 546, P, D and Admlty
  204
Samco Europe v MSC Prestige [2011] EWHC 1580 (Admlty), [2011] 2 Lloyd's Rep 579,
  [2011] All ER (D) 54 (Jul) 705–706, 729, 739, 771
Samco Europe v MSC Prestige [2011] EWHC 1656 (Admlty), [2011] NLJR 988, [2012]
  BLR 267, [2011] All ER (D) 55 (Jul) 203
Sameiet Stavos (O H Meling Rederi) v The Berostar (Owners) [1970] 2 Lloyd's Rep 403
  .... 127, 178
Samick Lines Co Ltd v Antonis P Lemos (Owners) [1985] AC 711, [1985] 1 All ER 695,
  [1985] 2 WLR 468, [1985] 1 Lloyd's Rep 283, 129 Sol Jo 171, HL
  111
Samsun Logix Corp v Oceantrade Corp [2007] EWHC 2372 (Comm), [2008] 1 All ER
  (Comm) 673, [2008] 1 Lloyd's Rep 450, [2007] ArbLR 50, [2007] All ER (D) 272
  (Oct) 964
Samuel v Jones (1862) 1 Mar LC 282, 7 LT 760 333
Samuel, The (1851) 15 Jur 407, 17 LTOS 204 .... 855, 884, 910–911, 924
San Demetrio, The (1941) 69 Ll L Rep 5, P, D and Admlty
  .... 855, 869
San Onofre, The [1917] P 96, 86 LJP 103, 14 Asp MLC 74, 116 LT 800, P, D and Admlty
  .... 177, 888
San Onofre, The [1922] P 243, 92 LJP 17, 16 Asp MLC 1, [1922] All ER Rep 720, 127 LT
  540, 38 TLR 707, CA 727, 763, 798
Sandefjord, The [1953] 2 Lloyd's Rep 557, P, D and Admlty
  .... 189, 869
Sandrina, The. See Gatoil International Inc v Arkwright-Boston Manufacturers Mutual
  Insurance Co, The Sandrina
Sans Pareil, HMS [1900] P 267, 69 LJP 127, 9 Asp MLC 78, 82 LT 606, 16 TLR 390, CA
  .... 770, 786
Sanshin Victory, The [1980] 2 Lloyd's Rep 359 698
Santa Anna, The (1863) 32 LJPM & A 198, 9 Jur NS 1205
  430
Santanderino, The. See Vanvert v Arrotegui, The Santanderino
Santiago, The (1900) 70 LJP 12, 9 Asp MLC 147, 83 LT 439, 17 TLR 22, P, D and
  Admlty 869, 906
Santipore, The (1854) 1 Ecc & Ad 231, 164 ER 134 .... 863, 910
Santos v Owners of the Baltic Carrier [2001] 1 Lloyd's Rep 689, [2001] All ER (D) 247
  (Feb) 153, 1013
Sappho, The (1871) LR 3 PC 690, 8 Moo PCCNS 66, 40 LJ Adm 47, 1 Asp MLC 65, 24
  LT 795, PC 510, 865, 869
Sappho, The (1873) 2 Asp MLC 4, 28 LT 825, PC 705
Sara, The. See Hamilton v Baker, The Sara
Sarah Bell, The (1845) 8 LT 440, 6 LT 371, 4 Notes of Cases 144
  924
Sarah Jane, The (1843) 2 Wm Rob 110, 166 ER 696, 3 LT 182
  .... 867, 885
Sarah, The (1862) Lush 549, 167 ER 248 811
Sarah, The (1878) 3 PD 39, 3 Asp MLC 542, 37 LT 831, P, D and Admlty
  855
Saratoga, The (1861) Lush 318, 167 ER 140 .... 855, 871
Sargasso, The [1912] P 192, 82 LJP 9, 12 Asp MLC 202, 107 LT 204, 28 TLR 444, P, D
  and Admlty 714
Sargasso, The. See Neste Chemicals SA v DK Line SA and Tokumaru Kaiun KK, The
  Sargasso
Sarpedon, The (Cargo ex) (1877) 3 PD 28, 3 Asp MLC 509, 26 WR 375, 37 LT 505, P, D
  and Admlty 866, 877, 914
Sarpen, The [1916] P 306, 85 LJP 209, 13 Asp MLC 370, [1916–17] All ER Rep 1132, 60
  Sol Jo 538, 114 LT 1011, 32 TLR 575, CA 868

PARA

Sarrio SA v Kuwait Investment Authority [1999] 1 AC 32, [1997] 4 All ER 929, [1997] 3
WLR 1143, [1998] 1 Lloyd's Rep 129, (1997) Times, 17 November, [1997] Lexis
Citation 5261, 141 Sol Jo LB 248, [1997] All ER (D) 71, HL
.... 99
Saul v St Andrews Steam Fishing Co Ltd, The St Chad [1965] 2 Lloyd's Rep 1, 109 Sol Jo
392, CA 220
Sauria, The and The Trent [1957] 1 Lloyd's Rep 396, CA
.... 153, 1013
Savage v British India Steam Navigation Co Ltd (1930) 46 TLR 294
.... 424
Savina, The [1976] 2 Lloyd's Rep 123, 120 Sol Jo 434, HL
.... 220
Saxicava, The [1924] P 131, 18 Ll L Rep 155, 93 LJP 66, 16 Asp MLC 324, 68 Sol Jo
666, 131 LT 342, 40 TLR 334, CA 189
Saxonia, The (1862) Lush 410, 31 LJPM & A 201, 8 Jur NS 315, 1 Mar LC 192, 10 WR
431, 167 ER 179, 6 LT 6, sub nom Hamburgh American Steam Navigation Co v
North of Scotland Banking Co, The Eclipse and The Saxonia 15 Moo PCC 262, PC
.... 710
Sayce v Ameer Ruler Sadig Mohammad Abbasi Bahawalpur State [1952] 2 QB 390, [1952]
2 All ER 64, 96 Sol Jo 395, [1952] 1 TLR 1457, CA 121
Scaramanga v Stamp (1880) 5 CPD 295, 49 LJQB 674, 4 Asp MLC 295, 28 WR 691, 42
LT 840, CA 431, 897
Scarcity, The and The Daniel M [1967] 2 Lloyd's Rep 498, P, D and Admlty
.... 204
Scarsdale, The [1906] P 103, 75 LJP 31, 10 Asp MLC 235, 54 WR 335, 94 LT 528, 22
TLR 255, CA; affd sub nom Board of Trade v Baxter, The Scarsdale [1907] AC 373,
76 LJP 147, 10 Asp MLC 525, 51 Sol Jo 70, 97 LT 526, 23 TLR 729, HL
.... 510
Sceptre, The (1876) 3 Asp MLC 269, 35 LT 429, P, D and Admlty
.... 136
Scheldestad, The (1933) 45 Ll L Rep 269, P, D and Admlty
.... 881
Schiffahrtsgesellschaft MS Merkur Sky MbH & Co KG v MS Leerort Nth Schiffahrts
GmbH & Co KG, The Leerort and The Zim Piraeus [2001] EWCA Civ 1055, [2001] 2
Lloyd's Rep 291, [2001] All ER (D) 356 (Jun) 996, 1003
Schiller, Cargo ex (1877) 2 PD 145, 3 Asp MLC 439, 36 LT 714, CA
.... 120, 864, 868, 886, 914, 923, 969
Schwan, The [1892] P 419, 7 Asp MLC 347, 69 LT 34, 8 TLR 425, CA
.... 788
Scicluna v Stevenson, The Rhondda (1883) 8 App Cas 549, 5 Asp MLC 114, 49 LT 210,
PC 700, 747
Scindia, The. See Kirby v Scindia (Owners), The Scindia
Scio, The (1867) LR 1 A & E 353, 2 Mar LC 527, 16 LT 642, HC
.... 321, 974, 983, 991
Scioto, The (1847) Daveis 359 736
Scotia, The (1890) 6 Asp MLC 541, 63 LT 324, P, D and Admlty
.... 733, 746, 761, 769
Scott v Scott (1818) 2 Stark 438, 171 ER 698, NP 782
Scottish Musician, The [1942] P 128, 72 Ll L Rep 284, 111 LJP 65, 167 LT 417, 58 TLR
299, P, D and Admlty 5
Scout, The (1872) LR 3 A & E 512, 41 LJ Adm 42, 1 Asp MLC 258, 20 WR 617, 26 LT
371, HC 867
Screw Collier Co v Webster (or Kerr) [1910] AC 165, 79 LJPC 57, HL
.... 700
Sea Nymph, The (1860) Lush 23, 167 ER 12 744
Sea Salvage, The (1912) Times, 9 December 861
Sea Spray, The [1907] P 133, 76 LJP 48, 10 Asp MLC 462, 96 LT 792, P, D and Admlty
.... 975–977, 982
Sea Tractor (Owners and/or Demise Charterers) v Tramp (Owners) [2007] EWHC 31
(Admlty), [2007] 2 Lloyd's Rep 363, [2007] All ER (D) 88 (Jan)
.... 849
Seacombe, The [1912] P 21, 81 LJP 36, 12 Asp MLC 137, 142, 56 Sol Jo 140, 106 LT
241, 246, 28 TLR 107, CA; affd sub nom Devonshire (Owners) v Barge Leslie
(Owners) [1912] AC 634, 12 Asp MLC 210, 107 LT 179, 28 TLR 551, sub nom The
Devonshire 81 LJP 94, 57 Sol Jo 10, HL 183, 599, 742, 775, 784
Seagrave v Parks [1891] 1 QB 551, 60 LJQB 355 187

PARA

Secony Bunker Oil Co Ltd v SS D'Vora (Owners), The D'Vora. See D'Vora, The, Socony
 Bunker Oil Co Ltd v SS D'Vora of Haifa (Owners)
Secret, The (1872) 1 Asp MLC 318, 26 LT 670, 6 ILT 146
 .... 734, 736, 789
Sedgepool, The [1956] 2 Lloyd's Rep 668, P, D and Admlty
 700
Sedgworth v Overend (1797) 7 Term Rep 279, 101 ER 974
 790
Sedulity, The [1956] 1 Lloyd's Rep 510, P, D and Admlty
 .... 735, 770
Segredo, The (otherwise The Eliza Cornish) (1853) 1 Ecc & Ad 36, 17 Jur 738, 164 ER 22,
 22 LTOS 36 .... 425, 440
Seismic Shipping Inc v Total E & P UK plc [2005] EWCA Civ 985, [2005] All ER (D) 461
 (Jul), sub nom Seismic Shipping Inc v Total E & P UK plc, The Western Regent [2005]
 2 All ER (Comm) 515, [2005] 2 Lloyd's Rep 359 .... 196, 199, 1002–1003, 1007
Seistan, The [1960] 1 All ER 32, [1960] 1 WLR 186, [1959] 2 Lloyd's Rep 607, 104 Sol Jo
 233, P, D and Admlty 224
Selat Arjuna, The (Owners)v Contship Success, The (Owners)[2000] 1 All ER (Comm) 905,
 [2000] Lexis Citation 2946, [2000] All ER (D) 518 707
Selina, The (1842) 2 Notes of Cases 18 .... 888, 979–982
Semco Salvage & Marine Pte Ltd v Lancer Navigation Co Ltd, The Nagasaki Spirit [1997]
 AC 455, [1997] 1 All ER 502, [1997] 2 WLR 298, [1997] 1 Lloyd's Rep 323, [1997]
 NLJR 218, (1997) Times, 10 February, 141 Sol Jo LB 43, HL
 879
Semiramis, The [1952] 2 Lloyd's Rep 86, P, D and Admlty
 183
Senat v Porter (1797) 7 Term Rep 158, 101 ER 908 430
Sennar, The. See DSV Silo-und Verwaltungsgesellschaft mbH v Sennar (Owners), The
 Sennar
Serafina, The (1864) Brown & Lush 277, 167 ER 362 431
Seraglio, The (1885) 10 PD 120, 54 LJP 76, 5 Asp MLC 421, 34 WR 32, 52 LT 865, 1
 TLR 446, P, D and Admlty 162, 164
Sergeant, The. See Hesselmoor, The and The Sergeant
Settlement Corpn v Hochschild [1966] Ch 10, [1965] 3 All ER 486, [1965] 3 WLR 1150,
 109 Sol Jo 920 101
Seymolicus, The [1909] P 109, 78 LJP 52, 11 Asp MLC 206, 100 LT 382, P, D and Admlty
 700
Shakkeborg, The [1911] P 245n, P, D and Admlty 739
Shallcross v Oldham (1862) 2 John & H 609, 10 WR 291, 70 ER 1202, 5 LT 824
 429
Shanklin, The (1932) 43 Ll L Rep 153, P, D and Admlty
 743
Shannon, The (1842) 1 Wm Rob 463, 7 Jur 380, 166 ER 645, 6 LT 581
 .... 734, 789
Sharp v Taylor (1849) 2 Ph 801, 41 ER 1153, 14 LTOS 1, Ct of Ch
 239
Sherbro, The (1883) 52 LJP 28, 5 Asp MLC 88, 48 LT 767, P, D and Admlty
 321
Shersby v Hibbert, The Duke of Manchester (1847) 6 Moo PCC 90, 13 ER 618, 5 Notes
 of Cases 470, PC 742
Shillito v Biggart [1903] 1 KB 683, 72 LJKB 294, 9 Asp MLC 396, 8 Com Cas 137, 51
 WR 479, 47 Sol Jo 354, 88 LT 426, 19 TLR 313 .... 332, 334
Shipping Controller v Athena (1923) 14 Ll L Rep 515, HL
 705
Shipton v Thornton (1838) 9 Ad & El 314, 8 LJQB 73, 1 Per & Dav 216, 1 Will Woll &
 H 710, 112 ER 1231, [1835–42] All ER Rep 62 436
Shizelle, The [1992] 2 Lloyd's Rep 444 318
Sickens v Irving (1859) 7 CBNS 165, 29 LJCP 25, 6 Jur NS 200, 141 ER 778
 428
Silesia, The (1880) 5 PD 177, 50 LJP 9, 4 Asp MLC 338, 29 WR 156, 43 LT 319, P, D
 and Admlty 899
Silia, The [1981] 2 Lloyd's Rep 534 93
Silver Bullion (1854) 2 Ecc & Ad 70, 164 ER 312, sub nom The Sir Robert Peel 8 LT 335
 .... 872, 884
Simpson v Fogo (1860) 1 John & H 18, 29 LJ Ch 657, 6 Jur NS 949, 8 WR 407, 70 ER
 644, sub nom Liverpool Bank v Foggo 2 LT 594 321

PARA

Simpson v Thomson (1877) 3 App Cas 279, 3 Asp MLC 567, 38 LT 1, HL
.... 780
Sims v Brittain (or Britten) (1832) 4 B & Ad 375, 1 Nev & MKB 594, 110 ER 496
.... 238
Singapore, The and The Hebe (1866) LR 1 PC 378, 4 Moo PCCNS 271, Holt Adm 124,
PC 220, 757
Singleton Abbey (SS) (Owners) v SS Paludina (Owners), The Paludina [1927] AC 16, 95
LJP 135, 17 Asp MLC 117, [1926] All ER Rep 220, 135 LT 707, HL
.... 143, 757, 795, 798
Sinquasi, The (1880) 5 PD 241, 50 LJP 5, 4 Asp MLC 383, 43 LT 768, P, D and Admlty
.... 599, 784
Sir Henry Webb, The (1849) 13 Jur 639, 7 LT 224 428
Sir Ralph Abercrombie, The. See Carmichael v Brodie, The Sir Ralph Abercrombie
Sir Robert Peel, The (1880) 4 Asp MLC 321, 43 LT 364, CA
.... 205
Sir Robert Peel, The. See Silver Bullion
Sisters, The (1875) 2 Asp MLC 589, 32 LT 837 172
Sisters, The (1876) 1 PD 117, 45 LJP 39, 3 Asp MLC 122, 24 WR 412, 34 LT 338, CA
.... 220, 762, 766
Sitarem, The (Owners) v Owners and/or demise charterers of the Spirit [2001] 2 All ER
(Comm) 837, [2001] 2 Lloyd's Rep 107, [2001] Lexis Citation 1390, [2001] All ER
(D) 143 (Apr) 707
Sivewright v Allen [1906] 2 KB 81, 70 JP 290, 75 LJKB 476, 10 Asp MLC 251, 11 Com
Cas 167, 54 WR 604, 50 Sol Jo 440, 94 LT 778, 22 TLR 482, DC
.... 487
Six Sisters, The [1900] P 302, 69 LJP 139, P, D and Admlty
.... 733
Skibladner, The (1877) 3 PD 24, 47 LJP 84, 3 Asp MLC 556, 38 LT 150, P, D and Admlty
.... 855, 906
Skipsea, The [1905] P 32, 74 LJP 34, 10 Asp MLC 91, 53 WR 538, 93 LT 181, P, D and
Admlty 751
Skrim, The (1914) 30 TLR 555, P, D and Admlty 716
Skylark, The. See Atle Marine v The Skylark (Owners), The Skylark
Slaney, The [1951] 2 Lloyd's Rep 538, P, D and Admlty
.... 189, 871
Slater v Reed and McGrath, The Varos [1980] 2 Lloyd's Rep 581, DC
.... 760
Smit International (Deutschland) GmbH v Mobius [2001] 2 All ER (Comm) 265, [2001]
Lexis Citation 2170, [2001] All ER (D) 26 (Jun) 1010
Smith v Bank of New South Wales, The Staffordshire (1872) LR 4 PC 194, 8 Moo PCCNS
443, 41 LJ Adm 49, 1 Asp MLC 365, 20 WR 557, 27 LT 46, PC
.... 435
Smith v Cocking [1959] 1 Lloyd's Rep 88, DC 1170
Smith v Dobson (1841) 3 Man & G 59, 3 Scott NR 336, 133 ER 1057, 3 LT 419
.... 741
Smith v Plummer (1818) 1 B & Ald 575, 106 ER 212 .... 968, 970
Smith v Readshaw (1781) 2 Park's Marine Insurances (8th Edn) 708
.... 5
Smith v St Lawrence Tow-Boat Co (1873) LR 5 PC 308, 2 Asp MLC 41, 21 WR 569, 28
LT 885, PC 598–599, 742
Smith v Voss (1857) 2 H & N 97, 26 LJ Ex 233, 5 WR 534, 157 ER 40, 29 LTOS 97,
Exch Ct 779
Smith v Zigurds SS Owners and E A Casper, Edgar & Co Ltd. See Zigurds, The
Smith's Dock Co Ltd v The St Merriel (Owners), The St Merriel [1963] P 247, [1963] 1 All
ER 537, [1963] 2 WLR 488, [1963] 1 Lloyd's Rep 63, P, D and Admlty
.... 93, 109, 126, 810, 974, 990
Smith Kline and French Laboratories Ltd v Bloch [1983] 2 All ER 72, [1983] 1 WLR 730,
127 Sol Jo 410 101
Smyrna, The cited in (1861) Lush 385 720
Smyrna, The. See Imperial Royal Privileged Danubian Steam Navigation Co v Greek and
Oriental Steam Navigation Co, The Smyrna
Snark, The [1900] P 105, 69 LJP 41, 9 Asp MLC 50, 48 WR 279, 44 Sol Jo 209, 82 LT
42, 16 TLR 160, CA 787, 945

PARA

Snia Viscosa Societa, etc v SS Yuri Maru. See Yuri Maru, The

Soares v Rahn, The Prince of Saxe Coburg (1838) 3 Moo PCC 1, 13 ER 1, 4 LT 28, 92,
PC 134

Sobieski, The [1949] P 313, [1949] 1 All ER 701, 82 Ll L Rep 370, 93 Sol Jo 237, 65 TLR
263, sub nom Layard v Esperance (Owners) and Sobieski (Owners) [1949] LJR 946,
CA 152, 220, 1013

Soblomsten, The (1866) LR 1 A & E 293, 36 LJ Adm 5, 2 Mar LC 436, 15 WR 591, 15
LT 393, HC 889, 985

Société Anonyme de Remorquage à Hélice v Bennetts [1911] 1 KB 243, 80 LJKB 228, 16
Com Cas 24, 27 TLR 77 793

Societe Maritme Caledonienne v The Cythera and Her Cargo [1965] 2 Lloyd's Rep 454,
NSW SC 861

Socrates, The and The Champion [1923] P 76, 92 LJP 51, 129 LT 159, P, D and Admlty;
revsd [1923] P 162, 93 LJP 38, CA 732, 774

Solace (No 2), The (1936) 55 Ll L Rep 201, P, D and Admlty
.... 148

Solway Prince, The [1896] P 120, 65 LJP 45, 8 Asp MLC 128, 74 LT 32, 12 TLR 184, P,
D and Admlty 868

Somes v British Empire Shipping Co (1860) 8 HL Cas 338, 30 LJQB 229, 6 Jur NS 761, 8
WR 707, 11 ER 459, [1843–60] All ER Rep 844, 2 LT 547, HL
.... 974, 990

Somes v Sugrue (1830) 4 C & P 276, 172 ER 703 439

Sophie, The (1842) 1 Wm Rob 368, 6 Jur 351, 166 ER 610, 3 LT 153, 1 Notes of Cases
393, HC 432

Southern Venturer, The [1953] 1 Lloyd's Rep 428, Ct of Sess
.... 906

Southport Corpn v Esso Petroleum Co Ltd [1953] 2 All ER 1204, [1953] 3 WLR 773; on
appeal [1954] 2 QB 182, [1954] 2 All ER 561, [1954] 3 WLR 200, 52 LGR 404,
[1954] 1 Lloyd's Rep 446, 118 JP 411, 99 Sol Jo 472, CA; affd sub nom Esso
Petroleum Co Ltd v Southport Corpn [1956] AC 218, [1955] 3 All ER 864, [1956] 2
WLR 81, 54 LGR 91, [1955] 2 Lloyd's Rep 655, 120 JP 54, 100 Sol Jo 32, HL
.... 205, 757, 788

Southport Corpn v Morriss [1893] 1 QB 359, 57 JP 231, 7 Asp MLC 279, 5 R 201, 41
WR 382, 68 LT 221, sub nom R v Southport Corpn and Morris 62 LJMC 47, DC
.... 229

Southwark, The [1962] 2 Lloyd's Rep 62, P, D and Admlty
.... 204

Soya Margareta, The, Owners of Cargo on Board Soya Lovisa v Owners of Soya
Margareta [1960] 2 All ER 756, [1961] 1 WLR 709, [1960] 1 Lloyd's Rep 675, 105
Sol Jo 406, P, D and Admlty 101

Soya, The [1956] 2 All ER 393, [1956] 1 Lloyd's Rep 557, sub nom Dirphys (Owners) v
Soya (Owners), The Soya [1956] 1 WLR 714, 100 Sol Jo 433, CA
.... 804

Spaight v Tedcastle (1881) 6 App Cas 217, 4 Asp MLC 406, 29 WR 761, 44 LT 589, HL
.... 598–599, 742, 767, 770

Spain v The Arantzazu Mendi [1939] AC 256, [1939] 1 All ER 719, 63 Ll L Rep 89, 108
LJP 55, 19 Asp MLC 263, 83 Sol Jo 356, 160 LT 513, 55 TLR 454, 2 BILC 198, HL
.... 86, 164

Spanish Republican Government v Abodi Mendi. See Abodi Mendi, The

Sparti, The [2000] 2 Lloyd's Rep 618 988

Sparto, The [1956] 1 Lloyd's Rep 400, P, D and Admlty
.... 707

Speedlink Vanguard and The European Gateway. See European Gateway, The

Spiliada Maritime Corpn v Cansulex Ltd, The Spiliada [1987] AC 460, [1986] 3 All ER
843, [1986] 3 WLR 972, [1987] 1 Lloyd's Rep 1, 130 Sol Jo 925, [1987] LS Gaz R
113, [1986] NLJ Rep 1137, [1987] LRC (Comm) 356, HL
.... 100–101

Spirit of the Age, The (1857) Sw 286, 166 ER 1141, 30 LTOS 189
.... 852

Spree, The [1893] P 147, 7 Asp MLC 397, 1 R 584, 69 LT 628, P, D and Admlty
.... 867

Spyros, The [1953] 1 Lloyd's Rep 501, P, D and Admlty
.... 705

Stackpoole v R (1875) IR 9 Eq 619, CA 115

PARA

Staffordshire, The. See Smith v Bank of New South Wales, The Staffordshire
Stanmore, The (1885) 10 PD 134, 54 LJP 89, 5 Asp MLC 441, 53 LT 10, CA
.... 697
Stanton v Redriff (1921) 6 Ll L Rep 348, P, D and Admlty
.... 769
Star of India, The (1876) 1 PD 466, 45 LJP 102, 3 Asp MLC 261, 25 WR 377, 35 LT 407,
P, D and Admlty 804
Star of Persia, The (1887) 6 Asp MLC 220, 57 LT 839, CA
.... 900
Star of the Isles, The (1938) 62 Ll L Rep 139, P, D and Admlty
.... 789
Statue of Liberty, The [1970] 2 Lloyd's Rep 151, CA; on appeal [1971] 2 Lloyd's Rep 277,
HL 220, 707
Steadfast, The (1922) 13 Ll L Rep 252, 39 TLR 96, P, D and Admlty
.... 147, 149
Steadman v Scholfield. See Steedman v Scofield
Steamship Mutual Underwriting Association (Bermuda) Ltd v Owners of the Cargo Lately
Laden on Board the Vessel 'Jutha Rajpruek' [2003] EWCA Civ 378, (2003) Times, 19
March, [2003] All ER (D) 127 (Mar) 97
Steedman v Scofield [1992] 2 Lloyd's Rep 163, sub nom Steadman v Scholfield [1992] 17
LS Gaz R 51, (1992) Times, 15 April, 136 Sol Jo LB 129
.... 110, 152, 691, 1013
Steel v Lester and Lilee (1877) 3 CPD 121, 47 LJQB 43, 3 Asp MLC 537, 26 WR 212, 37
LT 642, CPD 242
Steel v State Line Steamship Co (1877) 3 App Cas 72, 3 Asp MLC 516, [1874–80] All ER
Rep 145, 37 LT 333, HL 597
Steel & Co v A Scott & Co. See Strang, Steel & Co v A Scott & Co
Steel Barges. See Five Steel Barges
Steele & Co v Dixon (1876) 3 R 1003, 13 SLR 723 238
Steingrim, The (1930) 37 Ll L Rep 284, P, D and Admlty
.... 798
Stella Nova [1981] Lexis Citation 615 111
Stella, The (1867) LR 1 A & E 340, 36 LJ Adm 13, 2 Mar LC 505, 15 WR 936, 16 LT
335, HC 887
Stellar Chartering and Brokerage Inc v Efibanca-Ente Finanziario Interbancario SpA [1984]
1 WLR 27, [1984] 1 Lloyd's Rep 119, 128 Sol Jo 32, [1984] LS Gaz R 283, HL
.... 331
Stentor, The [1934] P 133, 49 Ll L Rep 9, 103 LJP 105, 18 Asp MLC 490, [1934] All ER
Rep 545, 152 LT 450, CA 222
Stephan J, The [1985] 2 Lloyd's Rep 344 .... 93, 158, 160
Stephens v Broomfield, The Great Pacific (1869) LR 2 PC 516, 6 Moo PCCNS 151, 38 LJ
Adm 45, 3 Mar LC 263, 17 WR 933, 16 ER 683, 21 LT 38, PC
.... 972
Stevens v Gourley, The Cleadon (1860) Lush 158, 14 Moo PCC 92, 15 ER 240, 167 ER
76, 5 LT 694, PC 784
Stiklestad, The [1926] P 205, 95 LJP 161, 17 Asp MLC 191, 136 LT 479, 42 TLR 720, P,
D and Admlty; affd (1926) 43 TLR 118, CA 863
Stilk v Myrick (1809) 2 Camp 317, 6 Esp 129, 170 ER 851, 170 ER 1168, NP
.... 471
Stinne Peter, The (1986, unreported) 126
Stolt Kestrel BV v Sener Petrol Denizcilik Ticaret AS (The Stolt Kestrel and The Niyazi S)
[2015] EWCA Civ 1035, [2016] 1 All ER (Comm) 843, [2016] 1 Lloyd's Rep 125, 165
NLJ 7674, [2015] All ER (D) 146 (Oct) 92, 152–153, 1013
Stone (Thomas) Shipping Ltd v Admiralty, The Albion [1953] P 117, [1953] 1 All ER 978,
[1953] 2 WLR 807, [1953] 1 Lloyd's Rep 239, 97 Sol Jo 262, CA
.... 717, 730, 742, 763, 784
Stoomschappy Nederland v P and O Steam Navigation Co (1880) 5 App Cas
876, 4 Asp MLC 360, 29 WR 173, 43 LT 610, HL 690, 739, 760–762, 770
Stoomvart Maatschappy Nederland v Peninsular and Oriental Steam Navigation Co, The
Khedive (1882) 7 App Cas 795, 52 LJP 1, 4 Asp MLC 567, 31 WR 249, [1881–5] All
ER Rep 342, 47 LT 198, HL 207, 772–773

PARA

Storm King and The United Kingdom (Owners) v The Minnehaha (Owners). See
    Minnehaha, The
Stormcock, The (1885) 5 Asp MLC 470, 53 LT 53, P, D and Admlty
.... 742
Stort v Clements (1792) Peake 107 .... 779, 781
Strang, Steel & Co v A Scott & Co (1889) 14 App Cas 601, 6 Asp MLC 419, 5 TLR 705,
    sub nom Steel & Co v A Scott & Co 59 LJPC 1, 38 WR 452, 61 LT 597, PC
.... 875
Stranna, The [1937] P 130, [1937] 2 All ER 383, 106 LJP 81, 19 Asp MLC 115, 157 LT
    462, 53 TLR 558, P, D and Admlty; affd [1938] P 69, [1938] 1 All ER 458, 60 Ll L
    Rep 51, 107 LJP 33, 43 Com Cas 175, 82 Sol Jo 112, 54 TLR 393, CA
.... 757
Strathfillan, SS (Owners) v SS Ikala (Owners), The Ikala [1929] AC 196, 32 Ll L Rep 159,
    98 LJP 49, 17 Asp MLC 555, 140 LT 177, HL 803–805
Strathgarry, The [1895] P 264, 64 LJP 59, 7 Asp MLC 573, 11 R 732, 72 LT 202, P, D
    and Admlty 204, 883–884, 898
Strathnaver, The (1875) 1 App Cas 58, 3 Asp MLC 113, 34 LT 148, PC
.... 79, 167, 855, 861
Stream Fisher, The [1927] P 73, 26 Ll L Rep 4, 96 LJP 29, 17 Asp MLC 159, [1926] All
    ER Rep 513, 136 LT 189, P, D and Admlty 975–976, 978
Strickland, Re, ex p Bland (1814) 2 Rose 91 974
Strong Wise Ltd v Esso Australia Resources Pty Ltd (The APL Sydney) [2010] FCA 240,
    [2010] 2 Lloyd's Rep 555, Aust FC 190, 195, 994, 998
Strout v Foster (1843) 1 Howard 89 736
Stumore, Weston & Co v Breen (1886) 12 App Cas 698, 56 LJQB 401, HL
.... 429
Sullivar, The [1965] 2 Lloyd's Rep 350, P, D and Admlty
.... 163
Sultan, The, Cargo ex (1859) 5 Jur NS 1060, Sw 504, 166 ER 1235
.... 134
Sunheath, The (1925) 22 Ll L Rep 361 116
Sunlight, The [1904] P 100, 73 LJP 25, 9 Asp MLC 509, 90 LT 32, P, D and Admlty
.... 705, 754–755
Sunniside, The (1883) 8 PD 137, 52 LJP 76, 5 Asp MLC 140, 31 WR 859, 49 LT 401, P,
    D and Admlty 814, 899, 904
Susan V Luckenbach, SS (Owners) v Admiralty Comrs, The Susan V Luckenbach [1951] P
    197, [1951] 1 All ER 753, sub nom Susan V Luckenbach, The 84 Ll L Rep 538, sub
    nom Admiralty Comrs v Susan V Luckenbach SS (Owners) [1951] 1 TLR 165, CA
.... 865
Svanfos, The [1919] P 189, 88 LJP 154, 63 Sol Jo 575, 35 TLR 488, P, D and Admlty
.... 118
Svein Jarl, The (1923) 14 Ll L Rep 400, 16 Asp MLC 159, 129 LT 255, [1923] All ER Rep
    Ext 745, P, D and Admlty 204
Swainston v Garrick (1833) 2 LJ Ex 255 429
Swan, Hunter and Wigham Richardson Ltd v France, Fenwick Tyne and Wear Co Ltd, The
    Albion. See Albion, The, France, Fenwick and Tyne and Wear Co Ltd v Swan, Hunter
    and Wigham Richardson Ltd
Swan, The (1839) 1 Wm Rob 68 .... 855, 865
Swanland, The (1855) 2 Ecc & Ad 107, 164 ER 333 757
Swanston v Lishman (1881) 4 Asp MLC 450, 45 LT 360, CA
.... 238
Sweet v The Owners of Blyth Lifeboat 'Edward Duke of Windsor' (2002) Times, 22
    February, [2002] All ER (D) 146 (Jan) 1013
Swift, The [1901] P 168, 70 LJP 47, 9 Asp MLC 244, 85 LT 346, 17 TLR 400, P, D and
    Admlty 765
Swiftsure, The. See Hudson and Humphrey v Barge Swiftsure (Owners), The Swiftsure
Sydney Cove, The (1815) 2 Dods 1, 165 ER 1396, HC 980
Sydney Cove, The (1815) 2 Dods 11 .... 127, 478, 970, 982
Sydney Express, The [1988] 2 Lloyd's Rep 257 168
Sykes v Beadon (1879) 11 Ch D 170, 48 LJ Ch 522, 27 WR 464, 40 LT 243
.... 239
Sylph, The (1854) 2 Ecc & Ad 75, 164 ER 315, sub nom The Meteor v The Sylph 5 LT
    462 .... 700, 710
Sylph, The (1857) Sw 233, 166 ER 1112 707
Sylph, The (1867) LR 2 A & E 24, 37 LJ Adm 14, 3 Mar LC 37, 17 LT 519, HC
.... 765

PARA

Sylvan Arrow, The [1923] P 220, 92 LJP 119, 16 Asp MLC 244, 130 LT 157, 39 TLR 655,
P, D and Admlty 92, 964, 967
Sylvester Hale, The (Schooner) (1873) 6 Benedict United States District Court Reporter 523
.... 692

T

Tacoma City, The [1991] 1 Lloyd's Rep 330, CA 127, 478, 970
Tafelberg, The (1941) 71 Ll L Rep 189, P, D and Admlty
.... 855
Tagus, The [1903] P 44, 72 LJP 4, 9 Asp MLC 371, 87 LT 598, 19 TLR 82, P, D and
Admlty 128, 169, 330, 981, 986
Talabot, The (1890) 15 PD 194, 6 Asp MLC 602, 63 LT 812, P, D and Admlty
.... 748
Talbot, The [1891] P 184, 7 Asp MLC 36, 64 LT 542, P, D and Admlty
.... 710
Talca, The (1880) 5 PD 169, 4 Asp MLC 226, 29 WR 123, 42 LT 61, P, D and Admlty
.... 240
Tanner v Heard (1857) 23 Beav 555, 3 Jur 427, 5 WR 420, 53 ER 219, 29 LTOS 257
.... 321
Tanner v Phillips (1872) 42 LJ Ch 125, 1 Asp MLC 448, 21 WR 68, 27 LT 480
.... 332
Tantalus (Master and Crew) v Telemachus, Her Cargo and Freight (Owners), The
Telemachus [1957] P 47, [1957] 1 All ER 72, [1957] 2 WLR 200, [1956] 2 Lloyd's
Rep 490, 35 ATC 497, 50 R & IT 319, [1957] TR 1, 101 Sol Jo 112, P, D and
Admlty 886
Tarbert, The [1921] P 372, 90 LJP 353, 15 Asp MLC 423, 125 LT 800, 37 TLR 831, P, D
and Admlty 863, 871
Tarrant v Ramage, The Salvital [1998] 1 Lloyd's Rep 185, [1997] 36 LS Gaz R 43, (1997)
Times, 31 July 626
Tartar, The (1822) 1 Hag Adm 1, 166 ER 1 425
Tasmania, The (1888) 13 PD 110, 57 LJP 49, 6 Asp MLC 305, 59 LT 263, P, D and
Admlty 92, 600, 782, 967
Taunton, The (1928) 31 Ll L Rep 119, CA 707
Taylor v Burger (1898) 8 Asp MLC 364, 78 LT 93, 14 TLR 228, HL
.... 754–755, 785
Taylor v Geelong Harbour Trusts Comrs and Howard Smith Ltd [1962] 1 Lloyd's Rep 143
.... 600
Tees, The (1862) Lush 505, 1 Mar LC 251 855
Teh Hu, The v Nippon Salvage Co of Tokyo [1970] P 106, [1969] 3 All ER 1200, [1969] 3
WLR 1135, [1969] 2 Lloyd's Rep 365, 113 Sol Jo 792 .... 207, 886
Telegraph, The, Valentine v Cleugh (1854) 8 Moo PCC 167, 1 Ecc & Ad 427, 164 ER 246,
24 LTOS 11, PC 736
Telemachus, The. See Tantalus (Master and Crew) v Telemachus, Her Cargo and Freight
(Owners), The Telemachus
Temple Bar (Owners) v Guildford (Owners), The Guildford [1956] P 364, [1956] 2 All ER
915, [1956] 3 WLR 474, 100 Sol Jo 569, sub nom The Guildford [1956] 2 Lloyd's
Rep 74, P, D and Admlty 143, 694, 763, 798
Tergeste, The [1903] P 26, 72 LJP 18, 9 Asp MLC 356, 87 LT 567, 19 TLR 63, P, D and
Admlty 126, 970, 974, 981–982, 984, 987, 990
Terneuzen, The, Marsh v Lensen Shipping Ltd [1938] P 109, [1938] 2 All ER 348, 60 Ll L
Rep 368, 107 LJP 60, 54 TLR 661, P, D and Admlty 487
Tervaete, The [1922] P 259, 91 LJP 213, 16 Asp MLC 48, [1922] All ER Rep 387, 67 Sol
Jo 98, 128 LT 176, 38 TLR 825, CA 964, 967
Testbank, The [1942] P 75, 72 Ll L Rep 6, 111 LJP 49, 167 LT 97, 58 TLR 164, sub nom
The Ceramic (Owners) v The Testbank (Owners) [1942] 1 All ER 281, CA
.... 771
Thacker v Moates (1831) 1 Mood & R 79, 174 ER 27 432
Thai-Europe Tapioca Service Ltd v Government of Pakistan, Ministry of Food and
Agriculture, Directorate of Agricultural Supplies (Imports and Shipping Wing) [1975] 3
All ER 961, [1975] 1 WLR 1485, [1976] 1 Lloyd's Rep 1, 119 Sol Jo 745
.... 86
Thames Iron Works Co v Patent Derrick Co (1860) 1 John & H 93, 29 LJ Ch 714, 6 Jur
NS 1013, 8 WR 408, 70 ER 676, 2 LT 208 .... 974, 990
Thames, The (1805) 5 Ch Rob 345, 165 ER 799 741

PARA

The City of London, Morgan v Sim. See Morgan v Sim, The London
The City of Seattle (1903) 9 Canadian Exchequer Reports 146
.... 720
Theodore, The (1858) Sw 351, 166 ER 1163, sub nom The Pilot v The Theodore 8 LT 335
.... 884
Theodoros, The [1923] P 26, 92 LJP 30, 39 TLR 86, P, D and Admlty
.... 204, 735
Theresa Libra, The (Owners) v MSC Pamela, The (Owners) [2013] EWHC 2792 (Admlty),
    [2013] 2 Lloyd's Rep 596, [2013] All ER (D) 175 (Sep) 152, 178, 1013
Thetford, The (1887) 6 Asp MLC 179, 57 LT 455, P, D and Admlty
.... 751
Thetis, HMS (1835) 3 Hag Adm 228, 166 ER 390 .... 122, 139
Thetis, The (1869) LR 2 A & E 365, 38 LJ Adm 42, 3 Mar LC 357, 22 LT 276
.... 117, 814
Thomas Allen, The (Owners) v Gow, The Thomas Allen (1866) 12 App Cas 118, 6 Asp
    MLC 99, 56 LT 285, 3 TLR 188, PC 900
Thomas Blyth, The (1860) Lush 16, 167 ER 8 899
Thomas Fielden, The (1862) 32 LJPM & A 61 .... 891, 898
Thomas Powell, The v The Cuba (1866) 2 Mar LC 344, 14 LT 603
.... 788
Thomaseverett, The [1981] 1 Lloyd's Rep 1, CA 694, 756
Thompson v Finden (1829) 4 C & P 158, 172 ER 651 238
Thompson v Smith (1815) 1 Madd 395, 56 ER 145 327
Thomson v Hart (1890) 18 R 3, 28 SLR 28, 2 White 539
.... 457
Thomson v Royal Exchange Assurance Co (1813) 1 M & S 30, 105 ER 11
.... 972
Thorley (Joseph) Ltd v Orchis Steamship Co Ltd [1907] 1 KB 660, 76 LJKB 595, 10 Asp
    MLC 431, 12 Com Cas 251, 51 Sol Jo 289, 96 LT 488, 23 TLR 338, CA
.... 437
Thornley, The (1843) 7 Jur 659, 1 LTOS 293 .... 736, 789
Thorogood v Van Den Berghs and Jurgens Ltd. See Thurogood v Van Den Berghs and
    Jurgens Ltd
Thuringia, The (1871) 41 LJ Adm 20, 1 Asp MLC 166, 25 LT 605
.... 149
Thuringia, The (1872) 41 LJ Adm 44, 1 Asp MLC 283, 26 LT 446
.... 727, 798
Thurogood v Van Den Berghs and Jurgens Ltd [1951] 2 KB 537, 49 LGR 504, 95 Sol Jo
    317, [1951] 1 TLR 557, sub nom Thorogood v Van Den Berghs and Jurgens Ltd
    [1951] 1 All ER 682, 115 JP 237, CA 793
Thuroklint (Owners) v Koningin Juliana (Owners), The Koningin Juliana [1975] 2 Lloyd's
    Rep 111, HL 771
Ticonderoga, The (1857) Sw 215, 166 ER 1103 .... 784, 967
Timandra, The, Georgia, SS or Vessel (Owners) v M/S or Vessel Timandra (Owners) [1956]
    2 All ER 531, [1956] 1 WLR 691, [1956] 1 Lloyd's Rep 466, 100 Sol Jo 437, P, D and
    Admlty 748
Tinto v Humber Conservancy Board and Lincolnshire Steam Trawler Mutual Insurance Co
    Ltd, The Manorbier Castle (1923) 15 Ll L Rep 164, CA
.... 763, 770, 787, 945
Titan, The (1906) 10 Asp MLC 350, 96 LT 93, P, D and Admlty
.... 763
Titan, The (1922) 13 Ll L Rep 428, P, D and Admlty 735
Titanic (1912) Times 31 July, p 8 739
Tjaskemolen (now named Visvliet) (No 2), The [1997] 2 Lloyd's Rep 476, [1996] Lexis
    Citation 3911 171–172
Tjaskemolen (now named Visvliet), The [1997] 2 Lloyd's Rep 465
.... 93, 306
Tojo Maru, The, NV Wijsmuller v Owners of Motor Tanker Tojo Maru (her cargo and
    freight) [1972] AC 242, [1971] 1 All ER 1110, [1971] 2 WLR 970, [1971] 1 Lloyd's
    Rep 341, 115 Sol Jo 325, HL 82, 117, 204, 856, 865
Tolla, The [1921] P 22, 90 LJP 103, 37 TLR 73, P, D and Admlty
.... 434
Tolten, The [1946] P 135, [1946] 2 All ER 372, 79 Ll L Rep 349, [1947] LJR 201, 175 LT
    469, 62 TLR 378, CA 110, 967
Toni, The [1974] 1 Lloyd's Rep 489, CA 204, 771

PARA

Topaz and Irapua, The [2003] EWHC 320 (Admlty), [2003] 2 Lloyd's Rep 19, [2003] All
ER (D) 52 (Mar) 183
Tovarisch, The [1930] P 1, 35 Ll L Rep 183, 99 LJP 23, 18 Asp MLC 58, 142 LT 372, 6
TLR 125, CA; affd sub nom SS Alcantra (Owners) v Sailing Ship Tovarisch (Owners),
The Tovarisch [1931] AC 121, 38 Ll L Rep 139, 100 LJP 46, 18 Asp MLC 182,
[1930] All ER Rep 559, 144 LT 230, 47 TLR 89, HL 220
Toward (Owners) v Turkistan (Owners) (1885) 13 R 342
.... 759
Tower Bridge, The [1936] P 30, 53 Ll L Rep 171, 105 LJP 33, 18 Asp MLC 594, [1935]
All ER Rep 635, 154 LT 565, 52 TLR 153, P, D and Admlty
.... 855, 861
Tower Field (Owners) v Workington Harbour and Dock Board. See Workington Harbour
and Dock Board v Towerfield (Owners)
Towerfield, The. See Workington Harbour and Dock Board v Towerfield (Owners)
Towle v The Great Eastern (1864) 2 Mar LC 148 .... 870, 907
Tradigrain SA v King Diamond Marine Ltd [2000] 2 All ER (Comm) 542, [2000] 2 Lloyd's
Rep 319, [2000] Lexis Citation 3093, [2000] All ER (D) 979
.... 964
Transit, The. See Glannibanta, The
Transoceanica Francesca and Nicos V, The [1987] 2 Lloyd's Rep 155
.... 207
Treherbert, The [1934] P 31, 47 Ll L Rep 274, 103 LJP 65, 18 Asp MLC 458, [1933] All
ER Rep 509, 151 LT 69, 50 TLR 120, CA 700, 707
Trelawney, The (1801) 3 Ch Rob 216n 84
Trelawney, The (1802) 4 Ch Rob 223, 165 ER 592 865
Trendtex Trading Corpn v Credit Suisse [1980] QB 629, [1980] 3 All ER 721, [1980] 3
WLR 367, 124 Sol Jo 396, CA; affd [1982] AC 679, [1981] 3 All ER 520, [1981] 3
WLR 766, [1981] Com LR 262, 125 Sol Jo 761, HL 100, 102
Trent, The. See Sauria, The and The Trent
Tres, The (1936) 55 Ll L Rep 16, P, D and Admlty 861
Tresco, The (1944) 77 Ll L Rep 514, P, D and Admlty 899
Trewhella v Rowe (1809) 11 East 435, 103 ER 1072 434
Tribels, The. See Athens Sky Cia Naviera SA v Port Service Corpn Ltd, The Tribels
Trident, The (1854) 1 Ecc & Ad 217, 164 ER 126 748
Trishna (Owners, Master and Crew) v Panther and Ericbank (Owners), The Panther and
The Ericbank [1957] P 143, [1957] 2 WLR 432, [1957] 1 Lloyd's Rep 57, 101 Sol Jo
209, sub nom The Panther and The Ericbank, Steam Barge Trishna (Owners) v Motor
Tug Panther (Owners) [1957] 1 All ER 641, P, D and Admlty
.... 599, 742, 774, 784
Troilus (Cargo Owners) v Glenogle (Owners, Master and Crew) [1951] AC 820, [1951] 2
All ER 40, [1951] 1 Lloyd's Rep 467, 95 Sol Jo 465, [1951] 2 TLR 22, HL
.... 125, 855, 861
Tronson v Dent (1853) 8 Moo PCC 419, 14 ER 159, PC
.... 443
Troubador, The (1866) LR 1 A & E 302, 2 Mar LC 475, 16 LT 156, HC
.... 331
True Blue, The (1843) 2 Wm Rob 176, 7 Jur 756, 166 ER 721, 3 LT 182, 2 Notes of
Cases 413 884
True Blue, The. See Papayanni v Hocquard, The True Blue
Trumpeter, The (1947) 80 Ll L Rep 263, P, D and Admlty
.... 894, 913
Trustees of Stokes Pension Fund v Western Power Distribution (South West) plc [2005]
EWCA Civ 854, [2005] 3 All ER 775, [2005] 1 WLR 3595, (2005) Times, 28 July,
[2006] 2 Costs LR 226, [2005] All ER (D) 107 (Jul) 203
Try Again, The (1908) Shipping Gazette, 2 June 700, 705–706
Tubantia, The [1924] P 78, 18 Ll L Rep 158, 93 LJP 148, 16 Asp MLC 346, [1924] All ER
Rep 615, 131 LT 570, 40 TLR 335, P, D and Admlty 3, 80, 86, 122, 139, 910, 913
Tuff v Warman (1857) 2 CBNS 740, 140 ER 607; affd (1858) 5 CBNS 573, 27 LJCP 322,
5 Jur NS 222, 6 WR 693, 141 ER 231, Ex Ch 767, 770
Tugela, The (1913) 30 TLR 101, P, D and Admlty 805
Turgot, The (1886) 11 PD 21, 5 Asp MLC 548, 34 WR 552, 54 LT 276, P, D and Admlty
.... 131, 433, 971
Turiddu, The [2000] ICR 354, [1999] 2 Lloyd's Rep 401
.... 127
Turliani, The (1875) 2 Asp MLC 603, 32 LT 841 432

PARA

Turner v Owen (1862) 3 F & F 176, 176 ER 79, NP 471
Turquoise, The [1908] P 148, 77 LJP 97, 11 Asp MLC 28, 98 LT 588, DC
.... 699, 720
Turret Court, The (1900) 69 LJP 117, P, D and Admlty 737, 761
Tuyuti, The [1984] QB 838, [1984] 2 All ER 545, [1984] 3 WLR 231, [1984] 2 Lloyd's
  Rep 51, 128 Sol Jo 498, [1984] LS Gaz R 1362 .... 158, 175
Twentje, The. See West Friesland, The
Two Ellens, The. See Johnson v Black, The Two Ellens
Two Friends, The (1799) 1 Ch Rob 271, 1 Eng Pr Cas 130, 165 ER 174
.... 869, 914
Two Friends, The (1844) 2 Wm Rob 349, 8 Jur 1011, 166 ER 786, 3 LT 246
.... 867
Tyne Improvement Comrs v Armement Anversois SA, The Brabo [1949] AC 326, [1949] 1
  All ER 294, [1949] LJR 435, 93 Sol Jo 180, 65 TLR 114, HL
.... 188

U

Uhla, The (1867) 37 LJ Adm 16n, 3 Mar LC 148, 19 LT 89
.... 735, 765
Ulster, The. See Laird v Brownlie, The Ulster
Umona, The [1914] P 141, 83 LJP 106, 12 Asp MLC 527, 111 LT 415, 30 TLR 498, P, D
  and Admlty 775–776, 784
Umtali, The (1938) 62 Ll L Rep 195, 19 Asp MLC 254, 160 LT 114, HL
.... 220
Undaunted, The (1860) Lush 90, 29 LJPM & A 176, 167 ER 47, 2 LT 520
.... 855, 863
Undaunted, The (1886) 11 PD 46, 55 LJP 24, 5 Asp MLC 580, 34 WR 686, 54 LT 542, P,
  D and Admlty 600, 783
Underwood v Robertson (1815) 4 Camp 138, 171 ER 44, NP
.... 438
Uniao Vencedora, The (otherwise The Gipsy) (1864) 33 LJPM & A 195, 2 Mar LC 146, 11
  LT 351 439
Union Dampfschiffsrhederei AG v SS Parisian [1907] AC 193, 76 LJPC 33, 10 Asp MLC
  365, 96 LT 335, 23 TLR 344, PC 705, 707
Union Lighterage Co Ltd v Sailing Barge Shamrock (1921) 6 Ll L Rep 154, P, D and
  Admlty 744
Union Steamship Co v Aracan (Owners), The American and The Syria (1874) LR 6 PC
  127, 43 LJ Adm 30, 2 Asp MLC 350, 22 WR 927, 31 LT 42, PC
.... 713, 784
Union, The (1860) 1 Lush 128, 30 LJPM & A 17, 167 ER 60, 3 LT 280
.... 980, 982, 986
Unique Mariner, The (No 2) [1979] 1 Lloyd's Rep 37 911
United British Steamship Co Ltd v Port of London Authority, The Framlington Court
  (1936) 56 Ll L Rep 200, P, D and Admlty 785
United Kingdom Lord High Admiral v M/V Josefina Thorden (Owners) and Cargo. See
  Admiralty Comrs v Josefina Thorden (Owners), The Josefina Thorden
United Salvage Pty Ltd v Louis Dreyfus Armateurs SNC (2007) 240 ALR 630
.... 878
United Service, The (1883) 9 PD 3, 53 LJP 1, 5 Asp MLC 170, 32 WR 565, 49 LT 701,
  CA 600
United States v St Louis and Mississippi Valley Transportation Co 184 US 247 (1902)
.... 736
United States Shipping Board v Laird Line Ltd [1924] AC 286, 93 LJPC 123, 16 Asp MLC
  302, 130 LT 552, [1923] All ER Rep Ext 850, HL 762
United States, The (1865) 2 Mar LC 166, 12 LT 33, PC
.... 731, 769
Unterweser Reederei GmbH v Zapata Off-Shore Co, The Chaparral [1968] 2 Lloyd's Rep
  158, CA 102
Upcerne, The [1912] P 160, 81 LJP 110, 12 Asp MLC 281, 107 LT 860, 28 TLR 370, DC
.... 690
Upton Castle, The [1906] P 147, 75 LJP 77, 10 Asp MLC 153, 93 LT 814, P, D and
  Admlty 716

PARA

Uranienborg, The [1936] P 21, 53 Ll L Rep 165, 105 LJP 10, 18 Asp MLC 591, [1935] All
ER Rep 70, 154 LT 664, 52 TLR 114, P, D and Admlty
.... 600
Utopia (Owners) v Primula (Owners and Master), The Utopia [1893] AC 492, 62 LJPC
118, 7 Asp MLC 408, 1 R 394, 70 LT 47, 9 TLR 542, PC
.... 92, 787, 945, 967

V

Vadne, The. See Bartlett v Admiralty, The Vadne
Valdes, The (1914) 31 TLR 144, P, D and Admlty 789
Valiant, The (1839) 1 Wm Rob 64, 166 ER 497, 7 LT 442, 803
.... 240
Valkyrie, The [1910] WN 138, P, D and Admlty 906
Valsesia, The [1927] P 115, 96 LJP 38, 17 Asp MLC 207, 136 LT 544, 43 TLR 144, P, D
and Admlty 598
Van Hasselt v Sack, Bremer & Co, The Twentje. See West Friesland, The
Van Omeron v Dowick (1809) 2 Camp 42, 170 ER 1075, NP
.... 442
Vanderplank v Miller (1828) Mood & M 169, 173 ER 1119
.... 735
Vandyck, The (1881) 7 PD 42, P, D and Admlty; affd (1882) 5 Asp MLC 17, 47 LT 694,
CA 813, 855, 866
Vanner v Frost (1870) 39 LJ Ch 626 238
Vanvert v Arrotegui, The Santanderino (1893) 3 Exch CR 378; affd (1894) 23 SCR 145
.... 700
Vardopulo v Vardopulo (1909) 53 Sol Jo 469, 25 TLR 518, CA
.... 101
Varmdo, The [1940] P 15, P, D and Admlty; affd [1940] P 137, 67 Ll L Rep 197, 109 LJP
85, 19 Asp MLC 370, 164 LT 14, 56 TLR 758, CA 700
Varna, The [1993] 2 Lloyd's Rep 253, (1993) Times, 22 April, CA
.... 161
Vasso (owners) v Vasso (cargo owners), The Vasso [1984] QB 477, [1984] 1 All ER 1126,
[1984] 2 WLR 570, [1984] 1 Lloyd's Rep 235, 128 Sol Jo 260
.... 93, 161
Vaughan v Taff Vale Rly Co (1860) 24 JP 453, 5 H & N 679, 29 LJ Ex 247, 6 Jur NS 899,
8 WR 549, 157 ER 1351, [1843–60] All ER Rep 474, 2 LT 394, Ex Ch
.... 760
Vechtstroom, The [1964] 1 Lloyd's Rep 118, P, D and Admlty
.... 694
Vectis, The [1929] P 204, 98 LJP 135, 17 Asp MLC 574, 140 LT 563, 45 TLR 384, P, D
and Admlty 733, 756
Velocity, The. See General Steam Navigation Co v Hedley, The Velocity
Velox, The [1906] P 263, 75 LJP 81, 10 Asp MLC 277, 95 LT 271, P, D and Admlty
.... 116, 874, 891
Venus, The (Cargo ex) (1866) LR 1 A & E 50, 12 Jur NS 379, 14 WR 466, HC
.... 177
Veraston, The [1920] P 12, 89 LJP 7, 14 Asp MLC 595, 122 LT 750, 36 TLR 30, P, D and
Admlty 802
Verena, The [1961] 2 Lloyd's Rep 127, CA 698
Veritas, The [1901] P 304, 70 LJP 75, 9 Asp MLC 237, 50 WR 30, [1900–3] All ER Rep
501, 45 Sol Jo 708, 85 LT 136, 17 TLR 721, P, D and Admlty
.... 110, 113, 169, 811, 967, 973, 975–977, 979, 982
Vernon City, The [1942] P 9, 58 TLR 15, P, D and Admlty; affd [1942] P 61, 72 Ll L Rep
223, 111 LJP 81, 167 LT 393, 58 TLR 142, CA 5
Vessel SA v CP Ships (UK) Ltd [2004] EWHC 3305 (Admlty), [2005] All ER (D) 423
(Mar), sub nom Denise (The) (Owners) v The Denise (Charterers) [2005] 2 All ER
(Comm) 47 .... 992, 1003
Vesta, The (1828) 2 Hag Adm 189, 166 ER 214 116
Vestland, The. See Richmond Shipping Ltd v Vestland D/S and A/S, The Vestland
Vianna, The (1858) Sw 405, 166 ER 1187 731
Vibilia, The (1838) 1 Wm Rob 1, 166 ER 474 435
Victor, The (1860) Lush 72, 28 LJPM & A 110, 167 ER 38, 2 LT 331
.... 811, 968
Victor, The (1865) 2 Mar LC 261, 13 LT 21 439

PARA

Victoria, The (1848) 3 Wm Rob 49, 166 ER 881, 4 LT 839, 6 Notes of Cases 176
.... 710
Victoria, The (1854) 7 Ir Jur 94 752
Victoria, The (1859) 5 Jur NS 204, Sw 408, 7 WR 330, 166 ER 1188
.... 240
Victoria, The (1876) 1 PD 280, 3 Asp MLC 230, 3 Char Pr Cas 460, 24 WR 596, 34 LT
    931, CA 219
Victoria, The (1887) 12 PD 105, 56 LJP 75, 6 Asp MLC 120, 35 WR 291, 56 LT 499, P, D
    and Admlty 110
Victory, The. See Antares II, The and The Victory
Vigilant, The [1921] P 312, 90 LJP 318, 15 Asp MLC 337, 125 LT 636, 37 TLR 709, P, D
    and Admlty 598
Vimeira (No 2), The. See Aiden Shipping Co Ltd v Interbulk Ltd, The Vimeira (No 2)
Vinalines Pioneer, The [2016] 1 Lloyd's Rep 278 110
Vindobala, The (1889) 14 PD 50, 58 LJP 51, 6 Asp MLC 376, 37 WR 409, 60 LT 657,
    CA 239–240, 244
Vine, The (1825) 2 Hag Adm 1, 166 ER 145 867
Viper, The [1926] P 37, 95 LJP 38, 17 Asp MLC 26, 135 LT 60, 42 TLR 314, DC
.... 735
Virgil, The (1843) 2 Wm Rob 201, 7 Jur 1174, 166 ER 730, 5 LT 122, 2 Notes of Cases
    499, HC 758, 788
Virgo, The (1876) 3 Asp MLC 285, 25 WR 397, 35 LT 519, P, D and Admlty
.... 789
Vishva Ajay, The [1989] 2 Lloyd's Rep 558 100
Vitruvia Steamship Co Ltd v Ropner Shipping Co Ltd 1923 SC 574, Ct of Sess; affd (1925)
    21 Ll L Rep 280, 1925 SC (HL) 1, HL 804
Vivid, The (1856) Sw 88, 4 WR 504, 166 ER 1034; affd sub nom Churchward v Palmer,
    The Vivid (1856) 10 Moo PCC 472, 4 WR 755, 14 ER 570, sub nom The Henry v
    The Vivid 5 LT 146, PC 740
Vivid, The (1873) 42 LJ Adm 57, 1 Asp MLC 601, 28 LT 375
.... 734
Vlierboom v Chapman (1844) 13 LJ Ex 384, 8 Jur 811, 13 M & W 230, 153 ER 96, Exch
    Ct 889
Vogiatzis v SS Fairport, The Fairport [1967] P 167, [1966] 2 All ER 1026, [1966] 3 WLR
    426, [1966] 2 Lloyd's Rep 7, 110 Sol Jo 385, P, D and Admlty
.... 130, 470, 478
Volant, The (1842) 1 Wm Rob 383, 6 Jur 540, 166 ER 616, 5 LT 185, 525, 7 LT 509, 1
    Notes of Cases 503 84
Volant, The (1864) Brown & Lush 321, 167 ER 385 321
Volcano, The (1844) 2 Wm Rob 337, 166 ER 782, 3 Notes of Cases 210
.... 734, 786
Von Freeden v Hull (1907) 75 LJKB 359, 10 Asp MLC 247, 94 LT 849, 22 TLR 358;
    revsd (1907) 76 LJKB 715, 10 Asp MLC 394, 96 LT 590, 23 TLR 335, CA
.... 240, 244
Voutakos v Tsavliris Salvage (International) Ltd, The Voutakos [2008] EWHC 1581
    (Admlty), [2009] 1 All ER (Comm) 1067, [2008] 2 Lloyd's Rep 516, [2008] All ER
    (D) 143 (Jul) 878
Vrede, The (1861) Lush 322, 30 LJPM & A 209, 167 ER 143
.... 870
Vrouw Margaretha, The (1801) 4 Ch Rob 103, 165 ER 551
.... 855

W

WH No 1 and The Knight Errant, The. See Comet, Lightship (Owners) v The WH No 1
    (Owners), The WH No 1 and The Knight Errant
WH Randall, The [1928] P 41, 29 Ll L Rep 234, 97 LJP 42, 17 Asp MLC 397, 138 LT
    459, CA 204
W J Guy & Son v Glen Line Ltd. See Glen Line Ltd v W J Guy & Sons, The Glenaffric
Waalstroom, The (1923) 17 Ll L Rep 53 757

PARA

Wagon Mound (No 2), The. See Overseas Tankship (UK) Ltd v Miller Steamship Co Pty,
  The Wagon Mound (No 2)
Wagon Mound, The. See Overseas Tankship (UK) Ltd v Morts Dock and Engineering Co
  Ltd, The Wagon Mound
Waikato (Cargo Owners) v New Zealand Shipping Co [1899] 1 QB 56, 68 LJQB 1, 8 Asp
  MLC 442, 4 Com Cas 10, 43 Sol Jo 41, 79 LT 326, 15 TLR 33, CA
  600
Wallsend, The [1907] P 302, 76 LJP 131, 10 Asp MLC 476, 96 LT 851, 23 TLR 356, P, D
  and Admlty 798
Walshe v Provan (1853) 22 LJ Ex 355, 8 Exch 843, 155 ER 1595, 1 CLR 823
  431
War Tempest v Plym (1921) 9 Ll L Rep 489, P, D and Admlty
  735
Ward v M'Corkill, The Minnehaha. See Minnehaha, The
Ward v Royal Exchange Shipping Co Ltd, ex p Harrison (1887) 6 Asp MLC 239, 58 LT
  174 .... 321, 334
Warkworth, The (1884) 9 PD 145, 53 LJP 65, 5 Asp MLC 326, 33 WR 112, 51 LT 558,
  CA 757
Warrior, The (1818) 2 Dods 288, 165 ER 1490, HC 80, 104, 440
Warrior, The (1862) Lush 476, 1 Mar LC 204, 167 ER 214, 6 LT 133
  .... 487, 869
Waterloo, The (1820) 2 Dods 433, 165 ER 1537, HC 865, 867
Watson v RCA Victor Co Inc (1934) 50 Ll L Rep 77, Sh Ct
  114
Watson and Parker v Gregory, The Cairo [1908] WN 230, 11 Asp MLC 161, 99 LT 940, P,
  D and Admlty 429, 971
Watt, The (1843) 2 Wm Rob 70, 166 ER 681, 6 LT 371
  .... 867, 870, 888
Waverley, The (1871) LR 3 A & E 369, 40 LJ Adm 42, 1 Asp MLC 47, 24 LT 713, HC
  884–885
Waziristan, The, Seirstad (Owners) v Hindustan Shipping Co Ltd [1953] 2 All ER 1213,
  [1953] 1 WLR 1446, [1953] 2 Lloyd's Rep 361, 97 Sol Jo 833, P, D and Admlty
  204
Webb v Thomson (1797) 1 Bos & P 5, 126 ER 746 5
Webster v Manchester, Sheffield and Lincolnshire Rly Co (1884) Bitt Rep in Ch 172
  184
Webster v Seekamp (1821) 4 B & Ald 352, 106 ER 966
  .... 427, 432
Weeks v Ross [1913] 2 KB 229, 77 JP 182, 82 LJKB 925, 12 Asp MLC 307, 23 Cox CC
  337, 108 LT 423, 29 TLR 369, DC 229
Wega, The [1895] P 156, 64 LJP 68, 7 Asp MLC 597, 11 R 726, 72 LT 332, 11 TLR 251,
  P, D and Admlty 720
Weguelin v Cellier (1873) LR 6 HL 286, 42 LJ Ch 758, 22 WR 26, HL
  334
Wellfield (Owners) v Adamson and Short, The Alfred (1884) 5 Asp MLC 214, 50 LT 511,
  P, D and Admlty 883
Wellington, The. See Adriatic, The
Wells v Gas Float Whitton No 2 (Owners), The Gas Float Whitton No 2. See Gas Float
  Whitton No 2, The
Werra, The (1886) 12 PD 52, 56 LJP 53, 6 Asp MLC 115, 35 WR 552, 56 LT 580, P, D
  and Admlty 881, 896–897
West Cock, The [1911] P 208, 80 LJP 97, 12 Asp MLC 57, 55 Sol Jo 329, 104 LT 736, 27
  TLR 301, CA 597, 600, 783
West Friesland, The (1859) 5 Jur NS 658, Sw 454, 166 ER 1213; revsd sub nom Van
  Hasselt v Sack, Bremer & Co, The Twentje (1860) 13 Moo PCC 185, 8 WR 423, 2 LT
  613, sub nom West Friesland, The Sw 456, 166 ER 1214, PC
  432
West Wales, The [1932] P 165, 43 Ll L Rep 504, 101 LJP 92, 18 Asp MLC 349, 148 LT
  80, P, D and Admlty 806
Westbourne, The (1889) 14 PD 132, 58 LJP 78, 6 Asp MLC 405, 38 WR 56, 61 LT 156, 5
  TLR 599, CA 884
Westburn, The (1896) 8 Asp MLC 130, 74 LT 200, P, D and Admlty
  871
Western Belle, The (1906) 10 Asp MLC 279, 95 LT 364, P, D and Admlty
  .... 735, 746, 761

PARA

Western Bulk Shipowning III A/S v Carbofer Maritime Trading ApS (The Western Moscow) [2012] EWHC 1224 (Comm), [2012] 2 All ER (Comm) 1140, [2012] 2 Lloyd's Rep 163, [2012] All ER (D) 134 (May) 964

Western Neptune v Philadelphia Express [2009] EWHC 1274 (Admlty), [2010] 2 All ER (Comm) 154, [2010] 1 Lloyd's Rep 158, [2009] All ER (D) 295 (Jun)
.... 697

Western Ocean, The (1870) LR 3 A & E 38, HC 321

Westfalen, Barque (Owners) v Admiralty Comrs (Steam Yacht Oriana II (Owners)) (1919) 1 Ll L Rep 527, HL 735

Westlake, Re, ex p Willoughby (1881) 16 Ch D 604, 29 WR 934, 44 LT 111
.... 974, 991

Westminster Bank Ltd v West of England SS Owners' Protection and Idemnity Association Ltd (1933) 46 Ll L Rep 101 171

Westminster, The (1841) 1 Wm Rob 229, 166 ER 558, 6 LT 868, 8 LT 153
.... 884, 888, 969

Westmorland, The (1841) 1 Wm Rob 216, 166 ER 553, 1 Notes of Cases 11
.... 510

Weston v Wright (1841) 10 LJ Ex 329, 5 Jur 197, 7 M & W 396, 151 ER 820, Exch Ct
.... 428

Westport, The (No 2), British Mexican Petroleum Co Ltd v Owners of Motor Ship or Vessel Westport [1965] 2 All ER 447, [1965] 1 WLR 871, [1965] 1 Lloyd's Rep 549, P, D and Admlty 178

Westport, The (No 3) [1966] 1 Lloyd's Rep 342, P, D and Admlty
.... 132

Westport, The (No 4) [1968] 2 Lloyd's Rep 559, P, D and Admlty
.... 130, 178

Westport, The, British Mexican Petroleum Co Ltd v Owners of Motor Ship or Vessel Westport [1965] 2 All ER 167, [1965] 1 WLR 796, [1965] 1 Lloyd's Rep 547, P, D and Admlty 178

Westrup v Great Yarmouth Steam Carrying Co (1889) 43 Ch D 241, 59 LJ Ch 111, 6 Asp MLC 443, 38 WR 505, 61 LT 714, 6 TLR 84, P, D and Admlty
.... 125, 966

Wharton v May (1799) 5 Ves 27, 31 ER 454, 34 ER 887
.... 101

White v Crisp (1854) 23 LJ Ex 317, 10 Exch 312, 2 WR 624, 156 ER 463, 2 CLR 1215, 23 LTOS 300 .... 787, 945

White v Ditchfield, The Meredith. See Meredith, The
White Star, The (1866) LR 1 A & E 68, HC 871

Whitlieburn, The (1900) 9 Asp MLC 154, 83 LT 748, 17 TLR 183, P, D and Admlty
.... 700

Whitwell v Perrin (1858) 4 CBNS 412, 140 ER 1144, 31 LTOS 134, sub nom The Feliza, Whitwell v Perren 7 LT 509 238

Wild Ranger, The (1862) Lush 553, 32 LJPM & A 49, 9 Jur NS 134, 1 Mar LC 275, 1 New Rep 132, 11 WR 255, 167 ER 249, 7 LT 725 3

Wild Ranger, The (1863) Brown & Lush 84, 2 New Rep 402, 167 ER 310
.... 991

Wilhelm Tell, The [1892] P 337, 61 LJP 127, 7 Asp MLC 329, 1 R 551, 41 WR 205, 69 LT 199, P, D and Admlty 904

Wilhelmine, The (1842) 7 LT 441, 1 Notes of Cases 376
.... 862

Wilhelmine, The (or The Whilelmine) (1842) 1 Wm Rob 335, 7 Jur 331, 166 ER 598, 2 Notes of Cases 213 159

Wilkes v Saunion (1877) 7 Ch D 188, 47 LJ Ch 150 333

Wilkinson v Barking Corpn [1948] 1 KB 721, [1948] 1 All ER 564, 46 LGR 169, 112 JP 215, [1948] LJR 1164, 92 Sol Jo 205, 64 TLR 230, CA
.... 906

Willem III, The (1871) LR 3 A & E 487, 1 Asp MLC 129, 20 WR 216, 25 LT 386, HC
.... 120–121, 860, 864, 874, 969

William Beckford, The (1801) 3 Ch Rob 355, 165 ER 492
.... 881

William F Safford, The (1860) Lush 69, 29 LJPM & A 109, 167 ER 37, 2 LT 301
.... 432, 980, 982

William Lindsay, The. See Doward v Lindsay, The William Lindsay
William Lushington, The (1850) 7 Notes of Cases 361 883

William, The (1858) Sw 346, 6 WR 871, 31 LTOS 345 981

Williamina, The (1878) 3 PD 97, P, D and Admlty 799

PARA

Williams v Allsup (1861) 10 CBNS 417, 30 LJCP 353, 8 Jur NS 57, 1 Mar LC 87, 142 ER
514, 4 LT 550 .... 321, 331

Williams v Chapman. See Iron Duke, The

Williams v Roffey Bros & Nicholls (Contractors) Ltd [1991] 1 QB 1, [1990] 1 All ER 512,
[1990] 2 WLR 1153, (1989) Times, 8 December, [1990] 12 LS Gaz R 36, [1989]
NLJR 1712, 48 BLR 75 471

Williamson v Hine [1891] 1 Ch 390, 60 LJ Ch 123, 39 WR 239, 63 LT 682, 7 TLR 130,
sub nom Williamson v Hine Bros 6 Asp MLC 559 238

Williamson v Page (1844) 1 Car & Kir 581, 174 ER 947
.... 427

Willis v Palmer (1860) 7 CBNS 340, 29 LJCP 194, 6 Jur NS 732, 8 WR 295, 141 ER 847,
2 LT 626 332

Wilson v Canada Shipping Co (1877) 2 App Cas 389, PC
.... 744

Wilson v Dickson (1818) 2 B & Ald 2, 106 ER 268 443

Wilson v R (1866) LR 1 PC 405, 4 Moo PCCNS 307, PC
.... 235

Wilson v Rankin (1865) LR 1 QB 162, 6 B & S 208, 35 LJQB 87, 2 Mar LC 287, 14 WR
198, 122 ER 1173, 13 LT 564, Ex Ch 428

Wilson v Wilson (1872) LR 14 Eq 32, 41 LJ Ch 423, 1 Asp MLC 265, 20 WR 436, 26 LT
346 .... 332, 334

Winestead, The [1895] P 170, 64 LJP 51, 7 Asp MLC 547, 11 R 720, 72 LT 91, 11 TLR
220, [1895–9] All ER Rep Ext 2183, P, D and Admlty 204

Winkfield, The [1902] P 42, 71 LJP 21, 9 Asp MLC 259, 50 WR 246, [1900–3] All ER
Rep 346, 46 Sol Jo 163, 85 LT 668, 18 TLR 178, CA 790

Winson, The. See China-Pacific SA v Food Corpn of India, The Winson

Winstanley, The [1896] P 297, 65 LJP 121, 8 Asp MLC 170, 75 LT 133, CA
.... 700, 770

Wirrall, The (1848) 3 Wm Rob 56, 166 ER 884, 6 Notes of Cases 199
.... 739

Wladyslaw Lokotiek, The [1978] 2 Lloyd's Rep 520 100

Woburn Abbey, The (1869) 38 LJ Adm 28, 3 Mar LC 240, 20 LT 621
.... 734–735

Wood v Smith, The City of Cambridge. See City of Cambridge, The

Woodarra, The (1921) 9 Ll L Rep 347, 66 Sol Jo 183, 38 TLR 160, P, D and Admlty
.... 189

Woodhorn, The (1891) 92 LT Jo 113 487

Woodrop-Sims, The (1815) 2 Dods 83, 165 ER 1422, HC
.... 767

Woosung, The (Cargo ex) (1876) 1 PD 260, 3 Asp MLC 239, 25 WR 1, 35 LT 8, CA
.... 884

Workington Harbour and Dock Board v Towerfield (Owners) [1951] AC 112, [1950] 2 All
ER 414, 66 (pt 2) TLR 387, sub nom Tower Field (Owners) v Workington Harbour
and Dock Board 84 Ll L Rep 233, sub nom The Towerfield 94 Sol Jo 517, HL
.... 429

World Beauty, Owners of Steam Tanker Andros Springs v Owners of Steam Tanker World
Beauty. See Andros Springs (Owners) v Owners of World Beauty, The World Beauty

World Harmony, Konstantinidis v World Tankers Corpn Inc. See Konstantinidis v World
Tankers Corpn, The World Harmony

World Harmony, The. See Konstantinidis v World Tankers Corpn, The World Harmony

World Star, The [1987] 1 Lloyd's Rep 452 .... 175, 178

Woron, The [1927] AC 906, 43 TLR 698, sub nom Canadian American Shipping Co v SS
Woron 28 Ll L Rep 21, 96 LJPC 137, 17 Asp MLC 322, 71 Sol Jo 649, 137 LT 747,
PC 217

Wright v Marwood (1881) 7 QBD 62, 50 LJQB 643, 4 Asp MLC 451, 29 WR 673, 45 LT
297, CA 437

Y

Yan Yean, The (1883) 8 PD 147, 52 LJP 67, 5 Asp MLC 135, 31 WR 950, 49 LT 187, P,
D and Admlty 204, 894

Yeo and Yeo v Tatem and Dwerryhouse Braginton, The Orient (1871) LR 3 PC 696, 8
Moo PCCNS 74, 40 LJ Adm 29, 1 Asp MLC 108, 20 WR 6, 17 ER 241, 24 LT 918,
PC 967

PARA

York, The [1929] P 178, 98 LJP 147, 17 Asp MLC 600, 141 LT 215, CA
.... 802
Yorkshireman, The (1827) 2 Hag Adm 30n 805
Young, ex p (1813) 2 Rose 78n, 2 Ves & B 242, 35 ER 311
.... 244
Young v Merchants' Marine Insurance Co Ltd [1932] 2 KB 705, 43 Ll L Rep 277, 101
    LJKB 567, 18 Asp MLC 341, 37 Com Cas 415, [1932] All ER Rep 928, 147 LT 236,
    48 TLR 579, CA 772
Young v The Scotia [1903] AC 501, 72 LJPC 115, 9 Asp MLC 485, 89 LT 374, PC
.... 969
Young Sid, The [1929] P 190, 33 Ll L Rep 302, 98 LJP 97, 18 Asp MLC 22, 141 LT 234,
    45 TLR 389, CA 204, 222
Yuille v B and B Fisheries (Leigh) Ltd and Bates, The Radiant [1958] 2 Lloyd's Rep 596, P,
    D and Admlty 196
Yuri Maru, The [1927] AC 906, 43 TLR 698, sub nom Snia Viscosa Societa, etc v SS Yuri
    Maru 28 Ll L Rep 21, 96 LJPC 137, 17 Asp MLC 322, 71 Sol Jo 649, 137 LT 747,
    PC 217
Yvonne, The and The Effra (1932) 43 Ll L Rep 252, P, D and Admlty
.... 720

Z

Zaanland, The. See Jessie, The and The Zaanland
Zafiro, The, John Carlbom & Co Ltd v Owners of Zafiro [1960] P 1, [1959] 2 All ER 537,
    [1959] 3 WLR 123, [1959] 1 Lloyd's Rep 359, 103 Sol Jo 509, P, D and Admlty
.... 126, 132, 973, 987, 989
Zaglebie Dobrowskie (No 2), The [1978] 1 Lloyd's Rep 573
.... 795
Zelo, The [1922] P 9, 91 LJP 57, 15 Asp MLC 428, 126 LT 351, 38 TLR 69, P, D and
    Admlty 110, 790, 814
Zephyr, The (1827) 2 Hag Adm 43, 166 ER 160 865
Zephyrus, The (1842) 1 Wm Rob 329, 6 Jur 304, 166 ER 596, 8 LT 153, 1 Notes of Cases
    338 863
Zeta, The (1875) LR 4 A & E 460, 44 LJ Adm 22, 3 Asp MLC 73, 24 WR 180, 33 LT
    477, P, D and Admlty 924, 935, 1160
Zeta, The. See Mersey Docks and Harbour Board v Turner, The Zeta
Ziemniak v ETPM Deep Sea Ltd [2003] EWCA Civ 636, [2003] 2 All ER (Comm) 283,
    [2003] 2 Lloyd's Rep 214, (2003) Times, 15 May, [2003] All ER (D) 67 (May)
.... 602
Zigurds, The [1932] P 113, 101 LJP 75, 18 Asp MLC 324, 148 LT 72, 48 TLR 556, P, D
    and Admlty; revsd [1933] P 87, 102 LJP 39, 148 LT 381, 49 TLR 193, CA; affd sub
    nom Smith v Zigurds SS Owners and E A Casper, Edgar & Co Ltd [1934] AC 209,
    103 LJP 28, 18 Asp MLC 475, 39 Com Cas 178, 150 LT 303, sub nom Zigurds, The
    47 Ll L Rep 267, [1933] All ER Rep 717, 50 TLR 162, HL
.... 321, 334, 983, 986
Zirje, The [1989] 1 Lloyd's Rep 493 153
Zodiac, The (1825) 1 Hag Adm 320, 166 ER 114 425
Zoe, The (1886) 11 PD 72, 55 LJP 52, 5 Asp MLC 583, 35 WR 61, 54 LT 879, P, D and
    Admlty 194, 991
Zollverein, The (1856) 2 Jur NS 429, Sw 96, 4 WR 555, 166 ER 1038, 27 LTOS 160
.... 2, 82, 739

Decisions of the European Court of Justice are listed below numerically. These decisions
are also included in the preceding alphabetical list.

PARA

C-351/89: Overseas Union Insurance Ltd v New Hampshire Insurance Co [1992] 1 QB
    434, [1992] 2 All ER 138, [1991] ECR I-3317, [1992] 2 WLR 586, [1992] 1 Lloyd's
    Rep 204, (1991) Times, 20 August, ECJ 99
C-406/92: Maciej Rataj, The, Tatry (cargo owners) v Maciej Rataj [1999] QB 515, [1994]
    ECR I-5439, [1999] 2 WLR 181, [1995] All ER (EC) 229, [1995] 1 Lloyd's Rep 302,
    (1994) Times, 28 December, [1995] IL Pr 81, ECJ 92, 95–96, 99

PARA

C-308/06: R (on the application of International Association of Independent Tanker
    Owners (Intertanko) v Secretary of State for Transport [2008] ECR I-4057, [2008] 3
    CMLR 203, [2008] 2 Lloyd's Rep 260, [2008] All ER (D) 04 (Jun), ECJ
    14
C-45/07: European Commission v Hellenic Republic [2009] ECR I-701, [2009] 2 CMLR
    995, [2009] 1 Lloyd's Rep 425, ECJ 12
C-188/07: Commune de Mesquer v Total France SA [2008] ECR I-4501, [2009] All ER
    (EC) 525, [2008] 3 CMLR 445, [2008] 2 Lloyd's Rep 672, [2009] PTSR 588, [2008]
    All ER (D) 308 (Jun), ECJ 14

SHIPPING AND MARITIME LAW

Vol 93

                                                                              PARA

1.   INTRODUCTION... 1
(1)   In general.. 1
      (i)   Scope of Title 1
      (ii)   English Private Maritime Law 2
      (iii)   Maritime Issues relating to War and Neutrality...................... 4
(2)   Conventions and Legislation 7
      (i)   International Conventions and Organisations......................... 7
      (ii)   EU Legislation 14
      (iii)   United Kingdom Legislation... 15
               A.   Existing Statute Law 15
               B.   Application of the Merchant Shipping Act 1995 to Certain
                     Descriptions of Ships etc 17
      (iv)   Cognate Law.. 24
(3)   Administration 36
      (i)   The Secretary of State and the Welsh Authorities................... 36
      (ii)   The Admiralty Registrar.. 45
      (iii)   Enforcement Officers and their Powers.............................. 46
               A.   Enforcement Officers.. 46
               B.   Powers of Inspection etc 47
               C.   Powers in connection with Improvement Notices and
                     Prohibition Notices... 51
      (iv)   Lighthouse Authorities 56
      (v)   Other Bodies and Agencies... 57
      (vi)   General Financial Provisions under the Merchant Shipping Act 1995 . 63
      (vii)   Funding of Maritime Services 66
      (viii)   Service of Documents under the Merchant Shipping Act 1995.......... 74
(4)   Shipping and Trading Interests 75
      (i)   Protection of Shipping etc Interests from Foreign Action........... 75
      (ii)   Protection of Coastal Shipping Services 77
      (iii)   Liner Conferences.. 78

2.   ADMIRALTY JURISDICTION OF THE HIGH COURT 79
(1)   The Jurisdiction 79
      (i)   Outline of the Jurisdiction.. 79
      (ii)   Origins of Jurisdiction.. 80
      (iii)   Present Jurisdiction 85
      (iv)   Procedural Matters 91
      (v)   Conflicts of Jurisdiction 95
               A.   In general 95
               B.   Effect of the Civil Jurisdiction and Judgments Act 1982 96
               C.   Stay of Proceedings under National Law...................... 100
(2)   Particular Subjects of Jurisdiction 104
      (i)   Possession or Ownership 104

                                                                                    PARA
(ii)   Co-ownership 106
(iii)   Mortgage or Charge 109
(iv)   Damage done by or to a Ship 110
(v)   Claims relating to Cargo or to Contracts of Carriage or Hire 111
(vi)   Loss of Life or Personal Injury 112
(vii)   Salvage 113
          A.   In general 113
          B.   Salvage of Property 115
          C.   Life Salvage 120
          D.   Salvage of Wreck and Derelict 122
(viii)   Towage and Pilotage 125
(ix)   Supplies, Repairs and Dock Charges 126
(x)   Wages and Disbursements 127
(xi)   General Average 133
(xii)   Bottomry 134
(xiii)   Forfeiture, Condemnation and Restoration of Ship or Goods 135
(xiv)   Droits of Admiralty 139
(3) Practice of the High Court 140
     (i)   The Admiralty Registrar 140
              A.   The Admiralty Registrar and Registry 140
              B.   References to the Registrar 143
     (ii)   Limitation of Time for Admiralty Claims 151
     (iii)   Admiralty Claims except Limitation Claims 157
              A.   In general 157
              B.   Commencement of Claims 158
                    (A)   Commencement of Claims in rem 158
                           (a)   The in rem Claim Form 158
                           (b)   Warrant of Arrest 161
                           (c)   Caution against Arrest 166
                           (d)   Acknowledgment of Service 168
                           (e)   Provision of Security 171
                           (f)   Dealings with Arrested Property 173
                           (g)   Survey, Appraisement or Sale of Ship subject
                                  to a Claim in rem 178
                           (h)   Claims in rem etc against the Crown 179
                    (B)   Commencement of Collision Claims 180
                           (a)   The Claim Form and Service 180
                           (b)   Collision Statement of Case 182
                           (c)   Stay of Proceedings in Collision Claims in rem. 185
                    (C)   Commencement of Claims in personam ('Other
                           Claims') 186
              C.   Procedure following Service 189
                    (A)   Particulars of Claim, Defence and Reply 189
                    (B)   Judgment in Default 190
     (iv)   Limitation Claims 194
              A.   Right to Limit Liability 194
              B.   Limitation Proceedings 196

PARA

(v)   Trial of Admiralty Claims and Post-trial Proceedings.................. 203
       A.   Offers to Settle 203
       B.   General Procedure relating to Trial............................. 204
       C.   Payments and Enforcement 207
(4) Other Courts having Admiralty Jurisdiction..................................... 209
     (i)   County Court.......................... 209
     (ii)   Court of Admiralty of the Cinque Ports................................ 210
     (iii) Other Admiralty Courts............................... 214
(5) Appeals... 218
     (i)   Appeals from the High Court............................. 218
       A.   Jurisdiction and Preliminary Proceedings..................... 218
       B.   Hearing and Decision 220
     (ii)   Appeals from Inferior Courts 223
     (iii) Pilotage Appeals 228

3.   MERCHANT SHIPS 229
(1) British Ships.. 229
(2) Ownership... 236
     (i)   Acquisition of Ownership 236
     (ii)   Rights of Ownership 237
     (iii) Liabilities.. 242
(3) The Register and Registration 245
     (i)   Registration: In general............................... 245
       A.   Entitlement to Register........................... 245
       B.   Registration Regulations 247
       C.   The Tonnage Regulations 248
       D.   Disclosure of Information....................................... 251
       E.   Private Law Provisions 252
       F.   Proceedings on Forfeiture 253
     (ii)   The Register of British Ships in the United Kingdom 254
     (iii) Qualification and Entitlement for Registration on Part I of the Register. 258
     (iv)   Qualification and Entitlement for Registration on Part II of the Register. 262
     (v)   Appointment of Representative Persons 267
     (vi)   Registration 269
       A.   Application for Registration 269
       B.   Survey and Measurement 276
       C.   Names 277
       D.   Official Number and Port of Choice 279
       E.   Carving and Marking 280
       F.   Completion of Registration 289
       G.   Certificates of Registry; Temporary Registration Documents
             for Fishing Vessels.. 298
       H.   Renewal of Registration....................................... 304
       I.   Transfers etc of Registered Ships 306
       J.   Notification of Changes.................................... 313
       K.   Change of Name; Transfer of Port of Choice.................... 315
       L.   Termination of Ship's Registration............................ 317
     (vii) Mortgages... 318
       A.   Creation of Mortgages 318

                                                                   PARA
       B.   Transfer and Transmission of Registered Mortgages 323
       C.   Mortgagee's Rights and Powers................................. 327
       D.   Discharge of Registered Mortgages..................... 335
  (viii) Provisional Registration 337
  (ix)   Transfers to, from or within the Register............................. 341
  (x)   Registration of Small Ships........................... 344
  (xi)   Ships Bareboat Chartered-in 357
  (xii) Miscellaneous Provisions relating to Registration...................... 369
       A.   Documents etc..................................... 369
       B.   Certificates of Registry 373
       C.   Removal of Marks 378
       D.   Fees Payable to Registrar 379
       E.   Re-measurement of Tonnage....................... 380

4. HOVERCRAFT... 381
(1) Hovercraft: In general 381
(2) Civil Liability.. 386
(3) Registration etc.. 387
  (i)   Application of Provisions................................... 387
  (ii)   Registration 390
  (iii) Certification and Maintenance 396
  (iv) Duties of Operator and Captain 402
  (v)   Safety etc... 410
  (vi) Fees... 417
  (vii) Births, Deaths and Missing Persons........................ 418

5. MASTERS AND CREWS 423
(1) Statutory and Common Law Framework............................ 423
(2) Masters 424
  (i)   Employment... 424
  (ii)   Master's Authority and Liability 427
  (iii) Master's Authority to Make Contracts 431
  (iv) Master's Authority to Hypothecate Ship and Freight 435
  (v)   Master's Authority to Tranship or Jettison Cargo..................... 436
  (vi) Master's Authority to Sell Ship or Cargo............................. 438
  (vii) Powers exercisable in the interests of Safety, Good Order and
       Discipline... 444
  (viii) Master's Duty to Assist Aircraft in Distress 446
  (ix) Master's Duty where he ceases to be Master during Voyage 447
(3) Engagement and Employment of Crews 448
  (i)   Minimum Age of Seafarers.............................. 448
       A.   United Kingdom Ships and Ships in United Kingdom Waters.. 448
       B.   Fishing Vessels, Ships of Traditional Build and
             Non-Commercial Vessels....................... 449
  (ii)   Seafarers' Employment Agreements and Crew Agreements............. 451
       A.   United Kingdom Ships and Ships in United Kingdom Waters.. 451
       B.   Ships of Traditional Build and Non-Commercial Vessels....... 457
  (iii) Medical Fitness Certification for Workers Aboard United Kingdom
       Ships.. 464

                                                                          PARA
(iv)   Discharge of Crews 468
(v)   Wages 470
           A.   Vessels and Seamen Generally 470
                 (A)   Entitlement to Wages 470
                 (B)   Payment and Account of Wages 473
                 (C)   Allotment of Wages 476
                 (D)   Proceedings for Recovery of Wages 478
                 (E)   Claims against Seamen's Wages for Maintenance etc of
                       Dependants 481
           B.   Additional Provisions relating to United Kingdom Ships and
                 Ships in United Kingdom Waters 482
           C.   Provisions applicable only to Ships of Traditional Build and
                 Non-Commercial Vessels 484
           D.   Provisions applicable only to Fishing Vessels 488
(vi)   Crew Accommodation 490
(vii)   Catering and Medical Care 492
           A.   United Kingdom Ships and Ships in United Kingdom Waters .. 492
           B.   Fishing Vessels, Ships of Traditional Build and
                 Non-Commercial Vessels 500
(viii)   Training, Certification and Manning 502
(ix)   Working Hours and Leave 511
           A.   Sea-Going Ships 511
           B.   Fishing Vessels 515
           C.   Ships operating on Inland Waterways 520
(x)   Inquiries into Fitness or Conduct of Officers and Seamen 524
           A.   Officers 524
           B.   Seamen other than Officers 530
           C.   Hearings and Appeals 536
           D.   Codes of Conduct 539
(xi)   Relief and Repatriation of Seamen 540
           A.   United Kingdom Ships and Ships in United Kingdom Waters .. 540
                 (A)   Repatriation 540
                 (B)   Compensation, Sick Pay, Disposal of Remains 544
           B.   Fishing Vessels, Ships of Traditional Build and
                 Non-Commercial Vessels 548
(xii)   Required Documentation 551
           A.   Official Log Books 551
           B.   Lists of Crew 553
           C.   British Seamen's Cards and Discharge Books 559
                 (A)   British Seamen's Cards 559
                 (B)   Discharge Books 565
                 (C)   Provisions relating to British Seamen's Cards and to
                       Discharge Books 570

6.   PILOTAGE AND TOWAGE 574
(1) Pilotage 574
     (i)   Pilotage Functions of Competent Harbour Authorities 574
           A.   In general 574

PARA

      B.   Provision of Pilotage Services 576

      C.   Compulsory Pilotage 580

      D.   Charging by Authorities.. 583

      E.   Agents and Joint Arrangements................................. 584

      F.   Accounts of Competent Harbour Authority 587

  (ii)   General Provisions concerning Pilotage................................. 588

      A.   Compulsory Pilotage 588

      B.   Rights of Pilots 590

      C.   Limitation of Liability.. 594

      D.   Deep Sea Pilotage 595

(2)   Towage 597

Volume 94

PARA

7.   SAFETY AND SECURITY AT SEA 601

(1)   Safety and Health on Ships... 601

  (i)   Submersible Apparatus 601

  (ii)   Construction and Survey 602

      A.   In general 602

      B.   Merchant Shipping 604

      C.   Fishing Vessels... 607

      D.   Vessels in Commercial Use for Sport or Pleasure 612

      E.   High Speed Craft 617

  (iii) Health and Safety... 626

      A.   In general 626

      B.   Safety Management Codes....................................... 627

      C.   Protection of Workers... 628

      D.   Navigation... 634

      E.   Equipment, Life-saving Appliances and Communications...... 638

      F.   Counting and Registering Passengers........................... 640

          (A)   Procedure for Counting and Registering Passengers ... 640

          (B)   Returns Required as to Passengers on Board, Births etc. 643

  (iv) Carriage of Dangerous Goods by Ship 645

  (v)   Carriage of Cargoes requiring Special Precautions...................... 649

      A.   In general 649

      B.   Bulk Cargoes other than Grain 655

      C.   Cargo Ships carrying Grain 657

  (vi) Special Provision for Ships receiving Transhipped Fish 658

(2)   Load Lines... 660

  (i)   Application of Provisions relating to Load Lines etc.................... 660

  (ii)   Freeboards 663

  (iii) Surveys and Certificates 664

  (iv) Load Lines and Marks 670

  (v)   Information for the Master.. 671

  (vi) Equivalents... 672

(3)   Temporary Exclusion Zones.. 673

(4)   Safety Directions 675

	PARA
(5) Port State Control	678
(6) Ship and Port Facility Security	684
8. COLLISIONS	690
(1) Prevention of Collisions	690
(i) Domestic and International Rules	690
(ii) Steering and Sailing	695
A. Conduct of Vessels in any Condition of Visibility	695
B. Conduct of Vessels in Sight of One Another	702
C. Conduct of Vessels in Restricted Visibility	709
(iii) Lights and Shapes	710
(iv) Sound and Light Signals	722
(2) Duties after Collision	727
(3) Rules of Good Seamanship	729
(i) Scope of Rules	729
(ii) Particular Conditions	731
(iii) Particular Classes of Vessels	742
(iv) Navigation in Rivers and Narrow Waters	747
(4) Negligence causing Damage; Fault	756
(i) Negligence causing Damage	756
(ii) Determination of Liability when Both Parties at Fault	767
(iii) Rule of Division of Loss in Proportion to Fault	771
(5) General Incidence and Extent of Liability	779
(i) Parties Liable	779
(ii) Inevitable Accident	788
(6) Rights and Remedies of Injured Parties	790
(i) Persons entitled to Recover	790
(ii) Measure of Damages	793
(iii) Rights in rem and Rights in personam; Limitation of Time	810
(7) Collision as affecting Salvage	813
9. ACCIDENT INVESTIGATIONS AND INQUIRIES	815
(1) Marine Accident Investigations	815
(2) Formal Investigations by Wreck Commissioner	830
(i) Provision for Formal Investigation	830
(ii) Procedure for Formal Investigation	831
(iii) Rehearings and Appeals	844
(3) Inquiries into and Reports on Deaths and Injuries	846
10. SALVAGE AND WRECK	849
(1) Salvage	849
(i) Law and Jurisdiction	849
(ii) Performance of Salvage Operations	855
(iii) Conditions for Salvage Reward	860
(iv) Who may be Eligible for Reward	866
(v) Who is Liable for Salvage Award	874
(vi) Fixing the Award	878
A. By the Court	878
B. By Agreement	883

PARA

    C.   Matters influencing the Award 886
(vii)   Apportionment of Award between Salvors 901
(viii) Enforcement, Payment and Security 913
(2) Wreck 923
(i)   Law and Jurisdiction 923
(ii)   Duty to Insure 930
(iii)   Dealing with Wrecks 934
    A.   Reporting, Locating and Marking 934
    B.   Removal 942
(iv)   Claimed and Unclaimed Wrecks 949
(v)   Liability for Costs and Powers of Sale 953
(vi)   Protection of Wreck of RMS Titanic 959

11. LIENS ON SHIPS, FREIGHT AND CARGO 964
(1) Maritime Liens 964
(2) Statutory and Possessory Liens 973
(3) Ranking of Liens 975
(4) Enforcement and Extinction of Liens 987

12. LIMITATION OF LIABILITY OF SHIPOWNERS ETC 992
(1) The Convention on Limitation of Liability for Maritime Claims 992
(i)   Right of Limitation under the Convention 992
(ii)   Limits of Liability under the Convention 998
(iii)   The Limitation Fund under the Convention 1003
(iv)   Scope of Application of the Convention 1007
(2) Exclusion and Apportionment of Liability for Loss or Damage 1009

13. LIGHTHOUSE AUTHORITIES 1017
(1) Authorities and Commissioners 1017
(2) Functions of the Secretary of State 1021
(3) Functions of General Lighthouse Authorities 1023
(4) Powers of Harbour Authorities as Local Lighthouse Authorities 1030
(5) Transfers between Lighthouse Authorities 1031
(6) Dues Leviable by Lighthouse Authorities 1033
(i)   General Light Dues 1033
(ii)   Local Light Dues 1038
(7) Finance and Administration 1039
(8) Exemptions from Taxes, Rates etc and Harbour Dues 1046
(9) Wrecks 1048

14. OFFENCES AND LEGAL PROCEEDINGS 1049
(1) Prosecution of Offences generally 1049
(i)   Time Limits 1049
(ii)   Bodies Corporate 1051
(iii)   Jurisdiction 1052
(iv)   Return of Offenders 1056
(v)   Special Evidential Provisions 1057
(2) Specific Offences 1062
(i)   Offences relating to Registration of Ships 1062

                                                                              PARA
     (ii)   Crew-related Offences 1073
             A.   Offences Committed in relation to Crew........................1073
             B.   Conduct-related Offences Committed by Crew 1102
                       (A)   General Conduct 1102
                       (B)   Alcohol and Drugs Offences 1105
     (iii)   Safety Offences 1109
             A.   Offences under General Safety Provisions......................1109
             B.   Offences relating to Use of Unsafe Ships etc 1140
     (iv)   Offences against Maritime Security 1147
             A.   Safety of Ships and Fixed Platforms...........................1147
             B.   Protection of Ships against Acts of Violence 1155
             C.   Extension of Maritime Security Provisions.....................1156
     (v)   Offences in respect of Salvage and Wreck 1157
     (vi)   Offences Committed in Wartime.......................................1167
     (vii)   Pilotage Offences 1168
     (viii) Obstruction of Enforcement Powers 1175
     (ix)   Improper Disclosures; Giving False Information 1182
     (x)   Damage to Lighthouses etc; False Lights 1183
(3) Barratry and Piracy 1185
(4) Civil Liability of Seamen for Offences 1187
(5) Detention of Ships 1190

7. SAFETY AND SECURITY AT SEA

(1) SAFETY AND HEALTH ON SHIPS

(i) Submersible Apparatus

601. Safety of submersible and supporting apparatus. The safety of submersible and supporting apparatus is controlled by regulations[1]. The regulations apply to any submersible or supporting apparatus operated within United Kingdom waters or launched or operated from, or comprising, a United Kingdom ship[2]. For these purposes, 'submersible apparatus' means any apparatus used, or designed for use, in supporting human life on or under the bed of any waters or elsewhere under the surface of any waters; 'supporting apparatus' means any apparatus used, or designed for use, in connection with the operation of any submersible apparatus; and 'apparatus' includes any vessel, vehicle or hovercraft, any structure, any diving plant or equipment and any other form of equipment[3].

1 See the Merchant Shipping (Diving Safety) Regulations 2002, SI 2002/1587 (made under the Merchant Shipping Act 1995 s 88(2), Sch 2) and, by virtue of the Interpretation Act 1978 s 17(2)(b), the Merchant Shipping (Registration of Submersible Craft) Regulations 1976, SI 1976/940; the Merchant Shipping (Submersible Craft Construction and Survey) Regulations 1981, SI 1981/1098; and the Merchant Shipping (Submersible Craft Operations) Regulations 1987, SI 1987/311. As to the Secretary of State see PARA 36. As to the power of the Secretary of State to make subordinate legislation under the Merchant Shipping Act 1995, including his power to appoint committees for the purpose of advising him when considering the making or alteration of any regulations etc, see PARA 39; and as to the Secretary of State's power to make regulations prescribing fees to be charged in respect of the issue or recording of any certificate, licence or other document see PARA 63.

   As to the powers of inspectors appointed under s 256(6) (see PARA 46) to serve improvement notices or prohibition notices where s 88 and Sch 2 (see PARA 601) and the provisions of any instrument of a legislative character having effect thereunder are being contravened, or where activities to which s 88 and Sch 2 apply are carried on so as to involve serious personal injury or serious pollution, see PARA 46 et seq.
2 Merchant Shipping Act 1995 s 88(1). As to the meaning of 'United Kingdom waters' see PARA 48 note 10. As to the meaning of 'United Kingdom ship' see PARA 230; as to the meaning of 'ship' see PARA 229; and as to the meaning of 'United Kingdom' see PARA 16 note 3.
3 Merchant Shipping Act 1995 s 88(4).

(ii) Construction and Survey

A. IN GENERAL

602. Provision regarding design, construction, etc of ships and their machinery and equipment. Safety regulations[1] concerned with the design, construction, maintenance, repair, alteration, inspection, surveying and marking of ships and their machinery and equipment have been made (or have effect as if so made[2]) with regard to:
- (1)   passenger ships[3];
- (2)   cargo ships[4];
- (3)   gas carriers[5];
- (4)   ships carrying dangerous or noxious liquid substances in bulk[6];
- (5)   other ships[7];
- (6)   small workboats and pilot boats[8];
- (7)   ro-ro passenger ships[9];
- (8)   fishing vessels[10];
- (9)   pleasure vessels[11]; and

(10)   high speed craft[12].

1   Ie regulations made under the Merchant Shipping Act 1995 ss 85, 86 (amended by the Merchant Shipping and Maritime Security Act 1997 s 8, 29(2), Sch 7 Pt 1; by the British Overseas Territories Act 2002 s 2(3); and by the Health Act 2006 s 5(4). In the Merchant Shipping Act 1995, regulations under s 85 are referred to as 'safety regulations': see s 313(1). A breach of safety regulations gives rise to a civil right of action: see *Ziemniak v ETPM Deep Sea Ltd* [2003] EWCA Civ 636, [2003] 2 All ER (Comm) 283, [2003] 2 Lloyd's Rep 214.

2   Ie by virtue of the Interpretation Act 1978 s 17(2)(b), the regulations mentioned in heads (1) to (10) in the text have effect as if made under the Merchant Shipping Act 1995 s 85 (see note 1).

3   See the Merchant Shipping (Passenger Ship Construction: Ships of Classes I, II and II(A)) Regulations 1998, SI 1998/2514, Pt II (regs 6–19) (Strength, Construction and Watertight Subdivision); Pt V (regs 37–47) (Stability and Shipside Markings); Pt VI (regs 48–51) (Bilge Pumping Arrangements); Pt VII (regs 52–61) (Electrical Equipment and Installations); Pt VIII (regs 62–78) (Boilers and Machinery); Pt IX (regs 79–84) (Miscellaneous Requirements); and Pt X (regs 85–89) (Miscellaneous Requirements for Ships with Special Category or Ro-Ro Cargo Spaces). For these purposes, passenger ships are arranged in Classes as follows:

    (1)   ships engaged on international voyages: Class I (Ships engaged on voyages any of which are long international voyages); Class II (Ships engaged on voyages any of which are short international voyages) (see reg 2(6)); and

    (2)   ships not engaged on international voyages: Class II(A) (Ships engaged on voyages of any kind other than international voyages, which are not ships of Classes III to VI(A) as defined in the Merchant Shipping (Passenger Ship Construction: Ships of Classes III to VI(A)) Regulations 1998, SI 1998/2515 (see heads (a) to (e) below); or ships of Classes A, B, C or D as defined in the Merchant Shipping (Passenger Ships on Domestic Voyages) Regulations 2000, SI 2000/2687 (see PARA 605 note 4) which are new ships, engaged on domestic voyages, for the purposes of those Regulations (see the Merchant Shipping (Passenger Ship Construction: Ships of Classes I, II and II(A)) Regulations 1998, SI 1998/2514, reg 2(6)).

See also the Merchant Shipping (Passenger Ship Construction: Ships of Classes III to VI(A)) Regulations 1998, SI 1998/2515, Pt II (regs 6–14) (Strength, Construction and Watertight Subdivision); Pt V (regs 30–39) (Stability, Survivability and Shipside Markings); Pt VI (regs 40–42) (Bilge Pumping Arrangements); Pt VII (regs 43–48) (Electrical Equipment and Installations); Pt VIII (regs 49–62) (Boilers and Machinery); Pt IX (regs 63–67) (Miscellaneous Requirements); and Pt X (regs 68–71) (Miscellaneous Requirements for Ships with Special Category or Ro-Ro Cargo Spaces). For these purposes, passenger ships are arranged in Classes as follows (see reg 2(6)(a)(i)):

    (a)   Class III (Ships engaged only on voyages in the course of which they are at no time more than 70 miles by sea from their point of departure and not more than 18 miles from the coast of the United Kingdom, and which are at sea only in favourable weather and during restricted periods);

    (b)   Class IV (Ships engaged only on voyages in Category A, B, C or D waters);

    (c)   Class V (Ships engaged only on voyages in Category A, B, or C waters);

    (d)   Class VI (Ships engaged only on voyages with not more than 250 passengers on board, to sea, or in Category A, B, C or D waters, in all cases in favourable weather and during restricted periods, in the course of which the ships are at no time more than 15 miles, exclusive of any Category A, B, C, or D waters, from their point of departure nor more than 3 miles from land);

    (e)   Class VI(A) (Ships carrying not more than 50 passengers for a distance of not more than 6 miles on voyages to or from isolated communities on the islands or coast of the United Kingdom and which do not proceed for a distance of more than 3 miles from land; subject to any conditions which the Secretary of State may impose).

Classes of ships under heads (a) to (e) do not include ships engaged on international voyages (see reg 2(6)(a)(ii)). For these purposes, 'Category A, B, C or D waters' means the waters specified as Category A, B, C or D waters in Merchant Shipping Notice 1776(M); and cognate expressions are to be construed accordingly; 'restricted period' means a period falling wholly from 1 April to 31 October (both dates inclusive) and between one hour before sunrise and one hour after sunset in the case of ships fitted with navigation lights conforming to the collision regulations and between sunrise and sunset in the case of any other ships; and 'sea' does not include any waters of Category A, B, C or D: see reg 2(6)(b).

See also the Merchant Shipping (Bridge Visibility) (Small Passenger Ships) Regulations 2005, SI 2005/2286. As to safety rules and standards in relation to passenger ships on domestic voyages see the Merchant Shipping (Passenger Ships on Domestic Voyages) Regulations 2000, SI

2000/2687; and PARA 605; and as to mandatory surveys for high speed passenger craft see the Merchant Shipping (Mandatory Surveys for Ro-Ro Ferry and High Speed Passenger Craft) Regulations 2001, SI 2001/152; and PARA 606.

4　See the Merchant Shipping (Cargo Ship Construction) Regulations 1997, SI 1997/1509. The Merchant Shipping (High Speed Craft) Regulations 2004, SI 2004/302, disapply the Merchant Shipping (Cargo Ship Construction) Regulations 1997, SI 1997/1509, to any vessel which has been examined, and in respect of which appropriate certificates have been issued, in accordance with the Code of Practice for the Safety of Large Commercial Sailing and Motor Vessels: see PARA 613. See also the Merchant Shipping (Additional Safety Measures for Bulk Carriers) Regulations 1999, SI 1999/1644.

5　See the Merchant Shipping (Gas Carriers) Regulations 1994, SI 1994/2464.

6　See the Merchant Shipping (Dangerous or Noxious Liquid Substances in Bulk) Regulations 1996, SI 1996/3010; and ENVIRONMENTAL QUALITY AND PUBLIC HEALTH vol 45 (2010) PARA 404 et seq.

7　See the Merchant Shipping (Passenger Ship Construction: Ships of Classes I, II and II(A)) Regulations 1998, SI 1998/2514 (see note 3).

8　See the Merchant Shipping (Small Workboats and Pilot Boats) Regulations 1998, SI 1998/1609 (amended by SI 2006/2055).

9　See the Merchant Shipping (Emergency Equipment Lockers for Ro/Ro Passenger Ships) Regulations 1988, SI 1988/2272; the Merchant Shipping (Passenger Ship Construction: Ships of Classes I, II and II(A)) Regulations 1998, SI 1998/2514 (see note 3); and the Merchant Shipping (Ro-Ro Passenger Ships) (Stability) Regulations 2004, SI 2004/2884. As to mandatory surveys for ro-ro ferries see the Merchant Shipping (Mandatory Surveys for Ro-Ro Ferry and High Speed Passenger Craft) Regulations 2001, SI 2001/152; and PARA 606.

10　See PARA 607 et seq.

11　See the Merchant Shipping (Vessels in Commercial Use for Sport or Pleasure) Regulations 1998, SI 1998/2771; and PARA 612 et seq.

12　See the Merchant Shipping (High-Speed Craft) Regulations 2004, SI 2004/302; and PARA 617 et seq.

603. Obligation of shipowners as to seaworthiness. In every contract of employment between the owner of a United Kingdom ship[1] and the master[2] of or any seaman[3] employed in the ship there is to be implied an obligation on the owner of the ship that[4]:

(1)　　the owner of the ship[5];
(2)　　the master of the ship[6]; and
(3)　　every agent charged with the loading of the ship, the preparing of the ship for sea, or the sending of the ship to sea[7],

must use all reasonable means to ensure the seaworthiness[8] of the ship for the voyage at the time when the voyage commences and to keep the ship in a seaworthy condition for the voyage during the voyage[9].

This obligation[10] applies notwithstanding any agreement to the contrary[11]; and no liability on the owner of a ship arises under this obligation[12] in respect of the ship being sent to sea in an unseaworthy state where, owing to special circumstances, the sending of the ship to sea in such a state was reasonable and justifiable[13].

1　As to the meaning of 'ship' see PARA 229; and as to the meaning of 'United Kingdom ship' see PARA 230. As to the meaning of 'United Kingdom' see PARA 16 note 3.
　　The Merchant Shipping Act 1995 s 42 (see the text and notes 2–13) applies to all United Kingdom ships: being concerned with matters with which the Merchant Shipping (Maritime Labour Convention) (Minimum Requirements for Seafarers etc) Regulations 2014, SI 2014/1613 and the Maritime Labour Convention (Cm 7049)) are not concerned (see PARA 423), these provisions are not limited to the vessels excluded from the scope of the Convention.

2　As to the meaning of 'master' see PARA 444 note 1.

3　As to the meaning of 'seaman' see PARA 457 note 5.

4　Merchant Shipping Act 1995 s 42(1).

5　Merchant Shipping Act 1995 s 42(1)(a).

6　Merchant Shipping Act 1995 s 42(1)(b).

7　Merchant Shipping Act 1995 s 42(1)(c).

8　For these purposes, 'seaworthy' means that the ship should be in a fit state as to repairs, equipment and crew, and in all other respects, to encounter the ordinary perils of the voyage: see *Dixon v*

Sadler (1839) 5 M & W 405 at 414. The master's negligence in not using with proper care the means of safety provided does not make the ship unseaworthy within the meaning of the Merchant Shipping Act 1995 s 42: see *Hedley v Pinkney & Sons Steamship Co Ltd* [1894] AC 222, HL.
9   Merchant Shipping Act 1995 s 42(1).
10 Ie under the Merchant Shipping Act 1995 s 42(1) (see the text and notes 1–9): see s 42(2).
11 Merchant Shipping Act 1995 s 42(2).
12 Ie under the Merchant Shipping Act 1995 s 42(1) (see the text and notes 1–9): see s 42(3).
13 Merchant Shipping Act 1995 s 42(3).

B.   MERCHANT SHIPPING

604.   Survey and certification. Safety regulations[1] concerned with the design, construction, maintenance, repair, alteration, inspection, surveying and marking of ships and their machinery and equipment have been made with regard to:
(1)   surveys of passenger ships[2];
(2)   surveys of cargo ship safety equipment[3];
(3)   surveys of cargo ship radio installations[4];
(4)   survey requirements for the structure, machinery and equipment of cargo ships[5];
(5)   the responsibilities of the owner and master[6];
(6)   the procedure to be adopted when the ship is deficient[7];
(7)   the issue and operation of certificates[8];
(8)   the prohibition on proceeding to sea without the appropriate documentation[9] or on proceeding on a voyage or excursion without the appropriate certificate[10];
(9)   the limit on the number of passengers on passenger ships[11];
(10)   penalties[12];
(11)   power of detention[13]; and
(12)   arbitration[14].
Regulations also make provision for the survey and certification of vessels in the context of ensuring that the United Kingdom discharges its responsibilities under the Maritime Labour Convention[15]. Provision is made with regard to:
(a)   surveys and certification of ships[16];
(b)   the issuing and operation of Maritime Labour Certificates and interim certificates[17];
(c)   declarations of Maritime Labour Compliance[18];
(d)   complaints prodcures[19];
(e)   arbitration[20];
(f)   offences and penalties[21]; and
(g)   inspection and detention[22].

1   As to the meaning of 'safety regulations' see PARA 602 note 1. The Merchant Shipping (Survey and Certification) Regulations 2015, SI 2015/580 (see the text and notes 2–14) apply to United Kingdom ships wherever they may be and to other ships whilst they are in United Kingdom waters, but not to fishing vessels, pleasure vessels, high speed craft to which the Merchant Shipping (High Speed Craft) Regulations 2004, SI 2004/302 (see PARA 617 et seq) apply, passenger ships to which the Merchant Shipping (Passenger Ships) (Safety Code for UK Categorised Waters) Regulations 2010, SI 2010/680 apply (ie ships operating only on inland waterways), vessels to which the Merchant Shipping (Technical Requirements for Inland Waterway Vessels) Regulations 2010, SI 2010/1075 apply, and to Class IX(A) and Class IX(A)(T) ships: Merchant Shipping (Survey and Certification) Regulations 2015, SI 2015/508, reg 5(1), (2). The Secretary of State may also grant exemptions from all or any of the provisions of the Merchant Shipping (Survey and Certification) Regulations 2015, SI 2015/508 on such terms (if any) as he may so specify and may, subject to giving reasonable notice, alter or cancel any such exemption: reg 5(3). As to the Secretary of State see PARA 36. For these purposes, 'pleasure vessel' means:
    (1)   any vessel which at the time it is being used is, in the case of a vessel wholly owned by an individual or individuals, used only for the sport or pleasure of the owner or the immediate family or friends of the owner or, in the case of a vessel owned by a body corporate, one on which the persons are employees or officers of the body corporate, or their immediate family or friends; and is on a voyage or excursion which is one for which the owner does not receive money for or in connection with operating the vessel or

carrying any person, other than as a contribution to the direct expenses of the operation of the vessel incurred during the voyage or excursion;

(2)   any vessel wholly owned by or on behalf of a members' club formed for the purpose of sport or pleasure which, at the time it is being used, is used only for the sport or pleasure of members of the club or their immediate family; and for the use of which any charges levied are paid into club funds and applied for the general use of the club; and

(3)   in the case of any vessel referred to in head (1) or head (2) no other payments are made by or on behalf of the users of the vessel, other than by the owner;

and, for these purposes, 'immediate family' means, in relation to an individual, the spouse or civil partner of the individual, and a relative of the individual or the relative's spouse or civil partner; and 'relative' means brother, sister, ancestor or lineal descendant: reg 3(1).

As to safety rules and standards in relation to passenger ships on domestic voyages see the Merchant Shipping (Passenger Ships on Domestic Voyages) Regulations 2000, SI 2000/2687; and PARA 605. As to mandatory surveys for ro-ro ferry and high speed passenger craft see the Merchant Shipping (Mandatory Surveys for Ro-Ro Ferry and High Speed Passenger Craft) Regulations 2001, SI 2001/152; and PARA 606.

2 See the Merchant Shipping (Survey and Certification) Regulations 2015, SI 2015/580, regs 6, 11.

3 See the Merchant Shipping (Survey and Certification) Regulations 2015, SI 2015/580, reg 7.

4 See the Merchant Shipping (Survey and Certification) Regulations 2015, SI 2015/580, reg 8.

5 See the Merchant Shipping (Survey and Certification) Regulations 2015, SI 2015/580, reg 9.

6 See the Merchant Shipping (Survey and Certification) Regulations 2015, SI 2015/580, reg 10.

7 See the Merchant Shipping (Survey and Certification) Regulations 2015, SI 2015/580, reg 12.

8 See the Merchant Shipping (Survey and Certification) Regulations 2015, SI 2015/580, regs 13–22.

9 See the Merchant Shipping (Survey and Certification) Regulations 2015, SI 2015/580, reg 23.

10 See the Merchant Shipping (Survey and Certification) Regulations 2015, SI 2015/580, reg 24.

11 See the Merchant Shipping (Survey and Certification) Regulations 2015, SI 2015/580, reg 25.

12 See the Merchant Shipping (Survey and Certification) Regulations 2015, SI 2015/580, reg 26.

13 See the Merchant Shipping (Survey and Certification) Regulations 2015, SI 2015/580, reg 27.

14 See the Merchant Shipping (Survey and Certification) Regulations 2015, SI 2015/580, reg 28.

15 As to the Maritime Labour Convention see PARA 423 note 1.

16 See the Merchant Shipping (Maritime Labour Convention) (Survey and Certification) Regulations 2013, SI 2013/1785, regs 5, 7, 9. The regulations implement the Maritime Labour Convention reg 5.1.

17 See the Merchant Shipping (Maritime Labour Convention) (Survey and Certification) Regulations 2013, SI 2013/1785, regs 6, 8, 10, 12.

18 See the Merchant Shipping (Maritime Labour Convention) (Survey and Certification) Regulations 2013, SI 2013/1785, reg 11.

19 See the Merchant Shipping (Maritime Labour Convention) (Survey and Certification) Regulations 2013, SI 2013/1785, regs 13, 18.

20 See the Merchant Shipping (Maritime Labour Convention) (Survey and Certification) Regulations 2013, SI 2013/1785, reg 14.

21 See the Merchant Shipping (Maritime Labour Convention) (Survey and Certification) Regulations 2013, SI 2013/1785, reg 15.

22 See the Merchant Shipping (Maritime Labour Convention) (Survey and Certification) Regulations 2013, SI 2013/1785, regs 16, 17, 19, 20.

605. Provision made in relation to passenger ships on domestic voyages.

Safety regulations[1] have made provision in relation to passenger ships engaged on domestic voyages[2] in respect of:

(1)   safety requirements[3];

(2)   the use of alternative construction processes, equipment and machinery[4];

(3)   stability requirements for ro-ro passenger ships[5];

(4)   safety requirements for persons with reduced mobility[6];

(5)   the Secretary of State's power to exempt classes of ships or individual ships from specified provisions of the regulations[7];

(6)   penalties for any contravention of the regulations[8], and the power to detain a ship that does not comply with the requirements of the regulations[9].

1 As to the meaning of 'safety regulations' see PARA 602 note 1.

2   For the purposes of the Merchant Shipping (Passenger Ships on Domestic Voyages) Regulations 2000, SI 2000/2687, passenger ships engaged on domestic voyages are arranged in Classes as follows (see reg 3(1)):

    (1)   Class A (ships engaged solely on domestic voyages other than ships of Class B, Class C and Class D);

    (2)   Class B (ships engaged solely on domestic voyages in the course of which they are at no time more than 20 miles from the line of the coast where shipwrecked persons can land, corresponding to the medium tide height);

    (3)   Class C (ships engaged solely on domestic voyages in sea areas where the probability of significant wave heights exceeding 2.5 metres is less than 10% over a one year period for all year round operation, or over a specific restricted period of the year for operation exclusively in such period, in the course of which they are at no time more than 15 miles from a place of refuge, nor more than 5 miles from the line of the coast where shipwrecked persons can land, corresponding to the medium tide height);

    (4)   Class D (ships engaged solely on domestic voyages in sea areas where the probability of significant wave heights exceeding 1.5 metres is less than 10% over a one year period for all year round operation, or over a specific restricted period of the year for operation exclusively in such period, in the course of which they are at no time more than 6 miles from a place of refuge, nor more than 3 miles from the line of the coast, where shipwrecked persons can land, corresponding to the medium tide height).

For the purposes of this classification of vessels, the Secretary of State must establish, and update when necessary, a list of sea areas under United Kingdom jurisdiction which includes the limits of zones for all year round operation and, where appropriate, for restricted periodical operation, and publish that list in its updated version in a Merchant Shipping Notice and in a public database available on the Internet site of the Maritime and Coastguard Agency: reg 3(2) (substituted by SI 2004/2883). Accordingly, for the purposes of rules or regulations made under the Merchant Shipping Act 1995, 'category A, B, C or D waters' respectively means the waters specified as Category A, B, C or D waters in Merchant Shipping Notice 1776(M): see the Merchant Shipping (Categorisation of Waters) Regulations 1992, SI 1992/2356, reg 3.

In relation to passenger ships of Class A, B, C or D of 24 metres or over in length engaged on domestic voyages, the following Regulations cease to apply (see the Merchant Shipping (Passenger Ships on Domestic Voyages) Regulations 2000, SI 2000/2687, reg 5 (amended by SI 2002/1473)):

    (a)   the Merchant Shipping (Passenger Ship Construction: Ships of Classes I, II and II(A)) Regulations 1998, SI 1998/2514 (see PARAS 602, 637);

    (b)   the Merchant Shipping (Passenger Ship Construction: Ships of Classes III to VI(A)) Regulations 1998, SI 1998/2515 (see PARAS 602, 637);

    (c)   the Merchant Shipping (Life-Saving Appliances for Ships Other Than Ships Of Classes III To VI(A)) Regulations 1999, SI 1999/2721 (see PARA 639);

    (d)   the Merchant Shipping (Life-Saving Appliances for Passenger Ships Of Classes III To VI(A)) Regulations 1999, SI 1999/2723 (see PARA 639);

    (e)   the Merchant Shipping (Fire Protection: Small Ships) Regulations 1998, SI 1998/1011 (see PARA 633);

    (f)   the Merchant Shipping (Fire Protection: Large Ships) Regulations 1998, SI 1998/1012 (see PARA 633);

    (g)   the Merchant Shipping (Radio Installations) Regulations 1998, SI 1998/2070 (see PARA 636); and

    (h)   the Merchant Shipping (Safety of Navigation) Regulations 2002, SI 2002/1473 (see PARA 634).

As to the application of the Merchant Shipping (Passenger Ships on Domestic Voyages) Regulations 2000, SI 2000/2687, see reg 4 (amended by SI 2004/302).

The Merchant Shipping (Passenger Ships on Domestic Voyages) Regulations 2000, SI 2000/2687, implemented Council Directive (EC) 98/18 (OJ L144, 15.05.1998, p 1) on Safety Rules and Standards for Passenger Ships (see now Council Directive (EC) 2009/45 (OJ L136, 25.6.2009, p 1))). As to mandatory surveys for ro-ro ferry and high speed passenger craft see the Merchant Shipping (Mandatory Surveys for Ro-Ro Ferry and High Speed Passenger Craft) Regulations 2001, SI 2001/152; and PARA 606.

3   See the Merchant Shipping (Passenger Ships on Domestic Voyages) Regulations 2000, SI 2000/2687, reg 6 (amended by SI 2003/771; SI 2004/2883; SI 2012/2636).

4   See the Merchant Shipping (Passenger Ships on Domestic Voyages) Regulations 2000, SI 2000/2687, SI 2000/2687, reg 7 (amended by SI 2012/2636).

5   See the Merchant Shipping (Passenger Ships on Domestic Voyages) Regulations 2000, SI 2000/2687, regs 7A, 7B (added by SI 2004/2883).

6 See the Merchant Shipping (Passenger Ships on Domestic Voyages) Regulations 2000, SI 2000/2687, reg 7C (added by SI 2004/2883).
7 See the Merchant Shipping (Passenger Ships on Domestic Voyages) Regulations 2000, SI 2000/2687, reg 8.
8 See the Merchant Shipping (Passenger Ships on Domestic Voyages) Regulations 2000, SI 2000/2687, reg 9 (amended by SI 2004/2883).
9 See the Merchant Shipping (Passenger Ships on Domestic Voyages) Regulations 2000, SI 2000/2687, reg 10.

606. Mandatory surveys for ro-ro ferry and high speed passenger craft.

Safety regulations[1] have made provision[2] in relation to ro-ro ferry and high speed passenger craft operating a regular service to or from a port in the United Kingdom, requiring the Maritime and Coastguard Agency[3] to:

(1)   carry out verifications in relation to the vessel[4];
(2)   carry out verifications in relation to the company operating the vessel, and the flag state of the vessel[5];
(3)   carry out an initial specific survey before the vessel begins operating on a regular service to or from a United Kingdom port[6];
(4)   carry out further surveys every year, or where the circumstances of the vessel change[7];
(5)   issue prevention of operation notices[8], or reports of inspection[9] or improvement notices requiring defects to be remedied[10];
(6)   comply with certain administrative requirements[11]; and
(7)   operate a shore-based navigational guidance system[12].

1 As to the meaning of 'safety regulations' see PARA 602 note 1.
2 See the Merchant Shipping (Mandatory Surveys for Ro-Ro Ferry and High Speed Passenger Craft) Regulations 2001, SI 2001/152, which implement, in part, Council Directive (EC) 1999/35 (OJ L138, 01.06.1999, p 1) on a system of mandatory surveys for the safe operation of regular ro-ro ferry and high-speed passenger craft services. The Merchant Shipping (Mandatory Surveys for Ro-Ro Ferry and High Speed Passenger Craft) Regulations 2001, SI 2001/152, apply to a ro-ro ferry or a high speed passenger craft which is operating a regular service to or from a port in the United Kingdom either on international voyages, or in sea areas covered by Class A as referred to in Council Directive (EC) 2009/45 (OJ L136, 25.6.2009, p 1) on Safety Rules and Standards for Passenger Ships art 4 (see PARA 605): see the Merchant Shipping (Mandatory Surveys for Ro-Ro Ferry and High Speed Passenger Craft) Regulations 2001, SI 2001/152, reg 3. As to the meaning of 'United Kingdom' see PARA 16 note 3. As to the safety rules and standards in relation to passenger ships on domestic voyages that have been implemented in the United Kingdom see the Merchant Shipping (Passenger Ships on Domestic Voyages) Regulations 2000, SI 2000/2687; and PARA 605.
3 For these purposes, 'Maritime and Coastguard Agency' means the Maritime and Coastguard Agency, an executive agency of the Department of Transport: the Merchant Shipping (Mandatory Surveys for Ro-Ro Ferry and High Speed Passenger Craft) Regulations 2001, SI 2001/152, reg 2(1). As to the Maritime and Coastguard Agency see PARA 57.
4 See the Merchant Shipping (Mandatory Surveys for Ro-Ro Ferry and High Speed Passenger Craft) Regulations 2001, SI 2001/152, reg 4. As to exemptions from reg 4 see reg 7.
5 See the Merchant Shipping (Mandatory Surveys for Ro-Ro Ferry and High Speed Passenger Craft) Regulations 2001, SI 2001/152, reg 5. As to exemptions from reg 5 see reg 7.
6 See the Merchant Shipping (Mandatory Surveys for Ro-Ro Ferry and High Speed Passenger Craft) Regulations 2001, SI 2001/152, reg 6. As to exemptions from reg 6 see reg 7.
7 See the Merchant Shipping (Mandatory Surveys for Ro-Ro Ferry and High Speed Passenger Craft) Regulations 2001, SI 2001/152, reg 8.
8 Ie notices preventing a vessel which does not meet the requirements of Council Directive (EC) 1999/35 (OJ L138, 01.06.1999, p 1) (see note 2) from operating: see the Merchant Shipping (Mandatory Surveys for Ro-Ro Ferry and High Speed Passenger Craft) Regulations 2001, SI 2001/152, reg 9. A prevention of operation notice served in accordance with reg 9 is treated as a prohibition notice for the purposes of the Merchant Shipping Act 1995 s 264 (see PARA 54), s 265 (see PARA 55) and s 266 (see PARA 1178): see the Merchant Shipping (Mandatory Surveys for Ro-Ro Ferry and High Speed Passenger Craft) Regulations 2001, SI 2001/152, reg 9. As to the costs of issuing prevention of operation notices see reg 12.
9 Ie where the defects to which the Merchant Shipping (Mandatory Surveys for Ro-Ro Ferry and High Speed Passenger Craft) Regulations 2001, SI 2001/152, reg 9 (see the text and note 8) might otherwise apply do not pose an immediate danger to the safety of the vessel, its crew and

passengers: see the Merchant Shipping (Mandatory Surveys for Ro-Ro Ferry and High Speed Passenger Craft) Regulations 2001, SI 2001/152, reg 10.

10 See the Merchant Shipping (Mandatory Surveys for Ro-Ro Ferry and High Speed Passenger Craft) Regulations 2001, SI 2001/152, reg 11. A notice issued in accordance with reg 11 is treated for the purposes of the Merchant Shipping Act 1995 s 261 (see PARA 51), s 263 (see PARA 53), s 264 (see PARA 54) and s 266 (see PARA 1178) as an improvement notice served under s 261: see the Merchant Shipping (Mandatory Surveys for Ro-Ro Ferry and High Speed Passenger Craft) Regulations 2001, SI 2001/152, reg 11.

11 See the Merchant Shipping (Mandatory Surveys for Ro-Ro Ferry and High Speed Passenger Craft) Regulations 2001, SI 2001/152, reg 13.

12 See the Merchant Shipping (Mandatory Surveys for Ro-Ro Ferry and High Speed Passenger Craft) Regulations 2001, SI 2001/152, reg 14.

C. FISHING VESSELS

607. Fishing vessel construction rules. Rules have been made ('fishing vessel construction rules') prescribing requirements for the hull, equipment and machinery of United Kingdom fishing vessels[1]. A surveyor of ships[2] may inspect any fishing vessel for the purpose of seeing that it complies with the fishing vessel construction rules[3]. If the rules are contravened[4] with respect to any vessel (or if a vessel is exempted[5] from any requirement subject to a condition and the condition is not complied with) the owner or master[6] of the vessel commits an offence[7]. However, a breach of the rules cannot, of itself, form the basis of a civil claim by a person who has suffered damage as a result of such a breach[8].

1 See the Fishing Vessels (Safety Provisions) Rules 1975, SI 1975/330 (having effect under the Merchant Shipping Act 1995 s 121(1)–(3)). As to the meaning of 'United Kingdom fishing vessel' see PARA 230. As to the meaning of 'fishing vessel' see PARA 230 note 9; and as to the meaning of 'United Kingdom' see PARA 16 note 3. Fishing vessels of less than 15 metres length are subject to the Fishing Vessels (Code of Practice for the Safety of Small Fishing Vessels) Regulations 2001, SI 2001/9; and fishing vessels of between 15 metres and 24 metres length are subject to the Fishing Vessels (Safety of 15–24 Metre Vessels) Regulations 2002, SI 2002/2201. Both these regulations require vessels to comply with codes of practice: see further FISHERIES AND AQUACULTURE vol 51 (2013) PARA 309. Fishing vessels of more than 24 metres length built on or after 1 January 1999 are subject to the Fishing Vessels (EC Directive on Harmonised Safety Regime) Regulations 1999, SI 1999/2998. As to the Secretary of State's power to make rules under the Merchant Shipping Act 1995 generally see PARA 39. As to the Secretary of State see PARA 36. Before making rules under Pt V Ch II (ss 121–127), the Secretary of State must consult with organisations in the United Kingdom appearing to him representative of persons who will be affected by the regulations or rules: see s 306(4); and PARA 39 note 1. As to the powers of inspectors appointed under s 256(6) (see PARA 46) to serve improvement notices or prohibition notices where s 121 and the provisions of any instrument of a legislative character having effect thereunder are being contravened, or where activities to which s 121 applies are carried on so as to involve serious personal injury or serious pollution, see PARA 46 et seq.

2 As to the meaning of 'surveyor of ships' see PARA 46 note 13.

3 Merchant Shipping Act 1995 s 121(4).

4 As to the meaning of 'contravention' see PARA 51 note 3.

5 Ie under the Merchant Shipping Act 1995 s 121(2): see s 121(5).

6 As to the meaning of 'master' see PARA 444 note 1.

7 See the Merchant Shipping Act 1995 s 121(5); and PARA 1111.

8 *Todd v Adam* [2002] EWCA Civ 509, [2002] 2 All ER (Comm) 97, [2002] 2 Lloyd's Rep 293 (a number of features of the Merchant Shipping Act 1995 s 121, when taken together, firmly indicated that a breach of rules issued pursuant to s 121 could not, of itself, form the basis of a civil claim:

  (1) the existence of criminal sanctions in s 121(5) indicated that the legislature had not intended a civil remedy to be available;

  (2) the statutory duty the claimants sought to enforce was not a duty which the legislature had imposed on any particular person;

  (3) the power to exempt certain vessels under s 121(2) means that any liability would not fall evenly;

  (4) it was unlikely that the legislature had intended the master or owner of a vessel with a valid certificate (see PARA 608 et seq) to be open to civil liability;

  (5) it was not likely that the legislature had intended to impose on masters or owners an absolute obligation in all events, even in the absence of negligence).

608. Fishing vessel survey rules. Rules have been made ('fishing vessel survey rules') for the surveying and periodical inspection of United Kingdom fishing vessels[1] for the purpose of ensuring their compliance with the requirements of the fishing vessel construction and equipment provisions[2].

1 As to the meaning of 'United Kingdom fishing vessel' see PARA 230. As to the meaning of 'fishing vessel' see PARA 230 note 9; and as to the meaning of 'United Kingdom' see PARA 16 note 3.

2 See the Fishing Vessels (Safety Provisions) Rules 1975, SI 1975/330 (having effect under the Merchant Shipping Act 1995 s 122(1)). For the purposes of Pt V Ch II (ss 121–127), 'fishing vessel construction and equipment provisions' means fishing vessel construction rules and rules or safety regulations relating to life-saving, radio and navigational equipment for fishing vessels: s 122(2). As to the meaning of 'safety regulations' see PARA 602 note 1; and as to the meaning of 'fishing vessel construction rules' see PARA 607. Fishing vessels of less than 15 metres length are subject to the Fishing Vessels (Code of Practice for the Safety of Small Fishing Vessels) Regulations 2001, SI 2001/9; and fishing vessels of between 15 metres and 24 metres length are subject to the Fishing Vessels (Safety of 15–24 Metre Vessels) Regulations 2002, SI 2002/2201. Both these regulations require vessels to comply with codes of practice: see further FISHERIES AND AQUACULTURE vol 51 (2013) PARA 309. Fishing vessels of more than 24 metres length built on or after 1 January 1999 are subject to the Fishing Vessels (EC Directive on Harmonised Safety Regime) Regulations 1999, SI 1999/2998. As to the Secretary of State's power to make rules under the Merchant Shipping Act 1995 generally see PARA 39. As to the Secretary of State see PARA 36. Before making rules under Pt V Ch II (ss 121–127), the Secretary of State must consult with organisations in the United Kingdom appearing to him representative of persons who will be affected by the regulations or rules: see s 306(4); and PARA 39 note 1. As to the powers of inspectors appointed under s 256(6) (see PARA 46) to serve improvement notices or prohibition notices where s 121 and the provisions of any instrument of a legislative character having effect thereunder are being contravened, or where activities to which s 121 applies are carried on so as to involve serious personal injury or serious pollution, see PARA 46 et seq.

609. Fishing vessel certificates confirming compliance with rules. If the Secretary of State[1] or any person authorised by him for the purpose is satisfied, on receipt of a declaration of survey in respect of a fishing vessel[2] surveyed under the fishing vessel survey rules[3], that the vessel complies with such of the requirements of the fishing vessel construction and equipment provisions[4] as are or will be applicable to the vessel, the Secretary of State or authorised person must, on the application of the owner, issue a certificate (a 'fishing vessel certificate') showing that the vessel complies with those requirements[5].

Fishing vessel survey rules may require, in the case of such fishing vessel certificate as may be specified in the rules, that the Secretary of State or person authorised to issue it must not issue the certificate unless satisfied that the vessel in respect of which it is to be issued is provided with the lights, shapes and means of making fog signals required by safety regulations[6] for the prevention of collisions[7].

A fishing vessel certificate must be in such form as may be prescribed by the fishing vessel survey rules[8]; and those rules may make provision for the duration, extension or cancellation of any such certificate and for the endorsement on it of information relating to the inspection, in accordance with the rules, of the vessel to which it relates and of any extension of the period for which the certificate was issued[9].

The Secretary of State may require a fishing vessel certificate which has expired or been cancelled, to be delivered up as he directs[10]; and, if the owner or skipper of the fishing vessel fails without reasonable excuse to comply with such a requirement, he commits an offence[11].

The owner or skipper of a fishing vessel to whom a fishing vessel certificate is issued must forthwith, on the receipt of the certificate by him (or his agent), cause a copy of it to be put up in some conspicuous place on board the vessel, so as to be legible to all persons on board, and to be kept so put up and legible while the certificate remains in force and the vessel is in use[12]. If the owner or skipper of a fishing vessel fails without reasonable excuse to comply with that requirement, he commits an offence[13].

If any person intentionally makes, or assists in making, or procures to be made, a false or fraudulent fishing vessel certificate, he commits an offence[14].

A fishing vessel certificate is admissible in evidence[15].

1   As to the Secretary of State see PARA 36.
2   As to the meaning of 'fishing vessel' see PARA 230 note 9.
3   As to the meaning of 'fishing vessel survey rules' see PARA 608.
4   As to the meaning of 'fishing vessel construction and equipment provisions' see PARA 608 note 2.
5   Merchant Shipping Act 1995 s 123(1). For this purpose, any requirement from which the vessel has been exempted under s 121(2) (see PARA 607) or any other provision of the Merchant Shipping Act 1995 is deemed not to be applicable to it: see s 123(1). For the purposes of ss 123–126, 'fishing vessel certificate' includes a certificate issued under the Fishing Vessels (Safety Provisions) Rules 1975, SI 1975/330, r 126B(1) (as to which see FISHERIES AND AQUACULTURE vol 51 (2013) PARA 309): r 126B(2) (added by SI 1999/2998).
    As to the Secretary of State's power to make regulations prescribing fees to be charged in respect of the issue or recording of any certificate, licence or other document see PARA 62. As to the powers of inspectors appointed under s 256(6) (see PARA 46) to serve improvement notices or prohibition notices where s 123 and the provisions of any instrument of a legislative character having effect thereunder are being contravened, or where activities to which s 123 applies are carried on so as to involve serious personal injury or serious pollution, see PARA 46 et seq.
6   As to the meaning of 'safety regulations' see PARA 602 note 1.
7   Merchant Shipping Act 1995 s 123(2). As to the safety regulations relating to the prevention of collisions see PARA 690 et seq.
8   Merchant Shipping Act 1995 s 123(3). As to the form of the fishing vessel certificate see the Fishing Vessels (Safety Provisions) Rules 1975, SI 1975/330, Sch 1; and the Fishing Vessels (EC Directive on Harmonised Safety Regime) Regulations 1999, SI 1999/2998, reg 10 (amended by SI 2003/1112).
9   Merchant Shipping Act 1995 s 123(3).
10 Merchant Shipping Act 1995 s 124(1).
11 See the Merchant Shipping Act 1995 s 124(2); and PARA 1112.
12 Merchant Shipping Act 1995 s 124(3).
13 See the Merchant Shipping Act 1995 s 124(4); and PARA 1112.
14 See the Merchant Shipping Act 1995 s 124(5); and PARA 1112.
15 See the Merchant Shipping Act 1995 s 124(7); and PARA 1112.

610. Prohibition on going to sea without appropriate certificate.

No fishing vessel[1] required to be surveyed under the fishing vessel survey rules[2] is to go to sea unless there are in force fishing vessel certificates[3] showing that the vessel complies with such of the requirements of the fishing vessel construction and equipment provisions[4] as are applicable to the vessel[5]. If a fishing vessel goes to sea in contravention[6] of this prohibition, the owner or skipper of the vessel commits an offence[7].

The skipper of any United Kingdom fishing vessel[8] must on demand produce to any officer of Revenue and Customs[9] or of the Secretary of State[10] any certificate required by the fishing vessels safety provisions[11]; and the fishing vessel, if in United Kingdom waters[12], may be detained until the certificate is so produced[13].

1   As to the meaning of 'fishing vessel' see PARA 230 note 9.
2   As to the meaning of 'fishing vessel survey rules' see PARA 608.
3   As to the meaning of 'fishing vessel certificate' see PARA 609.
4   As to the meaning of 'fishing vessel construction and equipment provisions' see PARA 608 note 2.
5   Merchant Shipping Act 1995 s 125(1).
6   As to the meaning of 'contravention' see PARA 51 note 3.
7   See the Merchant Shipping Act 1995 s 125(2); and PARA 1113. As to the powers of inspectors appointed under s 256(6) (see PARA 46) to serve improvement notices or prohibition notices where s 125 and the provisions of any instrument of a legislative character having effect thereunder are being contravened, or where activities to which s 125 applies are carried on so as to involve serious personal injury or serious pollution, see PARA 46 et seq.
8   As to the meaning of 'United Kingdom fishing vessel' see PARA 230.

9   As to the appointment of officers of Revenue and Customs see INCOME TAXATION vol 58 (2014)
    PARA 33.
10 As to the Secretary of State see PARA 36.
11 Ie any certificate required by the Merchant Shipping Act 1995 Pt V Ch II (ss 121–127) (see
    PARA 607 et seq): see s 125(3) (amended by the Merchant Shipping and Maritime Security Act
    1997 s 9, Sch 1 para 3; and by virtue of the Commissioners for Revenue and Customs Act 2005
    s 50(1), (2), (7)).
12 As to the meaning of 'United Kingdom waters' see PARA 48 note 10.
13 Merchant Shipping Act 1995 s 125(3) (as amended: see note 11). As to the detention of ships under
    the Merchant Shipping Act 1995 see PARA 1190.

**611. Requirement to give notice of alterations when a fishing vessel
certificate is in force.** Where a fishing vessel certificate[1] is in force in respect of
a fishing vessel[2] and:

(1)   the certificate shows compliance with requirements of the fishing vessel
        construction rules[3] and an alteration[4] is made in the vessel's hull,
        equipment or machinery which affects the efficiency thereof or the
        seaworthiness of the vessel[5]; or

(2)   the certificate shows compliance with requirements of the fishing vessel
        equipment provisions[6] and an alteration is made affecting the efficiency
        or completeness of the appliances or equipment which the vessel is
        required to carry by the fishing vessel equipment provisions[7],

the owner or skipper must, as soon as possible after the alteration is made, give
written notice containing full particulars of it to the Secretary of State[8] or, if the
certificate was issued by another person, to that person[9].

If the notice so required is not given as so required, the owner or skipper
commits an offence[10].

1   As to the meaning of 'fishing vessel certificate' see PARA 609.
2   As to the meaning of 'fishing vessel' see PARA 230 note 9.
3   As to the meaning of 'fishing vessel construction rules' see PARA 607.
4   For these purposes, 'alteration' in relation to anything includes the renewal of any part of it:
    Merchant Shipping Act 1995 s 126(3).
5   Merchant Shipping Act 1995 s 126(1)(a).
6   For these purposes, 'fishing vessel equipment provisions' means the provisions of the fishing vessel
    construction and equipment provisions other than the fishing vessel construction rules: Merchant
    Shipping Act 1995 s 126(3). As to the meaning of 'fishing vessel construction and equipment
    provisions' see PARA 608 note 2.
7   Merchant Shipping Act 1995 s 126(1)(b).
8   As to the Secretary of State see PARA 36.
9   Merchant Shipping Act 1995 s 126(1). As to the service of documents under the Merchant
    Shipping Act 1995 generally see s 291.
10 See the Merchant Shipping Act 1995 s 126(2); and PARA 1114.
        As to the powers of inspectors appointed under s 256(6) (see PARA 46) to serve improvement
    notices or prohibition notices where s 126 and the provisions of any instrument of a legislative
    character having effect thereunder are being contravened, or where activities to which s 126
    applies are carried on so as to involve serious personal injury or serious pollution, see PARA 46 et
    seq.

D.   VESSELS IN COMMERCIAL USE FOR SPORT OR PLEASURE

**612. Vessels to which the provisions regulating commercial use for sport
or pleasure apply.** The Merchant Shipping (Vessels in Commercial Use for Sport
or Pleasure) Regulations 1998[1] apply to:

(1)   any vessel used for sport or pleasure which is not a pleasure vessel[2];
(2)   United Kingdom vessels wherever they may be[3]; and
(3)   other vessels operating from United Kingdom ports whilst in United
        Kingdom waters[4].

The regulations do not apply to vessels carrying more than 12 passengers[5].

For these purposes, 'pleasure vessel' means:

(a)   any vessel which at the time it is being used is: (i) (in the case of a vessel wholly owned by an individual or individuals) used only for the sport or pleasure of the owner or the immediate family[6] or friends of the owner, or (in the case of a vessel owned by a body corporate) used only for sport or pleasure and where the persons on board the vessel are employees or officers of the body corporate, or their immediate family or friends[7]; and (ii) on a voyage or excursion which is one for which the owner does not receive money for or in connection with operating the vessel or carrying any person, other than as a contribution to the direct expenses of the operation of the vessel incurred during the voyage or excursion[8]; or

(b)   any vessel wholly owned by or on behalf of a members' club formed for the purpose of sport or pleasure which, at the time it is being used, is used only for the sport or pleasure of members of that club or their immediate family, and for the use of which any charges levied are paid into club funds and applied for the general use of the club[9]; and

(c)   in the case of any vessel referred to in head (a) or head (b) above, no other payments are made by or on behalf of users of the vessel, other than by the owner[10].

1   Ie the Merchant Shipping (Vessels in Commercial Use for Sport or Pleasure) Regulations 1998, SI 1998/2771 (see PARA 613 et seq): see reg 3(1).
2   Merchant Shipping (Vessels in Commercial Use for Sport or Pleasure) Regulations 1998, SI 1998/2771, reg 3(1).
3   Merchant Shipping (Vessels in Commercial Use for Sport or Pleasure) Regulations 1998, SI 1998/2771, reg 3(2)(a).
4   Merchant Shipping (Vessels in Commercial Use for Sport or Pleasure) Regulations 1998, SI 1998/2771, reg 3(2)(b).
5   Merchant Shipping (Vessels in Commercial Use for Sport or Pleasure) Regulations 1998, SI 1998/2771, reg 3(3).
6   For the purposes of this definition, 'immediate family' means, in relation to an individual, the spouse or civil partner of the individual, and a relative of the individual or the individual's spouse or civil partner, where 'relative' means brother, sister, ancestor or lineal descendant: Merchant Shipping (Vessels in Commercial Use for Sport or Pleasure) Regulations 1998, SI 1998/2771, reg 2(1) (definition amended by SI 2005/2114).
7   Merchant Shipping (Vessels in Commercial Use for Sport or Pleasure) Regulations 1998, SI 1998/2771, reg 2(1)(a)(i).
8   Merchant Shipping (Vessels in Commercial Use for Sport or Pleasure) Regulations 1998, SI 1998/2771, reg 2(1)(a)(ii).
9   Merchant Shipping (Vessels in Commercial Use for Sport or Pleasure) Regulations 1998, SI 1998/2771, reg 2(1)(b).
10 Merchant Shipping (Vessels in Commercial Use for Sport or Pleasure) Regulations 1998, SI 1998/2771, reg 2(1)(c).

613. Large commercial vessels to comply with the applicable safety code of practice. Large commercial vessels[1] must comply with the provisions of the Code of Practice for the Safety of Large Commercial Sailing and Motor Vessels[2]. Certain statutory instruments[3] do not apply to a vessel which has been examined, and in respect of which appropriate certificates have been issued, in accordance with the Code of Practice[4]. Where a vessel has been so examined and appropriate certificates issued, the vessel must not proceed or attempt to proceed to sea[5] unless:

(1)   the certificates are currently in force[6]; and

(2)   the vessel complies with the applicable requirements of the Code of
        Practice (including any requirements as to operation, manning and
        maintenance)[7].

1   As to the vessels generally to which the Merchant Shipping (Vessels in Commercial Use for Sport
    or Pleasure) Regulations 1998, SI 1998/2771, apply see PARA 612. Regulation 4 applies only to
    large vessels: reg 4(1)(a). For these purposes, 'large vessel' means a vessel which is not a small
    vessel, and 'small vessel' means a vessel of less than 24 metres in load line length or (in the case of
    a vessel the keel of which was laid or which was at a similar stage of construction before 21 July
    1968) less than 150 tons: reg 2(1). For the purposes of this definition, 'load line length' means (by
    virtue of reg 2(1)) the greater of the following distances (measured at and along the waterline):
        (1)   the distance between the foreside of the stem and the axis of the rudder stock; or
        (2)   a distance measured from the foreside of the stem, being 96% of the distance between
                that point and the aft side of the stern.
    The waterline referred to in this definition must be at 85% of the least moulded depth of the
    vessel and, in the case of a vessel having a rake of keel, the waterline must be parallel to the
    designed waterline: see reg 2(1). For these purposes, 'similar stage of construction' means (by
    virtue of reg 2(1)) a stage at which:
        (a)   construction identifiable with a specific vessel begins; and
        (b)   assembly of that vessel, comprising at least 1% of the estimated mass of all structural
                material has commenced; and 'tons' means gross tons, measured in accordance with the
                regulations for measuring tonnage which were in force on 20 July 1968.
    As to the tonnage regulations in force currently see PARA 248 et seq.
2   Merchant Shipping (Vessels in Commercial Use for Sport or Pleasure) Regulations 1998, SI
    1998/2771, reg 4(1)(b), (2). Accordingly, any provision of the Code of Practice expressed in the
    conditional (ie 'should') is a requirement: reg 4(2). References to Codes of Practice in the Merchant
    Shipping (Vessels in Commercial Use for Sport or Pleasure) Regulations 1998, SI 1998/2771, are
    references to the Codes of those names published (or treated as published) by the Maritime and
    Coastguard Agency, and include any document amending the same which the Secretary of State
    considers relevant from time to time: reg 2(2). 'Maritime and Coastguard Agency' means the
    Maritime and Coastguard Agency ('MCA'), an executive agency of the Department for Transport,
    which is responsible throughout the United Kingdom for implementing HM government's
    maritime safety policy: see reg 2(1). As to the Secretary of State see PARA 36; and as to the
    Maritime and Coastguard Agency generally see PARA 57. As to the penalties that apply to the
    contravention of any of the requirements set out in the Merchant Shipping (Vessels in Commercial
    Use for Sport or Pleasure) Regulations 1998, SI 1998/2771, see PARA 1109.
3   Ie the statutory instruments listed in the Merchant Shipping (Vessels in Commercial Use for Sport
    or Pleasure) Regulations 1998, SI 1998/2771, reg 4(3), Sch 1 (Sch 1 amended by SI 2016/353),
    which are:
        (1)   the Merchant Shipping (Cargo Ship Construction) Regulations 1997, SI 1997/1509 (as
                to which see PARA 602);
        (2)   the Merchant Shipping (Fire Protection: Small Ships) Regulations 1998, SI 1998/1011
                (as to which see PARA 633);
        (3)   the Merchant Shipping (Fire Protection: Large Ships) Regulations 1998, SI 1998/1012
                (as to which see PARA 633);
        (4)   the Merchant Shipping (Radio Installations) Regulations 1998, SI 1998/2070 (as to
                which see PARA 636);
        (5)   the Merchant Shipping (Load Line) Regulations 1998, SI 1998/2241 (as to which see
                PARA 660 et seq);
        (6)   the Merchant Shipping (Marine Equipment) Regulations 1999, SI 1999/1957 (revoked:
                see now the Merchant Shipping (Marine Equipment) Regulations 2016, SI 2016/1025;
                and PARA 638);
        (7)   the Merchant Shipping (Life-Saving Appliances For Ships Other Than Ships Of Classes
                III To VI(A)) Regulations 1999, SI 1999/2721 (as to which see PARA 639);
        (8)   the Merchant Shipping (Safety of Navigation) Regulations 2002, SI 2002/1473 (as to
                which see PARA 634);
        (9)   the Merchant Shipping (Maritime Labour Convention) (Minimum Requirements for
                Seafarers etc) Regulations 2014, SI 2014/1613 (see PARA 448);
        (10)   the Merchant Shipping (Survey and Certification) Regulations 2015, SI 2015/508 (as to
                which see PARA 604); and
        (11)   the Merchant Shipping (Standards of Training, Certification and Watchkeeping)
                Regulations 2015, SI 2015/782 (see PARAS 503–504).
4   Merchant Shipping (Vessels in Commercial Use for Sport or Pleasure) Regulations 1998, SI
    1998/2771, reg 4(3).

5   Any reference in the Merchant Shipping (Vessels in Commercial Use for Sport or Pleasure) Regulations 1998, SI 1998/2771, to 'proceeding to sea' includes a reference to proceeding on a voyage or excursion that does not involve going to sea: reg 2(3).
6   Merchant Shipping (Vessels in Commercial Use for Sport or Pleasure) Regulations 1998, SI 1998/2771, reg 4(4)(a).
7   Merchant Shipping (Vessels in Commercial Use for Sport or Pleasure) Regulations 1998, SI 1998/2771, reg 4(4)(b).

614. Small commercial vessels to comply with the applicable safety codes of practice.

Certain statutory instruments[1] do not apply to a small commercial vessel[2] which has been examined, and in respect of which a certificate has been issued, in accordance with the applicable Code of Practice[3], or to a vessel which is operating under the phase-in arrangements of the Code of Practice[4].

Where a vessel has been so examined and a small commercial vessel certificate issued, the vessel must not proceed or attempt to proceed to sea[5] unless:

(1)   the certificate is currently in force[6];
(2)   the vessel complies with the requirements of the relevant Code of Practice (including any requirements as to operation, manning and maintenance)[7]; and
(3)   the certificate is displayed in some conspicuous place on board or, if this is not reasonably practicable, is available for inspection on board[8].

Where a vessel is operating under the phase-in arrangements of a Code of Practice, it must not proceed or attempt to proceed to sea unless it meets the requirements for phase-in which are specified in the Code of Practice[9].

1   Ie the statutory instruments listed in the Merchant Shipping (Vessels in Commercial Use for Sport or Pleasure) Regulations 1998, SI 1998/2771, reg 5(3), Sch 2 (Sch 2 substituted by SI 2016/353), which are:
      (1)   the Merchant Shipping (Fire Protection: Small Ships) Regulations 1998, SI 1998/1011 (as to which see PARA 633);
      (2)   the Merchant Shipping (Load Line) Regulations 1998, SI 1998/2241 (as to which see PARA 660 et seq);
      (3)   the Merchant Shipping (Marine Equipment) Regulations 1999, SI 1999/1957 (revoked: see now the Merchant Shipping (Marine Equipment) Regulations 2016, SI 2016/1025);
      (4)   the Merchant Shipping (Life-Saving Appliances for Ships Other Than Ships Of Classes III To VI(A)) Regulations 1999, SI 1999/2721 (as to which see PARA 639);
      (5)   the Merchant Shipping (Safety of Navigation) Regulations 2002, SI 2002/1473 (as to which see PARA 634);
      (6)   the Merchant Shipping (Fire Protection) Regulations 2003, SI 2003/2950;
      (7)   the Merchant Shipping (Maritime Labour Convention) (Minimum Requirements for Seafarers etc) Regulations 2014, SI 2014/1613 (see PARA 448);
      (8)   the Merchant Shipping (Survey and Certification) Regulations 2015, SI 2015/508 (as to which see PARA 604); and
      (9)   the Merchant Shipping (Standards of Training, Certification and Watchkeeping) Regulations 2015, SI 2015/782 (see PARAS 503–504).
2   As to the vessels generally to which the Merchant Shipping (Vessels in Commercial Use for Sport or Pleasure) Regulations 1998, SI 1998/2771, apply see PARA 612. Regulation 5 applies only to small vessels: reg 5(1). As to the meaning of 'small vessel' see PARA 613 note 1.
3   For these purposes, 'Code of Practice' means 'The Safety of Small Commercial Sailing Vessels—A Code of Practice', or 'The Safety of Small Commercial Motor Vessels—A Code of Practice' or 'The Safety of Small Vessels in Commercial Use for Sport or Pleasure Operating from a Nominated Departure Point—A Code of Practice': see the Merchant Shipping (Vessels in Commercial Use for Sport or Pleasure) Regulations 1998, SI 1998/2771, reg 5(2)(a) (amended by SI 2000/482). As to references to Codes of Practice in the Merchant Shipping (Vessels in Commercial Use for Sport or Pleasure) Regulations 1998, SI 1998/2771, see PARA 613 note 2.
4   Merchant Shipping (Vessels in Commercial Use for Sport or Pleasure) Regulations 1998, SI 1998/2771, reg 5(3). For these purposes, 'phase-in arrangements of the Code of Practice' means such arrangements set out in the relevant paragraphs of a Code of Practice: see reg 5(2)(b). As to the penalties that apply to the contravention of any of the requirements set out in the Merchant Shipping (Vessels in Commercial Use for Sport or Pleasure) Regulations 1998, SI 1998/2771, see PARA 1109.

5   As to references in the Merchant Shipping (Vessels in Commercial Use for Sport or Pleasure)
    Regulations 1998, SI 1998/2771, to 'proceeding to sea' see PARA 613 note 5.
6   Merchant Shipping (Vessels in Commercial Use for Sport or Pleasure) Regulations 1998, SI
    1998/2771, reg 5(4)(a).
7   Merchant Shipping (Vessels in Commercial Use for Sport or Pleasure) Regulations 1998, SI
    1998/2771, reg 5(4)(b). For this purpose, any provision of the Code expressed in the conditional
    (ie 'should') is a requirement: see reg 5(4)(b).
8   Merchant Shipping (Vessels in Commercial Use for Sport or Pleasure) Regulations 1998, SI
    1998/2771, reg 5(4)(c).
9   Merchant Shipping (Vessels in Commercial Use for Sport or Pleasure) Regulations 1998, SI
    1998/2771, reg 5(5).

615. Power to permit equivalent provision to be made outside the regulations and codes.

Where the Merchant Shipping (Vessels in Commercial Use for Sport or Pleasure) Regulations 1998[1] or a Code of Practice[2] requires that a particular piece of equipment or machinery must be provided or carried in a vessel[3], or that any particular provision must be made, the Secretary of State[4] must permit any other piece of equipment or machinery to be provided or carried or any other provision to be made in that vessel if he is satisfied by trial thereof or otherwise that such other fitting, material, appliance or apparatus (or type thereof) or provision is at least as effective as that required by the Regulations[5] or the Code of Practice[6].

For these purposes, the results of verifications and tests carried out by the bodies and laboratories of other EEA states[7] offering suitable and satisfactory guarantees of technical and professional competence and independence are to be accepted[8].

1   Ie the Merchant Shipping (Vessels in Commercial Use for Sport or Pleasure) Regulations 1998, SI
    1998/2771 (see PARA 612 et seq): see reg 6.
2   Ie the safety codes of practice that apply to large commercial vessels (see PARA 613) and to small
    commercial vessels (see PARA 614).
3   Ie a vessel to which the Merchant Shipping (Vessels in Commercial Use for Sport or Pleasure)
    Regulations 1998, SI 1998/2771 apply (as to which see PARA 612): see reg 6.
4   As to the Secretary of State see PARA 36.
5   Ie by the Merchant Shipping (Vessels in Commercial Use for Sport or Pleasure) Regulations 1998,
    SI 1998/2771 (see PARA 612 et seq): see reg 6.
6   Merchant Shipping (Vessels in Commercial Use for Sport or Pleasure) Regulations 1998, SI
    1998/2771, reg 6.
7   As to the meanings of 'EEA state' and 'EEA Agreement' see the Interpretation Act 1978 Sch 1; and
    STATUTES AND LEGISLATIVE PROCESS vol 96 (2012) PARA 1210 (definition applied by the
    Merchant Shipping (Vessels in Commercial Use for Sport or Pleasure) Regulations 1998, SI
    1998/2771, reg 2(1) (amended by SI 2014/1614)).
8   Merchant Shipping (Vessels in Commercial Use for Sport or Pleasure) Regulations 1998, SI
    1998/2771, reg 7.

616. Offences and power to detain.

Contravention of any of the provisions governing the safety requirements that are applicable to commercially operated vessels[1] is an offence by the owner and master of the vessel[2]. In any case where a vessel does not so comply[3], the vessel is liable to be detained[4].

1   Ie contravention of any of the Merchant Shipping (Vessels in Commercial Use for Sport or
    Pleasure) Regulations 1998, SI 1998/2771 (see PARA 612 et seq): see reg 8(1); and PARA 1109.
2   See the Merchant Shipping (Vessels in Commercial Use for Sport or Pleasure) Regulations 1998,
    SI 1998/2771, reg 8(1); and PARA 1109.
3   Ie with the Merchant Shipping (Vessels in Commercial Use for Sport or Pleasure) Regulations
    1998, SI 1998/2771 (see PARA 612 et seq): see reg 9.
4   Merchant Shipping (Vessels in Commercial Use for Sport or Pleasure) Regulations 1998, SI
    1998/2771, reg 9. The Merchant Shipping Act 1995 s 284 (enforcing detention of ships) (see
    PARA 1190) has effect in relation to the vessel, subject to the modification that, for the words 'this
    Act' wherever they appear, there are to be substituted 'the Merchant Shipping (Vessels in
    Commercial Use for Sport or Pleasure) Regulations 1998': see reg 9.

E.   HIGH SPEED CRAFT

617.   Application of provisions. The Merchant Shipping (High Speed Craft) Regulations 2004[1] apply to every high speed craft[2] which meets all of the following criteria[3]:

(1)   it is either a United Kingdom high speed craft[4] or a non-United Kingdom high speed craft in United Kingdom waters[5];

(2)   it is constructed[6] on or after 1 January 1996, or was constructed before 1 January 1996 and repairs, alterations or modifications, or outfitting relating to it, of a major character are made on or after 1 January 1996[7];

(3)   it is (wholly or partly) sea-going or operating in any Category A, B, C or D waters[8]; and

(4)   it is:

(a)   a passenger craft[9] which does not proceed in the course of its voyage[10] more than four hours at operational speed[11] from a place of refuge[12] when fully laden[13];

(b)   a craft which is carrying passengers for hire or reward which is not a passenger craft and which does not proceed in the course of its voyage more than four hours at operational speed from a place of refuge when fully laden[14];

(c)   a cargo craft[15] of 500 gross tonnage[16] or more which does not proceed in the course of its voyage more than eight hours at operational speed from a place of refuge when fully laden[17]; or

(d)   a cargo craft of less than 500 gross tonnage which is carrying cargo for hire or reward and which does not proceed in the course of its voyage more than eight hours at operational speed from a place of refuge when fully laden[18].

The Merchant Shipping (High Speed Craft) Regulations 2004[19] do not apply to a high speed craft which is[20]:

(i)   a pleasure craft[21];

(ii)   a warship, naval auxiliary or other craft owned or operated by a state and used, for the time being, only on government non-commercial service[22];

(iii)   a craft not propelled by mechanical means[23];

(iv)   a wooden craft of primitive build[24];

(v)   a fishing craft[25];

(vi)   a craft which has been duly examined, and in respect of which appropriate certificates have been issued, in accordance with the safety codes of practice which are applicable to large and small commercial vessels[26];

(vii)   a craft which has been duly surveyed, certified and maintained in accordance with, and which complies with, the provisions of the Merchant Shipping (Small Workboats and Pilot Boats) Regulations 1998[27]; and

(viii)   a passenger ship[28] engaged on domestic voyages in sea areas of class B, C or D.

1   Ie the Merchant Shipping (High Speed Craft) Regulations 2004, SI 2004/302 (see PARA 618 et seq): see reg 3(1).

2   For these purposes, 'high speed craft' means a craft capable of a maximum speed in metres per second (m/s) equal to or exceeding 3.7 0.1667, where equals the volume of displacement corresponding to the design waterline (m), excluding craft the hull of which is supported clear above the water surface in non displacement mode by aerodynamic forces generated by ground effect; and 'craft' means ships and hovercraft: Merchant Shipping (High Speed Craft) Regulations 2004, SI 2004/302, reg 2(1).

3   Merchant Shipping (High Speed Craft) Regulations 2004, SI 2004/302, reg 3(1).

4   For these purposes, 'United Kingdom high speed craft' means a high speed craft which is a United Kingdom ship or a hovercraft registered in the United Kingdom: Merchant Shipping (High Speed Craft) Regulations 2004, SI 2004/302, reg 2(1). As to the meaning of 'United Kingdom' see PARA 16 note 3.

5   Merchant Shipping (High Speed Craft) Regulations 2004, SI 2004/302, reg 3(1)(a).

6   For these purposes, 'constructed' means a craft the keel of which is laid or which is at a similar stage of construction; and 'similar stage of construction' means a stage at which construction identifiable with a specific craft begins and assembly of that craft has commenced comprising at least 50 tonnes or 3% of the estimated mass of all structural material, whichever is the less: Merchant Shipping (High Speed Craft) Regulations 2004, SI 2004/302, reg 2(1).

7   Merchant Shipping (High Speed Craft) Regulations 2004, SI 2004/302, reg 3(1)(b).

8   Merchant Shipping (High Speed Craft) Regulations 2004, SI 2004/302, reg 3(1)(c). For these purposes, 'Category A, B, C or D waters' means waters specified as such in Merchant Shipping Notice 1776(M): see the Merchant Shipping (High Speed Craft) Regulations 2004, SI 2004/302, reg 2(1). 'Merchant Shipping Notice' means a notice described as such and issued by the Maritime and Coastguard Agency (an executive agency of the Department for Transport), and any reference to a particular Merchant Shipping Notice includes reference to any such document amending or replacing that Notice which is considered by the Secretary of State to be relevant from time to time: see reg 2(1). Merchant Shipping Notice 1776(M) (Categorisation of Waters: Notice to Owners, Operators and Masters) (March 2003) is published by the Maritime and Coastguard Agency and it categorises United Kingdom waters which are not regarded as 'sea' for the purposes of Merchant Shipping legislation (excepting marine pollution). As to the Secretary of State see PARA 36; and as to the Maritime and Coastguard Agency see PARA 57.

9   For these purposes, 'passenger craft' means craft carrying more than 12 passengers: Merchant Shipping (High Speed Craft) Regulations 2004, SI 2004/302, reg 2(1).

10   For these purposes, 'voyage' includes an excursion: Merchant Shipping (High Speed Craft) Regulations 2004, SI 2004/302, reg 2(1). References to proceeding to sea or on a voyage over water include proceeding on or over land, so far as such proceeding is part of that voyage: reg 2(4).

11   For these purposes, 'operational speed' means 90% of the maximum speed of which the craft is capable: Merchant Shipping (High Speed Craft) Regulations 2004, SI 2004/302, reg 2(1).

12   For these purposes, 'place of refuge' means any naturally or artificially sheltered area which may be used as a shelter by craft under conditions likely to endanger its safety: Merchant Shipping (High Speed Craft) Regulations 2004, SI 2004/302, reg 2(1).

13   Merchant Shipping (High Speed Craft) Regulations 2004, SI 2004/302, reg 3(1)(d)(i).

14   Merchant Shipping (High Speed Craft) Regulations 2004, SI 2004/302, reg 3(1)(d)(ii).

15   For these purposes, 'cargo craft' means a high speed craft, other than a passenger craft, which is capable of maintaining the main functions and safety systems of unaffected spaces after damage in any one compartment on board: Merchant Shipping (High Speed Craft) Regulations 2004, SI 2004/302, reg 2(1).

16   For these purposes, 'gross tonnage' means gross tonnage within the meaning of the Merchant Shipping (Tonnage) Regulations 1997, SI 1997/1510, reg 6 (as to which see PARA 248 et seq): Merchant Shipping (High Speed Craft) Regulations 2004, SI 2004/302, reg 2(1).

17   Merchant Shipping (High Speed Craft) Regulations 2004, SI 2004/302, reg 3(1)(d)(iii).

18   Merchant Shipping (High Speed Craft) Regulations 2004, SI 2004/302, reg 3(1)(d)(iv).

19   Ie the Merchant Shipping (High Speed Craft) Regulations 2004, SI 2004/302 (see PARA 618 et seq): see reg 3(2).

20   Merchant Shipping (High Speed Craft) Regulations 2004, SI 2004/302, reg 3(2).

21   Merchant Shipping (High Speed Craft) Regulations 2004, SI 2004/302, reg 3(2)(a). For these purposes, 'pleasure craft' means:

    (1)   any craft which is wholly owned by an individual or individuals and used only for the sport or pleasure of the owner or the immediate family or friends of the owner (or is owned by a body corporate and used only for the sport or pleasure of employees or officers of the body corporate, or their immediate family or friends) and is on a voyage which is one for which the owner does not receive money for or in connection with operating the craft or carrying any person, other than as a contribution to the direct expenses of the operation of the craft incurred during the voyage; or

    (2)   any craft which is wholly owned by or on behalf of a members' club formed for the purpose of sport or pleasure which, at the time it is being used, is used only for the sport or pleasure of members of that club or their immediate family; and for the use of which any charges levied are paid into club funds and applied for the general use of the club,

and no payments other than those mentioned are made by or on behalf of users of the craft, other than by the owner: reg 2(1). For the purposes of this definition, 'immediate family' means in relation to an individual, the spouse or civil partner of the individual, and a brother, sister, ancestor or lineal descendant of that individual or that individual's spouse or civil partner: see reg 2(1) (amended by SI 2005/2114). Where a high speed craft is managed by a person other than its owner (whether on behalf of the owner or some other person, or on his own behalf), a reference in the Merchant Shipping (High Speed Craft) Regulations 2004, SI 2004/302, to the owner must be construed as including a reference to that person: reg 2(1), (3).

22 Merchant Shipping (High Speed Craft) Regulations 2004, SI 2004/302, reg 3(2)(b).
23 Merchant Shipping (High Speed Craft) Regulations 2004, SI 2004/302, reg 3(2)(c).
24 Merchant Shipping (High Speed Craft) Regulations 2004, SI 2004/302, reg 3(2)(d).
25 Merchant Shipping (High Speed Craft) Regulations 2004, SI 2004/302, reg 3(2)(e).
26 Merchant Shipping (High Speed Craft) Regulations 2004, SI 2004/302, reg 3(2)(f). The text refers to examinations and certificates issued in accordance with one of the following documents referred to in the Merchant Shipping (Vessels in Commercial Use for Sport or Pleasure) Regulations 1998, SI 1998/2771, reg 4 (as to which see PARA 613) and reg 5 (as to which see PARA 614), or in accordance with any document amending one or more of those documents which is considered by the Secretary of State to be relevant from time to time (Merchant Shipping (High Speed Craft) Regulations 2004, SI 2004/302, reg 3(2)(f)), namely:
   (1)   the Code of Practice for Safety of Large Commercial Sailing and Motor Vessels (Merchant Shipping (High Speed Craft) Regulations 2004, SI 2004/302, reg 3(2)(f)(i));
   (2)   the Safety of Small Commercial Sailing Vessels – A Code of Practice (Merchant Shipping (High Speed Craft) Regulations 2004, SI 2004/302, reg 3(2)(f)(ii));
   (3)   the Safety of Small Commercial Motor Vessels – A Code of Practice (Merchant Shipping (High Speed Craft) Regulations 2004, SI 2004/302, reg 3(2)(f)(iii));
   (4)   the Safety of Small Vessels in Commercial Use for Sport or Pleasure Operating from a Nominated Departure Point - A Code of Practice (Merchant Shipping (High Speed Craft) Regulations 2004, SI 2004/302, reg 3(2)(f)(iv)).
27 Merchant Shipping (High Speed Craft) Regulations 2004, SI 2004/302, reg 3(2)(g). The text refers to a craft which has been surveyed, certified and maintained in accordance with, and which complies with, the Merchant Shipping (Small Workboats and Pilot Boats) Regulations 1998, SI 1998/1609, reg 5 (as to which see PARA 602): see the Merchant Shipping (High Speed Craft) Regulations 2004, SI 2004/302, reg 3(2)(g).
28 The text refers to a passenger ship when the displacement of that vessel corresponding to the design waterline is less than 500m3 and the maximum speed of that vessel, as defined in paragraph 1.4.30 of the High Speed Craft Code 1994 or, where applicable, paragraph 1.4.37 of the High Speed Craft Code 2000, is less than 20 knots: see the Merchant Shipping (High Speed Craft) Regulations 2004, SI 2004/302, reg 3(2)(h) (added by SI 2012/2636). As to the High Speed Craft Codes 1994 and 2000 see PARA 619 note 3.

618. Power to permit equivalent provision to be made outside the high speed craft regulations.

The Secretary of State[1] may grant exemptions from all or any of the provisions of the Merchant Shipping (High Speed Craft) Regulations 2004[2] (as may be specified in the exemption) for individual cases or classes of cases on such terms (if any) as he may specify, if he is satisfied that[3]:

   (1)   compliance with such provision is either impracticable or unreasonable in that case or class of cases[4]; and

   (2)   the exemption is subject to such conditions and limitations as will provide a level of safety equivalent to that provided by the provision or provisions from which exemption is being granted[5].

The Secretary of State may, on giving reasonable notice, alter or cancel any exemption so granted[6].

Any exemption so granted[7] and any such alteration or cancellation[8] must be given in writing and must specify the date on which it takes effect and the conditions (if any) on which it is given[9].

1 As to the Secretary of State see PARA 36.
2 Ie the Merchant Shipping (High Speed Craft) Regulations 2004, SI 2004/302 (see PARAS 617, 619 et seq): see reg 4(1).
3 Merchant Shipping (High Speed Craft) Regulations 2004, SI 2004/302, reg 4(1).
4 Merchant Shipping (High Speed Craft) Regulations 2004, SI 2004/302, reg 4(1)(a).
5 Merchant Shipping (High Speed Craft) Regulations 2004, SI 2004/302, reg 4(1)(b).
6 Merchant Shipping (High Speed Craft) Regulations 2004, SI 2004/302, reg 4(2). The text refers to any exemption granted under reg 4(1) (see the text and notes 1–5): see reg 4(2).
7 Ie under the Merchant Shipping (High Speed Craft) Regulations 2004, SI 2004/302, reg 4(1) (see the text and notes 1–5): see reg 4(3).

8 Ie under the Merchant Shipping (High Speed Craft) Regulations 2004, SI 2004/302, reg 4(2) (see the text and note 6): see reg 4(3).
9 Merchant Shipping (High Speed Craft) Regulations 2004, SI 2004/302, reg 4(3).

619. Secretary of State's power to grant approvals. The Secretary of State[1] may as respects a United Kingdom high speed craft[2] grant an approval for any thing in either the High Speed Craft Code 1994[3] or the High Speed Craft Code 2000[4] which requires the approval of the Government of the State whose flag the craft is entitled to fly[5]. The Secretary of State may, on giving reasonable notice, alter or cancel any approval so given[6].

Any approval so given[7] and any such alteration or cancellation[8] must be given in writing and must specify the date on which it takes effect and the conditions (if any) on which it is given[9].

1 As to the Secretary of State see PARA 36.
2 As to the meaning of 'United Kingdom high speed craft' see PARA 617 note 4. As to the meaning of 'United Kingdom' see PARA 16 note 3.
3 For these purposes, 'High Speed Craft Code 1994' means the International Code of Safety for High Speed Craft adopted by the Maritime Safety Committee of the International Maritime Organisation by resolution MSC36(63) of 20 May 1994 and amended by resolution MSC119(74), MSC 174(79), MSC 221(82) and MSC 259(84) and includes any document amending it which is considered by the Secretary of State to be relevant from time to time and is specified in a Merchant Shipping Notice: Merchant Shipping (High Speed Craft) Regulations 2004, SI 2004/302, reg 2(1) (definition substituted by SI 2012/2636). As to the meaning of 'Merchant Shipping Notice' see PARA 617 note 8.
4 For these purposes, 'High Speed Craft Code 2000' means (by virtue of the Merchant Shipping (High Speed Craft) Regulations 2004, SI 2004/302, reg 2(1) (definition substituted by SI 2012/2636)) the International Code of Safety for High Speed Craft 2000 adopted by the Maritime Safety Committee of the International Maritime Organisation by resolution MSC97(73) of 5 December 2000 and amended by resolutions MSC 175(79), MSC 260(84), MSC 27(85) and includes any document amending it which is considered by the Secretary of State to be relevant from time to time and is specified in a Merchant Shipping Notice; and
    (1) in relation to vessels built on or after 1 July 2002 but before 1 July 2008 it includes the amendments contained in paragraphs 1.2.2, 1.81, 1.9.1, 2.7.2, 13.8.2, and 14.15.10 of MSC 222(82); and
    (2) in relation to vessels built on or after 1 July 2008, it includes all the amendments contained in MSC 222(82).
5 Merchant Shipping (High Speed Craft) Regulations 2004, SI 2004/302, reg 5(1).
6 Merchant Shipping (High Speed Craft) Regulations 2004, SI 2004/302, reg 5(2). The text refers to any approval given under reg 5(1) (see the text and notes 1–5): see reg 5(2).
7 Ie under the Merchant Shipping (High Speed Craft) Regulations 2004, SI 2004/302, reg 5(1) (see the text and notes 1–5): see reg 5(3).
8 Ie under the Merchant Shipping (High Speed Craft) Regulations 2004, SI 2004/302, reg 5(2) (see the text and note 6): see reg 5(3).
9 Merchant Shipping (High Speed Craft) Regulations 2004, SI 2004/302, reg 5(3).

620. The high speed craft codes. A relevant high speed craft[1] which was constructed[2] on or after 1 January 1996 but before 1 July 2002 (or which was constructed before 1 January 1996 and to which repairs, alterations or modifications, or outfitting relating to it, of a major character were made on or after 1 January 1996 but before 1 July 2002) must comply with the High Speed Craft Code 1994[3], and the requirements specified in Merchant Shipping Notice 1672(M+F) (which relates to ship inspections and survey organisations) relevant to a high speed craft of its description[4].

A relevant high speed craft[5] which was constructed on or after 1 July 2002 (or which was constructed before 1 July 2002 and to which repairs, alterations or modifications, or outfitting relating to it, of a major character are made on or after 1 July 2002) must comply with the High Speed Craft Code 2000[6], and the requirements specified in Merchant Shipping Notice 1672(M+F) relevant to a high speed craft of its description[7].

United Kingdom high speed craft[8] and other high speed craft operating on a scheduled service from any port in the United Kingdom to any port in another member state (or vice versa) or operating on a voyage which is not an international voyage must[9] comply with the statutory requirements relating to marine equipment[10].

A relevant high speed craft[11] must, alternatively or additionally (as the case may be) to these requirements[12], comply with such requirements as apply in relation to a craft of its description which:

(1)   relate to the High Speed Craft Code 1994 or the High Speed Craft Code 2000 or to amendments from time to time of one of those Codes[13];

(2)   relate to all or any of the health and safety purposes in relation to which the Secretary of State may make regulations[14], which is considered by the Secretary of State to be relevant from time to time[15]; and

(3)   are specified as alternative or additional requirements in a Merchant Shipping Notice and relate to all or any of the purposes mentioned in head (2) above[16].

1   Ie a high speed craft to which the Merchant Shipping (High Speed Craft) Regulations 2004, SI 2004/302, apply (see PARA 617): see reg 6(1). Regulation 6(1) is subject to reg 6(2) (as to which see the text and notes 5–7) and reg 6(4) (as to which see the text and notes 8–10): see reg 6(1). As to the meaning of 'high speed craft' see PARA 617 note 2. As to offences under the Merchant Shipping (High Speed Craft) Regulations 2004, SI 2004/302, see PARA 1110.
2   As to the meaning of 'constructed' for these purposes see PARA 617 note 6.
3   Merchant Shipping (High Speed Craft) Regulations 2004, SI 2004/302, reg 6(1)(a). Having been made mandatory under reg 6, the language of the High Speed Craft Code 1994 is to be construed accordingly, and in particular 'should' must be construed as 'shall': reg 2(2). As to the meaning of 'High Speed Craft Code 1994' see PARA 619 note 3.
4   Merchant Shipping (High Speed Craft) Regulations 2004, SI 2004/302, reg 6(1)(b). The requirements specified in Merchant Shipping Notice 1672(M+F) are, in relation to craft to which reg 6(1) applies, approved standards relating to construction or maintenance relating to hull, machinery, electrical installations and control installations: reg 6(3)(a). As to the meaning of 'Merchant Shipping Notice' see PARA 617 note 8.
5   Ie a high speed craft to which the Merchant Shipping (High Speed Craft) Regulations 2004, SI 2004/302, apply (see PARA 617): see reg 6(2). Regulation 6(2) is subject to reg 6(4) (as to which see the text and notes 8–10): see reg 6(2).
6   Merchant Shipping (High Speed Craft) Regulations 2004, SI 2004/302, reg 6(2)(a). Having been made mandatory under reg 6, the language of the High Speed Craft Code 2000 is to be construed accordingly, and in particular 'should' must be construed as 'shall': reg 2(2). As to the meaning of 'High Speed Craft Code 2000' see PARA 619 note 4.
7   Merchant Shipping (High Speed Craft) Regulations 2004, SI 2004/302, reg 6(2)(b). The requirements specified in Merchant Shipping Notice 1672(M+F) are, in relation to craft to which reg 6(2) applies, requirements relating to hull, machinery, electrical installations and control installations which correspond to the requirements of the High Speed Craft Code 2000: reg 6(3)(b).
8   As to the meaning of 'United Kingdom high speed craft' see PARA 617 note 4. As to the meaning of 'United Kingdom' see PARA 16 note 3.
9   Ie in so far as it relates to equipment to which the Merchant Shipping (Marine Equipment) Regulations 2016, SI 2016/1957 (see PARA 638) apply: see the Merchant Shipping (High Speed Craft) Regulations 2004, SI 2004/302, reg 6(4).
10 Merchant Shipping (High Speed Craft) Regulations 2004, SI 2004/302, reg 6(4). The text refers to compliance with the requirements of the Merchant Shipping (Marine Equipment) Regulations 2016, SI 2016/1025 (see PARA 638): see the Merchant Shipping (High Speed Craft) Regulations 2004, SI 2004/302, reg 6(4) (amended by SI 2016/1025).
11 Ie a high speed craft to which the Merchant Shipping (High Speed Craft) Regulations 2004, SI 2004/302, apply (see PARA 617): see reg 6(5).
12 Ie the requirements set out in the Merchant Shipping (High Speed Craft) Regulations 2004, SI 2004/302, reg 6(1)–(4) (see the text and notes 1–10): see reg 6(5).
13 Merchant Shipping (High Speed Craft) Regulations 2004, SI 2004/302, reg 6(5)(a).

14 Ie all or any of the purposes set out in the Merchant Shipping Act 1995 s 85(1) (as to which see PARA 602 note 1): see the Merchant Shipping (High Speed Craft) Regulations 2004, SI 2004/302, reg 6(5)(b). As to the Secretary of State see PARA 36.
15 Merchant Shipping (High Speed Craft) Regulations 2004, SI 2004/302, reg 6(5)(b).
16 Merchant Shipping (High Speed Craft) Regulations 2004, SI 2004/302, reg 6(5)(c). The text refers to all or any of the purposes set out in the Merchant Shipping Act 1995 s 85(1): see the Merchant Shipping (High Speed Craft) Regulations 2004, SI 2004/302, reg 6(5)(c).

621. Safety requirements for persons with reduced mobility. In complying with the High Speed Craft Codes[1]:

(1)   a high speed craft[2] used for public transport and engaged on a voyage[3], in whole or in part in sea areas classified in accordance with Merchant Shipping Notice 1747(M)[4], which begins and ends in a port in the United Kingdom[5]; and

(2)   a United Kingdom high speed craft[6] used for public transport and engaged on a voyage, in whole or in part in classified sea areas[7], which begins and ends in ports within a member state other than the United Kingdom or begins and ends in ports within a state (other than the United Kingdom) which is an EEA state[8],

the keel of which was laid or which was at a similar stage of construction on or after 1 October 2004, must, where practicable, be constructed[9] and equipped, and display signs, based on the guidelines in Annex III to the EC Council Directive of 17 March 1998 on safety rules and standards for passenger ships[10].

However, in complying with the High Speed Craft Codes, a craft which falls within head (1) or head (2) above, the keel of which was laid or which was at a similar stage of construction before 1 October 2004 must, if undergoing modification, be constructed and equipped as respects that modification, and display signs as respects that modification, based on the guidelines in Annex III to the EC Council Directive of 17 March 1998 on safety rules and standards for passenger ships, only so far as is reasonable and practicable in economic terms[11].

The Secretary of State[12] must draw up a national action plan on how the guidelines in Annex III to the EC Council Directive of 17 March 1998 on safety rules and standards for passenger ships are to be applied to a high speed craft, the keel of which was laid or which was at a similar stage of construction before 1 October 2004 and which is used for public transport, as respects any modification of that craft[13].

1   Ie in complying with the Merchant Shipping (High Speed Craft) Regulations 2004, SI 2004/302, reg 6 (see PARA 620): see reg 7A(2) (reg 7A added by SI 2004/2883). As to offences under the Merchant Shipping (High Speed Craft) Regulations 2004, SI 2004/302, see PARA 1110.
2   As to the meaning of 'high speed craft' see PARA 617 note 2.
3   As to the meaning of 'voyage' see PARA 617 note 10.
4   As to the meaning of 'Merchant Shipping Notice' see PARA 617 note 8.
5   Merchant Shipping (High Speed Craft) Regulations 2004, SI 2004/302, reg 7A(1)(a) (as added: see note 1). As to the meaning of 'United Kingdom' see PARA 16 note 3.
6   As to the meaning of 'United Kingdom high speed craft' see PARA 617 note 4.
7   Ie sea areas classified in accordance with the Parliament and Council Directive (EC) 2009/45 (OJ L163, 25.6.2009, p 1) on safety rules and standards for passenger ships: see the Merchant Shipping (High Speed Craft) Regulations 2004, SI 2004/302, reg 7A(1)(b) (as added (see note 4); amended by SI 2012/2636).
8   Merchant Shipping (High Speed Craft) Regulations 2004, SI 2004/302, reg 7A(1)(b) (as added: see note 1). The text refers to a state which is a contracting party to the Agreement on the European Economic Area (Oporto, 2 May 1992; EC 7 (1992); Cm 2183) as adjusted by the Protocol (Brussels, 17 March 1993; EC 2 (1993); Cm 2183): see the Merchant Shipping (High Speed Craft) Regulations 2004, SI 2004/302, reg 7A(1)(b) (as so added).
9   As to the meaning of 'constructed' and 'similar stage of construction' for these purposes see PARA 617 note 6.
10 Merchant Shipping (High Speed Craft) Regulations 2004, SI 2004/302, reg 7A(2)(a) (as added: see note 1).

11 Merchant Shipping (High Speed Craft) Regulations 2004, SI 2004/302, reg 7A(2)(b) (as added: see note 1).
12 As to the Secretary of State see PARA 36.
13 Merchant Shipping (High Speed Craft) Regulations 2004, SI 2004/302, reg 7A(3) (as added: see note 1).

622. Risk assessment with reference to wash. A passage plan prepared in accordance with the High Speed Craft Code 1994[1] or the High Speed Craft Code 2000[2] (as applicable) must include a full risk assessment of the passage plan with respect to wash[3]. The risk assessment so required must:

(1) be carried out in accordance with generally recognised procedures for risk assessment[4];

(2) identify any likely areas of potentially hazardous wash, taking into account possible operating conditions and the classification of wash as sub-critical, critical or super-critical[5], and identify the operating restrictions necessary to reduce that potentially hazardous wash[6]; and

(3) be documented in the operating manual required by the High Speed Craft Code 1994 or the High Speed Craft Code 2000 (as applicable)[7].

1 As to the meaning of 'High Speed Craft Code 1994' see PARA 619 note 3. Having been made mandatory under the Merchant Shipping (High Speed Craft) Regulations 2004, SI 2004/302, reg 6 (see PARA 620), the language of the High Speed Craft Code 1994 is to be construed accordingly, and in particular 'should' must be construed as 'shall': see reg 2(2); and PARA 620 note 3.
2 As to the meaning of 'High Speed Craft Code 2000' see PARA 619 note 4. Having been made mandatory under the Merchant Shipping (High Speed Craft) Regulations 2004, SI 2004/302, reg 6 (see PARA 620), the language of the High Speed Craft Code 2000 is to be construed accordingly, and in particular 'should' must be construed as 'shall': see reg 2(2); and PARA 620 note 6.
3 Merchant Shipping (High Speed Craft) Regulations 2004, SI 2004/302, reg 7(1). 'Wash' is defined for these purposes by reg 2(1). As to offences under the Merchant Shipping (High Speed Craft) Regulations 2004, SI 2004/302, see PARA 1110.
4 Merchant Shipping (High Speed Craft) Regulations 2004, SI 2004/302, reg 7(2)(a).
5 Merchant Shipping (High Speed Craft) Regulations 2004, SI 2004/302, reg 7(2)(b)(i).
6 Merchant Shipping (High Speed Craft) Regulations 2004, SI 2004/302, reg 7(2)(b)(ii).
7 Merchant Shipping (High Speed Craft) Regulations 2004, SI 2004/302, reg 7(2)(c).

623. Passenger craft to operate in accordance with permit. A Permit to Operate which is issued as respects a passenger craft[1] by the Secretary of State[2] in accordance with the High Speed Craft Code 1994[3] or the High Speed Craft Code 2000[4] must state the maximum number of passengers which that craft is allowed to carry on board[5]. A Permit to Operate issued in this way[6] must set out, and be subject to, the operating restrictions identified in accordance with the risk assessment with reference to wash[7].

The owner[8] and master of a passenger craft must ensure that the craft does not carry more than the maximum number of passengers as stated in the craft's Permit to Operate[9].

1 As to the meaning of 'passenger craft' see PARA 617 note 9.
2 As to the Secretary of State see PARA 36.
3 As to the meaning of 'High Speed Craft Code 1994' see PARA 619 note 3; and see PARA 620 note 3.
4 As to the meaning of 'High Speed Craft Code 2000' see PARA 619 note 4; and see PARA 620 note 6.
5 Merchant Shipping (High Speed Craft) Regulations 2004, SI 2004/302, reg 8(1).
6 Ie in accordance with the Merchant Shipping (High Speed Craft) Regulations 2004, SI 2004/302, reg 8(1) (see the text and notes 1–5): see reg 8(2).
7 Merchant Shipping (High Speed Craft) Regulations 2004, SI 2004/302, reg 8(2). The text refers to the operating restrictions identified in accordance with reg 7 (as to which see PARA 622): see reg 8(2). As to the meaning of 'wash' see PARA 622 note 3.
8 As to references in the Merchant Shipping (High Speed Craft) Regulations 2004, SI 2004/302, to the owner see PARA 617 note 21.
9 Merchant Shipping (High Speed Craft) Regulations 2004, SI 2004/302, reg 8(3). As to offences under the Merchant Shipping (High Speed Craft) Regulations 2004, SI 2004/302, see PARA 1110.

624. Behaviour of persons on passenger craft. A person on board a high speed passenger craft[1] who is drunk and disorderly, and if he has paid a fare has had that fare returned or tendered to him, must, if so requested by the master or crew, leave the ship at any place in the United Kingdom[2] at which he can conveniently do so[3].

A person who is on board a high speed passenger craft must not, after being warned by the master or crew, molest or continue to molest any passenger[4].

A person who is on board a high speed passenger craft must not intentionally do or cause to be done anything in such a manner as to:

(1)   obstruct or damage any part of the machinery or equipment of that craft[5]; or

(2)   obstruct, impede or molest the master or crew, or any of them, in the navigation or management of the craft, or otherwise in the execution of their duty on or about the craft[6].

Any contravention of these provisions is an offence[7].

1   As to the meaning of 'passenger craft' see PARA 617 note 9.
2   As to the meaning of 'United Kingdom' see PARA 16 note 3.
3   Merchant Shipping (High Speed Craft) Regulations 2004, SI 2004/302, reg 9(1).
4   Merchant Shipping (High Speed Craft) Regulations 2004, SI 2004/302, reg 9(2).
5   Merchant Shipping (High Speed Craft) Regulations 2004, SI 2004/302, reg 9(3)(a).
6   Merchant Shipping (High Speed Craft) Regulations 2004, SI 2004/302, reg 9(3)(b).
7   See the Merchant Shipping (High Speed Craft) Regulations 2004, SI 2004/302, reg 10; and PARA 1110.

625. Offences and power to detain. Any contravention of the Merchant Shipping (High Speed Craft) Regulations 2004[1] in respect of a high speed craft[2] is an offence by both the owner[3] and the master of that craft[4]. In any case where a high speed craft does not so comply[5], the craft is liable to be detained[6].

1   Ie any contravention of the Merchant Shipping (High Speed Craft) Regulations 2004, SI 2004/302 (see PARA 617 et seq), other than reg 9 (as to which see PARA 624): see reg 10(1); and PARA 1110.
2   As to the meaning of 'high speed craft' see PARA 617 note 2.
3   As to references in the Merchant Shipping (High Speed Craft) Regulations 2004, SI 2004/302, to the owner see PARA 617 note 21.
4   See the Merchant Shipping (High Speed Craft) Regulations 2004, SI 2004/302, reg 10(1); and PARA 1110.
5   Ie with the Merchant Shipping (High Speed Craft) Regulations 2004, SI 2004/302 (see PARA 617 et seq): see reg 11.
6   Merchant Shipping (High Speed Craft) Regulations 2004, SI 2004/302, reg 11. The Merchant Shipping Act 1995 s 284(1)–(6), (8) (enforcing detention of ships) (see PARA 1190) has effect in relation to the craft, subject to the modification that, for the words 'this Act' wherever they appear, there are to be substituted 'the Merchant Shipping (High Speed Craft) Regulations 2004', and for the word 'ship' there were substituted 'high speed craft': see reg 11.

(iii) Health and Safety

A.   IN GENERAL

626. Health and safety: general duties. Regulations[1] have been made in order to give effect as respects shipping activities in the United Kingdom[2] to various EU Directives relating to the safety and health of workers at work[3]. Accordingly, it is the duty of the employer[4] of workers aboard a United Kingdom ship[5] to ensure the health and safety of workers and other persons so far as is reasonably practicable, having regard to the following principles[6]:

(1)   the avoidance of risks, which among other things include the combating of risks at source and the replacement of dangerous practices, substances or equipment by non-dangerous or less dangerous practices, substances or equipment[7];

(2)   the evaluation of unavoidable risks and the taking of action to reduce them[8];

(3)   the adoption of work patterns and procedures which take account of the capacity of the individual, especially in respect of the design of the workplace and the choice of work equipment, with a view in particular to alleviating monotonous work and to reducing any consequent adverse effect on workers' health and safety[9];

(4)   the adaptation of procedures to take account of new technology and other changes in working practices, equipment, the working environment and any other factors which may affect health and safety[10];

(5)   the adoption of a coherent approach to management of the vessel or undertaking, taking account of health and safety at every level of the organisation[11];

(6)   giving collective protective measures priority over individual protective measures[12];

(7)   the provision of appropriate and relevant information and instruction for workers[13].

The matters to which the duty extends include in particular[14]:

(a)   provision and maintenance of plant, machinery and equipment and systems of work that are, so far as is reasonably practicable, safe and without risk to health[15];

(b)   arrangements for ensuring, so far as is reasonably practicable, safety and absence of risk to health in connection with the risk to health in connection with the use, handling, storage and transport of articles and substances[16];

(c)   such arrangements as are appropriate, having regard to the nature of, and the substances used in, the activities and size of the operation, for the effective planning, organisation, control, monitoring and review of preventative and protective measures[17];

(d)   provision of such information, instruction, training and supervision as is necessary to ensure the health and safety of workers and of other persons aboard ship who may be affected by their acts or omissions[18];

(e)   maintenance of all places of work within the ship in a condition which is, so far as is reasonably practicable, safe and without risk to health[19];

(f)   arrangements to ensure, so far as is reasonably practicable, that no person has access to any area of the ship to which it is necessary to restrict access on grounds of health and safety unless the individual concerned has received adequate and appropriate health and safety instruction[20];

(g)   provision and maintenance of an environment for persons aboard ship that is, so far as is reasonably practicable, safe and without risk to health[21];

(h)   collaboration with any other persons upon whom a duty is imposed[22] or who have control of a matter to which a regulation relates to protect, so far as is reasonably practicable, the health and safety of all authorised persons aboard the ship or engaged in loading or unloading activities in relation to that ship[23].

A written statement must be prepared and, as often as may be appropriate, revised, of the employer's general policy with respect to health and safety and the organisation and arrangements for the time being in force for carrying out that policy, and this and any revisions must be brought to the notice of the workers[24].

A suitable and sufficient assessment must be made of the risks of the health and safety of workers arising in the course of their activities or duties, for the purpose of identifying groups of workers at particular risk in the performance of their duties and the measures to be taken to comply with the employer's duties[25]; and any significant findings of the assessment and any revision of it must be brought to the notice of workers[26].

Further provision is made in relation to:

(i) workers who include women with potential for child-bearing where the work is of a kind which could involve risk[27], by reason of her condition, to the health and safety of a new or expectant mother[28], or to that of her baby, from any process or working conditions, or physical, biological or chemical agents[29];

(ii) the provision to workers of such health surveillance as is appropriate having regard to the risks to their health and safety which are identified by the risk assessment[30];

(iii) the need, in entrusting tasks to workers, to take account of their capabilities as regards health and safety and to provide adequate and appropriate health and safety training and instruction where required[31];

(iv) special responsibilities for health and safety to be assigned (including the appointment of safety officers) and for consultation with workers to be effected on all matters relating to their health and safety[32]; and

(v) the general duties of workers in relation to health and safety[33].

No charge in respect of anything done or provided in pursuance of any of the above requirements may be levied or permitted to be levied on any worker[34].

No person may intentionally or recklessly interfere with or misuse anything provided in the interests of health and safety aboard a United Kingdom ship[35].

Contravention of the above requirements is an offence[36]; and provision is made for the detention of vessels[37].

These general duties in relation to health and safety are supplemented by requirements which relate to the provision of safety and/or health signs at work[38].

It is the duty of the employer of workers aboard a United Kingdom ship, so far as is reasonably practicable, also to take appropriate measures or provide means (including mechanical equipment) to avoid the need for manual handling of loads which involve a risk of workers being injured[39].

1   As to safety regulations generally see PARA 602 note 1. See also note 3.
2   As to the meaning of 'United Kingdom' see PARA 16 note 3.
3   The regulations so made are the Merchant Shipping and Fishing Vessels (Health and Safety at Work) Regulations 1997, SI 1997/2962 (supplemented by the Merchant Shipping and Fishing Vessels (Health and Safety at Work) (Work at Height) Regulations 2010, SI 2010/332), and the Directives to which they give effect, as mentioned in the text, are: Council Directive (EC) 89/391 (OJ L183, 29.06.1989, p 1) on the introduction of measures to encourage improvements in the safety and health of workers at work; Council Directive (EC) 91/383 (OJ L206, 29.07.1991, p 19) supplementing the measures to encourage improvements in the safety and health at work of workers with a fixed-duration employment relationship or a temporary employment relationship; and Council Directive (EC) 92/85 (OJ L348, 28.11.1992, p 1) on the introduction of measures to encourage improvements in the safety and health at work of pregnant workers and workers who have recently given birth or are breastfeeding. The regulations are made under the powers contained in the Merchant Shipping Act 1995 ss 85, 86 (see PARA 602 note 1) except in respect of their application to government ships (see the Merchant Shipping and Fishing Vessels (Health and Safety at Work) Regulations 1997, SI 1997/2962, reg 2(2); and note 5) and in respect of the provision of benefits to new or expectant mothers contained in reg 8 (see head (i) in the text) and reg 9 (see note 29), where the power is provided by the European Communities Act 1972 s 2(2).
4   It is the duty of every employer, and any other person upon whom a duty is imposed by the Merchant Shipping and Fishing Vessels (Health and Safety at Work) Regulations 1997, SI 1997/2962, to comply with the provisions of those regulations; and where such a person does not have control of the matter to which the regulation relates because he does not have responsibility for the operation of the ship, then any duty imposed by that regulation also extends to any person who has control of that matter: see reg 4 (amended by SI 1998/2411). As to workers on board a

United Kingdom ship not employed by the owner of the ship (or any other organisation or person such as the manager, or bareboat charterer, who has assumed the responsibility for operation of the ship from the owner) see the Merchant Shipping and Fishing Vessels (Health and Safety at Work) Regulations 1997, SI 1997/2962, regs 2(2), 13. A shipmaster is not excluded from the employer's general duty of care to his employee: *MacIver v J & A Gardner Ltd* 2001 SLT 585, OH.

5   For these purposes, 'United Kingdom ship' means (by virtue of the Merchant Shipping and Fishing Vessels (Health and Safety at Work) Regulations 1997, SI 1997/2962, reg 2(2)):

   (1)   a ship which either is registered in the United Kingdom or is not registered under the law of any country but is wholly owned by persons each of whom is a British citizen, a British overseas territories citizen or a British Overseas citizen or a body corporate which is established under the law of a part of the United Kingdom and has its principal place of business in the United Kingdom (Merchant Shipping Act 1995 s 85(2) (amended by virtue of the British Overseas Territories Act 2002 s 2(3));

   (2)   a ship which is a government ship within the meaning of the Merchant Shipping Act 1995 s 308(4) (see PARA 19 note 3); or

   (3)   a ship which is a hovercraft registered under the Hovercraft Act 1968 (see PARA 390 et seq).

   In connection with the application of the Merchant Shipping and Fishing Vessels (Health and Safety at Work) Regulations 1997, SI 1997/2962, see reg 3 (amended by SI 2015/1692; SI 2014/1616). As to the meaning of 'British citizen' see PARA 18 note 7; as to the meaning of 'British overseas territories citizen' see PARA 18 note 8; as to the meaning of 'British Overseas citizen' see PARA 18 note 9; as to the meaning of 'registered' see PARA 254 note 2; as to the meaning of 'ship' see PARA 229; and as to the meaning of 'United Kingdom' see PARA 16 note 3.

6   Merchant Shipping and Fishing Vessels (Health and Safety at Work) Regulations 1997, SI 1997/2962, reg 5(1) (amended by SI 2001/54).

7   Merchant Shipping and Fishing Vessels (Health and Safety at Work) Regulations 1997, SI 1997/2962, reg 5(1)(a).

8   Merchant Shipping and Fishing Vessels (Health and Safety at Work) Regulations 1997, SI 1997/2962, reg 5(1)(b).

9   Merchant Shipping and Fishing Vessels (Health and Safety at Work) Regulations 1997, SI 1997/2962, reg 5(1)(c).

10 Merchant Shipping and Fishing Vessels (Health and Safety at Work) Regulations 1997, SI 1997/2962, reg 5(1)(d).

11 Merchant Shipping and Fishing Vessels (Health and Safety at Work) Regulations 1997, SI 1997/2962, reg 5(1)(e).

12 Merchant Shipping and Fishing Vessels (Health and Safety at Work) Regulations 1997, SI 1997/2962, reg 5(1)(f).

13 Merchant Shipping and Fishing Vessels (Health and Safety at Work) Regulations 1997, SI 1997/2962, reg 5(1)(g).

14 Merchant Shipping and Fishing Vessels (Health and Safety at Work) Regulations 1997, SI 1997/2962, reg 5(2) (amended by SI 1998/2411). This provision is expressed to be without prejudice to the generality of the duty under the Merchant Shipping and Fishing Vessels (Health and Safety at Work) Regulations 1997, SI 1997/2962, reg 5(1) (see the text and notes 4–13): see reg 5(2) (as so amended).

15 Merchant Shipping and Fishing Vessels (Health and Safety at Work) Regulations 1997, SI 1997/2962, reg 5(2)(a).

16 Merchant Shipping and Fishing Vessels (Health and Safety at Work) Regulations 1997, SI 1997/2962, reg 5(2)(b).

17 Merchant Shipping and Fishing Vessels (Health and Safety at Work) Regulations 1997, SI 1997/2962, reg 5(2)(c).

18 Merchant Shipping and Fishing Vessels (Health and Safety at Work) Regulations 1997, SI 1997/2962, reg 5(2)(d).

19 Merchant Shipping and Fishing Vessels (Health and Safety at Work) Regulations 1997, SI 1997/2962, reg 5(2)(e).

20 Merchant Shipping and Fishing Vessels (Health and Safety at Work) Regulations 1997, SI 1997/2962, reg 5(2)(f).

21 Merchant Shipping and Fishing Vessels (Health and Safety at Work) Regulations 1997, SI 1997/2962, reg 5(2)(g).

22 Ie any other persons covered by the Merchant Shipping and Fishing Vessels (Health and Safety at Work) Regulations 1997, SI 1997/2962, reg 4 (see note 4): see reg 5(2)(h).

23 Merchant Shipping and Fishing Vessels (Health and Safety at Work) Regulations 1997, SI 1997/2962, reg 5(2)(h).

24 Merchant Shipping and Fishing Vessels (Health and Safety at Work) Regulations 1997, SI 1997/2962, reg 6(1). However, the written statement mentioned in reg 6(1) does not apply where five or fewer workers in aggregate are employed by the same employer, or associated employers, in a United Kingdom ship: see reg 6(2).

25 Ie under the Merchant Shipping and Fishing Vessels (Health and Safety at Work) Regulations 1997, SI 1997/2962: see reg 7(1).

26 Merchant Shipping and Fishing Vessels (Health and Safety at Work) Regulations 1997, SI 1997/2962, reg 7(1). As to the risk assessment see further reg 7(2)–(6) (amended by SI 2014/1616).

Although working in a war zone involved risks which could not all be guarded against by the exercise of reasonable care and skill, the owners of vessels which are operating in a war zone owe a qualified duty of care to members of the crew with regard to their safety; whatever the type of vessel, that duty requires the owners to provide written instructions as to specific types of risk to which the vessel is likely to be exposed and to give appropriate instruction and information as to how such risk might be reduced or eliminated: *Tarrant v Ramage, The Salvital* [1998] 1 Lloyd's Rep 185, (1997) Times, 31 July.

27 For these purposes, references to 'risk' in relation to risk from any infectious or contagious disease are references to a level of risk at work which is in addition to the level to which a new or expectant mother may be expected to be exposed outside the workplace: Merchant Shipping and Fishing Vessels (Health and Safety at Work) Regulations 1997, SI 1997/2962, reg 8(4).

28 For these purposes, 'new or expectant mother' means a worker who is either pregnant, or has given birth within the previous six months, or is breast-feeding: Merchant Shipping and Fishing Vessels (Health and Safety at Work) Regulations 1997, SI 1997/2962, reg 2(2).

29 See the Merchant Shipping and Fishing Vessels (Health and Safety at Work) Regulations 1997, SI 1997/2962, reg 8 (amended by SI 2015/21). As to circumstances where a new or expectant mother works at night see reg 9; and as to the notification that must be given to the employer or to the company before such action is required see the Merchant Shipping and Fishing Vessels (Health and Safety at Work) Regulations 1997, SI 1997/2962, reg 10.

30 See the Merchant Shipping and Fishing Vessels (Health and Safety at Work) Regulations 1997, SI 1997/2962, regs 11, 11A (reg 11A added by SI 2014/1616). The text refers to the risk assessment made under the Merchant Shipping and Fishing Vessels (Health and Safety at Work) Regulations 1997, SI 1997/2962, reg 7(1) (see the text and notes 25–26): see reg 11.

31 See the Merchant Shipping and Fishing Vessels (Health and Safety at Work) Regulations 1997, SI 1997/2962, reg 12.

32 See the Merchant Shipping and Fishing Vessels (Health and Safety at Work) Regulations 1997, SI 1997/2962, Pt IV (regs 14–20) (amended by SI 1998/2411; SI 2014/1616).

33 See the Merchant Shipping and Fishing Vessels (Health and Safety at Work) Regulations 1997, SI 1997/2962, Pt V (reg 21) (amended by SI 2014/1616).

34 See the Merchant Shipping and Fishing Vessels (Health and Safety at Work) Regulations 1997, SI 1997/2962, reg 22.

35 See the Merchant Shipping and Fishing Vessels (Health and Safety at Work) Regulations 1997, SI 1997/2962, reg 23.

36 See the Merchant Shipping and Fishing Vessels (Health and Safety at Work) Regulations 1997, SI 1997/2962, reg 24 (amended by SI 2015/1692; SI 2014/1616). Provision is made also for corporate offences (see the Merchant Shipping and Fishing Vessels (Health and Safety at Work) Regulations 1997, SI 1997/2962, reg 25 (amended by SI 1998/2411)); and for the burden of showing that compliance with a duty in the Merchant Shipping and Fishing Vessels (Health and Safety at Work) Regulations 1997, SI 1997/2962, was not reasonably practicable to be on the defendant (see reg 26). See also PARA 1115.

37 See the Merchant Shipping and Fishing Vessels (Health and Safety at Work) Regulations 1997, SI 1997/2962, regs 27, 27A, 27B, 28, 28A, 28B, 29, 30 (regs 27, 28, 29 amended, regs 27A, 27B, 28A, 28B added, by SI 2014/1616).

38 See the Merchant Shipping and Fishing Vessels (Safety Signs and Signals) Regulations 2001, SI 2001/3444, which give effect to Council Directive (EC) 92/58 (OJ L245, 26.08.1992, p 23) on the minimum requirements for the provision of safety and/or health signs at work. The Merchant Shipping and Fishing Vessels (Safety Signs and Signals) Regulations 2001, SI 2001/3444, are made under the powers contained in the Merchant Shipping Act 1995 ss 85, 86 except in respect of their application to government ships (see the Merchant Shipping and Fishing Vessels (Safety Signs and Signals) Regulations 2001, SI 2001/3444, reg 2(1)), where the power is provided by the European Communities Act 1972 s 2(2). See also the Merchant Shipping (Entry into Dangerous Spaces) Regulations 1988, SI 1988/1638.

The circumstances in which the Merchant Shipping and Fishing Vessels (Safety Signs and Signals) Regulations 2001, SI 2001/3444, apply are set out in terms which are similar to those governing the Merchant Shipping and Fishing Vessels (Health and Safety at Work) Regulations

1997, SI 1997/2962 (see note 5), although exclusions apply to signs used in relation to the supply of dangerous substances or equipment, for the transport of dangerous goods and for the regulation of transport: see the Merchant Shipping and Fishing Vessels (Safety Signs and Signals) Regulations 2001, SI 2001/3444, reg 3 (amended by SI 2015/21). The persons on whom duties are imposed are set out in the Merchant Shipping and Fishing Vessels (Safety Signs and Signals) Regulations 2001, SI 2001/3444, reg 4 (again in terms similar to the persons on whom general duties relating to health are imposed: see note 4). Safety signs must be provided where a risk assessment made under the Merchant Shipping and Fishing Vessels (Health and Safety at Work) Regulations 1997, SI 1997/2962, reg 7(1) (see the text and notes 25–26) indicates that risks cannot be avoided or adequately controlled in other ways: see the Merchant Shipping and Fishing Vessels (Safety Signs and Signals) Regulations 2001, SI 2001/3444, reg 5, Schedule. The employer must ensure that comprehensible and relevant information on the measures to be taken in connection with safety signs is provided to each worker; and that each worker receives suitable and sufficient instruction and training in the meaning of safety signs and the measures to be taken in connection with safety signs: see reg 6. As to enforcement see regs 7–13; and PARA 1115.

39 See the Merchant Shipping and Fishing Vessels (Manual Handling Operations) Regulations 1998, SI 1998/2857, which give effect as regards shipping activities in the United Kingdom to Council Directive (EC) 90/269 (OJ L269, 21.06.1990, p 9) on the minimum health and safety requirements for the manual handling of loads where there is a risk particularly of back injury to workers. The Merchant Shipping and Fishing Vessels (Manual Handling Operations) Regulations 1998, SI 1998/2857, are made under the powers contained in the Merchant Shipping Act 1995 ss 85, 86 except in respect of their application to government ships (see the Merchant Shipping and Fishing Vessels (Manual Handling Operations) Regulations 1998, SI 1998/2857, reg 2(2)), where the power is provided by the European Communities Act 1972 s 2(2).

The circumstances in which the Merchant Shipping and Fishing Vessels (Manual Handling Operations) Regulations 1998, SI 1998/2857, apply are set out in terms which are similar to those governing the Merchant Shipping and Fishing Vessels (Health and Safety at Work) Regulations 1997, SI 1997/2962 (see note 5): see the Merchant Shipping and Fishing Vessels (Manual Handling Operations) Regulations 1998, SI 1998/2857, reg 3. However, exclusions apply where the Manual Handling Operations Regulations 1992, SI 1992/2793 (see HEALTH AND SAFETY AT WORK vol 53 (2014) PARA 545) apply instead: see the Merchant Shipping and Fishing Vessels (Manual Handling Operations) Regulations 1998, SI 1998/2857, reg 3. The persons on whom duties are imposed are set out in reg 4 (again in terms similar to the persons on whom general duties relating to health are imposed: see note 4). The duty on employers is set out in the text (see reg 5); and every worker while at work must make full and proper use of any system of work provided for his use by his employer in accordance with reg 5 (see reg 6). As to enforcement see regs 7–13 (reg 13 amended by SI 1999/2205); and PARA 1115.

B.   SAFETY MANAGEMENT CODES

627. International and domestic safety management codes. Provision is made for implementing an international standard for the safe management and operation of ships (the 'ISM Code'), which establishes safety-management objectives and requires a safety management system and a policy for achieving these objectives to be established by shipowners and persons responsible for operating vessels[1]. Ship operating companies are required to comply with the Code as it applies to that company and to any ship owned by it or for which it has responsibility[2]. Smaller passenger ships operating in domestic waters are required to comply with the Safety Management Code for Domestic Passenger Ships[3] as it applies to that company and to any ship owned by it or for which it has operational responsibility[4].

1 See the International Management Code for the Safe Operation of Ships and for Pollution Prevention as adopted by the International Maritime Organisation (the 'IMO') by Resolution A.741 (18), which is implemented in respect of the EU by Council Regulation (EC) 336/2006 (OJ L64, 4.3.2006, p 1) on the implementation of the Safety Management Code with in the Community, and in respect of the United Kingdom by the Merchant Shipping (International Safety Management (ISM) Code) Regulations 2014, SI 2014/1512. As to the International Maritime Organisation (the 'IMO') see PARA 12.

2 See the Merchant Shipping (International Safety Management (ISM) Code) Regulations 2014, SI 2014/1512, reg 4–6.

3 Ie the Safety Management Code for Small Vessels set out in Merchant Shipping Notice 1754(M) (Safety Management Code for Domestic Passenger Ships of Classes III–VI (A)), which is

implemented in the United Kingdom by the Merchant Shipping (Domestic Passenger Ships) (Safety Management Code) Regulations 2001, SI 2001/3209.

4   See the Merchant Shipping (Domestic Passenger Ships) (Safety Management Code) Regulations 2001, SI 2001/3209, reg 5.

C.   PROTECTION OF WORKERS

628. Noise. Regulations impose duties on employers to protect the health and safety of workers who may be exposed to risk from noise as a result of their work[1]. In particular, provision is made for:

(1)   action values and limit values for daily and weekly exposure to noise[2];

(2)   risk assessment[3];

(3)   elimination or, where elimination is not reasonably practicable, reduction of exposure to noise, actions to be taken at action values and limit values, and a prohibition on exceeding limit values[4];

(4)   provision of individual hearing protection[5];

(5)   information, instruction and training[6];

(6)   health surveillance[7];

(7)   consultation with workers[8];

(8)   the grant of exemptions by the Secretary of State[9]; and

(9)   offences, detention, inspection and penalties[10].

1   See the Merchant Shipping and Fishing Vessels (Control of Noise at Work) Regulations 2007, SI 2007/3075. The regulations apply in relation to United Kingdom ships: reg 4(1). However, where a ship is being used in the course of public service activities or activities for the purpose of civil protection services, and characteristics peculiar to those activities inevitably conflict with a provision of the regulations, that provision does not apply in relation to that ship to the extent of that conflict: reg 4(2). In such a case, there is in relation to that ship a duty on the employer to ensure, so far as is reasonably practicable, the health and safety of workers who are or who are likely to be exposed to risks from noise as a result of their work: see reg 4(3).

The provisions of the Merchant Shipping and Fishing Vessels (Health and Safety at Work) Regulations 1997, SI 1997/2962 (see PARA 626) and the Merchant Shipping and Fishing Vessels (Provision and Use of Work Equipment) Regulations 2006, SI 2006/2183 (see PARA 638) continue to apply to activities to which the Merchant Shipping and Fishing Vessels (Control of Noise at Work) Regulations 2007, SI 2007/3075, apply, except where the latter regulations contain more stringent or specific provisions (when such provisions must apply instead): see reg 4(4). However, the Merchant Shipping and Fishing Vessels (Control of Noise at Work) Regulations 2007, SI 2007/3075, do not apply to activities to which the Control of Noise at Work Regulations 2005, SI 2005/1643 (see HEALTH AND SAFETY AT WORK vol 53 (2014) PARAS 574–581) apply: see the Merchant Shipping and Fishing Vessels (Control of Noise at Work) Regulations 2007, SI 2007/3075, reg 4(6).

2   See the Merchant Shipping and Fishing Vessels (Control of Noise at Work) Regulations 2007, SI 2007/3075, reg 5.

3   See the Merchant Shipping and Fishing Vessels (Control of Noise at Work) Regulations 2007, SI 2007/3075, reg 6.

4   See the Merchant Shipping and Fishing Vessels (Control of Noise at Work) Regulations 2007, SI 2007/3075, reg 7.

5   See the Merchant Shipping and Fishing Vessels (Control of Noise at Work) Regulations 2007, SI 2007/3075, reg 8.

6   See the Merchant Shipping and Fishing Vessels (Control of Noise at Work) Regulations 2007, SI 2007/3075, reg 9.

7   See the Merchant Shipping and Fishing Vessels (Control of Noise at Work) Regulations 2007, SI 2007/3075, reg 10.

8   See the Merchant Shipping and Fishing Vessels (Control of Noise at Work) Regulations 2007, SI 2007/3075, reg 11.

9   See the Merchant Shipping and Fishing Vessels (Control of Noise at Work) Regulations 2007, SI 2007/3075, reg 13.

10   See the Merchant Shipping and Fishing Vessels (Control of Noise at Work) Regulations 2007, SI 2007/3075, regs 12, 14–21.

629. Mechanical vibration. Regulations impose duties on employers to protect the health and safety of workers who may be exposed to risk from mechanical vibration as a result of their work[1]. In particular, provision is made for:

(1)   action values and limit values for daily exposure to hand-arm and whole body vibration[2];

(2)   risk assessment[3];

(3)   elimination or, where elimination is not reasonably practicable, reduction of exposure to mechanical vibration, actions to be taken at action values and limit values, and a prohibition on exceeding limit values[4];

(4)   provision of suitable and sufficient information, instruction and training (where required)[5];

(5)   health surveillance[6];

(6)   consultation with workers[7];

(7)   the grant of exemptions by the Secretary of State[8]; and

(8)   offences, detention, inspection and penalties[9].

1   See the Merchant Shipping and Fishing Vessels (Control of Vibration at Work) Regulations 2007, SI 2007/3077. The regulations apply in relation to United Kingdom ships: reg 4(1). However, where a ship is being used in the course of public service activities or activities for the purpose of civil protection services, and characteristics peculiar to those activities inevitably conflict with a provision of the regulations, that provision does not apply in relation to that ship to the extent of that conflict: reg 4(2). In such a case, there is in relation to that ship a duty on the employer to ensure, so far as is reasonably practicable, the health and safety of workers who are or who are likely to be exposed to risks from mechanical vibration as a result of their work: see reg 4(3).

     The provisions of the Merchant Shipping and Fishing Vessels (Health and Safety at Work) Regulations 1997, SI 1997/2962 (see PARA 626) and the Merchant Shipping and Fishing Vessels (Provision and Use of Work Equipment) Regulations 2006, SI 2006/2183 (see PARA 638) continue to apply to activities to which the Merchant Shipping and Fishing Vessels (Control of Vibration at Work) Regulations 2007, SI 2007/3077, apply, except where the latter regulations contain more stringent or specific provisions (when such provisions must apply instead): see reg 4(4). However, the Merchant Shipping and Fishing Vessels (Control of Vibration at Work) Regulations 2007, SI 2007/3077, do not apply to activities to which the Control of Vibration at Work Regulations 2005, SI 2005/1093 (see HEALTH AND SAFETY AT WORK vol 53 (2014) PARAS 558–561) apply: see the Merchant Shipping and Fishing Vessels (Control of Vibration at Work) Regulations 2007, SI 2007/3077, reg 4(6).

2   See the Merchant Shipping and Fishing Vessels (Control of Vibration at Work) Regulations 2007, SI 2007/3077, reg 5.

3   See the Merchant Shipping and Fishing Vessels (Control of Vibration at Work) Regulations 2007, SI 2007/3077, reg 6.

4   See the Merchant Shipping and Fishing Vessels (Control of Vibration at Work) Regulations 2007, SI 2007/3077, reg 7.

5   See the Merchant Shipping and Fishing Vessels (Control of Vibration at Work) Regulations 2007, SI 2007/3077, reg 8.

6   See the Merchant Shipping and Fishing Vessels (Control of Vibration at Work) Regulations 2007, SI 2007/3077, reg 9.

7   See the Merchant Shipping and Fishing Vessels (Control of Vibration at Work) Regulations 2007, SI 2007/3077, reg 10.

8   See the Merchant Shipping and Fishing Vessels (Control of Vibration at Work) Regulations 2007, SI 2007/3077, reg 12.

9   See the Merchant Shipping and Fishing Vessels (Control of Vibration at Work) Regulations 2007, SI 2007/3077, regs 11, 13–20.

630. Work at height. Employers of workers aboard ships are required to ensure that no person engages in any activity, including organisation, planning and supervision, in relation to work at height or work equipment for use in such work, unless that person is competent to do so or, if being trained, is being supervised by a person who is competent to supervise and do that activity[1].

1   See the Work at Height Regulations 2005, SI 2005/735; and HEALTH AND SAFETY AT WORK vol 53 (2014) PARA 546 et seq.

631. Carcinogens and mutagens, biological and chemical agents, asbestos, artificial optical radiation and electromagnetic fields. Regulations impose duties on employers to protect workers from to risks related to exposure to carcinogens and mutagens[1], biological agents[2], chemical agents[3], asbestos[4], artificial optical radiation[5] and electromagnetic fields[6] The regulations are concerned with:

(1)   the assessment of health risks[7];
(2)   reducing the use of, and limiting exposure to, harmful substances[8];
(3)   the provision of information to the Secretary of State[9];
(4)   ameliorating the risk of contamination[10];
(5)   the provision of information and training for workers and the keeping of at-risk workers under surveillance[11];
(6)   offences and penalties[12]; and
(7)   detention and inspection of ships[13].

1   Ie as defined in the Merchant Shipping and Fishing Vessels (Health and Safety at Work) (Carcinogens and Mutagens) Regulations 2007, SI 2007/3100, reg 2(1), Sch 1 (reg 2(1) amended by SI 2015/21).
2   Ie as defined and classified by the Merchant Shipping and Fishing Vessels (Health and Safety at Work) (Biological Agents) Regulations 2010, SI 2010/323, regs 2(1), 7.
3   Ie as defined by the Merchant Shipping and Fishing Vessels (Health and Safety at Work) (Chemical Agents) Regulations 2010, SI 2010/330, reg 2(1).
4   Ie as defined by the Merchant Shipping and Fishing Vessels (Health and Safety at Work) (Asbestos) Regulations 2010, SI 2010/2984, reg 2(1).
5   Ie as defined by the Merchant Shipping and Fishing Vessels (Health and Safety at Work) (Artificial Optical Radiation) Regulations 2010, SI 2010/2987, reg 2(1).
6   Ie as defined by the Merchant Shipping and Fishing Vessels (Health and Safety at Work) (Electromagnetic Fields) Regulations 2016, SI 2016/1026, reg 2(1), Schedule.
7   See the Merchant Shipping and Fishing Vessels (Health and Safety at Work) (Carcinogens and Mutagens) Regulations 2007, SI 2007/3100, regs 4, 16; the Merchant Shipping and Fishing Vessels (Health and Safety at Work) (Biological Agents) Regulations 2010, SI 2010/323, regs 6, 19–21; the Merchant Shipping and Fishing Vessels (Health and Safety at Work) (Chemical Agents) Regulations 2010, SI 2010/330, regs 6, 14; the Merchant Shipping and Fishing Vessels (Health and Safety at Work) (Asbestos) Regulations 2010, SI 2010/2984, regs 5, 20; the Merchant Shipping and Fishing Vessels (Health and Safety at Work) (Artificial Optical Radiation) Regulations 2010, SI 2010/2987, regs 6, 11; and the Merchant Shipping and Fishing Vessels (Health and Safety at Work) (Electromagnetic Fields) Regulations 2016, SI 2016/1026, regs 6–10, 23.
8   See the Merchant Shipping and Fishing Vessels (Health and Safety at Work) (Carcinogens and Mutagens) Regulations 2007, SI 2007/3100, regs 5, 6, 8–10, Schs 2, 3; the Merchant Shipping and Fishing Vessels (Health and Safety at Work) (Biological Agents) Regulations 2010, SI 2010/323, regs 8, 9; the Merchant Shipping and Fishing Vessels (Health and Safety at Work) (Chemical Agents) Regulations 2010, SI 2010/330, regs 7–9; the Merchant Shipping and Fishing Vessels (Health and Safety at Work) (Asbestos) Regulations 2010, SI 2010/2984, regs 6–12, 14; the Merchant Shipping and Fishing Vessels (Health and Safety at Work) (Artificial Optical Radiation) Regulations 2010, SI 2010/2987, reg 7; and the Merchant Shipping and Fishing Vessels (Health and Safety at Work) (Electromagnetic Fields) Regulations 2016, SI 2016/1026, regs 5, 7–10, 23.
9   See the Merchant Shipping and Fishing Vessels (Health and Safety at Work) (Carcinogens and Mutagens) Regulations 2007, SI 2007/3100, reg 7; the Merchant Shipping and Fishing Vessels (Health and Safety at Work) (Biological Agents) Regulations 2010, SI 2010/323, regs 10, 16.
10 See the Merchant Shipping and Fishing Vessels (Health and Safety at Work) (Carcinogens and Mutagens) Regulations 2007, SI 2007/3100, reg 11; the Merchant Shipping and Fishing Vessels (Health and Safety at Work) (Biological Agents) Regulations 2010, SI 2010/323, reg 11; the Merchant Shipping and Fishing Vessels (Health and Safety at Work) (Chemical Agents) Regulations 2010, SI 2010/330, reg 11; the Merchant Shipping and Fishing Vessels (Health and Safety at Work) (Artificial Optical Radiation) Regulations 2010, SI 2010/2987, regs 8, 9; and the Merchant Shipping and Fishing Vessels (Health and Safety at Work) (Asbestos) Regulations 2010, SI 2010/2984, reg 15.
11 See the Merchant Shipping and Fishing Vessels (Health and Safety at Work) (Carcinogens and Mutagens) Regulations 2007, SI 2007/3100, regs 12–15, Sch 4; the Merchant Shipping and Fishing Vessels (Health and Safety at Work) (Biological Agents) Regulations 2010, SI 2010/323, regs 12–15, 17, 18; the Merchant Shipping and Fishing Vessels (Health and Safety at Work) (Chemical Agents) Regulations 2010, SI 2010/330, regs 10, 12, 13; the Merchant Shipping and Fishing Vessels (Health and Safety at Work) (Asbestos) Regulations 2010, SI 2010/2984, regs 13, 16–19; the Merchant Shipping and Fishing Vessels (Health and Safety at Work) (Artificial Optical

Radiation) Regulations 2010, SI 2010/2987, reg 10; and the Merchant Shipping and Fishing Vessels (Health and Safety at Work) (Electromagnetic Fields) Regulations 2016, SI 2016/1026, regs 19–22.

12 See the Merchant Shipping and Fishing Vessels (Health and Safety at Work) (Carcinogens and Mutagens) Regulations 2007, SI 2007/3100, regs 17–19; the Merchant Shipping and Fishing Vessels (Health and Safety at Work) (Biological Agents) Regulations 2010, SI 2010/323, regs 22–24; the Merchant Shipping and Fishing Vessels (Health and Safety at Work) (Chemical Agents) Regulations 2010, SI 2010/330, regs 15–17; the Merchant Shipping and Fishing Vessels (Health and Safety at Work) (Asbestos) Regulations 2010, SI 2010/2984, regs 21–23; the Merchant Shipping and Fishing Vessels (Health and Safety at Work) (Artificial Optical Radiation) Regulations 2010, SI 2010/2987, regs 12, 13, 19; and the Merchant Shipping and Fishing Vessels (Health and Safety at Work) (Electromagnetic Fields) Regulations 2016, SI 2016/1026, regs 11, 12, 18.

13 See the Merchant Shipping and Fishing Vessels (Health and Safety at Work) (Carcinogens and Mutagens) Regulations 2007, SI 2007/3100, regs 20–23; the Merchant Shipping and Fishing Vessels (Health and Safety at Work) (Biological Agents) Regulations 2010, SI 2010/323, regs 25–29; the Merchant Shipping and Fishing Vessels (Health and Safety at Work) (Chemical Agents) Regulations 2010, SI 2010/330, regs 18–22; the Merchant Shipping and Fishing Vessels (Health and Safety at Work) (Asbestos) Regulations 2010, SI 2010/2984, regs 24–28; the Merchant Shipping and Fishing Vessels (Health and Safety at Work) (Artificial Optical Radiation) Regulations 2010, SI 2010/2987, regs 14–18; and the Merchant Shipping and Fishing Vessels (Health and Safety at Work) (Electromagnetic Fields) Regulations 2016, SI 2016/1026, regs 13–17.

632. Requirement to provide personal protective equipment and to use it properly. Personal protective equipment[1] must be used when risks cannot be avoided or reduced to an acceptable level by means of systems of work that are safe and without risk to health or by means of collective protection or by other means which are in use equally or more effective[2].

The employer must ensure[3]:

(1)   that the personal protective equipment required to be used[4] is provided, and such personal protective equipment must be suitable[5];

(2)   that an assessment is made to identify those circumstances where risk to the health and safety of individual workers at work cannot be avoided or reduced by other means, and to identify the characteristics required of personal protective equipment in order to provide protection to workers from that risk[6];

(3)   that personal protective equipment is provided[7] to a worker for his individual use[8], that appropriate instructions for the proper use and maintenance of any such personal protective equipment is readily available to any worker required to use that equipment, and is comprehensible to him[9], and that that personal protective equipment is properly stored and maintained, and is regularly inspected and, where appropriate, checked that it is in satisfactory working order[10];

(4)   that workers are provided with adequate and appropriate information, training and instruction[11].

The employer must take all reasonably practicable steps to ensure that any personal protective equipment so provided to workers[12] is used as instructed[13]; and every worker must use any personal protective equipment so provided to him and must follow any training in the use of the personal protective equipment which has been received by him and the instructions respecting that use, which also have been provided[14].

Any contravention of the requirements relating to the provision of personal protective equipment is an offence[15]; and, in any case where it is found in relation to a ship that there is a failure to comply with those requirements, the ship may be detained[16].

1   For these purposes, 'personal protective equipment' means all clothing and equipment designed to be worn or held by the worker for protection against one or more hazards likely to endanger his health or safety at work, and any addition or accessory designed for this purpose, with the exception of ordinary working clothes and uniforms which are not specifically designed to protect the health and safety of the worker, equipment provided for the purposes of fire-fighting or lifesaving, personal protective equipment worn or used by the military, the police and other public order agencies, personal protective equipment required for road transport, sports equipment, self-defence or deterrent equipment, or portable devices for detecting and signalling risk and nuisances: Merchant Shipping and Fishing Vessels (Personal Protective Equipment) Regulations 1999, SI 1999/2205, reg 2(2). 'Health and safety' includes the occupational health and safety of persons whilst on board the ship and whilst boarding or leaving the ship: reg 2(2).

2   Merchant Shipping and Fishing Vessels (Personal Protective Equipment) Regulations 1999, SI 1999/2205, reg 5.
   The Merchant Shipping and Fishing Vessels (Personal Protective Equipment) Regulations 1999, SI 1999/2205, apply to all activities of workers on United Kingdom ships except when the activity of a worker is on a public service vessel or a vessel engaged in search and rescue, and when the characteristics of that activity inevitably conflict with a provision of the regulations; and in such a case there is a duty on the employer so far as is reasonably practicable to ensure the health and safety of the worker when performing that activity: reg 3(1). The Merchant Shipping and Fishing Vessels (Personal Protective Equipment) Regulations 1999, SI 1999/2205, do not apply to or in relation to the activities of a worker which are covered by the Personal Protective Equipment at Work Regulations 1992, SI 1992/2966 (as to which see HEALTH AND SAFETY AT WORK vol 52 (2014) PARAS 485–491): Merchant Shipping and Fishing Vessels (Personal Protective Equipment) Regulations 1999, SI 1999/2205, reg 3(3). The provisions of reg 3(1), (3) apply to ships other than United Kingdom ships which are in United Kingdom waters: see reg 3(2). For these purposes, 'United Kingdom ship' means a ship which is a United Kingdom ship within the meaning of the Merchant Shipping Act 1995 s 85(2) (see PARA 591 note 4), is a government ship within the meaning of s 308(4) (see PARA 19 note 3), or is a hovercraft registered under the Hovercraft Act 1968 (see PARA 390 et seq): Merchant Shipping and Fishing Vessels (Personal Protective Equipment) Regulations 1999, SI 1999/2205, reg 2(2). 'Public service vessel' means any vessel operated by and on behalf of a public body while it is carrying out the authorised functions of that body: reg 2(2).

3   Where a person on whom a duty is imposed by any provision of the Merchant Shipping and Fishing Vessels (Personal Protective Equipment) Regulations 1999, SI 1999/2205, does not have control of the matter to which the regulation relates because he does not have responsibility for the operation of the ship, then any duty imposed by that regulation also extends to any person who has control of that matter: reg 4.

4   Ie under the Merchant Shipping and Fishing Vessels (Personal Protective Equipment) Regulations 1999, SI 1999/2205, reg 5 (see the text and notes 1–2): see reg 6(1).

5   Merchant Shipping and Fishing Vessels (Personal Protective Equipment) Regulations 1999, SI 1999/2205, reg 6(1). As to the meaning of 'suitable' for these purposes see reg 6(2). Personal protective equipment must be provided free of charge to the worker except that where use of the equipment is not exclusive to the work place, workers may be required to contribute towards the cost of personal protective equipment: reg 6(3).

6   Merchant Shipping and Fishing Vessels (Personal Protective Equipment) Regulations 1999, SI 1999/2205, reg 7(1). In accordance with the findings of such assessment as is mentioned in head (2) in the text, personal protective equipment which complies with the characteristics identified therein and which meets the standards specified as suitable under reg 6(2) (see note 5) must be provided: see reg 7(1). The assessment mentioned in head (2) in the text must be made before personal protective equipment is provided under the regulations (see reg 7(1)); and must be reviewed to take account of any changes to the factors on which it was based (reg 7(2)).

7   Ie under the Merchant Shipping and Fishing Vessels (Personal Protective Equipment) Regulations 1999, SI 1999/2205, reg 6(1) (see head (1) in the text): see reg 8(1).

8   Merchant Shipping and Fishing Vessels (Personal Protective Equipment) Regulations 1999, SI 1999/2205, reg 8(1). Equipment may be provided for the use of more than one person if it is adjustable to fit all sizes, easily accessible and kept in clearly marked places, and maintained in a hygienic condition and repaired, decontaminated and replaced as necessary, so that it will not create any health or hygiene problems: reg 8(2).

9   Merchant Shipping and Fishing Vessels (Personal Protective Equipment) Regulations 1999, SI 1999/2205, reg 8(3).

10 See the Merchant Shipping and Fishing Vessels (Personal Protective Equipment) Regulations 1999, SI 1999/2205, reg 8(4).
11 Merchant Shipping and Fishing Vessels (Personal Protective Equipment) Regulations 1999, SI 1999/2205, reg 9(1). The information, training and instruction provided in accordance with head (4) in the text may include the organisation of demonstrations in the wearing of personal protective equipment, in respect of the risks against which the personal protective equipment is designed to provide protection, the circumstances in which it is to be used, and the correct use, maintenance and storage of the equipment: see reg 9(1). The information, training and instruction so provided is not adequate and appropriate unless it is comprehensible to the persons to whom it is provided: reg 9(2).
12 Ie under the Merchant Shipping and Fishing Vessels (Personal Protective Equipment) Regulations 1999, SI 1999/2205, reg 6(1) (see head (1) in the text): see reg 10(1).
13 Merchant Shipping and Fishing Vessels (Personal Protective Equipment) Regulations 1999, SI 1999/2205, reg 10(1).
14 Merchant Shipping and Fishing Vessels (Personal Protective Equipment) Regulations 1999, SI 1999/2205, reg 10(2). The text refers to the training in the use of the personal protective equipment and the instructions respecting that use provided under reg 9 (see head (4) in the text): see reg 10(2).
15 See the Merchant Shipping and Fishing Vessels (Personal Protective Equipment) Regulations 1999, SI 1999/2205, regs 11–13; and PARA 1079.
16 See the Merchant Shipping and Fishing Vessels (Personal Protective Equipment) Regulations 1999, SI 1999/2205, regs 14–17; and PARA 1079. The provisions of regs 15–17 apply to ships other than United Kingdom ships which are in United Kingdom waters: see reg 3(2).

633. Fire precautions. Provision is made with respect to the steps to be taken to prevent, detect and deal with outbreaks of fire on a ship[1], dealing with fire prevention, fire appliances and structural fire protection on small and large passenger ships and tankers, and ships carrying dangerous goods[1].

1 See the Merchant Shipping (Fire Protection: Large Ships) Regulations 1998, SI 1998/1012; and the Merchant Shipping (Fire Protection: Small Ships) Regulations 1998, SI 1998/1011.
1 See the Merchant Shipping (Fire Protection: Large Ships) Regulations 1998, SI 1998/1012; and the Merchant Shipping (Fire Protection: Small Ships) Regulations 1998, SI 1998/1011.

D. NAVIGATION

634. General safety of navigation requirements. Regulations have been made[1] giving effect to the provisions of Chapter V of the International Convention for the Safety of Life at Sea 1974 (the 'SOLAS Convention'), which identifies certain navigation safety services which should be provided by contracting governments and sets forth provisions of an operational nature applicable in general to ships and other vessels on all voyages[2].

Accordingly, the application of various provisions contained in Chapter V of the SOLAS Convention is made compulsory (in relation to ships of qualifying descriptions)[3]. Provision is made for offences and penalties to apply where various requirements are contravened[4], and for the detention of a ship in any such case of non-compliance[5].

1 See the Merchant Shipping (Safety of Navigation) Regulations 2002, SI 2002/1473, which apply to all United Kingdom ships wherever they may be and to all other ships while they are within United Kingdom waters: reg 4(1). However, the regulations do not apply to warships or naval auxiliaries, to ships, other than United Kingdom ships, which are owned or operated by an EEA state and used only on government non-commercial service, to ships navigating solely the Great Lakes of North America and their connecting and tributary waters as far east as the lower exit of the St Lambert Lock at Montreal in the Province of Quebec, Canada, to passenger ships to which the Merchant Shipping (Passenger Ships) (Safety Code for UK Categorised Waters) Regulations 2010, SI 2010/680 (see PARA 604) apply, or vessels to which the Merchant Shipping (Technical Requirements for Inland Waterway Vessels) Regulations 2010, SI 2010/1075 (see PARA 604) apply: reg 4(2) (amended by SI 2004/2110; SI 2010/680; SI 2010/1075). Nor do the Merchant Shipping (Safety of Navigation) Regulations 2002, SI 2002/1473, apply to ships, other than United Kingdom ships, which are owned or operated by a contracting government and used only on government non-commercial service: reg 4(2A) (added by SI 2004/2110). Various individual regulations are disapplied in relation to various specific categories of ship: see the Merchant

Shipping (Safety of Navigation) Regulations 2002, SI 2002/1473, reg 4(2B)–(10) (reg 4(2B), (5A), (6A) added, reg 4(5) amended, by SI 2004/2110; Merchant Shipping (Safety of Navigation) Regulations 2002, SI 2002/1473, reg 4(4) amended by SI 2004/302).
    The Merchant Shipping (Safety of Navigation) Regulations 2002, SI 2002/1473, do not apply in relation to passenger ships of Class A, B, C or D of 24 metres or over in length engaged on domestic voyages: see the Merchant Shipping (Passenger Ships on Domestic Voyages) Regulations 2000, SI 2000/2687, reg 5; and PARA 605 note 4.

2   See the International Convention for the Safety of Life at Sea 1974 (London, 1 November 1974 to 1 July 1975; TS 46 (1980); Cmnd 7874), with Protocol (London, 1 June 1978 to 1 March 1979; TS 40 (1981); Cmnd 8277) (see PARA 7).

3   See the Merchant Shipping (Safety of Navigation) Regulations 2002, SI 2002/1473, reg 5 (amended by SI 2011/2978). Supplementary provision is made by reg 6, Sch 3. The Secretary of State may grant exemptions from various provisions of the SOLAS Convention Ch V (see the Merchant Shipping (Safety of Navigation) Regulations 2002, SI 2002/1473, regs 7, 8); and he may grant approvals, as respects a United Kingdom ship, where a regulation in the SOLAS Convention Ch V refers to any thing requiring the approval of the Administration, to be done to the satisfaction of the Administration, or to be acceptable to the Administration (see the Merchant Shipping (Safety of Navigation) Regulations 2002, SI 2002/1473, reg 9).

4   See the Merchant Shipping (Safety of Navigation) Regulations 2002, SI 2002/1473, reg 10, Sch 4; and PARA 1120.

5   See the Merchant Shipping (Safety of Navigation) Regulations 2002, SI 2002/1473, reg 11; and PARA 1120.

635. Procedure allowing radio stations to receive signals indicating dangers to navigation. Every person in charge of a controlled station for wireless telegraphy[1] must, on receiving the signal prescribed under safety regulations relating to dangers to navigation[2], which indicates that a message is about to be sent under those regulations, refrain from sending messages for a time sufficient to allow other stations to receive the message, and, if so required by the Secretary of State, must transmit the message in such manner as may be required by the Secretary of State[3]. Compliance with this requirement[4] is deemed to be a condition of every wireless telegraphy licence[5].

1   For these purposes, 'controlled station for wireless telegraphy' means such a station controlled by the Secretary of State or by the Office of Communications; 'controlled' includes controlled by means of a licence granted by the Office of Communications; and 'station for wireless telegraphy' has the same meaning as 'wireless telegraphy station' in the Wireless Telegraphy Act 2006 (as to which see BROADCASTING vol 4 (2011) PARA 510): Merchant Shipping Act 1995 s 91(7) (amended by the Communications Act 2003 Sch 17 para 132; and the Wireless Telegraphy Act 2006 Sch 7 para 15). As to the Secretary of State see PARA 36. As to the Office of Communications ('OFCOM') see TELECOMMUNICATIONS vol 97 (2015) PARA 2 et seq; and as to licences granted by OFCOM see BROADCASTING vol 4 (2011) PARA 724 et seq.

2   As to the Merchant Shipping (Safety of Navigation) Regulations 2002, SI 2002/1473, see PARA 634.

3   Merchant Shipping Act 1995 s 91(5) (amended by SI 2002/1473).

4   Ie compliance with the Merchant Shipping Act 1995 s 91(5) (see the text and notes 1–3): see s 91(6).

5   Merchant Shipping Act 1995 s 91(6). For these purposes, 'wireless telegraphy licence' has the same meaning as in the Wireless Telegraphy Act 2006 (see BROADCASTING vol 4 (2011) PARA 514): Merchant Shipping Act 1995 s 91(7) (definition added by the Wireless Telegraphy Act 2006 Sch 7 para 15).

636. Radio installations. The requirements relating to radio installations[1] to be complied with by ships[2] cover:
(1)   GMDSS ships[3]; and
(2)   non-GMDSS ships[4], including:
    (a)   VHF radiotelephony[5];
    (b)   radiotelephony[6];
    (c)   radiotelegraphy[7]; and
    (d)   radio equipment for lifeboats and survival craft[8].

There are also powers of enforcement[9]. Separate provision is made in relation to fishing vessels[10].

1   Ie the Merchant Shipping (Radio Installations) Regulations 1998, SI 1998/2070. For these purposes, 'radio installation' means any radio installation provided on board a ship in compliance with the Merchant Shipping (Radio Installations) Regulations 1998, SI 1998/2070, including its associated antennas, interconnecting circuits and, where appropriate, sources of electrical energy: reg 2. The regulations apply to sea-going United Kingdom ships wherever they may be (except while they are within the Great Lakes of North America and their connecting and tributary waters as far east as the lower exit of the St Lambert Lock at Montreal in the Province of Quebec, Canada) and to other seagoing ships while they are within United Kingdom waters: reg 3(1) (amended by SI 2000/2687). The Merchant Shipping (Radio Installations) Regulations 1998, SI 1998/2070, do not apply to troopships not registered in the United Kingdom, ships not propelled by mechanical means, pleasure vessels, fishing vessels, cargo ships of less than 300 tons, craft to which the Merchant Shipping (High Speed Craft) Regulations 2004, SI 2004/302 (see PARA 617 et seq) apply and ships which are passenger ships of Class A, B, C or D as defined in the Merchant Shipping (Passenger Ships on Domestic Voyages) Regulations 2000, SI 2000/2687 (see PARA 605 note 4), which are new ships, engaged on domestic voyages, for the purposes of those regulations: Merchant Shipping (Radio Installations) Regulations 1998, SI 1998/2070, reg 3(2) (amended by SI 2000/2687; SI 2004/302). Accordingly, the Merchant Shipping (Radio Installations) Regulations 1998, SI 1998/2070, have been revoked in relation to passenger ships of Class A, B, C or D of 24 metres or over in length engaged on domestic voyages (see the Merchant Shipping (Passenger Ships on Domestic Voyages) Regulations 2000, SI 2000/2687, reg 5; and PARA 605 note 4); and they do not apply to a commercial vessel which has been examined, and in respect of which a certificate has been issued, in accordance with the applicable Code of Practice, or to a vessel which is operating under the phase-in arrangements of the Code of Practice, as provided for under the Merchant Shipping (Vessels in Commercial Use for Sport or Pleasure) Regulations 1998, SI 1998/2771 (see PARAS 613, 614).

2   As to the Secretary of State's power to permit the provision of equivalent equipment and exemptions see the Merchant Shipping (Radio Installations) Regulations 1998, SI 1998/2070, reg 5; and as to the performance standards to be met by equipment that is required to be provided under the regulations see reg 6 (amended by SI 1999/1957; SI 2016/1025). Nothing in the Merchant Shipping (Radio Installations) Regulations 1998, SI 1998/2070, prohibits any ship, survival craft or person in distress from using any means at their disposal to attract attention, make known their position or obtain help: reg 4.

3   See the Merchant Shipping (Radio Installations) Regulations 1998, SI 1998/2070, Pt II (regs 7–20) which makes provision in relation to: functional requirements (reg 8); installation, location and control of radio equipment (reg 9); installation of a distress panel (reg 10); radio equipment to be provided for all sea areas (reg 11, Sch 1 (satellite EPIRBs)); additional radio equipment to be provided for area A1 ships (reg 12); additional radio equipment to be provided for area A2 ships (reg 13); additional radio equipment to be provided for area A3 ships (reg 14); additional radio equipment to be provided for area A4 ships (reg 15), radio watches (reg 16); sources of energy (reg 17); serviceability and maintenance requirements (reg 18, Sch 2 (equipment tests and reserve power checks)); radio personnel (reg 19); radio records (reg 20, Sch 3 (radio log)); and interpretation (reg 7). For these purposes, 'sea area A1' and 'sea area A2' mean an area specified as such in the Admiralty List of Radio Signals, being the document so entitled published by the Hydrographer of the Navy and any subsequent List containing the like information which the Hydrographer of the Navy considers relevant from time to time which replaces the Admiralty List of Radio Signals or replaces any subsequent List containing the like information (and a reference to any such List includes a reference to any Admiralty Notice to Mariners amending the same which the Hydrographer of the Navy considers relevant from time to time); 'sea area A3' means an area (excluding sea areas A1 and A2) within the coverage of an INMARSAT geostationary satellite in which continuous alerting is available; and 'sea area A4' means any area of the sea which is not sea area A1, A2 or A3: see reg 2. 'INMARSAT' means the Organisation established by the Convention on the International Maritime Satellite Organisation (with Operating Agreement) (London, 3 September 1976; TS 94 (1979); Cmnd 7722): see the Merchant Shipping (Radio Installations) Regulations 1998, SI 1998/2070, reg 2. As to the INMARSAT Convention see PARA 8; and TELECOMMUNICATIONS vol 97 (2015) PARA 56. 'GMDSS ship' means a ship to which the Merchant Shipping (Radio Installations) Regulations 1998, SI 1998/2070, Pt II applies; and 'GMDSS' means the Global Maritime Distress and Safety System: reg 2. GMDSS is the International Maritime Organisation's world-wide network of automated emergency communications for vessels at sea. As to the International Maritime Organisation see PARA 12.

4   See the Merchant Shipping (Radio Installations) Regulations 1998, SI 1998/2070, Pt III (regs 21–27) which makes provision in relation to: provision of radio installations (reg 22); interference

with reception and with other installations (reg 23); testing of equipment (reg 24, Sch 4 (equipment tests and battery and reserve power checks)); charging of batteries (reg 25); spare parts, tools and testing equipment (reg 26); serviceability and maintenance of radio installation (reg 27); and interpretation (reg 21 (amended by SI 2001/1638; SI 2011/1043)).

5 See the Merchant Shipping (Radio Installations) Regulations 1998, SI 1998/2070, Pt III (regs 28–32) which makes provision in relation to: VHF radiotelephone stations (reg 28); provision of antennas (reg 29); supply of electrical energy (reg 30); radiotelephone operators using the VHF radiotelephone installation (reg 31); and VHF radio watch (reg 32).

6 See the Merchant Shipping (Radio Installations) Regulations 1998, SI 1998/2070, Pt III (regs 33–39) which makes provision in relation to: radiotelephone stations (reg 33); provision of antennas (reg 34); the range of radiotelephone transmitters (reg 35); supply of electrical energy (reg 36); radiotelephone operators (reg 37, Sch 5 (additional knowledge and training requirements for radiotelephone operators and radio operators)); radio watch (reg 38); and the radio log in respect of radiotelephone ships (reg 39, Sch 6 (radio log in respect of radiotelephone ships) (reg 39 amended by SI 2001/1638)).

7 See the Merchant Shipping (Radio Installations) Regulations 1998, SI 1998/2070, Pt III (regs 40–47) which makes provision in relation to: radiotelegraph stations (reg 40); radiotelegraph operating rooms (reg 41); provision of antennas (reg 42); range of radiotelegraph transmitters (reg 43); supply of electrical energy (reg 44); radio officers (reg 45, Sch 5 (additional knowledge and training requirements for radiotelephone operators and radio operators) (reg 45 amended by SI 2001/1638)); radio watch (Merchant Shipping (Radio Installations) Regulations 1998, SI 1998/2070, reg 46); and radio log in respect of radiotelegraph ships (reg 47, Sch 7 (radio log in respect of radiotelegraph ships) (reg 47 amended by SI 2001/1638)).

8 See the Merchant Shipping (Radio Installations) Regulations 1998, SI 1998/2070, Pt III (reg 48).

9 See the Merchant Shipping (Radio Installations) Regulations 1998, SI 1998/2070, Pt IV (regs 49–51) which makes provision in relation to: the power to detain (reg 49); penalties (reg 50); and defences (reg 51).

10 See the Merchant Shipping (Radio) (Fishing Vessels) Regulations 1999, SI 1999/3210 (amended by SI 2002/2201); and FISHERIES AND AQUACULTURE vol 51 (2013) PARA 309.

637. Closing of openings in hulls etc. Before ships proceed on any voyage, they must comply with the relevant provisions relating to the closure of openings in hulls and watertight bulkheads below the bulkhead deck[1] and in enclosed superstructures and bulkheads above the bulkhead deck[2].

1 See the Merchant Shipping (Passenger Ship Construction: Ships of Classes I, II and II(A)) Regulations 1998, SI 1998/2514, Pt III (regs 20–26); and the Merchant Shipping (Passenger Ship Construction: Ships of Classes III to VI(A)) Regulations 1998, SI 1998/2515, Pt III (regs 15–20). Both the Merchant Shipping (Passenger Ship Construction: Ships of Classes I, II and II(A)) Regulations 1998, SI 1998/2514, and the Merchant Shipping (Passenger Ship Construction: Ships of Classes III to VI(A)) Regulations 1998, SI 1998/2515, have been revoked in relation to passenger ships of Class A, B, C or D of 24 metres or over in length engaged on domestic voyages: see the Merchant Shipping (Passenger Ships on Domestic Voyages) Regulations 2000, SI 2000/2687, reg 5; and PARA 605 note 4.

2 See the Merchant Shipping (Passenger Ship Construction: Ships of Classes I, II and II(A)) Regulations 1998, SI 1998/2514, Pt IV (regs 27–36) (amended by SI 2001/1638); and the Merchant Shipping (Passenger Ship Construction: Ships of Classes III to VI(A)) Regulations 1998, SI 1998/2515, Pt IV (regs 21–29). See note 1.

E. EQUIPMENT, LIFE-SAVING APPLIANCES AND COMMUNICATIONS

638. Safety requirements relating to ship's machinery and equipment. Regulations have been made imposing health and safety requirements with respect to:

(1) the provision and use of work equipment on merchant ships and fishing vessels[1];

(2) lifting operations and the provision and use of lifting equipment on merchant ships and fishing vessels[2]; and

(3) ensuring the safety of navigation (pursuant to which certain requirements are set down in relation to the equipment used in navigation)[3].

Separate provision is made to implement the EC Directive on Marine Equipment[4].

1　See the Merchant Shipping and Fishing Vessels (Provision and Use of Work Equipment) Regulations 2006, SI 2006/2183, which make provision in relation to: the circumstances in which the regulations apply (reg 4); the duties extended by the regulations to any person having control of a matter, eg by reason of having responsibility for operation of the ship (reg 5); requirements as to the suitability of work equipment (reg 6 (amended by SI 2008/2165)); the requirement for work equipment to be maintained in an efficient state and in good repair (Merchant Shipping and Fishing Vessels (Provision and Use of Work Equipment) Regulations 2006, SI 2006/2183, reg 7); the inspection of work equipment where its safety depends on the installation conditions (reg 8); the use of work equipment which involves a specific risk to health or safety (reg 9); information and instructions and training in the use of work equipment (regs 10, 11); the requirement for work equipment to be designed and constructed in accordance with specified requirements (reg 12, Schedule (amended by SI 2008/1597; SI 2013/1387)); the requirement for dangerous parts of ship's work equipment to have guards or protection devices (Merchant Shipping and Fishing Vessels (Provision and Use of Work Equipment) Regulations 2006, SI 2006/2183, reg 13), and for protection against electrical hazards (reg 14); the requirement for workers to be protected against specified hazards (reg 15) and from injury as a consequence of high or very low temperatures (reg 16); controls in relation to mobile work equipment (regs 17–21); the isolation of work equipment from sources of energy (reg 22); the stability of work equipment (reg 23); lighting (reg 24); maintenance operations (reg 25); markings (reg 26); warnings (reg 27); mobile work equipment (regs 28–33); the requirement for workers to comply with any instruction or training provided under the regulations (reg 34); and penalties, offences, inspections and detentions as well as compensation (regs 35–41).

2　See the Merchant Shipping and Fishing Vessels (Lifting Operations and Lifting Equipment) Regulations 2006, SI 2006/2184, which make provision in relation to: the circumstances in which the regulations apply (reg 4); the duties extended by the regulations to any person having control of a matter, eg by reason of having responsibility for operation of the ship (reg 5); requirements as to the strength of and stability of lifting equipment (reg 6); requirements as to lifting equipment for lifting persons (reg 7); the positioning and installation of permanently installed lifting equipment (reg 8); the requirement for lifting equipment to be marked with its safe working loads (reg 9); the requirement for lifting operations to be properly planned and supervised and for the employer to provide a safe system of work in specified circumstances (reg 10); the testing, examination and inspection of lifting equipment, and certificates and reports in relation to such matters (regs 11–15) (reg 11 amended by SI 2008/2166); requirements as to hatch covers used on a ship, which requires account to be taken of the principles and guidance in the Code of Safe Working Practices for Merchant Seamen (Merchant Shipping and Fishing Vessels (Lifting Operations and Lifting Equipment) Regulations 2006, SI 2006/2184, reg 16); the requirement for workers to comply with any reasonable instructions under reg 7, 10 or 16, as well as with any system of work provided by their employer in accordance with reg 10 (reg 17); and penalties, offences, inspections and detentions as well as compensation (regs 18–24).

3　In relation to navigation safety equipment see the Merchant Shipping (Safety of Navigation) Regulations 2002, SI 2002/1473; and PARA 634.

4　Ie Parliament and Council Directive (EU) 2014/90 (OJ L257, 28.08.2014, p 146) on marine equipment. As to the implementation referred to in the text see the Merchant Shipping (Marine Equipment) Regulations 2016, SI 2016/1025.

639. Life-saving routines, appliances and communications. Regulations have been made relating to:

(1)　emergency information for passengers[1];

(2)　minimum levels of training for seafarers, requiring the means for safe communication among the crew, between the crew and shore-based authorities, and between the crew and passengers on passenger ships and hovercraft in emergency situations[2];

(3)　life-saving appliances for different classes of ships[3]; and

(4)　musters and training[4].

1　See the Merchant Shipping (Emergency Information for Passengers) Regulations 1990, SI 1990/660.

2　See the Merchant Shipping (Minimum Standards of Safety Communications) Regulations 1997, SI 1997/529.

3   See the Merchant Shipping (Life-Saving Appliances For Ships Other Than Ships Of Classes III To VI(A)) Regulations 1999, SI 1999/2721; and the Merchant Shipping (Life-Saving Appliances For Passenger Ships Of Classes III To VI(A)) Regulations 1999, SI 1999/2723. Both the Merchant Shipping (Life-Saving Appliances For Ships Other Than Ships Of Classes III To VI(A)) Regulations 1999, SI 1999/2721, and the Merchant Shipping (Life-Saving Appliances For Passenger Ships Of Classes III To VI(A)) Regulations 1999, SI 1999/2723, are revoked in relation to passenger ships of Class A, B, C or D of 24 metres or over in length engaged on domestic voyages: see the Merchant Shipping (Passenger Ships on Domestic Voyages) Regulations 2000, SI 2000/2687, reg 5; and PARA 605 note 4. The Merchant Shipping (Life-Saving Appliances For Ships Other Than Ships Of Classes III To VI(A)) Regulations 1999, SI 1999/2721 do not apply to a commercial vessel which has been examined, and in respect of which a certificate has been issued, in accordance with the applicable Code of Practice, or to a vessel which is operating under the phase-in arrangements of the Code of Practice, as provided for under the Merchant Shipping (Vessels in Commercial Use for Sport or Pleasure) Regulations 1998, SI 1998/2771: see PARAS 613, 614.

4   See the Merchant Shipping (Musters, Training and Decision Support Systems) Regulations 1999, SI 1999/2722. Musters, fire-fighting and lifeboat drills prescribed by these regulations must be conducted in a manner which minimises the disturbance of rest periods and does not induce fatigue: see the Merchant Shipping (Hours of Work) Regulations 2002, SI 2002/2125, reg 5(3); and as to minimum hours of rest see PARA 511.

F.   COUNTING AND REGISTERING PASSENGERS

(A)   Procedure for Counting and Registering Passengers

640.   System for counting passengers on board. The owner of any passenger ship[1] must ensure that, in respect of any United Kingdom passenger ship when it leaves any landing point[2] and in respect of any other passenger ship when it leaves any landing point in the United Kingdom, there is a system capable of counting all persons[3] on board which[4]:

(1)   in the case of a passenger ship of Class II or II(A)[5], in respect of passengers, uses a system of individual passenger boarding cards[6];

(2)   conforms to the prescribed requirements[7] and the appropriate Merchant Shipping Notice[8]; and

(3)   is approved by the Secretary of State[9].

The system of counting so established[10] must be such that:

(a)   all persons boarding such a ship at a landing point at the beginning of a voyage[11] are counted individually on, or just prior to, boarding[12] and, as the case may be:

(i)   all persons disembarking at subsequent landing points, during the course of a voyage, are counted individually as they disembark[13];

(ii)   all persons boarding at subsequent landing points, during the course of a voyage, are counted individually on, or just prior to, boarding[14]; and

(iii)   the number of persons remaining on board at each landing point is determined[15]; or

(b)   the number of persons is determined and recorded according to an alternative method approved by the Secretary of State, which must be of equivalent effectiveness to the system set out in head (a) above[16];

If the counting system so established in respect of a passenger ship[17] includes a system of individual passenger boarding cards no passenger is to be permitted to board the ship unless he has been issued with an individual boarding card[18].

Immediately before a passenger ship leaves any landing point the total number of persons on board at that time as determined by means of the counting system must be communicated to the master of the ship and the passenger registrar[19].

If, in respect of any person on board a ship, any person has declared a need for special care or assistance in emergency situations, the owner must ensure that such information is properly recorded and communicated to the master of the ship[20].

No passenger ship is to leave any landing point if:

(A)   the total number of persons on board has not been communicated to the master of the ship and the passenger registrar[21] or the owner has not properly recorded and communicated to the master of the ship any person's declared need for special care or assistance in emergency situations[22]; or

(B)   the total number of persons on board the ship exceeds the number of persons the ship is permitted to carry[23].

The arrangements made in pursuance of the requirements for counting all persons on board[24] must be described in written instructions which are to be kept on board the ship at all times in the custody of the master[25].

Additional requirements apply to voyages of more than 20 miles[26]; and, in respect of any passenger ship which is not a Community ship[27] on any voyage from any landing point outside the territory of the European Community to the United Kingdom the owner must make specified information[28] readily available to the appropriate search and rescue services[29] for the purposes of search and rescue in the event of an emergency or in the aftermath of an accident involving the ship[30].

1   For these purposes, 'passenger ship' means any ship carrying more than 12 passengers; and 'ship' includes hovercraft: Merchant Shipping (Counting and Registration of Persons on Board Passenger Ships) Regulations 1999, SI 1999/1869, reg 3(1). Where a ship is managed or operated by a person other than the owner (whether on behalf of the owner or some other person, or on his own behalf), a reference to the owner is to be construed as including a reference to that other person: reg 3(2).
    The Merchant Shipping (Counting and Registration of Persons on Board Passenger Ships) Regulations 1999, SI 1999/1869, apply to any United Kingdom passenger ship wherever it may be and any other passenger ship while it is within United Kingdom waters: reg 4(1). However, the regulations do not apply to any ship of war, any troop ship, any pleasure yacht (unless it is or will be crewed and carry more than 12 passengers for commercial purposes), any passenger ship to which the Merchant Shipping (Passenger Ships) (Safety Code for UK Categorised Waters) Regulations 2010, SI 2010/680 (see PARA 604) apply, or any vessel to which the Merchant Shipping (Technical Requirements for Inland Waterway Vessels) Regulations 2010, SI 2010/1075 (see PARA 604) apply: reg 4(2) (amended by SI 2010/680; SI 2010/1075). For these purposes, 'United Kingdom passenger ship' means a passenger ship which is a United Kingdom ship: Merchant Shipping (Counting and Registration of Persons on Board Passenger Ships) Regulations 1999, SI 1999/1869, reg 3(1). As to the meaning of 'United Kingdom' see PARA 16 note 3.
    The regulations implement Council Directive (EC) 98/41 (OJ L188, 02.07.1998, p 35) on the registration of persons sailing on board passenger ships operating to or from ports of the Member States of the Community and the International Convention for the Safety of Life at Sea 1974 (London, 1 November 1974 to 1 July 1975; TS 46 (1980); Cmnd 7874), with Protocol (London, 1 June 1978 to 1 March 1979; TS 40 (1981); Cmnd 8277) (as to which see PARA 7) Ch III.
2   For these purposes, 'landing point' means any berth, excursion point, floating pier or stage, link span, pier, port, stop or anchorage point from or to where passengers are embarked or disembarked: Merchant Shipping (Counting and Registration of Persons on Board Passenger Ships) Regulations 1999, SI 1999/1869, reg 3(1).
3   For these purposes, 'person' means any person on board a ship irrespective of their age: Merchant Shipping (Counting and Registration of Persons on Board Passenger Ships) Regulations 1999, SI 1999/1869, reg 3(1).
4   Merchant Shipping (Counting and Registration of Persons on Board Passenger Ships) Regulations 1999, SI 1999/1869, reg 5(1). As to exemptions see PARA 642; and as to offences see PARA 1121.
5   Ie within the meaning of the Merchant Shipping (Passenger Ship Construction: Ships of Classes I, II and II(A)) Regulations 1998, SI 1998/2514 (see PARA 602 note 3): see the Merchant Shipping (Counting and Registration of Persons on Board Passenger Ships) Regulations 1999, SI 1999/1869, reg 5(1)(a).
6   Merchant Shipping (Counting and Registration of Persons on Board Passenger Ships) Regulations 1999, SI 1999/1869, reg 5(1)(a).

7　Ie the requirements of the Merchant Shipping (Counting and Registration of Persons on Board Passenger Ships) Regulations 1999, SI 1999/1869, reg 5(2)–(5) (see the text and notes 10–20): see reg 5(1)(b).

8　Merchant Shipping (Counting and Registration of Persons on Board Passenger Ships) Regulations 1999, SI 1999/1869, reg 5(1)(b). For these purposes, 'Merchant Shipping Notice' means a Notice described as such, issued by the Maritime and Coastguard Agency; and a reference to any particular Merchant Shipping Notice includes a reference to any document amending or replacing that Notice: reg 3(1). Accordingly, the text refers to Merchant Shipping Notice 1794(M+F): see the Merchant Shipping (Counting and Registration of Persons on Board Passenger Ships) Regulations 1999, SI 1999/1869, reg 5(1)(b). As to the Maritime and Coastguard Agency see PARA 57.

9　Merchant Shipping (Counting and Registration of Persons on Board Passenger Ships) Regulations 1999, SI 1999/1869, reg 5(1)(c). As to the Secretary of State see PARA 36.

10　Ie established by the Merchant Shipping (Counting and Registration of Persons on Board Passenger Ships) Regulations 1999, SI 1999/1869, reg 5(1) (see the text and notes 1–9): see reg 5(2).

11　For these purposes, 'voyage' includes an excursion: Merchant Shipping (Counting and Registration of Persons on Board Passenger Ships) Regulations 1999, SI 1999/1869, reg 3(1).

12　Merchant Shipping (Counting and Registration of Persons on Board Passenger Ships) Regulations 1999, SI 1999/1869, reg 5(2)(a).

13　Merchant Shipping (Counting and Registration of Persons on Board Passenger Ships) Regulations 1999, SI 1999/1869, reg 5(2)(a)(i).

14　Merchant Shipping (Counting and Registration of Persons on Board Passenger Ships) Regulations 1999, SI 1999/1869, reg 5(2)(a)(ii).

15　Merchant Shipping (Counting and Registration of Persons on Board Passenger Ships) Regulations 1999, SI 1999/1869, reg 5(2)(a)(iii).

16　Merchant Shipping (Counting and Registration of Persons on Board Passenger Ships) Regulations 1999, SI 1999/1869, reg 5(2)(b).

17　Ie established by the Merchant Shipping (Counting and Registration of Persons on Board Passenger Ships) Regulations 1999, SI 1999/1869, reg 5(1) (see the text and notes 1–9): see reg 5(3).

18　Merchant Shipping (Counting and Registration of Persons on Board Passenger Ships) Regulations 1999, SI 1999/1869, reg 5(3).

19　Merchant Shipping (Counting and Registration of Persons on Board Passenger Ships) Regulations 1999, SI 1999/1869, reg 5(4). For these purposes, 'passenger registrar' means the person appointed by the owner of a ship pursuant to reg 8(1)(b) (see PARA 651): reg 3(1). As to exemptions in respect of reg 5(4) particularly see PARA 642.

20　Merchant Shipping (Counting and Registration of Persons on Board Passenger Ships) Regulations 1999, SI 1999/1869, reg 5(5).

21　Ie if the requirements of the Merchant Shipping (Counting and Registration of Persons on Board Passenger Ships) Regulations 1999, SI 1999/1869, reg 5(4) (see the text and note 19) have not been complied with: see reg 5(6)(a).

22　Ie if the requirements of the Merchant Shipping (Counting and Registration of Persons on Board Passenger Ships) Regulations 1999, SI 1999/1869, reg 5(5) (see the text and note 20) have not been complied with: see reg 5(6)(a).

23　Merchant Shipping (Counting and Registration of Persons on Board Passenger Ships) Regulations 1999, SI 1999/1869, reg 5(6)(b).

24　Ie the requirements in the Merchant Shipping (Counting and Registration of Persons on Board Passenger Ships) Regulations 1999, SI 1999/1869, reg 5(1) (see the text and notes 1–9): see reg 5(7).

25　Merchant Shipping (Counting and Registration of Persons on Board Passenger Ships) Regulations 1999, SI 1999/1869, reg 5(7).

26　In respect of any United Kingdom passenger ship leaving any landing point either inside the territory of the EU on a voyage of more than 20 miles from that landing point, or outside the territory of the EU on an international voyage, and in respect of any other passenger ship leaving any landing point in the United Kingdom on a voyage of more than 20 miles from that landing point (Merchant Shipping (Counting and Registration of Persons on Board Passenger Ships) Regulations 1999, SI 1999/1869, reg 6(1) (amended by SI 2011/1043)), the owner must ensure that:

　　(1)　the information specified in heads (a) to (e) below is collected, in relation to each person on board, before the ship departs from the landing point (Merchant Shipping (Counting and Registration of Persons on Board Passenger Ships) Regulations 1999, SI 1999/1869, reg 6(2)(a)); and

(2)   that information is communicated to the passenger registrar within 30 minutes of the ship's departure from the landing point, and, in respect of any such information as is specified in head (e) below, communicated to the master of the ship before the ship leaves the landing point (reg 6(2)(b)).

For these purposes, 'mile' means a nautical mile of 1852 metres: reg 3(1). The information referred to in heads (1) and (2) above is, in relation to each person on board the ship:

(a)   family name (reg 6(3)(a));
(b)   forenames or initials (reg 6(3)(b));
(c)   gender (reg 6(3)(c));
(d)   an indication of the category of age (such category being either adult, child or infant) to which the person belongs or the age or the year of birth of the person (reg 6(3)(d)); and
(e)   if volunteered by a person, any information concerning the need for special care or assistance in emergency situations (reg 6(3)(e)).

If the information in relation to a person indicates the category of age to which the person belongs (see head (d) above) but does not indicate that person's age or year of birth, the information must be accompanied by an indication of the age range used to define each category, and the age range used must be the age range used by the system for the registration of the information established in accordance with reg 8(1) (see PARA 641): reg 6(4). For these purposes, 'international voyage' means a voyage from a country to which the International Convention for the Safety of Life at Sea 1974 (London, 1 November 1974 to 1 July 1975; TS 46 (1980); Cmnd 7874), with Protocol (London, 1 June 1978 to 1 March 1979; TS 40 (1981); Cmnd 8277) (as to which see PARA 7) applies to a port outside that country, or conversely: Merchant Shipping (Counting and Registration of Persons on Board Passenger Ships) Regulations 1999, SI 1999/1869, reg 3(1). As to exemptions in relation to reg 6(2) particularly see PARA 642.

A person must not, in connection with a system for counting the persons on board a passenger ship or collecting the information specified in reg 6(3), either knowingly or recklessly make any false statement liable or intended to lead to error in the determination of the total number of persons on board or in the collection of the information specified in reg 6(3), or falsify the information collected or transmitted to the passenger registrar: reg 10. As to offences see PARA 1121.

27 For these purposes, 'Community ship' means a ship which is registered in, or which is entitled to fly the flag of, a member state: Merchant Shipping (Counting and Registration of Persons on Board Passenger Ships) Regulations 1999, SI 1999/1869, reg 3(1). In any Act, 'member state' means a state which is a member of the European Communities: see the European Communities Act 1972 s 1(2), Sch 1 Pt II; and the Interpretation Act 1978 s 5, Sch 1.

28 Ie information as to the total number of persons on board the ship, and the information specified in the Merchant Shipping (Counting and Registration of Persons on Board Passenger Ships) Regulations 1999, SI 1999/1869, reg 6(3) (see note 25): see reg 7.

29 For these purposes, 'appropriate search and rescue services' means, in relation to a ship involved in an emergency, the search and rescue services for the area in which the ship is located; and 'search and rescue services' means the search and rescue services responsible for the initiation and co-ordination of all maritime search and rescue activity required to provide assistance in the event of an emergency involving a ship or its aftermath: Merchant Shipping (Counting and Registration of Persons on Board Passenger Ships) Regulations 1999, SI 1999/1869, reg 3(1).

30 Merchant Shipping (Counting and Registration of Persons on Board Passenger Ships) Regulations 1999, SI 1999/1869, reg 7.

641. System for registering passengers on board. The owner of a passenger ship[1] must[2]:

(1)   establish a system for the registration of the information collected in relation to persons[3] on board passenger ships[4] which is in accordance with the requirements of the appropriate Merchant Shipping Notice[5] and is approved by the Secretary of State[6];
(2)   appoint a shore-based passenger registrar[7] who is to be responsible for holding the information so collected[8] and for its transmission to appropriate search and rescue services[9] in the event of an emergency or in the aftermath of an accident involving the ship[10]; and
(3)   ensure that the information so collected[11] is at all times readily available for transmission to the appropriate search and rescue services for use in an emergency or in the aftermath of an accident involving the ship[12].

Any personal data which are collected solely for the purposes of counting and registering persons on board passenger ships[13] by an owner must be kept only for as long as is necessary for those purposes[14].

The Secretary of State may appoint persons to carry out checks on the proper functioning of registration systems so approved[15]; and, in performing such checks, the persons so appointed are entitled to board any ship to which the registration system relates and enter any premises of the passenger registrar[16], and they are to have access to any records and documents, including electronic and computer records, which comprise the owner's registration system[17].

1   Ie a passenger ship to which the Merchant Shipping (Counting and Registration of Persons on Board Passenger Ships) Regulations 1999, SI 1999/1869, reg 5 or reg 6 applies (see PARA 640): see reg 8(1). As to the meaning of 'passenger ship' and as to the meaning of references to the owner of a ship see PARA 640 note 1.
2   Merchant Shipping (Counting and Registration of Persons on Board Passenger Ships) Regulations 1999, SI 1999/1869, reg 8(1). As to exemptions see PARA 642; and as to offences see PARA 1121.
3   As to the meaning of 'person' for these purposes see PARA 640 note 3.
4   Ie information collected pursuant to the Merchant Shipping (Counting and Registration of Persons on Board Passenger Ships) Regulations 1999, SI 1999/1869 (see PARA 640): see reg 8(1)(a).
5   Merchant Shipping (Counting and Registration of Persons on Board Passenger Ships) Regulations 1999, SI 1999/1869, reg 8(1)(a)(i). The text refers to Merchant Shipping Notice 1794(M+F): see the Merchant Shipping (Counting and Registration of Persons on Board Passenger Ships) Regulations 1999, SI 1999/1869, reg 8(1)(a)(i). As to the meaning of 'Merchant Shipping Notice' see PARA 640 note 8.
6   Merchant Shipping (Counting and Registration of Persons on Board Passenger Ships) Regulations 1999, SI 1999/1869, reg 8(1)(a)(ii). As to the Secretary of State see PARA 36.
7   As to the meaning of 'passenger registrar' for these purposes see PARA 640 note 19.
8   Ie collected pursuant to the Merchant Shipping (Counting and Registration of Persons on Board Passenger Ships) Regulations 1999, SI 1999/1869 (see PARA 640): see reg 8(1)(b).
9   As to the meanings of 'appropriate search and rescue services' and 'search and rescue services' for these purposes see PARA 640 note 29.
10 Merchant Shipping (Counting and Registration of Persons on Board Passenger Ships) Regulations 1999, SI 1999/1869, reg 8(1)(b).
11 Ie collected pursuant to the Merchant Shipping (Counting and Registration of Persons on Board Passenger Ships) Regulations 1999, SI 1999/1869 (see PARA 640): see reg 8(1)(c).
12 Merchant Shipping (Counting and Registration of Persons on Board Passenger Ships) Regulations 1999, SI 1999/1869, reg 8(1)(c).
13 Ie collected solely pursuant to the Merchant Shipping (Counting and Registration of Persons on Board Passenger Ships) Regulations 1999, SI 1999/1869 (see PARA 640): see reg 8(2).
14 Merchant Shipping (Counting and Registration of Persons on Board Passenger Ships) Regulations 1999, SI 1999/1869, reg 8(2).
15 Merchant Shipping (Counting and Registration of Persons on Board Passenger Ships) Regulations 1999, SI 1999/1869, reg 8(3). The text refers to registration systems approved under the Merchant Shipping (Counting and Registration of Persons on Board Passenger Ships) Regulations 1999, SI 1999/1869, reg 8: see reg 8(3).
16 Merchant Shipping (Counting and Registration of Persons on Board Passenger Ships) Regulations 1999, SI 1999/1869, reg 8(4)(i).
17 Merchant Shipping (Counting and Registration of Persons on Board Passenger Ships) Regulations 1999, SI 1999/1869, reg 8(4)(ii).

642. Exemption from the requirements to count and register passengers on board.

The Secretary of State[1] may exempt any passenger ship[2] from the requirements of the provisions which require the counting and registration of persons[3] on board[4], subject to such conditions (if any) as he may specify, and may, subject to giving reasonable notice, alter or cancel any exemption so granted[5].

Without prejudice to this provision, the Secretary of State may exempt any passenger ship[6]:

(1)   leaving any landing point[7] within the United Kingdom[8] from the requirement[9] to communicate to the master of the ship and the passenger registrar[10] the total number of persons on board at that time,

in so far as that requirement applies as respects the passenger registrar if the ship is engaged, exclusively in a protected sea area[11], on a regular service[12] of less than one hour between calls at landing points[13]; or

(2)　from the requirements[14] placed on the owner of the ship[15] to collect and communicate additional information on persons in respect of any voyage[16] of more than 20 miles from the landing point[17]:

(a)　if, in respect of any United Kingdom passenger ship[18] leaving any landing point outside the territory of the EU on an international voyage[19], the scheduled voyages of the ship make it impracticable for such records to be prepared[20]; and

(b)　if, in respect of any passenger ship leaving any landing point within the United Kingdom, the ship sails exclusively in a protected sea area between two landing points or from and to the same landing point without calling at any intermediate landing point[21], or the ship is engaged on a regular community service[22].

1　As to the Secretary of State see PARA 36.
2　As to the meaning of 'passenger ship' for these purposes see PARA 640 note 1.
3　As to the meaning of 'person' for these purposes see PARA 640 note 3.
4　Ie from the requirements of the Merchant Shipping (Counting and Registration of Persons on Board Passenger Ships) Regulations 1999, SI 1999/1869 (see PARAS 640, 641): see reg 9(1).
5　Merchant Shipping (Counting and Registration of Persons on Board Passenger Ships) Regulations 1999, SI 1999/1869, reg 9(1).
6　Merchant Shipping (Counting and Registration of Persons on Board Passenger Ships) Regulations 1999, SI 1999/1869, reg 9(2).
7　As to the meaning of 'landing point' for these purposes see PARA 640 note 2.
8　As to the meaning of 'United Kingdom' see PARA 16 note 3.
9　Ie from the requirements of the Merchant Shipping (Counting and Registration of Persons on Board Passenger Ships) Regulations 1999, SI 1999/1869, reg 5(4) (see PARA 640): see reg 9(2)(a).
10　As to the meaning of 'passenger registrar' for these purposes see PARA 640 note 19.
11　For these purposes, 'protected sea area' means a sea area sheltered from open sea effects where a ship is at no time more than six miles from a place of refuge where shipwrecked persons can land and in which the proximity of search and rescue facilities is ensured: Merchant Shipping (Counting and Registration of Persons on Board Passenger Ships) Regulations 1999, SI 1999/1869, reg 3(1). As to the meaning of 'search and rescue services' for these purposes see PARA 640 note 29.
12　For these purposes, 'regular service' means a series of ship crossings operated so as to serve traffic between the same two or more ports either according to a published timetable, or with crossings so regular or frequent that they constitute a recognisable systematic series: Merchant Shipping (Counting and Registration of Persons on Board Passenger Ships) Regulations 1999, SI 1999/1869, reg 3(1).
13　Merchant Shipping (Counting and Registration of Persons on Board Passenger Ships) Regulations 1999, SI 1999/1869, reg 9(2)(a).
14　Ie from the requirements of the Merchant Shipping (Counting and Registration of Persons on Board Passenger Ships) Regulations 1999, SI 1999/1869, reg 6(2) (see PARA 640): see reg 9(2)(b).
15　As to the meaning of references to the owner of a ship see PARA 640 note 1.
16　As to the meaning of 'voyage' see PARA 640 note 11.
17　Merchant Shipping (Counting and Registration of Persons on Board Passenger Ships) Regulations 1999, SI 1999/1869, reg 9(2)(b).
18　As to the meaning of 'United Kingdom passenger ship' see PARA 640 note 1.
19　As to the meaning of 'international voyage' see PARA 640 note 26.
20　Merchant Shipping (Counting and Registration of Persons on Board Passenger Ships) Regulations 1999, SI 1999/1869, reg 9(2)(b)(i) (amended by SI 2011/1043).
21　Merchant Shipping (Counting and Registration of Persons on Board Passenger Ships) Regulations 1999, SI 1999/1869, reg 9(2)(b)(ii)(aa).
22　Merchant Shipping (Counting and Registration of Persons on Board Passenger Ships) Regulations 1999, SI 1999/1869, reg 9(2)(b)(ii)(bb). For these purposes, 'regular community service' means a regular service in a sea area where the annual probability of the significant wave height exceeding two metres is less than 10% and either the voyage does not exceed 30 miles or thereabouts from the point of departure, or the primary purpose of the service is to provide regular links to outlying communities for customary purposes: reg 3(1).

(B)   Returns Required as to Passengers on Board, Births etc

643.   Returns to be furnished by masters of ships as to passengers. The master[1] of every ship[2], whether or not a United Kingdom ship[3], which carries any passenger to a place in the United Kingdom from any place out of the United Kingdom, or from any place in the United Kingdom to any place out of the United Kingdom, must furnish to such person and in such manner as the Secretary of State directs[4] a return giving the total number of any passengers so carried, distinguishing, if so directed by the Secretary of State, the total number of any class of passengers so carried, and giving, if the Secretary of State so directs, such particulars with respect to passengers as may be for the time being required by the Secretary of State[5].

Any passenger must furnish the master of the ship with any information required by him for the purpose of the return[6].

If the master of a ship fails to make a return as required[7] (or if he makes a false return)[8], or if any passenger refuses to give any information required by the master of the ship for the purpose of the return so required (or, for that purpose, gives to the master information which he knows to be false, or recklessly gives to him information which is false)[9], the master or, as the case may be, passenger commits an offence[10].

1   As to the meaning of 'master' see PARA 444 note 1.
2   As to the meaning of 'ship' see PARA 229.
3   As to the meaning of 'United Kingdom ship' see PARA 230. As to the meaning of 'United Kingdom' see PARA 16 note 3.
4   As to the Secretary of State see PARA 36; and as to the Secretary of State's power to give directions under the Merchant Shipping Act 1995 generally see PARA 39.
5   Merchant Shipping Act 1995 s 107(1). As to the Secretary of State's power to require statistical returns in respect of carriage of goods and passengers by sea from any person carrying on business or trade in the maritime transport sector see PARA 42.
6   Merchant Shipping Act 1995 s 107(2).
7   Ie as required by the Merchant Shipping Act 1995 s 107(1), (2) (see the text and notes 1–6): see s 107(3)(a); and PARA 1123.
8   See the Merchant Shipping Act 1995 s 107(3)(a); and PARA 1123.
9   See the Merchant Shipping Act 1995 s 107(3)(b); and PARA 1123.
10 See the Merchant Shipping Act 1995 s 107(3); and PARA 1123.

644.   Requirement to register births and deaths on board ship. Where a child is born in a ship registered in the United Kingdom[1], the master of the ship must make a return of the birth[2]; and where:

(1)   any person dies in a ship registered in the United Kingdom[3]; or
(2)   any person employed in any such ship dies outside the United Kingdom[4],

the master of the ship must make a return of the death[5] and, as soon as practicable but no more than three days after the death, must notify the death to such person, if any, as the deceased may have named as his next of kin[6].

Where a citizen of the United Kingdom and Colonies[7] is born or dies in a ship not registered in the United Kingdom, and the ship thereafter calls at a port in the United Kingdom in the course of or at the end of the voyage during which the death occurs, the master of the ship must make a return of the birth or death[8].

Any return of a birth or of a death occurring in a ship registered in the United Kingdom[9] must be made by the master of the ship as soon as practicable, but within six months, after the birth or death to which it relates[10]; and:

(a)   in the case of a birth or death which occurs in the ship, must be made to a superintendent[11] or proper officer[12] for the place where the ship is at the time of the birth or death, or at which it next calls thereafter[13]; and

(b)   in the case of a death which occurs elsewhere than in a ship, must be made to a superintendent or proper officer for the place where the ship is when the master first becomes aware of the death or at which it next calls thereafter[14].

Any return of a birth or of a death of a citizen of the United Kingdom and Colonies occurring in a ship not registered in the United Kingdom but which thereafter calls at a port in the United Kingdom in the course of or at the end of the voyage[15] must be made by the master of the ship to a superintendent for that port in the United Kingdom before the ship leaves that port[16].

When a return of a birth or death duly made[17] has been transmitted to him, or when a record of a death (where the master is unable to act)[18] has been made by him, the Registrar General of Shipping and Seamen must send a copy of that return or record, certified by him or by a person authorised by him for that purpose to be a true copy, to the appropriate Registrar General[19]. The following births and deaths occurring outside the United Kingdom in circumstances where no return or record is otherwise required may also be recorded in the marine register by the appropriate Registrar General as he thinks fit, if he is satisfied that such a birth or death has occurred[20], namely:

(i)   any birth or death of a citizen of the United Kingdom and Colonies which occurs in a ship not registered in the United Kingdom[21];

(ii)   any death of a citizen of the United Kingdom and Colonies who has been employed in such a ship which occurs elsewhere than in the ship[22]; and

(iii)   any death of a person who has been employed in a ship registered in the United Kingdom which occurs elsewhere than in the ship[23].

The master of a ship who fails to comply with any of the provisions which require returns to be made as to births and deaths occurring in his ship[24] is guilty of an offence[25].

1   As to the meaning of 'United Kingdom' see PARA 16 note 3. The provisions of the Merchant Shipping (Returns of Births and Deaths) Regulations 1979, SI 1979/1577, except reg 4 (see the text and notes 7–8), and reg 10(1)(a) (see head (i) in the text) and reg 10(1)(b) (see head (ii) in the text) extend to ships which are sea-going ships (not registered in the United Kingdom or elsewhere) which are owned by a person resident in, or by a body corporate having a principal place of business in, the United Kingdom, and masters and seamen employed in them: reg 12(1) (amended by SI 1991/1366). However, in such a case, the particulars required to be contained in records or returns by the Merchant Shipping (Returns of Births and Deaths) Regulations 1979, SI 1979/1577, Sch 1 (see notes 10, 16) and Sch 2 (see notes 6, 16), as extended by reg 12(1), are subject to certain modifications: see reg 12(2). The Merchant Shipping (Returns of Births and Deaths) Regulations 1979, SI 1979/1577, have effect under the Merchant Shipping Act 1995 s 108 (amended by the British Overseas Territories Act 2002 s 2(3); and by the Coroners and Justice Act 2009 Sch 21 para 33).

2   Merchant Shipping (Returns of Births and Deaths) Regulations 1979, SI 1979/1577, reg 2. The return required as mentioned in the text must be made in accordance with regs 5, 6 (see the text and notes 9–16): see reg 2.

3   Merchant Shipping (Returns of Births and Deaths) Regulations 1979, SI 1979/1577, reg 3(a).

4   Merchant Shipping (Returns of Births and Deaths) Regulations 1979, SI 1979/1577, reg 3(b).

5   The return required by the Merchant Shipping (Returns of Births and Deaths) Regulations 1979, SI 1979/1577, reg 3 must be made in accordance with regs 5, 6 (see the text and notes 9–16): see reg 3.

6   Merchant Shipping (Returns of Births and Deaths) Regulations 1979, SI 1979/1577, reg 3. Where it appears to the Registrar General of Shipping and Seamen that the master of the ship cannot perform the duty imposed on him by virtue of reg 3 in respect of the death because he has himself died or is incapacitated or missing (reg 7); and either:

(1)   the death in question has been the subject of an inquest held by the coroner or a statutory inquiry held under the Merchant Shipping Act 1995 s 271 (see PARA 846), and the findings of the inquest or inquiry include a finding that the death occurred (Merchant Shipping (Returns of Births and Deaths) Regulations 1979, SI 1979/1577, reg 7(1)); or

(2)   a post-mortem examination has been made of the deceased's body and in consequence
the coroner is satisfied that an inquest is unnecessary (reg 7(2)),
then the Registrar General of Shipping and Seamen must record such of the information specified
in reg 7, Sch 2 (see note 10) as he may be able to obtain in the circumstances of death: reg 7.
However, in circumstances where:
(a)   an inquest is held on a dead body or touching a death or a post-mortem examination is
made of a dead body as a result of which the coroner is satisfied that an inquest is
unnecessary (reg 8(1)); and
(b)   it appears to the coroner that the death in question is such as is mentioned in reg 3(a)
(see head (1) in the text) or in reg 3(b) (see head (2) in the text), as extended by reg 12(1)
(see note 1) (reg 8(2)),
it is the duty of the coroner to send to the Registrar General of Shipping and Seamen particulars
in respect of the deceased of the kind specified in reg 8, Sch 3: reg 8. Accordingly, the particulars
that are required to be sent by coroners in respect of deaths under reg 8 relate to: the ship in which
death occurred or in which the deceased was employed; the deceased; and the Coroner's certificate:
see Sch 3. As to the Registrar General of Shipping and Seamen see PARA 62.
7   As to the meaning of 'colony' for the purposes of the British Nationality Act 1981 see BRITISH
NATIONALITY vol 4 (2011) PARA 415.
8   Merchant Shipping (Returns of Births and Deaths) Regulations 1979, SI 1979/1577, reg 4. The
return required as mentioned in the text must be made in accordance with regs 5, 6 (see the text
and notes 9–16): see reg 4.
9   Ie a return required to be made under the Merchant Shipping (Returns of Births and Deaths)
Regulations 1979, SI 1979/1577, reg 2 (see the text and notes 1–2) or reg 3 (see the text and notes
3–6): see reg 5(1).
10 Merchant Shipping (Returns of Births and Deaths) Regulations 1979, SI 1979/1577, reg 5(1).
Without prejudice to reg 5(1), and to the provisions of reg 13 (offences) (see PARA 1124), a return
of a birth or of a death required to be made under reg 2 (see the text and notes 1–2) or reg 3 (see
the text and notes 3–6) which is not made within the prescribed period or is made to a
superintendent or proper officer other than that specified in reg 5(1) (see heads (a), (b) in the text)
is not invalid by reason only that it is not made within that period or to that specified person: reg
5(3). A return of a birth or of a death required to be made under the Merchant Shipping (Returns
of Births and Deaths) Regulations 1979, SI 1979/1577, must be in writing, must be signed by the
master of the ship as informant, and must contain (in the case of a birth) the particulars specified
in Sch 1 (amended by SI 2009/1892) or (in the case of a death) the particulars specified in the
Merchant Shipping (Returns of Births and Deaths) Regulations 1979, SI 1979/1577, Sch 2, or in
either case so many of those particulars as the master may reasonably be able to obtain, having
regard to the circumstances of the birth or of the death: reg 6. Accordingly, the particulars that are
required to be contained in returns of births (or authorised to be recorded in the marine register)
relate to: the ship in which birth occurred; the child; the father; the mother; and the informant: see
Sch 1 (as so amended). The particulars that are required to be contained in returns or records of
deaths (or authorised to be recorded in the marine register) relate to: the ship in which death
occurred or in which the deceased was employed; the deceased; and the informant: see Sch 2.
11 As to the meaning of 'superintendent' see PARA 61 note 1.
12 As to the meaning of 'proper officer' see PARA 48 note 11.
13 Merchant Shipping (Returns of Births and Deaths) Regulations 1979, SI 1979/1577, reg 5(1)(a).
14 Merchant Shipping (Returns of Births and Deaths) Regulations 1979, SI 1979/1577, reg 5(1)(b).
15 Ie a return required to be made under the Merchant Shipping (Returns of Births and Deaths)
Regulations 1979, SI 1979/1577, reg 4 (see the text and notes 7–8): see reg 5(2).
16 Merchant Shipping (Returns of Births and Deaths) Regulations 1979, SI 1979/1577, reg 5(2).
Without prejudice to reg 5(2), and to the provisions of reg 13 (offences) (see PARA 1124), a return
of a birth or of a death required to be made under reg 4 (see the text and notes 7–8) which is not
made within the prescribed period or is made to a superintendent or proper officer other than that
specified in reg 5(2) is not invalid by reason only that it is not made within that period or to that
specified person: reg 5(3). A return of a birth or of a death required to be made under the Merchant
Shipping (Returns of Births and Deaths) Regulations 1979, SI 1979/1577, must be in writing, must
be signed by the master of the ship as informant, and must contain (in the case of a birth) the
particulars specified in Sch 1 (see note 10), or (in the case of a death) the particulars specified in
Sch 2 (see note 10), or in either case so many of those particulars as the master may reasonably be
able to obtain, having regard to the circumstances of the birth or of the death: reg 6.
17 Ie a return made in accordance with the Merchant Shipping (Returns of Births and Deaths)
Regulations 1979, SI 1979/1577, regs 5, 6 (see the text and notes 9–16): see reg 9.
18 Ie a record made in accordance with the Merchant Shipping (Returns of Births and Deaths)
Regulations 1979, SI 1979/1577, reg 7 (see note 6): see reg 9.
19 Merchant Shipping (Returns of Births and Deaths) Regulations 1979, SI 1979/1577, reg 9. The
appropriate Registrar General for the purposes of regs 9, 10 is the Registrar General for England
and Wales: see reg 11. As to the Registrar General of Births, Deaths and Marriages in England see

REGISTRATION CONCERNING THE INDIVIDUAL vol 88 (2012) PARA 334 et seq. As to the meanings of 'England' and 'Wales' see PARA 16 note 2.

20 See the Merchant Shipping (Returns of Births and Deaths) Regulations 1979, SI 1979/1577, reg 10(1), (2). In the case of a birth, such of the particulars specified in Sch 1 may be recorded in the marine register as he thinks fit: see reg 10(2)(a). In the case of a death, such of the particulars specified in Sch 2 may be so recorded as he thinks fit: see reg 10(2)(b).

21 Merchant Shipping (Returns of Births and Deaths) Regulations 1979, SI 1979/1577, reg 10(1)(a).
22 Merchant Shipping (Returns of Births and Deaths) Regulations 1979, SI 1979/1577, reg 10(1)(b).
23 Merchant Shipping (Returns of Births and Deaths) Regulations 1979, SI 1979/1577, reg 10(1)(c).
24 Ie the Merchant Shipping (Returns of Births and Deaths) Regulations 1979, SI 1979/1577, regs 2–6 (see the text and notes 1–16), or those regulations (except reg 4) as extended by reg 12 (see note 1): see reg 13; and PARA 1124.
25 See the Merchant Shipping (Returns of Births and Deaths) Regulations 1979, SI 1979/1577, reg 13; and PARA 1124.

(iv) Carriage of Dangerous Goods by Ship

645. Dangerous goods in general. Where any dangerous goods[1] have been sent or carried, or attempted to be sent or carried, on board any ship[2], whether or not a United Kingdom ship[3]:

(1) without being marked as required by safety regulations[4];
(2) without such notice having been given as is required by safety regulations[5];
(3) under a false description[6]; or
(4) with a false description of their sender or carrier[7],

any court having Admiralty jurisdiction[8] may declare the goods, and any package or receptacle in which they are contained, to be forfeited[9].

On a declaration of forfeiture being made, the goods are forfeited and they must be disposed of as the court directs[10].

The powers so conferred on the court[11] are exercisable notwithstanding that the owner of the goods[12]:

(a) has not committed any offence under safety regulations relating to dangerous goods[13];
(b) is not before the court[14]; and
(c) has no notice of the proceedings[15];

and notwithstanding that there is no evidence to show to whom the goods belong[16].

Nevertheless the court may, in its discretion, require such notice as it may direct to be given to the owner or shipper of the goods before they are forfeited[17].

1 For these purposes, 'dangerous goods' means goods designated as dangerous goods by safety regulations: Merchant Shipping Act 1995 s 87(5). As to the meaning of 'safety regulations' see PARA 602 note 1; and see the Merchant Shipping (Dangerous Goods and Marine Pollutants) Regulations 1997, SI 1997/2367, made under the Merchant Shipping Act 1995 s 85 and other powers (cited in PARA 646).
2 As to the meaning of 'ship' see PARA 229.
3 Merchant Shipping Act 1995 s 87(1). As to the meaning of 'United Kingdom ship' see PARA 230.
4 Merchant Shipping Act 1995 s 87(1)(a).
5 Merchant Shipping Act 1995 s 87(1)(b).
6 Merchant Shipping Act 1995 s 87(1)(c).
7 Merchant Shipping Act 1995 s 87(1)(d).
8 As to the Admiralty jurisdiction of the High Court generally see PARA 85 et seq.
9 Merchant Shipping Act 1995 s 87(1).
10 Merchant Shipping Act 1995 s 87(2).
11 Ie by the Merchant Shipping Act 1995 s 87(1), (2) (see the text and notes 1–10): see s 87(3).
12 Merchant Shipping Act 1995 s 87(3).
13 Merchant Shipping Act 1995 s 87(3)(a).
14 Merchant Shipping Act 1995 s 87(3)(b).
15 Merchant Shipping Act 1995 s 87(3)(c).

16 Merchant Shipping Act 1995 s 87(3).
17 Merchant Shipping Act 1995 s 87(4).

646. Handling, stowage, carriage of dangerous goods and marine pollutants by merchant shipping.

It is the duty of every operator[1], every employer of persons aboard a ship and every master of a ship to ensure that, so far as is reasonably practicable, when dangerous goods are being handled[2], stowed or carried on the ship nothing in the manner in which those goods are handled, stowed or carried as the case may be is such as might create a significant risk to the health and safety of any person[3].

It is the duty of every employee[4] aboard ship[5]:

(1)   to take reasonable care for the health and safety of himself and of other persons who may be affected by his acts or omissions in connection with the handling, stowage and carriage of dangerous goods in the ship[6]; and

(2)   as regards any duty or requirement imposed on the operator, or the employee's employer by the Merchant Shipping Act 1995 or any regulation or rule made thereunder with regard to the health and safety of persons aboard a ship[7], to cooperate with the operator or employer so far as is necessary to enable that duty or requirement to be performed or complied with in connection with the handling, stowage and carriage of dangerous goods in the ship[8].

In connection with the handling, stowage and carriage of dangerous goods in a United Kingdom ship, no person may intentionally or recklessly interfere with or misuse anything provided on, or disobey instructions displayed on, the ship in the interests of health or safety in pursuance of the Merchant Shipping Act 1995 or any regulation or rule made thereunder[9].

Further provision is made in relation to the carriage of packaged dangerous goods or packaged marine pollutants[10], the carriage of dangerous goods or marine pollutants in bulk[11], and spaces for the carriage of packaged goods and dangerous goods in solid form in bulk[12].

The Secretary of State[13] may grant exemptions from all or any of the provisions relating to such handling, stowage and carriage of dangerous goods and marine pollutants[14] (as may be specified in the exemption) for classes of cases or individual cases on such terms (if any) as he may so specify and may, subject to giving reasonable notice, alter or cancel any such exemption[15].

1   For these purposes, 'operator' in relation to a ship includes any owner, charterer, manager and agent of the ship: Merchant Shipping (Dangerous Goods and Marine Pollutants) Regulations 1997, SI 1997/2367, reg 2(1). The Merchant Shipping (Dangerous Goods and Marine Pollutants) Regulations 1997, SI 1997/2367, apply to ships carrying dangerous goods in bulk or packaged form or marine pollutants in packaged form (reg 5(1)); and they apply to United Kingdom ships wherever they may be and to other ships while they are within the United Kingdom waters (reg 5(2)). For these purposes, 'dangerous goods' means goods classified in the IMDG Code or in any other publication of the International Maritime Organisation ('IMO') referred to in the Merchant Shipping (Dangerous Goods and Marine Pollutants) Regulations 1997, SI 1997/2367, as dangerous for carriage by sea, and any other substance or article that the shipper has reasonable cause to believe might meet the criteria for such classification; and the expression includes residues in empty receptacles, empty tanks or cargo holds which have been used previously for the carriage of dangerous goods unless such receptacles, empty tanks or cargo holds have been cleaned and dried, purged, gas freed or ventilated as appropriate or, in the case of radioactive materials, have been both cleaned and adequately closed, and goods labelled, marked or declared as dangerous goods; but the expression does not include goods forming part of the equipment or stores of the ship in which they are carried; 'in bulk' means directly and without intermediate form of containment in a hold, tank or cargo space, which is a structural part of or permanently attached to a ship: reg 2(1). 'IMDG Code' means the 2010/11 edition of the IMO International Maritime Dangerous Goods Code: Merchant Shipping (Dangerous Goods and Marine Pollutants) Regulations 1997, SI 1997/2367, reg 2(1) (definition substituted by SI 2004/2110; amended by SI

2011/2616). For these purposes, 'marine pollutant' means a substance classified as such in the IMDG Code, or as a noxious liquid substance in the IBC Code, oil as defined in Annex I to the MARPOL Convention, excluding bunkers and ship's stores and any other substance, material or article that the shipper has reasonable cause to believe might meet the criteria for such classification: Merchant Shipping (Dangerous Goods and Marine Pollutants) Regulations 1997, SI 1997/2367, reg 2(1) (definition amended by SI 2004/2110). 'IBC Code' means the 2007 Edition of the IMO International Code for the Construction and Equipment of Ships Carrying Dangerous Chemicals in Bulk: Merchant Shipping (Dangerous Goods and Marine Pollutants) Regulations 1997, SI 1997/2367, reg 2(1) (definition amended by SI 2004/2110; SI 2011/2616). 'MARPOL Convention' means the International Convention for the Prevention of Pollution from Ships (London, 8 October to 2 November 1973; Misc 26 (1974); Cmnd 5748), with Protocol (London, 1 June 1978 to 31 May 1979; Misc 27 (1978); Cmnd 7347) (see PARA 7): Merchant Shipping (Dangerous Goods and Marine Pollutants) Regulations 1997, SI 1997/2367, reg 2(1) (definition added by SI 2004/2110; amended by SI 2011/2616). For these purposes, 'United Kingdom ship' means a ship or hovercraft which is registered under the Merchant Shipping Act 1995 Pt II (ss 8–23) (see PARA 245 et seq), is registered under the Hovercraft Act 1968 (as to which see PARA 390 et seq), is a government ship within the meaning of the Merchant Shipping Act 1995 s 308(4) (see PARA 19 note 3) used for commercial purposes, or is not registered under the law of any other country but is wholly owned by persons each of whom is a British citizen, a British overseas territories citizen or a British Overseas citizen, or is a body corporate which is established under the law of a part of the United Kingdom and has its principal place of business in the United Kingdom: Merchant Shipping (Dangerous Goods and Marine Pollutants) Regulations 1997, SI 1997/2367, reg 2(1) (definition amended by virtue of the British Overseas Territories Act 2002 s 2(3)). As to the meaning of 'British citizen' see BRITISH NATIONALITY vol 4 (2011) PARAS 406, 421–444; as to the meaning of 'British overseas territories citizen' see BRITISH NATIONALITY vol 4 (2011) PARAS 406, 445–458; and as to the meaning of 'British Overseas citizen' see BRITISH NATIONALITY vol 4 (2011) PARA 459 et seq. As to the meaning of 'United Kingdom' see PARA 16 note 3. As to the International Maritime Organisation see PARA 12.

2   For these purposes, 'handling' includes the operations of loading, unloading and transferring dangerous goods or marine pollutants and cleaning, purging, gasfreeing, ullaging, sounding, sampling and similar operations required for the carriage of such goods in a ship; and cognate expressions are to be construed accordingly: Merchant Shipping (Dangerous Goods and Marine Pollutants) Regulations 1997, SI 1997/2367, reg 2(1).

3   See the Merchant Shipping (Dangerous Goods and Marine Pollutants) Regulations 1997, SI 1997/2367, reg 6. If an employer, operator or master fails to comply with the requirements of reg 6 he commits an offence: see PARA 1125. As to the carriage of packaged irradiated nuclear fuel by sea see PARA 647; and as to the reporting requirements for ships carrying dangerous or polluting goods see PARA 648.

4   For these purposes, 'employee' means a person (including the master but excluding dock workers or shore-based repair or other workers temporarily employed on board the ship) employed either in the deck, engine, radio, medical or catering department of a ship, or in the provision of goods, services or entertainment on board: Merchant Shipping (Dangerous Goods and Marine Pollutants) Regulations 1997, SI 1997/2367, reg 2(1).

5   See the Merchant Shipping (Dangerous Goods and Marine Pollutants) Regulations 1997, SI 1997/2367, reg 7. If any employee aboard a ship carrying dangerous goods fails to comply with the requirements of reg 7 he commits an offence: see PARA 1125.

6   See the Merchant Shipping (Dangerous Goods and Marine Pollutants) Regulations 1997, SI 1997/2367, reg 7; and see note 5.

7   Ie a ship to which the Merchant Shipping (Dangerous Goods and Marine Pollutants) Regulations 1997, SI 1997/2367, apply (as to which see note 1): see reg 7.

8   See the Merchant Shipping (Dangerous Goods and Marine Pollutants) Regulations 1997, SI 1997/2367, reg 7; and see note 5.

9   See the Merchant Shipping (Dangerous Goods and Marine Pollutants) Regulations 1997, SI 1997/2367, reg 8. If any person aboard a ship carrying dangerous goods fails to comply with the requirements of reg 8 he commits an offence: see PARA 1125.

10 See the Merchant Shipping (Dangerous Goods and Marine Pollutants) Regulations 1997, SI 1997/2367, Pt II (regs 10–19), which makes provision in relation to: the dangerous goods declaration or marine pollutants declaration (reg 10 (amended by SI 2004/2110); SI 2011/2616); the preparation of goods for transport (the Merchant Shipping (Dangerous Goods and Marine Pollutants) Regulations 1997, SI 1997/2367, reg 11); Container or Vehicle Packing Certificates (reg 12); the required documentation which may be provided directly to the master or operator in the form of a paper document or by electronic data processing or electronic data interchange methods (reg 13); list, manifest or stowage plans (reg 14); the marking, labelling or placarding of

packaged goods (reg 15); the stowage of packaged goods on board ship (reg 16); cargo securing documentation (regs 17, 18); and the duty of operator and master to ensure that all employees are familiar with the essential actions to be taken in an emergency involving such packaged goods as are carried on the ship (reg 19). As to related offences see PARA 1125.

11 See the Merchant Shipping (Dangerous Goods and Marine Pollutants) Regulations 1997, SI 1997/2367, Pt III (regs 20–21), which makes provision in relation to: dangerous goods or marine pollutants handled or carried in bulk (reg 20 (amended by SI 2011/2616)); and the required documentation relating to such goods or pollutants (Merchant Shipping (Dangerous Goods and Marine Pollutants) Regulations 1997, SI 1997/2367, reg 21 (amended by SI 2004/2110; SI 2011/2616)). As to related offences see PARA 1125.

12 See the Merchant Shipping (Dangerous Goods and Marine Pollutants) Regulations 1997, SI 1997/2367, Pt IV (reg 22). As to related offences see PARA 1125.

13 As to the Secretary of State see PARA 36.

14 Ie from all or any of the provisions of the Merchant Shipping (Dangerous Goods and Marine Pollutants) Regulations 1997, SI 1997/2367 (see the text and notes 1–12): see reg 4.

15 See the Merchant Shipping (Dangerous Goods and Marine Pollutants) Regulations 1997, SI 1997/2367, reg 4.

647. Carriage of packaged irradiated nuclear fuel by sea.

Every ship carrying INF cargo[1] must be constructed, equipped, inspected and surveyed in accordance with the requirements of the INF Code[2]; and the operator[3] and master must ensure that a ship carrying INF cargo complies with the requirements of the INF Code[4].

The Secretary of State[5] must, on the application of the operator of a ship registered in the United Kingdom, if he is satisfied that the ship complies with the requirements of the INF Code, issue to the operator a Certificate of Fitness certifying compliance with the INF Code[6]; and an operator or master must not accept INF cargo for carriage in a ship which has not been issued with a Certificate of Fitness either by the Secretary of State[7], or by the administration of the state whose flag the ship is entitled to fly[8].

Any contravention by the operator or master of their duty to ensure that a ship carrying INF cargo complies with the requirements of the INF Code[9] or of their duty to refuse such cargo for carriage in a ship which has not been issued with such a Certificate of Fitness[10] is an offence for which each of them is liable[11]; and, in any case where a ship does not comply with those requirements, the ship may be detained[12].

1 For these purposes, 'INF cargo' means packaged irradiated nuclear fuel, plutonium and high-level radioactive wastes carried as cargo; 'high-level radioactive wastes' means liquid wastes resulting from the operation of the first stage extraction system or the concentrated wastes from subsequent extraction stages, in a facility for reprocessing irradiated nuclear fuel, or solids into which such liquid wastes have been converted; 'irradiated nuclear fuel' means material containing uranium, thorium or plutonium isotopes which has been used to maintain a self-sustaining nuclear chain reaction; and 'plutonium' means the resultant mixture of isotopes of that material extracted from the reprocessing of irradiated nuclear fuel: see the Merchant Shipping (Carriage of Packaged Irradiated Nuclear Fuel etc) (INF Code) Regulations 2000, SI 2000/3216, reg 2(1).

The Merchant Shipping (Carriage of Packaged Irradiated Nuclear Fuel etc) (INF Code) Regulations 2000, SI 2000/3216, apply to ships carrying INF cargo (reg 3(1)), in particular United Kingdom ships wherever they may be, and other ships which are in United Kingdom waters (reg 3(2)). In relation to hovercraft, the regulations have effect subject to the modification that for any reference to a ship or ships, there is respectively to be substituted a reference to a hovercraft or to hovercraft: reg 3(3). For these purposes, 'United Kingdom ship' means a ship or hovercraft which is registered under the Merchant Shipping Act 1995 Pt II (ss 8–23) (see PARA 245 et seq), is registered under the Hovercraft Act 1968 (as to which see PARA 390 et seq), is a government ship within the meaning of the Merchant Shipping Act 1995 s 308(4) (see PARA 19 note 3) used for commercial purposes, or is not registered under the law of any other country but is wholly owned by persons each of whom is a British citizen, a British overseas territories citizen or a British Overseas citizen, or is a body corporate which is established under the law of a part of the United Kingdom and has its principal place of business in the United Kingdom: Merchant Shipping (Carriage of Packaged Irradiated Nuclear Fuel etc) (INF Code) Regulations 2000, SI 2000/3216, reg 2(1) (definition amended by virtue of the British Overseas Territories Act 2002 s 2(3)). As to the meaning of 'British citizen' see BRITISH NATIONALITY vol 4 (2011) PARAS 406, 421–444; as to the meaning of 'British overseas territories citizen' see BRITISH NATIONALITY vol 4 (2011) PARAS 406, 445–458; and as to the meaning of 'British Overseas citizen' see BRITISH NATIONALITY vol 4 (2011) PARA 459 et seq. As to the meaning of 'United Kingdom' see PARA 16 note 3.

    As to the handling, stowage, carriage of dangerous goods and marine pollutants by merchant shipping generally see PARA 646; and as to the reporting requirements for ships carrying dangerous or polluting goods see PARA 648.

2 Merchant Shipping (Carriage of Packaged Irradiated Nuclear Fuel etc) (INF Code) Regulations 2000, SI 2000/3216, reg 4(1). For these purposes, 'INF Code' means the International Code for the Safe Carriage of Packaged Irradiated Nuclear Fuel, Plutonium and High-Level Radioactive Wastes on Board Ships adopted on 27 May 1999 by the Maritime Safety Committee of the International Maritime Organisation ('IMO') by resolution MSC 88(71) and set out in the Annex thereto: Merchant Shipping (Carriage of Packaged Irradiated Nuclear Fuel etc) (INF Code) Regulations 2000, SI 2000/3216, reg 2(1). As to the International Maritime Organisation see PARA 12.

3 For these purposes, 'operator' in relation to a ship includes any owner, charterer, manager and agent of the ship: Merchant Shipping (Carriage of Packaged Irradiated Nuclear Fuel etc) (INF Code) Regulations 2000, SI 2000/3216, reg 2(1).

4 Merchant Shipping (Carriage of Packaged Irradiated Nuclear Fuel etc) (INF Code) Regulations 2000, SI 2000/3216, reg 4(2).

5 As to the Secretary of State see PARA 36.

6 Merchant Shipping (Carriage of Packaged Irradiated Nuclear Fuel etc) (INF Code) Regulations 2000, SI 2000/3216, reg 4(3). For these purposes, 'Certificate of Fitness' means the International Certificate of Fitness for the Carriage of INF Cargo, as provided for in the INF Code: reg 2(1).

7 Ie as mentioned in the Merchant Shipping (Carriage of Packaged Irradiated Nuclear Fuel etc) (INF Code) Regulations 2000, SI 2000/3216, reg 4(3) (see the text and notes 5–6): see reg 5.

8 Merchant Shipping (Carriage of Packaged Irradiated Nuclear Fuel etc) (INF Code) Regulations 2000, SI 2000/3216, reg 5.

9 Ie where there is a breach of the Merchant Shipping (Carriage of Packaged Irradiated Nuclear Fuel etc) (INF Code) Regulations 2000, SI 2000/3216, reg 4(2) (see the text and notes 3–4): see reg 6; and PARA 1125.

10 Ie where there is a breach of the Merchant Shipping (Carriage of Packaged Irradiated Nuclear Fuel etc) (INF Code) Regulations 2000, SI 2000/3216, reg 5 (see the text and notes 7–8): see reg 6; and PARA 1125.

11 See the Merchant Shipping (Carriage of Packaged Irradiated Nuclear Fuel etc) (INF Code) Regulations 2000, SI 2000/3216, regs 6, 8; and PARA 1125.

12 See the Merchant Shipping (Carriage of Packaged Irradiated Nuclear Fuel etc) (INF Code) Regulations 2000, SI 2000/3216, reg 7; and PARA 1125.

648. Reporting requirements for ships carrying dangerous or polluting goods.

Before a United Kingdom ship[1], which is bound for a port which is not located in an EEA state[2] and is carrying dangerous goods[3] or harmful substances in packaged form[4], leaves a port which is not located in an EEA state, the operator of that ship must comply with specified requirements of the appropriate Merchant Shipping Notice[5] which conforms to the Consolidated European Reporting System ('CERS')[6]. Further provision is made in relation to the reporting of incidents[7] and for offences and penalties to apply in cases of contravention[8].

1 Ie a United Kingdom ship irrespective of size: see the Merchant Shipping (Reporting Requirements for Ships Carrying Dangerous or Polluting Goods) Regulations 1995, SI 1995/2498, reg 5(1) (reg 5 substituted by SI 2004/2110). For these purposes, 'United Kingdom ship' means a ship which is registered in the United Kingdom, or is not registered under the law of any country but is wholly owned by persons each of whom is a British Citizen, a British overseas territories citizen or a British Overseas citizen, or is a body corporate which is established under the law of any part of the United Kingdom and has its principal place of business in the United Kingdom: see the Merchant Shipping (Reporting Requirements for Ships Carrying Dangerous or Polluting Goods) Regulations 1995, SI 1995/2498, reg 2(4) (added by SI 2004/2110). As to the meaning of 'British citizen' see BRITISH NATIONALITY vol 4 (2011) PARAS 406, 421–444; as to the meaning of 'British overseas territories citizen' see BRITISH NATIONALITY vol 4 (2011) PARAS 406, 445–458; and as to the meaning of 'British Overseas citizen' see BRITISH NATIONALITY vol 4 (2011) PARA 459 et seq. As to the meaning of 'United Kingdom' see PARA 16 note 3.

    For these purposes, 'ship' includes a vessel of any type whatsoever operating in the marine environment or in other waters navigable by sea-going vessels and (without prejudice to the generality of the foregoing) includes submersible craft, floating craft and hovercraft: Merchant Shipping (Reporting Requirements for Ships Carrying Dangerous or Polluting Goods) Regulations 1995, SI 1995/2498, reg 2(2) (definition amended by SI 1999/2121). As to the ships to which the Merchant Shipping (Reporting Requirements for Ships Carrying Dangerous or Polluting Goods) Regulations 1995, SI 1995/2498, apply see reg 3 (substituted by SI 2005/1092;amended by SI 2008/3145; SI 2014/3306).

2   For these purposes, 'EEA state' means a member state, Norway, Iceland or Liechtenstein: Merchant Shipping (Reporting Requirements for Ships Carrying Dangerous or Polluting Goods) Regulations 1995, SI 1995/2498, reg 5(3) (as substituted: see note 1). In any Act, 'member state' means a state which is a member of the European Communities: see the European Communities Act 1972 s 1(2), Sch 1 Pt II; and the Interpretation Act 1978 s 5, Sch 1.

3   For these purposes, 'dangerous goods' means goods classified as such in the IMDG Code including radioactive materials as referred to in the INF Code, in the IGC-Code Ch 19 or in the IBC-Code Ch 17: Merchant Shipping (Reporting Requirements for Ships Carrying Dangerous or Polluting Goods) Regulations 1995, SI 1995/2498, reg 2(2) (definition amended by SI 1999/2121). 'IBC Code' means the 1998 edition of the International Maritime Organisation ('IMO') International Code for Construction and Equipment of Ships Carrying Dangerous Chemicals in Bulk: Merchant Shipping (Reporting Requirements for Ships Carrying Dangerous or Polluting Goods) Regulations 1995, SI 1995/2498, reg 2(2) (definition amended by SI 2004/2110). 'IGC Code' means the 1993 edition of the Code for the Construction and Equipment of Ships Carrying Liquefied Gases in Bulk published by the IMO: Merchant Shipping (Reporting Requirements for Ships Carrying Dangerous or Polluting Goods) Regulations 1995, SI 1995/2498, reg 2(2) (definition amended by SI 2004/2110). 'IMDG Code' means the 2002 edition of the International Maritime Dangerous Goods Code published by the IMO: Merchant Shipping (Reporting Requirements for Ships Carrying Dangerous or Polluting Goods) Regulations 1995, SI 1995/2498, reg 2(2) (definition amended by SI 2004/2110). 'INF Code' means the 2001 edition of the International Code for the Safe Carriage of Packaged Irradiated Nuclear Fuels, Plutonium and High-Level Radioactive Waste on Board Ships: Merchant Shipping (Reporting Requirements for Ships Carrying Dangerous or Polluting Goods) Regulations 1995, SI 1995/2498, reg 2(2) (definition substituted by SI 2004/2110). For the purposes of the Merchant Shipping (Reporting Requirements for Ships Carrying Dangerous or Polluting Goods) Regulations 1995, SI 1995/2498, reg 5, in relation to a ship, bunkers, stores and equipment for use on board that ship are not to be regarded as dangerous goods or harmful substances in packaged form: see reg 3(9) (reg 3 as substituted: see note 1). As to the International Maritime Organisation see PARA 12. As to the handling, stowage, carriage of dangerous goods and marine pollutants by merchant shipping generally see PARA 646; and as to the carriage of packaged irradiated nuclear fuel by sea see PARA 647.

4   For these purposes, 'harmful substances in packaged form' has the meaning given by MARPOL Annex III: Merchant Shipping (Reporting Requirements for Ships Carrying Dangerous or Polluting Goods) Regulations 1995, SI 1995/2498, reg 2(2) (definition added by SI 1999/2121). 'MARPOL' means the International Convention for the Prevention of Pollution from Ships (London, 8 October to 2 November 1973; Misc 26 (1974); Cmnd 5748), with Protocol (London, 1 June 1978 to 31 May 1979; Misc 27 (1978); Cmnd 7347) (see PARA 7): Merchant Shipping (Reporting Requirements for Ships Carrying Dangerous or Polluting Goods) Regulations 1995, SI 1995/2498, reg 2(2) (definition amended by SI 2005/1092).

5   For these purposes, 'Merchant Shipping Notice' means a Notice described as such, issued by the Secretary of State, and includes a reference to any document amending or replacing that Notice which is considered by the Secretary of State to be relevant from time to time and is specified in a Merchant Shipping Notice: Merchant Shipping (Reporting Requirements for Ships Carrying Dangerous or Polluting Goods) Regulations 1995, SI 1995/2498, reg 2(2) (definition amended by SI 1999/2121). As to the Secretary of State see PARA 36.

6   Merchant Shipping (Reporting Requirements for Ships Carrying Dangerous or Polluting Goods) Regulations 1995, SI 1995/2498, reg 5(2) (as substituted: see note 1). The text refers to the requirements of Merchant Shipping Notice 1817(M+F): see the Merchant Shipping (Reporting Requirements for Ships Carrying Dangerous or Polluting Goods) Regulations 1995, SI 1995/2498, reg 5(2) (as so substituted). Merchant Shipping Notice 1817(M+F) details the technical requirements applicable to ships and United Kingdom port authorities to comply with the Merchant Shipping (Vessel Traffic Monitoring and Reporting Requirements) Regulations 2004, SI 2004/2110, which amended the Merchant Shipping (Reporting Requirements for Ships Carrying Dangerous or Polluting Goods) Regulations 1995, SI 1995/2498, and implemented Parliament and Council Directive (EC(2002/59 (OJ L208, 05.08.2002, p 10) establishing a Community vessel traffic monitoring and information system. Accordingly, Merchant Shipping Notice 1817(M+F) concerns itself with the Consolidated European Reporting System ('CERS'), in particular as it relates to ship arrival and departure notifications (including additional requirements for ships

carrying dangerous or polluting goods) and the reporting requirements in the event of an accident or incident: see Merchant Shipping Notice 1817(M+F).

Any person duly authorised by the Secretary of State may inspect any ship to which the Merchant Shipping (Reporting Requirements for Ships Carrying Dangerous or Polluting Goods) Regulations 1995, SI 1995/2498, apply and, if he is satisfied that there is a failure to comply in relation to that ship with relation to the requirements of reg 5, he may detain the ship until such requirements are met: see reg 17; and PARA 1125.

The Secretary of State may require by notice in writing any person carrying on business or trade in the maritime transport sector to furnish, in the specified form and manner and within the specified time, periodical or other returns about cargo, passenger and vessel movement, certain particulars in relation to the transport of containers or ro-ro units, and information in relation to the vessel: see the Statistical Returns (Carriage of Goods and Passengers by Sea) Regulations 1997, SI 1997/2330; and PARA 42.

7   See the Merchant Shipping (Reporting Requirements for Ships Carrying Dangerous or Polluting Goods) Regulations 1995, SI 1995/2498, reg 9 (amended by SI 1999/2121; SI 2004/2110; SI 2005/1092); and see the Merchant Shipping (Reporting Requirements for Ships Carrying Dangerous or Polluting Goods) Regulations 1995, SI 1995/2498, reg 10 (supplementary reports); and reg 11 (amended by SI 2004/2110) (reporting procedures). For these purposes, 'incident' means damage, failure or breakdown which affects the safety of the ship, failure or breakdown of machinery or equipment which results in impairment of the safety of navigation, including any circumstances when a vessel is 'not under command', or any circumstances at sea which have caused actual damage or any other condition which affects the safety of any vessel or persons or which has or may cause damage or discharge into the marine environment: Merchant Shipping (Reporting Requirements for Ships Carrying Dangerous or Polluting Goods) Regulations 1995, SI 1995/2498, reg 2(2) (definition amended by SI 2005/1092). The Maritime and Coastguard Agency ('MCA') must, as necessary, broadcast within the relevant areas information about any incident notified under the Merchant Shipping (Reporting Requirements for Ships Carrying Dangerous or Polluting Goods) Regulations 1995, SI 1995/2498, reg 9, and information with regard to any vessel which poses a threat to other shipping: reg 19 (amended by SI 2004/2110). As to the Maritime and Coastguard Agency see PARA 57.

8   See the Merchant Shipping (Reporting Requirements for Ships Carrying Dangerous or Polluting Goods) Regulations 1995, SI 1995/2498, regs 15, 16 (offences); regs 17, 18 (inspection and detention of ships); and PARA 1125.

(v) Carriage of Cargoes requiring Special Precautions

A.   IN GENERAL

649. Cargo information. The shipper[1] must provide such information ('cargo information')[2] to the owner or master sufficiently in advance of loading as is necessary to enable them to ensure that[3]:

(1)   the different commodities to be carried are compatible with each other or suitably separated[4];

(2)   the cargo is suitable for the ship[5];

(3)   the ship is suitable for the cargo[6]; and

(4)   the cargo can be safely stowed and secured on board the ship and transported under all expected conditions during the intended voyage[7].

The information must be confirmed in writing and by appropriate shipping documents prior to loading the cargo on the ship[8].

In preparing cargo units for carriage by ships, the shipper (or, as the case may be, the forwarder[9]) must ensure that the gross mass of such units is in accordance with the gross mass declared on the shipping documents[10]. Where the shipper does not deliver the cargo to the ship or its agent he must provide the forwarder with such cargo information[11]; and if the shipper does not deliver the cargo to the ship or its agent it is the duty of the forwarder to provide the owner or master with the appropriate cargo information[12].

If a shipper or forwarder fails to provide appropriate cargo information as so required[13], or furnishes cargo information which he knows to be false or recklessly furnishes cargo information which is false, he is guilty of an offence[14]; and if an owner or master accepts for carriage, or takes or receives on board any cargo for which appropriate cargo information as so required[15] has not been furnished, he is guilty of an offence[16].

1   For these purposes, 'shipper' means any person who, whether as principal or agent for another, consigns goods for carriage by sea: Merchant Shipping (Carriage of Cargoes) Regulations 1999, SI 1999/336, reg 2(1). The Merchant Shipping (Carriage of Cargoes) Regulations 1999, SI 1999/336, apply to sea-going United Kingdom ships wherever they may be, and to sea-going ships which are not United Kingdom ships while they are within United Kingdom waters, when loaded or intended to be loaded with any cargo: reg 3(1). For these purposes, 'cargo' means any cargo which, owing to its particular hazard to ships or persons on board, may require special precautions, with the exception of liquids carried in bulk and gases carried in bulk: reg 2(1). 'In bulk', except in the context of roll-on roll-off cargo spaces, means directly and without intermediate form of containment in a hold, tank or cargo space forming a structural part of, or permanently attached to, a ship; and 'cargo space' means any space in the ship appropriated for the carriage of cargo: reg 2(1). 'Roll-on roll-off cargo spaces' means spaces not normally subdivided in any way and extending to either a substantial length or the entire length of the ship in which the goods (packaged or in bulk, in or on rail or road cars, vehicles (including road or rail tankers), trailers, containers, pallets, demountable tanks or in or on similar stowage units or other receptacles) can be loaded and unloaded normally in a horizontal direction; and 'container' means an article of transport equipment as defined in the International Convention for Safe Containers (Geneva, 2 December 1972; TS 40 (1979); Cmnd 7535) (CSC 1972) (as to which see PARA 7), published by the International Maritime Organisation ('IMO'): Merchant Shipping (Carriage of Cargoes) Regulations 1999, SI 1999/336, reg 2(1). As to the International Maritime Organisation see PARA 12.
        The Merchant Shipping (Carriage of Cargoes) Regulations 1999, SI 1999/336, apply to the carriage of all cargoes, but are subject to any requirements contained in the Merchant Shipping (Dangerous Goods and Marine Pollutants) Regulations 1997, SI 1997/2367 (as to which see PARA 646), in respect of the carriage of dangerous goods and marine pollutants (as defined in those regulations); and where any requirement in those regulations regulates an aspect of carriage provided for in the Merchant Shipping (Carriage of Cargoes) Regulations 1999, SI 1999/336, the Merchant Shipping (Dangerous Goods and Marine Pollutants) Regulations 1997, SI 1997/2367, apply to that extent, and not the Merchant Shipping (Carriage of Cargoes) Regulations 1999, SI 1999/336: reg 3(2). As to exemptions see PARA 654.
2   The cargo information referred to in the Merchant Shipping (Carriage of Cargoes) Regulations 1999, SI 1999/336, reg 4(1)(a) must include:
      (1)   in the case of general cargo and cargo carried in cargo units, a general description of the cargo, the gross mass of the cargo or cargo units and any relevant special properties of the cargo (reg 4(1)(b)(i));
      (2)   in the case of bulk cargoes, information on the stowage factor of the cargo, the trimming procedures, the likelihood of shifting including angle of repose, if applicable, and any other relevant special properties; and, in the case of a concentrate or other cargo which may liquefy, additional information in the form of a certificate indicating the moisture content of the cargo and its transportable moisture limit (reg 4(1)(b)(ii));
      (3)   in the case of bulk cargoes which are not classified in accordance with the SOLAS Convention reg VII/2, but have chemical properties that may create a potential hazard, information on the chemical properties in addition to that required by head (2) (reg 4(1)(b)(iii)).
        For these purposes, 'cargo unit' includes a cargo transport unit and means wheeled cargo, vehicle, container, flat, pallet, portable tank, packaged unit, or any other cargo, and loading equipment, or any part thereof, which belongs to the ship and which is not fixed to the ship; reg 2(1). 'Bulk cargo' means cargo carried in bulk; 'trimming' means any levelling of the material within a cargo space, either partial or total, by means of loading spouts or chutes, portable machinery, equipment or manual labour; 'cargoes which may liquefy' means cargoes which are subject to moisture migration and subsequent liquefaction if shipped with a moisture content in excess of the transportable moisture limit; 'moisture content' means the amount of moisture present in a particular sample expressed as a percentage by weight of the total wet weight of the sample; 'transportable moisture limit' means nine-tenths of the flow moisture point; 'flow moisture point' means the percentage moisture content (wet weight basis) at which a flow state develops under the methods of test in a representative sample of the material as prescribed by the Code of Safe Practice for Solid Bulk Cargoes (BC Code), published by the IMO; and 'flow state' means the condition when a mass of granular material is saturated with liquid to an extent that under

prevailing external forces such as vibration, impaction or ship's motion, it loses its internal shear strength and behaves as a liquid: Merchant Shipping (Carriage of Cargoes) Regulations 1999, SI 1999/336, reg 2(1). Any reference to a Code includes a reference to any document amending it which is considered by the Secretary of State to be relevant from time to time and is specified in a Merchant Shipping Notice: Merchant Shipping (Carriage of Cargoes) Regulations 1999, SI 1999/336, reg 2(3). For these purposes, 'Merchant Shipping Notice' means a Notice described as such, issued by the Department of Transport: Merchant Shipping (Carriage of Cargoes) Regulations 1999, SI 1999/336, reg 2(1). Any reference to a Merchant Shipping Notice includes a reference to any document amending it which is considered by the Secretary of State to be relevant from time to time and is specified in a Merchant Shipping Notice: Merchant Shipping (Carriage of Cargoes) Regulations 1999, SI 1999/336, reg 2(3). As to the Secretary of State see PARA 36.

'SOLAS Convention' means the International Convention for the Safety of Life at Sea 1974 (London, 1 November 1974 to 1 July 1975; TS 46 (1980); Cmnd 7874), with Protocol (London, 1 June 1978 to 1 March 1979; TS 40 (1981); Cmnd 8277) (as to which see PARA 7): Merchant Shipping (Carriage of Cargoes) Regulations 1999, SI 1999/336, reg 2(1). Any reference to a Convention includes a reference to any document amending it which is considered by the Secretary of State to be relevant from time to time and is specified in a Merchant Shipping Notice: Merchant Shipping (Carriage of Cargoes) Regulations 1999, SI 1999/336, reg 2(3).

3 Merchant Shipping (Carriage of Cargoes) Regulations 1999, SI 1999/336, reg 4(1)(a). Where a ship is operated by a person other than its owner, (whether on behalf of the owner or some other person, or on his own behalf) a reference to the owner must be construed as including a reference to that person: reg 2(5).

The Secretary of State may require by notice in writing any person carrying on business or trade in the maritime transport sector to furnish, in the specified form and manner and within the specified time, periodical or other returns about cargo, passenger and vessel movement, certain particulars in relation to the transport of containers or ro-ro units, and information in relation to the vessel: see the Statistical Returns (Carriage of Goods and Passengers by Sea) Regulations 1997, SI 1997/2330; and PARA 42.

4 Merchant Shipping (Carriage of Cargoes) Regulations 1999, SI 1999/336, reg 4(1)(a)(i).
5 Merchant Shipping (Carriage of Cargoes) Regulations 1999, SI 1999/336, reg 4(1)(a)(ii).
6 Merchant Shipping (Carriage of Cargoes) Regulations 1999, SI 1999/336, reg 4(1)(a)(iii).
7 Merchant Shipping (Carriage of Cargoes) Regulations 1999, SI 1999/336, reg 4(1)(a)(iv).
8 Merchant Shipping (Carriage of Cargoes) Regulations 1999, SI 1999/336, reg 4(2).
9 For these purposes, 'forwarder' means a person who receives the appropriate cargo information in preparation for eventual delivery of the cargo to the ship or its agent (and may include a cargo packer or consolidator); and 'appropriate cargo information' means information relevant to the cargo and its stowage and securing, which should specify in particular the precautions necessary for the safe carriage of that cargo by sea: Merchant Shipping (Carriage of Cargoes) Regulations 1999, SI 1999/336, reg 2(1).
10 Merchant Shipping (Carriage of Cargoes) Regulations 1999, SI 1999/336, reg 4(3).
11 Merchant Shipping (Carriage of Cargoes) Regulations 1999, SI 1999/336, reg 4(4).
12 Merchant Shipping (Carriage of Cargoes) Regulations 1999, SI 1999/336, reg 4(5).
13 Ie as required by the Merchant Shipping (Carriage of Cargoes) Regulations 1999, SI 1999/336, reg 4: see reg 4(6).
14 See the Merchant Shipping (Carriage of Cargoes) Regulations 1999, SI 1999/336, reg 4(6); and PARA 1126.
15 Ie as required by the Merchant Shipping (Carriage of Cargoes) Regulations 1999, SI 1999/336, reg 4: see reg 4(7).
16 See the Merchant Shipping (Carriage of Cargoes) Regulations 1999, SI 1999/336, reg 4(7); and PARA 1126.

650. Carriage of required documentation.

The owner and master of every ship[1], other than a ship engaged in the carriage of grain[2], must ensure that appropriate documentation, relevant to the cargo[3] and its stowage and securing, which should specify in particular the precautions necessary for the safe carriage of that cargo by sea, is carried on board[4].

The owner and master of every ship[5] carrying grain must ensure that the International Grain Code[6] is carried on board[7].

All passenger ships[8] and cargo ships[9] carrying cargoes other than solid bulk cargoes[10], except cargo ships of less than 500 tons[11] engaged on voyages which are not international voyages, must carry on board a Cargo Securing Manual[12].

An owner or master who contravenes the requirement to carry appropriate documentation[13], including the requirement to carry the International Grain Code[14], is guilty of an offence[15].

1 Ie every ship to which the Merchant Shipping (Carriage of Cargoes) Regulations 1999, SI 1999/336, apply: see reg 5(1). As to the application of the Merchant Shipping (Carriage of Cargoes) Regulations 1999, SI 1999/336, see PARA 649 note 1; and as to references to the owner see PARA 649 note 3.
2 For these purposes, 'grain' includes wheat, maize (corn), oats, rye, barley, rice, pulses, seeds and processed forms thereof whose behaviour is similar to that of grain in its natural state: Merchant Shipping (Carriage of Cargoes) Regulations 1999, SI 1999/336, reg 2(1). As to the carriage of grain generally see PARA 657.
3 As to the meaning of 'cargo' for these purposes see PARA 649 note 1.
4 Merchant Shipping (Carriage of Cargoes) Regulations 1999, SI 1999/336, reg 5(1). Such documentation may consist of one or more of the following Codes of Safe Practice:
    (1)   the Code of Safe Practice for Cargo Stowage and Securing adopted by the Organization by Resolution A.714(17) (1992 edition) (as amended in 1994 and 1995) (Merchant Shipping (Carriage of Cargoes) Regulations 1999, SI 1999/336, reg 5(2)(a));
    (2)   the Code of Safe Practice for Ships Carrying Timber Deck Cargoes adopted by the Organization by Resolution A.715(17) (1992 edition) (Merchant Shipping (Carriage of Cargoes) Regulations 1999, SI 1999/336, reg 5(2)(b)); and
    (3)   the Code of Safe Practice for Solid Bulk Cargoes (BC Code) adopted by the Organisation by Resolution A.434(XI) (1991 edition) (as amended in 1996) (Merchant Shipping (Carriage of Cargoes) Regulations 1999, SI 1999/336, reg 5(2)(c)).
    As to references made to Codes see PARA 649 note 2. As to exemptions see PARA 654.
5 Ie every ship to which the Merchant Shipping (Carriage of Cargoes) Regulations 1999, SI 1999/336, apply: see reg 5(3).
6 For these purposes, 'International Grain Code' means the International Code for the Safe Carriage of Grain in Bulk adopted by the Maritime Safety Committee of the International Maritime Organisation ('IMO') by resolution MSC 23(59) on 23 May 1991: Merchant Shipping (Carriage of Cargoes) Regulations 1999, SI 1999/336, reg 2(1). As to the International Maritime Organisation see PARA 12.
    In interpreting the International Grain Code, the requirements having been made mandatory under the Merchant Shipping (Carriage of Cargoes) Regulations 1999, SI 1999/336, reg 11 (as to which see PARA 657) the language thereof must be construed accordingly, the definitions set out in the Code apply, and references to the Administration are, in relation to United Kingdom ships, references to the Secretary of State, and references to the contracting government of the port of loading, in relation to all ships loading in the United Kingdom, are references to the Secretary of State: Merchant Shipping (Carriage of Cargoes) Regulations 1999, SI 1999/336, reg 2(6). As to the Secretary of State see PARA 36.
7 Merchant Shipping (Carriage of Cargoes) Regulations 1999, SI 1999/336, reg 5(3).
8 For these purposes, 'passenger ship' means a ship carrying more than 12 passengers: Merchant Shipping (Carriage of Cargoes) Regulations 1999, SI 1999/336, reg 2(1).
9 For these purposes, 'cargo ship' means a ship which is not a passenger ship, troop ship, pleasure vessel or fishing vessel, where 'pleasure vessel' has the same meaning as in the Merchant Shipping (Cargo Ship Construction) Regulations 1997, SI 1997/1509 (as to which generally see PARA 602): Merchant Shipping (Carriage of Cargoes) Regulations 1999, SI 1999/336, reg 2(1).
10 As to the meaning of 'bulk cargo' for these purposes see PARA 649 note 2.
11 For these purposes, 'tons' means gross tons: Merchant Shipping (Carriage of Cargoes) Regulations 1999, SI 1999/336, reg 2(1).
12 Merchant Shipping (Carriage of Cargoes) Regulations 1999, SI 1999/336, reg 5(4). 'Cargo Securing Manual' means a manual drawn up to the standard contained in the Maritime Safety Committee Circular of the IMO, MSC/Circ 745 (dated 13 June 1996), and approved, in the case of United Kingdom ships by the Secretary of State, or in the case of other ships by or on behalf of the flag state, where 'flag state' in relation to a ship means the state in which the ship is registered or, if unregistered, whose flag it is entitled to fly: Merchant Shipping (Carriage of Cargoes) Regulations 1999, SI 1999/336, reg 2(1).
13 Ie who contravenes the Merchant Shipping (Carriage of Cargoes) Regulations 1999, SI 1999/336, reg 5(1) (see the text and notes 1–4): see reg 5(5).
14 Ie who contravenes the Merchant Shipping (Carriage of Cargoes) Regulations 1999, SI 1999/336, reg 5(3) (see the text and notes 5–7): see reg 5(5).
15 See the Merchant Shipping (Carriage of Cargoes) Regulations 1999, SI 1999/336, reg 5(5); and PARA 1126.

651. Duties regarding stowage and securing. The owner[1] and master must ensure that[2]:

(1) cargo[3] and cargo units[4] carried on or under deck are loaded, stowed and secured so as to prevent as far as is practicable, throughout the voyage, damage or hazard to the ship and the persons on board, and loss of cargo overboard[5];

(2) appropriate precautions are taken during loading and transport of heavy cargoes or cargoes with abnormal physical dimensions to ensure that no structural damage to the ship occurs and to maintain adequate stability throughout the voyage[6];

(3) appropriate precautions are taken during loading and transport of cargo units on board ro-ro ships, especially with regard to the securing arrangements on board such ships and on the cargo units and with regard to the strength of the securing points and lashings[7]; and

(4) cargo on board all passenger ships[8] and cargo ships[9] carrying cargoes other than solid bulk cargoes[10] (except cargo ships of less than 500 tons[11] engaged on voyages which are not international voyages)[12] is stowed and secured throughout any voyage in accordance with the Cargo Securing Manual[13]; and

(5) cargo on board all such ships as are mentioned in head (4) above[14] with roll-on/roll-off cargo spaces[15], must be stowed and secured in accordance with the Cargo Securing Manual before the ship leaves a berth[16].

Where packaged goods have been packed into or onto a cargo unit, the shipper[17] or forwarder[18] of such goods must ensure that[19]:

(a) the cargo is packed and secured so as to prevent, throughout any voyage, damage or hazard to the ship and the persons on board[20]; and

(b) if the cargo unit is a container[21], it is not loaded to more than the maximum gross weight indicated on the Safety Approval Plate attached to the container in accordance with the International Convention for Safe Containers ('CSC') 1972[22].

An owner or master who contravenes the requirements of heads (1) to (5) above[23] is guilty of an offence[24]; and a shipper or forwarder who contravenes the requirements of head (a) or head (b) above[25] is guilty of an offence[26].

1 As to references to the owner see PARA 649 note 3.
2 Merchant Shipping (Carriage of Cargoes) Regulations 1999, SI 1999/336, reg 6(1). As to equivalents and exemptions see PARA 654.
3 As to the meaning of 'cargo' for these purposes see PARA 649 note 1.
4 As to the meaning of 'cargo unit' for these purposes see PARA 649 note 2.
5 Merchant Shipping (Carriage of Cargoes) Regulations 1999, SI 1999/336, reg 6(1)(a).
6 Merchant Shipping (Carriage of Cargoes) Regulations 1999, SI 1999/336, reg 6(1)(b).
7 Merchant Shipping (Carriage of Cargoes) Regulations 1999, SI 1999/336, reg 6(1)(c).
8 As to the meaning of 'passenger ship' see PARA 650 note 8.
9 As to the meaning of 'cargo ship' see PARA 650 note 9.
10 As to the meaning of 'bulk cargo' see PARA 649 note 2.
11 As to the meaning of 'tons' see PARA 650 note 11.
12 Ie all ships to which the Merchant Shipping (Carriage of Cargoes) Regulations 1999, SI 1999/336, reg 5(4) (see PARA 650) is applicable: see reg 6(1)(d).
13 Merchant Shipping (Carriage of Cargoes) Regulations 1999, SI 1999/336, reg 6(1)(d). As to the meaning of 'Cargo Securing Manual' see PARA 650 note 12.
14 Ie all ships to which the Merchant Shipping (Carriage of Cargoes) Regulations 1999, SI 1999/336, reg 5(4) (see PARA 650) is applicable: see reg 6(1)(e).
15 As to the meaning of 'roll-on/roll-off cargo spaces' see PARA 649 note 1.
16 Merchant Shipping (Carriage of Cargoes) Regulations 1999, SI 1999/336, reg 6(1)(e).
17 As to the meaning of 'shipper' see PARA 649 note 1.
18 As to the meaning of 'forwarder' see PARA 649 note 9.
19 Merchant Shipping (Carriage of Cargoes) Regulations 1999, SI 1999/336, reg 6(2).

20 Merchant Shipping (Carriage of Cargoes) Regulations 1999, SI 1999/336, reg 6(2)(a).

21 As to the meaning of 'container' see PARA 649 note 1.

22 Merchant Shipping (Carriage of Cargoes) Regulations 1999, SI 1999/336, reg 6(2)(b). The text refers to the International Convention for Safe Containers (Geneva, 2 December 1972; TS 40 (1979); Cmnd 7535) (CSC 1972) (as to which see PARA 7), published by the International Maritime Organisation ('IMO'): see the Merchant Shipping (Carriage of Cargoes) Regulations 1999, SI 1999/336, reg 6(2)(b). As to the International Maritime Organisation see PARA 12.

23 Ie an owner or master who contravenes the Merchant Shipping (Carriage of Cargoes) Regulations 1999, SI 1999/336, reg 6(1) (see the text and notes 1–16): see reg 6(3)(a).

24 See the Merchant Shipping (Carriage of Cargoes) Regulations 1999, SI 1999/336, reg 6(3)(a); and PARA 1126.

25 Ie a shipper or forwarder who contravenes the Merchant Shipping (Carriage of Cargoes) Regulations 1999, SI 1999/336, reg 6(2) (see the text and notes 17–22): see reg 6(3)(b).

26 See the Merchant Shipping (Carriage of Cargoes) Regulations 1999, SI 1999/336, reg 6(3)(b); and PARA 1126.

652. Requirement for oxygen analysis and gas detection equipment. In the case of a ship transporting or accepting for transport a bulk cargo[1] which is liable to emit a toxic or flammable gas, or cause oxygen depletion in the cargo hold[2], an appropriate instrument for measuring the concentration of gas or oxygen in the air must be provided together with detailed instructions for its use[3]. Such an instrument must be of a type approved by a certifying authority[4], and the crew are to be trained in its use[5].

An owner[6] of a ship which transports, or a master who accepts for carriage, such a bulk cargo without ensuring that this requirement for oxygen analysis and gas detection equipment has been complied with[7] is guilty of an offence[8].

1 As to the meaning of 'bulk cargo' see PARA 649 note 2; and as to the meaning of 'cargo' for these purposes see PARA 649 note 1.

2 For these purposes, 'cargo hold' means any hold in the ship appropriated for the carriage of cargo: Merchant Shipping (Carriage of Cargoes) Regulations 1999, SI 1999/336, reg 2(1).

3 Merchant Shipping (Carriage of Cargoes) Regulations 1999, SI 1999/336, reg 7(1). As to equivalents and exemptions see PARA 654.

4 For these purposes, 'Certifying Authority' means the Secretary of State or any other person or organisation authorised by the Secretary of State: Merchant Shipping (Carriage of Cargoes) Regulations 1999, SI 1999/336, reg 2(1). As to the Secretary of State see PARA 38. Any approval given pursuant to the Merchant Shipping (Carriage of Cargoes) Regulations 1999, SI 1999/336, must be given in writing and must specify the date when it is to come into force and the conditions (if any) on which it is given: reg 2(4).

5 Merchant Shipping (Carriage of Cargoes) Regulations 1999, SI 1999/336, reg 7(1).

6 As to references to the owner see PARA 660 note 3.

7 Ie an owner who fails to ensure that the Merchant Shipping (Carriage of Cargoes) Regulations 1999, SI 1999/336, reg 7(1) (see the text and notes 1–5) has been complied with: see reg 7(2).

8 See the Merchant Shipping (Carriage of Cargoes) Regulations 1999, SI 1999/336, reg 7(2); and PARA 1187.

653. Safe use of pesticides in ships. Where pesticides are used in cargo spaces[1], they must be used in accordance with the appropriate Merchant Shipping Notice[2].

If this requirement as to the safe use of pesticides in ships is not complied with[3], the owner[4] and master are each guilty of an offence[5].

1 As to the meaning of 'cargo space' see PARA 649 note 1.

2 Merchant Shipping (Carriage of Cargoes) Regulations 1999, SI 1999/336, reg 8(1). The text refers to Merchant Shipping Notice 1718(M) ('The Safe Use of Pesticides in Ships'): see the Merchant Shipping (Carriage of Cargoes) Regulations 1999, SI 1999/336, reg 8(1). As to the meaning of 'Merchant Shipping Notice' see PARA 649 note 2. The stated purpose of Merchant Shipping Notice 1718(M) is to specify: the requirements for the safe use of pesticides in cargo spaces on board ships when loaded or intended to be loaded with any cargo, with the exception of liquids in bulk or gases in bulk; and the relevant aspects of the International Maritime Organisation ('IMO') Recommendations on the Safe Use of Pesticides in Ships which are mandatory for these purposes. As to the International Maritime Organisation see PARA 12. As to equivalents and exemptions see PARA 654.

3   Ie if the Merchant Shipping (Carriage of Cargoes) Regulations 1999, SI 1999/336, reg 8(1) (see the text and notes 1–2) has not been complied with: see reg 8(2).
4   As to references to the owner see PARA 649 note 3.
5   See the Merchant Shipping (Carriage of Cargoes) Regulations 1999, SI 1999/336, reg 8(2); and PARA 1126.

654. Power to provide for equivalents and exemptions. Where there is a requirement[1] that a particular piece of equipment (or type thereof) is to be provided or carried in a ship (or that any particular provision is to be made) the certifying authority[2] may permit any other piece of equipment to be provided or carried (or any other provisions to be made in that ship) if he is satisfied by trials thereof or otherwise that such other piece of equipment or provision is at least as effective as that otherwise[3] required[4]. For these purposes, the results of verification and tests carried out by bodies or laboratories of other member states of the International Maritime Organisation[5] offering suitable and satisfactory guarantees of technical and professional competence and independence must be accepted[6].

The Secretary of State[7] may exempt any ship from all or any of the provisions relating to the carriage of cargoes[8] as may be specified in the exemption on such terms, if any, as he may specify and, on giving reasonable notice, he may also alter or cancel such an exemption[9].

1   Ie in the Merchant Shipping (Carriage of Cargoes) Regulations 1999, SI 1999/336, or in documentation referred to therein (see PARAS 649 et seq, 655 et seq): see reg 15(1).
2   As to the meaning of 'certifying authority' see PARA 652 note 4.
3   Ie otherwise required by the Merchant Shipping (Carriage of Cargoes) Regulations 1999, SI 1999/336, or information referred to therein: see reg 15(1).
4   Merchant Shipping (Carriage of Cargoes) Regulations 1999, SI 1999/336, reg 15(1).
5   As to the International Maritime Organisation see PARA 12.
6   Merchant Shipping (Carriage of Cargoes) Regulations 1999, SI 1999/336, reg 15(2).
7   As to the Secretary of State see PARA 36.
8   Ie from all or any of the provisions of the Merchant Shipping (Carriage of Cargoes) Regulations 1999, SI 1999/336: see reg 15(3).
9   Merchant Shipping (Carriage of Cargoes) Regulations 1999, SI 1999/336, reg 15(3).

B.   BULK CARGOES OTHER THAN GRAIN

655. Conditions to be met before bulk cargoes other than grain are loaded. Prior to loading a bulk cargo[1], the master must be in possession of stability information[2], containing comprehensive information on the ship's stability and on the distribution of cargo and ballast for the standard loading conditions[3].

The master must not accept for loading concentrates or other cargoes which may liquefy[4] unless[5]:

(1)   either the moisture content[6] of the cargo indicated in the certificate (which indicates both the moisture content of the cargo and its transportable moisture limit)[7] is less than its transportable moisture limit[8]; or

(2)   if the moisture content is above that limit, appropriate safety arrangements are made to the satisfaction of the certifying authority[9] to ensure adequate stability in the case of cargo shifting, and the ship has adequate structural integrity[10].

Prior to loading a bulk cargo which is not classified in accordance with the SOLAS Convention[11], but which has chemical properties that may create a potential hazard[12], appropriate special precautions for its safe carriage must be taken[13].

The owner[14] must ensure that the master is furnished with the stability information[15]; and the master must not accept cargo for loading unless:

(a)   he has in his possession the stability information[16];

(b)   he is satisfied by calculations that the proposed loading arrangements would ensure sufficient stability in accordance with the stability information so provided[17]; and

(c)   he is satisfied that, in the case of a bulk cargo which is not classified in accordance with the SOLAS Convention[18], but which has chemical properties that may create a potential hazard[19], the appropriate special precautions for its safe carriage that are required[20] have been taken[21].

An owner who contravenes the requirement to ensure that the master is furnished with the stability information[22] is guilty of an offence[23]; and a master who contravenes the conditions for accepting for loading concentrates or other cargoes which may liquefy[24] or who contravenes the conditions for accepting cargo which are set out in heads (a) to (c) above[25] is guilty of an offence[26].

1   As to the meaning of 'bulk cargo' see PARA 649 note 2; and as to the meaning of 'cargo' for these purposes see PARA 649 note 1.
2   Ie information provided pursuant to the Merchant Shipping (Load Line) Regulations 1998, SI 1998/2241, reg 32 (as to which see PARA 671): see the Merchant Shipping (Carriage of Cargoes) Regulations 1999, SI 1999/336, reg 9(1).
3   Merchant Shipping (Carriage of Cargoes) Regulations 1999, SI 1999/336, reg 9(1). As to equivalents and exemptions see PARA 654.
4   As to the meaning of 'cargoes which may liquefy' see PARA 649 note 2.
5   Merchant Shipping (Carriage of Cargoes) Regulations 1999, SI 1999/336, reg 9(2).
6   As to the meaning of 'moisture content' for these purposes see PARA 649 note 2.
7   Ie the certificate mentioned in the Merchant Shipping (Carriage of Cargoes) Regulations 1999, SI 1999/336, reg 4(1)(b) (see PARA 649): see reg 9(2)(i). As to the meaning of 'transportable moisture limit' for these purposes see PARA 649 note 2.
8   Merchant Shipping (Carriage of Cargoes) Regulations 1999, SI 1999/336, reg 9(2)(i).
9   As to the meaning of 'certifying authority' for these purposes see PARA 652 note 4.
10 Merchant Shipping (Carriage of Cargoes) Regulations 1999, SI 1999/336, reg 9(2)(ii).
11 Ie not classified in accordance with the SOLAS Convention reg VII/2: see the Merchant Shipping (Carriage of Cargoes) Regulations 1999, SI 1999/336, reg 9(3). As to the meaning of 'SOLAS Convention' see PARA 649 note 2.
12 Ie a bulk cargo referred to in the Merchant Shipping (Carriage of Cargoes) Regulations 1999, SI 1999/336, reg 4(1)(b)(iii) (see PARA 649): see reg 9(3).
13 Merchant Shipping (Carriage of Cargoes) Regulations 1999, SI 1999/336, reg 9(3).
14 As to references to the owner see PARA 649 note 3.
15 Merchant Shipping (Carriage of Cargoes) Regulations 1999, SI 1999/336, reg 9(4). The text refers to the stability information referred to in reg 9(1) (see the text and notes 1–3): see reg 9(4).
16 Merchant Shipping (Carriage of Cargoes) Regulations 1999, SI 1999/336, reg 9(5)(a). The text refers to the stability information referred to in reg 9(1) (see the text and notes 1–3): see reg 9(5)(a).
17 Merchant Shipping (Carriage of Cargoes) Regulations 1999, SI 1999/336, reg 9(5)(b). The text refers to the stability information provided under reg 9(1) (see the text and notes 1–3): see reg 9(5)(b).
18 Ie not classified in accordance with the SOLAS Convention reg VII/2: see the Merchant Shipping (Carriage of Cargoes) Regulations 1999, SI 1999/336, reg 9(5)(c).
19 Ie a bulk cargo referred to in the Merchant Shipping (Carriage of Cargoes) Regulations 1999, SI 1999/336, reg 4(1)(b)(iii) (see PARA 649): see reg 9(5)(c).
20 Ie required by the Merchant Shipping (Carriage of Cargoes) Regulations 1999, SI 1999/336, reg 9(3) (see the text and notes 11–13): see reg 9(5)(c).
21 Merchant Shipping (Carriage of Cargoes) Regulations 1999, SI 1999/336, reg 9(5)(c).
22 Ie an owner who contravenes the Merchant Shipping (Carriage of Cargoes) Regulations 1999, SI 1999/336, reg 9(4) (see the text and notes 14–15): see reg 9(6).
23 See the Merchant Shipping (Carriage of Cargoes) Regulations 1999, SI 1999/336, reg 9(6); and PARA 1126.
24 Ie a master who contravenes the Merchant Shipping (Carriage of Cargoes) Regulations 1999, SI 1999/336, reg 9(2) (see the text and notes 4–10): see reg 9(7).
25 Ie a master who contravenes the Merchant Shipping (Carriage of Cargoes) Regulations 1999, SI 1999/336, reg 9(5) (see the text and notes 16–21): see reg 9(7).

26 See the Merchant Shipping (Carriage of Cargoes) Regulations 1999, SI 1999/336, reg 9(7); and
PARA 1126.

656. Loading, unloading and stowage of bulk cargoes. To enable the
master to prevent excessive stresses in the ship's structure, it is the duty of the
owner[1] to ensure the ship is provided with a cargo loading manual, which must be
written in a language with which the ship's officers responsible for cargo
operations are familiar[2]. If this language is not English, the ship must be provided
with a manual written also in the English language[3]. The manual may consist of
one or more booklets and must, as a minimum, include[4]:

(1)   stability data[5];
(2)   ballasting and deballasting rates and capacities[6];
(3)   maximum allowable load per unit surface area of the tank top plating[7];
(4)   maximum allowable load per hold[8];
(5)   general loading and unloading instructions with regard to the strength
        of the ship's structure including any limitations on the most adverse
        operating conditions during loading, unloading, ballasting operations
        and the voyage[9];
(6)   any special restrictions such as limitations on the most adverse operating
        conditions imposed by the administration[10] (or organisation recognised
        by it, if applicable)[11]; and
(7)   where strength calculations are required, maximum permissible forces
        and moments on the ship's hull during loading, unloading and the
        voyage[12].

Before a solid bulk cargo[13] is loaded or unloaded, the master and the terminal
representative[14] must agree on a plan which:

(a)   ensures that the permissible forces and moments on the ship are not
        exceeded during loading or unloading[15]; and
(b)   includes the sequence, quantity and rate of loading or unloading[16],

taking into consideration the intended speed of loading or unloading, intended
number of pours and the deballasting or ballasting capability of the ship[17]. The
plan and any subsequent amendments thereto must be lodged with the
appropriate authority of the port state[18]. The master and terminal representative
must ensure that loading and unloading operations are conducted in accordance
with the plan so agreed[19].

It is the duty of the master to ensure that:

(i)   bulk cargoes are loaded and trimmed[20] reasonably level, as necessary, to
        the boundaries of the cargo space[21] so as to minimize the risk of shifting
        and to ensure that adequate stability will be maintained throughout the
        voyage[22];
(ii)   when bulk cargoes are carried in 'tween-decks, the hatchways of such
        'tween-decks are closed in those cases where the loading information
        indicates an unacceptable level of stress of the bottom structure if the
        hatchways are left open[23];
(iii)   the cargo is trimmed reasonably level and either extends from side to
        side or is secured by additional longitudinal divisions of sufficient
        strength[24];
(iv)   the safe load-carrying capacity of the 'tween-decks is observed to ensure
        that the deck-structure is not overloaded[25].

If during loading or unloading any of the limits of the ship referred to in heads
(1) to (7) above[26] are exceeded or are likely to become so if the loading or
unloading continues, the master has the right to suspend operation, and if he does
so he must notify accordingly the appropriate authority of the port state with

which the plan has been lodged[27]; and, where these circumstances apply[28], the master and the terminal representative must ensure that corrective action is taken[29].

When unloading cargo, the master and terminal representative must ensure that the unloading method does not damage the ship's structure[30].

The master must ensure that ship's personnel continuously monitor cargo operations[31].

Where possible, the ship's draught must be checked regularly during loading or unloading to confirm the tonnage figures supplied[32]; and each draught and tonnage observation must be recorded in a cargo log-book[33].

If significant deviations from the plan agreed for loading or unloading[34] are detected, cargo or ballast operations (or both) must be adjusted to ensure that the deviations are corrected[35].

An owner who contravenes the duty to ensure the ship is provided with a cargo loading manual[36] is guilty of an offence[37].

A master who contravenes the provisions which require a plan for loading or unloading the ship to be agreed[38], or who fails to ensure that loading and unloading operations are conducted in accordance with the plan so agreed[39], or who fails to ensure that cargoes are loaded and trimmed as necessary[40], or who fails to ensure that corrective action is taken where, during loading or unloading, any of the ship's limits[41] are exceeded or are likely to become so[42], or who fails to ensure that the unloading method does not damage the ship's structure[43], or who fails to monitor cargo operations as required or fails to ensure that deviations from the plan agreed for loading or unloading are corrected[44], is guilty of an offence[45].

A terminal representative in the United Kingdom who contravenes the provisions which require a plan for loading or unloading the ship to be agreed[46], or who fails to ensure that loading and unloading operations are conducted in accordance with the plan so agreed[47], or who fails to ensure that corrective action is taken where, during loading or unloading, any of the ship's limits[48] are exceeded or are likely to become so[49], or who fails to ensure that the unloading method does not damage the ship's structure[50], is guilty of an offence[51].

1   As to references to the owner see PARA 649 note 3.
2   Merchant Shipping (Carriage of Cargoes) Regulations 1999, SI 1999/336, reg 10(2). As to equivalents and exemptions see PARA 654.
3   Merchant Shipping (Carriage of Cargoes) Regulations 1999, SI 1999/336, reg 10(2).
4   Merchant Shipping (Carriage of Cargoes) Regulations 1999, SI 1999/336, reg 10(2).
5   Merchant Shipping (Carriage of Cargoes) Regulations 1999, SI 1999/336, reg 10(2)(a). Head (1) in the text refers to stability data, to the extent required by the Merchant Shipping (Load Line) Regulations 1998, SI 1998/2241, reg 32 (as to which see PARA 671): see the Merchant Shipping (Carriage of Cargoes) Regulations 1999, SI 1999/336, reg 10(2)(a).
6   Merchant Shipping (Carriage of Cargoes) Regulations 1999, SI 1999/336, reg 10(2)(b).
7   Merchant Shipping (Carriage of Cargoes) Regulations 1999, SI 1999/336, reg 10(2)(c).
8   Merchant Shipping (Carriage of Cargoes) Regulations 1999, SI 1999/336, reg 10(2)(d).
9   Merchant Shipping (Carriage of Cargoes) Regulations 1999, SI 1999/336, reg 10(2)(e).
10 'Administration', in relation to United Kingdom ships, means the Secretary of State: Merchant Shipping (Carriage of Cargoes) Regulations 1999, SI 1999/336, reg 2(1). As to the Secretary of State see PARA 36.
11 Merchant Shipping (Carriage of Cargoes) Regulations 1999, SI 1999/336, reg 10(2)(f).
12 Merchant Shipping (Carriage of Cargoes) Regulations 1999, SI 1999/336, reg 10(2)(g).
13 As to the meaning of 'bulk cargo' see PARA 649 note 2; and as to the meaning of 'cargo' for these purposes see PARA 649 note 1.
14 For the purposes of the Merchant Shipping (Carriage of Cargoes) Regulations 1999, SI 1999/336, reg 10, 'terminal representative' means an individual who represents the terminal or other facility where the ship is loading or unloading and who has responsibility for operations conducted by that

terminal or facility with regard to the particular ship: reg 10(1)(a). For these purposes, 'terminal' means any terminal, jetty, pier, floating structure or other works within a harbour at which ships can obtain shelter or ship and unship goods or passengers: reg 2(1).

15 Merchant Shipping (Carriage of Cargoes) Regulations 1999, SI 1999/336, reg 10(3)(i).

16 Merchant Shipping (Carriage of Cargoes) Regulations 1999, SI 1999/336, reg 10(3)(ii).

17 Merchant Shipping (Carriage of Cargoes) Regulations 1999, SI 1999/336, reg 10(3).

18 Merchant Shipping (Carriage of Cargoes) Regulations 1999, SI 1999/336, reg 10(3). For the purposes of reg 10(3) and reg 10(7) (as to which see the text and notes 26–30), the appropriate authority of a port in the United Kingdom is the harbour authority of that port; and if a terminal in the port is not operated by the harbour authority, then the operator of the terminal is the appropriate authority: reg 10(1)(b). 'Operator of the terminal' means the person under whose control the activities at the terminal are: reg 2(1). As to the meaning of 'United Kingdom' see PARA 16 note 3.

19 Merchant Shipping (Carriage of Cargoes) Regulations 1999, SI 1999/336, reg 10(6).

20 As to the meaning of 'trimming' for these purposes see PARA 649 note 2.

21 As to the meaning of 'cargo space' see PARA 649 note 1.

22 Merchant Shipping (Carriage of Cargoes) Regulations 1999, SI 1999/336, reg 10(4).

23 Merchant Shipping (Carriage of Cargoes) Regulations 1999, SI 1999/336, reg 10(5)(a).

24 Merchant Shipping (Carriage of Cargoes) Regulations 1999, SI 1999/336, reg 10(5)(b).

25 Merchant Shipping (Carriage of Cargoes) Regulations 1999, SI 1999/336, reg 10(5)(c).

26 Ie the limits of the ship referred to in the Merchant Shipping (Carriage of Cargoes) Regulations 1999, SI 1999/336, reg 10(2) (see the text and notes 1–12): see reg 10(7)(a).

27 Merchant Shipping (Carriage of Cargoes) Regulations 1999, SI 1999/336, reg 10(7)(a). As to the meaning of 'appropriate authority' for these purposes see note 17.

28 Ie where the Merchant Shipping (Carriage of Cargoes) Regulations 1999, SI 1999/336, reg 10(7)(a) (see the text and notes 26–27) applies: see reg 10(7)(b).

29 Merchant Shipping (Carriage of Cargoes) Regulations 1999, SI 1999/336, reg 10(7)(b).

30 Merchant Shipping (Carriage of Cargoes) Regulations 1999, SI 1999/336, reg 10(7)(c).

31 Merchant Shipping (Carriage of Cargoes) Regulations 1999, SI 1999/336, reg 10(8)(a).

32 Merchant Shipping (Carriage of Cargoes) Regulations 1999, SI 1999/336, reg 10(8)(b).

33 Merchant Shipping (Carriage of Cargoes) Regulations 1999, SI 1999/336, reg 10(8)(c).

34 Ie the plan agreed under the Merchant Shipping (Carriage of Cargoes) Regulations 1999, SI 1999/336, reg 10(3) (see the text and notes 13–18): see reg 10(8)(d).

35 Merchant Shipping (Carriage of Cargoes) Regulations 1999, SI 1999/336, reg 10(8)(d).

36 Ie an owner who contravenes the Merchant Shipping (Carriage of Cargoes) Regulations 1999, SI 1999/336, reg 10(2) (see the text and notes 1–12): see reg 10(9)(a).

37 See the Merchant Shipping (Carriage of Cargoes) Regulations 1999, SI 1999/336, reg 10(9)(a); and PARA 1126.

38 Ie a master who contravenes the Merchant Shipping (Carriage of Cargoes) Regulations 1999, SI 1999/336, reg 10(3) (see the text and notes 13–18): see reg 10(9)(b).

39 Ie a master who contravenes the Merchant Shipping (Carriage of Cargoes) Regulations 1999, SI 1999/336, reg 10(6) (see the text and note 19): see reg 10(9)(b).

40 Ie a master who contravenes the Merchant Shipping (Carriage of Cargoes) Regulations 1999, SI 1999/336, reg 10(4), (5) (see the text and notes 20–25): see reg 10(9)(b).

41 Ie the limits of the ship referred to in the Merchant Shipping (Carriage of Cargoes) Regulations 1999, SI 1999/336, reg 10(2) (see the text and notes 1–12): see reg 10(7)(a).

42 Ie a master who contravenes the Merchant Shipping (Carriage of Cargoes) Regulations 1999, SI 1999/336, reg 10(7)(b) (see the text and notes 28–29): see reg 10(9)(b).

43 Ie a master who contravenes the Merchant Shipping (Carriage of Cargoes) Regulations 1999, SI 1999/336, reg 10(7)(c) (see the text and note 30): see reg 10(9)(b).

44 Ie a master who contravenes the Merchant Shipping (Carriage of Cargoes) Regulations 1999, SI 1999/336, reg 10(8) (see the text and notes 31–35): see reg 10(9)(b).

45 See the Merchant Shipping (Carriage of Cargoes) Regulations 1999, SI 1999/336, reg 10(9)(b); and PARA 1126.

46 Ie a terminal representative in the United Kingdom who contravenes the Merchant Shipping (Carriage of Cargoes) Regulations 1999, SI 1999/336, reg 10(3) (see the text and notes 13–18): see reg 10(9)(c).

47 Ie a terminal representative in the United Kingdom who contravenes the Merchant Shipping (Carriage of Cargoes) Regulations 1999, SI 1999/336, reg 10(6) (see the text and note 19): see reg 10(9)(c).

48 Ie the limits of the ship referred to in the Merchant Shipping (Carriage of Cargoes) Regulations 1999, SI 1999/336, reg 10(2) (see the text and notes 1–12): see reg 10(7)(a).

49 Ie a terminal representative in the United Kingdom who contravenes the Merchant Shipping
   (Carriage of Cargoes) Regulations 1999, SI 1999/336, reg 10(7)(b) (see the text and notes 28–29):
   see reg 10(9)(c).
50 Ie a terminal representative in the United Kingdom who contravenes the Merchant Shipping
   (Carriage of Cargoes) Regulations 1999, SI 1999/336, reg 10(7)(c) (see the text and note 30): see
   reg 10(9)(c).
51 See the Merchant Shipping (Carriage of Cargoes) Regulations 1999, SI 1999/336, reg 10(9)(c); and
   PARA 1126.

C.   CARGO SHIPS CARRYING GRAIN

657.   Ships carrying grain to comply with the International Grain Code. A
ship carrying grain[1] must comply with the requirements of the International Grain
Code[2].

The owner[3] and master must ensure[4] that:
(1)   a ship loading grain complies with the International Grain Code[5]; and
(2)   subject to head (b) below, the ship has on board a document of
        authorisation as required by that Code[6].

Except when a ship may be in distress, the owner and master must not permit
a ship loaded with grain in bulk outside the United Kingdom[7] to enter any port in
the United Kingdom so laden, unless the ship has been loaded in accordance with
the International Grain Code[8].

No person may order the commencement of the loading of grain into a ship in
the United Kingdom unless he is satisfied that[9]:
(a)   the ship has on board a document of authorisation referred to in head
        (2) above[10]; or
(b)   the master has demonstrated to the satisfaction of the certifying
        authority that the ship will, in its proposed loading condition, comply
        with the appropriate requirements of the International Grain Code and
        has obtained a document to this effect signed by a surveyor of such a
        certifying authority[11].

An owner or master who fails to ensure that a ship loading grain complies with
the International Grain Code and has on board a document of authorisation as
required by that Code[12], or who permits a ship loaded in contravention of the
International Grain Code outside the United Kingdom to enter any port in the
United Kingdom so laden[13], is guilty of an offence[14].

A person who orders the commencement of the loading of grain into a ship in
the United Kingdom without satisfying himself first as to the conditions so
required (as set out in heads (a) and (b) above)[15] is guilty of an offence[16].

1   As to the meaning of 'grain' see PARA 650 note 2.
2   Merchant Shipping (Carriage of Cargoes) Regulations 1999, SI 1999/336, reg 11(1). As to the
    meaning of 'International Grain Code' see PARA 650 note 6. As to equivalents and exemptions see
    PARA 654.
3   As to references to the owner see PARA 649 note 3.
4   Ie without prejudice to the Merchant Shipping (Carriage of Cargoes) Regulations 1999, SI
    1999/336, reg 11(1) (see the text and notes 1–2) or any other requirement of the Merchant
    Shipping (Carriage of Cargoes) Regulations 1999, SI 1999/336: see reg 11(2).
5   Merchant Shipping (Carriage of Cargoes) Regulations 1999, SI 1999/336, reg 11(2)(a).
6   Merchant Shipping (Carriage of Cargoes) Regulations 1999, SI 1999/336, reg 11(2)(b). In the case
    of a United Kingdom ship, the document of authorisation must be issued by the certifying
    authority: see reg 11(2)(b). As to the meaning of 'certifying authority' see PARA 652 note 4.
7   As to the meaning of 'United Kingdom' see PARA 16 note 3.
8   Merchant Shipping (Carriage of Cargoes) Regulations 1999, SI 1999/336, reg 11(3).
9   Merchant Shipping (Carriage of Cargoes) Regulations 1999, SI 1999/336, reg 11(4).
10 Merchant Shipping (Carriage of Cargoes) Regulations 1999, SI 1999/336, reg 11(4)(a).
11 Merchant Shipping (Carriage of Cargoes) Regulations 1999, SI 1999/336, reg 11(4)(b).

12 Ie an owner or master who contravenes the Merchant Shipping (Carriage of Cargoes) Regulations 1999, SI 1999/336, reg 11(2) (see the text and notes 3–6): see reg 11(5).

13 Ie an owner or master who contravenes the Merchant Shipping (Carriage of Cargoes) Regulations 1999, SI 1999/336, reg 11(3) (see the text and notes 7–8): see reg 11(5).

14 See the Merchant Shipping (Carriage of Cargoes) Regulations 1999, SI 1999/336, reg 11(5); and PARA 1126.

15 Ie a person who contravenes the Merchant Shipping (Carriage of Cargoes) Regulations 1999, SI 1999/336, reg 11(4) (see the text and notes 9–11): see reg 11(6).

16 See the Merchant Shipping (Carriage of Cargoes) Regulations 1999, SI 1999/336, reg 11(6); and PARA 1126.

(vi) Special Provision for Ships receiving Transhipped Fish

658. Requirements to be met by ships in respect of which transhipment licences are in force. The Secretary of State[1] may, for all or any of the following purposes[2], that is to say:

(1)   the purpose of securing the safety of ships[3] in respect of which transhipment licences[4] are in force and persons on them[5];

(2)   the purpose of protecting the health of persons on such ships[6];

(3)   the purpose of securing the safety of any other persons or property[7]; and

(4)   the purpose of preventing or reducing pollution[8],

by regulations[9] prescribe requirements to be met by ships in respect of which transhipment licences are in force[10]. The matters with respect to which requirements may be so prescribed include, in particular, the construction and equipment of ships, the manning of ships and operational matters[11]; and such regulations may[12] apply in relation to a ship in respect of which a transhipment licence is in force any requirements contained in safety regulations[13], regulations relating to pollution[14], or any international agreement[15], whether or not those requirements would otherwise apply in relation to that ship[16].

1   As to the Secretary of State see PARA 36.
2   See the Merchant Shipping Act 1995 s 100F(1) (ss 100F, 100G added by the Merchant Shipping and Maritime Security Act 1997 s 11).
3   As to the meaning of 'ship' see PARA 229.
4   For these purposes, 'transhipment licence' means a licence under the Sea Fish (Conservation) Act 1967 s 4A (prohibition of transhipment of fish unless authorised by a licence) (see FISHERIES AND AQUACULTURE vol 51 (2013) PARAS 259, 260): Merchant Shipping Act 1995 s 100F(1) (as added: see note 2).
5   Merchant Shipping Act 1995 s 100F(3)(a) (as added: see note 2).
6   Merchant Shipping Act 1995 s 100F(3)(b) (as added: see note 2).
7   Merchant Shipping Act 1995 s 100F(3)(c) (as added: see note 2).
8   Merchant Shipping Act 1995 s 100F(3)(d) (as added: see note 2).
9   As to the power of the Secretary of State to make subordinate legislation under the Merchant Shipping Act 1995, including his power to appoint committees for the purpose of advising him when considering the making or alteration of any regulations etc, see PARA 39. At the date at which this volume states the law, no such regulations had been made under s 100F.
10 Merchant Shipping Act 1995 s 100F(2) (as added: see note 2). The obligation imposed by regulations under s 100F(2) is not enforceable except in accordance with s 100G (failure to comply with prescribed standards) (see PARA 659): s 100G(6) (as so added). However, s 100G(6) does not limit the powers conferred by s 258 (power to inspect ships and their equipment etc) (see PARA 48): see s 100G(6) (as so added).
11 Merchant Shipping Act 1995 s 100F(4) (as added: see note 2).
12 Ie without prejudice to the generality of the Merchant Shipping Act 1995 s 100F(2) (see the text and notes 9–10): see s 100F(5) (as added: see note 2).
13 Merchant Shipping Act 1995 s 100F(5)(a) (as added: see note 2). As to the meaning of 'safety regulations' see PARA 602 note 1.
14 Merchant Shipping Act 1995 s 100F(5)(b) (as added: see note 2). The text refers to regulations under s 128 (see ENVIRONMENTAL QUALITY AND PUBLIC HEALTH vol 45 (2010) PARA 360): see s 100F(5)(b) (as so added).

15 Merchant Shipping Act 1995 s 100F(5)(c) (as added: see note 2).
16 Merchant Shipping Act 1995 s 100F(5) (as added: see note 2).

659. Compliance with standards prescribed for ships in respect of which transhipment licences are in force. If it appears to the Secretary of State[1] that any requirement of regulations made by him either in relation to ships[2] in respect of which transhipment licences[3] are in force[4], or in relation to compulsory insurance or security[5], is being contravened in respect of such a ship[6], he may serve on the master[7] a notice[8], which specifies the contravention by reason of which it is given[9], and must:

(1)   prohibit the receiving by the ship of fish transhipped from another ship[10];
(2)   prohibit the processing of fish on the ship[11]; or
(3)   prohibit both such receiving and such processing[12].

The Secretary of State must revoke such a notice if he is satisfied that the contravention specified in it has been remedied[13].

If a transhipment licence ceases to be in force in respect of a ship to which such a notice relates, the notice is[14] revoked[15].

If without reasonable excuse the master of a ship causes or permits any prohibition imposed by such a notice[16] to be contravened in respect of the ship, he is guilty of an offence[17].

1 As to the Secretary of State see PARA 36.
2 As to the meaning of 'ship' see PARA 229.
3 As to the meaning of 'transhipment licence' see PARA 658 note 4.
4 Ie under the Merchant Shipping Act 1995 s 100F(2) (see PARA 658): see s 100G(1) (s 100G added by the Merchant Shipping and Maritime Security Act 1997 s 11). The obligation imposed by regulations under the Merchant Shipping Act 199 s 100F(2) is not enforceable except in accordance with s 100G (failure to comply with prescribed standards): s 100G(6) (as so added). However, s 100G(6) does not limit the powers conferred by s 258 (power to inspect ships and their equipment etc) (see PARA 48): see s 100G(6) (as so added).
5 Ie under the Merchant Shipping Act 1995 s 192A (see PARA 1016): see s 100G(1) (as added: see note 4). See further the Merchant Shipping (Compulsory Insurance: Ships Receiving Trans-shipped Fish) Regulations 1998, SI 1998/209; and PARA 1016.
6 Ie a ship in respect of which a transhipment licence is in force: see the Merchant Shipping Act 1995 s 100G(1) (as added: see note 4).
7 As to the meaning of 'master' see PARA 444 note 1.
8 Merchant Shipping Act 1995 s 100G(1) (as added: see note 4).
9 Merchant Shipping Act 1995 s 100G(2) (as added: see note 4).
10 Merchant Shipping Act 1995 s 100G(2)(a) (as added: see note 4).
11 Merchant Shipping Act 1995 s 100G(2)(b) (as added: see note 4).
12 Merchant Shipping Act 1995 s 100G(2)(c) (as added: see note 4).
13 Merchant Shipping Act 1995 s 100G(3) (as added: see note 4).
14 Ie by virtue of the Merchant Shipping Act 1995 s 100G(4): see s 100G(4) (as added: see note 4).
15 Merchant Shipping Act 1995 s 100G(4) (as added: see note 4).
16 Ie by a notice under the Merchant Shipping Act 1995 s 100G(2) (see the text and notes 9–12): see s 100G(5); and PARA 1127.
17 See the Merchant Shipping Act 1995 s 100G(5); and PARA 1127.

(2) LOAD LINES

(i) Application of Provisions relating to Load Lines etc

660. Application of the load lines provisions. The provisions relating to load lines[1] apply to United Kingdom ships wherever they may be and to other ships while they are within United Kingdom waters[2], except:

(1)   ships of war[3];
(2)   ships solely engaged in fishing[4];

(3)   pleasure vessels[5];
(4)   ships which do not go to sea[6]; and
(5)   ships under 80 net tons engaged solely in the coasting trade and not carrying cargo[7] which fall within one of the following classes[8], namely:
    (a)   tugs or salvage ships[9];
    (b)   hopper barges or dredgers[10];
    (c)   ships used by or on behalf of:
        (i)   a general or local lighthouse authority[i] for the purpose of the authority's functions as such[12];
        (ii)   a government department for fishery protection purposes, or an inshore fisheries and conservation authority[13] for the regulation of sea fisheries within its district[14];
        (iii)   a government department for fishery or scientific research[15]; or
        (iv)   the Secretary of State[16] for the purpose of ensuring safety in the use of firing ranges or weapons at sea[17]; and
    (d)   ships in respect of which passenger certificates are in force specifying limits beyond which the ship must not ply, and which operate solely within those limits[18].

1   Ie the Merchant Shipping (Load Line) Regulations 1998, SI 1998/2241: see reg 4(1). For these purposes, 'load line' means a mark on a ship indicating the maximum depth to which it may be loaded: reg 2(1).

2   Merchant Shipping (Load Line) Regulations 1998, SI 1998/2241, reg 4(1). As to exemptions granted under the Merchant Shipping (Load Line) Regulations 1998, SI 1998/2241, see PARA 661. As to the meaning of 'United Kingdom' see PARA 16 note 3.
    The Merchant Shipping (Load Line) Regulations 1998, SI 1998/2241, do not apply to large or small commercial vessels which have been examined, and in respect of which a certificate has been issued, in accordance with the applicable Code of Practice, or to a vessel which is operating under the phase-in arrangements of the applicable Code of Practice, pursuant to the Merchant Shipping (Vessels in Commercial Use for Sport or Pleasure) Regulations 1998, SI 1998/2771: see PARAS 613, 614.

3   Merchant Shipping (Load Line) Regulations 1998, SI 1998/2241, reg 4(1)(a).

4   Merchant Shipping (Load Line) Regulations 1998, SI 1998/2241, reg 4(1)(b).

5   Merchant Shipping (Load Line) Regulations 1998, SI 1998/2241, reg 4(1)(c). For these purposes, 'pleasure vessel' means:
    (1)   any ship which at the time it is being used is, in the case of a ship wholly owned by an individual or individuals, used only for the sport or pleasure of the owner or the immediate family or friends of the owner or, in the case of a ship owned by a body corporate, used only for sport or pleasure and on which the persons are employees or officers of the body corporate, or their immediate family or friends; and is on a voyage or excursion for which the owner does not receive money for or in connection with operating the ship or carrying any person, other than as a contribution to the direct expenses of the operation of the ship incurred during the voyage or excursion; or
    (2)   any ship wholly owned by or on behalf of a members' club formed for the purpose of sport or pleasure which, at the time it is being used, is used only for the sport or pleasure of members of the club or their immediate family; and for the use of which any charges levied are paid into club funds and applied for the general use of the club; and
    (3)   in the case of any ship referred to in head (1) or head (2) no other payments are made by or on behalf of the users of the ship, other than by the owner;
    and, for these purposes, 'immediate family' means, in relation to an individual, the spouse or civil partner of the individual, and a relative of the individual or the individual's spouse or civil partner; and 'relative' means brother, sister, ancestor or lineal descendant: reg 2(1) (definition amended by SI 2005/2114).

6   Merchant Shipping (Load Line) Regulations 1998, SI 1998/2241, reg 4(1)(d). For these purposes, 'sea' does not include Category A, B, C or D waters, where 'Category A, B, C or D waters' means the waters specified as such in Merchant Shipping Notice 1776(M): Merchant Shipping (Load Line) Regulations 1998, SI 1998/2241, reg 2(1). 'Merchant Shipping Notice' means a Notice described as such and issued by the Maritime and Coastguard Agency, and any reference to a particular Merchant Shipping Notice includes a reference to any Merchant Shipping Notice amending that Notice: reg 2(1). Accordingly, Merchant Shipping Notice 1776(M) (Categorisation

of Waters: Notice to Owners, Operators and Masters) (March 2003) is published by the Maritime and Coastguard Agency and categorises United Kingdom waters which are not regarded currently as 'sea' for the purposes of merchant shipping legislation (excepting marine pollution). As to the Maritime and Coastguard Agency see PARA 57.

7 A ship referred to in head (5) in the text falling within the class in head (d) in the text is excepted from the provisions of the Merchant Shipping (Load Line) Regulations 1998, SI 1998/2241, while carrying cargo in accordance with the terms, if any, of the ship's passenger certificate expressly authorising the carriage of cargo: reg 4(3).

8 Merchant Shipping (Load Line) Regulations 1998, SI 1998/2241, reg 4(1)(e) (amended by SI 2000/1335).

9 Merchant Shipping (Load Line) Regulations 1998, SI 1998/2241, reg 4(2)(a).

10 Merchant Shipping (Load Line) Regulations 1998, SI 1998/2241, reg 4(2)(b).

i As to lighthouse authorities see PARA 1017 et seq.

12 Merchant Shipping (Load Line) Regulations 1998, SI 1998/2241, reg 4(2)(c)(i).

13 For these purposes 'inshore fisheries and conservation authority' means an inshore fisheries and conservation authority for an inshore fisheries and conservation district established under the Marine and Coastal Access Act 2009 s 149(1) (see FISHERIES AND AQUACULTURE vol 51 (2013) PARA 227): Merchant Shipping (Load Line) Regulations 1998, SI 1998/2241, reg 2(1) (amended by SI 2011/603).

14 Merchant Shipping (Load Line) Regulations 1998, SI 1998/2241, reg 4(2)(c)(ii) (amended by SI 2011/603).

15 Merchant Shipping (Load Line) Regulations 1998, SI 1998/2241, reg 4(2)(c)(iii).

16 As to the Secretary of State see PARA 36.

17 Merchant Shipping (Load Line) Regulations 1998, SI 1998/2241, reg 4(2)(c)(iv).

18 Merchant Shipping (Load Line) Regulations 1998, SI 1998/2241, reg 4(2)(d). See note 7.

661. Exemptions from load line rules. The Secretary of State[1] may exempt from the provisions relating to load lines[2]:

(1) any ship which embodies features of a novel kind if the development of those features and their incorporation in ships engaged on international voyages[3] might be seriously impeded if the ship had to comply with all the requirements of the provisions relating to load lines[4];

(2) any ship plying on international voyages between near neighbouring ports if, in his opinion, the sheltered nature and condition of the voyages make it unreasonable or impracticable to apply the provisions relating to load lines, and if he is satisfied the government of the other country (or, as the case may be, of each of the other countries) concurs in that opinion[5].

The Secretary of State may also exempt from the provisions a ship which is not a Convention-size[6] ship or any other ship which does not ply on international voyages[7].

Where a United Kingdom ship does not normally ply on international voyages but is, in exceptional circumstances, required to undertake a single international voyage, the Secretary of State may exempt the ship while engaged on that voyage[8].

1 As to the Secretary of State see PARA 36.

2 Ie exempt from the Merchant Shipping (Load Line) Regulations 1998, SI 1998/2241 (see PARAS 660, 662 et seq): reg 5(1). As to the meaning of 'load line' see PARA 660 note 1. Any exemption conferred under reg 5 may be conferred subject to such conditions as the Secretary of State thinks fit; and, where any such exemption is conferred subject to conditions, the exemption is not to have effect unless those conditions are complied with: reg 5(4).

Where a ship is exempted under reg 5(1), an International Load Line Exemption Certificate in the form prescribed by the International Convention on Load Lines (London, 5 April to 4 July 1966; TS 58 (1968); Cmnd 3708), as amended by the 1988 Protocol (Cmnd 4419) Annex III must be issued in respect of the ship by the Secretary of State: reg 12(1) (substituted by SI 2000/1335). Except in so far as the nature or terms of any such exemption require the contrary, the ship must be assigned freeboards in accordance with the Merchant Shipping (Load Line) Regulations 1998, SI 1998/2241, reg 7 (see PARA 663), the ship is subject to surveys in accordance with reg 8 (see PARA 664), and regs 8–11 (see PARA 664 et seq) apply in relation to the Exemption Certificate as they apply in relation to an appropriate certificate, subject to the substitution, for references in those regulations to an Assigning Authority, of references to the Secretary of State: reg 12(3) (amended by SI 2000/1335). As to the meaning of 'Assigning Authority' see PARA 663 note 1. For these purposes, 'Exemption Certificate' means an International Load Line Exemption Certificate or a United Kingdom Load Line Exemption Certificate: Merchant Shipping (Load Line) Regulations 1998, SI 1998/2241, reg 2(1) (definition added by SI 2000/1335). 'International Load Line Exemption Certificate' means an International Load Line Exemption Certificate issued under the International Convention on Load Lines (London, 5 April to 4 July 1966; TS 58 (1968); Cmnd 3708) (the '1966 Convention'), as amended by the 1988 Protocol (Cmnd 4419): Merchant Shipping (Load Line) Regulations 1998, SI 1998/2241, reg 2(1) (definition added by SI 2000/1335). 'United Kingdom Load Line Exemption Certificate' means a certificate issued pursuant to the Merchant Shipping (Load Line) Regulations 1998, SI 1998/2241, reg 12(2) (see PARA 661 note 7): reg 2(1) (definition added by SI 2000/1335).

Any reference in the Merchant Shipping (Load Line) Regulations 1998, SI 1998/2241, to the 1966 Convention includes any amendment of it considered by the Secretary of State to be relevant from time to time, and specified in a Merchant Shipping Notice: Merchant Shipping (Load Line) Regulations 1998, SI 1998/2241, reg 2(3). As to the meaning of 'Merchant Shipping Notice' see PARA 660 note 6. As to the International Convention on Load Lines 1966 see PARA 7.

3 For these purposes, 'international voyage' means a voyage either between a port in the United Kingdom and a port outside the United Kingdom, or between a port in a Convention country (other than the United Kingdom) and a port in any other country or territory (whether a Convention country or not) which is outside the United Kingdom: Merchant Shipping (Load Line) Regulations 1998, SI 1998/2241, reg 2(1). As to the meaning of 'United Kingdom' see PARA 16 note 3. In determining for these purposes what are the ports between which a voyage is made no account is to be taken of any deviation by a ship from its intended voyage which is solely due to stress of weather or any other circumstance which neither the master nor the owner or the charterer (if any) of the ship could have prevented or forestalled: reg 2(2). For these purposes, 'Convention country' means a country or territory which is either a country the government of which is party to the International Convention on Load Lines (London, 5 April to 4 July 1966; TS 58 (1968); Cmnd 3708) (the '1966 Convention'), or to the 1966 Convention as amended by the 1988 Protocol (Cmnd 4419), or a territory to which the 1966 Convention, or the 1966 Convention as amended by the 1988 Protocol, extends: Merchant Shipping (Load Line) Regulations 1998, SI 1998/2241, reg 2(1) (definition amended by SI 2000/1335).

4 Merchant Shipping (Load Line) Regulations 1998, SI 1998/2241, reg 5(1)(a). See note 2.

5 Merchant Shipping (Load Line) Regulations 1998, SI 1998/2241, reg 5(1)(b). See note 2.

6 For these purposes, 'Convention-size' in relation to a ship, means in the case of an existing ship, of not less than 150 gross tons (ascertained in accordance with the law in force on 21 July 1968) and in the case of a new ship, of not less than 24 metres in length; 'new ship' means a ship whose keel is laid (or which is at a similar stage of construction) on or after the material date; and 'existing ship' means a ship which is not a new ship: Merchant Shipping (Load Line) Regulations 1998, SI 1998/2241, reg 2(1). 'Material date' for the purposes of the definitions of a 'new' and an 'existing' ship is, in relation to a ship whose parent country is a Convention country other than the United Kingdom, the date on which the 1966 Convention entered into force for that country and, in relation to any other ship, 21 July 1968: reg 2(1). 'Parent country', in relation to a ship, means the country or territory in which the ship is registered or, if the ship is not registered anywhere, it means the country or territory whose flag the ship flies: reg 2(1).

'Length' ('L'), in relation to a ship means the greater of the following distances:

(1)   96 per cent of the total length on a waterline at 85 per cent of the least moulded depth measured from the top of the keel; or

(2)   the length from the fore-side of the stern to the axis of the rudder stock on that waterline;

and where the stem contour is concave above the waterline at 85% of the least moulded depth, both the forward terminal of the total length and the fore-side of the stem respectively must be taken at the vertical projection to that waterline of the aftermost point of the stem contour above that waterline; in ships designed with a rake of keel, the waterline on which this length is measured must be parallel to the designed waterline: reg 2(1) (definition substituted by SI 2000/1335). As to the meanings of 'moulded depth' and 'rake of keel' for these purposes see the Merchant Shipping (Load Line) Regulations 1998, SI 1998/2241, reg 2(1).

7 Merchant Shipping (Load Line) Regulations 1998, SI 1998/2241, reg 5(2). See note 2. Where a ship is exempted under reg 5(2), a United Kingdom Load Line Exemption Certificate must be issued in respect of the ship by the Secretary of State which must state the conditions with which the ship is to comply, and which must be in the form prescribed in Merchant Shipping Notice 1752(M) Sch 8 (United Kingdom Load Line Certificates): Merchant Shipping (Load Line) Regulations 1998, SI 1998/2241, reg 12(2) (amended by SI 2000/1335). Except in so far as the nature or terms of any such exemption require the contrary, the ship must be assigned freeboards in accordance with the Merchant Shipping (Load Line) Regulations 1998, SI 1998/2241, reg 7 (see PARA 663), the ship is subject to surveys in accordance with reg 8 (see PARA 664), and regs 8–11 (see PARA 664 et seq) apply in relation to the Exemption Certificate as they apply in relation to an

appropriate certificate, subject to the substitution, for references in those regulations to an Assigning Authority, of references to the Secretary of State: reg 12(3) (as amended: see note 2).

8 Merchant Shipping (Load Line) Regulations 1998, SI 1998/2241, reg 5(3). See note 2. Where a ship is exempted under reg 5(3), an International Load Line Exemption Certificate in the form prescribed by the International Convention on Load Lines (London, 5 April to 4 July 1966; TS 58 (1968); Cmnd 3708), as amended by the 1988 Protocol (Cmnd 4419) must be issued in respect of the ship by the Secretary of State: reg 12(1) (as substituted: see note 2). Except in so far as the nature or terms of any such exemption require the contrary, the ship must be assigned freeboards in accordance with the Merchant Shipping (Load Line) Regulations 1998, SI 1998/2241, reg 7, is subject to surveys in accordance with reg 8, and regs 8–11 apply in relation to the Exemption Certificate as they apply in relation to an appropriate certificate, subject to the substitution, for references in those regulations to an Assigning Authority, of references to the Secretary of State: reg 12(3) (as amended: see note 2).

662. General compliance with load line rules. Subject to any exemption conferred under the provisions relating to load lines[1], a ship must not proceed, or attempt to proceed, to sea[2] unless:

(1)   it has been surveyed in accordance with the load lines rules[3];
(2)   it is marked with the appropriate marks[4];
(3)   it complies with the conditions of assignment applicable to it[5]; and
(4)   information as to the stability of the ship[6], or as to the loading and ballasting of any ship of more than 150 metres in length[7], is provided for the guidance of the master of the ship[8].

However, this requirement does not apply to a non-United Kingdom ship[9] in respect of which a valid Convention certificate[10] is produced[11].

A ship must not be so loaded that if the ship is in salt water and has no list the appropriate load line on each side of the ship is submerged[12] or, in any other case, so that the appropriate load line on each side of the ship would be submerged if the ship were in salt water and had no list[13]; and a ship must not proceed to sea when it is in contravention of this provision[14].

Before any ship proceeds to sea from any port in the United Kingdom[15], the master of that ship must produce to an officer of revenue and customs from whom a clearance[16] for the ship is demanded for an international voyage[17]:

(a)   in the case of a Convention-size ship[18], a valid Convention certificate[19]; or

(b)   in the case of any other ship, a United Kingdom Load Line Certificate[20] or a United Kingdom Load Line Exemption Certificate[21], which is in force in relation to the ship[22].

For these purposes[23], where a valid Convention certificate cannot be produced, the freeboard deck[24] and the freeboard must be determined in accordance with the provisions relating to load lines[25] and the appropriate load line is the maximum depth to which the ship may be loaded in salt water[26].

1 Ie subject to any exemption conferred under the Merchant Shipping (Load Line) Regulations 1998, SI 1998/2241 (see PARA 661): see reg 6(1). As to the meaning of 'load line' see PARA 660 note 1.
2 As to the meaning of 'sea' see PARA 660 note 6. As to penalties relating to the contravention of heads (1) to (4) in the text see PARA 1128.
3 Merchant Shipping (Load Line) Regulations 1998, SI 1998/2241, reg 6(1)(a). Head (1) in the text refers to a ship that has been surveyed in accordance with the Merchant Shipping (Load Line) Regulations 1998, SI 1998/2241 (as to which see PARA 664 et seq): see reg 6(1)(a).
4 Merchant Shipping (Load Line) Regulations 1998, SI 1998/2241, reg 6(1)(b). For these purposes, 'appropriate marks' means the appropriate load lines, the deck-line (as to which see reg 16; and PARA 670) and load-line mark (as to which see reg 17; and PARA 670): Merchant Shipping (Load Line) Regulations 1998, SI 1998/2241, reg 2(1). 'Appropriate load line' means the load line directed to be marked on a ship pursuant to reg 7(2)(b) (see PARA 663), or in the case of a ship not surveyed under the Merchant Shipping (Load Line) Regulations 1998, SI 1998/2241, pursuant to an International Load Line Certificate or an International Load Line Certificate (1966) which is in force, indicating the maximum depth to which the ship may be loaded in salt water in a particular zone or area and seasonal period: Merchant Shipping (Load Line) Regulations 1998, SI

1998/2241, reg 2(1) (definition amended by SI 2000/1335). 'International Load Line Certificate' means an International Load Line Certificate issued under the International Convention on Load Lines (London, 5 April to 4 July 1966; TS 58 (1968); Cmnd 3708) (the '1966 Convention'), as amended by the 1988 Protocol (Cmnd 4419); and 'International Load Line Certificate (1966)' means an International Load Line Certificate issued under the 1966 Convention before the relevant entry into force date, where 'relevant entry into force date' means the date when the 1988 Protocol enters into force in respect of the Government of the parent country of the ship in question: Merchant Shipping (Load Line) Regulations 1998, SI 1998/2241, reg 2(1) (all definitions added by SI 2000/1335). As to the International Convention on Load Lines 1966 see PARA 7; and as to any reference, in the Merchant Shipping (Load Line) Regulations 1998, SI 1998/2241, to the 1966 Convention see PARA 661 note 2.

5   Merchant Shipping (Load Line) Regulations 1998, SI 1998/2241, reg 6(1)(c). For these purposes, 'conditions of assignment' means the conditions relating to construction, arrangement and stability with which a ship must comply in order to be assigned freeboards: reg 2(1) (definition added by SI 2000/1335). 'Freeboard' means the distance measured vertically downwards at amidships (ie the middle of the ship's length) from the upper edge of the deck-line described in the Merchant Shipping (Load Line) Regulations 1998, SI 1998/2241, reg 16 (see PARA 670) to the position at which the upper edge of the load line appropriate to the freeboard is to be marked, where 'amidships' in relation to a ship means the middle of the ship's length (L): reg 2(1). As to the meaning of 'length (L)' see PARA 661 note 6. As to compliance with the applicable conditions of assignment of freeboards see PARA 663.

6   Ie the information required by the Merchant Shipping (Load Line) Regulations 1998, SI 1998/2241, reg 32 (as to which see PARA 671): see reg 6(1)(d).

7   Ie the information required by the Merchant Shipping (Load Line) Regulations 1998, SI 1998/2241, reg 33 (as to which see PARA 671): see reg 6(1)(d).

8   Merchant Shipping (Load Line) Regulations 1998, SI 1998/2241, reg 6(1)(d).

9   For these purposes, 'non-United Kingdom ship' means any ship other than a United Kingdom ship within the meaning of the Merchant Shipping Act 1995 s 85(2) (see PARA 602 note 1): Merchant Shipping (Load Line) Regulations 1998, SI 1998/2241, reg 2(1).

10 For these purposes, 'valid Convention certificate' means either an International Load Line Certificate (1966) or an International Load Line Exemption Certificate (1966), which is in force, or an International Load Line Certificate or an International Load Line Exemption Certificate, which is in force: Merchant Shipping (Load Line) Regulations 1998, SI 1998/2241, reg 2(1) (definition substituted by SI 2000/1335). As to the meaning of 'International Load Line Exemption Certificate' see PARA 661 note 2. 'International Load Line Exemption Certificate (1966)' means an International Load Line Exemption Certificate issued under the 1966 Convention before the relevant entry into force date (if any): Merchant Shipping (Load Line) Regulations 1998, SI 1998/2241, reg 2(1) (definition added by SI 2000/1335). As to the meanings of '1966 Convention' and 'relevant entry into force date' see note 4.

11 Merchant Shipping (Load Line) Regulations 1998, SI 1998/2241, reg 6(2). As to penalties relating to altering, falsely making or misusing certificates referred to in the Merchant Shipping (Load Line) Regulations 1998, SI 1998/2241, see PARA 1129.

12 Merchant Shipping (Load Line) Regulations 1998, SI 1998/2241, reg 6(3)(a). As to penalties relating to the contravention of reg 6(3)(a) see PARA 1128.

13 Merchant Shipping (Load Line) Regulations 1998, SI 1998/2241, reg 6(3)(b). As to penalties relating to the contravention of reg 6(3)(b) see PARA 1128.

14 Merchant Shipping (Load Line) Regulations 1998, SI 1998/2241, reg 6(4). As to penalties relating to the contravention of reg 6(4) see PARA 1128.

15 As to the meaning of 'United Kingdom' see PARA 16 note 3.

16 For these purposes, 'clearance' includes transire: Merchant Shipping (Load Line) Regulations 1998, SI 1998/2241, reg 2(1). A transire is a warrant from the custom-house to let goods pass: see CUSTOMS AND EXCISE vol 31 (2012) PARA 1061.

17 Merchant Shipping (Load Line) Regulations 1998, SI 1998/2241, reg 6(5) (amended by virtue of the Commissioners for Revenue and Customs Act 2005 s 50(1), (2), (7)). As to the meaning of 'international voyage' see PARA 661 note 3.

18 As to the meaning of 'Convention-size' in relation to a ship see PARA 661 note 6.

19 Merchant Shipping (Load Line) Regulations 1998, SI 1998/2241, reg 6(5)(a) (reg 6(5)(a), (b) substituted by SI 2000/1335).

20 For these purposes, 'United Kingdom Load Line Certificate' means a certificate issued under the Merchant Shipping (Load Line) Regulations 1998, SI 1998/2241, reg 9(1) (see PARA 665) other than an International Load Line Certificate (as to which see note 4): reg 2(1) (definition added by SI 2000/1335).

21 As to the meaning of 'United Kingdom Load Line Exemption Certificate' see PARA 661 note 2.

22 Merchant Shipping (Load Line) Regulations 1998, SI 1998/2241, reg 6(5)(b) (as substituted: see note 19).

23 Ie for the purpose of the Merchant Shipping (Load Line) Regulations 1998, SI 1998/2241, reg 6: see reg 6(6).

24 For these purposes, 'freeboard deck' means the deck from which the freeboards assigned to the ship are calculated, being:

    (1)   the uppermost complete deck exposed to weather and sea, which has permanent means of closing all openings open to the weather, and below which all openings in the sides of the ship are fitted with permanent means of watertight closing; or

    (2)   at the request of the owner and subject to the approval of the Secretary of State, a deck lower than that described in head (1) above, it being a complete and permanent deck which is continuous both in a fore and aft direction at least between the machinery space and peak bulkheads of the ship, and athwartships,

a deck which is stepped being taken to consist for this purpose of the lowest line of the deck and the continuation of that line parallel to the upper part of the deck: Merchant Shipping (Load Line) Regulations 1998, SI 1998/2241, reg 2(1) (definition amended by SI 2000/1335). 'Watertight', in relation to any part of the ship, means capable of preventing the passage of water in any direction: Merchant Shipping (Load Line) Regulations 1998, SI 1998/2241, reg 2(1). Any approval given pursuant to the Merchant Shipping (Load Line) Regulations 1998, SI 1998/2241, must be given in writing and must specify the date on which it takes effect and the conditions (if any) on which it is given: reg 2(5). As to the Secretary of State see PARA 36.

25 Ie in accordance with the Merchant Shipping (Load Line) Regulations 1998, SI 1998/2241: see reg 6(6).

26 Merchant Shipping (Load Line) Regulations 1998, SI 1998/2241, reg 6(6).

(ii) Freeboards

663. Assignment of freeboards and the conditions of assignment. The Assigning Authority[1] must assign freeboards[2] to a United Kingdom ship in accordance with the requirements of the provisions relating to load lines[3]. The Authority must:

    (1)   determine the particulars of the freeboards to be assigned[4];

    (2)   determine which load lines[5] are to be marked[6] on the sides of the ship[7];

    (3)   determine the position where the load lines, the deck-line and the load line mark are to be so marked[8]; and

    (4)   complete a copy of the record of particulars[9] relating to the conditions of assignment[10].

Various types of freeboards, including timber freeboards, may be assigned under the provisions[11]. The freeboards assigned to a new ship[12] must be determined in accordance with the relevant provisions of the appropriate Merchant Shipping Notice[13]; while the freeboards assigned to an existing ship[14] must be determined in accordance with the provisions applicable to the ship under the law in force immediately before 21 July 1968[15]. In either case, a freeboard so determined[16] is the minimum freeboard that may be assigned to the ship[17], although a greater than minimum freeboard (except a timber freeboard) may be assigned in certain circumstances[18].

Every ship to which freeboards are assigned under the load line provisions[19] must comply with the conditions of assignment[20] applicable to that ship which are set out in the relevant provisions of the appropriate Merchant Shipping Notice[21]. However, an existing ship may, instead of complying with these conditions[22], comply with such of the requirements relevant to the assignment of freeboards to ships as were applicable to the ship under the law in force immediately before 21 July 1968[23].

A ship ceases to comply with the conditions of assignment:

    (a)   if, at any time after the assignment of freeboards, there has been any alteration[24] of the hull, superstructures, fittings or appliances of the ship such that[25]:

(i)   a requirement relevant to the assignment of freeboards which is applicable to the ship[26] is not complied with[27]; or

(ii)   it differs in a material respect from the record of particulars[28]; or

(b)   if the record of particulars is not on board[29].

However, a ship is taken to comply with the conditions of assignment notwithstanding an alteration referred to in head (a) above if[30]:

(A)   amended freeboards appropriate to the condition of the ship have been assigned, the ship has been marked with these load lines and a new certificate issued to the owner of the ship accordingly[31]; or

(B)   the alteration has been inspected by a surveyor[32] on behalf of the Authority and that Authority is satisfied that the alteration is not such as to require any change in the freeboards assigned to the ship, and full particulars of the alteration together with the date and place of his inspection have been indorsed by the surveyor on the record of particulars[33].

1   For these purposes, 'Assigning Authority' means the Secretary of State or any person or organisation authorised by him for the purposes of the Merchant Shipping (Load Line) Regulations 1998, SI 1998/2241: reg 2(1). As to the Secretary of State see PARA 36.
2   As to the meaning of 'freeboard' see PARA 662 note 5.
3   Merchant Shipping (Load Line) Regulations 1998, SI 1998/2241, reg 7(1). The text refers to the provisions of the Merchant Shipping (Load Line) Regulations 1998, SI 1998/2241: see reg 7(1). As to the meaning of 'load line' see PARA 660 note 1.
4   Merchant Shipping (Load Line) Regulations 1998, SI 1998/2241, reg 7(2)(a).
5   Ie which of the load lines described in the Merchant Shipping (Load Line) Regulations 1998, SI 1998/2241, Pt III (regs 15–24) (as to which see PARA 670): see reg 7(2)(b).
6   Ie marked in accordance with the requirements of the Merchant Shipping (Load Line) Regulations 1998, SI 1998/2241, Pt III (as to which see PARA 670): see reg 7(2)(b).
7   Merchant Shipping (Load Line) Regulations 1998, SI 1998/2241, reg 7(2)(b).
8   Merchant Shipping (Load Line) Regulations 1998, SI 1998/2241, reg 7(2)(c). As to the deck-line and load-line mark see PARA 670.
9   The record of particulars must be provided on the ship in a form given in Merchant Shipping Notice 1752(M) Sch 3 (Record of particulars): Merchant Shipping (Load Line) Regulations 1998, SI 1998/2241, reg 27(1) (amended by SI 2000/1335). The record must be furnished by the Assigning Authority and be retained on board at all times: Merchant Shipping (Load Line) Regulations 1998, SI 1998/2241, reg 27(2). As to the meaning of 'Merchant Shipping Notice' see PARA 660 note 6.
10 Merchant Shipping (Load Line) Regulations 1998, SI 1998/2241, reg 7(2)(d).
11 The freeboards that can be assigned to a ship under the Merchant Shipping (Load Line) Regulations 1998, SI 1998/2241, are: the Summer freeboard; Tropical freeboard; Winter freeboard; Winter North Atlantic freeboard; Fresh Water freeboard and Tropical Fresh Water freeboard; and, in the case of ships carrying Timber, accordingly, Summer Timber freeboard; Winter Timber freeboard; Winter North Atlantic Timber freeboard; Tropical Timber freeboard; Fresh Water Timber freeboard and Tropical Fresh Water Timber freeboard: see the Merchant Shipping (Load Line) Regulations 1998, SI 1998/2241, reg 28.
12 Ie a ship whose keel is laid (or which is at a similar stage of construction) on or after the material date, being the date, in relation to a ship whose parent country is a Convention country other than the United Kingdom, on which the International Convention on Load Lines (London, 5 April to 4 July 1966; TS 58 (1968); Cmnd 3708) (the '1966 Convention') entered into force for that country and, in relation to any other ship, 21 July 1968: see the Merchant Shipping (Load Line) Regulations 1998, SI 1998/2241, reg 2(1); and PARA 661 note 6. As to the meaning of 'United Kingdom' see PARA 16 note 3. As to the International Convention on Load Lines 1966 see PARA 7; and as to any reference, in the Merchant Shipping (Load Line) Regulations 1998, SI 1998/2241, to the 1966 Convention see PARA 661 note 2.
13 See the Merchant Shipping (Load Line) Regulations 1998, SI 1998/2241, reg 29(1) (amended by SI 2000/1335). The text refers to the provisions of Merchant Shipping Notice 1752(M) Sch 4 (Freeboards), which take effect except as otherwise provided for in the Merchant Shipping (Load Line) Regulations 1998, SI 1998/2241, reg 30 (see the text and notes 16–18): see reg 29(1) (as so amended).
14 As to the meaning of 'existing ship' for these purposes see PARA 661 note 6.

15 Merchant Shipping (Load Line) Regulations 1998, SI 1998/2241, reg 29(2). However, if an existing ship has been so constructed or modified as to comply with all the conditions of assignment set out in Merchant Shipping Notice 1752(M) Sch 2 (conditions of assignment) applicable to a new ship of her type, and application is made for the assignment to her of freeboards determined in accordance with Sch 4 (Freeboards), such freeboards must be assigned to her: Merchant Shipping (Load Line) Regulations 1998, SI 1998/2241, reg 29(2) proviso (amended by SI 2000/1335). As to the significance of the date 21 July 1968 see note 12.

16 Ie a freeboard determined in accordance with the Merchant Shipping (Load Line) Regulations 1998, SI 1998/2241, reg 29 (see the text and notes 12–15): see reg 30(1).

17 Merchant Shipping (Load Line) Regulations 1998, SI 1998/2241, reg 30(1).

18 See the Merchant Shipping (Load Line) Regulations 1998, SI 1998/2241, reg 30(2), (3). Provision is also made for the correction of freeboards, once assigned, as a consequence of a variant deck-line marked pursuant to reg 16 (as to which see PARA 670): see reg 31 (amended by SI 2000/1335).

19 Ie under the Merchant Shipping (Load Line) Regulations 1998, SI 1998/2241: see reg 25(1) (reg 25 substituted by SI 2000/1335).

20 As to the meaning of 'conditions of assignment' for these purposes see PARA 662 note 5.

21 Merchant Shipping (Load Line) Regulations 1998, SI 1998/2241, reg 25(1) (as substituted: see note 19). The text refers to the conditions of assignment set out in Merchant Shipping Notice 1752(M) Sch 2 (conditions of assignment): see the Merchant Shipping (Load Line) Regulations 1998, SI 1998/2241, reg 25(1) (as so substituted).

22 Ie the conditions of assignment referred to in the Merchant Shipping (Load Line) Regulations 1998, SI 1998/2241, reg 25(1) (see the text and notes 19–21): see reg 25(2) (as substituted: see note 19).

23 Merchant Shipping (Load Line) Regulations 1998, SI 1998/2241, reg 25(2) (as substituted: see note 19). As to the significance of the date 21 July 1968 see note 12.

24 For these purposes, 'alteration' includes deterioration: Merchant Shipping (Load Line) Regulations 1998, SI 1998/2241, reg 2(1).

25 Merchant Shipping (Load Line) Regulations 1998, SI 1998/2241, reg 26(1)(a).

26 Ie under the Merchant Shipping (Load Line) Regulations 1998, SI 1998/2241, reg 25 (see the text and notes 19–23): see reg 26(1)(a)(i).

27 Merchant Shipping (Load Line) Regulations 1998, SI 1998/2241, reg 26(1)(a)(i).

28 Merchant Shipping (Load Line) Regulations 1998, SI 1998/2241, reg 26(1)(a)(ii). The text refers to the record of particulars provided in accordance with reg 27 (see note 9): see reg 26(1)(a)(ii).

29 Merchant Shipping (Load Line) Regulations 1998, SI 1998/2241, reg 26(1)(b). The text refers to the record of particulars which must be retained on board at all times in accordance with reg 27(2) (see note 9): see reg 26(1)(b).

30 Merchant Shipping (Load Line) Regulations 1998, SI 1998/2241, reg 26(2).

31 Merchant Shipping (Load Line) Regulations 1998, SI 1998/2241, reg 26(2)(a). As to penalties relating to altering, falsely making or misusing certificates referred to in the Merchant Shipping (Load Line) Regulations 1998, SI 1998/2241, see PARA 1129.

32 For these purposes, 'surveyor' means a surveyor appointed by the Secretary of State or an exclusive surveyor of any other Assigning Authority, an 'exclusive surveyor' being a surveyor appointed by and working exclusively for an Assigning Authority: Merchant Shipping (Load Line) Regulations 1998, SI 1998/2241, reg 2(1).

33 Merchant Shipping (Load Line) Regulations 1998, SI 1998/2241, reg 26(2)(b). The text refers to the record of particulars referred to in reg 27(1) (see note 9): see reg 26(2)(b).

(iii) Surveys and Certificates

664. The required initial survey, renewal survey and annual survey. A United Kingdom ship is subject to the following surveys[1]:

(1)   an initial survey before the ship is put into service, which must include a complete inspection of its structure and equipment[2], and must be such as to ensure that the arrangements, materials and scantlings comply fully with the requirements of the provisions relating to load lines[3];

(2)   a renewal survey at intervals not exceeding five years[4], which must be such as to ensure that the structure, equipment, arrangements, materials and scantlings comply fully with the requirements of the provisions relating to load lines[5];

(3)   an annual survey within the period of three months before or after each anniversary date of the appropriate certificate[6] to ensure that[7]:

    (a)   alterations[8] have not been made to the hull or superstructures which would affect the calculations determining the position of the load line[9];

    (b)   the fittings and appliances for the protection of openings, guard rails, freeing ports and means of access to crew's quarters are maintained in an effective condition[10];

    (c)   the appropriate marks[11] are correctly and permanently indicated[12]; and

    (d)   information as to the stability of the ship[13], or as to the loading and ballasting of any ship of more than 150 metres in length[14], is provided for the guidance of the master of the ship[15].

The owner and master must ensure that after any of the surveys referred to in heads (1) to (3) above has been completed, no material alteration is made to the ship, its structure and equipment, without the approval[16] of the Assigning Authority[17].

After a satisfactory annual survey referred to in head (3) above, the surveyor[18] must indorse the appropriate certificate[19] accordingly[20].

1   Merchant Shipping (Load Line) Regulations 1998, SI 1998/2241, reg 8(1).
2   Ie as required by the Merchant Shipping (Load Line) Regulations 1998, SI 1998/2241: see reg 8(1)(a).
3   Merchant Shipping (Load Line) Regulations 1998, SI 1998/2241, reg 8(1)(a). The text refers to the requirements of the provisions of the Merchant Shipping (Load Line) Regulations 1998, SI 1998/2241: see reg 8(1)(a). As to the meaning of 'load line' see PARA 660 note 1.
4   Ie except where the Merchant Shipping (Load Line) Regulations 1998, SI 1998/2241, reg 10(2)(a), (5), (6) or (7) (see PARA 667) (duration and extension of certificates) is applicable: see reg 8(1)(b) (amended by SI 2000/1335).
5   Merchant Shipping (Load Line) Regulations 1998, SI 1998/2241, reg 8(1)(b) (as amended: see note 4). The text refers to the requirements of the provisions of the Merchant Shipping (Load Line) Regulations 1998, SI 1998/2241: see reg 8(1)(b) (as so amended).
6   For these purposes, 'anniversary date', in relation to a certificate, means the day and the month of each year which corresponds to the date of the expiry of the certificate: Merchant Shipping (Load Line) Regulations 1998, SI 1998/2241, reg 2(1) (definition added by SI 2000/1335). 'Appropriate certificate' means, in the case of a Convention-size ship, an International Load Line Certificate or an International Load Line Certificate (1966), and, in the case of any other ship, a United Kingdom Load Line Certificate: Merchant Shipping (Load Line) Regulations 1998, SI 1998/2241, reg 2(1) (definition amended by SI 2000/1335). As to the meaning of 'Convention-size' in relation to a ship see PARA 661 note 6; as to the meanings of 'International Load Line Certificate' and 'International Load Line Certificate (1966)' see PARA 662 note 4; and as to the meaning of 'United Kingdom Load Line Certificate' see PARA 662 note 20. As to penalties relating to altering, falsely making or misusing certificates referred to in the Merchant Shipping (Load Line) Regulations 1998, SI 1998/2241, see PARA 1129.
7   Merchant Shipping (Load Line) Regulations 1998, SI 1998/2241, reg 8(1)(c) (substituted by SI 2000/1335).
8   As to the meaning of 'alteration' for these purposes see PARA 663 note 24.
9   Merchant Shipping (Load Line) Regulations 1998, SI 1998/2241, reg 8(1)(c)(i) (as substituted: see note 7).
10 Merchant Shipping (Load Line) Regulations 1998, SI 1998/2241, reg 8(1)(c)(ii) (as substituted: see note 7).
11 As to the meaning of 'appropriate marks' for these purposes see PARA 662 note 4.
12 Merchant Shipping (Load Line) Regulations 1998, SI 1998/2241, reg 8(1)(c)(iii) (as substituted: see note 7).
13 Ie the information required by the Merchant Shipping (Load Line) Regulations 1998, SI 1998/2241, reg 32 (as to which see PARA 671): see reg 8(1)(c)(iv) (as substituted: see note 7).
14 Ie the information required by the Merchant Shipping (Load Line) Regulations 1998, SI 1998/2241, reg 33 (as to which see PARA 671): see reg 8(1)(c)(iv) (as substituted: see note 7).
15 Merchant Shipping (Load Line) Regulations 1998, SI 1998/2241, reg 8(1)(c)(iv) (as substituted: see note 7).
16 Any approval given pursuant to the Merchant Shipping (Load Line) Regulations 1998, SI 1998/2241, must be given in writing and must specify the date on which it takes effect and the conditions (if any) on which it is given: reg 2(5).

17 Merchant Shipping (Load Line) Regulations 1998, SI 1998/2241, reg 8(2). As to the meaning of 'Assigning Authority' see PARA 663 note 1. As to penalties, in connection with any survey required by these provisions, for knowingly or recklessly furnishing false information see PARA 1129.

18 As to the meaning of 'surveyor' for these purposes see PARA 663 note 32.

19 Ie the International Load Line Certificate, the International Load Line Certificate (1966) or, as the case may be, the United Kingdom Load Line Certificate: see reg 8(3) (amended by SI 2000/1335).

20 Merchant Shipping (Load Line) Regulations 1998, SI 1998/2241, reg 8(3) (as amended: see note 19).

665. Issue of appropriate certificates. The Assigning Authority[1] must issue[2] an International Load Line Certificate[3] in the case of a Convention-size ship[4], or a United Kingdom Load Line Certificate[5] in respect of any other ship, in respect of a United Kingdom ship which has been duly surveyed and marked[6]. Whether the certificate is an International Load Line Certificate or a United Kingdom Load Line Certificate, it must be in the prescribed form[7].

Subject to any exemption conferred by or under the provisions relating to load lines[8], a ship must not proceed, or attempt to proceed, to sea[9] unless the appropriate certificate[10] is in force in respect of that ship[11].

Provision is made concerning the surveying of ships and the issuing of an International Load Line Certificate (or the endorsement of the appropriate certificate[12]) in respect of United Kingdom ships by the governments of other Convention countries[13], upon request by the Secretary of State[14]; and the surveying and issuing of an International Load Line Certificate by the Assigning Authority in respect of ships transferred from the registries of the governments of other countries to the United Kingdom registry, provided certain conditions are satisfied[15].

1 As to the meaning of 'Assigning Authority' see PARA 663 note 1.

2 Ie subject to the Merchant Shipping (Load Line) Regulations 1998, SI 1998/2241, reg 10 (see PARA 667) (duration and extension of certificates): see reg 9(1) (amended by SI 2000/1335).

3 As to the meaning of 'International Load Line Certificate' see PARA 662 note 4.

4 As to the meaning of 'Convention-size' in relation to a ship see PARA 661 note 6.

5 As to the meaning of 'United Kingdom Load Line Certificate' see PARA 662 note 20.

6 Merchant Shipping (Load Line) Regulations 1998, SI 1998/2241, reg 9(1) (as amended: see note 2). The text refers to a United Kingdom ship which has been duly surveyed and marked in accordance with the Merchant Shipping (Load Line) Regulations 1998, SI 1998/2241: see reg 9(1) (as so amended). As to penalties relating to altering, falsely making or misusing certificates referred to in the Merchant Shipping (Load Line) Regulations 1998, SI 1998/2241, see PARA 1129.

7 In the case of an International Load Line Certificate, the certificate must be in the form prescribed by the 1988 Protocol (Cmnd 4419) Annex III relating to the International Convention on Load Lines (London, 5 April to 4 July 1966; TS 58 (1968); Cmnd 3708) (the '1966 Convention'): see the Merchant Shipping (Load Line) Regulations 1998, SI 1998/2241, reg 9(2) (substituted by SI 2000/1335). In the case of a United Kingdom Load Line Certificate, the certificate must be in the form prescribed in Merchant Shipping Notice 1752(M) Sch 8 (United Kingdom Load Line Certificates): see the Merchant Shipping (Load Line) Regulations 1998, SI 1998/2241, reg 9(3) (amended by SI 2000/1335). As to the meaning of 'Merchant Shipping Notice' see PARA 660 note 6. As to the meaning of 'United Kingdom' see PARA 16 note 3. As to the International Convention on Load Lines 1966 see PARA 7; and as to any reference, in the Merchant Shipping (Load Line) Regulations 1998, SI 1998/2241, to the 1966 Convention see PARA 661 note 2.

8 Ie subject to any exemption conferred by or under the Merchant Shipping (Load Line) Regulations 1998, SI 1998/2241 (see PARA 661): see reg 9(4). As to the meaning of 'load line' see PARA 660 note 1.

9 As to the meaning of 'sea' see PARA 660 note 6.

10 As to the meaning of 'appropriate certificate' for these purposes see PARA 664 note 6.

11 Merchant Shipping (Load Line) Regulations 1998, SI 1998/2241, reg 9(4). As to penalties relating to the contravention of reg 9(4) see PARA 1128.

12 The appropriate certificate is endorsed in the case of an annual survey required under the Merchant Shipping (Load Line) Regulations 1998, SI 1998/2241, reg 8(1)(c) (as to which see PARA 664): see reg 9(5) (amended by SI 2000/1335).

13 As to the meaning of 'Convention country' for these purposes see PARA 661 note 3.

14 See the Merchant Shipping (Load Line) Regulations 1998, SI 1998/2241, reg 9(5) (as amended: see note 12). As to the Secretary of State see PARA 36.
15 See the Merchant Shipping (Load Line) Regulations 1998, SI 1998/2241, reg 9(6) (amended by SI 2000/1335). As to the survey of non-United Kingdom ships see PARA 666.

666. Issue of certificate following survey of non-United Kingdom ship. The Secretary of State[1] may, at the request of a government of a Convention country[2] survey a ship registered in that country and, if satisfied that the requirements of the International Convention on Load Lines 1966[3] are complied with and that a survey has been satisfactorily completed in accordance with the provisions relating to load lines[4], issue to the ship an International Load Line Certificate[5] and, where appropriate, indorse such certificates in accordance with the requirements of the 1966 Convention[6]. A certificate issued in accordance with such a request must contain a statement that it has been so issued and it has the same effect as if it was issued by that government and not by the Secretary of State[7].

A United Kingdom Load Line Certificate[8] may be issued to a non-United Kingdom ship[9] which has been surveyed and marked in accordance with the load line provisions[10]. A certificate issued in this way is subject to the same conditions and has the same effect as a similar certificate issued to a United Kingdom ship[11], except that any certificate so issued in respect of a ship registered in a Convention country is valid only so long as the ship is not plying on international voyages[12], and must be cancelled by the Secretary of State if he has reason to believe that the ship is plying on such voyages[13].

1 As to the Secretary of State see PARA 36.
2 As to the meaning of 'Convention country' for these purposes see PARA 661 note 3.
3 Ie the International Convention on Load Lines (London, 5 April to 4 July 1966; TS 58 (1968); Cmnd 3708) (the '1966 Convention') as amended by the 1988 Protocol (Cmnd 4419) relating to the Convention: see the Merchant Shipping (Load Line) Regulations 1998, SI 1998/2241, reg 2(1) (amended by SI 2000/1335). As to the International Convention on Load Lines 1966 see PARA 7; and as to any reference, in the Merchant Shipping (Load Line) Regulations 1998, SI 1998/2241, to the 1966 Convention see PARA 661 note 2.
4 Ie completed in accordance with the Merchant Shipping (Load Line) Regulations 1998, SI 1998/2241: see reg 14(1) (amended by SI 2000/1335). As to the meaning of 'load line' see PARA 660 note 1.
5 As to the meaning of 'International Load Line Certificate' see PARA 662 note 4.
6 Merchant Shipping (Load Line) Regulations 1998, SI 1998/2241, reg 14(1) (as amended: see note 4). As to penalties relating to altering, falsely making or misusing certificates referred to in the Merchant Shipping (Load Line) Regulations 1998, SI 1998/2241, see PARA 1129.
7 Merchant Shipping (Load Line) Regulations 1998, SI 1998/2241, reg 14(1) (as amended: see note 4).
8 As to the meaning of 'United Kingdom Load Line Certificate' see PARA 662 note 20.
9 As to the meaning of 'non-United Kingdom ship' see PARA 662 note 9.
10 Merchant Shipping (Load Line) Regulations 1998, SI 1998/2241, reg 14(2). The text refers to a non-United Kingdom ship which has been surveyed and marked in accordance with the Merchant Shipping (Load Line) Regulations 1998, SI 1998/2241: see reg 14(2).
11 Merchant Shipping (Load Line) Regulations 1998, SI 1998/2241, reg 14(3).
12 As to the meaning of 'international voyage' see PARA 661 note 3.
13 Merchant Shipping (Load Line) Regulations 1998, SI 1998/2241, reg 14(4).

667. Duration and extension of issued certificates. The duration of any certificate issued under the provisions relating to load lines[1] must not exceed five years[2] beginning with the date of completion of any initial or renewal survey[3]. However, this is subject to the following qualifications[4]:

(1) when the renewal survey[5] is completed within three months before the expiry of the existing certificate, the new certificate is valid for a period beginning with the date of completion of the renewal survey and ending on a date which does not exceed five years from the expiry of the existing certificate[6];

(2)   when the renewal survey[7] is completed after the expiry of the existing certificate, the new certificate is valid for a period beginning with the date of completion of the renewal survey and ending on a date which does not exceed five years from the expiry of the previous certificate[8];

(3)   when the renewal survey[9] is completed more than three months before the expiry of the existing certificate, the new certificate is valid for a period beginning with the date of completion of the renewal survey and ending on a date which does not exceed five years from the date of completion of the renewal survey[10];

(4)   if, after the renewal survey, a new certificate cannot be issued to the ship before the expiry of the existing certificate, the Assigning Authority may extend the validity of the existing certificate for a period not exceeding five months[11];

(5)   if, at the time when a certificate expires, a ship is not in a port in which it is to be surveyed, the Assigning Authority may extend the validity of the certificate, but this extension may be granted only where it appears proper and reasonable to the Assigning Authority to do so for the purpose of allowing the ship to complete its voyage to the port in which it is to be surveyed[12]; and

(6)   a certificate issued to a ship engaged on short voyages which has not already been extended[13] may be extended by the Assigning Authority for a period of not more than one month beginning with the date of its expiry[14].

In special circumstances, as determined by the Assigning Authority, a new certificate need not be dated from the expiry of the previous certificate before the extension was granted, as required by heads (1) to (3), (5) and (6) above; and, in these special circumstances, the new certificate is valid for a period ending on a date which is not more than five years from the date of completion of the renewal survey[15].

If an annual survey is completed before the period of three months specified in relation thereto[16] then:

(a)   a new anniversary date must be indorsed on the certificate, which must not be more than three months later than the date on which the annual survey was completed[17];

(b)   the subsequent annual survey[18] must be completed at the intervals prescribed in relation thereto[19] using the new anniversary date[20]; and

(c)   the expiry date of the certificate may remain unchanged provided one or more annual surveys are carried out so that the maximum prescribed intervals between the surveys[21] are not exceeded[22].

1   Ie under the Merchant Shipping (Load Line) Regulations 1998, SI 1998/2241: see reg 10(1) (reg 10 substituted by SI 2000/1335). As to the meaning of 'load line' see PARA 660 note 1. As to the issue of appropriate certificates see PARA 665. As to penalties relating to altering, falsely making or misusing certificates referred to in the Merchant Shipping (Load Line) Regulations 1998, SI 1998/2241, see PARA 1129.

2   Ie subject to the Merchant Shipping (Load Line) Regulations 1998, SI 1998/2241, reg 10(2), (4)–(6) (see heads (1) to (6) in the text): see reg 10(1) (as substituted: see note 1). If a certificate is issued for a period of less than five years, the Assigning Authority may extend the validity of the certificate beyond the expiry date to the maximum period specified in reg 10(1), provided that the annual surveys applicable when a certificate is issued for a period of five years are carried out as appropriate (as to which see PARA 664): reg 10(3) (as so substituted). As to the meaning of 'Assigning Authority' see PARA 663 note 1.

3   Merchant Shipping (Load Line) Regulations 1998, SI 1998/2241, reg 10(1) (as substituted: see note 1). The text refers to the initial survey that is required under reg 8(1)(a) (as to which see PARA 664) and the renewal survey that is required under reg 8(1)(b) (as to which see PARA 664): see reg 10(1) (as so substituted).

4   See note 2.

5   Ie the renewal survey that is referred to in the Merchant Shipping (Load Line) Regulations 1998, SI 1998/2241, reg 8(1)(b) (as to which see PARA 664): see reg 10(2)(a) (as substituted: see note 1).
6   Merchant Shipping (Load Line) Regulations 1998, SI 1998/2241, reg 10(2)(a) (as substituted: see note 1).
7   Ie the renewal survey that is referred to in the Merchant Shipping (Load Line) Regulations 1998, SI 1998/2241, reg 8(1)(b) (as to which see PARA 664): see reg 10(2)(b) (as substituted: see note 1).
8   Merchant Shipping (Load Line) Regulations 1998, SI 1998/2241, reg 10(2)(b) (as substituted: see note 1).
9   Ie the renewal survey that is referred to in the Merchant Shipping (Load Line) Regulations 1998, SI 1998/2241, reg 8(1)(b) (as to which see PARA 664): see reg 10(2)(c) (as substituted: see note 1).
10 Merchant Shipping (Load Line) Regulations 1998, SI 1998/2241, reg 10(2)(c) (as substituted: see note 1).
11 Merchant Shipping (Load Line) Regulations 1998, SI 1998/2241, reg 10(4) (as substituted: see note 1). The extension referred to in head (4) in the text must be indorsed on the certificate, and may only be granted where there have been no alterations in the structure, equipment, arrangements, materials or scantlings which affect the ship's freeboard: reg 10(4) (as so substituted). As to the meaning of 'alteration' for these purposes see PARA 663 note 24; and as to the meaning of 'freeboard' see PARA 662 note 5.
12 Merchant Shipping (Load Line) Regulations 1998, SI 1998/2241, reg 10(5) (as substituted: see note 1). Under head (5) in the text, no certificate may be extended for a period longer than three months beginning with the date of expiry, and a ship to which an extension is granted is not, on its arrival in the port in which it is to be surveyed, entitled by virtue of such extension to leave that port without having a new certificate: reg 10(5) (as so substituted). When the renewal survey is completed, the new certificate is valid for a period ending on a date which does not exceed five years from the expiry of the previous certificate before the extension was granted: reg 10(5) (as so substituted).
13 Ie under the Merchant Shipping (Load Line) Regulations 1998, SI 1998/2241, reg 10(3) (as to which see note 2), reg 10(4) (see head (4) in the text) or reg 10(5) (see head (5) in the text): see reg 10(6) (as substituted: see note 1).
14 Merchant Shipping (Load Line) Regulations 1998, SI 1998/2241, reg 10(6) (as substituted: see note 1). Under head (6) in the text, when the renewal survey is completed (as to which see PARA 664), the new certificate is valid for a period ending on a date which does not exceed five years from the expiry of the previous certificate before the extension was granted: reg 10(6) (as so substituted).
15 Merchant Shipping (Load Line) Regulations 1998, SI 1998/2241, reg 10(7) (as substituted: see note 1).
16 Ie before the period specified in the Merchant Shipping (Load Line) Regulations 1998, SI 1998/2241, reg 8(1)(c) (as to which see PARA 664): see reg 10(8) (as substituted: see note 1).
17 Merchant Shipping (Load Line) Regulations 1998, SI 1998/2241, reg 10(8)(a) (as substituted: see note 1).
18 Ie required by the Merchant Shipping (Load Line) Regulations 1998, SI 1998/2241, reg 8(1)(c) (as to which see PARA 664): see reg 10(8)(b) (as substituted: see note 1).
19 Ie prescribed by the Merchant Shipping (Load Line) Regulations 1998, SI 1998/2241, reg 8(1)(c) (as to which see PARA 664): see reg 10(8)(b) (as substituted: see note 1).
20 Merchant Shipping (Load Line) Regulations 1998, SI 1998/2241, reg 10(8)(b) (as substituted: see note 1).
21 Ie the maximum intervals between the surveys prescribed by the Merchant Shipping (Load Line) Regulations 1998, SI 1998/2241, reg 8(1)(c) (as to which see PARA 664): see reg 10(8)(c) (as substituted: see note 1).
22 Merchant Shipping (Load Line) Regulations 1998, SI 1998/2241, reg 10(8)(c) (as substituted: see note 1).

668. Certificates ceasing to be valid, and surrender and cancellation of certificates.

An appropriate certificate[1] issued in respect of a United Kingdom ship[2] ceases to be valid where[3]:

(1)   material alterations[4] have taken place in the hull or superstructures of the ship such as would necessitate the assignment of an increased freeboard[5];

(2)   the fittings and appliances for the protection of openings, guard rails, freeing ports and means of access to crew's quarters[6] are not maintained in an effective condition[7];

(3)   the certificate is not appropriately indorsed[8] to show that it has been the subject of an annual survey[9];

(4)   the structural strength of the ship is lowered to such an extent that the ship is unsafe[10];

(5)   a new certificate is issued in respect of the ship[11]; or

(6)   the ship ceases to be a United Kingdom ship[12].

The Secretary of State[13] may cancel an appropriate certificate issued in respect of a United Kingdom ship if he is satisfied that[14]:

(a)   the certificate was issued on false or erroneous information[15];

(b)   information on the basis of which freeboards were assigned to the ship was incorrect in a material particular[16]; or

(c)   the ship ceases to comply with the conditions of assignment relating to it[17].

However, where the Secretary of State proposes to cancel a certificate, he must first notify the owner in writing, specifying the grounds for the proposed cancellation[18]; and, unless he considers that urgent safety considerations so require[19], the Secretary of State must not cancel the certificate until the owner has been given a reasonable opportunity to make representations, and until the Secretary of State has considered any such representations made[20].

The Secretary of State may require any certificate duly issued[21] which has expired, ceased to be valid, or been cancelled, to be surrendered as he directs[22].

1   As to the meaning of 'appropriate certificate' for these purposes see PARA 664 note 6.
2   As to the issue of appropriate certificates see PARA 665.
3   Merchant Shipping (Load Line) Regulations 1998, SI 1998/2241, reg 11(1) (reg 11 substituted by SI 2000/1335). As to penalties relating to altering, falsely making or misusing certificates referred to in the Merchant Shipping (Load Line) Regulations 1998, SI 1998/2241, see PARA 1129.
4   As to the meaning of 'alteration' for these purposes see PARA 663 note 24.
5   Merchant Shipping (Load Line) Regulations 1998, SI 1998/2241, reg 11(1)(a) (as substituted: see note 3). As to the meaning of 'freeboard' see PARA 662 note 5. As to the assignment of freeboards see PARA 663.
6   Ie those fittings and appliances mentioned in the Merchant Shipping (Load Line) Regulations 1998, SI 1998/2241, reg 8(1)(c)(ii) (as to which see PARA 664): see reg 11(1)(b) (as substituted: see note 3).
7   Merchant Shipping (Load Line) Regulations 1998, SI 1998/2241, reg 11(1)(b) (as substituted: see note 3).
8   Ie in accordance with the requirements of the Merchant Shipping (Load Line) Regulations 1998, SI 1998/2241, reg 8(3) (as to which see PARA 664): see reg 11(1)(c) (as substituted: see note 3).
9   Merchant Shipping (Load Line) Regulations 1998, SI 1998/2241, reg 11(1)(c) (as substituted: see note 3). The text refers to a survey conducted in accordance with reg 8(1)(c) (as to which see PARA 664): see reg 11(1)(c) (as so substituted).
10 Merchant Shipping (Load Line) Regulations 1998, SI 1998/2241, reg 11(1)(d) (as substituted: see note 3).
11 Merchant Shipping (Load Line) Regulations 1998, SI 1998/2241, reg 11(1)(e) (as substituted: see note 3).
12 Merchant Shipping (Load Line) Regulations 1998, SI 1998/2241, reg 11(1)(f) (as substituted: see note 3).
13 As to the Secretary of State see PARA 36.
14 Merchant Shipping (Load Line) Regulations 1998, SI 1998/2241, reg 11(2) (as substituted: see note 3).
15 Merchant Shipping (Load Line) Regulations 1998, SI 1998/2241, reg 11(2)(a) (as substituted: see note 3).
16 Merchant Shipping (Load Line) Regulations 1998, SI 1998/2241, reg 11(2)(b) (as substituted: see note 3).
17 Merchant Shipping (Load Line) Regulations 1998, SI 1998/2241, reg 11(2)(c) (as substituted: see note 3). As to compliance with the applicable conditions of assignment of freeboards see PARA 663.
18 Merchant Shipping (Load Line) Regulations 1998, SI 1998/2241, reg 11(3) (as substituted: see note 3). The requirement that the notification referred to in reg 11(3) should be in writing is

satisfied where the text of the notification is transmitted by electronic means, is received in legible form, and is capable of being used for subsequent reference: reg 11(7) (as so substituted).

19 Merchant Shipping (Load Line) Regulations 1998, SI 1998/2241, reg 11(5) (as substituted: see note 3).
20 Merchant Shipping (Load Line) Regulations 1998, SI 1998/2241, reg 11(4) (as substituted: see note 3).
21 Ie any certificate issued under the Merchant Shipping (Load Line) Regulations 1998, SI 1998/2241: see reg 11(6) (as substituted: see note 3).
22 Merchant Shipping (Load Line) Regulations 1998, SI 1998/2241, reg 11(6) (as substituted: see note 3). A failure to surrender such a certificate that the Secretary of State requires and directs to be surrendered under reg 11(6) is an offence: see PARA 1129.

669. Publication of load line certificate and notification of draughts.

Where an appropriate certificate[1] or an exemption certificate[2] is issued[3] in respect of a United Kingdom ship, the owner and master of the ship must ensure that the certificate is kept legible and posted up in some conspicuous place on board the ship[4].

Before any United Kingdom ship leaves any dock, wharf, harbour or other place for the purpose of proceeding to sea[5], the master of the ship must[6] ensure a notice is posted up in some conspicuous place on board the ship, in a form and containing such particulars relating to the depth to which the ship is loaded as is specified in the relevant provisions of the appropriate Merchant Shipping Notice[7]. Where a notice has been posted up in this way[8], the master of the ship must cause it to be kept posted and legible until the ship arrives at some other dock, wharf, harbour or place[9].

1 As to the meaning of 'appropriate certificate' for these purposes see PARA 664 note 6.
2 As to the meaning of 'exemption certificate' for these purposes see PARA 661 note 2.
3 As to the issue of appropriate certificates see PARA 676; and as to exemptions generally see PARA 661.
4 Merchant Shipping (Load Line) Regulations 1998, SI 1998/2241, reg 13(1). As to penalties relating to the contravention of reg 13 see PARA 1128; and as to penalties relating to altering, falsely making or misusing certificates referred to in the Merchant Shipping (Load Line) Regulations 1998, SI 1998/2241, see PARA 1129.
5 As to the meaning of 'sea' see PARA 660 note 6.
6 Ie except where the ship is employed on a near-coastal voyage: see the Merchant Shipping (Load Line) Regulations 1998, SI 1998/2241, reg 13(4). For these purposes, 'near-coastal voyage' means a voyage during which the vessel is never more than 150 nautical miles from a safe haven in the United Kingdom, or never more than 30 nautical miles from a safe haven in the Republic of Ireland: reg 2(1). As to the meaning of 'United Kingdom' see PARA 16 note 3.
7 Merchant Shipping (Load Line) Regulations 1998, SI 1998/2241, reg 13(2) (amended by SI 2000/1335). The text refers to the form and particulars as specified in Merchant Shipping Notice 1752(M) Sch 7 (notice of load lines to be posted up before sailing): see the Merchant Shipping (Load Line) Regulations 1998, SI 1998/2241, reg 13(2) (as so amended). As to the meaning of 'Merchant Shipping Notice' see PARA 660 note 6. See note 4.
8 Ie in accordance with the Merchant Shipping (Load Line) Regulations 1998, SI 1998/2241, reg 13(2) (see the text and notes 5–7): see reg 13(3).
9 Merchant Shipping (Load Line) Regulations 1998, SI 1998/2241, reg 13(3). See note 4.

(iv) Load Lines and Marks

670. Specification of load lines and marks.

Provisions relating to load lines[1] make detailed specification as to the marking of deck-lines, load line marks and load lines[2], in particular:

(1)   the exact size and positioning of the deck-line[3];
(2)   the exact size and positioning of the load line mark[4];
(3)   the exact size, variant type and positioning of the load lines[5];
(4)   the exact size, variant type and positioning of timber load lines[6];
(5)   the exact positioning of each load line mark on each side of the ship[7]; and

(6)   the method of marking[8].

The appropriate load line[9] in respect of a ship at any particular zone or area and seasonal period must be ascertained in accordance with the relevant provisions of the appropriate Merchant Shipping Notice[10].

After the appropriate marks have been made on a ship, it is the duty of the owner and master to keep the ship so marked[11]; and the marks must not be concealed, removed, altered, defaced or obliterated except with the authority of the Assigning Authority[12].

1   Ie the Merchant Shipping (Load Line) Regulations 1998, SI 1998/2241, Pt III (regs 15–24): see reg 15 (amended by SI 2000/1335). As to the meaning of 'load line' see PARA 671 note 1.
2   See the Merchant Shipping (Load Line) Regulations 1998, SI 1998/2241, reg 15 (as amended: see note 1). As to the determination of lines to be marked see PARA 674.
3   See the Merchant Shipping (Load Line) Regulations 1998, SI 1998/2241, reg 16.
4   See the Merchant Shipping (Load Line) Regulations 1998, SI 1998/2241, reg 17. The identity of the Assigning Authority may be marked alongside the load line mark (which is a ring) either above the horizontal line which passes through the centre of the ring, or above and below it: see reg 24(1). As to the exact specification of such a mark see reg 24(2). As to the meaning of 'Assigning Authority' see PARA 674 note 1.
5   See the Merchant Shipping (Load Line) Regulations 1998, SI 1998/2241, reg 18.
6   See the Merchant Shipping (Load Line) Regulations 1998, SI 1998/2241, reg 19 (amended by SI 2000/1335).
7   See the Merchant Shipping (Load Line) Regulations 1998, SI 1998/2241, reg 21.
8   See the Merchant Shipping (Load Line) Regulations 1998, SI 1998/2241, reg 22 (amended by SI 2000/1335).
9   As to the meaning of 'appropriate load line' see PARA 673 note 4.
10   Merchant Shipping (Load Line) Regulations 1998, SI 1998/2241, reg 20 (amended by SI 2000/1335). The text refers to the provisions of Merchant Shipping Notice 1752(M) Sch 1 (appropriate load lines and seasonal zones, areas and periods): see the Merchant Shipping (Load Line) Regulations 1998, SI 1998/2241, reg 20 (as so amended). As to the meaning of 'Merchant Shipping Notice' see PARA 671 note 6.
      Where a passenger ship is marked with subdivision load lines, and the lowest of those lines is lower than the line which is the appropriate load line then that subdivision load line has effect as if it is the appropriate load line for the purposes of the Merchant Shipping (Load Line) Regulations 1998, SI 1998/2241 (see PARA 674): reg 7(3).
11   Merchant Shipping (Load Line) Regulations 1998, SI 1998/2241, reg 23(a). As to penalties relating to the contravention of reg 23(a) see PARA 1189.
12   Merchant Shipping (Load Line) Regulations 1998, SI 1998/2241, reg 23(b). As to penalties relating to the contravention of reg 23(b) see PARA 1189.

(v) Information for the Master

671. Information as to stability, loading and ballasting of ships. The owner of every ship[1] must provide, for the guidance of the master, information relating to the stability of the ship[2]. Such information must be in the form of a book which must be kept on the ship at all times in the custody of the master[3]. In the case of a United Kingdom ship, the information must include all matters specified in the relevant provisions of the appropriate Merchant Shipping Notice[4] and must be in the form required therein[5].

The information must be based on the determination of stability taken from an inclining test carried out in the presence of a surveyor[6]. The information must be amended whenever any alterations[7] are made to the ship or changes occur to it which will materially affect the information and, if necessary, the ship must be re-inclined[8]. However, the inclining test may be dispensed with if:
(1)   in the case of any ship, basic stability data is available from the inclining test of a sister ship and the Secretary of State (or, where applicable, the Assigning Authority) is satisfied that reliable stability information can be obtained from such data[9]; and

(2)   in the case of a ship specially designed for the carriage of liquids or ore in bulk (or of any class of such ships), the information available in respect of similar ships shows that the ship's proportions and arrangements will ensure more than sufficient stability in all probable loading conditions[10].

The owner of any ship of more than 150 metres in length[11] specially designed for the carriage of liquids or ore in bulk must provide, for the guidance of the master, information relating to the loading and ballasting of the ship[12]. This information must indicate the maximum stresses permissible for the ship and specify the manner in which the ship is to be loaded and ballasted to avoid the creation of unacceptable stresses in its structure[13].

1   Ie every ship to which the Merchant Shipping (Load Line) Regulations 1998, SI 1998/2241, apply (see PARA 660): see reg 32(1).
2   Merchant Shipping (Load Line) Regulations 1998, SI 1998/2241, reg 32(1).
3   Merchant Shipping (Load Line) Regulations 1998, SI 1998/2241, reg 32(1). Before the information is issued to the master, if it relates to a ship falling within Merchant Shipping Notice 1752(M) Sch 6 Pt II (ships in relation to which the Secretary of State's or the Assigning Authority's approval of the stability information is required), it must be approved either by the Secretary of State or by the Assigning Authority which assigned freeboards to the ship (Merchant Shipping (Load Line) Regulations 1998, SI 1998/2241, reg 32(5)(a) (amended by SI 2000/1335)); and if the information relates to any other ship it must be approved by the Secretary of State before being so issued (Merchant Shipping (Load Line) Regulations 1998, SI 1998/2241, reg 32(5)(b)). Any approval given pursuant to the Merchant Shipping (Load Line) Regulations 1998, SI 1998/2241, must be given in writing and must specify the date on which it takes effect and the conditions (if any) on which it is given: reg 2(5). As to the meaning of 'Assigning Authority' see PARA 663 note 1. As to the meaning of 'freeboard' see PARA 662 note 5. As to the assignment of freeboards see PARA 663.
4   Ie all matters specified in Merchant Shipping Notice 1752(M) Sch 6 (stability): see the Merchant Shipping (Load Line) Regulations 1998, SI 1998/2241, reg 32(2) (amended by SI 2000/1335). As to the meaning of 'Merchant Shipping Notice' see PARA 660 note 6.
5   Merchant Shipping (Load Line) Regulations 1998, SI 1998/2241, reg 32(2) (as amended: see note 4). The text refers to the requirement for the specified information to be in the form required by Merchant Shipping Notice 1752(M) Sch 6 (stability): see the Merchant Shipping (Load Line) Regulations 1998, SI 1998/2241, reg 32(2) (as so amended). The information must also be in accordance with the requirements of reg 32(3)–(5) (see the text and notes 6–9): reg 32(2) (as so amended).
6   Merchant Shipping (Load Line) Regulations 1998, SI 1998/2241, reg 32(3) (amended by SI 2000/1335). As to the meaning of 'surveyor' for these purposes see PARA 663 note 32. The surveyor is appointed by the Secretary of State or, in the case of a ship listed in Merchant Shipping Notice 1752(M) Sch 6 Pt II, by the Assigning Authority: Merchant Shipping (Load Line) Regulations 1998, SI 1998/2241, reg 32(3) (as so amended). As to the Secretary of State see PARA 36.
7   As to the meaning of 'alteration' for these purposes see PARA 663 note 24.
8   Merchant Shipping (Load Line) Regulations 1998, SI 1998/2241, reg 32(3) (as amended: see note 6).
9   Merchant Shipping (Load Line) Regulations 1998, SI 1998/2241, reg 32(4)(a) (amended by SI 2000/1335).
10   Merchant Shipping (Load Line) Regulations 1998, SI 1998/2241, reg 32(4)(b).
11   As to the meaning of 'length' for these purposes see PARA 672 note 6.
12   Merchant Shipping (Load Line) Regulations 1998, SI 1998/2241, reg 33(1).
13   Merchant Shipping (Load Line) Regulations 1998, SI 1998/2241, reg 33(2). In the case of a United Kingdom ship, reg 32(5) has effect in respect of information required under reg 33, and the information so approved must be included in the book referred in reg 32(1) (see the text and notes 1–3): reg 33(3).

(vi) Equivalents

672. Power to allow equivalents. The Assigning Authority[1] may, with the approval of the Secretary of State[2]:

(1)   allow any fitting, material, appliance or apparatus to be fitted in a ship, or allow other provisions to be made in a ship, in the place of any fitting, material, appliance, apparatus or provision respectively which is required under any of the provisions relating to load lines[3], if satisfied by trial or otherwise that it is at least as effective as that so required[4]; or

(2)   allow in an exceptional case departure from the requirements of any of the provisions relating to load lines[5] on condition that the freeboards to be assigned to the ship[6] are increased to such an extent as to satisfy the Secretary of State that the safety of the ship and protection afforded to the crew will be no less effective than would be the case if the ship fully complied with those requirements and there were no such increase of freeboards[7].

1   As to the meaning of 'Assigning Authority' see PARA 663 note 1.
2   Merchant Shipping (Load Line) Regulations 1998, SI 1998/2241, reg 34. As to the Secretary of State see PARA 36. Any approval given pursuant to the Merchant Shipping (Load Line) Regulations 1998, SI 1998/2241, must be given in writing and must specify the date on which it takes effect and the conditions (if any) on which it is given: reg 2(5).
3   Ie under any of the provisions of the Merchant Shipping (Load Line) Regulations 1998, SI 1998/2241: see reg 34(a). As to the meaning of 'load line' see PARA 660 note 1.
4   Merchant Shipping (Load Line) Regulations 1998, SI 1998/2241, reg 34(a).
5   Ie from the provisions of the Merchant Shipping (Load Line) Regulations 1998, SI 1998/2241: see reg 34(b).
6   As to the assignment of freeboards see PARA 663. As to the meaning of 'freeboard' see PARA 662 note 5.
7   Merchant Shipping (Load Line) Regulations 1998, SI 1998/2241, reg 34(b).

(3) TEMPORARY EXCLUSION ZONES

673. Power to establish temporary exclusion zones where a casualty is wrecked, damaged or in distress. Where a ship[1], structure or other thing (the 'relevant casualty')[2] is in United Kingdom waters[3], or in a part of the sea within which the jurisdiction and rights of the United Kingdom are exercisable for the purposes of the protection and preservation of the marine environment[4], and where the relevant casualty is wrecked, damaged or in distress[5], then, if it appears to the Secretary of State[6]:

(1)   that significant harm[7] will or may occur as a direct or indirect result of the relevant casualty being wrecked, damaged or in distress[8]; and

(2)   that, if access to an area around the relevant casualty were restricted[9], significant harm, or the risk of such harm, would be prevented or reduced[10],

he may by a direction[11] identify an area to which access is so restricted (a 'temporary exclusion zone')[12].

A temporary exclusion zone may not include any area which is neither within United Kingdom waters nor within a part of the sea within which the jurisdiction and rights of the United Kingdom are exercisable for the purposes of the protection and preservation of the marine environment[13].

If it appears to the Secretary of State at any time after a temporary exclusion zone is established that the zone is larger than is needed for the purpose of preventing or reducing significant harm, or the risk of such harm, he must by direction vary the direction establishing the zone accordingly[14].

A temporary exclusion zone may be identified[15] by reference to the position of the relevant casualty from time to time[16].

If it appears to the Secretary of State at any time after a temporary exclusion zone is established that the zone is not needed for the purpose of preventing or reducing significant harm, or the risk of such harm, he must by direction revoke the direction establishing the zone[17].

Where the Secretary of State gives a direction in relation to temporary exclusion zones[18], he must[19]:

(a)   as soon as practicable, publish it in such manner as he considers appropriate for bringing it to the attention of persons likely to be affected by it[20]; and

(b)   within the period of 24 hours from the giving of the direction, send a copy of it to the International Maritime Organisation[21].

1   As to the meaning of 'ship' see PARA 229.
2   Merchant Shipping Act 1995 s 100A(1) (s 100A added by the Merchant Shipping and Maritime Security Act 1997 s 1). For the purposes of the Merchant Shipping Act 1995 ss 100A, 100B, 'relevant casualty' means the ship, structure or other thing referred to in s 100A(1): see s 100A(1) (as so added).
3   As to the meaning of 'United Kingdom waters' see PARA 48 note 11. As to the meaning of 'United Kingdom' see PARA 16 note 3.
4   Merchant Shipping Act 1995 s 100A(1)(a) (as added: see note 2). The reference in the text to a part of the sea within which the jurisdiction and rights of the United Kingdom are exercisable for the purposes of the protection and preservation of the marine environment is to a part of the sea specified by virtue of the Merchant Shipping Act 1995 s 129(2)(b), providing for orders to specify areas of sea above any of the areas for the time being designated under the Continental Shelf Act 1964 s 1(7) (as to which see ENERGY AND CLIMATE CHANGE vol 44 (2011) PARA 1040) as waters within which the jurisdiction and rights of the United Kingdom are exercisable in accordance with the United Nations Convention on the Law of the Sea (Montego Bay, 10 December 1982 to 9 December 1984; TS 3 Misc 11 (1983); Cmnd 8941) (the 'United Nations Convention on the Law of the Sea 1982') (as to which see PARA 9) Pt XII (arts 192–237) (protection and preservation of the marine environment) (as to which see ENVIRONMENTAL QUALITY AND PUBLIC HEALTH vol 45 (2010) PARA 402 et seq): see the Merchant Shipping Act 1995 s 100A(1)(a) (as so added).
5   Merchant Shipping Act 1995 s 100A(1)(b) (as added: see note 2).
6   Merchant Shipping Act 1995 s 100A(2) (as added: see note 2). As to the Secretary of State see PARA 36.
7   For these purposes, 'significant harm' means either significant pollution in the United Kingdom, in United Kingdom waters or in a part of the sea specified by virtue of the Merchant Shipping Act 1995 s 129(2)(b) (as to which see note 4), or significant damage to persons or property: s 100A(3) (as added: see note 2).
8   Merchant Shipping Act 1995 s 100A(2)(a) (as added: see note 2).
9   Ie in accordance with the Merchant Shipping Act 1995 s 100B (see PARA 674): see s 100A(2)(b) (as added: see note 2)
10 Merchant Shipping Act 1995 s 100A(2)(b) (as added: see note 2).
11 As to the Secretary of State's power to make directions under the Merchant Shipping Act 1995 generally see PARA 39. As to directions given under s 100A see the text and notes 18–21.
12 Merchant Shipping Act 1995 s 100A(2) (as added: see note 2). However, s 100A(2) does not apply where an order under the Protection of Wrecks Act 1973 s 2 (see PARA 948) has effect in relation to the relevant casualty: Merchant Shipping Act 1995 s 100A(9) (added by the Merchant Shipping and Maritime Security Act 1997 s 1).
13 Merchant Shipping Act 1995 s 100A(4) (as added: see note 2). The reference in the text to a part of the sea within which the jurisdiction and rights of the United Kingdom are exercisable for the purposes of the protection and preservation of the marine environment is to a part of the sea specified by virtue of the Merchant Shipping Act 1995 s 129(2)(b) (see note 4): see s 100A(4) (as so added).
14 Merchant Shipping Act 1995 s 100A(5) (as added: see note 2). As to directions given under s 100A see the text and notes 18–21.
15 Ie subject to the Merchant Shipping Act 1995 s 100A(4), (5) (see the text and notes 13–14): see s 100A(6) (as added: see note 2).
16 Merchant Shipping Act 1995 s 100A(6) (as added: see note 2).
17 Merchant Shipping Act 1995 s 100A(7) (as added: see note 2). As to directions given under s 100A see the text and notes 18–21.
18 Ie under the Merchant Shipping Act 1995 s 100A: see s 100A(8) (as added: see note 2).
19 Merchant Shipping Act 1995 s 100A(8) (as added: see note 2).
20 Merchant Shipping Act 1995 s 100A(8)(a) (as added: see note 2).

21 Merchant Shipping Act 1995 s 100A(8)(b) (as added: see note 2). As to the International Maritime Organisation see PARA 12.

674. Control of movements affected by temporary exclusion zones. A direction establishing a temporary exclusion zone[1] may contain a statement to the effect that the direction is given for the purpose of preventing or reducing significant pollution (or the risk of significant pollution) in the United Kingdom[2], in United Kingdom waters[3], or in a part of the sea within which the jurisdiction and rights of the United Kingdom are exercisable for the purposes of the protection and preservation of the marine environment[4]. If a direction establishing a temporary exclusion zone contains a statement to such effect, no ship[5] may[6] enter or remain in the zone[7]. However, if such a direction establishing a temporary exclusion zone does not contain a statement to such effect, then[8]:

(1)   no ship may enter or remain in any part of the zone that is in United Kingdom waters[9]; and

(2)   no United Kingdom ship[10] may enter or remain in any part of the zone that is in a part of the sea within which the jurisdiction and rights of the United Kingdom are exercisable for the purposes of the protection and preservation of the marine environment[11].

A ship may, however, enter or remain in a temporary exclusion zone or a part of such a zone if it does so[12]:

(a)   in accordance with the direction establishing the zone[13];

(b)   with the consent of the Secretary of State[14]; or

(c)   in accordance with regulations made by the Secretary of State for these purposes[15].

A qualifying foreign ship[16] may enter a temporary exclusion zone or a part of such a zone if, in doing so, it is exercising the right of transit passage[17] through straits used for international navigation[18].

If a ship enters or remains in a temporary exclusion zone or a part of such a zone in contravention[19] of the restrictions in force[20], its owner and its master[21] are each guilty of an offence[22].

1   As to the meaning of 'temporary exclusion zone' see PARA 673.
2   As to the meaning of 'United Kingdom' see PARA 16 note 3.
3   As to the meaning of 'United Kingdom waters' see PARA 48 note 11.
4   Merchant Shipping Act 1995 s 100B(2) (s 100B added by the Merchant Shipping and Maritime Security Act 1997 s 1). The reference in the text to a part of the sea within which the jurisdiction and rights of the United Kingdom are exercisable for the purposes of the protection and preservation of the marine environment is to a part of the sea specified by virtue of the Merchant Shipping Act 1995 s 129(2)(b) (see PARA 673 note 4): see s 100B(2) (as so added).
5   As to the meaning of 'ship' see PARA 229.
6   Ie subject to the Merchant Shipping Act 1995 s 100B(4) (see the text and notes 12–15): see s 100B(1) (as added: see note 4).
7   Merchant Shipping Act 1995 s 100B(1) (as added: see note 4).
8   Merchant Shipping Act 1995 s 100B(3) (as added: see note 4). Heads (1) and (2) in the text are subject to s 100B(4), (5) (see the text and notes 12–18): see s 100B(3) (as so added).
9   Merchant Shipping Act 1995 s 100B(3)(a) (as added: see note 4).
10 As to the meaning of 'United Kingdom ship' see PARA 230.
11 Merchant Shipping Act 1995 s 100B(3)(b) (as added: see note 4). The reference in the text to a part of the sea within which the jurisdiction and rights of the United Kingdom are exercisable for the purposes of the protection and preservation of the marine environment is to a part of the sea specified by virtue of s 129(2)(b) (see PARA 673 note 4): see s 100B(3)(b) (as so added).
12 Merchant Shipping Act 1995 s 100B(4) (as added: see note 4).
13 Merchant Shipping Act 1995 s 100B(4)(a) (as added: see note 4). As to directions establishing a temporary exclusion zone see PARA 673.
14 Merchant Shipping Act 1995 s 100B(4)(b) (as added: see note 4). As to the Secretary of State see PARA 36.
15 Merchant Shipping Act 1995 s 100B(4)(c) (as added: see note 4). As to the power of the Secretary of State to make subordinate legislation under the Merchant Shipping Act 1995, including his

power to appoint committees for the purpose of advising him when considering the making or alteration of any regulations etc, see PARA 39. At the date at which this volume states the law, no such regulations had been made under s 100B.

16 As to the meaning of 'qualifying foreign ship' see PARA 18.
17 As to the meaning of 'right of transit passage' see PARA 69 note 11.
18 Merchant Shipping Act 1995 s 100B(5) (as added: see note 4). As to the meaning of 'straits used for international navigation' see PARA 69 note 12.
19 As to the meaning of 'contravention' see PARA 51 note 3.
20 Ie in contravention of the Merchant Shipping Act 1995 s 100B(1) (see the text and notes 5–7) or s 100B(3) (see the text and notes 8–11): see s 100B(6); and PARA 1130.
21 As to the meaning of 'master' see PARA 424.
22 See the Merchant Shipping Act 1995 s 100B(6); and PARA 1130.

(4) SAFETY DIRECTIONS

675. Secretary of State's power to give safety directions in respect of a ship. The Secretary of State[1] may give a direction in respect of a ship[2] if, in his opinion, an accident[3] has occurred to or in the ship[4], if, in his opinion, the accident has created a risk to safety or a risk of pollution by a hazardous substance[5], and if, in his opinion, the direction is necessary to remove or reduce the risk[6]. The direction may be given to:

(1)   the owner of the ship[7];
(2)   a person in possession of the ship[8];
(3)   the ship's master[9];
(4)   a ship's pilot[10];
(5)   the owner of a hazardous substance in the ship[11];
(6)   a salvor in possession of the ship[12];
(7)   a person who is the servant or agent of a salvor in possession and who is in charge of the salvage operation[13]; or
(8)   where the ship is in or has been directed to move into waters regulated or managed by a harbour authority[14], the harbour authority or harbour master[15].

The direction may require the person to whom it is given to take or refrain from taking any specified action in relation to the ship[16], anything which is or was in the ship[17], anything which forms or formed part of the ship[18], anything which is or was being towed by the ship[19], or a person on the ship[20]. In particular, the direction may require a person to ensure that:

(a)   a ship or other thing is moved or not moved[21];
(b)   a ship or other thing is moved or not moved to or from a specified area or over a specified route[22];
(c)   cargo is or is not unloaded or discharged[23];
(d)   a substance is or is not unloaded or discharged[24];
(e)   specified salvage measures are taken or not taken[25];
(f)   a person is put ashore or on board a ship[26].

The Secretary of State also may give such a direction in respect of a ship if, in his opinion, an accident has occurred to or in the ship[27], if, in his opinion, the accident has created a risk to safety or a risk of pollution by a hazardous substance[28], and if, in his opinion, the direction is necessary to remove or reduce the risk[29], and he may give the direction to a person in charge of coastal land or premises[30]. Such a direction must be given in writing (or, if that is not reasonably practicable, confirmed in writing as soon as is reasonably practicable)[31] and may require the person to whom it is given to grant access or facilities to or in relation to the ship or any person or thing which is or was on the ship[32]. In particular, such a direction may require a person:

(i)   to permit persons to land[33];

(ii)   to make facilities available for the undertaking of repairs or other works[34];

(iii)   to make facilities available for the landing, storage and disposal of cargo or other things[35].

However, before giving such a direction[36] in respect of land or premises, the Secretary of State must, unless he thinks that it is not reasonably practicable, give the person to whom he proposes to give the direction an opportunity to make representations, and consider any representations made[37].

The Secretary of State also may give a direction in respect of a ship[38] if in his opinion it is necessary for the purpose of securing the safety of the ship or of other ships[39], securing the safety of persons or property[40], or preventing or reducing pollution[41]. The direction may be given to the owner of the ship[42], to a person in possession of the ship[43], or to the master of the ship[44]; and may require the person to whom it is given to ensure that:

(A)   the ship is moved or not moved from a specified place or area in United Kingdom waters[45];

(B)   the ship is moved or not moved to a specified place or area in United Kingdom waters[46];

(C)   the ship is moved or not moved over a specified route in United Kingdom waters[47];

(D)   the ship is removed from United Kingdom waters[48].

A person acting on behalf of the Secretary of State may board a ship for the purpose of serving a safety direction[49] and may enter land or premises for that purpose also[50].

Where the Secretary of State proposes to give a safety direction[51] to a company or other body, and he thinks that the usual provisions as to service on a company[52] do not apply, he may serve the direction in such manner as he thinks most suitable[53].

A person to whom a safety direction is given[54] must comply with the direction[55], and he commits an offence if he fails so to comply[56]. A person to whom a safety direction is given also must try to comply with the direction in a manner which avoids risk to human life[57].

If a person intentionally obstructs another person who is acting on behalf of the Secretary of State in connection with the giving of such a direction[58], or who is complying with such a direction, that first-named person commits an offence[59].

1   As to the Secretary of State see PARA 36.
2   Ie under the Merchant Shipping Act 1995 s 108A(1), Sch 3A para 1: see Sch 3A para 1(1) (s 108A, Sch 3A added by the Marine Safety Act 2003 s 1(1), (2), Sch 1). As to the Secretary of State's power to make directions under the Merchant Shipping Act 1995 generally see PARA 39. A provision made by or by virtue of the Merchant Shipping Act 1995 (including one which creates an offence) has no effect in so far as it is inconsistent with the exercise by or on behalf of the Secretary of State of a power under Sch 3A, or would interfere with a person's compliance with a direction under Sch 3A, or would interfere with action taken by virtue of Sch 3A: s 108A(2) (as so added). However, nothing in Sch 3A is to be taken to prejudice any right or power of Her Majesty's government: Sch 3A para 23 (as so added).
    A direction under the Merchant Shipping Act 1995 Sch 3A para 1 or under Sch 3A para 2 (see the text and notes 27–37), in so far as it relates to a risk of pollution, may have effect in respect of a ship only if it is a United Kingdom ship, or is in United Kingdom waters or an area of the sea specified under s 129(2)(b): Sch 3A para 17 (as so added). For these purposes, 'pollution' means significant pollution in the United Kingdom, United Kingdom waters or an area of the sea specified under s 129(2)(b): Sch 3A para 22(1) (as so added). As to the meaning of 'United Kingdom ship' see PARA 230; as to the meaning of 'ship' see PARA 229; as to the meaning of 'United Kingdom' see PARA 16 note 3; and as to the meaning of 'United Kingdom waters' see PARA 48 note 11. The reference to an area of the sea specified under s 129(2)(b) is to an area of sea (so specified by order)

above any of the areas for the time being designated under the Continental Shelf Act 1964 s 1(7) (as to which see ENERGY AND CLIMATE CHANGE vol 44 (2011) PARA 1040) as waters within which the jurisdiction and rights of the United Kingdom are exercisable in accordance with the United Nations Convention on the Law of the Sea (Montego Bay, 10 December 1982 to 9 December 1984; TS 3 Misc 11 (1983); Cmnd 8941) (the 'United Nations Convention on the Law of the Sea 1982') (as to which see PARA 9) Pt XII (arts 192–237) (protection and preservation of the marine environment): see ENVIRONMENTAL QUALITY AND PUBLIC HEALTH vol 45 (2010) PARA 402 et seq.

Her Majesty may by Order in Council provide that a direction under the Merchant Shipping Act 1995 Sch 3A para 1 or under Sch 3A para 2, in so far as it relates to a risk of pollution, is to have effect in respect of a ship which is not a United Kingdom ship and is not in United Kingdom waters or an area of the sea specified under s 129(2)(b): Sch 3A para 18(1) (as so added). Such an order may be expressed to apply generally or only in specified circumstances, may make different provision for different circumstances, may provide for Sch 3A to have effect in cases to which the Order in Council applies with specified modifications, and may contain transitional or consequential provision (including provision amending an enactment): Sch 3A para 18(2) (as so added).

A direction under Sch 3A para 1 or under Sch 3A para 2, in so far as it relates to a risk of safety, may have effect in respect of a ship only if it is in United Kingdom waters and it is not a qualifying foreign ship, or if it is in United Kingdom waters and it is a qualifying foreign ship which in the Secretary of State's opinion is exercising neither the right of innocent passage nor the right of transit passage through straits used for international navigation: Sch 3A para 19 (as so added). For these purposes, 'risk to safety' means a risk to the safety of persons, property or anything navigating in or using United Kingdom waters: Sch 3A para 22(1) (as so added). As to the meaning of 'qualifying foreign ship' see PARA 18; as to the meaning of 'right of transit passage' see PARA 69 note 11; and as to the meaning of 'straits used for international navigation' see PARA 69 note 12.

A direction may not be given under Sch 3A para 1(2)(a)–(d) (see heads (1) to (4) in the text) or under Sch 3A para 3 (see the text and notes 38–48) in respect of a ship of Her Majesty's Navy or a government ship: Sch 3A para 21 (as so added). As to the meaning of 'government ship' see PARA 19 note 3.

A direction under Sch 3A may be varied or revoked by a further direction: Sch 3A para 10(1) (as so added). If the Secretary of State thinks that such a direction is wholly or partly no longer necessary for the purpose for which it was given, he must vary or revoke the direction as soon as is reasonably practicable: Sch 3A para 10(2) (as so added). Where the Secretary of State has given such a direction to a person he must consider any representations about varying or revoking the direction which are made to him by that person: Sch 3A para 10(3) (as so added).

3   For these purposes, 'accident' means a collision of ships, a stranding, another incident of navigation or another event (whether on board a ship or not) which results in material damage to a ship or its cargo or in an imminent threat of such material damage: Merchant Shipping Act 1995 Sch 3A para 22(1) (as added: see note 2).

4   Merchant Shipping Act 1995 Sch 3A para 1(1)(a) (as added: see note 2).

5   Merchant Shipping Act 1995 Sch 3A para 1(1)(b) (as added: see note 2). For these purposes, 'hazardous substance' means oil within the meaning given by s 151(1) (see ENVIRONMENTAL QUALITY AND PUBLIC HEALTH vol 45 (2010) PARA 425), any other substance which creates a hazard to human health, harms living resources or marine life, damages amenities or interferes with lawful use of the sea, and any other substance prescribed by order of the Secretary of State: Sch 3A para 22(1), (2) (as so added). As to the power of the Secretary of State to make subordinate legislation under the Merchant Shipping Act 1995, including his power to appoint committees for the purpose of advising him when considering the making or alteration of any regulations etc, see PARA 39. At the date at which this volume states the law, no such regulations had been made under Sch 3A but, by virtue of the Interpretation Act 1978 s 17(2)(b), the Merchant Shipping (Prevention of Pollution: Substances Other than Oil) (Intervention) Order 1997, SI 1997/1869, takes effect as if made under the Merchant Shipping Act 1995 Sch 3A para 22(2). Accordingly, the substances prescribed for the purposes of Sch 3A para 22(2) (substances other than oil) are those listed in the Merchant Shipping (Prevention of Pollution: Substances Other than Oil) (Intervention) Order 1997, SI 1997/1869, art 2, Schedule.

6   Merchant Shipping Act 1995 Sch 3A para 1(1)(c) (as added: see note 2). As to action which may be taken in lieu of a safety direction see PARA 676; and as to liabilities in respect of action taken in accordance with a safety direction see PARA 677.

7   Merchant Shipping Act 1995 Sch 3A para 1(2)(a) (as added: see note 2). For these purposes, 'owner', in relation to the ship to or in which an accident has occurred, includes its owner at the time of the accident: Sch 3A para 22(1) (as so added).

8   Merchant Shipping Act 1995 Sch 3A para 1(2)(b) (as added: see note 2).

9   Merchant Shipping Act 1995 Sch 3A para 1(2)(c) (as added: see note 2). As to the meaning of
    'master' see PARA 444 note 1.
10 Merchant Shipping Act 1995 Sch 3A para 1(2)(d) (as added: see note 2). For these purposes, 'pilot'
    means a person who does not belong to a ship but who has the conduct of it: Sch 3A para 22(1)
    (as so added).
11 Merchant Shipping Act 1995 Sch 3A para 1(2)(da) (Sch 3A as added (see note 2); Sch 3A para
    1(2)(da) added by SI 2004/2110).
12 Merchant Shipping Act 1995 Sch 3A para 1(2)(e) (as added: see note 2).
13 Merchant Shipping Act 1995 Sch 3A para 1(2)(f) (as added: see note 2).
14 For these purposes, 'harbour authority' has the meaning given by the Merchant Shipping Act 1995
    s 151(1) (see ENVIRONMENTAL QUALITY AND PUBLIC HEALTH vol 45 (2010) PARA 428):
    Sch 3A para 22(1) (as added: see note 2).
15 Merchant Shipping Act 1995 Sch 3A para 1(2)(g) (as added: see note 2). For these purposes,
    'harbour master' includes a dock master or pier master, and any person specially appointed by a
    harbour authority for the purpose of enforcing the provisions of Sch 3A in relation to the harbour:
    Sch 3A para 22(1) (as so added).
16 Merchant Shipping Act 1995 Sch 3A para 1(3)(a) (as added: see note 2). For these purposes,
    'action' includes omission: Sch 3A para 22(1) (as so added).
17 Merchant Shipping Act 1995 Sch 3A para 1(3)(b) (as added: see note 2).
18 Merchant Shipping Act 1995 Sch 3A para 1(3)(c) (as added: see note 2).
19 Merchant Shipping Act 1995 Sch 3A para 1(3)(d) (as added: see note 2).
20 Merchant Shipping Act 1995 Sch 3A para 1(3)(e) (as added: see note 2).
21 Merchant Shipping Act 1995 Sch 3A para 1(4)(a) (as added: see note 2).
22 Merchant Shipping Act 1995 Sch 3A para 1(4)(b) (as added: see note 2).
23 Merchant Shipping Act 1995 Sch 3A para 1(4)(c) (as added: see note 2).
24 Merchant Shipping Act 1995 Sch 3A para 1(4)(d) (as added: see note 2).
25 Merchant Shipping Act 1995 Sch 3A para 1(4)(e) (as added: see note 2).
26 Merchant Shipping Act 1995 Sch 3A para 1(4)(f) (as added: see note 2).
27 Merchant Shipping Act 1995 Sch 3A para 2(1)(a) (as added: see note 2).
28 Merchant Shipping Act 1995 Sch 3A para 2(1)(b) (as added: see note 2).
29 Merchant Shipping Act 1995 Sch 3A para 2(1)(c) (as added: see note 2).
30 Merchant Shipping Act 1995 Sch 3A para 2(2) (as added: see note 2). For these purposes, a person
    is in charge of land or premises if he is wholly or partly able to control the use made of the land
    or premises; 'coastal' means adjacent to or accessible from United Kingdom waters over which the
    public is permitted to navigate: Sch 3A para 2(3) (as so added). As to directions given under Sch 3A
    para 2 see note 2.
31 Merchant Shipping Act 1995 Sch 3A para 2(6) (as added: see note 2).
32 Merchant Shipping Act 1995 Sch 3A para 2(4) (as added: see note 2).
33 Merchant Shipping Act 1995 Sch 3A para 2(5)(a) (as added: see note 2).
34 Merchant Shipping Act 1995 Sch 3A para 2(5)(b) (as added: see note 2).
35 Merchant Shipping Act 1995 Sch 3A para 2(5)(c) (as added: see note 2).
36 Ie a direction under the Merchant Shipping Act 1995 Sch 3A para 2: see Sch 3A para 13 (as added:
    see note 2).
37 Merchant Shipping Act 1995 Sch 3A para 13 (as added: see note 2).
38 A direction under the Merchant Shipping Act 1995 Sch 3A para 3 may have effect in respect of a
    ship only if it is in United Kingdom waters and it is not a qualifying foreign ship, or if it is United
    Kingdom waters and is a qualifying foreign ship which in the Secretary of State's opinion is
    exercising neither the right of innocent passage nor the right of transit passage through straits used
    for international navigation: Sch 3A para 20(1) (as added: see note 2). See also note 48.
39 Merchant Shipping Act 1995 Sch 3A para 3(1)(a) (as added: see note 2).
40 Merchant Shipping Act 1995 Sch 3A para 3(1)(b) (as added: see note 2).
41 Merchant Shipping Act 1995 Sch 3A para 3(1)(c) (as added: see note 2).
42 Merchant Shipping Act 1995 Sch 3A para 3(2)(a) (as added: see note 2).
43 Merchant Shipping Act 1995 Sch 3A para 3(2)(b) (as added: see note 2).
44 Merchant Shipping Act 1995 Sch 3A para 3(2)(c) (as added: see note 2).
45 Merchant Shipping Act 1995 Sch 3A para 3(3)(a) (as added: see note 2).
46 Merchant Shipping Act 1995 Sch 3A para 3(3)(b) (as added: see note 2).
47 Merchant Shipping Act 1995 Sch 3A para 3(3)(c) (as added: see note 2).
48 Merchant Shipping Act 1995 Sch 3A para 3(3)(d) (as added: see note 2). However, a direction may
    not be given under Sch 3A para 3(3)(d) in respect of a United Kingdom ship: Sch 3A para 20(2)
    (as so added).
49 Ie for the purpose of serving a direction under the Merchant Shipping Act 1995 Sch 3A: see Sch 3A
    para 12 (as added: see note 2).

50 Merchant Shipping Act 1995 Sch 3A para 12 (as added: see note 2).
51 Ie a direction under the Merchant Shipping Act 1995 Sch 3A: see Sch 3A para 11(1) (as added (see note 2); Sch 3A para 11 substituted by SI 2009/1941).
52 Ie the Companies Act 2006 s 1139 (see COMPANIES vol 15 (2016) PARA 743).
53 Merchant Shipping Act 1995 Sch 3A para 11(2) (as added and substituted: see notes 2, 51).
54 Ie under the Merchant Shipping Act 1995 Sch 3A: see Sch 3A para 5 (as added: see note 2).
55 Merchant Shipping Act 1995 Sch 3A para 5(a) (as added: see note 2).
56 See the Merchant Shipping Act 1995 Sch 3A para 6; and PARA 1131.
57 Merchant Shipping Act 1995 Sch 3A para 5(b) (as added: see note 2).
58 Ie under the Merchant Shipping Act 1995 Sch 3A: see Sch 3A para 7; and PARA 1131.
59 See the Merchant Shipping Act 1995 Sch 3A para 7; and PARA 1131.

676. Action taken in lieu of safety direction. Where the Secretary of State[1] thinks that circumstances exist which would entitle him to give a safety direction in respect of a ship[2], but that the giving of a direction would not be likely to achieve a sufficient result[3], or where he has given such a direction[4] but, in his opinion, the direction has not achieved a sufficient result[5], he may take such action as appears to him necessary or expedient for the purpose for which the direction could have been given or was given[6]. In particular, the Secretary of State may:

(1)   authorise a person to enter land or make use of facilities[7];
(2)   do or authorise a person to do anything which the Secretary of State could require a person to do by a direction[8];
(3)   authorise a person to assume control of a ship[9];
(4)   make arrangements or authorise the making of arrangements for the sinking or destruction of a ship[10].

If a person intentionally obstructs another person who is taking such action[11], that first-named person commits an offence[12].

1   As to the Secretary of State see PARA 36.
2   Ie a direction under the Merchant Shipping Act 1995 s 108A(1), Sch 3A (see PARA 675): see Sch 3A para 4(1) (s 108A, Sch 3A added by the Marine Safety Act 2003 s 1(1), (2), Sch 1). As to the meaning of 'ship' see PARA 229. As to the Secretary of State's power to make directions under the Merchant Shipping Act 1995 generally see PARA 39; and as to directions made under Sch 3A specifically see PARA 675.
3   Merchant Shipping Act 1995 Sch 3A para 4(1) (as added: see note 2).
4   Ie under the Merchant Shipping Act 1995 s 108A(1), Sch 3A (see PARA 675): see Sch 3A para 4(2) (as added: see note 2).
5   Merchant Shipping Act 1995 Sch 3A para 4(2) (as added: see note 2).
6   Merchant Shipping Act 1995 Sch 3A para 4(3) (as added: see note 2). As to liabilities in respect of action taken in lieu of a safety direction see PARA 677.
7   Merchant Shipping Act 1995 Sch 3A para 4(4)(a) (as added: see note 2).
8   Merchant Shipping Act 1995 Sch 3A para 4(4)(b) (as added: see note 2).
9   Merchant Shipping Act 1995 Sch 3A para 4(4)(c) (as added: see note 2).
10 Merchant Shipping Act 1995 Sch 3A para 4(4)(d) (as added: see note 2).
11 Ie who is acting by virtue of the Merchant Shipping Act 1995 Sch 3A para 4 (see the text and notes 1–10): see Sch 3A para 7; and PARA 1131.
12 See the Merchant Shipping Act 1995 Sch 3A para 7; and PARA 1131.

677. Liabilities in respect of action taken in accordance with, or in lieu of, a safety direction. Where action ('remedial action') taken in accordance with a safety direction[1], or taken in lieu of such a direction[2], either:

(1)   was not reasonably necessary for the purpose for which the direction was given[3]; or
(2)   caused loss or damage which could not be justified by reference to that purpose[4],

the Secretary of State[5] must pay compensation to any person who suffered loss or damage as a result of the remedial action (whether it was taken by him or someone else)[6] and who applies to him for compensation[7]. In considering what is reasonably necessary or justifiable for the purposes of heads (1) and (2) above, account must be taken of[8]:

(a)   the extent of the risk to safety[9] or threat of pollution[10] which the direction was intended to address[11];

(b)   the likelihood of the remedial action being effective[12]; and

(c)   the extent of the loss or damage caused by the remedial action[13].

Where a safety direction is given in respect of a ship[14] to a person in respect of land or premises[15], or where the Secretary of State[16] takes, or authorises action, in lieu of such a direction[17], the following expenses may be recovered[18]:

(i)   the person to whom such a direction is given is entitled to recover the costs of his compliance with the direction from the ship's owner[19];

(ii)   a person in charge of coastal land or premises is entitled to recover from the ship's owner costs incurred by him as a result of action taken in lieu of a direction[20] in relation to that land or premises[21];

(iii)   the Secretary of State is entitled to recover from the owner of the ship:

       (A)   costs incurred in connection with the giving of a direction[22];

       (B)   costs incurred in connection with action taken in lieu of such a direction[23];

       (C)   costs incurred by the Secretary of State in making payments to a person on account of sums recoverable by that person under head (i) or (ii) above[24].

The Admiralty jurisdiction of the High Court[25] includes jurisdiction to hear and determine any claim so arising in relation to such expenses[26] or in relation to such compensation[27].

Where action is taken in respect of a ship which is under arrest (or in respect of anything in a ship which is under arrest), being action duly taken in accordance with a safety direction[28], or taken in lieu of such a direction[29], the action does not constitute contempt of court and does not give rise to civil liability on the part of the Admiralty Marshal[30].

1   Ie a direction under the Merchant Shipping Act 1995 s 108A(1), Sch 3A (see PARA 675): see Sch 3A para 14(1) (s 108A, Sch 3A added by the Marine Safety Act 2003 s 1(1), (2), Sch 1). As to the Secretary of State's power to make directions under the Merchant Shipping Act 1995 generally see PARA 39; and as to directions made under Sch 3A specifically see PARA 675.

2   Ie by a person who is acting by virtue of the Merchant Shipping Act 1995 Sch 3A para 4 (see PARA 676): see Sch 3A para 14(1) (as added: see note 1).

3   Merchant Shipping Act 1995 Sch 3A para 14(1)(a) (as added: see note 1).

4   Merchant Shipping Act 1995 Sch 3A para 14(1)(b) (as added: see note 1).

5   As to the Secretary of State see PARA 36.

6   Merchant Shipping Act 1995 Sch 3A para 14(2)(a) (as added: see note 1).

7   Merchant Shipping Act 1995 Sch 3A para 14(2)(b) (as added: see note 1).

8   Merchant Shipping Act 1995 Sch 3A para 14(3) (as added: see note 1).

9   As to the meaning of 'risk to safety' for these purposes see PARA 675 note 2.

10   As to the meaning of 'pollution' see PARA 675 note 2.

11   Merchant Shipping Act 1995 Sch 3A para 14(3)(a) (as added: see note 1).

12   Merchant Shipping Act 1995 Sch 3A para 14(3)(b) (as added: see note 1).

13   Merchant Shipping Act 1995 Sch 3A para 14(3)(c) (as added: see note 1).

14   As to the meaning of 'ship' see PARA 229.

15   Merchant Shipping Act 1995 Sch 3A para 15(1)(a) (as added: see note 1). The text refers to the circumstance where a direction is given to a person in respect of a ship under Sch 3A para 2 (see PARA 675): see Sch 3A para 15(1)(a) (as so added).

16   Ie relying on the Merchant Shipping Act 1995 Sch 3A para 4 (see PARA 676): see Sch 3A para 15(1)(b) (as added: see note 1).

17   Merchant Shipping Act 1995 Sch 3A para 15(1)(b) (as added: see note 1).

18   A right under any of heads (i) to (iii) in the text permits the recovery of costs only in so far as they are not recoverable under another enactment, by virtue of an agreement, or under the law relating to salvage: Merchant Shipping Act 1995 Sch 3A para 15(6) (as added: see note 1).

19 Merchant Shipping Act 1995 Sch 3A para 15(2) (as added: see note 1). The Secretary of State may make payments to a person on account of sums recoverable by that person under Sch 3A para 15(2): see Sch 3A para 15(4) (as so added). As to the meaning of 'owner' for these purposes see PARA 675 note 7.

20 Ie action taken by virtue of the Merchant Shipping Act 1995 Sch 3A para 4: see Sch 3A para 15(3) (as added: see note 1).

21 Merchant Shipping Act 1995 Sch 3A para 15(3) (as added: see note 1). The Secretary of State may make payments to a person on account of sums recoverable by that person under Sch 3A para 15(3): see Sch 3A para 15(4) (as so added).

22 Merchant Shipping Act 1995 Sch 3A para 15(5)(a) (as added: see note 1).

23 Merchant Shipping Act 1995 Sch 3A para 15(5)(b) (as added: see note 1). Head (B) in the text refers to costs incurred in connection with action taken under Sch 3A para 4: see Sch 3A para 15(5)(b) (as so added).

24 Merchant Shipping Act 1995 Sch 3A para 15(5)(c) (as added: see note 1). The text refers to costs incurred by the Secretary of State in making payments to a person under Sch 3A para 15(4) (see notes 19, 21): see Sch 3A para 15(5)(c) (as so added).

25 As to the Admiralty jurisdiction of the High Court generally see PARA 85 et seq.

26 Ie a claim arising under the Merchant Shipping Act 1995 Sch 3A para 15 (see notes 14–24): see Sch 3A para 16 (as added: see note 1).

27 Merchant Shipping Act 1995 Sch 3A para 16 (as added: see note 1). The text refers to a claim for compensation arising under Sch 3A para 14 (see notes 1–13): see Sch 3A para 16 (as so added).

28 Ie a direction under the Merchant Shipping Act 1995 Sch 3A: see Sch 3A para 24(1) (as added: see note 1).

29 Ie by a person who is acting by virtue of the Merchant Shipping Act 1995 Sch 3A para 4: see Sch 3A para 24(1) (as added: see note 1).

30 Merchant Shipping Act 1995 Sch 3A para 24(1) (as added: see note 1). As to the Admiralty Marshal see PARA 160 note 6.

(5) PORT STATE CONTROL

678. Shipping required to comply with international safety standards.
Ships using the ports of EU member states are required to comply with international standards for ship safety, pollution prevention and shipboard living and working conditions[1], and an EU-wide inspections regime has been established in order to enforce this requirement[2]. In a United Kingdom context the inspection requirements[3] apply to any ship and its crew calling at a port or anchorage in the United Kingdom[4] to engage in a ship/port interface[5] other than a British ship[6], a fishing vessel[7], a warship[8], a naval auxiliary[9], a wooden ship of primitive build[10], a government ship used for non-commercial purposes[11] or a pleasure yacht not engaged in trade[12].

1 In this context 'ship' means (by virtue of the Merchant Shipping (Port State Control) Regulations 2011, SI 2011/2601, reg 2(1)) a seagoing vessel (including hovercraft) to which one or more of the following conventions applies:
    (1)   the International Convention on Load Lines (London, 5 April to 4 July 1966; TS 58 (1968); Cmnd 3708);
    (2)   the International Convention for the Safety of Life at Sea 1974 (London, 1 November 1974 to 1 July 1975; TS 46 (1980); Cmnd 7874), with Protocol (London, 1 June 1978 to 1 March 1979; TS 40 (1981); Cmnd 8277);
    (3)   the International Convention for the Prevention of Pollution from Ships (London, 8 October to 2 November 1973; Misc 26 (1974); Cmnd 5748), with Protocol (London, 1 June 1978 to 31 May 1979; Misc 27 (1978); Cmnd 7347) ('MARPOL');
    (4)   the International Convention on Standards of Training, Certification and Watchkeeping for Seafarers 1978 (London, 1 December 1978 to 30 November 1979; TS 50 (1984); Cmnd 9266) (the 'STCW Convention');
    (5)   the Convention on the International Regulations for Preventing Collisions at Sea 1972 (London, 20 October 1972; TS 77 (1977); Cmnd 3678) ('COLREG');
    (6)   the International Convention on Tonnage Measurement of Ships 1969 (London, 23 June to 23 December 1969; TS 50 (1982); Cmnd 8716) ('ITC69');
    (7)   the Merchant Shipping (Minimum Standards) Convention 1976 (ILO No 147) (Cmnd 7183; and

(8)   the International Convention on Civil Liability for Oil Pollution Damage (Brussels, 29 November 1969 to 31 December 1970; TS 106 (1975); Cmnd 6183) with Protocol (London, 27 November 1992),

in so far as:

(a)   they relate to all or any of the purposes set out in Merchant Shipping Act 1985 s 85(1) (see PARA 602 note 1);

(b)   they are considered by the Secretary of State to be relevant from time to time; and

(c)   they are specified in a Merchant Shipping Notice,

and a reference to a Convention is a reference to any of the Conventions. As to the Secretary of State see PARA 36. 'Member state' includes an EEA state: reg 2(1). 'Merchant Shipping Notice' means a Notice described as such, issued by the Maritime and Coastguard Agency (see PARA 12), and reference to a specific Merchant Shipping Notice includes a reference to any document amending or replacing that notice which is considered by the Secretary of State to be relevant from time to time and is specified in a Merchant Shipping Notice: reg 2(1)/

2   See Parliament and Council Directive (EC) 2009/16 (OJ L131, 28.5.2009, p 57) on port state control, which is implemented in the United Kingdom by the Merchant Shipping (Port State Control) Regulations 2011, SI 2011/2601 and (in so far as relating to Parliament and Council Regulation (EU) 2015/757 (OJ L123, 19.5.2015, p 55) on the monitoring, reporting and verification of carbon dioxide emissions from maritime transport), by the Merchant Shipping (Monitoring, Reporting and Verification of Carbon Dioxide Emissions) and the Port State Control (Amendment) Regulations 2017, SI 2017/825. The EC Directive and the EU Regulations should be referred to for the interpretation of the applicable domestic Regulations: see the Merchant Shipping (Port State Control) Regulations 2011, SI 2011/2601, reg 2(1); and the Merchant Shipping (Monitoring, Reporting and Verification of Carbon Dioxide Emissions) and the Port State Control (Amendment) Regulations 2017, SI 2017/825, reg 2(2). The 2011 Regulations do not prejudice the additional requirements of the Conventions concerning notification and reporting procedures related to port State control: Merchant Shipping (Port State Control) Regulations 2011, SI 2011/2601, reg 9(12).

3   Ie the Merchant Shipping (Port State Control) Regulations 2011, SI 2011/2601, Pt 1 (regs 2–23) (see the text and notes 4–12; and PARAS 679–683).

4   As to the meaning of 'United Kingdom' see PARA 16 note 3. References in the Merchant Shipping (Port State Control) Regulations 2011, SI 2011/2601, to the United Kingdom include United Kingdom waters (reg 2(3)); as to the meaning of 'United Kingdom waters' see the Merchant Shipping Act 1995 s 313(2)(a); and PARA 48 note 11 (definition applied by the Merchant Shipping (Port State Control) Regulations 2011, SI 2011/2601, reg 2(1)).

5   Merchant Shipping (Port State Control) Regulations 2011, SI 2011/2601, reg 3(1).

6   Merchant Shipping (Port State Control) Regulations 2011, SI 2011/2601, reg 3(2)(a). As to the meaning of 'British ship' see the Merchant Shipping Act 1995 s 1; and PARA 230 (definition applied by the Merchant Shipping (Port State Control) Regulations 2011, SI 2011/2601, reg 2(1)).

7   Merchant Shipping (Port State Control) Regulations 2011, SI 2011/2601, reg 3(2)(b). 'Fishing vessel' means a vessel used for catching fish, whales, seals, walrus or other living resources of the sea: reg 2(1).

8   Merchant Shipping (Port State Control) Regulations 2011, SI 2011/2601, reg 3(2)(c).

9   Merchant Shipping (Port State Control) Regulations 2011, SI 2011/2601, reg 3(2)(d).

10 Merchant Shipping (Port State Control) Regulations 2011, SI 2011/2601, reg 3(2)(e).

11 Merchant Shipping (Port State Control) Regulations 2011, SI 2011/2601, reg 3(2)(f).

12 Merchant Shipping (Port State Control) Regulations 2011, SI 2011/2601, reg 3(2)(g).

679. Inspections. For these purposes[1] an 'inspection' is:

(1)   an initial inspection[2];

(2)   a more detailed inspection[3]; or

(3)   an expanded inspection[4].

In carrying out an inspection of a ship the inspector[5] must as a minimum carry out an initial inspection[6]. A more detailed inspection must be carried out when there are clear grounds for believing, after an initial inspection, that the condition of a ship or of its equipment or crew does not substantially meet the relevant requirements[7]. Certain high-risk ships[8] are eligible for expended inspections, which may include a more detailed inspection whenever there are clear grounds for believing that the condition of a ship or of its equipment or crew does not substantially meet the Convention requirements[9].

On completion of an initial inspection, a more detailed inspection or an expanded inspection, the inspector must draw up a report[10] and must provide the ship's master with a copy of the report[11].

Ships when in ports in the United Kingdom, and in the case of United Kingdom ships when elsewhere, are subject to inspection for the purpose of checking that the master and crew are familiar with essential procedures and operations relating to the safety of the ship[12].

1   Ie for the purposes of Parliament and Council Directive (EC) 2009/16 (OJ L131, 28.5.2009, p 57) on port state control, and the Merchant Shipping (Port State Control) Regulations 2011, SI 2011/2601: see PARA 678. An inspection in the United Kingdom of a ship, while not in a port, is considered an inspection for these purposes: reg 3(4). As to the meaning of 'ship' see PARA 678 note 1. When carrying out an inspection under these provisions, the inspector must make all possible efforts to avoid a ship being unduly detained or delayed: reg 9(13).
    The Secretary of State must in each calendar year ensure the carrying out of the United Kingdom's share of the total number of inspections to be carried out annually in accordance with Parliament and Council Directive (EC) 2009/16 (OJ L131, 28.5.2009, p 57): see the Merchant Shipping (Port State Control) Regulations 2011, SI 2011/2601, reg 4(1), (2). As to the Secretary of State see PARA 36. Port authorities are required to report all arrivals and departures to the Secretary of State: see reg 20. 'Port authority' means a harbour authority within the meaning of the Harbours Act 1964 (see PORTS AND HARBOURS vol 85 (2012) PARA 20) or if there is no such authority, the person having control of the operation of the port: Merchant Shipping (Port State Control) Regulations 2011, SI 2011/2601, reg 2(1). A port authority which contravenes reg 20 is guilty of an offence and liable on summary conviction to a fine: reg 23(6). As to the powers of magistrates' courts to issue fines on summary conviction see SENTENCING vol 92 (2015) PARA 176.
    It is a defence for a person charged under reg 23 to prove that they took all reasonable steps to avoid committing the offence (reg 23(7)(a)) and for a port authority charged under reg 23(6) with contravention of reg 20 to prove that it had been informed by the Secretary of State that the Secretary of State was not ready to receive the information to which reg 20 applies (reg 23(7)(b)).
2   Merchant Shipping (Port State Control) Regulations 2011, SI 2011/2601, reg 4(3)(a). 'Initial inspection' means a visit on board a ship by an inspector in order to check compliance with the relevant Conventions including at least the checks set out in Parliament and Council Directive (EC) 2009/16 (OJ L131, 28.5.2009, p 57) art 13.1: Merchant Shipping (Port State Control) Regulations 2011, SI 2011/2601, reg 2(1). As to the Conventions see PARA 678 note 1.
3   Merchant Shipping (Port State Control) Regulations 2011, SI 2011/2601, reg 4(3)(b). 'More detailed inspection' means an inspection where the ship, its equipment and crew as a whole or parts thereof are subjected to an in-depth examination covering the ship's construction, equipment, manning, living and working conditions and compliance with on-board operational procedures: reg 2(1).
4   Merchant Shipping (Port State Control) Regulations 2011, SI 2011/2601, reg 4(3)(c). 'Expanded inspection' means an inspection which covers at least the items listed in Parliament and Council Directive (EC) 2009/16 (OJ L131, 28.5.2009, p 57) Annex VII: Merchant Shipping (Port State Control) Regulations 2011, SI 2011/2601, reg 2(1).
5   'Inspector' means a person duly authorised by the Secretary of State to carry out inspections required by the Merchant Shipping (Port State Control) Regulations 2011, SI 2011/2601: reg 2(1). Provision is made in connection with the professional profile, qualifications etc of inspectors (see the Merchant Shipping (Port State Control) Regulations 2011, SI 2011/2601, reg 8) and in connection with the costs of inspections (see reg 22). A person who obstructs an inspector or any person assisting the inspector is guilty of an offence and liable on summary conviction to a fine: reg 23(4).
6   Merchant Shipping (Port State Control) Regulations 2011, SI 2011/2601, reg 5(1). If after an inspection complying with Parliament and Council Directive (EC) 2009/16 (OJ L131, 28.5.2009, p 57) art 13.1 has been carried out in any member state, deficiencies to be rectified in the ship's next port of call have been recorded in the inspection database, and that next port of call is in the United Kingdom, the inspector must, if carrying out an inspection of that ship, as a minimum comply with the requirements of art 13.1(b): Merchant Shipping (Port State Control) Regulations 2011, SI 2011/2601, reg 5(2).
7   Merchant Shipping (Port State Control) Regulations 2011, SI 2011/2601, reg 5(3). The 'Convention requirements' are the requirements of one of the Conventions listed in PARA 678 note 1. For the purposes of regs 4(3), 6(3), clear grounds exist when the inspector finds evidence which in the inspector's professional judgement warrants a more detailed inspection of the ship, its equipment or its crew and examples of clear grounds are set out in Parliament and Council

Directive (EC) 2009/16 (OJ L131, 28.5.2009, p 57) Annex V: Merchant Shipping (Port State Control) Regulations 2011, SI 2011/2601, reg 5(4).
8 Ie ships in the categories set out in Parliament and Council Directive (EC) 2009/16 (OJ L131, 28.5.2009, p 57) art 14.1: see the Merchant Shipping (Port State Control) Regulations 2011, SI 2011/2601, reg 6(1). Such ships must notify the Secretary of State of their intention to call at a port or anchorage in the United Kingdom: see reg 6(2), (6).
9 Merchant Shipping (Port State Control) Regulations 2011, SI 2011/2601, reg 6(3). The ship's owner or master must ensure that sufficient time is available in the operating schedule to allow the expanded inspection to be carried out (reg 6(4)) and, without prejudice to control measures required for security purposes, the ship must not leave the port or anchorage until the inspection is completed (reg 6(5)). 'Owner' includes, in relation to a ship, any operator, manager, charterer or agent of the ship: reg 2(1). Where a ship fails to give notification in breach of reg 6(2) or leaves a port or anchorage in breach of reg 6(5), the owner and master are each guilty of an offence and liable on summary conviction to a fine: reg 23(3).
10 Ie in accordance with Parliament and Council Directive (EC) 2009/16 (OJ L131, 28.5.2009, p 57) Annex IX.
11 Merchant Shipping (Port State Control) Regulations 2011, SI 2011/2601, reg 7.
12 Merchant Shipping (Port State Control) Regulations 2011, SI 2011/2601, reg 25(1). The Merchant Shipping Act 2005 s 258 (see PARA 48) applies in this context subject to modifications: see reg 25(2).

680. Rectification and detention.

A ship's owner[1] must satisfy the Secretary of State[2] that any deficiencies which are confirmed or revealed by an initial inspection, more detailed inspection or expanded inspection[3] are or will be[4] rectified in accordance with the Conventions[5]. Where such deficiencies are clearly hazardous to safety, health or the environment, the inspector[6] must[7] detain the ship, or require the stoppage of the operation in the course of which the deficiencies have been revealed[8]. A detention notice issued in these circumstances may include a direction that a ship must remain in a particular place, or must move to a particular anchorage or berth, and specify circumstances when the master of the ship may move that ship from a specified place for reasons of safety or prevention of pollution[9]. Failure to comply with such a direction is an offence[10].

Measures imposed by an inspector in these circumstances must not be lifted until the Secretary of State has established that the ship can, subject to any necessary conditions, proceed to sea or the operation be resumed without risk to the safety and health of passengers or crew, or risk to other ships, or without there being an unreasonable threat of harm to the marine environment[11]. In exceptional circumstances, where the overall condition of a ship is obviously substandard, the inspector may, in addition to detaining the ship, suspend the inspection of that ship until the responsible parties have taken the steps necessary to ensure that it complies with the Convention requirements[12]. Detained ships may, however, be allowed to proceed for repairs[13].

Provision is made for arbitration in detention matters and for the award of compensation for invalid detention[14]. The risk of port congestion must not be a consideration in a decision to detain a ship or to release a ship from detention[15].

1 As to the meaning of 'ship' see PARA 678 note 1; as to the meaning of 'owner' see PARA 679 note 9.
2 As to the Secretary of State see PARA 36.
3 As to inspections see PARA 679.
4 Ie in accordance with of one of the Conventions listed in PARA 678 note 1.
5 Merchant Shipping (Port State Control) Regulations 2011, SI 2011/2601, reg 9(1).
6 As to the meaning of 'inspector' see PARA 679 note 5.
7 Ie using powers of detention in Convention enactments (ie the Merchant Shipping Act 1995 and statutory instruments made thereunder (including statutory instruments made under an order made thereunder) which implement the Conventions as appropriate), or issuing a prohibition notice under the Merchant Shipping Act 1995 s 262 (see PARA 52), as the case may be: Merchant Shipping (Port State Control) Regulations 2011, SI 2011/2601, regs 2(1), 9(2). Without prejudice to any other requirement in the Convention enactments, when exercising professional judgement as to whether or not a ship should be detained the inspector must apply the criteria set out in

Parliament and Council Directive (EC) 2009/16 (OJ L131, 28.5.2009, p 57) on port state control Annex X: Merchant Shipping (Port State Control) Regulations 2011, SI 2011/2601, reg 9(5).
8 Merchant Shipping (Port State Control) Regulations 2011, SI 2011/2601, reg 9(2). A ship must be detained if it is not equipped with a functioning voyage data recorder system, when its use is compulsory in accordance with Parliament and Council Directive (EC) 2002/59 (OJ L208, 05.08.2002, p 10) establishing a Community vessel traffic monitoring: Merchant Shipping (Port State Control) Regulations 2011, SI 2011/2601, reg 9(6). If such deficiency cannot readily be rectified in the port of detention, the inspector may either allow the ship to proceed to the appropriate repair yard nearest to the port of detention where it is capable of being rectified and is to be so rectified, or require that the deficiency be rectified within a maximum period of 30 days: reg 9(7). Where a ship is detained, relevant authorities must be informed of the detention: see reg 9(9)–(11). Where a ship is a ship to which reg 9(7) applies and fails to proceed to the repair yard specified (reg 23(2)(c)(i)) or fails to comply with the requirement that the deficiency be rectified within 30 days (reg 23(2)(c)(ii)), the owner and master are each guilty of an offence, and liable on summary conviction to a fine (reg 23(2)(c)). As to the powers of magistrates' courts to issue fines on summary conviction see SENTENCING vol 92 (2015) PARA 176. See also reg 23(7)(a); and PARA 679 note 1 (defence of reasonable steps).
9 Merchant Shipping (Port State Control) Regulations 2011, SI 2011/2601, reg 9(3).
10 Subject to the Merchant Shipping (Port State Control) Regulations 2011, SI 2011/2601, 18 (power to permit ship to proceed to repair yard: see note 11), if there is any contravention of a direction made pursuant to reg 9(3) in respect of a ship, the owner and master are each guilty of an offence, and liable on summary conviction to a fine: reg 23(1).
11 Merchant Shipping (Port State Control) Regulations 2011, SI 2011/2601, reg 9(4).
12 Merchant Shipping (Port State Control) Regulations 2011, SI 2011/2601, reg 9(8). The 'Convention requirements' are the requirements of one of the Conventions listed in PARA 678 note 1.
13 Where deficiencies referred to in the Merchant Shipping (Port State Control) Regulations 2011, SI 2011/2601, reg 9(2) cannot be rectified in the port of inspection, an inspector may allow the ship to proceed without undue delay to the appropriate repair yard nearest to the port of detention, as chosen by the master and authorities concerned, where follow-up action can be taken, provided that the conditions determined by the competent authority of the flag administration and agreed by the inspector are complied with: reg 18(1). Such conditions must ensure that the ship can proceed without risk to the safety and health of passengers or crew, or risk to other ships, or without there being an unreasonable threat of harm to the marine environment: reg 18(2). Where a ship is permitted to leave a port pursuant to reg 18(1) but fails to proceed to the repair yard specified, the owner and master are each guilty of an offence, and liable on summary conviction to a fine: reg 23(2)(b).
14 See the Merchant Shipping (Port State Control) Regulations 2011, SI 2011/2601, reg 14(1), (3), (4), 15, 16, 24.
15 Merchant Shipping (Port State Control) Regulations 2011, SI 2011/2601, reg 9(14).

681. Prohibition on detained ships requiring repair entering United Kingdom port.

A ship[1] which has been detained by an EU member state and allowed to proceed to a repair yard[2], and proceeds to sea from any port or anchorage in any member state:

(1) without complying with the conditions determined by the competent authority of the member state in the port of inspection[3]; or

(2) without calling into the indicated repair yard[4],

must not enter any port or anchorage within the United Kingdom[5] until the owner[6] has provided evidence to the satisfaction of the competent authority[7] that the ship fully complies with all applicable Convention requirements[8]. Failure to comply with these requirements is an offence[9].

Certain vessels, flying the flags of states with provably poor safety records, may be refused entry to ports or anchorages in the United Kingdom[10].

1 As to the meaning of 'ship' see PARA 678 note 1.
2 Ie a ship which:
    (1) was detained in a port in a member state after an inspection revealed deficiencies clearly hazardous to safety, health or the environment (Merchant Shipping (Port State Control) Regulations 2011, SI 2011/2601, reg 17(2)(a)); or
    (2) was so detained and was allowed by the competent authority of the member state to proceed to the appropriate repair yard nearest to the port of detention (reg 17(2)(b)).

3   Merchant Shipping (Port State Control) Regulations 2011, SI 2011/2601, reg 17(1)(a).
4   Merchant Shipping (Port State Control) Regulations 2011, SI 2011/2601, reg 17(1)(b).
5   As to the meaning of 'United Kingdom' see PARA 678 note 4.
6   As to the meaning of 'owner' see PARA 679 note 9.
7   Ie the competent authority referred to in note 2.
8   Merchant Shipping (Port State Control) Regulations 2011, SI 2011/2601, reg 17(1). The 'Convention requirements' are the requirements of one of the Conventions listed in PARA 678 note 1.
9   Where a ship enters a port or anchorage in breach of the Merchant Shipping (Port State Control) Regulations 2011, SI 2011/2601, reg 17, the owner and master are each guilty of an offence, and liable on summary conviction to a fine: reg 23(2)(a). As to the powers of magistrates' courts to issue fines on summary conviction see SENTENCING vol 92 (2015) PARA 176. See also reg 23(7)(a); and PARA 679 note 1 (defence of reasonable steps).
10   See the Merchant Shipping (Port State Control) Regulations 2011, SI 2011/2601, regs 10–13, 14(2). Failure to comply with reg 10 is an offence: see reg 23(2)(a).

682. Duty to report anomalies. Where an authorised pilot[1] who is engaged in the berthing or unberthing of a ship[2] in the United Kingdom[3], or is engaged on such a ship bound for a port in the United Kingdom[4] or in transit through United Kingdom waters[5], learns, in the course of his normal duties, that there are apparent anomalies which may prejudice the safe navigation of the ship, or which may pose a threat of harm to the marine environment, he must immediately inform the appropriate authority[6]. If a port authority receives information from a pilot[7] or learns, in the course of its normal duties, that a ship within its port has apparent anomalies which may prejudice the safety of the ship or poses an unreasonable threat of harm to the marine environment, that authority must immediately inform the Secretary of State[8].

1   Ie a pilot who:
    (1)   is authorised under the Pilotage Act 1987 (see PARA 574 et seq) (Merchant Shipping (Port State Control) Regulations 2011, SI 2011/2601, reg 19(2)(a)); or
    (2)   boards the ship in the United Kingdom (reg 19(2)(b)).
    As to the meaning of 'United Kingdom' see PARA 678 note 4.
2   As to the meaning of 'ship' see PARA 678 note 1.
3   Merchant Shipping (Port State Control) Regulations 2011, SI 2011/2601, reg 19(1)(a).
4   Merchant Shipping (Port State Control) Regulations 2011, SI 2011/2601, reg 19(1)(b)(i).
5   Merchant Shipping (Port State Control) Regulations 2011, SI 2011/2601, reg 19(1)(b)(ii).
6   Merchant Shipping (Port State Control) Regulations 2011, SI 2011/2601, reg 19(3). If the pilot falls within reg 19(2)(a) (see note 1), the appropriate authority is the port authority which authorised the pilot (reg 19(3)(a)); in any other case, the appropriate authority is the Secretary of State (reg 19(3)(b)(i)) or the competent authority of a coastal member state (reg 19(3)(b)(ii)). As to the Secretary of State see PARA 36. The information which must be provided in accordance with reg 19(3) or (4) must be in electronic format whenever possible and must include: the ship's name, IMO number and call sign; the flag under which the ship is sailing; the previous port of call; the port of destination; and a description of the apparent anomalies: reg 19(5). As to the meaning of 'port authority' see PARA 679 note 1. A pilot who contravenes reg 19(3) is guilty of an offence and liable on summary conviction to a fine: reg 23(5). As to the powers of magistrates' courts to issue fines on summary conviction see SENTENCING vol 92 (2015) PARA 176. See also reg 23(7)(a); and PARA 679 note 1 (defence of reasonable steps).
7   Ie in accordance with the Merchant Shipping (Port State Control) Regulations 2011, SI 2011/2601, reg 19(3)(a) (see note 6).
8   Merchant Shipping (Port State Control) Regulations 2011, SI 2011/2601, reg 19(4). A port authority which contravenes reg 19(4) is guilty of an offence and liable on summary conviction to a fine: reg 23(6). See note 6.

683. Complaints. If a complaint relating to a ship[1] is submitted to the Secretary of State, the Secretary of State must make an assessment of it as quickly as possible to determine whether it is justified[2], and if the complaint is determined to be justified the Secretary of State must:
    (1)   inform the complainant of that conclusion and of any follow-up action taken with regard to the complaint[3];
    (2)   ensure that anyone directly concerned by that complaint can make their views known[4];

(3)	take such action as he considers necessary[5]; and
(4)	inform the administration of the ship's flag state, and the International Labour Organisation if appropriate, of the complaint and action taken[6].

If the complaint is determined not to be justified, the Secretary of State must inform the complainant of the reasons for this conclusion[7].

1	As to the meaning of 'ship' see PARA 678 note 1. The identity of the complainant must not be revealed to the master or owner of the ship concerned by the Secretary of State or by an inspector: Merchant Shipping (Port State Control) Regulations 2011, SI 2011/2601, reg 21(4). As to the meaning of 'owner' see PARA 679 note 9. As to the Secretary of State see PARA 36. As to the meaning of 'inspector' see PARA 679 note 5. An inspector interviewing any members of the crew of the ship concerning the complaint must ensure confidentiality during such interviews and report on such interviews to the Secretary of State: reg 21(5).
2	Merchant Shipping (Port State Control) Regulations 2011, SI 2011/2601, reg 21(1).
3	Merchant Shipping (Port State Control) Regulations 2011, SI 2011/2601, reg 21(2)(a).
4	Merchant Shipping (Port State Control) Regulations 2011, SI 2011/2601, reg 21(2)(b).
5	Merchant Shipping (Port State Control) Regulations 2011, SI 2011/2601, reg 21(2)(c).
6	Merchant Shipping (Port State Control) Regulations 2011, SI 2011/2601, reg 21(2)(d).
7	Merchant Shipping (Port State Control) Regulations 2011, SI 2011/2601, reg 21(3).

(6) SHIP AND PORT FACILITY SECURITY

684. Application of the ship and port facility security regulations. The ship and port facility security regulations[1] apply to:
(1)	the following types of United Kingdom ships[2] and non-United Kingdom ships[3] in United Kingdom waters[4] when engaged on international voyages[5], and their companies[6]:
	(a)	passenger ships including high speed craft which carry more than 12 passengers[7];
	(b)	cargo ships, including high speed craft, of 500 gross tonnage and upwards[8];
	(c)	mobile offshore drilling units[9],
(2)	Class A passenger ships[10] operating domestic services within United Kingdom waters and their companies[11];
(3)	port facilities serving the ships specified in heads (1) and (2) above[12].
The ship and port facility security regulations[13] do not apply to:
(i)	ships of war and troop ships[14];
(ii)	cargo ships of less than 500 gross tonnage[15];
(iii)	ships not propelled by mechanical means[16];
(iv)	wooden ships of primitive build[17];
(v)	pleasure yachts not engaged in trade[18];
(vi)	fishing vessels[19]; and
(vii)	vessels not engaged in commercial activities[20].

1	Ie the Ship and Port Facility (Security) Regulations 2004, SI 2004/1495, which implement Parliament and Council Regulation (EC) 725/2004 (OJ L129, 29.04.2004, p 6) on enhancing ship and port facility security (see the Ship and Port Facility (Security) Regulations 2004, SI 2004/1495, reg 3). Certain expressions used in the Ship and Port Facility (Security) Regulations 2004, SI 2004/1495, are defined by reference to Parliament and Council Regulation (EC) 725/2004 (OJ L129, 29.04.2004, p 6) and the SOLAS Convention (as to which see note 5): see the Ship and Port Facility (Security) Regulations 2004, SI 2004/1495, reg 2(2), (3), Schedule.
2	For these purposes, 'United Kingdom ship' has the same meaning as in the Merchant Shipping Act 1995 s 85(2) (as to which see PARA 602 note 1): Ship and Port Facility (Security) Regulations 2004, SI 2004/1495, reg 2(1).
3	For these purposes, 'Non-United Kingdom ship' means a ship other than a United Kingdom ship: Ship and Port Facility (Security) Regulations 2004, SI 2004/1495, reg 2(1).
4	For these purposes, 'United Kingdom waters' means the sea or other waters within the seaward limits of the territorial sea of the United Kingdom: Ship and Port Facility (Security) Regulations

2004, SI 2004/1495, reg 2(1). As to the meaning of 'United Kingdom' see PARA 17 note 3. As to the territorial sea generally see INTERNATIONAL RELATIONS LAW vol 61 (2010) PARA 123.

5   For these purposes, 'international voyage' means a voyage from a country to which the SOLAS Convention applies to a port outside such country, or conversely; and 'SOLAS Convention' means the International Convention for the Safety of Life at Sea 1974 (London, 1 November 1974 to 1 July 1975; TS 46 (1980); Cmnd 7874) ('SOLAS Convention'), with Protocol (London, 1 June 1978 to 1 March 1979; TS 40 (1981); Cmnd 8277) (as to which see PARA 7) as amended from time to time, in so far as those amendments are integrated in Community maritime legislation in accordance with Parliament and Council Regulation (EC) 725/2004 (OJ L129, 29.04.2004, p 6) art 10 (integration of amendments to international instruments): Ship and Port Facility (Security) Regulations 2004, SI 2004/1495, reg 2(1).

6   Ship and Port Facility (Security) Regulations 2004, SI 2004/1495, reg 4(1)(a).

7   Ship and Port Facility (Security) Regulations 2004, SI 2004/1495, reg 4(1)(a)(i).

8   Ship and Port Facility (Security) Regulations 2004, SI 2004/1495, reg 4(1)(a)(ii).

9   Ship and Port Facility (Security) Regulations 2004, SI 2004/1495, reg 4(1)(a)(iii).

10   For these purposes, 'Class A passenger ships' are passenger ships within the meaning of Council Directive (EC) 98/18 (OJ L144, 15.05.1998, p 1) on Safety Rules and Standards for Passenger Ships art 4 (see PARA 605), in which 'Class A' means a passenger ship engaged on domestic voyages other than voyages covered by Classes B, C and D in art 4: Ship and Port Facility (Security) Regulations 2004, SI 2004/1495, reg 2(1).

11   Ship and Port Facility (Security) Regulations 2004, SI 2004/1495, reg 4(1)(b). 'Domestic shipping' means any transport service by ship in sea areas from a port facility of the United Kingdom to the same port facility or another port facility within the United Kingdom: reg 2(1).

12   Ship and Port Facility (Security) Regulations 2004, SI 2004/1495, reg 4(1)(c).

13   Ie the Ship and Port Facility (Security) Regulations 2004, SI 2004/1495: see reg 4(2).

14   Ship and Port Facility (Security) Regulations 2004, SI 2004/1495, reg 4(2)(a).

15   Ship and Port Facility (Security) Regulations 2004, SI 2004/1495, reg 4(2)(b).

16   Ship and Port Facility (Security) Regulations 2004, SI 2004/1495, reg 4(2)(c).

17   Ship and Port Facility (Security) Regulations 2004, SI 2004/1495, reg 4(2)(d).

18   Ship and Port Facility (Security) Regulations 2004, SI 2004/1495, reg 4(2)(e).

19   Ship and Port Facility (Security) Regulations 2004, SI 2004/1495, reg 4(2)(f).

20   Ship and Port Facility (Security) Regulations 2004, SI 2004/1495, reg 4(2)(g).

685. Powers of inspection exercisable in relation to ships and port facilities.

A duly authorised officer[1] has the power[2], on production, if required, of his credentials, to inspect[3]:

   (1)   any United Kingdom ship[4];
   (2)   any non-United Kingdom ship[5] while in a port facility[6];
   (3)   any non-United Kingdom ship in United Kingdom waters[7] which has communicated its intention to enter a port in the United Kingdom[8];
   (4)   any United Kingdom port facility[9].

A duly authorised officer inspecting a ship or a port facility has the following powers[10]:

   (a)   to subject any property found by him on the ship, or any apparatus or equipment installed on the ship which is required by or approved in the relevant ship security plan to such tests[11];
   (b)   to subject any part of the port facility or any property found by him in the port facility, or any apparatus or equipment installed in the port facility which is required by or approved in the relevant port facility security plan to such tests[12];
   (c)   to take such steps to ascertain what practices or procedures are being followed in relation to security, or to test the effectiveness of any practice or procedure relating to security[13]; or
   (d)   to require the company, or the company security officer, or the ship security officer, or the master of the ship, or the port facility security officer, or the owner of the port facility security plan, or person acting on behalf of any of those persons to furnish to him such information[14],

to be exercised as the duly authorised officer may consider necessary for the purpose for which the inspection is carried out[15].

A duly authorised officer, for the purpose of exercising any power so conferred on him[16] in relation to a ship or in relation to a port facility, may[17]:

(i)   for the purpose of inspecting a ship, go on board and take all such steps as are necessary to ensure that it is not moved[18]; or

(ii)   for the purpose of inspecting a port facility, enter any building or works in the port facility or enter any land in the port facility[19].

However, the powers conferred under heads (i) and (ii) above do not include power for a duly authorised officer to use force for the purpose of going on board any ship, entering any building or works or entering any land[20].

Any person who, without reasonable excuse, fails to comply with a requirement imposed on him under head (d) above, or who, in furnishing any information so required makes a statement which he knows to be false in a material particular, or recklessly makes a statement which is false in a material particular, commits an offence[21].

1   For these purposes, 'duly authorised officer' means either an inspector or a surveyor appointed under the Merchant Shipping Act 1995 s 256 (as to which see PARA 46), or an 'authorised person' within the meaning of the Aviation and Maritime Security Act 1990 s 46(1) (see PORTS AND HARBOURS vol 85 (2012) PARA 126): Ship and Port Facility (Security) Regulations 2004, SI 2004/1495, reg 2(1). A person who intentionally obstructs a duly authorised officer acting in the exercise of a power duly conferred upon him (as to which see the text and notes 2–15), or who falsely pretends to be a duly authorised officer, commits an offence: see reg 12; and PARA 1132.

2   Ie for the purpose of enabling a duly authorised officer to verify that ships and port facilities are in compliance with the requirements of Parliament and Council Regulation (EC) 725/2004 (OJ L129, 29.04.2004, p 6) on enhancing ship and port facility security (as to which see PARA 684) or of of ascertaining whether any enforcement notice is being or has been complied with: see the Ship and Port Facility (Security) Regulations 2004, SI 2004/1495, reg 6(1). As to enforcement notices see PARA 689.

The following persons are required to submit to such inspections of ships and port facilities that are conducted pursuant to Parliament and Council Regulation (EC) 725/2004 (OJ L129, 29.04.2004, p 6) art 9 (implementation and conformity checking):

(1)   the company (Ship and Port Facility (Security) Regulations 2004, SI 2004/1495, reg 7(1)(a));

(2)   the company security officer (reg 7(1)(b));

(3)   the ship security officer (reg 7(1)(c));

(4)   the master of a ship (reg 7(1)(d));

(5)   the port facility security officer (reg 7(1)(e)); and

(6)   the owner of the port facility security plan (reg 7(1)(f)).

For these purposes, 'master' includes every person, except a pilot, having command or charge of a ship, 'owner of the port facility security plan' means the person who submits the port facility security plan or the person on whose behalf that plan is submitted to the Secretary of State for approval under the ISPS Code Pt A section 16.2; and 'ISPS Code' means the International Ship and Port Facility Security Code (see PARA 684) as amended from time to time, in so far as those amendments are integrated in Community maritime legislation in accordance with Parliament and Council Regulation (EC) 725/2004 (OJ L129, 29.04.2004, p 6) art 10: Ship and Port Facility (Security) Regulations 2004, SI 2004/1495, reg 2(1). As to the meaning of 'SOLAS Convention' see PARA 684 note 5.

The persons referred to in heads (1) to (6) above must take all necessary steps to remedy any shortcomings identified following such an inspection as are notified to them in writing by the Secretary of State, and must do so within such period as may be required in the notification: Ship and Port Facility (Security) Regulations 2004, SI 2004/1495, reg 7(2). As to the Secretary of State see PARA 36.

3   Ship and Port Facility (Security) Regulations 2004, SI 2004/1495, reg 6(1).

4   Ship and Port Facility (Security) Regulations 2004, SI 2004/1495, reg 6(1)(a). As to the meaning of 'United Kingdom ship' see PARA 684 note 2.

5   As to the meaning of 'non-United Kingdom ship' see PARA 684 note 3.

6   Ship and Port Facility (Security) Regulations 2004, SI 2004/1495, reg 6(1)(b).

7   As to the meaning of 'United Kingdom waters' see PARA 684 note 4.

8   Ship and Port Facility (Security) Regulations 2004, SI 2004/1495, reg 6(1)(c).

9   Ship and Port Facility (Security) Regulations 2004, SI 2004/1495, reg 6(1)(d).

10 Ship and Port Facility (Security) Regulations 2004, SI 2004/1495, reg 6(2).

11 Ship and Port Facility (Security) Regulations 2004, SI 2004/1495, reg 6(2)(a).
12 Ship and Port Facility (Security) Regulations 2004, SI 2004/1495, reg 6(2)(b).
13 Ship and Port Facility (Security) Regulations 2004, SI 2004/1495, reg 6(2)(c).
14 Ship and Port Facility (Security) Regulations 2004, SI 2004/1495, reg 6(2)(d).
15 Ship and Port Facility (Security) Regulations 2004, SI 2004/1495, reg 6(2).
16 Ie by the Ship and Port Facility (Security) Regulations 2004, SI 2004/1495, reg 6(1), (2) (see the
    text and notes 1–15): see reg 6(3).
17 Ship and Port Facility (Security) Regulations 2004, SI 2004/1495, reg 6(3).
18 Ship and Port Facility (Security) Regulations 2004, SI 2004/1495, reg 6(3)(a).
19 Ship and Port Facility (Security) Regulations 2004, SI 2004/1495, reg 6(3)(b).
20 Ship and Port Facility (Security) Regulations 2004, SI 2004/1495, reg 6(4).
21 See the Ship and Port Facility (Security) Regulations 2004, SI 2004/1495, reg 6(5); and PARA 1132.

686. Retention of records related to ship and port facility security. The
master[1] is responsible for ensuring that records of activities, as specified in Part A
of the ISPS Code[2], and which are addressed in the ship security plan, are kept on
board the ship for a period of at least three years from the date of the activity
taking place[3].

Any declaration of security which is completed in respect of a ship or port
facility must be retained for a period of at least three years after it was last used[4]:

(1)   in respect of ships, on board the ship by the master[5]; and
(2)   in respect of port facilities, by the port facility security officer[6].

1 As to the meaning of 'master' see PARA 685 note 2.
2 Ie the activities specified in the ISPS Code Pt A section 10.1: see the Ship and Port Facility (Security)
   Regulations 2004, SI 2004/1495, reg 17. As to the meaning of 'ISPS Code' see PARA 685 note 2.
3 Ship and Port Facility (Security) Regulations 2004, SI 2004/1495, reg 17.
4 Ship and Port Facility (Security) Regulations 2004, SI 2004/1495, reg 18(1).
5 Ship and Port Facility (Security) Regulations 2004, SI 2004/1495, reg 18(1)(a). In the case of ships,
   any completed declaration of security relating to one of its last ten calls at port facilities must be
   retained on board the ship by the master for as long as it relates to any of those last ten calls, even
   where the period over which those calls extend exceeds the minimum three-year period referred to
   in reg 18(1) (see the text and notes 4–5): reg 18(2).
6 Ship and Port Facility (Security) Regulations 2004, SI 2004/1495, reg 18(1)(b).

687. Procedure for making amendments to security plans. In accordance
with the ISPS Code[1], the Secretary of State[2] must decide (and thereafter must
notify companies and owners of port facility security plans, in writing, of) the
changes or amendments to the relevant approved ship security plan or port facility
security plan that must first be submitted to him for approval before they are
implemented in respect of those ships and port facilities[3]. Any changes or
amendments notified in this way[4] must not be implemented by the companies or
owners of port facility security plans without first obtaining the approval of the
Secretary of State[5].

1 As to the meaning of 'ISPS Code' see PARA 685 note 2.
2 As to the Secretary of State see PARA 36.
3 Ship and Port Facility (Security) Regulations 2004, SI 2004/1495, reg 19(1).
4 Ie the changes or amendments referred to in the Ship and Port Facility (Security) Regulations 2004,
   SI 2004/1495, reg 19(1) (see the text and notes 1–3): see reg 19(2).
5 Ship and Port Facility (Security) Regulations 2004, SI 2004/1495, reg 19(2).

688. Detention notices; the procedure relating to objections. Where a duly
authorised officer[1] proposes to detain a ship pursuant to control and compliance
measures[2], he must serve on the master[3] of the ship a notice (a 'detention notice')[4].
A detention notice must specify the steps that the duly authorised officer requires
to be taken in respect of the ship in order to secure its release from detention[5], and
must require the master to take steps to ensure that the ship does not proceed to
sea while the detention notice is in force[6].

The master of a ship in respect of which a detention notice is served may object
to the notice in writing to the Secretary of State[7]. On receipt of an objection to a
detention notice, the Secretary of State must:

(1)   consider the objection[8];
(2)   allow the person making the objection and the duly authorised officer who gave the notice an opportunity to make written or oral representations to the Secretary of State or a person appointed by him[9];
(3)   confirm, modify or cancel the notice[10]; and
(4)   give notice of his decision in writing to the person who made the objection and to the duly authorised officer who served the notice[11].

The Secretary of State must include in his decision a finding as to whether in relation to any of the matters specified in respect of a ship in a detention notice, there was or was not a valid basis for the detention of the ship[12]. A detention notice in respect of a ship continues in force until a duly authorised officer cancels it by notice in writing[13] or until the Secretary of State cancels it under head (3) above[14]. A person commits an offence if without reasonable excuse he fails to comply with a requirement of a detention notice[15].

Where, having considered an objection in respect of a detention notice relating to a ship[16], the Secretary of State finds that there was no valid basis for the detention, the owner of the ship is entitled, on application, to receive compensation for such loss or damage suffered by him which is directly attributable to the detention of the ship[17]. Such a claim for compensation must be made in writing to the Secretary of State within three months beginning with the date the Secretary of State serves notice of his decision under head (4) above[18]. Any person claiming compensation in this way[19] must provide all such information and supplementary information in respect of the loss or damage incurred as the Secretary of State may at any time reasonably require and must verify the same in any such manner, including the production of original documents in his possession or control, as may be reasonably required[20].

1   As to the meaning of 'duly authorised officer' for these purposes see PARA 685 note 1.
2   Ie pursuant to the control and compliance measures specified in the SOLAS Convention Ch XI-2 reg 9: see the Ship and Port Facility (Security) Regulations 2004, SI 2004/1495, reg 8(1). As to the meaning of 'SOLAS Convention' see PARA 684 note 5.
3   As to the meaning of 'master' see PARA 685 note 2.
4   Ship and Port Facility (Security) Regulations 2004, SI 2004/1495, reg 8(1). The detention notice must state that the duly authorised officer is detaining the ship because he has grounds for believing that:
    (1)   the ship is not in compliance with the SOLAS Convention Ch XI-2 (Ship and Port Facility (Security) Regulations 2004, SI 2004/1495, reg 8(1)(a));
    (2)   the ship is not in compliance with the ISPS Code Pt A (Ship and Port Facility (Security) Regulations 2004, SI 2004/1495, reg 8(1)(b)); or
    (3)   there has been a failure to make available for inspection a valid International Ship Security Certificate or a valid Interim International Ship Security Certificate issued under the ISPS Code Pt A (Ship and Port Facility (Security) Regulations 2004, SI 2004/1495, reg 8(1)(c)).
    As to the meaning of 'ISPS Code' see PARA 685 note 2. As to the service of notices (including by means of electronic communication) under the Ship and Port Facility (Security) Regulations 2004, SI 2004/1495, see reg 20 (amended by SI 2006/2190).
5   Ship and Port Facility (Security) Regulations 2004, SI 2004/1495, reg 8(2).
6   Ship and Port Facility (Security) Regulations 2004, SI 2004/1495, reg 8(3).
7   Ship and Port Facility (Security) Regulations 2004, SI 2004/1495, reg 8(4). As to the Secretary of State see PARA 36.
8   Ship and Port Facility (Security) Regulations 2004, SI 2004/1495, reg 8(5)(a).
9   Ship and Port Facility (Security) Regulations 2004, SI 2004/1495, reg 8(5)(b).
10 Ship and Port Facility (Security) Regulations 2004, SI 2004/1495, reg 8(5)(c).
11 Ship and Port Facility (Security) Regulations 2004, SI 2004/1495, reg 8(5)(d).
12 Ship and Port Facility (Security) Regulations 2004, SI 2004/1495, reg 8(6).
13 Ship and Port Facility (Security) Regulations 2004, SI 2004/1495, reg 8(7)(a).
14 Ship and Port Facility (Security) Regulations 2004, SI 2004/1495, reg 8(7)(b).
15 See the Ship and Port Facility (Security) Regulations 2004, SI 2004/1495, reg 8(8); and PARA 1132.

16 Ie under the Ship and Port Facility (Security) Regulations 2004, SI 2004/1495, reg 8 (see the text and notes 1–15): see reg 9(1).
17 Ship and Port Facility (Security) Regulations 2004, SI 2004/1495, reg 9(1). Any compensation granted under reg 9 is payable by the Secretary of State (reg 9(5)); and any disputed question as to the right to (or the amount of) any compensation payable under reg 9 must be referred to a single arbitrator appointed by agreement between the parties for that question to be decided by him (reg 9(4)).
18 Ship and Port Facility (Security) Regulations 2004, SI 2004/1495, reg 9(2).
19 Ie under the Ship and Port Facility (Security) Regulations 2004, SI 2004/1495, reg 9: see reg 9(3).
20 Ship and Port Facility (Security) Regulations 2004, SI 2004/1495, reg 9(3).

689. Enforcement notices; the procedure relating to objections. Where it appears to a duly authorised officer[1] that any of the following persons[2], namely:

(1)   the company[3];
(2)   the company security officer[4];
(3)   the ship security officer[5];
(4)   the master[6] of a ship[7];
(5)   the port facility security officer[8];
(6)   the owner of the port facility security plan[9]; or
(7)   any person who carries on port operations in a port facility[10],

has failed to comply with the relevant specified requirements of the SOLAS Convention[11], the ISPS Code[12], or the ship and port facility security regulations[13], that duly authorised officer may serve a notice (an 'enforcement notice') on that person[14]. An enforcement notice:

(a)   must state the matters which appear to the duly authorised officer to constitute a failure to comply with the requirements duly specified in the SOLAS Convention, in the ISPS Code, or in the ship and port facility security regulations[15];

(b)   may be framed so as to afford the person on whom it is served a choice between different ways of complying with the requirements set out in the notice[16];

(c)   must specify the steps which the duly authorised officer requires to be taken (or the activity or the activities which the duly authorised officer requires to cease) in order to achieve compliance with the specified requirements mentioned in head (a) above[17];

(d)   must specify the date on which it is to take effect and takes effect on that date[18]; and

(e)   must specify the period at the end of which any steps are required to have been taken (or any activities are required to have ceased) and may specify different periods for different steps or activities[19].

Any person who without reasonable excuse fails to comply with an enforcement notice served on him is guilty of an offence[20].

A person on whom an enforcement notice is served may serve on the Secretary of State a notice in writing of his objection to the enforcement notice[21]. The grounds of objection to an enforcement notice are:

(i)   that the steps required by the notice to be taken as mentioned in heads (a) to (e) above[22] have been complied with[23];

(ii)   that the matters stated in the enforcement notice in accordance with head (a) above do not constitute a failure to comply with the requirements mentioned there[24];

(iii)   that any requirement of the notice is unnecessary for complying with the specified requirements[25] and should be dispensed with or, having regard to the terms of those requirements, is excessively onerous or inconvenient and should be modified in a manner specified in the notice of objection[26].

An objection to an enforcement notice must be served on the Secretary of State within seven days of the date on which the enforcement notice was served[27].

Where the person on whom an enforcement notice is served serves a notice objecting to the enforcement notice[28], the Secretary of State must consider the grounds of the objection and, if so required by the objector, must afford to him an opportunity of appearing before and being heard by a person appointed by the Secretary of State for the purpose[29]. The Secretary of State must then serve on the objector a notice in writing either confirming the enforcement notice as originally served[30], or confirming it subject to one or more modifications specified in the notice[31], or cancelling the enforcement notice[32]. An enforcement notice to which an objection has been made may not take effect until it has been so confirmed (with or without modification) by such a notice[33].

An enforcement notice served on any person may be revoked by a notice served on him by a duly authorised officer, and may be varied by a further enforcement notice served on him by a duly authorised officer[34].

1   As to the meaning of 'duly authorised officer' for these purposes see PARA 685 note 1.
2   See the Ship and Port Facility (Security) Regulations 2004, SI 2004/1495, reg 13(1).
3   Ship and Port Facility (Security) Regulations 2004, SI 2004/1495, reg 13(2)(a).
4   Ship and Port Facility (Security) Regulations 2004, SI 2004/1495, reg 13(2)(b).
5   Ship and Port Facility (Security) Regulations 2004, SI 2004/1495, reg 13(2)(c).
6   As to the meaning of 'master' see PARA 685 note 2.
7   Ship and Port Facility (Security) Regulations 2004, SI 2004/1495, reg 13(2)(d).
8   Ship and Port Facility (Security) Regulations 2004, SI 2004/1495, reg 13(2)(e).
9   Ship and Port Facility (Security) Regulations 2004, SI 2004/1495, reg 13(2)(f).
10 Ship and Port Facility (Security) Regulations 2004, SI 2004/1495, reg 13(2)(g).
11 Ie the requirements of the SOLAS Convention Ch XI-2: see the Ship and Port Facility (Security) Regulations 2004, SI 2004/1495, reg 13(1)(a). As to the meaning of 'SOLAS Convention' see PARA 684 note 5.
12 Ie the requirements of the ISPS Code Pt A or of the ISPS Code Pt B para 1.12, 6.1, 8.3, 8.5, 8.7–8.10, 13.6, 13.7, 18.5 or 18.6: see the Ship and Port Facility (Security) Regulations 2004, SI 2004/1495, reg 13(1)(b), (c). As to the meaning of 'ISPS Code' see PARA 685 note 2.
13 Ie the requirement to submit to an inspection and to rectify any shortcomings identified following such an inspection in accordance with the Ship and Port Facility (Security) Regulations 2004, SI 2004/1495, reg 7 (see PARA 685) (see reg 13(1)(d)); or the requirement to submit specified changes or amendments to a ship security plan or a port facility security plan to the Secretary of State for approval in accordance with reg 19 (see PARA 687) (reg 13(1)(e)). As to the Secretary of State see PARA 36.
14 See the Ship and Port Facility (Security) Regulations 2004, SI 2004/1495, reg 13(1). As to the service of notices (including by means of electronic communication) under the Ship and Port Facility (Security) Regulations 2004, SI 2004/1495, see reg 20 (amended by SI 2006/2190).
15 Ship and Port Facility (Security) Regulations 2004, SI 2004/1495, reg 14(1). Head (a) in the text refers to a failure to comply with the requirements specified in reg 13 (see the text and notes 1–14): see reg 14(1).
16 Ship and Port Facility (Security) Regulations 2004, SI 2004/1495, reg 14(2). An enforcement notice requiring a person not to cause or permit anything to be done must be construed as requiring him to take all such steps as in any particular circumstances are practicable and necessary to prevent that thing from being done: reg 14(7).
17 Ship and Port Facility (Security) Regulations 2004, SI 2004/1495, reg 14(3). Head (c) in the text refers to compliance with the requirements specified in reg 13 (see the text and notes 1–14): see reg 14(3).
18 Ship and Port Facility (Security) Regulations 2004, SI 2004/1495, reg 14(4).
19 Ship and Port Facility (Security) Regulations 2004, SI 2004/1495, reg 14(5). Where different periods apply to different steps or activities, references in the Ship and Port Facility (Security)

Regulations 2004, SI 2004/1495, to the period for compliance with an enforcement notice, in relation to any step or activity, are to the period at the end of which the step is required to have been taken or the activity is required to have ceased: reg 14(6).

20 See the Ship and Port Facility (Security) Regulations 2004, SI 2004/1495, reg 15; and PARA 1132.
21 Ship and Port Facility (Security) Regulations 2004, SI 2004/1495, reg 16(1).
22 Ie the steps required to be taken for the purposes of the Ship and Port Facility (Security) Regulations 2004, SI 2004/1495, reg 13 (see the text and notes 1–14): see reg 16(2)(a).
23 Ship and Port Facility (Security) Regulations 2004, SI 2004/1495, reg 16(2)(a).
24 Ship and Port Facility (Security) Regulations 2004, SI 2004/1495, reg 16(2)(b) (substituted by SI 2005/1434). The text refers to the requirements specified in the Ship and Port Facility (Security) Regulations 2004, SI 2004/1495, reg 13 (see the text and notes 1–14): see reg 16(2)(b) (as so substituted).
25 Ie the requirements specified in the Ship and Port Facility (Security) Regulations 2004, SI 2004/1495, reg 13 (see the text and notes 1–14): see reg 16(2)(c).
26 Ship and Port Facility (Security) Regulations 2004, SI 2004/1495, reg 16(2)(c).
27 Ship and Port Facility (Security) Regulations 2004, SI 2004/1495, reg 16(3). A person making an objection to an enforcement notice under reg 16 must submit to the Secretary of State (either when making the objection or within the seven days referred to in reg 16(3)) a statement in writing specifying the grounds on which he is objecting to the enforcement notice, and providing such further information as may be appropriate: reg 16(4).
28 Ie under the Ship and Port Facility (Security) Regulations 2004, SI 2004/1495, reg 16(1) (see the text and note 21): see reg 16(5).
29 Ship and Port Facility (Security) Regulations 2004, SI 2004/1495, reg 16(5).
30 Ship and Port Facility (Security) Regulations 2004, SI 2004/1495, reg 16(5)(a).
31 Ship and Port Facility (Security) Regulations 2004, SI 2004/1495, reg 16(5)(b).
32 Ship and Port Facility (Security) Regulations 2004, SI 2004/1495, reg 16(5)(c).
33 Ship and Port Facility (Security) Regulations 2004, SI 2004/1495, reg 16(6).
34 Ship and Port Facility (Security) Regulations 2004, SI 2004/1495, reg 16(7).

8. COLLISIONS

(1) PREVENTION OF COLLISIONS

(i) Domestic and International Rules

690. Meaning of 'collision' and application of the Collision Regulations.
Liability for collision — ie, damage sustained by a ship as a result of another ship
coming into contact with her[1]— and matters relating to the prevention and
avoidance of collision generally, are governed by the Collision Regulations[2], with
which all United Kingdom ships, hovercraft and seaplanes and non-United
Kingdom ships, hovercraft and seaplanes in United Kingdom waters[3] are required
to comply[4].

1 *Everard v Kendall* (1870) LR 5 CP 428; *The Normandy* [1904] P 187, 9 Asp MLC 568, DC; *The
   Upcerne* [1912] P 160, 12 Asp MLC 281. Damage done by a ship to a pier or other structure on
   land is not damage by collision for this purpose: cf *The Normandy*; *Gartland Steamship Co and
   Lablanc v R* [1960] 1 Lloyd's Rep 388 (Can SC). As to collisions with piers see PARA 765. As to
   the interpretation of a collision clause in a marine insurance policy see INSURANCE vol 60 (2011)
   PARAS 336–338.
2 Ie the International Regulations for Preventing Collisions at Sea (London, 20 October 1972; TS 77
   (1977); Cmnd 6962) (as to which see PARA 7). It would seem that it is also the purpose of the
   Collision Regulations to minimise the results of collision: see *Stoomvaart Maatschappy Nederland
   v Peninsular and Oriental Steam Navigation Co* (1880) 5 App Cas 876 at 903, 904, HL, per Lord
   Watson. See also *Barnes v The Charterers of the Motor Vessel (The Snow Bunting)* [2012] 2
   Lloyd's Rep 647.
3 The Merchant Shipping (Distress Signals and Prevention of Collisions) Regulations 1996, SI
   1996/75 (see also PARA 726) apply (by virtue of reg 2(1)) to:
   (1)   United Kingdom ships, wherever they may be, and other ships while within the United
          Kingdom or the territorial waters thereof; and
   (2)   seaplanes registered in the United Kingdom and on the surface of water anywhere, and
          other seaplanes on the surface of water in the United Kingdom or the territorial waters
          thereof.
   As to the meaning of 'United Kingdom' see PARA 16 note 3. For these purposes, 'ships'
   includes hovercraft: reg 2(2). In connection with vessels and seaplanes in this context see PARA 691
   note 2. As to the territorial sea generally see INTERNATIONAL RELATIONS LAW vol 61 (2010)
   PARA 123; and WATER AND WATERWAYS vol 100 (2009) PARA 31.
4 Vessels to which the Merchant Shipping (Distress Signals and Prevention of Collisions)
   Regulations 1996, SI 1996/75 apply must comply with the Collision Regulations rr 1–36, Annexes
   I–III (as to which see PARA 690 et seq): see the Merchant Shipping (Distress Signals and Prevention
   of Collisions) Regulations 1996, SI 1996/75, reg 4(1). The provisions of the Collision Regulations
   relating to distress signals (ie r 37, Annex IV) are also directly applied to such vessels: see the
   Merchant Shipping (Distress Signals and Prevention of Collisions) Regulations 1996, SI 1996/75,
   reg 3; and PARA 726. There are limited exemptions for certain older vessels: see reg 4(2); and the
   Collision Regulations r 38. The Secretary of State may also exempt any ship or description of ships
   from all or any of the provisions of the Merchant Shipping (Distress Signals and Prevention of
   Collisions) Regulations 1996, SI 1996/75, which relate to the number, position, range or arc of
   visibility of lights or shapes, as well as the disposition and characteristics of sound-signalling
   appliances if he is satisfied that compliance with such provision is either impractical or
   unreasonable in the case of that ship or description of ships in such terms, if any, as he may specify
   and may, subject to giving reasonable notice, alter or cancel any such exemption: reg 5. As to the
   Secretary of State see PARA 36.
   For the purposes of the Merchant Shipping (Distress Signals and Prevention of Collisions)
   Regulations 1996, SI 1996/75, 'International Regulations' means the Collision Regulations as
   amended by Resolutions A464(XII), A626(15), A678(16) and A736(18) of the International
   Maritime Organization ('IMO'), and by any further Resolutions of the IMO which the Secretary
   of State notifies by Merchant Shipping Notice that he considers relevant from time to time:
   Merchant Shipping (Distress Signals and Prevention of Collisions) Regulations 1996, SI 1996/75,
   reg 1(3). 'Merchant Shipping Notice' means a Notice described as such and issued by the Maritime
   and Coastguard Agency: reg 1(3). Accordingly, Merchant Shipping Notice 1781(M) sets out the
   Collision Regulations as amended by Resolutions A464(XII), A626(15), A678(16), A736(18) and
   A.910(22) of the IMO, and Merchant Shipping Notice 1781(M), and the rules referred to in it,

form an integral part of the Merchant Shipping (Distress Signals and Prevention of Collisions) Regulations 1996, SI 1996/75: see Merchant Shipping Notice 1781(M) Introduction paras 1–3. The application of the Rules contained in the Collision Regulations is limited, through the Merchant Shipping (Distress Signals and Prevention of Collisions) Regulations 1996, SI 1996/75, to the vessels or ships as defined in the Merchant Shipping Act 1995; and application to craft falling outside of this definition is subject to a Maritime and Coastguard Agency opinion of what it considers to be good conduct and practice by the owners, operators and those in charge of such craft: see Merchant Shipping Notice 1781(M) Introduction para 4. As to the International Maritime Organisation see PARA 12; as to the Maritime and Coastguard Agency see PARA 57.

691. Scope of the rules. The Collision Regulations[1] apply to all vessels[2] upon the high seas and in all waters connected therewith navigable by sea-going vessels[3]. Nothing in those rules interferes with the operation of special rules duly made by an appropriate authority for roadsteads, harbours, rivers, lakes or inland waterways connected with the high seas and navigable by sea-going vessels; but such special rules must conform as closely as possible to the Collision Regulations[4]. If there is conflict between a local rule and one of the rules of the Collision Regulations, the local rule prevails[5]. Where local rules make no provision at all, they are to be supplemented by the Collision Regulations, but this is not to be done where a local rule provides adequately for a situation although differently from the general regulations[6]. A local rule which has not been duly made by a competent authority may nevertheless represent a standard of care to which seamen should conform[7]; and well-recognised practice and long usage may give such a rule the force of law[8].

Nothing in the rules interferes with the operation of any special rules made by the government of any state with respect to additional station or signal lights, shapes or whistle signals for ships of war and vessels proceeding under convoy, or with respect to additional station or signal lights for fishing vessels engaged in fishing[9] as a fleet[10]. These additional station or signal lights, shapes or whistle signals must, so far as possible, be such that they cannot be mistaken for any light, shape or signal authorised elsewhere under the rules[11].

Traffic separation schemes may be adopted by the International Maritime Organisation[12] for the purpose of the rules[13].

Whenever the government concerned has determined that a vessel of any special construction or purpose cannot comply fully with the provisions of any of the rules with respect to the number, position, range or arc of visibility of lights or shapes[14], as well as to the disposition and characteristics of sound-signalling appliances[15], such vessel must comply with such other provisions in regard to the number, position, range or arc of visibility of lights or shapes, as well as to the disposition and characteristics of sound-signalling appliances, as her government has determined to be the closest possible compliance with the rules in respect of that vessel[16].

1 Ie the International Regulations for Preventing Collisions at Sea (London, 20 October 1972; TS 77 (1977); Cmnd 6962): see PARA 690.
2 For these purposes, 'vessel' includes every description of water craft, including non-displacement craft, wing-in-ground (WIG) craft and seaplanes, used or capable of being used as a means of transportation on water (Collision Regulations r 3(a)); 'seaplane' includes any aircraft designed to manoeuvre on the water (r 3(e)); and 'wing-in-ground (WIG) craft' means a multimodal craft which, in its main operational mode, flies in close proximity to the surface by utilizing surface-effect action (r 3(m)).
   The Collision Regulations, whilst not applying to a jet-ski, contain a standard of care to which the driver of a jet-ski should conform: see *Steedman v Scofield* [1992] 2 Lloyd's Rep 163. As to fishing boats and collision regulations see FISHERIES AND AQUACULTURE vol 51 (2013) PARA 376.
3 Collision Regulations r 1(a). As to exemptions see reg 38; and PARA 690 note 4.
4 Collision Regulations r 1(b).
5 *The Carlotta* [1899] P 223, 8 Asp MLC 544.

6 *The Carlotta* [1899] P 223, 8 Asp MLC 544; *The Bitinia* [1912] P 186, 12 Asp MLC 237 (affd 82 LJP 8, CA); *The Ceylon* [1920] P 187, 15 Asp MLC 100.
7 *The Humbergate* [1952] 1 Lloyd's Rep 168.
8 *Imperial Royal Privileged Danubian Steam Navigation Co v Greek and Oriental Steam Navigation Co, The Smyrna* (1864) 2 Moo PCCNS 435.
9 For these purposes, 'vessel engaged in fishing' means any vessel fishing with nets, lines, trawls or other fishing apparatus which restrict manoeuvrability, but does not include a vessel fishing with trolling lines or other fishing apparatus which do not restrict manoeuvrability: Collision Regulations r 3(d).
10 Collision Regulations r 1(c).
11 Collision Regulations r 1(c).
12 As to the International Maritime Organisation see PARA 12.
13 Collision Regulations r 1(d). As to traffic separation schemes see PARA 701.
14 As to lights and shapes see PARA 710 et seq.
15 As to sound-signalling equipment see PARA 722 et seq.
16 Collision Regulations r 1(e).

692. Construction of the rules.

The Collision Regulations[1] are issued for the guidance of seafarers and are to be construed literally and with seamanlike knowledge[2]. They are not to be construed according to the strictest and nicest interpretation of language but are to be given the same kind of reasonable and business interpretation as in an Act of Parliament which regulates some large trade or business[3].

1 Ie the International Regulations for Preventing Collisions at Sea (London, 20 October 1972; TS 77 (1977); Cmnd 6962): see PARA 690.
2 *The Libra* (1881) 6 PD 139 at 142, 4 Asp MLC 439 at 440, CA; *The Dunelm* (1884) 9 PD 164, 5 Asp MLC 304, CA.
3 *The Dunelm* (1884) 9 PD 164 at 171, 5 Asp MLC 304 at 308, CA. As the Collision Regulations are of an international character, they have in many cases been judicially construed in the courts of foreign countries: see eg *The Sylvester Hale (The Schooner)* (1873) 6 Benedict United States District Court Reporter 523 (where it was said to be of paramount importance that they should be understood alike by all nations).

693. Responsibility under the rules.

Nothing in the Collision Regulations[1] exonerates any vessel[2] (or her owner, master or crew) from the consequences of any neglect to comply with the rules or of the neglect of any precaution which may be required by the ordinary practice of seamen, or by the special circumstances of the case[3].

In construing and complying with the rules, due regard must be had to all dangers of navigation and collision and to any special circumstances, including the limitations of the vessels involved, which may make a departure from the rules necessary to avoid immediate danger[4].

1 Ie the International Regulations for Preventing Collisions at Sea (London, 20 October 1972; TS 77 (1977); Cmnd 6962): see PARA 690.
2 As to the meaning of 'vessel' for these purposes see PARA 691 note 2.
3 Collision Regulations r 2(a). See *Owners and/or demise charterers of the MV Eleftheria v Owners and/or demise charterers of the MV Hakki Deval* [2006] EWHC 2809 (Admlty). As to the rules of good seamanship see PARA 729 et seq.
4 Collision Regulations r 2(b).

694. Infringement of the rules and breaches of duty.

Although a ship may have infringed the Collision Regulations[1], the onus is on the party setting up a case of negligence against the ship to prove breach of duty and damage[2].

When radar is installed, there is a duty to use it at common law[3] and under the rules of the Collision Regulations, proper use must be made of radar, if fitted and operational, to obtain early warning of the risk of collision[4]. The use of radar may justify a speed that would otherwise be excessive[5]. Radar must be used in an intelligent and seamanlike manner, and failure so to use it is negligence[6]. Where, however, there is clear visibility, failure to make radar observations on the alteration of another vessel's course is not necessarily negligence[7]. Failure to obtain the information available from a port radar installation when navigating in a river in fog has been held to be negligence[8].

1 Ie the International Regulations for Preventing Collisions at Sea (London, 20 October 1972; TS 77 (1977); Cmnd 6962): see PARA 690.

2 See *SS Heranger (Owners) v SS Diamond (Owners)* [1939] AC 94 at 104, 62 Ll L Rep 204 at 211, HL (where the actual default in question was merely a breach of the rules of good seamanship). See also *SS Heranger (Owners) v SS Diamond (Owners)* at 100 and at 209. However, the court considered to be incorrect the view (which had been expressed in *The Aeneas* [1935] P 128 at 131, 18 Asp MLC 571 at 575, on the authority of certain cases decided before the Maritime Conventions Act 1911 (repealed)) that those guilty of a breach of a rule contained in the collision regulations or a local rule must show affirmatively that their default did not contribute to the collision or the resulting loss: *SS Heranger (Owners) v SS Diamond (Owners)* at 104, 105 and at 211, 212. The grounds for holding this view to be incorrect were that it was contrary to:

    (1)   the principle that only faults which contribute to the accident are to be taken into account in apportioning liability under what is now the Merchant Shipping Act 1995 s 187 (see PARA 800); and

    (2)   the general principle of the law of negligence that the claimant must show both breach of duty and consequent damage (*SS Heranger (Owners) v SS Diamond (Owners)* at 104 and at 211).

    For instances of cases decided before the Maritime Conventions Act 1911 (repealed), in which no statutory presumption of fault was applicable but breach of collision regulations or local rules was treated as throwing on those in default the burden of exonerating themselves, see *The Fenham* (1870) LR 3 PC 212 at 216; *Cayzer, Irvine & Co, SS Clan Sinclair (Owners) v Carron Co, SS Margaret (Owners)* (1884) 9 App Cas 873 at 886, 887, 5 Asp MLC 371 at 374, 375, HL. Cf *The Raithwaite Hall* (1874) 2 Asp MLC 210 at 212; and *Cayzer, Irvine & Co, SS Clan Sinclair (Owners) v Carron Co, SS Margaret (Owners)* at 882, 883 and at 373. For an instance since the passing of the Maritime Conventions Act 1911 (repealed), in which it was suggested that the onus was on a wrongdoer to show that his default had not contributed to the collision, see *SS Haugland (Owners) v SS Karamea (Owners)* [1922] 1 AC 68 at 75, 15 Asp MLC 430 at 432, HL (onus on vessel failing to give whistle signal to show that it would not have been heard); but cf *Haugland (Owners) v Karamea (Owners)* at 74, 77 and at 432, 433. As to the burden of proof in collision cases and the circumstances in which it may shift to the defendant see further PARA 757.

3 See *The Lady Gwendolen; Arthur Guiness Son and Co (Dublin) Ltd v Owners of Motor Vessel Freshfield* [1965] 2 All ER 283.

4 See the Collision Regulations r 7(b); and PARA 697.

5 *The Kurt Arlt SS Petrel (Owners) v SS Kurt Arlt (Owners)* [1962] 2 All ER 27, [1962] 1 Lloyd's Rep 31, sub nom *Petrel (Owners) v Kurt Arlt (Owners), The Kurt Arlt* [1962] 1 WLR 439. As to the use of radar to determine a safe speed see the Collision Regulations r 6(b); and PARA 696.

6 *The Anna Salen* [1954] 1 Lloyd's Rep 475 at 488; *The Nora* [1956] 1 Lloyd's Rep 617; *The Guildford* (as reported in [1956] 2 Lloyd's Rep 74 at 80); *The Evje* [1960] 2 Lloyd's Rep 221. See also *The British Aviator* (1965) 109 Sol Jo 215, CA (collision caused by defective radar observations).

7 *The Thomaseverett* [1981] 1 Lloyd's Rep 1, CA.

8 *The Indus* [1957] 1 Lloyd's Rep 335; *The Vechtstroom* [1964] 1 Lloyd's Rep 118.

(ii) Steering and Sailing

A.   CONDUCT OF VESSELS IN ANY CONDITION OF VISIBILITY

695. Requirement to maintain a proper look-out. Under the Collision Regulations[1], every vessel[2] must at all times maintain a proper look-out[3] by sight and hearing as well as by all available means appropriate in the prevailing circumstances and conditions so as to make a full appraisal of the situation and of the risk of collision[4].

This rule applies in any condition of visibility[5].

1 Ie the International Regulations for Preventing Collisions at Sea (London, 20 October 1972; TS 77 (1977); Cmnd 6962): see PARA 690.

2 As to the meaning of 'vessel' for these purposes see PARA 691 note 2.

3 As to the rules of good seamanship concerning the keeping of a look-out see PARA 739.

4   Collision Regulations r 5. As to the risk of collision see PARA 697.
5   Collision Regulations r 4. As to the conduct of vessels in restricted visibility see PARA 709.

696.   Safe speed. Under the Collision Regulations[1] every vessel[2] must at all times proceed at a safe speed[3] so that she can take proper and effective action to avoid collision[4] and be stopped within a distance appropriate to the prevailing circumstances and conditions[5]. This rule applies in any condition of visibility[6].

In determining a safe speed, the following factors must be among those taken into account by all vessels[7]:

(1)   the state of visibility[8];

(2)   the traffic density including concentrations of fishing vessels or any other vessels[9];

(3)   the manoeuvrability of the vessel with special reference to stopping distance and turning ability in the prevailing conditions[10];

(4)   at night the presence of background light such as from shore lights or from back scatter of her own lights[11];

(5)   the state of wind, sea and current, and the proximity of navigational hazards[12];

(6)   the draught in relation to the available depth of water[13].

The following additional factors must be taken into account by vessels with operational radar[14]:

(a)   the characteristics, efficiency and limitations of the radar equipment[15];

(b)   any constraints imposed by the radar range scale in use[16];

(c)   the effect on radar detection of the sea state, weather and other sources of interference[17];

(d)   the possibility that small vessels, ice and other floating objects may not be detected by radar at an adequate range[18];

(e)   the number, location and movement of vessels detected by radar[19];

(f)   the more exact assessment of the visibility that may be possible when radar is used to determine the range of vessels or other objects in the vicinity[20].

1   Ie the International Regulations for Preventing Collisions at Sea (London, 20 October 1972; TS 77 (1977); Cmnd 6962): see PARA 690.
2   As to the meaning of 'vessel' for these purposes see PARA 691 note 2.
3   As to the rules of good seamanship concerning speed see PARA 740.
4   As to rules under the Collision Regulations regarding action taken to avoid collision see PARA 698.
5   Collision Regulations r 6.
6   Collision Regulations r 4. As to the conduct of vessels in restricted visibility see PARA 709.
7   Collision Regulations r 6(a).
8   Collision Regulations r 6(a)(i).
9   Collision Regulations r 6(a)(ii). As to the meaning of 'vessel engaged in fishing' for these purposes see PARA 691 note 9.
10 Collision Regulations r 6(a)(iii).
11 Collision Regulations r 6(a)(iv).
12 Collision Regulations r 6(a)(v).
13 Collision Regulations r 6(a)(vi).
14 Collision Regulations r 6(b). As to radar generally see PARA 694.
15 Collision Regulations r 6(b)(i).
16 Collision Regulations r 6(b)(ii).
17 Collision Regulations r 6(b)(iii).
18 Collision Regulations r 6(b)(iv).
19 Collision Regulations r 6(b)(v).
20 Collision Regulations r 6(b)(vi).

697.   Risk of collision. Under the Collision Regulations[1] every vessel[2] must use all available means appropriate to the prevailing circumstances and conditions to determine if risk of collision exists[3]. If there is any doubt, such risk is deemed to exist[4]. This rule applies in any condition of visibility[5].

Proper use must be made of radar equipment[6], if fitted and operational, including long-range scanning to obtain early warning of the risk of collision and radar plotting or equivalent systematic observation of detected objects[7]. Assumptions must not be made on the basis of scanty information, especially scanty radar information[8].

In determining if the risk of collision exists[9], the following considerations must be among those taken into account[10]:

(1)   risk of collision is deemed to exist if the compass bearing of an approaching vessel does not appreciably change[11];

(2)   such risk may sometimes exist even when an appreciable bearing change is evident, particularly when approaching a very large vessel or a tow or when approaching a vessel at close range[12].

1   Ie the International Regulations for Preventing Collisions at Sea (London, 20 October 1972; TS 77 (1977); Cmnd 6962): see PARA 690.
2   As to the meaning of 'vessel' for these purposes see PARA 691 note 2.
3   Collision Regulations r 7(a). On the duty to avoid collision see *Owners, Demise Charterers and Time Charterers of the Ship 'Western Neptune' v Owners and Demise Charterers of the Ship 'Philadelphia Express' (St Louis Express)* [2009] EWHC 1274 (Admlty), [2010] 2 All ER (Comm) 154 (large vessel or tow). Cf *The Stanmore* (1885) 10 PD 134, 5 Asp MLC 441, CA (where it was held that, if it is probable that a vessel has done something to cause a risk of collision, such a risk should be assumed to exist). As to action to avoid collision see PARA 698.
4   Collision Regulations r 7(a). The rules of the Collision Regulations are designed not only to prevent collisions but also to prevent even the risk of collisions: see *The Beryl* (1884) 9 PD 137 at 140, 5 Asp MLC 321 at 323, CA.
5   Collision Regulations r 4. As to the conduct of vessels in restricted visibility see PARA 709.
6   As to radar generally see PARA 694.
7   Collision Regulations r 7(b).
8   Collision Regulations r 7(c).
9   The question whether risk of collision exists is a matter partly of nautical experience and partly of law: see *The Mangerton* (1856) Sw 120.
10 Collision Regulations r 7(d).
11 Collision Regulations r 7(d)(i).
12 Collision Regulations r 7(d)(ii).

698. Action to avoid collision. Under the Collision Regulations[1], any action taken to avoid collision must, if the circumstances of the case admit, be positive, made in ample time and with due regard to the observance of good seamanship[2]. Any alteration of course and/or speed to avoid collision must, if the circumstances of the case admit, be large enough to be readily apparent to another vessel[3] observing visually or by radar[4]; a succession of small alterations of course and/or speed should be avoided[5]. If there is sufficient sea room, alteration of course alone may be the most effective action to avoid a close-quarters situation[6] provided that it is made in good time, is substantial and does not result in another close-quarters situation[7].

Action taken to avoid collision with another vessel must be such as to result in passing at a safe distance[8]. The effectiveness of the action must be carefully checked until the other vessel is finally past and clear[9].

If necessary to avoid collision or allow more time to assess the situation, a vessel must slacken her speed or take all way off by stopping or reversing her means of propulsion[10].

A vessel which is required[11] not to impede the passage or safe passage of another vessel must, when required by the circumstances of the case, take early action to allow sufficient sea room for the safe passage of the other vessel[12]. A vessel required not to impede the passage or safe passage of another vessel is not relieved of this obligation if approaching the other vessel so as to involve risk of collision and must, when taking action, have full regard to the action which may be required[13] by the steering and sailing rules[14]. A vessel the passage of which is not to be impeded remains fully obliged to comply with the steering and sailing rules[15] when the two vessels are approaching one another so as to involve risk of collision[16].

This rule applies in any condition of visibility[17].

1 Ie the International Regulations for Preventing Collisions at Sea (London, 20 October 1972; TS 77 (1977); Cmnd 6962): see PARA 690.
2 Collision Regulations r 8(a). In addition, any action so taken must be in accordance with the rules of Pt B (rr 4–19) (steering and sailing rules) (see PARAS 695–697, 699 et seq): see r 8(a). As to the rules of good seamanship in particular see PARA 729 et seq.
3 As to the meaning of 'vessel' for these purposes see PARA 691 note 2.
4 Collision Regulations r 8(b). As to radar generally see PARA 694. See also *The Sanshin Victory* [1980] 2 Lloyd's Rep 359.
5 Collision Regulations r 8(b).
6 What constitutes a close-quarters situation depends on the size, characteristics and speed of the ships concerned: see *The Verena* [1961] 2 Lloyd's Rep 127 at 133, CA, per Willmer LJ.
7 Collision Regulations r 8(c).
8 Collision Regulations r 8(d).
9 Collision Regulations r 8(d).
10 Collision Regulations r 8(e). As to what is a safe speed see PARA 696.
11 Ie by any of the rules of the Collision Regulations: see r 8(f)(i).
12 Collision Regulations r 8(f)(i).
13 Ie by the rules of the Collision Regulations Pt B (rr 4–19): see r 8(f)(ii).
14 Collision Regulations r 8(f)(ii).
15 Ie the Collision Regulations Pt B: see r 8(f)(iii).
16 Collision Regulations r 8(f)(iii).
17 Collision Regulations r 4. As to the conduct of vessels in restricted visibility see PARA 709.

699. The narrow channel rule. Under the Collision Regulations[1] a vessel[2] proceeding along the course of a narrow channel[3] or fairway[4] must keep as near to the outer limit of the channel or fairway which lies on her starboard side as is safe and practicable[5]. A vessel of less than 20 metres in length[6] or a sailing vessel[7] must not impede the passage of a vessel which can safely navigate only within a narrow channel or fairway[8]. A vessel engaged in fishing[9] must not impede the passage of any other vessel navigating within a narrow channel or fairway[10].

A vessel must not cross a narrow channel or fairway if such crossing impedes the passage of a vessel which can safely navigate only within such channel or fairway[11]. The latter vessel may use the appropriate sound signal[12] if in doubt as to the intention of the crossing vessel[13].

In a narrow channel or fairway, when overtaking[14] can take place only if the vessel to be overtaken has to take action to permit safe passing, the vessel intending to overtake must indicate her intention by sounding the appropriate signal[15]. The vessel to be overtaken must, if in agreement, sound the appropriate signal[16] and take steps to permit safe passing[17]. If in doubt, she may sound the signals appropriate for that circumstance instead[18].

A vessel nearing a bend or an area of a narrow channel or fairway where other vessels may be obscured by an intervening obstruction must navigate with particular alertness and caution and must sound the appropriate warning signal[19].

Any vessel must, if the circumstances of the case admit, avoid anchoring in a narrow channel[20].

This rule applies in any condition of visibility[21].

1 Ie the International Regulations for Preventing Collisions at Sea (London, 20 October 1972; TS 77 (1977); Cmnd 6962): see PARA 690.
2 As to the meaning of 'vessel' for these purposes see PARA 691 note 2.

3   As to the meaning of 'narrow channel' see PARA 700.
4   Wherever there is an open navigable passage used by vessels proceeding up and down a river or channel, that may be said to be a 'fairway': see *The Blue Bell* [1895] P 242 at 264, 7 Asp MLC 601 at 602, DC. See also *The Clutha Boat 147* [1909] P 36, 11 Asp MLC 199; and *The Lake Farragut* [1921] P 305. Cf *The Turquoise* [1908] P 148, 11 Asp MLC 28 (where a vessel lying moored outside another vessel at a wharf was held not to be in or near a fairway).
5   Collision Regulations r 9(a). This rule is known as the 'narrow channel rule'. See *Pelopidas (owners) v TRSL Concord (owners)* [1999] 2 Lloyd's Rep 675, [1999] 2 All ER (Comm) 737 (in apportioning liability, the preponderate feature of the lead up to collision was a breach of the Collision Regulations r 9). In connection with the operation of Collision Regulations r 9 see *The Nordlake and The Seaeagle* [2015] EWHC 3605 (Admlty), [2016] 1 Lloyd's Rep 656, [2016] 2 All ER (Comm) 449.
6   For these purposes, 'length' of a vessel means her length overall: Collision Regulations r 3(j).
7   For these purposes, 'sailing vessel' means any vessel under sail provided that propelling machinery, if fitted, is not being used: Collision Regulations r 3(c).
8   Collision Regulations r 9(b).
9   As to the meaning of 'vessel engaged in fishing' see PARA 691 note 9.
10   Collision Regulations r 9(c).
11   Collision Regulations r 9(d).
12   Ie the signal prescribed in the Collision Regulations r 34(d) (see PARA 723): see r 9(d).
13   Collision Regulations r 9(d).
14   Collision Regulations r 9 does not relieve the overtaking vessel of her obligation under r 13 (overtaking) (see PARA 703): r 9(e)(ii).
15   Collision Regulations r 9(e)(i). The appropriate signal referred to in the text is that prescribed in r 34(c)(i) (see PARA 723): see r 9(e)(i).
16   Ie the signal prescribed by the Collision Regulations r 34(c)(ii) (see PARA 723): see r 9(e)(i).
17   Collision Regulations r 9(e)(i).
18   Collision Regulations r 9(e)(i). The appropriate signals referred to in the text are those prescribed in r 34(d) (see PARA 723): see r 9(e)(i).
19   Collision Regulations r 9(f). The appropriate signal referred to in the text is that prescribed in r 34(e) (see PARA 723): see r 9(f).
20   Collision Regulations r 9(g).
21   Collision Regulations r 4. As to the conduct of vessels in restricted visibility see PARA 709.

700.   Meaning of 'narrow channel'.

Prima facie, 'narrow channel'[1] means a channel bounded on either side by land, so that a vessel[2] cannot navigate in any great width between the two banks; it is opposed to 'at sea'[3]. A narrow channel must have two boundaries which are close to one another; a stretch of water which on one side is open to an indefinite extent cannot be a narrow channel[4]. The court will not lay down what particular width or length will constitute a narrow channel[5], but, while a narrow channel is of necessity comparatively small in breadth, it may also be very short in length[6]. An entrance between the piers of a harbour has more than once been held to be a narrow channel[7]. In view of its object, which is the prevention of risk of collision[8], there is as much reason to apply the 'narrow channel rule'[9] to such an entrance as to a longer channel[10].

When such an entrance or opening is a narrow channel, the duty to keep to the starboard side applies in so much of the water inside and outside of the entrance as is required for manoeuvring for the entrance[11].

Although physical conditions remain the same, the alteration in lights and other marks which affect navigation sometimes makes a part of a large piece of water into a narrow channel[12].

There have been many decisions of the courts, both domestic and overseas, as to whether particular waters are narrow channels[13]. In some instances, while not deciding that certain waters were a narrow channel, the courts have held that vessels should navigate in them as if the narrow channel rule applied[14].

The narrow channel rule is to be construed with reasonable latitude. Some allowance has to be made for tide, locality and wind and for the case of a vessel being in tow[15]. Although the court might be of the opinion that the vessel might have kept 50 yards closer to the proper shore of the river, it may refuse to look at a question of a few yards more or less[16].

1 For particular waters which have been held to be narrow channels see the text and notes 7, 12–17.
2 As to the meaning of 'vessel' for the purposes of the Collision Regulations see PARA 691 note 2. As to the Collision Regulations (ie the International Regulations for Preventing Collisions at Sea (London, 20 October 1972; TS 77 (1977); Cmnd 6962)) see PARA 690.
3 *The Florence Nightingale and The Maeander* (1863) 1 Mar LC 301, PC, per Dr Lushington. See *Nautical Challenge Ltd v Evergreen Marine (UK) Ltd* [2017] EWHC 453 (Admlty).
4 *The Treherbert* [1934] P 31 at 46, 47, 18 Asp MLC 458 at 468, CA.
5 *Scicluna v Stevenson, The Rhondda* (1883) 8 App Cas 549 at 552, 5 Asp MLC 114 at 117, PC. Whether a space of water is a narrow channel may be entirely a question of fact: *Australian Steam Navigation Co v Smith & Sons* (1889) 14 App Cas 318, PC.
6 *The Kaiser Wilhelm der Grosse* [1907] P 259 at 263, 10 Asp MLC 504 at 506, CA.
7 See *The Kaiser Wilhelm der Grosse* [1907] P 259, 10 Asp MLC 504, CA.
8 As to the risk of collision see PARA 697.
9 Ie the Collision Regulations r 9(a) (as to which see PARA 699).
10 *The Kaiser Wilhelm der Grosse* [1907] P 259 at 264, 10 Asp MLC 504 at 506, CA. The question whether the rule applies to an opening between buoys or lightships does not depend on whether there is a dredged channel there or not: *The Kaiser Wilhelm der Grosse*.
11 *The Kaiser Wilhelm der Grosse* [1907] P 36 at 44, 10 Asp MLC 361 at 364 per Gorell Barnes P; *The Knaresbro* (1900) [1907] P 38n. Even apart from the narrow channel rule, a vessel going out of or coming into a narrow harbour entrance ought not to cross the entrance so close as not to leave room for vessels going the other way, but ought to make a wide sweep so as to leave them a fairway: *The Harvest* (1886) 11 PD 90, 6 Asp MLC 5, CA. In a harbour where there was a rule to the effect that a vessel when proceeding out or in should be kept to the right of mid-channel and two buoys really marked the entrance to the channel, although there was sufficient water for vessels to go outside the buoys, it was held that a vessel ought to round in so as to enter either on the right side of the channel marked by the buoys, or outside the right-hand buoy: *The Winstanley* [1896] P 297, 8 Asp MLC 170, CA.
12 *The Gustafsberg* [1905] P 10 at 19, 10 Asp MLC 61 at 65.
13 See eg *The Florence Nightingale, The Maeander* (1863) 1 Mar LC 301, PC; *The Cuba v McMillan* (1869) 26 SCR 651; *Scicluna v Stevenson, The Rhondda* (1883) 8 App Cas 549, 5 Asp MLC 114, PC; *The Clydach* (1884) 5 Asp MLC 336; *The Brooklyn City* (1885) 2 Pritchard's Admiralty Digest (3rd Edn) 2371; *The Leverington* (1886) as reported in 6 Asp MLC 7, CA; *Australian Steam Navigation Co v Smith & Sons* (1889) 14 App Cas 318, PC; *The Santanderino* (1893) 3 Exch CR 378; *SS Diana v SS Clieveden, The Clieveden* [1894] AC 625 at 629, PC *The Minnie* [1894] P 336, 7 Asp MLC 521, CA; *The Corennie* [1894] P 338n; *The Oporto* [1897] P 249, CA; *The Knaresbro* (1900) [1907] P 38n; *The Gustafsberg* [1904] P 10 at 20, 10 Asp MLC 61 at 65; *SS Calvin Austin v Lovitt* (1905) 35 SCR 616; *The Ashton* [1905] P 21, 10 Asp MLC 88; *The Glengariff* [1905] P 106, 10 Asp MLC 103; *The Assaye* [1905] P 289 at 291, 10 Asp MLC 183 at 184; *The Kaiser Wilhelm der Grosse* [1907] P 259, 10 Asp MLC 504, CA; *The Red Cross* (1907) 10 Asp MLC 521; *Bryce v Canadian Pacific Rly Co* (1908) 13 BCR 446; *The Try Again* (1908) Shipping Gazette, 2 June; *The Whitlieburn* (1900) 9 Asp MLC 154; *The Prince Leopold de Belgique* [1909] P 103, 11 Asp MLC 203; *The Seymolicus* [1909] P 109, 11 Asp MLC 206; *The Corinthian* [1909] P 260 at 265, 266, 11 Asp MLC 208 at 211, CA; *Screw Collier Co v Webster (or Kerr)* [1910] AC 165, HL; *Clyde Navigation Trustees v Wilhelmsen* 1915 SC 392; *The Ravenna* [1918] P 297, CA; *Dredger No 9 (Owners) v Wheatear* (1920) 3 Ll L Rep 229; *Admiral Codrington v Canadian Raider* (1921) 9 Ll L Rep 477; *The Fiumana* (1931) 39 Ll L Rep 32 at 34; *The Varmdo* [1940] P 15 (affd [1940] P 137, 19 Asp MLC 370, CA; *The Anna Salen* [1954] 1 Lloyd's Rep 475; *The Edison Mariner* [1955] 1 Lloyd's Rep 235; *The Sedgepool* [1956] 2 Lloyd's Rep 668.
14 *The Ashton* [1905] P 21, 10 Asp MLC 88; *The Try Again* (1908) Shipping Gazette, 2 June; *The Corinthian* [1909] P 260 at 266, 11 Asp MLC 208 at 211.
15 *The La Plata* (1857) Sw 220 at 222; revsd Sw 298, PC. See also *The Ravenna* [1918] P 297, CA; *The Prinses Juliana* [1936] P 139 at 152, [1936] 1 All ER 685 at 660, 18 Asp MLC 614 at 619 (local byelaw which required vessel navigating against tide to ease speed and, if necessary, wait before rounding bend; state of tide and length of vessel taken into account).
16 *The Sylph* (1854) 2 Ecc & Ad 75 at 81.

701. Traffic separation schemes. Special provisions of the Collision Regulations[1] apply to traffic separation schemes adopted by the International Maritime Organisation[2].

Accordingly, a vessel using a traffic separation scheme must[3]:

(1)   proceed in the appropriate traffic lane in the general direction of traffic flow for that lane[4];

(2)   so far as practicable keep clear of a traffic separation line or separation zone[5];

(3)   normally join or leave a traffic lane at the termination of the lane, but, when joining or leaving from the side, must do so at as small an angle to the general direction of traffic flow as practicable[6].

A vessel must, so far as practicable, avoid crossing traffic lanes, but, if obliged to do so, must cross on a heading as nearly as practicable at right angles to the general direction of traffic flow[7].

A vessel must not use an inshore traffic zone when she can safely use the appropriate traffic lane within the adjacent traffic separation scheme[8]; but vessels of less than 20 metres in length[9], sailing vessels[10] and vessels engaged in fishing[11] may use the inshore traffic zone[12]. A vessel may[13] use an inshore traffic zone when en route to or from a port, offshore installation or structure, pilot station or any other place situated within the inshore traffic zone, or to avoid immediate danger[14].

A vessel, other than a crossing vessel or a vessel joining or leaving a lane, must not normally enter a separation zone or cross a separation line[15], except:

(a)   in cases of emergency to avoid immediate danger[16];

(b)   to engage in fishing within a separation zone[17].

A vessel navigating in areas near the termination of traffic separation schemes must do so with particular caution[18]; and a vessel must so far as practicable avoid anchoring in a traffic separation scheme or in areas near its terminations[19]. A vessel not using a traffic separation scheme must avoid it by as wide a margin as is practicable[20]. A vessel engaged in fishing must not impede the passage of any vessel following a traffic lane[21]. A vessel of less than 20 metres in length or a sailing vessel must not impede the safe passage of a power-driven vessel[22] following a traffic lane[23].

A vessel restricted in her ability to manoeuvre[24] when engaged in an operation for:

(i)   the maintenance of safety of navigation in a traffic separation scheme[25]; or

(ii)   the laying, servicing or picking up of a submarine cable, within a traffic separation scheme[26],

is exempted from complying with the traffic separation provisions[27] to the extent necessary to carry out the operation[28].

This rule applies in any condition of visibility[29].

1   Ie the International Regulations for Preventing Collisions at Sea (London, 20 October 1972; TS 77 (1977); Cmnd 6962): see PARA 690.

2   Collision Regulations r 10(a). As to the International Maritime Organisation see PARA 12. However, nothing in r 10 relieves any vessel of her obligation under any other rule of the Collision Regulations: see r 10(a). As to the meaning of 'vessel' for these purposes see PARA 691 note 2.
    The traffic separation schemes which are referred to in r 10(a) are the schemes listed in Notice to Mariners No 17 and marked with an asterisk in the margin: Merchant Shipping (Distress Signals and Prevention of Collisions) Regulations 1996, SI 1996/75, reg 1(4); Merchant Shipping Notice 1781(M) Introduction para 7(1). For these purposes, 'Notice to Mariners' means an Admiralty Notice to Mariners published by the Hydrographer of the Navy (Merchant Shipping (Distress Signals and Prevention of Collisions) Regulations 1996, SI 1996/75, reg 1(3)); and 'Hydrographer of the Navy' means the person for the time being appointed to that office by the Admiralty Board (reg 1(3)). 'Notice to Mariners No 17' means (by virtue of reg 1(4)) Notice to Mariners No 17 in the Annual Summary of Admiralty Notices to Mariners of 1989 and any subsequent Notice to Mariners containing like material which the Hydrographer of the Navy considers relevant from time to time, being a Notice to Mariners which:

(1)   replaces Admiralty Notice to Mariners No 17; or
(2)   replaces any subsequent Notice to Mariners containing the like material;
and a reference to any such subsequent Notice to Mariners includes a reference to any Notice to Mariners amending the same which the Hydrographer of the Navy considers relevant from time to time.

3 Collision Regulations r 10(b).
4 Collision Regulations r 10(b)(i).
5 Collision Regulations r 10(b)(ii).
6 Collision Regulations r 10(b)(iii).
7 Collision Regulations r 10(c).
8 Collision Regulations r 10(d)(i).
9 As to the meaning of 'length' see PARA 699 note 6.
10 As to the meaning of 'sailing vessel' see PARA 699 note 7.
11 As to the meaning of 'vessel engaged in fishing' see PARA 691 note 9.
12 Collision Regulations r 10(d)(i).
13 Ie notwithstanding the Collision Regulations r 10(d)(i) (see the text and notes 8–12): see r 10(d)(ii).
14 Collision Regulations r 10(d)(ii).
15 Collision Regulations r 10(e).
16 Collision Regulations r 10(e)(i).
17 Collision Regulations r 10(e)(ii).
18 Collision Regulations r 10(f).
19 Collision Regulations r 10(g).
20 Collision Regulations r 10(h).
21 Collision Regulations r 10(i).
22 For these purposes, 'power-driven vessel' means any vessel propelled by machinery: Collision Regulations r 3(b).
23 Collision Regulations r 10(j).
24 For these purposes, 'vessel restricted in her ability to manoeuvre' means a vessel which from the nature of her work is restricted in her ability to manoeuvre as required by the rules of the Collision Regulations and is, therefore, unable to keep out of the way of another vessel: r 3(g). The term 'vessels restricted in their ability to manoeuvre' includes but is not limited to:
      (1)   a vessel engaged in laying, servicing or picking up a navigation mark, submarine cable or pipe-line (r 3(g)(i));
      (2)   a vessel engaged in dredging, surveying or underwater operations (r 3(g)(ii));
      (3)   a vessel engaged in replenishment or transferring persons, provisions or cargo while underway (r 3(g)(iii));
      (4)   a vessel engaged in the launching or recovery of aircraft (r 3(g)(iv));
      (5)   a vessel engaged in mine-clearance operations (r 3(g)(v));
      (6)   a vessel engaged in a towing operation such as severely restricts the towing vessel and her tow in their ability to deviate from their course (r 3(g)(vi)).
      'Underway' means that a vessel is not at anchor, or made fast to the shore, or aground: r 3(i).
25 Collision Regulations r 10(k).
26 Collision Regulations r 10(l).
27 Ie exempted from complying with Collision Regulations r 10: see r 10(k), (l).
28 See Collision Regulations r 10(k), (l).
29 Collision Regulations r 4. As to the conduct of vessels in restricted visibility see PARA 709.

B.   CONDUCT OF VESSELS IN SIGHT OF ONE ANOTHER

702. Rules applicable to sailing vessels. Under the Collision Regulations[1], when two sailing vessels[2] are approaching one another, so as to involve risk of collision[3], one of them must keep out of the way of the other[4], as follows:
      (1)   when each has the wind on a different side, the vessel which has the wind on the port side must keep out of the way of the other[5];
      (2)   when both have the wind on the same side, the vessel which is to windward[6] must keep out of the way of the vessel which is to leeward[7];
      (3)   if a vessel with the wind on the port side sees a vessel to windward and cannot determine with certainty whether the other vessel has the wind on the port or on the starboard side, she must keep out of the way of the other[8].

This rule applies only to vessels in sight of one another[9].

1　Ie the International Regulations for Preventing Collisions at Sea (London, 20 October 1972; TS 77 (1977); Cmnd 6962): see PARA 690.
2　As to the meaning of 'sailing vessel' see PARA 699 note 7; and as to the meaning of 'vessel' for these purposes see PARA 691 note 2.
3　As to the risk of collision see PARA 697.
4　See the Collision Regulations r 12(a). The rules in Pt B (Steering and Sailing Rules) Section II (Conduct of vessels in sight of one another) (rr 11–18) (see also PARAS 703–708) must be strictly complied with; however, vessels are not prevented from taking sufficiently early action ahead of the point in time at which those rules come into effect: Merchant Shipping Notice 1781(M) Introduction para 6.
　　As to the conduct of power-driven vessels see PARAS 704, 705; and as to the conduct of vessels in restricted visibility see PARA 709.
5　Collision Regulations r 12(a)(i).
6　For these purposes, the windward side is deemed to be the side opposite to that on which the mainsail is carried or, in the case of a square-rigged vessel, the side opposite to that on which the largest fore-and-aft sail is carried: Collision Regulations r 12(b).
7　Collision Regulations r 12(a)(ii).
8　Collision Regulations r 12(a)(ii).
9　Collision Regulations r 11. For these purposes, vessels are deemed to be in sight of one another only when one can be observed visually from the other: Collision Regulations r 3(k).

703.　Overtaking rules. Under the Collision Regulations[1] any vessel[2] overtaking any other must keep out of the way of the vessel being overtaken[3]. A vessel is deemed to be overtaking when coming up[4] with another vessel from a direction more than 22.5 degrees abaft her beam (that is, in such a position with reference to the vessel she is overtaking, that at night she would be able to see only the sternlight[5] of that vessel but neither of her sidelights)[6]. When a vessel is in any doubt as to whether she is overtaking another, she must assume that this is the case and act accordingly[7].

Any subsequent alteration of the bearing between the two vessels does not make the overtaking vessel a crossing vessel[8] or relieve her of the duty of keeping clear of the overtaken vessel until she is finally past and clear[9].

This rule applies only to vessels in sight of one another[10].

1　Ie the International Regulations for Preventing Collisions at Sea (London, 20 October 1972; TS 77 (1977); Cmnd 6962): see PARA 690.
2　As to the meaning of 'vessel' for these purposes see PARA 691 note 2.
3　Collision Regulations r 13(a). This rule applies notwithstanding anything contained in Pt B Section I (rr 4–10) (Conduct of vessels in any conditions of visibility) (see PARAS 695–701) and Section II (Conduct of vessels in sight of one another) (rr 11–18) (see also PARAS 702, 704–708): see r 13(a). See *The Frosta* [1973] 2 Lloyd's Rep 348; and as to the duty of the vessel being overtaken see PARA 707.
　　The rules in the Collision Regulations Pt B (Steering and Sailing Rules) Section II must be strictly complied with; however, vessels are not prevented from taking sufficiently early action ahead of the point in time at which those rules come into effect: Merchant Shipping Notice 1781(M) Introduction para 6.
4　A vessel is deemed to be 'coming up' with another when there is some proximity in space between them even though there is no risk of collision at that time: *The Nowy Sacz* [1979] QB 236 at 246, 247, [1978] 2 All ER 297 at 303, [1977] 2 Lloyd's Rep 91 at 96, CA (overruling *The Banshee* (1887) 6 Asp MLC 221, CA, and *The Manchester Regiment* [1938] P 117, 60 Ll L Rep 279).
5　As to the meaning of 'sternlight' see PARA 711 note 7.
6　Collision Regulations r 13(b). As to the meaning of 'sidelights' see PARA 711 note 6.
7　Collision Regulations r 13(c).
8　Ie within the meaning of the Collision Regulations: see r 13(d). As to the rule applicable in a crossing situation see PARA 705.
9　Collision Regulations r 13(d).
10　Collision Regulations r 11. As to when vessels are deemed to be in sight of one another see PARA 702 note 9.

704.　Head-on situation. Under the Collision Regulations[1], when two power-driven vessels[2] are meeting on reciprocal or nearly reciprocal courses so as to involve risk of collision[3], each must alter her course to starboard so that each pass on the port side of the other[4]. Such a situation is deemed to exist when a vessel sees the other ahead or nearly ahead and by night she could see the masthead lights[5] of the other in a line or nearly in a line and/or both sidelights[6] and by day she observes the corresponding aspect of the other vessel[7]. When a vessel is in any doubt as to whether such a situation exists, she must assume that it does exist and act accordingly[8].

This rule applies only to vessels in sight of one another[9].

1 Ie the International Regulations for Preventing Collisions at Sea (London, 20 October 1972; TS 77 (1977); Cmnd 6962): see PARA 690.
2 As to the meaning of 'vessel' for these purposes see PARA 691 note 2. As to the meaning of 'power-driven vessel' see PARA 701 note 22. As to the rules applicable to sailing vessels see PARA 702.
3 As to the risk of collision see PARA 697.
4 Collision Regulations r 14(a). The rules in Pt B (Steering and Sailing Rules) Section II (Conduct of vessels in sight of one another) (rr 11–18) (see also PARAS 702–703, 704–708) must be strictly complied with; however, vessels are not prevented from taking sufficiently early action ahead of the point in time at which those rules come into effect: Merchant Shipping Notice 1781(M) Introduction para 6.
5 As to the meaning of 'masthead light' see PARA 711 note 5.
6 As to the meaning of 'sidelights' see PARA 711 note 6.
7 Collision Regulations r 14(b).
8 Collision Regulations r 14(c).
9 Collision Regulations r 11. As to when vessels are deemed to be in sight of one another see PARA 702 note 9.

705. The crossing rule. Under the Collision Regulations[1], when two power-driven vessels[2] are crossing[3] so as to involve risk of collision[4], the vessel which has the other on her own starboard side must keep out of the way and, if the circumstances of the case admit, must avoid crossing ahead of the other vessel[5]. This rule applies only to vessels in sight of one another[6].

If two vessels are on courses which, if maintained, will bring them to the same point at, or nearly at, the same moment, they are crossing for the purpose of this rule; but vessels are not so crossing if the course which is reasonably to be attributed to either vessel would keep her clear of the other[7]. Thus if, as a result of their both following the winding curves of the river, two vessels find themselves momentarily on courses which would, if pursued, cross, the crossing rule does not apply[8].

Where two vessels are on crossing courses in open waters or the sea and each knows that the other is going to alter her course at about the same place but there is nothing that definitely settles where they will alter course, the crossing rule nevertheless applies. In such circumstances, however, as a matter of good seamanship the give-way vessel should give way clearly, presenting the stand-on vessel with the clearest indication that the give-way vessel means to get out of the way[9]. The fact that two vessels on crossing courses are both manoeuvring to take up a pilot is not of itself a special circumstance[10] justifying departure from the crossing rule[11].

The crossing rule does not apply if it is not possible for the give-way vessel under the rule to appreciate that the other vessel is on a crossing course[12] and it seems that, if two vessels are within sight of one another and one of them, without observing the other, by her manoeuvres creates a situation in which the crossing rule would apply, the vessel creating the situation is not entitled to rely on the rule[13].

Whether the crossing rule applies to the case of a vessel coming out of a dock into a river in which another vessel is passing up or down depends on whether or not the vessels sight one another at such a distance that they can each of them reasonably act under the crossing rule and so avoid collision[14]. When two vessels are approaching one another at a forked intersection in a narrow channel and bear from one another as if on crossing courses, it appears that they will be governed not by the crossing rule but by the narrow channel rule[15], if it is reasonable to assume that their courses will not in fact cross or that one vessel will pass well ahead or astern of the other[16]. Where, however, the course of one vessel intersects the course of the other so that both will meet at about the point of intersection, both the 'narrow channel rule' and the 'crossing rule' apply, so that normally each vessel ought to keep to the starboard side of the channel[17] in which she is and it is the duty of the vessel which has the other on her starboard side to keep out of the way[18] and not to cross ahead[19] of the other vessel and the duty of the other vessel[20] to keep her course and speed[21].

1   Ie the International Regulations for Preventing Collisions at Sea (London, 20 October 1972; TS 77 (1977); Cmnd 6962): see PARA 690.
2   As to the meaning of 'vessel' for these purposes see PARA 691 note 2. As to the meaning of 'power-driven vessel' see PARA 701 note 22. As to the rules applicable to sailing vessels see PARA 702.
3   For the rules as to overtaking and meeting head on see PARAS 703, 704.
4   As to the risk of collision see PARA 697.
5   Collision Regulations r 15. The rules in Pt B (Steering and Sailing Rules) Section II (Conduct of vessels in sight of one another) (rr 11–18) (see also PARAS 702–704, 706–708) must be strictly complied with; however, vessels are not prevented from taking sufficiently early action ahead of the point in time at which those rules come into effect: Merchant Shipping Notice 1781(M) Introduction para 6. In connection with the Collision Regulations r 15 see *Nautical Challenge Ltd v Evergreen Marine (UK) Ltd* [2017] EWHC 453 (Admlty); and see also *Samco Europe v MSC Prestige* [2011] EWHC 1580 (Admlty), [2011] 2 Lloyd's Rep 579.
6   Collision Regulations r 11. As to when vessels are deemed to be in sight of one another see PARA 702 note 9.
7   *Normandie (Owners of Norwegian SS) v Pekin (Owners of British SS), The Pekin* [1897] AC 532 at 536–537, 8 Asp MLC 367 at 368, PC; *SS Albano v Allan Line SS Co Ltd, Union Dampfschiffsrhederei AG v SS Parisian* [1907] AC 193 at 205, 10 Asp MLC 365 at 369, PC. Vessels continue to be crossing vessels until the crossing is completed: see *Orduna (Owners) v Shipping Controller* [1921] 1 AC 250, HL (where it was held that vessels were still crossing vessels, although the green light of one, after being originally observed on the port bow of the other, had passed to ahead or slightly to starboard of the bow of the first vessel); *Shipping Controller v Athena* (1923) 14 Ll L Rep 515 at 517, HL, per Lord Sumner (commenting on *Orduna (Owners) v Shipping Controller*).
8   *General Steam Navigation Co v Hedley, The Velocity* (1869) LR 3 PC 44; *Malcolmson v General Steam Navigation Co, The Ranger and The Cologne* (1872) LR 4 PC 519, 1 Asp MLC 484; *Normandie (Owners of Norwegian SS) v Pekin (Owners of British SS), The Pekin* [1897] AC 532, 8 Asp MLC 367, PC; *The Olympic and HMS Hawke* (1914) (as reported in 84 LJP 49 at 52, 12 Asp MLC 580 at 584, HL). It seems also that the crossing rule does not apply if two vessels are momentarily on crossing courses as a result of one of them altering course to avoid another vessel or an obstacle: see *The Oceano* (1878) 3 PD 60 at 63, CA. If one vessel is in fact crossing the river so that she will cross the course of the other and there is risk of collision, the crossing rule applies, unless it is ousted by a local rule: *The Oceano* (1878) 3 PD 60 at 63, CA; cf *The Esk and The Niord* (1870) LR 3 PC 436 at 442, 1 Asp MLC 1 at 3 (where the question whether the vessels, when they first sighted each other, were crossing vessels was left undecided). As to the relationship between the rules contained in the Collision Regulations and local rules see PARA 690.
9   *The Karemea* [1921] P 76 at 88, 15 Asp MLC 318 at 323. See also *The Homer* [1973] 1 Lloyd's Rep 501, CA.
10 Ie within the meaning of the Collision Regulations r 2, regarding allocations of responsibility (see PARA 693).
11 *SS Albano v Allan Line SS Co Ltd, Union Dampfschiffsrhederei AG v SS Parisian* [1907] AC 193 at 206, 10 Asp MLC 365 at 370, PC; *The Ada, The Sappho* (1873) 2 Asp MLC 4, PC.
12 *Lorentzen, as Director of Shipping and Curator of the Royal Norwegian Government v The Alcoa Rambler* [1949] AC 236, 82 Ll L Rep 359, PC.
13 *The Spyros* [1953] 1 Lloyd's Rep 501 at 509. See also *The Boynton* (1898) 14 TLR 173.
14 *The Gulf of Suez* [1921] P 318, 15 Asp MLC 328, CA; and see *The Sunlight* [1904] P 100, 9 Asp MLC 509; and *The Llanelly* [1914] P 40, 12 Asp MLC 485. In coming out of a dock a vessel ought

to navigate with the greatest possible caution: *The Llanelly* at 43 and at 486. When two steam vessels, one going out and the other coming in, have to pass each other near the entrance of a canal or harbour where the 'narrow channel rule' (see PARA 728) applies, it appears that the 'crossing rule' does not apply, even though for a time the two vessels seem to be on crossing courses: *The Kaiser Wilhelm der Grosse* [1907] P 36 at 44, 10 Asp MLC 361 at 364 (on appeal [1907] P 259 at 263, 10 Asp MLC 504 at 506, CA). A vessel crossing a channel towards the entrance to a dock is not excused from keeping out of the way, under the crossing rule, of a vessel coming down the channel, on the grounds that she herself is bound for the dock and is carrying the appropriate docking signal: *The St Audries* (1886) 5 Asp MLC 552. The crossing rule may not apply in a confined space of water: *The Red Cross* (1907) 10 Asp MLC 521. See also *The Hazelmere* [1911] P 69, 11 Asp MLC 536, CA.

15 Ie the Collision Regulations r 9 (see PARA 699).

16 *Normandie (Owners of Norwegian SS) v Pekin (Owners of British SS), The Pekin* [1897] AC 532 at 537, 8 Asp MLC 367 at 368, PC. If one vessel comes to the point of intersection reasonably in advance of the other, it appears that as a matter of good seamanship she should keep on whereas the other should wait until she has passed. If both vessels approach the point of intersection at the same time, they must act reasonably and it would be reasonable for the one with the tide against her to wait: *The Prince Leopold de Belgique* [1909] P 103 at 106, 11 Asp MLC 203 at 205.

17 Ie under the 'narrow channel rule' (see PARA 699).

18 Ie under the 'crossing rule' (see the text and notes 1–6).

19 See the Collision Regulations r 15; and the text and notes 1–5.

20 See PARA 707.

21 *The Ashton* [1905] P 21, 10 Asp MLC 88; cf *The Try Again* (1908) Shipping Gazette, 2 June.

706. Action by give-way vessel.

Under the Collision Regulations[1], every vessel[2] which is directed to keep out of the way of another vessel[3] must, so far as possible, take early and substantial action to keep well clear[4].

This rule applies only to vessels in sight of one another[5].

1 Ie the International Regulations for Preventing Collisions at Sea (London, 20 October 1972; TS 77 (1977); Cmnd 6962): see PARA 690.

2 As to the meaning of 'vessel' for these purposes see PARA 691 note 2.

3 See eg the Collision Regulations r 13 (overtaking vessel to keep out of way of other) (see PARA 703) and r 15 (vessel with other on starboard side when crossing to keep out of way) (see PARA 705).

4 Collision Regulations r 16. The rules in Pt B (Steering and Sailing Rules) Section II (Conduct of vessels in sight of one another) (rr 11–18) (see also PARAS 702–705, 707–708) must be strictly complied with; however, vessels are not prevented from taking sufficiently early action ahead of the point in time at which those rules come into effect: Merchant Shipping Notice 1781(M) Introduction para 6. As to action by a stand-on vessel see PARA 707. In connection with the taking of avoiding action see *Samco Europe v MSC Prestige* [2011] EWHC 1580 (Admlty), [2011] 2 Lloyd's Rep 579.

5 Collision Regulations r 11. As to when vessels are deemed to be in sight of one another see PARA 702 note 9.

707. Action by stand-on vessel.

Under the Collision Regulations[1], where one of two vessels[2] is to keep out of the way[3], the other (the 'stand-on' vessel) must keep her course and speed[4]. The duty of the stand-on vessel to keep her course and speed does not come into force until it is the duty of the give-way vessel to keep out of the way and that duty does not arise until there is risk of collision[5] within the meaning of the collision rules[6], or a close proximity between vessels in an overtaking situation[7].

The stand-on vessel may, however, take action to avoid collision by her manoeuvre alone, as soon as it becomes apparent to her that the vessel required to keep out of the way is not taking appropriate action in compliance with the Collision Regulations[8]. When, from any cause, the vessel required to keep her course and speed finds herself so close that collision cannot be avoided by the action of the give-way vessel alone, she must take such action as will best aid[9] to avoid collision[10].

A power-driven vessel[11] which takes action[12] in a crossing situation[13] to avoid collision with another power-driven vessel must not, if the circumstances of the case admit, alter course to port for a vessel on her own port side[14].

This rule applies only to vessels in sight of one another[15]; and it does not relieve the give-way vessel of her obligation[16] to keep out of the way[17].

1   Ie the International Regulations for Preventing Collisions at Sea (London, 20 October 1972; TS 77 (1977); Cmnd 6962): see PARA 690.
2   As to the meaning of 'vessel' for these purposes see PARA 691 note 2.
3   See eg the Collision Regulations r 13 (overtaking vessel to keep out of way of other) (see PARA 703) and r 15 (vessel with other on starboard side when crossing to keep out of way) (see PARA 705).
4   Collision Regulations r 17(a)(i). For these purposes, 'course and speed' means course and speed in following the nautical manoeuvre in which, to the knowledge of the other vessel, the stand-on vessel is at the time engaged: *The Roanoke* [1908] P 231 at 239, 11 Asp MLC 253 at 257, CA, per Lord Alverstone CJ; and see eg *The Afrika* (1937) 57 Ll L Rep 215 at 220, 221, PC (vessel engaged in coming to anchor); *The Taunton* (1928) 31 Ll L Rep 119 at 120. Thus it means the course and speed which the vessel would take naturally and independently of the presence of the other vessel, as the proper method of her navigation at the particular time and place: *The Roanoke* at 247 and at 259 per Kennedy LJ; and see *The Karamea* [1921] P 76, 15 Asp MLC 318, CA (affd sub nom *Haughland (Owners) v Karamea (Owners)* [1922] 1 AC 68, 15 Asp MLC 430, HL) (two crossing ships making for the same buoy where both would make an eight point turn).
    In ordinary circumstances, when no alteration of course or speed is required by the manoeuvre which the vessel is carrying out, the first duty of the stand-on vessel under the Collision Regulations r 17 is not to make any alteration in either, but to keep her course and speed as long as this will enable the other vessel to keep out of the way: cf *The Ranza* (1898) 79 LJP 21n; *The Huntsman* (1911) 11 Asp MLC 606.
    The rules in the Collision Regulations Pt B (Steering and Sailing Rules) Section II (Conduct of vessels in sight of one another) (rr 11–18) (see also PARAS 702–706, 708) must be strictly complied with; however, vessels are not prevented from taking sufficiently early action ahead of the point in time at which those rules come into effect: Merchant Shipping Notice 1781(M) Introduction para 6.
5   As to the risk of collision see PARA 697.
6   *The Bellanoch* [1907] P 170 at 180, CA; *The Roanoke* [1908] P 231 at 241, 245, 11 Asp MLC 253 at 257, 258, CA. See also *The Norma* (1876) 3 Asp MLC 272, PC (schooner altered course when steamer two miles off; manoeuvre innocent); *The Sylph* (1857) Sw 233; *Great Ship Co v Sharples, The Great Eastern* (1864) 3 Moo PCCNS 31; *The Manchester Regiment* [1938] P 117 at 129, 130, 60 Ll L Rep 279; *The Statue of Liberty* [1971] 2 Lloyd's Rep 277, HL. A vessel which would normally be the give-way vessel and which is not under command and has hoisted the appropriate shapes (see PARA 717) is not thereby converted into a stand-on vessel for the purposes of the Collision Regulations r 17, but the other ship has a duty arising from the duty of good seamanship to keep out of her way: *Mendip Range (Owners) v Radcliffe* [1921] 1 AC 556, 15 Asp MLC 242, HL. See also *Orduna (Owners) v Shipping Controller* [1921] 1 AC 250, HL; *The Fancy* [1917] P 13, 13 Asp MLC 603 (patrol steamer when intercepting a steamship not relieved of her obligations under the crossing rule, but other vessel also to blame for altering course and speed).
7   See *The Nowy Sacz* [1979] QB 236, [1978] 2 All ER 297, [1977] 2 Lloyd's Rep 91, CA; and PARA 703.
8   Collision Regulations r 17(a)(ii).
9   The liability of the stand-on vessel is to be judged on the supposition that she is only aiding action by the other vessel and she is not to be held to blame because of the other vessel's inaction: see *The Sparto* [1956] 1 Lloyd's Rep 400 at 407. The action which as a rule will best aid to avert collision is to go full speed astern: *Peter Pan v Mendocino* (1921) 6 Ll L Rep 519 at 521, 522; *Kitano Maru (Owners) v Otranto (Owners), The Otranto* [1931] AC 194, 18 Asp MLC 193, HL.
10 Collision Regulations r 17(b). Prior to the Collision Regulations, which gave the vessel discretionary power to take action to avoid collision (see r 17(a)(ii); and the text and note 8) it was a matter of some difficulty for the officer in charge of a stand-on vessel to determine when the time had arrived for him to take action, although latitude was allowed to him: *SS Albano v Allan Line SS Co Ltd, Union Dampfschiffsrhederei AG v SS Parisian* [1907] AC 193 at 207, 10 Asp MLC 365 at 370, PC; *The Huntsman* (1911) 11 Asp MLC 606 at 608; and see also *Compagnie des Forges et d'Hormecourt v Gibson & Co, The Eidsvaag v The Gala* 1920 SC 247 (action to avert collision justified); *The Treherbert* [1934] P 31, 18 Asp MLC 458, CA; *The Sparto* [1956] 1 Lloyd's Rep 400 at 407. It is quite impossible to determine mathematically the point at which the stand-on vessel must act; the rules have to be construed so that persons may act reasonably upon them: *The Ranza* (1898) 79 LJP 21n; and see *Kitano Maru (Owners) v Otranto (Owners), The Otranto* [1931] AC 194, 18 Asp MLC 193, HL. If the officer in charge is found to have been watching the other vessel and doing his best to make up his mind when to act, he ought not to be held to blame for waiting a moment too long before acting or acting too soon: *The Ranza* (1898)

79 LJP 21n at 22; *The Huntsman* (1911) 11 Asp MLC 606; *The Sparto* [1956] 1 Lloyd's Rep 400 at 407. See also *Owners of the Mineral Dampier v Owners of the Hanjin Madras* [2001] EWCA Civ 1278, [2001] 2 All ER (Comm) 805, [2001] 2 Lloyd's Rep 419; and *Owners of the Selat Arjuna v Owners of the Contship Success* [2000] 1 All ER (Comm) 905, CA (in both cases, stand-on vessel not liable for failing to take correct avoiding action); and *Owners of the Sitarem v Owners and/or demise charterers of the Spirit* [2001] 2 All ER (Comm) 837, [2001] 2 Lloyd's Rep 107 (vessel not complying with her obligation to take early action to keep out of the way nonetheless was manifestly a much smaller vessel able to manoeuvre more readily than the other vessel).

11 As to the meaning of 'power-driven vessel' see PARA 701 note 22.
12 Ie action in accordance with the Collision Regulations r 17(a)(ii) (see the text and note 8): see r 17(c).
13 As to the meaning of a 'crossing situation' see PARA 705.
14 Collision Regulations r 17(c).
15 Collision Regulations r 11. As to when vessels are deemed to be in sight of one another see PARA 702 note 9.
16 Ie under the Collision Regulations r 16 (see PARA 706): see r 17(d).
17 Collision Regulations r 17(d).

708. Responsibilities between vessels. Except where the rules of the Collision Regulations[1] relating to narrow channels[2], traffic separation schemes[3] and overtaking[4] otherwise require[5]:

(1)   a power-driven vessel[6] underway[7] must keep out of the way[8] of:
        (a)   a vessel not under command[9];
        (b)   a vessel restricted in her ability to manoeuvre[10];
        (c)   a vessel engaged in fishing[11];
        (d)   a sailing vessel[12];
(2)   a sailing vessel underway must keep out of the way of:
        (a)   a vessel not under command[13];
        (b)   a vessel restricted in her ability to manoeuvre[14];
        (c)   a vessel engaged in fishing[15];
(3)   a vessel engaged in fishing when underway must, so far as possible, keep out of the way of:
        (a)   a vessel not under command[16];
        (b)   a vessel restricted in her ability to manoeuvre[17].

Any vessel other than a vessel not under command or a vessel restricted in her ability to manoeuvre must, if the circumstances of the case admit, avoid impeding the safe passage of a vessel constrained by her draught[18], exhibiting the appropriate[19] signals[20]. A vessel constrained by her draught must navigate with particular caution having full regard to her special condition[21].

A seaplane[22] on the water must, in general, keep well clear of all vessels and avoid impeding their navigation[23]. In circumstances, however, where risk of collision[24] exists, she must comply with the steering and sailing rules[25].

A wing-in-ground (WIG) craft[26] must, when taking off, landing and in flight near the surface, keep well clear of all other vessels and avoid impeding their navigation[27]; and such a craft operating on the water surface must comply with the steering and sailing rules[28] as a power-driven vessel[29].

This rule applies only to vessels in sight of one another[30].

1 Ie the International Regulations for Preventing Collisions at Sea (London, 20 October 1972; TS 77 (1977); Cmnd 6962): see PARA 690.
2 Ie the Collision Regulations r 9 (see PARA 699): see r 18.
3 Ie the Collision Regulations r 10 (see PARA 701): see r 18.
4 Ie the Collision Regulations r 13 (see PARA 703): see r 18.
5 Collision Regulations r 18. The rules in Pt B (Steering and Sailing Rules) Section II (Conduct of vessels in sight of one another) (rr 11–18) (see also PARAS 702–707) must be strictly complied with; however, vessels are not prevented from taking sufficiently early action ahead of the point in time at which those rules come into effect: Merchant Shipping Notice 1781(M) Introduction para 6.

6   As to the meaning of 'power-driven vessel' see PARA 701 note 22; and as to the meaning of 'vessel' for these purposes see PARA 691 note 2.
7   As to the meaning of 'underway' see PARA 701 note 24.
8   As to the duty to keep out of the way see PARA 706.
9   Collision Regulations r 18(a)(i). For these purposes, 'vessel not under command' means a vessel which through some exceptional circumstance is unable to manoeuvre as required by the rules of the Collision Regulations and is, therefore, unable to keep out of the way of another vessel: r 3(f).
10 Collision Regulations r 18(a)(ii). As to the meaning of 'vessel restricted in her ability to manoeuvre' see PARA 701 note 24.
11 Collision Regulations r 18(a)(iii). As to the meaning of 'vessel engaged in fishing' see PARA 691 note 9.
12 Collision Regulations r 18(a)(iv). As to the meaning of 'sailing vessel' see PARA 699 note 7. A power-driven vessel may perform her duty of keeping out of the way of a sailing vessel by decreasing her speed or by altering her course so as to pass astern; but she should not alter her course to a sailing vessel approaching from a distance at night if she cannot see her lights owing to their improper position or otherwise and is in doubt as to the course the sailing vessel is pursuing and on which side she is going to pass; a prudent master of a power-driven vessel, if in doubt as to the course of the sailing vessel and if it is necessary to act, ought to wait by slackening speed or stopping until he can ascertain her course: *Beal v Marchais, The Bougainville and The James C Stevenson* (1873) LR 5 PC 316 at 323, 2 Asp MLC 1 at 3.
13 Collision Regulations r 18(b)(i).
14 Collision Regulations r 18(b)(ii).
15 Collision Regulations r 18(b)(iii).
16 Collision Regulations r 18(c)(i).
17 Collision Regulations r 18(c)(ii).
18 For these purposes, 'vessel constrained by her draught' means a power-driven vessel which, because of her draught in relation to the available depth and width of navigable water, is severely restricted in her ability to deviate from the course she is following: Collision Regulations r 3(h).
19 Ie the signals prescribed by the Collision Regulations r 28 (see PARA 718): see r 18(d)(i).
20 Collision Regulations r 18(d)(i).
21 Collision Regulations r 18(d)(ii).
22 As to the meaning of 'seaplane' see PARA 691 note 2.
23 Collision Regulations r 18(e).
24 As to the risk of collision see PARA 697.
25 Collision Regulations r 18(e). The text refers to the rules in Pt B (rr 4–19) (see also PARAS 695–707, 709): see r 18(e).
26 As to the meaning of 'wing-in-ground (WIG) craft' see PARA 691 note 2.
27 Collision Regulations r 18(f)(i).
28 Ie the rules in the Collision Regulations Pt B: see r 18(f)(ii).
29 Collision Regulations r 18(f)(ii).
30 Collision Regulations r 11. As to when vessels are deemed to be in sight of one another see PARA 702 note 9.

C.   CONDUCT OF VESSELS IN RESTRICTED VISIBILITY

709. Vessels proceeding in restricted visibility. Special provisions of the Collision Regulations[1] apply to vessels[2] not in sight of one another[3] when navigating in or near an area of restricted visibility[4].

Every vessel must proceed at a safe speed[5] adapted to the prevailing circumstances and conditions of restricted visibility[6]. A power-driven vessel[7] must have her engines ready for immediate manoeuvre[8].

Every vessel must have due regard to the prevailing circumstances and conditions of restricted visibility when complying with the rules relating to the conduct of vessels in any conditions of visibility[9].

A vessel which detects, by radar[10] alone, the presence of another vessel must determine if a close-quarters situation[11] is developing and/or risk of collision[12] exists[13]. If so, she must take avoiding action[14] in ample time, provided that, when such action consists of an alteration of course, so far as possible the following must be avoided[15]:

(1)   an alteration of course to port for a vessel forward of the beam, other than for a vessel being overtaken[16];

(2)   an alteration of course towards a vessel abeam or abaft the beam[17].

Except where it has been determined that a risk of collision does not exist, every vessel which hears apparently forward of her beam the fog signal[18] of another vessel, or which cannot avoid a close-quarters situation with another vessel forward of her beam, must reduce her speed to the minimum at which she can be kept on her course[19]. She must, if necessary, take all her way off and in any event navigate with extreme caution until danger of collision is over[20].

1   Ie the International Regulations for Preventing Collisions at Sea (London, 20 October 1972; TS 77 (1977); Cmnd 6962): see PARA 690.
2   As to the meaning of 'vessel' for these purposes see PARA 691 note 2.
3   As to when vessels are deemed to be in sight of one another see PARA 702 note 9; and as to the conduct of vessels in sight of one another see PARAS 702–708.
4   Collision Regulations r 19(a). For these purposes, 'restricted visibility' means any condition in which visibility is restricted by fog, mist, falling snow, heavy rainstorms, sandstorms or any other similar causes: r 3(l). See *Owners of the Ship 'Bulk Atalanta' v Owners of the Ship 'Forest Pioneer'* [2007] EWHC 84 (Comm).
    The rules in the Collision Regulations Pt B (Steering and Sailing Rules) section III (Conduct of vessels in restricted visibility) (r 19) must be strictly complied with; however, vessels are not prevented from taking sufficiently early action ahead of the point in time at which those rules come into effect: Merchant Shipping Notice 1781(M) Introduction para 6.
5   As to what is a safe speed see PARA 696.
6   Collision Regulations r 19(b).
7   As to the meaning of 'power-driven vessel' see PARA 701 note 22.
8   Collision Regulations r 19(b).
9   Collision Regulations r 19(c). The text refers to the rules of Pt B Section I (rr 4–10) (see PARAS 695–701): see r 19(c).
10 As to radar generally see PARA 694.
11 As to what constitutes a close-quarters situation see PARA 698 note 6.
12 As to the risk of collision see PARA 697.
13 Collision Regulations r 19(d).
14 As to action to avoid collision see PARA 698.
15 Collision Regulations r 19(d).
16 Collision Regulations r 19(d)(i). As to conduct of vessels during overtaking see PARA 703.
17 Collision Regulations r 19(d)(ii).
18 As to sound signals in restricted visibility see PARA 724.
19 Collision Regulations r 19(e).
20 Collision Regulations r 19(e).

(iii) Lights and Shapes

710. Application of rules concerning lights and shapes. The rules of the Collision Regulations[1] concerning lights and shapes[2] must be complied with in all weathers[3].

The rules concerning lights[4] must be complied with from sunset to sunrise and during such times no other lights may be exhibited, except such lights as cannot be mistaken for the lights specified in the rules[5] or do not impair their visibility or distinctive character, or interfere with the keeping of a proper look-out[6]. The lights so prescribed[7] must, if carried, also be exhibited from sunrise to sunset in restricted visibility[8] and may be exhibited in all other circumstances when it is deemed necessary[9].

The rules concerning shapes must be complied with by day[10].

1   Ie the International Regulations for Preventing Collisions at Sea (London, 20 October 1972; TS 77 (1977); Cmnd 6962): see PARA 690.
2   Ie the Collision Regulations Pt C (rr 20–31) (see also PARA 711 et seq): see r 20(a). The lights and shapes specified in Pt C must comply with the provisions of Annex I (Positioning and technical details of lights and shapes): r 20(e).
3   Collision Regulations r 20(a).
4   As to the visibility of lights see PARA 711.

5 Ie the lights specified in the Collision Regulations: see r 20(b).
6 Collision Regulations r 20(b). As to the keeping of a look-out see PARA 695. The rules as to lights
   are in general not satisfied by equivalents, or by anything less than a close and literal adherence to
   what they prescribe: *The Emperor and The Lady of the Lake* (1865) Holt Adm 37 at 38, PC. In
   special circumstances, a vessel may be excused for showing unusual lights: *The Buckhurst* (1881)
   6 PD 152, 4 Asp MLC 484; *The Merchant Prince* (1885) 10 PD 139, 5 Asp MLC 520; *The
   Faedrelandet* [1895] P 205, 8 Asp MLC 1, CA. For an unsuccessful effort to justify a wrong light
   by custom see *The Talbot* [1891] P 184, 7 Asp MLC 36. A vessel which has lost or damaged her
   lights owing to bad weather, collision or otherwise is bound to replace them as soon as she
   reasonably can: *The Aurora, The Robert Ingham* (1861) Lush 327; *The Saxonia, The Eclipse*
   (1862) Lush 410, PC; *The Kjobenhavn* (1874) 2 Asp MLC 213, PC. It is no excuse for the absence
   of lights that they were unnecessary owing to bright moonlight (*The City of London, Morgan v
   Sim* (1857) Sw 245, PC) or that they were being trimmed (*The Victoria* (1848) 3 Wm Rob 49; *The
   CM Palmer, The Larnax* (1873) 2 Asp MLC 94, PC) or went out by accident (*The Rob Roy* (1849)
   3 Wm Rob 190; *The Sylph* (1854) 2 Ecc & Ad 75; *The Hibernia* (1874) 2 Asp MLC 454, PC).
7 Ie prescribed by the Collision Regulations: see r 20(c).
8 As to the meaning of 'restricted visibility' see PARA 709 note 4.
9 Collision Regulations r 20(c).
10 Collision Regulations r 20(d).

711. Visibility of lights. The lights prescribed in the rules of the Collision
Regulations relating to lights and shapes[1] must be of a specified intensity[2] so as to
be visible at various prescribed minimum ranges[3], as follows:

(1)   in vessels of 50 metres or more in length[4], the prescribed minimum
       ranges are: for a masthead light[5], six miles; for a sidelight[6], three miles;
       for a sternlight[7], three miles; for a towing light[8], three miles; for a white,
       red, green or yellow all-round[9] light, three miles[10];

(2)   in vessels of 12 metres or more in length but less than 50 metres in
       length, the prescribed minimum ranges are: for a masthead light, five
       miles (except that, where the length of the vessel is less than 20 metres,
       it is three miles); for a sidelight, two miles; for a sternlight, two miles; for
       a towing light, two miles; for a white, red, green or yellow all-round
       light, two miles[11];

(3)   in vessels of less than 12 metres in length, the prescribed minimum
       ranges are: for a masthead light, two miles; for a sidelight, one mile; for
       a sternlight, two miles; for a towing light, two miles; for a white, red,
       green or yellow all-round light, two miles[12];

(4)   in inconspicuous, partly submerged vessels or objects being towed, the
       prescribed range is, for a white all-round light, three miles[13].

1 Ie prescribed in the International Regulations for Preventing Collisions at Sea (London, 20 October
   1972; TS 77 (1977); Cmnd 6962) (see PARA 690) Pt C (rr 20–31) (see also PARAS 710, 712 et seq):
   see r 22.
2 Ie lights prescribed in the Collision Regulations Pt C (see also PARAS 710, 712 et seq) must have
   an intensity as specified in Annex I Section 8: see r 22. As to the application of Annex I see
   PARA 710 note 2.
3 Collision Regulations r 22. As to the application of these provisions see PARA 710.
4 As to the meaning of 'length' see PARA 699 note 6.
5 For these purposes, 'masthead light' means a white light placed over the fore and aft centreline of
   the vessel showing an unbroken light over an arc of the horizon of 225 degrees and so fixed as to
   show the light from right ahead to 22.5 degrees abaft the beam on either side of the vessel:
   Collision Regulations r 21(a).
6 For these purposes, 'sidelights' means a green light on the starboard side and a red light on the port
   side each showing an unbroken light over an arc of the horizon of 112.5 degrees and so fixed as
   to show the light from the right ahead to 22.5 degrees abaft the beam on its respective side; but
   in a vessel of less than 20 metres in length the sidelights may be combined in one lantern carried
   on the fore and aft centreline of the vessel: Collision Regulations r 21(b).
7 For these purposes, 'sternlight' means a white light placed as nearly as practicable at the stern
   showing an unbroken light over an arc of the horizon of 135 degrees and so fixed as to show the
   light 67.5 degrees from right aft on each side of the vessel: Collision Regulations r 21(c).
8 For these purposes, 'towing light' means a yellow light having the same characteristics as the
   sternlight as defined in the Collision Regulations r 21(c) (see note 7): r 21(d).

9   For these purposes, 'all-round light' means a light showing an unbroken light over an arc of the
    horizon of 360 degrees: Collision Regulations r 21(e).
10 Collision Regulations r 22(a).
11 Collision Regulations r 22(b).
12 Collision Regulations r 22(c).
13 Collision Regulations r 22(d).

712.   Lights required by power-driven vessels underway. Under the rules of
the Collision Regulations relating to lights and shapes[1], a power-driven vessel[2]
underway[3] must exhibit[4]:
(1)   a masthead light[5] forward[6];
(2)   a second masthead light abaft of and higher than the forward one,
         except that a vessel of less than 50 metres in length[7] is not obliged to
         exhibit such light but may do so[8];
(3)   sidelights[9];
(4)   a sternlight[10].
An air-cushion vessel when operating in the non-displacement mode must, in
addition to the lights prescribed in heads (1) to (4) above, exhibit an all-round[11]
flashing[12] yellow light[13]; and a wing-in-ground (WIG) craft[14] only when taking off,
landing and in flight near the surface must, in addition to the lights prescribed in
heads (1) to (4) above, exhibit a high intensity all-round flashing red light[15].
A power-driven vessel of less than 12 metres in length may, in lieu of the lights
prescribed in heads (1) to (4) above, exhibit an all-round white light and
sidelights[16].
A power-driven vessel of less than seven metres in length whose maximum
speed does not exceed seven knots may, in lieu of the lights prescribed in heads (1)
to (4) above, exhibit an all-round white light and must, if practicable, also exhibit
sidelights[17].
The masthead light or all-round white light on a power-driven vessel of less
than 12 metres in length may be displaced from the fore and aft centreline of the
vessel if centreline fitting is not practicable, provided that the sidelights are
combined in one lantern which must be carried on the fore and aft centreline of
the vessel or located as nearly as practicable in the same fore and aft line as the
masthead light or the all-round white light[18].

1   Ie the International Regulations for Preventing Collisions at Sea (London, 20 October 1972; TS 77
    (1977); Cmnd 6962) (see PARA 690) Pt C (rr 20–31) (see also PARAS 710–711, 713 et seq). As to
    the application of these provisions see PARA 710. As to the positioning and technical details of
    lights and shapes see Annex I; and PARA 710 note 2; and as to the required visibility of the
    prescribed lights see PARA 711.
2   As to the meaning of 'power-driven vessel' see PARA 701 note 22; and as to the meaning of 'vessel'
    for these purposes see PARA 691 note 2.
3   As to the meaning of 'underway' see PARA 701 note 24.
4   Collision Regulations r 23(a).
5   As to the meaning of 'masthead light' see PARA 711 note 5.
6   Collision Regulations r 23(a)(i).
7   As to the meaning of 'length' see PARA 699 note 6.
8   Collision Regulations r 23(a)(ii).
9   Collision Regulations r 23(a)(iii). As to the meaning of 'sidelights' see PARA 711 note 6.
10 Collision Regulations r 23(a)(iv). As to the meaning of 'sternlight' see PARA 711 note 7.
11 As to the meaning of 'all-round light' see PARA 711 note 9.
12 For these purposes, 'flashing light' means a light flashing at regular intervals at a frequency of 120
    flashes or more per minute: Collision Regulations r 21(f).
13 Collision Regulations r 23(b).
14 As to the meaning of 'wing-in-ground (WIG) craft' see PARA 691 note 2.
15 Collision Regulations r 23(c).
16 Collision Regulations r 23(d)(i).
17 Collision Regulations r 23(d)(ii).
18 Collision Regulations r 23(d)(iii).

713. Lights and shapes required by vessels towing and pushing. Under the rules of the Collision Regulations relating to lights and shapes[1], a power-driven vessel[2], when towing[3], must exhibit[4]:

(1)   two masthead lights[5] forward in a vertical line, or, when the length of the tow, measuring from the stern of the towing vessel to the after end of the tow, exceeds 200 metres, three such lights in a vertical line[6];

(2)   sidelights[7];

(3)   a sternlight[8];

(4)   a towing light[9] in a vertical line above the sternlight[10];

(5)   when the length of the tow exceeds 200 metres, a diamond shape where it can best be seen[11].

When a pushing vessel and a vessel being pushed ahead are rigidly connected in a composite unit, they are to be regarded as a power-driven vessel and exhibit the appropriate lights[12].

A power-driven vessel, when pushing ahead or towing alongside, except in the case of a composite unit, must exhibit[13]:

(a)   two masthead lights forward in a vertical line[14];

(b)   sidelights[15];

(c)   a sternlight[16].

Where, from any sufficient cause, it is impracticable for a vessel not normally engaged in towing operations to display the lights prescribed in heads (1) to (5) above[17] or in heads (a) to (c) above[18], such vessel is not required to exhibit those lights when engaged in towing another vessel in distress or otherwise in need of assistance[19]. All possible measures must be taken to indicate the nature of the relationship between the towing vessel and the vessel being towed[20], in particular by illuminating the towline[21].

1   Ie the International Regulations for Preventing Collisions at Sea (London, 20 October 1972; TS 77 (1977); Cmnd 6962) (see PARA 690) Pt C (rr 20–31) (see also PARAS 710–712, 714 et seq). As to the application of these provisions see PARA 710. As to the positioning and technical details of lights and shapes see Annex I; and PARA 710 note 2; and as to the required visibility of the prescribed lights see PARA 711.
2   As to the meaning of 'power-driven vessel' see PARA 701 note 22; and as to the meaning of 'vessel' for these purposes see PARA 691 note 2.
3   The purpose of the lights required to be carried by vessels, when towing, is to warn other vessels that the vessel towing is incumbered and not in all respects in control of her movements: *Union Steamship Co v Aracan (Owners), The American and The Syria* (1874) LR 6 PC 127 at 131, 2 Asp MLC 350 at 360. A tug towing a vessel up to her anchor should exhibit the towing lights: *The Romance* [1901] P 15, 9 Asp MLC 149.
4   Collision Regulations r 24(a). A power-driven vessel to which r 24(a) applies must also comply with r 23(a)(ii) (see PARA 712): see r 24(d).
5   As to the meaning of 'masthead light' see PARA 711 note 5.
6   Collision Regulations r 24(a)(i). Head (1) in the text applies instead of r 23(a)(i), (ii) (see PARA 712): see r 24(a)(i).
7   Collision Regulations r 24(a)(ii). As to the meaning of 'sidelights' see PARA 711 note 6.
8   Collision Regulations r 24(a)(iii). As to the meaning of 'sternlight' see PARA 711 note 7.
9   As to the meaning of 'towing light' see PARA 711 note 8.
10 Collision Regulations r 24(a)(iv).
11 Collision Regulations r 24(a)(v).
12 Collision Regulations r 24(b). The text refers to the appropriate lights that are prescribed by r 23 (see PARA 712): see r 24(b).
13 Collision Regulations r 24(c). A power-driven vessel to which r 24(c) applies must also comply with r 23(a)(ii) (see PARA 712): see r 24(d).
14 Collision Regulations r 24(c)(i). Head (a) in the text applies to a power-driven vessel instead of r 23(a)(i), (ii) (see PARA 712): see r 24(c)(i).
15 Collision Regulations r 24(c)(ii).
16 Collision Regulations r 24(c)(iii).
17 Ie the lights prescribed in the Collision Regulations r 24(a) (see the text and notes 1–11): see r 24(i).

18 Ie the lights prescribed in the Collision Regulations r 24(c) (see the text and notes 13–16): see r 24(i).
19 Collision Regulations r 24(i).
20 Ie as authorised by the Collision Regulations r 36 (see PARA 725): see r 24(i).
21 Collision Regulations r 24(i).

714. Lights and shapes required by vessels being towed or pushed. Under the rules of the Collision Regulations relating to lights and shapes[1], a vessel[2] or object being towed[3] must exhibit[4]:

(1)   sidelights[5];
(2)   a sternlight[6];
(3)   when the length of the tow exceeds 200 metres, a diamond shape where it can best be seen[7].

Any number of vessels being towed alongside or pushed in a group must be lighted as one vessel[8]; however:

(a)   a vessel being pushed ahead, not being part of a composite unit, must exhibit, at the forward end, sidelights[9];
(b)   a vessel being towed alongside must exhibit a sternlight and, at the forward end, sidelights[10].

An inconspicuous, partly submerged vessel or object, or combination of such vessels or objects being towed, must exhibit[11]:

(i)   if it is less than 25 metres in breadth[12], one all-round white light[13] at or near the forward end and one at or near the after end, except that dracones need not exhibit a light at or near the forward end[14];
(ii)   if it is 25 metres or more in breadth, two additional all-round white lights at or near the extremities of its breadth[15];
(iii)   if it exceeds 100 metres in length[16], additional all-round white lights between the lights prescribed in heads (i) and (ii) above so that the distance between the lights does not exceed 100 metres[17];
(iv)   a diamond shape at or near the aftermost extremity of the last vessel or object being towed and, if the length of the tow exceeds 200 metres, an additional diamond shape where it can best be seen and located as far forward as is practicable[18].

Where from any sufficient cause it is impracticable for a vessel or object being towed to exhibit the lights or shapes prescribed in heads (1) to (3) above[19] or in heads (i) to (iv) above[20], all possible measures must be taken to light the vessel or object towed or at least to indicate the presence of such vessel or object[21].

1 Ie the International Regulations for Preventing Collisions at Sea (London, 20 October 1972; TS 77 (1977); Cmnd 6962) (see PARA 690) Pt C (rr 20–31) (see also PARAS 710–713, 715 et seq). As to the application of these provisions see PARA 710. As to the positioning and technical details of lights and shapes see Annex I; and PARA 710 note 2; and as to the required visibility of the prescribed lights see PARA 711.
2 As the meaning of 'vessel' for these purposes see PARA 691 note 2.
3 Ie other than a vessel or object being towed as mentioned in the Collision Regulations r 24(g) (see the text and notes 11–18): see r 24(e).
   A dumb barge lashed alongside a tug underway is probably a vessel being towed: see *The Lighter (No 3)* (1902) 18 TLR 322, PC (where it seems to have been assumed that the dumb barge was being towed). In view of the special provision now made as to lights for vessels being pushed (see PARA 713), the question might perhaps arise whether a vessel lashed alongside another was being towed or pushed. A vessel being drawn up to her anchor by a tug is not being towed: *The Romance* [1901] P 15, 9 Asp MLC 149. The tug must carry towing lights: see PARA 713. A tug which merely has a rope fast to a vessel with the intention of towing her at a future time is not towing: *The Sargasso* [1912] P 192, 12 Asp MLC 202.
4 Collision Regulations r 24(e).
5 Collision Regulations r 24(e)(i). As to the meaning of 'sidelights' see PARA 711 note 6.
6 Collision Regulations r 24(e)(ii). As to the meaning of 'sternlight' see PARA 711 note 7.
7 Collision Regulations r 24(e)(iii).

8   Collision Regulations r 24(f).
9   Collision Regulations r 24(f)(i).
10 Collision Regulations r 24(f)(ii).
11 Collision Regulations r 24(g).
12 For these purposes, 'breadth' of a vessel means her greatest breadth: Collision Regulations r 3(j).
13 As to the meaning of 'all-round light' see PARA 711 note 9.
14 Collision Regulations r 24(g)(i).
15 Collision Regulations r 24(g)(ii).
16 As to the meaning of 'length' see PARA 699 note 6.
17 Collision Regulations r 24(g)(iii).
18 Collision Regulations r 24(g)(iv).
19 Ie the lights or shapes prescribed in the Collision Regulations r 24(e) (see the text and notes 1–7):
    see r 24(h).
20 Ie the lights or shapes prescribed in the Collision Regulations r 24(g) (see the text and notes
    11–18): see r 24(h).
21 Collision Regulations r 24(h).

715. Lights and shapes required by sailing vessels underway and vessels under oars. Under the rules of the Collision Regulations relating to lights and shapes[1], a sailing vessel[2] underway[3] must exhibit[4]:
(1)   sidelights[5];
(2)   a sternlight[6].
In a sailing vessel of less than 20 metres in length[7], the lights prescribed by heads (1) and (2) above may be combined in one lantern carried at or near the top of the mast where it can best be seen[8].
A sailing vessel underway may, in addition to the lights prescribed by heads (1) and (2) above, exhibit at or near the top of the mast, where they can best be seen, two all-round lights[9] in a vertical line, the upper being red and the lower green, but these lights must not be exhibited in conjunction with the combined lantern[10].
A sailing vessel of less than seven metres in length must, if practicable, also exhibit the prescribed lights[11] but, if she does not, she must have ready at hand an electric torch or lighted lantern showing a white light which must be exhibited in sufficient time to prevent collision[12].
A vessel under oars may exhibit the prescribed lights for sailing vessels[13] but, if she does not, she must have ready at hand an electric torch or lighted lantern showing a white light which must be exhibited in sufficient time to prevent collision[14].
A vessel proceeding under sail, when also being propelled by machinery, must exhibit forward where it can best be seen a conical shape, apex downwards[15].

1   Ie the International Regulations for Preventing Collisions at Sea (London, 20 October 1972; TS 77
    (1977); Cmnd 6962) (see PARA 690) Pt C (rr 20–31) (see also PARAS 710–714, 716 et seq). As to
    the application of these provisions see PARA 710. As to the positioning and technical details of
    lights and shapes see Annex I; and PARA 710 note 2; and as to the required visibility of the
    prescribed lights see PARA 711.
2   As to the meaning of 'sailing vessel' see PARA 699 note 7.
3   As to the meaning of 'underway' see PARA 701 note 24.
4   Collision Regulations r 25(a).
5   Collision Regulations r 25(a)(i). As to the meaning of 'sidelights' see PARA 711 note 6.
6   Collision Regulations r 25(a)(ii). As to the meaning of 'sternlight' see PARA 711 note 7.
7   As to the meaning of 'length' see PARA 699 note 6.
8   Collision Regulations r 25(b).
9   As to the meaning of 'all-round light' see PARA 711 note 9.
10 Collision Regulations r 25(c). The 'combined lantern' referred to is that permitted by r 25(b) (see
    the text and notes 7–8): see r 25(c).
11 Ie the lights prescribed in the Collision Regulations r 25(a) or (b) (see the text and notes 1–8): see
    r 25(d)(i).
12 Collision Regulations r 25(d)(i). As to the risk of collision see PARA 697; and as to action taken
    to avoid collision see PARA 698.

13 Ie the lights prescribed in the Collision Regulations r 25: see r 25(d)(ii).
14 Collision Regulations r 25(d)(ii).
15 Collision Regulations r 25(e).

716. Lights and shapes required by fishing vessels. Under the rules of the Collision Regulations relating to lights and shapes[1], a vessel engaged in fishing[2], whether underway[3] or at anchor, must exhibit only the lights and shapes prescribed as follows[4]:

(1)   a vessel, when engaged in trawling[5], must exhibit[6]:

    (a)   two all-round lights[7] in a vertical line, the upper being green and the lower white, or a shape consisting of two cones with their apexes together in a vertical line one above the other[8];

    (b)   a masthead light[9] abaft of and higher than the all-round green light, although a vessel of less than 50 metres in length is not obliged to exhibit such a light but may do so[10];

    (c)   when making way through the water, in addition to the lights prescribed in heads (a) and (b) above, sidelights[11] and a sternlight[12];

(2)   a vessel engaged in fishing, other than trawling, must exhibit[13]:

    (a)   two all-round lights in a vertical line, the upper being red and the lower white, or a shape consisting of two cones with apexes together in a vertical line one above the other[14];

    (b)   when there is outlying gear extending more than 150 metres horizontally from the vessel, an all-round white light or a cone apex upwards in the direction of the gear[15];

    (c)   when making way through the water, in addition to the lights prescribed in heads (a) and (b) above, sidelights and a sternlight[16]; and

(3)   the additional signals which are prescribed[17] must be exhibited by a vessel engaged in fishing in close proximity to other vessels engaged in fishing[18].

A vessel, when not engaged in fishing, must not exhibit the lights or shapes so prescribed[19], but only those prescribed for a vessel of her length[20].

1   Ie the International Regulations for Preventing Collisions at Sea (London, 20 October 1972; TS 77 (1977); Cmnd 6962) (see PARA 690) Pt C (rr 20–31) (see also PARAS 710–715, 717 et seq). As to the application of these provisions see PARA 710. As to the positioning and technical details of lights and shapes see Annex I; and PARA 710 note 2; and as to the required visibility of the prescribed lights see PARA 711.
2   As to the meaning of 'vessel engaged in fishing' see PARA 691 note 9.
3   As to the meaning of 'underway' see PARA 701 note 24.
4   Collision Regulations r 26(a).
5   For these purposes, 'trawling' means the dragging through the water of a dredge net or other apparatus used as a fishing appliance: see the Collision Regulations r 26(b). 'Engaged in trawling' is not the same as trawling, but seems to cover the work of fishing with a trawl from the first shooting until in any case the trawl is got aboard again: *The Cockatrice* [1908] P 182 at 188, 11 Asp MLC 50 at 52. 'Engaged in trawling' even covers the interval after the trawl has been got aboard and before the vessel shoots again if she is going to shoot immediately on the same ground (*The Cockatrice* at 188 and at 52), or if she is hove-to, with the work of trawling not yet completed (*The Picton* [1910] P 46, 11 Asp MLC 358); but, if the vessel decides to go off to another spot to trawl, then, as soon as she is under command and in a position to go full steam ahead, she ought to shift her lights and put up the underway lights (*The Upton Castle* [1906] P 147, 10 Asp MLC 153; *The Cockatrice* at 188 and at 52; *The Skrim* (1914) 30 TLR 555).
6   Collision Regulations r 26(b).
7   As to the meaning of 'all-round light' see PARA 711 note 9.
8   Collision Regulations r 26(b)(i).
9   As to the meaning of 'masthead light' see PARA 711 note 5.
10   Collision Regulations r 26(b)(ii).
11   As to the meaning of 'sidelights' see PARA 711 note 6.
12   Collision Regulations r 26(b)(iii). As to the meaning of 'sternlight' see PARA 711 note 7.

13 Collision Regulations r 26(c).
14 Collision Regulations r 26(c)(i).
15 Collision Regulations r 26(c)(ii).
16 Collision Regulations r 26(c)(iii).
17 Ie the additional signals prescribed in the Collision Regulations Annex II (Additional signals for
    fishing vessels fishing in close proximity): see r 26(d).
18 Collision Regulations r 26(d).
19 Ie prescribed in the Collision Regulations r 26 (see heads (1) to (3) in the text): see r 26(e).
20 Collision Regulations r 26(e). As to the meaning of 'length' see PARA 699 note 6.

717. Lights and shapes required by vessels not under command or restricted in their ability to manoeuvre. Under the rules of the Collision Regulations relating to lights and shapes[1], a vessel not under command[2] must exhibit[3]:

(1)   two all-round red lights[4] in a vertical line where they can best be seen[5];
(2)   two balls or similar shapes in a vertical line where they can best be seen[6];
(3)   when making way through the water, in addition to the lights prescribed in heads (1) and (2) above, sidelights[7] and a sternlight[8].

A vessel restricted in her ability to manoeuvre[9], except a vessel engaged in mine-clearance operations, must exhibit[10]:

(a)   three all-round lights in a vertical line where they can best be seen, the highest and lowest of these lights being red and the middle light white[11];
(b)   three shapes in a vertical line where they can best be seen, the highest and lowest of these shapes being balls and the middle one a diamond[12];
(c)   when making way through the water, a masthead light[13] or lights, sidelights and a sternlight, in addition to the lights prescribed in head (a) above[14];
(d)   when at anchor, in addition to the lights or shapes prescribed in heads (a) and (b) above, the appropriate light, lights or shapes[15] for vessel at anchor[16].

A power-driven vessel[17] engaged in a towing operation such as severely restricts the towing vessel and her tow in their ability to deviate from their course must, in addition to the lights or shapes otherwise prescribed in relation to towing[18], exhibit the lights or shapes prescribed in heads (a) and (b) above[19].

A vessel engaged in dredging or underwater operations, when restricted in her ability to manoeuvre, must exhibit the lights and shapes prescribed in heads (a) to (c) above and must in addition, when an obstruction exists, exhibit[20]:

(i)   two all-round red lights or two balls in a vertical line to indicate the side on which the obstruction exists[21];
(ii)   two all-round green lights or two diamonds in a vertical line to indicate the side on which another vessel may pass[22];
(iii) when at anchor, the lights or shapes prescribed in heads (i) and (ii) above instead of the lights or shape normally exhibited[23] by vessels at anchor[24].

Whenever the size of a vessel engaged in diving operations makes it impracticable to exhibit the shapes prescribed in heads (i) to (iii) above, the following must be exhibited[25]:

(A)   three all-round lights in a vertical line where they can best be seen, the highest and lowest of these lights being red and the middle light white[26];
(B)   a rigid replica of the International Code flag 'A' not less than one metre in height; and measures must be taken to ensure its all-round visibility[27].

A vessel engaged in mine-clearance operations must, in addition to the lights prescribed for a power-driven vessel[28] or to the lights or shape prescribed for a vessel at anchor[29], as appropriate, exhibit three all-round green lights or three balls, one of these lights or shapes being exhibited at or near the foremast head and one at each end of the fore yard[30]. These lights or shapes indicate that it is dangerous for another vessel to approach within 1,000 metres of the mine-clearance vessel[31].

Vessels of less than 12 metres in length[32], except those engaged in diving operations, are not required to exhibit the lights and shapes so prescribed[33].

The signals so prescribed[34] are not signals of vessels in distress and requiring assistance[35], for which other provision is made[36].

1   Ie the International Regulations for Preventing Collisions at Sea (London, 20 October 1972; TS 77 (1977); Cmnd 6962) (see PARA 690) Pt C (rr 20–31) (see also PARAS 710–716, 718 et seq). As to the application of these provisions see PARA 710. As to the positioning and technical details of lights and shapes see Annex I; and PARA 710 note 2; and as to the required visibility of the prescribed lights see PARA 711.

2   As to the meaning of 'vessel not under command' see PARA 708 note 9; and as to the meaning of 'vessel' see PARA 691 note 2. Whether a vessel is not under command is a question of fact which depends upon the actual condition of the vessel and not upon the belief of the person in charge of her: *Mendip Range (Owners) v Radcliffe* [1921] 1 AC 556, 15 Asp MLC 242, HL. The fact that tugs are attached to a vessel in tow is not necessarily enough to prevent the tow being out of command: *Thomas Stone Shipping Ltd v The Admiralty, The Albion* [1953] P 117, [1953] 1 All ER 978, CA.

3   Collision Regulations r 27(a).

4   As to the meaning of 'all-round light' see PARA 711 note 9.

5   Collision Regulations r 27(a)(i).

6   Collision Regulations r 27(a)(ii).

7   As to the meaning of 'sidelights' see PARA 711 note 6.

8   Collision Regulations r 27(a)(iii). As to the meaning of 'sternlight' see PARA 711 note 7.

9   As to the meaning of 'vessel restricted in her ability to manoeuvre' see PARA 701 note 24. As to the lights to be exhibited by a vessel engaged in a towing operation which renders her unable to deviate from her course see the Collision Regulations r 27(c) (see the text and notes 17–19); and see PARA 713.

10   Collision Regulations r 27(b).

11   Collision Regulations r 27(b)(i).

12   Collision Regulations r 27(b)(ii).

13   As to the meaning of 'masthead light' see PARA 711 note 5.

14   Collision Regulations r 27(b)(iii).

15   Ie the light, lights or shape prescribed by the Collision Regulations r 30 (see PARA 720): see r 27(b)(iv).

16   Collision Regulations r 27(b)(iv).

17   As to the meaning of 'power-driven vessel' see PARA 701 note 22.

18   Ie prescribed by the Collision Regulations r 24(a) (see PARA 713): see r 27(c).

19   Collision Regulations r 27(c).

20   Collision Regulations r 27(d).

21   Collision Regulations r 27(d)(i).

22   Collision Regulations r 27(d)(ii).

23   Ie the lights or shape as prescribed by the Collision Regulations r 30 (see PARA 720): see r 27(d)(iii).

24   Collision Regulations r 27(d)(iii).

25   Collision Regulations r 27(e).

26   Collision Regulations r 27(e)(i).

27   Collision Regulations r 27(e)(ii).

28   Ie in the Collision Regulations r 23 (see PARA 712): see r 27(f).

29   Ie in the Collision Regulations r 30 (see PARA 720): see r 27(f).

30   Collision Regulations r 27(f).

31   Collision Regulations r 27(f).

32   As to the meaning of 'length' see PARA 699 note 6.

33   Collision Regulations r 27(g). The text refers to the lights and shapes prescribed in r 27: see r 27(g).

34   Ie in the Collision Regulations r 27: see r 27(h).

35   Collision Regulations r 27(h).

36   Signals of vessels in distress and requiring assistance are contained in the Collision Regulations Annex IV (Distress Signals) (see PARA 726): see r 27(h).

718. Lights required by vessels constrained by their draught. Under the rules of the Collision Regulations relating to lights and shapes[1], a vessel constrained by her draught[2] may, in addition to the lights prescribed for power-driven vessels[3], exhibit where they can best be seen three all-round red lights[4] in a vertical line, or a cylinder[5].

1 Ie the International Regulations for Preventing Collisions at Sea (London, 20 October 1972; TS 77 (1977); Cmnd 6962) (see PARA 690) Pt C (rr 20–31) (see also PARAS 710–717, 719 et seq). As to the application of these provisions see PARA 710. As to the positioning and technical details of lights and shapes see Annex I; and PARA 710 note 2; and as to the required visibility of the prescribed lights see PARA 711.
2 As to the meaning of 'vessel constrained by her draught' see PARA 708 note 18; and as to the meaning of 'vessel' see PARA 691 note 2.
3 Ie the lights prescribed by the Collision Regulations r 23 (see PARA 712): see r 28. As to the meaning of 'power-driven vessel' see PARA 701 note 22.
4 As to the meaning of 'all-round light' see PARA 711 note 9.
5 Collision Regulations r 28.

719. Lights and shapes required by pilot vessels. Under the rules of the Collision Regulations relating to lights and shapes[1], a vessel[2] engaged on pilotage duty[3] must exhibit[4]:
(1)   at or near the masthead, two all-round lights[5] in a vertical line, the upper being white and the lower red[6];
(2)   when underway[7], in addition, sidelights[8] and a sternlight[9];
(3)   when at anchor, in addition to the lights prescribed in head (1) above, the light, lights or shape prescribed[10] for vessels at anchor[11].

A pilot vessel, when not engaged on pilotage duty, must exhibit the lights or shapes prescribed for a similar vessel of her length[12].

1 Ie the International Regulations for Preventing Collisions at Sea (London, 20 October 1972; TS 77 (1977); Cmnd 6962) (see PARA 690) Pt C (rr 20–31) (see also PARAS 710–718, 720, 721). As to the application of these provisions see PARA 710. As to the positioning and technical details of lights and shapes see Annex I; and PARA 710 note 2; and as to the required visibility of the prescribed lights see PARA 711.
2 As to the meaning of 'vessel' see PARA 691 note 2.
3 As to pilotage generally see PARA 574 et seq.
4 Collision Regulations r 29(a).
5 As to the meaning of 'all-round light' see PARA 711 note 9.
6 Collision Regulations r 29(a)(i).
7 As to the meaning of 'underway' see PARA 701 note 24.
8 As to the meaning of 'sidelights' see PARA 711 note 6.
9 Collision Regulations r 29(a)(ii). As to the meaning of 'sternlight' see PARA 711 note 7.
10 Ie in the Collision Regulations r 30 (see PARA 720): see r 29(a)(iii).
11 Collision Regulations r 29(a)(iii).
12 Collision Regulations r 29(b). As to the meaning of 'length' see PARA 699 note 6.

720. Lights and shapes required by anchored vessels and vessels aground. Under the rules of the Collision Regulations relating to lights and shapes[1], a vessel[2] at anchor[3] must exhibit where it can best be seen[4]:
(1)   in the fore part, an all-round white light[5] or one ball[6];
(2)   at or near the stern and at a lower level than the light prescribed in head (1) above, an all-round white light[7].

A vessel of less than 50 metres in length[8] may exhibit an all-round white light where it can best be seen instead of the lights prescribed in heads (1) and (2) above[9].

A vessel at anchor may, and a vessel of 100 metres and more in length must, also use the available working or equivalent lights to illuminate her decks[10].

A vessel aground[11] must exhibit the usual lights prescribed[12] and in addition, where they can best be seen[13]:
(a)   two all-round red lights in a vertical line[14];
(b)   three balls in a vertical line[15].

A vessel of less than seven metres in length, when at anchor, not in or near a narrow channel[16], fairway[17] or anchorage (or where other vessels normally navigate) is not required to exhibit the usual prescribed[18] lights or shape[19].

A vessel of less than 12 metres in length, when aground, is not required to exhibit the lights or shapes prescribed in heads (a) and (b) above[20].

1 Ie the International Regulations for Preventing Collisions at Sea (London, 20 October 1972; TS 77 (1977); Cmnd 6962) (see PARA 690) Pt C (rr 20–31) (see also PARAS 710–719, 721). As to the application of these provisions see PARA 710. As to the positioning and technical details of lights and shapes see Annex I; and PARA 710 note 2; and as to the required visibility of the prescribed lights see PARA 711.
2 As to the meaning of 'vessel' see PARA 691 note 2.
3 A vessel is (per *The Dunelm* (1884) 9 PD 164 at 171, 5 Asp MLC 304 at 308, CA) 'at anchor' when either:
    (1)   she is held by her own anchor or some equivalent eg a heavy stone; or
    (2)   she is fast to moorings which are secured by an anchor or some equivalent.
    When a vessel has her anchor down, she is 'at anchor' only if she is held by and under the control of her anchor: *The Esk* (1869) LR 2 A & E 350 at 353. For cases in which vessels were held to have been 'at anchor' see *The Wega* [1895] P 156, 7 Asp MLC 597 (vessel failed to take in sidelights immediately she was brought up by anchor); *The Romance* [1901] P 15, 9 Asp MLC 149 (vessel still at anchor, although being moved by tug up to anchor, before being towed away); *The Palembang* [1929] P 246, 18 Asp MLC 45 (vessel at anchor although using engines to avoid another vessel). For cases in which vessels were held not to have been 'at anchor' see *The Esk* (vessel pulling up anchor and no longer held by it); *The Indian Chief* (1888) 14 PD 24, 6 Asp MLC 362 (barge dredging down river with anchor down to check her way; cf *The Smyrna* (1860) cited in *The George* Arkle (1861) Lush 382 at 385, PC); *The Faedrelandet* [1895] P 205, 8 Asp MLC 1, CA (vessel riding gale with anchor chains out and anchors unshackled); *The Yvonne and The Effra* (1932) 43 Ll L Rep 252 (vessel turning with anchor down but not held by it); cf *The Buckhurst* (1881) 6 PD 152, 4 Asp MLC 484 (vessel carrying anchor light after parting from anchors; collision inevitable, whatever lights carried). A vessel moored to a wharf is not at anchor: *The City of Seattle* (1903) 9 Canadian Exchequer Reports 146; *The Turquoise* [1908] P 148, 11 Asp MLC 28 (vessel lying outside another vessel at wharf).
4 Collision Regulations r 30(a).
5 As to the meaning of 'all-round light' see PARA 711 note 9.
6 Collision Regulations r 30(a)(i).
7 Collision Regulations r 30(a)(ii).
8 As to the meaning of 'length' see PARA 699 note 6.
9 Collision Regulations r 30(b).
10 Collision Regulations r 30(c).
11 A vessel dragging through mud was judged not to be aground in *The Bellanoch* [1907] P 170 at 174, CA (on appeal on another point [1907] AC 269, HL).
12 Ie the lights prescribed by the Collision Regulations r 30(a) or (b) (see the text and notes 1–9): see r 30(d).
13 Collision Regulations r 30(d).
14 Collision Regulations r 30(d)(i).
15 Collision Regulations r 30(d)(ii).
16 As to the meaning of 'narrow channel' see PARA 700.
17 As to the meaning of 'fairway' see PARA 699 note 4.
18 Ie the lights or shape prescribed by the Collision Regulations r 30(a) or (b) (see the text and notes 1–9): see r 30(e).
19 Collision Regulations r 30(e).
20 Collision Regulations r 30(f).

721. Lights and shapes required by seaplanes or wing-in-ground craft.
Where it is impracticable for a seaplane[1] or a wing-in-ground (WIG) craft[2] to exhibit lights and shapes of the characteristics or in the positions prescribed in the rules of the Collision Regulations relating to lights and shapes[3], it must exhibit lights and shapes as closely similar in characteristics and position as is possible[4].

1 As to the meaning of 'seaplane' see PARA 691 note 2.
2 As to the meaning of 'wing-in-ground (WIG) craft' see PARA 691 note 2.
3 Ie the International Regulations for Preventing Collisions at Sea (London, 20 October 1972; TS 77 (1977); Cmnd 6962) (see PARA 690) Pt C (rr 20–31) (see also PARAS 710–720). As to the

application of these provisions see PARA 710. As to the positioning and technical details of lights and shapes see Annex I; and PARA 710 note 2; and as to the required visibility of the prescribed lights see PARA 711.
4 Collision Regulations r 31.

(iv) Sound and Light Signals

722. Equipment for sound signals. Under the rules of the Collision Regulations[1] a vessel[2] of 12 metres or more in length[3] must be provided with a whistle[4], a vessel of 20 metres or more in length must be provided with a bell in addition to a whistle, and a vessel of 100 metres or more in length must, in addition, be provided with a gong, the tone and sound of which cannot be confused with that of the bell[5].

A vessel of less than 12 metres in length is not obliged to carry the sound signalling appliances so prescribed[6] but, if she does not, she must be provided with some other means of making an efficient sound signal[7].

1 Ie the International Regulations for Preventing Collisions at Sea (London, 20 October 1972; TS 77 (1977); Cmnd 6962): see PARA 690.
2 As to the meaning of 'vessel' for these purposes see PARA 691 note 2.
3 As to the meaning of 'length' see PARA 699 note 6.
4 For these purposes, 'whistle' means any sound signalling appliance capable of producing the prescribed blasts and which complies with the specifications of the Collision Regulations Annex III (Technical details of sound signal appliances): r 32(a). See also note 5.
5 Collision Regulations r 33(a). The whistle, bell and gong referred to in the text must comply with the specifications in Annex III: see r 33(a). The bell or gong or both may be replaced by other equipment having the same respective sound characteristics, provided that manual sounding of the required signals is always possible: see r 33(a).
6 Ie prescribed in the Collision Regulations r 33(a): see r 33(b).
7 Collision Regulations r 33(b).

723. Manoeuvring and warning signals. Under the rules of the Collision Regulations[1], when vessels[2] are in sight of one another[3], a power-driven vessel[4] underway[5], when manoeuvring as authorised or required by the rules of the Collision Regulations[6], must indicate that manoeuvre by the following signals on her whistle[7]: one short blast[8] to mean 'I am altering my course to starboard'; two short blasts to mean 'I am altering my course to port'; three short blasts to mean 'I am operating astern propulsion'[9].

Any vessel may supplement the whistle signals so prescribed[10] by light signals, repeated as appropriate, whilst the manoeuvre is being carried out[11]. The light signals have the following significance[12]: one flash[13] to mean 'I am altering my course to starboard'; two flashes to mean 'I am altering my course to port'; three flashes to mean 'I am operating astern propulsion'[14].

When in sight of one another in a narrow channel[15] or fairway[16], a vessel intending to overtake another must[17] indicate her intention by the following signals on her whistle[18]: two prolonged blasts[19] followed by one short blast to mean 'I intend to overtake you on your starboard sides'; two prolonged blasts followed by two short blasts to mean 'I intend to overtake you on your port side'[20].

The vessel about to be overtaken must[21] indicate her agreement by the following signal on her whistle, that is to say one prolonged, one short, one prolonged and one short blast, in that order[22].

When vessels in sight of one another are approaching each other and from any cause either vessel fails to understand the intentions or actions of the other, or is in doubt whether sufficient action is being taken by the other to avoid collision[23], the vessel in doubt must immediately indicate such doubt by giving at least five short and rapid blasts on the whistle[24]. Such signal may be supplemented by a light signal of at least five short and rapid flashes[25].

A vessel nearing a bend or an area of a channel or fairway where other vessels may be obscured by an intervening obstruction must sound one prolonged blast[26]. Such signal must be answered with a prolonged blast by any approaching vessel that may be within hearing around the bend or behind the intervening obstruction[27].

If whistles are fitted on a vessel at a distance apart of more than 100 metres, one whistle only must be used for giving manoeuvring and warning signals[28].

1 Ie the International Regulations for Preventing Collisions at Sea (London, 20 October 1972; TS 77 (1977); Cmnd 6962): see PARA 690.
2 As to the meaning of 'vessel' for these purposes see PARA 691 note 2.
3 As to when vessels are deemed to be in sight of one another see PARA 702 note 9.
4 As to the meaning of 'power-driven vessel' see PARA 701 note 22.
5 As to the meaning of 'underway' see PARA 701 note 24.
6 Ie by the rules of the Collision Regulations (see PARA 690 et seq): see r 34(a).
7 Collision Regulations r 34(a). As to the meaning of 'whistle' see PARA 722 note 4.
8 For these purposes, 'short blast' means a blast of about one second's duration: Collision Regulations r 32(b).
9 Collision Regulations r 34(a).
10 Ie prescribed by the Collision Regulations r 34(a) (see the text and notes 1–9): see r 34(b).
11 Collision Regulations r 34(b). The light used for this signal must, if fitted, be an all-round white light, visible at a minimum range of five miles, and must comply with the provisions of Annex I (Positioning and technical details of lights and shapes): r 34(b)(iii). As to the meaning of 'all-round light' see PARA 711 note 9.
12 Collision Regulations r 34(b)(i).
13 The duration of each flash must be about one second; the interval between flashes must be about one second; and the interval between successive signals must be not less than ten seconds: Collision Regulations r 34(b)(ii).
14 Collision Regulations r 34(b)(i).
15 As to the meaning of 'narrow channel' see PARA 700.
16 As to the meaning of 'fairway' see PARA 699 note 4.
17 Ie in compliance with the Collision Regulations r 9(e)(i) (see PARA 699): see r 34(c)(i).
18 Collision Regulations r 34(c)(i).
19 For these purposes, 'prolonged blast' means a blast of from four to six seconds' duration: Collision Regulations r 32(c).
20 Collision Regulations r 34(c)(i).
21 Ie when acting in compliance with the Collision Regulations r 9(e)(i) (see PARA 699): see r 34(c)(ii).
22 Collision Regulations r 34(c)(ii).
23 As to action to avoid collision see PARA 698.
24 Collision Regulations r 34(d).
25 Collision Regulations r 34(d).
26 Collision Regulations r 34(e). See also PARA 699.
27 Collision Regulations r 34(e).
28 Collision Regulations r 34(f).

724. Sound signals in restricted visibility. Under the rules of the Collision Regulations[1], the following signals must be used in or near an area of restricted visibility[2], whether by day or night, as prescribed[3]:

(1) a power-driven vessel[4] making way through the water must sound at intervals of not more than two minutes one prolonged blast[5];

(2) a power-driven vessel underway[6] but stopped and making no way through the water must sound at intervals of not more than two minutes two prolonged blasts in succession with an interval of about two seconds between them[7];

(3) a vessel not under command[8], a vessel restricted in her ability to manoeuvre[9], a vessel constrained by her draught[10], a sailing vessel[11], a vessel engaged in fishing[12] and a vessel engaged in towing[13] or pushing

another vessel must, instead of the signals prescribed in head (1) or (2) above, sound at intervals of not more than two minutes three blasts in succession, that is one prolonged followed by two short blasts[14];

(4)   a vessel engaged in fishing, when at anchor[15], and a vessel restricted in her ability to manoeuvre when carrying out her work at anchor, must, instead of the signals prescribed in head (7) below sound the signal prescribed in head (3) above[16];

(5)   a vessel towed[17] or, if more than one vessel is towed, the last vessel of the tow, if manned, must at intervals of not more than two minutes sound four blasts in succession, namely one prolonged followed by three short blasts; and when practicable, this signal must be made immediately after the signal made by the towing vessel[18];

(6)   when a pushing vessel and a vessel being pushed ahead are rigidly connected in a composite unit, they are regarded as a power-driven vessel and must give the signals prescribed in head (1) or (2) above[19];

(7)   a vessel at anchor must at intervals of not more than one minute ring the bell[20] rapidly for about five seconds; in a vessel of 100 metres or more in length[21] the bell must be sounded in the forepart of the vessel and, immediately after the ringing of the bell, the gong[22] must be sounded rapidly for about five seconds in the after part of the vessel[23];

(8)   a vessel aground[24] must give the bell signal and, if required, the gong signal prescribed in head (7) above and must, in addition, give three separate and distinct strokes on the bell immediately before and after the rapid ringing of the bell[25];

(9)   a vessel of 12 metres or more but less than 20 metres in length is not obliged to give the bell signals prescribed in heads (7) and (8) above, but, if she does not, she must make some other efficient sound signal at intervals of not more than two minutes[26];

(10)   a vessel of less than 12 metres in length is not obliged to give the above-mentioned signals but, if she does not, must make some other efficient sound signal at intervals of not more than two minutes[27];

(11)   a pilot vessel, when engaged on pilotage duty, may, in addition to the signals prescribed in head (1), (2) or (7) above, sound an identity signal consisting of four short blasts[28].

1   Ie the International Regulations for Preventing Collisions at Sea (London, 20 October 1972; TS 77 (1977); Cmnd 6962): see PARA 690.
2   As to the meaning of 'restricted visibility' see PARA 709 note 4.
3   See the Collision Regulations r 35.
4   As to the meaning of 'power-driven vessel' see PARA 701 note 22. As to the meaning of 'vessel' see PARA 691 note 2.
5   Collision Regulations r 35(a). As to the meaning of 'prolonged blast' see PARA 723 note 19.
6   As to the meaning of 'underway' see PARA 701 note 24.
7   Collision Regulations r 35(b).
8   As to the meaning of 'vessel not under command' see PARA 708 note 9.
9   As to the meaning of 'vessel restricted in her ability to manoeuvre' see PARA 701 note 24.
10 As to the meaning of 'vessel constrained by her draught' see PARA 708 note 18.
11 As to the meaning of 'sailing vessel' see PARA 699 note 7.
12 As to the meaning of 'vessel engaged in fishing' see PARA 691 note 9.
13 As to towing see PARA 713.
14 Collision Regulations r 35(c). As to the meaning of 'short blast' see PARA 723 note 8.
15 As to the meaning of 'vessel at anchor' see PARA 720 note 3.
16 Collision Regulations r 35(d).
17 As to the meaning of 'vessel being towed' see PARA 714 note 3.
18 Collision Regulations r 35(e).
19 Collision Regulations r 35(f).
20 As to the bell see PARA 722.
21 As to the meaning of 'length' see PARA 699 note 6.
22 As to the gong see PARA 722.

23 Collision Regulations r 35(g). A vessel at anchor may, in addition, sound three blasts in succession, namely one short, one prolonged and one short blast, to give warning of her position and of the possibility of collision to an approaching vessel: see r 35(g).

24 As to vessels aground see PARA 720 note 11.

25 Collision Regulations r 35(h). A vessel aground may in addition sound an appropriate whistle signal: see r 35(h).

26 Collision Regulations r 35(i).

27 Collision Regulations r 35(j).

28 Collision Regulations r 35(k). As to pilotage generally see PARA 574 et seq.

725. Signals to attract attention.

Under the rules of the Collision Regulations[1], if necessary to attract the attention of another vessel[2], any vessel may make light[3] or sound[4] signals that cannot be mistaken for any signal authorised elsewhere in the rules of the Collision Regulations[5], or may direct the beam of her searchlight in the direction of the danger, in such a way as not to embarrass any vessel[6]. Any light to attract the attention of another vessel must be such that it cannot be mistaken for any aid to navigation; and, for these purposes, the use of high intensity intermittent or revolving lights, such as strobe lights, must be avoided[7].

1 Ie the International Regulations for Preventing Collisions at Sea (London, 20 October 1972; TS 77 (1977); Cmnd 6962): see PARA 690.

2 As to the meaning of 'vessel' for these purposes see PARA 691 note 2.

3 As to the lights and shapes required to be carried on vessels see PARA 710 et seq.

4 As to sound and light signals see PARA 722 et seq.

5 See PARA 690 et seq.

6 Collision Regulations r 36.

7 Collision Regulations r 36.

726. Distress signals.

Under the rules of the Collision Regulations[1] when a vessel[2] is in distress and requires assistance, she must use or exhibit the signals prescribed as follows[3], the signals, to be so used or exhibited either together or separately, in order to indicate distress and need of assistance[4]:

(1)   a gun or other explosive signal fired at intervals of about a minute[5];

(2)   a continuous sounding with any fog-signalling apparatus[6];

(3)   rockets or shells, throwing red stars fired one at a time at short intervals[7];

(4)   a signal made by radiotelegraphy or by any other signalling method consisting of the group . . . — — — . . . (SOS) in the Morse Code[8];

(5)   a signal sent by radiotelephony consisting of the spoken word 'Mayday'[9];

(6)   the International Code Signal of distress indicated by NC[10];

(7)   a signal consisting of a square flag having above or below it a ball or anything resembling a ball[11];

(8)   flames on the vessel, as from a burning tar barrel, oil barrel etc[12];

(9)   a rocket parachute flare or a hand flare showing a red light[13];

(10)   a smoke signal giving off orange-coloured smoke[14];

(11)   slowly and repeatedly raising and lowering arms outstretched to each side[15];

(12)   the radiotelegraph alarm signal[16];

(13)   the radiotelephone alarm signal[17];

(14)   signals transmitted by emergency position-indicating radio beacons ('EPIRBs')[18];

(15)   approved signals transmitted by radiocommunication systems, including survival craft radar transponders[19].

The use or exhibition of any of the signals set out in heads (1) to (15) above, except for the purpose of indicating distress and need of assistance, and the use of other signals which may be confused with any of the above signals, is prohibited[20].

In a United Kingdom context[21], no signal of distress must be used by any vessel unless the master of the vessel so orders[22]; and the master must not order any signal of distress to be used by his vessel unless he is satisfied:

(a)   that his vessel is in serious and imminent danger, or that another ship or an aircraft or person is in serious and imminent danger and cannot send that signal[23]; and

(b)   that the vessel in danger, whether his own vessel or another vessel, or the aircraft or person in danger, as the case may be, requires immediate assistance in addition to any assistance then available[24].

The master of a vessel which has sent any signal of distress by means of radio or other means must cause that signal to be revoked by all appropriate means as soon as he is satisfied that the vessel or aircraft to which or the person to whom the signal relates is no longer in need of such assistance[25].

1   Ie the International Regulations for Preventing Collisions at Sea (London, 20 October 1972; TS 77 (1977); Cmnd 6962): see PARA 690.

2   As to the meaning of 'vessel' for these purposes see PARA 691 note 2.

3   See the Collision Regulations r 37. The text refers to the signals described in Annex IV (Distress Signals) (see heads (1) to (15) in the text): see r 37. For these purposes, attention is drawn to the relevant sections of the International Code of Signals, the Merchant Ship Search and Rescue Manual and the following signals:

    (1)   a piece of orange-coloured canvas with either a black square and circle or other appropriate symbol (for identification from the air) (Annex IV para 3(a));

    (2)   a dye marker (Annex IV para 3(b)).

   The reference to the International Code of Signals is a reference to the International Code of Signals (1985) published by the International Maritime Organisation: Merchant Shipping (Distress Signals and Prevention of Collisions) Regulations 1996, SI 1996/75, reg 1(7); Merchant Shipping Notice 1781(M) Introduction para 7(3). The reference to the Merchant Ship Search and Rescue Manual is a reference to the manual of that name published in 1986 by the International Maritime Organisation: Merchant Shipping (Distress Signals and Prevention of Collisions) Regulations 1996, SI 1996/75, reg 1(7). Such references include references to any document amending either of those publications which is considered by the Secretary of State to be relevant from time to time and is specified in a Merchant Shipping Notice: Merchant Shipping (Distress Signals and Prevention of Collisions) Regulations 1996, SI 1996/75, reg 1(7). As to the International Maritime Organisation (the 'IMO') see PARA 12; and as to the Secretary of State see PARA 36. As to the meaning of 'Merchant Shipping Notice' see PARA 690 note 4.

4   Collision Regulations Annex IV para 1. The signals of distress which must be used by United Kingdom ships, wherever they may be, and other ships while within the United Kingdom or the territorial waters thereof (ie the vessels to which the Merchant Shipping (Distress Signals and Prevention of Collisions) Regulations 1996, SI 1996/75, apply by virtue of reg 2(1)(a) (see PARA 690 note 3)) are those set out in the Collision Regulations Annex IV: Merchant Shipping (Distress Signals and Prevention of Collisions) Regulations 1996, SI 1996/75, reg 3(1). As to the meaning of 'ships' see PARA 690 note 3.

5   Collision Regulations Annex IV para 1(a).

6   Collision Regulations Annex IV para 1(b).

7   Collision Regulations Annex IV para 1(c).

8   Collision Regulations Annex IV para 1(d).

9   Collision Regulations Annex IV para 1(e).

10 Collision Regulations Annex IV para 1(f).

11 Collision Regulations Annex IV para 1(g).

12 Collision Regulations Annex IV para 1(h).

13 Collision Regulations Annex IV para 1(i).

14 Collision Regulations Annex IV para 1(j).

15 Collision Regulations Annex IV para 1(k).

16 Collision Regulations Annex IV para 1(l).

17 Collision Regulations Annex IV para 1(m).

18 Collision Regulations Annex IV para 1(n).

   The Merchant Shipping (EPIRB Registration) Regulations 2000, SI 2000/1850, provide that EPIRBs carried on United Kingdom ships and hovercraft must be registered with the competent authority in a member state of the International Telecommunication Union; and that, in the United Kingdom, the competent authority is HM Coastguard: see the Merchant Shipping (EPIRB Registration) Regulations 2000, SI 2000/1850.

19 Collision Regulations Annex IV para 1(o).

20 Collision Regulations Annex IV para 2.

21 Ie in the context of the Merchant Shipping (Distress Signals and Prevention of Collisions) Regulations 1996, SI 1996/75 (see note 4).

22 Merchant Shipping (Distress Signals and Prevention of Collisions) Regulations 1996, SI 1996/75, reg 3(2).

23 Merchant Shipping (Distress Signals and Prevention of Collisions) Regulations 1996, SI 1996/75, reg 3(3)(a).

24 Merchant Shipping (Distress Signals and Prevention of Collisions) Regulations 1996, SI 1996/75, reg 3(3)(b).

25 Merchant Shipping (Distress Signals and Prevention of Collisions) Regulations 1996, SI 1996/75, reg 3(4).

(2) DUTIES AFTER COLLISION

727. Duty of ship to assist the other in case of collision. In every case of collision between two ships[1], it is the duty of the master[2] of each ship, if and so far as he can do so without danger[3] to his own ship, crew and passengers, if any[4]:

(1)   to render[5] to the other ship, its master, crew and passengers, if any, such assistance as may be practicable[6], and may be necessary to save them from any danger caused by the collision, and to stay by the other ship until he has ascertained that it has no need of further assistance[7]; and

(2)   to give to the master of the other ship the name of his own ship and also the names of the ports[8] from which it comes and to which it is bound[9].

The failure of the master of a ship to comply with this duty[10] does not raise any presumption of law that the collision was caused by his wrongful act, neglect or default[11]. However, if the master fails without reasonable excuse to comply with the duty[12], he commits an offence[13]; and, if he is a certified officer, an inquiry into his conduct may be held[14] and his certificate cancelled or suspended[15].

Compliance with the statutory duty of rendering assistance after a collision does not prevent the assistance so given ranking as voluntary services for salvage purposes[16].

1   As to the meaning of 'ship' see PARA 229.

2   The duties imposed on the master of a ship by the Merchant Shipping Act 1995 s 92(1) apply to the masters of United Kingdom ships and to the masters of foreign ships when in United Kingdom waters: s 92(2). As to the meaning of 'master' see PARA 444 note 1. As to the meaning of 'foreign', in relation to a ship, see PARA 18 note 2; as to the meaning of 'United Kingdom ship' see PARA 230; and as to the meaning of 'United Kingdom waters' see PARA 48 note 10.

3   It seems that a reasonable apprehension that delay may result in capture by an enemy may excuse a vessel from staying to render assistance when that assistance may be rendered by the approaching enemy: *The Thuringia* (1872) 1 Asp MLC 283 at 292. Where, after a collision for which one vessel was solely to blame, the other vessel rendered assistance to her, although assistance could not be rendered without danger, and there was, therefore, no statutory duty to assist, and the vessel rendering assistance suffered damage in doing so, her owners were held not entitled to recover in a collision action from the owners of the ship assisted in respect of the damage suffered by their ship while rendering assistance, since that damage was not the direct result of the negligence which caused the collision, although the position might have been different if there had been a statutory duty to assist: *The San Onofre* [1922] P 243, 16 Asp MLC 1, CA. As to damages in collision actions see PARA 793 et seq.

4   Merchant Shipping Act 1995 s 92(1).

5   The duty to render arises only if there is danger from the collision. In the case of probable danger to life, the duty is to stay by until the extent of the danger can be ascertained: *The Queen of the Orwell* (1863) 7 LT 839.

6   This may consist of sending a ship's boat when more direct assistance would be impossible or dangerous: see *The Adriatic* (1875) 3 Asp MLC 16. Even when no other assistance can be given, it seems that at least the distress signals of the other vessel must be acknowledged: *The Emmy Haase* (1884) 9 PD 81, 5 Asp MLC 216.
7   Merchant Shipping Act 1995 s 92(1)(a). As to the duty to assist ships and hovercraft in distress see the International Convention for the Safety of Life at Sea 1974 (London, 1 November 1974 to 1 July 1975; TS 46 (1980); Cmnd 7874), with Protocol (London, 1 June 1978 to 1 March 1979; TS 40 (1981); Cmnd 8277) (see PARA 7), especially Ch V, which is given effect by the Merchant Shipping (Safety of Navigation) Regulations 2002, SI 2002/1473 (as to which see PARA 634). As to the duty to assist aircraft in distress see PARA 446.
8   As to the meaning of 'port' see PARA 46 note 12.
9   Merchant Shipping Act 1995 s 92(1)(b).
10 Ie a failure to comply with the provisions of the Merchant Shipping Act 1995 s 92: see s 92(3).
11 Merchant Shipping Act 1995 s 92(3).
12 Ie if the master fails without reasonable excuse to comply with the Merchant Shipping Act 1995 s 92: see s 92(4); and PARA 1135.
13 See the Merchant Shipping Act 1995 s 92(4); and PARA 1135.
14 As to inquiries into the conduct of an officer see PARA 524 et seq.
15 See the Merchant Shipping Act 1995 s 92(4); and PARA 1135.
16 See PARA 868. A vessel cannot, however, claim for salvage services if she was to blame for the collision: see *The Harvest Home* [1904] P 409, 10 Asp MLC 19 (where a tug which was to blame was held entitled to claim remuneration for towing the damaged vessel).

728. Required entry in log following accident, collision etc. Where there is loss of life or major injury to any person on board, or any person is lost from, a ship or a ship's boat, or where a ship is lost or presumed to be lost (or is abandoned or materially damaged) or where a ship strands or is in collision, or where a ship is disabled or where any material damage is caused by a ship, a description of the casualty and the place where (or the position of the ship when) it occurred must be entered in the official log[1]. The entry must be signed by the master and witnessed by a member of the crew[2].

1   See the Merchant Shipping (Official Log Books) Regulations 1981, SI 1981/569, regs 3, 4, Schedule Pt I para 12 (Schedule Pt I para 12 column 1 substituted by SI 1991/2145). As to the official log book see PARAS 551–552.
2   See the Merchant Shipping (Official Log Books) Regulations 1981 Schedule Pt I para 12 columns 2, 3.

(3) RULES OF GOOD SEAMANSHIP

(i) Scope of Rules

729. Matters to which the rules relate. The rules of good seamanship extend over the whole range of conditions in the working of a vessel from the time of launching and getting underway until she returns to her anchorage in port or moorings in a dock[1]. There are special rules of good seamanship for the manoeuvring of sailing ships and other vessels[2], and for cases of fog and heavy weather[3], and for navigation in rivers and other inland waters[4]. The question of what is good seamanship is one of fact to be decided on a consideration of all the relevant circumstances[5].

1   See PARA 731 et seq. Even though a vessel may have infringed a rule of good seamanship, it seems that a party alleging negligence against her must prove both breach of duty and damage: see PARA 694. As to negligence causing damage see PARA 756 et seq.
2   See PARA 742 et seq.
3   See PARA 732.
4   See PARA 747 et seq.
5   *SS Heranger (Owners) v SS Diamond (Owners)* [1939] AC 94 at 100, 62 Ll L Rep 204 at 209, HL. On good seamanship and use of VHF communication see *Samco Europe v MSC Prestige* [2011] EWHC 1580 (Admlty), [2011] 2 Lloyd's Rep 579.

730. Relationship between the rules of good seamanship and the collision regulations. In any case where one of the rules contained in the Collision Regulations[1] applies, and the obligation imposed by that rule differs from the obligation which, in the absence of such a rule, would be imposed by good seamanship, the rule must be observed[2]. In general, however, the duty to observe good seamanship has been preserved by the Collision Regulations[3]. Moreover, the rules of good seamanship normally[4] embody the obligations to be observed by persons in charge of vessels in circumstances for which the Collision Regulations make no provision[5], or in other cases where those Regulations do not apply.

1 Ie the International Regulations for Preventing Collisions at Sea (London, 20 October 1972; TS 77 (1977); Cmnd 6962): see PARA 690.
2 A difference may exist between the obligation contained in the Collision Regulations r 8(e) (see PARA 698) to slacken speed and take all way off if necessary to avoid collision and the practice of good seamanship to keep way on the ship to make her more manageable.
3 See the Collision Regulations r 2(a); and PARA 693.
4 Cases to which the Collision Regulations do not apply may be governed by local rules: see PARA 690.
5 Cf *Thomas Stone Ltd v Admiralty, The Albion* [1953] P 117, [1953] 1 All ER 978, [1953] 1 Lloyd's Rep 239, CA.

(ii) Particular Conditions

731. Launching of vessel. When a vessel is to be launched, those in charge of her are bound to give customary[1] or reasonable[2] notice of the launching, to prevent damage to vessels in the neighbourhood. This notice should be given by hoisting flags, by having boats in attendance to warn passing vessels[3], by giving written notices or otherwise. Those in charge are also bound to take customary[4] or reasonable[5] precautions to prevent damage to other vessels, by keeping a good look-out, by having a tug or tugs in attendance and otherwise. The burden of proving such notice and such precautions lies on those in charge, even when they are defendants[6]. There are also, however, obligations on those in charge of passing vessels to keep out of the way[7]. A vessel at anchor in the track of a launch is bound to get out of the way if she has warning and the offer of a tug to move her[8]. If she refuses, those in charge of the launch may be justified in risking the chance of damaging her to avoid serious risk to life and property which would result from postponement[9].

1 *The Vianna* (1858) Sw 405 at 406 (the custom of the place is the main matter for attention).
2 *The Blenheim* (1846) 2 Wm Rob 421 (where it was held that what is reasonable notice depends on local considerations and other circumstances; notice of the day is not sufficient; the time should be stated more definitely).
3 *The Vianna* (1858) Sw 405 at 407; *The George Roper* (1883) 8 PD 119, 5 Asp MLC 134 (breach of duty for the tug not to warn approaching vessels).
4 Eg having the harbour master present: see *The United States* (1865) 12 LT 33, PC.
5 *The George Roper* (1883) 8 PD 119 at 120, 5 Asp MLC 134.
6 *The Glengarry* (1874) 2 PD 235n, 2 Asp MLC 230.
7 *The United States* (1865) 12 LT 33, PC (where the vessel being launched was to blame for not signalling, and the other vessel was to blame for being there negligently).
8 *The Cachapool* (1881) 7 PD 217, 4 Asp MLC 502. This is so even if her anchor is foul and she will incur expense by slipping it: see *Frances (Owners) v Highland Loch (Owners), The Highland Loch* [1912] AC 312, 12 Asp MLC 106, HL.
9 *Frances (Owners) v Highland Loch (Owners), The Highland Loch* [1912] AC 312, 12 Asp MLC 106, HL (where it was dangerous to postpone the launch because the shores and keel blocks had been removed and the vessel could at any time have taken charge and gone off on her own account).

732. Special weather conditions. It may be exceedingly imprudent to move a large vessel, without the use of her engines, by means of a tug in a river at night in anything like thick weather[1], and an owner may be held liable for a collision if his vessel gets underway unnecessarily in bad weather with other vessels about her[2]. In a dense fog, it may be improper for her to be underway at all[3].

Apart from the rules contained in the Collision Regulations[4] as to conduct in fog or other conditions restricting visibility[5], a vessel may be to blame for neglecting such precautions as good seamanship dictates to guard against dangers arising from special weather[6]. Thus a steamship with three hands on board which broke from her moorings in a gale has been held to blame for not having her anchor ready to let go, and for her master and more of her crew not being on board[7]. A steamship, properly moored but dashed into by another vessel in heavy weather and broken adrift, was also held to blame for collision with a third vessel, among other reasons, for having her chains improperly unbent from her anchors, so that no anchor could be let go[8]. The master of a vessel has been held at fault for not having a sufficient crew on board in heavy weather to protect her against the ordinary incidents of peril which a competent seaman would guard against[9].

1   *The Borussia* (1856) Sw 94; cf *The Socrates and The Champion* [1923] P 162, CA.
2   *The Carrier Dove* (1863) Brown & Lush 113, PC.
3   See PARA 709.
4   Ie the International Regulations for Preventing Collisions at Sea (London, 20 October 1972; TS 77 (1977); Cmnd 6962): see PARA 690.
5   Ie the Collision Regulations r 19: see PARA 709. As to sound signals in restricted visibility see PARA 724.
6   As to standing close in bad weather see PARA 741.
7   *The Kepler* (1875) 2 PD 40 (where a steamship was moored in a place which required every precaution, and there was a byelaw requiring her not to be left without a responsible person on board). As to the duty to have the anchor ready see PARA 733.
8   *The Pladda* (1876) 2 PD 34.
9   *The Excelsior* (1868) LR 2 A & E 268 at 272 (where the master was unable to move to another pier as requested by the harbour master because he had insufficient crew).

733. Carrying and dropping anchor.

A power-driven vessel ought to have both anchors ready to let go when navigating in port past other vessels, where the existence of an exceptional current is known to be possible[1]. Such a vessel[2] or a sailing vessel[3] may, however, be excused for not dropping her anchor in time to prevent a collision. In a river, a vessel should carry her anchor as far as possible so as not to expose other vessels to damage by it[4]. Whether she is underway or moored, her owners will be liable for damage done by the improper projection of the anchor at night[5] although not in daytime, if the other vessel could with ordinary care have avoided it[6].

1   *The City of Peking v Compagnie des Messageries Maritimes, The City of Peking* (1888) 14 App Cas 40, 6 Asp MLC 396, CA. Similarly, a vessel at anchor in a strong tideway may be found in fault if her second anchor is so placed that it cannot be let go at once, where by so letting go she might have avoided a collision: *The Jessie and The Zaanland* [1917] P 138, 14 Asp MLC 139.
2   *The CM Palmer, The Larnax* (1873) 2 Asp MLC 94, PC.
3   *The Elizabeth, The Adalia* (1870) 22 LT 74; cf *The Peerless* (1860) Lush 30 (affd sub nom *Prouse v European and American Steam Shipping Co, The Peerless* (1860) Lush 103); *Doward v Lindsay, The William Lindsay* (1873) LR 5 PC 338, 2 Asp MLC 118 (defence of inevitable accident).
4   *The Six Sisters* [1900] P 302. As to navigation in rivers generally see PARA 747 et seq.
5   *The Margaret* (1881) 6 PD 76, 4 Asp MLC 375, CA. The vessel may be only partly to blame if a man ought to have been on the other vessel who would have prevented the damage: *The Scotia* (1890) 6 Asp MLC 541; *The Dunstanborough* (1891) [1892] P 363n.
6   *The Monte Rosa* [1893] P 23, 7 Asp MLC 326 (collision with tug). See also *The Vectis* [1929] P 204, 17 Asp MLC 574. As to coming up to anchor see PARA 734.

734. Coming to anchor and foul berth.

A vessel intending to come to anchor ought to make preparations[1], choosing her time[2] and easing her speed[3], and ought to see carefully that all is clear around her[4]. If the vessel is anchoring in a river, she should round to against the strength of the tide[5], and give any necessary warning before putting herself across the line of navigation[6].

When one vessel anchors near another, there should be sufficient space left for swinging to the anchor, so that in ordinary circumstances the two vessels cannot come together. A berth such that sufficient space is not left is a foul berth[7]. It is improper to anchor directly ahead or directly astern of another vessel, in the direction of the tides or prevailing winds, unless at so great a distance as will allow time for either vessel to take measures to avoid collision in the event of either driving from her anchors[8]. When a vessel has given another a foul berth, she has no right to demand that the other should take extraordinary precautions[9], and, when the difficulty calls for instant decision, the other may not be to blame for an error of judgment[10].

1   She should, if necessary, get tug assistance: see PARA 738. As to carrying and dropping anchor see PARA 733.
2   Cf *Bibby v Boissevaim, The Egyptian* (1863) 1 Moo PCCNS 373.
3   Cf *The Ceres* (1857) Sw 250 at 252. A sailing vessel should shorten sail in time before bringing up near other vessels: cf *The Neptune the Second* (1814) 1 Dods 467; *The Secret* (1872) 1 Asp MLC 318. As to rules governing speed generally see PARA 740.
4   *The Ceres* (1857) Sw 250; *The Annot Lyle* (1886) 11 PD 114, 6 Asp MLC 50, CA.
5   *The Shannon* (1842) 1 Wm Rob 463 at 471.
6   *The Queen Victoria* (1891) 7 Asp MLC 9, CA; *The Philotaxe* (1877) 3 Asp MLC 512.
7   *The Northampton* (1853) 1 Ecc & Ad 152 at 160. Cf *The Woburn Abbey* (1869) 3 Mar LC 240 (foul berth, though collision not for some days); *The Innisfail, The Secret* (1876) 3 Asp MLC 337 (foul berth and hurricane; inevitable accident).
8   *The Cumberland* (1836) Stuart's Vice Admiralty Court Cases Lower Canada 75 at 79. A vessel has been held to blame for coming to anchor in a bay during bad weather two cables ahead of another (*The Volcano* (1844) 2 Wm Rob 337), but a cable's length was held a clear berth in the Mersey (*The Princeton* (1878) 3 PD 90, 3 Asp MLC 562).
9   *The Vivid* (1873) 1 Asp MLC 601.
10 *Mary Tug Co v British India Steam Navigation Co, The Meanatchy* [1897] AC 351, PC.

735.   Precautions while vessel at anchor or moored alongside etc.

A vessel at anchor[1] ought to have a competent person on watch to see that the anchor light[2] is duly exhibited, and also do everything in his power to avert or minimise a collision[3]. While a ship at anchor is not entirely free from duties towards a ship underway, the ship at anchor ought not to alter her position or heading until it is apparent to her that the ship underway cannot by her own unaided action avoid a collision[4]. She must take proper precautions to prevent driving in heavy weather[5], or in a tideway[6]. It may be her duty to shift her berth[7], or to slip and put to sea[8]. A vessel coming last to a tier has been held in fault for not hauling out from it in bad weather, that being the only means of avoiding damage to a vessel alongside[9]. Moreover, when one vessel is lying on shore or in dock, and a second vessel is voluntarily placed where damage will occur if some probable event arises which it is not possible to control, the owners of the second vessel will be responsible[10]. The owners will be liable if a vessel moors where she will take the ground and heel over and damage another vessel[11]. A vessel in dock with mooring ropes across the dock must keep a vigilant look-out for ships moving in the dock at tide time so that the obstruction may be readily removed[12].

1   As to the meaning of 'vessel at anchor' see PARA 720 note 3.
2   As to lights for vessels at anchor under the Collision Regulations see PARA 720. As to the Collision Regulations (ie the International Regulations for Preventing Collisions at Sea (London, 20 October 1972; TS 77 (1977); Cmnd 6962)) see PARA 690.
3   *Mary Tug Co v British India Steam Navigation Co, The Meanatchy* [1897] AC 351, PC. See also *Vanderplank v Miller* (1828) Mood & M 169; *Lake Seward* (1829) 4 C & P 106; *The Sedulity* [1956] 1 Lloyd's Rep 510 (steering vessel in charge of inexperienced deck-hand). Two persons have been considered sufficient look-out for an anchor watch: *The Christiana* (1849) 7 Notes of Cases 2 at 6. A ship moored to buoys in the Tyne was held to blame for not having an anchor watch: *The Pladda* (1876) 2 PD 34 at 39. A single watchman may suffice for a ship in a dock: *The Excelsior* (1868) LR 2 A & E 268 at 271. As to look-out generally see PARA 739.

4　*The Viper* [1926] P 37 at 40, 41, 17 Asp MLC 26 at 27, DC. As to rules under the Collision Regulations regarding action taken to avoid collision see PARA 698.

5　A single anchor may suffice for a vessel intending to stop for only one tide (*The Gipsey King* (1847) 2 Wm Rob 537), but not in a gale (*The Maggie Armstrong v The Blue Bell* (1865) 2 Mar LC 318). Cf *Argus v Volga* (1922) 11 Ll L Rep 102 (where in bad weather a vessel was held not to be negligent in lying to a single anchor). Persons who give the use of mooring appliances for value warrant their fitness (*Allen v Quebec Warehouse Co* (1886) 12 App Cas 101, PC), and port authorities which permit their use treat them as sufficient (*Doward v Lindsay, The William Lindsay* (1873) LR 5 PC 338 at 343, 2 Asp MLC 118 at 120). Sixty fathoms were found an improperly short cable for a vessel of 1,489 tons in the Mersey in a strong wind and tide: *The City of Cambridge* (1874) LR 4 A & E 161 (affd sub nom *Wood v Smith, The City of Cambridge* LR 5 PC 451, 2 Asp MLC 239); cf *The Peerless* (1860) Lush 30 (affd sub nom *Prowse v European and American Steam Shipping Co, The Peerless* (1860) Lush 103, PC (catching of cable on windlass an inevitable accident)). A ship has been held to blame for not getting a rope fast, when necessary, to a pier-head 800 feet off (*The Lyn* (1883) Pritchard's Admiralty Digest (3rd Edn) 291), and for not striking her top gear and yards (*The Ruby Queen* (1861) Lush 266; *The Excelsior* (1868) LR 2 A & E 268). See also *Manley v Kyles* (1923) 16 Ll L Rep 272 (where a vessel lying at buoys was negligent not to have her anchor out to avoid being set on the bank); *The Titan* (1922) 13 Ll L Rep 428 (standard of care required when floating crane left in river full of ships). As to inevitable accident see further PARA 788.

6　*Westfalen (Owners) v Oriana II (Owners)* (1919) 1 Ll L Rep 527.

7　*The Woburn Abbey* (1869) 3 Mar LC 240; *The British Holly* (1924) 20 Ll L Rep 237 (where a steamer lying alongside another steamer failed to move in bad weather).

8　*The Uhla* (1867) 19 LT 89.

9　*The Patriotto v The Rival* (1860) 2 LT 301. As to conduct in bad weather generally see PARA 732.

10　*The Lidskjalf* (1856) Sw 117 at 119 (where a vessel heeled over as the tide fell, damaging a neighbouring vessel); *The Jacob* (1860) 12 Ir Jur 379. A barge ought not to be adrift in a dock like the Surrey Commercial Dock Basin, and at tide time when vessels are moving in and out ought not to be unattended: *War Tempest v Plym* (1921) 9 Ll L Rep 489.

11　*The Jacob* (1860) 12 Ir Jur 379; *The Indian v The Jessie* (1865) 2 Mar LC 217 (damage to barge); *The Western Belle* (1906) 10 Asp MLC 279 (damage to moorings); but see *Dalton v Denton* (1857) 1 CBNS 672.

12　*The Theodoros, The Blidensol* [1923] P 26.

736. Keeping clear of vessel at anchor.

It is the duty of every vessel seeing another at anchor[1], whether in a proper or improper place, and whether properly or improperly anchored[2], to take reasonable care to avoid a collision if practicable and consistent with her own safety[3]. A ship brought up in an exposed position has been held not to contribute to a collision with a ship driving into her[4]. It appears, however, that a vessel may be so lying at anchor as to require more than ordinary care to avoid her[5]. There is a similar duty to keep clear of a sailing vessel which is compelled at the moment to go about[6], or of a vessel engaged in fishing, or of other disabled vessels[7]. There is a statutory duty not to run foul of any lightship, buoy or beacon[8].

1　As to the meaning of 'vessel at anchor' see PARA 720 note 3.

2　For the rules of good seamanship concerning coming to anchor see PARA 734.

3　Cf *The Girolamo* (1834) 3 Hag Adm 169 at 173; *The Batavier* (1845) 2 Wm Rob 407; *The Lochlibo* (1850) 3 Wm Rob 310; *The Duna* (1860) 12 Ir Jur 384; *The Anne* (1860) 12 Ir Jur 360; *The Secret* (1872) 1 Asp MLC 318. Where a ship is weighing anchor, there is a duty on a vessel underway to keep clear: *HMS Trawler Argon II v Porthcawl (Owners)* (1920) 2 Ll L Rep 370. As to the burden of proof in such cases see PARA 757.

4　*The Despatch* (1860) Lush 98, PC.

5　*The Telegraph, Valentine v Cleugh* (1854) 1 Ecc & Ad 427 at 429, PC; cf *The Bothnia* (1860) Lush 52. In various American cases, the vessel at anchor has been held in such circumstances to have caused or contributed to the collision: see *Strout v Foster* (1843) 1 Howard 89; *The Scioto* (1847) Daveis 359; *The Clara* (1880) 12 Otto 200; *United States v St Louis and Mississippi Valley Transportation Co* 184 US 247 (1902). Cf *The Eurymedon* [1938] P 41, [1938] 1 All ER 122, 59 Ll L Rep 214, CA (vessel at anchor in improper position). An anchor which will form an obstruction in the fairway of a navigable river must be buoyed: *The Harkaway* [1928] P 199, 17 Asp MLC 503.

6　See PARA 744.

7   See the Collision Regulations r 18(a), (b); and PARA 708. As to the Collision Regulations (ie the International Regulations for Preventing Collisions at Sea (London, 20 October 1972; TS 77 (1977); Cmnd 6962)) see PARA 690. As to the duty to keep clear of a vessel in stays see PARA 744. In cases where a vessel has been unmanageable a collision has sometimes been held accidental: *The John Buddle* (1847) 5 Notes of Cases 387; *The Thornley* (1843) 7 Jur 659.

8   See the Merchant Shipping Act 1995 s 219(2); and PARA 1183. As to lighthouses and lightships see further PARA 1017 et seq.

737. Steering gear.

A vessel using power-operated steering gear and navigating in crowded waters has been held to blame in some instances for not having her hand gear ready in case of a breakdown[1].

1   *The Merchant Prince* [1892] P 179, 7 Asp MLC 208, CA; *The Turret Court* (1900) 69 LJP 117. See also the cases as to steering gear cited in PARA 789 note 8. As to the statutory requirements that must be met in the provision and use of equipment for navigation purposes generally see PARA 602 et seq.

738. Tug assistance.

A vessel may be held to blame for manoeuvring without taking tug assistance when it is available and reasonably necessary. For example, a power-driven vessel getting up her anchors off Dover in a gale without tug assistance was liable for damage caused when she was driven ashore[1], and a sailing vessel was liable for damage caused when trying to bring up ahead of another vessel in the Downs after losing one anchor and without using available tug assistance[2].

1   *The Gertor* (1894) 7 Asp MLC 472. As to precautions for special weather conditions see PARA 732; and as to carrying and dropping anchor see PARA 733.

2   *The Annot Lyle* (1886) 11 PD 114, 6 Asp MLC 50, CA. As to tugs and tows generally see PARA 742.

739. Officers and watch on look-out.

It is a lack of due care for a senior officer on watch to give up charge to a junior officer and go below while his vessel is actually manoeuvring for another vessel which is drawing near to her[1]. To constitute a good look-out[2] on a ship, there must be a sufficient number of persons stationed for the purpose, who must know and be able to discharge that duty[3]. As a rule, except doubtless in the case of very small vessels, there ought to be a lookout forward[4] besides the officer on the bridge, even on a fine day[5]. Sometimes the proper place for the look-out is, not forward, but on the bridge[6]. The crow's nest may be a proper place for a look-out[7].

In deciding what is a proper look-out, the state of the weather and the proximity of vessels must be considered. The greater the necessity for the look-out owing to thick weather or otherwise, the more vigilant it should be. It is no excuse for a bad look-out to urge that no vigilance could have prevented the collision[8]. It has been held that a power-driven vessel proceeding at high speed in a crowded thoroughfare, or in fog, ought to have a double look-out forward[9]. It is a lack of due care for the look-out forward to be engaged on other duties, for example clearing the anchor[10]. There is no necessity as a rule for a vessel at sea at night, if she has a fixed stern light, to look out for vessels astern[11], but there may be if there is reason to suppose that a vessel so approaching does not see her[12]. Failure to have any look-out is a breach of the Collision Regulations[13], and it is no excuse that it was immaterial because the vessel had to keep her course[14].

It is the duty of a vessel towing another to keep a look-out for both[15], but this does not relieve the tow from keeping a good look-out, and even a pilot cutter being towed alongside a ship in tow of a tug has been held liable for not doing so[16].

In a river, the duty of a look-out as to reporting lights is different from the duty in the open sea, because to report every light in a river would mean confusion. The duty is to report every material light[17].

The look-out is stationed to see what vessels or obstacles are in the channel, and his attention is properly directed to this, and not elsewhere, for example to the Blue Peter of a vessel in a basin and just coming out[18]. If visibility is deceptive, it may be proper for the person in charge of the navigation of a vessel to make use of binoculars[19].

Failure to appreciate that the vessel is dragging her anchor constitutes a bad look-out[20].

1   *Stoomvaart Maatschappy Nederland v Pensinsular and Oriental Steam Navigation Co* (1880) 5 App Cas 876 at 880, 896, 897, 4 Asp MLC 360 at 361, 366, HL. See also *The Arthur Gordon, The Independence* (1861) Lush 270 at 280, PC (where a ship in tow was held at fault for tug being left, while the tug master was at breakfast, in charge of a sailor, as he was not competent and failed to manoeuvre soon enough for another vessel).

2   As to the burden of proof of a good look-out see PARA 757 note 12. VHF communication is no replacement for a proper look out: see *Samco Europe v MSC Prestige* [2011] EWHC 1580 (Admlty), [2011] 2 Lloyd's Rep 579.

3   *The George* (1845) 2 Wm Rob 386; *The Manchester Regiment* [1938] P 117, 60 Ll L Rep 279. As to anchor watch see PARA 735; and as to having a bargeman on a dumb barge in a river see PARA 746.

4   The look-out ought to be astern if the vessel is proceeding stem first: *The Juno* (1894) 7 Asp MLC 506 at 507.

5   *The Glannibanta* (1876) 1 PD 283 at 290, CA. See also *Netherlands Steam Boat Co v Styles, The Batavier* (1854) 9 Moo PCC 286; *London and Edinburgh Shipping Co v Eaton, The Iona* (1867) 2 Mar LC 479 at 481, PC; *The Hector* (1883) 52 LJP 47, 5 Asp MLC 101, CA; *The St Angus* [1938] P 225, 61 Ll L Rep 168.

6   Even where a river rule provided for a look-out at the bow, it was said that the proper place for the look-out in the circumstances was on the bridge instead, and that a pilot and two other persons there were a sufficient look-out: *Clyde Navigation Co v Barclay* (1876) 1 App Cas 790 at 797, 798, 3 Asp MLC 390 at 392, HL.

7   *The Bethania* (1 November 1910, unreported), CA, per Lord Alverstone CJ (ship in the English Channel off Beachy Head).

8   *The Mellona* (1847) 3 Wm Rob 7 at 11–13 (the duty to keep a good look-out is especially incumbent in hazy weather); *The Nevada* (1872) 1 Asp MLC 477; *The Milanese* (1881) Pritchard's Admiralty Digest (3rd Edn) 222, HL; but see *The Claudio* (1924) 18 Ll L Rep 442 (where the absence of look-out on the fo'c'sle head was held not to have contributed to the collision).

9   *The Europa* (1850) 14 Jur 627; *The Germania* (1869) 3 Mar LC 269, PC. See also *The Iron Duke* (1845) 4 Notes of Cases 94 (affd sub nom *Williams v Chapman* (1846) 4 Notes of Cases 585n, PC); *Londonderry (Owners) v Dolbadarn Castle (Owners)* (1845) 4 Notes of Cases, Supplement xxxi.

10 *The Bold Buccleugh* (1853) Pritchard's Admiralty Digest (3rd Edn) 221.

11 *The City of Brooklyn* (1876) 1 PD 276 at 279, 3 Asp MLC 230 at 233, CA; *The Reiher* (1881) 4 Asp MLC 478; cf *The Earl Spencer* (1875) LR 4 A & E 431, 2 Asp MLC 523; affd 3 Asp MLC 4, PC.

12 *The Anglo–Indian* (1875) 3 Asp MLC 1, PC. If a vessel is proceeding stern first, there is a duty to keep a look-out astern: see PARA 749.

13 See the Collision Regulations r 5; and PARA 695. As to the Collision Regulations (ie the International Regulations for Preventing Collisions at Sea (London, 20 October 1972; TS 77 (1977); Cmnd 6962)) see PARA 690.

14 *The Craigellachie* [1909] P 1 at 5, 11 Asp MLC 103 at 105 (dissented from on a different point in *The Grovehurst* [1910] P 316, 11 Asp MLC 440, CA).

15 *The Jane Bacon* (1878) 27 WR 35, CA.

16 *The Harvest Home* [1905] P 177, 10 Asp MLC 19, CA. A vessel sailing so close to another as to obstruct her own look-out has been held to blame: *The Zollverein* (1856) Sw 96 at 97. As to tugs and tows generally see PARA 742.

17 *The Shakkeborg* [1911] P 245n. In river rules it is sometimes prescribed that a master of a small steamer is to stand on the bridge, and in such a case he has been found to blame for bad look-out through not doing so: *The Wirrall* (1848) 3 Wm Rob 56 at 62, 64. As to navigating in rivers generally see PARA 747 et seq.

18 *James Moss & Co v African Steamship Co, The Calabar* (1868) LR 2 PC 238 at 242.

19 *The Gorm* [1961] 1 Lloyd's Rep 196 at 199. See also *The Hibernia* (1874) 2 Asp MLC 454 at 460, PC, and Lord Mersey's Report as regards *The Titanic* (1912) Times 31 July, p 8.

20 *The Gerda Toft* [1953] 2 Lloyd's Rep 249.

740. Speed. No particular speed by power-driven vessels or other vessels can be said absolutely to be dangerous, and whether any given speed is dangerous or not must depend on the weather, locality, sea room and other facts[1]. Fog or clear, light or dark, no power-driven vessel has a right to navigate at such a speed that it is impossible for her to prevent damage by taking all precautions at the moment she sees damage to be possible or probable[2]. When a vessel's lights are obscured by her own smoke so as to prevent her from seeing or being seen by ships approaching, it is negligence for her to proceed at full speed[3].

1 *The Europa* (1850) 14 Jur 627 at 630; *The Milan* (1861) Lush 388. For the factors to be taken into consideration in determining a safe speed under the Collision Regulations see r 6(a), (b); and PARA 696. As to the Collision Regulations (ie the International Regulations for Preventing Collisions at Sea (London, 20 October 1972; TS 77 (1977); Cmnd 6962)) see PARA 690.
2 *The Europa* (5 December 1851) PC (cited in Pritchard's Admiralty Digest (3rd Edn) 223; and in *The Pennsylvania* (1874) 2 Asp MLC 378). Cf *The Europa* (1850) 14 Jur 627; *The Great Eastern* (1864) 11 LT 5 at 8, PC; *The Kaiser Wilhelm II* (1915) 85 LJP 26, CA. For the requirement of the Collision Regulations that speed must be adapted for the prevailing conditions, especially in fog or other conditions restricting visibility, see r 19; and PARA 709. Where a speed for steamers is prescribed by byelaw, it means speed over the ground and not through the water: *The RL Alston* (1882) 8 PD 5, 5 Asp MLC 43, CA (decided under the Tees rule).
3 *The Rona, The Ava* (1873) 2 Asp MLC 182, PC; and see *The Puffin* (1925) 21 Ll L Rep 10 (vessel zigzagging to avoid her own smoke). It is no excuse for a vessel going at excessive speed that she is under contract to carry government mails at a higher speed: see *The Vivid* (1856) Sw 88; affd sub nom *Churchward v Palmer, The Vivid* 10 Moo PCC 472.

741. Standing close and speaking. A vessel ought not to stand so close to another in bad weather that, if she is struck by a squall, there will be a collision[1]. Thus, if a vessel tries to pass in a narrow space between vessels unnecessarily, she will be to blame for a collision which results from her doing so[2]. A ship which approaches another to speak to her does so at her own risk[3], and a sailing vessel ought not to run alongside another for this purpose while running before the wind[4].

In the case of a fishing ground, even a sailing vessel has been held to blame for crossing the ground at excessive speed[5], and power-driven vessels which choose to pass through a fleet of fishing vessels ought to regulate their speed so as to be able to keep out of the way of incumbered fishing vessels[6].

In a river[7], power-driven vessels must proceed only at a speed compatible with the safety of other vessels, and they have been held to blame for swamping other vessels by their wash[8].

It is the duty of a power-driven vessel under the Collision Regulations and generally as a matter of good seamanship to slacken speed, or stop, or reverse, in order to avoid collision[9].

1 *The Globe* (1848) 6 Notes of Cases 275. As to precautions in bad weather conditions see PARA 732.
2 *The Schwalbe* (1861) Lush 239, PC. As to vessels proceeding in convoy see *Port Chalmers v Kerry Range* (1921) 9 Ll L Rep 137 at 139.
3 *HMS Bellerophon* (1874) 3 Asp MLC 58. A pilot cutter ought to anticipate that a steamer wanting a pilot will take off her way and that, to do so, she will reverse her engines, and the cutter ought not to put herself so close to the steamer that, if the steamer does reverse, a collision is inevitable: *Pansy v Inchbrayock* (1921) 6 Ll L Rep 150.
4 *The Thames* (1805) 5 Ch Rob 345.
5 *The Pepperell* (1855) Sw 12.
6 *The Picton* [1910] P 46, 11 Asp MLC 358. A speed of nine knots in such a case has been held excessive with a bad look-out (*The Picton*), but not with a good one. See also *The Rose* (1843) 2 Wm Rob 1; *The Columbus* (1848) Pritchard's Admiralty Digest (3rd Edn) 239 (duty of vessel with a fair wind not to disturb a smack engaged in fishing); *The Margaret v The Tuscar* (1866) 15 LT 86; *Murphy v Palgreave* (1869) 21 LT 209 (where a steamer bore down on a yawl boat moored on a fishing ground, and touched her without damage; and three men who jumped overboard, in reasonable fear of their lives, recovered damages); *The Pacific* (1884) 9 PD 124, 5 Asp MLC 263. As to the duty to keep out of the way of fishing vessels imposed on other vessels by the Collision

Regulations see r 18; and PARA 708. As to the Collision Regulations (ie the International Regulations for Preventing Collisions at Sea (London, 20 October 1972; TS 77 (1977); Cmnd 6962)) see PARA 690.

7   As to navigation in rivers generally see PARA 747 et seq.
8   *The Batavier* (1854) 1 Ecc & Ad 378 at 382 (affd sub nom *Netherlands Steam Boat Co v Styles, The Batavier* 9 Moo PCC 286); *The Aruba* (1930) 37 Ll L Rep 225 (where in a narrow channel a vessel ahead was known to be in trouble; it was held unseamanlike to approach too close to her at full speed). Where, however, the sinking of a barge was due partly to the swell and partly to her being moored in a very exposed place, she could not formerly recover at common law owing to her contributory negligence (see *The Duke of Cornwall* (1862) Pritchard's Admiralty Digest (3rd Edn) 226), nor could she if her sinking was partly due to her being improperly trimmed (cf *Luxford v Large* (1832) 5 C & P 421; *Smith v Dobson* (1841) 3 Scott NR 336). See also *The Portia* (1932) 44 Ll L Rep 295 (where the speed of ten knots was held to be excessive in passing the entrance to a draw dock in Woolwich Reach of the River Thames); *The Ausonia* (1933) 45 Ll L Rep 71 (where 15 knots was held not to be too high a speed to pass a barge properly equipped and battened down in Sea Reach). As to damage to barges by steamers see PARA 746.
9   See the Collision Regulations r 8(e); and PARA 698.

(iii) Particular Classes of Vessels

742. Tug and tow. When one vessel is in tow of another[1], the tug and tow owe certain duties towards each other and other vessels to prevent a collision. When, as is usual when a tug is towing barges[2] in a river, the tug controls the navigation and her master and crew are not the employees of the owners of the tow[3], the duty of those on board the tow towards the tug appears to be substantially confined to following her manoeuvres[4], and the tow is entitled to act on the belief that the tug will be reasonably well navigated[5].

In the case of a ship in tow of a tug at sea or in a river[6], it seems that, in the absence of special provisions in the contract of towage, the tow normally[7] controls the navigation in order to avoid a divided command, and also because the pilot, if there is one, takes his station on the tow and the officers of the tow are usually of a higher class and better able to direct the navigation than those of the tug[8].

The question of the relation between the tow and the tug is, however, one of fact, not law[9]. Even where the general direction is to be given by those on the tow, they are not constantly to interfere, and those in charge of the tug must use their judgment and not constantly expect orders from the tow[10]. When, however, there is a pilot on the tow, he is bound to give the tug proper directions and the tug is bound to obey them[11]. If the tug does not get orders, she is responsible for the direction of the course[12]. It is the duty of those on the tow[13] to check the tug, and of those on the tug[14] to warn the tow, if they know that the course which is set is dangerous. It is, in general, the duty of the tow to follow all the tug's manoeuvres[15], and, when other vessels are likely to be met, to have the means ready of slipping or cutting the tow rope[16].

1   As to the meaning of 'being towed' see PARA 714 note 3.
2   As to dumb barges see further PARA 746.
3   As to when the tug or tow takes control, and as to the liabilities of the tug and tow towards one another and third persons, see further PARAS 597 et seq, 783–784.
4   *The Jane Bacon* (1878) 27 WR 35, CA. When a tug sounds the regulation whistles, the tow need not sound her whistle (*The Marmion* (1913) 29 TLR 646); but see now the Collision Regulations r 35(e); and PARA 724. As to the Collision Regulations (ie the International Regulations for Preventing Collisions at Sea (London, 20 October 1972; TS 77 (1977); Cmnd 6962)) see PARA 690.
5   *Comet Lightship (Owners) v The WH No 1 (Owners) and The Knight Errant* [1911] AC 30, 11 Asp MLC 497, HL.
6   *The Isca* (1886) 12 PD 34 at 35, 6 Asp MLC 63 at 65.
7   Cf *Thomas Stone Shipping Ltd v The Admiralty, The Albion* as reported in [1953] P 117 at 133, CA (normal relationship of tug and tow was to prevail).

8   *The Niobe* (1888) 13 PD 55 at 59, 6 Asp MLC 300 at 302. See also *The Mary* (1879) 5 PD 14 at
     16, 4 Asp MLC 183 at 184. See also PARA 599.
9   *The Isca* (1886) 12 PD 34 at 35, 6 Asp MLC 63 at 65; cf *Devonshire (Owners) v Leslie (Owners)*
     [1912] AC 634 at 656, 12 Asp MLC 210 at 213, HL. A ship in tow at night with a long hawser
     was held not to be under a duty to direct the movements of the tug: see *The Stormcock* (1885) 5
     Asp MLC 470.
10   *The Isca* (1886) 12 PD 34 at 35, 6 Asp MLC 63 at 65; and see *Trishna (Owners, Master and Crew)
     v Panther and Ericbank (Owners), The Panther and the Ericbank* [1957] P 143 at 147, [1957] 1
     All ER 641 at 647, [1957] 1 Lloyd's Rep 57 at 66 (pilot on ship could not be expected to direct
     engine movements of stern tug).
11   *The Duke of Sussex* (1841) 1 Wm Rob 270; *The Christina* (1848) 3 Wm Rob 27; *The Energy*
     (1870) LR 3 A & E 48 (order to try to ship the tow rope); *Smith v St Lawrence Tow-Boat Co*
     (1873) LR 5 PC 308, 2 Asp MLC 41 (orders to stop in fog); *Spaight v Tedcastle* (1881) 6 App Cas
     217, 4 Asp MLC 406, HL.
12   *The Altair* [1897] P 105 at 115, 8 Asp MLC 224 at 229. See also *The Robert Dixon* (1879) 5 PD
     54 at 58, 4 Asp MLC 246 at 248, CA.
13   *The Altair* [1897] P 105 at 116, 8 Asp MLC 224 at 229, 230. As to the duty to keep a look-out
     see PARA 739.
14   *Shersby v Hibbert, The Duke of Manchester* (1847) 5 Notes of Cases 470, PC. See also *Maridive
     VII v Key Singapore, The Key Singapore* [2004] EWHC 2227 (Comm), [2005] 1 All ER (Comm)
     99, [2005] 1 Lloyd's Rep 91 (tugs towing a rig required to provide salvage services to the tow;
     fact-sensitive nature of any analysis of responsibility emphasised).
15   *The Jane Bacon* (1878) 27 WR 35, CA.
16   *The Jane Bacon* (1878) 27 WR 35, CA. As to the tug casting off the tow cf *The Annapolis, The
     Golden Light, The HM Hayes* (1861) Lush 355, PC; as to two vessels being in tow of a tug, and
     one being damaged by the grounding of the other without fault of the tug, see *Harris v Anderson*
     (1863) 14 CBNS 499; and as to the contract of towage see PARA 597 et seq.

743. Tug and tow manoeuvring for other vessels.

Many of the ordinary
obligations of a power-driven vessel as regards manoeuvring for other vessels are
shared by a tug and her tow, because to a great extent they partake of the nature
of such a vessel[1]. However, when it would have been the duty of an ordinary
vessel, on approaching another vessel so as to involve risk of collision, to stop her
engines, a tug with a ship in tow has been held excused for not stopping them
when she was going extremely slowly[2]. A tug with a vessel in tow may be subject
to the general duty, applicable to power driven vessels underway, to keep out of
the way of a sailing vessel[3].

1   *The Lord Bangor* [1896] P 28 at 33, 8 Asp MLC 217 at 218. See also *The Knarwater* (1894) 63
     LJP 65, CA. As to special care to be taken by a tug lashed alongside her tow see *The Shanklin*
     (1932) 43 Ll L Rep 153; *Rio Verdi (Owners) v Abaris (Owners)* (1920) 2 Ll L Rep 411 (where it
     was held to be negligent to use an unduly long scope of towing hawser in Falmouth harbour).
2   *The Lord Bangor* [1896] P 28, 8 Asp MLC 217. As to risk of collision see PARA 697.
3   See the Collision Regulations r 18(a); and PARA 708. As to the Collision Regulations (ie the
     International Regulations for Preventing Collisions at Sea (London, 20 October 1972; TS 77
     (1977); Cmnd 6962)) see PARA 690. If, however, the tug is a vessel restricted in her ability to
     manoeuvre, the sailing vessel must keep out of her way: r 18(b). As to the meaning of 'vessel
     restricted in her ability to manoeuvre' for these purposes see PARA 701 note 24.

744. Sailing vessels.

One general rule as regards sailing vessels[1] is that, when a
vessel is in stays or in the act of going about, she becomes for the time being
unmanageable, and in this case it is the duty of another vessel which ought
otherwise to have kept her course to execute any practical manoeuvre which
would prevent collision[2]. However, when a vessel goes about very near to another,
and without giving any indication from which that other can be warned in time
to prepare to give room, the damage may arise from the fault of those in charge
of the vessel going about at such an improper time or place[3].

When a vessel which ought to keep out of the way of another has thrown
herself into stays, she ought still to take any reasonable steps to avoid collision[4].
When a sailing vessel beating up a river has gone as near one shore as she can
safely go so as to avoid collision with vessels at anchor, she is entitled to go about
without warning to other vessels; and it is the duty of a power-driven vessel

coming up astern to know, from her position and the state of her sails, that she is going about, and to keep out of her way[5]. It is the duty of a sailing vessel following another to go about when the leading vessel is compelled to go about[6].

A sailing vessel is entitled to wear instead of staying, but ought not to resort to the extraordinary operation of wearing unless she is sure that she has room to do so safely[7].

A vessel hove-to[8] should exercise more than ordinary care not to obstruct navigation[9]. Heaving-to in the track of ships and lying with helm lashed alee may be negligence[10].

In manoeuvring for other vessels, it is the duty of a sailing vessel to use her sails to assist her helm when necessary[11].

1 For the rule contained in the Collision Regulations for determining which of two approaching sailing vessels is to give way to the other see r 12; and PARA 702; and for the duty of a power-driven vessel to keep out of the way of a sailing vessel see r 18; and PARA 708. As to the Collision Regulations (ie the International Regulations for Preventing Collisions at Sea (London, 20 October 1972; TS 77 (1977); Cmnd 6962)) see PARA 690. As to the meaning of 'vessel restricted in her ability to manoeuvre' for these purposes see PARA 701 note 24.
2 *The Ida v The Wasa Nicolaistadt* (1806) 15 LT 103; *Wilson v Canada Shipping Co* (1877) 2 App Cas 389, PC.
3 *The Leonidas* (1841) 1 SVAR 226 at 229; *The Mobile* (1856) Sw 69 (on appeal Sw 127, PC). The burden of proof is first on the vessel to show that she is in stays (which is almost the same as at anchor), and then on the other vessel to show that the first vessel was improperly in stays or otherwise: *The Sea Nymph* (1860) Lush 23. A vessel has a duty to take a proper survey of the sea around her before going into stays: *The Allan v The Flora* (1866) 2 Mar LC 386.
4 *The Kingston-by-Sea* (1849) 3 Wm Rob 152 at 158 (through making her pay off before the wind, by squaring the mainyard); *Wilson v Canada Shipping Co* (1877) 2 App Cas 389, PC (by getting sternway on her).
5 *The Palatine* (1872) 1 Asp MLC 468. The vessel in stays, when the state of her canvas is not visible to the other vessel, should warn the other vessel in sufficient time: *Wilson v Canada Shipping Co* (1877) 2 App Cas 389, PC. The sailing craft tacking in a narrow channel has to behave reasonably, and under proper conditions an overtaking tug with barges in tow may go ahead: *Union Lighterage Co Ltd v Sailing Barge Shamrock* (1921) 6 Ll L Rep 154. As to navigation in rivers generally see PARA 747 et seq.
6 *The Priscilla* (1870) LR 3 A & E 125; cf *The Annie* [1909] P 176 at 179, 11 Asp MLC 213 at 214. As to not standing too close in a time of squalls cf *The Plato v The Perseverance* (1865) Holt Adm 262; and see PARA 741.
7 *The Falkland, The Navigator* (1863) Brown & Lush 204, PC.
8 As to coming to anchor and precautions while at anchor see PARAS 734, 735.
9 *The Eleanor v The Alma* (1865) 2 Mar LC 240.
10 *The Attila* (1879) 5 QLR 340.
11 *The Lady Anne* (1850) 15 Jur 18; *The James* (1856) Sw 55, 60, PC; *The Ulster* (1862) 1 Mar LC 234, PC (duty of schooner to run her outer jib to assist in turning her head); *The Marpesia* (1872) LR 4 PC 212, 1 Asp MLC 261 (assist helm by hauling in head-sheets and letting go lee braces, if there is time).

745. Dangerous vessels. If a ship is fitted with a latent instrument of danger, for example a ram on a warship, those who have control of it are bound to take all reasonable precautions to ensure that it shall not cause damage to other vessels, for example by giving notice of it. The obligation to give notice is, however, dependent on having a reasonable opportunity to do so; and there is no obligation to give it unless there is a reasonable probability of danger to the other vessel from want of it[1]. Vessels carrying explosives or petroleum are subject to special byelaws while in most harbours or canals[2].

1 *HMS Bellerophon* (1874) 3 Asp MLC 58.
2 See EXPLOSIVES vol 47 (2014) PARA 511.

746. Dumb barges. A dumb barge[1] in a river, in the absence of any rule of the road, regulation or custom to prevent it, may navigate on either side of the river[2], and in the deep water, even though she thereby obstructs larger vessels, having as much right as they to the advantage of a swift stream[3]. There is no duty imposed by statute on a dumb barge to get out of the way of a steamer; on the contrary, it is the steamer's duty to keep out of her way[4].

In fog, a dumb barge which has no duty to carry an anchor and no means of bringing up is entitled to keep going until she comes into contact with something to which she can make fast[5].

Whether a barge when not underway ought to have a man in charge of her depends on the circumstances. One important factor is whether it is usual in the circumstances to have a man in charge, but this is not conclusive[6]. The principle of the cases as regards barges, even when in dock, has been that it is negligence not to have a man in charge if there are dangers likely to be incurred which he could prevent, and which are so obvious that they ought to be prevented. The same principle applies wherever a barge is situated, whenever a man should be present on account of the run of the river or exposure of the barge[7].

1   A dumb barge is a barge without sails or helm: *The Barge T-429* [1957] 1 Lloyd's Rep 135 at 137. It is a barge which, with the exception of two small cabins at the ends, is altogether undecked and open for the reception of cargo: *Helios A/S v Ekman & Co* [1897] 2 QB 83 at 87, CA.
2   *The Owen Wallis* (1874) LR 4 A & E 175 at 177, 2 Asp MLC 206 at 207. As to navigation in rivers generally see PARA 747 et seq.
3   *The Ralph Creyke* (1886) 6 Asp MLC 19. There is nothing negligent in one keel driving up river on the flood tide lashed to another keel, they together taking up no more room than a steamship: *The Ralph Creyke*.
4   *The Owen Wallis* (1874) LR 4 A & E 175 at 177, 2 Asp MLC 206 at 207. As to the duty to get out of the way see the Collision Regulations r 18 (cited in PARA 708); and as to damage to barges by the swell of steamers see PARA 741. As to the Collision Regulations (ie the International Regulations for Preventing Collisions at Sea (London, 20 October 1972; TS 77 (1977); Cmnd 6962)) see PARA 690.
5   *The Rose of England* (1888) 6 Asp MLC 304, PC.
6   *The Scotia* (1890) 6 Asp MLC 541; *The Western Belle* (1906) 10 Asp MLC 279 (absence of man not negligence).
7   *The Western Belle* (1906) 10 Asp MLC 279. A dumb barge at night with her head fast to another barge at a tier is in fault for swinging athwart the fairway of a river with no one on board to show a light or warn approaching vessels: *The St Aubin* [1907] P 60, 10 Asp MLC 298 (barge alone to blame). When a barge was fast by her head rope in dock, with her stern swinging out as an obstacle, but there was plenty of light, and a tug coming down the dock struck her, the absence of a bargeman was held to have nothing to do with the collision: *The Hornet* [1892] P 361, 7 Asp MLC 262, PC. Where a barge was moored in barge roads and out of the track, and it was not usual to have a man on board, his absence was held not to be negligence, even though, if on board, he might have averted the damage: *The Western Belle* (1906) 10 Asp MLC 279. Where, however, a steamer and barge were moored in dock at night, and the steamer got underway and her propeller struck the barge, and a bargeman would have avoided the accident, his absence was held to be negligence contributing to the collision, although it was not usual to have a man on a barge in dock: see *The Scotia* (1890) 6 Asp MLC 541; cf *The Dunstanborough* (1891) [1892] P 363n (absence negligent); and see *Lack v Seward* (1829) 4 C & P 106 (where the plaintiff could not recover at common law if the accident would have been avoided but for the negligence of his men in not being on board a barge when it was lying in a dangerous place); *The Barge T-429* [1957] 1 Lloyd's Rep 135 (where a dumb barge, left unattended when a storm was approaching, broke from her moorings and collided with a schooner, and the onus was on her owners to rebut negligence).

(iv) Navigation in Rivers and Narrow Waters

747.   Tide and current. When an exceptional current or tide occurs at a place at distant intervals, but may occur at any time, a cautious seaman is bound to keep in view its possibility and be prepared for it; and, if those in charge of a vessel are caught unprepared by such a current because they think that there is no possibility of it, they will be at fault[1]. Where an eddy noted in the charts prevented a vessel's rudder from acting, so that a collision occurred, but the necessity for using the wheel arose from the other vessel proceeding along the wrong side of a channel and suddenly coming out, the first vessel had a right to expect that the coast would be clear and was held not to blame[2].

1 *The City of Peking Compagnie des Messageries Maritimes, The City of Peking* (1888) 14 App Cas 40, 6 Asp MLC 396, PC. Those who allege an unusual eddy as excusing them should give positive evidence of it; it is not enough to say that a strong eddy must have caught the vessel, otherwise she would have come round: *The Polynésien* [1910] P 28 at 31, 11 Asp MLC 354 at 357.
2 *Scicluna v Stevenson, The Rhondda* (1883) 8 App Cas 549, 5 Asp MLC 114, PC. As to the 'narrow channel rule' see PARA 699.

748. Waiting at a bend. In a tidal river where there is a sharp bend, a power-driven vessel having the tide against her should ease her engines and wait under the point until another vessel coming with the tide has cleared her[1]. Where a power-driven vessel coming up with the tide failed to answer her wheel at a sharp and dangerous bend in the river owing to the eddy, another such vessel coming down against the tide was held to blame for the collision, owing to her not having waited for the first vessel to clear the bend[2]. A power-driven vessel proceeding down a difficult reach in a river against the flood tide in darkness and poor visibility ought to navigate with great care and great caution, because on a flood tide vessels will probably be met, and she has a special duty to keep a good look-out[3].

1 *The Talabot* (1890) 15 PD 194, 6 Asp MLC 602 (where the rule as to waiting was applied, although there was also a rule that the vessels should pass port to port). See also *The Prinses Juliana* [1936] P 139, [1936] 1 All ER 685, 18 Asp MLC 614 (where both a harbour byelaw which required a vessel navigating against the tide to ease and, if necessary, wait, and the narrow channel rule, which requires vessels to keep to starboard and pass port to port, were applicable): *The Timandra, Georgia (Owners) v Timandra (Owners)* [1956] 2 All ER 531, [1956] 1 WLR 691, [1956] 1 Lloyd's Rep 466. As to the 'narrow channel rule' under the Collision Regulations see r 9(a); and PARA 699. As to the Collision Regulations (ie the International Regulations for Preventing Collisions at Sea (London, 20 October 1972; TS 77 (1977); Cmnd 6962)) see PARA 690. As to the duty under those rules to signal before rounding a bend see PARA 723.
   In *The Smyrna* (1864) 11 LT 74, PC, it was held that, in the absence of any regulations governing the matter, common prudence required that a vessel ascending a bend in the Danube with a strong current should place herself out of the strength of the current, so as to allow full swing to the descending vessels.
2 *The Ezardian* [1911] P 92, 11 Asp MLC 602.
3 *The Trident* (1854) 1 Ecc & Ad 217 at 220, 223. As to the duty to keep a look-out see PARA 739; and as to precautions in special weather conditions see PARA 732.

749. Dredging up stern first. A power-driven vessel proceeding up river with a strong tide and approaching a bend may be held to blame for not swinging round and dredging up stern first, according to local practice, in order to avoid excessive speed[1]. Any vessel proceeding up river stern first at night should exhibit a stern light to down-coming vessels[2] and should keep a look-out up river[3], and, if a power-driven vessel, should give some signal[4] to prevent a mistake by down-coming vessels[5]. When a keel with her mast lowered, lashed to another keel, was driving up the deep water channel of a river on the flood tide, it was held that both keels should have dredged up, so that, by keeping the anchor on the ground, they could practically steer themselves and by letting the anchor hold could bring themselves to a standstill[6].

1 *The Frankfort* [1910] P 50, 11 Asp MLC 326, CA. As to the duty to wait at a bend see PARA 748.
2 Cf *The Indian Chief* (1888) 14 PD 24, 6 Asp MLC 362. As to the meaning of 'stern light' under the Collision Regulations see PARA 711 note 7. As to the Collision Regulations (ie the International Regulations for Preventing Collisions at Sea (London, 20 October 1972; TS 77 (1977); Cmnd 6962)) see PARA 690.
3 As to the duty to keep a look-out see PARA 739.
4 Eg a prolonged blast on her whistle (*The Juno* (1894) 7 Asp MLC 506); or three short blasts (*The Battersea* (1912) Shipping Gazette, 14 February). As to the meaning of 'short blast' under the Collision Regulations see PARA 723 note 8; and as to the meaning of 'prolonged blast' under those Regulations see PARA 723 note 19.

5   *The Juno* (1894) 7 Asp MLC 506.
6   *The Ralph Creyke* (1886) 6 Asp MLC 19. As to a duty to dredge up river if underway in a dense
    fog cf *The Aguadillana* (1889) 6 Asp MLC 390.

750. Warping; smelling the ground. If a vessel chooses to use a particular
mode of going down river at a time which makes it difficult for her to escape
collision, she must bear the consequences of a contingency to which she has
exposed herself. Accordingly, when a steamship was warping down river against
the flood, it was held to be no excuse that she was incapable of getting out of the
way[1].

When those in charge of a vessel are navigating a river where they know there
is a risk of her smelling the ground, they ought, if necessary by occasionally
stopping their engines, to keep her so well under control as to be able to avoid
collision with other vessels in case she smells the ground and fails to answer her
wheel[2].

1   *The Hope* (1843) 2 Wm Rob 8. As to the 'narrow channel rule' under the Collision Regulations
    see r 9(a); and PARA 699. As to the Collision Regulations (ie the International Regulations for
    Preventing Collisions at Sea (London, 20 October 1972; TS 77 (1977); Cmnd 6962)) see
    PARA 690.
2   *The Ralph Creyke* (1886) 6 Asp MLC 19. As to precautions to be taken to allow for tide and
    current see PARA 747.

751. Crossing or turning in a river. It is not uncommon to have a byelaw in
a river to the effect that a vessel crossing must keep out of the way of other traffic[1].
Such a rule does not mean that, if two vessels come into collision, the one which
is crossing is necessarily to blame[2]. The whole river belongs to everybody and
nobody has an exclusive occupation of the road. If a vessel is properly
endeavouring to get to the other side of the river as soon as practicable, and is
doing that in a proper way, she is merely making a legitimate use of the river[3]. The
crossing vessel may cross if there is the time and opportunity to do so without
hampering another vessel, and the other vessel which sees a vessel about to cross
must act reasonably with regard to her, and, if the crossing vessel wants a little
more room to assist her in crossing, must give it.

The weight of responsibility for the operation at the outset is, however,
principally on the vessel crossing, in that she must see whether she has room to
cross[4]. Where one vessel about to cross is near a second vessel which must act for
her if she crosses, those on the first vessel ought to make up their minds at once
whether to cross or not and indicate their intention in an unmistakable way[5].
Similarly, a burden is sometimes placed on a vessel turning in a river either not to
cause damage to other vessels[6] but to complete her turn in a proper manner, using
no more water than is necessary[7], or, if a power-driven vessel, to give certain
sound signals[8]. A vessel has been found at fault for trying to turn around too
sharply across the course of another vessel in the Bosporus[9].

1   As to the application of the crossing rule for narrow channels contained in the Collision
    Regulations see r 9(d); and PARA 699. As to the Collision Regulations (ie the International
    Regulations for Preventing Collisions at Sea (London, 20 October 1972; TS 77 (1977); Cmnd
    6962)) see PARA 690.
2   *The Thetford* (1887) 6 Asp MLC 179 (decided under the Rules for the Navigation of the River
    Tyne).
3   *The Thetford* (1887) 6 Asp MLC 179 at 180.
4   *Hogstad v Coombe Dingle* (1921) 8 Ll L Rep 153 at 155; *The Oldekerk* [1974] 1 Lloyd's Rep 95.
    Under Thames rules, it is the duty of a vessel which is about to cross into the main stream of traffic
    to observe, before she does so, what traffic is approaching in the main stream and not to cross the
    stream before it is safe to do so: *Hogstad v Coombe Dingle*.
5   *The Skipsea* [1905] P 32 at 37, 41, 10 Asp MLC 91 at 93, 94.
6   See eg the Tyne Rules 1884 art 22.
7   *The Australmead* [1924] P 36, 16 Asp MLC 247.

8   As to sound signals under the Collision Regulations see PARAS 722–726. Signals should be
    sounded repeatedly: *The Lillois* [1955] 1 Lloyd's Rep 383. The vessel having given the turning
    signal must not put herself athwart the stream and continue to come on athwart: *The Australmead*
    [1924] P 36, 16 Asp MLC 247 (decided on the former Humber Rules 1910 art 14).
9   *Chittagong (Owners) v Kostroma (Owners)* [1901] AC 597, 9 Asp MLC 252, PC.

752.   Anchoring in fairway.

A vessel is justified in anchoring[1] in the fairway[2] of
a river if overtaken by a dense fog, but those in charge ought to move her as soon
as they reasonably can[3]. It is improper for a vessel to anchor so that she lies
athwart the fairway[4], but, when a vessel is compelled by damage from a collision
occasioned by no fault of hers to drop her anchor, it is not negligent to drop it in
the fairway in what would otherwise have been an improper place[5]. It is not
necessarily unlawful in fine weather to anchor in a river in the track of a ferry
boat[6]. A vessel which lays out her anchor in the fairway of a navigable river, and
thereby creates danger for other craft, is under a duty to mark the anchor by a
buoy or otherwise[7].

1   As to coming to anchor and precautions while at anchor see PARAS 734, 735.
2   As to the meaning of 'fairway' see PARA 699 note 4.
3   *The Aguadillana* (1889) 6 Asp MLC 390 at 391. As to special weather conditions see PARA 732.
4   *The Eurymedon* [1938] P 41, [1938] 1 All ER 122, 59 Ll L Rep 214, CA.
5   *The Kjobenhavn* (1874) 2 Asp MLC 213, PC. A vessel anchoring near a channel where there are
    a number of vessels passing must exhibit lights, whether required by harbour regulations or not:
    The Victoria (1854) 7 Ir Jur 94.
6   *The Lancashire* (1874) LR 4 A & E 198 at 200, 2 Asp MLC 202 at 204.
7   *The Harkaway* [1928] P 199, 17 Asp MLC 503.

753.   Aground in the fairway.

Apart from any regulations[1], those in charge of
a vessel aground at night in the fairway[2] of a navigable channel are bound to take
proper means to apprise other vessels of her position[3]. A vessel at anchor in a fog
which neglects to give prescribed signals[4] may be partly at fault for the collision,
even if the other vessel had no right to be underway[5].

1   Ie apart from the Collision Regulations r 20 (see PARA 739) and any local regulations. As to the
    Collision Regulations (ie the International Regulations for Preventing Collisions at Sea (London,
    20 October 1972; TS 77 (1977); Cmnd 6962)), which make allowance for certain categories of
    local rules, see PARA 690.
2   As to the meaning of 'fairway' see PARA 699 note 4.
3   *The Industrie* (1871) LR 3 A & E 303 at 308, 1 Asp MLC 17 at 18, 19 (no light shown); *The
    Bromsgrove* [1912] P 182, 12 Asp MLC 196. A steamship in the Firth of Clyde suddenly stopping
    to anchor ought to signal by whistle to vessels approaching from astern, even though she is
    carrying a stern light: *The Queen Victoria* (1891) 7 Asp MLC 9, CA.
4   Ie prescribed by a byelaw or by the Collision Regulations r 35 (sound signals in restricted visibility)
    (as to which see PARA 724).
5   *The Clutha Boat 147* [1909] P 36 at 42, 11 Asp MLC 199 at 201. See also *The Blue Bell* [1895]
    P 242, 7 Asp MLC 601, DC; *The Lake Farragut* [1921] P 305. As to the right of a vessel to be
    underway in a fog see PARA 732.

754.   Incoming vessel to wait for outgoing.

When an incoming and an
outgoing vessel are approaching the entrance to a dock or harbour[1] so as to reach
it at about the same time, and there is not room for them to pass each other there,
it is the ordinary rule that the incoming vessel should wait to enter until the
outgoing vessel has got clear[2]. Where a vessel is coming out of dock to turn up or
down river, another vessel is entitled to take for granted that she will resort to all
the means proper for the purpose; and, if a vessel, for example by not running up
her jib, fails to take such means, and so causes a collision, she is to blame for it[3].

1   The entrance to a harbour may be a narrow channel for the purposes of the Collision Regulations
    see PARA 700. As to the Collision Regulations (ie the International Regulations for Preventing
    Collisions at Sea (London, 20 October 1972; TS 77 (1977); Cmnd 6962)) see PARA 690.
2   *Taylor v Burger* (1898) 8 Asp MLC 364, HL. Cf *The Henry Morton* (1874) 2 Asp MLC 466 at
    467, PC (duty to stop or go under the stern of outgoing vessel); and see *The Hazelmere* [1911] P
    69, 11 Asp MLC 536, CA; *Balaena v Cairngarth* (1921) 6 Ll L Rep 354 (River Mersey).

3   *Laird v Brownlie, The Ulster* (1862) 1 Moo PCCNS 31 at 41. Cf *The Mourne* [1901] P 68, 9 Asp MLC 155 (where a vessel, having already begun to swing to port before coming out of dock, was held not bound to give the signal for an alteration of course to port, nor to stop her engines, on seeing another vessel); *The Sunlight* [1904] P 100, 9 Asp MLC 509 (where the out-coming vessel was held at fault while in the half-tide lock for not seeing the lights of the vessels in the river and for not easing her engines and starboarding). When there is a regulation as to a vessel lying off at a specified distance, if there are several vessels waiting to enter, this is intended to preserve order among those competing for entrance, and is not intended to excuse the erratic and dangerous movements of another vessel: *Richelieu and Ontario Navigation Co v Taylor* [1910] AC 170 at 174, 11 Asp MLC 315 at 317, PC. See also *The Oldekerk* [1974] 1 Lloyd's Rep 95. As to the application of the crossing rule contained in the Collision Regulations r 15 to a vessel coming out of a dock see PARA 705.

755. Obeying orders of dock master or harbour master. It is the duty of a harbour master or dock master[1] to consider the interests of all the shipping under his care, and he is entitled to order a vessel to move from her berth if a second vessel, which is disabled, absolutely requires the protection of this berth, while the first vessel can with care do without it, even if in the interests of the first vessel alone to move would be injudicious[2]. The harbour master is under a duty to give warning to those in charge of a vessel of a concealed danger, the existence of which they cannot reasonably be expected to know[3]. A dock master has authority to give directions to a vessel which is coming into dock[4], and to order a ship to leave the premises of the dock authority[5]. The primary duty of those in charge of a vessel is obedience to the orders of the harbour master or dock master; it is not their duty in any doubtful case to consider whether the order is right or wrong. If however, it is certain that a disaster will happen by obeying an order, then, and then only, ought it to be disobeyed[6].

1   As to the powers of a harbour master with regard to the control of shipping see PORTS AND HARBOURS vol 85 (2012) PARA 91 et seq. 'Harbour master' for this purpose includes a dock master.
2   *The Excelsior* (1868) LR 2 A & E 268. In such a case, the master of the vessel ought to move her, and may be in fault if he has not sufficient crew on board to protect his vessel against ordinary perils: *The Excelsior*. See also PORTS AND HARBOURS vol 85 (2012) PARA 91.
3   *Robertson v Portpatrick and Wigtownshire Joint Committee* 1919 SC 293.
4   *Reney v Kirkcudbright Magistrates* [1892] AC 264 at 269, 7 Asp MLC 221 at 222. See also PORTS AND HARBOURS vol 85 (2012) PARA 92.
5   *The Sunlight* [1904] P 100 at 112, 9 Asp MLC 509 at 512.
6   *Taylor v Burger* (1898) 8 Asp MLC 364 at 365, HL; *Cory & Son Ltd v France, Fenwick & Co Ltd* [1911] 1 KB 114, 11 Asp MLC 499, CA. When a signal was given for a sailing vessel to enter a narrow channel leading to a dock, a tug was held to blame for entering the channel to pick up a buoy and thereby obstructing the sailing vessel and causing a collision: *The Effort* (1847) 5 Notes of Cases 279; *The Rockabill* [1937] P 93, [1937] 1 All ER 191, 56 Ll L Rep 149, CA. As to liability when a vessel acting under the orders of a harbour master or dock master is involved in a collision see PARA 785.

(4) NEGLIGENCE CAUSING DAMAGE; FAULT

(i) Negligence causing Damage

756. Cause of action. The ordinary case of negligence causing damage by collision is that of one vessel coming into collision with another vessel. In these circumstances, in order to establish a right of action against the owner of a vessel, the court must decide that:

(1)   there was a collision;
(2)   damage was done by it; and
(3)   the collision or damage was caused wholly or in part by the fault of the owner or a person for whose act or omission he is responsible[1].

Impact of two vessels without damage gives no right of action[2], but, if the defendant's negligence has caused the damage, although not the collision, he will be at least partly at fault[3]. Impact and damage without fault on the part of those in charge of a vessel give no right of action in rem against the vessel[4], and the damage is then either an inevitable accident or is due to the fault of the other party or some other person[5].

Special arrangements have been made[6] as regards the settlement of claims in respect of death or personal injury in connection with the operation of vessels of visiting forces in the United Kingdom or its territorial waters[7].

1   *The Margaret* (1881) 6 PD 76 at 79, 4 Asp MLC 375, CA; *The Thomaseverett* [1981] 1 Lloyd's Rep 1, CA. As to the prevention of collisions see PARA 690 et seq.
2   *The Margaret* (1881) 6 PD 76, 4 Asp MLC 375, CA. Cf *Overseas Tankship (UK) Ltd v Morts Dock and Engineering Co Ltd, The Wagon Mound* [1961] AC 388 at 425, [1961] 1 All ER 404 at 415, [1961] 1 Lloyd's Rep 1 at 11, PC (no liability in tort until damage done).
3   *The Margaret* (1881) 6 PD 76 at 79, 4 Asp MLC 375 at 377, CA. The defendant will not, however, be liable for his anchor wrongly projecting, even if it is the instrument of damage, provided that the claimant's vessel could see it and with ordinary care avoid it: *The Monte Rosa* [1893] P 23, 7 Asp MLC 326. The defendant may be only partly at fault if there ought to have been a crew member on the other vessel who ought to have veered the vessel away: *The Dunstanborough* (1891) [1892] P 363n; and see *The Vectis* [1929] P 204, 17 Asp MLC 574. Where a collision is caused by the fault of one vessel and the damage resulting is augmented by the fault of the other, both must be held to blame: *The Kaiser Wilhelm II* (1915) 85 LJP 26, CA. As to the division of liability between both parties see PARA 767 et seq.
4   *Morgan v Castlegate Steamship Co, The Castlegate* [1893] AC 38 at 52, 7 Asp MLC 284 at 288, HL. In a claim made in respect of a collision the property is not treated as the delinquent per se: *Morgan v Castlegate Steamship Co, The Castlegate* at 52, 288. As to actions in rem for damage done by or to a ship see PARA 810.
5   As to incidence of liability see PARA 779 et seq; and as to inevitable accident particularly see PARAS 788, 789.
6   Ie under the Visiting Forces Act 1952 s 9 (settlement of claims against visiting forces): see ARMED FORCES vol 3 (2011) PARA 419.
7   See the London Gazette dated 4 June 1954 p 3338; the Law Society's Gazette dated June 1954 p 241.

757. Burden of proof. In the case of collision between vessels, the burden of proof usually at first rests on the claimant[1], even if the defendant has broken one of the Collision Regulations[2], or even if he alleges inevitable accident[3] or admits that he is partly at fault[4].

Where the evidence on both sides is nicely balanced and conflicting, the court will be guided by the probabilities of the cases set up[5]. The reasonable way to do so is to analyse the facts in order to ascertain the principal subject of inquiry on which the case hinges, and to endeavour to arrive at a satisfactory conclusion as to the testimony upon that matter[6].

The claimant cannot succeed, however, if the case is left in doubt[7], and it is for him to adduce preponderating evidence[8].

It is prima facie evidence of negligence for a vessel to drag her anchor or break adrift from her moorings[9] and for a barge to sink and get into such a position that a steamer alongside her sits on her[10]. Where, on the undisputed evidence of the circumstances leading up to a collision, a prima facie case of negligence is made out against a ship, it is not sufficient rebuttal to show that her steering gear jammed. It must be shown that the jamming could not have been avoided by the exercise of reasonable care and skill, or at any rate that all reasonable care and skill was used to prevent the jamming and that the gear might reasonably have jammed from a cause which could not have been prevented by such care and skill[11].

The defendant in a collision case is usually bound to prove those facts which are peculiarly or exclusively within his knowledge[12].

1　*The Bolina* (1844) 3 Notes of Cases 208 at 210. As to the burden of proof of consequential damage see the dictum of Hill J in *The Waalstroom* (1923) 17 Ll L Rep 53, approved by Bankes LJ in *The Paludina* [1925] P 40 at 43, 16 Asp MLC 453 at 455. As to the burden of proof generally see CIVIL PROCEDURE vol 12 (2015) PARA 702 et seq.
2　As to contraventions of the Collision Regulations see PARA 1134. As to the Collision Regulations (ie the International Regulations for Preventing Collisions at Sea (London, 20 October 1972; TS 77 (1977); Cmnd 6962)) see PARA 690.
3　*The Otter* (1874) LR 4 A & E 203, 2 Asp MLC 208. As to inevitable accident see PARAS 788, 789.
4　*The Cadeby* [1909] P 257, 11 Asp MLC 285.
5　*The Mary Stewart* (1844) 2 Wm Rob 244.
6　*The Singapore and The Hebe* (1866) LR 1 PC 378.
7　*The City of London* (1857) Sw 300 at 302, PC. If the defendant gives a reasonable explanation consistent with the accident happening without his negligence, the burden of proof is shifted back to the claimant: see *The Kite* [1933] P 154, 46 Ll L Rep 83; *The Mulbera* [1937] P 82, 57 Ll L Rep 31; cf *The Stranna* [1937] P 130 at 147, [1937] 2 All ER 383 at 391, 19 Asp MLC 115 at 120 (affd without reference to burden of proof [1938] P 69, [1938] 1 All ER 458, 60 Ll L Rep 51, CA). See also the text and note 9.
8　*The Ligo* (1831) 2 Hag Adm 356.
9　*London v Exeter City and Sea Serpent* (1922) 12 Ll L Rep 423; *The Barge T-429* [1957] 1 Lloyd's Rep 135; cf *The Aralia* (1949) 82 Ll L Rep 884 (where the defendants provided a reasonable explanation of how the accident might have occurred without negligence on their part and the burden of proof shifted back to the claimants).
10　*The Princess* [1929] P 287, 18 Asp MLC 56.
11　*The Llanover* (1945) 79 Ll L Rep 159 at 163. See also *The Warkworth* (1884) 9 PD 145, 5 Asp MLC 326, CA; *The European* (1885) 10 PD 99, 5 Asp MLC 417; *The Merchant Prince* [1892] P 179, 7 Asp MLC 208, CA; *The Calderon* (1912) Times, 26 March; *The Louis Sheid* [1958] 1 Lloyd's Rep 606 at 615 (where there had been three previous failures of steering). Cf *Esso Petroleum Ltd v Southport Corpn* [1956] AC 218, [1955] 3 All ER 864, [1955] 2 Lloyd's Rep 655, HL. As to liability for not having hand gear ready see PARA 737; and as to the defence of inevitable accident on the ground of a failure of machinery consistent with the exercise of reasonable care and skill see PARA 789.
12　*The John Harley v The William Tell* (1865) 2 Mar LC 290. The burden of proof of good look-out on a vessel on a dark night is on those on board who allege it, and not on those who were not on board. Where a vessel which was moored complained that a second vessel was improperly moored and drifted down on her, and the defence was that the second vessel was properly moored in a gale and that there was no negligence, the burden of proof that the second vessel was properly moored lay on those who alleged it: *The John Harley v The William Tell*. Cf *The Swanland* (1855) 2 Ecc & Ad 107 (where the burden of proof as to his lights was held to lie on the plaintiff, partly because their state was a matter peculiarly within his knowledge).

758. Rules as to proof. The court generally follows ascertained lines in drawing conclusions as to testimony in collision cases. When the certain facts of a case, for example weather, description of vessels, courses, time, and place, which are admitted or indisputably proved, are ascertained, the doubtful facts are to be fitted in with them as far as possible[1]. It is a rule in collision cases not to attribute perjury, if it is possible to avoid doing so[2]. Although on nautical points the court is assisted by the opinion and advice of nautical assessors[3] whose duty it is to be guided in matters of nautical experience by their own knowledge[4], the court is not bound to take the advice of its nautical assessors but must make up its own mind on questions of nautical skill and seamanship[5].

1　*The Carron* (1853) 1 Ecc & Ad 91 at 92. As to the burden of proof in collision cases see PARA 757.
2　*The Clarence* (1853) 1 Ecc & Ad 206 at 213; *The Alice and The Princess Alice* (1868) LR 2 PC 245; *The Glannibanta* (1876) 1 PD 283, sub nom *The Transit* 3 Asp MLC 233, CA; *Gannet (Owners) v Algoa (Owners), The Gannet* [1900] AC 234, 9 Asp MLC 43, HL; *The Olympic and HMS Hawke* [1913] P 214 at 258, CA (affd [1915] AC 385, 12 Asp MLC 580, HL). The court does not as a rule pay great attention to evidence of conversations after a collision, devoting its consideration to testimony of the facts other than of these uncertain colloquies (*The Dundee* (1821) Times, 5 December per Lord Stowell) or admissions (*The Virgil* (1843) 2 Wm Rob 201 at 203).

3   See *The City of Berlin* [1908] P 110, 11 Asp MLC 4, CA. As to the role of assessors generally see
    PARA 205; as to particular questions to nautical assessors see *The Beryl* (1884) 9 PD 137 at 142,
    143, 5 Asp MLC 321 at 324, CA; *The New Pelton* [1891] P 258, 7 Asp MLC 81; and as to the
    form of questions for assessors see *Admiralty Comrs v Ausonia (Owners)* (1920) 2 Ll L Rep 123.
4   *The Gazelle* (1842) 1 Wm Rob 471 at 474. As to how far the court should be guided by the
    nautical assessors, and as to decision on questions of testimony resting with the court, see *The Aid*
    (1881) 6 PD 84, 4 Asp MLC 432, CA (county court); *The Beryl* (1884) 9 PD 137 at 141, 5 Asp
    MLC 321 at 324, CA; *Gannet (Owners) v Algoa (Owners), The Gannet* [1900] AC 234, 9 Asp
    MLC 43, HL. Assessors advising the Court of Appeal do not speak with any greater authority than
    those advising the court below: *The Fina Canada* [1962] 2 Lloyd's Rep 445 at 454, CA, per
    Willmer LJ.
5   *Australia (Owners) v Nautilus (Cargo Owners), The Australia* [1927] AC 145, 17 Asp MLC 86,
    HL. See also *Melanie (Owners) v San Onofre (Owners)* (1919) [1927] AC 162n; *Artemisia
    (Owners) v Douglas (Owners)* [1927] AC 164n, HL; *The Marinegra* [1959] 2 Lloyd's Rep 65 at
    76–78, CA, per Willmer LJ (a dissenting judgment) (on appeal [1960] 2 Lloyd's Rep 1, HL). See
    also CIVIL PROCEDURE vol 12 (2015) PARA 921.

759. Negligence in construction, equipment or manning. The simplest case
of negligence on the part of an owner of a vessel causing damage by collision is
negligence in constructing or equipping or manning her[1]. Vessels have been held
to blame for a collision owing to their not being built or equipped or loaded with
reasonable care[2]. As regards the officers of a ship, certificates are required in some
cases for the master, mates, engineers and radio officers[3]. The number of hands
required depends on circumstances. There ought to be a sufficient crew on board
even in harbour to protect a ship against the ordinary incidents of peril which a
competent seaman would foresee[4].

1   As to the incidence of liability see PARA 779 et seq.
2   Eg in the case of a vessel not safely navigable owing to her improper trim (*The Argo* (1859) Sw
    462), or not having a proper mast to carry her light (*The Hirondelle* (1905) 22 TLR 146, CA) or
    having defective steering gear (see PARA 737), although this will be excused if the defect was
    consistent with the exercise of all reasonable care and skill to prevent defects (see PARA 788).
    Where breakdowns have occurred, it is negligent to omit regular checks on equipment: *The Louis
    Sheid* [1958] 1 Lloyd's Rep 606 at 615. A vessel may be to blame for having too light an anchor
    (*The Massachusetts* (1842) 1 Wm Rob 371) or no mechanical foghorn (*The Love Bird* (1881) 6
    PD 80, 4 Asp MLC 427). As to the equipment required by the rules of the Collision Regulations
    see PARA 711 (lights); and PARA 722 (sound signals). As to the Collision Regulations (ie the
    International Regulations for Preventing Collisions at Sea (London, 20 October 1972; TS 77
    (1977); Cmnd 6962)) see PARA 690.
3   See PARA 502 et seq. As to officers and watch on look-out see PARA 739.
4   *The Excelsior* (1868) LR 2 A & E 268 at 272. As to crewing in special weather conditions see
    PARA 732. However, see also *Toward (Owners) v Turkistan (Owners)* (1885) 13 R 342. A vessel
    on a trial trip need not be officered and manned as on a voyage, but she should have a sufficient
    crew for the temporary purpose of navigating safely: *Clyde Navigation Co v Barclay* (1876) 1 App
    Cas 790 at 794, 800, 3 Asp MLC 390 at 391, 393, HL. A rowing barge in the Thames with two
    hands is properly manned: *The Minna* (1868) LR 2 A & E 97. As to when a crew member is
    required on a barge in a river see PARA 746.

760. Negligence in navigation. Negligence in navigation, as regards other
vessels, is failure to exercise that attention and vigilance which is needed for their
security[1], and which, if neglected so as to become, however unintentionally, the
cause of damage to a vessel, amounts to a breach of duty, giving a right of action[2].
In such circumstances negligence is failure to exercise reasonable care and
reasonable skill[3], reasonable care being sometimes more than ordinary care, and
reasonable skill being possibly in an emergency less than ordinary skill[4].
Negligence in navigation includes not only failure to exercise reasonable care and
reasonable skill in the usual sense, but also failure to exercise reasonable foresight[5]
and ordinary nerve[6].

1   As to the rules contained in the Collision Regulations for the purpose of preventing collisions see
    PARA 690 et seq (collision regulations); and PARA 758 et seq (rules of good seamanship). As to the
    Collision Regulations (ie the International Regulations for Preventing Collisions at Sea (London,
    20 October 1972; TS 77 (1977); Cmnd 6962)) see PARA 690.

2 *The Dundee* (1823) 1 Hag Adm 109 at 120. The word 'navigate' is not a concept which is restricted to steering a vessel; it incorporates the idea of navigating her in the sense of directing her course and being responsible for it: *Slater v Reed and McGrath, The Varos* [1980] 2 Lloyd's Rep 581, DC.

3 *Stoomvaart Maatschappy Nederland v Peninsular and Oriental Steam Navigation Co* (1880) 5 App Cas 876 at 891, 4 Asp MLC 360 at 365, HL. Negligence is the absence of care according to the circumstances: see *Vaughan v Taff Vale Rly Co* (1860) 5 H & N 679 at 688, Ex Ch; *Grill v General Iron Screw Collier Co* (1866) LR 1 CP 600 at 612. As to the meaning of 'reasonable care' and 'reasonable skill' see PARA 761.

4 As to the exercise of skill in sudden difficulty see PARA 762.

5 *Doward v Lindsay, The William Lindsay* (1873) LR 5 PC 338 at 343, 2 Asp MLC 118 at 120.

6 *Stoomvaart Maatschappy Nederland v Peninsular and Oriental Steam Navigation Co* (1880) 5 App Cas 876 at 888, 4 Asp MLC 360 at 364, HL (ordinary care, skill and nerve).

761. Meaning of 'reasonable care' and 'reasonable skill'.

'Reasonable care' and 'reasonable skill' mean as a rule ordinary care and ordinary skill[1]. Where the circumstances of the case are such as often occur, it is important to see whether it is or is not usual to do the thing alleged to have been neglected, for example to have a man in charge of a barge in dock[2]. The degree of care required, however, varies according to the circumstances, and more than ordinary care is sometimes required. For example, there is a duty to take special precautions when using a delicate instrument[3].

'Ordinary skill' means the skill which would ordinarily be shown by a seaman of competent skill and experience in the circumstances[4]. Failure to do the very best thing, or to show extraordinary skill or presence of mind, does not create a right of action[5].

1 Negligence is thus usually described as failure to exercise ordinary care and skill. As to the standard of care in negligence generally see NEGLIGENCE vol 78 (2010) PARAS 21–23.

2 *The Western Belle* (1906) 10 Asp MLC 279. The fact that the act complained of is usually done is, however, by no means conclusive disproof of negligence: see *The Scotia* (1890) 6 Asp MLC 541. As to whether it is negligence not to have a man in charge of a barge in dock see PARA 746.

3 *The Turret Court* (1900) 69 LJP 117 (where it was held that a master using steam steering gear ought to have had the hand gear ready).

4 *Inman v Reck, The City of Antwerp and The Friedrich* (1868) LR 2 PC 25 at 34. As to the exercise of a particular skill see NEGLIGENCE vol 78 (2010) PARA 23.

5 See *Stoomvaart Maatschappy Nederland v Peninsular and Oriental Steam Navigation Co* (1880) 5 App Cas 876 at 888, 4 Asp MLC 360 at 365, HL. See also *The Bywell Castle* (1879) 4 PD 219 at 227, 4 Asp MLC 207 at 211, CA. As to the exercise of skill in sudden difficulty see PARA 762.

762. Degree of skill required in sudden difficulty.

When one vessel by a wrongful act suddenly puts another in a difficulty, the same amount of skill is not to be expected from the other vessel as in other circumstances[1]. In such a case, a mistake by the other vessel in the agony of collision is not to be held to have in any way caused it[2]. It is not enough in such circumstances to show an act or omission by the officer in charge of the other vessel by reason of which the collision actually occurred[3]. His conduct is entitled to favourable consideration[4].

A person may not do the right thing, and may even do the wrong thing, and yet not be guilty of neglect of his duty, which is not absolutely to do right at all events, but only to take reasonable care and use reasonable skill[5]. When a person is suddenly and without warning thrown into a critical position, due allowance must be made for this, but not too much[6].

So, when a sudden change of circumstances takes place which brings one of the rules contained in the Collision Regulations[7] into operation, even though the thing prescribed is not done by the person in charge, yet the rule can hardly be said to be infringed by him until he knows or ought to have known of the change of circumstances[8]. The officer in charge of a vessel placed suddenly in a difficulty by the fault of another vessel must have time (although it may be a very short time) for thought[9]. When vessels have to manoeuvre for one another, and one hails the other to alter her wheel, it appears that she cannot complain of the alteration[10]; or, if the hail is not to alter the wheel, it becomes the duty of the hailing vessel, even if not so before, to take action to avoid the other vessel[11].

1 *The Bywell Castle* (1879) 4 PD 219, 4 Asp MLC 207, CA. See also *Admiralty (HMS P31) v Bretagne* (1921) 7 Ll L Rep 127.
2 *The Nor* (1874) 2 Asp MLC 264 at 266, PC; *The Fagerstrand* (1929) 33 Ll L Rep 67.
3 *The Sisters* (1876) 1 PD 117 at 120, 3 Asp MLC 122 at 124, CA. See also *The Elizabeth, The Adalia* (1870) 22 LT 74 (where a schooner following up river a steamer which suddenly grounded was held not to blame for not dropping her anchor, although it was a proper thing to do); *The CM Palmer, The Larnax* (1873) 2 Asp MLC 94, PC (where the master of a vessel in a sudden emergency was held not to blame because it did not occur to him to let go his anchor, even supposing it would have averted the collision). When, however, a ship of 2,256 tons gross, laden with iron ore, lay at anchor to a single anchor in the Downs, she was held liable for a collision after she had been broken adrift by another vessel for failing to let go her second anchor and for not having her second anchor so placed that it could be let go at once: *The Jessie and The Zaanland* [1917] P 138, 14 Asp MLC 139. As to coming to anchor and precautions while at anchor see PARAS 734, 735; and as to the incidence of liability see PARA 779 et seq.
4 *Mary Tug Co v British India Steam Navigation Co, The Meanatchy* [1897] AC 351 at 357, PC.
5 *Stoomvaart Maatschappy Nederland v Peninsular and Oriental Steam Navigation Co* (1880) 5 App Cas 876 at 891, 4 Asp MLC 360 at 365, HL. As to the meaning of 'reasonable care' and 'reasonable skill' see PARA 761.
6 As to the standard of care in an emergency see NEGLIGENCE vol 78 (2010) PARA 21.
7 Ie the International Regulations for Preventing Collisions at Sea (London, 20 October 1972; TS 77 (1977); Cmnd 6962): see PARA 690.
8 *Stoomvaart Maatschappy Nederland v Peninsular and Oriental Steam Navigation Co* (1880) 5 App Cas 876 at 894, 4 Asp MLC 360 at 366, HL.
9 *The Emmy Haase* (1884) 9 PD 81, 5 Asp MLC 216; *Kwang Tung (Owner) v Ngapoota (Owners), The Ngapoota* [1897] AC 391, PC; *Hoek van Holland Maatschappij v Clyde Shipping Co* (1902) 5 F 227; and see *United States Shipping Board v Laird Line Ltd* [1924] AC 286, 16 Asp MLC 302, HL; cf PARA 707.
10 Cf *The James Watt* (1844) 2 Wm Rob 270 at 275. Blame may be attached to a vessel which wrongly hails another vessel to alter her wheel: *Maddox v Fisher, The Independence* (1861) 14 Moo PCC 103 at 109.
11 *The Carolus* (1837) 3 Hag Adm 343n. As to rules under the Collision Regulations regarding action taken to avoid collision see PARA 698.

763. Collateral negligence immaterial. It is not necessarily negligent to risk doing damage to another vessel intentionally. Thus, persons have been held justified in risking damage to one vessel by launching another, in order to avoid the more serious risk to life and property by postponement[1]. Moreover, the breach of duty must be connected with the damage as cause and effect to afford the right of action[2]. For example, even though a vessel lying at a pontoon is a trespasser, her owners will not be liable for damage done by her to the pontoon owing to another vessel wrongly striking her[3]. The nature of the accident and what the neglect is should be looked at, and it must be proved[4] that the actual transgression was to some extent the cause of the accident, for, even if blame is attributable to an act, one must guard against assuming that it was, therefore, the cause of the accident[5], and not merely collateral negligence. The defendant is, however, responsible for the reasonably foreseeable consequences of his negligence[6], both on the navigation of his own vessel and of other vessels[7].

1 *Frances (Owners) v Highland Loch (Owners), The Highland Loch* [1912] AC 312, 12 Asp MLC 106, HL (where the master of the vessel damaged had received warning of the launch but had failed to move his vessel out of the way) (see PARA 731).
2 As to establishing the cause of action see PARA 756.
3 *The Titan, The Rambler* (1906) 10 Asp MLC 350.
4 As to the burden of proof see PARA 757.
5 *Cayzer, Irvine & Co, SS Clan Sinclair (Owners) v Carron Co, SS Margaret (Owners)* (1884) 9 App Cas 873 at 881, 882, 5 Asp MLC 371 at 373, HL.
6 As to foreseeability of damage as the test of liability see DAMAGES vol 29 (2014) PARA 409 et seq.

7   *Romney Marsh (Bailiffs) v Trinity House* (1870) LR 5 Exch 204 (affd (1872) LR 7 Exch 247, Ex
Ch); *The City of Lincoln* (1889) 15 PD 15, 6 Asp MLC 475, CA (where the defendants were liable
for the grounding of a vessel due to the loss of charts etc in a collision caused by the defendants);
The Gertor (1894) 7 Asp MLC 472 at 473 (where the defendants, through not taking a tug in a
gale, were held liable for the cost of the subsequent damage done by their vessel); *The Port Victoria*
[1902] P 25, 9 Asp MLC 314 (where it was held that a steamship driven to slip her cable to avoid
a collision could recover the loss); *The Jessie and The Zaanland* [1917] P 138, 14 Asp MLC 139
(cited in PARA 762 note 3). Cf *The Douglas* (1882) 7 PD 151, 5 Asp MLC 15, CA (where there
was a collision with the wreck of a vessel sunk by collision and unlighted without fault of the
owners; the fact that the wreck had been sunk through the negligence of the owners' employees did
not render them liable in respect of the collision); *The Manorbier Castle* (1922) 15 Ll L Rep 164
(where a negligently lighted wreck was run into by a steamer the pilot of which knew the position
of the wreck, and the steamer was found alone to blame). As to liability for collision with wrecks
see PARA 787. Reasonable but mistaken conduct of another person may be a consequence for
which the defendant is liable: *The Oropesa* [1943] P 32, [1943] 1 All ER 211, CA (launching of
boat in rough weather by master of damaged vessel); *Thomas Stone Shipping Ltd v The Admiralty,
The Albion* [1952] 1 Lloyd's Rep 38 at 62, 63 (damage through improper use of engines by vessel
after collision) (on appeal [1953] P 117, [1953] 1 All ER 978, [1953] 1 Lloyd's Rep 239, CA);
Temple Bar (Owners) v Guildford (Owners), The Guildford [1956] P 364, [1956] 2 All ER 915,
[1956] 2 Lloyd's Rep 74 (refusal of offer to tow). The defendant may also be liable for damage
suffered by a third person in seeking, in accordance with a statutory duty, to render assistance to
those on board a vessel in danger of sinking through the negligence of those in charge of the
defendants' vessel: *The Gusty and The Daniel M* [1940] P 159, 19 Asp MLC 366; cf *The San
Onofre* [1922] P 243, 16 Asp MLC 1, CA. As to statutory duties to render assistance see
PARAS 446, 727; and as to the effect upon liability for negligence of intervening action by the
claimant or a third party see generally DAMAGES vol 29 (2014) PARAS 369, 371.

764. Care and skill afloat and ashore.
There is no difference between the rules of the Court of Admiralty and the rules of courts of common law as to what amounts to negligence causing damage by collision[1], but there are differences in the application of the rules because of the distinction between ships and land vehicles in their power to stop and manoeuvre and the distance over which a look-out must be kept[2].

1   As to establishing the cause of action see PARA 756; and as to the burden of proof see PARA 757.
    As to the Admiralty jurisdiction of the High Court of Justice generally see PARA 85 et seq.
2   *Cayzer, Irvine & Co, SS Clan Sinclair (Owners) v Carron Co, SS Margaret (Owners)* (1884) 9 App
    Cas 873 at 882, 5 Asp MLC 371 at 373, HL. As to liability for negligence see generally
    NEGLIGENCE vol 78 (2010) PARA 1 et seq; and as to keeping a look-out see PARA 739.

765. Damage other than to a ship.
In addition to the ordinary case of collision between two vessels[1], there are cases of negligence or fault on the part of an owner of a vessel or his employees[2] causing damage by the vessel colliding with, or some part of it striking, property other than a vessel, for example a pier[3], or a person who is not on board a vessel[4].

1   As to the prevention of collisions see PARA 690 et seq (ie under the International Regulations for
    Preventing Collisions at Sea (London, 20 October 1972; TS 77 (1977); Cmnd 6962)); and
    PARA 729 et seq (common law cases reflecting customary rules of good seamanship).
2   As to the incidence of liability see PARA 779 et seq.
3   See eg *The Excelsior* (1868) LR 2 A & E 268 (damage to pier); *The Swift* [1901] P 168, 9 Asp MLC
    244 (damage to oyster beds). Cf *The Albert Edward* (1875) 44 LJ Adm 49 (where a vessel was held
    not liable for damage to a mooring dolphin as it ought to have been stronger); *The Bien* [1911] P
    40, 11 Asp MLC 558 (where river conservators, and not the owner of a vessel, were liable for
    damage where a wrecked vessel was placed by the order of the conservators' harbour master on
    an oyster bed); *The Oxford v The James and Ann* (1922) 10 Ll L Rep 119 (where the master was
    ignorant of the existence of a ferry cable, and so was not negligent). As to liability for damage
    caused by a vessel acting under the orders of a harbour master see PARA 785; and as to the
    circumstances in which a vessel may ground in a fishery see *Colchester Corpn v Brooke* (1845) 7
    QB 339; and FISHERIES AND AQUACULTURE vol 51 (2013) PARAS 374, 375. As to liability for
    damage to works under the Harbours, Docks, and Piers Clauses Act 1847, and as to the remedy
    for such damage, see ss 74, 75; and PORTS AND HARBOURS vol 85 (2012) PARA 155. Although
    damage caused by a ship striking an object other than a ship is not damage by collision (see
    PARA 690), the Admiralty jurisdiction of the High Court and the existing Admiralty jurisdiction
    of the county court extend to damage caused to or by ships on their striking things other than
    ships: see the Senior Courts Act 1981 s 20(2)(d), (e) (see PARA 110); *The Uhla* (1867) 3 Mar LC

148 (breakwater); *Mersey Docks and Harbour Board v Turner, The Zeta* [1893] AC 468, 7 Asp
MLC 369, HL (pier); *The Swift* [1901] P 168, 9 Asp MLC 244 (oyster beds). As to the power to
enforce a claim against a ship in rem see *The Swift*; the Senior Courts Act 1981 s 21(3); and
PARA 93. As to Admiralty jurisdiction generally see PARA 85 et seq; and as to damage by a ship
to foreign land see CONFLICT OF LAWS vol 19 (2011) PARA 691.

4   See *The Sylph* (1867) LR 2 A & E 24 (injury to diver). As to claims for personal injuries see
PARA 777.

766. Damage to another vessel without collision. There are cases where, by
the fault of those in charge of a vessel, damage is done to another vessel without
coming into collision with her, as, for example by causing a collision between her
and a third vessel[1], or compelling her to go out of the fairway and run aground[2],
or negligently dragging down on her so as to compel her to slip her anchor and
chain and put to sea to avoid collision[3].

1   *The Sisters* (1876) 1 PD 117, 3 Asp MLC 122, CA. A defendant is liable for the reasonably
foreseeable consequences of his negligence: see PARA 763.
2   *The Industrie* (1871) LR 3 A & E 303, 1 Asp MLC 17. See also *Owners of Bow Spring v Owners
of Manzanillo II* [2004] EWCA Civ 1007, [2005] 1 All ER (Comm) 53n, [2005] 1 WLR 144,
[2005] 1 Lloyd's Rep 1 (tanker deliberately beached herself just outside the northern by-pass
channel of the Suez Canal to avoid risk of collision with dredger but the decision to beach was held
to be a hurried and ill-considered over-reaction and the tanker was judged 50% to blame for any
damage incurred to itself). As to the meaning of 'fairway' see PARA 699 note 4.
3   *The Port Victoria* [1902] P 25, 9 Asp MLC 314. As to a power-driven vessel damaging other craft
by her wash see PARA 741.

(ii) Determination of Liability when Both Parties at Fault

767. Principles of liability. When there is fault or negligence attributable to the
owners of both vessels concerned in a collision[1]:

(1)   if one party's fault has not even partly caused the damage[2] by collision,
        then, if he is the claimant, he can recover in full for the damage to his
        vessel caused by the other party, and, if he is the defendant, he is not
        liable for the damage to the other vessel[3];

(2)   if the fault of each party has partly caused[4] the damage by the collision,
        both vessels are to blame, and each party is liable to make good the
        damage of the other party in proportion to the degree in which his vessel
        was in fault[5];

(3)   if one party's fault has solely caused the damage by collision, then, if he
        is the claimant, he cannot recover for the damage to his vessel and, if he
        is the defendant, he is liable for the whole of the damage to the other
        vessel[6].

1   The principles stated in the text apply mutatis mutandis where more than two vessels are
concerned: cf PARA 774. As to the incidence of liability see PARA 779 et seq.
2   Negligence which renders a party liable as defendant (or affects his right to recover in full if
claimant) is sometimes referred to as negligence which 'directly causes' or 'directly contributes' to
the damage: see eg *Tuff v Warman* (1857) 2 CBNS 740 at 743; *The Bernina (2)* (1887) 12 PD 58
at 61–63, 6 Asp MLC 75 at 77, 78, CA. As to the necessity for causation see PARA 763.
3   See *The Woodrop-Sims* (1815) 2 Dods 83 at 85 (approved in *Hay v Le Neve* (1824) 2 Sh Sc
App 395, HL); *Spaight v Tedcastle* (1881) 6 App Cas 217 at 219, 4 Asp MLC 406 at 407, HL;
Cayzer, Irvine & Co, SS Clan Sinclair (Owners) v Carron Co, SS Margaret (Owners) (1884) 9 App
Cas 873 at 880, 881, 5 Asp MLC 371 at 373, HL. As to the measure of damages see PARA 793
et seq.
4   It is possible that each party may be negligent, and yet that the acts of negligence may be too trivial
or indirect to be held to be a cause of the damage, which will then, so far as these parties are
concerned, be an inevitable accident: see PARAS 788, 789.
5   See the Merchant Shipping Act 1995 s 187; and PARA 1010 et seq. As to the liability to make good
the damage when more than two vessels have been at fault see PARA 774.
6   See *Cayzer, Irvine & Co, SS Clan Sinclair (Owners) v Carron Co, SS Margaret (Owners)* (1884)
9 App Cas 873 at 881, 5 Asp MLC 371 at 373, HL. See also *The Woodrop-Sims* (1815) 2 Dod
83 at 85 (approved in *Hay v Le Neve* (1824) 2 Sh Sc App 395, HL).

768. Negligence causing damage. Whether one or more negligent acts have caused or partly caused certain damage by collision is generally not a question of law but a question of fact[1]. Thus, when the particular events have been ascertained, the conclusion that the act was or was not the cause or part cause of the damage should be drawn according to the general good sense of ordinary persons[2].

1   See *Cayzer, Irvine & Co, SS Clan Sinclair (Owners) v Carron Co, SS Margaret (Owners)* (1884) 9 App Cas 873 at 881, 5 Asp MLC 371 at 373, HL. As to causation in tort generally see DAMAGES vol 29 (2014) PARA 364 et seq; and as to the burden of proof in collision cases see PARA 757.
2   See *Hero (Owners) v Admiralty Comrs* [1912] AC 300 at 304, 12 Asp MLC 108 at 109, HL (the negligence of one vessel 'in the ordinary plain common sense of the business' contributed to the damage by collision). See also *Admiralty Comrs v SS Volute* [1922] 1 AC 129 at 144, 15 Asp MLC 530 at 537, HL. As to the assistance given to the court by nautical assessors see PARA 758.

769. Simultaneous negligence. Where both vessels have been simultaneously negligent at or up to the last moment before the collision, the usual question is whether the act of negligence on each side was in itself so substantial[1] and so related[2] to the damage by the collision as to amount to a cause of it[3]. When both vessels have thus been simultaneously negligent at or up to the last moment, and when the negligent act of each is substantial and directly related to the collision damage, each vessel is held to have partly caused the damage, and the judgment is that both are to blame[4].

1   See *The Argo* (1900) 9 Asp MLC 74, CA.
2   See *Fanny M Carvill (Owners) v Peru (Owners), The Fanny M Carvill* (1875) 13 App Cas 455n, 2 Asp MLC 565, PC.
3   As to the test of foreseeability of damage see DAMAGES vol 29 (2014) PARA 409 et seq; and as to establishing the cause of action see PARA 756.
4   See eg *The United States* (1865) 12 LT 33, PC (cited in PARA 731 note 7); *The Agra and The Elizabeth Jenkins* (1867) LR 1 PC 501 (failure of one sailing vessel to keep out of the way and of the other to keep her course); *The Roslie* (1880) 5 PD 245, 4 Asp MLC 384 (failure of one sailing vessel to keep out of way and of the other to take action to avoid imminent collision); *The Margaret* (1881) 6 PD 76, 4 Asp MLC 375, CA (moored vessel partly to blame for collision damage because her anchor was improperly projecting at night) (cited in PARA 733). Cf *The Monte Rosa* [1893] P 23, 7 Asp MLC 326 (where the collision was in daylight (see PARA 770 note 7)). See also *The Scotia* (1890) 6 Asp MLC 541; *The Dunstanborough* [1892] P 363n; *The Clutha Boat 147* [1909] P 36, 11 Asp MLC 199 (vessel at anchor in fog to blame for not sounding fog signal; other vessel at fault for being underway and going too fast); *The Frankfort* [1910] P 50, 11 Asp MLC 326, CA (collision in river; excessive speed by one vessel and wrong manoeuvre and failure to signal on part of other); and see *Stanton v Redriff* (1921) 6 Ll L Rep 348; *The Eurymedon* [1938] P 41, [1938] 1 All ER 122, 59 Ll L Rep 214, CA (vessel anchored in improper position athwart fairway; other vessel negligent in failing to appreciate that lights seen were anchor lights); *Boy Andrew (Owners) v St Rognvald (Owners)* [1948] AC 140, [1947] 2 All ER 350, 80 Ll L Rep 559, HL (simultaneous faulty navigation of overtaking and overtaken vessel); *Cunard White Star Line Ltd v Admiralty Comrs, The Queen Mary* [1949] WN 75, 82 Ll L Rep 303, HL (negligence of escorted vessel and escort); *The Hurst* [1952] 1 Lloyd's Rep 96 (barge adrift unattended; attempt to pass between barge and other vessels). As to the principles of liability where two parties are at fault see PARA 767 et seq; and as to the division of loss where both are at fault see PARA 771 et seq.

770. Antecedent and subsequent negligence. Where, as in a large number of collisions at sea[1], one vessel has been negligent at the last moment before collision and the other vessel's negligence has taken place before that, the decision as to whether each act was or was not a cause of the collision is more difficult[2].

It must be considered how far the subsequent act should be treated as connected with or independent of the antecedent act, and the importance of each has to be contrasted in connection with the resulting damage[3]. Where a clear line can be drawn, the subsequent negligence is the only one to look to[4]. If one party has actually observed the negligence of the other party or could by reasonable care have become aware of it, and could by reasonable care[5] have avoided causing damage, he is solely responsible for the damage[6]. It is a question of fact in each case whether the negligence of the initial wrongdoer could have been avoided by the other party[7].

There may, however, be cases where the two acts of negligence come so closely together, and the second act is so much mixed up with the state of things brought about by the first act, that the party secondly negligent, while not held free from blame, may invoke the prior negligence as being part of the cause of the collision so as to make it a case of contribution[8]; and there may be cases where the collision was caused wholly by the antecedent negligence, the subsequent negligence being then too slight a factor to be reckoned as a cause[9].

1   *Stoomvaart Maatschappy Nederland v Peninsular and Oriental Steam Navigation Co* (1880) 5 App Cas 876 at 903, 4 Asp MLC 360 at 367, HL. As to the prevention of collisions see PARA 690 et seq (ie under the International Regulations for Preventing Collisions at Sea 1972); and PARA 729 et seq (common law cases reflecting customary rules of good seamanship).
2   As to the burden of proof in collision cases see PARA 757.
3   When there has been antecedent and subsequent negligence, it will not be sufficient, in order to prove that the other party partly caused the damage, to show that, if he in some earlier stage of navigation had done something which he ought to have done, a different situation would have resulted: see *Spaight v Tedcastle* (1881) 6 App Cas 217 at 219, 4 Asp MLC 406 at 407, HL, per Lord Selborne LC.
4   *Admiralty Comrs v SS Volute (Owners)* [1922] 1 AC 129 at 144, 15 Asp MLC 530 at 537, HL. See also eg *Spaight v Tedcastle* (1881) 6 App Cas 217, 4 Asp MLC 406, HL (negligence by tow and subsequent negligence by tug); *The Hornet* [1892] P 361, 7 Asp MLC 262 (where the absence of the person in charge of a moored barge did not contribute to the collision); *The Kate* (1936) 54 Ll L Rep 120 at 124 (where a moored barge obstructed a lock entrance, but was plainly visible to a steamer which got underway in the lock and ran into the barge); *The Arabert* [1959] 1 Lloyd's Rep 63, CA (where a vessel engaged in turning in a river was run into by another). In such a case the party held responsible is said to have been subsequently and severably negligent: *Admiralty Comrs v SS Volute* at 136 and at 535; and see DAMAGES vol 29 (2014) PARA 388.
5   As to the meaning of 'reasonable care' and 'reasonable skill' see PARA 761.
6   *The Eurymedon* [1938] P 41 at 49, 50, [1938] 1 All ER 122 at 126, 59 Ll L Rep 214 at 217, CA. See also *Dowell v General Steam Navigation Co* (1855) 5 E & B 195 at 206; *Tuff v Warman* (1858) 5 CBNS 573 at 585; *Spaight v Tedcastle* (1881) 6 App Cas 217 at 226, 4 Asp MLC 406 at 409, HL; *Cayzer, Irvine & Co, SS Clan Sinclair (Owners) v Carron Co, SS Margaret (Owners)* (1884) 9 App Cas 873 at 887, 5 Asp MLC 371 at 375, HL; *The Bernina (2)* (1887) 12 PD 58 at 61, 62, 6 Asp MLC 75 at 77, CA.
7   *The Hero* [1911] P 128 at 151, 12 Asp MLC 10 at 17, 18, CA. See eg *Krysia Maritime Inc v Intership Ltd* [2008] EWHC 1523 (Admlty), [2008] All ER (D) 08 (Jul) (rope attached to fender that was free in the water was a hazard or danger to all vessels approaching the barge but it had been unseamanlike for the master of the other vessel to manoeuvre so that there was a danger that his vessel might have hit the side of the barge; 30% liability attributed to claimant).
    For instances in which the person subsequently negligent was held wholly responsible for the damage see *Cayzer, Irvine & Co SS Clan Sinclair (Owners) v Carron Co, SS Margaret (Owners)* (1884) 9 App Cas 873, 5 Asp MLC 371, HL (where a steamship negligently failed to wait before rounding the point of a river and a second steamship was subsequently negligent by trying recklessly to run between the first-mentioned steamship and a third vessel when there was insufficient room). Cf *The Ovingdean Grange* [1902] P 208, 9 Asp MLC 295, CA (cited in note 8); *The Monte Rosa* [1893] P 23, 7 Asp MLC 326 (where a tug which in daylight by negligent navigation came into collision with a steamer and suffered damage from the steamer's anchor which was improperly projecting was held solely to blame); contrast *The Margaret* (1881) 6 PD 76, 4 Asp MLC 375, CA; *Carse v North British Steam Packet Co* (1895) 22 R 475 (where a steamer ran down a boat moored in an improper place); *The Winstanley* [1896] P 297, 8 Asp MLC 170, CA (where a steamer on her wrong side of a channel collided with a steamer which had regained her right side); *HMS Sans Pareil* [1900] P 267, 9 Asp MLC 78, CA (where a tug and tow improperly attempted to cross ahead of a squadron of warships, but a warship could by ordinary diligence have avoided collision and was solely responsible for it: for comment on this decision see *Admiralty Comrs v SS Volute* [1922] 1 AC 129 at 141, 15 Asp MLC 530 at 536, HL); *Memnon v Paulsboro* (1920) 5 Ll L Rep 250, CA (where one vessel had been going at excessive speed in fog but had stopped and reversed on hearing another vessel's fog whistle, and the other vessel alone was to blame for the collision); *The Manorbier Castle* (1922) 15 Ll L Rep 164 (where a vessel

which collided with a wreck was solely to blame, although wreck-marking lights were negligently displayed); *Anglo-Newfoundland Development Co Ltd v Pacific Steam Navigation Co* [1924] AC 406, 16 Asp MLC 385, HL (where a vessel was solely to blame where she held her course and attempted to pass another vessel after a warning that the river was blocked by the other vessel). See also note 4.

8   *Admiralty Comrs v SS Volute* [1922] 1 AC 129 at 144, 15 Asp MLC 530 at 537. See also *Hay v Le Neve* (1824) 2 Sh Sc App 395 (vessel at anchor with no light; other vessel ought to have had a better look-out and so avoided her; both vessels partly caused collision); *The Ovingdean Grange* [1902] P 208, 9 Asp MLC 295, CA (manoeuvring in river; second vessel, by failing to stop before rounding point, placed first vessel in difficulty; first vessel, through failure in look-out, collided with second; both vessels to blame; cf *Cayzer, Irvine & Co, SS Clan Sinclair (Owners) v Carron Co, SS Margaret (Owners)* (1884) 9 App Cas 873, 5 Asp MLC 371, HL); *The Hero (Owners) v Admiralty Comrs* [1912] AC 300, 12 Asp MLC 108, HL (where there was a collision between a merchant vessel and one of a flotilla of warships, and it was held that the collision was partly caused by the merchant vessel's negligence in steering across the warships' course and partly by the subsequent manoeuvres of the warship with which she collided); *The Sedulity* [1956] 1 Lloyd's Rep 510 (one vessel left at anchor exhibiting misleading light and in charge of inexperienced person although she had tendency to sheer; approaching vessel thereby embarrassed, but, if she had kept good look-out, would have realised nature of light and that first vessel was sheering); *The Nordlake and The Seaeagle* [2015] EWHC 3605 (Admlty), [2016] 1 Lloyd's Rep 656, [2016] 2 All ER (Comm) 449 (several vessels committing several faults in close proximity to one another). Cf *The Eurymedon* [1938] P 41, [1938] 1 All ER 122, 59 Ll L Rep 214, CA (where the negligence of both parties was held to have continued up to the time of the collision). As to the duty of a vessel underway to avoid a collision with a vessel at anchor see PARA 736; and as to the division of loss in proportion to fault see PARA 771 et seq.

9   See eg *The Bywell Castle* (1879) 4 PD 219 at 222, 223, 227, 228, 4 Asp MLC 207 at 209, 210, 211, 212, CA; cf *Stoomvaart Maatshappy Nederland v Peninsular and Oriental Steam Navigation Co* (1880) 5 App Cas 876 at 888, 889, 4 Asp MLC 360 at 364, HL. As to the position where one vessel by a wrongful act puts another in a position of difficulty see PARA 762. Where a wharfinger had a mast projecting from his wharf over a river and the bowsprit of a vessel at an adjoining wharf descended on the mast with the falling tide and damaged it, the wharfinger was held not to be entitled to recover damages: *Dalton v Denton* (1857) 1 CBNS 672. In cases where the antecedent negligence is held to have caused the damage, it is sometimes referred to as the 'causa causans' or 'real cause': see *Lloyd v General Iron Screw Collier Co* (1864) 3 H & C 284 at 291, although in that case an antecedent act which was an efficient cause in the ordinary sense was compared with a subsequent natural event which was not strictly an efficient cause because it lacked the element of human responsibility. See also *Chartered Mercantile Bank of India v Netherlands India Steam Navigation Co* (1883) 10 QBD 521 at 531, 5 Asp MLC 65 at 67–68, CA.

(iii) Rule of Division of Loss in Proportion to Fault

771.   Rule as to division of loss. Where, by the fault[1] of two or more ships[2], damage or loss is caused to one or more of those ships, to their cargoes or freight[3] or to any property on board, the liability[4] to make good the damage or loss is in proportion to the degree in which each ship was in fault[5]. If, in any such case, having regard to all the circumstances, it is not possible to establish different degrees of fault, the liability must be apportioned equally[6].

Nothing in the above provisions:

(1)   operates so as to render any ship liable for any loss or damage to which the fault of the ship has not contributed[7];

(2)   affects the liability of any person under a contract of carriage[8] or any contract, or is to be construed as imposing any liability upon any person from which he is exempted by any contract or any provision of law, or as affecting the right of any person to limit his liability in the manner provided by law[9].

1   The fact that the owners of one ship do not allege any fault against the other is immaterial if the court finds on the evidence that the fault existed: *The Mimosa* [1944] WN 74. As to the determination of liability see PARAS 767–770.
2   As to the meaning of 'ship' see PARA 229.

3 For these purposes, 'freight' includes passage money and hire: Merchant Shipping Act 1995 s 187(6).

4 The Merchant Shipping Act 1995 s 187 applies to persons other than the owners of a ship who are responsible for the fault of the ships, as well as to the owners of a ship; and, where, by virtue of any charter or demise, or for any other reason, the owners are not responsible for the navigation and management of the ship, s 187 applies to the charterers or other persons for the time being so responsible instead of the owners: s 187(3).

5 Merchant Shipping Act 1995 s 187(1). 'Damage' and 'loss' include the plural, and liability for different heads of damage arising from the same event may be apportioned on different bases: *Carlsholm (Owners) v Calliope (Owners), The Calliope* [1970] P 172 at 182, [1970] 1 All ER 624 at 638, [1970] 1 Lloyd's Rep 84 at 99 per Brandon J. References to damage or loss caused by the fault of a ship include references to any salvage or other expenses, consequent upon that fault, recoverable at law by way of damages: Merchant Shipping Act 1995 s 187(7). As to other expenses which are recoverable see *The Napier Star* [1939] P 330, 64 Ll L Rep 197 (costs in defending claims for loss of life and personal injuries); and see PARA 799 et seq. The Merchant Shipping Act 1995 s 187 is not confined to damage by collision: cf *The Batavier III* (1925) 134 LT 155, 16 Asp MLC 563 (damage by swell caused by excessive speed). The Merchant Shipping Act 1995 s 187 has, however, no application to a case in which a vessel strikes and damages a structure on land: cf *Gartland Steamship Co and Lablanc v R* [1960] 1 Lloyd's Rep 388 (Can SC); and see *The Rockabill* [1937] P 93, [1937] 1 All ER 191, 56 Ll L Rep 149, CA. As to rights of cargo owners and passengers see PARA 776. As to liability for damage done to harbours see PORTS AND HARBOURS vol 85 (2012) PARA 155.

The words 'in which each ship was in fault' must be construed as meaning 'in which each ship was at fault, causing or contributing to the collision': *The Peter Benoit* (1915) 84 LJP 87, CA (affd 13 Asp MLC 203, 114 LT 147, HL); *SS Haugland (Owners) v SS Karamea (Owners)* [1922] 1 AC 68 at 71, 15 Asp MLC 430 at 431, HL; *Miraflores (Owners) v George Livanos (Owners)* [1967] 1 AC 826, [1967] 1 All ER 672, [1967] 1 Lloyd's Rep 191, HL (where a collision between two ships partly caused the grounding of a third, and the liability of each vessel had to be assessed by comparison of her fault with the fault of each of the other vessels considered separately); *The Eglantine, Credo and Inez* [1990] 2 Lloyd's Rep 390, CA; *Samco Europe v MSC Prestige* [2011] EWHC 1580 (Admlty), [2011] 2 Lloyd's Rep 579 (both parties liable in proportion); *The Nordlake and The Seaeagle* [2015] EWHC 3605 (Admlty), [2016] 1 Lloyd's rep 656, [2016] 2 All ER (Comm) 449 (several vessels committing several faults). There is, however, no rule or principle, applicable to collision cases or analogous types of case in the Admiralty Court where there was no counterclaim (see PARA 204 note 16), that a claimant who was at fault under the Merchant Shipping Act 1995 s 187(1), (2) should recover his costs in proportion to the liability to the defendant: *Krysia Maritime Inc v Intership Ltd* [2008] EWHC 1880 (Admlty), [2008] All ER (D) 12 (Aug). As to costs in Admiralty proceedings generally see PARA 204; and as to the time limit for proceedings to enforce a claim or lien against a ship or her owners in respect of damage or loss caused see PARA 812.

6 Merchant Shipping Act 1995 s 187(2). See *The Anneliese, Arietta S Livanos (Owners) v Anneliese (Owners)* [1970] 2 All ER 29n, [1970] 1 Lloyd's Rep 355, CA. See also *The Kaiser Wilhelm II* (1915) as reported in 31 TLR 615, CA (where damage was apportioned equally, and it was ordered that, as one of the ships concerned was owned by enemy aliens, no payment was to be made under the judgment until the end of the war or until further order). The appellate court will not lightly interfere with the judge below on the apportionment of liability unless it disagrees with him on the facts: *The Peter Benoit* (1915) 13 Asp MLC 203, 114 LT 147, HL; *The Karamea* [1921] P 76, 15 Asp MLC 318 (affd sub nom *SS Haugland (Owners) v SS Karamea (Owners)* [1922] 1 AC 68, 15 Asp MLC 430); *The Clara Camus* (1925) 134 LT 50, 16 Asp MLC 570, CA (on appeal (1926) 136 LT 291, 17 Asp MLC 171, HL); *Kitano Maru (Owners) v Otranto (Owners), The Otranto* [1931] AC 194 at 204, 18 Asp MLC 193 at 196, HL; *The Umtali* (1938) 62 Ll L Rep 195, HL; *British Fame (Owners) v Macgregor (Owners), The Macgregor* [1943] AC 197, [1943] 1 All ER 33, 74 Ll L Rep 82, HL (not approving on this point *The Testbank* [1942] P 75, sub nom *The Ceramic (Owners) v The Testbank (Owners)* [1942] 1 All ER 281, CA); *The Lucile Bloomfield, Ronda (Owners) v SS Lucile Bloomfield (Owners)* [1967] 2 All ER 633n, [1967] 1 WLR 697n, [1967] 1 Lloyd's Rep 341, CA; *The Toni* [1974] 1 Lloyd's Rep 489, CA; *Thuroklint (Owners) v Königin Juliana (Owners), The Königin Juliana* [1975] 2 Lloyd's Rep 111, HL; *The Djerada* [1976] 2 Lloyd's Rep 40, CA; *MIOM 1 Ltd v Sea Echo ENE* [2010] EWHC 3180 (Admlty), [2010] All ER (D) 113 (Dec). See also note 5. As to Admiralty appeals generally see PARA 218 et seq.

7 Merchant Shipping Act 1995 s 187(4).

8 See PARA 776.

9 Merchant Shipping Act 1995 s 187(5). As to limitation of liability see PARAS 767, 992 et seq.

772. Working out of division of loss between shipowners. In working out
the division of loss under the statutory provision regarding apportionment of
liability[1], all the damages caused to the owner[2] of each ship which he has to share
with the owner of the other ship have first to be ascertained[3].

When the divisible damages of the first owner have been thus ascertained, the
liability of the second owner to make good his proportion of these first damages
is only a provisional liability according to established principles, and it is not a
debt due from him to the first owner[4]. The divisible damages of the second owner
must also be ascertained. Then the proportion of the first damages due from the
second owner has to be set against the proportion of the second damages due from
the first owner, and the smaller sum has to be deducted from the larger, and the
balance is a debt due from one owner to the other. There is only one liability, and
there can be only one payment[5]. Thus, in the simple case of both ships being found
equally to blame, the owner who has suffered the greater damages is entitled to
receive from the second owner half those damages, less half the damages which
the second owner has sustained[6].

1 Ie the Merchant Shipping Act 1995 s 187 (see PARA 771). As to the determination of liability see
   PARA 767 et seq.
2 As to the meaning of 'owner' for these purposes see PARA 771 note 4.
3 As to the mode of ascertainment see PARA 110 et seq. The divisible damages include damages or
   loss caused to his vessel or her cargo or freight, passage money or hire and also any salvage or other
   expenses consequent on the fault of his vessel recoverable from him by way of damages: see
   PARA 771.
4 So the second owner could not recover this sum from his insurers under a 'running down clause'
   not providing for settlement on the principle of cross-liabilities: see *London Steamship Owners'
   Insurance Co v Grampian Steamship Co* (1890) 24 QBD 663, 6 Asp MLC 506, CA.
5 *London Steamship Owners' Insurance Co v Grampian Steamship Co* (1890) 24 QBD 663 at 667,
   6 Asp MLC 506 at 507, CA.
6 See *Stoomvaart Maatschappy Nederland v Peninsular and Oriental Steam Navigation Co* (1882)
   7 App Cas 795, 4 Asp MLC 567, HL; *Young v Merchants' Marine Insurance Co Ltd* [1932] 2 KB
   705 at 707, 18 Asp MLC 341 at 343, CA.

773. Limitation of liability. Either owner can proceed to limit[1] his liability[2],
and pay into court the sum due from him in case of such limitation. In such a case
the owner of the ship who is entitled to receive the larger payment towards his
damages, and to whom, therefore, a balance is due, can prove against the fund for
the amount of the balance[3].

1 Ie under the Merchant Shipping Act 1995 s 185 (see PARA 992).
2 See the Merchant Shipping Act 1995 s 187; and PARA 771.
3 *Stoomvaart Maatschappy Nederland v Peninsular and Oriental Steam Navigation Co* (1882) 7
   App Cas 795, 4 Asp MLC 567, HL. As to the rule of division of loss see PARA 771; and as to the
   determination of liability see PARAS 767–770.

774. More than two ships in fault. Where more than two ships have been in
collision, and they have all been in fault, statutory liability to make good the
damage or loss will be distributed among them in proportion to the degree in
which each ship was in fault[1]. Thus, when a tug, tow and third vessel are all in
fault for a collision between any two of them, each vessel must normally be
allotted its own proportion of the damages[2]. It may be a great disadvantage to one
vessel in such a case to allow judgment to go by default in an action by one of the
others[3].

1 See the Merchant Shipping Act 1995 s 187; and PARA 771.
2 *Trishna (Owners, Master and Crew) v Panther (Owners), The Panther and The Ericbank* [1957]
   P 143, [1957] 1 All ER 641, [1957] 1 Lloyd's Rep 57 (tug and third vessel damaged; tow and third
   vessel each to blame to the extent of one-quarter and tug to blame to extent of one-half),
   distinguishing *The Socrates and The Champion* [1923] P 76 (revsd on the facts [1923] P 162, CA)
   (where, the tug and tow having been held in fault for jointly participating in a negligent operation,
   the court refused to apportion liability between them and held them jointly and severally liable for

half of the third vessel's damage); *Miraflores (Owners) v George Livanos (Owners)* [1967] 1 AC 826, [1967] 1 All ER 672, [1967] 1 Lloyd's Rep 191, HL; *The Eglantine, Credo and Inez* [1990] 2 Lloyd's Rep 390, CA. For decisions before the Maritime Conventions Act 1911 (repealed) cf *The Englishman and The Australia* [1894] P 239, 7 Asp MLC 603 (cited in PARA 784 note 3); *The Harvest Home* [1905] P 177, 10 Asp MLC 118, CA. As to the incidence of liability for collisions involving tug and tow see PARAS 783, 784; and as to the rules of good seamanship concerning tug and tow see PARA 742.

3   See *The Morgengry and The Blackcock* [1900] P 1, 8 Asp MLC 591, CA (an action against a tow and a tug where the decree went by default against the tow; the action proceeded against the tug, and both the plaintiffs' vessel and the tug were held to be to blame, and the plaintiffs were held to be entitled to the proceeds of sale of the tow and half their damage (see PARA 771) from the tug owners, the proceeds and the half not exceeding the whole of the plaintiffs' loss). See also *The Nordlake and The Seaeagle* [2015] EWHC 3605 (Admlty), [2016] 1 Lloyd's Rep 656, [2016] 2 All ER (Comm) 449.

775. Third innocent vessel.

Where, by the fault of two vessels, a collision is caused between one of them and a third innocent vessel, the statutory provision as to division of liability[1] does not directly[2] apply to an action by the owners of the innocent vessel against either or both of the wrong-doing vessels for the full amount of their damages[3].

1   Ie the Merchant Shipping Act 1995 s 187 (see PARA 771).
2   As to the determination of liability see PARAS 767–770; and as to the right of contribution see PARA 778.
3   See *The Cairnbahn* [1914] P 25 at 28, 12 Asp MLC 455 at 456 (on appeal at 39 and at 460) (where an innocent tow was damaged owing to the joint equal negligence of the tug and a third vessel, and, although judgment was entered against both the tug and the third vessel, the tow owners recovered damages in full against the owners of the third vessel); *The Koursk* [1924] P 140, 16 Asp MLC 374, CA (where, as a result of separate negligent acts by two vessels, a collision took place between one of the two and a third vessel, and the third vessel was allowed to bring separate actions against each of the negligent vessels). The same rule existed before the Maritime Conventions Act 1911 (repealed): see *Devonshire (Owners) v Barge Leslie (Owners)* [1912] AC 634, 12 Asp MLC 210. It appears that, according to the International Convention for the Unification of Certain Rules of Law respecting Collisions (Brussels, 23 September 1910; TS 4 (1913); Cd 6677) art 4, it was provided that even to innocent third parties a vessel was only to be liable in proportion to the degree in which she was in fault: see Roscoe and Robertson's *Maritime Conventions Act 1911* p 8. The Maritime Conventions Act 1911 (repealed) was passed to enable this Convention to be carried into effect, but in the above respect it appears not to have done so. In *The Cairnbahn*, the only collision was between the innocent vessel and one of the wrongdoing vessels, but the same rule applies if the collision was the result of a collision between the two wrong-doing vessels. As to the law on this point before the Maritime Conventions Act 1911 (repealed) see *The Frankland* [1901] P 161, 9 Asp MLC 196. See further *The Umona* [1914] P 141, 12 Asp MLC 527 (where in an action by a tow which had been damaged owing to the joint negligence of the tug and a third vessel, both of which were found to blame, it was held that the tow was not an innocent tow, as the owners of the tug were at the time of the collision, as bailees for hire, the owners of the tow). As to the measure of damages recoverable by the owner of the cargo on the tow see PARA 776; and as to the general incidence of liability see PARA 779 et seq.

776. Rights of cargo owners and others.

Where cargo in one vessel is damaged by a collision with another vessel by the fault of both of them[1], the cargo owner is by statute only entitled to recover in tort from each vessel a proportion of his loss corresponding to the degree to which that vessel was to blame for the collision[2]. It would seem that he is entitled to recover in full in contract against the owner of the vessel carrying his cargo, but any right of recovery against that owner may be qualified by the contract of carriage contained, for example, in the charterparty or bill of lading[3].

It seems that in similar circumstances the right of the master or a member of the crew to recover damages for lost effects[4] or the right of a passenger to recover his passage money[5] or to recover for damage or loss of luggage[6] against the owner of the other vessel is similarly limited by the statutory provision as to division of loss[7] where the claim is in tort.

1   As to the determination of liability when both vessels at fault see PARAS 767–770.

2   See the Merchant Shipping Act 1995 s 187; and PARA 771. See also *The Umona* [1914] P 141, 12 Asp MLC 527 (where, a third vessel being held three-quarters to blame and the tug one-quarter, the owner of the cargo in the tow was held only entitled to recover three-quarters of his damage as the owners of the tug were treated as owners of the tow). As to the application of the rule as to apportionment of loss to a cargo owner's right to recover in respect of a contribution to general average expenses see PARA 808.

3   See the Merchant Shipping Act 1995 s 187(5) (cited in PARA 771); and *The Giacinto Motta* [1977] 2 Lloyd's Rep 221 (where an exception clause was held to extend to an indirect claim by a party who had had to pay the party who suffered the actual loss).

4   As to this right see *The Petrel* [1893] P 320.

5   Cf the Merchant Shipping Act 1995 s 187(6) (cited in PARA 771), which defines 'freight' as including passage money and hire.

6   Cf the Merchant Shipping Act 1995 s 187(1) (cited in PARA 771), which refers to 'any property on board'.

7   Ie limited by the Merchant Shipping Act 1995 s 187 (see PARA 771).

777. Loss of life and personal injuries.

Where loss of life or personal injuries are suffered by any person on board a ship[1] owing to the fault of that ship and of any other ship or ships, the liability of the owners[2] of the ships is joint and several[3].

However, nothing in these provisions is to be construed as depriving any person of any right of defence on which he might otherwise have relied in an action brought against him by the person injured, or any person or persons entitled to sue in respect of such loss of life, or affects the right of any person to limit his liability in the manner provided by law[4].

1   As to the meaning of 'ship' see PARA 229.

2   The Merchant Shipping Act 1995 s 188 applies to persons other than the owners of a ship who are responsible for the fault of the ships, as well as to the owners of a ship; and, where, by virtue of any charter or demise, or for any other reason, the owners are not responsible for the navigation and management of the ship, s 188 applies to the charterers or other persons for the time being so responsible instead of the owners: ss 187(3), 188(2).

3   Merchant Shipping Act 1995 s 188(1). References to damage or loss caused by the fault of a ship include references to any salvage or other expenses, consequent upon that fault, recoverable at law by way of damages: ss 187(7), 188(4). As to the determination of liability see PARA 767; as to actions in respect of death or personal injuries see PARA 792; and as to the time limit for actions by persons on board one vessel or their representatives against the owners of another vessel see PARA 812.

4   Merchant Shipping Act 1995 s 188(3).

778. Loss of life or personal injuries; right of contribution.

Where loss of life or personal injuries are suffered by any person on board a ship[1] owing to the fault of that ship and any other ship or ships, and a proportion of the damages is recovered against the owners[2] of one of the ships which exceeds the proportion in which the ship was in fault, they may recover by way of contribution the amount of the excess from the owners of the other ship or ships to the extent to which those ships were respectively in fault[3].

In addition to any other remedy provided by law, the persons entitled to any contribution recoverable under these provisions have, for the purposes of recovering it, the same rights and powers as the persons entitled to sue for damages in the first instance[4].

Nothing in these provisions authorises the recovery of any amount which could not, by reason of any statutory or contractual limitation of, or exemption from, liability, or which could not for any other reason, have been recovered in the first instance as damages by the persons entitled to sue therefor[5].

When by the fault of two vessels a collision is caused between one of them and a third innocent vessel, the owner of one of the two vessels in fault who has been compelled to pay damages in full to the innocent vessel can recover against the owner of the other vessel in fault a proportion, not only of the damage to his own vessel, but also of the damages which he has paid to the owner of the innocent vessel[6], but he cannot recover any proportion of the costs of unsuccessfully disputing his liability to the owner of the innocent vessel[7].

1 As to the meaning of 'ship' see PARA 229.
2 The Merchant Shipping Act 1995 s 189 applies to persons other than the owners of a ship who are responsible for the fault of the ships, as well as to the owners of a ship; and, where, by virtue of any charter or demise, or for any other reason, the owners are not responsible for the navigation and management of the ship, s 189 applies to the charterers or other persons for the time being so responsible instead of the owners: ss 187(3), 189(2).
3 Merchant Shipping Act 1995 s 189(1). See *Miraflores (Owners) v George Livanos (Owners)* [1967] 1 AC 826, [1967] 1 All ER 672, [1967] 1 Lloyd's Rep 19, HL. As to the time limit for proceedings for contribution founded on Admiralty jurisdiction see PARA 151; and as to the determination of liability see PARA 767.
4 Merchant Shipping Act 1995 s 189(4).
5 Merchant Shipping Act 1995 s 189(3). See also *The Cedric* [1920] P 193, 15 Asp MLC 285 (where no contribution was recoverable where the owners of the vessel against whom contribution was sought were protected by foreign law); *The Molière* [1925] P 27, 16 Asp MLC 470 (where it was held that the provisions as to contribution did not apply to statutory compensation payable independently of fault of the shipowners).
6 *The Cairnbahn* [1914] P 25, 12 Asp MLC 455, CA.
7 *The Cairnbahn (No 2)* (1913) 29 TLR 559; affd (1914) 30 TLR 309, CA. The costs of fighting claims for loss of life or personal injuries are, however, apportionable under the Merchant Shipping Act 1995 s 187: see *The Napier Star* [1939] P 330, 64 Ll L Rep 197; and PARA 771.

(5) GENERAL INCIDENCE AND EXTENT OF LIABILITY

(i) Parties Liable

779. Personal liability. The person who by his negligent act or omission causes a ship to collide and do damage is liable for the damage caused by that negligent act or omission[1].

1 *Stort v Clements* (1792) Peake 107 (where the pilot (defendant) escaped liability); *Nicholson v Mounsey and Symes* (1812) 15 East 384 (where the captain of naval ship was held not liable for the negligence of his lieutenant); *Lawson v Dumlin* (1850) 9 CB 54 (where the pilot (defendant) was held liable); *Smith v Voss* (1857) 2 H & N 97 (similar case). As to the prevention of collisions see PARA 690 et seq (ie under the International Regulations for Preventing Collisions at Sea 1972) and PARA 729 et seq (common law cases reflecting customary rules of good seamanship). As to the cause of action in negligence see PARA 756; as to the burden of proof in collision cases see PARA 757; and as to limitation of liability see PARA 992 et seq.

780. Vicarious liability of owner. In accordance with the general principles of employment law, the owner of a ship is liable for damage caused by the negligence of his employees[1] on board the ship when they are acting within the scope of their employment[2]. If there is no evidence as to who is the employer of the person in charge of a ship, it seems that the burden is on the owner to show that the person in charge was not his employee[3].

The liability of the owner as a rule, in Admiralty as at common law, rests on his responsibility for the acts of his employees and agents, and does not depend on the ownership of the vessel[4]. In some cases, however, the legislature has imposed a liability on the owner of a ship as owner for damage done by her[5].

1 As to the liability of an owner for the negligence of a compulsory pilot see PARA 579.
2 As to the liability of an employer to third persons for the torts of his employee see TORT vol 97 (2015) PARA 800. A question may arise whether the general or temporary employer of an employee is liable for the employee's act: see eg *Martin v Temperley* (1843) 4 QB 298 (where the owner was liable for the act of a hired waterman); *The Louise* (1901) 18 TLR 19, DC (where a gang moving a ship in a dock were held to be the employees of the dock company). As to chartered ships see PARA 782; and as to tugs and tow see PARA 784. As to the cause of action in negligence see PARA 756.

3   See *Joyce v Capel* (1838) 8 C & P 370; *Hibbs v Ross* (1866) LR 1 QB 534. A person wrongfully registered as managing owner is not necessarily held out as the agent of the registered owner of shares in a ship: *Frazer v Cuthbertson* (1880) 6 QBD 93 at 98. The burden lies on the owner because the relevant facts are peculiarly within his knowledge: *Hibbs v Ross* at 543; and see CIVIL PROCEDURE vol 12 (2015) PARA 705. As to the burden of proof in collision cases see PARA 757.

4   *Hibbs v Ross* (1866) LR 1 QB 534. At common law, the owner would not be liable merely because he was the owner or without showing that those navigating the vessel were his employees: *River Wear Comrs v Adamson* (1877) 2 App Cas 743 at 751, 3 Asp MLC 521 at 522, HL. The owner of a ship is liable to an action for damages, not because he is the owner, but because he is the employer of the captain and crew, whose negligence in the course of their employment occasioned the damage: *Simpson v Thomson* (1877) 3 App Cas 279 at 293, 3 Asp MLC 567 at 572, HL. As to the liability of owners as such see PARAS 242–244; and as to the liability of a ship to maritime liens when in the hands of charterers or other persons allowed to use her see PARA 967.

5   See the Harbours, Docks, and Piers Clauses Act 1847 s74; and PORTS AND HARBOURS vol 85 (2012) PARA 155.

781. Liability of master. The master is liable for damage arising from his own negligence[1] or breach of contract made with the owner of cargo shipped on his vessel[2]. He is not, however, liable for the damage done by an act of the crew or of the pilot, whether done in the course of their duty to the shipowner or not, unless ordered by him[3].

1   See PARA 779.

2   As to contracts for the carriage of goods see CARRIAGE AND CARRIERS vol 7 (2015) PARA 206 et seq.

3   *Stort v Clements* (1792) Peake 107; *M'Manus v Crickett* (1800) 1 East 106; *Bowcher v Noidstrom* (1809) 1 Taunt 568 (where the master was not liable for wilful injury to another ship done by one of his crew without his privity or direction, but by order of the pilot); *Aldrich v Simmons* (1816) 1 Stark 214 (where it was held that the captain could not be responsible to the owner for the pilot's misconduct); *Blaikie v Stembridge* (1860) 6 CBNS 894 (where a stevedore appointed by the charterer, but paid by and acting under the master's orders, was held not to be the employee or agent of the master so as to render him responsible); *Oakley v Speedy* (1879) 4 Asp MLC 134 (where, with a compulsory pilot in charge, a master was held not criminally liable for a breach of the regulations in the absence of proof that he wrongfully interfered with the navigation). As to a master's liability see also PARA 429; and as to the liability of the shipowner see PARA 780.

782. Chartered ship. Where a collision is due to the negligence[1] of the crew the owner of the vessel is liable in personam if the vessel is under time or voyage charter (since then the crew continues to be employed by the owner), but not if she is bareboat chartered (since the bareboat charterer himself crews the ship)[2]. The ship is liable in rem in any case[3].

1   As to establishing the cause of action in negligence see PARA 756.

2   See eg *Scott v Scott* (1818) 2 Stark 438 (it seems that the owner of a barge is not liable for the negligence of the employees of another person to whom he has lent it); *Fenton v City of Dublin Steam Packet Co* (1838) 8 Ad & El 835 (where the owners kept their own crew on board and were to keep the vessel in good order, and they were held liable for the crew's negligence, although the crew were to be paid by the charterer); *Dalyell v Tyrer* (1858) EB & E 899 (where a passenger who had contracted for a passage with the lessee of a ferry was held entitled to recover from the owners of a tug, hired by the lessee for one day, for injury arising from negligence of the tug's crew); *Hodgkinson v Fernie* (1857) 2 CBNS 415 (it seems that the owner of a vessel hired by the government is not responsible for damage resulting from the master's obedience to the order of the officer commanding the expedition); *Baumwoll Manufactur von Carl Scheibler v Furness* [1893] AC 8, 7 Asp MLC 263, HL. As to when a charterparty amounts to a demise of the ship see eg *Associated Portland Cement Manufacturers (1910) Ltd v Ashton* [1915] 2 KB 1, 13 Asp MLC 40, CA; and CARRIAGE AND CARRIERS vol 7 (2015) PARAS 211–213.

3   See *The Father Thames* [1979] 2 Lloyd's Rep 364. See also *The Lemington* (1874) 2 Asp MLC 475 (where a chartered vessel was held liable in an action in rem for collision, as the crew were the employees of the charterers, who were *pro hac vice* owners); *The Tasmania* (1888) 13 PD 110, 6 Asp MLC 305 (where a chartered tug was held not liable in an action in rem for a collision with her tow, as the charterers had contracted with the owners of the tow to be free from the liability). See also PARA 967. As to the liability of shipowners see PARA 780.

783. Collision between tug and tow. In case of a collision between a tug and her tow causing damage[1], a liability arises in favour of the one and against the other if the collision is due to the other not fulfilling her duties under the contract of towage[2].

In the absence of agreement to the contrary[3], there is in a contract of towage an implied warranty by the owners of the tug that she is fit for her service[4]. It is also implied that her crew, tackle and equipment will be equal to the work to be accomplished in the weather and other circumstances reasonably to be expected, and that reasonable skill, care and energy will be shown in accomplishing the work[5].

Further, it is implied that neither party will negligently create unnecessary risk to the other or increase any risk incidental to the service[6]. The tug owners are not responsible if the towing becomes impossible through no fault of theirs[7]; nor can they recover compensation from the owners of the tow for damage incurred by the tug owing to dangerous circumstances without misconduct of the tow[8]. The owners of the tow are liable for damage arising to the tug from improper orders of the tow, for example to get connection[9].

1   As to the duty to prevent collision between tug and tow see PARA 742.
2   As to the contract of towage generally see PARA 597 et seq.
3   As to conditions relieving the tug from liability see PARA 600.
4   *The Undaunted* (1886) 11 PD 46, 5 Asp MLC 580; *The West Cock* [1911] P 208 at 217, 12 Asp MLC 57, CA; *The Maréchal Suchet* [1911] P 1 at 12, 11 Asp MLC 553. A contract for a named tug, however, excludes any implied warranty: *Robertson v Amazon Tug and Lighterage Co* (1881) 4 Asp MLC 496, CA; *Point Anne Quarries v The MF Whalen* (1922) 39 TLR 37, PC.
5   *The Robert Dixon* (1879) 4 PD 121 (affd 5 PD 54, 4 Asp MLC 246, CA); *The Maréchal Suchet* [1911] P 1, 11 Asp MLC 553; cf *Preston Corpn v Biornstad, The Ratata* [1898] AC 513, 8 Asp MLC 427, HL (where a harbour authority undertook to tow a number of vessels up a tidal river with hired tugs). The main burden of keeping the tug clear of the tow lies on the tug, whether in making fast (*Harmony v Faraday* (1920) 5 Ll L Rep 177; *Contest v Age* (1923) 17 Ll L Rep 172; *Assistance v Lagarto* (1923) 17 Ll L Rep 264), or in manoeuvring during the towage service (*Alexandra (Newport and South Wales) Docks and Rly Co (Lady Tredegar) v Cape Colony* (1920) 4 Ll L Rep 116). As to negligence in the construction, equipment or manning of a vessel see PARA 759; and as to the exercise of reasonable care and skill see PARA 761.
6   *The Julia* (1860) Lush 224 at 231, PC; and see *Harmony v Northborough* (1923) 15 Ll L Rep 119 (where a vessel was held to blame for working her engines while her tug was making fast on her quarter). See further PARA 598.
7   *The Maréchal Suchet* [1911] P 1 at 12, 11 Asp MLC 553 at 556.
8   *The Julia* (1860) Lush 224, PC. As to the position where damage has been caused by the fault of both vessels see PARAS 767–770; and as to the division of loss in proportion to fault see PARA 771 et seq.
9   See note 8.

784. Collision of tug or tow with a third vessel. In case of a collision with a third vessel, the owners of the tug and the tow are normally responsible for damage caused by their own negligence or the negligent navigation of their respective vessels[1]. Where there have been defects in equipping or planning the operation, both the persons responsible for the care of the tow and the owners of the tug may share responsibility[2]. The owners of the tow are responsible, to the exclusion of the tug owners, for injury caused to third persons by the negligence of the tug only if the relation of employer and employee in fact exists between the owners of the tow and those in charge of the tug in relation to the negligent act or omission complained of[3].

As against third persons, the question whether those in charge of the tug are the employees of the owners of the tow is not concluded by the terms of the contract of towage, but depends[4] on who has control of the manner in which the work of the tug is done in relation to the relevant act or omission[5].

Where the general control of navigation is in the tow, although the motive power is in the tug, the owners of the tow are liable for an act or omission by the tug within the scope of the general control of the pilot or officer in charge of the tow[6], but are not normally liable for negligence by the tug in a matter falling outside such control and within the discretion of the tug master, such as the detail of a manoeuvre of the tug[7]. Where the control of navigation is in the tug[8], the owners of the tow are not normally liable to third persons for the negligence of the tug[9] unless the tug and tow are in the same ownership[10].

1   As to negligence causing damage generally see PARA 756 et seq; as to the distribution of liability where the tug, tow and the third vessel have all been at fault see PARA 774; and as to the rights of the owner of the third vessel where his vessel and the tug have both been to blame for a collision in respect of which the owners of the tow have recovered against him see *The Cairnbahn* (1914) 29 TLR 60; and PARA 778.

2   *Thomas Stone Shipping Ltd v Admiralty, The Albion* [1953] P 117, [1953] 1 All ER 978, [1953] 1 Lloyd's Rep 239, CA.

3   *The Quickstep* (1890) 15 PD 196 at 199, 6 Asp MLC 603 at 604; *Devonshire (Owners) v Barge Leslie (Owners)* [1912] AC 634, 12 Asp MLC 210, HL. As to the liability of shipowners generally see PARA 780. Certain cases in which it was suggested that the owners of the tow were liable for the negligence of the tug in all cases (see eg *The Ticonderoga* (1857) Sw 215) or that the owners of the tow and the owners of the tug might both be liable for the tug's negligence merely on the ground that the relationship of employer and employee existed between tow and tug (see *The Englishman and The Australia* [1894] P 239, 7 Asp MLC 603), can no longer be considered authoritative.

4   Ie in accordance with the general principle which determines whether the general employer or the temporary employer is liable for the torts of an employee temporarily hired by one employer to another: see TORT vol 97 (2015) PARA 801.

5   *Trishna (Owners, Master and Crew) v Panther and Ericbank (Owners), The Panther and The Ericbank* [1957] P 143 at 147–149, [1957] 1 All ER 641 at 647, 648, [1957] 1 Lloyd's Rep 57 at 67. See also eg *The Adriatic and The Wellington* (1914) 30 TLR 699. As to the contract of towage generally see PARA 597 et seq; and as to the relation between tug and tow see PARA 742.

6   See *Stevens v Gourley, The Cleadon* (1860) 14 Moo PCC 92 at 97; *Union Steamship Co v Aracan (Owners), The American and The Syria* (1874) LR 6 PC 127 at 132, 2 Asp MLC 350 at 361; cf *Trishna (Owners, Master and Crew) v Panther and Ericbank (Owners), The Panther and The Ericbank* [1957] P 143 at 148, 149, [1957] 1 All ER 641 at 648, [1957] 1 Lloyd's Rep 57 at 67. As to the circumstances in which the tug controls the navigation see PARAS 599, 742.

7   *Trishna (Owners, Master and Crew) v Panther and Ericbank (Owners), The Panther and The Ericbank* [1957] P 143, [1957] 1 All ER 641, [1957] 1 Lloyd's Rep 57; and see *The Niobe* (1888) 13 PD 55 at 60, 6 Asp MLC 300 at 302. *The Sinquasi* (1880) 5 PD 241, 4 Asp MLC 383 cannot now be considered an authority to the contrary.

8   This is usually the case when a tug is towing barges in a river: see PARA 742.

9   *Union Steamship Co v Aracan (Owners), The American and The Syria* (1874) LR 6 PC 127, 2 Asp MLC 350 (ship towing another at sea); *The Quickstep* (1890) 15 PD 196, 6 Asp MLC 603; *The Comet (Owners) WH No 1 (Owners), The WH No 1 and The Knight Errant* [1911] AC 30, 11 Asp MLC 497; *The Adriatic and The Wellington* (1914) 30 TLR 699, HL (cases of tugs towing barges in rivers); and see *Devonshire (Owners) v Barge Leslie (Owners)* [1912] AC 634, 12 Asp MLC 210, HL. The tug owners may, however, be entitled under the terms of the contract of towage to be indemnified by the owners of the tow against liability to third persons: see *The Riverman* [1928] P 33, 17 Asp MLC 344; and see generally PARA 600.

10 *The Umona* [1914] P 141 at 145, 12 Asp MLC 527 at 529; *The Ran, The Graygarth* [1922] P 80, 15 Asp MLC 517, CA (explaining and distinguishing *Union SS Co v Aracan (Owners), The American and The Syria* (1874) LR 6 PC 127, 2 Asp MLC 350, as regards the effect of common ownership).

785. Vessel acting under orders of harbour or dock master. When a collision is caused by those on board a vessel following the orders of a harbour master or dock master, given within the limits of his jurisdiction[1], the owner of the ship is not normally liable for the damage caused by the collision[2]. The orders of such an official have, however, to be executed with care, and, whether the order is properly given or not, the shipowner will be liable in the event of negligence on the part of the master or crew[3]. An official who has given a negligent order is personally liable for the damage resulting from it. The harbour or dock authority is also in general liable if the harbour master or dock master giving the order gave it within the scope of his authority[4]. Harbour authorities are entitled in certain circumstances to limit their liability[5].

1　As to the statutory powers of a harbour or dock master with regard to the control of shipping see PORTS AND HARBOURS vol 85 (2012) PARA 91 et seq; and as to the duty to obey the orders of a harbour master or dock master see PARA 755.

2　*The Bilbao* (1860) Lush 149; *Reney v Kirkcudbright Magistrates* [1892] AC 264, 7 Asp MLC 221, HL; *Taylor v Burger* (1898) 8 Asp MLC 364, HL; *The Mystery* [1902] P 115, 9 Asp MLC 281, CA. As to the vicarious liability of shipowners see PARA 780.

3　*The Excelsior* (1868) LR 2 A & E 268; *The Belgic* (1875) 2 PD 57n, 3 Asp MLC 348; *The Framlingham Court* (1936) 56 Ll L Rep 200. Cf *The Rockabill* [1937] P 93 at 102, [1937] 1 All ER 191 at 193, 56 Ll L Rep 149 at 152, CA (where Greer LJ described a dock master's order as a 'conditional order', ie an order to come ahead subject to a good look-out being kept). As to negligence causing damage see PARA 756 et seq.

4　See PORTS AND HARBOURS vol 85 (2012) PARA 146 et seq.

5　See the Merchant Shipping Act 1995 s 191; and PARA 1014.

786. National ships. When one of Her Majesty's ships by the negligence of the person in charge of her collides with another vessel, causing damage[1], the person whose negligence caused the collision is liable for the damage resulting from his negligence, but his superior officers are not liable unless they were privy to the negligence[2].

An action in personam generally lies against the Crown for damage caused by the negligence of those in charge of a Crown ship[3], but proceedings in rem do not lie against a Crown ship[4].

Foreign and Commonwealth states are immune from proceedings in rem against their ships[5], unless they are in use for commercial purposes[6]. Vessels, other than commercial vessels[7], owned by a foreign state are also immune from arrest[8].

1　As to negligence causing damage see PARA 756 et seq; and as to personal liability see PARA 779.

2　*The Mentor* (1799) 1 Ch Rob 179 (where it was held that an action does not lie against the admiral of a station for the destruction of a vessel, after hostilities have been declared to cease, by a ship acting under the admiral's general orders; the action must be against the immediate wrongdoer); *The Volcano* (1844) 2 Wm Rob 337 (where the commander of one of Her Majesty's ships was condemned in a cause of damage); *The Birkenhead* (1848) 3 Wm Rob 75 (a similar case); *HMS Bellerophon* (1874) 3 Asp MLC 58 (no obligation on officer in charge of ship to give notice of her ram, where no reasonable ground for apprehending danger); *HMS Sans Pareil* [1900] P 267, 9 Asp MLC 78, CA; *Hero (Owners) v Admiralty Comrs* [1912] AC 300, 12 Asp MLC 108, HL (both vessels held to blame); and see *HMS Archer* [1919] P 1 (limitation of action against naval officer). As to the vicarious liability of shipowners see PARA 780.

3　As to the application of provisions limiting the period within which action may be brought see PARA 812.

4　See PARA 179.

5　See the State Immunity Act 1978 s 1; and CIVIL PROCEDURE vol 11 (2015) PARA 474.

6　See the State Immunity Act 1978 s 10(1), (2); and INTERNATIONAL RELATIONS LAW vol 61 (2010) PARA 254.

7　See the State Immunity Act 1978 s 13(4); and INTERNATIONAL RELATIONS LAW vol 61 (2010) PARA 257.

8　See the State Immunity Act 1978 s 13(2)(b); and INTERNATIONAL RELATIONS LAW vol 61 (2010) PARA 257.

787. Collision with wreck. Where a wreck is a danger to navigation, the owner or person in charge of it is under a duty[1] to mark or light the wreck for the protection of other shipping and may be liable in negligence[2] for damage consequent on his failure to take reasonable care to do so[3].

If, however, a conservancy or harbour or other authority having power to light the wreck has been sufficiently notified of the wreck, and has undertaken the duty of marking and lighting it, the fact that the owner does not ensure that it is lighted is not negligence on his part[4]. It seems that, if an owner of a wreck properly abandons it or transfers possession and control of it to another person, any subsequent failure to mark or light the wreck is not negligence on his part[5].

If the wreck is not abandoned either to the harbour authority or otherwise, and the owner himself employs a contractor to mark the position of the wreck or raise it, and the contractor acts negligently in marking or in raising it so as to cause damage, the owner is liable for the damage[6].

1 See *White v Crisp* (1854) 10 Exch 312 (vessel foundered in Bristol Channel).
2 Negligence after the sinking of the wreck, with which the text is concerned, must be distinguished from negligence causing the sinking which may lead to responsibility to a harbour or other authority for damage or for expenses of removal of the wreck: see PARAS 1008–1009; and PORTS AND HARBOURS vol 85 (2012) PARA 92.
3 As to negligence causing damage generally see PARA 756 et seq. As to the meaning of 'reasonable care' in this context see PARA 761.
4 *The Douglas* (1882) 7 PD 151 at 158, 5 Asp MLC 15 at 16, CA (vessel sunk in the Thames); *Utopia (Owners) v Primula (Owners and Masters), The Utopia* [1893] AC 492, 7 Asp MLC 408, PC (vessel sunk in the Straits of Gibraltar); *The Snark* [1900] P 105, 9 Asp MLC 50, CA (possession, management and control of barge sunk in Thames not transferred). As to delegation of duties cf *The Jersey* [1942] P 119. As to instances of insufficient lighting see further PARA 945 note 7.
5 See *Utopia (Owners) v Primula (Owners and Master), The Utopia* [1893] AC 492 at 498, 7 Asp MLC 408 at 410, PC. The passage referred to must not be read to mean that by abandoning a wreck an owner of a ship can escape damage for his negligence before the abandonment: see *Dee Conservancy Board v McConnell* [1928] 2 KB 159 at 166, 17 Asp MLC 433 at 436, CA. Negligence in lighting a wreck after it has been abandoned by its owner to a conservancy authority is not negligence of the owners, nor are they then under a duty to light the wreck: *The Manorbier Castle* (1922) 16 Asp MLC 151 at 154.
6 *The Snark* [1900] P 105, 9 Asp MLC 50, CA; cf *Penny v Wimbledon UDC* [1899] 2 QB 72, CA; and *The Jersey* [1942] P 119 at 126, 127. As to vicarious liability of shipowners for the acts of employees see PARA 780.

(ii) Inevitable Accident

788. Defence of inevitable accident. A collision is said to be the result of an inevitable accident if it could not have been prevented by the exercise of reasonable care and ordinary skill[1].

Where the defendant has prima facie caused the collision, in order to prove that the collision was an inevitable accident[2] he must show that it's occurrence was consistent with the exercise on his part of reasonable care and skill, and that he exercised reasonable care and skill[3]. It is no excuse for a master that he could not prevent the accident when it occurred, if he neglected to use precautionary measures which would have rendered the accident less probable[4].

1 *The Virgil* (1843) 2 Wm Rob 201 at 205; *The Europa* (1850) 14 Jur 627, DC; *The Lochlibo* (1850) 3 Wm Rob 310 at 318; *The Thomas Powell v The Cuba* (1866) 14 LT 603 (extraordinary skill or extraordinary diligence not expected, but that degree of skill and that degree of diligence which is generally found in persons who discharge their duty); *The Marpesia* (1872) LR 4 PC 212 at 220, 1 Asp MLC 261 at 264, 265; *The Schwan, The Alabano* [1892] P 419, 7 Asp MLC 347, CA; *Lamington v Wentworth* (1922) 12 Ll L Rep 259. As to the meaning of 'reasonable care' and 'reasonable skill' see PARA 761. As to the prevention of collisions see PARA 690 et seq (ie under the International Regulations for Preventing Collisions at Sea 1972) and PARA 729 et seq (common law cases reflecting customary rules of good seamanship). As to the circumstances in which the defence arises see PARA 789.
2 As to the burden of proof in collision cases generally see PARA 757.
3 See *The Llanover* (1945) 79 Ll L Rep 159 at 163; *Southport Corpn v Esso Petroleum Co Ltd* [1954] 2 QB 182 at 193, 194, [1954] 2 All ER 561 at 568, 569, [1954] 1 Lloyd's Rep 446 at 453, 454, CA (on appeal [1956] AC 218, [1955] 3 All ER 864, [1955] 2 Lloyd's Rep 655, HL); *The Louis Sheid* [1958] 1 Lloyd's Rep 606 at 615. In these cases, the courts did not adopt the severer test suggested in *The Merchant Prince* [1892] P 179 at 189, 7 Asp MLC 208 at 211, CA, per Fry LJ

(that the defendants must show the actual cause, or all possible causes, of the accident, and in either case that the result could not have been avoided by reasonable care and skill). See also *The Calderon* (1912) Times, 26 March.

4   *The Virgil* (1843) 2 Wm Rob 201; *The Marpesia* (1872) LR 4 PC 212, 1 Asp MLC 261; *The Pladda* (1876) 2 PD 34 at 38. As to the determination of liability when both parties at fault see PARAS 767–770.

789.   Circumstances in which defence may arise. The defence of inevitable accident[1] may arise in cases of storm[2] or fog[3] or unusual local circumstances[4], or where a vessel goes ashore[5] or is disabled by a prior collision[6], or, if a sailing vessel, is disabled by loss of gear[7], or a steamer by failure of steering gear or machinery[8], or otherwise.

1   As to the defence of inevitable accident see PARA 788.
2   *The Pladda* (1876) 2 PD 34 (proper precautions not taken in a storm; cables unchained from anchors, and no look-out on deck); *The Star of the Isles* (1938) 62 Ll L Rep 139, Ct of Sess. See also *R (owner of The Adolph Woermann) v The Hessa* (1922) 10 Ll L Rep 734, CA.
3   *The Marpesia* (1872) LR 4 PC 212, 1 Asp MLC 261 (sailing vessels in fog; inevitable accident); *The Nador* [1909] P 300, 11 Asp MLC 283 (inevitable accident; vessel at anchor in dense fog, and her light not seen, and bell not heard by steamship, in time to avoid her); cf *The Rosetta* (1888) 6 Asp MLC 310 (inability to hear sound in fog not necessarily negligence). See also *The Shannon* (1842) 1 Wm Rob 463 (collision in Sea Reach due to the darkness of the night); *The Valdes* (1914) 31 TLR 144 (defence of inevitable accident unsuccessful).
4   *The Secret* (1872) 1 Asp MLC 318 (harbour entrance found obstructed; proper precautions as regards shortening sail, anchor etc not taken); *The City of Peking Compagnie des Messageries Maritimes, The City of Peking* (1888) 14 App Cas 40, 6 Asp MLC 396, PC (exceptional current ought to have been anticipated; port anchor not ready, and delay with starboard anchor); *The Boucau* [1909] P 163, 11 Asp MLC 240 (accident caused by combination of less water than usual, strong breeze and flood, held inevitable); *The Polynésien* [1910] P 28, 11 Asp MLC 354 (abnormal current alleged, but not proved). See also *The Cardiff Hall* [1918] P 56, 14 Asp MLC 328 (ships navigating without lights under Admiralty orders); *Eva v Knutenborg* (1921) 9 Ll L Rep 494 (breaking of dock gates).
5   *The Thornley* (1843) 7 Jur 659 (vessel ashore could not let go anchor).
6   *The Aimo, The Amelia* (1873) 2 Asp MLC 96, PC (inevitable accident; vessel with duty to keep out of the way disabled from doing so by prior collision); cf *The Kjobenhavn* (1874) 2 Asp MLC 213, PC. As to liability for antecedent and subsequent negligence see PARA 770.
7   *The Calcutta, Calcutta (Owners) v Emma (Owners)* (1869) 21 LT 768, PC (where a ship partly disabled by carrying away her fore tack was held not to have done all she should).
8   *The Peerless* (1860) Lush 30 at 103, PC (chain catching on windlass held to be a pure accident); *Doward v Lindsay, The William Lindsay* (1873) LR 5 PC 338, 2 Asp MLC 118 (inevitable accident; mooring buoy broke in a storm; anchor let go, but windlass jammed by accident); *The Virgo* (1876) 3 Asp MLC 285 (inevitable accident; latent defect in steam steering gear); *The Indus* (1886) 12 PD 46, 6 Asp MLC 105, CA (machinery alleged to be out of order, but not so proved, as it worked well before and after); *The Branksome Hall* (1934) 48 Ll L Rep 43 (inevitable accident not proved; unexplained opening of mooring shackle). The failure must be shown to have been consistent with the exercise of reasonable care and skill to prevent it: see PARAS 757, 788.

(6) RIGHTS AND REMEDIES OF INJURED PARTIES

(i) Persons entitled to Recover

790.   Owners of damaged ship. The beneficial or registered owners of the damaged ship may sue for the damage done to her[1], and so also may the bailees of a ship[2]. The owners of the damaged ship may also sue for damage done to the cargo, as they are bailees of her[3]. If there is any doubt as to who is entitled to receive the damages, they should be paid into the Admiralty Registry, and the parties rightly claiming them can then establish their right[4].

Charterers are not entitled to recover damages for economic loss caused by the vessel being out of use[5].

1   *The Ilos* (1856) Sw 100. As to ownership generally see PARA 236 et seq; and as to part owners see *Sedgworth v Overend* (1797) 7 Term Rep 279; and PARA 244. Sub-charterers have been held entitled to sue for loss of bill of lading freight: see *The Okehampton* [1913] P 173, 12 Asp MLC 428, CA. As to the right of salvors to sue for damage done to a wreck whilst in their possession see *The Zelo* [1922] P 9, 15 Asp MLC 428; and PARA 814. As to apportionment of liability to make good damage or loss where both vessels are at fault see PARAS 767–770; as to the measure of damages see PARA 793 et seq; and as to limitation of liability see PARA 992 et seq.
2   *The Minna* (1868) LR 2 A & E 97. See also *The Rosalind* (1920) 90 LJP 126; and PARA 796 note 3.
3   *The Winkfield* [1902] P 42, 9 Asp MLC 259, CA. See further *The Joannis Vatis* [1922] P 92, 15 Asp MLC 506, CA. In this regard see also the Torts (Interference with Goods) Act 1977 s 8; and TORT vol 97 (2015) PARA 656. As to loss by cargo owners see PARA 808.
4   *The Ilos* (1856) Sw 100; *The Minna* (1868) LR 2 A & E 97. As to the Admiralty Registry see PARA 142.
5   See *Candlewood Navigation Corpn Ltd v Mitsui OSK Lines Ltd; The Mineral Transporter, The Ibaraki Maru* [1986] AC 1, [1985] 2 All ER 935, PC.

791.   Owners of cargo or other property in ship. Owners of cargo and other property are entitled to sue the owners of the vessel carrying it for breach of contract to carry it safely[1], or for damage caused to it by negligence[2], although their right to do so is subject to any valid term in the contract of carriage or statutory provision which abrogates or qualifies the right[3]. Cargo owners and others can also as a rule recover against the owners of a vessel whose negligent navigation has caused a collision between her and the vessel carrying the cargo[4], although their right to recover where both vessels were at fault is limited[5].

1   As to the shipowner's liability as common carrier see CARRIAGE AND CARRIERS vol 7 (2015) PARA 261.
2   As to negligence causing damage see PARA 756 et seq.
3   As to exceptions of collision, negligence etc, and the Hague-Visby Rules see CARRIAGE AND CARRIERS vol 7 (2015) PARA 368 et seq.
4   See PARA 808.
5   See PARA 776.

792.   Personal injuries or death. Persons on board a vessel may at common law sue the owners of the vessel carrying them or another vessel for personal injuries arising from a collision caused by the negligence of those for whom the owners were responsible[1]. Sea carriers are also liable for personal injury or death under the Athens Convention[2].

By statute, the personal representatives of an innocent person on board a vessel whose death was caused by a collision due to the fault of that vessel or another vessel may sue the owner of the vessel at fault to recover damages[3]. The right of action against a vessel other than that which carried the person who suffered injury or death exists even though the vessel which carried him was also at fault[4], and in such a case the liability of the owners of the vessels is joint and several[5]. In the case of passengers, however, the rights of action against the owners of the vessel which carried them may depend on the terms of their contract[6].

1   As to negligence causing damage see PARA 756 et seq; as to the vicarious liability of shipowners see PARA 780; and as to the measure of damages for personal injuries and death see DAMAGES vol 29 (2014) PARA 434 et seq.
2   Ie the Convention relating to the Carriage of Passengers and their Luggage by Sea (Athens, 13 December 1974; TS 40 (1987); Cm 202), as amended by the 2002 Protocol (London, 1 November 2002; TS 14 (2014)), as applied and augmented in the EU by Parliament and Council Regulation (EC) 392/2009 (OJ L131, 28.5.2009, p 24) on the liability of carriers of passengers by sea in the event of accidents ('the EU Carriage by Sea Regulation'): see CARRIAGE AND CARRIERS vol 7 (2015) PARAS 635–650.
3   See the Fatal Accidents Act 1976 ss 1–2; and NEGLIGENCE vol 78 (2010) PARA 24 et seq. As to the limitation of time for proceedings cf PARA 812; and as to the survival of causes of action vested

in a person before his death see the Law Reform (Miscellaneous Provisions) Act 1934 s 1(1); and
WILLS AND INTESTACY vol 103 (2016) PARA 1277 et seq.
4   *Mills v Armstrong, The Bernina* (1888) 13 App Cas 1, 6 Asp MLC 257, HL; *The Esso Malaysia*
[1975] QB 198, [1974] 2 All ER 705, [1974] 2 Lloyd's Rep 143 (collision between two foreign
ships outside United Kingdom territorial waters).
5   See PARA 777. As to the right of contribution see PARA 778.
6   See CARRIAGE AND CARRIERS vol 7 (2015) PARA 627 et seq; cf PARA 776.

(ii) Measure of Damages

793.   General principles. Subject to the statutory provisions as to limitation of
liability[1] and certain other exceptions[2], the fundamental principle governing the
measure of damages is the payment of full compensation[3]. The injured party is
entitled to be put, as far as practicable, into the same condition as if the injury had
not been suffered. He is to have the full value of the property lost[4]. The wrongdoer
is, however, it seems, liable only for such damage as a reasonable person should
have foreseen as the consequence of the wrongful act[5]. The injured party is bound
to prove that he has sustained the loss which he alleges, and he must supply the
means for ascertaining its amount[6]. If the injured party can reasonably mitigate
the damage done by the collision, he is bound ordinarily to do so[7].

1   As to which see PARA 992 et seq.
2   Eg the rule that, where two ships are each to blame for the collision, the innocent owner of cargo
on one vessel can recover from the owner of the other vessel only in proportion to the fault of that
vessel: see PARA 776.
3   *The Dundee* (1923) 1 Hag Adm 109 at 120; *The Liesbosch, Dredger (owners) v Edison Steamship
(owners)* [1933] AC 449, 18 Asp MLC 380, HL. As to the measure of damages generally see
DAMAGES vol 29 (2014) PARA 408 et seq.
4   *The Clarence* (1850) 3 Wm Rob 283 at 285; *The Clyde* (1856) Sw 23 at 24. The injured party
cannot recover more than is sufficient to place him in the position which he would have occupied
if there had been no collision: *The Lady Emerald* (1932) 44 Ll L Rep 176. See further PARA 796.
5   *Overseas Tankship (UK) Ltd v Morts Dock and Engineering Co Ltd, The Wagon Mound* [1961]
AC 388, [1961] 1 All ER 404, [1961] 1 Lloyd's Rep 1, PC, distinguished on the facts in *Overseas
Tankship (UK) Ltd v Miller Steamship Co Pty Ltd, The Wagon Mound (No 2)* [1967] 1 AC 617,
[1966] 2 All ER 709, [1966] 1 Lloyd's Rep 657, PC; but see *Re Polemis and Furness, Withy & Co
Ltd* [1921] 3 KB 560, 15 Asp MLC 398, CA. See also *Thurogood v Van Den Berghs and Jurgens
Ltd* [1951] 2 KB 537 at 552, 555, [1951] 1 All ER 682 at 690, 692, CA, per Asquith LJ. A person
cannot escape liability, however indirect the damage, if he foresees or could reasonably have
foreseen the intervening events which led to its being done: *Overseas Tankship (UK) Ltd v Morts
Dock and Engineering Co Ltd, The Wagon Mound* at 426 and at 416. See also *The Gertor* (1894)
7 Asp MLC 472 (damage following on breaking of tow rope was consequence of tow's failure to
obtain tug's assistance earlier); *HMS London* [1914] P 72, 12 Asp MLC 405 (delay through strike
in repair of vessel damaged by negligence; damages recoverable for loss of use of vessel during
strike because loss was 'direct' and 'natural' consequence of negligence or, alternatively, strike was
reasonably foreseeable); *The Liesbosch, Dredger (owners) v Edison Steamship (owners)* [1933] AC
449, 18 Asp MLC 380, HL (cited in PARA 796 note 6). Cf *Anglo-Algerian Steamship Co Ltd v
Houlder Line Ltd* [1908] 1 KB 659, 11 Asp MLC 45 (negligent damage by defendants' ship to
dock gates; plaintiffs not entitled to recover damages for loss suffered through detention of their
ship outside dock while gates were repaired); *Société Anonyme de Remorquage à Hélice v Bennetts*
[1911] 1 KB 243 (tug sunk by negligence of third person; tug owner not entitled to recover from
third person for loss of towage remuneration). See generally DAMAGES vol 29 (2014) PARA 409
et seq.
6   *The Clarence* (1850) 3 Wm Rob 283. As to the burden of proof see PARA 795.
7   *The Mediana* [1899] P 127 at 137, 8 Asp MLC 493 at 500, CA. The burden of proof that the
claimant has failed in his duty is on the defendant: see *The Bharatkhand* [1952] 1 Lloyd's Rep 470.
As to mitigation of damages generally see DAMAGES vol 29 (2014) PARA 378 et seq.

794.   Nature of indemnity. If the settlement of the indemnification is attended
with any difficulty, the party at fault must, in certain circumstances, bear the
inconvenience[1]. The injured party may derive a greater benefit than

indemnification; for example, in case of repairs and supply of new articles, the wrongdoer, unlike the insurer, is not entitled to a deduction of one-third new for old[2].

1 As to the measure of damages see PARA 793.
2 *The Gazelle* (1844) 2 Wm Rob 279 at 281; *The Egyptian* (1864) 2 Mar LC 56 at 58. As to the loss for which insurers are liable see INSURANCE vol 60 (2011) PARA 397 et seq.

795. Burden of proof. The burden is always on the claimant who claims damages to prove that the damage was caused by the negligence of the defendant[1]. When the claimant has made out a prima facie case that the damage claimed is occasioned by the collision, the burden of proof then shifts to the defendant to show that the damage was not so occasioned, for example by showing that it is to be attributable to another or a concurrent cause for which the claimant is responsible[2].

1 *The Paludina* [1925] P 40 at 50, 16 Asp MLC 453 at 457, CA; affd sub nom *Singleton Abbey (Owners) v Paludina (Owners)* [1927] AC 16, 17 Asp MLC 117, HL. Cf PARA 798. As to negligence causing damage see PARA 756 et seq; and as to the burden of proof in collision cases particularly see PARA 757.
2 *The Egyptian* (1864) 2 Mar LC 56 at 58 (damage alleged to have been caused by severe weather preceding collision); *The Bharatkhand* [1952] 1 Lloyd's Rep 470 (alleged failure to take steps to mitigate damage); *The Fritz Thyssen; Owners of Motor Vessel Mitera Marigo v Owners of Motorship Or Vessel Fritz Thyssen* [1967] 1 All ER 628 (repeated and unreasonable refusal of assistance which could have saved vessel); *The Zaglebie Dobrowskie (No 2)* [1978] 1 Lloyd's Rep 573 (failure of crew to take preventive measures); and see CIVIL PROCEDURE vol 12 (2015) PARA 704. As to the determination of liability when both parties at fault see PARAS 767–770; and as to the division of loss in proportion to fault see PARA 771 et seq.

796. Damages in case of total loss. If a vessel is totally lost by the collision, the measure of damages is the value of the vessel to her owners as a going concern at the time and place of the loss, and, in assessing that value, regard must be had to her pending engagements, whether profitable or unprofitable[1]. If the vessel was not under a profitable contract, the shipowner is normally entitled to the market value of the vessel at the time when and at the place where she was sunk[2], and interest on this until payment[3]. If the vessel was earning freight, the owner is entitled to the probable value of the ship at the end of her voyage, and of the freight which she would have earned on that voyage and under any further engagements contracted for, subject to proper allowances[4]. When a vessel is lost while proceeding in ballast to a loading port under a charterparty, the damages are measured in the same way[5]. If she was not a freight-earning vessel but was under other profitable contract, the owner is entitled to her value as a profit-earning vessel at the time and place of her loss[6].

1 See *The Liesbosch, Dredger (owners) v Edison Steamship (owners)* [1933] AC 449, 18 Asp MLC 380, HL, disapproving the view stated in *The Columbus* (1849) 3 Wm Rob 158 at 164 (that, whether or not a ship was profit-earning, only the market value could be allowed). As to damages when the vessel is not lost see PARA 799.
2 *The Clyde* (1856) Sw 23. As to valuation in absence of market value see PARA 797.
3 *The Northumbria* (1869) LR 3 A & E 6 at 12, DC; *The Kong Magnus* [1891] P 223, 7 Asp MLC 64. In general, prospective earnings otherwise than under fixed engagements cannot be taken into account (*The Philadelphia* [1917] P 101, 14 Asp MLC 68, CA), but this rule has been held not to apply to a pleasure vessel employed on inland waters in one small defined area whose seasonable employment at scheduled rates could be fairly accurately determined by what actually occurred in the case of other craft belonging to the same owner (*The Fortunity Four of Hearts (Owners) v Fortunity (Owners)* [1960] 2 All ER 64, [1961] 1 WLR 351, [1960] 1 Lloyd's Rep 252). A bailee in possession is entitled to recover from a wrongdoer the market value of the chattel at the time of the loss, with interest from that date until payment: see *The Rosalind* (1920) 90 LJP 126. As to interest see further PARA 809.
4 *The Philadelphia* [1917] P 101, 14 Asp MLC 68, CA; and see *SS Baron Vernon v SS Metagama* 1927 SC 498 (10% off estimated profit deducted for contingencies); cf *The Northumbria* (1869) LR 3 A & E 6 at 12; *The Racine* [1906] P 273, 10 Asp MLC 300, CA; *The Empress of Britain* (1913) 29 TLR 423. References in these cases to the value of the vessel at the end of her voyage

must be regarded merely as indicating that wear and tear during the voyage is to be taken into account: see *The Philadelphia* at 110–111 and 73. The value of prospective freights cannot, however, be simply added to the market value of the vessel as a free vessel, as the owner would then be getting his damages twice over: *The Liesbosch, Dredger (owners) v Edison Steamship (owners)* [1933] AC 449 at 454, 18 Asp MLC 380 at 383, HL. Where the market value allowed is based on that of a comparable vessel whose value is enhanced by the virtual certainty of future profitable employment, no further sum is allowable for future trading profits other than the profit which the vessel would have made if she had completed the voyage on which she was lost: *The Llanover* [1947] P 80, 80 Ll L Rep 433.

5   *The Kate* [1899] P 165, 8 Asp MLC 539, as explained in *The Philadelphia* [1917] P 101, 14 Asp MLC 68, CA.
6   *The Liesbosch, Dredger (owners) v Edison Steamship (owners)* [1933] AC 449, 18 Asp MLC 380, HL (where the measure of damages was held to be the value of the dredger, which was under a profitable contract, to the owners as a profit-earning dredger at the time and place of her loss; this included:
    (1)   a capital sum covering the market value of a comparable substitute, costs of adaptation etc, and compensation for loss in carrying out the contract over period of delay, but excluding loss due to the financial poverty of the owners; and
    (2)   interest on that capital from the date of the loss).

797. Valuation in absence of market value.
In the absence of a market value for a vessel, the test is what she was fairly worth to her owners as a going concern at the time and place of the loss[1]. The opinion of competent persons who knew the vessel is the best evidence of her value, but the evidence of professional valuers is also of weight. Elements to be considered in such a valuation are the original cost of the vessel, her age, her condition, the profits she earned[2] and the market price of similar vessels.

1   *The Harmonides* [1903] P 1; *The Liesbosch, Dredger (owners) v Edison Steamship (owners)* [1933] AC 449, 18 Asp MLC 380, HL. See also the salvage cases cited in PARA 976 note 1. As to the measure of damages in cases of total loss of vessel see PARA 796.
2   *The Iron-Master* (1859) Sw 441.

798. Loss after collision.
There is no presumption of law that damage suffered by a vessel after a collision must be deemed to be the result of the collision unless the owner of the vessel whose negligence caused the collision proves the contrary[1].

However, in particular circumstances, damage, for example the stranding of the damaged vessel, may be of such a kind and follow so immediately on the collision that it is to be assumed that the damage was caused by the collision unless it is proved that there was some other cause[2]. The cost of raising a vessel sunk in a harbour or river is recoverable as damages in a collision action if the authority has the power to charge the owners with the cost and if the charges are reasonable[3]. Although the principle of constructive total loss[4] has no direct relation to collision liabilities, there may be cases where the proper mode of measuring the damages would be to assess them on the same basis as for a constructive total loss and then the defendant is entitled to the wreck[5].

1   As to negligence causing damage see PARA 756 et seq; and as to the burden of proof in collision cases see PARA 757 (negligence) and PARA 795 (damages).
2   *The Paludina* [1925] P 40 at 48, 49, 16 Asp MLC 453 at 457, CA; affd sub nom *Singleton Abbey (Owners) v Paludina (Owners), The Paludina* [1927] AC 16, 17 Asp MLC 117, HL. See also *The Mellona* (1847) 3 Wm Rob 7; *The Blenheim* (1854) 1 Ecc & Ad 285 (unreasonable abandonment); *The Linda* (1857) Sw 306 (salvage after improper abandonment); *The Pensher* (1857) Sw 211; *The Flying Fish* (1865) Brown & Lush 436 (where the partial damage became a total loss owing to the plaintiff's negligence, and the defendants were held liable for the partial damage); *The George and Richard* (1871) LR 3 A & E 466, 1 Asp MLC 50 (driving ashore and loss of life due to collision); *The Thuringia* (1872) 1 Asp MLC 283; *The Hansa* (1887) 6 Asp MLC 268; *The City of Lincoln* (1889) 15 PD 15, 6 Asp MLC 475, CA (stranding resulting from collision); *The Bruxellesville* [1908] P 312, 11 Asp MLC 24 (subsequent loss not due to collision); *The San Onofre* [1922] P 243, 16 Asp MLC 1, CA; *The Marigola* (1929) 34 Ll L Rep 217 (where subsequent stranding was due to the precipitate action of the master of the plaintiff's vessel); *The Steingrim* (1930) 37 Ll L

Rep 284 (reasonable abandonment). See also *Temple Bar (Owners) v Guildford (Owners), The Guildford* [1956] P 364, [1956] 2 All ER 915; *Mitera Marigo (Owners) v Fritz Thyssen (Owners), The Fritz Thyssen* [1968] P 255 at 261n, [1967] 3 All ER 117n, [1967] 2 Lloyd's Rep 199, CA (where the sinking was not a direct result of the collision as assistance was refused). The defendants are entitled to a diminution of damages only if those in charge of the claimant's vessel were guilty of negligence, as opposed to mere error of judgment, amounting to a novus actus interveniens which caused the extra damage: see *SS Baron Vernon v SS Metagama* 1928 SC (HL) 21. As to reasonable human conduct not breaking the chain of causation see the cases cited in PARA 763 note 7; and DAMAGES vol 29 (2014) PARA 371.

3   *The Harrington* (1888) 13 PD 48, 6 Asp MLC 282; *The Emerald, The Greta Holme* [1896] P 192, 8 Asp MLC 138, CA (revsd on other grounds sub nom *No 7 Steam Sand Pump Dredger (Owners) v Greta Holme (Owners), The Greta Holme* [1897] AC 596, 8 Asp MLC 317, HL); *The Wallesend* [1907] P 302, 10 Asp MLC 476; but see *Steamship Enterprises of Panama Inc, Liverpool (Owners) v Ousel (Owners), The Liverpool (No 2)* [1963] P 64, [1960] 3 All ER 307, [1960] 2 Lloyd's Rep 66, CA (where a claim by an authority for removal expenses against the owners of a negligent ship was allowed and a claim by the owners of a wreck in respect of contingent statutory liability for wreck-saving expenses was disallowed). As to the power to raise vessels see PORTS AND HARBOURS vol 85 (2012) PARA 92.
4   See INSURANCE vol 60 (2011) PARA 434 et seq.
5   *The Columbus* (1849) 3 Wm Rob 158. See also *The Empress Eugenie* (1860) Lush 138.

799.   Vessel damaged but not lost.

When the ship is damaged but not lost[1], the damages recoverable generally consist of salvage[2] or towage[3], repairs (including dock dues)[4], crew's wages and other expenses of the vessel during repair, and loss of profit[5]. Where a ship has been temporarily repaired, and it is proved with reasonable certainty that, although permanent repairs have not been effected, they will be effected, her owners are entitled to recover a sum in respect of the prospective permanent repairs and of the prospective loss of time occupied in effecting them[6].

Salvage expenses incurred by reason of a collision are recoverable from the wrongdoer[7], as is towage[8].

1   As to damages recoverable when the ship is lost see PARA 796.
2   As to salvage generally see PARA 849 et seq.
3   As to towage generally see PARA 597 et seq.
4   As to the cost of repairs see PARA 800.
5   As to the general principles governing the measure of damages see PARA 793.
6   *The Kingsway* [1918] P 344, 14 Asp MLC 509, CA.
7   *The Pensher* (1857) Sw 211; *The Williamina* (1878) 3 PD 97 at 99. The claimant's costs in the action against his vessel by the salvors are usually recoverable (*The Legatus* (1856) Sw 168); but see *The British Commerce* (1884) 9 PD 128, 5 Asp MLC 335 (where commission on bail was not recoverable).
8   *HMS Inflexible* (1857) Sw 200.

800.   Cost of repairs.

The owner is entitled to a complete repair of all the damage done, even though the result may be to render the vessel worth more than she was before the collision[1]. The cost of the repairs recoverable is the cost at the nearest convenient port at which the repairs could have been executed[2]. The owner is entitled to recover the cost of the repairs even though he does not actually repair the vessel[3], or even though he sells her unrepaired to the shipbreakers[4]. The estimated cost of repairs is often the simplest way of calculating the loss which has to be made good[5]. The owner is not, however, entitled to the renewal of rotten parts discovered by the opening up for collision repairs, even though such parts might otherwise have lasted for years[6]. There is no claim for the cost of repairs out of all proportion to the value of the vessel[7].

1   *The Pactolus* (1856) Sw 173; *The Bernina* (1886) 6 Asp MLC 65. See also *The Kingsway* [1918] P 344, 14 Asp MLC 590, CA. The fees of a surveyor acting on behalf of a shipowner may be allowed even though he was engaged and paid by the insurers, but not fees for mere surveillance for them: *The Molière* [1925] P 27, 16 Asp MLC 470. As to a damaged vessel which was already

in poor condition see *Kamal XXVI (owners and/or demise charterers) v Ariela (owners)* [2009] EWHC 177 (Comm), [2009] All ER (D) 90 (Feb). As to interest see *The Napier Star* [1933] P 136, 18 Asp MLC 400; and PARA 809.

2   *Beucker v Aberdeen Steam Trawling and Fishing Co Ltd* 1910 SC 655; *The Admiralty v Aberdeen Steam Trawling and Fishing Co Ltd* 1910 SC 553. Damages may be awarded in the currency best compensating the claimant, having regard to the currency in which he generally operates or with which he has the closest connection: *Eleftherotria (Owners) v Despina R (Owners), The Despina R* [1979] AC 685, [1979] 1 All ER 421, [1979] 1 Lloyd's Rep 1, HL.

3   *The Endeavour* (1890) 6 Asp MLC 511.

4   *The London Corpn* [1935] P 70, 18 Asp MLC 535, CA; *Porter v George Robb & Sons Ltd* 1961 SLT (Sh Ct) 14.

5   See generally PARA 822; and DAMAGES vol 29 (2014) PARAS 412, 415.

6   *The Princess* (1885) 5 Asp MLC 451.

7   See *The Minnehaha* (1921) 6 Ll L Rep 12; *The Argonaftis* [1989] 2 Lloyd's Rep 487.

801.   Dry-docking. Dues paid for dry-docking a vessel for collision repairs are recoverable[1]. Even where her owners take the opportunity to do other work on the vessel when the collision repairs are being done, the whole of the dock dues are recoverable from the wrongdoer, if the amount paid for the hire of the dock is not increased by the owners' work[2]. If there are two collisions and the vessel would have had to be dry-docked for the damage caused by the first collision, and the repairs of the damage caused by the two collisions are carried out concurrently so that no extra dues become payable, it seems that the first wrongdoer only is liable for the dock dues[3]. Where neither the collision repairs nor the owners' repairs are immediately necessary, the cost of dry-docking must be apportioned[4].

1   As to the measure of damages generally see PARA 793; and as to cost of repairs see PARA 800.

2   *Ruabon Steamship Co v London Assurance* [1900] AC 6, 9 Asp MLC 2, HL; *The Acanthus* [1902] P 17, 9 Asp MLC 276; cf *The Alfred* (1850) 3 Wm Rob 232 at 239; *Admiralty Comrs v SS Chekiang* [1926] AC 637, 17 Asp MLC 74, HL (damages for delay); *The Ferdinand Retzlaff* [1972] 2 Lloyd's Rep 120 (where the defendants were held not to be entitled to credit for the saving of time in bringing forward the special survey and owners' repairs to the time when the collision repairs were being carried out since these operations had not increased the cost of the collision repairs or the time occupied in them).

3   *Carslogie Steamship Co Ltd v Royal Norwegian Government* [1952] AC 292, [1952] 1 All ER 20, [1951] 2 Lloyd's Rep 441, HL, disapproving on this point *The Haversham Grange* [1905] P 307, 10 Asp MLC 156, CA.

4   *The Royal Fusilier* (1926) 25 Ll L Rep 566.

802.   Detention of ship. The shipowner is entitled to the expenses of detention of his vessel[1], and the amount of profit lost[2]. Both these heads of damages depend on time, and the shipowner is only entitled to such period of time as is shown to have been necessary allowing for reasonable dispatch[3]. Where there have been two collisions, and the second collision has caused no extra detention beyond what would have been caused by the first, the second wrongdoer is not liable for any part of the loss caused by the detention[4]. The wrongdoer is not liable if the detention would in any case have been necessary owing to weather damage suffered by the claimant's vessel after the collision[5].

1   *HMS Inflexible* (1857) Sw 200. As to the expenses of detention see PARA 803.

2   *HMS Inflexible* (1857) Sw 200; *HMS London* [1914] P 72, 12 Asp MLC 405 (cited in PARA 822 note 5). As to the loss of profits caused by detention see PARA 804. Where there neither has been nor can be detention during repairs, the owner suffers no loss by reason of detention: see *The Glenfinlas* [1918] P 363n, 14 Asp MLC 594n (ship lost) (approved in *The Kingsway* [1918] P 344, 14 Asp MLC 590, CA; and in *The York* [1929] P 178, 17 Asp MLC 600, CA (repairs effected during period when already prevented from trading by contract of sale requiring preparation of ship for inspection; no loss due to detention)). Damages have been held to be recoverable for loss of time waiting for the next convoy in time of war (*The Veraston* [1920] P 12, 14 Asp MLC 595), but not damages for delay caused by a government order unconnected with the collision (*The Charles le Borgne* [1920] P 15 note 1; *The Kafue* [1920] P 15 note 2). As to the measure of the loss in case of a non-trading vessel, eg one owned by a foreign state or public authority, see PARA 806.

3   *The City of Buenos Aires* (1871) 1 Asp MLC 169; *The Ferdinand Retzlaff* [1972] 2 Lloyd's Rep 120. The fact that the owners take the opportunity of the period of detention to do other repairs

which have not actually become a necessity is no ground for reducing the wrongdoer's liability: *Admiralty Comrs v SS Chekiang* [1926] AC 637, 17 Asp MLC 74, HL.

4   *The Haversham Grange* [1905] P 307, 10 Asp MLC 156, CA, approved on this point in *Carslogie Steamship Co Ltd v Royal Norwegian Government* [1952] AC 292, [1952] 1 All ER 20, [1951] 2 Lloyd's Rep 441, HL. Where the claimant loses a government subsidy as a result of the detention, this is part of his loss: *The Daressa* [1971] 1 Lloyd's Rep 60. As to the determination of liability when more than one party is at fault see PARAS 767–770.

5   *Carslogie Steamship Co Ltd v Royal Norwegian Government* [1952] AC 292, [1952] 1 All ER 20, [1951] 2 Lloyd's Rep 441, HL. If there is an intention, even without a final decision, to carry out repairs rendered necessary before the collision took place, the time which would have been spent on them is excluded: *The Hassel* [1962] 2 Lloyd's Rep 139.

803.   Expenses of detention.

The burden of proving that there has been any loss by detention rests on the claimant[1]. Two things are necessary, namely loss and reasonable proof of the amount[2]. The ordinary expenses of a vessel in port are allowed, including the master's and crew's wages and maintenance where necessarily incurred, fuel and stores consumed, and other matters[3]. It may, however, be that the insurance premium, if the vessel is long in port, will be subject to a deduction[4].

1   *Strathfillan (Owners) v Ikala (Owners)* [1929] AC 196 at 209, 17 Asp MLC 555 at 560, HL. As to the burden of proof see PARA 757 (negligence); and PARA 795 (damages). As to liability for detention see PARA 802.

2   *The Clarence* (1850) 3 Wm Rob 283 at 286. As to loss of profits see PARA 804.

3   Cf eg *Admiralty Comrs v SS Chekiang* [1926] AC 637, 17 Asp MLC 74, HL; *The Hebridean Coast, Lord Citrine (Owners) v Hebridean Coast (Owners)* [1961] AC 545, [1961] 1 All ER 82, [1960] 2 Lloyd's Rep 423, HL (cited in PARA 806 note 3); *The Ferdinand Retzlaff* [1972] 2 Lloyd's Rep 120.

4   As to marine insurance see INSURANCE vol 60 (2011) PARA 238 et seq.

804.   Loss of profits by detention.

A ship is a thing by the use of which money may ordinarily be earned, and, for the purpose of determining what profits, if any, were lost by detention, the question is what use the shipowner would, but for the collision, have had of his ship, and what profits would have been earned by such use, excluding elements of uncertain or speculative or special character[1]. Where the ship is under a charterparty[2] which is lost in consequence of the collision, the charterparty is admissible evidence to prove that the ship has been thrown out of employment, but, in the absence of any charterparty, other evidence may equally establish the loss of employment[3].

Where there is a charterparty for the voyage, this may afford a measure of the profits lost, although there is no rigid rule that the calculation is to be based on the charterparty current at the date of the collision; where there is no charterparty but a reasonable certainty of employment[4], the matter is more at large[5]. The usual evidence given is as to the two or three previous voyages of the vessel[6], and sometimes as to a subsequent voyage.

Damages are not necessarily confined to loss of profits during the actual period during which the ship is laid up for repairs but may include loss of earnings under any engagement for a future voyage which she had secured at the time of the collision[7].

The loss of profit may consist of a loss of profit on the sale of goods which the owner would have carried in his vessel[8]. A fishing vessel has been allowed damages for loss due to interruption of fishing, as proved by the catches made by other vessels[9]; and a whaling vessel which loses her season is as much entitled to recover for her loss of employment as a vessel carrying cargo[10]. Loss of fishing in general, however, has been held to be too problematical[11]. In all cases of loss of employment proper deductions must be made from the gross amount which would have been earned, for the expenses which would have been incurred in earning it[12], and the saving of wear and tear to the vessel[13].

1   *The Argentino* (1888) 13 PD 191 at 201, 6 Asp MLC 348 at 351, CA; affd (1889) 14 App Cas 519, 6 Asp MLC 433, HL. As to foreseeability as a requirement for damages see PARA 793; as to liability for detention see PARA 802; and as to the expenses of detention see PARA 803.

2   As to charterparties generally see CARRIAGE AND CARRIERS vol 7 (2015) PARA 208 et seq.

3   *The Argentino* (1888) 13 PD 191 at 202, 6 Asp MLC 348 at 352, CA (affd (1889) 14 App Cas 519, 6 Asp MLC 433, HL); *The Hebridean Coast, Lord Citrine (Owners) v Hebridean Coast (Owners)* [1961] AC 545 at 563, [1960] 2 All ER 85 at 95, [1960] 1 Lloyd's Rep 227 at 240, CA, per Devlin LJ (affd [1961] AC 545 at 570, [1961] 1 All ER 82, [1960] 2 Lloyd's Rep 423, HL).

4   It has been suggested that it would now be sufficient to show merely a probability of earning a profit: *The Hebridean Coast, Lord Citrine (Owners) v Hebridean Coast (Owners)* [1961] AC 545 at 562, [1960] 2 All ER 85 at 94, [1960] 1 Lloyd's Rep 227 at 239, CA (affd [1961] AC 545 at 570, [1961] 1 All ER 82, [1960] 2 Lloyd's Rep 423, HL).

5   *The Argentino* (1888) 13 PD 191 at 203, 6 Asp MLC 348 at 352, CA (affd (1889) 14 App Cas 519, 6 Asp MLC 433, HL); *The Soya* [1956] 2 All ER 393, [1956] 1 Lloyd's Rep 557, sub nom *Dirphys (Owners) v Soya (Owners), The Soya* [1956] 1 WLR 714, CA; and see *Re Mersey Docks and Harbour Board and Admiralty Comrs* [1920] 3 KB 223, 15 Asp MLC 24, DC; *Admiralty Comrs v SS Valeria (Owners)* [1922] 2 AC 242, 16 Asp MLC 25, HL (where charterers were allowed loss of profits on commercial freight plus working expenses instead of actual out-of-pocket expenses, which included cost of hire, cases of non-freight-earning vessels being distinguished); *Vitruvia Steamship Co Ltd v Ropner Shipping Co Ltd* 1923 SC 574 (affd 1925 SC (HL) 1) (where damages were allowed at an agreed-on daily rate although the vessel had been able to complete her voyage under her charterparty and although no specific loss due to the delay had been proved); *The Soya* (where the vessel duly completed her current charterparty, but was delayed in reaching the Far East where at the time exceptionally high freight rates prevailed; loss of profits through delay in reaching the Far East were speculative, and the loss was held to be rightly assessed by reference to the profits being earned at the time of the collision); *Owners of the Ship Front Ace v Owners of the Ship Vicky 1* [2008] EWCA Civ 101, [2008] 2 All ER (Comm) 42 (no binding authority for the proposition that the 'ballast/laden' basis is the appropriate methodology to be adopted in all cases where a claimant loses a fixture as a result of a collision; calculation of loss of profit depends upon the facts of the particular case). A useful but not obligatory way of assessing damage where there is no charterparty is to take (subject to an allowance for contingencies if need be) an appropriate rate of hire for the period, to deduct the cost of earning the hire so far as not incurred and to award the balance: *The Hebridean Coast, Lord Citrine (Owners) v Hebridean Coast (Owners)* [1961] AC 545 at 563, [1960] 2 All ER 85 at 95, [1960] 1 Lloyd's Rep 227 at 239, CA (affd [1961] AC 545 at 570, [1961] 1 All ER 82, [1960] 2 Lloyd's Rep 423, HL).

6   Cf *The Hebe* (1847) 2 Wm Rob 530 at 536.

7   *The Argentino* (1889) 14 App Cas 519, 6 Asp MLC 433, HL; *The Soya* [1956] 2 All ER 393, [1956] 1 Lloyd's Rep 557, sub nom *Dirphys (Owners) v Soya (Owners), The Soya* [1956] 1 WLR 714, CA.

8   *Strathfillan (Owners) v Ikala (Owners)* [1929] AC 196, 17 Asp MLC 555, HL (where, on a reference to assess damages (reported sub nom *The Ikala* (1929) 35 Ll L Rep 191, CA), the Court of Appeal refused to interfere with a calculation based on the cost of hiring a similar ship, even though it did not appear that any ship had been hired to replace the damaged ship, since the damages awarded were not on any basis of calculation excessive). For comment on this case see *The Hebridean Coast, Lord Citrine (Owners) v Hebridean Coast (Owners)* [1961] AC 545, [1961] 1 All ER 82, [1960] 2 Lloyd's Rep 423, HL.

9   *The Risoluto* (1883) 8 PD 109, 5 Asp MLC 93.

10 *The Argentino* (1888) 13 PD 191 at 202, 6 Asp MLC 348 at 352; affd sub nom *Gracie (Owners) v Argentino (Owners), The Argentino* (1889) 14 App Cas 519, 6 Asp MLC 433, HL.

11 *The Anselma de Larringa* (1913) 29 TLR 587.

12 *The Gazelle* (1844) 2 Wm Rob 279 at 284.

13 *The Star of India* (1876) 1 PD 466 at 472, 3 Asp MLC 261 at 263.

805.   Use of another vessel. Where, in order to carry out a charterparty, the shipowner hires another vessel to take the place of the vessel detained, the amount paid for the hire of the substituted vessel generally constitutes the measure of his loss[1]. Where the shipowner substitutes another vessel of his own for the vessel detained, he is entitled to be paid for reasonable losses thus incurred, but no compensation will be due for time during which the substituted vessel would have been unemployed[2].

1   *The Yorkshireman* (1827) 2 Hag Adm 30n; and see *The Tugela* (1913) 30 TLR 101 (addition for loss of use of damaged vessel beyond period of time of substituted vessel allowed). As to the right of shipowners not engaged in trading for profit to claim the cost of hiring see PARA 806. Even though there may be no sufficient positive evidence of any chartering effected for the purpose of supplying the loss of a particular ship, it seems that the circumstances proved may be such that a court may be justified in drawing the inference that a proportion of the chartered tonnage did in fact supply that loss: *Strathfillan (Owners) v Ikala (Owners), The Ikala* [1929] AC 196 at 211, 17 Asp MLC 555 at 561, HL. Cf *The Hebridean Coast, Lord Citrine (Owners) v Hebridean Coast (Owners)* [1961] AC 545, [1961] 1 All ER 82, [1960] 2 Lloyd's Rep 423, HL (where such an inference could not be drawn); *Beechwood Birmingham Ltd v Hoyer Group UK Ltd* [2010] EWCA Civ 647, [2011] QB 357, [2011] 1 All ER (Comm) 460 (analogous situation relating to car hire). As to liability for detention see PARA 802; and as to the loss of profits see PARA 804.

2   *The Black Prince* (1862) Lush 568; *The City of Peking v Compagnie des Messageries Maritimes, The City of Peking* (1890) 15 App Cas 438, 6 Asp MLC 572, PC; *Andros Springs (Owners) v World Beauty (Owners), The World Beauty* [1970] P 144, sub nom *The World Beauty, Owners of Steam Trawler Andros Springs v Owners of Steam Tanker World Beauty* [1969] 3 All ER 158, [1969] 1 Lloyd's Rep 350, CA.

806. Damages recoverable by foreign state or public authority.

General damages are recoverable for loss of use of a vessel, although the owners are a foreign state, or a public authority which is not authorised to use it for profit like a private individual[1]. There is no absolute rule as to the method of assessing such damages, which must depend on the facts of the case[2]. In some cases, damages have been assessed on a percentage of the capital value of the ship[3]; in other cases, damages have been held to be assessable on the operating cost or the cost of maintaining a spare ship[4]. Where another vessel has been hired to do the work of the damaged vessel, the owners of the damaged vessel may claim as special damages the cost of hiring, even though they are not engaged in trading for profit[5].

1   *No 7 Steam Sand Pump Dredger (Owners) v Greta Holme (Owners), The Greta Holme* [1897] AC 596, 8 Asp MLC 317, HL; *Mediana (Owners) v Comet (Owners, Master and Crew), The Mediana* [1900] AC 113, 9 Asp MLC 41, HL; *Mersey Docks and Harbour Board v Marpessa (Owners)* [1907] AC 241, HL; *The Astrakhan* [1910] P 172, 11 Asp MLC 390; cf *The Bodlewell* [1907] P 286, 10 Asp MLC 479 (vessel worked at a loss for the time; damages not allowed, except expenses); and see DAMAGES vol 29 (2014) PARA 419. The principle extends to men-of-war: see eg *Admiralty Comrs v SS Chekiang* [1926] AC 637, sub nom *The Chekiang* 17 Asp MLC 74, HL. Cf *Beechwood Birmingham Ltd v Hoyer Group UK Ltd* [2010] EWCA Civ 647, [2011] QB 357, [2011] 1 All ER (Comm) 460 (analogous situation relating to car hire). As to liability for detention see PARA 802; and as to loss of profits by detention see PARA 804.

2   *Admiralty Comrs v SS Chekiang* [1926] AC 637, sub nom *The Chekiang* 17 Asp MLC 74, HL; *Admiralty Comrs v Susquehanna (Owners), The Susquehanna* [1926] AC 655 at 662, 17 Asp MLC 81 at 83, HL; and see *Clyde Navigation Trustees v Bowring Steamship Co Ltd* 1929 SC 715 (hopper barge; allowed cost of reasonably efficient second-hand hopper barge, plus cost of adaptation for the special purpose for which it was intended, plus loss of use, plus interest); *The West Wales* [1932] P 165, 18 Asp MLC 349 (damage to warship; allowance to be made for use of Admiralty dry dock and cranes; as regards loss of use, the estimated life of the ship, annual depreciation and cost of maintenance must be considered); *The Luimneach* (1936) 54 Ll L Rep 5, CA. As to the general principles of assessing damages see PARA 793.

3   *Admiralty Comrs v SS Chekiang* [1926] AC 637, sub nom *The Chekiang* 17 Asp MLC 74, HL (5% on capital value, plus pay and allowances of officers and crew); *Admiralty Comrs v Susquehanna (Owners), The Susquehanna* [1926] AC 655 at 663, 664, 17 Asp MLC 81 at 84, HL (Admiralty oil tanker); *The Hebridean Coast, Lord Citrine (Owners) v Hebridean Coast (Owners)* [1961] AC 545, [1961] 1 All ER 82, [1960] 2 Lloyd's Rep 423, HL (collier of Central Electricity Generating Board; 7% on capital value allowed, plus allowances for depreciation, maintenance charges and consumption of stores).

4   *Mediana (Owners) v Comet (Owners), The Mediana* [1900] AC 113, 9 Asp MLC 41, HL (cost of maintaining spare lightship); *Mersey Docks and Harbour Board v Marpessa (Owners)* [1907] AC 241, HL (dredger; operating cost); and see *The Hebridean Coast, Lord Citrine (Owners) v Hebridean Coast (Owners)* [1961] AC 545, [1961] 1 All ER 82, [1960] 2 Lloyd's Rep 423, HL.

5   *Mersey Docks and Harbour Board v Marpessa (Owners)* [1907] AC 241 at 244, HL; and see *The Hebridean Coast, Lord Citrine (Owners) v Hebridean Coast (Owners)* [1961] AC 545, [1961] 1 All ER 82, [1960] 2 Lloyd's Rep 423, HL (where no specific vessel had been chartered as replacement tonnage). Cf *The St Charles* (1927) 17 Asp MLC 399, CA (where the plaintiffs were allowed (inter alia) a sum for loss of use of another vessel to which the cargo was transhipped). As to liability where another vessel has been hired to fulfil obligations see PARA 805. Even where it cannot be inferred that tonnage was chartered to replace the damaged vessel, it seems that there may be cases in which the owners of that vessel have been put to extra expenses and in which damages may appropriately be ascertained by reference to the sums which the owners of the damaged vessel were paying for chartered tonnage, less the expenses saved by not using the damaged vessel: see *The Hebridean Coast, Lord Citrine (Owners) v Hebridean Coast (Owners)* at 579, 86 and 428.

807. Other expenses. It seems that the shipowner can recover from the wrongdoer the whole of any general average expenses[1], notwithstanding the liability of the cargo owners for their share, although, if a cargo owner has an independent claim and exerts it in time in competition with the shipowner's claim, his claim will prevail[2]. He can recover expenses which he has had to pay for repatriation of seamen if the law of the flag puts that burden on him[3], and any special expenses which he has properly incurred to mitigate his loss[4].

1   As to general average expenses see CARRIAGE AND CARRIERS vol 7 (2015) PARA 606 et seq.
2   *Morrison Steamship Co Ltd v Greystoke Castle (Cargo Owners)* [1947] AC 265, [1946] 2 All ER 696, HL, not approving *The Marpessa* [1891] P 403, 7 Asp MLC 155. See also *The Kumanovo* [1998] 2 Lloyd's Rep 301, [1998] All ER (D) 14 (Jan) (agency 'uplift'). As to the measure of damages see PARA 793; and as to cargo owner's loss see PARA 808.
3   *The Craftsman* [1906] P 153, 10 Asp MLC 274. Cf the Merchant Shipping Act 1995 ss 73–76 (see PARA 548 et seq).
4   Eg extra costs to save delay (*The Normandy* (1900) 16 TLR 567), but not pensions paid by way of gratuity for which the shipowner is not legally liable (*The Amerika* (1913) 12 Asp MLC 478; affd sub nom *Admiralty Comrs v SS Amerika* [1917] AC 38, 13 Asp MLC 558, HL). As to mitigation of loss see DAMAGES vol 29 (2014) PARA 378 et seq.

808. Cargo owner's loss. A cargo owner who has lost his goods carried in one vessel in consequence of a collision due to the negligent navigation of another vessel[1] is, as a rule[2], entitled to recover from the owner of the other vessel the value of the goods at the place and time and in the state at and in which they ought to have been delivered to the cargo owner[3]. This value is the market price of the goods, if there is a market at that place. If not, such value has to be calculated, taking into account among other matters the cost price, the expenses of transit, and the importer's profit[4]. Wherever circumstances admit of calculations as to the time of arrival being made with reasonable certainty, damages for loss of market due to late delivery are recoverable[5]. Where general average expenses[6] are incurred by the carrying vessel, a cargo owner has a direct right of action in respect of his contribution to such expenses against the owner of another vessel whose negligent navigation has caused or contributed to the collision[7].

1   As to negligence giving rise to damage see PARA 756 et seq; and as to the right of cargo owners to recover see PARA 791.
2   As to the position where the vessel on which the cargo was carried is partly to blame for the collision see PARA 776.
3   As to the measure of damages for breach of contract see CARRIAGE AND CARRIERS vol 7 (2015) PARA 778 et seq.
4   *The Notting Hill* (1884) 9 PD 105 at 110, 5 Asp MLC 241 at 245, CA; cf *Rodocanachi v Milburn* (1886) 18 QBD 67, 6 Asp MLC 100, CA; *The Activ* (1901) 17 TLR 351 (the sound value at port of destination, after deducting proceeds of forced sale).
5   *Dunn v Bucknall Bros, Dunn v Donald Currie & Co* [1902] 2 KB 614 at 622, 623, 9 Asp MLC 336 at 339, CA; *Koufos v C Czarnikow Ltd, The Heron II* [1969] 1 AC 350, [1967] 3 All ER 686, [1967] 2 Lloyd's Rep 457, HL (fact that sugar prices fluctuate was known so that loss due to delay was foreseeable).
6   As to the nature of general average expenses see CARRIAGE AND CARRIERS vol 7 (2015) PARA 606 et seq.

7   *Morrison Steamship Co Ltd v Greystoke Castle (Cargo Owners)* [1947] AC 265, [1946] 2 All ER
    696, HL; and see *The Toward* (1899) Shipping Gazette, 8 May; *The Minnetonka* [1905] P 206, 10
    Asp MLC 142, CA (right to recover substituted expenses). The right to recover is subject to the
    statutory provisions as to apportionment of loss where both vessels are to blame: see *Morrison
    Steamship Co Ltd v Greystoke Castle (Cargo Owners)*; and see PARA 771 et seq.

809.   Interest. Interest until payment is usually allowed on all claims proved, as
being a part of the damages[1]. If the ship is totally lost and is in ballast, interest
generally runs from the date of her loss[2]. If, however, she is without cargo but
under charter and a sum in respect of freight is allowed, interest runs from the
date at which she might be expected to receive the freight[3], and, if she is loaded,
interest runs from the date on which she would probably have ended her voyage
and earned freight[4]. If the ship is damaged but not lost, interest is usually allowed
from the date on which the repair bill is paid[5].

1   *The Crathie* [1897] P 178, 8 Asp MLC 256; *The Kong Magnus* [1891] P 223, 7 Asp MLC 64; *The
    Joannis Vatis (No 2)* [1922] P 213, 16 Asp MLC 13; *The Berwickshire* [1950] P 204, [1950] 1 All
    ER 699 (where interest was allowed for the whole period between the collision and judgment
    although the plaintiff was an enemy alien for part of the period). Interest is not allowed on items
    of damage, eg estimated repairs and estimated demurrage in respect of which no expenditure or
    loss has yet been incurred: *The Napier Star* [1933] P 136, 64 Ll L Rep 197. As to the general
    discretion of all courts to award interest see CIVIL PROCEDURE vol 12A (2015) PARA 1235 et seq;
    FINANCIAL INSTRUMENTS AND TRANSACTIONS vol 49 (2015) PARA 94; and as to the measure
    of damages generally see PARA 793.
2   *The Northumbria* (1869) LR 3 A & E 6. As to damages where the vessel is totally lost see
    PARA 796.
3   *The Kate* [1899] P 165, 8 Asp MLC 539.
4   *The Northumbria* (1869) LR 3 A & E 6. As to the payment of freight see CARRIAGE AND
    CARRIERS vol 7 (2015) PARA 568 et seq.
5   *The Hebe* (1847) 2 Wm Rob 530. As to damages where the vessel is not lost see PARA 799. Interest
    awarded by the Admiralty Court on damages for collision and included in the total award of
    damages is interest of money (see INCOME TAXATION vol 58 (2014) PARA 505): *The Norseman*
    [1957] P 224, [1957] 2 All ER 660, [1957] 1 Lloyd's Rep 503.

(iii) Rights in rem and Rights in personam; Limitation of Time

810.   Admiralty jurisdiction in rem and in personam. The Admiralty
jurisdiction of the High Court[1] extends to any claim for damage done by or
received by a ship, any claim for loss of life or personal injury[2] in consequence of
a defect in a ship or the wrongful act, neglect or default of her owners, charterers
etc or of any persons for whom they are responsible, in her navigation or
management, and any claim for loss of or damage to goods carried in a ship[3].

   An action in rem[4] lies where there is a maritime lien or other charge on a ship[5].
Irrespective of the existence of such lien, if the claim arises in connection with a
ship, and if the person who would be liable on the claim in an action in personam
was, when the cause of action arose, the owner or charterer of, or in possession
or control of, the ship, an action in rem lies against that ship, or any other ship,
if in either case at the time when the action is brought the ship is beneficially
owned as respects all the shares in her by that person[6].

   An action in personam in respect of a claim for damage, loss of life or personal
injury arising out of a collision between ships, or out of the carrying out or failure
to carry out a manoeuvre by one or more of two or more ships, or out of
non-compliance with the Collision Regulations[7] by one or more of two or more
ships, lies in a court in England or Wales only if the defendant has his habitual
residence or place of business in England or Wales, or the cause of action arose
within inland waters of England or Wales or the limits of a port there, or an action

arising out of the same incident or series of incidents is proceeding, or has been
determined, in the court[8].

1 As the Admiralty jurisdiction of the High Court see the Senior Courts Act 1981 ss 20–24; and
PARA 85 et seq.
2 As to damages for personal injuries see PARA 792.
3 See the Senior Courts Act 1981 s 20(1), (2)(d)–(g); and PARA 93 et seq. As to negligence in the
construction of ships see PARA 759; as to negligence in navigation see PARA 760; as to the parties
liable see PARA 779 et seq; and as to damage to cargo see PARAS 791, 808.
4 As to Admiralty actions in rem see PARA 92 et seq.
5 See the Senior Courts Act 1981 s 21(3); and PARA 93. A possessory lien by ship repairers is not
an 'other charge': *Smith's Dock Co Ltd v St Merriel (Owners), The St Merriel* [1963] P 247, [1963]
1 All ER 537, [1963] 1 Lloyd's Rep 63.
6 See the Senior Courts Act 1981 s 21(4); and PARA 93. See also *Smith's Dock Co Ltd v St Merriel
(Owners), The St Merriel* [1963] P 247, [1963] 1 All ER 537; *I Congreso del Partido* [1978] QB
500, [1978] 1 All ER 1169, [1977] 1 Lloyd's Rep 536 (revsd [1983] 1 AC 244, [1981] 2 All ER
1064, [1981] 2 Lloyd's Rep 367, HL). In the case of a ship chartered by demise, the demise
charterer is the beneficial owner: *Medway Drydock and Engineering Co Ltd v MV Andrea Ursula,
The Andrea Ursula* [1973] QB 265, [1971] 1 All ER 821, [1971] 1 Lloyd's Rep 145.
7 Ie the International Regulations for Preventing Collisions at Sea (London, 20 October 1972; TS 77
(1977); Cmnd 6962): see PARA 690.
8 See the Senior Courts Act 1981 s 22(1), (2); and PARA 94. See also *Konstantinidis v World Tankers
Corpn Inc, The World Harmony* [1967] P 341, sub nom *The World Harmony, Konstantinidis v
World Tankers Corpn Inc* [1965] 2 All ER 139, [1965] 1 Lloyd's Rep 244.

811. Maritime lien. There is a maritime lien[1] against a ship and her freight for
all damage by collision done by that ship which is caused by the negligence of the
employees, either of the owners[2] or of those in whom the control of the ship is
vested with the consent of the owners, within the scope of their employment[3].
Every such lien may be carried into effect, when opportunity offers, by the arrest
of the ship in an action in rem[4].

The object is the satisfaction of the claim of the injured party out of the
property seized, and, if the owners do not acknowledge service, the proceedings
only enforce the lien against the property that is the subject of the claim (the res);
but, if they do acknowledge service, the proceedings are a means of enforcing
against them the complete claim[5].

The maritime lien against the freight may be enforced by arrest of the cargo to
make the owners pay the amount into court[6].

A maritime lien exists against any vessel doing damage by collision[7], and
whether the collision was on the high seas or within the limits of a port[8].

1 As to maritime liens see PARA 964 et seq.
2 As to the vicarious liability of shipowners see PARA 780.
3 As to negligence causing damage see PARA 756 et seq; as to the incidence of liability see PARA 779
et seq; and as to liens for damage done by a ship see PARA 967.
4 As to the procedure of arrest see PARA 161 et seq; and as to actions in rem for damage done by
or to a ship see especially PARA 810.
5 *The Dictator* [1892] P 304 at 313, 320, 7 Asp MLC 251 at 254, 256; *The Gemma* [1899] P 285,
8 Asp MLC 585, CA; and see *The Dupleix* [1912] P 8, 12 Asp MLC 122; *The Joannis Vatis (No
2)* [1922] P 213, 16 Asp MLC 13; and PARA 92.
6 *The Flora* (1866) LR 1 A & E 45; *The Roecliff* (1869) LR 2 A & E 363 at 364; and as to freight cf
The Victor (1860) Lush 72; *The Leo* (1862) Lush 444; *The Orpheus* (1871) LR 3 A & E 308.
Freight collected and paid into a bank cannot be arrested, nor can a warrant be issued for the arrest
of freight apart from the warrant to arrest the ship or cargo: *The Kaleten* (1914) 30 TLR 572. As
to the lien on freight see PARA 968.
7 *The Sarah* (1862) Lush 549 (vessel without masts or sails and usually propelled by a pole).
8 See *The Veritas* [1901] P 304 at 311, 9 Asp MLC 237 at 241.

812. Limitation of time for proceedings. An action to enforce any claim or
lien against a ship[1] or her owners in respect of damage or loss caused by the fault
of that ship to another ship, her cargo or freight or any property on board her, or
for damages for loss of life or personal injury caused by the fault of that ship to

any person on board another ship, must normally be begun within two years of the date when the damage or loss was caused or the loss of life or injury was suffered[2].

1   As to the meaning of 'ship' see PARA 229. As to maritime liens see PARA 964 et seq.
2   See the Merchant Shipping Act 1995 s 190(1), (3); and PARA 1013. As to the time limit for proceedings for contribution founded on Admiralty jurisdiction see PARA 151; and as to the enforcement of maritime liens see PARA 991 et seq. As to damages for personal injuries see PARA 792; and as to damages for loss of or damage to vessel see PARA 793 et seq.

(7) COLLISION AS AFFECTING SALVAGE

813. Assistance after collision. If salvage services[1] were rendered necessary by the faulty navigation of the salving vessel, it seems that neither the owner nor the crew can obtain a salvage reward[2]. When two vessels have been in collision and are in danger from one another, and one of them is towed away from the other, salvage may be payable by both to the salvor[3].

1   As to salvage generally see PARA 849 et seq.
2   As to salvage reward see PARAS 860 et seq, 866.
3   *The Vandyck* (1881) 7 PD 42 (affd (1882) 5 Asp MLC 17, CA); *The Emilie Galline* [1903] P 106, 9 Asp MLC 401; *The Port Caledonia and The Anna* [1903] P 184, 9 Asp MLC 479. As to the measure of damages generally see PARA 793 et seq.

814. Damage received during salvage. When a vessel is damaged by collision without her own fault, while rendering salvage services[1], it is necessary to ascertain the amount of the damages sustained and to award this as part of the salvage remuneration, but, where this cannot be ascertained, the salvage award must be assessed on a liberal scale taking the damages sustained into account[2].

If the salving vessel negligently collides with and damages the vessel which she is salving, her owners do not necessarily forfeit their right to a salvage award, but they have to pay for the damage by the collision[3]. The owners of the salving vessel are liable for the damage caused, as the master was acting within the scope of his authority in attempting to salve[4].

The salvage expenses of a vessel damaged by collision through the negligence of another vessel, although ordinarily recoverable from the owners of the wrongdoing vessel[5] cannot be recovered if the salvage is chargeable to improper abandonment[6].

Where another vessel negligently collides with a wreck whilst salvors are in possession, the salvors are entitled to sue for damages done to it; the owners and salvors of the wreck between them are entitled to recover the whole value, such value being dependent on whether the salvage operations would have been successful[7]. A claim may be made for loss of salvage where a vessel engaged in performing salvage services is sunk by the negligence of another vessel[8].

1   As to salvage see PARA 851 et seq.
2   *The Mud Hopper (No 4)* (1879) 4 Asp MLC 103; *The Sunniside* (1883) 8 PD 137, 5 Asp MLC 140; *Baku Standard (Owners) v Angèle (Owners)* [1901] AC 549, 9 Asp MLC 197, PC. See further PARA 899.
3   See PARA 895. As to the measure of damages see PARA 793 et seq.
4   *The Thetis* (1869) LR 2 A & E 365. As to the vicarious liability of shipowners see PARA 780.
5   A probable but discretionary outlay for towage, if there had been no collision, cannot be deducted from the salvage expenses: see *HMS Inflexible* (1857) Sw 200.
6   *The Linda* (1857) Sw 306. As to intervention in the salvage action by the wrongdoer see *The Diana* (1874) 2 Asp MLC 366. As to whether costs in the salvage action are recoverable from the wrongdoer see *The Legatus* (1856) Sw 168; *The British Commerce* (1884) 9 PD 128, 5 Asp MLC 335.

7 *The Zelo* [1922] P 9, 15 Asp MLC 428.
8 *The Betsey Caines* (1826) 2 Hag Adm 28.

9. ACCIDENT INVESTIGATIONS AND INQUIRIES

(1) MARINE ACCIDENT INVESTIGATIONS

815. Appointment of marine accident inspectors. The Secretary of State[1] must, for the purpose of the investigation of any such accidents[2] as are mentioned in heads (1) and (2) below, namely[3]:

    (1)   any accident involving a ship or ship's boat[4] where, at the time of the accident, the ship is a United Kingdom ship[5] or the ship (or, in a case of an accident involving a ship's boat, that boat) is within United Kingdom waters[6]; and

    (2)   such other accidents involving ships or ships' boats as the Secretary of State may determine[7],

appoint such number of persons as he may determine to be inspectors of marine accidents; and he must appoint one of those persons to be Chief Inspector of Marine Accidents[8].

1   As to the Secretary of State see PARA 36.
2   As to the meaning of 'accident' see PARA 816. See also note 4.
3   Merchant Shipping Act 1995 s 267(1). The text refers to any such accidents as are mentioned in s 267(2) (see heads (1) and (2) in the text): see s 267(1).
4   For these purposes, references to an accident involving a ship or ship's boat include references to an accident occurring on board a ship or ship's boat (and any reference to a ship or ship's boat involved in an accident is to be construed accordingly): Merchant Shipping Act 1995 s 267(10)(a). 'Ship's boat' includes a life-raft: s 267(10)(b). As to the meaning of 'ship' see PARA 229.
5   As to the meaning of 'United Kingdom ship' see PARA 230.
6   Merchant Shipping Act 1995 s 267(1), (2)(a). As to the meaning of 'United Kingdom waters' see PARA 48 note 10.
7   Merchant Shipping Act 1995 s 267(1), (2)(b).
8   Merchant Shipping Act 1995 s 267(1). Any inspector of marine accidents has, for the purpose of discharging any functions conferred on him by or under s 267, the powers conferred on an inspector by s 259 (see PARA 49): s 267(8). Nothing in s 267 limits the powers of any authority under s 252 (see PARA 939), s 253 (see PARA 945) and s 254 (see PARA 1048): s 267(9). The Chief Inspector of Marine Accidents or, as the case may be, inspectors of marine accidents generally, must discharge such functions in addition to those conferred by or under s 267(1), (2) (see also the text and notes 1–7) and by or under s 267(3)–(6) (see PARA 816) as the Secretary of State may determine: s 267(7).

816. Meaning of 'accident'. For the purposes of those provisions of the Merchant Shipping Act 1995[1], and the regulations made thereunder[2], which govern the reporting and investigation of marine accidents, 'accident' means a marine casualty[3], a very serious marine casualty[4], a serious marine casualty[5] or a marine incident[6]. An 'accident' does not include a deliberate act or omission with the intention to cause harm to the safety of a ship, an individual or the environment[7].

1   Ie the Merchant Shipping Act 1995 s 267 (see PARA 815): see the Merchant Shipping (Accident Reporting and Investigation) Regulations 2012, SI 2012/1743, reg 3(1) (made under the Merchant Shipping Act 1995 s 267(3)–(6)). The Merchant Shipping (Accident Reporting and Investigation) Regulations 2012, SI 2012/1743, implement Parliament and Council Directive (EC) 2009/18 (OJ L131, 28.5.2009, p 114) establishing the fundamental principles governing the investigation of accidents in the maritime transport sector. Provision is made for the periodic review of the regulations by the Secretary of State: see reg 20. As to the Secretary of State see PARA 36.
2   Ie the Merchant Shipping (Accident Reporting and Investigation) Regulations 2012, SI 2012/1743 (see also PARA 821 et seq): see reg 3(1). As to the application of the regulations so made see PARA 821.
3   Merchant Shipping (Accident Reporting and Investigation) Regulations 2012, SI 2012/1743, reg 3(1)(a). As to the meaning of 'marine casualty' see PARA 817.
4   Merchant Shipping (Accident Reporting and Investigation) Regulations 2012, SI 2012/1743, reg 3(1)(b). As to the meaning of 'very serious marine casualty' see PARA 818.
5   Merchant Shipping (Accident Reporting and Investigation) Regulations 2012, SI 2012/1743, reg 3(1)(c). As to the meaning of 'serious marine casualty' see PARA 819.

6 Merchant Shipping (Accident Reporting and Investigation) Regulations 2012, SI 2012/1743, reg 3(1)(d). As to the meaning of 'marine incident' see PARA 820.
7 Merchant Shipping (Accident Reporting and Investigation) Regulations 2012, SI 2012/1743, reg 3(2).

817. Meaning of 'marine casualty'. For the purpose of the reporting and investigation of marine accidents[1] a 'marine casualty' is an event or sequence of events that has resulted in any of the following and has occurred directly by or in connection with the operation of a ship involving:

(1)   the death of, or serious injury[2] to, a person[3];
(2)   the loss of a person from a ship[4];
(3)   the loss, presumed loss or abandonment of a ship[5];
(4)   material damage to a ship[6];
(5)   the stranding or disabling of a ship, or the involvement of a ship in a collision[7];
(6)   material damage to marine infrastructure external of a ship, that could seriously endanger the safety of the ship, another ship or any individual[8]; or
(7)   pollution, or the potential for such pollution to the environment caused by damage to a ship or ships[9].

1 Ie for the purposes described in PARA 816.
2 'Serious injury' means (by virtue of the Merchant Shipping (Accident Reporting and Investigation) Regulations 2012, SI 2012/1743, reg 2(1)):
   (1)   any fracture, other than to a finger, thumb or toe;
   (2)   any loss of a limb or part of a limb;
   (3)   dislocation of the shoulder, hip, knee or spine;
   (4)   loss of sight, whether temporary or permanent;
   (5)   penetrating injury to the eye;
   (6)   any injury to a person employed or carried in a ship which occurs on board or during access which results in incapacitation for more than three consecutive days excluding the day of the accident; and
   (7)   any other injury leading to hypothermia or unconsciousness, requiring resuscitation, or requiring admittance to a hospital or other medical facility as an in-patient for more than 24 hours.
   'Incapacitation' means a person's inability to undertake his full range of normal activities: Merchant Shipping (Accident Reporting and Investigation) Regulations 2012, SI 2012/1743, reg 2(1).
3 Merchant Shipping (Accident Reporting and Investigation) Regulations 2012, SI 2012/1743, reg 3(1)(a)(i).
4 Merchant Shipping (Accident Reporting and Investigation) Regulations 2012, SI 2012/1743, reg 3(1)(a)(ii).
5 Merchant Shipping (Accident Reporting and Investigation) Regulations 2012, SI 2012/1743, reg 3(1)(a)(iii).
6 Merchant Shipping (Accident Reporting and Investigation) Regulations 2012, SI 2012/1743, reg 3(1)(a)(iv).
7 Merchant Shipping (Accident Reporting and Investigation) Regulations 2012, SI 2012/1743, reg 3(1)(a)(v).
8 Merchant Shipping (Accident Reporting and Investigation) Regulations 2012, SI 2012/1743, reg 3(1)(a)(vi).
9 Merchant Shipping (Accident Reporting and Investigation) Regulations 2012, SI 2012/1743, reg 3(1)(a)(vii).

818. Meaning of 'very serious marine casualty'. For the purpose of the reporting and investigation of marine accidents[1] a 'very serious marine casualty' is an event or sequence of events that has resulted in any of the following and has occurred directly by or in connection with the operation of a ship involving:

(1)   the total loss of a ship[2];
(2)   loss of life[3]; or
(3)   severe pollution[4].

1 Ie for the purposes described in PARA 816.

2   Merchant Shipping (Accident Reporting and Investigation) Regulations 2012, SI 2012/1743, reg 3(1)(b)(i).
3   Merchant Shipping (Accident Reporting and Investigation) Regulations 2012, SI 2012/1743, reg 3(1)(b)(ii).
4   Merchant Shipping (Accident Reporting and Investigation) Regulations 2012, SI 2012/1743, reg 3(1)(b)(iii). 'Severe pollution' has the same meaning as that set out by the International Maritime Organisation: reg 2(1). As to the International Maritime Organisation see PARA 12.

819.   Meaning of 'serious marine casualty'. For the purpose of the reporting and investigation of marine accidents[1] a 'serious marine casualty' is an event or sequence of events that has occurred directly by or in connection with the operation of a ship but which does not qualify as a very serious marine casualty[2], that involves:

(1)   fire[3];
(2)   explosion[4];
(3)   collision[5];
(4)   grounding[6];
(5)   contact[7];
(6)   heavy weather damage[8]; or
(7)   ice damage, or a suspected hull defect[9],

resulting in any of the following:

(a)   the immobilization of the main engines[10];
(b)   extensive accommodation damage[11];
(c)   severe structural damage including penetration of the hull under water rendering the ship unfit to proceed[12];
(d)   pollution[13]; or
(e)   a breakdown that necessitates towage or shore assistance[14].

1   Ie for the purposes described in PARA 816.
2   As to the meaning of 'very serious marine casualty' see PARA 818.
3   Merchant Shipping (Accident Reporting and Investigation) Regulations 2012, SI 2012/1743, reg 3(1)(c)(i).
4   Merchant Shipping (Accident Reporting and Investigation) Regulations 2012, SI 2012/1743, reg 3(1)(c)(ii).
5   Merchant Shipping (Accident Reporting and Investigation) Regulations 2012, SI 2012/1743, reg 3(1)(c)(iii).
6   Merchant Shipping (Accident Reporting and Investigation) Regulations 2012, SI 2012/1743, reg 3(1)(c)(iv).
7   Merchant Shipping (Accident Reporting and Investigation) Regulations 2012, SI 2012/1743, reg 3(1)(c)(v).
8   Merchant Shipping (Accident Reporting and Investigation) Regulations 2012, SI 2012/1743, reg 3(1)(c)(vi).
9   Merchant Shipping (Accident Reporting and Investigation) Regulations 2012, SI 2012/1743, reg 3(1)(c)(vii).
10 Merchant Shipping (Accident Reporting and Investigation) Regulations 2012, SI 2012/1743, reg 3(1)(c)(aa).
11 Merchant Shipping (Accident Reporting and Investigation) Regulations 2012, SI 2012/1743, reg 3(1)(c)(bb).
12 Merchant Shipping (Accident Reporting and Investigation) Regulations 2012, SI 2012/1743, reg 3(1)(c)(cc).
13 Merchant Shipping (Accident Reporting and Investigation) Regulations 2012, SI 2012/1743, reg 3(1)(c)(dd).
14 Merchant Shipping (Accident Reporting and Investigation) Regulations 2012, SI 2012/1743, reg 3(1)(c)(ee).

820.   Meaning of 'marine incident'. For the purpose of the reporting and investigation of marine accidents[1] a 'marine incident' is an event or sequences of events other than those resulting in a marine casualty, a very serious marine casualty or a serious marine casualty[2], which has occurred directly in connection with the operation of a ship that endangered, or if not corrected would endanger the safety of a ship, its occupants or any other person or the environment[3].

1   Ie for the purposes described in PARA 816.
2   Ie an event other than those listed in the Merchant Shipping (Accident Reporting and Investigation) Regulations 2012, SI 2012/1743, reg 3(1)(a)–(c) (see PARAS 817–819).
3   Merchant Shipping (Accident Reporting and Investigation) Regulations 2012, SI 2012/1743, reg 3(1)(d).

821. Application of provisions relating to the reporting and investigation of marine accidents. The provisions relating to the reporting and investigation of marine accidents[1] apply to accidents involving or occurring on board[2]:
(1)   any United Kingdom ship[3]; and
(2)   any other ship within the United Kingdom or United Kingdom waters[4].
However, an investigation may also be held[5] into an accident involving or occurring on board a ship which is not a United Kingdom ship and which at the time of the accident was not within the United Kingdom or United kingdom waters, if the Secretary of State[6] so determines[7].

1   Ie the provisions described in PARA 816.
2   Merchant Shipping (Accident Reporting and Investigation) Regulations 2012, SI 2012/1743, reg 4(1).
3   Merchant Shipping (Accident Reporting and Investigation) Regulations 2012, SI 2012/1743, reg 4(1)(a). For these purposes, 'United Kingdom ship' means a ship registered in the United Kingdom or a ship that is not registered under the law of any state but is eligible for registration in the United Kingdom under the Merchant Shipping Act 1995: Merchant Shipping (Accident Reporting and Investigation) Regulations 2012, SI 2012/1743, reg 2(1). As to the meaning of 'United Kingdom' see PARA 16 note 3. As to the registration of ships in the United Kingdom under the Merchant Shipping Act 1995 see PARA 245 et seq.
    Although head (1) in the text applies generally, the Merchant Shipping (Accident Reporting and Investigation) Regulations 2012, SI 2012/1743, reg 6 (see PARA 823) does not apply in relation to:
    (1)   a pleasure vessel (reg 4(1)(a)(i));
    (2)   a recreational craft which is hired on a bareboat basis (reg 4(1)(a)(ii)); or
    (3)   any other craft or boat, other than one carrying passengers, which is in commercial use in a harbour or on an inland waterway and is less than 8 metres overall in length (reg 4(1)(a)(iii)),
unless, in the case of a craft or boat mentioned in head (2) or head (3) above, the accident involves any of the following: explosion, fire, death, serious injury, capsize of a power-driven craft or boat, or severe pollution (see reg 4(1)(a)). As to the meaning of 'serious injury' see PARA 817 note 2. As to the meaning of 'severe pollution' see PARA 818 note 4. For these purposes, 'hired on a bareboat basis' means hired without a professional master, skipper or crew: see reg 4(3). 'Pleasure vessel' means:
    (a)   any vessel which is wholly owned by an individual or individuals and used only for the sport or pleasure of the owner or the immediate family or friends of the owner, or is owned by a body corporate and used only for the sport or pleasure of employees or officers of the body corporate, or their immediate family or friends; and is on a voyage or excursion which is one for which the owner is not paid for or in connection with operating the vessel or carrying any person, other than as a contribution to the direct expenses of the operation of the vessel incurred during the voyage or excursion; or
    (b)   any vessel which is wholly owned by or on behalf of a members' club formed for the purpose of sport or pleasure which, at the time it is being used, is used only for the sport or pleasure of members of the club or their immediate family, and for the use of which any charges levied are paid into club funds and applied for the general use of the club; and
    (c)   in the case of any vessel referred to in head (a) or head (b) above, no payments other than those mentioned are made by or on behalf of the users of the vessel, other than by the owner;
and, for these purposes, 'immediate family' means, in relation to an individual, the husband, wife or civil partner of the individual, and a brother, sister, ancestor or lineal descendant of that individual or that individual's husband, wife or civil partner: reg 2(1). Where a ship is managed by a person other than by the owner (whether on behalf of the owner or some other person, or on their own behalf), a reference in the Merchant Shipping (Accident Reporting and Investigation) Regulations 2012, SI 2012/1743, to the 'owner' is construed as including a reference to that person: reg 2(2).

4   Merchant Shipping (Accident Reporting and Investigation) Regulations 2012, SI 2012/1743, reg 4(1)(b). Although head (2) in the text applies generally, reg 6 and reg 10(1)–(3) (see PARA 827) only apply in relation to such a ship as in mentioned in head (2) in the text if:

    (1)   the ship is within the jurisdiction of a harbour master or Queen's harbour master appointed, or required to be appointed, under any enactment (reg 4(1)(b)(i));

    (2)   the ship is employed in carrying passengers to or from a port in the United Kingdom or a place mentioned in head (1) above (reg 4(1)(b)(ii)); or

    (3)   an inspector, or other person acting on behalf of the Chief Inspector, requires that any of the evidence mentioned in reg 10(1) or (2) be preserved (reg 4(1)(b)(iii)).

     For these purposes, 'inspector' means an inspector of marine accidents appointed by the Secretary of State under the Merchant Shipping Act 1995 s 267(1) (see PARA 815) and in the context of the investigation or a particular accident includes any person appointed to investigate that accident under the Merchant Shipping (Accident Reporting and Investigation) Regulations 2012, SI 2012/1743, reg 11(2) (see PARA 825): reg 2(1). 'Chief Inspector' means the Chief Inspector of Marine Accidents appointed by the Secretary of State under the Merchant Shipping Act 1995 s 267(1) and any Deputy Chief Inspector: Merchant Shipping (Accident Reporting and Investigation) Regulations 2012, SI 2012/1743, reg 2(1).

5   Ie under the Merchant Shipping (Accident Reporting and Investigation) Regulations 2012, SI 2012/1743, reg 8 (see PARA 824): see reg 4(2).

6   As to the Secretary of State see PARA 36.

7   Merchant Shipping (Accident Reporting and Investigation) Regulations 2012, SI 2012/1743, reg 4(2).

822. Objective of a marine investigation.

The sole objective of the investigation of an accident[1], under the provisions which govern the reporting and investigation of marine accidents[2], is the prevention of future accidents through the ascertainment of its causes and circumstances[3]. It is not the purpose of such an investigation to determine liability nor, except so far as is necessary to achieve the objective, to apportion blame[4].

1   As to the meaning of 'accident' for these purposes see PARA 816.

2   Ie the provisions described in PARA 816.

3   Merchant Shipping (Accident Reporting and Investigation) Regulations 2012, SI 2012/1743, reg 5(1).

4   Merchant Shipping (Accident Reporting and Investigation) Regulations 2012, SI 2012/1743, reg 5(2).

823. Duty to notify accidents and serious injuries.

When an accident[1] occurs, the following persons associated with the ship must notify the Chief Inspector[2] as soon as is practicable following the accident and by the quickest means available[3]:

    (1)   the master or, if he has not survived, the senior surviving officer[4]; and

    (2)   the ship's owner[5], unless he has ascertained to his satisfaction that the master or senior surviving officer has reported the accident in accordance with head (1) above[6].

In addition to any notification so made[7], the following persons must notify the Chief Inspector as soon as is practicable and by the quickest means available any accident of which they are aware[8]:

    (a)   in the case of an accident within or adjacent to the limits of any harbour, the harbour authority for that harbour[9];

    (b)   in the case of an accident on any inland waterway in the United Kingdom, the person, authority or body having responsibility for that waterway[10]; or

    (c)   an official of the Maritime and Coastguard Agency[11] in respect of an accident within United Kingdom waters[12].

Any person making such a report to the Chief Inspector[13] must, in so far as is practicable, include the following information[14]:

    (i)   name of ship and its International Maritime Organisation[15], official or fishing vessel number[16];

    (ii)   type of ship[17];

    (iii)   date and time of the accident[18];

(iv)   latitude and longitude or geographical position in which the accident occurred[19];

(v)   name and port of registry of any other ship involved[20];

(vi)   number of people killed or seriously injured and associated type or types of casualty[21];

(vii) brief details of the accident including ship, cargo or other damage[22];

(viii) if the ship is fitted with a voyage data recorder[23], the make and model of the recorder[24];

(ix)   ports of departure and destination[25];

(x)   Traffic separation scheme if appropriate[26];

(xi)   place on board[27]; and

(xii) the nature of any pollution that occurs as a result of an accident[28].

In addition to making such notification[29], the persons specified in heads (1), (2), (a) and (b) above, must, so far as is reasonably practicable, ensure that the circumstances of every accident are examined and that a report giving the findings of such examination, stating any measures taken or proposed to prevent a recurrence, must be provided to the Chief Inspector as soon as is practicable[30].

Failure to comply with certain of the above requirements is an offence[31].

1   As to the meaning of 'accident' for these purposes see PARA 816.
2   As to the meaning of 'Chief Inspector' see PARA 821 note 4.
    Any notice or other document required or authorised by any provision of the Merchant Shipping (Accident Reporting and Investigation) Regulations 2012, SI 2012/1743, to be served on or given to any person may be served or given:
    (1)   by delivering it to that person (reg 18(a));
    (2)   by leaving it at their usual or last-known residence or place of business, whether in the United Kingdom or elsewhere (reg 18(b));
    (3)   by sending it to them by post at that address (reg 18(c)); or
    (4)   by sending it to them by facsimile, or other means which produces a document containing a text of the communication, or by electronic mail in which event the document shall be regarded as having been served when it is sent (reg 18(d)). As to the service and giving of notices see PARA 823 note 2.
3   Merchant Shipping (Accident Reporting and Investigation) Regulations 2012, SI 2012/1743, reg 6(1). In connection with the application of reg 6 see PARA 821 notes 3, 4.
4   Merchant Shipping (Accident Reporting and Investigation) Regulations 2012, SI 2012/1743, reg 6(1)(a). For these purposes, 'senior surviving officer' means the senior surviving officer in the deck department and, if there is no surviving officer in the deck department, whoever is the senior surviving officer between the senior surviving engineer officer or the senior surviving electro-technical officer: reg 2(1).
5   In connection with the meaning of 'owner' see PARA 821 note 3.
6   Merchant Shipping (Accident Reporting and Investigation) Regulations 2012, SI 2012/1743, reg 6(1)(b).
7   Ie under the Merchant Shipping (Accident Reporting and Investigation) Regulations 2012, SI 2012/1743, reg 6(1) (see the text and notes 1–6): see reg 6(2).
8   Merchant Shipping (Accident Reporting and Investigation) Regulations 2012, SI 2012/1743, reg 6(2).
9   Merchant Shipping (Accident Reporting and Investigation) Regulations 2012, SI 2012/1743, reg 6(2)(a).
10 Merchant Shipping (Accident Reporting and Investigation) Regulations 2012, SI 2012/1743, reg 6(2)(b).
11 As to the Maritime and Coastguard Agency see PARA 57.
12 Merchant Shipping (Accident Reporting and Investigation) Regulations 2012, SI 2012/1743, reg 6(2)(c).
13 Ie pursuant to either the Merchant Shipping (Accident Reporting and Investigation) Regulations 2012, SI 2012/1743, reg 6(1) (see the text and notes 1–6) or reg 6(2) (see the text and notes 7–12): see reg 6(3).
14 Merchant Shipping (Accident Reporting and Investigation) Regulations 2012, SI 2012/1743, reg 6(3).
15 As to the International Maritime Organisation see PARA 12.

16 Merchant Shipping (Accident Reporting and Investigation) Regulations 2012, SI 2012/1743, Schedule para (a).
17 Merchant Shipping (Accident Reporting and Investigation) Regulations 2012, SI 2012/1743, Schedule para (b).
18 Merchant Shipping (Accident Reporting and Investigation) Regulations 2012, SI 2012/1743, Schedule para (c).
19 Merchant Shipping (Accident Reporting and Investigation) Regulations 2012, SI 2012/1743, Schedule para (d).
20 Merchant Shipping (Accident Reporting and Investigation) Regulations 2012, SI 2012/1743, Schedule para (e).
21 Merchant Shipping (Accident Reporting and Investigation) Regulations 2012, SI 2012/1743, Schedule para (f).
22 Merchant Shipping (Accident Reporting and Investigation) Regulations 2012, SI 2012/1743, Schedule para (g).
23 For these purposes, 'Voyage data recorder' means the electronic or mechanical equipment which may be installed on a ship to record key navigational and control information: Merchant Shipping (Accident Reporting and Investigation) Regulations 2012, SI 2012/1743, reg 2(1).
24 Merchant Shipping (Accident Reporting and Investigation) Regulations 2012, SI 2012/1743, Schedule para (h).
25 Merchant Shipping (Accident Reporting and Investigation) Regulations 2012, SI 2012/1743, Schedule para (i).
26 Merchant Shipping (Accident Reporting and Investigation) Regulations 2012, SI 2012/1743, Schedule para (j).
27 Merchant Shipping (Accident Reporting and Investigation) Regulations 2012, SI 2012/1743, Schedule para (k).
28 Merchant Shipping (Accident Reporting and Investigation) Regulations 2012, SI 2012/1743, Schedule para (l).
29 Ie under the Merchant Shipping (Accident Reporting and Investigation) Regulations 2012, SI 2012/1743, reg 6(1)–(3) (see the text and notes 1–28): see reg 6(4) (amended by SI 2013/2882).
30 Merchant Shipping (Accident Reporting and Investigation) Regulations 2012, SI 2012/1743, reg 6(4) (as amended: see note 29).
31 A person is guilty of an offence, punishable on summary conviction by a fine, if:
    (1)   being a person mentioned in the Merchant Shipping (Accident Reporting and Investigation) Regulations 2012, SI 2012/1743, reg 6(1), (2)(a) or (b) (see the text and notes 1–10), they fail without reasonable cause to report an accident as required by reg 6 (reg 19(1)(a));
    (2)   being such a person, they fail without reasonable cause to provide information as required by reg 6(3) (see the text and notes 11–14) (reg 19(1)(b)); or
    (3)   they falsely claim to have any additional information or new evidence pertaining to any accident (reg 19(1)(c)).
    As to the powers of magistrates' courts to issue fines on summary conviction see SENTENCING vol 92 (2015) PARA 176.

824. Safety investigations and preliminary assessments.

A 'safety investigation' is[1] an investigation or inquiry into an accident[2] conducted with the objective of preventing future accidents; and a 'preliminary assessment' is a preparatory evaluation by the Chief Inspector[3] which is intended to establish the likely causes and circumstances of an accident with a view to deciding whether or not a safety investigation should be undertaken[4]. In the case of a serious marine casualty[5], in relation to a qualifying vessel[6], the Chief Inspector must carry out a preliminary assessment in order to decide whether or not to undertake a safety investigation[7].

The Chief Inspector must ensure a safety investigation is carried out in relation to any accident[8] that is a very serious marine casualty[9] as regards a qualifying vessel[10]; may decide to undertake a safety investigation in relation to an accident that is a serious marine casualty having carried out[11] a preliminary assessment[12]; and may carry out a safety investigation in relation to an accident that is a marine casualty[13]. Where the Chief Inspector has received an accident notification[14] he must decide whether or not a safety investigation should be carried out[15].

Notwithstanding a decision not to investigate, the Chief Inspector may at any subsequent time undertake a safety investigation if satisfied that there is a good reason in the interests of future safety to do so[16]. He may also re-open a safety investigation if, following its completion, new and important evidence is discovered which in his opinion could have a material effect on any safety recommendations made[17].

1   Ie for the purposes of the provisions described in PARA 816.
2   As to the meaning of 'accident' for these purposes see PARA 816.
3   As to the meaning of 'Chief Inspector' see PARA 821 note 4.
4   Merchant Shipping (Accident Reporting and Investigation) Regulations 2012, SI 2012/1743, reg 2(1). For the purposes of a preliminary assessment the powers in the Merchant Shipping Act 1995 s 259 (powers of inspectors: see PARA 49) apply: Merchant Shipping (Accident Reporting and Investigation) Regulations 2012, SI 2012/1743, reg 7(4).
5   As to the meaning of 'serious marine casualty' see PARA 819.
6   Ie vessel covered by Parliament and Council Directive (EC) 2009/18 (OJ L131, 28.5.2009, p 114) establishing the fundamental principles governing the investigation of accidents in the maritime transport sector (see PARA 816 note 1).
7   Merchant Shipping (Accident Reporting and Investigation) Regulations 2012, SI 2012/1743, reg 7(1). When carrying out a preliminary assessment the Chief Inspector must take into account, but need not be limited to:
    (1)   the seriousness of the accident (Merchant Shipping (Accident Reporting and Investigation) Regulations 2012, SI 2012/1743, reg 7(2)(a));
    (2)   the type of vessel and or cargo involved (reg 7(2)(b));
    (3)   the potential for the findings of a safety investigation to lead to the prevention of future accidents (reg 7(2)(c)).
    In relation to any preliminary assessment which the Chief Inspector has conducted under reg 7 the Chief Inspector must decide, having regard to the objective set out in reg 5 (see PARA 822), whether it is appropriate in the circumstances to conduct a safety investigation leading to the publication of a report: reg 11(8). Where the Chief Inspector decides not to undertake a safety investigation into a serious marine casualty in relation to a vessel covered by Parliament and Council Directive (EC) 2009/18 (OJ L131, 28.5.2009, p 114), the reasons for that decision must be recorded and notified to the European Commission: Merchant Shipping (Accident Reporting and Investigation) Regulations 2012, SI 2012/1743, reg 7(3).
8   In the case of an accident to which the Merchant Shipping (Accident Reporting and Investigation) Regulations 2012, SI 2012/1743, reg 3 (see PARA 816) applies, the Chief Inspector may decide not to carry out a safety investigation if satisfied, or it is otherwise established to his satisfaction, that any loss of life resulted from suicide or natural causes or any serious injury resulted from attempted suicide, and in such circumstances the Chief Inspector may discontinue any safety investigation which has already been commenced: reg 8(8).
9   As to the meaning of 'very serious marine casualty' see PARA 818.
10 Merchant Shipping (Accident Reporting and Investigation) Regulations 2012, SI 2012/1743, reg 8(1).
11 Ie in accordance with the Merchant Shipping (Accident Reporting and Investigation) Regulations 2012, SI 2012/1743, reg 7(1), (2) (see the text and note 1–7).
12 Merchant Shipping (Accident Reporting and Investigation) Regulations 2012, SI 2012/1743, reg 8(2). Before deciding whether a safety investigation should be carried out and if so, what form it should take, the Chief Inspector may obtain such information as he considers necessary concerning the accident and any remedial action taken as a result: reg 8(6). Any person mentioned in reg 6(1) or (2) (see PARA 823), as well as any other person who is in possession of information requested by an inspector for the purposes of reg 8(6), must provide such information to the best of their ability and knowledge: reg 8(7).
13 Merchant Shipping (Accident Reporting and Investigation) Regulations 2012, SI 2012/1743, reg 8(4). As to the meaning of 'marine casualty' see PARA 820.
14 Ie notification under the Merchant Shipping (Accident Reporting and Investigation) Regulations 2012, SI 2012/1743, reg 6(1) or (2) or a report under reg 6(4) (see PARA 823). As to the service and giving of notices see PARA 823 note 2.
15 Merchant Shipping (Accident Reporting and Investigation) Regulations 2012, SI 2012/1743, reg 8(5). The Chief Inspector must publish details of his decision as soon as is reasonably practical, in such manner as is seen fit: reg 8(5).
16 Merchant Shipping (Accident Reporting and Investigation) Regulations 2012, SI 2012/1743, reg 9(1).

17 Merchant Shipping (Accident Reporting and Investigation) Regulations 2012, SI 2012/1743, reg
    9(2). Any safety investigation may be re-opened either in whole or as to any part of it and a
    re-opened investigation is subject to and conducted in accordance with the provisions of the
    Merchant Shipping (Accident Reporting and Investigation) Regulations 2012, SI 2012/1743: reg
    9(3).

825. Conduct of safety investigations. A safety investigation[1] must be started
as promptly as is practicable by the Chief Inspector[2] after an accident[3], occurs,
and in any event no later than two months after the Chief Inspector is notified of
its occurrence[4]. The investigation must include but is not limited to:

    (1)   the collection and analysis of evidence[5];

    (2)   the identification of causal factors[6]; and

    (3)   where appropriate, the making of safety recommendations[7].

If the Chief Inspector decides[8] that a safety investigation must be carried out,
it must be undertaken by one or more inspectors at such times and places and in
such manner as appear to them most conducive to achieving the objective[9] of a
safety investigation[10]. A safety investigation may extend to cover, but need not be
limited to:

    (a)   all events and circumstances preceding the accident together with
            subsequent events and circumstances[11];

    (b)   issues involving salvage and pollution connected with the accident[12];
            and

    (c)   the conduct of search and rescue operations[13],

if in the opinion of the Chief Inspector they are relevant to future safety[14].

The Chief Inspector may subsequently decide to discontinue a safety
investigation of any accident (whether or not it involves a qualifying vessel[15]) at
any time[16].

Provision is made for witness anonymity and confidentiality[17].

1   See PARA 824.
2   As to the meaning of 'Chief Inspector' see PARA 821 note 4.
3   As to the meaning of 'accident' for these purposes see PARA 816.
4   Merchant Shipping (Accident Reporting and Investigation) Regulations 2012, SI 2012/1743, reg
    8(10). As to notifications see reg 6; and PARA 823. Public notice that a safety investigation has
    been commenced may be given in such manner as the Chief Inspector may think fit, and may invite
    any persons who so desire to present relevant evidence to an Inspector in such a manner and within
    such a time as is specified in the notice: reg 8(9). As to the service and giving of notices see
    PARA 823 note 2.
5   Merchant Shipping (Accident Reporting and Investigation) Regulations 2012, SI 2012/1743, reg
    8(3)(a).
6   Merchant Shipping (Accident Reporting and Investigation) Regulations 2012, SI 2012/1743, reg
    8(3)(b).
7   Merchant Shipping (Accident Reporting and Investigation) Regulations 2012, SI 2012/1743, reg
    8(3)(c).
8   Ie in accordance with the Merchant Shipping (Accident Reporting and Investigation) Regulations
    2012, SI 2012/1743, reg 8(2), (4), (5) (see PARA 824).
9   Ie the objective set out in the Merchant Shipping (Accident Reporting and Investigation)
    Regulations 2012, SI 2012/1743, reg 5 (see PARA 822).
10 Merchant Shipping (Accident Reporting and Investigation) Regulations 2012, SI 2012/1743, reg
    11(1). When the Chief Inspector is conducting a safety investigation into an accident he must take
    into account the provisions of the IMO guidelines on the fair treatment of seafarers (ie the
    Resolution and guidelines on fair treatment of seafarers in the event of a maritime accident): regs
    2(1), 11(11). The Chief Inspector may also appoint one or more persons who are not inspectors
    appointed under Merchant Shipping Act 1995 for the purpose of carrying out an investigation in
    circumstances where inspectors appointed under the Act are not conveniently available or where
    the persons appointed have special qualifications or experience, and such persons will have the
    powers conferred on an inspector by ss 259, 267(8) (see PARAS 49, 815): Merchant Shipping
    (Accident Reporting and Investigation) Regulations 2012, SI 2012/1743, reg 11(2).
        Every person required to attend before an inspector must be allowed the reasonable expenses
    of attending, payable by the Secretary of State: reg 11(4). As to the Secretary of State see PARA 36.

Any person (not being a solicitor or other professional legal adviser acting solely on behalf of the person required to attend) who has been allowed by an inspector to be present, or who has been nominated to be present by a person required to attend, at a witness interview before an inspector, may at any time be excluded from being present by the inspector with the agreement of the Chief Inspector, if both the inspector and Chief Inspector have substantial reason to believe that his presence would hamper the investigation with the result that the objective in reg 5 (see PARA 822) is likely to be hindered and future safety thereby endangered, and the Chief Inspector is satisfied, having regard to all the circumstances, that it is proper to exclude that person: reg 11(5). As to the meaning of 'inspector' see PARA 821 note 4. Where a person nominated to be present has been excluded in this way, the person required to attend may be entitled to nominate another person to be present at the witness interview in place of the excluded person and the same conditions as to their continued presence then apply to that other person: reg 11(6). An inspector may record a witness interview of any person who is assisting a safety investigation carried out in accordance with the Merchant Shipping (Accident Reporting and Investigation) Regulations 2012, SI 2012/1743, in any manner that he considers reasonable: reg 11(12).

11 Merchant Shipping (Accident Reporting and Investigation) Regulations 2012, SI 2012/1743, reg 11(3)(a).
12 Merchant Shipping (Accident Reporting and Investigation) Regulations 2012, SI 2012/1743, reg 11(3)(b).
13 Merchant Shipping (Accident Reporting and Investigation) Regulations 2012, SI 2012/1743, reg 11(3)(c).
14 Merchant Shipping (Accident Reporting and Investigation) Regulations 2012, SI 2012/1743, reg 11(3).
15 Ie vessel covered by Parliament and Council Directive (EC) 2009/18 (OJ L131, 28.5.2009, p 114) establishing the fundamental principles governing the investigation of accidents in the maritime transport sector (see PARA 816 note 1).
16 Merchant Shipping (Accident Reporting and Investigation) Regulations 2012, SI 2012/1743, reg 11(9). The Inspector must make any reasons for discontinuation publicly available: reg 11(9). Regulation 11(9) will not apply to the safety investigation of an accident involving a qualifying vessel that is a very serious marine casualty or a serious marine casualty, where following a preliminary assessment undertaken in accordance with reg 7(1), (2) (see PARA 824) a decision is made to conduct a safety investigation: reg 11(10). As to the meanings of 'very serious marine casualty' and 'serious marine casualty' see PARAS 818, 819.
17 Subject to reg 13, the names, addresses or any other details of anyone who has given evidence to an inspector must not be disclosed (reg 13(1)); and, unless the high court orders otherwise, the following documents or records must not be made available for purposes other than the investigation:

    (1)   all declarations or statements taken from persons by an inspector or supplied to him in the course of his investigation, together with any notes or recordings of witness interviews (subject to the proviso that a person who has given a declaration or statement to an inspector in the course of an investigation may make available a copy of his declaration or statement to another person as he sees fit) (reg 13(2)(a), (3));
    (2)   medical or confidential information regarding persons involved in an accident (reg 13(2)(b));
    (3)   any report made under reg 6(4) (see PARA 823) concerning the circumstances of an accident or serious injury (reg 13(2)(c));
    (4)   copies of the report other than the final report (except as mentioned in reg 14(4)(a), (5) or (12) (see PARA 828) (reg 13(2)(d));
    (5)   all correspondence received by the Chief Inspector from parties involved in a safety investigation (reg 13(2)(d));
    (6)   evidence from voyage data recorders (reg 13(2)(e));
    (7)   the notes made by an inspector or person appointed under reg 11(2) (see note 10), whether written or held electronically along with any recordings or photographs (reg 13(2)(f));
    (8)   all communications between persons having been involved in the operation of the ship or ships (reg 13(2)(g)); and
    (9)   Inspector's opinions expressed in the analysis of information (reg 13(2)(h)).

As to the meaning of 'voyage data recorder' see PARA 823 note 23.
However, any independent technical analysis commissioned by the Chief Inspector, and opinions expressed in such analysis, may be made publicly available if he considers it appropriate to do so: reg 13(4).
No order for disclosure of the documents or records listed in heads (1) to (9) above may be made by the court unless it is satisfied, having regard to the views of the Chief Inspector, that the interests of justice in disclosure outweigh any prejudice, or likely prejudice, to:
    (a)   the investigation into the accident to which the document or record relates (reg 13(5)(a));

(b)   any future accident investigation undertaken in the United Kingdom (reg 13(5)(b)); or
(c)   relations between the United Kingdom and any other state, or international organisation (reg 13(5)(c)).

Copies of information obtained from a voyage data recorder or from other recording systems, pertinent to the accident, including voice recordings (other than any recordings mentioned in head (1) above), video recordings and other electronic or magnetic recordings and any transcripts made from such information or recordings, may be provided at the discretion of the Chief Inspector to the police or other official authorities: reg 13(7). Information obtained from a voyage data recorder may be provided at the discretion of the Chief Inspector to the ship's owner: reg 13(8) (added by SI 2013/2882). In connection with the meaning of 'owner' see PARA 821 note 3.

The provisions of the Merchant Shipping (Accident Reporting and Investigation) Regulations 2012, SI 2012/1743, reg 13 are without prejudice to any rule of law which authorises or requires the withholding of any document or record or part thereof on the ground that disclosure of it would be injurious to the public interest: reg 13(6).

If any person without reasonable cause discloses or permits to be disclosed any information in contravention of reg 13(1), or makes available any documents or records in contravention of reg 13(2), they are guilty of an offence and liable on summary conviction to a fine: reg 19(3). As to the powers of magistrates' courts to issue fines on summary conviction see SENTENCING vol 92 (2015) PARA 176.

826.   Co-operation with other states. A safety investigation[1] commenced by the Chief Inspector[2] must, where appropriate, be conducted in co-operation with another member State[3] or another Substantially Interested State[4], and a Substantially Interested State is allowed to participate in a safety investigation led by the Chief Inspector at any stage of that investigation by mutual agreement[5]. Where a safety investigation has been commenced[6], the Chief Inspector and any other States involved must agree in the shortest possible time which of them is to lead the investigation[7] and the procedures to be adopted for the purposes of it[8]: where a Substantially Interested State has been allowed to participate in a safety investigation and no such agreement[9] has occurred then the Chief Inspector and such other member States or Substantially Interested States, or both must:

(1)   conduct parallel safety investigations[10];
(2)   exchange evidence and information with each other for the purposes, as far as possible, of reaching shared conclusions[11]; and
(3)   in the case of two member States conducting parallel safety investigations, notify the European Commission of the reasons for doing so[12].

The Chief Inspector may delegate the whole or any part of a safety investigation to another member State by mutual agreement with the member State[13]. Where an investigation[14] involves a ro-ro ferry or a high-speed passenger craft[15], the Chief Inspector must enable an EEA State to participate or co-operate in accordance with the IMO Code[16].

1   As to the meaning of 'safety investigation' see PARA 824.
2   Ie under the Merchant Shipping (Accident Reporting and Investigation) Regulations 2012, SI 2012/1743, reg 8: see PARA 824. As to the meaning of 'Chief Inspector' see PARA 821 note 4. When the Chief Inspector is requested to assist another member State in a safety investigation in which the United Kingdom is not involved then the costs of any such assistance provided must be agreed between them: reg 11(13).
3   Merchant Shipping (Accident Reporting and Investigation) Regulations 2012, SI 2012/1743, reg 12(1)(a).
4   Merchant Shipping (Accident Reporting and Investigation) Regulations 2012, SI 2012/1743, reg 12(1)(b). For these purposes a Substantially Interested State has equal rights and access to witnesses and evidence involved in a safety investigation (reg 12(4)(a)) and any representations that it may make to the lead investigating State must be taken into consideration for the purposes of the investigation (reg 12(4)(b)). For these purposes, reg 12(4)(a) applies only if the Chief Inspector is satisfied that the Substantially Interested State will comply with the provisions of Parliament and Council Directive (EC) 2009/18 (OJ L131, 28.5.2009, p 114) establishing the fundamental principles governing the investigation of accidents in the maritime transport sector (see PARA 816 note 1) art 9: Merchant Shipping (Accident Reporting and Investigation) Regulations 2012, SI 2012/1743, reg 12(5).

5 Merchant Shipping (Accident Reporting and Investigation) Regulations 2012, SI 2012/1743, reg 12(2).
6 Ie under the Merchant Shipping (Accident Reporting and Investigation) Regulations 2012, SI 2012/1743, reg 12(1) (see the text and notes 1–4).
7 Merchant Shipping (Accident Reporting and Investigation) Regulations 2012, SI 2012/1743, reg 12(3)(a).
8 Merchant Shipping (Accident Reporting and Investigation) Regulations 2012, SI 2012/1743, reg 12(3)(b).
9 Ie no agreement in accordance with the Merchant Shipping (Accident Reporting and Investigation) Regulations 2012, SI 2012/1743, 12(3)(a).
10 Merchant Shipping (Accident Reporting and Investigation) Regulations 2012, SI 2012/1743, reg 12(6)(a).
11 Merchant Shipping (Accident Reporting and Investigation) Regulations 2012, SI 2012/1743, reg 12(6)(b).
12 Merchant Shipping (Accident Reporting and Investigation) Regulations 2012, SI 2012/1743, reg 12(6)(c). As to the service and giving of notices see PARA 823 note 2.
13 Merchant Shipping (Accident Reporting and Investigation) Regulations 2012, SI 2012/1743, reg 12(7).
14 Ie an investigation conducted under the Merchant Shipping (Accident Reporting and Investigation) Regulations 2012, SI 2012/1743.
15 Ie a ro-ro ferry or high speed passenger craft to which Council Directive (EC) 1999/35 of 29 April 1999 (OJ L138, 01.06.1999, p 1) on a system of mandatory surveys for the safe operation of regular ro-ro ferry and high-speed passenger craft services applies (see PARA 603): see the Merchant Shipping (Accident Reporting and Investigation) Regulations 2012, SI 2012/1743, reg 11(1). Accordingly, for these purposes, 'ro-ro ferry' and 'high speed passenger craft' have the meanings given to them by Council Directive (EC) 1999/35 (OJ L138, 01.06.1999, p 1): see the Merchant Shipping (Accident Reporting and Investigation) Regulations 2012, SI 2012/1743, reg 2(1).
16 Merchant Shipping (Accident Reporting and Investigation) Regulations 2012, SI 2012/1743, reg 12(8). 'IMO Code' means the Code for the Investigation of Marine Casualties and Incidents adopted by the International Maritime Organisation by means of Assembly Resolution A.849(20) of 27 November 1997: see the Merchant Shipping (Accident Reporting and Investigation) Regulations 2012, SI 2012/1743, reg 2(1). As to the International Maritime Organisation see PARA 12. When a ro-ro ferry or high-speed passenger craft is involved in an accident in:
    (1)   United Kingdom waters a safety investigation must be started by the Chief Inspector (reg 12(9)(a)); or
    (2)   if the accident occurred outside of United Kingdom waters and outside the territorial waters of another member State the Chief Inspector must start a safety investigation if the United Kingdom was the last point of departure (reg 12(9)(b)).
In the case of an accident to which reg 12(9)(b) applies the United Kingdom remains responsible for the safety investigation unless it has been agreed with any other substantially interested member State, that the other member State will be responsible for leading the safety investigation.

827. **Preservation of evidence.** Following an accident[1] involving a United Kingdom ship[2] which is reportable[3], the following persons[4], namely the master (or, if he has not survived, the senior surviving officer)[5] and the ship's owner[6] (unless he has ascertained to his satisfaction that the master or senior surviving officer has duly reported the accident)[7], must so far as is practicable ensure that all[8]:

    (1)   charts[9];
    (2)   log books[10];
    (3)   recorded information relating to the period preceding, during and after an accident, howsoever recorded or retained, including information from a voyage data recorder[11] and video recorders[12]; and
    (4)   all documents or other records which might reasonably be considered pertinent to the accident[13],

are kept and that no alteration is made to any recordings or entries in them[14].

In the case of an accident involving a United Kingdom ship[15], the persons referred to above must also ensure that:

(a)   all information from a voyage data recorder or recording system relating to the circumstances of an accident is saved and preserved, in particular by taking steps, where necessary, to prevent such information from being overwritten[16]; and

(b)   any other equipment which might reasonably be considered pertinent to the investigation of the accident is so far as practicable left undisturbed[17].

The duty to ensure that documents, information or records are kept and not altered[18] and to ensure that information is saved and preserved, or that equipment is left undisturbed[19], continues until[20]:

(i)   published information is received from the Chief Inspector[21] that no safety investigation is to take place or that the investigation has been completed[22];

(ii)   30 days have passed since the Chief Inspector received an accident report[23] and no notice has been published by the Chief Inspector that he has decided to investigate the matter[24]; or

(iii)   the Chief Inspector or an inspector carrying out the investigation gives written notification that they are no longer required[25].

Following an accident in United Kingdom waters involving a ship which is not a United Kingdom ship, the persons referred to above must comply with the duty to ensure that documents, information or records are kept and not altered, or to ensure that information is saved and preserved, or that equipment is left undisturbed[26], if requested to do so by or on behalf of the Chief Inspector[27].

An inspector may, pending investigation, prohibit persons from gaining access to, or interfering with, any ship, ship's boat[28] or other equipment involved in an accident[29]. Following an accident, the Chief Inspector may, if it is considered reasonably necessary for the collection or preservation of evidence in connection with any safety investigation (including a preliminary examination[30]) relating to the accident, require any of the master (or, if he has not survived, the senior surviving officer) and the ship's owner to ensure that a ship is accessible to any inspector engaged in the investigation of such accident, until the process of collecting or preserving the evidence has been completed to the inspector's satisfaction[31].

Failure to comply with these requirements is an offence[32].

1   As to the meaning of 'accident' for these purposes see PARA 816.
2   Ie an accident to which the Merchant Shipping (Accident Reporting and Investigation) Regulations 2012, SI 2012/1743, reg 4 (see PARA 821) applies: reg 10(1). As to the meaning of 'United Kingdom ship' see PARA 821 note 3.
3   Ie under the Merchant Shipping (Accident Reporting and Investigation) Regulations 2012, SI 2012/1743, reg 6 (see PARA 823): see reg 10(1). As to the application of the regulations generally see PARA 821; and as to the application of reg 10 in particular see PARA 821 note 4. As to penalties for contravention see PARA 1128.
4   Ie the persons mentioned in the Merchant Shipping (Accident Reporting and Investigation) Regulations 2012, SI 2012/1743, reg 9(3) (see heads (1) and (2) in the text): see reg 9(1).
5   Merchant Shipping (Accident Reporting and Investigation) Regulations 2012, SI 2012/1743, reg 10(3)(a). As to the meaning of 'senior surviving officer' see PARA 823 note 4.
6   In connection with the meaning of 'owner' see PARA 821 note 3.
7   See the Merchant Shipping (Accident Reporting and Investigation) Regulations 2012, SI 2012/1743, reg 10(3)(b).
8   Merchant Shipping (Accident Reporting and Investigation) Regulations 2012, SI 2012/1743, reg 10(1).
9   Merchant Shipping (Accident Reporting and Investigation) Regulations 2012, SI 2012/1743, reg 10(1)(a).
10   Merchant Shipping (Accident Reporting and Investigation) Regulations 2012, SI 2012/1743, reg 10(1)(b).

11 As to the meaning of 'voyage data recorder' see PARA 823 note 23.

12 Merchant Shipping (Accident Reporting and Investigation) Regulations 2012, SI 2012/1743, reg 10(1)(c).

13 Merchant Shipping (Accident Reporting and Investigation) Regulations 2012, SI 2012/1743, reg 10(1)(d).

14 Merchant Shipping (Accident Reporting and Investigation) Regulations 2012, SI 2012/1743, reg 10(1). Any document, record or information mentioned in reg 10, properly required by an inspector to be produced for the purposes of a safety investigation (whether on board the ship involved or otherwise) may be retained by the inspector until the safety investigation is completed: reg 11(7). As to the meaning of 'inspector' see PARA 821 note 4.

15 See note 2.

16 Merchant Shipping (Accident Reporting and Investigation) Regulations 2012, SI 2012/1743, reg 10(2)(a).

17 Merchant Shipping (Accident Reporting and Investigation) Regulations 2012, SI 2012/1743, reg 10(2)(b).

18 Ie under the Merchant Shipping (Accident Reporting and Investigation) Regulations 2012, SI 2012/1743, reg 10(1) (see the text and notes 1–14): see reg 9(4).

19 Ie under the Merchant Shipping (Accident Reporting and Investigation) Regulations 2012, SI 2012/1743, reg 10(2) (see the text and notes 15–17): see reg 9(4).

20 Merchant Shipping (Accident Reporting and Investigation) Regulations 2012, SI 2012/1743, reg 9(4).

21 As to the meaning of 'Chief Inspector' see PARA 821 note 4.

22 Merchant Shipping (Accident Reporting and Investigation) Regulations 2012, SI 2012/1743, reg 10(4)(a).

23 Ie the report referred to in the Merchant Shipping (Accident Reporting and Investigation) Regulations 2012, SI 2012/1743, reg 6(1) (see PARA 823): see reg 10(4)(b).

24 Merchant Shipping (Accident Reporting and Investigation) Regulations 2012, SI 2012/1743, reg 10(4)(b).

25 Merchant Shipping (Accident Reporting and Investigation) Regulations 2012, SI 2012/1743, reg 10(4)(c).

26 Ie the requirements of the Merchant Shipping (Accident Reporting and Investigation) Regulations 2012, SI 2012/1743, reg 10(1), (2) (see the text and notes 1–17): see reg 10(5).

27 Merchant Shipping (Accident Reporting and Investigation) Regulations 2012, SI 2012/1743, reg 10(5).

28 'Ship's boat' includes a life-raft, painting punt and any boat normally carried by a ship: Merchant Shipping (Accident Reporting and Investigation) Regulations 2012, SI 2012/1743, reg 2(1).

29 Merchant Shipping (Accident Reporting and Investigation) Regulations 2012, SI 2012/1743, reg 10(6).

30 As to the meaning of 'preliminary examination' see PARA 824.

31 Merchant Shipping (Accident Reporting and Investigation) Regulations 2012, SI 2012/1743, reg 10(7). The Chief Inspector must not require a ship to which reg 4(1)(a), (b) or (c) apply to remain in United Kingdom waters any longer than is necessary for the collection or preservation, as the case may be, of such evidence and must take all reasonable steps to ensure that such evidence is collected or preserved expeditiously: reg 10(8). No such requirement is to be made unless the Chief Inspector has reasonable grounds for concern that if a ship to which reg 4(1)(a), (b) or (c) apply leaves United Kingdom waters, access to it, to any member of the crew, or to any evidence on board relating to the investigation, may subsequently be denied to him or any inspector conducting such investigation: reg 10(9).

32 If any person fails without reasonable cause to comply with any requirement, duty or prohibition in the Merchant Shipping (Accident Reporting and Investigation) Regulations 2012, SI 2012/1743, reg 10(1), (2), (6) or (7) (see the text and notes 1–31), they are guilty of an offence and liable on summary conviction to a fine: reg 19(2). As to the powers of magistrates' courts to issue fines on summary conviction see SENTENCING vol 92 (2015) PARA 176.

828. Reports. The Chief Inspector[1] must submit to the Secretary of State[2] a report of any safety investigation[3], and must make every effort to make such a report publicly available in the shortest possible time or within 12 months of the date of an accident[4] being notified to the Chief Inspector[5]. Where the Chief Inspector is of the view that a safety investigation will not have the potential to lead to the prevention of future accidents then a simplified report may be published in such manner as the Chief Inspector thinks fit[6]. No person may[7] disclose any information which has been furnished[8] to them[9] or permit such information to be disclosed, except with the prior consent in writing of the Chief Inspector, to any other[10] person[11].

A copy of the report when made publicly available must be given by the Chief Inspector to:

(1) any person who has been served[12] with a notice[13];

(2) those persons or bodies to whom recommendations have been addressed in that report[14];

(3) the Secretary of State[15];

(4) the IMO[16];

(5) any person or organisation whom the Chief Inspector considers may find the report useful or of interest[17]; and

(6) the European Commission, where the report pertains to Directive vessels[18] or where the Chief Inspector deems it appropriate[19].

The Chief Inspector may from time to time publish collective short reports of accidents which have not been the subject of a published[20] report[21], and may submit a report to the Secretary of State on any matter arising from the Chief Inspector's analysis of marine accident investigations[22].

1   As to the meaning of 'Chief Inspector' see PARA 821 note 4.

2   As to the Secretary of State see PARA 36.

3   Merchant Shipping (Accident Reporting and Investigation) Regulations 2012, SI 2012/1743, reg 14(1). As to the meaning of 'safety investigation' (ie an investigation conducted in accordance with reg 11) see PARA 824. A report in relation to an accident to which Parliament and Council Directive (EC) 2009/18 (OJ L131, 28.5.2009, p 114) establishing the fundamental principles governing the investigation of accidents in the maritime transport sector (see PARA 816 note 1) applies must contain but need not be limited to:

(1) the information set out in Annex 1 of the Directive (Merchant Shipping (Accident Reporting and Investigation) Regulations 2012, SI 2012/1743, reg 14(3)(a));

(2) conclusions relating to the facts of the evidence (reg 14(3)(b));

(3) where the facts cannot be clearly established, analysis and professional judgement to determine the probable facts (reg 14(3)(c)); and

(4) recommendations for future safety where appropriate (reg 14(3)(d)).

If any part of any document or analysis it contains (ie any part of any publication produced by the Chief Inspector as a result of a safety investigation) is based on information obtained in accordance with an inspector's powers under the Merchant Shipping Act 1995 ss 259, 267(8) (see PARAS 49, 815), that part is inadmissible in any judicial proceedings whose purpose or one of whose purposes is to attribute or apportion liability or blame unless a Court, having regard to the factors mentioned in the Merchant Shipping (Accident Reporting and Investigation) Regulations 2012, SI 2012/1743, reg 13(5)(b) or (c), determines otherwise: reg 14(14), (15). Where any inspector is required to attend judicial proceedings (ie any civil or criminal proceedings before any Court, or person having by law the power to hear, receive and examine evidence on oath) the inspector is not required to provide opinion evidence or analysis of information provided to them, or to provide information obtained in accordance with an inspector's powers under the Merchant Shipping Act 1995 ss 259, 267(8) where the purpose or one of the purposes of those proceedings is to attribute or apportion liability or blame unless a Court, having regard to all the factors mentioned in the Merchant Shipping (Accident Reporting and Investigation) Regulations 2012, SI 2012/1743, reg 13(5)(b) or (c) determines otherwise: reg 14(16), (17).

4   As to the meaning of 'accident' for these purposes see PARA 816.

5   Merchant Shipping (Accident Reporting and Investigation) Regulations 2012, SI 2012/1743, reg 14(2)(a). In the case of a report to which Parliament and Council Directive (EC) 2009/18 (OJ L131, 28.5.2009, p 114) applies, if it is not possible to produce such a report within that 12-month period, an interim report must be published within 12 months of the date of the accident being notified to the Chief Inspector: Merchant Shipping (Accident Reporting and Investigation) Regulations 2012, SI 2012/1743, reg 14(2)(b). For the purposes of reg 14(2) a report may be published in such manner as the Chief Inspector sees fit: reg 14(9). A report must not be made publicly available until the Chief Inspector has:

(1) served a notice under the Merchant Shipping (Accident Reporting and Investigation) Regulations 2012, SI 2012/1743, upon any person who, or organisation which, could be adversely affected by the report or, if that person is deceased, upon such person or

persons as appear to the Chief Inspector, at the time it is proposed to serve notice in accordance with these provisions, as best to represent the interests and reputation of the deceased in the matter (reg 14(4)(a)); and

(2)   considered the representations relating to the facts or analysis contained in the report which may be made to the Chief Inspector in accordance with reg 14(6) (which requires that the representations referred to in reg 14(4)(b) must be in writing and must be served on the Chief Inspector within 30 days of service of the notice referred to in reg 14(4)(b) or within such further period as may be allowed under reg 17 (see below)) by or on behalf of the persons served with such notice, or reg 14(7) (which provides that When a Substantially Interested State requests the Chief Inspector to supply it with a draft safety investigation report the Chief Inspector must not do so unless that State has agreed, in writing to comply with the provisions of Chapter 13 of the IMO Code (reg 14(4)(b));

and the report must be amended in such manner as the Chief Inspector thinks fit (reg 14(4). The notice referred to in reg 14(4)(a) must be accompanied by a draft copy of the report: reg 14(5). The Chief Inspector may extend the period of 30 days prescribed in reg 14(6), if he considers that there are good reasons to do so having regard to the requirements in reg 14(2) for a report of a safety investigation to be made available in the shortest time possible: reg 17(1). This power may be exercised notwithstanding that the prescribed period has expired: reg 17(3).

In connection with the admissibility of reports in other proceedings see *The Speedlink Vanguard and the European Gateway* [1987] QB 206, [1986] 3 All ER 554; *Hoyle v Rogers* [2014] EWCA Civ 257, [2015] QB265, [2014] 3 All ER 550.

6   Merchant Shipping (Accident Reporting and Investigation) Regulations 2012, SI 2012/1743, reg 14(9).

7   Ie subject to a court order under the Merchant Shipping (Accident Reporting and Investigation) Regulations 2012, SI 2012/1743, reg 13 (see PARA 825 note 17).

8   Ie furnished to them in accordance with the Merchant Shipping (Accident Reporting and Investigation) Regulations 2012, SI 2012/1743, reg 14(4) (see the text and notes 1–5) (reg 14(10)(a)) or which has otherwise been furnished to them by or on behalf of the Chief Inspector in advance of the publication of a report and whose confidentiality is protected by reg 13 (reg 14(10)(b)). If any person without reasonable cause discloses or permits to be disclosed any information in contravention of reg 14(10), they are guilty of an offence and liable on summary conviction to a fine: reg 19(3). As to the powers of magistrates' courts to issue fines on summary conviction see SENTENCING vol 92 (2015) PARA 176.

9   Merchant Shipping (Accident Reporting and Investigation) Regulations 2012, SI 2012/1743, reg 14(10)(a).

10   Ie except to such advisers as are necessary in order to make representations to the Chief Inspector referred to in the Merchant Shipping (Accident Reporting and Investigation) Regulations 2012, SI 2012/1743, reg 14(4)(b) (see note 5), and those advisers must be similarly be subject to the duty not to disclose the information or permit it to be disclosed: reg 14(10).

11   Merchant Shipping (Accident Reporting and Investigation) Regulations 2012, SI 2012/1743, reg 14(10). Where an inquest or fatal accident inquiry is to be held following an accident which has been subject to a safety investigation, a draft report may be made available in confidence to the coroner or procurator fiscal by the Chief Inspector: reg 14(13).

12   Ie in accordance with the Merchant Shipping (Accident Reporting and Investigation) Regulations 2012, SI 2012/1743, reg 14(4)(a) (see note 5).

13   Merchant Shipping (Accident Reporting and Investigation) Regulations 2012, SI 2012/1743, reg 14(11)(a). As to the service and giving of notices see PARA 823 note 2.

14   Merchant Shipping (Accident Reporting and Investigation) Regulations 2012, SI 2012/1743, reg 14(11)(b).

15   Merchant Shipping (Accident Reporting and Investigation) Regulations 2012, SI 2012/1743, reg 14(11)(c).

16   Merchant Shipping (Accident Reporting and Investigation) Regulations 2012, SI 2012/1743, reg 14(11)(d). As to the International Maritime Organisation see PARA 12.

17   Merchant Shipping (Accident Reporting and Investigation) Regulations 2012, SI 2012/1743, reg 14(11)(e). Data will be provided to the European Marine Casualty Information Platform ('EMCIP') in accordance with the requirements of Parliament and Council Directive (EC) 2009/18 (OJ L131, 28.5.2009, p 114) art 17: Merchant Shipping (Accident Reporting and Investigation) Regulations 2012, SI 2012/1743, regs 2(1), 14(12) (reg 2(1) amended by SI 2013/2882).

18   'Directive vessel' means a vessel covered by the scope of Parliament and Council Directive (EC) 2009/18 (OJ L131, 28.5.2009, p 114): Merchant Shipping (Accident Reporting and Investigation) Regulations 2012, SI 2012/1743, reg 2(1).

19 Merchant Shipping (Accident Reporting and Investigation) Regulations 2012, SI 2012/1743, reg 14(11)(f).

20 Ie a report published under the Merchant Shipping (Accident Reporting and Investigation) Regulations 2012, SI 2012/1743, reg 14(1) (see the text and notes 1–3).

21 Merchant Shipping (Accident Reporting and Investigation) Regulations 2012, SI 2012/1743, reg 15(1).

22 Merchant Shipping (Accident Reporting and Investigation) Regulations 2012, SI 2012/1743, reg 15(2).

829. Recommendations as to how future marine accidents may be prevented.

The Chief Inspector[1] may at any time make recommendations as to how future accidents[2] may be prevented[3]. The actions recommended must be addressed to those persons or bodies who, in the opinion of the Chief Inspector, are most fitted to implement them[4]; and recommendations must be made publicly available if the Chief Inspector considers that to do so is in the interests of safety or preventing pollution[5].

Any person to whom a recommendation is addressed must without delay[6]:

(1)   take that recommendation into consideration[7];

(2)   send to the Chief Inspector:

    (a)   details of the measures, if any, he has taken or proposes to take to implement the recommendation and the timetable for securing that implementation[8]; or

    (b)   an explanation as to why the recommendation is not to be the subject of measures to be taken to implement it[9], and

(3)   give notice to the Chief Inspector if at any time any information provided to the Chief Inspector in pursuance of head (2)(a) above concerning the measures he proposes to take or the timetable for securing their implementation is rendered inaccurate by any change of circumstances[10].

The Chief Inspector must, annually or at such other intervals as he sees fit, make information publicly available in respect of the matters, including any explanation mentioned in heads (2) and (3) above, which have been communicated to him, and he must inform the Secretary of State of those matters[11]. However, the Chief Inspector must not publish such information unless notification has been sent to all persons mentioned in the information and the Chief Inspector has considered any representations relating to the information which may be made to him[12] by or on behalf of any person so notified, and amended the information in such manner as he thinks fit[13].

1   As to the meaning of 'Chief Inspector' see PARA 821 note 4.

2   As to the meaning of 'accident' for these purposes see PARA 816.

3   Merchant Shipping (Accident Reporting and Investigation) Regulations 2012, SI 2012/1743, reg 16(1). Without prejudice to reg 16(1), if the Chief Inspector is of the view that at any stage of a safety investigation, urgent action is required to be taken so as to prevent the risk of further accidents occurring then he may inform the European Commission as soon as possible as regards what urgent action should be taken by member States or other States or other relevant parties: reg 16(8).

4   Merchant Shipping (Accident Reporting and Investigation) Regulations 2012, SI 2012/1743, reg 16(2).

5   Merchant Shipping (Accident Reporting and Investigation) Regulations 2012, SI 2012/1743, reg 16(3).

6   Merchant Shipping (Accident Reporting and Investigation) Regulations 2012, SI 2012/1743, reg 16(4).

7   Merchant Shipping (Accident Reporting and Investigation) Regulations 2012, SI 2012/1743, reg 16(4)(a).

8   Merchant Shipping (Accident Reporting and Investigation) Regulations 2012, SI 2012/1743, reg 16(4)(b)(i). Any such details or timetable must be provided to the Chief Inspector within 28 days following receipt of the recommendation: reg 16(4)(b). The Chief Inspector has the power to

extend the period of 28 days prescribed in reg 16(4), where he considers it appropriate to do so: reg 17(2). This power may be exercised notwithstanding that the prescribed period has expired: reg 17(3).

9　Merchant Shipping (Accident Reporting and Investigation) Regulations 2012, SI 2012/1743, reg 16(4)(b)(ii). Any such explanation must be provided to the Chief Inspector within 28 days following receipt of the recommendation: reg 16(4)(b). See reg 17(2), (3); and note 8.

10　Merchant Shipping (Accident Reporting and Investigation) Regulations 2012, SI 2012/1743, reg 16(4)(c). As to the service and giving of notices see PARA 823 note 2.

11　Merchant Shipping (Accident Reporting and Investigation) Regulations 2012, SI 2012/1743, reg 16(5). As to the Secretary of State see PARA 36.

12　Any representations made in accordance with the Merchant Shipping (Accident Reporting and Investigation) Regulations 2012, SI 2012/1743, reg 16(6), must be in writing and must be served on the Chief Inspector within 30 days of receipt of the notification referred to in reg 16(6) or within such further period as may be allowed under reg 17 (see note 8): reg 16(7).

13　Merchant Shipping (Accident Reporting and Investigation) Regulations 2012, SI 2012/1743, reg 16(6).

(2)　FORMAL INVESTIGATIONS BY WRECK COMMISSIONER

(i)　Provision for Formal Investigation

830. Provision for formal investigation into accident to be held by a wreck commissioner. Where any accident[1] has occurred, the Secretary of State[2] may, whether or not an investigation into it has been carried out by marine inspectors[3], cause a formal investigation into the accident to be held by a wreck commissioner[4].

A wreck commissioner holding a formal investigation must conduct it in accordance with the rules[5]; and those rules must require the assistance of one or more assessors[6] and, if any question as to the cancellation or suspension of an officer's certificate is likely, the assistance of not less than two assessors[7].

If, as a result of the investigation, the wreck commissioner is satisfied, with respect to any officer, of any of the following matters[8], that is say:

(1)　that the officer is unfit to discharge his duties, whether by reason of incompetence or misconduct or for any other reason[9];

(2)　that the officer has been seriously negligent in the discharge of his duties[10]; or

(3)　that the officer has failed to comply with his duty[11] to assist in case of collision[12],

and, if it is a matter mentioned in heads (1) or (2) above, is further satisfied that it caused or contributed to the accident, he may cancel or suspend any certificate issued to the officer[13] or censure him; and, if he cancels or suspends the certificate, the officer must deliver it forthwith to him or to the Secretary of State[14]. If a person fails to deliver a cancelled or suspended certificate as so required, he is guilty of an offence[15].

Where a certificate has been so cancelled or suspended, the Secretary of State, if of the opinion that the justice of the case requires it, may reissue the certificate or, as the case may be, reduce the period of suspension and return the certificate, or may grant a new certificate of the same or a lower grade in place of the cancelled or suspended certificate[16].

The wreck commissioner may make such awards as he thinks just with regard to the costs of the investigation and of any parties at the investigation, and with regard to the parties by whom those costs are to be paid; and any such award of the wreck commissioner may, on the application of any party named in it, be made an order of the High Court[17]. Any costs directed by an award to be paid are to be assessed in the High Court[18].

The wreck commissioner must make a report on the investigation to the Secretary of State[19].

1 As to the meaning of 'accident' for these purposes see the Merchant Shipping (Accident Reporting and Investigation) Regulations 2012, SI 2012/1743, reg 3; and PARA 816 (definition applied by the Merchant Shipping Act 1995 s 268(1)).
2 As to the Secretary of State see PARA 36.
3 Ie under the Merchant Shipping Act 1995 s 267 (see PARA 815): see s 268(1). As to the appointment of marine accident inspectors see PARA 815.
4 Merchant Shipping Act 1995 s 268(1)(a). As to the appointment of wreck commissioners see PARA 59. The Magistrates' Courts Act 1980 s 97(1), (3), (4) (see MAGISTRATES vol 71 (2013) PARA 572), which provides for the attendance of witnesses and the production of evidence, applies in relation to a formal investigation held by a wreck commissioner as if the wreck commissioner were a magistrates' court and the investigation a complaint; and the wreck commissioner has power to administer oaths for the purposes of the investigation: Merchant Shipping Act 1995 s 268(3).
  The Merchant Shipping Act 1995 ss 268–270 and the Merchant Shipping (Formal Investigations) Rules 1985, SI 1985/1001 apply in relation to hovercraft as they apply in relation to ships, and for that purpose have effect subject to the modifications set out in the Hovercraft (Application of Enactments) Order 1989, SI 1989/1350, art 2, Sch 1: see art 2. See also PARA 382.
5 Ie in accordance with rules under the Merchant Shipping Act 1995 s 270(1) (see PARA 831 et seq): see s 268(2).
6 As to the role of assessors generally see PARA 205.
7 Merchant Shipping Act 1995 s 268(2).
8 Ie any of the matters mentioned in the Merchant Shipping Act 1995 s 61(1)(a)–(c) (see heads (1) to (3) in the text): see s 268(5).
9 See the Merchant Shipping Act 1995 s 61(1)(a); and PARA 524.
10 See the Merchant Shipping Act 1995 s 61(1)(b); and PARA 524.
11 Ie under the Merchant Shipping Act 1995 s 92 (see PARA 756): see s 61(1)(c); and PARA 524.
12 See the Merchant Shipping Act 1995 s 61(1)(c); and PARA 524.
13 Ie under the Merchant Shipping Act 1995 s 47 (see PARA 503): see s 268(5).
14 Merchant Shipping Act 1995 s 268(5).
15 See the Merchant Shipping Act 1995 s 268(6); and PARA 1085.
16 Merchant Shipping Act 1995 s 268(7).
17 Merchant Shipping Act 1995 s 268(8).
18 Merchant Shipping Act 1995 s 268(9)(a).
19 Merchant Shipping Act 1995 s 268(10).

(ii) Procedure for Formal Investigation

831. Wreck commissioners and assessors. Where it appears to the Secretary of State[1] that a formal investigation[2] should be held into the circumstances or causes of, or into any particular matter relating to, an accident, he may direct that a formal investigation be held and conducted in accordance with the rules which govern such investigations[3] by a wreck commissioner[4]. The wreck commissioner must be assisted by one or more assessors appointed by the Lord Chancellor[5].

The Lord Chancellor must maintain a list of assessors who have the required qualifications[6] and may at any time add or withdraw the name of any person to or from the list[7].

If any question as to the cancellation or suspension of an officer's[8] certificate is likely to arise, the wreck commissioner must be assisted by not less than two assessors[9]:

(1)   two of whom must be, in the case of a master or deck officer, mercantile marine masters[10];

(2)   one of whom must be, in the case of a marine engineer officer, a mercantile marine engineer, and one a mercantile marine master[11];

(3)   one of whom must be, in the case of a fishing vessel officer, a mercantile marine master and one a fishing vessel skipper[12];

and in any such case where a question as to the cancellation or suspension of an officer's certificate is likely to arise, wherever possible at least one of the assessors appointed must have had experience in the same capacity and in the same type of ship as the officer concerned[13].

1   As to the Secretary of State see PARA 36.
2   For these purposes, 'formal investigation' means a formal investigation into an accident under the Merchant Shipping Act 1995 s 268 (see PARA 830): Merchant Shipping (Formal Investigations) Rules 1985, SI 1985/1001, r 2(1) (definition amended by SI 1990/123) (having effect under the Merchant Shipping Act 1995 s 270). As to the meaning of 'accident' see the Merchant Shipping (Accident Reporting and Investigation) Regulations 2012, SI 2012/1743, reg 3; and PARA 816 (definition applied by the Merchant Shipping (Formal Investigations) Rules 1985, SI 1985/1001, r 2(1) (definition substituted by SI 1990/123)). These provisions also apply in relation to hovercraft: see PARA 830 note 4.
3   Ie in accordance with the Merchant Shipping (Formal Investigations) Rules 1985, SI 1985/1001 (see PARA 832 et seq): see the Merchant Shipping (Formal Investigations) Rules 1985, SI 1985/1001, r 4(1) (amended by SI 1990/123).
4   Merchant Shipping (Formal Investigations) Rules 1985, SI 1985/1001, r 4(1) (as amended: see note 3). For these purposes, 'wreck commissioner' means, in the case of a formal investigation to be held in England and Wales, a wreck commissioner appointed for that purpose by the Lord Chancellor: r 2(1). As to the meanings of 'England' and 'Wales' see PARA 16 note 2. As to the appointment of wreck commissioners see PARA 59. As to the Lord Chancellor see CONSTITUTIONAL AND ADMINISTRATIVE LAW vol 20 (2014) PARA 255 et seq.
5   Merchant Shipping (Formal Investigations) Rules 1985, SI 1985/1001, r 4(1) (as amended: see note 3). As to the role of assessors generally see PARA 205.
6   The qualifications so required are (by virtue of the Merchant Shipping (Formal Investigations) Rules 1985, SI 1985/1001, r 4(2), Schedule):
    (1)   in the case of a mercantile marine master, he must:
        (a)   be in possession of a Certificate of Competency (Deck Officer) (Class 1) (Master Mariner) (or its equivalent) and have had command of a United Kingdom registered vessel for at least two years; and
        (b)   have a wide knowledge of all modern aids to navigation,
    (2)   in the case of a mercantile marine engineer, he must:
        (a)   be in possession of a Certificate of Competency (Marine Engineer Officer) (Class 1) (or its equivalent) and have been the Chief Engineer Officer of a United Kingdom registered ship for at least two years; and
        (b)   have a wide knowledge of matters relating to marine engineering,
    (3)   in the case of a fishing vessel skipper, he must:
        (a)   be in possession of a Skipper's (Full) Certificate and have had command of a fishing vessel for at least two years; and
        (b)   have a wide knowledge of fishing vessels and their operation,
    (4)   in the case of the Royal Navy, he must either:
        (a)   have had rank of Admiral or Captain and two years' service in command of one or Her Majesty's ships at sea;
        (b)   have had rank of Commander and two years' service in that rank in one of Her Majesty's ships at sea; or
        (c)   have had rank of Lieutenant-Commander and two years' service in that rank as an appropriate specialist in one of Her Majesty's ships at sea, and
    (5)   in the case of a person of special skill or knowledge, he must be:
        (a)   a naval architect; or
        (b)   a person with special skills or knowledge, including managerial experience.
    In each case apart from that relating to a person of special skill or knowledge, the person must also not be more than 70 years of age: Schedule.
7   Merchant Shipping (Formal Investigations) Rules 1985, SI 1985/1001, r 4(2).
8   For these purposes, 'officer' means an officer qualified for the purposes of the Merchant Shipping Act 1995 s 47 (see PARA 503) and includes a master, skipper, mate, second hand, deck officer, marine engineer officer and radio officer: Merchant Shipping (Formal Investigations) Rules 1985, SI 1985/1001, r 2(1).
9   Merchant Shipping (Formal Investigations) Rules 1985, SI 1985/1001, r 4(3).
10 Merchant Shipping (Formal Investigations) Rules 1985, SI 1985/1001, r 4(3)(a).
11 Merchant Shipping (Formal Investigations) Rules 1985, SI 1985/1001, r 4(3)(b).

12 Merchant Shipping (Formal Investigations) Rules 1985, SI 1985/1001, r 4(3)(c).
13 Merchant Shipping (Formal Investigations) Rules 1985, SI 1985/1001, r 4(4).

832. Remittance of case to the Attorney General. Where the Secretary of State[1] has directed a formal investigation[2] to be held, he must remit the case to the Attorney General[3], and thereafter the preparation and presentation of the case must be conducted by the Treasury Solicitor under the direction of the Attorney General[4]; the Chief Inspector of Marine Accidents must render such assistance to the wreck commissioner[5] and to the Attorney General as is in his power[6].

1 As to the Secretary of State see PARA 36.
2 As to the meaning of 'formal investigation' see PARA 831 note 2.
3 As to the Attorney General see CONSTITUTIONAL AND ADMINISTRATIVE LAW vol 20 (2014) PARA 273.
4 Merchant Shipping (Formal Investigations) Rules 1985, SI 1985/1001, r 4A (added by SI 1990/123). These provisions also apply in relation to hovercraft: see PARA 830 note 4.
5 As to the meaning of 'wreck commissioner' see PARA 831 note 4.
6 Merchant Shipping (Formal Investigations) Rules 1985, SI 1985/1001, r 4A (as added: see note 4).

833. Notice of investigation; parties to the investigation. When the Secretary of State[1] causes a formal investigation[2] to be held, the Attorney General[3] must cause a notice (a 'notice of investigation') to be served on any persons, including the Department of Transport[4], who in the opinion of the Attorney General ought to be made a party[5]; and any such person upon whom a notice of investigation has been served is a party to the formal investigation[6]. The Attorney General must be a party to the formal investigation[7].

The notice of investigation must contain a statement of the facts giving rise to the formal investigation and a statement of the questions which the Attorney General intends to raise at the formal investigation[8]. At any time before or during the hearing of the formal investigation the Attorney General may amend, add to or omit any of the questions contained in the notice of investigation[9].

The Attorney General must, as far as practicable, cause every party to the formal investigation to be given not less than 30 days' notice of the time of and the date when and the place where the hearing of the formal investigation will commence, provided that such notice is not required to be given to any person who is made a party[10] after the date of the hearing has been fixed[11].

If at any time during the preparation for the formal investigation it appears likely to the Attorney General that the conduct of any person will be in issue, the Attorney General must cause that person to be notified to that effect[12].

Service of any notice or other document so issued[13] may be effected either personally or by registered post or by the recorded delivery service to the person's last known address[14].

Any person who is not already a party to a formal investigation may, with the leave of the wreck commissioner[15], become a party to the formal investigation[16]. Application for such leave may be made to the wreck commissioner at any time before or during the formal investigation[17].

1 As to the Secretary of State see PARA 36.
2 As to the meaning of 'formal investigation' see PARA 831 note 2.
3 As to the Attorney General see CONSTITUTIONAL AND ADMINISTRATIVE LAW vol 20 (2014) PARA 273.
4 As to the Department of Transport see ROAD TRAFFIC vol 89 (2011) PARA 38.
5 Merchant Shipping (Formal Investigations) Rules 1985, SI 1985/1001, r 5(1) (r 5(1)–(4) amended by SI 1990/123). These provisions also apply in relation to hovercraft: see PARA 830 note 4.
6 Merchant Shipping (Formal Investigations) Rules 1985, SI 1985/1001, r 5(1) (as amended: see note 5).
7 Merchant Shipping (Formal Investigations) Rules 1985, SI 1985/1001, r 5(1) (as amended: see note 5).

8   Merchant Shipping (Formal Investigations) Rules 1985, SI 1985/1001, r 5(2) (as amended: see note 5).
9   Merchant Shipping (Formal Investigations) Rules 1985, SI 1985/1001, r 5(2) (as amended: see note 5).
10 Ie pursuant to the Merchant Shipping (Formal Investigations) Rules 1985, SI 1985/1001, r 6 (see the text and notes 15–17): see r 5(3) (as amended: see note 5).
11 Merchant Shipping (Formal Investigations) Rules 1985, SI 1985/1001, r 5(3) (as amended: see note 5). Any period of time specified in the Merchant Shipping (Formal Investigations) Rules 1985, SI 1985/1001, by reference to days is exclusive of the first day and inclusive of the last day unless the last day falls on a Saturday, Sunday, Christmas Day, Good Friday or any day appointed by law to be a bank holiday in that part of the United Kingdom where the formal investigation is to be held, in which case the time is to be reckoned exclusively of that day also: r 2(2).
12 Merchant Shipping (Formal Investigations) Rules 1985, SI 1985/1001, r 5(4) (as amended: see note 5).
13 Ie under the Merchant Shipping (Formal Investigations) Rules 1985, SI 1985/1001, r 5: see r 5(5).
14 Merchant Shipping (Formal Investigations) Rules 1985, SI 1985/1001, r 5(5).
15 As to the meaning of 'wreck commissioner' see PARA 831 note 4.
16 Merchant Shipping (Formal Investigations) Rules 1985, SI 1985/1001, r 6.
17 Merchant Shipping (Formal Investigations) Rules 1985, SI 1985/1001, r 6.

834. Admission of evidence to formal investigation. Without prejudice to the admission of documents as secondary evidence allowed by statute or otherwise, statements, statutory declarations, any report of an investigation into the accident[1], the subject of a formal investigation[2], conducted by an inspector[3] and other written evidence must, unless the wreck commissioner[4] considers it unjust, be admitted as evidence at the formal investigation[5].

A party may give to any other party notice in writing to admit any documents, saving all just exceptions, and in case of neglect or refusal to admit after such notice, the party so neglecting or refusing is liable for all the costs of proving the documents, whatever may be the result, unless the wreck commissioner is of opinion that the refusal to admit was reasonable[6]; and no costs of proving any document may be allowed unless such notice has been given, except where the omission to give the notice has, in the opinion of an officer by whom the costs are assessed, caused a saving of expense[7].

1   As to the meaning of 'accident' see PARA 831 note 2.
2   As to the meaning of 'formal investigation' see PARA 831 note 2.
3   Ie pursuant to the Merchant Shipping Act 1995 s 267 (see PARA 815): see the Merchant Shipping (Formal Investigations) Rules 1985, SI 1985/1001, r 7(1) (amended by SI 1990/123).
4   As to the meaning of 'wreck commissioner' see PARA 831 note 4.
5   Merchant Shipping (Formal Investigations) Rules 1985, SI 1985/1001, r 7(1) (as amended: see note 3). These provisions also apply in relation to hovercraft: see PARA 830 note 4.
6   Merchant Shipping (Formal Investigations) Rules 1985, SI 1985/1001, r 7(2).
7   Merchant Shipping (Formal Investigations) Rules 1985, SI 1985/1001, r 7(2).

835. Meeting preliminary to commencement of formal investigation. At any time before the date appointed for the commencement of the formal investigation[1] the wreck commissioner[2] may hold a preliminary meeting at which any direction may be given or any preliminary or interim order as to the procedure may be made[3].

1   As to the meaning of 'formal investigation' see PARA 831 note 2.
2   As to the meaning of 'wreck commissioner' see PARA 831 note 4.
3   Merchant Shipping (Formal Investigations) Rules 1985, SI 1985/1001, r 7(3). These provisions also apply in relation to hovercraft: see PARA 830 note 4.

836. Holding of formal investigation. At the time and place appointed for the commencement of the formal investigation[1], the wreck commissioner[2] may proceed with the formal investigation whether the parties upon whom a notice of investigation[3] has been served, or a person who has applied to become a party[4], or any of them, are present or not, provided that, where the party concerned has been served with the notice of investigation by, the wreck commissioner must not proceed with the formal investigation in his absence unless satisfied that the party has been duly served[5].

The wreck commissioner must hold the formal investigation in public save to the extent to which he is of opinion that, in the interest of justice or for other good and sufficient reason in the public interest, any part of the evidence, or any argument relating thereto, should be heard in private[6].

1 As to the meaning of 'formal investigation' see PARA 831 note 2.
2 As to the meaning of 'wreck commissioner' see PARA 831 note 4.
3 As to the meaning of 'notice of investigation' see PARA 833.
4 Ie pursuant to the Merchant Shipping (Formal Investigations) Rules 1985, SI 1985/1001, r 6: see PARA 833. These provisions also apply in relation to hovercraft: see PARA 830 note 4.
5 Merchant Shipping (Formal Investigations) Rules 1985, SI 1985/1001, r 7(4). The text refers to the party being duly served in accordance with the requirements of r 5(5) (see PARA 833): see r 7(4).
6 Merchant Shipping (Formal Investigations) Rules 1985, SI 1985/1001, r 7(5).

837. Opening statements in formal investigation; written statements. The formal investigation[1] must commence with an opening statement by the Attorney General[2], followed at the discretion of the wreck commissioner[3] with brief speeches on behalf of the other parties[4]. The proceedings must continue with the production and examination of witnesses on behalf of the Attorney General; and the Attorney General may adduce documentary evidence[5]. These witnesses may be cross-examined by the parties in such order as the wreck commissioner may direct and then be re-examined on behalf of the Attorney General[6]. The Attorney General must then cause to be stated the questions relating to the accident[7] and to the conduct of persons connected with the accident upon which the opinion of the wreck commissioner is desired[8]. In framing the questions for the opinion of the wreck commissioner, the Attorney General may make such modifications in, additions to, or omissions from, the questions as set out in the notice of investigation[9] or subsequent notices[10] as, having regard to the evidence which has been given, the Attorney General may think fit[11].

Any other party to the formal investigation is entitled to make a further opening statement, to give evidence, to adduce documentary evidence, to call witnesses, to cross-examine any witnesses called by any other party and to address the wreck commissioner in such order as the wreck commissioner may direct[12]. The Attorney General may also produce and examine further witnesses who may be cross-examined by the parties and re-examined by the Attorney General[13].

A party who does not appear in person at a formal investigation and is not represented may make representations in writing to the wreck commissioner and such written representations may be read out at the formal investigation by or on behalf of the wreck commissioner[14].

1 As to the meaning of 'formal investigation' see PARA 831 note 2.
2 As to the Attorney General see CONSTITUTIONAL AND ADMINISTRATIVE LAW vol 20 (2014) PARA 273.
3 As to the meaning of 'wreck commissioner' see PARA 831 note 4.
4 Merchant Shipping (Formal Investigations) Rules 1985, SI 1985/1001, r 7(6) (amended by SI 1990/123). These provisions also apply in relation to hovercraft: see PARA 830 note 4.
5 Merchant Shipping (Formal Investigations) Rules 1985, SI 1985/1001, r 7(6) (as amended: see note 4).
6 Merchant Shipping (Formal Investigations) Rules 1985, SI 1985/1001, r 7(6) (as amended: see note 4).
7 As to the meaning of 'accident' see PARA 831 note 2.
8 Merchant Shipping (Formal Investigations) Rules 1985, SI 1985/1001, r 7(6) (as amended: see note 4).
9 As to the meaning of 'notice of investigation' see PARA 833.
10 Ie referred to in the Merchant Shipping (Formal Investigations) Rules 1985, SI 1985/1001, r 5(2) (see PARA 833): see r 7(6) (as amended: see note 4).

11 Merchant Shipping (Formal Investigations) Rules 1985, SI 1985/1001, r 7(6) (as amended: see note 4).
12 Merchant Shipping (Formal Investigations) Rules 1985, SI 1985/1001, r 8(1) (amended by SI 1990/123).
13 Merchant Shipping (Formal Investigations) Rules 1985, SI 1985/1001, r 8(1) (as amended: see note 12).
14 Merchant Shipping (Formal Investigations) Rules 1985, SI 1985/1001, r 8(2).

838. Conduct of formal investigation. Every formal investigation[1] must be conducted in such manner that, if substantial criticism[2] is made against any person, that person has an opportunity of making his defence either in person or otherwise[3].

1 As to the meaning of 'formal investigation' see PARA 831 note 2.
2 For these purposes, 'substantial criticism' means criticism which in the opinion of the wreck commissioner is substantial criticism: Merchant Shipping (Formal Investigations) Rules 1985, SI 1985/1001, r 2(1).
3 Merchant Shipping (Formal Investigations) Rules 1985, SI 1985/1001, r 9. These provisions also apply in relation to hovercraft: see PARA 830 note 4.

839. Addresses to the wreck commissioner after taking of evidence. Any of the parties who desires so to do may, after completion of the taking of evidence, address the wreck commissioner[1] upon the evidence; and the Attorney General[2] may address the wreck commissioner in reply upon the whole case[3]. After this address in reply upon the whole case, at the discretion of the wreck commissioner, an officer[4] of whose conduct substantial criticism[5] has been made during the formal investigation[6] may be permitted or invited to make a final statement as to why, in the event of a finding that his conduct caused or contributed to the accident, his certificate of competency should not be cancelled or suspended, or as to why he should not be censured[7].

1 As to the meaning of 'wreck commissioner' see PARA 831 note 4.
2 As to the Attorney General see CONSTITUTIONAL AND ADMINISTRATIVE LAW vol 20 (2014) PARA 273.
3 Merchant Shipping (Formal Investigations) Rules 1985, SI 1985/1001, r 10 (amended by SI 1990/123).
4 As to the meaning of 'officer' see PARA 831 note 8.
5 As to the meaning of 'substantial criticism' see PARA 838 note 2.
6 As to the meaning of 'formal investigation' see PARA 831 note 2.
7 Merchant Shipping (Formal Investigations) Rules 1985, SI 1985/1001, r 10 (as amended: see note 3). As to officer's certificates in general see PARA 507 et seq.

840. Adjournment of formal investigation. The wreck commissioner[1] may adjourn the formal investigation[2] from time to time and from place to place; and, where an adjournment is asked for by any party to the formal investigation, the wreck commissioner may impose such terms as to payment of costs as he thinks just as a condition of granting the adjournment[3].

1 As to the meaning of 'wreck commissioner' see PARA 831 note 4.
2 As to the meaning of 'formal investigation' see PARA 831 note 2.
3 Merchant Shipping (Formal Investigations) Rules 1985, SI 1985/1001, r 11. These provisions also apply in relation to hovercraft: see PARA 830 note 4.

841. Result of formal investigation. At the end of the formal investigation[1] the wreck commissioner[2] must:

(1)   in any case where an officer's[3] certificate is in issue, give his decision concerning the certificate in public[4];

(2)   whether or not a certificate is in issue, make a report on the case to the Secretary of State[5] including his and the assessor's, or assessors', findings as to the reasons for the accident[6] or as to any particular matter relating thereto, or as to the conduct or any person implicated therein, and the reason for suspending or cancelling any officer's certificate[7].

1 As to the meaning of 'formal investigation' see PARA 831 note 2.

2 As to the meaning of 'wreck commissioner' see PARA 831 note 4.
3 As to the meaning of 'officer' see PARA 831 note 8.
4 Merchant Shipping (Formal Investigations) Rules 1985, SI 1985/1001, r 12(a) (substituted by SI 1990/123). As to officer's certificates in general see PARA 490 et seq. These provisions also apply in relation to hovercraft: see PARA 830 note 4.
5 As to the Secretary of State see PARA 36.
6 As to the meaning of 'accident' see PARA 831 note 2.
7 Merchant Shipping (Formal Investigations) Rules 1985, SI 1985/1001, r 12(b).

842. Reports of formal investigation. Each assessor[1] must either sign the report with or without reservations, or state in writing his dissent therefrom and his reasons for such dissent; and such dissent and reasons, if any, must be forwarded to the Secretary of State[2] with the report[3]. The Secretary of State must, unless in the interests of justice or otherwise in the public interest there are good reasons to the contrary, cause each party to the formal investigation[4] to be given a copy of the whole or, where appropriate, the relevant part of the report[5].

Further copies of the report must not be released until the Secretary of State is satisfied that the parties have had reasonable time to receive and read their copies[6].

1 As to the appointment of assessors for these purposes see PARA 831.
2 As to the Secretary of State see PARA 36.
3 Merchant Shipping (Formal Investigations) Rules 1985, SI 1985/1001, r 13 (amended by SI 1990/123). As to the report that must be forwarded to the Secretary of State see PARA 841. These provisions also apply in relation to hovercraft: see PARA 830 note 4.
4 As to the meaning of 'formal investigation' see PARA 831 note 2.
5 Merchant Shipping (Formal Investigations) Rules 1985, SI 1985/1001, r 13 (as amended: see note 3).
6 Merchant Shipping (Formal Investigations) Rules 1985, SI 1985/1001, r 13 (as amended: see note 3).

843. Costs. Where the wreck commissioner[1] makes any award as to the costs of the investigation and of any of the parties at the investigation, or with regard to the parties by whom those costs are to be paid, he must state in a report his reasons for making such an award[2].

1 As to the meaning of 'wreck commissioner' see PARA 831 note 4.
2 Merchant Shipping (Formal Investigations) Rules 1985, SI 1985/1001, r 14 (substituted by SI 1990/123). As to the wreck commissioner's report see PARA 841. These provisions also apply in relation to hovercraft: see PARA 830 note 4.

(iii) Rehearings and Appeals

844. Rehearing of and appeal from investigations. Where a formal investigation has been held[1], the Secretary of State[2] may order the whole or part of the case to be reheard[3]; and he must do so if there appear to him to be grounds for suspecting that a miscarriage of justice may have occurred[4]. Such an order may provide for the rehearing to be by a wreck commissioner[5] or by the High Court[6]; and any such rehearing which is not held by the High Court must be conducted in accordance with the rules[7] relating to marine investigations and appeals[8].

Where the wreck commissioner holding the investigation has decided to cancel or suspend the certificate of any person or has found any person at fault, then, if no application for an order to rehear the formal investigation[9] has been made, or if such an application has been refused, that person or any other person who, having an interest in the investigation, has appeared at the hearing and is affected by the decision or finding, may appeal to the High Court[10]. Also, where a certificate has been so cancelled or suspended, the Secretary of State, if of the opinion that the justice of the case requires it, may reissue the certificate or, as the case may be, reduce the period of suspension and return the certificate, or may grant a new certificate of the same or a lower grade in place of the cancelled or suspended certificate[11].

The discretion to be exercised in relation to the incidence of the costs of participation of a party to a formal investigation or rehearing of the formal investigation must have regard to the application of relevant public policy factors[12].

1 Ie under the Merchant Shipping Act 1995 s 268 (see PARA 830): see s 269(1).
2 As to the Secretary of State see PARA 36.
3 See the Merchant Shipping Act 1995 s 269(1). In the case of *Re M/V Derbyshire* (1999) Times, 28 October, the effect of an order issued under the Merchant Shipping Act 1995 s 269 for a rehearing of the formal investigation ('RFI') in respect of 'the whole case' was held to have the effect of initiating a complete re- investigation into the 'accident' involving the loss of the vessel, treating 'accident' as having the same meaning as it would for the purpose of s 268 (as to which see PARA 830 note 1).
    The Merchant Shipping Act 1995 ss 268–270 apply in relation to hovercraft as they apply in relation to ships, and for that purpose have effect subject to the modifications set out in the Hovercraft (Application of Enactments) Order 1989, SI 1989/1350, art 2, Sch 1: see art 2. See also PARA 382.
4 Merchant Shipping Act 1995 s 269(1)(b) (amended by the Deregulation Act 2015 s 55(b)).
5 As to the appointment of wreck commissioners see PARA 59.
6 Merchant Shipping Act 1995 s 269(2)(a). This provision applies only if the investigation was held in England or Wales: see s 269(2)(a). As to the meanings of 'England' and 'Wales' see PARA 16 note 2.
7 Ie the Merchant Shipping (Formal Investigations) Rules 1985, SI 1985/1001 (made under the Merchant Shipping Act 1995 s 270(1)) (see PARA 831): see s 269(3).
8 Merchant Shipping Act 1995 s 269(3). The provisions of s 268 (see PARA 830) apply in relation to a rehearing of an investigation by a wreck commissioner as they apply in relation to the holding of an investigation: s 269(3).
9 Ie under the Merchant Shipping Act 1995 s 269(1) (see the text and notes 1–5): see s 269(4).
10 Merchant Shipping Act 1995 s 269(4). This provision applies only if the investigation was held in England or Wales: see s 269(4).
11 Merchant Shipping Act 1995 ss 268(7), 269(5).
12 *Re-hearing of the formal Investigation into the loss of the MV Derbyshire* [2003] 1 All ER (Comm) 784.

845. Procedure. Any rehearing of a formal investigation[1] which is not held by the High Court must be conducted in accordance with the provisions of rules governing formal investigations[2].

1 Ie pursuant to the Merchant Shipping Act 1995 s 269(1) (see PARA 844): see the Merchant Shipping (Formal Investigations) Rules 1985, SI 1985/1001, r 15. For these purposes, 'rehearing' means a rehearing of a formal investigation: r 2(1). As to the meaning of 'formal investigation' see PARA 831 note 2. These provisions also apply in relation to hovercraft: see PARA 830 note 4.
2 Merchant Shipping (Formal Investigations) Rules 1985, SI 1985/1001, r 15. The text refers to a rehearing to be conducted in accordance with the provisions of the Merchant Shipping (Formal Investigations) Rules 1995, SI 1995/1001 (see PARA 831 et seq): see r 15.

(3) INQUIRIES INTO AND REPORTS ON DEATHS AND INJURIES

846. Inquiries into deaths of crew members and others. Where:

(1)   any person dies in a United Kingdom ship[1] or in a boat or life-raft from such a ship[2]; or

(2)   the master[3] of, or a seaman[4] employed in, such a ship dies in a country outside the United Kingdom[5],

an inquiry into the cause of the death must be held by a superintendent[6] or proper officer[7] at the next port[8] where the ship calls after the death and where there is a superintendent or proper officer, or at such other place as the Secretary of State[9] may direct[10].

Where it appears to the Secretary of State that:

(a)   in consequence of an injury sustained or a disease contracted by a person when he was the master of or a seaman employed in a United Kingdom ship, he ceased to be employed in the ship and subsequently died[11]; and

(b)   the death occurred in a country outside the United Kingdom during the period of one year beginning with the day on which he so ceased[12],

the Secretary of State may arrange for an inquiry into the cause of the death to be held by a superintendent or proper officer[13].

Where it appears to the Secretary of State that a person may:

(i)   have died in a United Kingdom ship or in a boat or life-raft from such a ship[14]; or

(ii)   have been lost from such a ship, boat or life-raft and have died in consequence of being so lost[15],

the Secretary of State may arrange for an inquiry to be held by a superintendent or proper officer into whether the person died as mentioned above and, if the superintendent or officer finds that he did, into the cause of the death[16].

The superintendent or proper officer holding the inquiry has, for the purpose of the inquiry, the powers conferred[17] on an inspector[18].

The person holding the inquiry must make a report of his findings to the Secretary of State who must make the report available[19]:

(A)   if the person to whom the report relates was employed in the ship and a person was named as his next of kin in the crew agreement[20] or list of the crew in which the name of the person to whom the report relates last appeared, to the person so named[21];

(B)   in any case, to any person requesting it who appears to the Secretary of State to be interested[22].

However, no such inquiry may be held[23] where a coroner's inquest is to be held[24].

1   As to the meaning of 'ship' see PARA 229; and as to the meaning of 'United Kingdom ship' see PARA 230. As to the meaning of 'United Kingdom' see PARA 16 note 3.
2   Merchant Shipping Act 1995 s 271(1)(a).
3   As to the meaning of 'master' see PARA 444 note 1.
4   As to the meaning of 'seaman' see PARA 457 note 5.
5   Merchant Shipping Act 1995 s 271(1)(b).
6   As to the meaning of 'superintendent' see PARA 61 note 1. As to the appointment of superintendents see PARA 61.
7   As to the meaning of 'proper officer' see PARA 48 note 12.
8   As to the meaning of 'port' see PARA 46 note 12.
9   As to the Secretary of State see PARA 36.
10 Merchant Shipping Act 1995 s 271(1). As to the Secretary of State's power to give directions see PARA 39.
11 Merchant Shipping Act 1995 s 271(2)(a).
12 Merchant Shipping Act 1995 s 271(2)(b).
13 Merchant Shipping Act 1995 s 271(2). This provision is subject to s 271(6) (see the text and notes 23–24): see s 271(2).
14 Merchant Shipping Act 1995 s 271(3)(a).
15 Merchant Shipping Act 1995 s 271(3)(b).
16 Merchant Shipping Act 1995 s 271(3). This provision is subject to s 271(6) (see the text and notes 23–24): see s 271(3).
17 Ie by the Merchant Shipping Act 1995 s 259 (see PARA 49): see s 271(4).

18 Merchant Shipping Act 1995 s 271(4).
19 Merchant Shipping Act 1995 s 271(5).
20 As to the meaning of 'crew agreement' see PARA 457.
21 Merchant Shipping Act 1995 s 271(5)(a).
22 Merchant Shipping Act 1995 s 271(5)(b).
23 Ie under the Merchant Shipping Act 1995 s 271: see s 271(6).
24 Ie where an investigation is to be conducted under the Coroners and Justice Act 2009 Pt 1 (ss 1–50)
    (see CORONERS vol 24 (2010) PARA 90 et seq) or under corresponding Scotland or Northern
    Ireland legislation: Merchant Shipping Act 1995 s 271(6) (amended by the Coroners and Justice
    Act 2009 Sch 21 para 34).

847. Reports of and inquiries into injuries. Where the master[1] or a member
of the crew of a United Kingdom fishing vessel[2] is injured during a voyage, an
inquiry into the cause and nature of the injury may be held by a superintendent[3]
or proper officer[4].

The superintendent or proper officer holding such an inquiry has, for the
purposes of the inquiry, the powers conferred[5] on a Departmental inspector[6] and
he must make a report of his findings to the Secretary of State[7].

1 As to the meaning of 'master' see PARA 444 note 1.
2 As to the meaning of 'United Kingdom fishing vessel' see PARA 230.
3 As to the meaning of 'superintendent' see PARA 61 note 1. As to the appointment of
   superintendents see PARA 61.
4 Merchant Shipping Act 1995 s 272(1). As to the meaning of 'proper officer' see PARA 48 note 12.
   As to the powers of inspectors appointed under s 256(6) (see PARA 46) to serve improvement
   notices or prohibition notices where s 272 and the provisions of any instrument of a legislative
   character having effect thereunder are being contravened, or where activities to which s 272
   applies are carried on so as to involve serious personal injury or serious pollution, see PARA 46 et
   seq.
5 Ie by the Merchant Shipping Act 1995 s 259 (see PARA 49): see s 272(2).
6 As to the meaning of 'Departmental officer' see PARA 47 note 11.
7 Merchant Shipping Act 1995 s 272(2).

848. Transmission of particulars of deaths on ships. Where:
(1)   an inquest is held into a death[1]; or
(2)   an investigation[2] into a person's death is discontinued[3] on grounds that
        the cause of death has been revealed by a post-mortem examination[4],
and it appears to the coroner that the death in question constitutes[5] the death of
a person occurring in a ship or of a person employed in a ship, it is the duty of the
coroner to send to the Registrar General of Shipping and Seamen[6] particulars in
respect of the deceased of a kind prescribed by regulations made by the Secretary
of State[7].

1 Merchant Shipping Act 1995 s 273(1)(a) (s 273(1) renumbered and amended, s 273(2) added, by
   the Coroners and Justice Act 2009 Sch 21 para 35). As to coroner's inquests generally see
   CORONERS vol 24 (2010) PARA 121 et seq.
2 Ie an investigation under the Coroners and Justice Act 2009 Pt 1 (ss 1–50) (see CORONERS vol 24
   (2010) PARA 90 et seq).
3 Ie under the Coroners and Justice Act 2009 s 4 (see CORONERS vol 24 (2010) PARA 118).
4 Merchant Shipping Act 1995 s 273(2)(a) (as added: see note 1).
5 Ie is such as is mentioned in the Merchant Shipping Act 1995 s 108(2) (required returns as to
   deaths on ship etc) (see PARA 644) or in s 108(2) as extended, with or without amendments, by
   virtue of s 307 (see PARA 17): see s 273(1)(b).
6 As to the Registrar General of Shipping and Seamen see PARA 62.
7 Merchant Shipping Act 1995 s 273(1) (renumbered: see note 1). As to the Secretary of State see
   PARA 36.
       At the date at which this volume states the law no such regulations had been made under s 273
   but, by virtue of the Interpretation Act 1978 s 17(2)(b), the Merchant Shipping (Returns of Births
   and Deaths) Regulations 1979, SI 1979/1577 (see PARA 644) have effect as if so made. As to the
   power of the Secretary of State to make subordinate legislation under the Merchant Shipping Act
   1995, including his power to appoint committees for the purpose of advising him when
   considering the making or alteration of any regulations etc, see PARA 39.

10. SALVAGE AND WRECK

(1) SALVAGE

(i) Law and Jurisdiction

849. 'Salvage'. 'Salvage' may signify either the service rendered by a salvor or the reward payable to him for his service[1]. For the purposes of the Merchant Shipping Act 1995[2], 'salvage' includes, subject to the Salvage Convention[3], all expenses properly incurred by the salvor[4] in the performance of the salvage services[5].

Liability for death or personal injury resulting from negligence cannot be excluded or restricted in a contract of marine salvage[6].

1   The law of salvage which is here discussed is sometimes termed 'civil salvage', to distinguish it from 'prize salvage' (or 'salvage recapture'), which is payment in respect of ships, aircraft or goods belonging to a British subject which are recaptured after having been taken as prize by the enemy: see PRIZE vol 85 (2012) PARA 640 et seq. The term 'salvage' is also applied to the salved property in matters relating to insurance: see eg INSURANCE vol 60 (2011) PARA 614 et seq. As to the expenses of the salvor see PARA 899.
2   Ie the Merchant Shipping Act 1995 Pt IX (ss 224–255) (see PARA 850 et seq): see s 255(1).
3   Ie the International Convention on Salvage 1989 (London, 28 April 1989; Cm 1526): see PARA 851.
4   For these purposes, 'salvor' means, in the case of salvage services rendered by the officers or crew or part of the crew of any ship belonging to Her Majesty, the person in command of the ship: Merchant Shipping Act 1995 s 255(1). As to the meaning of 'ship' see PARA 229. As to government ships see PARA 19.
5   Merchant Shipping Act 1995 s 255(1). Cf the meaning of 'salvage operation' in the Salvage Convention (see PARA 850). In connection with 'salvage' (as distinct from 'towage') see *Owners and/or Demise Charterers of the tug 'Sea Tractor', her Master, Officers and Crew v Owners of the Ship 'Tramp'* [2007] EWHC 31 (Admlty), [2007] All ER (D) 88 (Jun).
6   See the Unfair Contract Terms Act 1977 ss 1(2), 2(1), Sch 1 para 2(a); and CONTRACT vol 22 (2012) PARA 416.

850. 'Salvage operation'. For the purposes of the Salvage Convention[1], 'salvage operation' means any act or activity undertaken to assist a vessel[2] or any other property[3] in danger[4] in navigable waters or in any other waters whatsoever[5].

1   Ie the International Convention on Salvage 1989 (London, 28 April 1989; Cm 1526): see PARA 851.
2   For these purposes, 'vessel' means any ship or craft or any structure capable of navigation: see the International Convention on Salvage 1989 art 1(b). In this context, see also *Gas Float Whitton No 2* [1895] P 301, DC; on appeal [1896] P 42, 8 Asp MLC 110, CA; affd sub nom *Wells v Gas Float Whitton No 2 (Owners), The Gas Float Whitton No 2* [1897] AC 337, 8 Asp MLC 272, HL (cited in PARA 860). As to the exclusion of platforms and drilling units on location see PARA 851; as to the exclusion of state-owned vessels see PARA 851; and as to the reservation in the case of maritime cultural property of prehistoric, archaeological or historic interest situated on the sea bed see PARA 851.
3   For these purposes, 'property' means any property not permanently and intentionally attached to the shoreline and includes freight at risk: Salvage Convention 1989 art 1(c).
4   As to danger to property at common law see PARAS 861, 862.
5   Salvage Convention art 1(a). Thus, under art 1(a) salvage is not restricted to tidal waters. The provisions of the Salvage Convention do not, however, apply to a salvage operation which takes place in inland waters of the United Kingdom and in which all the vessels involved are of inland navigation, and to a salvage operation which takes place in inland waters of the United Kingdom and in which no vessel is involved: see the Merchant Shipping Act 1995 Sch 11 Pt II para 2; and PARA 851. It is submitted, therefore, that the decision in *The Goring* [1988] AC 831, [1988] 1 All ER 641, [1988] 1 Lloyd's Rep 397, HL (salvage in non-tidal waters) still applies.

851. The Salvage Convention. The provisions of the Salvage Convention[1] have the force of law[2] in the United Kingdom[3]. There is no authority in point as to whether the Convention entirely supersedes the common law of salvage[4]: it is apprehended that it would still be correct for English courts to refer to the pre-existing principles of salvage law in interpreting and applying the Convention[5], provided that, in doing so, the courts proceed on the basis that the Convention now represents the law and that pre-existing common law principles are to be considered in relation to the Convention and not vice versa[6].

The Convention does not apply to:

(1)　　fixed or floating platforms or mobile offshore drilling units when such platforms or units are on location engaged in the exploration, exploitation or production of sea-bed mineral resources[7]; or

(2)　　warships or other non-commercial vessels[8] owned or operated by a state and entitled, at the time of salvage operations[9], to sovereign immunity under generally recognised principles of international law unless that state decides otherwise[10],

and does not affect any provisions of national law or any international Convention relating to salvage operations by or under the control of public authorities[11]. Nevertheless, salvors carrying out such salvage operations are entitled to avail themselves of the rights and remedies provided for in the Convention in respect of salvage operations[12].

The provisions of the Salvage Convention also do not apply:

(a)　　to a salvage operation which takes place in inland waters[13] of the United Kingdom and in which all the vessels[14] involved are of inland navigation[15]; and

(b)　　to a salvage operation which takes place in inland waters of the United Kingdom and in which no vessel is involved[16].

1　Ie the International Convention on Salvage 1989 (London, 28 April 1989; Cm 1526). The Convention was open for signature at the headquarters of the International Maritime Organisation (IMO) from 1 July 1989 to 30 June 1990 and thereafter remains open for accession: see art 28. As to the IMO see PARA 12. The Convention entered into force on 1 July 1996, one year after the date on which 15 states had expressed their consent to be bound by it: see art 29. The Convention may be denounced by any state party at any time after the expiry of one year from the date on which that Convention enters into force for that state: see art 31. A conference for the purpose of revising or amending the Convention may be convened by the IMO: see art 32. Procedural provision as to ratification, acceptance, approval, accession, denunciation, amendment etc is made by arts 33, 34.

　　The relevant provisions of the Salvage Convention (apart from arts 28–34: see note 1) are set out in the Merchant Shipping Act 1995 s 224(1), Sch 11 Pt I (arts 1–27) (see PARA 852 et seq). The provisions of s 224(2), Sch 11 Pt II (paras 1–7) (see PARA 852 et seq) have effect in connection with the Salvage Convention, and the Merchant Shipping Act 1995 s 224(1) has effect subject to the provisions of Sch 11 Pt II (paras 1–7): s 224(2). However, nothing in either s 224(1) or s 224(2) affects any rights or liabilities arising out of any salvage operations started or other acts done before 1 January 1995: s 224(4). As respects any period before the entry into force of the Salvage Convention, any reference therein to a state party to the Salvage Convention was to be read as a reference to the United Kingdom: s 224(6). In connection with salvage under the Merchant Shipping Act 1995 generally see Pt IX Ch I (ss 224–230); and PARA 852 et seq. If it appears to Her Majesty in Council that the government of the United Kingdom has agreed to any revision of the Salvage Convention, She may by Order in Council make such modifications of Sch 11 Pt I or Pt II as She considers appropriate in consequence of the revision (s 224(3)); but nothing in any modification so made affects any rights or liabilities arising out of any salvage operations started or other acts done before the day on which the modification comes into force (s 224(5)). At the date at which this volume states the law, no such Orders in Council had been made and none has effect as if so made. As to the making of Orders under the Merchant Shipping Act 1995 generally see PARA 41.

　　The Salvage Convention 1989 replaced the International Convention for the Unification of Certain Rules of Law respecting Assistance and Salvage at Sea 1910 (Brussels, 23 September 1910; TS 4 (1913); Cd 6677) (the 'Salvage Convention 1910'). It seems to have been well recognised that the 1910 Convention reflected the general principles of English salvage law already being applied by the Admiralty courts in England: see eg the references to the Salvage Convention 1910 art 1 in *The Goring* [1988] AC 831 at 836, [1988] 1 All ER 641 at 646, [1988] 1 Lloyd's Rep 397 at 402, HL (salvage in non-tidal waters). In connection with the operation of the Convention see *Ministry* of *Trade of the Republic of Iraq v Tsavliris Salvage (International) Ltd, The Altair* [2008] EWHC 612 (Comm), [2008] 2 Lloyd's Rep 90, [2008] All ER (D) 14 (Apr).

2 As to the meaning of 'having the force of law' cf *The Hollandia* [1983] 1 AC 565, [1982] 3 All ER 1141, sub nom *The Morviken* [1983] 1 Lloyd's Rep 1, HL.

3 Merchant Shipping Act 1995 s 224(1). As to the meaning of 'United Kingdom' see PARA 16 note 3.

4 For a review of the law of salvage see *The Goring* [1988] AC 831 at 834 et seq, [1988] 1 All ER 641 at 643 et seq, [1988] 1 Lloyd's Rep 397 at 399 et seq, HL, per Lord Brandon of Oakbrook.

5 Ie following *Pepper (Inspector of Taxes) v Hart* [1993] AC 593, [1993] 1 All ER 42, HL; and see STATUTES AND LEGISLATIVE PROCESS vol 96 (2012) PARA 1122. Where statutory provisions are ambiguous, it is legitimate, in resolving any ambiguity, to have recourse to the travaux préparatoires of the Convention: *Gatoil International Inc v Arkwright-Boston Manufacturers Mutual Insurance Co* [1985] AC 255, [1985] 1 All ER 129, sub nom *The Sandrina* [1985] 1 Lloyd's Rep 181, HL.

6 As to treaty Acts and their interpretation generally see STATUTES AND LEGISLATIVE PROCESS vol 96 (2012) PARAS 635, 1128.

7 Salvage Convention art 3.

8 As to the meaning of 'vessel' see PARA 850 note 2. This exclusion is without prejudice to the International Convention on Salvage 1989 art 5 (salvage operations by or under the control of public authorities) (see PARA 851): see art 4(1).

9 As to the meaning of 'salvage operation' see PARA 850.

10 Salvage Convention art 4(1). Where a state party decides to apply the Convention to such warships or other vessels, it must notify the Secretary General of the International Maritime Organisation (IMO) specifying the terms and conditions of such application: arts 1(f), (g), 4(2). As to salvage claims by and against the Crown see PARA 854. State immunity is governed by the State Immunity Act 1978: see INTERNATIONAL RELATIONS LAW vol 61 (2010) PARA 242 et seq.

11 Salvage Convention art 5(1).

12 Salvage Convention art 5(2). The extent to which a public authority under a duty to perform salvage operations may avail itself of the rights and remedies provided for in the Convention is to be determined by the law of the state where such authority is situated: art 5(3).

13 For these purposes, 'inland waters' does not include any waters within the ebb and flow of the tide at ordinary spring tides or the waters of any dock which is directly or (by means of one or more other docks) indirectly, connected with such waters: Merchant Shipping Act 1995 Sch 11 Pt II para 2(2).

14 As to the meaning of 'vessel' under the Convention see PARA 850 note 2.

15 Merchant Shipping Act 1995 Sch 11 Pt II para 2(1)(a). This amounts to a reservation made by the United Kingdom pursuant to the powers conferred by the Salvage Convention art 30.

16 Merchant Shipping Act 1995 Sch 11 Pt II para 2(1)(b). See note 15.

852. Jurisdiction regarding salvage claims.

The Salvage Convention[1] applies whenever judicial or arbitral proceedings[2] relating to matters dealt with in the Convention are brought in a state party[3]. The Admiralty jurisdiction of the High Court[4] includes jurisdiction to hear and determine any claim under the Convention, under any contract for or in relation to salvage services or in the nature of salvage not falling within either of those two categories, or any corresponding claim in connection with an aircraft[5]. The jurisdiction extends to all ships, whether British or not and whether registered or not and wherever the residence or domicile of their owners may be, and to all claims wherever arising (including, in the case of cargo or wreck salvage, claims in respect of cargo or wreck found on land)[6].

Nothing in the Merchant Shipping Act 1995 provisions relating to salvage[7] prejudices or affects any jurisdiction or powers of Lord Warden or any officers of the Cinque ports[8] or of any court of those ports or of any court having concurrent jurisdiction within the boundaries of those ports; and disputes as to salvage arising without those boundaries are to be determined[9] in the manner in which they have been hitherto determined[10].

All salvage claims[11] must be started in the Admiralty Court[12]; the power to apportion amongst the salvors the amount of salvage remuneration was and is incident to the jurisdiction of the Admiralty Court in claims for salvage[13].

1 Ie the International Convention on Salvage 1989 (London, 28 April 1989; Cm 1526): see PARA 851.

2   For these purposes, references to judicial proceedings are references to proceedings, in England and Wales, in the High Court or the county court; and any reference to the tribunal having jurisdiction, so far as it refers to judicial proceedings, is to be construed accordingly: Merchant Shipping Act 1995 Sch 11 Pt II para 6. As to the meanings of 'England' and 'Wales' see PARA 16 note 2.

3   Salvage Convention art 2. An Order in Council made for these purposes and declaring that any state specified in the Order is a party to the Salvage Convention in respect of a specified country is conclusive evidence, subject to the provisions of any subsequent Order made for these purposes, that the state is a party to the Salvage Convention in respect of that country: Merchant Shipping Act 1995 Sch 11 Pt II para 7(1). For these purposes, 'country' includes territory: Sch 11 Pt II para 7(2). At the date at which this volume states the law, no such Order in Council had been made and none has effect as if so made.

     The Convention applies save to the extent that a contract otherwise provides expressly or by implication: see art 6; and PARA 853. As to salvage controlled by public authorities see PARA 851; and as to apportionment between salvors, where the law of the flag of the vessel applies, see PARA 901.

4   As to the Admiralty jurisdiction of the High Court of Justice generally see PARA 85 et seq. As to the Admiralty jurisdiction of the High Court in relation to salvage etc see PARAS 113–114. As to the mode of exercise of this jurisdiction see the Senior Courts Act 1981 s 21; and PARAS 93–94. As to the assignment of business to the Admiralty Court see PARA 91. The Admiralty jurisdiction of the High Court extends also to hovercraft: see PARA 87.

5   See the Senior Courts Act 1981 s 20(1)(a), (2)(j); and PARA 113. In connection with jurisdiction see *Ministry of Trade of the Republic of Iraq v Tsavliris Salvage (International) Ltd, The Altair* [2008] EWHC 612 (Comm), [2008] 2 Lloyd's Rep 90, [2008] All ER (D) 14 (Apr).

6   See the Senior Courts Act 1981 s 20(7); and PARA 86.

7   Ie the Merchant Shipping Act 1995 Pt IX (ss 224–255): see s 314(3), Sch 14 para 11.

8   As to the boundaries of the jurisdiction of the Lord Warden of the Cinque ports see the Cinque Ports Act 1821 s 18; and PARA 210.

9   Ie subject to the Salvage Convention as set out in the Merchant Shipping Act 1995 s 224(1), Sch 11 (see PARA 851 et seq): see Sch 14 para 11.

10 Merchant Shipping Act 1995 Sch 14 para 11.

11 For these purposes, 'admiralty claim' means a claim within the Admiralty jurisdiction of the High Court as set out in the Senior Courts Act 1981 s 20 (see PARA 85 et seq): see CPR 61.1(2)(a); and PARA 91 note 3.

12 See CPR 61.2(1)(d); and PARA 91. For these purposes, 'Admiralty Court' means the Admiralty Court of the Queen's Bench Division of the High Court of Justice: see CPR 61.1(2)(b); and PARA 91 note 3.

13 The court's power to apportion the amount of salvage remuneration amongst the salvors is now derived from the Merchant Shipping Act 1995 s 229(1)–(3): see PARA 903. The apportionment of salvage reward may be requested in the course of or promptly after the close of an ordinary salvage action by parties interested in the reward: see eg *The Firethorn* (1948) 81 Ll L Rep 178. Reasonable time will be allowed to a seaman: *The Spirit of the Age* (1857) Sw 286 at 287.

853. Salvage contracts and the Lloyd's Open Form.

The Salvage Convention[1] applies to any salvage operations[2] save to the extent that a contract otherwise provides expressly or by implication[3]. The master[4] has the authority to conclude contracts for salvage operations on behalf of the owner of the vessel[5]; and the master or the owner of the vessel has the authority to conclude such contracts on behalf of the owner of the property[6] on board the vessel[7].

Under the Salvage Convention a contract or any terms thereof may be annulled or modified if:

(1)   the contract has been entered into under undue influence or the influence of danger and its terms are inequitable[8]; or

(2)   the payment[9] under the contract is in an excessive degree too large or too small for the services actually rendered[10].

The Lloyd's Standard Form of Salvage Agreement, also known as 'Lloyd's Open Form' ('LOF'), is a standard contract for the performance of salvage services incorporating Lloyd's Standard Salvage and Arbitration Clauses (the 'LSSA Clauses'), and providing a framework for the collection of security to protect a salvor's claim and arbitration machinery to determine the contractors' remuneration or special compensation (or both) in the event that salvors and the owners of the salved vessel cannot agree on the payment for successful services[11].

1 Ie the International Convention on Salvage 1989 (London, 28 April 1989; Cm 1526): see PARA 851.
2 As to the meaning of 'salvage operation' see PARA 850. As to salvage controlled by public authorities see PARA 851.
3 Salvage Convention art 6(1). Nothing in these provisions affects the application of art 7 (see the text and notes 8–10) nor duties to prevent or minimise damage to the environment: art 6(3). For these purposes, 'damage to the environment' means substantial physical damage to human health or to marine life or resources in coastal or inland waters or areas adjacent thereto, caused by pollution, contamination, fire, explosion or similar major incidents: art 1(d).
4 As to the meaning of 'master' see PARA 444 note 1.
5 Salvage Convention art 6(2). As to the meaning of 'vessel' see PARA 850 note 2. As to the master's authority to sign a reasonable salvage contract see *The Unique Mariner* [1978] 1 Lloyd's Rep 438. Any restriction on the application of the Salvage Convention art 6(2) concerning agents would import a practical difficulty and an area of uncertainty into a beneficial provision of an international convention, designed to encourage certainty and remove or reduce delay and haggling, and could leave salvors potentially exposed to the vagaries of ship owners' corporate structures: *Ministry of Trade of the Republic of Iraq v Tsavliris Salvage (International) Ltd, The Altair* [2008] EWHC 612 (Comm), [2008] 2 Lloyd's Rep 90, [2008] All ER (D) 14 (Apr).
6 As to the meaning of 'property' see PARA 850 note 3.
7 Salvage Convention art 6(2), reversing the effect of *Industrie Chimiche Italia Centrale and Cerealfin SA v Alexander G Tsavliris & Sons Maritime Co, Panchristo Shipping Co SA and Bula Shipping Corpn, The Choko Star* [1990] 1 Lloyd's Rep 516, CA.
8 Salvage Convention art 7(a).
9 For these purposes, 'payment' means any reward, remuneration or compensation due under the Salvage Convention: art 1(e).
10 Salvage Convention art 7(b).
11 The latest version of LOF, which is approved and published by the Council of Lloyd's, is dated 9 May 2011 ('LOF 2011').

854. Salvage claims against the Crown; Crown rights of salvage and regulation thereof. Subject to the statutory provisions relating to the exclusion of proceedings in rem against the Crown[1], so far as consistent with the Salvage Convention[2], the law relating to civil salvage[3], whether of life or property, except for the provisions relating to the sale of detained property by the receiver[4], the apportionment of salvage under £5,000 by the receiver[5] and the apportionment of salvage by the court[6], apply in relation to salvage services in assisting any of Her Majesty's ships[7], or in saving life therefrom, or in saving any cargo or equipment belonging to Her Majesty in right of Her government in the United Kingdom, in the same manner as if the ship, cargo or equipment belonged to a private person[8].

Where salvage services are rendered by or on behalf of Her Majesty, whether in right of Her government in the United Kingdom or otherwise, Her Majesty is entitled to claim salvage in respect of those services to the same extent as any other salvor, and has the same rights and remedies in respect of those services as any other salvor[9].

No claim for salvage services by the commander or crew, or part of the crew, of any of Her Majesty's ships may be finally adjudicated upon without the consent of the Secretary of State[10] to the prosecution of the claim[11]; and any document purporting to give the consent of the Secretary of State for those purposes and to be signed by an officer of the Ministry of Defence is evidence of that consent[12]. If a claim is prosecuted without the consent so required, the claim must be dismissed with costs[13].

1 Ie the Crown Proceedings Act 1947 s 29 (see PARA 179): see the Merchant Shipping Act 1995 s 230(1). As to Admiralty claims in rem generally see PARA 158 et seq.
2 Ie the International Convention on Salvage 1989 (London, 28 April 1989; Cm 1526): see PARA 851.
3 As to the meaning of 'salvage' see PARA 849.
4 Ie the Merchant Shipping Act 1995 s 225 (see PARA 887): see s 230(1).

5   Ie the Merchant Shipping Act 1995 s 226 (see PARA 919): see s 230(1).
6   Ie the Merchant Shipping Act 1995 s 227 (see PARA 920): see s 230(1).
7   For these purposes, 'Her Majesty's ships' has the same meaning as in the Merchant Shipping Act
    1995 s 192 (see PARA 1015 note 7): s 230(7). As to the meaning of 'ship' see PARA 229.
8   Merchant Shipping Act 1995s 230(1).
9   Merchant Shipping Act 1995s 230(2).
10 As to the Secretary of State see PARA 36.
11 Merchant Shipping Act 1995s 230(3).
12 Merchant Shipping Act 1995s 230(4).
13 Merchant Shipping Act 1995s 230(5).

(ii) Performance of Salvage Operations

855. How salvage services may be rendered. Salvage services may be rendered in many different ways. They include: towing[1], piloting[2], navigating[3] or standing by[4] a vessel in danger; landing[5] or transhipping[6] cargo or persons belonging to that vessel; floating a stranded vessel[7]; raising a sunken vessel[8] or cargo[9]; saving a derelict[10] or wreck[11]; setting in motion[12], fetching[13] or bringing[14] assistance to a vessel in danger; giving advice or information in order to save a vessel from a local danger[15]; supplying officers or crew[16] or tackle[17] to a vessel in need of them; rescuing persons who have had to take to the boats[18]; removing a vessel from a danger such as a vessel or wreck which has fouled her[19], an ice floe[20] or an impending collision[21]; putting out a fire on board[22]; saving property or life from a vessel on fire[23]; removing a vessel or cargo from a position in which it is in imminent danger of catching fire[24]; protecting or rescuing a vessel, her cargo or persons on board from pirates or plunderers[25]; recovering and restoring a captured ship[26] or the recovery of a vessel from capture by revolutionaries[27]; and dispatching an aircraft to search for and transmit the position of a derelict vessel[28].

1   *The Ellora* (1862) Lush 550; *The Madras* [1898] P 90, 8 Asp MLC 397; *The Kangaroo* [1918] P
    327; *Troilus (Cargo Owners) v Glenogle (Owners, Master and Crew)* [1951] AC 820, [1951] 2 All
    ER 40, [1951] 1 Lloyd's Rep 467, HL; *The Ilo* [1982] 1 Lloyd's Rep 39.
2   *The Anders Knape* (1879) 4 PD 213, 4 Asp MLC 142; *The Tafelberg* (1941) 71 Ll L Rep 189.
3   *Newman v Walters* (1804) 3 Bos & P 612; *The Le Jonet* (1872) LR 3 A & E 556, 1 Asp MLC 438;
    The San Demetrio (1941) 69 Ll L Rep 5.
4   *The Undaunted* (1860) Lush 90 at 92; *The Guernsey Coast* (1950) 83 Ll L Rep 483.
5   *The Favorite* (1844) 2 Wm Rob 255.
6   *The Columbia* (1838) 3 Hag Adm 428; *The Erato* (1888) 13 PD 163, 6 Asp MLC 334.
7   *The Inchmaree* [1899] P 111, 8 Asp MLC 486; *The Cayo Bonito* [1904] P 310, 9 Asp MLC 603;
    The Queen Elizabeth (1949) 82 Ll L Rep 803.
8   *The Catherine* (1848) 6 Notes of Cases, Supp. xliii.
9   *The Cadiz and The Boyne* (1876) 3 Asp MLC 332.
10 *The Janet Court* [1897] P 59, 8 Asp MLC 223. As to the meaning of 'derelict' see PARA 923.
11 *The Samuel* (1851) 15 Jur 407. As to the meaning of 'wreck' see PARA 923.
12 *The Marguerite Molinos* [1903] P 160, 9 Asp MLC 424; *The Cayo Bonito* [1904] P 310, 9 Asp
    MLC 603 (launchers of a lifeboat).
13 *The Sarah* (1878) 3 PD 39, 3 Asp MLC 542.
14 *The Undaunted* (1860) Lush 90.
15 *The Eliza* (1862) Lush 536; *The Strathnaver* (1875) 1 App Cas 58 at 62, 63, 3 Asp MLC 113 at
    115, PC; but see *The Vrouw Margaretha* (1801) 4 Ch Rob 103 at 104 per Lord Stowell; *The Little
    Joe* (1860) Lush 88 at 89 per Dr Lushington (where it was doubted whether this service was a
    salvage service); *The Tower Bridge* [1936] P 30, 53 Ll L Rep 171; *The American Farmer* (1947)
    80 Ll L Rep 672.
16 *The Skibladner* (1877) 3 PD 24, 3 Asp MLC 556.
17 *The Prince of Wales* (1848) 6 Notes of Cases 39.
18 *The Cairo* (1874) LR 4 A & E 184, 2 Asp MLC 257; *The Carrie* [1917] P 224, 14 Asp MLC 321.
19 *The Vandyck* (1881) 7 PD 42 (affd (1882) 5 Asp MLC 17, CA); cf *The Emilie Galline* [1903] P
    106, 9 Asp MLC 401; *The Port Caledonia and the Anna* [1903] P 184, 9 Asp MLC 479; *The Ovre
    and the Conde de Zubiria* (1920) 2 Ll L Rep 21.
20 *The Swan* (1839) 1 Wm Rob 68.
21 *The Saratoga* (1861) Lush 318.

22 *The City of Newcastle* (1894) 7 Asp MLC 546; *The F D Lambert* [1917] P 232n, 14 Asp MLC 278; *The Flore* (1929) 34 Ll L Rep 172; *The Belgia* (1941) 71 Ll L Rep 21.
23 *The Eastern Monarch* (1860) Lush 81; *The Elkhound* (1931) 39 Ll L Rep 15.
24 *The Tees, The Pentucket* (1862) Lush 505; *The Demosthenes* (1926) 26 Ll L Rep 99.
25 *The Calypso* (1828) 2 Hag Adm 209; *The Erato* (1888) 13 PD 163, 6 Asp MLC 334.
26 *The Henry* (1810) Edw 192.
27 *The Lomonosoff* [1921] P 97.
28 *The American Farmer* (1947) 80 Ll L Rep 672.

856. Duties of salvor, owner and master. Under the Salvage Convention[1] the salvor owes a duty to the owner of the vessel[2] or other property[3] in danger[4]:

(1)   to carry out the salvage operations[5] with due care[6];
(2)   in performing the duty specified in head (1) above, to exercise due care to prevent or minimise damage to the environment[7];
(3)   whenever circumstances reasonably require, to seek assistance from other salvors[8]; and
(4)   to accept the intervention of other salvors when reasonably requested to do so by the owner or master[9] of the vessel or other property in danger, provided that the amount of his reward is not prejudiced should it be found that such a request was unreasonable[10].

The owner and master of the vessel or the owner of other property in danger owe a duty to the salvor[11]:

(a)   to co-operate fully with him during the course of the salvage operations[12];
(b)   in so doing, to exercise due care to prevent or minimise damage to the environment[13]; and
(c)   when the vessel or other property has been brought to a place of safety, to accept redelivery when reasonably requested by the salvor to do so[14].

1   Ie the International Convention on Salvage 1989 (London, 28 April 1989; Cm 1526): see PARA 851.
2   As to the meaning of 'vessel' see PARA 850 note 2.
3   As to the meaning of 'property' see PARA 850 note 3.
4   Salvage Convention art 8(1). Article 8 follows the common law principles established in *Tojo Maru (Owners) v Bureau Wijsmuller NV, The Toju Maru* [1972] AC 242, [1971] 1 All ER 1110, [1971] 1 Lloyd's Rep 341, HL (cited in PARA 851).
5   As to the meaning of 'salvage operation' see PARA 850.
6   Salvage Convention art 8(1)(a).
7   Salvage Convention art 8(1)(b). As to the meaning of 'damage to the environment' see PARA 853 note 3.
8   Salvage Convention art 8(1)(c).
9   As to the meaning of 'master' see PARA 444 note 1.
10   Salvage Convention art 8(1)(d).
11   Salvage Convention art 8(2).
12   Salvage Convention art 8(2)(a).
13   Salvage Convention art 8(2)(b).
14   Salvage Convention art 8(2)(c).

857. Rights of coastal states to protect coastline etc from pollution. Nothing in the Salvage Convention[1] affects the right of the coastal state concerned to take measures in accordance with generally recognised principles of international law to protect its coastline or related interests from pollution or the threat of pollution following upon a maritime casualty or acts relating to such a casualty which may reasonably be expected to result in major harmful consequences, including the right of a coastal state to give directions in relation to salvage operations[2].

1   Ie the International Convention on Salvage 1989 (London, 28 April 1989; Cm 1526): see PARA 851.
2   Salvage Convention art 9. As to the meaning of 'salvage operation' see PARA 850.

858. Duty to render assistance under Salvage Convention. Under the Salvage Convention[1] every master[2] is bound, so far as he can do so without serious danger to his vessel[3] and persons thereon, to render assistance to any person in danger of being lost at sea[4]. The master of a vessel who fails to comply with this duty commits an offence[5]. Compliance by the master of a vessel with that duty does not affect his right or the right of any other person to a payment[6] under the Convention or under any contract[7]. States parties to the Convention[8] must adopt the measures necessary to enforce that duty[9].

1 Ie the International Convention on Salvage 1989 (London, 28 April 1989; Cm 1526): see PARA 851.
2 As to the meaning of 'master' see PARA 444 note 1.
3 As to the meaning of 'vessel' see PARA 850 note 2.
4 Salvage Convention art 10(1). As to assistance to persons in danger at sea see further PARA 858. As to the effect of the duty to assist see *The Beaverford (Owners) v The Kafiristan (Owners)* [1938] AC 136, sub nom *The Kafiristan* [1937] 3 All ER 747, 58 Ll L Rep 317, HL (cited in PARA 868).
5 See the Merchant Shipping Act 1995 Sch 11 Pt II para 3(1); and PARA 1135. The owner of the vessel incurs no liability for any breach of the duty of the master so imposed: Salvage Convention art 10(3).
6 As to the meaning of 'payment' under the Convention see PARA 853 note 9.
7 Merchant Shipping Act 1995 Sch 11 Pt II para 3(2).
8 As to the making of Orders in Council declaring which states are parties to the Salvage Convention see PARA 852 note 3.
9 Salvage Convention art 10(2).

859. Co-operation between salvors, other interested parties and public authorities. Under the Salvage Convention[1] a state party[2] must, whenever regulating or deciding upon matters relating to salvage operations[3] such as admittance to ports of vessels[4] in distress or the provision of facilities to salvors, take into account the need for co-operation between salvors, other interested parties and public authorities in order to ensure the efficient and successful performance of salvage operations for the purpose of saving life or property[5] in danger as well as preventing damage to the environment[6] in general[7].

1 Ie the International Convention on Salvage 1989 (London, 28 April 1989; Cm 1526): see PARA 851.
2 As to the making of Orders in Council declaring which states are parties to the Salvage Convention see PARA 852 note 3.
3 As to the meaning of 'salvage operation' see PARA 850.
4 As to the meaning of 'vessel' see PARA 850 note 2.
5 As to the meaning of 'property' see PARA 850 note 3.
6 As to the meaning of 'damage to the environment' see PARA 853 note 3.
7 Salvage Convention art 11.

(iii) Conditions for Salvage Reward

860. Property the subject of salvage service. No property other than maritime property[1] can be the subject of a salvage service. 'Maritime property' consists of a vessel[2], her equipment, cargo or wreck. 'Cargo' includes all merchandise on board the salved vessel[3]. It does not include, so far as regards the liability to arrest and contribution to salvage reward, the personal effects of the master or crew[4], or the clothes or personal effects of passengers, whether on the person, or taken on board by them for their daily use[5], or, it would seem, ship's provisions[6].

Freight in the course of being earned by the carriage of the cargo, that is to say freight at risk, is the subject of salvage if it is earned in consequence of salvage service[7].

1 *Gas Float Whitton No 2* [1895] P 301, DC (on appeal [1896] P 42, 8 Asp MLC 110, CA; affd sub nom *Wells v Gas Float Whitton No 2 (Owners), The Gas Float Whitton No 2* [1897] AC 337, 8

Asp MLC 272, HL). See also *The Raft of Timber* (1844) 2 Wm Rob 251; *Palmer v Rouse* (1858) 3 H & N 505.

2   See *Gas Float Whitton No 2* [1895] P 301, DC (on appeal [1896] P 42, 8 Asp MLC 110, CA; affd sub nom *Wells v Gas Float Whitton No 2 (Owners), The Gas Float Whitton No 2* [1897] AC 337, 8 Asp MLC 272, HL); but see also the wide definition of 'vessel' in the International Convention on Salvage 1989 (London, 28 April 1989; Cm 1526) (the 'Salvage Convention') art 1(b) (cited in PARA 850 note 2). As to the operation of pre-existing common law together with the Merchant Shipping Act 1995 and the Salvage Convention see PARA 851.

3   As to whether 'cargo' should include goods in tow see *Wells v Gas Float Whitton No 2 (Owners)* [1897] AC 337 at 345, 8 Asp MLC 272 at 274, HL.

4   See 1 Beawes's *Lex Mercatoria* (6th Edn) (Chitty) p 242.

5   *The Willem III* (1871) LR 3 A & E 487, 1 Asp MLC 129.

6   Cf *Brown v Stapyleton* (1827) 4 Bing 119.

7   See PARA 888.

861. Danger requisite. The essence of a salvage service is that it is a service rendered to property or life in danger[1]. The requisite degree of danger is a real and appreciable danger. It must not be merely fanciful, but it need not be immediate or absolute[2]. It is sufficient if at the time of the service the situation of the subject of the service is such as to cause reasonable apprehension on the part of the person in charge of it[3]. The danger may arise from the condition of the salved vessel[4], or of her crew[5], from her position, or from the master's want of skill or his ignorance of the locality or of local conditions[6].

A service which begins as salvage is not necessarily transformed into towage[7] because on the voyage the ship is towed past, or into, ports at which she could be in safety[8].

1   See generally PARA 112 et seq. As to the operation of pre-existing common law together with the Merchant Shipping Act 1995 and the International Convention on Salvage 1989 (London, 28 April 1989; Cm 1526) (the 'Salvage Convention') see PARA 851.

2   *The Charlotte* (1848) 3 Wm Rob 68 at 71 per Dr Lushington (approved in *The Strathnaver* (1875) 1 App Cas 58 at 65, 3 Asp MLC 113 at 116, PC); and see *The Phantom* (1866) LR 1 A & E 58 at 60 per Dr Lushington; *The Calyx* (1910) 27 TLR 166; cf *The Sea Salvage* (1912) Times, 9 December. The dictum in *Akerblom v Price* (1881) 7 QBD 129 at 135, 4 Asp MLC 441 at 444, CA, per Brett LJ, that 'it is essential that the ship should be in imminent danger of being lost' may be explained as referring only to the case before him, a salvage claim by a pilot, to which special considerations apply (see PARA 869). For an extreme case see *The Batavier* (1853) 1 Ecc & Ad 169.

3   See the cases cited in note 2.

4   *The Ella Constance* (1864) 33 LJPM & A 189 at 191 (want of fuel); *The Cythera* [1965] 2 Lloyd's Rep 454 (NSW) (danger of vessel being stolen).

5   *The Aglaia* (1888) 13 PD 160, 6 Asp MLC 337 (crew suffering from frostbite).

6   *The Eugenie* (1844) 3 Notes of Cases 430 at 431; *The Lomonosoff* [1921] P 97; *The Tower Bridge* [1936] P 30, 53 Ll L Rep 171; *The Tres* (1936) 55 Ll L Rep 16.

7   As to towage generally see PARA 597 et seq.

8   *Troilus (Cargo Owners) v Glenogle (Owners, Master and Crew)* [1951] AC 820, [1951] 2 All ER 40, [1951] 1 Lloyd's Rep 467, HL.

862. Evidence of danger. The burden of proving the presence of danger rests upon those who claim as salvors[1]. The conduct of those on board the salved ship in giving signals of distress or in accepting help may be evidence of the presence of danger[2]. However, the views of experienced personnel on board the salved vessel are relevant only in so far as they shed light on the attitude which would have been adopted by a reasonably prudent and skilful person in charge of the venture; they are not dispositive of the issue of danger which has to be decided objectively[3].

Where signals of distress are wrongfully used, compensation is recoverable for any labour undertaken, or risk or loss incurred, by reason of persons accepting and acting on the prescribed signals of distress[4], and persons who are induced by ambiguous signals to proceed to the assistance of a vessel which is damaged or in danger are entitled to claim as salvors[5].

1   *The Wilhelmine* (1842) 1 Notes of Cases 376 at 378. See also *The Calyx* (1910) 27 TLR 166. As to the operation of pre-existing common law together with the Merchant Shipping Act 1995 and the International Convention on Salvage 1989 (London, 28 April 1989; Cm 1526) (the 'Salvage Convention') see PARA 851.
2   *The Bomarsund* (1860) Lush 77; cf *The Elswick Park* [1904] P 76, 9 Asp MLC 481.
3   *The Hamtun (owners) v The St John (owners)* [1999] 1 Lloyd's Rep 883, [1999] 1 All ER (Comm) 587.
4   As to the prescribed signals of distress and their use see PARA 726.
5   *The Mary* (1843) 1 Wm Rob 448 at 452, 453; *The Racer* (1874) 2 Asp MLC 317; *The Aglaia* (1888) 13 PD 160, 6 Asp MLC 337.

863.   Useful result. Under the Salvage Convention[1] salvage operations[2] which have had a useful result give right to a reward[3], and except as otherwise provided, no payment[4] is due under the Convention if the salvage operations have had no useful result[5]. This preserves the principle known in English common law[6] as the 'requirement of success' whereby to obtain a salvage reward[7] the salvor has, as a general rule, to show that his service has been successful[8]. Services, however meritorious, which do not contribute to the ultimate success give no right to reward[9].

Under the common law, salvage reward is given for benefits actually conferred, not for a service attempted to be rendered[10]. The claimant need not, however, prove that his service alone would have produced the ultimate safety of the subject of the service; it is sufficient for him to show that he materially contributed to its ultimate safety[11], and, where there is a doubt whether a service has contributed to the ultimate safety, the court inclines to the view that the service has so contributed[12]. No salvage reward is recoverable, however meritorious and hazardous the service may have been, and even though the property or lives in danger may have been ultimately preserved, if, at the termination of the service, the subject of the service has been left in a position not less dangerous than that in which it was at the commencement of the service, or the value at the conclusion of the service was no greater than at the commencement[13]. The mere fact that the claimant brought the ship to a spot where the ultimate salvor found her is not of itself a contribution to the ultimate success[14].

1   Ie the International Convention on Salvage 1989 (London, 28 April 1989; Cm 1526): see PARA 851.
2   As to the meaning of 'salvage operation' see PARA 850.
3   Salvage Convention art 12(1). The Convention provisions relating to the rights of salvors (ie Ch III (arts 12–19): see PARA 878 et seq) apply, notwithstanding that the salved vessel and the vessel undertaking the salvage operations belong to the same owner: art 12(3). As to the meaning of 'vessel' see PARA 850 note 2. Article 12(3), which permits a claim for salvage even where the service is provided by a sister ship, constitutes a change from English common law: cf *The Caroline* (1861) Lush 334; *The Goring* [1988] AC 831, [1988] 1 All ER 641, [1988] 1 Lloyd's Rep 397, HL.
4   As to the meaning of 'payment' see PARA 853 note 9.
5   Salvage Convention art 12(2). Quaere whether the common law principle of 'engaged services' (ie that where a service has been rendered at the request of the master or other person in charge of a vessel in danger in circumstances from which a promise to pay for the service can be implied, a salvage reward is payable for that service if the vessel is ultimately saved, even though the service did not contribute to its ultimate safety: see eg *The Undaunted* (1860) Lush 90; *The Helvetia* (1894) 8 Asp MLC 264n; *The Cambrian* (1897) 8 Asp MLC 263; *The Dart* (1899) 8 Asp MLC 122 at 481 at 482, 483 (explaining the decision in *The Melpomene* (1873) LR 4 A & E 129, 2 Asp MLC 122 on the same grounds); *The Stiklestad* [1926] P 205, 17 Asp MLC 191 (affd 43 TLR 118, CA); *The Tarbert* [1921] P 372, 15 Asp MLC 423; *The Loch Tulla* (1950) 84 Ll L Rep 62; *The Alenquer, The Rene* [1955] 1 Lloyd's Rep 101) is still good law; and see note 3.
6   As to the operation of pre-existing common law together with the Merchant Shipping Act 1995 and the Salvage Convention see PARA 851.

7 As to salvage rewards see PARA 883 et seq.
8 See also the principle of 'No Cure, No Pay'; and PARA 883 et seq.
9 *Melanie (Owners) v San Onofre (Owners)* [1925] AC 246 at 262, 16 Asp MLC 479 at 484, HL.
10 *The Zephyrus* (1842) 1 Wm Rob 329 at 330; *The EU* (1853) 1 Ecc & Ad 63 at 65; and see *The Killeena* (1881) 6 PD 193 at 198, 4 Asp MLC 472 at 473; *The Camellia* (1883) 9 PD 27 at 29, 5 Asp MLC 197 at 199; *The City of Chester* (1884) 9 PD 182 at 202, 5 Asp MLC 311 at 319, CA; *The Dart* (1899) 8 Asp MLC 481 at 482, 483; *Melanie (Owners) v San Onofre (Owners)* [1925] AC 246, 16 Asp MLC 479, HL.
11 *The Jonge Bastiaan* (1804) 5 Ch Rob 322; *The Atlas* (1862) Lush 518, PC; *The Camellia* (1884) 9 PD 27, 5 Asp MLC 197; *The Hestia* [1895] P 193, 7 Asp MLC 599; *The August Korff* [1903] P 166, 9 Asp MLC 428; *The Kangaroo* [1918] P 327.
12 *The EU* (1853) 1 Ecc & Ad 63; *The Santipore* (1854) 1 Ecc & Ad 231.
13 *The Cheerful* (1885) 11 PD 3, 5 Asp MLC 525; *The Benlarig* (1888) 14 PD 3, 6 Asp MLC 360; *The Lepanto* [1892] P 122, 7 Asp MLC 192; *The Dart* (1899) 8 Asp MLC 481; *The Tarbert* [1921] P 372, 15 Asp MLC 423.
14 *Melanie (Owners) v San Onofre (Owners)* [1925] AC 246 at 263, 16 Asp MLC 479 at 484, HL.

864. Salvage of persons. Under the Salvage Convention[1] a salvor of human life, who has taken part in the services rendered on the occasion of the accident giving rise to salvage, is entitled to a fair share of the payment[2] awarded to the salvor for salving the vessel[3] or other property[4] or preventing or minimising damage to the environment[5]. No remuneration is due from persons whose lives are saved, but nothing in these provisions[6] affects the provisions of national law on this subject[7].

At common law, it was held that where no property had been saved and life alone had been preserved from destruction, no suit for a salvage reward could be maintained in the Admiralty Court, one reason being that there could be no proceedings in rem, which was the ancient foundation of the salvage suit[8]. Where, however, both life and property had been saved it was the practice to give an enhanced award, the enhancement being a reflection of the value of the services rendered in the saving of life[9].

In circumstances where:

(1)   services are rendered wholly or in part in United Kingdom waters[10] in saving life from a vessel of any nationality or elsewhere in saving life from any United Kingdom ship[11]; and

(2)   either the vessel and other property are destroyed or the sum to which the salvor[12] is entitled under the Convention[13] is less than a reasonable amount for the services rendered in saving life[14],

the Secretary of State[15] may, if he thinks fit, pay to the salvor such sum or, as the case may be, such additional sum as he thinks fit in respect of the services rendered in saving life[16].

1 Ie the International Convention on Salvage 1989 (London, 28 April 1989; Cm 1526): see PARA 851.
2 As to the meaning of 'payment' see PARA 853 note 9.
3 As to the meaning of 'vessel' see PARA 850 note 2.
4 As to the meaning of 'property' see PARA 850 note 3.
5 Salvage Convention art 16(2). As to the meaning of 'damage to the environment' see PARA 853 note 3. In certain circumstances, a salvor might have obtained a true life salvage award under the Merchant Shipping Act 1894 ss 544–546 (repealed)) where, even though he himself had rendered no salvage services to ships and cargo (*The Bosworth (No 3)* [1962] 1 Lloyd's Rep 483), some property was preserved (*Nourse v Liverpool Sailing Ship Owners Mutual Protection and Indemnity Association* [1896] 2 QB 16, CA; *The Bosworth (No 2)* [1960] 1 All ER 729, [1961] 1 WLR 319, [1960] 1 Lloyd's Rep 173, CA). See also *The Schiller (Cargo ex)* (1877) 2 PD 145, CA (where the property salved was recovered by divers long after the life services were rendered). It is apprehended that the former practice of the Admiralty Court is now good law and that there can be no claim for life salvage unless some property is also saved: see the Salvage Convention art 16(2).
6 Ie nothing in the Salvage Convention art 16: see art 16(1).

7   Salvage Convention art 16(1). As to recourse for life salvage payments see further PARA 864.
     Article 16(1) must be read in the light of the duty under art 10: see PARA 858. There are no
     principles of English common law which conflict with art 16(1).
8   *The Fusilier* (1865) Brown & Lush 341 at 344 per Dr Lushington; and see *The Aid* (1822) 1 Hag
     Adm 83. As to the Admiralty jurisdiction of the High Court of Justice generally see PARA 85 et seq;
     and as to claims in rem generally see PARA 92 et seq. As to the operation of pre-existing common
     law together with the Merchant Shipping Act 1995 and the Salvage Convention see PARA 851.
9   See *The Bosworth (No 3)* [1962] 1 Lloyd's Rep 483; *The Bosworth (No 2)* [1960] 1 All ER 729,
     [1961] 1 WLR 319, [1960] 1 Lloyd's Rep 173, CA; *The Fusilier* (1865) Brown & Lush 341; *The
     Johannes* (1860) Lush 182; *The Willem III* (1871) LR 3 A & E 487, 1 Asp MLC.
10   As to the meaning of 'United Kingdom waters' see PARA 48 note 10. As to the meaning of 'United
     Kingdom' see PARA 16 note 3.
11   Merchant Shipping Act 1995 Sch 11 Pt II para 5(1)(a). As to the meaning of 'United Kingdom ship'
     see PARA 230; and as to the meaning of 'ship' see PARA 229.
12   As to the meaning of 'salvor' see PARA 849 note 4.
13   Ie under the Salvage Convention art 16(2) (see the text and notes 1–5).
14   Merchant Shipping Act 1995 Sch 11 Pt II para 5(1)(b).
15   As to the Secretary of State see PARA 36.
16   Merchant Shipping Act 1995 Sch 11 Pt II para 5(2). As to life salvage see also PARA 120 et seq.

865. Disqualifications. Under the Salvage Convention[1] a salvor may be
deprived of the whole or part of the payment due, to the extent that the salvage
operations[2] have become necessary or more difficult because of fault or neglect on
his part or if the salvor has been guilty of fraud or other dishonest conduct[3].
Services rendered notwithstanding the express and reasonable prohibition of the
owner or master[4] of the vessel[5] or the owner of any other property[6] in danger
which is not and has not been on board the vessel do not give rise to payment
under the Convention[7].

At common law the owner, charterer and crew of the salving vessel may be
disqualified from claiming a salvage reward[8]. The owner or the charterer, as the
case may be, of the salving vessel is not entitled to claim a salvage reward against
the salved vessel if he is also the owner of the salved vessel, or her charterer where
the charterparty amounts to a demise[9]; but he can still claim against the cargo[10] on
board the salved vessel[11], unless by the terms of his contract of carriage of the
cargo on the salved vessel he is liable for loss or damage to it, and the salvage
service rendered was necessary to save it from loss or damage[12]. If, however, only
some of part owners of the salving vessel are interested in the salved vessel, the
others are entitled to claim a salvage reward[13]. The inability of the owner or
charterer of the salving vessel to claim a salvage reward, whether against the ship
or against the cargo, in these circumstances, does not affect the right to a salvage
reward of the master or the crew of the salving vessel[14].

If the salvage services were rendered necessary by the faulty navigation of the
salving vessel, neither the owner nor the crew can obtain a salvage reward[15]; and
in that case no distinction is made between those who were and those who were
not responsible for the negligent navigation[16]. Where, however, a vessel has been
damaged by collision with a second vessel, caused by the negligence of the second
vessel, and is salved by a third vessel, the owner as well as the crew of the salving
vessel may be entitled to claim as salvors, even though the owner is also the owner
of the vessel at fault for the collision[17].

Where by the custom of a particular trade, or with regard to vessels of a
particular port, or by special agreement, the salving and salved vessels are bound
to give mutual protection[18], no salvage reward is recoverable.

1   Ie the International Convention on Salvage 1989 (London, 28 April 1989; Cm 1526): see
     PARA 851.
2   As to the meaning of 'salvage operation' see PARA 850.
3   Salvage Convention art 18. The extent to which a salvor may be deprived of salvage remuneration
     will depend upon the causative potency of his fault in causing the salvage operations to become

necessary or more difficult: see *Maridive VII v Key Singapore, The Key Singapore* [2004] EWHC 2227 (Comm), [2005] 1 All ER (Comm) 99, [2005] 1 Lloyd's Rep 91 (those on board the towed rig and those on board the tugs were held to be equally at fault for the failure to heave which necessitated salvage operations; reward apportioned accordingly). As to the general duties of the salvor see PARA 856. See also *Tojo Maru (Owners) v Bureau Wijsmuller NV, The Toju Maru* [1972] AC 242, [1971] 1 All ER 1110, [1971] 1 Lloyd's Rep 341, HL (salvors' liability to counterclaim).

4   As to the meaning of 'master' see PARA 444 note 1.

5   As to the meaning of 'vessel' see PARA 850 note 2.

6   As to the meaning of 'property' see PARA 850 note 3.

7   Salvage Convention art 19.

8   As to salvage rewards see PARA 883 et seq. As to the operation of pre-existing common law together with the Merchant Shipping Act 1995 and the Salvage Convention see PARA 851.

9   *The Maria Jane* (1850) 14 Jur 857; *The Collier* (1866) LR 1 A & E 83. The Salvage Convention permits a claim for salvage, even where the service is provided by a sister ship: see PARA 863.

10   As to the meaning of 'cargo' for salvage purposes see PARA 860.

11   *The Miranda* (1872) LR 3 A & E 561, 1 Asp MLC 440; *The Laertes (Cargo ex)* (1887) 12 PD 187, 6 Asp MLC 174; *The August Korff* [1903] P 166, 9 Asp MLC 428.

12   *The Glenfruin* (1885) 10 PD 103, 5 Asp MLC 413.

13   *The Caroline* (1861) Lush 334. See also *The Glenfruin* (1885) 10 PD 103, 5 Asp MLC 413.

14   *The Sappho* (1871) LR 3 PC 690, 1 Asp MLC 65. See also *The Glenfruin* (1885) 10 PD 103, 5 Asp MLC 113. Claims by seamen against a salved vessel which belongs to the owner of their own vessel are, however, not looked upon favourably unless the services rendered by them were of a serious nature: *The Agamemnon* (1883) 5 Asp MLC 92; *The Leon Blum* [1915] P 90 at 103 (affd [1915] P 290, 13 Asp MLC 273, CA).

15   *The Capella (Cargo ex)* (1807) LR 1 A & E 356. See also *The Altair* [1897] P 105, 8 Asp MLC 224; *The Harvest Home* [1904] P 409, 10 Asp MLC 19. Cf *The Beaverford (Owners) v The Kafiristan (Owners)* [1938] AC 136 at 149, [1937] 3 All ER 747 at 754, 755 (revsg sub nom *The Kafiristan* [1937] P 63, [1937] 1 All ER 40, CA) where Lord Wright expressed some doubt of 'the logic or equity' of the decision in *The Capella (Cargo ex)* and stated that, if the rule laid down in that case is at all sound, it is at any rate excluded where the ship which is the instrument of the salvage is a different ship from that which is the instrument of the negligent collision. See also the text and note 10.

16   *The Duc d'Aumale (No 2)* [1904] P 60, 9 Asp MLC 502. See notes 8, 10.

17   *The Beaverford (Owners) v The Kafiristan (Owners)* [1938] AC 136, sub nom *The Kafiristan* [1937] 3 All ER 747, 58 Ll L Rep 317, HL (approving *The Glengaber* (1872) 1 Asp MLC 401, and distinguishing *The Glenfruin* (1885) 10 PD 103, 5 Asp MLC 413); *Susan V Luckenbach (Owners) v Admiralty Comrs, The Susan V Luckenbach* [1951] P 197, [1951] 1 All ER 753, 84 Ll L Rep 538, CA (colliding and salving vessels under control of different departments of the Crown). See note 8.

18   *The Swan* (1839) 1 Wm Rob 68 at 70. This defence succeeded in *The Zephyr* (1827) 2 Hag Adm 43 (Honduras trade), *The Harriot* (1842) 1 Wm Rob 439 (South Sea whaling trade), and *The Maria Jane* (1850) 14 Jur 857 (African trade). It failed in *The Waterloo* (1820) 2 Dods 433 (vessels of the East India Company), and *The Swan* (northern whaling fisheries). In *The Africa* (1854) 1 Ecc & Ad 299, Dr Lushington doubted whether such a custom could prevail with regard to services rendered by a steamship. Strict proof of the custom or agreement will be required: *The Waterloo* at 436; and see CUSTOM AND USAGE vol 32 (2012) PARA 77 et seq. In the absence of proof of custom or special agreement, there may still be a connection 'between two ships which, though it would not bar a claim for salvage, might affect the quantum': *The Collier* (1866) LR 1 A & E 83 at 86. See also *The Trelawney* (1802) 4 Ch Rob 223 at 227, 228; *Clan Steam Trawling Co Ltd v Aberdeen Steam Trawling and Fishing Co Ltd* 1908 SC 651.

(iv) Who may be Eligible for Reward

866.   The right to salvage reward at common law. Maritime law[1] differs from common law in that at common law work and labour voluntarily done or money voluntarily expended by one person to preserve or benefit property which he knows to be that of another does not create any lien on the property saved or benefited, or create any obligation to repay the expenditure[2].

The common law courts would not entertain an action for salvage unless the salvor could prove a contract of employment, express or implied[3], under which reward was due and on which, accordingly, the salvor could recover quantum meruit in the absence of an agreement as to the amount of reward[4]. The right of the salvor in maritime law to salvage reward does not depend on contract, but on the obligation which that law imposes on the owner of property saved, or on persons who have had a benefit arising out of the saving of the property, to remunerate the salvor[5], although the right often does arise out of, or is accompanied by, contract[6].

A salvage service rendered to property so circumstanced that a prudent owner of the property would accept the service creates of itself a title to salvage reward[7]; and the fact that an express contract for the performance of salvage services has been entered into by the salvor, who has failed to carry it out, does not preclude him from obtaining salvage reward, if the service rendered by him contributed to some extent to the ultimate safety of the property in danger[8].

To maintain a claim for salvage reward it is not sufficient that services in the nature of salvage services have been rendered. It is necessary to show that the property in danger, or some part of it, has been ultimately saved, whether the result has been achieved with the aid of the salvage service or by other means[9]; for, if no part of the property in danger is ultimately saved, no salvage reward is recoverable unless by special agreement salvage reward is to be paid independently of the ultimate safety of the property in danger[10].

1 As to the nature of maritime law see PARAS 1–3.
2 *Falcke v Scottish Imperial Insurance Co* (1886) 34 ChD 234 at 248, 249, CA; and see CONTRACT vol 22 (2012) PARA 218; RESTITUTION vol 88 (2012) PARA 415. As to the operation of pre-existing common law together with the Merchant Shipping Act 1995 and the International Convention on Salvage 1989 (London, 28 April 1989; Cm 1526) (the 'Salvage Convention') see PARA 851.
3 *Lipson v Harrison* (1853) 2 WR 10 (need to establish implied contract). As to contracts of employment generally see EMPLOYMENT vol 39 (2014) PARA 1 et seq.
4 *Newman v Walters* (1804) 3 Bos & P 612.
5 *Five Steel Barges* (1890) 15 PD 142 at 146, 6 Asp MLC 580 at 582 per Hannen P; *The Hestia* [1895] P 193, 7 Asp MLC 599; *The Port Victor (Cargo ex)* [1901] P 243 at 247, 249, 9 Asp MLC 163 at 165, 166.
6 As to agreements for salvage see also PARA 883 et seq.
7 *The Vandyck* (1881) 7 PD 42 (affd (1882) 5 Asp MLC 17, CA); *The Liffey* (1887) 6 Asp MLC 255 (services rendered to a vessel which the salvor believed to be his own); *The Auguste Legembre* [1902] P 123, 9 Asp MLC 279 (services declined by master of salved vessel); and see *The Emilie Galline* [1903] P 106, 9 Asp MLC 401; *The Port Caledonia and The Anna* [1903] P 184, 9 Asp MLC 479; *The Kangaroo* [1918] P 327 (services accepted under protest while under convoy). As to salvage charges recoverable under a policy of marine insurance see INSURANCE vol 60 (2011) PARAS 400, 422.
8 *The Hestia* [1895] P 193, 7 Asp MLC 599.
9 *The Sarpedon (Cargo ex)* (1877) 3 PD 28, 3 Asp MLC 509; *The Renpor* (1883) 8 PD 115, 5 Asp MLC 98, CA; *The Elton* [1891] P 265 at 269; *The Port Victor (Cargo ex)* [1901] P 243 at 255–256, 9 Asp MLC 182 at 184, CA. As to the requirement of successful service see PARA 863.
10 See PARA 883.

867. Requirement of personal services. The general rule at common law is that all those, and only those, who render personal[1] services in the performance of a salvage service are entitled to a salvage reward[2]. To this rule there are, however, certain exceptions.

The rule of personal service does not extend to the associates of the actual salvors or to the owners of the salving vessel. Members of the crew of a vessel[3], including a vessel engaged in public service[4], who remain on board during the performance of salvage services by other members of the crew, taking no part, but willing, if called upon, to take a part in the services, are entitled to a share in the salvage reward[5]. The owner of the salving vessel is also entitled to a salvage award for the use of his vessel[6].

The charterer may stand in the position of the owner of the salving vessel in this respect; whether he does so or not depends on the terms of the charterparty. If the charterparty amounts to a demise of the vessel[7], or contains an express provision entitling the charterer to a salvage reward, he is entitled to share as charterer in the reward[8]; otherwise he is not[9].

1   *The Charlotte* (1848) 3 Wm Rob 68 at 72 per Dr Lushington. Thus, a coastguard officer merely sending off sailors to a vessel in danger (*The Vine* (1825) 2 Hag Adm 1), or a person who merely hires labourers to assist in unloading a stranded vessel (*The Watt* (1843) 2 Wm Rob 70), is not a salvor. See also *HMS Thetis* (1833) 3 Hag Adm 14 at 41, 42, 61. As to the operation of pre-existing common law together with the Merchant Shipping Act 1995 and the International Convention on Salvage 1989 (London, 28 April 1989; Cm 1526) (the 'Salvage Convention') see PARA 851.
2   As to salvage reward see PARA 883 et seq.
3   This exception applies only to those who properly constitute the crew (*The Coriolanus* (1890) 15 PD 103, 6 Asp MLC 514 (cattlemen); *The Minneapolis* [1902] P 30, 9 Asp MLC 270 (horsemen)), but it includes the non-navigating members of the crew such as the doctor, stewardesses, bakers and other persons of a like description (see *The Spree* [1893] P 147, 7 Asp MLC 397; *The Dunottar Castle* [1902] WN 70; *The Minneapolis*).
4   The Crown may claim salvage to the same extent as any other salvor: see the Merchant Shipping Act 1995 s 230(2); and PARA 854. As to salvage services by Her Majesty's ships see ARMED FORCES vol 3 (2011) PARA 449.
5   *The Sarah Jane* (1843) 2 Wm Rob 110. See also *Banda and Kirwee Booty* (1866) LR 1 A & E 109 at 135, 250 (right of all crew to share in naval prize bounty). As to the apportionment of reward see PARAS 851–852, 904 et seq.
6   *The Vine* (1825) 2 Hag Adm 1; *The Norden* (1853) 1 Ecc & Ad 185; *The Two Friends* (1844) 2 Wm Rob 349. Where the salving vessel is herself the principal instrument in effecting the service, as is now generally the case, the owner receives the largest share of the reward: see PARA 905.
7   *Elliott Steam Tug Co Ltd v Admiralty Comrs, Page v Admiralty Comrs* [1921] 1 AC 137, 15 Asp MLC 81, HL; and see ENVIRONMENTAL QUALITY AND PUBLIC HEALTH vol 45 (2010) PARAS 446, 480.
8   *The Maria Jane* (1850) 14 Jur 857 at 858; *The Collier* (1866) LR 1 A & E 83 at 85.
9   *The Waterloo* (1820) 2 Dods 433; *The Scout* (1872) LR 3 A & E 512, 1 Asp MLC 258.

868.   Voluntariness. Under the Salvage Convention[1] no payment[2] is due unless the services rendered exceed what can be reasonably considered as due performance of a contract entered into before the danger arose[3]. This is a restatement of the position at common law[4] whereby, subject to certain exceptions[5], the salvor's service must be voluntary as between the salvors and the owners of the salved vessel[6], but it may be the subject of special agreement[7]. If it is rendered under a general contractual obligation, in pursuance of official duty or solely in the interest of self-preservation, it is not a salvage service[8]. Thus, no claim as salvors may ordinarily[9] be made by the owner, master, crew and pilot of the salved vessel, or of a tug towing the salved vessel under a contract of towage, the ship's agent, government officials acting within the scope of their duties, and passengers on board the salved vessel for services rendered by them. Insurers who incur expenses which come within the suing and labouring clause of the policy[10] and persons who are employed under contract with third persons to do work in saving property may likewise be disqualified from obtaining a salvage reward[11] for their services[12].

1   Ie the International Convention on Salvage 1989 (London, 28 April 1989; Cm 1526): see PARA 851.
2   As to the meaning of 'payment' see PARA 853 note 9.
3   Salvage Convention art 17.
4   As to the operation of pre-existing common law together with the Merchant Shipping Act 1995 and the Salvage Convention see PARA 851.
5   The statutory duty under the Merchant Shipping Act 1995 s 92 (see PARA 727) whereby those on board a ship which has been in collision with another ship are required to stand by the other ship and afford assistance does not prevent the assistance so given from ranking as a voluntary service: see *The Hannibal, The Queen* (1867) LR 2 A & E 53; *Melanie (Owners) v San Onofre (Owners)* [1925] AC 246 at 261, 262, 16 Asp MLC 479 at 483, HL (approved in *The Beaverford (Owners) v The Kafiristan (Owners)* [1938] AC 136, [1937] 3 All ER 747, 58 Ll L Rep 317, HL).

6	*The Sarpen* [1916] P 306, 13 Asp MLC 370, CA. It is immaterial that the salvor has been ordered by someone who has control to carry out the salvage operations: *The Kangaroo* [1918] P 327; and see PARA 867.

7	See PARA 866.

8	*The Neptune* (1824) 1 Hag Adm 227 at 236 per Lord Stowell; *The Schiller (Cargo ex)* (1877) 2 PD 145 at 149, 3 Asp MLC 439 at 442, CA, per Brett LJ; *Clan Steam Trawling Co v Aberdeen Steam Trawling and Fishing Co* 1908 SC 651; *The Carrie* [1917] P 224, 14 Asp MLC 321; *The FD Lambert* [1917] P 232n, 14 Asp MLC 278; *The Lomonosoff* [1921] P 97; and see also PARA 933 et seq.

9	As to the circumstances in which these classes of persons will be treated as salvors see PARA 933 et seq.

10	*Crouan v Stanier* [1904] 1 KB 87. As to the suing and labouring clause, and as to the charges covered by it, see INSURANCE vol 60 (2011) PARA 411 et seq.

11	As to salvage rewards see PARA 943 et seq.

12	*The Solway Prince* [1896] P 120, 8 Asp MLC 128 (where the claimants were persons who had entered into such a contract with the insurers of the vessel); *The Pinna* (1912) Times, 29 November (persons contracting with canal company). Lifeboatmen employed to render services in saving life may be in this position: see PARA 940.

869. Crews and pilots. At common law[1] the crew of a salved vessel may claim a salvage reward as salvors if, prior to the performance of their services, their contracts of service have been terminated[2]. Termination of the contract of service may take place through discharge of the seamen by the master[3], or abandonment[4] or hostile capture[5] of the vessel.

There must be special circumstances of danger attending the performance of the pilot's duties[6] in order to justify a claim by him as a salvor[7]. They may exist at the beginning of the pilotage service[8] or they may supervene afterwards[9]. Whenever they occur, they must be of such a character as to make it unjust that the pilot should be paid otherwise than by a salvage reward[10]. The burden of showing that pilotage services were converted into salvage services rests strongly on the pilot[11].

Where a pilot is called on in any emergency to perform services outside his duties as pilot, as, for example, rendering assistance to a vessel outside his pilotage district, or doing work other than pilotage, he is entitled to be treated as an ordinary salvor[12].

1	As to the operation of pre-existing common law together with the Merchant Shipping Act 1995 and the International Convention on Salvage 1989 (London, 28 April 1989; Cm 1526) see PARA 851.

2	*The Sappho* (1871) LR 3 PC 690 at 694, 1 Asp MLC 65 at 66.

3	*The Warrior* (1862) Lush 476. The discharge will be valid even though improperly given by the master provided that there is no fraud on the part of the crew in accepting it: see *The Warrior* at 482.

4	The abandonment must be final, in good faith, and ordered by the master in consequence of danger: *The Florence* (1852) 16 Jur 572; *The Le Jonet* (1872) LR 3 A & E 556, 1 Asp MLC 438; *The Portreath* [1923] P 155, 16 Asp MLC 227; *The San Demetrio* (1941) 69 Ll L Rep 5; *The Albionic* [1942] P 81, 72 Ll L Rep 91, CA. Whether there has been abandonment depends on the facts of each case: *The Albionic*.

5	*The Two Friends* (1799) 1 Ch Rob 271 at 278; *The Governor Raffles* (1815) 2 Dods 14 at 17, 18 (where Lord Stowell expressed the view that, while hostile capture did, mutiny did not discharge the contract of service). See the doubts expressed in *The Florence* (1852) 16 Jur 572, and *Beale v Thompson* (1803) 3 Bros & P 405 at 430.

6	As to pilotage see PARA 574 et seq.

7	*The Rosehaugh* (1854) 1 Ecc & Ad 267; *The Æolus* (1873) LR 4 A & E 29 at 31, 1 Asp MLC 516 at 578; *The Monarch* (1886) 12 PD 5, 6 Asp MLC 90; *The Aglaia* (1888) 13 PD 160, 6 Asp MLC 337; *The Ilo* [1982] 1 Lloyd's Rep 39 (where services were rendered by a pilot who co-ordinated the actions of the tugs). For the general principles affecting claims by pilots see *The Joseph Harvey* (1799) 1 Ch Rob 306; *Akerblom v Price* (1881) 7 QBD 129, 4 Asp MLC 441, CA.

8	*The Jonge Andries* (1857) Sw 226; affd sub nom *Halsey v Albertuszen, The Jonge Andries* Sw 303, PC.

9	*Newman v Walters* (1804) 3 Bos & P 612 at 616.

10 *Akerblom v Price* (1881) 7 QBD 129, CA; *The Bedeburn* [1914] P 146, 12 Asp MLC 530; cf *The Santiago* (1900) 9 Asp MLC 147.
11 *The Æolus* (1873) LR 4 A & E 29 at 31, 1 Asp MLC 516 at 519.
12 *The Hebe* (1844) 2 Wm Rob 246; *The Sandefjord* [1953] 2 Lloyd's Rep 557.

870. Ship's agents and passengers. At common law[1] a ship's agent who renders services in assisting to save the vessel or her cargo may, in spite of his contractual obligation, obtain a salvage reward[2]. The admission of such claim is based on public policy[3]. His claim may, it seems, be entertained even where he has incurred no personal risk and has made no extraordinary exertion[4].

A passenger who remains on board a vessel in danger, being bound by a moral duty as well as by the interest of self-preservation to work for the safety of the vessel, is not entitled to claim as a salvor, unless he elects to remain on board and render assistance where he has the means of leaving, or unless he renders some special service, as, for example, taking command of the vessel[5].

1 As to the operation of pre-existing common law together with the Merchant Shipping Act 1995 and the International Convention on Salvage 1989 (London, 28 April 1989; Cm 1526) see PARA 851.
2 *The Happy Return* (1828) 2 Hag Adm 198; *The Favorite* (1844) 2 Wm Rob 255; *The Purissima Concepcion* (1849) 3 Wm Rob 181; *The Honor (Cargo ex)* (1866) LR 1 A & E 87; *The Kate B Jones* [1892] P 366, 7 Asp MLC 332. In *The Watt* (1843) 2 Wm Rob 70, *The Lively* (1848) 3 Wm Rob 64 and *The Crusader* [1907] P 15, 10 Asp MLC 353 (on appeal [1907] P 196, 10 Asp MLC 442, CA), the claim was rejected.
3 *The Purissima Concepcion* (1849) 3 Wm Rob 181 per Dr Lushington.
4 See *The Happy Return* (1828) 2 Hag Adm 198; *The Purissima Concepcion* (1849) 3 Wm Rob 181; *The Honor (Cargo ex)* (1866) LR 1 A & E 87.
5 *Newman v Walters* (1804) 3 Bos & P 612 (taking command of a vessel on the rocks); *The Branston* (1826) 2 Hag Adm 3n; *The Vrede* (1861) Lush 322. See also *Towle v The Great Eastern* (1861) 2 Mar LC 148 (devising and rigging temporary steering gear); *The Merrimac* (1868) 18 LT 92 (soldiers on troopships by organised efforts prevented ships from sinking).

871. Tugs under towage contract. As regards salvage at common law[1], the position of a tug under a contract[2] to tow the salved vessel is very similar to that of the pilot of the salved vessel[3], in that circumstances existing at the beginning of the towage service or supervening afterwards may convert a towage into a salvage service. If, when the towage contract was entered into, material facts affecting the danger of the tow or the danger or the difficulty of the towage service such as make it unjust to expect the towage service to be undertaken at a towage rate were not disclosed to the owner of the tug or his representative making the contract, the towage contract is disregarded and the service is treated as a salvage service[4]. If, also, during the towage the tow becomes in danger, through no fault of the tug, and the tug then renders services in the nature of salvage services such as could not reasonably be held to be within the intention of the parties, by means of which the ship is brought into a place of safety, the towage contract is superseded by the right to salvage reward[5]; but a slight departure from the way in which the towage contract was to be performed does not convert towage services into salvage services[6], and the strictest proof of the circumstances which lead to such a claim is required[7].

It makes no difference that the tug has acted under a sub-contract, and not under a direct contract between the owner of the tug and the owner of the tow[8].

1 As to the operation of pre-existing common law together with the Merchant Shipping Act 1995 and the International Convention on Salvage 1989 (London, 28 April 1989; Cm 1526) see PARA 851.
2 As to contracts of towage generally see PARA 597 et seq.
3 *The Saratoga* (1861) Lush 318 at 321.
4 *Akerblom v Price* (1881) 7 QBD 129 at 132, 4 Asp MLC 441 at 443, CA. Cf *The Kingalock* (1854) 1 Ecc & Ad 263; *The Canova* (1866) LR 1 A & E 54.
5 See *The Minnehaha* (1861) Lush 335, PC; *The Annapolis* (1861) Lush 355, PC; *The White Star* (1866) LR 1 A & E 68; *The Five Steel Barges* (1890) 15 PD 142, 6 Asp MLC 580; *The Liverpool*

[1893] P 154, 7 Asp MLC 340; *The Westburn* (1896) 8 Asp MLC 130; *The Emilie Galline* [1903] P 106, 9 Asp MLC 401; *The Aboukir* (1905) 21 TLR 200; *The Glenmorven* [1913] P 141 (towage contract expressly stating 'no claim to be made for salvage' superseded). See also *The Liverpool* at 160 per Gorell Barnes J, for a statement of the proposition to be found in the cases; and *The Leon Blum* [1915] P 90 (affd [1915] P 290, 13 Asp MLC 273, CA).

6 *The Domby* (1941) 69 Ll L Rep 161; *The Slaney* [1951] 2 Lloyd's Rep 538.
7 *The Galatea* (1858) Sw 349; *The Minnehaha* (1861) Lush 335 at 348, PC; *The Liverpool* [1893] P 154 at 164, 7 Asp MLC 340 at 342; *The Maréchal Suchet* [1911] P 1, 11 Asp MLC 553. It seems that an engaged tug which takes on board the master and crew is not so far acting outside her duty that she can claim life salvage: *The Tarbert* [1921] P 372, 15 Asp MLC 423.
8 *The Texaco Southampton* [1983] 1 Lloyd's Rep 94, NSW CA.

872. Public officers, coastguards and foyboatmen. At common law[1], magistrates and other persons holding a public office or appointment may obtain a salvage reward[2] only in respect of services clearly outside the scope of their official duties[3]. Employees of a public authority having a statutory duty to remove obstructions to navigation are not thereby excluded from claiming reward in respect of services beyond their ordinary duties as employees of that authority[4]. Officers and men of Her Majesty's Coastguard have duties with regard to watching for vessels in distress off the coasts, to initiate search and rescue measures for ships in distress and to render life-saving assistance by mustering or informing life-saving organisations and other authorities able to help[5]. If, however, they render services of the nature of salvage services beyond the scope of their official duties, they are entitled to be treated as ordinary salvors in respect of those services[6].

Foyboatmen performing services involving considerable risk to themselves in conditions in which they would not normally be prepared to ply their ordinary trade may be entitled to salvage reward in respect of those services[7].

1 As to the operation of pre-existing common law together with the Merchant Shipping Act 1995 and the International Convention on Salvage 1989 (London, 28 April 1989; Cm 1526) see PARA 851.
2 As to salvage rewards see PARA 883 et seq.
3 *The Aquila* (1798) 1 Ch Rob 37 at 46–49 per Sir W Scott (dismissing the claim of a magistrate); *The Purissima Concepcion* (1849) 3 Wm Rob 181 at 184.
4 See *The Mars* (1948) 81 Ll L Rep 452 (salvage services to barges by employees of the Port of London Authority). See also *The Citos* (1925) 22 Ll L Rep 275 (employees of lighthouse authority removing salved vessel from fairway); *Bostonian (Owners, Master and Crew) v Gregerso (Owners), The Gregerso* [1973] QB 274, [1971] 1 All ER 961, [1971] 2 Lloyd's Rep 220 (where a port authority was not entitled to salvage where it was exercising its statutory powers to remove a vessel obstructing a port).
5 See 574 HC Official Report (5th series), written answers, col 55. As to Her Majesty'sCoastguard see PARA 58; and as to remuneration for coastguard services see PARA 936.
6 *The Charlotta* (1831) 2 Hag Adm 361; *The London Merchant* (1837) 3 Hag Adm 394; *Silver Bullion* (1854) 2 Ecc & Ad 70.
7 *The MacGregor Laird* [1953] 2 Lloyd's Rep 259. The foyboatmen service provides assistance to a vessel from shore-based seamen, eg in running lines from ship to shore.

873. Lifeboat crews. At common law[1] the members of lifeboat crews are paid for services rendered in saving life by the Royal National Lifeboat Institution[2]. If, however, when they reach a vessel in distress, their services are required for the salvage of property alone, they are entitled to rank as salvors in respect of those services, being treated as having borrowed the lifeboat for the services, and are liable for any damage to the lifeboat occasioned by the salvage services[3]. In that case lifeboatmen who merely assist in launching the lifeboat may be entitled to reward[4].

1 As to the operation of pre-existing common law together with the Merchant Shipping Act 1995 and the International Convention on Salvage 1989 (London, 28 April 1989; Cm 1526) see PARA 851.

2 See the salvage regulations by the institution set out in *The Cayo Bonito* [1904] P 310; *The Marlborough* (1943) 76 Ll L Rep 102. See also *The Guernsey Coast* (1950) 83 Ll L Rep 483; *The Africa Occidental* [1951] 2 Lloyd's Rep 107.
3 *The Auguste Legembre* [1902] P 123, 9 Asp MLC 279; *The Cayo Bonito* [1904] P 310, 9 Asp MLC 603; *The Corcrest* (1946) 80 Ll L Rep 78; *The Ocean Hound* (1950) 84 Ll L Rep 5. The burden of showing that their position has changed from that of salvors of life to that of salvors of property rests on the lifeboatmen: *The Marguerite Molinos* [1903] P 160, 9 Asp MLC 424 (where the claim failed).
4 *The Cayo Bonito* [1904] P 310, 9 Asp MLC 603. As to salvage rewards see PARA 883 et seq.

(v) Who is Liable for Salvage Award

874. Liability to contribute. At common law all property which has benefited by the salvage services, generally the ship, freight, and cargo[1], except the wearing apparel and personal effects of the crew and passengers on board the salved vessel[2], contributes to the salvage reward[3]. Each part of the salved property contributes rateably according to its value, without regard to the degree of risk from which or difficulty with which that part has been salved as compared with the rest of the salved property[4], although, where the various interests in the salved property have been exposed to different degrees of risk, the court in its discretion may make a separate award in respect of each portion of the salved property[5]. The liability to contribute is not limited to the legal ownership of the salved property. It falls also on persons who have merely an interest in the salved property and whose interest has been saved by means of the salvage service[6]. Contribution is enforceable by or against the Crown as if the Crown were a private person[7].

1 As to the meaning of 'cargo' for salvage purposes see PARA 860. As to fixing the salvage award under the International Convention on Salvage 1989 (London, 28 April 1989; Cm 1526) (the 'Salvage Convention') see PARA 878. As to the Convention, and the operation of pre-existing common law alongside the Convention provisions and the Merchant Shipping Act 1995 see PARA 851.
2 *The Willem III* (1871) LR 3 A & E 487, 1 Asp MLC 129.
3 *The Fleece* (1850) 3 Wm Rob 278 at 282; *The Fusilier* (1865) Brown & Lush 341 at 352, PC. Where under a charterparty risks of war were taken by the charterers and salvage services were rendered to the vessel exposed to sea and war risks, the charterers were held to be liable for the proportion of the award attributable to war risks: *Pyman Steamship Co v Admiralty Comrs* [1919] 1 KB 49, 14 Asp MLC 364, CA.
4 *The Jonge Bastiaan* (1804) 5 Ch Rob 322; *The Longford* (1881) 6 PD 60, 4 Asp MLC 385 (specie); *The Chateaubriand* [1916] WN 105.
5 *The Velox* [1906] P 263, 10 Asp MLC 277.
6 *The Five Steel Barges* (1890) 15 PD 142, 6 Asp MLC 580; *The Port Victor (Cargo ex)* [1901] P 243, 9 Asp MLC 182, CA; *Holman & Sons Ltd v Merchants' Marine Insurance Co Ltd* [1919] 1 KB 383, 14 Asp MLC 433 (underwriter's proportion); *The Meandros* [1925] P 61, 16 Asp MLC 476.
7 See the Crown Proceedings Act 1947 s 4; and CROWN AND CROWN PROCEEDINGS vol 29 (2014) PARA 85 et seq.

875. Contribution as between cargo owner and shipowner. Where the salved cargo has not been benefited by the salvage services, as happens where the freight exceeds the value of the salved cargo[1], or where the services were rendered necessary by an actionable fault on the part of the shipowner or his employees[2], the cargo owner is entitled to require the shipowner to discharge the whole burden of the salvage reward; and in either of these cases, if the cargo owner has had to pay the shipowner for salvage, he may recover the amount so paid[3].

In all other cases the cargo owner is equally liable with the shipowner for payment of the reward, and, if the shipowner pays the cargo owner's share, he has a lien on the cargo for that amount[4].

1 *Cox v May* (1815) 4 M & S 152. As to the meaning of 'cargo' for salvage purposes see PARA 860. As to fixing the salvage award under the International Convention on Salvage 1989 (London, 28

April 1989; Cm 1526) (the 'Salvage Convention') see PARA 878. As to the Convention, and the operation of pre-existing common law alongside the Convention provisions and the Merchant Shipping Act 1995 see PARA 851.

2   *Prehn v Bailey, The Ettrick* (1881) 6 PD 127, 4 Asp MLC 465, CA. See also *Strang, Steel & Co v A Scott & Co* (1889) 14 App Cas 601 at 608, 6 Asp MLC 419 at 421, PC.

3   *The Princess Royal* (1870) LR 3 A & E 41.

4   *Briggs v Merchant Traders' Ship Loan and Insurance Association* (1849) 13 QB 167; *Cox v May* (1815) 4 M & S 152; *The Geestland* [1980] 1 Lloyd's Rep 628.

876.   Liability proportioned. Each interest is liable only for its proportionate share of the salvage reward[1], unless the salvors and the master of the salved vessel have entered into a binding salvage agreement fixing the amount of the reward, in which case the shipowner is liable for the whole of the reward due under the agreement[2].

1   *The Raisby* (1885) 10 PD 114, 5 Asp MLC 473; *The Mary Pleasants* (1857) Sw 224. See also *The Elton* [1891] P 265, 7 Asp MLC 66. In practice, the shipowner often pays the whole reward in the first instance, protecting himself by security from the cargo owner or relying on his lien on the cargo while it remains in his possession for the cargo owner's proportion: *Hingston v Wendt* (1876) 1 QBD 367, 3 Asp MLC 126; *The Prinz Heinrich* (1888) 13 PD 31 at 34, 6 Asp MLC 273 at 276.
    As to fixing the salvage award under the International Convention on Salvage 1989 (London, 28 April 1989; Cm 1526) (the 'Salvage Convention') see PARA 878. As to the Convention, and the operation of pre-existing common law alongside the Convention provisions and the Merchant Shipping Act 1995 see PARA 851.

2   The liability is both in rem and in personam: *The Cumbrian* (1887) 6 Asp MLC 151; *The Prinz Heinrich* (1888) 13 PD 31, 6 Asp MLC 273.

877.   Life salvage. For salvage reward for the saving of life[1], the ship, freight and cargo contributed rateably so far as they had been preserved[2]. If the vessel is saved but the cargo is lost, the shipowner is alone liable for payment of a salvage reward. Conversely, if the vessel is lost, but lives and cargo are saved, and no freight is payable, a salvage reward is payable wholly by the cargo owner[3].

1   As to the salvage of persons see the International Convention on Salvage 1989 (London, 28 April 1989; Cm 1526) (the 'Salvage Convention') art 16; and PARA 864. As to fixing the salvage award under the Convention see PARA 878. As to the Convention, and the operation of pre-existing common law alongside the Convention provisions and the Merchant Shipping Act 1995 see PARA 851.

2   See the Merchant Shipping Act 1894 ss 544–546 (repealed).

3   *The Sarpedon (Cargo ex)* (1877) 3 PD 28, 3 Asp MLC 509.

(vi) Fixing the Award

A.   BY THE COURT

878.   Convention principles and criteria. The reward under the Salvage Convention[1] must be fixed with a view to encouraging salvage operations[2], taking into account the following criteria without regard to the order in which they are presented below[3]:

(1)   the salved value of the vessel[4] and other property[5];

(2)   the skill and efforts of the salvors in preventing or minimising damage to the environment[6];

(3)   the measure of success[7] obtained by the salvor[8];

(4)   the nature and degree of the danger[9];

(5)   the skill and efforts of the salvors in salving the vessel, other property and life[10];

(6)   the time used and expenses and losses incurred by the salvors[11];

(7)   the risk of liability and other risks run by the salvors or their equipment[12];

(8)   the promptness of the services rendered[13];

(9)   the availability and use of vessels or other equipment intended for salvage operations[14];

(10)   the state of readiness and efficiency of the salvor's equipment and the value thereof[15].

Payment of a reward fixed according to these provisions[16] must be made by all of the vessel and other property interests in proportion to their respective salved values[17]. A state party[18] may, however, in its national law provide that the payment of a reward has to be made by one of these interests, subject to a right of recourse of this interest against the other interests for their respective shares[19]. Nothing in these provisions[20] prevents any right of defence[21].

The rewards, exclusive of any interest and recoverable legal costs that may be payable thereon, must not exceed the salved value of the vessel and other property[22].

1   Ie the International Convention on Salvage 1989 (London, 28 April 1989; Cm 1526): see PARA 851.
2   As to the meaning of 'salvage operation' see PARA 850. As to the principle of encouraging salvage operations see eg *The Rilland* [1979] 1 Lloyd's Rep 455 at 458 (cited in PARAS 886–881). As to the encouragement principle and the application of the moderating principle in a case involving high value cargo see *Ocean Crown (owners) v Five Oceans Salvage Consultants Ltd* [2009] EWHC 3040 (Admlty), [2010] 2 All ER (Comm) 931. Commercial towage rates are relevant to the determination of a salvage award but every case must be determined on its facts: see *Owners of the vessel 'Voutakos' v Tsavliris Salvage (International) Ltd; The Voutakos* [2008] EWHC 1581 (Admlty), [2009] 1 All ER (Comm) 1067, [2008] 2 Lloyd's Rep 516.
3   Salvage Convention art 13(1). As to the reward see PARA 880. The criteria in art 13 must form the basis for any decision of the receiver of wrecks under the Merchant Shipping Act 1995 s 228(4) (see PARA 902) and for any decision of the court under s 229 (see PARA 903).
4   As to the meaning of 'vessel' see PARA 850 note 2.
5   Salvage Convention art 13(1)(a). As to the meaning of 'property' see PARA 850 note 3.
6   Salvage Convention art 13(1)(b). As to the meaning of 'damage to the environment' see PARA 853 note 3. See also *United Salvage Pty Ltd v Louis Dreyfus Armateurs SNC* (2007) 240 ALR 630 (damage to be considered must be substantial and not possible, remote or hypothetical).
7   Cf the Salvage Convention art 12, where the expression 'useful result' rather than 'success' is used: see PARA 863. Thus, the existing case law on the measure of success continues to be good law: see PARA 863.
8   Salvage Convention art 13(1)(c).
9   Salvage Convention art 13(1)(d). See also *United Salvage Pty Ltd v Louis Dreyfus Armateurs SNC* (2007) 240 ALR 630 (danger to human life and the risk of loss, injury or damage must be assessed in relation to the salved property).
10 Salvage Convention art 13(1)(e).
11 Salvage Convention art 13(1)(f).
12 Salvage Convention art 13(1)(g).
13 Salvage Convention art 13(1)(h).
14 Salvage Convention art 13(1)(i).
15 Salvage Convention art 13(1)(j).
16 Ie fixed according to the Salvage Convention art 13(1) (see the text and notes 1–15): see art 13(2).
17 Salvage Convention art 13(2). As to personal liability to pay salvage remuneration see also PARA 116.
18 As to the making of Orders in Council declaring which states are parties to the Salvage Convention see PARA 852 note 3.
19 Salvage Convention art 13(2).
20 Ie the Salvage Convention art 13: see art 13(2).
21 Salvage Convention art 13(2).
22 Salvage Convention art 13(3).

879. Special compensation. If the salvor, under the Salvage Convention[1], has carried out salvage operations[2] in respect of a vessel[3] which by itself or its cargo threatened damage to the environment[4] and has failed to earn a reward[5] at least equivalent to the special compensation assessable in accordance with the following provisions, he is entitled to special compensation from the owner of that vessel equivalent to his expenses[6].

If, in such circumstances, the salvor by his salvage operations has prevented or minimised damage to the environment, the special compensation so payable by the owner to the salvor may be increased up to a maximum of 30% of the expenses incurred by the salvor[7]. However, the tribunal, if it deems it fair and just to do so and bearing in mind the relevant criteria for fixing the reward[8], may increase such special compensation further, but in no event must the total increase be more than 100% of the expenses incurred by the salvor[9].

The total special compensation assessed under these provisions[10] must be paid only if and to the extent that such compensation is greater than any reward recoverable by the salvor[11] under the usual criteria[12].

If the salvor has been negligent and has thereby failed to prevent or minimise damage to the environment, he may be deprived of the whole or part of any special compensation so due[13].

Nothing in the special compensation provisions[14] affects any right of recourse on the part of the owner of the vessel[15].

1 Ie the International Convention on Salvage 1989 (London, 28 April 1989; Cm 1526): see PARA 851.
2 As to the meaning of 'salvage operation' see PARA 850.
3 As to the meaning of 'vessel' see PARA 850 note 2.
4 As to the meaning of 'damage to the environment' see PARA 853 note 3.
5 Ie under the Salvage Convention art 13 (see PARA 878): see art 14(1).
6 Salvage Convention art 14(1). For these purposes, 'salvor's expenses' means the out-of-pocket expenses reasonably incurred by the salvor in the salvage operation and a fair rate for equipment and personnel actually and reasonably used in the salvage operation, taking into consideration the criteria set out in art 13(1)(h)–(j) (see PARA 878): art 14(3). As to special compensation see further PARA 880.
  For the purposes of art 14(3), 'expenses . . . incurred' by a salvor denotes amounts either disbursed or borne, not earned as profits. Accordingly, an award of special compensation under art 14(2) is intended to recompense or reimburse a salvor for his expenses in the event that his direct and standby costs exceed his salvage reward under art 13 and is not intended to yield or be a source of profit. It follows that salvors entitled to special compensation for protecting the environment are entitled to a fair rate of expense which is comprehensive of indirect or overhead expenses, including the additional cost of having resources on standby and instantly available but not including a profit element: *Semco Salvage and Marine Pte Ltd v Lancer Navigation Co Ltd, The Nagasaki Spirit* [1997] AC 455, [1997] 1 All ER 502, [1997] 1 Lloyd's Rep 323, HL.
7 Salvage Convention art 14(2).
8 Ie the relevant criteria set out in the Salvage Convention art 13(1): see art 14(2).
9 Salvage Convention art 14(2).
10 Ie under the Salvage Convention art 14: see art 14(4).
11 Ie under the Salvage Convention art 13: see art 14(4).
12 Salvage Convention art 14(4).
13 Salvage Convention art 14(5). The text refers to special compensation due under art 14: see art 14(5).
14 Ie nothing in the Salvage Convention art 14: see art 14(6).
15 Salvage Convention art 14(6).

880. The reward and special compensation; the common understanding.

In fixing a reward under the Salvage Convention[1] and in assessing special compensation under the Convention[2], the court or arbitrator is under no duty to fix a reward up to the maximum salved value of the vessel[3] and other property[4] before assessing the special compensation to be paid[5].

1 Ie under the International Convention on Salvage 1989 (London, 28 April 1989; Cm 1526) art 13 (see PARA 878): As to the Convention, and its operation together with the Merchant Shipping Act 1995, see PARA 851.
2 Ie under the Salvage Convention art 14 (see PARA 879).
3 As to the meaning of 'vessel' under the Convention see PARA 850 note 2.
4 As to the meaning of 'property' under the Convention see PARA 850 note 3.
5 Merchant Shipping Act 1995 Sch 11 Pt II para 4.

881.   Assessment by the court. At common law, in assessing the reward[1], the court endeavours to combine liberality to the salvor with justice to the owner of the salved property[2]. It regards not merely the work done in the performance of the salvage service[3], but the general interests of navigation and commerce[4]. Thus, it looks with favour on salvage services rendered by ships built and maintained for salvage services[5]. Because one of the main reasons why salvage remuneration is high is that, unless the vessel in danger is saved, no remuneration is payable at all, salvors who have acted under an agreement which entitled them to remuneration independently of success are not rewarded on the liberal scale applicable to other salvors[6].

1   As to the criteria for fixing the reward see the International Convention on Salvage 1989 (London, 28 April 1989; Cm 1526) (the 'Salvage Convention') art 13; and PARA 878. As to the Convention and the relationship between it and the pre-existing common law see PARA 851.
2   *HMS Thetis* (1833) 3 Hag Adm 14 at 62. As to the difficulty of assessing salvage rewards in times of inflation see *The Ilo* [1982] 1 Lloyd's Rep 39 at 42 per Sheen J; and *The Helenus and The Montagua* [1982] 2 Lloyd's Rep 261 at 265 per Sheen J.
3   *The Charlotte* (1848) 3 Wm Rob 68 at 71 per Dr Lushington ('the many and diverse ingredients of a salvage service'). There is divergence of judicial opinion as to the relative importance of these circumstances. Chief importance was attached in *The William Beckford* (1801) 3 Ch Rob 355 at 356 per Lord Stowell to the risk to salvors; in *The London Merchant* (1837) 3 Hag Adm 394 at 395 per Sir J Nicholl to the risk to salved property; in *The Werra* (1886) 12 PD 52 at 53, 6 Asp MLC 115 at 117 per Hannen J to the value of salved property; in *The City of Chester* (1884) 9 PD 182 at 202, 5 Asp MLC 311 at 319, CA, per Lindley LJ to the risk to salvors and salved property and the value of salved property.
4   *The William Beckford* (1801) 3 Ch Rob 355 at 356 per Lord Stowell; *The Industry* (1835) 3 Hag Adm 203 at 204 per Sir J Nicholl; *The City of Chester* (1884) 9 PD 182 at 203, 5 Asp MLC 311 at 319, CA, per Lindley LJ; *The Rilland* [1979] 1 Lloyd's Rep 455; *The Ilo* [1982] 1 Lloyd's Rep 39 at 42 per Sheen J.
5   See eg *The Glengyle* [1898] P 97, 8 Asp MLC 341, CA (affd [1898] AC 519, 8 Asp MLC 436, HL) (award of £19,000 on a salved value of £76,596); *The Scheidestad* (1933) 45 Ll L Rep 269 (award of £6,000 for services by two salvage vessels to an abandoned vessel on values of £8,900).
6   *The Lepanto* [1892] P 122, 7 Asp MLC 192; *The Kate B Jones* [1892] P 366, 7 Asp MLC 332; *The Edenmore* [1893] P 79, 7 Asp MLC 334.

882.   Finality of salvage award. Once made, a salvage award is generally final[1]. If, after an award has been made, it is found that a miscalculation has been made as to the values, the court has power to reopen and readjust its award[2], but the power is exercised with great caution[3].

1   As to the criteria for fixing the reward see the International Convention on Salvage 1989 (London, 28 April 1989; Cm 1526) (the 'Salvage Convention') art 13; and PARA 878. As to the Convention and the relationship between it and the pre-existing common law see PARA 851.
2   *The James Armstrong* (1875) LR 4 A & E 380, 3 Asp MLC 46 (where the cargo owner contributed upon the value of the cargo without deducting freight due on delivery and the freight was assessed too low).
3   *The Georg* [1894] P 330, 7 Asp MLC 476 (where readjustment claimed on the ground that the selling price of the salved property proved lower than the assessed value was refused).

B.   BY AGREEMENT

883.   Agreements in general. At common law[1] an agreement may be made fixing the amount to be paid to the salvor for his services, but leaving untouched all the other conditions necessary to support a salvage reward, one of which is the preservation of some part at least of the property in peril[2], unless by a special agreement a salvage reward is to be paid independently of the ultimate safety of the property in danger[3]. The usual agreement to render salvage services is on a 'No cure, No pay' basis[4].

The agreement need not be in writing[5], but it must be clearly proved[6]. It must state the services to be performed and the reward for them[7]. An agreement merely to refer to arbitration does not oust the jurisdiction of the court[8]. When duly proved, the agreement is prima facie binding, and the burden of proof lies on the party trying to set it aside[9]. There may be special circumstances in which the master or other person in charge of the property in danger is justified in binding the owner to pay for assistance[10] independently of the ultimate safety of the property; such an agreement is a valid salvage agreement[11].

1   As to the operation of pre-existing common law together with the Merchant Shipping Act 1995 and the International Convention on Salvage 1989 (London, 28 April 1989; Cm 1526) see PARA 851.
2   See eg *The Hestia* [1895] P 193 at 199, 7 Asp MLC 599 at 600.
3   *Wellfield (Owners) v Adamson and Short, The Alfred* (1884) 5 Asp MLC 214. Cf *The Prinz Heinrich* (1888) 13 PD 31 at 34, 6 Asp MLC 273 at 276; *The Edenmore* [1893] P 79, 7 Asp MLC 334; *The Strathgarry* [1895] P 264, 8 Asp MLC 19.
4   Where services are rendered under 'No cure, No pay' terms, they give rise to a maritime lien: *The Goulandris* [1927] P 182, 17 Asp MLC 209. As to the maritime liens for salvage services see PARAS 968, 969, 979.
5   *The Graces* (1844) 2 Wm Rob 294; *The Arthur* (1862) 6 LT 556 at 558; *The Cumbrian* (1887) 6 Asp MLC 151.
6   *The Graces* (1844) 2 Wm Rob 294 at 297.
7   *The William Lushington* (1850) 7 Notes of Cases 361 at 363.
8   *The Purissima Concepcion* (1849) 3 Wm Rob 181; and see *The City of Calcutta* (1898) 8 Asp MLC 442, CA.
9   *The Helen and George* (1858) Sw 368 at 369; *The Medina* (1876) 2 PD 5 at 7, 3 Asp MLC 305 at 306, CA; *Akerblom v Price* (1881) 7 QBD 129 at 132, 133, 4 Asp MLC 441 at 443, CA.
10 *Wellfield (Owners) v Adamson and Short, The Alfred* (1884) 5 Asp MLC 214. Cf *The Prinz Heinrich* (1888) 13 PD 31, 6 Asp MLC 273; *The Edenmore* [1893] P 79, 7 Asp MLC 334. As to the effect of such an agreement on an award see PARA 852.
11 *Admiralty Comrs v Valverda (Owners)* [1938] AC 173, [1938] 1 All ER 162, 59 Ll L Rep 231, HL.

884. Setting aside salvage agreement. At common law[1] an agreement as to the amount to be paid to the salvor may be set aside if it has been obtained by fraud[2], or by misstatement or non-disclosure, whether intentional or not[3], of a material fact, affecting, or not unlikely to affect, the danger of the property, or the risk, difficulty or duration of the salvage service[4]. Salvors are not held bound by an agreement where supervening circumstances, without the fault of either party, render the performance of the agreed service impossible, or where the service actually rendered was of a wholly different character from the agreed service[5].

An agreement may also be set aside as being inequitable where the reward fixed by it is exorbitant[6] or inadequate[7]. Where exorbitancy is the ground of a claim to set aside the agreement, the existence of circumstances showing that the master of the salved vessel was virtually compelled to enter into the agreement, although by no means essential[8], is an important factor in obtaining the avoidance of the agreement[9]. The court does not, however, set aside an agreement merely because it would have awarded a rather larger or smaller sum than that fixed by the agreement, or because, in the events that happened, the services were more or less dangerous, difficult or time-consuming than was anticipated by either party at the time of the making of the agreement[10], or because the salved value turns out to be less than the agreed salvage remuneration[11].

A settlement made after services have been performed is not binding on the salvor if the reward to be paid is very inadequate, and either the salvor did not appreciate the value of his services[12] or the circumstances in which the settlement was made are not satisfactorily explained[13] or show that it was made against authority[14].

The agreement may be cancelled by mutual consent[15], evidenced by express agreement between the parties[16] or by conduct from which the consent will be inferred[17]. The burden of proof of cancellation lies on the party setting it up[18].

1   As to the operation of pre-existing common law together with the Merchant Shipping Act 1995 and the International Convention on Salvage 1989 (London, 28 April 1989; Cm 1526) see PARA 851.
2   *The Henry* (1851) 15 Jur 183; *The Helen and George* (1858) Sw 368 at 369. For examples see *The Crus V* (1862) Lush 583 (bribe to agents of salved vessel); *The Generous* (1868) LR 2 A & E 57 (bribe to master of salving vessel); *The Kolpino* (1904) 73 LJP 29 at 30 (bribe to master of salved vessel). As to an agreement for salvage of a ship and not her cargo see *The Westminster* (1841) 1 Wm Rob 229 at 235.
3   *The Kingalock* (1854) 1 Ecc & Ad 263 at 265; *The Canova* (1866) LR 1 A & E 54.
4   *The Kingalock* (1854) 1 Ecc & Ad 263. For examples of concealment of facts held in the circumstances to be immaterial see *The Henry* (1851) 15 Jur 183 (value of salved cargo); *The Jonge Andries* (1857) Sw 226 (affd Sw 303, PC); *The Canova* (1866) LR 1 A & E 54 (illness of some of salved crew). As to misrepresentation and fraud see MISREPRESENTATION vol 76 (2013) PARA 701 et seq.
5   *The Westbourne* (1889) 14 PD 132, 6 Asp MLC 405, CA; and see *The Hestia* [1895] P 193, 7 Asp MLC 599. As to impossibility of performance and frustration see CONTRACT vol 22 (2012) PARA 467 et seq.
6   *The Henry* (1851) 15 Jur 183; *The Theodore* (1858) Sw 351; *The Woosung (Cargo ex)* (1876) 1 PD 260 at 270, 3 Asp MLC 239 at 241, CA; *Akerblom v Price* (1881) 7 QBD 129 at 132, 133, 4 Asp MLC 441 at 443, CA; *The Strathgarry* [1895] P 264 at 270, 8 Asp MLC 19 at 21. In *The Crusader* [1907] P 15, 10 Asp MLC 353 (on appeal [1907] P 196, 10 Asp MLC 442, CA), the agreement was set aside, although it was the deliberate choice of the master of the salved ship.
7   *The Phantom* (1866) LR 1 A & E 58; and see *The Henry* (1851) 15 Jur 183.
8   *The True Blue* (1843) 2 Wm Rob 176 at 179; *Akerblom v Price* (1881) 7 QBD 129 at 132–133, 4 Asp MLC 441 at 443, CA; but see *The Woosung (Cargo ex)* (1876) 1 PD 260 at 263, 264, 3 Asp MLC 239 at 240, 241, CA. Cf *The Rialto* [1891] P 175 at 178, 179, 7 Asp MLC 35 at 36.
9   *The Medina* (1876) 2 PD 5, 3 Asp MLC 305, CA; *The Mark Lane* (1890) 15 PD 135, 6 Asp MLC 540; *The Rialto* [1891] P 175, 7 Asp MLC 35; *The Altair* [1897] P 105, 8 Asp MLC 224; *The Port Caledonia and The Anna* [1903] P 184, 9 Asp MLC 479.
10 *The True Blue* (1843) 2 Wm Rob 176 at 180; *The Cato* (1866) 35 LJ Adm 116 at 117; *The Waverley* (1871) LR 3 A & E 369, 1 Asp MLC 47; *The Strathgarry* [1895] P 264 at 271, 8 Asp MLC 19 at 21.
11 *The Inna* [1938] P 148, 60 Ll L Rep 414.
12 *Silver Bullion* (1854) 2 Ecc & Ad 70.
13 *The Macgregor Laird* [1867] WN 308.
14 *The Hermione* [1922] P 162, 15 Asp MLC 493.
15 *The Repulse* (1845) 2 Wm Rob 396 at 397.
16 *The Africa* (1854) 1 Ecc & Ad 299.
17 *The Samuel* (1851) 15 Jur 407.
18 *The Betsey* (1843) 2 Wm Rob 167 at 172.

885. Person bound by an agreement as to amount. At common law[1] the owner of the salved ship is generally bound by an agreement as to amount entered into by the master[2], the master having an implied authority to bind his owner for all that is reasonably necessary for the successful navigation of the ship[3]. The shipowner is not bound by it, however, where he was easily accessible and gave no authority to the master to enter into it[4], or where in the circumstances the agreement was not reasonably necessary[5], or where the terms of the agreement show that it is not for the benefit of the shipowner[6]. The implied authority to bind the owner is limited to the master or other person properly acting in command of the ship. To support such an agreement made by any other person strict proof of agency is required[7].

The owner[8] of the salving vessel, at least where he is not accessible and the master has no means of communicating with him[9], and the crew[10] are bound by a salvage agreement made by the master with regard to future services[11]. They are not bound by an agreement made by him after services have been performed in respect of which a right to a salvage reward has arisen[12]. The owner of the salving vessel has the same limited power to bind the master and crew by a salvage agreement, that is to say he can bind them by agreement as to future, but not as to past services[13]. If a salvage agreement is entered into by the master affecting both past and future services, that part of it which relates to the past services will be set aside, and the rest will be given effect to if it is otherwise valid[14].

The owner of cargo on board the salved vessel is not bound by a salvage agreement made by the master, unless he is acting as the agent of the cargo owner[15] and it is open to him to dispute the reasonableness of the reward fixed by it[16].

Where salvage services are performed by a number of different salvors or sets of salvors, the mere accident of co-operation gives none of the salvors an implied agency to contract with the representatives of the salved vessel on behalf of his co-salvors[17].

1   As to the operation of pre-existing common law together with the Merchant Shipping Act 1995 and the International Convention on Salvage 1989 (London, 28 April 1989; Cm 1526) see PARA 851.
2   *The Henry* (1851) 15 Jur 183; *The Africa* (1854) 1 Ecc & Ad 299; *The Waverley* (1871) LR 3 A & E 369, 1 Asp MLC 47. Under the Salvage Convention, the master has the authority to conclude contracts for salvage operations on behalf of the owner of the vessel: see art 6(1); and PARA 853.
3   *Anderson v Ocean Steamship Co* (1884) 10 App Cas 107 at 116, 5 Asp MLC 401 at 404, HL; *Beldon v Campbell* (1851) 6 Exch 886. See also *The Leon Blum* [1915] P 90 (affd [1915] P 290, 13 Asp MLC 273, CA). As to the authority and liability of masters generally see PARA 427 et seq.
4   *The Elise* (1859) Sw 436 at 440; and see *Beldon v Campbell* (1851) 6 Exch 886.
5   *The Mariposa* [1896] P 273, 8 Asp MLC 159; *The Renpor* (1883) 8 PD 115 at 118, 5 Asp MLC 98 at 100, CA.
6   Eg an agreement to save lives without property: *The Mariposa* [1896] P 273 at 280, 8 Asp MLC 159 at 161. See also *The Kilmaho* (1900) 16 TLR 155, CA (agreement to pay where no liability). As to the master's power to his owner to submit the amount of reward to arbitration see *The City of Calcutta* (1898) 8 Asp MLC 442, CA.
7   In *The Crus V* (1862) Lush 583, the master of a ship in distress on a foreign coast and ignorant of the language was held to be entitled to delegate his authority to make a salvage agreement to the vice-consul of the flag to which the ship belonged.
8   *The Britain* (1839) 1 Wm Rob 40 at 43; *The Africa* (1854) 1 Ecc & Ad 299 at 300. As to the master's power to bind his owner to submit the amount to arbitration see *The City of Calcutta* (1898) 8 Asp MLC 442, CA.
9   *The Elise* (1859) Sw 436 at 440.
10 See *The Elise* (1859) Sw 436; *The Macgregor Laird* [1867] WN 308; *The Nasmyth* (1885) 10 PD 41, 5 Asp MLC 364; and *The Inchmaree* [1899] P 111, 8 Asp MLC 486, explaining *The Britain* (1839) 1 Wm Rob 40, and *The Sarah Jane* (1843) 2 Wm Rob 110 (where the crew was held not to be so bound).
11 *The Inchmaree* [1899] P 111, 8 Asp MLC 486. See also *The Margery* [1902] P 157, 9 Asp MLC 304, DC; *The Friesland* [1904] P 345, 10 Asp MLC 9.
12 See note 11.
13 *The Inchmaree* [1899] P 111, 8 Asp MLC 486.
14 *Anderson v Ocean Steamship Co* (1884) 10 App Cas 107 at 117, 5 Asp MLC 401 at 404, HL.
15 *China-Pacific SA v Food Corpn of India, The Winson* [1979] 2 All ER 35, [1979] 1 Lloyd's Rep 167.
16 *The Friesland* [1904] P 345, 10 Asp MLC 9. Where both salving and salved vessels are insured in associations under the articles of which salvage reward is to be mutually settled by committees of the associations, the arrangement does not bind the master and crew: *The Margery* [1902] P 157, 9 Asp MLC 304.
17 *The Charlotte* (1848) 3 Wm Rob 68 at 74.

C.   MATTERS INFLUENCING THE AWARD

886. Common law principles. At common law the amount of the salvage reward[1] is limited to the value of the property or the interest in property salved[2]. Subject to that limitation, the amount of the reward, unless it is fixed by agreement[3], is in the discretion of the court[4], and, except in cases of absolute necessity, the court which tries the case should also assess the remuneration[5].

As a general rule, where the owner of the salved property appears, the court will not award the salvor more than one-half of the value of the salved property, whether the property is derelict[6] or not[7]. A variation in the exchange rate of a currency is not a relevant factor to take into account in fixing the award for salvage services[8]. The court has power to award interest on a salvage award whether the salvage services were or were not performed under a special contract[9].

1   As to the criteria for fixing the reward see the International Convention on Salvage 1989 (London, 28 April 1989; Cm 1526) (the 'Salvage Convention') art 13; and PARA 878. As to the Convention and the relationship between it and the pre-existing common law see PARA 851.
     A salvor's claim survives in favour of his personal representative: *The Marquis of Huntly* (1835) 3 Hag Adm 246; *The Anna Helena* (1883) 5 Asp MLC 142.
2   *The Schiller (Cargo ex)* (1877) 2 PD 145, 3 Asp MLC 439, CA. Tax liability on the reward is not relevant: see *Island Tug and Barge Ltd v SS Makedonia (Owners), The Makedonia* [1958] 1 QB 365, [1958] 1 All ER 236, [1957] 2 Lloyd's Rep 575. See also *The Frisia* [1960] 1 Lloyd's Rep 90 at 94, 96, CA, per Hodson LJ and Devlin LJ; cf *Tantalus (Master and Crew) v Telemachus (Owners), The Telemachus* [1957] P 47, [1957] 1 All ER 72, [1957] 2 Lloyd's Rep 490, and *The Frisia* at 95 per Willmer LJ.
3   As to agreements see PARAS 883–885.
4   *The Ewell Grove* (1835) 3 Hag Adm 209 at 221; *The Cuba* (1860) Lush 14 at 15; *The City of Chester* (1884) 9 PD 182 at 187, 5 Asp MLC 311 at 313, 314, CA.
5   *Melanie (Owners) v San Onofre (Owners)* [1925] AC 246 at 256, 16 Asp MLC 479 at 482, HL.
6   For examples of awards in cases of a derelict exceeding one-half see *The Rasche* (1873) LR 4 A & E 127; *The Boiler ex Elephant* (1891) 64 LT 543, CA (where judgment was allowed to go by default, and there were charges which reduced the sum ultimately received by the salvors); *The Louisa* [1906] P 145, 10 Asp MLC 256 (where the whole of the net proceeds of sale of ship and cargo were awarded).
7   See, however, *The Erato* (1888) 13 PD 163, 6 Asp MLC 334. In *The Mercator* (1910) 26 TLR 450, where the owners appeared but did not put in a defence, the whole value was awarded.
8   *Teh Hu (Owners) and Owners of her Cargo and Freight v Nippon Salvage Co Ltd, The Teh Hu* [1970] P 106, [1969] 3 All ER 1200, [1969] 2 Lloyd's Rep 365, CA.
9   *The Aldora* [1975] QB 748, [1975] 2 All ER 69, [1975] 1 Lloyd's Rep 617; *The Rilland* [1979] 1 Lloyd's Rep 455. The right of the salvor to interest on any payment due under the Salvage Convention (ie the International Convention on Salvage 1989 (London, 28 April 1989; Cm 1526): see PARA 851) must be determined according to the law of the State in which the tribunal seized of the case is situated: art 24.

887. Valuation of property by receiver.

In the absence of agreement, the value of the salved property is usually assessed[1] at the time and place when and where the salvage operations ended[2]. Where any dispute as to salvage[3] arises, the receiver[4] may, on the application of either party, appoint a valuer to value the property[5].

When the valuation has been made, the receiver must give copies of it to both parties[6]. A copy of the valuation purporting to be signed by the valuer, and to be certified as a true copy by the receiver, is admissible as evidence in any subsequent proceedings[7].

There must be paid in respect of the valuation by the person applying for it such fee as the Secretary of State[8] may direct[9].

1   In assessing the value, allowance is made for any salvage reward ordered by another court to be paid to other salvors out of the proceeds of the salved property: *The Antilope* (1873) LR 4 A & E 33, 1 Asp MLC 513.
2   *The George Dean* (1857) Sw 290; *The Stella* (1867) LR 1 A & E 340; *The Georg* [1894] P 330, 7 Asp MLC 476; *The Germania* [1904] P 131, 9 Asp MLC 538.
3   As to the meaning of 'salvage' see PARA 849.
4   For these purposes, 'receiver' means a receiver of wrecks appointed under the Merchant Shipping Act 1995 s 248 (see PARA 929): s 255(1).
5   Merchant Shipping Act 1995 s 225(1). Section 225 is excluded by s 230 (salvage claims against the Crown): see PARA 854. As to the operation of the Merchant Shipping Act 1995 together with the

International Convention on Salvage 1989 (London, 28 April 1989; Cm 1526) (the 'Salvage Convention') and the common law see PARA 851.

6 Merchant Shipping Act 1995 s 225(2).
7 Merchant Shipping Act 1995 s 225(3). As to admissibility of documents in evidence generally see PARA 1059.
8 As to the Secretary of State see PARA 36.
9 Merchant Shipping Act 1995 s 225(4). As to the Secretary of State's power to give directions see PARA 39.

888. Value of ship, cargo and freight. The value of the ship is her value in her damaged condition on the completion of the salvage service[1]. In assessing it, deduction may be made for charges and expenses which have been incurred by the owners in connection with the ship subsequently to the inception of the salvor's interest and which have proved beneficial to that interest[2].

In assessing the value of cargo[3] an allowance may be made for reasonable and proper expenses of the discharge, storage and sale of the cargo[4], but not for prepaid freight[5], primage[6] or insurance[7] or a gratuity to the master of the carrying vessel[8].

Freight which was at risk at the time of the salvage service may be included in the value of the cargo or assessed separately. If the cargo owner has paid a salvage reward in respect of both cargo and freight at risk assessed together and has not paid the freight, he may deduct from the freight when it is payable to the shipowner the amount which he has paid in respect of salvage of freight. If he has paid the freight, he can recover the amount which he has paid in respect of salvage of freight from the shipowner[9].

1 *The Hohenzollern* [1906] P 339, 10 Asp MLC 296; *The Castor* [1932] P 142, 18 Asp MLC 312 (where prospective earnings under an existing charterparty were taken into consideration in assessing the value of the salved vessel); *The Kaffir Prince* [1917] P 26. See, however, *The San Onofre* [1917] P 96, 14 Asp MLC 74; *Lady Duncannon (Owners) v Eisenach (Owners)* [1936] 1 All ER 855, 19 Asp MLC 28.
    As to fixing the salvage award under the International Convention on Salvage 1989 (London, 28 April 1989; Cm 1526) (the 'Salvage Convention') see PARA 878. As to the Convention, and the operation of pre-existing common law alongside the Convention provisions and the Merchant Shipping Act 1995 see PARA 851.
2 *The Selina* (1842) 2 Notes of Cases 18 (crew's wages after service began and bottomry bond taken up by salvors); *The Watt* (1843) 2 Wm Rob 70 (owners unloaded cargo after vessel beached). Deduction was refused in *The Selina*, in respect of crew's wages before salvage service, and in *The Fleece* (1850) 3 Wm Rob 278 in respect of cost of prosecuting wreckers who took forcible possession of the ship.
3 As to the meaning of 'cargo' for salvage purposes see PARA 860.
4 This includes custom house charges, weighing, brokerage and commission: *The Peace* (1856) Sw 115 at 116.
5 *The Charlotte Wylie* (1846) 2 Wm Rob 495 at 497; *The Fleece* (1850) 3 Wm Rob 278 at 282.
6 *The Fleece* (1850) 3 Wm Rob 278.
7 *The Fleece* (1850) 3 Wm Rob 278.
8 *The Peace* (1856) Sw 115.
9 *The Charlotte Wylie* (1846) 2 Wm Rob 495 at 497; *The Fleece* (1850) 3 Wm Rob 278 at 282. See also *The Westminster* (1841) 1 Wm Rob 229 at 233.

889. Whether salvage service ends at port of destination. Where the salvage service continues until the salved vessel reaches the port of destination, the whole net freight unpaid and at risk when the salvage service commenced, and preserved to the shipowner by the service, contributes to the salvage reward[1]. Where the salvage service ends at a place other than the port of destination, and the cargo is not carried on to its destination, the following rules govern contribution:

(1)   if the cargo owner has prevented the shipowner from carrying it on, the whole freight is earned and, therefore, contributes[2];

(2)   if the cargo owner, having a choice, elects to take delivery of the cargo where it is[3], the whole[4] or a pro rata freight[5], according to the express or implied agreement on delivery, is due to the shipowner and has to be brought into contribution; and

(3)   if the failure to carry the cargo on is not due to the intervention or election of the cargo owner, no freight is due, and there is, therefore, no freight to contribute.

Where the cargo is carried on to the port of destination from the place where the salvage service ended, the contributory value of the freight is the estimated proportion of the freight in respect of the voyage up to the point where the service ended[6], less an allowance in respect of the shipowner's expenses incurred in the further transit[7].

Where the salvage service ends at a place which is not the port of destination and where there is no market for the cargo, and the cargo is carried on to its destination and sold there, the value may be assessed by allowing a pro rata freight to the place where the salvage service ended and deducting from the proceeds of sale a percentage of freight and other charges in respect of the voyage from that place to the port of destination[8].

1   It may be valued separately or with the cargo.
2   *The Galam (Cargo ex)* (1863) 33 LJPM & A 97, PC. As to fixing the salvage award under the International Convention on Salvage 1989 (London, 28 April 1989; Cm 1526) (the 'Salvage Convention') see PARA 878. As to the Convention, and the operation of pre-existing common law alongside the Convention provisions and the Merchant Shipping Act 1995 see PARA 851.
3   *Hunter v Prinsep* (1808) 10 East 378; *Vlierboom v Chapman* (1844) 13 M & W 230; *Hopper v Burness* (1876) 1 CPD 137, 3 Asp MLC 149; *Metcalfe v Britannia Ironworks Co* (1877) 2 QBD 423, 3 Asp MLC 407, CA.
4   *Christy v Row* (1808) 1 Taunt 300.
5   *The Soblomsten* (1866) LR 1 A & E 293; *Mitchell v Darthez* (1836) 2 Bing NC 555.
6   *The Norma* (1860) Lush 124. This is a departure from the common law doctrine that freight is not apportionable: cf *The Dorothy Foster* (1805) 6 Ch Rob 88.
7   *The Norma* (1860) Lush 124 at 127; *The James Armstrong* (1875) 3 Asp MLC 46 at 49.
8   *The George Dean* (1857) Sw 290 at 291.

890. Derelict. In the case of a derelict[1], if the vessel is not taken by the salvors to her port of destination, and her owners have taken no steps to carry the cargo[2] on, the cargo owner is entitled to delivery of the cargo without payment of any freight[3], and in that case there is no freight to contribute.

Recovery of the derelict by the shipowner at the port of discharge, after the cargo owner has exercised his right of treating the abandonment of the ship as a determination of the contract of carriage, does not revive the contract of carriage, and no freight is due from the cargo owner[4].

1   As to the meaning of 'derelict' see PARA 923.
2   As to the meaning of 'cargo' for salvage purposes see PARA 860.
3   *The Kathleen* (1874) LR 4 A & E 269, 2 Asp MLC 367; *The Cito* (1881) 7 PD 5, 4 Asp MLC 468, CA. See also *The Argonaut* (1883) unreported, CA; *Bradley v H Newson, Sons & Co* [1919] AC 16, 14 Asp MLC 340, HL. As to fixing the salvage award under the International Convention on Salvage 1989 (London, 28 April 1989; Cm 1526) (the 'Salvage Convention') see PARA 878. As to the Convention, and the operation of pre-existing common law alongside the Convention provisions and the Merchant Shipping Act 1995 see PARA 851.
4   *The Arno* (1895) 8 Asp MLC 5, CA.

891. Danger to life and property. Apart from the general considerations already mentioned[1], at common law the first consideration which affects the amount of the reward is the existence of danger to life, whether on board the salving or the salved vessel, arising either from the position from which the salved property has been rescued or from the performance of the salvage service[2].

The degree of danger from which property has been salved has a great influence on the amount of the reward[3]. Danger may arise from various causes, for example the character and condition of the salved vessel and her cargo, the number, capacity and condition of the crew, the nature of the locality, the master's knowledge of it, the risk of attack by enemy vessels[4], the season of the year, the state and prospect of the weather and the absence of other means of salvage. The greatest danger generally attaches to derelict[5] property.

In some cases of derelict[6], as much as one-half or thereabouts[7], and in a few cases of exceptional character more than one-half, of the value of the salved property has been awarded[8], and the award is often one-third of the salved value, unless the salved value is very large[9].

1   See PARA 886. As to the criteria for fixing the reward see the International Convention on Salvage 1989 (London, 28 April 1989; Cm 1526) (the 'Salvage Convention') art 13; and PARA 878. As to the Convention and the relationship between it and the pre-existing common law see PARA 851.
2   *The Thomas Fielden* (1862) 32 LJPM & A 61 at 62. See also *The Buffalo* (1937) 58 Ll L Rep 302 at 306. As to salvage of persons see the International Convention on Salvage 1989 art 16; and PARA 864.
3   See eg *The Krypton* [1954] 2 Lloyd's Rep 451. As to separate awards where ship, cargo and freight have been exposed to different degrees of danger see *The Velox* [1906] P 263, 10 Asp MLC 277 (cargo of herrings).
4   See *The Carrie* [1917] P 224, 14 Asp MLC 321; *The Rambler v The Kotka* [1917] 2 IR 406, CA; *The Athamas* (1917) 14 Asp MLC 276.
5   As to the meaning of 'derelict' see PARA 923.
6   The former practice was to award one-half (see *The Blenden Hall* (1814) 1 Dods 414 at 421; *The Effort* (1834) 3 Hag Adm 165 at 167), but now the fact of the salved property being derelict is merely an ingredient to be considered in assessing the reward (see *Papayanni v Hocquard, The True Blue* (1866) LR 1 PC 250 at 256; *The Anna Helena* (1883) 5 Asp MLC 142; *The Janet Court* [1897] P 59 at 62, 63, 8 Asp MLC 223 at 224 (three special elements usually present in the case of a derelict are the high degree of danger to property salved special difficulty of approaching and aiding her and necessity of supplying part of salvor's crew to work her)).
7   See *The Livietta* (1883) 8 PD 24, 5 Asp MLC 132; *The Janet Court* [1897] P 59, 8 Asp MLC 223.
8   See PARA 886 note 6.
9   See eg *The Amérique* (1874) LR 6 PC 468, 2 Asp MLC 460 (£18,000 on a value of £190,000).

892. Value of property salved. At common law the value of the salved property[1] is an important consideration in the assessment of reward[2], but it will not raise the reward out of due proportion to the services rendered[3]. If the value is large, the amount of the reward is usually a smaller proportion to the value than if the value is small[4]. As, however, the small value of salved property often renders it impossible to give an adequate reward[5], when the value is large, a liberal reward is generally given in order to encourage the performance of salvage services[6].

1   The salved value of the vessel and other property is one of the criteria to be taken into account when fixing the reward: see the International Convention on Salvage 1989 (London, 28 April 1989; Cm 1526) (the 'Salvage Convention') art 13(1)(a); and PARA 878. As to the Convention and the relationship between it and the pre-existing common law see PARA 851.
2   *The Amérique* (1874) LR 6 PC 468 at 475, 2 Asp MLC 460 at 465; *The City of Chester* (1884) 9 PD 182 at 202, 5 Asp MLC 311 at 319, CA. As to the valuation of the salved property see PARA 887.
3   *The Amérique* (1874) LR 6 PC 468 at 475, 2 Asp MLC 460 at 465; *The Glengyle* [1898] P 97 at 103, 8 Asp MLC 341 at 345, CA; *The Queen Elizabeth* (1949) 82 Ll L Rep 803.
4   *The Amérique* (1874) LR 6 PC 468, 2 Asp MLC 460; *The City of Chester* (1884) 9 PD 182, 5 Asp MLC 311, CA.
5   See *The Erato* (1888) 13 PD 163, 6 Asp MLC 334.
6   *The Earl of Eglinton* (1855) Sw 7 at 8.

893. Care, skill and knowledge of salvors. The salvor is required to show the reasonable degree of care, skill and knowledge to be expected in the circumstances[1] from a person in his position[2]; and, if through the absence of it the owner of the salved property suffers loss, the reward is less than it otherwise would be[3]. Where, however, there are any mitigating circumstances such as a sudden emergency, allowance may be made for them in measuring the degree of care, skill and knowledge required, and the fact that resulting damage arose in rendering assistance which was invited by the salvor may be taken into consideration[4].

1   As to the duties of the salvor and of the owner and master see the International Convention on Salvage 1989 (London, 28 April 1989; Cm 1526) (the 'Salvage Convention') art 8; and PARA 856. As to the Convention and the relationship between it and the pre-existing common law see PARA 851.
2   *The Lockwoods* (1845) 9 Jur 1017 at 1018. Breach of the duty to use reasonable care and skill involves liability to the potential claimant, and the principles as to standard of care recognised by the Admiralty courts are the same as those of the common law courts: *Anglo-Saxon Petroleum Co Ltd v Damant* [1947] KB 794, [1947] 2 All ER 465, 80 Ll L Rep 459, CA.
3   See *The Rosalie* (1853) 1 Ecc & Ad 188 (damage caused by ignorance); *The Perla* (1857) Sw 230 (bringing a derelict into an unsafe harbour); *The Magdalen* (1861) 31 LJPM & A 22; *The Dwina* [1892] P 58, 7 Asp MLC 173 (collision between salved and salving vessels); *The Alenquer, The Rene* [1955] 1 Lloyd's Rep 101 (salvor deprived of right to reward by unseamanlike action). In *The Dwina*, the full amount of damage was deducted.
4   *The CS Butler, The Baltic* (1874) 2 Asp MLC 237 at 238, 239.

894. Misconduct by salvors. Misconduct on the part of salvors[1] diminishes the reward and may cause forfeiture of all claim to reward[2], but criminal misconduct by the master and crew does not affect the owners, if they have not been privy to it[3]. The burden of proof of misconduct lies upon those who allege it, and strict proof of it is required[4]. In order to affect the reward, the misconduct need not have occasioned actual damage[5].

1   As to the duties of the salvor and of the owner and master see the International Convention on Salvage 1989 (London, 28 April 1989; Cm 1526) (the 'Salvage Convention') art 8; and PARA 856. As to the Convention and the relationship between it and the pre-existing common law see PARA 851.
2   *The Magdalen* (1861) 31 LJPM & A 22; *The Atlas* (1862) Lush 518, PC. For examples see also *The Dantzic Packet* (1837) 3 Hag Adm 383, and *The Martha* (1859) Sw 489 (interfering with additional salvors); *The Yan-Yean* (1883) 8 PD 147, 5 Asp MLC 135 (refusing to take the master of the vessel on board her and to accept a tug's services); *The Capella* [1892] P 70, 7 Asp MLC 158 (improperly retaining possession of ship and cargo). In *The Pinnas* (1888) 6 Asp MLC 313 and *The Trumpeter* (1947) 80 Ll L Rep 263 (improperly refusing to surrender possession of the salved property), the salvors were deprived of costs: see PARA 913. See also *The Clan Sutherland* [1918] P 332 (theft of salved property). As to maritime liens created by salvage services see PARAS 968, 969, 979.
3   *The Kenora* [1921] P 90.
4   *The Atlas* (1862) Lush 518 at 529, CA.
5   *The Glory* (1849) 13 Jur 991; *The Marie* (1882) 7 PD 203 at 205, 5 Asp MLC 27 at 28.

895. Negligence of salvors. Where actual loss or damage results from want of the requisite care, skill or knowledge[1], or misconduct, the reward, if it is not reduced by the amount of such loss or damage[2], will be diminished by an amount proportionate to the degree of negligence, unskilfulness, ignorance or misconduct proved[3].

The court takes a lenient view of the conduct of salvors, and is slow to find them guilty of negligence, as the policy of the law is to encourage the rendering of salvage services, but the court will make such a finding in a proper case[4]. The owners may bring a claim or counterclaim for negligence against the salvors for damage caused to the vessel during the salvage operation even where this has achieved more good than harm[5].

1   As to the required degree of care and skill see PARA 893. As to the duties of the salvor and of the owner and master see the International Convention on Salvage 1989 (London, 28 April 1989; Cm 1526) (the 'Salvage Convention') art 8; and PARA 856. As to the Convention and the relationship between it and the pre-existing common law see PARA 851.
2   See PARA 894; and see eg *The CS Butler, The Baltic* (1874) 2 Asp MLC 237; *The Dwina* [1892] P 58, 7 Asp MLC 173.

3   *The Cape Packet* (1848) 3 Wm Rob 122 at 125; *The Perla* (1857) Sw 230 at 231; *The Clan Sutherland* [1918] P 332. See also *Maridive VII v Key Singapore, The Key Singapore* [2004] EWHC 2227 (Comm), [2005] 1 All ER (Comm) 99, [2005] 1 Lloyd's Rep 91 (tugs towing a rig required to provide salvage services to the tow; fact-sensitive nature of any analysis of responsibility emphasised).
4   *The St Blane* [1974] 1 Lloyd's Rep 557.
5   *Tojo Maru (Owners) v NV Bureau Wijsmuller, The Tojo Maru* [1972] AC 242, [1971] 1 All ER 1110, [1971] 1 Lloyds Rep 342, HL.

896. Value of salving property. The value of the property employed in the salvage service[1] is an important element in the assessment of the reward at common law[2]. It is not, however, the measure of limit of the reward[3]. Where the value is small, it has little influence. The value of the cargo on board affects the reward only in so far as it increases the risk and responsibilities of the owner of the salving vessel[4].

1   The state of readiness and efficiency of the salvor's equipment and the value thereof are among the criteria to be taken into account when fixing the reward: see the International Convention on Salvage 1989 (London, 28 April 1989; Cm 1526) (the 'Salvage Convention') art 13(1)(j); and PARA 878. As to the Convention and the relationship between it and the pre-existing common law see PARA 851.
2   *The City of Chester* (1884) 9 PD 182, 5 Asp MLC 311, CA; *The Werra* (1886) 12 PD 52 at 54, 6 Asp MLC 115 at 117.
3   *The Fusilier* (1865) Brown & Lush 341 at 350, PC.
4   Cf *Carmichael v Brodie, The Sir Ralph Abercrombie* (1867) LR 1 PC 454.

897. Risk to salving property. Intimately connected with the value of the salving property and its influence on the reward is the risk to which the salving property is exposed by the performance of the salvage service[1]; and this is an important consideration at common law[2].

Apart from the actual danger to the salving property, there are certain risks and responsibilities incurred by the salvor which are considered in the assessment of the reward. They may include the risk of forfeiture of a policy of insurance, contractual liability to the owners of cargo on board the salving vessel through deviation to save property[3], and the responsibility involved in the use of Her Majesty's ships and passenger ships for salvage service[4].

Where any serious risk or responsibility is found to have been involved in the performance of the salvage service, special consideration is shown to the claim of the master of the salving vessel as well as to that of the owner[5].

1   The risk of liability and other risks run by the salvors or their equipment are among the criteria to be taken into account when fixing the reward: see the International Convention on Salvage 1989 (London, 28 April 1989; Cm 1526) (the 'Salvage Convention') art 13(1)(g); and PARA 878. As to the Convention and the relationship between it and the pre-existing common law see PARA 851.
2   *The City of Chester* (1884) 9 PD 182, 5 Asp MLC 311, CA; *The Werra* (1886) 12 PD 52, 6 Asp MLC 115; *The Rambler v The Kotka* [1917] 2 IR 406 (Ir CA).
3   *Carmichael v Brodie, The Sir Ralph Abercrombie* (1867) LR 1 PC 454; *Scaramanga v Stamp* (1880) 5 CPD 295, 4 Asp MLC 295, CA; *The Farnley Hall* (1881) 4 Asp MLC 499, CA; *The Edenmore* [1893] P 79, 7 Asp MLC 334. Deviation to save life does not involve risk to insurance or liability to owners of cargo: see *Scaramanga v Stamp*.
4   *The Martin Luther* (1857) Sw 287 at 289.
5   See PARA 906.

898. Duration of services. The length of the salvage operations[1] has not, in general, been a very important element for consideration at common law, unless the services were dangerous or invoked protracted exertion[2]. The additional loss or expense incurred by salvors by reason of the duration of their services has, however, been taken into consideration in the assessment of the reward[3].

The labour involved in the salvage service is an important element only so far as it is accompanied by the exercise of skill, or by danger or responsibility[4].

1 The time used and expenses and losses incurred by the salvors are among the criteria to be taken into account when fixing the reward: see the International Convention on Salvage 1989 (London, 28 April 1989; Cm 1526) (the 'Salvage Convention') art 13(1)(f); and PARA 878. As to the Convention and the relationship between it and the pre-existing common law see PARA 851.
2 *The Thomas Fielden* (1862) 32 LJPM & A 61 at 62; *The Strathgarry* [1895] P 264 at 270, 8 Asp MLC 19 at 20.
3 See PARA 899.
4 Thus, the seaman ordinarily receives less than the officer: see PARA 906.

899. Salvor's losses or expenses. In assessing the amount of the salvage reward the expenses and losses incurred by the salvor are usually taken into account[1]. Those losses and expenses may be given in the form of a separate award, but the common practice is to include them in the general award[2]. The losses and expenses which are dealt with in this manner include expenses reasonably incurred in bringing the salved property into a place of safety[3], and expenses such as the cost of repairing damage[4], loss by detention during repairs[5], depreciation in value of the salving vessel[6], penalties under contract[7], and loss of profits[8], caused by the performance of the salvage service[9]. If the damage which necessitated repairs occurred during the salvage service, the inference is that the damage resulted directly from the service, and the burden of proof lies on those who dispute it[10].

1 The time used and expenses and losses incurred by the salvors are among the criteria to be taken into account when fixing the reward: see the International Convention on Salvage 1989 (London, 28 April 1989; Cm 1526) (the 'Salvage Convention') art 13(1)(f); and PARA 878. As to the Convention and the relationship between it and the pre-existing common law see PARA 851.
2 See eg *The Lycaon* (1949) 82 Ll L Rep 691.
3 *The Le Jonet* (1872) LR 3 A & E 556, 1 Asp MLC 438 (hire of men to pump). See also *The Pinnas* (1888) 6 Asp MLC 313 at 314.
4 *The James Armstrong* (1875) 3 Asp MLC 46; *The Mud Hopper No 4* (1879) 4 Asp MLC 103; *The Sunniside* (1883) 8 PD 137, 5 Asp MLC 140; *Bird v Gibb, The De Bay* (1883) 8 App Cas 559, 5 Asp MLC 156, PC; *Baku Standard (Owners) v Angèle (Owners)* [1901] AC 549, 9 Asp MLC 197, PC; *The Fairport* [1912] P 168, 12 Asp MLC 165.
5 See the cases cited in note 4.
6 *Bird v Gibb, The De Bay* (1883) 8 App Cas 559, 5 Asp MLC 156, PC.
7 *The Silesia* (1880) 5 PD 177, 4 Asp MLC 338.
8 As to loss of profits in the case of fishing vessels see *The Salacia* (1829) 2 Hag Adm 262 at 270; *The Sunniside* (1883) 8 PD 137, 5 Asp MLC 140; *The Fairport* [1912] P 168, 12 Asp MLC 165. As to other vessels see *Bird v Gibb, The De Bay* (1883) 8 App Cas 559, 5 Asp MLC 156, PC; *The Edenmore* [1893] P 79, 7 Asp MLC 334; *The Bremen* (1906) 10 Asp MLC 229; *The Cato* (1930) 37 Ll L Rep 33 at 37; *The Comitas* (1934) 49 Ll L Rep 43 at 50; *The St Melante* (1947) 80 Ll L Rep 588; *The Tresco* (1944) 77 Ll L Rep 514; *The Perfective* (1949) 82 Ll L Rep 873; *The Ebor Jewel* (1949) 83 Ll L Rep 64.
9 No interest is allowed: *Bird v Gibb, The De Bay* (1883) 8 App Cas 559, 5 Asp MLC 156, PC.
10 *The Thomas Blyth* (1860) Lush 16; *Baku Standard (Owners) v Angèle (Owners)* [1901] AC 549 at 552, 9 Asp MLC 197 at 199.

900. Grounds of appeal. If the reward fixed by the court is made the subject of appeal, whether on the ground of excess or inadequacy, as a general rule it will be disturbed only where it is shown that the court below has erred in principle or has misapprehended the facts[1]. An award may, however, be altered on appeal on the ground of exorbitancy or inadequacy if it is clearly shown to be so greatly in excess as to be unjust to the owners of the salved property or so inadequate as to be unfair to the salvors[2]. If an unsuccessful appeal to the Court of Appeal is followed by an appeal to the Supreme Court, the case must be very exceptional to induce the Supreme Court to interfere[3].

Where a salvage action has been wrongly dismissed, the Court of Appeal, reversing that decision, may, if the facts are before it, itself award the amount of the salvage reward[4].

1   *The Star of Persia* (1887) 6 Asp MLC 220 at 221, CA. See also eg *The Amérique* (1874) LR 6 PC 468, 2 Asp MLC 460 (reduction of reward, undue weight being given to salved value); *Bird v Gibb, The De Bay* (1883) 8 App Cas 559, 5 Asp MLC 156, PC (reduction of award on ground of erroneous view of evidence and too high a remuneration for services); *The Accomac* [1891] P 349, 7 Asp MLC 153, CA (increase of reward on grounds of underrating danger and difficulties); *The Port Hunter* [1910] P 343, 11 Asp MLC 492, CA (reduction of reward on grounds of undue weight given to value of salved property). See also *The Rambler v The Kotka* [1917] 2 IR 406 (Ir CA). As to adjustment see PARA 882.
2   *The Clarisse* (1856) Sw 129 at 134, PC (approved in *Arnold v Cowie, The Glenduror* (1871) LR 3 PC 589, 1 Asp MLC 31); *The Amérique* (1874) LR 6 PC 468, 2 Asp MLC 460; *Thomas Allen (Owners) v Gow, The Thomas Allen* (1886) 12 App Cas 118, PC. See also the judgments, to substantially the same effect, in *The Lancaster* (1883) 9 PD 14, 5 Asp MLC 174, CA; *The Star of Persia* (1887) 6 Asp MLC 220, CA; *The Accomac* [1891] P 349, 7 Asp MLC 153, CA; *The Glengyle* [1898] P 97, CA (affd [1898] AC 519, 8 Asp MLC 436, HL); *The Port Hunter* [1910] P 343, 11 Asp MLC 492, CA. Inadequacy is as good an objection to an award as exorbitancy: *The Chetah* (1868) LR 2 PC 205 at 210, 211; *The Cruiser v The Taquary* 1913 SC 1107. For examples of successful and unsuccessful appeals against awards see Kennedy's *Law of Salvage* (5th Edn) pp 1337–1340. See also *The Frisia* [1960] 1 Lloyd's Rep 90, CA.
3   *The Glengyle* [1898] AC 519 at 520, 8 Asp MLC 436 at 437, HL.
4   *The Minnehaha* (1861) Lush 335, PC.

(vii) Apportionment of Award between Salvors

901. Criteria for apportionment under Salvage Convention. Under the Salvage Convention[1] the apportionment of a reward[2] between salvors must be made on the basis of the usual criteria[3] for fixing the reward[4]. The apportionment between the owner, master[5] and other persons in the service of each salving vessel[6] must be determined by the law of the flag of that vessel[7]. If the salvage has not been carried out from a vessel, the apportionment must be determined by the law governing the contract between the salvor and his servants[8].

1   Ie the International Convention on Salvage 1989 (London, 28 April 1989; Cm 1526): see PARA 851.
2   Ie under the Salvage Convention art 13 (see PARA 878): see art 15(1).
3   Ie the criteria contained in the Salvage Convention art 13: see art 15(1).
4   Salvage Convention art 15(1).
5   As to the meaning of 'master' see PARA 444 note 1.
6   As to the meaning of 'vessel' see PARA 850 note 2.
7   Salvage Convention art 15(2).
8   Salvage Convention art 15(2).

902. Apportionment of salvage under £5,000 by receiver. Where:

(1)   the aggregate amount of salvage[1] payable in respect of salvage services rendered in United Kingdom waters[2] has been finally determined and does not exceed £5,000[3]; but

(2)   a dispute arises as to the apportionment of the amount among several claimants[4],

the person liable to pay the amount may apply to the receiver[5] for leave to pay it to him[6].

The receiver must, if he thinks fit, receive the amount and, if he does, he must give the person paying it a certificate stating the amount paid and the services in respect of which it is paid[7]. Such a certificate is a full discharge and indemnity to the person by whom it was paid, and to his vessel[8], cargo, equipment and effects against the claims of all persons in respect of the services mentioned in the certificate[9].

The receiver must with all convenient speed distribute any amount so received by him[10] among the persons entitled to it, on such evidence, and in such shares and proportions, as he thinks fit[11]. Any such decision by the receiver must be made on the basis of the criteria for fixing the reward contained in the Salvage Convention[12].

The receiver may retain any money which appears to him to be payable to any person who is absent[13].

A distribution so made by a receiver[14] is final and conclusive as against all persons claiming to be entitled to any part of the amount distributed[15].

1   As to the meaning of 'salvage' see PARA 849.
2   As to the meaning of 'United Kingdom waters' see PARA 48 note 10. As to the meaning of 'United Kingdom' see PARA 16 note 3.
3   Merchant Shipping Act 1995 s 228(1)(a). As to the operation of the Merchant Shipping Act 1995 together with the International Convention on Salvage 1989 (London, 28 April 1989; Cm 1526) (the 'Salvage Convention') and the common law see PARA 851.
4   Merchant Shipping Act 1995 s 228(1)(b). As to apportionment by the court where the aggregate amount exceeds £5,000 see PARA 903. As to the Admiralty jurisdiction of the High Court in relation to the salvage of property see also PARA 115 et seq.
5   As to the meaning of 'receiver' see PARA 887 note 4.
6   Merchant Shipping Act 1995 s 228(1).
7   Merchant Shipping Act 1995 s 228(2).
8   As to the meaning of 'vessel' see PARA 919 note 5.
9   Merchant Shipping Act 1995 s 228(3).
10   Ie under the Merchant Shipping Act 1995 s 228: see s 228(4).
11   Merchant Shipping Act 1995 s 228(4).
12   Merchant Shipping Act 1995 s 228(5). The text refers to the criteria contained in the International Convention on Salvage 1989 (London, 28 April 1989; Cm 1526) art 13 (see PARA 878): see the Merchant Shipping Act 1995 s 228(5). As to the Salvage Convention generally see PARA 851.
13   Merchant Shipping Act 1995 s 228(6).
14   Ie under the Merchant Shipping Act 1995 s 228: see s 228(7).
15   Merchant Shipping Act 1995 s 228(7).

903. Apportionment by the court. Where:
   (1)   the aggregate amount of salvage[1] payable in respect of salvage services rendered in United Kingdom waters[2] has been finally determined and exceeds £5,000[3]; or
   (2)   the aggregate amount of salvage payable in respect of salvage services rendered outside United Kingdom waters (of whatever amount) has been finally determined[4]; but
   (3)   in either case, any delay or dispute arises as to the apportionment of the amount[5],
the court[6] may cause the amount of salvage to be apportioned among the persons entitled to it in such manner as it thinks just[7]. Any such decision of the court must be made on the basis of the criteria for fixing the reward in the Salvage Convention[8].

For the purpose of making that apportionment, the court may:
   (a)   appoint any person to carry that apportionment into effect[9];
   (b)   compel any person in whose hands or under whose control the amount may be to distribute it or to pay it into court to be dealt with as the court directs[10]; and
   (c)   issue such process as it thinks fit[11].

1   As to the meaning of 'salvage' see PARA 849.
2   As to the meaning of 'United Kingdom waters' see PARA 48 note 10. As to the meaning of 'United Kingdom' see PARA 16 note 3.
3   Merchant Shipping Act 1995 s 229(1)(a). As to the operation of the Merchant Shipping Act 1995 together with the International Convention on Salvage 1989 (London, 28 April 1989; Cm 1526) (the 'Salvage Convention') and the common law see PARA 851.

4 Merchant Shipping Act 1995 s 229(1)(b).
5 Merchant Shipping Act 1995 s 229(1)(c).
6 For these purposes, 'court' means the High Court: Merchant Shipping Act 1995 s 229(4).
7 Merchant Shipping Act 1995 s 229(1). As to apportionment by the receiver where the aggregate amount does not exceed £5,000 see PARA 902. As to the Admiralty jurisdiction of the High Court in relation to the salvage of property see also PARA 115 et seq.
   In *The Nicolaou Georgios* [1952] 2 Lloyd's Rep 215, where the amount had been determined by an arbitrator, who had also made an apportionment, and a dispute arose as to the apportionment, the salvage award was made a rule of court, and an inquiry was directed before the registrar to determine into which classes of the apportionment certain members of the crew fell.
8 Merchant Shipping Act 1995 s 229(2). The text refers to the criteria contained in the International Convention on Salvage 1989 (London, 28 April 1989; Cm 1526) art 13 (see PARA 878): see the Merchant Shipping Act 1995 s 228(5). As to the Salvage Convention generally see PARA 851.
9 Merchant Shipping Act 1995 s 229(3)(a).
10 Merchant Shipping Act 1995 s 229(3)(b).
11 Merchant Shipping Act 1995 s 229(3)(c).

904. Agreements for apportionment. At common law, an agreement between salvors as to the apportionment of the salvage reward amongst themselves, whether made before[1] or after[2] the services have begun, is binding on them if it has been made fairly and honestly[3], and the court will not set aside such an agreement merely because it would not have made the same apportionment[4]. At the same time, the court is careful to protect seamen from improvident arrangements[5], and sets aside those agreements whenever they are shown to be inequitable[6].

A seaman is prevented by statute from abandoning by agreement any right he may have or obtain in the nature of salvage[7], whether the agreement is made before or after the performance of the salvage service[8]. This does not, however, affect such of the terms of any agreement[9] made with the seamen belonging to a ship which is to be employed on salvage service, with regard to the salvage remuneration to be paid to them[10]; such an agreement, if it is equitable and honestly made, will be binding upon them[11], but must be strictly proved[12].

An agreement for the division of salvage rewards may be implied from the usage of a particular locality or occupation[13]. Such an agreement will be upheld only if it is equitable[14].

1 *The James Armstrong* (1875) 3 Asp MLC 46; *The Sunniside* (1883) 8 PD 137, 5 Asp MLC 140; *The Wilhelm Tell* [1892] P 337, 7 Asp MLC 329.
2 *The Afrika* (1880) 5 PD 192, 4 Asp MLC 266.
3 *The Enchantress* (1860) Lush 93; *The Afrika* (1880) 5 PD 192 at 196, 4 Asp MLC 266 at 268.
4 *The Afrika* (1880) 5 PD 192, 4 Asp MLC 266. As to apportionment under the Merchant Shipping Act 1995 and the International Convention on Salvage 1989 (London, 28 April 1989; Cm 1526) (the 'Salvage Convention') see PARAS 901–903. As to the Convention, and the operation of pre-existing common law alongside the Convention provisions, see PARA 851.
5 *The Wilhelm Tell* [1892] P 337 at 348, 7 Asp MLC 329 at 331.
6 *The Beulah* (1842) 1 Wm Rob 477; *The Louisa* (1843) 2 Wm Rob 22.
7 See the Merchant Shipping Act 1995 s 39(1); and PARA 479. An agreement between owner and crew that before division of the salvage reward the owner is to be entitled to deduct from the amount of the reward the cost of repairing damage sustained by the salved vessel in the service is void as being inconsistent with the statutory provision: *The Saltburn* (1894) 7 Asp MLC 474; and see *The Wilhelm Tell* [1892] P 337, 7 Asp MLC 329; *The Leon Blum* [1915] P 290, 13 Asp MLC 273, CA.
8 *The Rosario* (1876) 2 PD 41 at 45, 3 Asp MLC 334 at 336.
9 The agreement need not be in writing: *The Pride of Canada* (1863) Brown & Lush 208.
10 See the Merchant Shipping Act 1995 s 39(2); and PARA 479. A vessel is not within the exception merely because its articles contain a provision regulating the division of salvage rewards: *The Wilhelm Tell* [1892] P 337, 7 Asp MLC 329 (trawler).
11 *The Ganges* (1869) LR 2 A & E 370.
12 *The Pride of Canada* (1863) Brown & Lush 208; *Nicholson v Leith Salvage and Towage Co Ltd* 1923 SC 409.
13 *The Enchantress* (1860) Lush 93 at 97.
14 See note 13.

905.   Apportionment to owners. At common law, where the principal means of effecting the salvage service has been the salving vessel, her owners receive the largest share of the salvage reward, and their share is even larger where the salving vessel and her cargo were valuable and were exposed to great risk by the performance of the services[1]. Where the salvage service has been effected chiefly by the services of the crew, and the salving vessel and her cargo have not been exposed to any serious risk, the crew are entitled to the larger share in the reward[2]. Where the salving vessel is the chief instrument in effecting the salvage, the share of the owners in a salvage reward has been generally approximate to three-quarters of the whole award[3], but there is no rule of practice on the point[4]. The apportionment depends on the particular circumstances of each case[5], and there are many examples of variation in apportionment to owners[6].

1   Cf *The Enchantress* (1860) Lush 93 at 96. As to apportionment under the Merchant Shipping Act 1995 and the International Convention on Salvage 1989 (London, 28 April 1989; Cm 1526) (the 'Salvage Convention') see PARAS 901–903. As to the Convention, and the operation of pre-existing common law alongside the Convention provisions, see PARA 851.
2   *The Jane* (1831) 2 Hag Adm 338 at 343; *The Nicolina* (1843) 2 Wm Rob 175.
3   Before 1870, one-half was the most given; from 1870 to 1883, it was usually two-thirds, and since 1883 it has been usually three-quarters.
4   See *SS Nestor (Owners) v Mungana (Owners), The Mungana* [1936] 3 All ER 670.
5   *The Gipsy Queen* [1895] P 176 at 177, 7 Asp MLC 586, CA.
6   See Kennedy's *Law of Salvage* (5th Edn) p 1221 et seq.

906.   Shares of master, officers and crew. At common law the master of the salving ship usually receives a special apportionment by reason of the special responsibility which he undertakes in the performance of a salvage service[1]. The share given to him varies according to the degree of responsibility cast on him. It has often been from one-half to one-third of the balance of the award after deducting the sum apportioned to the owners. There is, however, no rule of practice governing his share[2].

Officers and crew generally share in the sum for salvage awarded to them collectively according to their ratings subject to an exception in favour of navigating officers with ratings lower than that of engineers, who are allowed to rank for the purpose of salvage as of the same ratings as engineers[3]. Special rewards may be given to officers or members of the crew who have rendered special services[4].

1   *The Martin Luther* (1857) Sw 287 at 289, 290; *The Charles* (1872) LR 3 A & E 536 at 538, 1 Asp MLC 296 at 298. As to apportionment under the Merchant Shipping Act 1995 and the International Convention on Salvage 1989 (London, 28 April 1989; Cm 1526) (the 'Salvage Convention') see PARAS 901–903. As to the Convention, and the operation of pre-existing common law alongside the Convention provisions, see PARA 851.
2   *The Gipsy Queen* [1895] P 176 at 177, 7 Asp MLC 586, CA.
3   *The Birnam* (1907) 10 Asp MLC 462. The crew includes 'runners', or men engaged for a single 'run', who may share on the basis of the rating of the persons whose posts they are filling (*The Persia* [1902] WN 210; but see *The Rasche* (1873) LR 4 A & E 127 (where they were treated as ABs)); and apprentices, with regard to whom there is no special scale of reward (*The Hope* (1838) 3 Hag Adm 423 (shares of seamen of lowest rank); *The Beulah* (1842) 1 Wm Rob 477 (one-half of ABs' shares); *The George Dean* (1857) Sw 290 (two-thirds of ABs' shares); *The Rasche* (1873) LR 4 A & E 127 (ABs' shares); *The Punta Lara* (1910) 26 TLR 268 (OSs' shares); *The Valkyrie* [1910] WN 138 (ABs' shares)). In *The Empire Gulf* [1948] P 168, [1948] 1 All ER 564, 81 Ll L Rep 255, the award was held apportionable according to basic rates of pay, war bonus thus disregarded. See also *The Southern Venturer* [1953] 1 Lloyd's Rep 428; *The New Australia* [1958] 2 Lloyd's Rep 35 (where the mate ranked as equivalent to the chief engineer).
4   See eg *The Golondrina* (1867) LR 1 A & E 334; *The Rasche* (1873) LR 4 A & E 127; *The Skibladner* (1877) 3 PD 24, 3 Asp MLC 556; *The Santiago* (1900) 9 Asp MLC 147; *The Minneapolis* [1902] P 30, 9 Asp MLC 270; *The Clan Sutherland* [1918] P 332.

907.   Shares of associates and passengers. At common law the shares of the associates[1] of the actual salvors depend on the amount of additional labour and danger imposed on them through the services of the actual salvors[2]. The amount of the reward of passengers who become entitled to salvage reward depends on the nature and circumstances of the services[3].

1   The rule of personal service does not extend to the associates: see PARA 867.
2   The non-navigating members of the crew were given in *The Spree* [1893] P 147, 7 Asp MLC 397, one-half shares, according to their ratings; in *The Dunottar Castle* [1902] WN 70, and *The Minneapolis* [1902] P 30, 9 Asp MLC 270, one-third shares, according to their actual rating. In *The Punta Lara* (1910) 26 TLR 268 a stewardess was refused any share.
    As to apportionment under the Merchant Shipping Act 1995 and the International Convention on Salvage 1989 (London, 28 April 1989; Cm 1526) (the 'Salvage Convention') see PARAS 901–903. As to the Convention, and the operation of pre-existing common law alongside the Convention provisions, see PARA 851.
3   See *The Hope* (1838) 3 Hag Adm 423 (shares of ABs); *The Perla* (1857) Sw 230 (foreign master and seamen passengers on salving vessel given ABs' shares, the master taking a double share). For very special services see *Newman v Walters* (1804) 3 Bos & P 612; *Towle v The Great Eastern* (1861) 2 Mar LC 148 (US District Court of Admiralty).

908.   Officers and men of the Royal Navy and other services. At common law officers and men of the Royal Navy can obtain an apportionment from the court, but, if an apportionment is not made by the court, the distribution of salvage is regulated by the naval prize proclamation in force at the time[1]. Similarly, officers and men of Her Majesty's Coastguard and of revenue boats may either obtain an apportionment by the court or rely on rules laid down by the Secretary of State for the distribution of salvage among them[2]. Lifeboat crews who become entitled to rank as salvors may obtain an apportionment from the court[3].

1   See ARMED FORCES vol 3 (2011) PARA 447; and *The Mary Ann* (1823) 1 Hag Adm 158 at 161. As to apportionment under the Merchant Shipping Act 1995 and the International Convention on Salvage 1989 (London, 28 April 1989; Cm 1526) (the 'Salvage Convention') see PARAS 901–903. As to the Convention, and the operation of pre-existing common law alongside the Convention provisions, see PARA 851.
2   As to the Secretary of State see PARA 36.
3   See PARA 873.

909.   Independent salvors. At common law, where persons who perform salvage services are independent salvors, as distinguished from members of a crew or others who act in association, the apportionment to them is determined by consideration of the risk, labour, skill, responsibility and value of their respective services[1].

Where salvage services have been performed by several independent sets of salvors, then, if their services have been contemporaneous, their shares of a salvage award are determined by the principles applicable to the assessment of the whole award. Where a tender is made and the circumstances are within the knowledge of the salved vessel, independent salvors may require the defendant to apportion the sum tendered[2]. Accordingly, a set of salvors who save both life and property usually receive a higher apportionment than a set of salvors who have salved property only[3].

1   See eg *Nicolaas Witzen* (1837) 3 Hag Adm 369. As to apportionment under the Merchant Shipping Act 1995 and the International Convention on Salvage 1989 (London, 28 April 1989; Cm 1526) (the 'Salvage Convention') see PARAS 901–903. As to the Convention, and the operation of pre-existing common law alongside the Convention provisions, see PARA 851.
2   *The Burnock* (1914) 12 Asp MLC 490. See also *The Athamas* (1917) 14 Asp MLC 276. In *The Bosworth* [1960] 1 All ER 146, [1961] 1 WLR 312, [1959] 2 Lloyd's Rep 537, the court in the exercise of its discretion would not relieve the defendants of making an apportionment of the lump sum tendered
3   *The Clarisse* (1856) Sw 129, PC; *The Anna Helena* (1883) 5 Asp MLC 142.

910.   First and second sets of salvors. At common law, where the salvage services have not been contemporaneous, but subsequently to the inception of the services another set of salvors, with the consent of the first set, have joined in the services or have succeeded the first set, who, after rendering some assistance, have been compelled by circumstances, through no fault of their own, to abandon the services, special favour is usually shown to the first set of salvors: the object of so doing being to encourage promptitude in the rendering of salvage services and willingness to accept additional assistance where such assistance is advisable[1]. If a second set of salvors dispossesses the original salvors against the will of the original salvors and while they are willing to continue their services, the second set of salvors are entitled to no reward unless they can prove that there was no reasonable probability that the services of the first salvors would have met with success[2]; in default of such proof the whole reward is given to the first salvors[3]. If however, the second set of salvors in dispossessing the first set acted under an honest and not unreasonable, although mistaken, belief that their interference was necessary, they may receive some reward, and in that case the original salvors are entitled to the same reward which they would have been awarded if they had completed the salvage service[4].

Where the services of the original salvors have been intermittent, and during an interval in the performance of them a second set of salvors have intervened against their wishes and rendered beneficial services, the second set of salvors receive a reward, although, if the interference of the second salvors is accompanied by the exercise of force, the reward is very much reduced[5].

1 *The Santipore* (1854) 1 Ecc & Ad 231; *The EU* (1853) 1 Ecc & Ad 63. As to apportionment under the Merchant Shipping Act 1995 and the International Convention on Salvage 1989 (London, 28 April 1989; Cm 1526) (the 'Salvage Convention') see PARAS 901–903. As to the Convention, and the operation of pre-existing common law alongside the Convention provisions, see PARA 851.
2 The burden of proof is on the second set of salvors: *The Eugene* (1834) 3 Hag Adm 156 at 160.
3 *The Fleece* (1850) 3 Wm Rob 278 at 280; *The Samuel* (1851) 15 Jur 407 at 409, 410 (approving *The Blenden Hall* (1814) 1 Dods 414). See also *The Pickwick* (1852) 16 Jur 669.
4 *The Maria* (1809) Edw 175; *The Charlotta* (1831) 2 Hag Adm 361; *The Tubantia* [1924] P 78, 18 Ll L Rep 158.
5 *The Clarisse* (1856) Sw 129, PC.

911. Intervention. At common law if the property in danger was not derelict[1] and was in charge of the owner or the master or other representative of the owner, and that person accepted the services of salvors, a second set of salvors intervening without any invitation or necessity receive no reward[2]. Original salvors have no right, however, to insist on the continuance of their services or to refuse additional assistance in defiance of the wishes of the owner of the property in danger or his representative or of the interests in the property[3].

Unless the property in danger is strictly derelict, the salvors are bound to submit to the orders of the owner of the property or his representative[4]. If they fail to do so, the reward is diminished or perhaps forfeited altogether[5]. Even in the case of derelict property, where the salvor has a vested interest and a right of exclusive possession[6], the first salvors may not refuse further assistance if the interests of the property demand it[7]. If they are dispossessed or superseded by the orders of the owner of the property in peril or his representative while they are able and willing to complete the salvage service, they receive a liberal reward[8], and the court is not very careful to inquire whether the dispossession or supersession was necessary and proper[9]. If the intervention of the second salvors was necessary for the safety of the property, the first salvors are liberally rewarded for any beneficial services rendered by them[10].

1 As to the meaning of 'derelict' see PARA 923. As to apportionment under the Merchant Shipping Act 1995 and the International Convention on Salvage 1989 (London, 28 April 1989; Cm 1526) (the 'Salvage Convention') see PARAS 901–903. As to the Convention, and the operation of pre-existing common law alongside the Convention provisions, see PARA 851.
2 *The Glasgow Packet* (1844) 2 Wm Rob 306 at 313; *The Fleece* (1850) 3 Wm Rob 278 at 281; *The Barefoot* (1850) 14 Jur 841 at 842; *The Samuel* (1851) 15 Jur 407 at 410.

3   *The Champion* (1863) Brown & Lush 69 at 71. For a case where refusal to allow intervention of
    the master of the salved ship was held to be justified see *The Elise* [1899] WN 54.
4   See note 3.
5   *The Dantzic Packet* (1837) 3 Hag Adm 383 (forcibly excluding assistance); *The Glasgow Packet*
    (1844) 2 Wm Rob 306 (insisting on continuing services dispensed with). See also *The Capella*
    [1892] P 70, 7 Asp MLC 158.
6   *Cossman v West, Cossman v British America Assurance Co* (1887) 13 App Cas 160 at 181, 6 Asp
    MLC 233 at 238, PC.
7   *The Cambria* (1848) 2 Pritchard's Admiralty Digest (3rd Edn) 1822.
8   *The Maude* (1876) 3 Asp MLC 338; *The Unique Mariner (No 2)* [1979] 1 Lloyd's Rep 37 (where
    the salvor was held to be entitled to payment for services rendered and compensation for the loss
    of opportunity to complete the salvage).
9   *The Maasdam* (1893) 7 Asp MLC 400 at 401.
10 *The Pickwick* (1852) 16 Jur 669; *The Magdalen* (1861) 31 LJPM & A 22; *The American Farmer*
    (1947) 80 Ll L Rep 672.

912.   Misconduct of salvors. At common law the misconduct of one set of
salvors does not affect the right of another set to obtain reward, unless they were
involved in the misconduct[1].

1   *The Neptune* (1842) 1 Wm Rob 297; *The Scindia* (1866) LR 1 PC 241. See PARA 894. As to
    apportionment under the Merchant Shipping Act 1995 and the International Convention on
    Salvage 1989 (London, 28 April 1989; Cm 1526) (the 'Salvage Convention') see PARAS 901–903.
    As to the Convention, and the operation of pre-existing common law alongside the Convention
    provisions, see PARA 851.

(viii)   Enforcement, Payment and Security

913.   Rights in rem. The salvor has a possessory lien on the salved property
which will be recognised in a court of common law[1], and he also has in Admiralty,
independently of possession, a maritime lien on the salved property[2]. No
proceedings in rem may, however, be instituted against any of Her Majesty's ships
or aircraft, or cargo or other property belonging to the Crown[3].

The remedy in rem is so complete that any attempt on the salvor's part to retain
exclusive possession of the salved property, except where the property is derelict[4],
or he can show that otherwise he would lose the security for his reward[5], or that
he is justified by special circumstances[6], may be visited by the court with a
diminution of the reward[7] or the loss of the costs of his action[8] or, in an extreme
case, the forfeiture of all title to reward[9].

In the case of derelict property, the first salvor in possession has ordinarily an
exclusive right to possession until his claim has been satisfied; he is also entitled
to a declaration as to possession, an injunction restraining naval salvors from
interfering with the property, and damages[10], but he may prejudice and even
forfeit his claim if he insists on retaining possession and in the circumstances of
the case the court is of opinion that he has no right to do so[11].

1   *Hartfort v Jones* (1698) 1 Ld Raym 393. Possessory liens (also sometimes described as common
    law liens) are now usually referred to as legal liens: see LIEN vol 68 (2016) PARAS 802, 817 et seq.
    As to the operation of the pre-existing common law together with the International Convention on
    Salvage 1989 (London, 28 April 1989; Cm 1526) (the 'Salvage Convention') see PARA 851.
2   See PARA 112. As to maritime liens for salvage services see PARAS 968, 969, 979.
3   See the Crown Proceedings Act 1947 s 29(1); and PARA 179. As to Admiralty claims in rem
    generally see PARA 158 et seq.
4   *Cossman v West, Cossman v British America Assurance Co* (1887) 13 App Cas 160 at 181, 6 Asp
    MLC 233 at 239, PC. Cf *The Gertrude* (1861) 30 LJPM & A 130. As to the meaning of 'derelict'
    see PARA 923.
5   *The Glasgow Packet* (1844) 2 Wm Rob 306 at 312, 313.
6   *The Orbona* (1853) 1 Ecc & Ad 161 at 165; *The Pinnas* (1888) 6 Asp MLC 313; *The Elise* [1899]
    WN 54.
7   *The Glasgow Packet* (1844) 2 Wm Rob 306.

8 *The Pinnas* (1888) 6 Asp MLC 313; *The Trumpeter* (1947) 80 Ll L Rep 263.
9 *The Barefoot* (1850) 14 Jur 841; *The Champion* (1863) Brown & Lush 69; *The Capella* [1892] P 70, 7 Asp MLC 158.
10 *Cossman v West, Cossman v British America AssuranceCo* (1887) 13 App Cas 160, 6 Asp MLC 233, PC; *The Tubantia* [1924] P 78, 18 Ll L Rep 158.
11 *The Lady Worsley* (1855) 2 Ecc & Ad 253 at 255.

914.   Rights in personam. In addition to the right of action in rem[1], the salvor also possesses in Admiralty a right of action in personam[2] against the owners of the salved property[3], but limited, in the absence of special contract[4], to cases where property[5] or an interest in property[6] has been saved to the person sued and to the extent of such property or interest.

1 See PARA 913.
2 See PARA 104 et seq. See also *The Two Friends* (1799) 1 Ch Rob 271 at 277; *The Schiller (Cargo ex)* (1877) 2 PD 145 at 149, 3 Asp MLC 439 at 441, CA; *The Five Steel Barges* (1890) 15 PD 142 at 146, 6 Asp MLC 580 at 582; *The Elton* [1891] P 265, 7 Asp MLC 66; *The Port Victor (Cargo ex)* [1901] P 243, 9 Asp MLC 182, CA. As to the operation of the pre-existing common law together with the International Convention on Salvage 1989 (London, 28 April 1989; Cm 1526) (the 'Salvage Convention') see PARA 851.
3 *The Sarpedon (Cargo ex)* (1877) 3 PD 28 at 34, 3 Asp MLC 509 at 510; *The Prinz Heinrich* (1888) 13 PD 31 at 34, 6 Asp MLC 273 at 276.
4 *The Sarpedon (Cargo ex)* (1877) 3 PD 28 at 34, 3 Asp MLC 509 at 510; *The Renpor* (1883) 8 PD 115 at 117, 5 Asp MLC 98 at 100, CA; *The Elton* [1891] P 265 at 269, 7 Asp MLC 66 at 67; *The Port Victor (Cargo ex)* [1901] P 243 at 255, 256, 9 Asp MLC 182 at 184, CA.
5 *The Five Steel Barges* (1890) 15 PD 142 at 146, 6 Asp MLC 580 at 582; *The Port Victor (Cargo ex)* [1901] P 243 at 249, 255, 9 Asp MLC 182 at 183, 184, CA.
6 *The Schiller (Cargo ex)* (1877) 2 PD 145 at 157, 3 Asp MLC 439 at 444, CA; *Admiralty Comrs v Josefina Thorden (Owners), The Josefina Thorden* [1945] 1 All ER 344.

915.   Maritime lien. Nothing in the Salvage Convention[1] affects the salvor's maritime lien[2] under any international Convention or national law[3].

The salvor may not enforce his maritime lien when satisfactory security for his claim, including interest and costs, has been duly tendered or provided[4].

1 Ie the International Convention on Salvage 1989 (London, 28 April 1989; Cm 1526): see PARA 851.
2 As to maritime liens see PARA 964 et seq.
3 Salvage Convention art 20(1).
4 Salvage Convention art 20(2).

916.   Duty to provide security. Upon the request of the salvor, a person liable for a payment[1] due under the Salvage Convention[2] must provide satisfactory security for the claim, including interest and costs of the salvor[3].

The owner of the salved vessel[4] must[5] use his best endeavours to ensure that the owners of the cargo provide satisfactory security for the claims against them including interest and costs before the cargo is released[6].

The salved vessel and other property[7] must not, without the consent of the salvor, be removed from the port or place at which they first arrive after the completion of the salvage operations[8] until satisfactory security has been put up for the salvor's claim against the relevant vessel or property[9].

1 As to the meaning of 'payment' see PARA 853 note 9.
2 Ie the International Convention on Salvage 1989 (London, 28 April 1989; Cm 1526): see PARA 851.
3 Salvage Convention art 21(1).
4 As to the meaning of 'vessel' see PARA 850 note 3.
5 Ie without prejudice to the Salvage Convention art 21(1) (see the text and notes 1–3): see art 21(2).
6 Salvage Convention art 21(2).
7 As to the meaning of 'property' see PARA 850 note 3.
8 As to the meaning of 'salvage operation' see PARA 850.
9 Salvage Convention art 21(3).

917. Interim payment. The tribunal having jurisdiction over the claim of the salvor under the Salvage Convention[1] may, by interim decision, order that the salvor is to be paid on account such amount as seems fair and just, and on such terms including terms as to security where appropriate, as may be fair and just according to the circumstances of the case[2].

In the event of such an interim payment, the security provided[3] is to be reduced accordingly[4].

1 Ie the International Convention on Salvage 1989 (London, 28 April 1989; Cm 1526): see PARA 851.
2 Salvage Convention art 22(1).
3 Ie under the Salvage Convention art 21 (see PARA 916): see art 22(2).
4 Salvage Convention art 22(2).

918. Limitation of actions. Any action relating to payment under the Salvage Convention[1] is time-barred if judicial proceedings[2] or arbitral proceedings have not been instituted within a period of two years[3]. The limitation period commences on the day on which the salvage operations[4] are terminated[5].

The person against whom a claim is made may at any time during the running of the limitation period extend that period by a declaration to the claimant[6]. This period may in the like manner be further extended[7].

An action for indemnity by a person liable may be instituted even after the expiration of the limitation period so provided for[8], if brought within the time allowed by the law of the state where proceedings are instituted[9].

1 Ie the International Convention on Salvage 1989 (London, 28 April 1989; Cm 1526): see PARA 851.
2 As to the meaning of 'judicial proceedings' see PARA 892 note 2.
3 Salvage Convention art 23(1).
4 As to the meaning of 'salvage operation' see PARA 850.
5 Salvage Convention art 23(1).
6 Salvage Convention art 23(2).
7 Salvage Convention art 23(2).
8 Ie provided for in the Salvage Convention art 23(1), (2) (see the text and notes 1–7): see art 23(3).
9 Salvage Convention art 23(3). The test as to when proceedings have been commenced is determined according to the lex fori: see *Dresser UK Ltd v Falcongate Freight Management Ltd* [1992] QB 502, [1992] 2 All ER 450, CA; and PARA 99. As to the lex fori see CONFLICT OF LAWS vol 19 (2011) PARA 313.

919. Detention of property liable to salvage by receiver. Where salvage[1] is due to any person[2], the receiver[3] must[4]:

(1) if the salvage is due in respect of services rendered in assisting a vessel[5], or in saving life from a vessel, or in saving the cargo and equipment of a vessel, detain the vessel and cargo or equipment[6]; and

(2) if the salvage is due in respect of the saving of any wreck[7], and the wreck is not sold as unclaimed[8], detain the wreck[9].

The receiver must detain the vessel and the cargo and equipment, or the wreck, as the case may be, until payment is made for salvage, or process is issued for the arrest or detention of the property by the court[10]. However, the receiver may release any property so detained if security is given[11]:

(a) to his satisfaction[12]; or

(b) where the claim for salvage exceeds £5,000, and any question is raised as to the sufficiency of the security, to the satisfaction of the court[13].

Any security so given for salvage to an amount exceeding £5,000 may be enforced by the court in the same manner as if bail had been given in that court[14].

1 As to the meaning of 'salvage' see PARA 849.
2 Ie under the Merchant Shipping Act 1995 Pt IX Ch I (ss 224–230): see s 226(1). The words 'due to any person under' in s 226(1) appear to cover any salvage which the Merchant Shipping Act

1995 contemplates being awarded by the court mentioned in it, the jurisdiction of which is compared or recognised by it: see *The Fulham* [1898] P 206 at 213, 8 Asp MLC 425 at 427 (discussing equivalent provision made under the Merchant Shipping Act 1894). As to the operation of the Merchant Shipping Act 1995 together with the International Convention on Salvage 1989 (London, 28 April 1989; Cm 1526) (the 'Salvage Convention') and the common law see PARA 851.
3 As to the meaning of 'receiver' see PARA 887 note 4.
4 Merchant Shipping Act 1995 s 226(1). Section 226 is excluded by s 230 (salvage claims against the Crown): see PARA 854. Nothing in the Senior Courts Act 1981 ss 20–23 (Admiralty jurisdiction) (see PARA 85 et seq) affects the provisions of the Merchant Shipping Act 1995 s 226: see the Senior Courts Act 1981 s 24(2)(b); and PARA 85.
5 For these purposes, 'vessel' includes any ship or boat, or any other description of vessel used in navigation: Merchant Shipping Act 1995 s 255(1). As to the meaning of 'ship' see PARA 229.
6 Merchant Shipping Act 1995 s 226(1)(a). See *Ministry of Trade of the Republic of Iraq v Tsavliris Salvage (International) Ltd, The Altair* [2008] EWHC 612 (Comm), [2008] 2 Lloyd's Rep 90, [2008] All ER (D) 14 (Apr) (freezing injunction).
7 As to the meaning of 'wreck' see PARA 923.
8 Ie under the Merchant Shipping Act 1995 Pt IX Ch I: see s 226(1)(b).
9 Merchant Shipping Act 1995 s 226(1)(b).
10 Merchant Shipping Act 1995 s 226(2). For these purposes, 'court' means the High Court: s 226(5). As to the sale of detained property see PARA 920.
11 Merchant Shipping Act 1995 s 226(3).
12 Merchant Shipping Act 1995 s 226(3)(a).
13 Merchant Shipping Act 1995 s 226(3)(b). After release salvors may not detain or arrest the property: *The Lady Katherine Barham* (1861) Lush 404.
14 Merchant Shipping Act 1995 s 226(4).

920. Sale of detained property by receiver.

The receiver[1] may sell any detained property[2] if the persons liable to pay the salvage[3] in respect of which the property is detained are aware of the detention, in the following cases[4], namely:
(1) where the amount is not disputed, and payment of the amount due is not made within 20 days after the amount is due[5];
(2) where the amount is disputed, but no appeal lies from the first court to which the dispute is referred, and payment is not made within 20 days after the decision of the first court[6];
(3) where the amount is disputed and an appeal lies from the decision of the first court to some other court, and within 20 days of the decision of the first court neither payment of the sum due is made nor proceedings are commenced for an appeal[7].

The proceeds of sale of detained property must, after payment of the expenses of the sale, be applied by the receiver in payment of the expenses, fees and salvage and any excess must be paid to the owners of the property or any other persons entitled to it[8].

1 As to the meaning of 'receiver' see PARA 887 note 4.
2 For these purposes, 'detained property' means property detained by the receiver under the Merchant Shipping Act 1995 s 226(2) (see PARA 919): s 227(4). As to the operation of the Merchant Shipping Act 1995 together with the International Convention on Salvage 1989 (London, 28 April 1989; Cm 1526) (the 'Salvage Convention') and the common law see PARA 851.
3 As to the meaning of 'salvage' see PARA 849.
4 Merchant Shipping Act 1995 s 227(1). Section 227 is excluded by s 230 (salvage claims against the Crown): see PARA 854.
5 Merchant Shipping Act 1995 s 227(2)(a).
6 Merchant Shipping Act 1995 s 227(2)(b).
7 Merchant Shipping Act 1995 s 227(2)(c).
8 Merchant Shipping Act 1995 s 227(3).

921. Prohibition on seizure of state-owned and humanitarian cargoes.

Unless the state owner consents, no provision of the Salvage Convention[1] may be used as a basis for the seizure, arrest or detention by any legal process of, nor for any proceedings in rem against, non-commercial cargoes owned by a state and entitled, at the time of the salvage operations[2], to sovereign immunity under generally recognised principles of international law[3].

No provision of the Convention may be used as a basis for the seizure, arrest or detention of humanitarian cargoes donated by a state, if such state has agreed to pay for salvage services rendered in respect of such humanitarian cargoes[4].

1 Ie the International Convention on Salvage 1989 (London, 28 April 1989; Cm 1526): see PARA 851.
2 As to the meaning of 'salvage operation' see PARA 850.
3 Salvage Convention art 25. State immunity is governed by the State Immunity Act 1978: see INTERNATIONAL RELATIONS LAW vol 61 (2010) PARA 242 et seq.
4 Salvage Convention art 26.

922. Publication of arbitral awards. Under the Salvage Convention[1], states parties[2] must encourage, as far as possible and with the consent of the parties, the publication of arbitral awards made in salvage cases[3].

1 Ie the International Convention on Salvage 1989 (London, 28 April 1989; Cm 1526): see PARA 851.
2 As to the making of Orders in Council declaring which states are parties to the Salvage Convention see PARA 852 note 3.
3 Salvage Convention art 27.

(2) WRECK

(i) Law and Jurisdiction

923. 'Maritime casualty' and 'wreck'. For the purposes of the Wrecks Convention[1] 'maritime casualty' means a collision of ships[2], stranding or other incident of navigation, or other occurrence on board a ship or external to it, resulting in material damage or imminent threat of material damage to a ship or its cargo[3]; and 'wreck', following upon a maritime casualty, means:

(1)   a sunken or stranded ship[4];
(2)   any part of a sunken or stranded ship, including any object that is or has been on board such a ship[5];
(3)   any object that is lost at sea from a ship and that is stranded, sunken or adrift at sea[6]; or
(4)   a ship that is about, or may reasonably be expected, to sink or to strand, where effective measures to assist the ship or any property in danger are not already being taken[7].

At common law 'wreck' may be defined as property cast ashore within the ebb and flow of the tide after shipwreck[8]; and the property must be a ship, her cargo or a portion of it[9]. Jetsam, flotsam and lagan or ligan[10] are not wreck at common law so long as they remain in or upon the sea, but, if they are cast up on the shore, they become wreck[11]. For the purposes of the statutory provisions relating to salvage and wreck[12], however, 'wreck' includes jetsam, flotsam, lagan and derelict found in or on the shores of the sea or any tidal water[13]. Fishing boats or fishing gear lost or abandoned at sea and either found or taken possession of within United Kingdom waters[14] or found or taken possession of beyond those waters and brought within those waters are treated as wreck for the purposes of the statutory provisions relating to salvage and wreck[15]; and 'wreck' includes any hovercraft[16] or any part of it or its cargo found sunk, stranded or abandoned in or on any navigable water[17] or on or over the foreshore or place where the tide normally ebbs or flows[18].

1   Ie the International Convention on the Removal of Wrecks (Nairobi, 18 May 2007; Cm 8243): see PARA 926.
2   In the context of the Wrecks Convention 'ships means a seagoing vessel of any type whatsoever and includes hydrofoil boats, air-cushion vehicles, submersibles, floating craft and floating platforms, except when such platforms are on location engaged in the exploration, exploitation or production of seabed mineral resources: art 1.2.
3   Wrecks Convention art 1.3.
4   Wrecks Convention art 1.4(a).
5   Wrecks Convention art 1.4(b).
6   Wrecks Convention art 1.4(c).
7   Wrecks Convention art 1.4(d).
8   Ie *wreckum maris significat illa bona quae naufragio ad terram appelluntur:* see *Sir Henry Constable's Case* (1601) 5 Co Rep 106a. On rights to wreck see *Crown Estate Comrs v Roberts* [2008] EWHC 1302 (Ch), [2008] 1 EGLR 129; and see further CROWN AND CROWN PROCEEDINGS vol 29 (2014) PARA 184 et seq. A raft of timber is not a wreck (*Nicholson v Chapman* (1793) 2 Hy Bl 254), nor are planks of timber moored in a river which have broken adrift (*Palmer v Rouse* (1858) 3 H & N 505), nor a gas buoy which has become adrift (*Wells v Gas Float Whitton No 2 (Owners)* [1897] AC 337, 8 Asp MLC 272, HL), none having formed part of a vessel, her apparel or cargo. See also *The Schiller (Cargo ex)* (1877) 2 PD 145 at 147, 3 Asp MLC 439 at 441, CA.
9   *Palmer v Rouse* (1858) 3 H & N 505. As to the meaning of 'cargo' for salvage purposes see PARA 860.
10   'Flotsam' is where a ship is wrecked and the goods float on the sea; 'jetsam' where they are cast into the sea in order to lighten the ship and sink; and 'ligan' where they are cast into the sea attached to a buoy to mark the spot; and in all cases it is necessary that the ship should perish: see *Sir Henry Constable's Case* (1601) 5 Co Rep 106a; *The Gas Float Whitton No 2* [1896] P 42 at 51, CA (on appeal sub nom *Wells v Gas Float Whittin No 2 (Owners)* [1897] AC 337, HL).
11   *Sir Henry Constable's Case* (1601) 5 Co Rep 106a; *R v Two Casks of Tallow* (1837) 3 Hag Adm 294 at 298; *The Pauline* (1845) 2 Wm Rob 358.
12   Ie in the Merchant Shipping Act 1995 Pt IX (ss 224–255): see s 255(1). Note that this definition applies only to Pt IX and not to the provisions relating to the Wrecks Convention (ie Pt 9A (ss 255A–255U)).
13   Merchant Shipping Act 1995 s 255(1). As to the meaning of 'derelict' see PARA 924. For these purposes, 'tidal water' means any part of the sea and any part of a river within the ebb and flow of the tide at ordinary spring tides, and not being a harbour: s 255(1). As to the meaning of 'harbour' see PARA 49 note 5. As to the common law meaning of 'wreck' in relation to the provisions for wages of seamen on termination of service by wreck or loss or the ship see PARA 470 note 2.
14   As to the meaning of 'United Kingdom waters' see PARA 48 note 10.
15   See the Merchant Shipping Act 1995 s 255(2). The purposes referred to in the text are those of Pt IX: see s 255(1).
16   As to the meaning of 'hovercraft' see PARA 381.
17   For these purposes, 'navigable water' means any water which is in fact navigable by ships or vessels, whether or not the tide ebbs and flows there, and whether or not there is a public right of navigation in that water: Hovercraft (Application of Enactments) Order 1972, SI 1972/971, art 3(1).
18   See the Hovercraft (Application of Enactments) Order 1972, SI 1972/971, art 8(1). This extended meaning of 'wreck' does not, however, apply to the claims of any admiral, vice-admiral, lord of the manor, or any person other than Her Majesty and her royal successors to unclaimed wreck for his own use: see art 8(1).

924. 'Derelict'. At common law 'derelict' is property, whether vessel or cargo[1], abandoned at sea by those in charge of it without hope on their part of recovering or intention of returning to it[2]. A vessel is not derelict which is only left temporarily by her master and crew with the intention of returning to her[3], even though the management of the vessel may have passed into the hands of salvors[4]. A vessel deserted by her master and crew with the intention of abandoning her does not, however, cease to be derelict because they subsequently change their intention and try to recover her[5]. Whenever the question arises whether a vessel is derelict or not, the test to be applied is the intention and expectation of the master and crew at the time of quitting her, and, in the absence of direct evidence, that is determined by consideration of all the circumstances of the case[6].

1   *R v Property Derelict* (1825) 1 Hag Adm 383; *R v Forty Nine Casks of Brandy* (1836) 3 Hag Adm 257 at 270; *The Samuel* (1851) 15 Jur 407 at 410; *The Coromandel* (1857) Sw 205; *The Boiler ex Elephant* (1891) 64 LT 543, CA.
2   *The Aquila* (1798) 1 Ch Rob 37 at 40; *The Gertrude* (1861) 30 LJPM & A 130 at 131; *Cossman v West, Cossman v British America Assurance* Co (1887) 13 App Cas 160 at 180, 181, 6 Asp MLC 233 at 239, PC; *The Carrie* [1917] P 224, 14 Asp MLC 321; *Bradley v H Newsom, Sons & Co* [1919] AC 16, 14 Asp MLC 340, HL.
3   *The Aquila* (1798) 1 Ch Rob 37; *The Lepanto* [1892] P 122, 7 Asp MLC 192.
4   *Cossman v West, Cossman v British America Assurance* Co (1887) 13 App Cas 160, 6 Asp MLC 233, PC; *The Lepanto* [1892] P 122, 7 Asp MLC 192.
5   *The Sarah Bell* (1845) 4 Notes of Cases 144 at 146.
6   See eg *The John and Jane* (1802) 4 Ch Rob 216; *The Cosmopolitan* (1848) 6 Notes of Cases, Supp xvii, xx-xxvii; *The Pickwick* (1852) 16 Jur 669 at 670; *The Zeta* (1875) LR 4 A & E 460, 3 Asp MLC 73; *The American Farmer* (1947) 80 Ll L Rep 672.

925. 'Hazard'. For the purposes of the Wrecks Convention[1] 'hazard' means any condition or threat that poses a danger or impediment to navigation or may reasonably be expected to result in major harmful consequences to the marine environment, or damage to the coastline or related interests[2] of one or more states[3]. When determining whether a wreck poses a hazard, the following criteria should be taken into account by the affected state[4]:

(1)   the type, size and construction of the wreck[5];
(2)   depth of the water in the area[6];
(3)   tidal range and currents in the area[7];
(4)   particularly sensitive sea areas identified and, as appropriate, designated in accordance with guidelines adopted by the IMO[8], or a clearly defined area of the exclusive economic zone where special mandatory measures have been[9] adopted[10];
(5)   proximity of shipping routes or established traffic lanes[11];
(6)   traffic density and frequency[12];
(7)   type of traffic[13];
(8)   nature and quantity of the wreck's cargo, the amount and types of oil (such as bunker oil and lubricating oil) on board the wreck and, in particular, the damage likely to result should the cargo or oil be released into the marine environment[14];
(9)   vulnerability of port facilities[15];
(10)   prevailing meteorological and hydrographical conditions[16];
(11)   submarine topography of the area[17];
(12)   height of the wreck above or below the surface of the water at lowest astronomical tide[18];
(13)   acoustic and magnetic profiles of the wreck[19];
(14)   proximity of offshore installations, pipelines, telecommunications cables and similar structures[20]; and
(15)   any other circumstances that might necessitate the removal of the wreck[21].

1   Ie the International Convention on the Removal of Wrecks (Nairobi, 18 May 2007; Cm 8243): see PARA 926.
2   'Related interests' means the interests of a coastal state directly affected or threatened by a wreck, such as:
    (1)   maritime coastal, port and estuarine activities, including fisheries activities, constituting an essential means of livelihood of the persons concerned (Wrecks Convention art 1.6(a));
    (2)   tourist attractions and other economic interests of the area concerned (art 1.6(b));
    (3)   the health of the coastal population and the wellbeing of the area concerned, including conservation of marine living resources and of wildlife (art 1.6(c)); and
    (4)   offshore and underwater infrastructure (art 1.6(d)).
3   Wrecks Convention art 1.5.

4   'Affected state' means the state in whose Convention area the wreck is located: Wrecks Convention
     art 1.10. As to the meaning of 'wreck' see PARA 923. In determining for the purposes of the
     Merchant Shipping Act 1995 Pt 9A (ss 255A–255U, Sch 11ZA) whether a wreck poses a hazard
     the Secretary of State must take into account the matters set out in the Wrecks Convention art 6:
     Merchant Shipping Act 1995 s 255R(5) (Pt 9A added by the Wreck Removal Convention Act 2011
     s 1, Schedule).
5   Wrecks Convention art 6(a).
6   Wrecks Convention art 6(b).
7   Wrecks Convention art 6(c).
8   As to the IMO (the International Maritime Organisation) see PARA 12.
9   Ie pursuant to the United Nations Convention on the Law of the Sea (Montego Bay, 10 December
     1982 to 9 December 1984; TS 3 Misc 11 (1983); Cmnd 8941) (the 'United Nations Convention
     on the Law of the Sea 1982') art 211, para 6.
10   Wrecks Convention art 6(d).
11   Wrecks Convention art 6(e).
12   Wrecks Convention art 6(f).
13   Wrecks Convention art 6(g).
14   Wrecks Convention art 6(h).
15   Wrecks Convention art 6(i).
16   Wrecks Convention art 6(j).
17   Wrecks Convention art 6(k).
18   Wrecks Convention art 6(l).
19   Wrecks Convention art 6(m).
20   Wrecks Convention art 6(n).
21   Wrecks Convention art 6(o). As to the meaning of 'removal' see PARA 942.

926. The Wrecks Convention and the Merchant Shipping Act 1995. The
United Kingdom is a signatory to the Wrecks Convention[1], which has been
incorporated into statute law[2]. The Convention's objective is to enable state
parties to take measures, in accordance with the Convention, in relation to the
removal of a wreck[3] which poses a hazard in the Convention area[4]. Measures so
taken must be proportionate to the hazard[5], must not go beyond what is
reasonably necessary to remove a wreck which poses a hazard, and must cease as
soon as the wreck has been removed[6]. Measures must not unnecessarily interfere
with the rights and interests of other states including the state of the ship's
registry[7], and of any person, physical or corporate, concerned[8].

There is no authority in point as to whether the Convention entirely supersedes
the common law relating to wreck: it is apprehended that it would still be correct
for English courts to refer to pre-existing principles in interpreting and applying
the Convention[9], provided that, in doing so, the courts proceed on the basis that
the Convention now represents the law and that pre-existing common law
principles are to be considered in relation to the Convention and not vice versa[10].

Matters not covered by the Wrecks Convention are dealt with under the
Merchant Shipping Act 1995[11].

1   Ie the International Convention on the Removal of Wrecks (Nairobi, 18 May 2007; Cm 8243):
     Merchant Shipping Act 1995 s 255A(1)(a) (Pt 9A (ss 255A–255U, Sch 11ZA) added by the Wreck
     Removal Convention Act 2011 s 1, Schedule). The Convention opened for signature at the
     headquarters of the International Maritime Organisation (IMO) from 19 November 2007 to 18
     November 2008 and thereafter remains open for accession: see art 17. As to the IMO see PARA 12.
     The Convention entered into force on 14 April 2015, one year after the date on which 10 states
     had expressed their consent to be bound by it: see art 18; and as to the maintenance and languages
     of the Convention see arts 20, 21. The Convention may be denounced by any state party at any
     time after the expiry of one year from the date on which that Convention enters into force for that
     state: see art 19. Provision is made for the amendment of the Convention (see art 14) and for the
     settlement of disputes between states parties about the interpretation or application of the
     Convention (see art 15 (which is subject to modification by art 4.4(a)(iii)). Nothing in the
     Convention prejudices the rights and obligations of any state under the United Nations
     Convention on the Law of the Sea (Montego Bay, 10 December 1982 to 9 December 1984; TS 3
     Misc 11 (1983); Cmnd 8941) (see PARA 9) and under the customary international law of the sea:
     Wrecks Convention art 16.

If Her Majesty by Order in Council declares that any state specified in the Order is a party to the Wrecks Convention, the Order is, while in force, conclusive evidence of that fact: Merchant Shipping Act 1995 s 255R(7) (as so added). The Secretary of State may by order amend Pt 9A to reflect any amendment of the Wrecks Convention: see the Merchant Shipping Act 1995 s 255U (as so added). At the date at which this volume states the law no such Order had been made.

2   The Convention is set out in the Merchant Shipping Act 1995 s 255A(2), Sch 11ZA (as added: see note 1).
3   As to the meaning of 'removal' see PARA 942; as to the meaning of 'wreck' see PARA 923.
4   Wrecks Convention art 2.1. As to the meaning of 'hazard', and the determination of a hazard, see PARA 925. In connection with the measures to be taken see PARAS 934–941. As to the 'Convention area' see PARA 927.
5   Wrecks Convention art 2.2.
6   Wrecks Convention art 2.3.
7   'State of the ship's registry' means, in relation to a registered ship, the state of registration of the ship and, in relation to an unregistered ship, the state whose flag the ship is entitled to fly: Wrecks Convention art 1.11.
8   Wrecks Convention art 2.4.
9   Ie following *Pepper (Inspector of Taxes) v Hart* [1993] AC 593, [1993] 1 All ER 42, HL; and see STATUTES AND LEGISLATIVE PROCESS vol 96 (2012) PARA 1122. Where statutory provisions are ambiguous, it is legitimate, in resolving any ambiguity, to have recourse to the travaux préparatoires of the Convention: *Gatoil International Inc v Arkwright-Boston Manufacturers Mutual Insurance Co* [1985] AC 255, [1985] 1 All ER 129, sub nom *The Sandrina* [1985] 1 Lloyd's Rep 181, HL.
10   As to treaty Acts and their interpretation generally see STATUTES AND LEGISLATIVE PROCESS vol 96 (2012) PARAS 635, 1128.
11   Ie the Merchant Shipping Act 1995 Pt IX (ss 224–255).

927. Geographical application of the Wrecks Convention, and the 'Convention area'.

The Wrecks Convention[1] applies to all wrecks in the Convention area[2], that is, the exclusive economic zone of a state party, established in accordance with international law or, if a state party has not established such a zone, an area beyond and adjacent to the territorial sea of that state determined by that state in accordance with international law and extending not more than 200 nautical miles from the baselines from which the breadth of its territorial sea is measured[3]. A state party may extend the application of the Convention to wrecks located within its territory, including the territorial sea[4]. The Secretary of State must from time to time by order describe the United Kingdom's Convention area[5].

The application of the Convention within the Convention area does not entitle a state party to claim or exercise sovereignty or sovereign rights over any part of the high seas[6].

1   Ie the International Convention on the Removal of Wrecks (Nairobi, 18 May 2007; Cm 8243): see PARA 926.
2   Wrecks Convention art 3.1.
3   Wrecks Convention art 1.1.
4   Wrecks Convention art 3.2. The state party must notify the Secretary-General accordingly, at the time of expressing its consent to be bound by the Convention or at any time thereafter: art 3.2. When a state party has made a notification to apply the Convention to wrecks located within its territory, including the territorial sea, it is without prejudice to the rights and obligations of that state to take measures in relation to wrecks located in its territory, including the territorial sea, other than locating, marking and removing them in accordance with the Convention: art 3.2. The provisions of arts 10–12 (see PARAS 953–954) do not apply to any measures so taken other than those referred to in art 7–9: art 2.2. When a state party has made such a notification art 2.4 (see note 5), arts 9.1, 9.5, 9.7–9.10 (see PARAS 941–944) do not apply in its territory, including the territorial sea, and art 15 (see PARA 926) applies with modifications: art 4.4. When a state party has made such a notification, the 'Convention area' of the affected state includes the territory, including the territorial sea, of that state party: see art 3.3; and as to the mechanism for notifications see arts 3.4, 3.5. As to the meaning of 'affected state' see PARA 925 note 4. As to the meaning of 'removing' see PARA 942.

5   Merchant Shipping Act 1995 s 255R(6) (Pt 9A (ss 255A–255U, Sch 11ZA) added by the Wreck
     Removal Convention Act 2011 s 1, Schedule). See the Merchant Shipping (United Kingdom Wreck
     Convention Area) Order 2015, SI 2015/172. As to the Secretary of State see PARA 36.
6   Wrecks Convention art 2.4. When a state party has made a notification under art 3.2 extending the
     application of the Convention to wrecks located within its territory (see note 4), art 2.4 does not
     apply with its territory: art 4.4(a)(i).

928.   Matters excluded from scope of the Wrecks Convention.

The Wrecks Convention[1] does not apply in the context of measures taken[2] to prevent and ameliorate the effects of pollution[3]. The Convention, and the United Kingdom statutory provisions implementing it[4], also do not apply to any warship or other ship owned or operated by a state and used, for the time being, only on Government non-commercial service, unless that state decides otherwise[5].

1   Ie the International Convention on the Removal of Wrecks (Nairobi, 18 May 2007; Cm 8243): see
     PARA 926.
2   Ie measures taken under the International Convention relating to Intervention on the High Seas in
     Cases of Oil Pollution Casualties (Brussels, 29 November 1969) or the Protocol relating to
     Intervention on the High Seas in Cases of Marine Pollution by Substances other than Oil which
     constitutes attachment 2 to the final act of the International Conference on Marine Pollution
     signed in London on 2 November 1973.
3   Wrecks Convention art 4.1.
4   Ie the Merchant Shipping Act 1995 Pt 9A (ss 255A–255U, Sch 11ZA).
5   Wrecks Convention art 4.2; Merchant Shipping Act 1995 s 255S(1), (2) (Pt 9A added by the Wreck
     Removal Convention Act 2011 s 1, Schedule). Where a state party decides to apply the Wrecks
     Convention to its warships or other ships as described in art 4.2, it must notify the
     Secretary-General, thereof, specifying the terms and conditions of such application: art 4.3.

929.   Secretary of State's functions as to wreck; appointment of receiver of wreck.

The Secretary of State[1] has the general superintendence throughout the United Kingdom[2] of all matters relating to wreck[3].

The Secretary of State may, with the consent of the Treasury[4], appoint one or more persons to be receiver of wreck for the purposes of the statutory provisions relating to salvage and wreck[5], and a receiver so appointed must discharge such functions as are assigned to him by the Secretary of State[6].

Such public notice of appointments to the office of receiver must be given as appears to the Secretary of State to be appropriate[7].

1   As to the Secretary of State see PARA 36.
2   As to the meaning of 'United Kingdom' see PARA 16 note 3.
3   Merchant Shipping Act 1995 s 248(1). As to the meaning of 'wreck' see PARA 923.
4   As to the Treasury see CONSTITUTIONAL AND ADMINISTRATIVE LAW vol 20 (2014)
     PARAS 262–265.
5   Ie for the purposes of the Merchant Shipping Act 1995 Pt IX (ss 224–255): see s 248(2).
6   Merchant Shipping Act 1995 s 248(2). There must be paid to the receiver the expenses properly
     incurred by him in the discharge of his functions and also, in respect of such matters as may be
     prescribed by regulations made by the Secretary of State, such fees as may be so prescribed; but the
     receiver is not entitled to any other remuneration: Merchant Shipping Act 1995 s 249(1), (2). At
     the date at which this volume states the law, no such regulations had been made and none have
     effect as if so made. As to the power of the Secretary of State to make subordinate legislation under
     the Merchant Shipping Act 1995, including his power to appoint committees for the purpose of
     advising him when considering the making or alteration of any regulations etc, see PARA 39. The
     receiver has, in addition to all other rights and remedies for the recovery of those expenses and fees,
     the same rights and remedies in respect of those expenses and fees as a salvor has in respect of
     salvage due to him: s 249(3). As to the meaning of 'salvor' see PARA 849 note 4. Whenever any
     dispute arises as to the amount payable to the receiver in respect of expenses or fees, that dispute
     must be determined by the Secretary of State whose decision is final: s 249(4).
7   Merchant Shipping Act 1995 s 248(3).

(ii) Duty to Insure

930. Compulsory insurance and other financial security. The registered owner[1] of a ship of 300 gross tonnage and above and flying the flag of a state party to the Wrecks Convention is required to maintain insurance or other financial security, such as a guarantee of a bank or similar institution, to cover liability under the Convention in an amount equal to the limits of liability under the applicable national or international limitation regime[2]. A certificate attesting that insurance or other financial security is in force in accordance with the provisions of the Convention must be issued to each ship of 300 gross tonnage and above by the appropriate authority of the state of the ship's registry[3] after determining that the above requirements have been complied with[4]. With respect to a ship registered in a state party, such certificate must be issued or certified by the appropriate authority of the state of the ship's registry; with respect to a ship not registered in a state party it may be issued or certified by the appropriate authority of any state party[5]. The certificate must be carried on board the ship and a copy must be deposited with the authorities who keep the record of the ship's registry or, if the ship is not registered in a state party, with the authorities issuing or certifying the certificate[6].

A state party may not permit any ship entitled to fly its flag to which these provisions apply to operate at any time unless a certificate has been[7] issued[8].

1 'Registered owner' means the person or persons registered as the owner of the ship or, in the absence of registration, the person or persons owning the ship at the time of the maritime casualty: Wrecks Convention art 1.8. However, in the case of a ship owned by a state and operated by a company which in that state is registered as the operator of the ship, 'registered owner' means such company: art 1.8; Merchant Shipping Act 1995 s 255S(6) (Pt 9A (ss 255A–255U, Sch 11ZA) added by the Wreck Removal Convention Act 2011 s 1, Schedule). As to the Wrecks Convention (ie the International Convention on the Removal of Wrecks (Nairobi, 18 May 2007; Cm 8243) see PARAS 926–928.
2 Wrecks Convention art 12.1. The amount must in all cases not exceed an amount calculated in accordance with the Convention on Limitation of Liability for Maritime Claims (London, 1 to 19 November 1976; TS 13 (1990); Cm 955) art 6(1)(b) (see PARA 998).
3 As to the meaning of 'state of the ship's registry' see PARA 926 note 7.
4 Wrecks Convention art 12.2. If insurance or other financial security is not maintained in respect of a ship owned by a state party, the provisions of art 12 relating thereto are not applicable to such ship, but the ship must carry a certificate issued by the appropriate authority of the state of registry, stating that it is owned by that state and that the ship's liability is covered within the limits prescribed in art 2.1: art 12.14. Such a certificate must follow as closely as possible the model prescribed by art 12.2: art 12.14.
5 Wrecks Convention art 12.2. Further provision in connection with the form, issuance and validity of certificates is made by arts 12.3–12.4, 12.6–12.8.
6 Wrecks Convention art 12.5. Notwithstanding the provisions of art 12.5, a state party may notify the Secretary-General of the IMO that, for the purposes of art 12.12 (see PARA 931), ships are not required to carry on board or to produce the certificate required by art 12.2, when entering or leaving a port in its territory, or arriving at or leaving from an offshore facility in its territorial sea, provided that the state party which issues the certificate required by art 12.2 has notified the Secretary-General that it maintains records in an electronic format, accessible to all states parties, attesting the existence of the certificate and enabling states parties to discharge their obligations under art 12.12: art 12.13. If the Secretary of State has given, or proposes to give, notice under art 12.13 he may by order make such amendments of the Merchant Shipping Act 1995 Pt 9A as he thinks necessary or expedient for giving effect to the notice: see s 255Q (as added: see note 1). As to the Secretary of State see PARA 36. At the date at which this volume states the law no such order had been made.
7 Ie under the Wrecks Convention art 12.2 or art 12.14.
8 Wrecks Convention art 12.11.

931. Duty of state party to ensure that registered chips are insured. Each state party to the Wrecks Convention[1] must ensure, under its national law, that insurance or other security[2] is in force in respect of any ship of 300 gross tonnage and above, wherever registered, entering or leaving a port in its territory, or arriving at or leaving from an offshore facility in its territorial sea[3]. It is accordingly provided that a United Kingdom ship[4] with a gross tonnage of 300 or more[5] may not enter or leave a port in the United Kingdom or elsewhere[6] unless the ship has wreck removal insurance[7] and the Secretary of State[8] has certified that it has wreck removal insurance[9]; and that a foreign ship may not enter or leave a port in the United Kingdom unless it has wreck removal insurance[10] and there is a certificate confirming that it has wreck removal insurance[11]. Such certification[12] is referred to as a 'wreck removal insurance certificate'[13], and the master[14] of any ship which is required to have a wreck removal insurance certificate before entering or leaving a port must ensure that the certificate is carried on board[15].

1 Ie the International Convention on the Removal of Wrecks (Nairobi, 18 May 2007; Cm 8243): see PARAS 926–928.
2 Ie to the extent required by the Wrecks Convention art 12.1 (see PARA 930).
3 Wrecks Convention art 12.12. This is subject to arts 21.1–12.11, 12.13–12.14: see PARAS 930, 954.
4 As to the meaning of 'United Kingdom ship' see PARA 230; and as to the meaning of 'ship' see PARA 229.
5 For these purposes the gross tonnage of a ship is to be calculated in the manner prescribed by order under the Merchant Shipping Act 1995 Sch 7 Pt II para 5(2) (see PARA 998): s 255J(1), (2)(a) (Pt 9A (ss 255A–255U, Sch 11ZA) added by the Wreck Removal Convention Act 2011 s 1, Schedule).
6 References in the Merchant Shipping Act 1995 Pt 9A to entering or leaving a port in a state include references to arriving at or leaving an offshore facility in the territorial sea of that state (except in s 255L): s 255R(3) (as so added).
7 Merchant Shipping Act 1995 s 255J(6) (as added: see note 5). 'Wreck removal insurance' means a contract of insurance or other security satisfying the requirements of the Wrecks Convention art 12 (see PARA 930): Merchant Shipping Act 1995 s 255J(7) (as so added).
8 As to the Secretary of State see PARA 36.
9 Merchant Shipping Act 1995 s 255J(2)(b) (as added: see note 5).
10 Merchant Shipping Act 1995 s 255J(3)(a) (as added: see note 5).
11 Merchant Shipping Act 1995 s 255J(3)(b) (as added: see note 5). For a ship registered in a foreign Wrecks Convention State the certificate must be one that has been issued by or under the authority of the government of that state: s 255J(4) (as so added). 'Wrecks Convention State' means a state which is a party to the Wrecks Convention: s 255A(1)(a) (as so added). For a foreign ship registered in any other state the certificate must be one that has been issued by the Secretary of State or by or under the authority of the government of a Wrecks Convention State: s 255J(5) (as so added). References in Pt 9A to ships registered in a state include unregistered ships entitled to fly the flag of that state: s 255R(4) (as so added).
12 Ie a certificate under the Merchant Shipping Act 1995 s 255J(2)(b) or (3)(b) (see the text and notes 9, 11).
13 Merchant Shipping Act 1995 s 255J(7) (as added: see note 5). In connection with applications for certificates and terms of issue see PARA 932.
14 As to the meaning of 'master' see PARA 444 note 1.
15 Merchant Shipping Act 1995 s 255M(1), (2) (as added: see note 5). The master of the ship must, on request, produce the certificate to an officer of Revenue and Customs, an officer of the Secretary of State and, if the ship is a United Kingdom ship, a proper officer: s 255M(3) (as so added). As to the Commissioners for Her Majesty's Revenue and Customs see CUSTOMS AND EXCISE vol 31 (2012) PARA 921 et seq. As to the meaning of 'proper officer' see PARA 48 note 12.

932. Terms of issue of wreck removal insurance certificates. Where the registered owner[1] applies to the Secretary of State[2] for a wreck removal insurance certificate[3] the Secretary of State must (where the application is in respect of a United Kingdom ship[4]) or may (where the application is in respect of a foreign ship registered in a state other than a Wrecks Convention State[5]) issue the certificate[6] if satisfied that the ship has wreck removal insurance in place for the period to which the certificate will relate[7] and that the obligations of the person providing the wreck removal insurance will be met[8].

The Secretary of State may make regulations about the cancellation and delivery up of wreck removal insurance certificates so issued[9]. A person who fails to deliver up a certificate in accordance with the regulations is guilty of an offence[10].

1 As to the meaning of 'registered owner' see PARA 930 note 1.

2 As to the Secretary of State see PARA 36.

3 As to wreck removal insurance and wreck removal insurance certificates see PARA 931.

4 Merchant Shipping Act 1995 s 255N(1)(a) (Pt 9A (ss 255A–255U, Sch 11ZA) added by the Wreck Removal Convention Act 2011 s 1, Schedule). As to the meaning of 'United Kingdom ship' see PARA 230; and as to the meaning of 'ship' see PARA 229.

5 Merchant Shipping Act 1995 s 255N(1)(b), (3) (as added: see note 4). As to the meaning of 'Wrecks Convention State', and as to references to ships registered in a state, see PARA 931 note 11.

6 The Secretary of State must send a copy of a certificate issued in respect of a United Kingdom ship to the Registrar General of Shipping and Seamen (Merchant Shipping Act 1995 s 255N(4) (as added: see note 4)) and must make such certificates available for public inspection (s 255N(5) (as so added)).

7 Merchant Shipping Act 1995 s 255N(2)(a) (as added: see note 4).

8 Merchant Shipping Act 1995 s 255N(2)(b) (as added: see note 4).

9 Merchant Shipping Act 1995 s 255O(1) (as added: see note 4). At the date at which this volume states the law no such regulations had been made.

10 Merchant Shipping Act 1995 s 255O(2) (as added: see note 4). A person guilty of the offence is liable on summary conviction to a fine: s 255O(3) (as so added). As to the powers of magistrates' courts to issue fines on summary conviction see SENTENCING vol 92 (2015) PARA 176.

933. Contravention of compulsory insurance and certification provisions.

The master[1] and operator of a ship[2] (other than ship which is owned by a Wrecks Convention State[3]) are each guilty of an offence if the ship enters or leaves a port[4] in contravention of the compulsory insurance provisions[5] or anyone attempts to navigate the ship into or out of a port in contravention thereof[6], and the master of a ship is guilty of an offence if he fails to comply with the certification[7] provisions[8]. A ship may be detained if anyone attempts to navigate it out of a port in contravention[9] of the compulsory insurance provisions[10].

1 As to the meaning of 'master' see PARA 444 note 1.

2 As to the meaning of 'ship' see PARA 229.

3 The Merchant Shipping Act 1995 s 255K does not apply to a ship (an 'exempt ship') that is owned by a Wrecks Convention State: s 255S(3) (Pt 9A (ss 255A–255U, Sch 11ZA) added by the Wreck Removal Convention Act 2011 s 1, Schedule). As to the Wrecks Convention (ie the International Convention on the Removal of Wrecks (Nairobi, 18 May 2007; Cm 8243)) see PARAS 926–928. As to the meaning of 'Wrecks Convention State', and as to references to ships registered in a state, see PARA 931 note 11. An exempt ship must have a certificate issued by the government of the state concerned and stating that the ship is owned by that State and that any liability under the Merchant Shipping Act 1995 s 255G (see PARA 953) will be met up to the limits prescribed by the Wrecks Convention art 12.1 (compulsory insurance: see PARA 930): Merchant Shipping Act 1995 s 255S(4) (as so added). The master of the ship must ensure that the certificate is carried on board (ss 255M(2), 255S(5) (as so added)) and must, on request, produce the certificate to an officer of Revenue and Customs, an officer of the Secretary of State and, if the ship is a United Kingdom ship, a proper officer: s 255M(3) (as so added). As to the Commissioners for Her Majesty's Revenue and Customs see CUSTOMS AND EXCISE vol 31 (2012) PARA 921 et seq. As to the meaning of 'proper officer' see PARA 48 note 12. Failure to comply with these s 255M(3), (3) is an offence punishable on summary conviction by a fine: s 255M(4), (5) (as so added). As to the powers of magistrates' courts to issue fines on summary conviction see SENTENCING vol 92 (2015) PARA 176.

4 As to references to entering or leaving a port see PARA 931 note 6.

5 Ie in contravention of the Merchant Shipping Act 1995 s 255J (see the text and notes 4–10).

6 Merchant Shipping Act 1995 s 255K(1) (as added: see note 3). A person guilty of an offence under s 255K is liable on summary conviction, or on conviction on indictment, to a fine: s 255K(2) (as so added; amended by SI 2015/664).

7 Ie the provisions of the Merchant Shipping Act 1995 s 255M(1)–(3) (see PARA 931).

8 Merchant Shipping Act 1995 s 255M(4) (as added: see note 3). A person guilty of an offence under s 255M is liable on summary conviction to a fine: s 255M(5) (as so added)

9 See note 5.

10 Merchant Shipping Act 1995 s 255L (as added: see note 3).

(iii) Dealing with Wrecks

A.   REPORTING, LOCATING AND MARKING

934.   Duty of persons responsible for wrecked vessel to report it. Where an
accident[1] results in a wreck[2] in a Convention area[3], the persons responsible for any
United Kingdom ship[4] involved in the accident must report the wreck without
delay[5]. If the wreck is in the United Kingdom's Convention area, it must be
reported to the Secretary of State[6]; if it is in the Convention area of any other state,
it must be reported to the government of that state[7]. Such reports are required to
provide (so far as it is known) the name and the principal place of business of the
registered owner[8] and all the relevant information necessary for the affected state
to determine whether the wreck poses a hazard[9], including:

(1)   the precise location of the wreck[10];
(2)   the type, size and construction of the wreck[11];
(3)   the nature of the damage to, and the condition of, the wreck[12];
(4)   the nature and quantity of the cargo, in particular any hazardous and
         noxious substances[13]; and
(5)   the amount and types of oil, including bunker oil and lubricating oil, on
         board[14].

Failure to comply with the reporting requirement is an offence[15].

1   'Accident' means a collision of ships, a stranding, another incident of navigation or another event
     (whether on board a ship or not) which results in material damage to a ship or its cargo or in an
     imminent threat of material damage to a ship or its cargo: Merchant Shipping Act 1995 s 255R(2)
     (Pt 9A (ss 255A–255U, Sch 11ZA) added by the Wreck Removal Convention Act 2011 s 1,
     Schedule). As to the meaning of 'ship' see PARA 229.
2   As to the meaning of 'wreck' see PARA 923.
3   As to the 'Convention area' see PARA 927.
4   As to the meaning of 'United Kingdom ship' see PARA 230. The master and operator of a ship are
     responsible for it: Merchant Shipping Act 1995 s 255B(4) (as added: see note 1). If one of the
     persons responsible for a ship makes such a report the others are no longer under a duty to make
     a report: s 255B(6) (as so added). 'Operator of the ship' means the owner of the ship or any other
     organisation or person such as the manager, or the bareboat charterer, who has assumed the
     responsibility for operation of the ship from the owner of the ship and who, on assuming such
     responsibility, has agreed to take over all duties and responsibilities established under the
     International Safety Management Code: Wrecks Convention art 1.9. As to the Wrecks Convention
     (ie the International Convention on the Removal of Wrecks (Nairobi, 18 May 2007; Cm 8243) see
     PARAS 926–928.
5   Merchant Shipping Act 1995 s 255B(1) (as added: see note 1). These provisions implement the
     Wrecks Convention art 5, which requires that a state party must require the master and the
     operator of a ship flying its flag to report to the affected state without delay when that ship has
     been involved in a maritime casualty resulting in a wreck (art 5.1). To the extent that the reporting
     obligation under art 5 has been fulfilled either by the master or the operator of the ship, the other
     is not obliged to report: art 5.1. As to the meaning of 'affected state' see PARA 925 note 4. As to
     the meaning of 'maritime casualty' see PARA 923.
6   Merchant Shipping Act 1995 s 255B(2) (as added: see note 1).
7   Merchant Shipping Act 1995 s 255B(3) (as added: see note 1).
8   As to the meaning of 'registered owner' see PARA 930 note 1.
9   Ie in accordance with the Wrecks Convention art 6 (see PARA 925). As to the meaning of 'hazard',
     and the determination of a hazard, see PARA 925.
10   Wrecks Convention art 5.2(a); Merchant Shipping Act 1995 s 255B(5) (as added: see note 1).
11   Wrecks Convention art 5.2(b).
12   Wrecks Convention art 5.2(c).
13   Wrecks Convention art 5.2(d).
14   Wrecks Convention art 5.2(e).
15   Merchant Shipping Act 1995 s 255B(7) (as added: see note 1). A person guilty of an offence under
     s 255B is liable on summary conviction, or on conviction on indictment, to a fine: s 255B(8) (as
     so added; amended by SI 2015/664). As to the powers of magistrates' courts to issue fines on
     summary conviction see SENTENCING vol 92 (2015) PARA 176.

935. Duties of finder of wreck. If any person finds or takes possession of any wreck[1] in United Kingdom waters[2], or finds or takes possession of any wreck outside United Kingdom waters and brings it within those waters, he must[3]:

(1)	if he is the owner of it, give notice to the receiver[4] stating that he has found or taken possession of it and describing the marks by which it may be recognised[5];

(2)	if he is not the owner of it, give notice to the receiver that he has found or taken possession of it and, as directed by the receiver, either hold it to the receiver's order or deliver it to the receiver[6].

If any person fails without reasonable excuse so to comply[7], he is liable on summary conviction to a fine[8].

1	As to the meaning of 'wreck' see PARA 923.
2	As to the meaning of 'United Kingdom waters' see PARA 48 note 10. As to the meaning of 'United Kingdom' see PARA 16 note 3.
3	Merchant Shipping Act 1995 s 236(1). Section 236 is directed towards a criminal and improper detention by which it is sought to practise a fraud upon the Crown or the owner and not towards salvors who have restored the property to the owners: *The Zeta* (1875) LR 4 A & E 460, 3 Asp MLC 73. It does not apply to salvors who remain in possession for the safety of the vessel (*The Glynoeron* (1905) 21 TLR 648) or to a person who takes possession of a stranded vessel under the bona fide belief that it is his property by purchase or otherwise (*The Liffey* (1887) 58 LT 351, 6 Asp MLC 255).
4	As to the meaning of 'receiver' see PARA 887 note 4. As to the giving of notices under the Merchant Shipping Act 1995 see PARA 74.
5	Merchant Shipping Act 1995 s 236(1)(a).
6	Merchant Shipping Act 1995 s 236(1)(b).
7	Ie to comply with the Merchant Shipping Act 1995 s 236(1) (see the text and notes 1–6): see s 236(2); and PARA 1160.
8	See the Merchant Shipping Act 1995 s 236(2); and PARA 1160. Such a person as is mentioned in the text, if he is not the owner of the wreck, is liable also to civil penalties and the forfeit of salvage rights under s 236: see s 236(2); and PARA 1160.

936. Duties and powers of receiver and customs officers on being notified of wreck. On being informed of a vessel[1] which is wrecked, stranded or in distress in United Kingdom waters[2] the receiver[3] must,

(1)	forthwith proceed to the place where the vessel is[4];

(2)	take command of all persons present[5]; and

(3)	assign such duties and give such directions to each person as he thinks fit for the preservation of the vessel and of the lives of the shipwrecked persons[6].

However, in doing so, the receiver must not interfere between the master[7] and crew of the vessel in reference to the management of the vessel unless he is requested to do so by the master[8].

The receiver may, for the purpose of the preservation of shipwrecked persons or of the vessel, cargo[9] and equipment:

(a)	require such persons as he thinks necessary to assist him[10];

(b)	require the master, or other person having the charge, of any vessel near at hand to give such assistance with his men, or vessel, as may be in his power[11]; and

(c)	require the use of any vehicle that may be near at hand[12].

If any person intentionally disobeys the direction of the receiver, or refuses without reasonable excuse to comply with any requirement so made, he is liable to a fine[13].

The Commissioners for Revenue and Customs must, subject to taking security for the protection of the revenue in respect of the goods[14]:

(i)   permit all goods saved from any ship[15] stranded or wrecked on its homeward voyage to be forwarded to the port[16] of its original destination[17]; and

(ii)   permit all goods saved from any ship stranded or wrecked on her outward voyage to be returned to the port at which they were shipped[18].

1   As to the meaning of 'vessel' see PARA 919 note 5.

2   The statutory provisions relating to vessels in distress (ie the Merchant Shipping Act 1995 ss 231–235 (see the text and notes 3–12; and PARAS 946–958) apply where a United Kingdom or foreign vessel is wrecked, stranded or in distress at any place on or near the coasts of the United Kingdom or any tidal water within United Kingdom waters: s 231(1). As to the meaning of 'United Kingdom ship' see PARA 230. As to the meaning of 'foreign', in relation to a ship, see PARA 18 note 2. As to the meaning of 'on or near the coast' see *The Fulham* [1898] P 206 at 213, 8 Asp MLC 425 at 426, 427 (on appeal [1899] P 251, 8 Asp MLC 559, CA). As to the meaning of 'United Kingdom' see PARA 16 note 3. As to the meaning of 'tidal water' see PARA 923 note 13. As to the meaning of 'United Kingdom waters' see PARA 48 note 10.

3   As to the meaning of 'receiver' see PARA 887 note 4. Where any function is conferred on the receiver by any of the Merchant Shipping Act 1995 ss 232–235, that function may be discharged by any officer of Revenue and Customs or any principal officer of the coastguard: s 231(2) (amended by virtue of the Commissioners for Revenue and Customs Act 2005 s 50(1), (2), (7)). As to Her Majesty's Coastguard see PARA 58. As to the appointment of officers of Revenue and Customs see INCOME TAXATION vol 58 (2014) PARA 33. An officer discharging any such functions of the receiver is to be treated, with respect to any goods or articles belonging to a vessel the delivery of which to the receiver is required by any of the statutory provisions relating to wreck (ie the Merchant Shipping Act 1995 Pt IX Ch II (ss 231–247)) as the agent of the receiver: s 231(3). However, an officer discharging such functions is neither entitled to any fees payable to receivers (s 231(4)(a)) nor deprived of any right to salvage (s 231(4)(b)) to which he would otherwise be entitled (s 231(4)).

Where services are rendered by any officers or men of the coastguard service in watching or protecting shipwrecked property, the owner of the property must pay in respect of those services remuneration according to a scale fixed by the Secretary of State: s 250(1). As to the Secretary of State see PARA 36; and as to the Secretary of State's power to appoint committees for the purpose of advising him when considering the making or alteration of any scales see PARA 39. As to Her Majesty's Coastguard see PARA 58. The scale fixed by the Secretary of State must not exceed the scale by which remuneration to officers and men of the coastguard for extra duties in the ordinary service of the Commissioners of Revenue and Customs is for the time being regulated: s 250(4) (amended by virtue of the Commissioners for Revenue and Customs Act 2005 s 50(1), (2), (7)). Such remuneration:

(1)   is recoverable by the same means (s 250(3)(a));
(2)   must be paid to the same persons (s 250(3)(b)); and
(3)   must be accounted for and applied in the same manner (s 250(3)(c)),

as fees received by the receiver under s 249 (see PARA 929): see s 250(3). However, no liability in respect of those services so arises where:

(a)   the services have been declined by the owner of the property or his agent at the time they were tendered (s 250(2)(a)); or
(b)   salvage has been claimed and awarded for the services (s 250(2)(b)).

As to the meaning of 'salvage' see PARA 849.

4   Merchant Shipping Act 1995 s 232(1), (2)(a) (ss 232(2), 233(1) amended, s 233(1A) added, by the Merchant Shipping and Maritime Security Act 1997 s 21(1), (2), Sch 6 para 14)

5   Merchant Shipping Act 1995 s 232(2)(b).

6   Merchant Shipping Act 1995 s 232(2)(c). For these purposes, 'shipwrecked persons', in relation to a vessel, means persons belonging to the vessel: s 231(5).

7   As to the meaning of 'master' see PARA 444 note 1.

8   Merchant Shipping Act 1995 s 232(3).

9   As to the meaning of 'cargo' for salvage purposes see PARA 860.

10   Merchant Shipping Act 1995 s 233(1)(a) (as amended: see note 4). Section 233(1) is subject to s 233(1A): see s 233(1) (as so amended). Accordingly, the receiver may not under s 233(1) impose any requirement on the master or other person having the charge of a vessel owned or operated by the Royal National Lifeboat Institution: s 233(1A) (as so added).

11   Merchant Shipping Act 1995 s 233(1)(b) (as amended: see note 4).

12   Merchant Shipping Act 1995 s 233(1)(c) (as amended: see note 4).

13   See the Merchant Shipping Act 1995 ss 232(4), 233(2); and PARAS 1157, 1158.

14   For these purposes, 'goods' includes wares and merchandise: Merchant Shipping Act 1995 s 251(3).

15   As to the meaning of 'ship' see PARA 229.

16 As to the meaning of 'port' see PARA 46 note 12.
17 See the Merchant Shipping Act 1995 s 251(1) (amended by virtue of the Commissioners for Revenue and Customs Act 2005 s 50(1), (2), (7)).
18 See the Merchant Shipping Act 1995 s 251(2) (amended by virtue of the Commissioners for Revenue and Customs Act 2005 s 50(1), (2), (7)).

937. Receiver to give notice of wreck on taking possession. Where the receiver[1] takes possession of any wreck[2], he must, within 48 hours[3]:

(1) make a record describing the wreck and any marks by which it is distinguished[4]; and

(2) if, in his opinion, the value of the wreck exceeds £5,000, also transmit a similar description to the chief executive officer of Lloyd's in London[5].

1 As to the meaning of 'receiver' see PARA 887 note 4.
2 As to the meaning of 'wreck' see PARA 923.
3 Merchant Shipping Act 1995 s 238(1).
4 Merchant Shipping Act 1995 s 238(1)(a). The record made by the receiver under s 238(1)(a) must be kept by him available for inspection by any person during reasonable hours without charge: s 238(2).
5 Merchant Shipping Act 1995 s 238(1)(b). The notice sent under s 238(1)(b) must be posted by the chief executive officer of Lloyd's in some conspicuous position for inspection: s 238(3).

938. Locating and marking of wrecks. Under the Wrecks Convention[1], upon becoming aware of a wreck[2], the affected state[3] must use all practicable means, including the good offices of states and organisations, to warn mariners and the states concerned of the nature and location of the wreck as a matter of urgency[4]. If the affected state has reason to believe that a wreck poses a hazard[5], it must ensure that all practicable steps are taken to establish the precise location of the wreck[6], and if that state determines that a wreck constitutes a hazard, it must ensure that all reasonable steps are taken to mark the wreck[7].

Where an accident[8] results in a wreck in the United Kingdom's Convention area[9] the Secretary of State[10] must ensure that the United Kingdom complies with these requirements[11], and the Secretary of State may, for those purposes, direct[12] any of the following to take specified steps in relation to the wreck if it is within their area:

(1) a general lighthouse authority[13];

(2) a harbour authority[14];

(3) a conservancy authority[15].

An authority to whom a direction is given must comply with it[16].

1 Ie the International Convention on the Removal of Wrecks (Nairobi, 18 May 2007; Cm 8243): see PARAS 926–928.
2 As to the meaning of 'wreck' see PARA 923.
3 As to the meaning of 'affected state' see PARA 925 note 4.
4 Wrecks Convention art 7.1.
5 As to the meaning of 'hazard', and the determination of a hazard, see PARA 925.
6 Wrecks Convention art 7.2.
7 Wrecks Convention art 8.1. In marking the wreck, all practicable steps must be taken to ensure that the markings conform to the internationally accepted system of buoyage in use in the area where the wreck is located: art 8.2. The affected state must promulgate the particulars of the marking of the wreck by use of all appropriate means, including the appropriate nautical publications: art 8.3.
8 As to the meaning of 'accident' see PARA 934 note 1.
9 As to the geographical application of the Wrecks Convention, and the United Kingdom's 'Convention area', see PARA 941.
10 As to the Secretary of State see PARA 36.
11 Ie complies with the United Kingdom's obligations under the Wrecks Convention arts 7, 8 (see the text and notes 1–7): Merchant Shipping Act 1995 s 255C(1), (2) (Pt 9A (ss 255A–255U, Sch 11ZA) added by the Wreck Removal Convention Act 2011 s 1, Schedule).
12 A direction may require an authority to exercise or not to exercise a power under the Merchant Shipping Act 1995 s 252 or s 253 within their area (and for this purpose a general lighthouse

authority has the powers conferred by s 253 throughout their area): s 255C(4) (as added: see note 11). A direction must be in writing or, where it is not reasonably practicable to give it in writing, must be confirmed in writing as soon as reasonably practicable: s 255C(6) (as so added).

13 Merchant Shipping Act 1995 s 255C(3)(a) (as added: see note 11). As to general lighthouse authorities see PARA 1017. Costs incurred by a general lighthouse authority in complying with a direction under s 255C are be paid out of the General Lighthouse Fund if or to the extent that they are not recovered under s 255G (see PARA 953); but s 213 (see PARA 1041) applies as if they were expenses of the authority falling within s 213(1) other than establishment expenses: s 255I (as so added).

14 Merchant Shipping Act 1995 s 255C(3)(b) (as added: see note 11). As to the meaning of 'harbour authority' see PARA 69 note 4.

15 Merchant Shipping Act 1995 s 255C(3)(c) (as added: see note 11). As to the meaning of 'conservancy authority' see PARA 72 note 2.

16 Merchant Shipping Act 1995 s 255C(7) (as added: see note 11).

939. Powers of harbor, conservancy and general lighthouse authorities to mark wrecks in waters under their control. Where any vessel[1] is sunk, stranded or abandoned in, or in or near any approach to, any harbour[2] or tidal water[3] under the control of a harbour authority or conservancy authority[4] in such a manner as, in the opinion of the authority, to be, or be likely to become, an obstruction or danger to navigation or to lifeboats engaged in lifeboat service in that harbour or water or approach thereto, that authority may[5] mark the location of the vessel or part of the vessel and any other property[6] to which the power extends until it is raised, removed or destroyed[7]. The authority may alternatively raise, remove or destroy such wreck[8], and may sell the vessel or part thereof to reimburse its costs[9].

1 As to the meaning of 'vessel' see PARA 919 note 5.
2 As to the meaning of 'harbour' see PARA 49 note 5.
3 As to the meaning of 'tidal water' see PARA 923 note 13.
4 As to the meaning of 'harbour authority' see PARA 69 note 4; as to the meaning of 'conservancy authority' see PARA 72 note 2. The provisions of the Merchant Shipping Act 1995 s 252 are without prejudice to any other powers of a harbour or conservancy authority: see s 252(10). If any question arises between a harbour authority or conservancy authority and a general lighthouse authority as to their respective powers under s 252 or s 253 (see also PARAS 945, 957) in relation to any place in or near an approach to a harbour or tidal water, that question must, on the application of either authority, be referred to the Secretary of State for his decision (s 254(1)); and any such decision of the Secretary of State is final (s 254(2)).
5 Merchant Shipping Act 1995 s 252(1).
6 Ie every article or thing or collection of things being or forming part of the equipment, cargo, stores or ballast of the vessel: Merchant Shipping Act 1995 s 252(3).
7 Merchant Shipping Act 1995 s 252(2)(b) (amended by the Marine Navigation Act 2013 s 11(1)).
8 See PARA 945.
9 See PARA 957.

940. Receiver's powers of entry. Where the receiver[1] has reason to believe that:

(1)   any wreck[2] is being concealed by or is in the possession of some person who is not the owner of it[3]; or

(2)   any wreck is being otherwise improperly dealt with[4],

he may apply to a justice of the peace for a search warrant[5].

Where a search warrant is so granted to the receiver, the receiver may, by virtue of the warrant[6]:

(a)   enter any house, or other place (wherever situated) or any vessel[7]; and

(b)   search for, seize and detain any wreck found there[8].

If any seizure of wreck is so made[9] in consequence of information given by any person to the receiver, the person giving the information is entitled, by way of salvage[10], to such sum, not exceeding £100, as the receiver may allow[11].

1 As to the meaning of 'receiver' see PARA 887 note 4.
2 As to the meaning of 'wreck' see PARA 923.
3 Merchant Shipping Act 1995 s 247(1)(a).

4   Merchant Shipping Act 1995 s 247(1)(b).
5   Merchant Shipping Act 1995 s 247(1). As to justices of the peace see MAGISTRATES vol 71 (2013) PARA 401 et seq; and as to applications for a search warrant see POLICE AND INVESTIGATORY POWERS vol 84A (2013) PARA 450 et seq.
6   Merchant Shipping Act 1995 s 247(2).
7   Merchant Shipping Act 1995 s 247(2)(a). As to the meaning of 'vessel' see PARA 919 note 5.
8   Merchant Shipping Act 1995 s 247(2)(b).
9   Ie under the Merchant Shipping Act 1995 s 247: see s 247(3).
10 As to the meaning of 'salvage' see PARA 849.
11 Merchant Shipping Act 1995 s 247(3).

941. Co-operation and consultation between states. Under the Wrecks Convention[1], if the affected state[2] determines that a wreck[3] constitutes a hazard[4], that state must immediately inform the state of the ship's registry[5] and the registered owner[6] and proceed to consult the state of the ship's registry and other states affected by the wreck regarding measures to be taken in relation to the wreck[7].

States parties must endeavour to co-operate when the effects of a maritime casualty[8] resulting in a wreck involve a state other than the affected state[9].

1   Ie the International Convention on the Removal of Wrecks (Nairobi, 18 May 2007; Cm 8243): see PARAS 926–928.
2   As to the meaning of 'affected state' see PARA 925 note 4. When a state party to the Wrecks Convention has made a notification under art 3.2 extending the application of the Convention to wrecks located within its territory (see PARA 927), art 9.1 (see the text and notes 3–7) does not apply with its territory: art 4.4(a)(ii).
3   As to the meaning of 'wreck' see PARA 923.
4   As to the meaning of 'hazard', and the determination of a hazard, see PARA 925.
5   As to the meaning of 'state of the ship's registry' see PARA 926 note 7. The information referred to in the Wrecks Convention art 9 must be provided by the affected state to the registered owner identified in the reports referred to in art 5.2 (see PARA 934): art 9.11. As to the meaning of 'registered owner' see PARA 930 note 1.
6   Wrecks Convention art 9.1(a). As to the meaning of 'registered owner' see PARA 930 note 1. As to the Wrecks Convention (ie the International Convention on the Removal of Wrecks (Nairobi, 18 May 2007; Cm 8243) see PARAS 926–928.
7   Wrecks Convention art 9.1(b).
8   As to the meaning of 'maritime casualty' see PARA 923.
9   Wrecks Convention art 2.5.

B.   REMOVAL

942. Duty of registered owner to remove wreck, and issue of wreck removal notice. 'Removal' means any form of prevention, mitigation or elimination of the hazard[1] created by a wreck[2]. Under the Wrecks Convention the registered owner[3] must remove a wreck determined to constitute a hazard[4], and when a wreck has been determined to constitute a hazard, the registered owner, or other interested party, must provide the competent authority of the affected state[5] with evidence[6] of insurance or other financial security[7].

Where a ship[8] has been involved in an accident[9] as a result of which it or anything from it has become a wreck in the United Kingdom's Convention area[10], and the Secretary of State[11] has determined that the wreck poses a hazard[12], the Secretary of State must take all reasonable steps to give a notice (a 'wreck removal notice')[13] requiring the registered owner to comply with:

(1)   the obligation[14] to remove a wreck[15]; and
(2)   the obligation[16] to provide evidence of insurance or other security[17].

A registered owner who fails, without reasonable excuse, to comply with a notice by the specified deadline is guilty of an offence[18].

1   As to the meaning of 'hazard', and the determination of a hazard, see PARA 925.

2 Wrecks Convention art 1.7. 'Remove', 'removed' and 'removing' are construed accordingly: art 1.7. As to the Wrecks Convention (ie the International Convention on the Removal of Wrecks (Nairobi, 18 May 2007; Cm 8243) see PARAS 926–928. As to the meaning of 'wreck' see PARA 923.
3 As to the meaning of 'registered owner' see PARA 930 note 1.
4 Wrecks Convention art 9.2.
5 As to the meaning of 'affected state' see PARA 925 note 4. When the removal referred to in art 9.2 has commenced, the affected state may intervene in the removal only to the extent necessary to ensure that the removal proceeds effectively in a manner that is consistent with considerations of safety and protection of the marine environment: art 9.5. When a state party to the Convention has made a notification under art 3.2 extending the application of the Convention to wrecks located within its territory (see PARA 927), arts 9.5, 9.9 do not apply with its territory: art 4.4(a)(ii).
6 Ie as required by the Wrecks Convention art 12 (see PARA 954).
7 Wrecks Convention art 9.3.
8 As to the meaning of 'ship' see PARA 229.
9 As to the meaning of 'accident' see PARA 934 note 1.
10 Merchant Shipping Act 1995 s 255D(1)(a) (Pt 9A (ss 255A–255U, Sch 11ZA) added by the Wreck Removal Convention Act 2011 s 1, Schedule). As to the geographical application of the Wrecks Convention, and the United Kingdom's 'Convention area', see PARA 941.
11 As to the Secretary of State see PARA 36.
12 Merchant Shipping Act 1995 s 255D(1)(b) (as added: see note 10).
13 The notice must be in writing and must specify the deadline set under the Wrecks Convention art 9.6(a) for the removal of the wreck, and inform the registered owner of the other matters set out in art 9.6(b), (c): Merchant Shipping Act 1995 s 255D(3) (as added: see note 10).
14 Ie the obligation imposed on registered owners by the Wrecks Convention art 9.2 (see the text and notes 1–4).
15 Merchant Shipping Act 1995 s 255D(2) (as added: see note 10). Section 255D(2) implements the requirement under the Wrecks Convention art 9.9 that states parties are required to take appropriate measures under their national law to ensure that their registered owners comply with art 9.2, 9.3.
16 Ie the obligation imposed on registered owners and other interested parties by the Wrecks Convention art 9.3 (see the text and notes 5–7).
17 Merchant Shipping Act 1995 s 255D(2) (as added: see note 10). See note 14.
18 Merchant Shipping Act 1995 s 255D(4) (as added: see note 10). A registered owner guilty of an offence under s 255D is liable on summary conviction, or on conviction on indictment, to a fine: s 255D(5) (as so added; amended by SI 2015/664). As to the powers of magistrates' courts to issue fines on summary conviction see SENTENCING vol 92 (2015) PARA 176.

943. Imposition of conditions about wreck removal. If the Secretary of State[1] has given a registered owner[2] a wreck removal notice[3] he may impose conditions[4] as to the removal[5] of the wreck[6] in accordance with the Wrecks Convention[7], which provides that the registered owner may contract with any salvor or other person to remove the wreck determined to constitute a hazard[8] on behalf of the owner and that before such removal commences, the affected state[9] may lay down conditions for such removal only to the extent necessary to ensure that the removal proceeds in a manner that is consistent with considerations of safety and protection of the marine environment[10]. A registered owner who fails, without reasonable excuse, to comply with a condition is guilty of an offence[11].

1 As to the Secretary of State see PARA 36.
2 As to the meaning of 'registered owner' see PARA 930 note 1.
3 As to the meaning of 'wreck removal notice' see PARA 942.
4 A condition is imposed by giving notice of it to the registered owner: Merchant Shipping Act 1995 s 255E(3) (Pt 9A (ss 255A–255U, Sch 11ZA) added by the Wreck Removal Convention Act 2011 s 1, Schedule).
5 As to the meaning of 'removal' see PARA 942.
6 As to the meaning of 'wreck' see PARA 923.
7 Ie in accordance with the Wrecks Convention art 9.4: Merchant Shipping Act 1995 s 255E(1), (2) (as added: see note 4). As to the Wrecks Convention (ie the International Convention on the Removal of Wrecks (Nairobi, 18 May 2007; Cm 8243) see PARAS 926–928.
8 As to the meaning of 'hazard', and the determination of a hazard, see PARA 925.
9 As to the meaning of 'affected state' see PARA 925 note 4.

10 Wrecks Convention art 9.4. When the removal referred to in art 9.4 has commenced, the affected
    state may intervene in the removal only to the extent necessary to ensure that the removal proceeds
    effectively in a manner that is consistent with considerations of safety and protection of the marine
    environment: art 9.5. When a state party to the Convention has made a notification under art 3.2
    extending the application of the Convention to wrecks located within its territory (see PARA 927),
    the power conferred on the registered owner by art 9.4 is subject to the national law of the affected
    state: see art 4.4(b).
        States parties to the Wrecks Convention give their consent to the affected state to act under arts
    9.4, 9.5, where required: art 9.10. When a state party to the Convention has made a notification
    under art 3.2 extending the application of the Convention to wrecks located within its territory
    (see PARA 927), arts 9.5, 9.10 do not apply with its territory: art 4.4(a)(ii).
11 Merchant Shipping Act 1995 s 255E(4) (as added: see note 4). A registered owner guilty of an
    offence under s 255E is liable on summary conviction, or on conviction on indictment, to a fine:
    s 255E(5) (as so added; amended by SI 2015/664). As to the powers of magistrates' courts to issue
    fines on summary conviction see SENTENCING vol 92 (2015) PARA 176.

944. Deadlines for wreck removal and state intervention in urgent cases.

Under the Wrecks Convention[1] the affected state[2] must set a reasonable deadline
within which the registered owner[3] must[4] remove[5] the wreck[6], and if the registered
owner does not remove the wreck within such deadline, or cannot be contacted,
the affected state may remove the wreck[7]. The affected state may also remove a
wreck where it intends to intervene immediately in circumstances[8] where the
hazard becomes particularly severe[9]. Accordingly, the Secretary of State[10] may
remove a wreck in the United Kingdom's Convention area[11] in the circumstances
described above[12] or direct[13] that a general lighthouse authority[14], a harbour
authority[15] or a conservancy authority[16] exercise such power[17]. An authority to
whom a direction is given must comply with it[18].

1 Ie the International Convention on the Removal of Wrecks (Nairobi, 18 May 2007; Cm 8243): see
   PARAS 926–928.
2 As to the meaning of 'affected state' see PARA 925 note 4. When a state party to the Wrecks
   Convention has made a notification under art 3.2 extending the application of the Convention to
   wrecks located within its territory (see PARA 927), arts 9.7, 9.8, 9.10 (see the text and notes 3–9)
   do not apply with its territory: art 4.4(a)(ii).
3 As to the meaning of 'registered owner' see PARA 930 note 1.
4 Ie taking into account the nature of the hazard determined in accordance with the Wrecks
   Convention art 6 (see PARA 925).
5 As to the meaning of 'remove' see PARA 942.
6 Wrecks Convention art 9.6(a). The affected state must inform the registered owner in writing of
   the deadline it has set and specify that, if the registered owner does not remove the wreck within
   that deadline, it may remove the wreck at the registered owner's expense: art 9.6(b). As to the
   meaning of 'wreck' see PARA 923.
       The information referred to in art 9 must be provided by the affected state to the registered
   owner identified in the reports referred to in art 5.2 (see PARA 934): art 9.11. States parties to the
   Convention give their consent to the affected state to act under arts 9.6–9.8, where required: art
   9.10.
7 Wrecks Convention art 9.7. Removal under art 9.7 or art 9.8 must be by the most practical and
   expeditious means available, consistent with considerations of safety and protection of the marine
   environment: arts 9.7. 9.8.
8 Ie in circumstances where immediate action is required and the affected state has informed the state
   of the ship's registry and the registered owner accordingly: Wrecks Convention art 9.8. As to the
   meaning of 'state of the ship's registry' see PARA 926 note 7.
9 Wrecks Convention art 9.8. See note 7. The affected state must inform the registered owner in
   writing that it intends the remove the wreck in these circumstances: art 9.6(c).
10 As to the Secretary of State see PARA 36.
11 As to the geographical application of the Wrecks Convention, and the United Kingdom's
   'Convention area', see PARA 941.
12 Merchant Shipping Act 1995 s 255F(1) (Pt 9A (ss 255A–255U, Sch 11ZA) added by the Wreck
   Removal Convention Act 2011 s 1, Schedule).
13 A direction may be given to an authority only in relation to a wreck within the authority's area:
   Merchant Shipping Act 1995 s 255F(3) (as added: see note 12). A direction must be in writing or
   where it is not reasonably practicable to give it in writing, must be confirmed in writing as soon
   as reasonably practicable: s 255F(5) (as so added).

14 Merchant Shipping Act 1995 s 255F(2)(a) (as added: see note 12). As to general lighthouse authorities see PARA 1017. Costs incurred by a general lighthouse authority in complying with a direction under s 255F are be paid out of the General Lighthouse Fund if or to the extent that they are not recovered under s 255G (see PARA 953); but s 213 (see PARA 1041) applies as if they were expenses of the authority falling within s 213(1) other than establishment expenses: s 255I (as so added).
15 Merchant Shipping Act 1995 s 255F(2)(b) (as added: see note 12). As to the meaning of 'harbour authority' see PARA 69 note 4.
16 Merchant Shipping Act 1995 s 255F(2)(c) (as added: see note 12). As to the meaning of 'conservancy authority' see PARA 72 note 2.
17 Merchant Shipping Act 1995 s 255F(2) (as added: see note 12).
18 Merchant Shipping Act 1995 s 255F(6) (as added: see note 12).

945. Powers of harbour, conservancy and general lighthouse authorities to raise, remove and destroy wrecks in waters under their control.

Where any vessel[1] is sunk, stranded or abandoned in, or in or near any approach to, any harbour[2] or tidal water[3] under the control of a harbour authority or conservancy authority[4] in such a manner as, in the opinion of the authority, to be, or be likely to become, an obstruction or danger to navigation or to lifeboats engaged in lifeboat service in that harbour or water or approach thereto, that authority may[5] take possession of, and raise, remove or destroy the whole or any part of the vessel and any other property[6] to which the power extends[7]. The authority may alternatively mark the location of the wreck until it is raised, removed or destroyed[8], and may sell the vessel or part thereof to reimburse its costs[9].

Where any vessel is sunk, stranded or abandoned in any fairway or on the seashore or on or near any rock, shoal or bank in the United Kingdom[10] or any of the adjacent seas or islands[11], and there is no harbour or conservancy authority having power to raise, remove or destroy the vessel[12], the general lighthouse authority[13] for the place in or near which the vessel is situated has, if in the authority's opinion the vessel is, or is likely to become, an obstruction or danger to navigation or to lifeboats engaged in lifeboat service in relation thereto, the same powers in relation thereto as those conferred[14] on harbour and conservancy authorities in relation to wrecks[15].

1 As to the meaning of 'vessel' see PARA 919 note 5.
2 As to the meaning of 'harbour' see PARA 49 note 5.
3 As to the meaning of 'tidal water' see PARA 923 note 13.
4 As to the meaning of 'harbour authority' see PARA 69 note 4; as to the meaning of 'conservancy authority' see PARA 72 note 2. As to the powers of these authorities see also PARA 945 note 4.
5 Merchant Shipping Act 1995 s 252(1).
6 As to the 'other property' in this context see PARA 939 note 7.
7 Merchant Shipping Act 1995 s 252(2)(a). Where the owners, although in possession, have transferred the management and control of a wreck to a wreck-raising authority, they are not liable and the wreck is not liable for any collision which may happen through subsequent insufficient lighting and buoying (*White v Crisp* (1854) 10 Exch 312; *The Douglas* (1882) 7 PD 151, 5 Asp MLC 15, CA; *Utopia (Owners) v Primula (Owners), The Utopia* [1893] AC 492, 7 Asp MLC 408, PC. Cf *Brown v Mallett* (1848) 5 CB 599 at 618; *Kidston v M'Arthur and Clyde Navigation Trustee* (1878) 5 R 936 (control not transferred); *The Snark* [1900] P 105, 9 Asp MLC 50, CA (liability of owner for negligence of independent contractor)), but the authority may be liable for its own negligence (*Dormont v Furness Rly Co* (1883) 11 QBD 496, 5 Asp MLC 127; *Mersey Docks Trustees v Gibbs* (1886) LR 1 HL 93; *Gilbert v Trinity House Corpn* (1886) 17 QBD 795, DC; *The Manorbier Castle* (1922) 16 Asp MLC 151 at 154).
8 See PARA 939.
9 See PARA 957.
10 As to the meaning of 'United Kingdom' see PARA 16 note 3.
11 Merchant Shipping Act 1995 s 253(1)(a).
12 Merchant Shipping Act 1995 s 253(1)(b).
13 As to the meaning of 'general lighthouse authority' see PARA 1017.
14 Ie conferred by the Merchant Shipping Act 1995 s 252 (see the text and notes 1–9; and PARAS 939, 957): see s 253(1).

15 Merchant Shipping Act 1995 s 253(1). As to the powers of lighthouse authorities in relation to wrecks see also PARA 1048.

946. Power to use adjoining land in case of vessel in distress. Where a vessel[1] is wrecked, stranded or in distress in United Kingdom waters[2] all persons may, for the purpose of:

(1)   rendering assistance to the vessel[3];

(2)   saving the lives of shipwrecked persons[4]; or

(3)   saving the cargo or equipment of the vessel[5],

pass and repass over any adjoining land without being subject to interruption by the owner or occupier and deposit on the land any cargo or other article recovered from the vessel[6]. The right of passage so conferred[7] is a right of passage with or without vehicles[8]; but no right of passage is so conferred[9] where there is some public road equally convenient[10].

The rights so conferred[11] must be so exercised as to do as little damage as possible[12]; and any damage sustained by an owner or occupier of land in consequence of the exercise of such rights is a charge on the vessel, cargo or articles in respect of or by which the damage is caused[13]. Any amount payable in respect of such damage must, in case of dispute, be determined and is, in default of payment, recoverable in the same manner as the amount of salvage[14] is determined and recoverable under the statutory provisions relating to salvage and wreck[15].

If the owner or occupier of any land:

(a)   impedes or hinders any person in the exercise of the rights so conferred[16];

(b)   impedes or hinders the deposit on the land of any cargo or other article recovered from the vessel[17]; or

(c)   prevents or attempts to prevent any cargo or other article recovered from the vessel from remaining deposited on the land for a reasonable time until it can be removed to a safe place of public deposit[18],

he is liable to a fine[19].

1   As to the meaning of 'vessel' see PARA 919 note 5.
2   These provisions apply where a United Kingdom or foreign vessel is wrecked, stranded or in distress at any place on or near the coasts of the United Kingdom or any tidal water within United Kingdom waters: see PARA 936 note 2.
3   Merchant Shipping Act 1995 s 234(1)(a).
4   Merchant Shipping Act 1995 s 234(1)(b). As to the meaning of 'shipwrecked persons' see PARA 936 note 6.
5   Merchant Shipping Act 1995 s 234(1)(c). As to the meaning of 'cargo' for salvage purposes see PARA 860.
6   Merchant Shipping Act 1995 s 234(1).
7   Ie by the Merchant Shipping Act 1995 s 234(1) (see the text and notes 1–6): see s 234(2).
8   Merchant Shipping Act 1995 s 234(2).
9   Ie by the Merchant Shipping Act 1995 s 234(1) (see the text and notes 1–6): see s 234(3).
10 Merchant Shipping Act 1995 s 234(3).
11 Ie by the Merchant Shipping Act 1995 s 234(1) (see the text and notes 1–6): see s 234(4).
12 Merchant Shipping Act 1995 s 234(4).
13 Merchant Shipping Act 1995 s 234(5).
14 As to the meaning of 'salvage' see PARA 849.
15 Merchant Shipping Act 1995 s 234(6). The text refers to the provisions of Pt XI (ss 224–255): see s 234(6).
16 See the Merchant Shipping Act 1995 s 234(7)(a); and PARA 1159. The text refers to the rights conferred by s 234: see s 234(7)(a); and PARA 1159.
17 See the Merchant Shipping Act 1995 s 234(7)(b); and PARA 1159.
18 See the Merchant Shipping Act 1995 s 234(7)(c); and PARA 1159.
19 See the Merchant Shipping Act 1995 s 234(7); and PARA 1159.

947. Provisions as respect cargo etc washed on shore or otherwise lost or taken. Where a vessel[1] is wrecked, stranded, or in distress at any place on or near the coasts[2] of the United Kingdom[3] or any tidal water[4] within United Kingdom waters[5], any cargo[6] or other articles belonging to or separated from the vessel which are washed on shore or otherwise lost or taken from the vessel must be delivered to the receiver[7].

If any person, whether the owner or not:

(1)   conceals or keeps possession of any such cargo or article[8]; or

(2)   refuses to deliver any such cargo or article to the receiver or to any person authorised by the receiver to require delivery[9],

he is liable on summary conviction to a fine[10]; and the receiver or any person authorised by him may take any such cargo or article, if necessary by force, from any person who refuses to deliver it[11].

1   As to the meaning of 'vessel' see PARA 919 note 5.
2   As to the meaning of 'on or near the coast' see *The Fulham* [1898] P 206 at 213, 8 Asp MLC 425 at 426, 427 (on appeal [1899] P 251, 8 Asp MLC 559, CA).
3   As to the meaning of 'United Kingdom' see PARA 16 note 3.
4   As to the meaning of 'tidal water' see PARA 923 note 6.
5   As to the meaning of 'United Kingdom waters' see PARA 48 note 10.
6   As to the meaning of 'cargo' for salvage purposes see PARA 860.
7   Merchant Shipping Act 1995 s 237(1). As to the meaning of 'receiver' see PARA 887 note 4.
8   See the Merchant Shipping Act 1995 s 237(2)(a); and PARA 1161.
9   See the Merchant Shipping Act 1995 s 237(2)(b); and PARA 1161.
10   See the Merchant Shipping Act 1995 s 237(2); and PARA 1161.
11   See the Merchant Shipping Act 1995 s 237(3); and PARA 1161.

948. Prohibition on approaching dangerous wrecks. If the Secretary of State[1] is satisfied with respect to a vessel lying wrecked in United Kingdom waters[2] that:

(1)   because of anything contained in it, the vessel is in a condition which makes it a potential danger to life or property[3]; and

(2)   on that account it ought to be protected from unauthorised interference[4],

he may by order designate an area round the vessel as a 'prohibited area'[5].

Such an order must identify the vessel and the place where it is lying[6]; and:

(a)   the prohibited area must be all within such distance of the vessel as is specified by the order, excluding any area above high water mark of ordinary spring tides[7]; and

(b)   the distance specified for the purposes of head (a) above must be whatever the Secretary of State thinks appropriate to ensure that unauthorised persons are kept away from the vessel[8].

A person who without due authority enters a prohibited area commits an offence[9].

1   As to the Secretary of State see PARA 36. Functions of the Secretary of State under the Protection of Wrecks Act 1973 are transferred so as to be exercisable in relation to Wales by the Welsh Ministers, except for those functions under s 2: see the National Assembly for Wales (Transfer of Functions) Order 1999, SI 1999/672, art 2, Sch 1; and PARA 1011 note 2. As to the meaning of 'Wales' see PARA 17 note 2.
2   For these purposes, 'United Kingdom waters' means any part of the sea within the seaward limits of United Kingdom territorial waters and includes any part of a river within the ebb and flow of ordinary spring tides; and 'sea' includes any estuary or arm of the sea: see the Protection of Wrecks Act 1973 s 3(1). As to the extent of the territorial and non-territorial sea (or waters) generally see INTERNATIONAL RELATIONS LAW vol 61 (2010) PARA 123 et seq. As to the meaning of 'United Kingdom' see PARA 16 note 3.
3   Protection of Wrecks Act 1973 s 2(1)(a).
4   Protection of Wrecks Act 1973 s 2(1)(b).

5 See the Protection of Wrecks Act 1973 ss 2(1), 3(2). The Secretary of State must revoke an order made under s 2 designating a prohibited area if he is satisfied that the vessel in question is no longer in a condition which makes it a potential danger to life or property: s 3(2)(b). As such orders are local in nature, they are not noted in this work.
6 Protection of Wrecks Act 1973 s 2(2).
7 Protection of Wrecks Act 1973 s 2(2)(a).
8 Protection of Wrecks Act 1973 s 2(2)(b).
9 See PARA 1166.

(iv) Claimed and Unclaimed Wrecks

949. Claims of owners to wreck. The owner of any wreck[1] in the possession of the receiver[2] who establishes his claim to the wreck to the satisfaction of the receiver within one year from the time when the wreck came into the receiver's possession is, on paying the salvage[3], fees and expenses due, entitled to have the wreck delivered or the proceeds of sale paid to him[4].

Where:

(1)   a foreign ship[5] has been wrecked on or near the coasts[6] of the United Kingdom[7]; or

(2)   any articles belonging to or forming part of or of the cargo[8] of a foreign ship which has been wrecked on or near the coasts of the United Kingdom are found on or near the coast or are brought into any port[9],

the appropriate consular officer[10] is to be treated, in the absence of the owner and of the master[11] or other agent of the owner, as the agent of the owner for the purposes of the custody and disposal of the wreck and such articles[12].

1 As to the meaning of 'wreck' see PARA 923.
2 As to the meaning of 'receiver' see PARA 887 note 4.
3 As to the meaning of 'salvage' see PARA 849.
4 Merchant Shipping Act 1995 s 239(1). Delivery of wreck, and payment of the proceeds of sale of wreck, under Pt IX Ch II (ss 231–247) discharges the receiver from all liability in respect of the delivery or payment: s 244(1). Delivery of wreck by the receiver does not, however, prejudice or affect any question which may be raised by third parties concerning the right or title to the wreck or concerning the title to the soil of the place at which the wreck was found: s 244(2).
5 As to the meaning of 'ship' see PARA 229; and as to the meaning of 'foreign', in relation to a ship, see PARA 18 note 2.
6 As to the meaning of 'on or near the coast' see *The Fulham* [1898] P 206 at 213, 8 Asp MLC 425 at 426–427 (on appeal [1899] P 251, 8 Asp MLC 559, CA).
7 Merchant Shipping Act 1995 s 239(2)(a). As to the meaning of 'United Kingdom' see PARA 16 note 3.
8 As to the meaning of 'cargo' for salvage purposes see PARA 860.
9 Merchant Shipping Act 1995 s 239(2)(b). As to the meaning of 'port' see PARA 46 note 12.
10 For these purposes, 'appropriate consular officer', in relation to a foreign ship, means the consul general of the country to which the ship or, as the case may be, the owners of the cargo may have belonged or any consular officer of that country authorised for the purpose by any treaty or arrangement with that country: Merchant Shipping Act 1995 s 239(3). As to the meaning of 'consular officer' for these purposes see PARA 48 note 12.
11 As to the meaning of 'master' see PARA 444 note 1.
12 Merchant Shipping Act 1995 s 239(2).

950. Right of Crown to unclaimed wreck. Her Majesty and Her Royal successors are entitled to all unclaimed wreck[1] found in the United Kingdom[2] or in United Kingdom waters[3] except in places where Her Majesty or any of Her Royal predecessors has granted the right to any other person[4].

1 As to the meaning of 'wreck' see PARA 923.
2 As to the meaning of 'United Kingdom' see PARA 16 note 3.
3 As to the meaning of 'United Kingdom waters' see PARA 48 note 10.
4 Merchant Shipping Act 1995 s 241. On rights to wreck see *Crown Estate Comrs v Roberts* [2008] EWHC 1302 (Ch), [2008] 1 EGLR 129.

951. Notice of unclaimed wreck to be given to persons entitled. Any person who is entitled to unclaimed wreck[1] found at any place in the United Kingdom[2] or in United Kingdom waters[3] must give the receiver[4] a statement containing the particulars of his entitlement and specifying an address to which notices may be sent[5].

Where a statement has been so given to the receiver and the entitlement is proved to the satisfaction of the receiver, the receiver must, on taking possession of any wreck found at a place to which the statement refers, within 48 hours, send to the specified address a description of the wreck and of any marks distinguishing it[6].

1   As to the meaning of 'wreck' see PARA 923. As to the right of the Crown to unclaimed wreck see PARA 950.
2   As to the meaning of 'United Kingdom' see PARA 16 note 3.
3   As to the meaning of 'United Kingdom waters' see PARA 48 note 10.
4   As to the meaning of 'receiver' see PARA 887 note 4.
5   Merchant Shipping Act 1995 s 242(1).
6   Merchant Shipping Act 1995 s 242(2).

952. Disposal of wreck unclaimed after one year. Where, as respects any wreck[1] found in the United Kingdom[2] or in United Kingdom waters[3] and in the possession of the receiver[4]:

(1)   no owner establishes a claim to it within one year after it came into the receiver's possession[5]; and

(2)   the wreck is claimed by any person who has delivered the required statement[6] and has proved to the satisfaction of the receiver his entitlement to receive unclaimed wreck found at the place where the wreck was found[7],

the wreck must, on payment of all expenses, costs, fees and salvage[8] due in respect of it, be delivered to that person[9].

Alternatively, such wreck may be sold by the receiver[10].

1   As to the meaning of 'wreck' see PARA 923.
2   As to the meaning of 'United Kingdom' see PARA 16 note 3.
3   As to the meaning of 'United Kingdom waters' see PARA 48 note 10.
4   As to the meaning of 'receiver' see PARA 887 note 4.
5   Merchant Shipping Act 1995 s 243(1). As to the right of the Crown to unclaimed wreck see PARA 950.
6   Ie the statement required by the Merchant Shipping Act 1995 s 242 (see PARA 951): see s 243(2).
7   Merchant Shipping Act 1995 s 243(2).
8   As to the meaning of 'salvage' see PARA 849.
9   Merchant Shipping Act 1995 s 243(2). Delivery of wreck discharges the receiver from liability in respect of delivery: see PARA 949 note 4.
10 See PARA 956.

(v) Liability for Costs and Powers of Sale

953. Costs and exclusions. Under the Wrecks Convention[1] the registered owner is liable for the costs of locating, marking and removing the wreck[2] unless he proves that the maritime casualty[3] that caused the wreck:

(1)   resulted from an act of war, hostilities, civil war, insurrection, or a natural phenomenon of an exceptional, inevitable and irresistible character[4];

(2)   was wholly caused by an act or omission done with intent to cause damage by a third party[5]; or

(3)   was wholly caused by the negligence or other wrongful act of any Government or other authority responsible for the maintenance of lights or other navigational aids in the exercise of that function[6].

The registered owner is not, however, liable under the Convention for any such costs if, and to the extent that, liability for such costs would be in conflict with specified anti-pollution measures[7].

Accordingly, where a ship[8] has been involved in an accident[9] as a result of which it or anything from it has become a wreck in the United Kingdom's Convention area[10], and costs have been incurred[11] in connection with the location, marking and removal of the wreck[12], the person who incurred the costs is entitled to recover them from the ship's registered owner[13] unless the owner proves that a Convention exception[14] applies[15]. The owner is not, however, liable for costs under these provisions if or to the extent that liability would conflict with one of the specified anti-pollution measures[16] or any other provision specified by order made by the Secretary of State[17].

An action to recover costs under these provisions is subject to a limitation period of six years from the date of the accident[18].

1 Ie the International Convention on the Removal of Wrecks (Nairobi, 18 May 2007; Cm 8243): see PARAS 926–928. Nothing in the Wrecks Convention affects the right of the registered owner to limit liability under any applicable national or international regime, such as the Convention on Limitation of Liability for Maritime Claims (London, 1 to 19 November 1976; TS 13 (1990); Cm 955) art 6(1)(b) (see PARA 998) (Wrecks Convention art 10.2); and nothing in art 10 prejudices any right of recourse against third parties (art 10.4). As to the meaning of 'registered owner' see PARA 930 note 1.

2 Ie under the costs under the Wrecks Convention arts 7, 8, 9 respectively (see PARAS 938–944). As to the meaning of 'removing' see PARA 942. As to the meaning of 'wreck' see PARA 923. No claim for the costs referred to in art 10.1 may be made against the registered owner otherwise than in accordance with the provisions of the Convention: art 10.3. This is without prejudice to the rights and obligations of a state party that has made a notification under art 3.2 (see PARA 927), in relation to wrecks located in its territory, including the territorial sea, other than locating, marking and removing in accordance with the Convention: art 10.3.

3 As to the meaning of 'maritime casualty' see PARA 923.

4 Wrecks Convention art 10.1(a).

5 Wrecks Convention art 10.1(b).

6 Wrecks Convention art 10.1(c).

7 Ie the registered owner is not liable under the Wrecks Convention for the costs mentioned in art 10.1 (see the text and notes 1–6) if, and to the extent that, liability for such costs would be in conflict with:

    (1)   the International Convention on Civil Liability for Oil Pollution Damage (Brussels, 29 November 1969 to 31 December 1970; TS 106 (1975); Cmnd 6183) (see ENVIRONMENTAL QUALITY AND PUBLIC HEALTH vol 45 (2010) PARA 441 et seq) (Wrecks Convention art 11.1(a));

    (2)   the Convention on Liability and Compensation for Damage in Connection with the Carriage of Hazardous and Noxious Substances by Sea 1996 (London, 3 May 1996; Misc 5 (1997); Cm 3580) (see ENVIRONMENTAL QUALITY AND PUBLIC HEALTH vol 45 (2010) PARA 472 et seq) (Wrecks Convention art 11.1(b));

    (3)   the Convention on Third Party Liability in the Field of Nuclear Energy (Paris, 29 July 1960; TS 69 (1968); Cmnd 3755) (see ENERGY AND CLIMATE CHANGE vol 44 (2011) PARA 769) or the Vienna Convention on Civil Liability for Nuclear Damage and an Optional Protocol concerning the Compulsory Settlement of Disputes (Vienna, 21 May 1963; Misc 9 (1964); Cmnd 2333) (see ENERGY AND CLIMATE CHANGE vol 44 (2011) PARA 771) or national law governing or prohibiting limitation of liability for nuclear damage (Wrecks Convention art 11.1(c)); or

    (4)   the International Convention on Civil Liability for Bunker Oil Pollution Damage (London, 23 March 2001; Misc 8 (2005); Cm 6693) (Wrecks Convention art 11.1(c)),

provided that the relevant convention is applicable and in force. To the extent that measures under the Wrecks Convention are considered to be salvage under applicable national law or an international convention, such law or convention applies to questions of the remuneration or compensation payable to salvors to the exclusion of the rules of the Wrecks Convention: art 11.2.

8 As to the meaning of 'ship' see PARA 229.

9 As to the meaning of 'accident' see PARA 934 note 1.

10 Merchant Shipping Act 1995 s 255G(1)(a) (Pt 9A (ss 255A–255U, Sch 11ZA) added by the Wreck Removal Convention Act 2011 s 1, Schedule). As to the geographical application of the Wrecks Convention, and the United Kingdom's 'Convention area', see PARA 941.

11 Ie costs have been incurred complying with the Merchant Shipping Act 1995 s 255C (see PARA 938) or s 255F (see PARA 944).

12 Merchant Shipping Act 1995 s 255G(1)(b) (as added: see note 10).

13 As to the meaning of 'registered owner' see PARA 930 note 1. Where the registered owner of each of two or more ships is liable for costs under these provisions but the costs for which each is liable cannot reasonably be separated, the registered owners are jointly liable for the total costs: Merchant Shipping Act 1995 s 255G(4) (as added: see note 10). Section 255 does not prevent the exercise of the right (if any) to limit liability by virtue of s 185 (see PARA 992): s 255G(5) (as so added).

14 Ie an exception set out in the Wrecks Convention art 10.1(a), (b) or (c) (see the text and notes 1–6).

15 Merchant Shipping Act 1995 s 255G(2) (as added: see note 10). In proceedings against a Wrecks Convention State for the recovery of costs under s 255G the state is treated as having submitted to the jurisdiction of the court in which the proceedings are brought; but this does not authorise execution against the property of a state: s 255S(7) (as so added). As to the meaning of 'Wrecks Convention State', and as to references to ships registered in a state, see PARA 931 note 11. Nothing in Pt 9A affects any claim, or the enforcement of any claim, a person incurring any liability under Pt 9A may have against any other person in respect of that liability: s 255T (as so added).

16 Ie a convention listed in the Wrecks Convention art 11.1 (see the text and note 7) or an enactment implementing such a convention: Merchant Shipping Act 1995 s 255G(3)(a), (b) (as added: see note 10).

17 See the Merchant Shipping Act 1995 s 255G(3)(c), (6), (7) (as added: see note 10). As to the Secretary of State see PARA 36. At the date at which this volume states the law no such order had been made.

18 See the Wrecks Convention art 13, which provides that rights to recover costs under the Convention are extinguished unless an action is brought within three years from the date when the hazard has been determined in accordance with the Convention, and that in no case may an action be brought after six years from the date of the maritime casualty that resulted in the wreck (that six-year period running, in the case of a maritime casualty consisting of a series of occurrences, from the date of the first occurrence); and the Merchant Shipping Act 1995 s 255H (as added: see note 10), which provides that an action to recover costs under s 255G may not be brought after the end of whichever of the following ends earlier: the period of 3 years beginning with the date on which a wreck removal notice was given in respect of the wreck, and the period of 6 years beginning with the date of the accident which resulted in the wreck. As to the meaning of 'maritime casualty' see PARA 923.

954. Claims for costs. Any claim for costs arising under the Wrecks Convention[1] may be brought directly against the insurer or other person providing financial security for the registered owner's liability[2]. In such a case the defendant may invoke the defences (other than the bankruptcy or winding up of the registered owner[3]) that the registered owner would have been entitled to invoke, including limitation of liability under any applicable national or international regime[4]. Furthermore, even if the registered owner is not entitled to limit liability, the defendant may limit liability to an amount equal to the amount of the insurance or other financial security required[5] to be maintained[6]. Moreover, the defendant may invoke the defence that the maritime casualty[7] was caused by the wilful misconduct of the registered owner, but the defendant may not invoke any other defence which the defendant might have been entitled to invoke in proceedings brought by the registered owner against the defendant[8]. The defendant must in any event have the right to require the registered owner to be joined in the proceedings[9].

1 Ie the International Convention on the Removal of Wrecks (Nairobi, 18 May 2007; Cm 8243): see PARAS 926–928.

2 Wrecks Convention art 12.11. As to the provision of insurance and other financial security see PARA 930.

3 As to the meaning of 'registered owner' see PARA 930 note 1.

4 Wrecks Convention art 12.11.

5 Ie under the Wrecks Convention art 12.1 (see PARA 930).

6 Wrecks Convention art 12.11.

7 As to the meaning of 'maritime casualty' see PARA 923.

8 Wrecks Convention art 12.11.

9 Wrecks Convention art 12.11.

955. Third party rights against insurers. Where a ship[1] has been involved in an accident[2] as a result of which it or anything from it has become a wreck[3] in the United Kingdom's Convention area[4], at the time of the accident the ship had wreck removal insurance[5], and there is a wreck removal insurance certificate in relation to the insurance[6], a person who is entitled to recover costs[7] from the ship's registered owner[8] may recover them from the insurer[9]. It is a defence for the insurer to prove that the accident was caused by the wilful misconduct of the ship's registered owner[10], and the insurer may also rely on any defences available[11] to the registered owner[12].

1   As to the meaning of 'ship' see PARA 229.
2   As to the meaning of 'accident' see PARA 934 note 1.
3   As to the meaning of 'wreck' see PARA 923.
4   Merchant Shipping Act 1995 s 255P(1)(a) (Pt 9A (ss 255A–255U, Sch 11ZA) added by the Wreck Removal Convention Act 2011 s 1, Schedule). As to the geographical application of the Wrecks Convention, and the United Kingdom's 'Convention area', see PARA 941.
5   Merchant Shipping Act 1995 s 255P(1)(b) (as added: see note 4). As to wreck removal insurance and wreck removal insurance certificates see PARA 931.
6   Merchant Shipping Act 1995 s 255P(1)(b) (as added: see note 4).
7   Ie under the Merchant Shipping Act 1995 s 255G (see PARA 953).
8   As to the meaning of 'registered owner' see PARA 930 note 1.
9   Merchant Shipping Act 1995 s 255P(2) (as added: see note 4). 'Insurer' means the person providing the insurance or other security: s 255J(7) (as so added). The Third Parties (Rights against Insurers) Act 1930 (see INSURANCE vol 60 (2011) PARAS 651–655) and the Third Parties (Rights against Insurers) Act 2010 (see INSURANCE vol 60 (2011) PARAS 657–665) do not apply in relation to any wreck removal insurance to which a wreck removal insurance certificate relates: Merchant Shipping Act 1995 s 255P(7) (as so added). The insurer may limit liability in respect of claims made under these provisions to the same extent as the registered owner may limit liability by virtue of s 185 (or would be able to limit liability by virtue of s 185 (see PARA 992) if it were not for Sch 7 Pt II para 3) (see PARA 994): s 255P(5) (as so added). However an insurer may limit liability whether or not the accident is caused by an act or omission mentioned in the Convention on Limitation of Liability for Maritime Claims (London, 1 to 19 November 1976; TS 13 (1990); Cm 955) art 4 (see PARA 995): Merchant Shipping Act 1995 s 255P(6) (as so added).
10 Merchant Shipping Act 1995 s 255P(3) (as added: see note 4).
11 Ie including defences under the Merchant Shipping Act 1995 s 255H (see PARA 953 note 18).
12 Merchant Shipping Act 1995 s 255P(4) (as added: see note 4).

956. Powers of receiver to sell wreck. The receiver[1] may at any time sell any wreck[2] in his possession if, in his opinion[3]:

(1)   it is under the value of £5,000[4];
(2)   it is so much damaged or of so perishable a nature that it cannot with advantage be kept[5]; or
(3)   it is not of sufficient value to pay for storage[6].

The receiver may also sell any wreck in his possession before the end of the year, calculated from the time when the wreck came into his possession[7], if[8]:

(a)   in his opinion it is unlikely that any owner will establish a claim to the wreck within that year[9]; and
(b)   no statement has been given to the receiver[10] in relation to the place where the wreck was found[11].

Where, as respects any wreck found in the United Kingdom[12] or in United Kingdom waters[13] and in the possession of the receiver:

(i)   no owner establishes a claim to it within one year after it came into the receiver's possession[14]; and
(ii)   the wreck is not duly claimed by any person[15],

the receiver must sell the wreck and, after making the required deductions[16] and paying to the salvors[17] the amount of salvage such as the Secretary of State directs generally or in the particular case[18], pay the proceeds as directed[19].

1   As to the meaning of 'receiver' see PARA 887 note 4.

2 As to the meaning of 'wreck' see PARA 923. The proceeds of sale must, after defraying the expenses of the sale, be held by the receiver for the same purposes and subject to the same claims, rights and liabilities as if the wreck had remained unsold: Merchant Shipping Act 1995 s 240(2) (s 240(2) amended, s 240(1A), (3) added, by the Merchant Shipping and Maritime Security Act 1997 s 22).
3 Merchant Shipping Act 1995 s 240(1).
4 Merchant Shipping Act 1995 s 240(1)(a).
5 Merchant Shipping Act 1995 s 240(1)(b).
6 Merchant Shipping Act 1995 s 240(1)(c).
7 Ie the year referred to in the Merchant Shipping Act 1995 239(1) (see PARA 949): see s 240(1A) (as added: see note 2). As to the proceeds of sale see note 2. Where the receiver sells any wreck in a case falling within heads (a) and (b) in the text, he may make to the salvors an advance payment, of such amount as he thinks fit and subject to such conditions as he thinks fit, on account of any salvage that may become payable to them in accordance with s 243(5) (see PARA 952): s 240(3) (as so added). As to the Secretary of State see PARA 36.
8 Merchant Shipping Act 1995 s 240(1A) (as added: see note 2).
9 Merchant Shipping Act 1995 s 240(1A)(a) (as added: see note 2).
10 Ie under the Merchant Shipping Act 1995 s 242(1) (see PARA 951): see s 240(1A)(b) (as added: see note 2).
11 Merchant Shipping Act 1995 s 240(1A)(b) (as added: see note 2).
12 As to the meaning of 'United Kingdom' see PARA 16 note 3.
13 As to the meaning of 'United Kingdom waters' see PARA 48 note 10.
14 Merchant Shipping Act 1995 s 243(1). As to the right of the Crown to unclaimed wreck see PARA 950.
15 Ie in accordance with the Merchant Shipping Act 1995 s 242 (see PARA 951): see s 243(3).
16 The deductions are:
    (1)   the expenses of the sale (Merchant Shipping Act 1995 s 243(4)(a));
    (2)   any other expenses incurred by the receiver (s 243(4)(b)); and
    (3)   his fees (s 243(4)(c).
17 As to the meaning of 'salvor' see PARA 849 note 4.
18 Merchant Shipping Act 1995 s 243(5). As to the Secretary of State see PARA 36; and as to the Secretary of State's power to give directions see PARA 39.
19 Merchant Shipping Act 1995 s 243(3). The proceeds of sale, after making the deductions and salvage payments referred to in the text, must be paid by the receiver for the benefit of Her Majesty:
    (1)   if the wreck is claimed in right of the Duchy of Lancaster, to the receiver-general of the duchy or his deputies as part of its revenues (s 243(6)(a));
    (2)   if the wreck is claimed in right of the Duchy of Cornwall, to the receiver-general of the duchy or his deputies as part of its revenues (s 243(6)(b)); and
    (3)   in any other case, into the Consolidated Fund (s 243(6)(c)).
    Payment of the proceeds of sale discharges the receiver from all liability in respect of the payment: see PARA 949 note 4. As to the Duchies of Lancaster and Cornwall see CROWN AND CROWN PROCEEDINGS vol 29 (2014) PARAS 214 et seq, 232 et seq. As to payments to be made into the Consolidated Fund under the Merchant Shipping Act 1995 see PARA 64. As to the Consolidated Fund generally see CONSTITUTIONAL AND ADMINISTRATIVE LAW vol 20 (2014) PARA 480 et seq.

957. Powers of harbor, conservancy and lighthouse authorities to sell vessels in order to reimburse costs.

Where a harbor, conservancy or general lighthouse authority[1] has raised, removed, destroyed or marked a wreck in waters under its control[2] it may sell, in such manner as it thinks fit, the vessel[3] or part of the vessel so raised or removed and any other property[4] recovered in the exercise of the removal or marking[5] powers[6] and reimburse itself, out of the proceeds of the sale, for the expenses incurred by it in relation to the sale[7]. Any surplus of the proceeds of a sale under these provisions must be held by the authority on trust for the persons entitled thereto[8]. Except in the case of property which is of a perishable nature or which would deteriorate in value by delay, no sale may be made under these provisions until at least seven days' notice of the intended sale has been given by advertisement in a local newspaper circulating in or near the area over which the authority has control[9]; and, at any time before any property is sold under these provisions, the owner of the property is entitled to have it delivered to him on payment of its fair market value[10]. Any proceeds of sale arising under these provisions from the sale of a vessel and any other property recovered from the vessel are to be treated as a common fund[11].

Where a general lighthouse authority has incurred expenses in its exercise of removal powers[12] in relation to any vessel, then:

(1)   if the proceeds of any sale made[13] in connection with the exercise of those powers in relation to the vessel are insufficient to reimburse the authority for the full amount of those expenses, the authority may recover the amount of the deficiency from the owner of the vessel at the time of the sinking, stranding or abandonment of the vessel (the 'relevant person')[14]; or

(2)   if there is no such sale, the authority may recover the full amount of those expenses from the relevant person[15].

Any expenses so incurred which are not recovered by the authority either out of the proceeds of any such sale or in accordance with head (1) or head (2) above must be paid out of the General Lighthouse Fund[16].

1   As to the meaning of 'harbour authority' see PARA 69 note 4; as to the meaning of 'conservancy authority' see PARA 72 note 2; as to the meaning of 'general lighthouse authority' see PARA 1017. As to the powers of these authorities see also PARA 939 note 4.
2   Ie pursuant to the powers set out in PARAS 945, 939.
3   As to the meaning of 'vessel' see PARA 919 note 5.
4   As to the 'other property' in this context see PARA 945 note 6.
5   Ie the powers conferred by the Merchant Shipping Act 1995 s 252(2)(a), (b) (see PARAS 945, 939).
6   Merchant Shipping Act 1995 s 252(2)(c). The power set out s 252(2)(c) is subject to s 252(5), (6) (see the text and notes 9–10): see s 252(2)(c).
7   Merchant Shipping Act 1995 ss 252(2)(d), 253(1).
8   Merchant Shipping Act 1995 s 252(4).
9   Merchant Shipping Act 1995 s 252(5).
10 Merchant Shipping Act 1995 s 252(6). The market value of property for the purposes of s 252(6) is that agreed on between the authority and the owner or, failing agreement, that determined by a person appointed for the purpose by the Secretary of State (s 252(7)); and the sum so paid to the authority in respect of any property is to be treated, for the purposes of these provisions, as the proceeds of sale of the property (s 252(8)). As to the Secretary of State see PARA 36.
11 Merchant Shipping Act 1995 s 252(9).
12 Ie the powers under the Merchant Shipping Act 1995 s 253(1): see PARA 945.
13 Ie under the Merchant Shipping Act 1995 s 252 (see PARA 945): see s 253(2)(a).
14 Merchant Shipping Act 1995 s 253(2)(a), (4).
15 Merchant Shipping Act 1995 s 253(2)(b).
16 Merchant Shipping Act 1995 s 253(3). However, the provisions of s 213 (see PARA 1041) apply to those expenses as if they were expenses of the authority falling within s 213(1) other than establishment expenses: see s 253(3). As to the General Lighthouse Fund see PARA 1039.

958. Liability for damage in case of plundered vessel.

Where a vessel[1] is wrecked, stranded or in distress in United Kingdom waters[2], and the vessel or any part of its cargo[3] and equipment is plundered, damaged or destroyed by persons in circumstances in which those persons commit the offence of riot[4], compensation must be made to the owner of the vessel, cargo or equipment[5]. Where the vessel, cargo or equipment is not within a police area, the plundering, damage or destruction is to be treated[6] as taking place within the nearest police area[7].

1   As to the meaning of 'vessel' see PARA 919 note 5.
2   These provisions apply where a United Kingdom or foreign vessel is wrecked, stranded or in distress at any place on or near the coasts of the United Kingdom or any tidal water within United Kingdom waters: see PARA 936 note 2.
3   As to the meaning of 'cargo' for salvage purposes see PARA 860.
4   As to the offence of riot see CRIMINAL LAW vol 26 (2016) PARA 550.
5   Merchant Shipping Act 1995 s 235(1). Compensation must be made by the appropriate local policing body (as defined by the Riot Compensation Act 2016 s 1(3): see POLICE AND INVESTIGATORY POWERS) in the manner provided by the Riot Compensation Act 2016 with respect to claims for compensation thereunder: Merchant Shipping Act 1995 s 235(2), (2A) (s 235(2) amended, s 235(2A) added, by the Riot Compensation Act 2016 s 10(2)).

6   Ie for the purposes of the Merchant Shipping Act 1995 s 235(2) (see note 5).
7   Merchant Shipping Act 1995 s 235(3).

(vi) Protection of Wreck of RMS Titanic

959. International agreement to protect wreck. As from a day to be appointed, provision is made for protecting and preserving the wreck of RMS Titanic and its artifacts[1], pursuant to an agreement made between the governments of the United Kingdom, the United States of America, Canada and France[2]. Any person wishing to carry out activities in the area of the wreck[3] must either be licensed by the Secretary of State[4] to carry out those activities[5] or authorised so to do by a state party to the Agreement other than the United Kingdom[6]. It is an offence to carry out unlicensed or unauthorised activities[7], and the activities that are licensed or authorised to be carried out are closely regulated[8]. Provision is also made for the enforcement of the restrictions[9].

1   'Artifacts' means the cargo of RMS Titanic and other contents, including those associated objects that are scattered in its vicinity and any portion of the hull: Protection of Wrecks (RMS Titanic) Order 2003, SI 2003/2496, art 2.
2   Ie the Agreement between the United Kingdom, the United States of America, Canada and the Republic of France, concerning the shipwrecked vessel RMS Titanic (Cm 5798). The agreement is given effect in United Kingdom law by the Protection of Wrecks (RMS Titanic) Order 2003, SI 2003/2496, which was made under the Merchant Shipping and Maritime Security Act 1997 s 24(1), (2), (7) and which comes into force on the date, to be notified in the London, Edinburgh and Belfast Gazettes, on which the Agreement concerning the shipwrecked vessel RMS Titanic enters into force in respect of the United Kingdom (see the Protection of Wrecks (RMS Titanic) Order 2003, SI 2003/2496, art 1(2) (not yet in force)).
3   Ie the area within one kilometre of the point 41° 43–84'N 49° 57–23'W (the 'designated area'): Protection of Wrecks (RMS Titanic) Order 2003, SI 2003/2496, art 3 (not yet in force).
4   As to the Secretary of State see PARA 36.
5   See the Protection of Wrecks (RMS Titanic) Order 2003, SI 2003/2496, arts 4, 5; and PARAS 960–961.
6   An authorisation granted by the appropriate authority of a state party to the Agreement (other than the United Kingdom) in accordance with the provisions of that Agreement is a 'relevant authorisation' for these purposes: Protection of Wrecks (RMS Titanic) Order 2003, SI 2003/2496, art 2 (not yet in force).
7   See the Protection of Wrecks (RMS Titanic) Order 2003, SI 2003/2496, arts 4, 6–9; and PARA 962.
8   See the Protection of Wrecks (RMS Titanic) Order 2003, SI 2003/2496, Schedule; and PARA 960 note 7.
9   See the Protection of Wrecks (RMS Titanic) Order 2003, SI 2003/2496, art 10; and PARA 963.

960. Licensing of activities in area of wreck. As from the appointed day[1] the Secretary of State may grant a licence[2] to authorise a project to carry out the following activities:

(1)   entry into the hull sections of RMS Titanic, including entry using equipment constructed or adapted for any purpose of diving or salvage operations[3];

(2)   activities aimed at the artifacts[4] from RMS Titanic found outside the hull of RMS Titanic (other than activities relating to the conservation or curation of artifacts)[5].

The Secretary of State may grant such a licence only in relation to a project which:

(a)   is justified by educational, scientific or cultural interests, including the need to protect the integrity of RMS Titanic and/or its artifacts from a significant threat[6]; and

(b)   complies with the Rules Concerning Activities Aimed at the RMS Titanic and/or its Artifacts[7].

Subject to the same conditions as apply as respects the granting of a licence[8], the Secretary of State may vary a licence[9].

1 These provisions have yet to be brought into force: see PARA 959.
2 As to the Secretary of State see PARA 36. As to the conditions under which a licence may be granted see PARA 961. It is an offence to carry out the applicable activities without a licence: see PARA 962. The Secretary of State may grant a licence only after he has provided copies of the application for the licence to the relevant national authorities of the other state parties to the Agreement concerning the shipwrecked vessel RMS Titanic (see PARA 959) and taken into account any comments received from those authorities within 90 days following the provision of those copies: Protection of Wrecks (RMS Titanic) Order 2003, SI 2003/2496, art 5(3) (not yet in force).
3 Protection of Wrecks (RMS Titanic) Order 2003, SI 2003/2496, arts 4(2)(a), 5(1) (not yet in force).
4 As to the meaning of 'artifacts' see PARA 959 note 1.
5 Protection of Wrecks (RMS Titanic) Order 2003, SI 2003/2496, art 4(2)(b) (not yet in force).
6 Protection of Wrecks (RMS Titanic) Order 2003, SI 2003/2496, art 5(2)(a) (not yet in force).
7 Protection of Wrecks (RMS Titanic) Order 2003, SI 2003/2496, art 5(2)(b) (not yet in force). The Rules are set out in the Schedule, and cover such areas as: project design; funding; timetable, objectives, methodologies and techniques; professional qualifications; documentation; conservation; safety; reporting and curation; and presentation of the results.
8 As to these see PARA 961.
9 Protection of Wrecks (RMS Titanic) Order 2003, SI 2003/2496, art 5(5) (not yet in force).

961. Contents of licence. As from the appointed day[1] a licence for the carrying out of activities in the area of the wreck of RMS Titanic[2]:

(1)   must require the project to be carried out in accordance with the Rules Concerning Activities Aimed at the RMS Titanic and/or its Artifacts[3];

(2)   must contain a condition that non-intrusive public access consistent with the Agreement[4] may not be precluded by the activities licensed[5]; and

(3)   may contain such other conditions and restrictions as the Secretary of State[6] considers appropriate[7].

Any person who knowingly contravenes any requirement, condition or restriction of a licence[8] which relates to:

(a)   the conservation, curation or keeping together of artifacts[9], or relating to the provision of public access to artifacts[10]; or

(b)   the reporting of the results to the Secretary of State and the publication of the results[11],

is guilty of an offence[12].

1 These provisions have yet to be brought into force: see PARA 959.
2 Ie a licence granted under the Protection of Wrecks (RMS Titanic) Order 2003, SI 2003/2496, art 5 (see PARA 960).
3 Protection of Wrecks (RMS Titanic) Order 2003, SI 2003/2496, art 5(4)(a) (not yet in force). The Rules are set out in the Schedule: see PARA 960 note 7.
4 Ie the Agreement concerning the shipwrecked vessel RMS Titanic (see PARA 959).
5 Protection of Wrecks (RMS Titanic) Order 2003, SI 2003/2496, art 5(4)(b) (not yet in force).
6 As to the Secretary of State see PARA 36.
7 Protection of Wrecks (RMS Titanic) Order 2003, SI 2003/2496, art 5(4)(c) (not yet in force).
8 See note 2.
9 As to the meaning of 'artifacts' see PARA 959 note 1.
10 Protection of Wrecks (RMS Titanic) Order 2003, SI 2003/2496, art 6(2) (not yet in force).
11 Protection of Wrecks (RMS Titanic) Order 2003, SI 2003/2496, art 6(3) (not yet in force).
12 Protection of Wrecks (RMS Titanic) Order 2003, SI 2003/2496, art 6(2), (3) (not yet in force). Such person is liable on summary conviction to a fine: art 6(2), (3) (not yet in force). As to the powers of magistrates' courts to issue fines on summary conviction see SENTENCING vol 92 (2015) PARA 176. As to enforcement see PARA 963.
  Where an offence under the Protection of Wrecks (RMS Titanic) Order 2003, SI 2003/2496, which is committed by a body corporate is proved to have been committed with the consent or connivance of, or to be attributable to any neglect on the part of, a director, manager, secretary or other similar officer of the body corporate, or any person who was purporting to act in any such capacity, he, as well as the body corporate, is guilty of that offence and liable to be proceeded

against and punished accordingly: art 7(1) (not yet in force). For this purpose 'director', in relation to any body corporate whose affairs are managed by its members, means any member of the body: art 7(2) (not yet in force).

No proceedings for an offence under any order under the Protection of Wrecks (RMS Titanic) Order 2003, SI 2003/2496, may be instituted except by or with the consent of the Director of Public Prosecutions: Merchant Shipping and Maritime Security Act 1997 s 24(6)(a). In any proceedings for such an offence a document signed by or on behalf of the Secretary of State stating whether or not a relevant authorisation has been granted, and (where such an authorisation has been granted) its terms, is admissible as evidence for the purposes of determining whether activities have been carried out without, or contrary to any provision of, such an authorization: art 8(1) (not yet in force). As to the meaning of 'relevant authorisation' see PARA 959 note 6. Nothing in art 8(1) makes a document admissible as evidence in proceedings for an offence except in a case where and to the like extent to which oral evidence to the like effect would have been admissible in those proceedings (except in the case of proceedings before a magistrates' court inquiring into an offence as examining justices) (art 8(2), (4)(a) (not yet in force)) and nothing in art 8(1) makes a document admissible as evidence in proceedings for an offence:

(1)   unless a copy of it has, not less than seven days before the hearing or trial, been served on the person charged with the offence (art 8(3)(a) (not yet in force)); or

(2)   (except in the case of proceedings before a magistrates' court inquiring into an offence as examining justices) if that person, not later than three days before the hearing or trial or within such further time as the court may in special circumstances allow, serves a notice on the prosecutor requiring attendance at the trial of the person who signed the document (art 8(3)(b), (4)(b) (not yet in force)).

A document required by art 8(3)(a) to be served on a person charged with an offence under the Protection of Wrecks (RMS Titanic) Order 2003, SI 2003/2496, may be served on that person by delivering it to him, by leaving it at his proper address or by sending it by post to him at his proper address: art 9(1) (not yet in force). If the person charged with an offence is the master of a ship the document may be served:

(a)   where there is a master, by leaving it for him on board the ship with the person appearing to be in command or charge of the ship (art 9(2)(a) (not yet in force));

(b)   where there is no master, on the managing owner of the ship, or if there is no managing owner, on any agent of the owner, or where no such agent is known or can be found, by fixing a copy of the document on the outside of the ship in a position in which it may reasonably be expected to be seen (art 9(2)(b) (not yet in force)).

A document required by art 8(3)(a) to be served on a person charged with an offence under the Protection of Wrecks (RMS Titanic) Order 2003, SI 2003/2496, may in the case of a body corporate, be served on the secretary or clerk of that body (art 9(3)(a) (not yet in force)), and in the case of a partnership, be served on a partner or person having the control or management of the partnership business (art 9(3)(b) (not yet in force)).

For the purposes of art 9(3) and the Interpretation Act 1978 s 7 (service of documents by post: see STATUTES AND LEGISLATIVE PROCESS vol 96 (2012) PARA 1219) in its application to the Protection of Wrecks (RMS Titanic) Order 2003, SI 2003/2496, art 9, the proper address of any person on whom a document under art 8(1) is to be served is his last known address, except that:

(i)   in the case of a body corporate or its secretary or clerk it is the address of the registered or principal office of that body (art 9(4)(a) (not yet in force)); and

(ii)   in the case of a partnership or a person having the control or management of the partnership business, it is the principal office of the partnership (art 9(4)(b) (not yet in force)),

and for the purposes of art 9(4) the principal office of a company registered outside the United Kingdom or of a partnership carrying on business outside the United Kingdom is its principal office in the United Kingdom (art 9(4) (not yet in force)).

962. Offence of carrying out unlicensed or unauthorised activities. As from the appointed day[1] a person may not in the designated area[2] carry out any of the licensable activities[3], or cause or permit any other person to carry out any of those activities:

(1)   without a licence granted[4] by the Secretary of State[5];

(2)   contrary to any requirement, condition or restriction of such a licence[6]; or

(3)   without, or contrary to any provision of, a relevant authorisation[7].

A person who contravenes this prohibition is guilty of an offence[8].

1   These provisions have yet to be brought into force: see PARA 959.
2   As to the meaning of 'designated area' see PARA 959 note 3.

3　As to the licensable activities see the Protection of Wrecks (RMS Titanic) Order 2003, SI 2003/2496, art 4(2); and PARA 960.

4　Ie a licence granted in accordance with the Protection of Wrecks (RMS Titanic) Order 2003, SI 2003/2496 (see paRAS 960–961).

5　Protection of Wrecks (RMS Titanic) Order 2003, SI 2003/2496, art 4(1)(a) (not yet in force). As to the Secretary of State see PARA 36.

6　Protection of Wrecks (RMS Titanic) Order 2003, SI 2003/2496, art 4(1)(b) (not yet in force).

7　Protection of Wrecks (RMS Titanic) Order 2003, SI 2003/2496, art 4(1)(c) (not yet in force). As to the meaning of 'relevant authorisation' see PARA 959 note 6.

8　Protection of Wrecks (RMS Titanic) Order 2003, SI 2003/2496, art 6(1) (not yet in force). Such person is liable on summary conviction to a fine: art 6(1) (not yet in force). As to the powers of magistrates' courts to issue fines on summary conviction see SENTENCING vol 92 (2015) PARA 176. In connection with offences see PARA 961 note 12; as to enforcement see PARA 963.

963. Criminal liability and enforcement.

No person may be guilty of an offence under the United Kingdom statutory provision for protecting and preserving the wreck of RMS Titanic and its artifacts[1] unless:

(1)　the acts or omissions which constitute the offence are committed in the United Kingdom[2], in United Kingdom waters[3] or on board a United Kingdom ship[4]; or

(2)　in a case where those acts or omissions are committed in international waters[5] but not on board a United Kingdom ship, that person is a British citizen, a British overseas territories citizen or a British Overseas citizen[6], a person who[7] is a British subject[8], a British National (Overseas)[9], a British protected person[10], or a registered[11] company[12].

Any such offence is, for the purpose only of conferring jurisdiction on any court, deemed to have been committed in any place where the offender may for the time being be[13].

As from the appointed day[14] a person so authorised by the Secretary of State[15] may at any reasonable time board and search any ship[16] if he has reason to suspect that the statutory provision for protecting and preserving the wreck of RMS Titanic and its artifacts[17] is not complied with, and may take possession of and detain anything found in the course of that search for so long as is necessary for all or any of the following purposes:

(a)　to examine it[18];

(b)　to ensure that it is not tampered with before his examination of it is completed[19];

(c)　to ensure that it is available for use as evidence in any proceedings for an offence[20].

1　Ie under the Protection of Wrecks (RMS Titanic) Order 2003, SI 2003/2496: see PARA 959. As to such offences see PARAS 961–962.

2　As to the meaning of 'United Kingdom' see PARA 16 note 3.

3　In this context 'United Kingdom waters' means the sea or other waters within the seaward limits of the territorial sea of the United Kingdom): Merchant Shipping and Maritime Security Act 1997 s 24(8). As to the extent of the territorial and non-territorial sea (or waters) generally see INTERNATIONAL RELATIONS LAW vol 61 (2010) PARA 123 et seq.

4　Merchant Shipping and Maritime Security Act 1997 s 24(3)(a). In this context 'ship' includes any description of vessel used in navigation (s 24(8)); and 'United Kingdom ship' means a ship which is registered in the United Kingdom (s 24(4)(a)) or is not registered under the law of any country but is wholly owned by persons each of whom is either a British citizen, a British overseas territories citizen or a British Overseas citizen, a person who under the British Nationality Act 1981 is a British subject, a British National (Overseas) (within the meaning of the British Nationality Act 1981), a British protected person (within the meaning of the British Nationality Act 1981), or a company registered under the Companies Act 2006 (Merchant Shipping and Maritime Security Act 1997 s 24(3)(b)(i)–(v), (4)(b) (s 24(3)(b)(i) amended by the British Overseas Territories Act 2002 s 2(3); Merchant Shipping and Maritime Security Act 1997 s 24(3)(b)(v) substituted by SI 2009/1941)). As to British citizenship see BRITISH NATIONALITY vol 4 (2011) PARAS 406, 421–444; as to British overseas territories citizenship see BRITISH NATIONALITY vol

4 (2011) PARAS 406, 445–458); as to British Overseas citizenship see BRITISH NATIONALITY vol 4 (2011) PARA 459 et seq; as to British subjects under the British Nationality Act 1981 see BRITISH NATIONALITY vol 4 (2011) PARAS 407, 469–470; as to British Nationals (Overseas) within the meaning of the British Nationality Act 1981 see BRITISH NATIONALITY vol 4 (2011) PARAS 406, 465–467; as to British protected persons within the meaning of the British Nationality Act 1981 see BRITISH NATIONALITY vol 4 (2011) PARAS 408, 476–480; as to the registration of companies under the Companies Act 2006 see COMPANIES vol 14 (2016) PARA 21 et seq.

5   In this context 'international waters' means any part of the sea outside the seaward limits of the territorial sea of any country or territory: Merchant Shipping and Maritime Security Act 1997 s 24(8).

6   Merchant Shipping and Maritime Security Act 1997 s 24(3)(b)(i) (as amended: see note 4).

7   Ie under the British Nationality Act 1981: see note 4.

8   Merchant Shipping and Maritime Security Act 1997 s 24(3)(b)(ii).

9   Merchant Shipping and Maritime Security Act 1997 s 24(3)(b)(iii). See note 4.

10 Merchant Shipping and Maritime Security Act 1997 s 24(3)(b)(iv). See note 4.

11 Ie a company registered under the Companies Act 2006: see note 4.

12 Merchant Shipping and Maritime Security Act 1997 s 24(3)(b)(v) (as substituted: see note 4).

13 Merchant Shipping and Maritime Security Act 1997 s 24(5).

14 These provisions have yet to be brought into force: see PARA 959.

15 A person appointed by the Secretary of State under the Merchant Shipping Act 1995 s 256(1) or (6) (see PARA 46) to be an inspector, and any commissioned naval officer, is a person authorised by the Secretary of State in accordance with these provisions: Protection of Wrecks (RMS Titanic) Order 2003, SI 2003/2496, art 10(2) (not yet in force). As to the Secretary of State see PARA 36.

16 The powers conferred by these provisions are conferred in relation to any ship which is in United Kingdom waters and any United Kingdom ship which is in international waters: Protection of Wrecks (RMS Titanic) Order 2003, SI 2003/2496, art 10(1) (not yet in force). As to the meaning of 'United Kingdom waters' see PARA 48 note 10. As to the meaning of 'United Kingdom ship' see PARA 230; and as to the meaning of 'ship' see PARA 229.

17 Ie the Protection of Wrecks (RMS Titanic) Order 2003, SI 2003/2496: see PARA 959.

18 Protection of Wrecks (RMS Titanic) Order 2003, SI 2003/2496, art 10(3)(a) (not yet in force).

19 Protection of Wrecks (RMS Titanic) Order 2003, SI 2003/2496, art 10(3)(b) (not yet in force).

20 Ie an offence under the Protection of Wrecks (RMS Titanic) Order 2003, SI 2003/2496 (see PARAS 961, 962): art 10(3)(c) (not yet in force).

11. LIENS ON SHIPS, FREIGHT AND CARGO

(1) MARITIME LIENS

964. Nature and extent. A maritime lien is a claim or privilege on a maritime property (most often a ship or her apparel or cargo, or any combination of those, and referred to, especially historically, as the 'res') in respect of service done to it or damage caused by it[1]. Such a lien does not import or require possession of the property against which the claim is brought or privilege claimed, for it is a claim or privilege on the property to be carried into effect by legal process[2]. A maritime lien travels with the property into whosesoever possession it may come, even though the property may have been purchased without notice of the lien[3] or may have been seized by the sheriff under a writ of control issued at the instance of execution creditors[4]. A maritime lien is inchoate from the moment the claim or privilege attaches, and, when called into effect by the legal process of a proceeding in rem, relates back to the period when it first attached[5].

There can be no maritime lien on a res which is not a ship or her apparel or cargo[6] and, if a lien has attached to a maritime res which is sold by the owner, there is no lien against the proceeds of sale since the lien travels with the property against which the claim is brought or privilege claimed[7]. A maritime lien only attaches to the particular property in respect of which the claim arises and not to any other property of the owner[8]. An owner's lien over cargoes or subfreights is contractual only, having no independent root in Admiralty, common law, equity or statute, and creates a right only as between the parties to the contract in which it is contained[9].

A maritime lien does not attach when the subject property belongs to the Crown or is owned by a foreign state[10]. Nothing in the Crown Proceedings Act 1947[11] authorises proceedings in rem in respect of any claim against the Crown, or the arrest, detention or sale of any of Her Majesty's ships, or of any cargo or other property belonging to the Crown, or gives to any person any lien on any such ship, cargo or other property[12].

Where a ship is under requisition by the Crown or a foreign state, no lien attaches in respect of damage done by her whilst under requisition[13]; but, where salvage services are rendered to a ship under requisition and her owners derive some benefit from those services, a maritime lien does attach, although it is unenforceable whilst the ship remains under requisition[14].

1 *Harmer v Bell, The Bold Buccleugh* (1852) 7 Moo PCC 267 at 284 (approved in *Currie v M'Knight* [1897] AC 97 at 106, 8 Asp MLC 193 at 195, HL); *The Ripon City* [1897] P 226 at 241, 242, 8 Asp MLC 304 at 310, 311 per Gorell Barnes J. See also PARA 83. The law relating to maritime liens is the same in England and Scotland (*Currie v M'Knight*), and applies to hovercraft and property connected with hovercraft, notwithstanding that the hovercraft is on land at any relevant time (see the Hovercraft Act 1968 s 2(2); and PARA 383).
   Damage giving rise to any claim under the Nuclear Installations Act 1965, in respect of any occurrence which constitutes a breach of duty under ss 7–11, does not give rise to a lien or other right in respect of any ship or aircraft: see s 14; and ENERGY AND CLIMATE CHANGE vol 44 (2011) PARA 901.

2 *Harmer v Bell, The Bold Buccleugh* (1852) 7 Moo PCC 267; *The Ripon City* [1897] P 226, 8 Asp MLC 304; *The Tervaete* [1922] P 259 at 270, 16 Asp MLC 48 at 55, CA.

3 *Harmer v Bell, The Bold Buccleugh* (1852) 7 Moo PCC 267; *The Nymph* (1856) Sw 86; *The Ripon City* [1897] P 226 at 241, 8 Asp MLC 304 at 310. Thus, even where a ship is let under a charterparty by demise, the res remains with the owner: *The Father Thames* [1979] 2 Lloyd's Rep 364.

4 *The James W Elwell* [1921] P 351, 15 Asp MLC 418; *The Ile de Ceylan* [1922] P 256, 16 Asp MLC 23. As to writs of control generally see CIVIL PROCEDURE vol 12A (2015) PARA 1379 et seq.

5   *Harmer v Bell, The Bold Buccleugh* (1852) 7 Moo PCC 267 at 284; *Hamilton v Baker, The Sara*
    (1889) 14 App Cas 209 at 216, 6 Asp MLC 413 at 414, HL, per Lord Halsbury LC; *The Tervaete*
    [1922] P 259 at 270, 16 Asp MLC 48 at 55, CA, per Scrutton LJ.
6   *Wells v Gas Float Whitton No 2 (Owners), The Gas Float Whitton No 2* [1897] AC 337, 8 Asp
    MLC 272, HL.
7   *The Optima* (1905) 10 Asp MLC 147, DC. It is otherwise where the sale takes place under the
    order of the court, because the court holds the proceeds subject to all liens which may be proved
    to exist against the res: see *The Optima* at 148 per Gorell Barnes P.
8   *The Beldis* [1936] P 51, 18 Asp MLC 598, CA. In certain circumstances, there may, however, exist
    a statutory right to proceed in rem against another ship beneficially owned by the same person as
    the ship in respect of which the claim arose: see the Senior Courts Act 1981 s 21(4); and PARA 93.
9   See *Samsun Logix Corpn v Oceantrade Corpn, Deval Denizeilik VE Ticaret AS v Oceantrade
    Corpn* [2007] EWHC 2372 (Comm), [2008] 1 All ER (Comm) 673, [2008] 1 Lloyd's Rep 450
    (applying *Tradigrain SA v King Diamond Marine Ltd, The Spiros C* [2000] 2 All ER (Comm) 542,
    [2000] 2 Lloyd's Rep 319, CA); *Dry Bulk Handy Holding Inc v Fayette International Holdings
    Ltd; The Bulk Chile* [2013] EWCA Civ 184, [2013] 2 All ER (Comm) 185; *Western Bulk
    Shipowning III A/S v Carbofer Maritime Trading ApS; The Western Moscow.* [2012] EWHC 1224
    (Comm), [2012] 2 All ER (Comm) 1140; *Bank of Tokyo-Mitsubishi UFJ Ltd v Owners of the MV
    Sanko Mineral* [2014] EWHC 3927 (Admlty), [2014] All ER (D) 14 (Dec).
10 *The Constitution* (1879) 4 PD 39, 4 Asp MLC 79; *The Parlement Belge* (1880) 5 PD 197, 4 Asp
    MLC 234, CA; *The Tervaete* [1922] P 259, 16 Asp MLC 48, CA.
11 As to the Crown Proceedings Act 1947 generally see CROWN AND CROWN PROCEEDINGS vol 29
    (2014) PARA 85 et seq.
12 Crown Proceedings Act 1947 s 29(1). As to Admiralty claims in rem generally see PARA 158 et seq.
    Where proceedings in rem have been instituted in the reasonable belief that the ship, cargo or
    property did not belong to the Crown, the court, if satisfied of this, may on terms order the
    proceedings to be treated as if in personam against the Crown or other person to be sued: see the
    Crown Proceedings Act 1947 s 29(2); and PARA 179. References in whatever terms in s 29 to ships,
    vessels or boats or activities or places connected with them include references to hovercraft or
    activities connected with hovercraft: Hovercraft (Application of Enactments) Order 1972, SI
    1972/971, art 4, Sch 1 Pt A. See also the Senior Courts Act 1981 s 24(2)(c); and PARA 85.
13 *The Sylvan Arrow* [1923] P 220, 16 Asp MLC 244.
14 *The Meandros* [1925] P 61, 16 Asp MLC 476. As to salvage generally see PARA 849 et seq.

965. Extent of judgment in rem.

When a judgment in rem is pronounced in respect of a maritime lien, it binds all the world to the extent that it enables the holder of the maritime lien to enforce the judgment against the property in respect of which the claim is brought (or privilege claimed), irrespective of the personal liability of the person into whose possession the property may have come[1].

A judgment in rem of a foreign court of competent jurisdiction in respect of a maritime lien is regarded by the English courts as conclusive and binding against all the world, even though a maritime lien would not have arisen in the same circumstances under English law[2]. A judgment in rem of a foreign court of competent jurisdiction will be enforced in the English courts by an action in rem; but a judgment in personam of a foreign court of competent jurisdiction will not be enforced in the English courts by an action in rem, even though in the same circumstances there would be a maritime lien under English law[3].

1   A maritime lien travels with the res into whosesoever possession it may come, even though the res
    may have been purchased without notice of the lien: see PARA 1014. As to enforcement of liens see
    PARA 1037 et seq. As to Admiralty claims in rem generally see PARA 158 et seq.
2   *Minna Craig Steamship Co v Chartered Mercantile Bank of India, London and China* [1897] 1 QB
    460, 8 Asp MLC 241, CA. See also *Castrique v Imrie* (1870) LR 4 HL 414; and CONFLICT OF
    LAWS vol 19 (2011) PARAS 416, 434, 438, 439.
3   *The City of Mecca* (1879) 5 PD 28, 4 Asp MLC 187; on appeal (1881) 6 PD 106, 4 Asp MLC 412,
    CA (where the Court of Appeal reversed the decision at first instance on the ground that the
    judgment of the foreign court was not a judgment in rem).

966. Maritime liens recognised by English law.

The maritime liens recognised by English law are those in respect of bottomry and respondentia bonds[1], salvage of property[2], seamen's wages[3], damage[4] and a salvor's rights under any international convention or national law[5]. A maritime lien has been held not to exist in respect of towage[6], the supply of goods, materials etc[7] or insurance contributions[8]. It is doubtful whether a maritime lien exists in respect of pilotage dues[9].

Statutory rights and remedies similar to those enjoyed by the holder of a maritime lien, and enforced in similar manner, include claims in respect of the wages, disbursements and liabilities of the master of a ship[10]; claims in respect of damage to land caused by persons rendering services to a vessel wrecked, stranded or in distress[11]; claims in respect of the fees and expenses of a receiver of wreck[12]; and claims in respect of the expenses of a local authority incurred on account of the burial or destruction of the carcase of any animal or carcase thrown or washed from any vessel[13].

1 As to bottomry and respondentia bonds see PARA 972. See also PARA 133.
2 As to salvage see PARA 849 et seq.
3 As to seamen's wages see PARAS 127, 970.
4 As to damage see also PARAS 109, 977.
5 See PARAS 915, 969.
6 *Westrup v Great Yarmouth Steam Carrying Co* (1889) 43 ChD 241, 6 Asp MLC 443.
7 *Northcote v The Henrich Björn (Owners), The Henrich Björn* (1886) 11 App Cas 270, 6 Asp MLC 1, HL; *The Cella* (1888) 13 PD 82, CA; *The James W Elwell* [1921] P 351, 15 Asp MLC 418. See also PARA 983 note 1.
8 *Cassa Nazionale della Previdenza Marinara v Proceeds of the Sale of the Italian SS Acrux, The Acrux* [1965] P 391, [1965] 2 All ER 323, [1965] 1 Lloyd's Rep 565. As to an insurance agent's lien on a maritime insurance policy see the Marine Insurance Act 1906 s 53; and INSURANCE vol 60 (2011) PARA 277.
9 See PARA 970 note 2; and see PARA 125.
10 See the Merchant Shipping Act 1995 s 41; and PARAS 480, 971. As to the Admiralty jurisdiction in this respect see PARA 127 et seq. In effect, this provision gives the master of a vessel a maritime lien: *The Ripon City* [1897] P 226 at 232, 234, 242, 247, 8 Asp MLC 304 at 308, 311, 312 per Gorrell Barnes J. See also *Morgan v Castlegate Steamship Co, The Castlegate* [1893] AC 38 at 46, 7 Asp MLC 284 at 285, HL, per Lord Herschell.
11 See the Merchant Shipping Act 1995 s 234(5), (6); and PARA 946.
12 See the Merchant Shipping Act 1995 s 249(3); and PARA 887.
13 See the Animal Health Act 1981 s 57; and ANIMALS vol 2 (2017) PARA 455.

967. Lien for damage done by a ship. The lien for damage done by a ship arises when damage is done by the ship[1] to another ship or property[2], whether on the high seas or within the limits of a port[3], through some wrongful act of navigation of the ship from want of skill or from negligence of the persons by whom she is navigated, being at the time of the damage[4] her owners or the employees of her owners, or having the possession and control of her by their authority[5].

Thus, charterers who have the control, or any persons who are allowed to have possession, of a ship for the purpose of using or employing her in the ordinary manner are deemed to have authority to subject her to liens, and so to make her liable for their negligence[6]; but the presumption is not absolute and may be rebutted by showing that the person navigating the ship did not derive any authority from the owners[7], or that the injured party is precluded by the terms of a contract from recovering against them[8].

Where the person in charge or possession of the ship has no such authority, express or implied, no lien arises. Thus, there is no lien for an act of a person in possession of the ship done in asserting a right claimed by him not as an employee or on behalf of the owner[9].

1 The damage must be mediately or immediately caused by an act of navigation. Thus, where the crew of one ship cut the moorings of another ship, as a result of which that other ship was damaged, no lien attached to the first ship: *Currie v M'Knight* [1897] AC 97, 8 Asp MLC 193, HL, approving *Harmer v Bell, The Bold Buccleugh* (1852) 7 Moo PCC 267. A lien cannot be enforced against the property of a foreign sovereign state: *The Parlement Belge* (1880) 5 PD 197, 4 Asp

MLC 234, CA; *The Jassy* [1906] P 270, 10 Asp MLC 278. A lien against a foreign sovereign cannot exist at all: *The Tervaete* [1922] P 259 at 274, 16 Asp MLC 48 at 57, CA, per Atkin LJ.
2 *The Merle* (1874) 2 Asp MLC 402; *Mersey Docks and Harbour Board v Turner, The Zeta* [1893] AC 468, 7 Asp MLC 369, HL (damage to a ship by collision with a pier-head); *The Veritas* [1901] P 304, 9 Asp MLC 237 (damage to a landing stage); *The Tolten* [1946] P 135, sub nom *United Africa Co Ltd v Tolten (Owners), The Tolten* [1946] 2 All ER 372, CA (damage to a wharf).
3 *The Veritas* [1901] P 304, 9 Asp MLC 237.
4 *The Parlement Belge* (1880) 5 PD 197 at 218, 4 Asp MLC 234 at 244, CA; *Utopia (Owners) v Primula (Owners and Master), The Utopia* [1893] AC 492, 7 Asp MLC 408, PC.
5 *The Ripon City* [1897] P 226 at 245, 8 Asp MLC 304 at 312. See also PARA 811.
6 *The Ripon City* [1897] P 226 at 244, 8 Asp MLC 304 at 311. See also *The Ticonderoga* (1857) Sw 215 (where damage was done by a ship when in the possession and under the full control of charterers); *The Ruby Queen* (1861) Lush 266; *The Lemington* (1874) 2 Asp MLC 475 (where damage was done by a yacht in the hands of yacht agents for sale); *The Tasmania* (1888) 13 PD 110 at 118, 6 Asp MLC 305 at 309; *The Sylvan Arrow* [1923] P 220, 16 Asp MLC 244 (where Hill J reviewed all the authorities on this subject).
7 *The Sylvan Arrow* [1923] P 220, 16 Asp MLC 244 (where damage was done by a vessel requisitioned and controlled by the United States government).
8 *The Tasmania* (1888) 13 PD 110 at 118, 6 Asp MLC 305 at 309.
9 *Yeo v Tatem, The Orient* (1871) LR 3 PC 696, 1 Asp MLC 108; *The Parlement Belge* (1880) 5 PD 197 at 218, 4 Asp MLC 234 at 244, CA, per Brett LJ; *Morgan v Castlegate Steamship Co, The Castlegate* [1893] AC 38 at 52, 7 Asp MLC 284 at 288, HL, per Lord Watson. See also *The Halley* (1868) LR 2 PC 193; cf *The Ruby Queen* (1861) Lush 266; *The Ripon City* [1897] P 226, 8 Asp MLC 304.

968. Property to which lien attaches. The moment the damage is done by the ship the lien attaches to her hull, tackle, apparel, furniture and freight[1]. It does not originate in possession and it follows the ship into whosesoever possession she may pass[2], and continues even after the ship is wrecked and may be enforced against the wreck[3]. The lien on freight may, however, only be enforced together with the enforcement of a lien on the ship, being consequential to that lien[4]. A lien arising out of damage caused in a collision between vessels is normally unenforceable after two years[5].

1 *The Alexander* (1812) 1 Dods 278 at 282 per Sir W Scott (sails and rigging); *The Dundee* (1823) 1 Hag Adm 109 at 124 per Lord Stowell (fishing gear); *The Victor* (1860) Lush 72; *The Leo* (1862) Lush 444 (freight); *The Mary Ann* (1865) LR 1 A & E 8 at 11 per Dr Lushington; *The Roecliff* (1869) LR 2 A & E 363.
2 *The Mellona* (1848) 3 Wm Rob 16 at 21 per Dr Lushington; *Dean v Richards, The Europa* (1863) 2 Moo PCCNS 1. A subsequent owner cannot be made liable to the extent of the freight earned by the ship at the time of the collision: *The Mellona* at 25, 26 per Dr Lushington.
3 *The Neptune* (1824) 1 Hag Adm 227; *Harmer v Bell, The Bold Buccleugh* (1852) 7 Moo PCC 267; *The Annie* (1886) 12 PD 50, 6 Asp MLC 117.
4 *Smith v Plummer* (1818) 1 B & Ald 575 at 582 per Lord Ellenborough CJ; *Morgan v Castlegate Steamship Co, The Castlegate* [1893] AC 38, 7 Asp MLC 284, HL. Thus, freight collected and paid into a bank cannot be arrested: *The Kaleten* (1914) 30 TLR 572.
5 See PARA 991.

969. Salvage of property. The lien for salvage is created by the rendering of salvage services to a maritime res or, in certain circumstances, by the saving of life[1] from a ship[2]. The lien attaches to the ship, freight and cargo severally but not jointly, and each is liable to contribute towards the salvage in proportion to its value[3], but cannot, except in cases of express agreement, be made liable for the salvage due from the other[4]. The lien accrues immediately upon the performance of the salvage services[5] and attaches to the salved vessel, her cargo and freight where freight has been saved[6]. It is unaffected by any change in the ownership or possession of the salved property[7], and the benefit of it can be lost only by the laches of the salvor[8]. A lien for salvage services rendered is normally unenforceable after two years[9].

1 Nothing in the Salvage Convention (ie the International Convention on Salvage 1989 (London, 28 April 1989; Cm 1526): see PARA 851) affects the salvor's maritime lien under any international convention or national law: see art 20(1); and PARA 915. The salvor may not, however, enforce

his maritime lien when satisfactory security for his claim, including interest and costs, has been duly tendered or provided: see art 20(2); and PARA 915. As to the right to salvage for saving life see PARA 864.

2   See *Bligh v Simpson, The Fusilier* (1865) Brown & Lush 341 at 344, PC, per Dr Lushington; *The Schiller (Cargo ex)* (1877) 2 PD 145 at 149, 3 Asp MLC 439 at 422, CA, per Brett LJ. See also PARA 114 (Admiralty jurisdiction in respect of salvage of aircraft). The maritime res in salvage must be a ship or part of a ship or her apparel or cargo (*Falcke v Scottish Imperial Insurance Co* (1886) 34 ChD 234 at 248, CA, per Bowen LJ; *Wells v Gas Float Whitton No 2 (Owners), The Gas Float Whitton No 2* [1897] AC 337, 8 Asp MLC 272, HL), but does not include ships or property of the Crown or of a foreign state, even though the property is carried in a private vessel, or private property on board a foreign warship which for public purposes is taking care of it (*The Constitution* (1879) 4 PD 39, 4 Asp MLC 79; *The Parlement Belge* (1880) 5 PD 197, 4 Asp MLC 234, CA; cf *The Bertie* (1886) 6 Asp MLC 26 (where a lien was enforced against the ship and freight where she carried government stores)); or wearing apparel of the passengers, master and crew, and effects for their daily use (*The Willem III* (1871) LR 3 A & E 487, 1 Asp MLC 129).

3   *The Westminster* (1841) 1 Wm Rob 229 at 233 per Dr Lushington; *The Charlotte Wylie* (1846) 2 Wm Rob 495. The lien cannot be enforced if the ship belongs to the Crown (*Young v SS Scotia* [1903] AC 501, 9 Asp MLC 485, PC), or is under requisition by the Crown (*The Broadmayne* [1916] P 64, 13 Asp MLC 356, CA), but is enforceable after the ship is released from requisition (*The Meandros* [1925] P 61, 16 Asp MLC 476).

4   *The Westminster* (1841) 1 Wm Rob 229; *The Charlotte Wylie* (1846) 2 Wm Rob 495 at 497 per Dr Lushington; *The Pyrennee* (1863) Brown & Lush 189; *The Raisby* (1885) 10 PD 114, 5 Asp MLC 473; *The Prinz Heinrich* (1888) 13 PD 31, 6 Asp MLC 273; *The Cumbrian* (1887) 6 Asp MLC 151.

5   *The Mary Anne* (1865) LR 1 A & E 8 at 11 per Dr Lushington.

6   *The Westminster* (1841) 1 Wm Rob 229; *The Charlotte Wylie* (1846) 2 Wm Rob 495.

7   *The Nymphe* (1856) Sw 86 at 87 per Dr Lushington.

8   *The Royal Arch* (1857) Sw 269 at 285 per Dr Lushington; *The Goulandris* [1927] P 182 at 195, 17 Asp MLC 209 at 215 per Bateson J.

9   See PARA 991.

970. Seamen's wages.

The lien for the wages[1] of the master and seamen[2] attaches to the ship and freight and every part of it[3], provided that the wages have been earned on board the ship[4] under an ordinary mariner's contract[5]. It does not affect the right to the lien that the master and crew were engaged by some person who had no right to engage them, so long as they have earned the wages on the ship[6]. This lien is not dependent on the earning of freight[7], but, if it does not attach to the ship, it cannot attach to the freight, for a lien on freight is consequential to the lien on the ship[8]. The lien for wages travels with the res into whosesoever possession it may come[9].

1   'Wages' includes subsistence money, viaticum (ie any sort of travel allowance), compensation for wrongful dismissal, money allowance instead of food, and a bonus to a master to stand by a ship and bring her home: *The Madonna d'Idra* (1811) 1 Dods 37 at 40; *Phillips v Highland Rly Co, The Ferret* (1883) 8 App Cas 329, 5 Asp MLC 94, PC; *The Tergeste* [1903] P 26, 9 Asp MLC 356; *The British Trade* [1924] P 104, 16 Asp MLC 296; *Cassa Nazionale della Previdenza Marinara v Proceeds of Sale of Italian SS Acrux, The Acrux* [1965] P 391, [1965] 2 All ER 323, [1965] 1 Lloyd's Rep 565. As to claims for severance pay and wages in lieu of notice see *The Tacoma City* [1990] 1 Lloyd's Rep 408.

2   As to who may sue for, and the recovery of, such wages see PARAS 127–132, 484 et seq. See also *Ross v Walker* (1765) 2 Wils 264 at 265. It is doubtful whether a pilot has a lien: *The Ambatielos, The Cephalonia* [1923] P 68, 16 Asp MLC 120; but cf *The Dowthorpe* (1843) 2 Wm Rob 73; and *La Constancia* (1846) 4 Notes of Cases 512.

3   *The Neptune* (1824) 1 Hag Adm 227 at 238 per Lord Stowell. See also *The Sydney Cove* (1815) 2 Dods 11 at 13 per Lord Stowell; *Bank of America National Trust and Savings Association v Epidavros Gulf Shipping Co SA, The Cape Sounion* [1990] 2 Lloyd's Rep 329.

4   *Morgan v Castlegate Steamship Co, The Castlegate* [1893] AC 38 at 52, 7 Asp MLC 284 at 288, HL, per Lord Watson.

5   A lien attaches only in respect of an ordinary contract of employment. As to the contract of employment generally see EMPLOYMENT vol 39 (2014) PARA 1 et seq.
     The scope of a master's lien for wages is the same as that of a seaman: *The Ever Success* [1999] 1 Lloyd's Rep 824. Under a special contract, neither a master nor a seaman has a lien for wages or for damages for wrongful dismissal: *The Sydney Cove* (1815) 2 Dods 11; *The British Trade*

[1924] P 104, 16 Asp MLC 296; *The Great Eastern* (1867) LR 1 A & E 384. In *The British Trade* it was, however, conceded that wages under a special contract, so far as earned on board, conferred a lien.

6 *Phillips v Highland Rly Co, The Ferret* (1883) 8 App Cas 329, 5 Asp MLC 94, PC (seamen earning wages under person attempting to steal ship); *The Edwin* (1864) Brown & Lush 281 (master appointed by person fraudulently in possession).

7 See *Hawkins v Twizell* (1856) 5 E & B 883.

8 *Smith v Plummer* (1818) 1 B & Ald 575 at 582 per Lord Ellenborough CJ; *Morgan v Castlegate Steamship Co, The Castlegate* [1893] AC 38, 7 Asp MLC 284, HL.

9 *The Nymph* (1856) Sw 86 at 87 per Dr Lushington; *The Fairport* (1882) 8 PD 48 at 55, 5 Asp MLC 62 at 63.

971. Disbursements and liabilities. Disbursements and liabilities properly made or incurred by a master on account of a ship give him a lien on the ship, which may be enforced in the same way as his lien for wages[1]; but the only disbursements and liabilities which can create this lien are those made by the master by virtue of his general authority and in the ordinary course of his employment, and for which he can pledge the owner's credit[2].

1 See the Merchant Shipping Act 1995 s 41; and PARA 480; *Morgan v Castlegate Steamship Co, The Castlegate* [1893] AC 38 at 46, 7 Asp MLC 284 at 286, HL, per Lord Herschell; *The Ripon City* [1897] P 226 at 232, 234, 242, 247, 8 Asp MLC 304 at 308, 311, 312 per Gorell Barnes J. The costs of a master in unsuccessfully defending an action on a dishonoured bill of exchange drawn by him on his owners for fuel supplied are not liabilities properly incurred unless the defence was reasonably necessary in the interest of the ship: *The Elmville (No 2)* [1904] P 422, 10 Asp MLC 23.

2 *The Ripon City* [1897] P 226, 8 Asp MLC 304. It is not necessary that the master should have been appointed by the real owners; it is sufficient if he was appointed by persons whom the owners have allowed to have possession and control of the ship: *The Turgot* (1886) 11 PD 21, 5 Asp MLC 548; *Morgan v Castlegate Steamship Co, The Castlegate* [1893] AC 38, 7 Asp MLC 284, HL; *The Orienta* [1895] P 49, 7 Asp MLC 529, CA; *The Cairo, Watson and Parker v Gregory* (1908) 11 Asp MLC 161. As to the power of a master to bind ship and cargo see PARA 435.

972. Bottomry and respondentia. As soon as a bottomry or respondentia bond[1] is executed, a lien attaches to the property hypothecated, and continues to attach until the total destruction of the property[2]. The lien for a bottomry bond travels with the property in respect of which the claim is brought (or privilege claimed), into whosesoever possession it may come[3].

1 As to bottomry and respondentia generally, and as to the hypothecation of the cargo, see PARAS 133, 435.

2 *Thomson v Royal Exchange Assurance Co* (1813) 1 M & S 30; *Stephen v Broomfield, The Great Pacific* (1869) LR 2 PC 516.

3 *The Nymph* (1856) Sw 86 at 87 per Dr Lushington.

(2) STATUTORY AND POSSESSORY LIENS

973. Statutory lien. A statutory lien attaches when property is arrested in a claim in rem under Admiralty jurisdiction[1]. The Admiralty jurisdiction of the High Court, including the cases in which that jurisdiction may be invoked by an action in personam, is defined by the Senior Courts Act 1981[2].

A statutory lien arising when property is arrested in an Admiralty claim in rem is of no avail against any subsisting charge on the property or against a purchaser in good faith for value[3].

Harbour and dock authorities generally have a right under their own private statute to detain vessels in respect of damage to the harbour or dock works[4], to detain and sell a ship in respect of dock and harbour dues[5] and to take possession

of and remove and sell wrecks and other obstructions and out of the proceeds to
reimburse themselves for the conservancy expenses incurred[6].

1　*The Cella* (1888) 13 PD 82, 6 Asp MLC 293, CA; *John Carlbom & Co Ltd v Zafiro (Owners),
　　The Zafiro* [1960] P 1, [1959] 2 All ER 537, [1959] 1 Lloyd's Rep 359; *Richmond Shipping Ltd
　　v D/S and A/S Vestland, The Vestland* [1980] 2 Lloyd's Rep 171. As to Admiralty claims in rem
　　generally see PARA 158 et seq.
2　See the Senior Courts Act 1981 ss 20, 21; and PARA 81 et seq.
3　*Giovanni Dapueto v James Wyllie & Co, The Pieve Superiore* (1874) LR 5 PC 482, 2 Asp MLC
　　319, PC; *The Aneroid* (1877) 2 PD 189; *The James W Elwell* [1921] P 351, 15 Asp MLC 418
　　(where a ship had been seized in execution by the sheriff at the instance of judgment creditors and
　　claims in rem were instituted by the suppliers of goods, materials etc and by the master for wages;
　　it was held that the suppliers of goods, materials etc had no rights at all until they arrested the res
　　and had, therefore, to be postponed to the execution creditors, but that, as the ship when seized
　　by the sheriff was incumbered with the master's lien for wages, the master's claim had priority over
　　the claim of the execution creditors).
4　The right arises where the authority's special Act incorporates the Harbours, Docks, and Piers
　　Clauses Act 1847 s 74 (see PORTS AND HARBOURS vol 85 (2012) PARA 155), or includes similar
　　provisions. The mere right to detain does not involve a right to sell and has been held to amount
　　to a possessory lien: see *The Veritas* [1901] P 304, 9 Asp MLC 237; *Mersey Docks and Harbour
　　Board v Hay, The Countess* [1923] AC 345, 490, 16 Asp MLC 161, HL. As to possessory liens see
　　PARA 974.
5　See the Harbours, Docks, and Piers Clauses Act 1847 s 44; and PORTS AND HARBOURS vol 85
　　(2012) PARA 77.
6　See the Harbours, Docks, and Piers Clauses Act 1847 s 56; and PORTS AND HARBOURS vol 85
　　(2012) PARA 92; the Merchant Shipping Act 1995 s 252; and PARA 939.

974. Possessory lien. A possessory lien is the right of a person in whose
possession a ship or her appurtenances is or are to retain possession of her or them
until payment or discharge of a debt or obligation due to that person in respect of
her[1]. Such a right belongs to one who repairs, alters or otherwise bestows labour
or skill on a ship, and retains possession of her[2]. There is no power to realise the
security, even though expenses and inconvenience must be incurred in keeping it[3].

1　Possessory liens (also sometimes described as common law liens) are now usually referred to as
　　legal liens: see LIEN vol 68 (2016) PARAS 802, 817 et seq. See also the Torts (Interference with
　　Goods) Act 1977 s 12 (bailee's power of sale of uncollected goods); and BAILMENT AND PLEDGE
　　vol 4 (2011) PARA 173.
2　*Re Strickland, ex p Bland* (1814) 2 Rose 91; *Franklin v Hosier* (1821) 4 B & Ald 341; *Smith's
　　Dock Co Ltd v The St Merriel (Owners), The St Merriel* [1963] P 247, [1963] 1 All ER 537, [1963]
　　1 Lloyd's Rep 63; *Delantera Amadora SA v Bristol Channel Shiprepairers Ltd and Swansea Dry
　　Dock, The Katingaki* [1976] 2 Lloyd's Rep 372 (where the lien extended to the cost of materials
　　and work done, but did not cover dock charges or loss or damage to business); *Fraser v Equatorial
　　Shipping Co Ltd and Equatorial Lines Ltd, The Ijaola* [1979] 1 Lloyd's Rep 103, DC (where a
　　consulting engineer was entitled to retain engine parts against advance payments because he had
　　incurred personal liability by hiring sub-contractors); *Metall Market OOO v Vitorio Shipping Co
　　Ltd; The Lehmann Timber* [2013] EWCA Civ 650, [2013] 2 All ER (Comm) 585; *Babcock Fitzroy
　　Ltd v The Ship M/V Southern Pasifika* [2012] NZHC 1254, [2012] 2 Lloyd's Rep 423. It is not
　　necessary in the case of repairs effected under a contract that they should be completed before the
　　right to retain possession accrues: *The Tergeste* [1903] P 26, 9 Asp MLC 356. A ship may be under
　　the control and in possession of a repairer in a public dock: *The Rellim* (1922) 39 TLR 41. See also
　　Re Westlake, ex p Willoughby (1881) 16 ChD 604; *Earle's Shipbuilding and Engineering Co v
　　Aktieselskabet D/S Gefion and Forth Shipbuilding and Engineering Co* (1922) 10 Ll L Rep 305,
　　CA. The mere fact that a repairer keeps some of his employees working on board, or leaves some
　　of his plant or tools on board, after the vessel has left his premises does not, however, necessarily
　　mean that he has retained such possession as will justify a possessory lien: see *The Scio* (1867) LR
　　1 A & E 353; *Olsen Ugelstad v GT Gray & Co* (1921) 9 Ll L Rep 565. See also *The Gregos* [1985]
　　2 Lloyd's Rep 347.
3　*Somes v British Empire Shipping Co* (1860) 8 HL Cas 338; *Thames Iron Works Co v Patent
　　Derrick Co* (1860) 1 John & H 93. The holder of a possessory lien cannot voluntarily give up
　　possession and still retain his rights as a possessory lien holder, nor has the court power to make
　　a declaration to the contrary effect: *The Gaupen* (1925) 22 Ll L Rep 57; *The Ally* [1952] 2 Lloyd's
　　Rep 427.

(3) RANKING OF LIENS

975. Priority of liens generally. It would seem that the determination of the priority of liens over one another rests on no rigid application of any rules but on the principle that equity must be done to the parties in the circumstances of each particular case[1]. There is, however, a general order of priority, and there are certain general rules which, in the absence of special circumstances, the court tends to apply. As to the general order of priority, the right of a dock and harbour authority exercising its powers under the Harbours, Docks, and Piers Clauses Act 1847[2], or under the similar provisions of its special Act, to detain a ship in respect of damage to dock works[3], or to detain and sell a ship in respect of dock and harbour dues[4], or to take possession of and sell a wreck in respect of conservancy charges[5], overrides all maritime liens.

Next in order of priority are maritime liens; these usually rank above mortgages[6] and statutory liens. A mortgage generally has precedence over a statutory lien. A possessory lien ranks after all liens which have attached before, and before all liens which attach after, the possessory lien holder has taken possession of the ship[7].

1 *The Stream Fisher* [1927] P 73 at 82, 26 Ll L Rep 4 at 7; *The Elin* (1883) 8 PD 39, 5 Asp MLC 120 (on appeal 8 PD 129 at 130, 5 Asp MLC 120 at 122, CA, per Brett MR).
2 See PARA 973.
3 *The Veritas* [1901] P 304, 9 Asp MLC 237; *Mersey Docks and Harbour Board v Hay, The Countess* [1923] AC 345 at 374, 16 Asp MLC 161 at 170, HL, per Lord Atkinson.
4 *The Emilie Millon* [1905] 2 KB 817, 10 Asp MLC 162, CA; *Mersey Docks and Harbour Board v Hay, The Countess* [1923] AC 345, 16 Asp MLC 161, HL; *Corps v Paddle Steamer Queen of the South (Owners) (Port of London Authority intervening), The Queen of the South* [1968] P 449, [1968] 1 All ER 1163, [1968] 1 Lloyd's Rep 182. The exercise of a statutory power of sale is not within the ambit of priorities. Priorities are first considered after any reimbursement has taken place, and operate in relation to the residue, if any, paid into court to the ultimate benefit of claimants who have sufficient priority: *The Charger, British Transport Docks Board v Owners of Proceeds of Sale of SS or Vessels Charger, Probe, Vigia, Dideki, Surveyor, Constellation, Errol and Regency* [1966] 3 All ER 117 at 119, [1966] 1 Lloyd's Rep 670 at 672 per Karminski J (where a claim in respect of dock dues for priority over mortgagees against the proceeds of sale of ships by a harbour authority which had not exercised its power to detain and sell under the Harbours, Docks, and Piers Clauses Act 1847 s 44 (as to which see PORTS AND HARBOURS vol 85 (2012) PARA 77) was rejected).
5 *The Sea Spray* [1907] P 133, 10 Asp MLC 462. In *The Veritas* [1901] P 304, 9 Asp MLC 237, it seems to have been admitted that the right was paramount and good against all the world including the holders of the maritime liens.
6 As to the priority of mortgagees see PARA 321.
7 As to the enforcement of liens see PARA 987 et seq.

976. Priority of maritime liens generally. Maritime liens are of two classes:
(1)   those arising ex delicto; and
(2)   those arising ex contractu or quasi ex contractu, such as wages, bottomry and salvage.

Although all maritime liens, whether arising ex delicto or ex contractu or quasi ex contractu, are the same[1], in practice they usually rank according to two broad principles. First, liens arising ex delicto, in the absence of laches, rank as between themselves pari passu[2], but in priority to liens arising ex contractu[3], except a subsequent lien for salvage[4]. Secondly, as a general rule, maritime liens arising ex contractu or quasi ex contractu, that is to say those for master's wages, disbursements and liabilities, seamen's wages, bottomry[5] and salvage, are payable in the inverse order of their attachment on the property in respect of which the claim is brought (or privilege claimed)[6], although as between themselves masters' wages and seamen's wages rank pari passu[7].

1   *The Stream Fisher* [1927] P 73 at 79, 26 Ll L Rep 4 at 6 per Bateson J. See *Bankers Trust International Ltd v Todd Shipyards Corpn, The Halcyon Isle* [1981] AC 221, [1980] 3 All ER 197, PC; *Reiter Petroleum Inc v The Ship 'Sam Hawk'* [2016] FCAFC 26, [2016] 2 Lloyd's Rep 639.
2   *The Stream Fisher* [1927] P 73, 26 Ll L Rep 4.
3   *The Aline* (1839) 1 Wm Rob 111; *The Benares* (1850) 7 Notes of Cases, Supp 1; *The Linda Flor* (1857) Sw 309; *The Veritas* [1901] P 304, 9 Asp MLC 237.
4   *The Sea Spray* [1907] P 133, 10 Asp MLC 462; *The Inna* [1938] P 148, 60 Ll L Rep 414. See also *The Georg* [1894] P 330, 7 Asp MLC 476, and *The Elin* (1883) 8 PD 39, 5 Asp MLC 120 (on appeal 8 PD 129, 5 Asp MLC 120 at 122, CA), in which cases it seems to have been admitted by the damage claimants that they ranked after claimants for subsequent salvage.
5   *The Rhadamanthe* (1813) 1 Dods 201; cf *The Exeter* (1799) 1 Ch Rob 173 (where, although the bonds were given at different dates, they were paid pro rata on the grounds that the bonds had been given on one advertisement and the bondholders had acted in privity and concert). As to priority of several loans on bottomry see PARA 980.
6   *The Hope* (1873) 1 Asp MLC 563. See also *The Veritas* [1901] P 304 at 312, 313, 9 Asp MLC 237 at 241 per Gorell Barnes J.
7   See PARA 982.

977. Damage. The lien for damage has priority over wages, whether earned before or after the collision[1], and over a prior bottomry bond, but not over a subsequent bottomry bond to the extent of the increased value of the vessel where the bond is given by a stranger who has advanced money for repairs[2]. Such a lien also has priority over prior salvage[3], but not over subsequent salvage services because they have preserved the property for the claimants in respect of damage[4].

1   *The Linda Flor* (1857) Sw 309; *The Duna* (1861) 1 Mar LC 159; *The Elin* (1883) 8 PD 39, 5 Asp MLC 120 (on appeal 8 PD 129, 5 Asp MLC 120 at 122, CA); *The Chimera* (1852) cited in *The Elin* at 131. This rule applies even to the crews of foreign ships claiming for wages earned subsequently to the collision. It is not based on the rule as to priority of liens ex delicto (see PARA 976), but on the Admiralty equitable doctrine that it is unjust to the owners of the damaged ship to allow the fund to be diminished by the payment of wages when the members of the crew have a remedy in personam, which the owners of the damaged ship may not have. The position may be different in the case of a bankrupt owner: see *The Linda Flor* at 310 per Dr Lushington.
2   *Harmer v Bell, The Bold Buccleugh* (1852) 7 Moo PCC 267 at 285; *The Aline* (1839) 1 Wm Rob 111 at 118. As to the ranking of damages liens, wages liens and liens secured under letters of undertaking see *Owners of the Carbonnade v Owners of the Ruta; Harding (Owner of the Luta II) v Owners of the Luta* [2000] 1 All ER (Comm) 847, [2000] 1 WLR 2068, [2000] 1 Lloyd's Rep 359.
3   *The Veritas* [1901] P 304, 9 Asp MLC 237.
4   *A-G v Norstedt* (1816) 3 Price 97; *The Galam (Cargo ex)* (1863) Brown & Lush 167 at 181, PC; *The Elin* (1883) 8 PD 39, 5 Asp MLC 120 (on appeal 8 PD 129, 5 Asp MLC 120 at 122, CA); *The Sea Spray* [1907] P 133, 10 Asp MLC 462 (expenses of wreck-raising authority); *The Inna* [1938] P 148, 60 Ll L Rep 414. See also PARA 976 note 4.

978. Several actions for damage arising against one ship. Where several claimants seek to satisfy liens for damage against property in respect of which the claim is brought (or privilege claimed), whether arising out of the same collision or out of several collisions, their respective liens, in the absence of laches, rank pari passu without regard to the various times when they attached[1]. This result is not affected by the fact that the various claimants obtain their decrees on different dates; the claimant who obtains the first decree is no longer in a specially privileged position, as in modern practice the decree is always made subject to any question of priorities being subsequently determined[2].

1   *The Stream Fisher* [1927] P 73, 26 Ll L Rep 4.
2   *The Stream Fisher* [1927] P 73 at 83, 26 Ll L Rep 4 at 8 per Bateson J; cf *The Africano* [1894] P 141, 7 Asp MLC 427; *The James W Elwell* [1921] P 351, 15 Asp MLC 418.

979. Salvage. The lien for salvage[1] ranks before all other liens which attached before the service was rendered, because the salvage service has saved the property for the benefit of the persons interested[2]. Thus, it has priority over the lien for wages earned before[3] the service[4], or for damage done before the service[5], but is postponed to subsequent liens[6].

Claims for salvage of property take priority in the inverse order of attachment[7]; but, where the efforts of different sets of salvors are directed to a common object and not to separate salvages, their claims will rank pari passu[8].

1 Nothing in the Salvage Convention (ie the International Convention on Salvage 1989 (London, 28 April 1989; Cm 1526): see PARA 851) affects the salvor's maritime lien under any international convention or national law: see art 20(1); and PARA 915. The salvor may not, however, enforce his maritime lien when satisfactory security for his claim, including interest and costs, has been duly tendered or provided: see art 20(2); and PARA 915.

2 *A-G v Norstedt* (1816) 3 Price 97; *The Galam (Cargo ex)* (1863) Brown & Lush 167 at 181; *The Elin* (1883) 8 PD 39, 5 Asp MLC 120 (on appeal 8 PD 129, 5 Asp MLC 120 at 122, CA); *The Veritas* [1901] P 304, 9 Asp MLC 237.

3 A salvage lien also has priority over a lien for wages earned after the service: *The Lyrma (No 2)* [1978] 2 Lloyd's Rep 30.

4 *The Sabina* (1842) 7 Jur 182.

5 *The Inna* [1938] P 148, 60 Ll L Rep 414; *The Elin* (1883) 8 PD 39, 5 Asp MLC 120 (on appeal 8 PD 129, 5 Asp MLC 120 at 122, CA).

6 *The Selina* (1842) 2 Notes of Cases 18; *The Edina* (1855) 4 WR 91; *The Veritas* [1901] P 304, 9 Asp MLC 237.

7 *The Veritas* [1901] P 304, 9 Asp MLC 237.

8 *The Russland* [1924] P 55 at 60, 16 Asp MLC 288 at 291 per Hill J.

980. Bottomry. Liens for bottomry[1] take precedence in the inverse order of the dates of execution[2] except that, where several bond-holders acting in privity and concert give bonds on different dates, the bonds will be paid pro rata[3]. A bottomry bond takes precedence over a master's lien for wages earned and disbursements incurred on a previous voyage to that during which the bottomry bond is given[4], claims for the supply of goods, materials etc[5], a mortgage made during the voyage upon which the bond was executed if enforced within a reasonable time[6], prior salvage[7] and over prior damage to the extent only of the increased value of the ship when the money has been advanced to effect the repair of such damage[8].

It is postponed to the master's lien for wages earned and disbursements incurred after the date of the bond[9], to seamen's wages, subsistence money and viaticum whenever earned[10], to subsequent damage[11], and to subsequent salvage[12].

1 As to bottomry generally see PARAS 133, 435.

2 *The Rhadamanthe* (1813) 1 Dods 201; *The Sydney Cove* (1815) 2 Dods 1; *The Betsey* (1813) 1 Dods 289; *The Eliza* (1833) 3 Hag Adm 87.

3 *The Exeter* (1799) 1 Ch Rob 173.

4 *The Hope* (1873) 1 Asp MLC 563.

5 *The William F Safford* (1860) Lush 69 (this is so even though the claim has been pronounced for before the bond was put in suit). See also PARA 983 note 1.

6 *The Royal Arch* (1857) Sw 269; *The Helgoland* (1859) Sw 491.

7 *The Selina* (1842) 2 Notes of Cases 18.

8 *The Aline* (1839) 1 Wm Rob 111 at 118.

9 *The Salcia* (1862) Lush 545; *The Hope* (1873) 1 Asp MLC 563 at 567.

10 *The Madonna d'Idra* (1811) 1 Dods 37 at 40; *The Union* (1860) 1 Lush 128; *The Constancia* (1866) 15 WR 183; cf *The Jonathan Goodhue* (1859) Sw 524; *The Janet Wilson* (1857) Sw 261.

11 *The Aline* (1839) 1 Wm Rob 111.

12 *The William F Safford* (1866) Lush 69.

981. Master's lien for wages and disbursements. The master's lien for wages and disbursements has priority over a bottomry bond given before the wages are earned[1] unless the master is personally liable on the bond[2], over salvage rendered before the wages were earned[3], over a shipwright's possessory lien to the extent that the master's lien originated before the shipwright took possession[4], and, where the master's lien has already attached, over the claim of a judgment creditor who is in possession of the property in respect of which the claim is brought (or privilege claimed), by reason of execution levied by the sheriff under a writ of control[5], over the fees and expenses of a sheriff incurred in seizing a ship under a writ of control[6], and over a mortgage[7], unless the master has guaranteed payment of it[8].

The master's lien for disbursements ranks on the same footing as his lien for wages[9]. Claims by successive masters for disbursements rank pari passu, and not in the inverse order of their attachment on the property in respect of which the claim is brought (or privilege claimed)[10].

The master's claim for wages ranks pari passu with the seamen's claim for wages[11]; but the master's lien is postponed to a bottomry bond given after the wages earned[12], to subsequent salvage[13], to damage[14], and, when the master is part owner and ordered the repairs or gave the instructions, to the claim of a person who has supplied goods, materials etc[15], and to a solicitor's lien for costs[16].

1 *The Salacia* (1862) Lush 545. See also *The Hope* (1873) 1 Asp MLC 563 at 567.
2 *The William* (1858) Sw 346; *The Jonathan Goodhue* (1859) Sw 524.
3 *The Selina* (1842) 2 Notes of Cases 18; *The Mons* [1932] P 109, 43 Ll L Rep 151.
4 *The Gustaf* (1862) Lush 506; *The Immacolata Concezione* (1883) 9 PD 37, 5 Asp MLC 208; *The Tergeste* [1903] P 26, 9 Asp MLC 356 (the lien for wages includes subsistence money and viaticum).
5 *The James W Elwell* [1921] P 351, 15 Asp MLC 418. As to writs of control generally see CIVIL PROCEDURE vol 12A (2015) PARA 1379 et seq.
6 *The Ile de Ceylan* [1922] P 256, 16 Asp MLC 23.
7 *The Feronia* (1868) LR 2 A & E 65; *The Tagus* [1903] P 44, 9 Asp MLC 371. The master of a foreign ship has priority in England for all his wages and disbursements, even though by the lex loci his rights are limited to the debts incurred on the last voyage; he is also entitled in respect of wages as a seaman whilst acting as supercargo, and for disbursements made to crew on account of wages: *The Tagus*.
8 *The Bangor Castle* (1896) 8 Asp MLC 156.
9 *The Mons* [1932] P 109, 43 Ll L Rep 151.
10 *The Mons* [1932] P 109, 43 Ll L Rep 151.
11 *The Royal Wells* [1985] QB 86, [1984] 3 All ER 193, [1984] 2 Lloyd's Rep 255.
12 *The Hope* (1873) 1 Asp MLC 563.
13 *The Selina* (1842) 2 Notes of Cases 18; *The Mons* [1932] P 109, 43 Ll L Rep 151.
14 *The Linda Flor* (1857) Sw 309; *The Panthea* (1871) 1 Asp MLC 133; *The Elin* (1883) 8 PD 39, 5 Asp MLC 120 (on appeal 8 PD 129, 5 Asp MLC 120 at 122, CA).
15 *The Jenny Lind* (1872) LR 3 A & E 529, 1 Asp MLC 294; *The Eva* [1921] P 454, 15 Asp MLC 424. See also PARA 983 note 1.
16 *The Heinrich* (1872) LR 3 A & E 505, 1 Asp MLC 260.

982. Seamen's lien for wages. The seamen's lien for wages takes priority over a bottomry bond whenever given[1], over the claim of a mortgagee[2], over a claim for goods, materials etc supplied to the ship[3], over towage[4], and over a shipwright's possessory lien to the extent of the wages earned up to the time the vessel is put into the hands of the shipwright[5]; but their claim for wages ranks pari passu with the master's claim for wages[6].

The seamen's lien is postponed to a damage lien[7], to salvage rendered after the wages are earned[8], to a shipwright's lien from the time he had possession[9], and to the claim of a dock or harbour authority in respect of dock and harbour dues[10], damage to dock or harbour works[11] or conservancy charges for the removal of wrecks and other obstructions[12].

1 *The Madonna d'Idra* (1811) 1 Dods 37 at 40; *The Sydney Cove* (1815) 2 Dods 11; *The Union* (1860) Lush 128; *The William F Safford* (1860) Lush 69; cf *The Jonathan Goodhue* (1859) Sw 524; *The Janet Wilson* (1857) Sw 261. As to the priority ranking of wages claims as a maritime lien see *The Ruta* [2000] ICR 1024 at 1028, [2000] 1 Lloyd's Rep 359.
2 *The Prince George* (1837) 3 Hag Adm 376.
3 *The Queen (No 2)* (1869) 19 LT 706.
4 *The Andalina* (1886) 12 PD 1, 6 Asp MLC 62.

5   *The Immacolata Concezione* (1883) 9 PD 37, 5 Asp MLC 208 (the lien for wages includes subsistence money and viaticum); *The Tergeste* [1903] P 26, 9 Asp MLC 356.

6   *The Royal Wells* [1985] QB 86, [1984] 3 All ER 193, [1984] 2 Lloyd's Rep 255.

7   *The Benares* (1850) 7 Notes of Cases, Supp 1; *The Linda Flor* (1857) Sw 309; *The Elin* (1883) 8 PD 39, 5 Asp MLC 120 (on appeal 8 PD 129 at 130, 5 Asp MLC 120 at 122, CA).

8   *The Sabina* (1842) 7 Jur 182 (and see apparently the same case reported as *The Selina* (1842) 2 Notes of Cases 18); *The Gustaf* (1862) Lush 506. The priority of wages earned after a salvage service does not seem to have been determined. In *The Mons* [1932] P 109, 43 Ll L Rep 151, the order of priority was expressly stated to be in accordance with an admission by the salvors.

9   *The Gustaf* (1862) Lush 506; *The Immacolata Concezione* (1883) 9 PD 37, 5 Asp MLC 208; *The Tergeste* [1903] P 26, 9 Asp MLC 356.

10 *The Emilie Millon* [1905] 2 KB 817, 10 Asp MLC 162, CA (a dock company which is authorised to detain a ship until the rates are paid can do so notwithstanding that there are maritime liens on the ship before she entered the dock); *Mersey Docks and Harbour Board v Hay, The Countess* [1923] AC 345, 16 Asp MLC 161, HL; *The Charger, British Transport Docks Board v Owners of Proceeds of Sale of SS or Vessels Charger, Probe, Vigia, Dideki, Surveyor, Constellation, Errol and Regency* [1966] 3 All ER 117, [1966] 1 Lloyd's Rep 670 (where a claim for priority in respect of dock dues by a harbour authority which had not exercised its power to sell a vessel under the Harbours, Docks, and Piers Clauses Act 1847 s 44 (as to which see PORTS AND HARBOURS vol 85 (2012) PARA 77) was rejected). See PARA 975.

11 *The Veritas* [1901] P 304, 9 Asp MLC 237; *Mersey Docks and Harbour Board v Hay, The Countess* [1923] AC 345, 16 Asp MLC 161, HL.

12 *The Sea Spray* [1907] P 133, 10 Asp MLC 462.

983. Supply of goods, materials etc.

The statutory lien for the supply of goods and materials to, and the repair of, a ship and disbursements made by a master, shipper, charterer or agent on account of a ship[1] as a general rule ranks after maritime liens but takes priority over a master's lien for wages and disbursements when supplied by the order of a master who is part owner of the ship[2]. It is postponed to a mortgage[3], to execution creditors at whose instance the sheriff has seized the property in respect of which the claim is brought (or privilege claimed) before the person supplying the goods, materials etc has arrested it[4], and to the solicitor's costs in defending an action brought against the ship before the goods etc were supplied[5].

Where there are several claims for the supply of goods, materials etc, they rank equally and are paid pro rata, provided that the holder of the lien is not guilty of laches in prosecuting his claim, because, when a ship is sold, the court holds the property not only for the first claimant but for all creditors of the same class who assert their claims before an unconditional decree is pronounced[6]. A claimant who supplies goods, materials etc to a ship which is already under arrest obtains no right to priority over other claimants for such supply, unless the goods, materials etc which he supplies are supplied with the sanction of the court[7]. The mere fact that claimants who have maritime liens (and thus have an interest in the preservation of the property in respect of which the claim is brought or privilege claimed) are benefited by the supply of goods, materials etc is not enough to give those claiming for the supply of goods, materials etc priority over those with maritime liens[8]. Nor will those claiming for the supply of goods, materials etc secure priority merely because their services have increased the value of the property[9].

1   See the Senior Courts Act 1981 s 20(2)(m), (n), (p); and PARAS 126, 127. The term 'necessaries' used to describe similar claims in earlier legislation (see eg the Supreme Court of Judicature (Consolidation) Act 1925 s 22(1)(a)(vii) (repealed)) is not used in the Senior Courts Act 1981. For a definition of 'necessaries' see *The Riga* (1872) LR 3 A & E 516, 1 Asp MLC 246. See also *The River Rima* [1987] 3 All ER 1, [1987] 2 Lloyd's Rep 106, CA; affd [1988] 2 All ER 641, [1988] 1 WLR 758, [1988] 2 Lloyd's Rep 193, HL. The supply of goods and materials to and the repair of a ship do not confer a maritime lien: *The Two Ellens* (1872) LR 4 PC 161; *Northcote v The Henrich Björn (Owners), The Henrich Björn* (1886) 11 App Cas 270, 6 Asp MLC 1, HL; *The Cella* (1888) 13 PD 82, CA; *The James W Elwell* [1921] P 351, 15 Asp MLC 418.

2 *The Jenny Lind* (1872) LR 3 A & E 529, 1 Asp MLC 294; *The Eva* [1921] P 454, 15 Asp MLC 424. As to merger of claim for necessaries in a bottomry bond see *The Elpis* (1872) LR 4 A & E 1, 1 Asp MLC 472.
3 *The Scio* (1867) LR 1 A & E 353; *The Zigurds* [1932] P 113, 18 Asp MLC 324 (where the mortgagee had priority over foreign necessaries men, ship repairers and stevedores). Where the mortgage is a foreign one, even though by the foreign law the claim for the supply of goods etc would be preferred, nevertheless in an English action the claim for the supply of goods etc will be postponed, since the law to be applied in distributing the proceeds is the lex fori: *The Colorado* [1923] P 102, 16 Asp MLC 145, CA; *Bankers Trust International Ltd v Todd Shipyards Corpn, The Halcyon Isle* [1981] AC 221, [1980] 3 All ER 197, PC. As to the lex fori see CONFLICT OF LAWS vol 19 (2011) PARA 313.
4 *The James W Elwell* [1921] P 351, 15 Asp MLC 418.
5 *The Heinrich* (1872) LR 3 A & E 505, 1 Asp MLC 260.
6 *The Africano* [1894] P 141, 7 Asp MLC 427; *The James W Elwell* [1921] P 351, 15 Asp MLC 418.
7 *The Rene* (1922) 16 Asp MLC 24; cf *The Zigurds* [1932] P 113 at 129, 18 Asp MLC 324 at 330.
8 *The Russland* [1924] P 55, 16 Asp MLC 288.
9 *The Zigurds* [1932] P 113, 18 Asp MLC 324.

984. Possessory lien. Possessory liens take priority over all claims arising after the ship is taken into possession, but are postponed to those liens which were created before that time, as the holder of the lien is presumed to have taken the ship into his possession with the obligations then upon her[1]. The mere fact that claimants with maritime liens have benefited by the work of the repairers is not, however, a sufficient reason why those maritime liens should be postponed to the repairers' possessory lien[2]. The statutory possessory lien of a dock or harbour authority overrides all maritime liens[3].

1 *The Gustaf* (1862) Lush 506 (salvage); *The Immacolata Concezione* (1883) 9 PD 37, 5 Asp MLC 208 (wages, subsistence money and viaticum); *The Tergeste* [1903] P 26, 9 Asp MLC 356 (wages, subsistence money and viaticum); see also *Babcock Fitzroy Ltd v The Ship M/V Southern Pasifika* [2012] NZHC 1254, [2012] 2 Lloyd's Rep 423. Possessory liens (also sometimes described as common law liens) are now usually referred to as legal liens: see LIEN vol 68 (2016) PARAS 802, 817 et seq.
2 *The Russland* [1924] P 55 at 59, 16 Asp MLC 288 at 291 per Hill J; cf *The Aline* (1839) 1 Wm Rob 111 at 118.
3 *Mersey Docks and Harbour Board v Hay, The Countess* [1923] AC 345, 16 Asp MLC 161, HL. See also PARA 975.

985. Solicitor's lien for costs. The solicitor's lien[1] for costs takes priority over claims for goods, materials etc supplied after the inception of the lien[2], and to the master's claim for wages when he is part owner and has instructed the solicitor[3]. It is postponed to the expense of sending home a shipwrecked foreign crew incurred by a foreign consul[4].

1 This lien is given by the Solicitors Act 1974 s 73: see LEGAL PROFESSIONS vol 66 (2015) PARA 783. As to the duties of the Admiralty court in making charging orders see *The Birnam Wood* [1907] P 1, 10 Asp MLC 325, CA (decided on similar provisions of the Solicitors Act 1860 s 28 (repealed)).
2 *The Soblomsten* (1866) LR 1 A & E 293; *The Heinrich* (1872) LR 3 A & E 505, 1 Asp MLC 260; and see PARA 983 note 1.
3 *The Heinrich* (1872) LR 3 A & E 505, 1 Asp MLC 260.
4 *The Constancia* (1866) 15 WR 183; *The Livietta* (1883) 8 PD 209 at 213, 5 Asp MLC 151 at 153.

986. Mode of determination of claims. While the rights of claimants may be determined by the lex loci or the law of the flag of the ship, all questions of priority of liens or claims are determined in England by the lex fori[1].

1 *The Union* (1860) Lush 128; *The Tagus* [1903] P 44, 9 Asp MLC 371; *The Colorado* [1923] P 102, 16 Asp MLC 145, CA; *The Zigurds* [1932] P 113, 18 Asp MLC 324 (revsd on another point [1933] P 87, CA; affd sub nom *Smith v Zigurds SS Owners and EA Casper, Edgar & Co Ltd* [1934] AC 209, 18 Asp MLC 475, HL). See also *Bankers Trust International Ltd v Todd Shipyards Corpn, The Halcyon Isle* [1981] AC 221, [1980] 3 All ER 197, PC; *Reiter Petroleum Inc v The Ship 'Sam Hawk'* [2016] FCAFC 26, [2016] 2 Lloyd's Rep 639. As to the lex fori see

CONFLICT OF LAWS vol 19 (2011) PARA 313. See also CONFLICT OF LAWS vol 19 (2011) PARA 326.

(4) ENFORCEMENT AND EXTINCTION OF LIENS

987. Enforcement of maritime liens. Maritime liens are enforced by a proceeding in rem[1], followed by the arrest, and if necessary by the sale, of the property in respect of which the claim is brought (or privilege claimed)[2]. To enforce such a lien, a court having Admiralty jurisdiction will seize the ship and forcibly dispossess those who claim to detain her or her apparel[3]. The court will seize and sell a ship even though she is in the possession of the holder of a possessory lien[4] or the sheriff at the instance of execution creditors[5]. Out of the proceeds of the sale the various claimants will be satisfied according to such rules of priority as are applicable to the case[6], the holder of the possessory lien retaining such rights of priority as he had while in possession[7] and the rights of the execution creditors being enforced[8]. Where the property in question belongs to a company registered in England and Wales which is being wound up by the court, that property may not be arrested after the commencement of the winding up[9]; and the proper procedure for enforcing a maritime lien in such an instance is by proceeding in the winding up, in which the maritime lien will have the same priority over other debts as if proceedings had been instituted in rem[10].

1 See the Senior Courts Act 1981 s 21(3); and PARA 93. See *Babcock Fitzroy Ltd v The Ship M/V Southern Pasifika* [2012] NZHC 1254, [2012] 2 Lloyd's Rep 423.
2 *Harmer v Bell, The Bold Buccleugh* (1852) 7 Moo PCC 267.
3 *The Harmonie* (1841) 1 Wm Rob 178.
4 *The Gustaf* (1862) Lush 506; *The Immacolata Concezione* (1883) 9 PD 37, 5 Asp MLC 208; *The Tergeste* [1903] P 26, 9 Asp MLC 356. Possessory liens (also sometimes described as common law liens) are now usually referred to as legal liens: see LIEN vol 68 (2016) PARAS 802, 817 et seq.
5 *The James W Ewell* [1921] P 351, 15 Asp MLC 418.
6 Even in the case of insolvency, maritime liens retain their priority over other debts: *The Orelia* (1833) 3 Hag Adm 75 at 83 per Sir John Nicholl.
7 *The Gustaf* (1862) Lush 506; *The Immacolata Concezione* (1883) 9 PD 37, 5 Asp MLC 208; *The Tergeste* [1903] P 26, 9 Asp MLC 356.
8 *The James W Ewell* [1921] P 351, 15 Asp MLC 418.
9 See COMPANIES vol 14 (2016) PARA 419.
10 *Re Australian Direct Steam Navigation Co* (1875) LR 20 Eq 325. The arrest of a vessel is not an execution against the goods of a company within the meaning of the Insolvency Act 1986 s 183 (see COMPANY AND PARTNERSHIP INSOLVENCY vol 17 (2011) PARA 840); and a person who already has notice of a meeting at which a resolution for the voluntary winding up of a company is to be proposed may become a secured creditor by arresting a ship in an action in rem and is entitled to the benefit of such arrest as against the liquidator subsequently appointed: *John Carlbom & Co Ltd v Zafiro (Owners), The Zafiro* [1960] P 1, [1959] 2 All ER 537, [1959] 1 Lloyd's Rep 359.

988. Transfer of maritime liens. As a general rule, maritime liens (other than the lien for bottomry[1]) are not transferable[2]; but a court having Admiralty jurisdiction has in some cases allowed persons who have, with the sanction of the court, paid off claims against a ship to have the same advantages as to priorities as the person had whose claim they have satisfied[3]. A foreign consul may in the name of his government have certain rights against a fund in court for the recovery of the expenses of repatriating seamen[4]; but a person who advances money to salvors has no lien on an award[5].

1 *The Rebecca* (1804) 5 Ch Rob 102 at 104; *The Catherine* (1847) 3 Wm Rob 1 at 2. As to the lien for bottomry see PARA 980.
2 *The Petone* [1917] P 198, 14 Asp MLC 283; *The Sparti* [2000] 2 Lloyd's Rep 618. As to the restrictions on forfeiture or assignment of seamen's wages and on his right to salvage see PARAS 474, 479.
3 In some early cases, persons who had paid off claims without the sanction of the court were allowed to avail themselves of the priority enjoyed by those whose claims they had satisfied. In *The*

Cornelia Henrietta (1866) LR 1 A & E 51, Dr Lushington laid down the rule that these payments must be made with the sanction of the court if the priority of the claim satisfied was to be claimed by the person satisfying the claim. Hill J exhaustively reviewed all the previous authorities in *The Petone* [1917] P 198, 14 Asp MLC 283, and in view of this judgment it would appear that the cases where parties paid on claims without the sanction of the court and then availed themselves of the priority enjoyed by the person whose claim had been satisfied would no longer be followed. As to the Admiralty jurisdiction of the High Court of Justice generally see PARA 85 et seq.

4   *The Livietta* (1883) 8 PD 209, 5 Asp MLC 132.
5   *The Louisa* (1848) 3 Wm Rob 99.

989.   Enforcement of statutory liens.

Statutory liens which owe their inception to a proceeding in rem and the arrest of maritime property are enforced by sale of that property, subject to the same conditions as apply to the satisfaction of maritime liens[1].

1   *The Cella* (1888) 13 PD 82, 6 Asp MLC 293, CA; *John Carlbom & Co Ltd v Zafiro (Owners), The Zafiro* [1960] P 1, [1959] 2 All ER 537, [1959] 1 Lloyd's Rep 359.

990.   Enforcement of possessory liens.

The holder of a possessory lien[1] may continue to hold the property until his claims are paid, even though to do so entails expense[2]. If, however, he is dispossessed by a court having Admiralty jurisdiction[3], then out of the proceeds of the ship he will be paid his claim according to the rules as to priorities[4].

1   Possessory liens (also sometimes described as common law liens) are now usually referred to as legal liens: see LIEN vol 68 (2016) PARAS 802, 817 et seq.
2   *Thames Iron Works Co v Patent Derrick Co* (1860) 1 John & H 93; *Somes v British Empire Shipping Co* (1860) 8 HL Cas 338; *Mulliner v Florence* (1878) 3 QBD 484, CA; *The Gaupen* (1925) 22 Ll L Rep 57; *The Ally* [1952] 2 Lloyd's Rep 427; *Smith's Dock Co Ltd v St Merriel (Owners), The St Merriel* [1963] P 247, [1963] 1 All ER 537, [1963] 1 Lloyd's Rep 63. See *Metall Market OOO v Vitorio Shipping Co Ltd; The Lehmann Timber* [2013] EWCA Civ 650, [2013] 2 All ER (Comm) 585.
3   As to the Admiralty jurisdiction of the High Court of Justice generally see PARA 85 et seq.
4   *The Gustaf* (1862) Lush 506; *The Immacolata Concezione* (1883) 9 PD 37, 5 Asp MLC 208; *The Tergeste* [1903] P 26, 9 Asp MLC 356. As to the ranking of liens generally see PARA 975 et seq.

991.   Extinction of liens.

Claims to enforce liens are liable to be statute-barred. No action is normally maintainable to enforce a lien against a ship or her owners in respect of damage or loss caused by the fault of that ship to another ship, its cargo or freight or any property on board her, or for damages for loss of life or personal injury caused by the fault of that ship to any person on board another ship, unless proceedings are brought within the period of two years from the date when the damage or loss was caused or the loss of life or injury was suffered[1]. In certain cases, the court may, however, extend the time limit for bringing such proceedings[2].

Maritime liens, other than those for collisions between vessels and salvage and for seamen's wages, are not limited to any time for enforcement, but travel with the ship into whosesoever possession she may come[3], but may be lost through lack of reasonable diligence in enforcing them[4].

A maritime or statutory lien is extinguished by giving bail or a guarantee to prevent the arrest or secure the release of the property in an action to enforce the lien[5], by the arrest and sale of the ship in an action in rem by a court of competent jurisdiction, whether English or foreign[6], by assignment without the sanction of the court[7], and by failure to bring the claim arising from it within the time ordained by the court in limitation proceedings[8].

Possessory liens are extinguished by payment, by yielding up possession, or by arrest of the ship by a court of competent authority[9].

1   See the Merchant Shipping Act 1995 s 190(1), (3); and PARA 1013. As to the application of s 190 to Crown ships see PARA 1015.

2	See the Merchant Shipping Act 1995 s 190(5), (6); and PARA 1013.
3	*Harmer v Bell, The Bold Buccleugh* (1852) 7 Moo PCC 267; *The Charles Amelia* (1868) LR 2 A
	& E 330; *Johnson v Black, The Two Ellens* (1872) LR 4 PC 161, 1 Asp MLC 208; *The Kong
	Magnus* [1891] P 223, 7 Asp MLC 64; *The Goulandris* [1927] P 182, 17 Asp MLC 209; and see
	PARA 964.
4	*The Jacob* (1802) 4 Ch Rob 245 (bottomry); *The Rebecca* (1804) 5 Ch Rob 102 (bottomry); *The
	Royal Arch* (1857) Sw 269 (bottomry); *The Fairport* (1882) 8 PD 48, 5 Asp MLC 62 (master's
	disbursements). See *Metall Market OOO v Vitorio Shipping Co Ltd; The Lehmann Timber* [2013]
	EWCA Civ 650, [2013] 2 All ER (Comm) 585 (possessory lien).
5	The effect of giving bail is to release the property in respect of which the claim is brought (or
	privilege claimed) altogether from the action: *The Kalamazoo* (1851) 15 Jur 885; *The Wild Ranger*
	(1863) Brown & Lush 84; *The Joannis Vatis (No 2)* [1922] P 213, 16 Asp MLC 13; *The Point
	Breeze* [1928] P 135, 17 Asp MLC 462; and see PARAS 171, 172.
6	*The Charles Amelia* (1868) LR 2 A & E 330; *Castrique v Imrie* (1870) LR 4 HL 414. Where a ship
	was sold under the authority of the Egyptian court by the assignees of a bankrupt owner, the sale
	was held not to be the equivalent to a sale in an action in rem but was a sale 'cum onere', and the
	maritime lien which had previously attached in respect of salvage services was held not to have
	been extinguished by the sale: *The Goulandris* [1927] P 182, 17 Asp MLC 209.
7	*The Petone* [1917] P 198, 14 Asp MLC 283.
8	The court may, however, in its discretion allow such a claim to be proved after the time fixed, but
	before the court has distributed the fund: *The Zoe* (1886) 11 PD 72, 5 Asp MLC 583.
9	*The Scio* (1867) LR 1 A & E 353; *Re Westlake, ex p Willoughby* (1881) 16 ChD 604. See also
	PARA 974. Possessory liens (also sometimes described as common law liens) are now usually
	referred to as legal liens: see LIEN vol 68 (2016) PARAS 802, 817 et seq.

12. LIMITATION OF LIABILITY OF SHIPOWNERS ETC

(1) THE CONVENTION ON LIMITATION OF LIABILITY FOR MARITIME CLAIMS

(i) Right of Limitation under the Convention

992. Legislative framework. The provisions of the Convention on Limitation of Liability for Maritime Claims[1] (the 'Convention') have the force of law[2] in the United Kingdom[3]. They apply in relation to Her Majesty's ships as they apply in relation to other ships[4]; but they do not apply to any liability in respect of loss of life or personal injury caused to, or loss of or damage to any property of, a person who is on board the ship[5] in question or employed in connection with that ship or with the salvage operations[6] in question if[7]:

(1)   he is so on board or employed under a contract of service governed by the law of any part of the United Kingdom[8]; and

(2)   the liability arises from an occurrence which took place on or after 1 January 1996[9].

1   Ie the Convention on Limitation of Liability for Maritime Claims (London, 1 to 19 November 1976; TS 13 (1990); Cm 955) (as to which see PARA 7). The provisions of the Convention are set out in the Merchant Shipping Act 1995 Sch 7 Pt I (arts 1–15, 18) (see PARA 993 et seq) and are referred to therein, and in Sch 7 Pt II (paras 1–13) (see PARA 993 et seq), as the 'Convention': see s 185(1). The provisions of Sch 7 Pt II have effect in connection with the Convention; and the Merchant Shipping Act 1995 s 185(1) has effect subject to the provisions of Pt II: s 185(2).
     Her Majesty may by Order in Council make such modifications of Sch 7 Pt I and Sch 7 Pt II as She considers appropriate in consequence of the revision of the Convention by the Protocol (2 May 1996) amending the Convention (the '1996 Protocol'): Merchant Shipping Act 1995 s 185(2A) (s 185(2A)–(2E), (5) added by the Merchant Shipping and Maritime Security Act 1997 s 15). If it appears to Her Majesty in Council that the government of the United Kingdom has agreed to any further revision of the Convention or to any revision of the 1996 Protocol art 8, She may by Order in Council make such modifications of the Merchant Shipping Act 1995 Sch 7 Pt I and Sch 7 Pt II, and of s 185(2C), (2D), as She considers appropriate in consequence of the revision: s 185(2B) (as so added). A draft of an Order in Council proposed to be made by virtue of s 185(2A) or s 185(2B) is not to be submitted to Her Majesty in Council unless it has been approved by a resolution of each House of Parliament: s 185(5) (as so added).
     The Secretary of State may by order make such amendments of Sch 7 Pt I and Sch 7 Pt II as appear to him to be appropriate for the purpose of giving effect to any amendment of a relevant limit which is adopted in accordance with the 1996 Protocol art 8: Merchant Shipping Act 1995 s 185(2C) (as so added). For these purposes, a 'relevant limit' means any of the limits for the time being specified in either of the following provisions of the Convention, namely art 6(1) and art 7(1): Merchant Shipping Act 1995 s 185(2D) (as so added). No modification made by virtue of s 185(2A), (2B) or (2C) may affect any rights or liabilities arising out of an occurrence which took place before the day on which the modification comes into force: s 185(2E) (as so added). At the date at which this volume states the law, no order relevant to the material set out in this title had been made under s 185(2C)–(2E). As to the Secretary of State see PARA 36; and as to the making of orders by the Secretary of State under the Merchant Shipping Act 1995 generally see PARA 39.

2   As to the meaning of 'having the force of law' cf *The Hollandia* [1983] 1 AC 565, [1982] 3 All ER 1141, sub nom *The Morviken* [1983] 1 Lloyd's Rep 1, HL.

3   Merchant Shipping Act 1995 s 185(1). As to the meaning of 'United Kingdom' see PARA 16 note 3. The Convention on Limitation of Liability for Maritime Claims does not limit the jurisdiction of the Admiralty Court, which is governed by the Senior Courts Act 1981: see *Vessel SA v CP Ships (UK) Ltd, sub nom Denise (The) (Owners) v The Denise (Charterers)* [2004] EWHC 3305 (Admlty), [2005] 2 All ER (Comm) 47 (owner was entitled to invoke the jurisdiction of the court to seek a decree of limitation even in circumstances where there was no claim (as yet) brought against it in the jurisdiction). As to the Admiralty jurisdiction of the High Court of Justice generally see PARA 85 et seq.
     An Order in Council made for the purposes of the Merchant Shipping Act 1995 Sch 7 Pt II para 13 and declaring that any state specified in the Order is a party to the Convention as amended by the 1996 Protocol is conclusive evidence, subject to the provisions of any subsequent Order made

for those purposes, that the state is a party to the Convention as amended by the 1996 Protocol: Merchant Shipping Act 1995 Sch 7 Pt II para 13 (substituted by SI 1998/1258). At the date at which this volume states the law, no such Order in Council had effect.

Nothing in the Pilotage Act 1987 s 22(3) or (4) (see PARA 594) affects any liability which may be limited under the Merchant Shipping Act 1995 s 185 (see the Pilotage Act 1987 s 22(7); and PARA 594); nor does anything in the Convention relating to the Carriage of Passengers and their Luggage by Sea (Athens, 13 December 1974; TS 40 (1987); Cm 202) affect the operation of the Merchant Shipping Act 1995 s 185 (see the Carriage of Passengers and their Luggage by Sea art 12; and CARRIAGE AND CARRIERS vol 7 (2015) PARA 643).

4   Merchant Shipping Act 1995 s 185(3). As to the meaning of 'ship' see PARA 229. As to the meaning of 'Her Majesty's ships' see the Crown Proceedings Act 1947 s 38(2); and CROWN AND CROWN PROCEEDINGS vol 29 (2014) PARA 86. As to the application of the Merchant Shipping Act 1995 s 185 to the Crown and its ships see PARA 1015.

5   For this purpose, 'ship' has the same meaning as in the Convention (see PARA 993 note 2): see the Merchant Shipping Act 1995 s 185(4).

6   For these purposes, 'salvage operations' has the same meaning as in the Convention (see PARA 993 note 3): see the Merchant Shipping Act 1995 s 185(4).

7   Merchant Shipping Act 1995 s 185(4).

8   Merchant Shipping Act 1995 s 185(4)(a). Although historically employment law originated in what was termed the law of master and servant, the modern terminology adopted is that of 'employer' and 'employee'; and 'contract of employment' is used rather than the older phrase 'contract of service' (save that the latter phrase is still used in social security and related legislation): see EMPLOYMENT vol 39 (2014) PARA 1 et seq.

9   Merchant Shipping Act 1995 s 185(4)(b). The date of 1 January 1996 is that on which the Merchant Shipping Act 1995 was commenced: see s 316(2).

993. Persons entitled to limit liability under the Convention.

Under the Convention on Limitation of Liability for Maritime Claims[1], shipowners[2] and salvors[3] may limit their liability[4] for claims that the Convention makes subject to limitation[5]. If any such claims are made against any person for whose act, neglect or default the shipowner or salvor is responsible, such person is entitled to avail himself of the limitation of liability provided for in the Convention[6].

An insurer of liability for claims subject to limitation[7] is entitled to the benefits of the Convention to the same extent as the assured himself[8].

The act of invoking limitation of liability does not constitute an admission of liability[9].

1   Ie the Convention on Limitation of Liability for Maritime Claims (London, 1 to 19 November 1976; TS 13 (1990); Cm 955): see PARA 992.

2   For these purposes, 'shipowner' means the owner, charterer, manager or operator of a sea-going ship: Convention on Limitation of Liability for Maritime Claims art 1(2). As to what amounts to a 'shipowner' for these purposes see also *Metvale Ltd v Monsanto International Sarl, The MSC Napoli* [2008] EWHC 3002 (Admlty), [2009] 1 All ER (Comm) 1158 (slot charterer). References in the Convention and in the Merchant Shipping Act 1995 Sch 7 Pt II paras 1–10 (see PARA 994 et seq) to a ship include references to any structure, whether completed or in course of completion, launched and intended for use in navigation as a ship or part of a ship: see Sch 7 Pt II para 12.

3   For these purposes, 'salvor' means any person rendering services in direct connection with salvage operations; and 'salvage operations' also includes operations referred to in art 2(1)(d), (e), (f) (see PARA 994): art 1(3).

4   Ie in accordance with the rules of the Convention (see PARA 994 et seq): art 1(1).

5   Convention on Limitation of Liability for Maritime Claims art 1(1). The claims that are made subject to limitation under the Convention are set out in art 2 (see PARA 994): see art 1(1).

The right to limit liability under the Convention applies in relation to any ship whether sea-going or not; and the meaning of 'shipowner' in art 1(2) (see note 2) is to be construed accordingly: Merchant Shipping Act 1995 Sch 7 Pt II paras 1, 2 (Sch 7 Pt II para 2 amended by SI 1998/1258). The Merchant Shipping Act 1995 Sch 7 Pt II para 2 is subject to Sch 7 Pt II para 6 (see PARA 999): see Sch 7 Pt II para 2 (as so amended). In the Convention, the liability of a shipowner includes liability in an action brought against the vessel herself: art 1(5).

A charterer's ability to limit liability pursuant to the Merchant Shipping Act 1995 depends on the type of claim that is brought against him rather than the capacity in which he was acting when his liability arose: *CMA CGM SA v Classica Shipping Co Ltd* [2004] EWCA Civ 114, [2004] 1 All ER (Comm) 865, [2004] 1 Lloyd's Rep 460. See also *Blue Nile Shipping Co Ltd v Iguana Shipping and Finance Inc* [2004] EWHC 1506 (Admlty), [2004] 2 Lloyd's Rep 469, [2004] All ER (D) 305

(Jun) (it mattered not that it was the owners who were seeking to limit against claims brought by charterers rather than the other way around; the issue turned on the scope of the claims that were subject to limitation and not the class of persons entitled to limit); *Metvale Ltd v Monsanto International Sarl, The MSC Napoli* [2008] EWHC 3002 (Admlty), [2009] 1 All ER (Comm) 1158 (slot charterer within definition of 'shipowner' and entitled to limit liability); *Bahamas Oil Refining Co International Ltd v Owners of the Cape Bari Tankschiffahrts GmbH & Co KG (Bahamas)* [2016[UKPC 20, [2016] All ER (D) 125 (Jul) (shipowner's entitlement to contract out of statutory limitation right).

6   Convention on Limitation of Liability for Maritime Claims art 1(4).
7   Ie in accordance with the rules of the Convention (see PARA 994 et seq): art 1(6).
8   Convention on Limitation of Liability for Maritime Claims art 1(6).
9   Convention on Limitation of Liability for Maritime Claims art 1(7).

994. Claims subject to limitation under the Convention.

Under the Convention on Limitation of Liability for Maritime Claims[1], the following claims, whatever the basis of liability may be, may be subject to limitation of liability[2]:

(1)   claims in respect of loss of life or personal injury or loss of or damage to property (including damage to harbour works, basins and waterways and aids to navigation), occurring on board or in direct connection with the operation of the ship[3] or with salvage operations[4], and consequential loss resulting therefrom[5];

(2)   claims in respect of loss resulting from delay in the carriage by sea of cargo, passengers or their luggage[6];

(3)   claims in respect of other loss resulting from infringement of rights other than contractual rights, occurring in direct connection with the operation of the ship or salvage operations[7];

(4)   claims in respect of the raising, removal, destruction or the rendering harmless of a ship which is sunk, wrecked, stranded or abandoned, including anything that is or has been on board such ship[8];

(5)   claims in respect of the removal, destruction or the rendering harmless of the cargo of the ship[9];

(6)   claims of a person other than the person liable in respect of measures taken in order to avert or minimise loss for which the person liable may limit his liability in accordance with the Convention, and further loss caused by such measures[10].

Claims set out in heads (1) to (6) above may be subject to limitation of liability even if brought by way of recourse or for indemnity under a contract or otherwise[11]. Claims set out in heads (4) to (6) above may not, however, be subject to limitation of liability to the extent that they relate to remuneration under a contract with the person liable[12].

1   Ie the Convention on Limitation of Liability for Maritime Claims (London, 1 to 19 November 1976; TS 13 (1990); Cm 955): see PARA 992.
2   Convention on Limitation of Liability for Maritime Claims art 2(1). Article 2(1) is subject to art 3 (claims excepted from limitation) (see PARA 995) and art 4 (see PARA 996) (conduct barring limitation): see art 2(1). See *Blue Nile Shipping Co Ltd v Iguana Shipping and Finance Inc* [2004] EWHC 1506 (Admlty), [2004] 2 Lloyd's Rep 469, [2004] All ER (D) 305 (Jun) (cited in PARA 993 note 5).
3   As to the meaning of references to a ship see PARA 993 note 2. The loss of the ship itself is not a loss of property 'occurring . . . in direct connection with the operation of the ship' for the purposes of the Convention on Limitation of Liability for Maritime Claims art (2)1(a): *Aegean Sea Traders Corpn v Repsol Petroleo SA* [1998] 2 Lloyd's Rep 39. Nor does the loss of freight fall within the Convention on Limitation of Liability for Maritime Claims art 2(1)(a): *Aegean Sea Traders Corpn v Repsol Petroleo SA*. See also *Strong Wise Ltd v Esso Australia Resources Pty Ltd (The 'APL Sydney')* [2010] FCA 240, [2010] 2 Lloyd's Rep 555, Aust FC (what amounts to a 'distinct occasion'). See also note 7. As to recourse claims in respect of damage caused by oil pollution see *Aegean Sea Traders Corpn v Repsol Petroleo SA.*
4   As to the meaning of 'salvage operations' see PARA 993 note 3.
5   Convention on Limitation of Liability for Maritime Claims art 2(1)(a). See note 2.
6   Convention on Limitation of Liability for Maritime Claims art 2(1)(b). See note 2.

7   Convention on Limitation of Liability for Maritime Claims art 2(1)(c). See note 2. Loss of freight
    does not fall within art 2(1)(c): *Aegean Sea Traders Corporation v Repsol Petroleo SA* [1998] 2
    Lloyd's Rep 39. See also note 3.
8   Convention on Limitation of Liability for Maritime Claims art 2(1)(d). See note 2. The right to
    limit liability for claims under art 2(1)(d) does not apply to the law of the United Kingdom unless
    provision has been made by an order of the Secretary of State for the setting up and management
    of a fund to be used for the making to harbour or conservancy authorities of payments needed to
    compensate them for the reduction, in consequence of art 2(1)(d), of amounts recoverable by them
    in claims of the kind mentioned in head (4) in the text, and to be maintained by contributions from
    such authorities raised and collected by them in respect of vessels in like manner as other sums so
    raised by them: Merchant Shipping Act 1995 Sch 7 Pt II paras 1, 3(1). Such an order may contain
    such incidental and supplemental provisions as appear to the Secretary of State to be necessary or
    expedient: Sch 7 Pt II para 3(2). However, at the date at which this volume states the law, no such
    order had been made and none has effect as if so made. As to the meaning of 'harbour authority'
    see PARA 69 note 4; and as to the meaning of 'conservancy authority' see PARA 72 note 2. As to
    the Secretary of State see PARA 36; and as to the making of orders by the Secretary of State under
    the Merchant Shipping Act 1995 generally see PARA 39.
9   Convention on Limitation of Liability for Maritime Claims art 2(1)(e). See note 2.
10 Convention on Limitation of Liability for Maritime Claims art 2(1)(f). See note 2.
11 Convention on Limitation of Liability for Maritime Claims art 2(2). See *The Breydon Merchant*
    [1992] 1 Lloyd's Rep 373 (under the Convention on Limitation of Liability for Maritime Claims,
    shipowners were entitled to limit their liability in respect of claims listed in art 2 whether such
    liability arose in contract, tort or by statute).
12 Convention on Limitation of Liability for Maritime Claims art 2(2).

995. Claims excepted from limitation under the Convention. The rules of
the Convention on Limitation of Liability for Maritime Claims[1] do not apply to[2]:
    (1)   claims for salvage[3] or contribution in general average[4];
    (2)   claims for oil pollution damage[5];
    (3)   claims subject to any international convention or national legislation
            governing or prohibiting limitation of liability for nuclear damage[6];
    (4)   claims against the shipowner[7] of a nuclear ship for nuclear damage[8];
    (5)   claims by servants of the shipowner or salvor[9] whose duties are
            connected with the ship[10] or the salvage operations[11], including claims
            of their heirs, dependants or other persons entitled to make such claims,
            if under the law governing the contract of service between the shipowner
            or salvor and such servants the shipowner or salvor is not entitled to
            limit his liability in respect of such claims, or if he is by such law only
            permitted to limit his liability to an amount greater than that provided
            for in the general limits[12] of liability[13].

Claims for damage within the meaning of the International Convention on
Liability and Compensation for Damage in Connection with the Carriage of
Hazardous and Noxious Substances by Sea 1996[14], which arise from occurrences
taking place after that Convention has effect in relation to the United Kingdom[15],
are also excluded from the Convention on Limitation of Liability for Maritime
Claims[16].

1   Ie the Convention on Limitation of Liability for Maritime Claims (London, 1 to 19 November
    1976; TS 13 (1990); Cm 955): see PARA 992.
2   Convention on Limitation of Liability for Maritime Claims art 3.
3   Ie including, if applicable, any claim for special compensation under the International Convention
    on Salvage 1989 (London, 28 April 1989; Cm 1526) art 14 (see PARA 879): see the Convention
    on Limitation of Liability for Maritime Claims art 3(a) (substituted by SI 1998/1258).
4   Convention on Limitation of Liability for Maritime Claims art 3(a) (as substituted: see note 3).
    Only claims by the salvor against the shipowner are exempt: *The Breydon Merchant* [1992] 1
    Lloyd's Rep 373.
5   Convention on Limitation of Liability for Maritime Claims art 3(b). Head (2) in the text refers to
    claims for oil pollution damage within the meaning of the International Convention on Civil
    Liability for Oil Pollution Damage (Brussels, 29 November 1969 to 31 December 1970; TS 106
    (1975); Cmnd 4403) or of any amendment or Protocol thereto which is force (see PARA 8): see the
    Convention on Limitation of Liability for Maritime Claims art 3(b). Accordingly, the claims

excluded from the Convention by art 3(b) are claims in respect of any liability incurred under the Merchant Shipping Act 1995 s 153 (as to which see ENVIRONMENTAL QUALITY AND PUBLIC HEALTH vol 45 (2010) PARA 445): Sch 7 Pt II para 4(2).

6   Convention on Limitation of Liability for Maritime Claims art 3(c). The claims excluded from the Convention by art 3(c) are claims made by virtue of any of the Nuclear Installations Act 1965 ss 7–11 (see ENERGY AND CLIMATE CHANGE vol 44 (2011) PARA 892 et seq): Sch 7 Pt II para 4(3).

7   As to the meaning of 'shipowner' see PARA 993 note 2.

8   Convention on Limitation of Liability for Maritime Claims art 3(d).

9   As to the meaning of 'salvor' see PARA 993 note 3.

10 As to the meaning of references to a ship see PARA 993 note 2.

11 As to the meaning of 'salvage operations' see PARA 993 note 3.

12 Ie provided for in the Convention on Limitation of Liability for Maritime Claims art 6 (see PARA 998): see art 3(e).

13 Convention on Limitation of Liability for Maritime Claims art 3(e). As to the 'contract of service' see PARA 992 note 8. In connection with contracting out see also *Bahamas Oil Refining Company International Ltd v Owners of the Cape Bari Tankschiffahrts GMBH & Co KG (Bahamas)* [2016] UKPC 20.

14 Ie the International Convention on Liability and Compensation for Damage in Connection with the Carriage of Hazardous and Noxious Substances by Sea 1996 (London, 3 May 1996; Misc 5 (1997); Cm 3580) or any amendment of or Protocol to that Convention (as to which see ENVIRONMENTAL QUALITY AND PUBLIC HEALTH vol 45 (2010) PARA 472 et seq): see the Merchant Shipping Act 1995 Sch 7 Pt II para 4(1) (substituted by SI 1998/1258). The text of the International Convention on Liability and Compensation for Damage in Connection with the Carriage of Hazardous and Noxious Substances by Sea 1996, excluding the annexes, is set out in the Merchant Shipping Act 1995 s 182A(2), Sch 5A: see ENVIRONMENTAL QUALITY AND PUBLIC HEALTH vol 45 (2010) PARA 474 et seq.

15 Ie which arise from occurrences which take place after the coming into force of the first Order in Council made by Her Majesty under the Merchant Shipping Act 1995 s 182B (power to give effect to the Convention) (see ENVIRONMENTAL QUALITY AND PUBLIC HEALTH vol 45 (2010) PARA 472 et seq): see Sch 7 Pt II para 4(1) (as substituted: see note 14).

16 Merchant Shipping Act 1995 Sch 7 Pt II para 4(1) (as substituted: see note 14).

996. Conduct barring limitation under the Convention.

Under the Convention on Limitation of Liability for Maritime Claims[1], a person liable is not entitled to limit his liability if it is proved[2] that the loss resulted from his personal act or omission, committed with the intent to cause such loss, or recklessly and with knowledge that such loss would probably result[3].

1   Ie the Convention on Limitation of Liability for Maritime Claims (London, 1 to 19 November 1976; TS 13 (1990); Cm 955): see PARA 992.

2   The policy of the Convention on Limitation of Liability for Maritime Claims is on the one hand to make it more difficult to deny limitation of liability and on the other to fix much higher limits of liability: see *The Breydon Merchant* [1992] 1 Lloyd's Rep 373 at 376 per Sheen J.

3   Convention on Limitation of Liability for Maritime Claims art 4. Article 4 requires actual knowledge; 'shut-eye' knowledge is not sufficient: *MSC Mediterranean Shipping Co SA v Delumar BVBA* [2000] 2 All ER (Comm) 458, [2000] 2 Lloyd's Rep 399 (absent any allegation of intent, the person challenging the right to limit must establish both reckless conduct and knowledge that the relevant loss would probably result, these two requirements being cumulative). See also *Schiffahrtsgesellschaft MS Merkur Sky MbH & Co KG v MS Leerort Nth Schiffahrts GmbH & Co KG, The Leerort and The Zim Piraeus* [2001] EWCA Civ 1055, [2001] 2 Lloyd's Rep 291 (the knowledge or foresight required is of the very loss that has in fact occurred, and not just loss of that type); *Peracomo Inc v Telus Communications Co (The 'Realice')* [2014] 2 Lloyd's Rep 315; *Kairos Shipping Ltd v Enka & Co Llc, The Atlantick Confidence* [2014] EWCA Civ 217, [2014] 1 All ER (Comm) 909 (deliberate acts of sabotage). However, see *Margolle v Delta Maritime Co Ltd* [2002] EWHC 2452 (Admlty), [2003] 1 All ER (Comm) 102, [2003] 1 Lloyd's Rep 203 (where a master, contrary to regulations, steers his vessel against the flow of traffic in a busy shipping lane, it can be inferred that he has the relevant knowledge that loss will probably result).

997. Counterclaims under the Convention.

Under the Convention on Limitation of Liability for Maritime Claims[1], where a person entitled to limitation of liability[2] has a claim against the claimant arising out of the same occurrence, their respective claims must be set off against each other and the provisions of the Convention only apply to the balance, if any[3].

1	Ie the Convention on Limitation of Liability for Maritime Claims (London, 1 to 19 November 1976; TS 13 (1990); Cm 955): see PARA 992.
2	Ie in accordance with the rules of the Convention on Limitation of Liability for Maritime Claims (see PARAS 993 et seq, 998 et seq): see art 5.
3	Convention on Limitation of Liability for Maritime Claims art 5.

(ii) Limits of Liability under the Convention

998. General limits of liability under the Convention. Under the Convention on Limitation of Liability for Maritime Claims[1], the limits of liability for claims arising on any distinct occasion, other than in respect of claims arising on any distinct occasion for loss of life or personal injury to passengers of a ship[2], must be calculated as follows[3]:

(1)	in respect of claims for loss of life or personal injury:
 (a)	two million units of account[4] for a ship[5] with a tonnage not exceeding 2,000 tons[6];
 (b)	for a ship with a tonnage in excess thereof, the following amount in addition to that mentioned in head (1)(a) above, that is to say, for each ton from 2,001 to 30,000 tons, 800 units of account, for each ton from 30,001 to 70,000 tons, 600 units of account, and, for each ton in excess of 70,000 tons, 400 units of account[7];
(2)	in respect of any other claims:
 (a)	one million units of account for a ship with a tonnage not exceeding 2,000 tons[8];
 (b)	for a ship with a tonnage in excess thereof, the following amount in addition to that mentioned in head (2)(a) above, that is to say, for a ship with a tonnage in excess of 2,000 tons, the additional amounts are, for each ton from 2,001 to 30,000 tons, 400 units of account, for each ton from 30,001 to 70,000 tons, 300 units of account, and, for each ton in excess of 70,000 tons, 200 units of account[9].

Where the amount calculated in accordance with head (1) above is insufficient to pay the claims mentioned therein in full, the amount calculated in accordance with head (2) above must be available for payment of the unpaid balance of claims under head (1) above and such unpaid balance ranks rateably with claims mentioned under head (2) above[10].

The limits of liability for any salvor[11] not operating from any ship or for any salvor operating solely on the ship to, or in respect of which he is rendering salvage services, must be calculated according to a tonnage of 1,500 tons[12].

In the application of the general limits of liability[13] to a ship with a tonnage less than 300 tons[14], those limits have effect as if head (1)(a) above referred to one million units of account and as if head (2)(a) above referred to 500,000 units of account[15].

1	Ie the Convention on Limitation of Liability for Maritime Claims (London, 1 to 19 November 1976; TS 13 (1990); Cm 955): see PARA 992.
2	Ie other than claims mentioned in the Convention on Limitation of Liability for Maritime Claims art 7 (see PARA 999): see art 6(1) (substituted by SI 1998/1258). As to the meaning of 'claims for loss of life or personal injury to passengers of a ship' for these purposes see PARA 999 note 2. In connection with what amounts to a 'distinct occasion' see *Strong Wise Ltd v Esso Australia Resources Pty Ltd (The 'APL Sydney')* [2010] FCA 240, [2010] 2 Lloyd's Rep 555, Aust FC.
3	Convention on Limitation of Liability for Maritime Claims art 6(1) (as substituted: see note 2). As to the modification of art 6 in relation to ships with a tonnage of less than 300 tons see notes 13–15; and as to the calculation of gross tonnage see note 14. As to the conversion into sterling of units of account see PARA 1000.

4   As to units of account see PARA 1000.
5   As to the meaning of references to a ship see PARA 993 note 2.
6   Convention on Limitation of Liability for Maritime Claims art 6(1)(a)(i) (as substituted: see note 2).
7   Convention on Limitation of Liability for Maritime Claims art 6(1)(a)(ii) (as substituted: see note 2).
8   Convention on Limitation of Liability for Maritime Claims art 6(1)(b)(i) (as substituted: see note 2).
9   Convention on Limitation of Liability for Maritime Claims art 6(1)(b)(ii) (as substituted: see note 2).
10 Convention on Limitation of Liability for Maritime Claims art 6(2).
11 As to the meaning of 'salvor' see PARA 993 note 3.
12 Convention on Limitation of Liability for Maritime Claims art 6(4).
13 Ie in the application of the Convention on Limitation of Liability for Maritime Claims art 6 (see the text and notes 1–12): see the Merchant Shipping Act 1995 Sch 7 Pt II para 5(1) (amended by SI 1998/1258).
14 For these purposes, a ship's tonnage is its gross tonnage calculated in such manner as may be prescribed by an order made by the Secretary of State: Merchant Shipping Act 1995 Sch 7 Pt II para 5(2). Any such order must, so far as appears to the Secretary of State to be practicable, give effect to the regulations in the International Convention on Tonnage Measurement of Ships (London, 23 June to 23 December 1969; TS 50 (1982); Cmnd 8716) Annex 1 (as to which see PARAS 7, 248 et seq): see the Merchant Shipping Act 1995 Sch 7 Pt II para 5(3). As to the Secretary of State see PARA 36; and as to the making of orders by the Secretary of State under the Merchant Shipping Act 1995 generally see PARA 39. At the date at which this volume states the law, no such order had been made but, by virtue of the Interpretation Act 1978 s 17(2)(b), the Merchant Shipping (Liability of Shipowners and Others) (Calculation of Tonnage) Order 1986, SI 1986/1040, has effect as if so made. Accordingly, for the purposes of the Convention on Limitation of Liability for Maritime Claims art 6 and the Merchant Shipping Act 1995 Sch 7 Pt II para 5, the gross tonnage of a ship must be calculated in accordance with the Merchant Shipping (Tonnage) Regulations 1997, SI 1997/1510 (as to which see PARA 248 et seq): Merchant Shipping (Liability of Shipowners and Others) (Calculation of Tonnage) Order 1986, SI 1986/1040, art 2(1). In the case of a ship of which, at the time when the limitation is claimed, the tonnage has not yet been and cannot be ascertained in accordance with the Merchant Shipping (Liability of Shipowners and Others) (Calculation of Tonnage) Order 1986, SI 1986/1040, art 2(1), the best evidence available of the measurements of the ship must be used in so calculating the tonnage of the ship: art 2(2).
15 Merchant Shipping Act 1995 Sch 7 Pt II para 5(1) (as amended: see note 13).

999. Limit for passenger claims under the Convention.

Under the Convention on Limitation of Liability for Maritime Claims[1], in respect of claims arising on any distinct occasion for loss of life or personal injury to passengers of a ship[2], the limit of liability of the shipowner[3] thereof is an amount of 175,000 units of account[4] multiplied by the number of passengers which the ship is authorised to carry according to the ship's certificate[5].

1   Ie the Convention on Limitation of Liability for Maritime Claims (London, 1 to 19 November 1976; TS 13 (1990); Cm 955): see PARA 992.
2   For these purposes, 'claims for loss of life or personal injury to passengers of a ship' means any such claims brought by or on behalf of any person carried in that ship under a contract of passenger carriage or who, with the consent of the carrier, is accompanying a vehicle or live animals which are covered by a contract for the carriage of goods: Convention on Limitation of Liability for Maritime Claims art 7(2). In art 7(2), the reference to 'claims brought [. . .] on behalf of a person' includes a reference to any claim in respect of the death of a person under the Fatal Accidents Act 1976 (as to which see NEGLIGENCE vol 78 (2010) PARA 24 et seq): Merchant Shipping Act 1995 Sch 7 Pt II para 6(2). As to the meaning of references to a ship see PARA 993 note 2.
3   As to the meaning of 'shipowner' see PARA 993 note 2.
4   As to units of account, and as to the conversion into sterling of units of account, see PARA 1000.
5   Convention on Limitation of Liability for Maritime Claims art 7(1) (substituted by SI 1998/1258). The Convention on Limitation of Liability for Maritime Claims art 7 does not apply in respect of any sea-going ship, and has effect in respect of any ship which is not sea-going as if art 7(1) were to read 'in respect of claims arising on any distinct occasion for loss of life or personal injury to passengers of a ship, the limit of liability of the shipowner thereof, in respect of each passenger, is an amount of 175,000 units of account': Merchant Shipping Act 1995 Sch 7 Pt II para 6(1) (substituted by SI 1998/1258).

1000. Unit of account used in the Convention. Under the Convention on Limitation of Liability for Maritime Claims[1], the unit of account that is referred to for the purposes of setting limits of liability[2] is the special drawing right as defined by the International Monetary Fund[3]. The amounts payable under the Convention[4] must be converted into the national currency of the state in which limitation is sought[5], according to the value of that currency at the date the limitation fund[6] has been constituted, payment is made, or security is given which under the law of that state is equivalent to such payment[7].

Accordingly, for the purpose of converting the amounts payable under the Convention[8] from special drawing rights into sterling, one special drawing right is to be treated as equal to such a sum in sterling as the International Monetary Fund has fixed as being the equivalent of one special drawing right for[9]:

(1)　　the relevant date[10]; or

(2)　　if no sum has been so fixed for that date, the last preceding date for which a sum has been so fixed[11].

A certificate given by or on behalf of the Treasury[12] stating:

(a)　　that a particular sum in sterling has been fixed as mentioned in head (1) above for a particular date[13]; or

(b)　　that no sum has been so fixed for that date and that a particular sum in sterling has been so fixed for a date which is the last preceding date for which a sum has been so fixed[14],

is conclusive evidence of those matters; and a document purporting to be such a certificate must, in any proceedings, be received in evidence and, unless the contrary is proved, is deemed to be such a certificate[15].

1　Ie the Convention on Limitation of Liability for Maritime Claims (London, 1 to 19 November 1976; TS 13 (1990); Cm 955): see PARA 992.
2　Ie the unit of account referred to in the Convention on Limitation of Liability for Maritime Claims art 6 (see PARA 998) and art 7 (see PARA 999): see art 8.
3　Convention on Limitation of Liability for Maritime Claims art 8. As to the International Monetary Fund see INTERNATIONAL RELATIONS LAW vol 61 (2010) PARA 533.
4　Ie the amounts mentioned in the Convention on Limitation of Liability for Maritime Claims arts 6, 7: see art 8.
5　As to Orders in Council which are made declaring that any state specified in the Order is a party to the Convention on Limitation of Liability for Maritime Claims, as amended by the 1996 Protocol, see PARA 992 note 3.
6　As to the limitation fund see PARA 1003 et seq.
7　Convention on Limitation of Liability for Maritime Claims art 8.
8　Ie the amounts mentioned in the Convention on Limitation of Liability for Maritime Claims arts 6, 7: see the Merchant Shipping Act 1995 Sch 7 Pt II para 7(1).
9　Merchant Shipping Act 1995 Sch 7 Pt II para 7(1).
10　Merchant Shipping Act 1995 Sch 7 Pt II para 7(1)(a).
11　Merchant Shipping Act 1995 Sch 7 Pt II para 7(1)(b).
12　As to the Treasury see CONSTITUTIONAL AND ADMINISTRATIVE LAW vol 20 (2014) PARAS 262–265.
13　Merchant Shipping Act 1995 Sch 7 Pt II para 7(2)(a).
14　Merchant Shipping Act 1995 Sch 7 Pt II para 7(2)(b).
15　Merchant Shipping Act 1995 Sch 7 Pt II para 7(2).

1001. Aggregation of claims under the Convention. Under the Convention on Limitation of Liability for Maritime Claims[1], the general limits of liability[2] apply to the aggregate of all claims which arise on any distinct occasion[3]:

(1)　　against the owner, charterer, manager or operator of a sea-going ship[4] and any person for whose act, neglect or default he or they are responsible[5]; or

(2)　　against the shipowner[6] of a ship rendering salvage services from that ship and the salvor[7] or salvors operating from such ship and any person for whose act, neglect or default he or they are responsible[8]; or

(3)   against the salvor or salvors who are not operating from a ship or who
        are operating solely on the ship to, or in respect of which, the salvage
        services are rendered and any person for whose act, neglect or default he
        or they are responsible[9].

The limits of liability for passenger claims[10] apply to the aggregate of all claims
subject thereto which may arise on any distinct occasion against the owner,
charterer, manager or operator of a sea-going ship[11] in respect of the ship[12] and
any person for whose act, neglect or default he or they are responsible[13].

1 Ie the Convention on Limitation of Liability for Maritime Claims (London, 1 to 19 November
   1976; TS 13 (1990); Cm 955): see PARA 992.
2 Ie the limits of liability determined in accordance with the Convention on Limitation of Liability
   for Maritime Claims art 6 (see PARA 998): see art 9(1).
3 Convention on Limitation of Liability for Maritime Claims art 9(1).
4 Ie the person or persons mentioned in the Convention on Limitation of Liability for Maritime
   Claims art 1(2) (see PARA 993 note 2): see art 9(1). As to the meaning of references to a ship see
   PARA 993 note 2.
5 Convention on Limitation of Liability for Maritime Claims art 9(1)(a).
6 As to the meaning of 'shipowner' see PARA 993 note 2.
7 As to the meaning of 'salvor' see PARA 993 note 3.
8 Convention on Limitation of Liability for Maritime Claims art 9(1)(b).
9 Convention on Limitation of Liability for Maritime Claims art 9(1)(c).
10 Ie the limits of liability determined in accordance with the Convention on Limitation of Liability
   for Maritime Claims art 7 (see PARA 999): see art 9(2).
11 Ie the person or persons mentioned in the Convention on Limitation of Liability for Maritime
   Claims art 1(2) (see PARA 993 note 2): see art 9(2).
12 Ie claims referred to in the Convention on Limitation of Liability for Maritime Claims art 7 (see
   PARA 999): see art 9(2).
13 Convention on Limitation of Liability for Maritime Claims art 9(2).

1002. Limitation of liability without constitution of a limitation fund.

Under the Convention on Limitation of Liability for Maritime Claims[1], limitation
of liability may be invoked notwithstanding that a limitation fund[2] has not been
constituted[3].

If limitation of liability is invoked without the constitution of a limitation fund,
the provisions relating to the distribution of that fund[4] apply correspondingly[5].

Questions of procedure arising under these rules[6] must be decided in
accordance with the national law of the state party[7] in which action is brought[8].

1 Ie the Convention on Limitation of Liability for Maritime Claims (London, 1 to 19 November
   1976; TS 13 (1990); Cm 955): see PARA 992.
2 Ie as mentioned in the Convention on Limitation of Liability for Maritime Claims art 11 (see
   PARA 1003): see art 10(1).
3 Convention on Limitation of Liability for Maritime Claims art 10(1). It seems that art 10, which
   is in a separate chapter of the Convention from art 11 (constitution of the fund), grants a
   free-standing entitlement to limit irrespective of whether there was ever a fund constituted; and
   there is nothing in the Civil Procedure Rules to support the opposite contention: see *The Western
   Regent (Owners) v The Western Regent (Charterers)* [2005] EWHC 460 (Admlty), [2005] 2 All
   ER (Comm) 51.
4 Ie the provisions of the Convention on Limitation of Liability for Maritime Claims art 12 (see
   PARA 1004): see art 10(2).
5 Convention on Limitation of Liability for Maritime Claims art 10(2).
6 Ie under the rules of the Convention on Limitation of Liability for Maritime Claims art 10: see art
   10(3).
7 As to Orders in Council which are made declaring that any state specified in the Order is a party
   to the Convention on Limitation of Liability for Maritime Claims, as amended by the 1996
   Protocol, see PARA 992 note 3.
8 Convention on Limitation of Liability for Maritime Claims art 10(3).

(iii) The Limitation Fund under the Convention

1003. Constitution of the limitation fund. Under the Convention on Limitation of Liability for Maritime Claims[1], any person alleged to be liable may constitute a fund with the court[2] or other competent authority in any state party[3] in which legal proceedings are instituted in respect of claims subject to limitation[4]. The fund must be constituted in the sum of such of the amounts payable[5] as are applicable to claims for which that person may be liable, together with interest thereon[6] from the date of the occurrence giving rise to the liability until the date of the constitution of the fund[7]. A fund may be constituted either by depositing the sum, or by producing a guarantee acceptable under the legislation of the state party where the fund is constituted and considered to be adequate by the court or other competent authority[8]. Any fund thus constituted is available only for the payment of claims in respect of which limitation of liability can be invoked[9].

Where a fund is so constituted with the court[10] for the payment of claims arising out of any occurrence, the court may stay any proceedings relating to any claim arising out of that occurrence which are pending against the person by whom the fund has been constituted[11].

1 Ie the Convention on Limitation of Liability for Maritime Claims (London, 1 to 19 November 1976; TS 13 (1990); Cm 955): see PARA 992.
2 References in the Convention and in the Merchant Shipping Act 1995 Sch 7 Pt II paras 1–10 (see note 1) to the court are references to the High Court: Sch 7 Pt II para 11.
3 As to Orders in Council which are made declaring that any state specified in the Order is a party to the Convention on Limitation of Liability for Maritime Claims, as amended by the 1996 Protocol, see PARA 992 note 3.
4 Convention on Limitation of Liability for Maritime Claims art 11(1). A fund constituted by one of the persons mentioned in art 9(1)(a)–(c), or in art 9(2) (see PARA 1001) or his insurer, is deemed constituted by all persons mentioned in art 9(1)(a)–(c), or in art 9(2), respectively: art 11(3). See *Metvale Ltd v Monsanto International Sarl, The MSC Napoli* [2008] EWHC 3002 (Admlty), [2009] 1 All ER (Comm) 1158 (limitation fund deemed constituted by defendant charterers who were entitled to limit their liability); *Kairos Shipping Ltd v Enka & Co Llc, The Atlantick Confidence* [2014[EWCA Civ 217, [2014] 1 All ER (Comm) 909.
    As to the situation where limitation is obtained before liability is even established see *Bouygues Offshore SA v Caspian Shipping Co* [1998] 2 Lloyd's Rep 461, CA; *Vessel SA v CP Ships (UK) Ltd*, sub nom *Denise (The) (Owners) v The Denise (Charterers)* [2004] EWHC 3305 (Admlty), [2005] 2 All ER (Comm) 47. See also *Schiffahrtsgesellschaft MS Merkur Sky MbH & Co KG v MS Leerort Nth Schiffahrts GmbH & Co KG, The Leerort and The Zim Piraeus* [2001] EWCA Civ 1055, [2001] 2 Lloyd's Rep 291 (judge had been correct to conclude that decree of limitation should not have been delayed to permit one of the cargo owners to pursue further discovery on a case that was doomed to failure). As to whether the entitlement to constitute a fund could arise when proceedings begin by way of arbitration in London had proceeded to an award see *ICL Shipping Ltd v Chin Tai Steel Enterprise Co Ltd, The ICL Vikraman* [2003] EWHC 2320 (Comm), [2004] 1 All ER (Comm) 246, [2004] 1 WLR 2254, [2004] 1 Lloyd's Rep 21 (arbitration proceedings are legal proceedings for the purpose of the Convention on Limitation of Liability for Maritime Claims art 11(1)).
    As to the relationship between art 10 (limitation of liability without constitution of a limitation fund) (see PARA 1002) and art 11(1) see *Seismic Shipping Inc v Total E&P UK plc, The Western Regent* [2005] EWCA Civ 985, [2005] 2 All ER (Comm) 515, [2005] 2 Lloyd's Rep 359 (affg *The Western Regent (Owners) v The Western Regent (Charterers)* [2005] EWHC 460 (Admlty), [2005] 2 All ER (Comm) 51).
5 Ie the amounts set out in the Convention on Limitation of Liability for Maritime Claims art 6 (see PARA 998) or art 7 (see PARA 999): see art 11(1).
6 The Secretary of State may, with the concurrence of the Treasury, by order prescribe the rate of interest for the purposes of the Convention on Limitation of Liability for Maritime Claims art 11(1): Merchant Shipping Act 1995 Sch 7 Pt II para 8(1). In exercise of this power the Secretary of State, with the concurrence of the Treasury, has made the Merchant Shipping (Liability of Shipowners and Others) (New Rate of Interest) Order 2004, SI 2004/931. Accordingly, the rate of interest for the purposes of the Convention on Limitation of Liability for Maritime Claims art 11(1) is the prescribed rate from 31 December 2003, where the occurrence takes place before 1 September 1999 (but the fund is constituted on or after 1 September 1999) or where the occurrence takes place on or after 1 September 1999: Merchant Shipping (Liability of Shipowners and Others)

(New Rate of Interest) Order 2004, SI 2004/931, art 4. For these purposes, 'prescribed rate' means 1% more than the base rate quoted from time to time by the Bank of England or the rate of interest set by any body which may supersede it and where there is more than one such rate, the lowest of them: art 2. As to the Secretary of State see PARA 36; and as to the making of orders by the Secretary of State under the Merchant Shipping Act 1995 generally see PARA 39. As to the Treasury see CONSTITUTIONAL AND ADMINISTRATIVE LAW vol 20 (2014) PARAS 262–265.
7   Convention on Limitation of Liability for Maritime Claims art 11(1).
8   Convention on Limitation of Liability for Maritime Claims art 11(2). Notwithstanding the previous long-standing practice of constituting a limitation fund by means of a payment into court, the effect of express wording of art 11(2) was that a limitation fund could be constituted by means of the production of a guarantee: *Kairos Shipping Ltd v Enka & Co Llc, The Atlantick Confidence* [2014] EWCA Civ 217, [2014] 1 All ER (Comm) 909.
9   Convention on Limitation of Liability for Maritime Claims art 11(1).
10 Ie in accordance with the Convention on Limitation of Liability for Maritime Claims art 11(1) (see the text and notes 1–9): see the Merchant Shipping Act 1995 Sch 7 Pt II para 8(3).
11 Merchant Shipping Act 1995 Sch 7 Pt II para 8(3). As to the persons by whom the fund has been constituted see note 4.

1004. Distribution of the limitation fund. Under the Convention on Limitation of Liability for Maritime Claims[1], the limitation fund[2] must be distributed[3] among the claimants in proportion to their established claims against the fund[4].

If, before the fund is distributed, the person liable, or his insurer, has settled a claim against the fund, such person acquires by subrogation, up to the amount he has paid, the rights which the person so compensated would have enjoyed under the Convention[5]. Such right of subrogation may also be exercised by other persons in respect of any amount of compensation which they may have paid, but only to the extent that such subrogation is permitted under the applicable national law[6].

Where the person liable or any other person establishes that he may be compelled to pay, at a later date, in whole or in part any such amount of compensation with regard to which such person would have enjoyed a right of subrogation[7] had the compensation been paid before the fund was distributed, the court[8] or other competent authority of the state where the fund has been constituted may order that a sufficient sum be provisionally set aside to enable such person at such later date to enforce his claim against the fund[9].

1   Ie the Convention on Limitation of Liability for Maritime Claims (London, 1 to 19 November 1976; TS 13 (1990); Cm 955): see PARA 992.
2   As to the constitution of the limitation fund see PARA 1003.
3   Ie subject to the provisions of the Convention on Limitation of Liability for Maritime Claims art 6(1), (2) (see PARA 998) or art 7 (see PARA 999): see art 12(1).
4   Convention on Limitation of Liability for Maritime Claims art 12(1). No lien or other right in respect of any ship or property affects the proportions in which under art 12 the limitation fund is distributed among several claimants: Merchant Shipping Act 1995 Sch 7 Pt II para 9. As to the meaning of references to a ship see PARA 993 note 2.
5   Convention on Limitation of Liability for Maritime Claims art 12(2).
6   Convention on Limitation of Liability for Maritime Claims art 12(3).
7   Ie pursuant to the Convention on Limitation of Liability for Maritime Claims art 12(2), (3) (see the text and notes 5–6): see art 12(4).
8   As to the meaning of references to the court see PARA 1003 note 2.
9   Convention on Limitation of Liability for Maritime Claims art 12(4).

1005. Bar to other actions once limitation fund has been constituted. Where, under the Convention on Limitation of Liability for Maritime Claims[1], a limitation fund has been constituted[2], any person having made a claim against the fund is barred from exercising any right in respect of such a claim against any other assets of a person by or on behalf of whom the fund has been constituted[3].

After a limitation fund has been constituted[4], any ship[5] or other property, belonging to a person on behalf of whom the fund has been constituted, which has been arrested or attached within the jurisdiction of a state party[6] for a claim which may be raised against the fund, or any security given, may be released by order of the court[7] or other competent authority of such state[8]. However, such release must always be ordered if the limitation fund has been constituted:

(1) at the port where the occurrence took place, or, if it took place out of port, at the first port of call thereafter[9]; or

(2) at the port of disembarkation in respect of claims for loss of life or personal injury[10]; or

(3) at the port of discharge in respect of damage to cargo[11]; or

(4) in the state where the arrest is made[12].

These rules[13] apply only if the claimant may bring a claim against the limitation fund before the court administering that fund and the fund is actually available and freely transferable in respect of that claim[14].

1 Ie the Convention on Limitation of Liability for Maritime Claims (London, 1 to 19 November 1976; TS 13 (1990); Cm 955): see PARA 992.
2 Ie in accordance with the Convention on Limitation of Liability for Maritime Claims art 11 (see PARA 1003): see art 13(1).
3 Convention on Limitation of Liability for Maritime Claims art 13(1).
4 Ie in accordance with the Convention on Limitation of Liability for Maritime Claims art 11: see art 13(2).
5 As to the meaning of references to a ship see PARA 993 note 2.
6 As to Orders in Council which are made declaring that any state specified in the Order is a party to the Convention on Limitation of Liability for Maritime Claims, as amended by the 1996 Protocol, see PARA 992 note 3.
7 As to the meaning of references to the court see PARA 1003 note 2.
8 Convention on Limitation of Liability for Maritime Claims art 13(2). Where the release of a ship or other property is ordered under art 13(2), the person on whose application it is ordered to be released is deemed to have submitted to the jurisdiction of the court to adjudicate on the claim for which the ship or property was arrested or attached: Merchant Shipping Act 1995 Sch 7 Pt II para 10. See *ICL Shipping Ltd v Chin Tai Steel Enterprise Co Ltd, The ICL Vikraman* [2003] EWHC 2320 (Comm), [2004] 1 All ER (Comm) 246, [2004] 1 WLR 2254, [2004] 1 Lloyd's Rep 21 (security in form of letter of undertaking to pay any damages awarded not required to be released as proceedings still current in state which was not party to the Convention).
9 Convention on Limitation of Liability for Maritime Claims art 13(2)(a).
10 Convention on Limitation of Liability for Maritime Claims art 13(2)(b).
11 Convention on Limitation of Liability for Maritime Claims art 13(2)(c).
12 Convention on Limitation of Liability for Maritime Claims art 13(2)(d).
13 Ie the rules of the Convention on Limitation of Liability for Maritime Claims art 13(1), (2) (see the text and notes 1–12): see art 13(3).
14 Convention on Limitation of Liability for Maritime Claims art 13(3).

1006. Governing law for the constitution and distribution of limitation fund.

Under the Convention on Limitation of Liability for Maritime Claims[1], the rules relating to the constitution and distribution of a limitation fund[2], and all rules of procedure in connection therewith, are governed[3] by the law of the state party[4] in which the fund is constituted[5].

1 Ie the Convention on Limitation of Liability for Maritime Claims (London, 1 to 19 November 1976; TS 13 (1990); Cm 955): see PARA 992.
2 As to the constitution of a limitation fund see PARA 1003; and as to the distribution of a limitation fund see PARA 1004.
3 Ie subject to the provisions of the Convention on Limitation of Liability for Maritime Claims Ch III (arts 11–14) (see PARAS 1053–1055): see art 14.
4 As to Orders in Council which are made declaring that any state specified in the Order is a party to the Convention on Limitation of Liability for Maritime Claims, as amended by the 1996 Protocol, see PARA 992 note 3.
5 Convention on Limitation of Liability for Maritime Claims art 14. Note that the effect of Parliament and Council Regulation (EC) 864/2007 (OJ L199, 31.7.2007, p 40) ('the Rome II Regulation') art 28 (see CONFLICT OF LAWS vol 19 (2011) PARA 648) is that the Convention on Limitation of Liability for Maritime Claims art 14 prevails over the Rome II Regulation.

(iv) Scope of Application of the Convention

1007. General application of the Convention. The Convention on Limitation of Liability for Maritime Claims[1] applies whenever any person who is entitled to limit liability[2] seeks to limit his liability before the court[3] of a state party[4] or seeks to procure the release of a ship[5] or other property or the discharge of any security given within the jurisdiction of any such state[6].

A state party may regulate by specific provisions of national law the system of limitation of liability to be applied to vessels which are, according to the law of that state, ships intended for navigation on inland waterways[7], or ships of less than 300 tons[8]. However, a state party which makes use of such an option must inform the depositary of the limits of liability adopted in its national legislation, or of the fact that there are none[9].

Notwithstanding the limit of liability prescribed for passenger claims[10], a state party may regulate by specific provisions of national law the system of liability to be applied to claims for loss of life or personal injury to passengers of a ship, provided that the limit of liability is not lower than that so prescribed[11]. However, a state party which makes use of such an option must inform the Secretary General of the International Maritime Organisation[12] of the limits of liability adopted, or of the fact that there are none[13].

1 Ie the Convention on Limitation of Liability for Maritime Claims (London, 1 to 19 November 1976; TS 13 (1990); Cm 955): see PARA 992.
2 Ie any person referred to in the Convention on Limitation of Liability for Maritime Claims art 1 (see PARA 993): see art 15(1) (renumbered by SI 1998/1258).
3 As to the meaning of references to the court see PARA 1003 note 2.
4 As to Orders in Council which are made declaring that any state specified in the Order is a party to the Convention on Limitation of Liability for Maritime Claims, as amended by the 1996 Protocol, see PARA 992 note 3.
5 As to the meaning of references to a ship see PARA 993 note 2.
6 Convention on Limitation of Liability for Maritime Claims art 15(1) (as renumbered: see note 2). For general comments on the application of the Convention on Limitation of Liability for Maritime Claims see *The Herceg Novi (owners) v Ming Galaxy (owners)* [1998] 4 All ER 238, [1998] 2 Lloyd's Rep 454, CA (collision occurring in the Straits of Singapore when Singapore still held to the earlier Convention of 1957). See also *Seismic Shipping Inc v Total E&P UK plc, The Western Regent* [2005] EWCA Civ 985, [2005] 2 All ER (Comm) 515, [2005] 2 Lloyd's Rep 359 (limitation proceedings could be brought in England where underlying proceedings instituted in Texas).
7 Convention on Limitation of Liability for Maritime Claims art 15(2)(a) (art 15(2) added by SI 1998/1258).
8 Convention on Limitation of Liability for Maritime Claims art 15(2)(b) (as added: see note 7).
9 Convention on Limitation of Liability for Maritime Claims art 15(2) (as added: see note 7).
10 Ie the limits of liability determined in accordance with the Convention on Limitation of Liability for Maritime Claims art 7(1) (see PARA 999): see art 15(3bis) (added by SI 1998/1258).
11 Convention on Limitation of Liability for Maritime Claims art 15(3bis) (as added: see note 10).
12 As to the International Maritime Organisation see PARA 12.
13 Convention on Limitation of Liability for Maritime Claims art 15(3bis) (as added: see note 10).

1008. Reservations under the Convention. Under the Convention on Limitation of Liability for Maritime Claims[1], any state[2] may, at the time of signature, ratification, acceptance, approval or accession, or at any time thereafter, reserve the right to exclude[3]:

    (1)   the right to make subject to limitation[4]:

        (a)   claims in respect of the raising, removal, destruction or the rendering harmless of a ship[5] which is sunk, wrecked, stranded or abandoned, including anything that is or has been on board such ship[6]; or

        (b)   claims in respect of the removal, destruction or the rendering harmless of the cargo of the ship[7]; and

(2)   claims for damage within the meaning of the International Convention on Liability and Compensation for Damage in Connection with the Carriage of Hazardous and Noxious Substances by Sea 1996[8], or of any amendment or Protocol thereto[9].

No other reservations are admissible to the substantive provisions of the Convention on Limitation of Liability for Maritime Claims[10].

1   Ie the Convention on Limitation of Liability for Maritime Claims (London, 1 to 19 November 1976; TS 13 (1990); Cm 955): see PARA 992.
2   As to Orders in Council which are made declaring that any state specified in the Order is a party to the Convention on Limitation of Liability for Maritime Claims, as amended by the 1996 Protocol, see PARA 992 note 3.
3   Convention on Limitation of Liability for Maritime Claims art 18(1) (art 18 added by SI 1998/1258).
4   Head (1) in the text refers to the right to exclude the application of the Convention on Limitation of Liability for Maritime Claims art 2(1)(d), (e) (see PARA 994): see art 18(1)(a) (as added: see note 3).
5   As to the meaning of references to a ship see PARA 993 note 2.
6   See the Convention on Limitation of Liability for Maritime Claims arts 2(1)(d), 18(1)(a) (art 18(1)(a) as added: see note 3).
7   See the Convention on Limitation of Liability for Maritime Claims arts 2(1)(e), 18(1)(a) (art 18(1)(a) as added: see note 3).
8   Ie the International Convention on Liability and Compensation for Damage in Connection with the Carriage of Hazardous and Noxious Substances by Sea 1996 (London, 3 May 1996; Misc 5 (1997); Cm 3580) (as to which see ENVIRONMENTAL QUALITY AND PUBLIC HEALTH vol 45 (2010) PARA 472 et seq): see the Convention on Limitation of Liability for Maritime Claims art 18(1)(b) (as added: see note 3). The text of the International Convention on Liability and Compensation for Damage in Connection with the Carriage of Hazardous and Noxious Substances by Sea 1996, excluding the annexes, is set out in the Merchant Shipping Act 1995 s 182A(2), Sch 5A: see ENVIRONMENTAL QUALITY AND PUBLIC HEALTH vol 45 (2010) PARA 474 et seq.
9   Convention on Limitation of Liability for Maritime Claims art 18(1)(b) (as added: see note 3).
10 Convention on Limitation of Liability for Maritime Claims art 18(1) (as added: see note 3).

(2) EXCLUSION AND APPORTIONMENT OF LIABILITY FOR LOSS OR DAMAGE

1009. General exclusions. The owner[1] of a United Kingdom ship[2] is not liable for any loss or damage in the following cases[3], namely:
(1)   where any property on board the ship is lost or damaged by reason of fire on board the ship[4]; or
(2)   where any gold, silver, watches, jewels or precious stones on board the ship are lost or damaged by reason of theft, robbery or other dishonest conduct and their nature and value were not at the time of shipment declared by their owner or shipper to the owner or master[5] of the ship in the bill of lading or otherwise in writing[6].

Where the loss or damage arises from anything done or omitted by any person in his capacity of master or member of the crew or, otherwise than in that capacity, in the course of his employment as a servant of the owner of the ship, the liability of the following persons is also excluded[7], namely:
(a)   the master, member of the crew or servant[8]; and
(b)   in a case where the master or member of the crew is the servant of a person whose liability would not otherwise be so excluded[9], the person whose servant he is[10].

These provisions[11] do not exclude the liability of any person for any loss or damage resulting from any personal act or omission of his, committed with the intent to cause such loss, or recklessly and with knowledge that such loss would probably result[12].

1 For these purposes, 'owner', in relation to a ship, includes any part owner and any charterer, manager or operator of the ship: Merchant Shipping Act 1995 s 186(5). As to the meaning of 'ship' see PARA 229.

2 As to the meaning of 'United Kingdom ship' see PARA 230. The Merchant Shipping Act 1995 s 186 applies in relation to Her Majesty's ships as they apply in relation to other ships: s 186(4). As to the meaning of 'Her Majesty's ships' see the Crown Proceedings Act 1947 s 38(2); and CROWN AND CROWN PROCEEDINGS vol 29 (2014) PARA 86. As to the application of the Merchant Shipping Act 1995 s 186 to the Crown and its ships see PARA 1015.

3 Merchant Shipping Act 1995 s 186(1). The provisions of s 186(1) are subject to s 186(3) (see the text and notes 11–12): see s 186(1). Nothing in the Pilotage Act 1987 s 22(3) or (4) (see PARA 594) affects any liability which may be excluded under the Merchant Shipping Act 1995 s 186 (see the Pilotage Act 1987 s 22(7); and PARA 594); nor does anything in the Merchant Shipping Act 1995 s 186 relieve a person of any liability imposed on him by the Convention relating to the Carriage of Passengers and their Luggage by Sea (Athens, 13 December 1974; TS 40 (1987); Cm 202) (see art 13; and CARRIAGE AND CARRIERS vol 7 (2015) PARA 645).

4 Merchant Shipping Act 1995 s 186(1)(a). See note 3.

5 As to the meaning of 'master' see PARA 444 note 1.

6 Merchant Shipping Act 1995 s 186(1)(b). See note 3.

7 Merchant Shipping Act 1995 s 186(2). The text refers to the provisions of s 186(1) (see the text and notes 1–6) excluding liability, subject to s 186(3) (see the text and notes 11–12), in the circumstances set out in s 186(2): see s 186(2).

8 Merchant Shipping Act 1995 s 186(2)(a). See note 7.

9 Ie would not be excluded by the Merchant Shipping Act 1995 s 186(1) (see the text and notes 1–6), apart from s 186(2): see s 186(2)(b). See note 7.

10 Merchant Shipping Act 1995 s 186(2)(b). See note 7.

11 Ie the Merchant Shipping Act 1995 s 186: see s 186(3).

12 Merchant Shipping Act 1995 s 186(3). The text refers to the liability of any person for any loss or damage resulting from any such personal act or omission of his as is mentioned in the Convention on Limitation of Liability for Maritime Claims (London, 1 to 19 November 1976; TS 13 (1990); Cm 955) art 4 (conduct barring limitation) (see PARA 996): see the Merchant Shipping Act 1995 s 186(3).

1010. Damage or loss: apportionment of liability.

Where, by the fault of two or more ships[1], damage or loss is caused[2] to one or more of those ships, to their cargoes or freight[3], or to any property on board, the liability to make good the damage or loss is in proportion to the degree in which each ship was in fault[4]. If, in any such case, having regard to all the circumstances, it is not possible to establish different degrees of fault, the liability must be apportioned equally[5].

These rules as to apportionment[6] apply to persons other than the owners of a ship who are responsible for the fault of the ships, as well as to the owners of a ship; and, where, by virtue of any charter or demise, or for any other reason, the owners are not responsible for the navigation and management of the ship, these rules apply to the charterers or other persons for the time being so responsible instead of the owners[7].

However, nothing in these provisions which govern apportionment of liability[8]:

(1)   operates so as to render any ship liable for any loss or damage to which the fault of the ship has not contributed[9];

(2)   affects the liability of any person under a contract of carriage or any contract, or is to be construed as imposing any liability upon any person from which he is exempted by any contract or by any provision of law, or as affecting the right of any person to limit his liability in the manner provided by law[10].

1 As to the meaning of 'ship' see PARA 229. The provisions of the Merchant Shipping Act 1995 s 187 are to be read as if references to ships include references to hovercraft: see the Hovercraft (Civil Liability) Order 1986, SI 1986/1305, art 7; and PARA 386.

2	For these purposes, references to damage or loss caused by the fault of a ship include references to any salvage or other expenses, consequent upon that fault, recoverable at law by way of damages: Merchant Shipping Act 1995 s 187(7).

3	For these purposes, 'freight' includes passage money and hire: Merchant Shipping Act 1995 s 187(6).

4	Merchant Shipping Act 1995 s 187(1). As to the application of s 187 to the Crown and its ships see PARA 1015. As to the time limit for proceedings see PARA 1013.

5	Merchant Shipping Act 1995 s 187(2).

6	Ie the Merchant Shipping Act 1995 s 187: see s 187(3).

7	Merchant Shipping Act 1995 s 187(3).

8	Ie nothing in the Merchant Shipping Act 1995 s 187: see s 187(4), (5).

9	Merchant Shipping Act 1995 s 187(4).

10	Merchant Shipping Act 1995 s 187(5). See *Smit International (Deutschland) GmbH v Josef Mobius* [2001] 2 All ER (Comm) 265 (apportionment of risk and responsibility governed by contractual terms).

1011. Loss of life or personal injuries; joint and several liability.

Where loss of life or personal injuries are suffered by any person on board a ship[1] owing to the fault of that ship[2] and of any other ship or ships, the liability of the owners[3] of the ships is joint and several[4].

However, nothing in the provisions which govern such liability[5] may be construed as depriving any person of any right of defence on which he might otherwise[6] have relied in an action brought against him by the person injured, or any person or persons entitled to sue in respect of such loss of life, or affects the right of any person to limit his liability in the manner provided by law[7].

1	As to the meaning of 'ship' see PARA 229. The provisions of the Merchant Shipping Act 1995 s 188 are to be read as if references to ships include references to hovercraft: see the Hovercraft (Civil Liability) Order 1986, SI 1986/1305, art 7; and PARA 386.

2	For these purposes, references to damage or loss caused by the fault of a ship include references to any salvage or other expenses, consequent upon that fault, recoverable at law by way of damages: Merchant Shipping Act 1995 s 187(7), applied by s 188(4).

3	The rules contained in the Merchant Shipping Act 1995 s 188 apply to persons other than the owners of a ship who are responsible for the fault of the ships, as well as to the owners of a ship; and, where, by virtue of any charter or demise, or for any other reason, the owners are not responsible for the navigation and management of the ship, s 188 applies to the charterers or other persons for the time being so responsible instead of the owners: s 187(3), applied by s 188(2).

4	Merchant Shipping Act 1995 s 188(1). As to the application of s 188 to the Crown and its ships see PARA 1015. As to the time limit for proceedings see PARA 1013.

5	Ie nothing in the Merchant Shipping Act 1995 s 188: see s 188(3).

6	Ie apart from the Merchant Shipping Act 1995 s 188: see s 188(3).

7	Merchant Shipping Act 1995 s 188(3).

1012. Loss of life or personal injuries; right of contribution.

Where loss of life or personal injuries are suffered by any person on board a ship[1] owing to the fault of that ship and any other ship or ships, and a proportion of the damages is recovered against the owners[2] of one of the ships which exceeds the proportion in which the ship was in fault, they may recover by way of contribution the amount of the excess from the owners of the other ship or ships to the extent to which those ships were respectively in fault[3].

However, nothing in these provisions governing the right of contribution[4] authorises the recovery of any amount which could not, by reason of any statutory or contractual limitation of, or exemption from, liability, or which could not for any other reason, have been recovered in the first instance as damages by the persons entitled to claim therefor[5].

In addition to any other remedy provided by law, the persons entitled to any contribution so recoverable[6] have, for the purposes of recovering it, the same rights and powers as the persons entitled to claim for damages in the first instance[7].

1   As to the meaning of 'ship' see PARA 229. The provisions of the Merchant Shipping Act 1995 s 189 are to be read as if references to ships include references to hovercraft: see the Hovercraft (Civil Liability) Order 1986, SI 1986/1305, art 7; and PARA 386.
2   The rules contained in the Merchant Shipping Act 1995 s 189 apply to persons other than the owners of a ship who are responsible for the fault of the ships, as well as to the owners of a ship; and, where, by virtue of any charter or demise, or for any other reason, the owners are not responsible for the navigation and management of the ship, s 189 applies to the charterers or other persons for the time being so responsible instead of the owners: s 187(3), applied by s 189(2).
3   Merchant Shipping Act 1995 s 189(1). As to the application of s 189 to the Crown and its ships see PARA 1015. As to the time limit for proceedings see PARA 1013.
4   Ie nothing in the Merchant Shipping Act 1995 s 189: see s 189(3).
5   Merchant Shipping Act 1995 s 189(3).
6   Ie recoverable under the Merchant Shipping Act 1995 s 189: see s 189(4).
7   Merchant Shipping Act 1995 s 189(4).

1013.   General time limits for proceedings to enforce claim or lien against a ship or her owners.

No proceedings to enforce any claim or lien against a ship[1] or her owners[2]:

(1)   in respect of damage or loss caused by the fault of that ship to another ship, its cargo or freight or any property on board it[3]; or

(2)   for damages for loss of life or personal injury caused by the fault of that ship to any person on board another ship[4],

may be brought after the period of two years from the date when[5]:

(a)   the damage or loss was caused[6]; or

(b)   the loss of life or injury was suffered[7].

Nor may any proceedings relating to multiple fault[8], to enforce any contribution in respect of any overpaid proportion of any damages for loss of life or personal injury, be brought after the period of one year from the date of payment[9].

Any court having jurisdiction in such proceedings[10] may, however, in accordance with rules of court, extend the period allowed for bringing proceedings to such extent and on such conditions as it thinks fit[11].

Any such court, if satisfied that there has not been during any period allowed for bringing proceedings any reasonable opportunity of arresting the defendant ship[12], either:

(i)   within the jurisdiction of the court[13]; or

(ii)   within the territorial sea of the country to which the claimant's ship belongs or in which the claimant resides or has his principal place of business[14],

must extend the period allowed for bringing proceedings to an extent sufficient to give a reasonable opportunity of so arresting the ship[15].

1   As to the meaning of 'ship' see PARA 229. The provisions of the Merchant Shipping Act 1995 s 190 are to be read as if references to ships include references to hovercraft: see the Hovercraft (Civil Liability) Order 1986, SI 1986/1305, art 7; and PARA 386. In *Steedman v Schofield* [1992] 2 Lloyd's Rep 163, a claim for damages against the operator of a jet-ski was held not to be time-barred by the Maritime Conventions Act 1911 s 8 (repealed) (now the Merchant Shipping Act 1995 s 190). Although s 190 is derived from the Maritime Conventions Act 1911 s 8 (repealed), there are significant differences. In particular, the Act of 1911 did not specify that the extent of fault was immaterial (see note 3). Any cases which are cited in the footnotes to this paragraph and which are based on the Maritime Conventions Act 1911 s 8 (repealed) should, therefore, be treated with some caution when interpreting provisions of the Merchant Shipping Act 1995 s 190.
2   See the Merchant Shipping Act 1995 s 190(1). For this purpose, 'owners' includes any person responsible for the fault of the vessel, and charterers are to be substituted for owners where the owners are not responsible for navigation and management: see *HMS Archer* [1919] P 1; *The Sobieski* [1949] P 313, [1949] 1 All ER 701, CA. See notes 1, 3. As to the application of s 190 to the Crown and its ships see PARA 1015.

3   Merchant Shipping Act 1995 s 190(1)(a). 'Fault' includes fault in the management of the ship: *John Franetovich & Co v Ministry of Defence, The Norwhale* [1975] QB 589, [1975] 1 Lloyd's Rep 610. The extent of the fault is immaterial for the purposes of the Merchant Shipping Act 1995 s 190: s 190(2). However, because s 190(2) applies only to claims which fall within s 190, claims which arise on board a ship and which lie against owners of that ship are not affected: *The Niceto de Larringa* [1966] P 80, [1965] 2 All ER 930. See note 1.

4   Merchant Shipping Act 1995 s 190(1)(b). See note 3. Other passenger claims will be governed by the Convention relating to the Carriage of Passengers and their Luggage by Sea (Athens, 13 December 1974; TS 40 (1987); Cm 202) (the 'Athens Convention') art 16 (as to which see CARRIAGE AND CARRIERS vol 7 (2015) PARA 648).

5   See the Merchant Shipping Act 1995 s 190(3). The provisions of s 190(3) are subject to s 190(5), (6) (see the text and notes 10–15): see s 190(3). The time limit provided by s 190 applies to counterclaims and cross-claims: *The Fairplay XIV* [1939] P 57, 65 Ll L Rep 108. See also *The Gniezno* [1968] P 418, [1967] 2 All ER 738, [1967] 1 Lloyd's Rep 441. A decree of limitation of liability does not override the two year period and rival claimants are therefore entitled to object to claims of persons who have not commenced proceedings within the statutory period, but, where limitation decrees are made, this may be a good reason for not issuing a claim form, so that in general an extension of time will be granted: see *The Disperser* [1920] P 228 at 235, 15 Asp MLC 112 at 114 per Hill J. See also note 11. The Merchant Shipping Act 1995 is complied with if the claim form is issued within two years, even though it is not served: see *The Espanoleto* [1920] P 223, 15 Asp MLC 287. The protection afforded by the Merchant Shipping Act 1995 s 190 is not waived by acknowledging service of a claim form: see *The Llandovery Castle* [1920] P 119; *The Alnwick* [1965] P 357, [1965] 2 All ER 569, [1965] 1 Lloyd's Rep 320, CA. See note 1.

6   Merchant Shipping Act 1995 s 190(3)(a). See note 7.

7   Merchant Shipping Act 1995 s 190(3)(b). See *The Caliph* [1912] P 213, 82 LJP 27 (where it was held that a claim could be brought within two years under the Maritime Conventions Act 1911 s 8 (repealed) (see now the Merchant Shipping Act 1995 s 190), notwithstanding that the Fatal Accidents Act 1846 (repealed) (see now the Fatal Accidents Act 1976) provided that the action had to be brought within 12 months (now three years) (see NEGLIGENCE vol 78 (2010) PARA 28)). See note 1.

    As to the distinction between heads (a) and (b) in the text see *Sweet v The Owners of Blyth Lifeboat 'Edward Duke of Windsor'* (2002) Times, 22 February, [2002] All ER (D) 146 (Jan) (on the true construction of the Merchant Shipping Act 1995 s 190(3)(b), it was possible for time not to begin to run in respect of a personal injury until after the date on which the relevant accident occurred, if in the particular case psychiatric symptoms had not been apparent until after the date of the accident; the wording of s 190(3)(b) provided for the two year period to begin to run from the date when the injury 'was suffered', which contrasted with s 190(3)(a), which provided that the period began when the damage or loss to a vessel or cargo 'was caused').

8   Ie proceedings under any of the Merchant Shipping Act 1995 s 187 (see PARA 1010), s 188 (see PARA 1011) or s 189 (see PARA 1012): see s 190(4).

9   Merchant Shipping Act 1995 s 190(4). The provisions of s 190(4) are subject to s 190(5), (6) (see the text and notes 10–15): see s 190(4).

10 Ie proceedings under the Merchant Shipping Act 1995 s 190(3) (see the text and notes 1–7) or under s 190(4) (see the text and notes 8–9): see s 190(5).

11 Merchant Shipping Act 1995 s 190(5). Although no rules have been made under s 190 (see also PARAS 152, 153), it is thought that the court's discretion is not thereby affected. This was the position under the Maritime Conventions Act 1911 (repealed): see *HMS Archer* [1919] P 1.

    Accordingly, in an application for an extension of time, there is a two stage test: the court must first consider the question of fact as to whether good reason for the extension has been demonstrated by the claimants and only if the claimant has established good reason should the court proceed to exercise its discretion, taking into account the balance of hardship, as to whether such an extension should be granted: *The Al Tabith and The Alanfushi* [1995] 2 Lloyd's Rep 336, CA (distinguishing *The Zirje* [1989] 1 Lloyd's Rep 493); *Stolt Kestrel BV v Sener Petrol Denizcilik Ticaret AS; CDE SA v Sure Wind Marine Ltd* [2015] EWCA Civ 1035, [2015] All ER (D) 146 (Oct) (two-stage test continues to apply: see also *Owners of the Ship Theresa Libra v Owners of the Ship MSC Pamela* [2013] EWHC 2792 (Admlty), [2013] All ER (D) 175 (Sep)). Mere oversight on the part of the claimant in failing to protect the time limit was not a good reason: *The Al Tabith and The Alanfushi*. There is much case law under the Maritime Conventions Act 1911 (repealed) as to how the discretion is to be exercised but these all need now to be considered in light of the two stage test in *The Al Tabith and The Alanfushi*. The exercise of the discretion ought not to be interfered with except on substantial grounds: *The Arraiz* (1924) 132 LT 715, 16 Asp MLC 451, CA. The claim will be allowed to proceed if satisfactory grounds are shown for the delay (*The Cambric* [1912] WN 272), but the party who wishes to have time extended must show substantial reasons why the other party should be deprived of the right to limitation of action which the law gives (see *The Kashmir* [1923] P 85 at 89, 16 Asp MLC 81 at 83, CA). The discretion has been exercised where the claimant was induced by correspondence with the defendants' solicitors to delay whilst awaiting settlement of liability in the collision action arising from the same incident: *The Vadne* [1959] 2 Lloyd's Rep 480. In the exercise of its discretion, the court has allowed a statement of claim in a salvage action to be amended to include allegations of further services arising out of the same occurrence: *The Katcher I* [1969] P 65, [1968] 3 All ER 344, [1968] 2 Lloyd's Rep 232. As to the exercise of discretion see also *The Alnwick* [1965] P 357, [1965] 2 All ER 569, [1965] 1 Lloyd's Rep 320, CA; *The Disperser* [1920] P 228, 15 Asp MLC 112. Applications for an extension have been dismissed where the delay was due to difficulty in ascertaining the amount of the claim (*The James Westoll* [1923] P 94n, 16 Asp MLC 453n, CA), where agreement had been reached on liability but there was no binding agreement to waive the time limit and there was undue delay (*The Sauria and The Trent* [1957] 1 Lloyd's Rep 396, CA), where the claimant was ignorant that she had a claim (*The Kashmir*), where a deliberate decision was taken not to start proceedings (*The Lu Shan* [1991] 2 Lloyd's Rep 386), where unsuccessful proceedings were first taken against another ship (*The PLM 8* [1920] P 236, 15 Asp MLC 51), where the institution of proceedings was postponed while diplomatic representations were made (*HMS Archer*), where owners elected not to sue in the United Kingdom and let time run out (*The Nedenes* (1925) 23 Ll L Rep 57), where the matter had been allowed to go to sleep and any claim by the defendant against third parties was also statute barred (*The Hesselmorr, The Sergeant* [1951] 1 Lloyd's Rep 146) and where proceedings were not allowed to run while the parties were in negotiations (see *The Albany and The Marie Josaine* [1983] 2 Lloyd's Rep 195; and see *The Mouna* [1991] 2 Lloyd's Rep 221, CA). In connection with the operation of agreed extensions see *The 'Pearl of Jebel Ali' and The 'Pride of Al Salam 95'* [2009] EWHC 1365 (Admlty), 2009] 2 Lloyd's Rep 484. See note 1.

12 Merchant Shipping Act 1995 s 190(6). The test of whether there has been any reasonable opportunity to arrest a vessel is to be determined objectively, without regard to whether steps have actually been taken in an attempt to arrest in a particular jurisdiction: *Santos v Owners of the Baltic Carrier* [2001] 1 Lloyd's Rep 689. A period of ten days during which a ship is under requisition has been held not to constitute reasonable opportunity: *The Largo Law* (1920) 123 LT 560. The Merchant Shipping Act 1995 s 190 has no application to cases in which the defendant vessel is permanently immune from arrest: *HMS Archer* [1919] P 1. See note 1.

13 Merchant Shipping Act 1995 s 190(6)(a).

14 Merchant Shipping Act 1995 s 190(6)(b).

15 Merchant Shipping Act 1995 s 190(6).

1014. General liability of harbour or conservancy authority etc.

The liability of a harbour authority[1], a conservancy authority[2] or the owners of any dock or canal[3] for any loss or damage caused to any ship[4], or to any goods, merchandise or other things whatsoever on board any ship is limited[5] by reference to the tonnage of the largest United Kingdom ship[6] which, at the time of the loss or damage is, or within the preceding five years has been, within the area over which the harbour authority, conservancy authority or owners of the dock or canal discharges or discharge any functions[7].

Such limitation of liability[8] relates to the whole of any losses and damages which may arise on any one distinct occasion, although such losses and damages may be sustained by more than one person, and applies whether the liability arises at common law or under any general or local or private Act, and notwithstanding anything contained in such an Act[9].

These provisions[10] do not exclude the liability of a harbour authority, a conservancy authority or the owners of a dock or canal for any loss or damage resulting from any such personal act or omission[11] committed with the intent to cause such loss, or recklessly and with knowledge that such loss would probably result[12]; but nothing in these provisions imposes any liability for any loss or damage where no liability otherwise exists[13].

1 As to the meaning of 'harbour authority' see PARA 69 note 4.

2 As to the meaning of 'conservancy authority' see PARA 72 note 2.

3 For these purposes, 'owners of any dock or canal' includes any authority or person having the control and management of any dock or canal, as the case may be; and 'dock' includes wet docks

and basins, tidal docks and basins, locks, cuts, entrances, dry docks, graving docks, gridirons, slips, quays, wharves, piers, stages, landing places and jetties: Merchant Shipping Act 1995 s 191(9).

4   As to the meaning of 'ship' see PARA 229.
5   Ie in accordance with the Merchant Shipping Act 1995 s 191(5): see s 191(2). Accordingly, the limit of liability must be ascertained by applying to the ship by reference to which the liability is to be determined the method of calculation specified in the Convention on Limitation of Liability for Maritime Claims (London, 1 to 19 November 1976; TS 13 (1990); Cm 955) art 6(1)(b), read with the Merchant Shipping Act 1995 s 185(2), Sch 7 Pt II para 5(1), (2) (see PARA 1008): s 191(5).
6   As to the meaning of 'United Kingdom ship' see PARA 230.
7   See the Merchant Shipping Act 1995 s 191(1), (2). For these purposes, a ship is not to be treated as having been within the area over which a harbour authority or conservancy authority discharges any functions by reason only that it has been built or fitted out within the area, or that it has taken shelter within or passed through the area on a voyage between two places both situated outside that area, or that it has loaded or unloaded mails or passengers within the area: s 191(7).
      The Convention on Limitation of Liability for Maritime Claims art 11 (see PARA 1003) and art 12 (see PARA 1004) and the Merchant Shipping Act 1995 Sch 7 Pt II para 8 (see PARA 1003) and Sch 7 Pt II para 9 (see PARA 1004) apply for the purposes of s 191: s 191(6). As to the application of s 191 to the Crown and its ships see PARA 1015.
8   Ie the limitation of liability under the Merchant Shipping Act 1995 s 191: see s 191(3).
9   Merchant Shipping Act 1995 s 191(3).
10   Ie the provisions of the Merchant Shipping Act 1995 s 191: see s 191(4).
11   Ie any such personal act or omission as is mentioned in the Convention on Limitation of Liability for Maritime Claims art 4 (see PARA 996): see the Merchant Shipping Act 1995 s 191(4).
12   Merchant Shipping Act 1995 s 191(1), (4).
13   Merchant Shipping Act 1995 s 191(8).

1015.   General application of liability provisions to Crown and its ships.

The provisions relating to the limitation of liability for maritime claims[1], exclusion of liability[2], apportionment of liability for damage or loss[3], joint and several liability for loss of life or personal injuries[4], the right of contribution for loss of life or personal injuries[5] and the time limit for proceedings against the owners or the ship[6] apply in the case of Her Majesty's ships[7] as they apply in relation to other ships; and the provisions relating to the limitation of liability of a harbour or conservancy authority or the owners of a dock or canal[8] apply to the Crown in its capacity as such an authority or owner[9].

1   Ie the Merchant Shipping Act 1995 s 185 (see PARA 992): see s 192(1).
2   Ie the Merchant Shipping Act 1995 s 186 (see PARA 1009): see s 192(1).
3   Ie the Merchant Shipping Act 1995 s 187 (see PARA 1010): see s 192(1).
4   Ie the Merchant Shipping Act 1995 s 188 (see PARA 1011): see s 192(1).
5   Ie the Merchant Shipping Act 1995 s 189 (see PARA 1012): see s 192(1).
6   Ie the Merchant Shipping Act 1995 s 190 (see PARA 1013), except s 190(6) (which allows for extension of time to arrest a defendant ship in certain circumstances): see s 192(1).
7   For these purposes, 'Her Majesty's ships' means (by virtue of the Merchant Shipping Act 1995 s 192(2)):
      (1)   ships of which the beneficial interest is vested in Her Majesty;
      (2)   ships which are registered as government ships;
      (3)   ships which are for the time being demised or sub-demised to or in the exclusive possession of the Crown,
      but it does not include any ship in which Her Majesty is interested otherwise than in right of Her government in the United Kingdom unless that ship is for the time being demised or sub-demised to Her Majesty in right of Her government in the United Kingdom or in the exclusive possession of Her Majesty in that right. As to the meaning of 'ship' see PARA 229; and as to the meaning of 'government ship' see PARA 19 note 3.
8   Ie the Merchant Shipping Act 1995 s 191 (see PARA 1014): see s 192(1).
9   Merchant Shipping Act 1995 s 192(1).

1016.   Compulsory insurance etc for ships receiving trans-shipped fish.

The owner, charterer and master of a ship, in respect of which a transhipment licence[1] is in force, must ensure that there is in force in respect of the ship, while it is in United Kingdom waters, a contract of insurance which is sufficient for these purposes[2] and which insures the owner against the following liabilities[3], namely:

(1) any liability[4] for pollution caused by oil (other than oil from tankers or bunker oil etc)[5];

(2) any liability for the costs of any operation to remove or render harmless the ship, or any article which had been on the ship, taken under the powers conferred on harbour and conservancy authorities[6] in relation to wrecks[7], or under the powers conferred on general lighthouse authorities[8] in relation to wrecks[9], or taken under corresponding powers under any statutory provision of local application[10];

(3) any liability for payment of salvage awards[11] and special compensation[12] under the International Convention on Salvage 1989[13]; and

(4) any liability for the cost of providing relief to, and of repatriating, seamen left behind or shipwrecked[14].

However, in place of a contract of insurance, there may be in force such other form of security which is sufficient for these purposes[15] and which will enable the owner to meet the liabilities mentioned in heads (1) to (4) above[16].

Any contravention of the requirements to have compulsory insurance in place (or to have such other form of security which meets those same requirements)[17] is an offence[18].

These requirements[19] are without prejudice to any entitlement to limit liability for maritime claims[20] and contracts of insurance and security may be limited accordingly[21].

Where a person is so required[22] to ensure that there is in force a contract of insurance or other security, documentary evidence of compliance with this requirement must be carried in the ship[23]; and the master and any other officer on the ship must produce on demand such documentary evidence to any relevant inspector[24]. Any contravention of the requirements to carry or to produce on demand such documents[25] is an offence[26].

1 For these purposes, 'transhipment licence' means a licence under the Sea Fish (Conservation) Act 1967 s 4A (prohibition of transhipment of fish unless authorised by a licence) (see FISHERIES AND AQUACULTURE vol 51 (2013) PARA 259): Merchant Shipping (Compulsory Insurance: Ships Receiving Trans-shipped Fish) Regulations 1998, SI 1998/209, reg 2 (made under the Merchant Shipping Act 1995 s 192A (added by the Merchant Shipping and Maritime Security Act 1997 s 31(4); amended by SI 2015/664)). As to the general requirements to be met by ships in respect of which transhipment licences are in force see PARAS 658, 659.

2 Ie a contract of insurance complying with the Merchant Shipping (Compulsory Insurance: Ships Receiving Trans-shipped Fish) Regulations 1998, SI 1998/209, reg 6: see reg 4(1). Accordingly, a contract of insurance, or other security (see the text and notes 15–16), is sufficient for the purpose of the Merchant Shipping (Compulsory Insurance: Ships Receiving Trans-shipped Fish) Regulations 1998, SI 1998/209, only if it satisfies all requirements (whether as to the person issuing it, the amount of compensation available, or for any other reason) as is specified in Merchant Shipping Notice No MSN 1711: see the Merchant Shipping (Compulsory Insurance: Ships Receiving Trans-shipped Fish) Regulations 1998, SI 1998/209, reg 6. For these purposes, 'Merchant Shipping Notice MSN No 1711' means the Notice described as such, issued by the Secretary of State, and includes a reference to any document amending or replacing it which is considered by the Secretary of State to be relevant from time to time: Merchant Shipping (Compulsory Insurance: Ships Receiving Trans-shipped Fish) Regulations 1998, SI 1998/209, reg 2. As to the Secretary of State see PARA 36. Merchant Shipping Notice 1711(M+F) ('Compulsory Insurance for Ships receiving trans-shipped Fish') specifies the forms of insurance and security satisfying the requirement of the Merchant Shipping (Compulsory Insurance: Ships Receiving Trans-shipped Fish) Regulations 1998, SI 1998/209; specifies the format of documentary evidence of compliance with the regulations which must be carried on board the ship; and provides information on the enforcement of the regulations.

3 See the Merchant Shipping (Compulsory Insurance: Ships Receiving Trans-shipped Fish) Regulations 1998, SI 1998/209, regs 3, 4(1).

4 Ie under the Merchant Shipping Act 1995 s 154 (see ENVIRONMENTAL QUALITY AND PUBLIC HEALTH vol 45 (2010) PARA 444): see the Merchant Shipping (Compulsory Insurance: Ships Receiving Trans-shipped Fish) Regulations 1998, SI 1998/209, reg 5(a).

5 Merchant Shipping (Compulsory Insurance: Ships Receiving Trans-shipped Fish) Regulations 1998, SI 1998/209, reg 5(a).

6 As to the meaning of 'conservancy authority' see PARA 72 note 2; and as to the meaning of 'harbour authority' see PARA 69 note 4.

7 Ie the powers conferred by the Merchant Shipping Act 1995 s 252 (see PARA 939): see the Merchant Shipping (Compulsory Insurance: Ships Receiving Trans-shipped Fish) Regulations 1998, SI 1998/209, reg 5(b).

8 As to the meaning of 'general lighthouse authority' see PARA 1017.

9 Ie the powers conferred by the Merchant Shipping Act 1995 s 253 (see PARA 945): see the Merchant Shipping (Compulsory Insurance: Ships Receiving Trans-shipped Fish) Regulations 1998, SI 1998/209, reg 5(b).

10 Merchant Shipping (Compulsory Insurance: Ships Receiving Trans-shipped Fish) Regulations 1998, SI 1998/209, reg 5(b).

11 Ie under the International Convention on Salvage 1989 (London, 28 April 1989; Cm 1526) art 12 (see PARA 903) or under art 13 (see PARA 878): see the Merchant Shipping (Compulsory Insurance: Ships Receiving Trans-shipped Fish) Regulations 1998, SI 1998/209, reg 5(c).

12 Ie under the International Convention on Salvage 1989 art 14 (see PARA 879): see the Merchant Shipping (Compulsory Insurance: Ships Receiving Trans-shipped Fish) Regulations 1998, SI 1998/209, reg 5(c).

13 Merchant Shipping (Compulsory Insurance: Ships Receiving Trans-shipped Fish) Regulations 1998, SI 1998/209, reg 5(c).

14 Merchant Shipping (Compulsory Insurance: Ships Receiving Trans-shipped Fish) Regulations 1998, SI 1998/209, reg 5(d). As to the relief and repatriation of seamen see PARA 548 et seq.

15 Ie which complies with the Merchant Shipping (Compulsory Insurance: Ships Receiving Trans-shipped Fish) Regulations 1998, SI 1998/209, reg 6 (see note 2): see reg 4(2).

16 Merchant Shipping (Compulsory Insurance: Ships Receiving Trans-shipped Fish) Regulations 1998, SI 1998/209, reg 4(2).

17 Ie any contravention of the Merchant Shipping (Compulsory Insurance: Ships Receiving Trans-shipped Fish) Regulations 1998, SI 1998/209, reg 4 (see the text and notes 1–16): see reg 8(1).

18 See the Merchant Shipping (Compulsory Insurance: Ships Receiving Trans-shipped Fish) Regulations 1998, SI 1998/209, reg 8(1); and PARA 1127.

19 Ie the Merchant Shipping (Compulsory Insurance: Ships Receiving Trans-shipped Fish) Regulations 1998, SI 1998/209, reg 4(1), (2) (see the text and notes 1–16): see reg 4(3).

20 Ie the entitlement to limit liability provided by the Merchant Shipping Act 1995 s 185 (see PARA 992): see the Merchant Shipping (Compulsory Insurance: Ships Receiving Trans-shipped Fish) Regulations 1998, SI 1998/209, reg 4(3).

21 Merchant Shipping (Compulsory Insurance: Ships Receiving Trans-shipped Fish) Regulations 1998, SI 1998/209, reg 4(3).

22 Ie under the Merchant Shipping (Compulsory Insurance: Ships Receiving Trans-shipped Fish) Regulations 1998, SI 1998/209: see reg 7(1).

23 Merchant Shipping (Compulsory Insurance: Ships Receiving Trans-shipped Fish) Regulations 1998, SI 1998/209, reg 7(1). Such documentary evidence must be in the form specified in Merchant Shipping Notice 1711(M+F) (see note 2): see the Merchant Shipping (Compulsory Insurance: Ships Receiving Trans-shipped Fish) Regulations 1998, SI 1998/209, reg 7(1).

24 Merchant Shipping (Compulsory Insurance: Ships Receiving Trans-shipped Fish) Regulations 1998, SI 1998/209, reg 7(2). The reference in the text to any relevant inspector is to any person mentioned in the Merchant Shipping Act 1995 s 258(1)(a), (b) or (c) (see PARA 48): see the Merchant Shipping (Compulsory Insurance: Ships Receiving Trans-shipped Fish) Regulations 1998, SI 1998/209, reg 7(2).

25 Ie any contravention of the Merchant Shipping (Compulsory Insurance: Ships Receiving Trans-shipped Fish) Regulations 1998, SI 1998/209, reg 7 (see the text and notes 22–24): see reg 8(2).

26 See the Merchant Shipping (Compulsory Insurance: Ships Receiving Trans-shipped Fish) Regulations 1998, SI 1998/209, reg 8(2); and PARA 1127.

13. LIGHTHOUSE AUTHORITIES

(1) AUTHORITIES AND COMMISSIONERS

1017. Meanings of 'general lighthouse authorities' and 'local lighthouse authorities'. For the purposes of the Merchant Shipping Act 1995 provisions which relate to lighthouses[1]:

    (1)   the Trinity House[2], as respects England and Wales[3] and the adjacent seas and islands[4];

    (2)   the Commissioners of Northern Lighthouses[5], as respects Scotland and the adjacent seas and islands[6]; and

    (3)   the Commissioners of Irish Lights[7], as respects Northern Ireland and the adjacent seas and islands[8],

are the 'general lighthouse authority'[9].

For the purposes of the Merchant Shipping Act 1995 provisions which relate to lighthouses[10]:

    (a)   each statutory harbour authority[11], as respects its area[12]; and

    (b)   any other existing local lighthouse authority, as respects its area[13],

are the 'local lighthouse authority'[14].

1 Ie for the purposes of the Merchant Shipping Act 1995 Pt VIII (ss 193–223) (see also PARA 1018 et seq): see s 193(1). For these purposes, 'lighthouse' includes any floating and other light exhibited for the guidance of ships, and also any sirens and any other description of fog signals, and also any addition to a lighthouse of any improved light, or any siren, or any description of fog signal (s 223(1)); and any reference to a lighthouse includes its appurtenances (s 223(2)). As to the meaning of 'ship' see PARA 229.

2 As to the meaning of 'Trinity House' see PARA 1018. Subject to the Merchant Shipping Act 1995 Sch 14 para 9(1), the Trinity House is also the general lighthouse authority as respects Gibraltar and, subject to Sch 14 para 9(2), the Channel Islands, and the seas adjacent thereto: s 193(5). Section 193(5) ceases to have effect on such day or days as the Secretary of State by order appoints: Sch 14 para 9(1). Accordingly, until that day, the powers of the Trinity House under Pt VIII with respect to lighthouses, buoys and beacons in the islands of Guernsey or Jersey, other than their powers under s 204 (see PARA 1032) and s 220 (see PARA 1184), may not be exercised without the consent of Her Majesty in Council (Sch 14 para 9(2)); and any such Order in Council must be laid before Parliament (Sch 14 para 9(4)). Until that day, no dues for any lighthouse, buoy or beacon erected or placed in or near the islands of Guernsey, Jersey, Sark or Alderney may be levied in the islands of Guernsey or Jersey without the consent of the States of those Islands respectively: Sch 14 para 9(3). As to the Secretary of State see PARA 36; and as to the making of orders by the Secretary of State under the Merchant Shipping Act 1995 generally see PARA 39.

    For these purposes, 'buoys and beacons' includes all other marks and signs of the sea (s 223(1)); and any reference to a buoy or beacon includes its appurtenances (s 223(2)). The Secretary of State may by order provide that references or a particular reference to a buoy or beacon in Pt VIII are or is to be construed as including, in such circumstances as are specified in the order, equipment of a kind so specified which is intended as an aid in the navigation of ships: s 223(3). In exercise of the powers so conferred by s 223(3), the Secretary of State has made the General Lighthouse Authorities (Beacons: Maritime Differential Correction Systems) Order 1997, SI 1997/3016, and the General Lighthouse Authorities (Beacons: Automatic Identification System) Order 2006, SI 2006/1977; and, by virtue of the Interpretation Act 1978 s 17(2)(b), the General Lighthouse Authorities (Beacons: Hyperbolic Systems) Order 1986, SI 1986/2285, and the General Lighthouse Authorities (Beacons: Hyperbolic Systems) Order 1991, SI 1991/347, have effect as if so made.

3 As to the meanings of 'England' and 'Wales' see PARA 16 note 2.

4 Merchant Shipping Act 1995 s 193(1)(a). In s 193(1) references to the 'seas' include seas in an area specified by virtue of s 129(2)(b) (see ENVIRONMENTAL QUALITY AND PUBLIC HEALTH vol 45 (2010) PARA 362): Merchant Shipping Act 1995 s 193(6) (added by the Marine Navigation Act 2013 s 8(1)).

5 As to the Commissioners of Northern Lighthouses see PARA 1019. Subject to the Merchant Shipping Act 1995 Sch 14 para 9(1) (as to which see note 2), the Commissioners of Northern Lighthouses are also the general lighthouse authority as respects the Isle of Man, and the seas adjacent thereto: see s 193(5) (prospectively repealed: see note 2).

6 Merchant Shipping Act 1995 s 193(1)(b).

7 As to the meaning of 'Commissioners of Irish Lights' see PARA 1020.
8 Merchant Shipping Act 1995 s 193(1)(c).
9 Merchant Shipping Act 1995 s 193(1).
10 Ie for the purposes of the Merchant Shipping Act 1995 Pt VIII (see also PARA 1018 et seq): see s 193(2).
11 As to the meaning of 'statutory harbour authority' see PARA 69 note 4.
12 Merchant Shipping Act 1995 s 193(2)(a) (amended by the Merchant Shipping and Maritime Security Act 1997 Sch 6 para 6(a)). For these purposes, 'area' means:
    (1)   in relation to a general lighthouse authority specified in s 193(1)(a), (b) or (c) (see heads (1) to (3) in the text), the area specified therein as the area of that authority (s 193(4)(a));
    (2)   in relation to a statutory harbour authority, the area or areas inside the limits within which the authority's statutory powers and duties as a harbour authority are exercisable (s 193(4)(b) (amended by the Merchant Shipping and Maritime Security Act 1997 ss 29(1), 31(3), Sch 6 para 6(b))); and
    (3)   in relation to any other existing local lighthouse authority, the existing area over which its authority extends in relation to lighthouses, buoys and beacons (Merchant Shipping Act 1995 s 193(4)(c));
and, for the purposes of s 193(2)(b) (see head (b) in the text) and s 193(4)(c) (see head (3) above), 'existing' means existing for the purposes of the Merchant Shipping Act 1894 immediately before the repeal of that Act by the Merchant Shipping Act 1995 (ss 193(4), 223(1)).
13 Merchant Shipping Act 1995 s 193(2)(b).
14 Merchant Shipping Act 1995 s 193(2).

1018. The Trinity House. For the purposes of the Merchant Shipping Act 1995 provisions which relate to lighthouses[1], the 'Trinity House' means the master, wardens and assistants of the guild, fraternity or brotherhood of the most glorious and undivided Trinity and of St Clement in the parish of Deptford Strond in the county of Kent, commonly called the corporation of the Trinity House of Deptford Strond[2].
The Trinity House was incorporated by royal charter in 1514[3].

1 Ie for the purposes of the Merchant Shipping Act 1995 Pt VIII (ss 193–223): see s 223(1). As to the meaning of 'lighthouse' see PARA 1017 note 1. Employees of the Trinity House Lighthouse Service are eligible for membership of superannuation schemes under the Superannuation Act 1972 (see s 1, Sch 1; the Superannuation (Admission to Schedule 1 to the Superannuation Act 1972) Order 2014, SI 2014/555, art 1(d); and CONSTITUTIONAL AND ADMINISTRATIVE LAW vol 20 (2014) PARA 298), the Trinity House scheme having been closed (see the Public Service Pensions Act 2013 s 31, Sch 10 para 13).
2 See the Merchant Shipping Act 1995 s 223(1).
3 See Letters Patent of Henry VIII dated 20 May 1514, confirmed by Letters Patent of James II dated 8 July 1685.

1019. The Commissioners of Northern Lighthouses. The Commissioners of Northern Lighthouses continue to exist under that name as a body corporate constituted as follows[1].
The following persons holding the following offices constitute the Commissioners of Northern Lighthouses, that is to say[2]:
    (1)   the Lord Advocate and the Solicitor-General for Scotland[3];
    (2)   the lords provosts of Edinburgh, Glasgow and Aberdeen, and the conveners of the councils for Highland and Argyll and Bute[4];
    (3)   the sheriffs principal of all the sheriffdoms in Scotland[5];
    (4)   a person nominated by the Lieutenant Governor of the Isle of Man and appointed by the Secretary of State[6];
    (5)   any person elected under head (a) or head (b) below[7];
    (6)   a person appointed by the Secretary of State (in addition to the person nominated under head (4) above)[8]; and
    (7)   a person appointed by the Scottish Ministers[9].
The Commissioners may elect, as members of their body:
    (a)   the convener of any council whose area includes any part of the coasts of Scotland[10];

(b)   not more than three other persons, but a person may not be so elected unless either he appears to the Commissioners to have special knowledge and experience of nautical matters or three persons who so appear are members of that body[11].

A person appointed by the Secretary of State under head (4) above, or a person appointed by the Commissioners under head (b) above, holds office for three years, but is eligible for re-appointment[12].

Any five of the Commissioners constitute a quorum[13]; and the Commissioners constituting a quorum have power to do all such matters and things as might be done by the whole body[14].

1   See the Merchant Shipping Act 1995 s 193(3), Sch 8 para 1(1). The Commissioners of Northern Lighthouses are eligible for membership of superannuation schemes under the Superannuation Act 1972 (see s 1, Sch 1; the Superannuation (Admission to Schedule 1 to the Superannuation Act 1972) Order 2014, SI 2014/555, art 1(b); and CONSTITUTIONAL AND ADMINISTRATIVE LAW vol 20 (2014) PARA 298), the Commissioners' own scheme having been closed (see the Public Service Pensions Act 2013 s 31, Sch 10 para 8).
2   See the Merchant Shipping Act 1995 Sch 8 para 1(2).
3   See the Merchant Shipping Act 1995 Sch 8 para 1(2)(a).
4   See the Merchant Shipping Act 1995 Sch 8 para 1(2)(b).
5   See the Merchant Shipping Act 1995 Sch 8 para 1(2)(c).
6   See the Merchant Shipping Act 1995 Sch 8 para 1(2)(d). As to the Secretary of State see PARA 38.
7   See the Merchant Shipping Act 1995 Sch 8 para 1(2)(e).
8   See the Merchant Shipping Act 1995 Sch 8 para 1(2)(f) (Sch 8 paras 1(2)(f), (g) added, Sch 8 para 2(2) amended, by the Scotland Act 2016 s 55)).
9   See the Merchant Shipping Act 1995 Sch 8 para 1(2)(g) (as added: see note 8).
10   See the Merchant Shipping Act 1995 Sch 8 para 2(1).
11   See the Merchant Shipping Act 1995 Sch 8 para 2(2) (as amended: see note 8).
12   See the Merchant Shipping Act 1995 Sch 8 para 3.
13   See the Merchant Shipping Act 1995 Sch 8 para 4(1).
14   See the Merchant Shipping Act 1995 Sch 8 para 4(2).

1020.   The Commissioners of Irish Lights. For the purposes of the Merchant Shipping Act 1995 provisions which relate to lighthouses[1], the 'Commissioners of Irish Lights' means the body incorporated by that name under the local Act of the session held in the thirtieth and thirty-first years of the reign of Queen Victoria intituled 'An Act to alter the constitution of the Corporation for preserving and improving the port of Dublin and for other purposes connected with that body and with the Port of Dublin Corporation'[2].

1   Ie for the purposes of the Merchant Shipping Act 1995 Pt VIII (ss 193–223) (see also PARAS 1068 et seq, 1072 et seq): see s 223(1). As to the meaning of 'lighthouse' see PARA 1068 note 1.
2   See the Merchant Shipping Act 1995 s 223(1). The Commissioners of Irish Lights are eligible for membership of superannuation schemes under the Superannuation Act 1972 (see s 1, Sch 1; the Superannuation (Admission to Schedule 1 to the Superannuation Act 1972) Order 2014, SI 2014/555, art 1(a); and CONSTITUTIONAL AND ADMINISTRATIVE LAW vol 20 (2014) PARA 298), the Commissioners' own scheme having been closed (see the Public Service Pensions Act 2013 s 31, Sch 10 para 4). In connection with pensions see also the Pensions Increase (Commissioners of Irish Lights) Regulations 2014, SI 2014/563.

(2) FUNCTIONS OF THE SECRETARY OF STATE

1021.   Returns and information to the Secretary of State. Every general lighthouse authority[1] and its officers must give to the Secretary of State[2] all such returns, explanations or information in relation to the lighthouses[3], buoys or beacons[4] within its area[5] and its management as the Secretary of State requires[6].

1   As to the meaning of 'general lighthouse authority' see PARA 1017.
2   As to the Secretary of State see PARA 36.
3   As to the meaning of 'lighthouse' see PARA 1017 note 1.

4   As to the meaning of 'buoys and beacons' see PARA 1017 note 2.
5   As to the meaning of 'area' see PARA 1017 note 12.
6   Merchant Shipping Act 1995 s 194.

1022. Powers of inspection by the Secretary of State. The Secretary of State[1], on complaint that any lighthouse[2], buoy or beacon[3] under the management of a general lighthouse authority[4], or any work connected with it, is inefficient, improperly managed or unnecessary, may authorise any persons appointed by him to inspect the lighthouse, buoy or beacon or any connected work[5].

A person so authorised may inspect the lighthouse, buoy or beacon and may make any inquiries which he thinks fit as to the lighthouse, buoy or beacon and its management[6].

All officers and others having the care, or concerned in the management, of any lighthouse, buoy or beacon in relation to which such powers of inspection[7] are being exercised must furnish any information and explanations in relation to it and its management which the person inspecting it requires[8].

1   As to the Secretary of State see PARA 36.
2   As to the meaning of 'lighthouse' see PARA 1017 note 1.
3   As to the meaning of 'buoys and beacons' see PARA 1017 note 2.
4   As to the meaning of 'general lighthouse authority' see PARA 1017.
5   Merchant Shipping Act 1995 s 200(1).
6   Merchant Shipping Act 1995 s 200(2).
7   Ie powers under the Merchant Shipping Act 1995 s 200: see s 200(3).
8   Merchant Shipping Act 1995 s 200(3).

(3) FUNCTIONS OF GENERAL LIGHTHOUSE AUTHORITIES

1023. General function of management of lighthouses etc. The general lighthouse authorities[1] have[2] the superintendence and management of all lighthouses[3], buoys and beacons[4] within their respective areas[5].

The general lighthouse authorities continue[6] to hold and maintain all property vested in them on 1 January 1996 in the same manner and for the same purpose as before[7].

1   As to the meaning of 'general lighthouse authority' see PARA 1017.
2   Ie subject to the provisions of the Merchant Shipping Act 1995 ss 196–223 and to the powers and rights of any local lighthouse authority: see s 195(1). As to the meaning of 'local lighthouse authority' see PARA 1017.
3   As to the meaning of 'lighthouse' see PARA 1017 note 1.
4   As to the meaning of 'buoys and beacons' see PARA 1017 note 2.
5   Merchant Shipping Act 1995 s 195(1). As to the meaning of 'area' see PARA 1017 note 12.
6   Ie subject to the provisions of the Merchant Shipping Act 1995 ss 196–223: see s 195(2).
7   Merchant Shipping Act 1995 s 195(2). The date of 1 January 1996 is that on which the Merchant Shipping Act 1995 was commenced: see s 316(2).

1024. Joint discharge of functions of general lighthouse authorities. Two or more general lighthouse authorities[1] may discharge any of their functions jointly[2]; and for that purpose:

(1)   those authorities may share any part of their respective establishments[3]; and

(2)   any of them may, in the area[4] of another and on that other's behalf, execute any works or do any other thing which the authority has power to execute or do in its own area[5];

and any enactment relating to the functions in question or to the authorities by which or the areas in which those functions are to be discharged is to be construed accordingly[6].

Any expenses incurred by any of the general lighthouse authorities in pursuance of the above provisions must be apportioned between that authority and the other authority concerned in such manner as may be agreed between them or, in default of agreement, determined by the Secretary of State[7].

1   As to the meaning of 'general lighthouse authority' see PARA 1017.
2   Merchant Shipping Act 1995 s 196(1).
3   Merchant Shipping Act 1995 s 196(1)(a).
4   As to the meaning of 'area' see PARA 1017 note 12.
5   Merchant Shipping Act 1995 s 196(1)(b).
6   Merchant Shipping Act 1995 s 196(1).
7   Merchant Shipping Act 1995 s 196(2). As to the Secretary of State see PARA 36.

1025. General powers of general lighthouse authority. A general lighthouse authority[1] has power, within its area[2]:

(1)   to erect or place any lighthouse[3], with all requisite works, roads and appurtenances[4];
(2)   to add to, alter, or remove any lighthouse[5];
(3)   to erect or place any buoy or beacon[6], or alter or remove any buoy or beacon[7];
(4)   to vary the character of any lighthouse or the mode of exhibiting lights therein[8].

However, a general lighthouse authority must not, in the area of a statutory harbour authority[9]:

(a)   erect or place any lighthouse, works, roads or appurtenances under head (1) above[10]; or
(b)   erect or place any buoy or beacon under head (3) above[11],

except in pursuance of a direction given by the Secretary of State[12]. The Secretary of State may give such a direction to a general lighthouse authority if he considers it appropriate to do so in the interests of general navigation[13].

Where any improved light or beacon, or any siren or any description of fog signal has been added to an existing lighthouse, the light or beacon, siren or fog signal may be treated[14] as if it were a separate lighthouse[15].

A general lighthouse authority may acquire any land which may be necessary for the exercise of its statutory powers under heads (1) to (4) above, for the maintenance of its works or for the residence of the light keepers[16]; and a general lighthouse authority may sell or lease any land belonging to it[17].

1   As to the meaning of 'general lighthouse authority' see PARA 1017.
2   Merchant Shipping Act 1995 s 197(1). Section 197(1) is subject to s 197(2) (see the text and notes 9–12): see s 197(1). As to the meaning of 'area' see PARA 1017 note 12.
3   As to the meaning of 'lighthouse' see PARA 1017 note 1.
4   Merchant Shipping Act 1995 s 197(1)(a).
5   Merchant Shipping Act 1995 s 197(1)(b).
6   As to the meaning of 'buoys and beacons' see PARA 1017 note 2.
7   Merchant Shipping Act 1995 s 197(1)(c).
8   Merchant Shipping Act 1995 s 197(1)(d).
9   Merchant Shipping Act 1995 s 197(2) (amended by the Merchant Shipping and Maritime Security Act 1997 s 29(1), Sch 6 para 7). As to the meaning of 'statutory harbour authority' see PARA 69 note 4.
10   Merchant Shipping Act 1995 s 197(2)(a).
11   Merchant Shipping Act 1995 s 197(2)(b).
12   Merchant Shipping Act 1995 s 197(2). As to the Secretary of State see PARA 36; and as to the Secretary of State's power to give directions under the Merchant Shipping Act 1995 see PARA 39.
13   Merchant Shipping Act 1995 s 197(3).
14   Ie for the purposes of the Merchant Shipping Act 1995 Pt VIII (ss 193–223) (lighthouses): see s 197(4).
15   Merchant Shipping Act 1995 s 197(4).

16 Merchant Shipping Act 1995 s 197(5). For the purposes of the acquisition of land by a general
    lighthouse authority under s 197(5), if the land is in England and Wales, the provisions of the
    Compulsory Purchase Act 1965 Pt I (ss 1–32) (so far as applicable) apply, except ss 4–8, 27, 31
    (see COMPULSORY ACQUISITION OF LAND): see the Merchant Shipping Act 1995 s 197(6)(a).
    As to the meanings of 'England' and 'Wales' see PARA 16 note 2.
        As to permitted development for the purposes of the functions of a general or local lighthouse
    authority see the Town and Country Planning (General Permitted Development) Order 1995, SI
    1995/418, art 3(1), Sch 2 Pt 17 Class I (lighthouse undertakings); and PLANNING vol 81 (2010)
    PARAS 486, 487.
17 Merchant Shipping Act 1995 s 197(7) (amended by the Merchant Shipping and Maritime Security
    Act 1997 s 19(1)).

1026. Commercial activities. A general lighthouse authority[1] may enter into
agreements for the use by others of it's assets ('hire agreements')[2] and for the
provision by it of consultancy or other services ('service agreements')[3]; however an
authority may enter into such an agreement only if satisfied that it is not likely to
prejudice the discharge of their general[4] functions[5] and the Secretary of State
consents[6]. Where an authority enter or seek to enter into hire or service
agreements expenditure of the authority incurred in connection with the
agreements, and with the Secretary of State's consent, must be paid out of the
General Lighthouse Fund[7] and sums received by the authority under the
agreements must be paid into the General Lighthouse Fund[8].

1 As to the meaning of 'general lighthouse authority' see PARA 1017.
2 Merchant Shipping Act 1995 s 197A(1)(a) (s 197A added by the Marine Navigation Act 2013 s
   9(1)). An authority must send a copy of any hire or service agreement to the Secretary of State:
   Merchant Shipping Act 1995 s 197A(5) (as so added). As to the Secretary of State see PARA 36.
3 Merchant Shipping Act 1995 s 197A(1)(b) (as added: see note 2). See note 2.
4 Ie functions under the Merchant Shipping Act 1995 s 195 (see PARA 1023).
5 Merchant Shipping Act 1995 s 197A(2)(a) (as added: see note 2).
6 Merchant Shipping Act 1995 s 197A(2)(b) (as added: see note 2). Consent under s 197A may be
   subject to conditions, may be general or specific, and may be prospective or retrospective: s
   197A(6) (as so added).
7 Merchant Shipping Act 1995 s 197A(3)(a) (as added: see note 2). As to the General Lighthouse
   Fund see PARA 1039. The Secretary of State may consent to expenditure in acquiring an asset for
   the purpose of entering into hire agreements only if he thinks that the expenditure is merely
   preparatory or subsidiary to hire agreements in respect of other assets (such as in the case of
   acquiring one asset to be used with another or to be used in fitting, maintaining or converting
   another): s 197A(4) (as so added).
8 Merchant Shipping Act 1995 s 197A(3)(b) (as added: see note 2).

1027. Inspection of local lighthouses. It is the duty of the general lighthouse
authority[1] for any area[2], or of any person authorised by that authority for the
purpose, to[3]:
    (1)   inspect all lighthouses[4], buoys and beacons[5] situated within its area but
            belonging to or under the management of any local lighthouse
            authority[6]; and
    (2)   make such inquiries about them and their management as it thinks fit[7].
All officers and others having the care, or concerned in the management, of any
such local lighthouses, buoys or beacons must furnish all such information and
explanations concerning them as the general lighthouse authority requires[8].
    All local lighthouse authorities and their officers must give to the general
lighthouse authority all such returns, explanations or information concerning the
lighthouses, buoys and beacons under their management and the management of
them as the general lighthouse authority may require[9].
    The general lighthouse authority must:
    (a)   communicate to each local lighthouse authority the results of its
            inspection of its lighthouses, buoys and beacons[10]; and

(b)   make to the Secretary of State[11] general reports of the results of the inspection of local lighthouses, buoys and beacons[12].

1 As to the meaning of 'general lighthouse authority' see PARA 1017.
2 As to the meaning of 'area' see PARA 1017 note 12.
3 Merchant Shipping Act 1995 s 198(1).
4 As to the meaning of 'lighthouse' see PARA 1017 note 1.
5 As to the meaning of 'buoys and beacons' see PARA 1017 note 2.
6 Merchant Shipping Act 1995 s 198(1)(a). As to the meaning of 'local lighthouse authority' see PARA 1017.
7 Merchant Shipping Act 1995 s 198(1)(b).
8 Merchant Shipping Act 1995 s 198(2).
9 Merchant Shipping Act 1995 s 198(3).
10 Merchant Shipping Act 1995 s 198(4)(a).
11 As to the Secretary of State see PARA 36.
12 Merchant Shipping Act 1995 s 198(4)(b).

1028. Control of local lighthouse authorities. A general lighthouse authority[1] may, within its area[2], with the consent of the Secretary of State[3], direct a local lighthouse authority[4]:

(1)   to lay down buoys[5];
(2)   to remove or discontinue any lighthouse[6], buoy or beacon[7]; or
(3)   to make any variation in the character of any lighthouse, buoy or beacon or in the mode of exhibiting lights in any lighthouse, buoy or beacon[8];

but the authority must not give a direction without first giving due notice of its intention to do so[9]. Such a direction must be given in writing; and it is the duty of a local lighthouse authority to which such a direction is given to comply with it[10].

A local lighthouse authority must not, without the consent of the general lighthouse authority:

(a)   erect or place any lighthouse, buoy or beacon[11];
(b)   remove or discontinue any lighthouse, buoy or beacon[12];
(c)   vary the character of any lighthouse, buoy or beacon or the mode of exhibiting lights in any lighthouse, buoy or beacon[13].

Nothing in these provisions[14] applies to local buoys and beacons placed or erected for temporary purposes[15].

1 As to the meaning of 'general lighthouse authority' see PARA 1017.
2 As to the meaning of 'area' see PARA 1017 note 12.
3 As to the Secretary of State see PARA 36.
4 Merchant Shipping Act 1995 s 199(1). As to the meaning of 'local lighthouse authority' see PARA 1017.
5 Merchant Shipping Act 1995 s 199(1)(a). As to the meaning of 'buoys and beacons' see PARA 1017 note 2.
6 As to the meaning of 'lighthouse' see PARA 1017 note 1.
7 Merchant Shipping Act 1995 s 199(1)(b).
8 Merchant Shipping Act 1995 s 199(1)(c).
9 Merchant Shipping Act 1995 s 199(1). As to service of documents under the Merchant Shipping Act 1995 see PARA 74.
10 Merchant Shipping Act 1995 s 199(3).
11 Merchant Shipping Act 1995 s 199(2)(a).
12 Merchant Shipping Act 1995 s 199(2)(b).
13 Merchant Shipping Act 1995 s 199(2)(c).
14 Ie nothing in the Merchant Shipping Act 1995 s 199: see s 199(4).
15 Merchant Shipping Act 1995 s 199(4).

1029. Disclosure of information to general lighthouse authorities. No obligation as to secrecy or other restriction on the disclosure of information (whether imposed by statute or otherwise) prevents a Minister of the Crown[1] from disclosing to a general lighthouse authority[2], or to a person appointed by a general lighthouse authority to collect general light dues[3], information for the purpose of enabling or assisting the authority to discharge its functions under the Merchant Shipping Act 1995 provisions[4] which relate to lighthouses[5].

Information so obtained by any person must not be disclosed by him to any other person, except where the disclosure is made to a general lighthouse authority, or to a person appointed by such an authority to collect general light dues, or for the purposes of any legal proceedings arising out of the Merchant Shipping Act 1995 provisions[6] which relate to lighthouses[7].

1   As to the meaning of 'Minister of the Crown' see PARA 72 note 6.
2   As to the meaning of 'general lighthouse authority' see PARA 1017.
3   As to the meaning of 'general light dues' see PARA 1033.
4   Ie the Merchant Shipping Act 1995 Pt VIII (ss 193–223): see s 222A(1) (s 222A added by the Merchant Shipping and Maritime Security Act 1997 s 20). As to the meaning of 'lighthouse' see PARA 1017 note 1.
5   Merchant Shipping Act 1995 s 222A(1) (as added: see note 4).
6   Ie the Merchant Shipping Act 1995 Pt VIII: see s 222A(2) (as added: see note 4).
7   Merchant Shipping Act 1995 s 222A(2) (as added: see note 4).

(4) POWERS OF HARBOUR AUTHORITIES AS LOCAL LIGHTHOUSE AUTHORITIES

1030. Powers of harbour authorities. Every statutory harbour authority[1] has power to carry out harbour operations[2], consisting of the marking or lighting of a harbour[3] or any part of a harbour, either within the authority's area[4] or on harbour land[5].

1   As to the meaning of 'statutory harbour authority' see PARA 69 note 4.
2   For these purposes, 'harbour operations' has the same meaning as in the Harbours Act 1964 (see PORTS AND HARBOURS vol 85 (2012) PARA 19): Merchant Shipping Act 1995 s 201(3).
3   As to the meaning of 'harbour' see PARA 49 note 5.
4   As to the meaning of 'area' see PARA 1017 note 12.
5   Merchant Shipping Act 1995 s 201(1), (2) (s 201(1) amended by the Merchant Shipping and Maritime Security Act 1997 ss 29(1), 31(3), Sch 6 para 8). For these purposes, 'harbour land' has the same meaning as in the Harbours Act 1964 (see PORTS AND HARBOURS vol 85 (2012) PARA 19): Merchant Shipping Act 1995 s 201(3).

(5) TRANSFERS BETWEEN LIGHTHOUSE AUTHORITIES

1031. Individual transfers of local lighthouses to harbour authorities. A general lighthouse authority[1] may, at any time, with the consent of the Secretary of State[2], transfer to a statutory harbour authority[3] any lighthouse[4], buoy or beacon[5] held by the general lighthouse authority which is situated in the area[6] of that harbour authority or on land adjacent to that area or any part of it and which appears to the general lighthouse authority to be of benefit solely or mainly to ships[7] within, or entering or leaving, that harbour authority's area[8].

1   As to the meaning of 'general lighthouse authority' see PARA 1017.
2   As to the Secretary of State see PARA 36.
3   As to the meaning of 'statutory harbour authority' see PARA 69 note 4.
4   As to the meaning of 'lighthouse' see PARA 1017 note 1.
5   As to the meaning of 'buoys and beacons' see PARA 1017 note 2.
6   As to the meaning of 'area' see PARA 1017 note 12.
7   As to the meaning of 'ship' see PARA 229.
8   Merchant Shipping Act 1995 s 203 (amended by the Merchant Shipping and Maritime Security Act 1997 ss 29(1), 31(3), Sch 6 para 10).

1032. Surrender of local lighthouses. A local lighthouse authority[1] may, if it thinks fit, surrender or sell any lighthouse[2], buoy or beacon[3] held by it to the general lighthouse authority[4] within whose area[5] it is situated[6]; and that general lighthouse authority may, with the consent of the Secretary of State[7], accept or purchase it[8]. However, the Secretary of State must not give his consent for these purposes in any case where the local lighthouse authority concerned is a statutory harbour authority[9] unless he considers that the maintenance of the lighthouse, buoy or beacon in question is in the interests of general navigation[10].

1   As to the meaning of 'local lighthouse authority' see PARA 1017.
2   As to the meaning of 'lighthouse' see PARA 1017 note 1.
3   As to the meaning of 'buoys and beacons' see PARA 1017 note 2.
4   As to the meaning of 'general lighthouse authority' see PARA 1017.
5   As to the meaning of 'area' see PARA 1017 note 12.
6   Merchant Shipping Act 1995 s 204(1).
7   As to the Secretary of State see PARA 36.
8   Merchant Shipping Act 1995 s 204(1).
9   As to the meaning of 'statutory harbour authority' see PARA 69 note 4.
10 Merchant Shipping Act 1995 s 204(2) (amended by the Merchant Shipping and Maritime Security Act 1997 ss 29(1), 31(3), Sch 6 para 11).

(6) DUES LEVIABLE BY LIGHTHOUSE AUTHORITIES

(i) General Light Dues

1033. Light dues leviable by general lighthouse authorities. A general lighthouse authority[1] may demand, take and recover[2] dues which it may levy in respect of lighthouses[3], buoys or beacons[4] under its management[5] ('general light dues')[6], and it may for that purpose appoint persons to collect them[7]. General light dues may be levied only by reference to the voyages made by ships[8] or by way of periodical payments[9]; and they are payable in respect of all ships whatever, except ships belonging to Her Majesty and ships exempted[10] from payment[11]. The amounts which may be levied are specified in regulations[12].

Every person appointed by a general lighthouse authority to collect general light dues must collect all such dues payable at the port at which he is so appointed or, as the case may be, such of those dues as he is appointed to collect, whether they are collected on account of that authority or on account of one of the other general lighthouse authorities[13].

Any person appointed by a general lighthouse authority to collect general light dues must pay over to that authority, or as that authority directs, the whole of the general light dues received by him[14].

A general lighthouse authority receiving dues, whether itself or from a collector, must keep accounts of the dues and must cause the dues to be remitted to the Secretary of State[15], or as he directs, and in such manner as he directs[16].

1   As to the meaning of 'general lighthouse authority' see PARA 1017.
2   Ie in accordance with the Merchant Shipping Act 1995 s 205: see s 205(1).
3   As to the meaning of 'lighthouse' see PARA 1017 note 1.
4   As to the meaning of 'buoys and beacons' see PARA 1017 note 2.
5   As to the general function of management of lighthouses see PARA 1023.
6   In the Merchant Shipping Act 1995 Pt VIII (ss 193–223) (lighthouses), 'general light dues' has the meaning given by s 205(1): see s 223(1).
7   Merchant Shipping Act 1995 s 205(1), (2).
8   As to the meaning of 'ship' see PARA 229.
9   Merchant Shipping Act 1995 s 205(3).
10 Ie in pursuance of the Merchant Shipping Act 1995 s 205(5) (see the text and notes 12–14): see s 205(4).

11 Merchant Shipping Act 1995 s 205(4).
12 See the Merchant Shipping (Light Dues) Regulations 1997, SI 1997/562 (made under the Merchant Shipping Act 1995 s 205(5), (6)).
13 Merchant Shipping Act 1995 s 205(7).
14 Merchant Shipping Act 1995 s 205(8).
15 As to the Secretary of State see PARA 36.
16 Merchant Shipping Act 1995 s 205(9) (amended by the Merchant Shipping and Maritime Security Act 1997 ss 29(1), 31(3), Sch 6 para 12). As to the power of the Secretary of State to give directions under the Merchant Shipping Act 1995 see PARA 39.

1034. Information to determine light dues. A general lighthouse authority[1] may, for the purpose of determining whether any and, if so, what general light dues[2] are payable in respect of any ship[3], require any relevant authority[4] or any person who is liable to pay general light dues in respect of the ship, to furnish to the general lighthouse authority such information in that authority's or person's possession or control relating to the arrival or departure of the ship at or from any port[5] within its area[6] as it may reasonably require for that purpose[7].

A general lighthouse authority may require any relevant authority to furnish to it such information in the relevant authority's possession or control relating to the movements within the relevant authority's area of ships or ships of any class or description for the purpose of determining whether any and, if so, what general light dues are payable in respect of the ships[8].

The powers so conferred on a general lighthouse authority[9] are also available to the person appointed by it to collect dues at a port[10].

It is the duty of a relevant authority or person of whom a requirement for information is so made[11] to furnish information as soon as is reasonably practicable[12].

1 As to the meaning of 'general lighthouse authority' see PARA 1017.
2 As to the meaning of 'general light dues' see PARA 1033.
3 As to the meaning of 'ship' see PARA 229.
4 For these purposes, 'relevant authority' means a harbour authority, the Commissioners for Revenue and Customs and a conservancy authority: Merchant Shipping Act 1995 s 206(5) (amended by virtue of the Commissioners for Revenue and Customs Act 2005 s 50(1), (2), (7)). As to the meaning of 'harbour authority' see PARA 69 note 4; and as to the meaning of 'conservancy authority' see PARA 72 note 2. As to the Commissioners for Revenue and Customs see INCOME TAXATION vol 58 (2014) PARA 33.
5 As to the meaning of 'port' see PARA 46 note 12.
6 As to the meaning of 'area' see PARA 1017 note 12.
7 Merchant Shipping Act 1995 s 206(1).
8 Merchant Shipping Act 1995 s 206(2).
9 Ie by the Merchant Shipping Act 1995 s 206(1), (2) (see the text and notes 1–8): see s 206(3).
10 Merchant Shipping Act 1995 s 206(3).
11 Ie under any of the Merchant Shipping Act 1995 s 206(1), (2) or (3) (see the text and notes 1–10): see s 206(4).
12 Merchant Shipping Act 1995 s 206(4).

1035. Recovery of general light dues. The following persons are liable to pay general light dues[1] in respect of any ship[2] in respect of which such dues are payable[3], namely:

(1)   the owner or master[4]; or
(2)   such consignees or agents of the owner or master as have paid, or made themselves liable to pay, any other charge on account of the ship in the port[5] of her arrival or discharge[6].

General light dues so payable in respect of any ship may, in England and Wales[7], be recovered summarily as a civil debt[8].

Any consignee or agent, not being the owner or master of the ship, who is so made liable[9] for the payment of general light dues in respect of any ship may, out of any money received by him on account of the ship or belonging to its owner, retain the amount of all general light dues paid by him, together with any reasonable expenses he may have incurred by reason of the payment of the dues or his liability to pay them[10].

1   As to the meaning of 'general light dues' see PARA 1033.
2   As to the meaning of 'ship' see PARA 229.
3   Merchant Shipping Act 1995 s 207(1).
4   Merchant Shipping Act 1995 s 207(1)(a). As to the meaning of 'master' see PARA 444 note 1.
5   As to the meaning of 'port' see PARA 46 note 12.
6   Merchant Shipping Act 1995 s 207(1)(b).
7   As to the meanings of 'England' and 'Wales' see PARA 16 note 2.
8   Merchant Shipping Act 1995 s 207(2).
9   Ie by the Merchant Shipping Act 1995 s 207: see s 207(4).
10   Merchant Shipping Act 1995 s 207(4).

1036. Distress on ship for general light dues. If the owner or master[1] of any ship[2] fails, on demand of the appointed collector, to pay the general light dues[3] in respect of the ship, the collector may enter the ship and distrain the goods or any equipment or other thing belonging to, or on board, the ship and detain that distress until those dues are paid[4].

If payment of the dues so demanded is not made within the period of five days following the distress, the collector may, at any time during the continuance of the non-payment, cause the distress to be independently appraised and thereupon sold by public auction[5].

The collector must apply the proceeds of the sale in payment of:

(1)   the general light dues due[6]; and
(2)   all reasonable expenses incurred by him[7],

and he must pay the surplus, if any, on demand to the owner or master of the ship[8].

The remedy so conferred[9] is in addition to any other remedy available to the collector or the general lighthouse authority[10] by which he was appointed[11].

1   As to the meaning of 'master' see PARA 444 note 1.
2   As to the meaning of 'ship' see PARA 229.
3   As to the meaning of 'general light dues' see PARA 1033.
4   Merchant Shipping Act 1995 s 208(1).
5   Merchant Shipping Act 1995 s 208(2).
6   Merchant Shipping Act 1995 s 208(3)(a).
7   Merchant Shipping Act 1995 s 208(3)(b). Head (2) in the text refers to all reasonable expenses incurred by the collector under s 208: see s 208(3)(b).
8   Merchant Shipping Act 1995 s 208(3).
9   Ie by the Merchant Shipping Act 1995 s 208: see s 208(4).
10   As to the meaning of 'general lighthouse authority' see PARA 1017.
11   Merchant Shipping Act 1995 s 208(4).

1037. Receipt for general light dues and its production. A receipt for general light dues[1] must be given to the person paying them by the authority or person receiving them from him[2].

A ship[3] may be detained at any port[4] until the receipt for any general light dues due in respect of the ship is produced to the proper officer of Revenue and Customs[5] or the person appointed to collect general light dues at the port[6].

1   As to the meaning of 'general light dues' see PARA 1033.
2   Merchant Shipping Act 1995 s 209(1).
3   As to the meaning of 'ship' see PARA 229.
4   As to the meaning of 'port' see PARA 46 note 12.
5   As to the appointment of officers of Revenue and Customs see INCOME TAXATION vol 58 (2014) PARA 33.
6   Merchant Shipping Act 1995 s 209(2) (amended by virtue of the Commissioners for Revenue and Customs Act 2005 s 50(1), (2), (7)). As to enforcing the detention of ships generally see PARA 1190.

(ii) Local Light Dues

1038. Light dues leviable by local lighthouse authorities. A local lighthouse authority[1], which is not a statutory harbour authority[2], may demand, take and recover in respect of every ship[3] which enters or leaves the port[4], harbour[5] or estuary in which is situated any lighthouse[6], buoy or beacon[7] over which it has authority, and which passes the lighthouse, buoy or beacon and derives benefit from it, such charges as the authority thinks fit[8].

The same persons are liable to pay charges leviable by a local lighthouse authority (which is not a statutory harbour authority) in respect of lighthouses, buoys or beacons over which it has authority ('local light dues')[9] as are liable[10] to pay general light dues[11]; and local light dues may be recovered in the same manner as general light dues may[12] be recovered[13].

A list showing the local light dues leviable by a local lighthouse authority must be kept at the authority's office and must be open there during reasonable hours for inspection by any person without charge[14]; and copies of the list must be kept for sale there at such reasonable price, if any, as the authority determines[15]. A copy of the list so kept by a local lighthouse authority must be supplied by it to the Secretary of State without charge[16].

No local light due may be levied by a local lighthouse authority if, at the time at which it is leviable, the authority is in default in compliance with its obligation[17] to keep a list of dues or the light due is not shown in the list kept there at that time[18].

All local light dues must be applied by the authority by which they are levied for the purpose of the construction, placing, maintenance and improvement of the lighthouses, buoys or beacons in respect of which the dues are levied, and for no other purpose[19].

The local lighthouse authority to which any local light dues are paid must keep a separate account of the receipt and expenditure of those dues[20].

1 As to the meaning of 'local lighthouse authority' see PARA 1017.
2 As to the meaning of 'statutory harbour authority' see PARA 69 note 4.
3 As to the meaning of 'ship' see PARA 229.
4 As to the meaning of 'port' see PARA 46 note 12.
5 As to the meaning of 'harbour' see PARA 49 note 5.
6 As to the meaning of 'lighthouse' see PARA 1017 note 1.
7 As to the meaning of 'buoys and beacons' see PARA 1017 note 2.
8 Merchant Shipping Act 1995 s 210(2) (amended by the Merchant Shipping and Maritime Security Act 1997 ss 29(1), 31(3), Sch 6 para 13).
9 The Harbours Act 1964 s 31 (rights of objection to ship, passenger and goods dues) (see PORTS AND HARBOURS vol 85 (2012) PARA 72) applies in relation to local light dues subject, however, to the modifications specified in the Merchant Shipping Act 1995 s 210(8), Sch 10: s 210(8).
10 Ie under the Merchant Shipping Act 1995 s 207 (see PARA 1035): see s 210(3).
11 Merchant Shipping Act 1995 s 210(1), (3) (s 210(1) amended by the Merchant Shipping and Maritime Security Act 1997 s 31(3), Sch 6 para 13). As to the meaning of 'general light dues' see PARA 1033.
12 Ie under the Merchant Shipping Act 1995 s 207 and s 208 (see PARA 1036): see s 210(4).
13 Merchant Shipping Act 1995 s 210(4).
14 Merchant Shipping Act 1995 s 210(5).
15 Merchant Shipping Act 1995 s 210(5).
16 Merchant Shipping Act 1995 s 210(7). As to the Secretary of State see PARA 36.
17 Ie under the Merchant Shipping Act 1995 s 210(5) (see the text and notes 14–15): see s 210(6).
18 Merchant Shipping Act 1995 s 210(6).
19 Merchant Shipping Act 1995 s 210(9).
20 Merchant Shipping Act 1995 s 210(10).

(7) FINANCE AND ADMINISTRATION

1039. General Lighthouse Fund; expenses and receipts. The General Lighthouse Fund is administered by the Secretary of State[1]. The following must be paid out of that Fund:

(1)   any expenses incurred by general lighthouse authorities[2] in connection with the discharge of their functions under the Merchant Shipping Act 1995 provisions which relate to lighthouses[3] and, in the case of the Commissioners of Irish Lights[4] as respects their functions in the Republic of Ireland, under the corresponding Part of the Merchant Shipping Act 1894[5], but subject to the statutory provisions[6] relating to estimates and accounts of expenses[7];

(2)   any expenses, whether of a capital nature or not, incurred by the Secretary of State in pursuance of any international agreement relating to the provision of an electronic position-fixing system intended as an aid to the navigation of ships or incurred by him preliminary to his entering into such an agreement[8];

(3)   such sums as the Secretary of State may determine as sums appearing to him to represent the amount or estimated amount of any expenses incurred or likely to be incurred by him in connection with the administration of the Fund[9];

(4)   any expenses incurred by the Secretary of State in maintaining the Sombrero lighthouse in the Leeward Islands[10];

(5)   any other sums made payable out of the Fund by any other provision of Part VIII[11] or Part IX[12] of the Merchant Shipping Act 1995[13].

The following must be paid into that Fund:

(a)   all general light dues[14] and other sums received by or accruing to any of the general lighthouse authorities by virtue of, or in connection with the discharge of their functions under, Part VIII of the Merchant Shipping Act 1995[15] and, in the case of the Commissioners of Irish Lights as respects their functions in the Republic of Ireland, under the corresponding Part of the Merchant Shipping Act 1894[16];

(b)   any sums received by the Secretary of State in pursuance of any such agreement as is mentioned in head (2) above in respect of expenses incurred by him in pursuance of the agreement or in respect of expenses incurred by any of the general lighthouse authorities which are payable[17] out of the Fund[18];

(c)   any other sums made payable into the Fund by any other provision of Part VIII[19] or Part IX[20] of the Merchant Shipping Act 1995[21].

The accounts of the Fund for each year must be examined by the Comptroller and Auditor General[22] who must send a copy of the accounts certified by him to the Secretary of State[23]; and the Secretary of State must lay copies of the accounts before each House of Parliament[24].

1   See the Merchant Shipping Act 1995 s 211(1). As to the Secretary of State see PARA 36. The General Lighthouse Fund was established under the Merchant Shipping (Mercantile Marine Fund) Act 1898 on the abolition of the Mercantile Marine Fund: see s 1 (repealed). There must continue to be paid out of the General Lighthouse Fund under the Merchant Shipping Act 1995 s 211 any expenditure incurred by the government of the United Kingdom in pursuance of the arrangement made with the government of Sri Lanka on 27 February 1976 for the transfer of certain lighthouses off the coast of that country: s 314(3), Sch 14 para 9(5).

2   As to the meaning of 'general lighthouse authority' see PARA 1017.

3   Ie the Merchant Shipping Act 1995 Pt VIII (ss 193–223): see s 211(2)(a). As to the meaning of 'lighthouse' see PARA 1017 note 1.

4   As to the meaning of 'Commissioners of Irish Lights' see PARA 1020.

5   Ie the Merchant Shipping Act 1894 Pt XI (ss 634–669) (repealed): see s 211(2)(a).

6   Ie the Merchant Shipping Act 1995 s 213 (see PARA 1041): see s 211(2)(a).

7　Merchant Shipping Act 1995 s 211(2)(a).
8　Merchant Shipping Act 1995 s 211(2)(b).
9　Merchant Shipping Act 1995 s 211(2)(c).
10　Merchant Shipping Act 1995 s 211(2)(d).
11　Ie the Merchant Shipping Act 1995 Pt VIII: see s 211(2)(e).
12　Ie the Merchant Shipping Act 1995 Pt IX (ss 224–255) (salvage and wreck) (see PARA 849 et seq): see s 211(2)(e).
13　Merchant Shipping Act 1995 s 211(2)(e).
14　As to the meaning of 'general light dues' see PARA 1033.
15　Ie the Merchant Shipping Act 1995 Pt VIII: see s 211(3)(a).
16　Merchant Shipping Act 1995 s 211(3)(a). As to the corresponding Part of the Merchant Shipping Act 1894 mentioned in the text see note 5.
17　Ie by virtue of the Merchant Shipping Act 1995 s 211(2) (see the text and notes 2–13): see s 211(3)(b).
18　Merchant Shipping Act 1995 s 211(3)(b).
19　Ie the Merchant Shipping Act 1995 Pt VIII: see s 211(3)(c).
20　Ie the Merchant Shipping Act 1995 Pt IX: see s 211(3)(c).
21　Merchant Shipping Act 1995 s 211(3)(c).
22　As to the Comptroller and Auditor General see CONSTITUTIONAL AND ADMINISTRATIVE LAW vol 20 (2014) PARA 494 et seq.
23　Merchant Shipping Act 1995 s 211(4).
24　Merchant Shipping Act 1995 s 211(5).

1040. Establishments of general lighthouse authorities. The Secretary of State[1] may determine[2]:

(1)　the establishments to be maintained by each of the general lighthouse authorities[3] on account of the services of lighthouses[4], buoys and beacons[5];

(2)　the annual or other sums to be paid out of the General Lighthouse Fund[6] in respect of those establishments or to members of the general lighthouse authority for England and Wales[7].

If it appears that any part of the establishments of the general lighthouse authorities is maintained for other purposes as well as for the purposes of their duties as general lighthouse authorities, the Secretary of State may determine the portion of the expenses of those establishments to be paid out of the General Lighthouse Fund[8].

An increase in any establishment or part of an establishment determined in this way[9] may not be made without the consent of the Secretary of State[10].

1　As to the Secretary of State see PARA 36.
2　Merchant Shipping Act 1995 s 212(1).
3　As to the meaning of 'general lighthouse authority' see PARA 1017.
4　As to the meaning of 'lighthouse' see PARA 1017 note 1.
5　Merchant Shipping Act 1995 s 212(1)(a). As to the meaning of 'buoys and beacons' see PARA 1017 note 2.
6　As to the General Lighthouse Fund see PARA 1039.
7　Merchant Shipping Act 1995 s 212(1)(b).
8　Merchant Shipping Act 1995 s 212(2).
9　Ie determined under Merchant Shipping Act 1995 s 212: see s 212(3).
10　Merchant Shipping Act 1995 s 212(3).

1041. Estimates or accounts of expenses to the Secretary of State. An expense of a general lighthouse authority[1] in respect of the services of lighthouses[2], buoys and beacons[3] must not be paid out of the General Lighthouse Fund[4], or allowed in account, unless it has been allowed as part of the establishment expenses[5] or an estimate or account of it has been approved by the Secretary of State[6].

For the purpose of approval by the Secretary of State, each of the general lighthouse authorities must submit to him an estimate of all expenses to be incurred by them in respect of lighthouses, buoys and beacons, other than expenses allowed[7] on account of their establishments[8]; but, in a case where it is necessary for a general lighthouse authority, in providing for any sudden emergency, to incur any such expense without waiting for the approval of the Secretary of State, the authority must as soon as possible submit to him a full account of the expense incurred[9].

The Secretary of State must consider any estimates and accounts so submitted to him[10] and may approve them either with or without modification[11].

1 As to the meaning of 'general lighthouse authority' see PARA 1017.
2 As to the meaning of 'lighthouse' see PARA 1017 note 1.
3 As to the meaning of 'buoys and beacons' see PARA 1017 note 2.
4 As to the General Lighthouse Fund see PARA 1039.
5 Ie under the Merchant Shipping Act 1995 s 212 (see PARA 1040): see s 213(1).
6 Merchant Shipping Act 1995 s 213(1). As to the Secretary of State see PARA 36.
7 Ie under the Merchant Shipping Act 1995 s 212: see s 213(2).
8 Merchant Shipping Act 1995 s 213(2).
9 Merchant Shipping Act 1995 s 213(3).
10 Ie under the Merchant Shipping Act 1995 s 213: see s 213(4).
11 Merchant Shipping Act 1995 s 213(4).

1042. Pension rights of certain employees. There are payable to or in respect of persons whose salaries are paid out of the General Lighthouse Fund[1] such pensions, allowances and gratuities as may be determined in accordance with[2]:

(1) in the case of such of those persons as are employed by the Secretary of State, arrangements made by him[3]; and

(2) in the case of other such persons, arrangements made by a general lighthouse authority[4] and approved by the Secretary of State[5];

and those benefits are to be charged on and payable out of that Fund[6].

1 As to the General Lighthouse Fund see PARA 1039.
2 Merchant Shipping Act 1995 s 214(1) (s 214(1) renumbered, s 214(2) added, by the Public Service Pensions Act 2013 Sch 8 para 21). Where pensions, allowances and gratuities to or in respect of persons whose salaries are paid out of the General Lighthouse Fund are payable otherwise than under the Merchant Shipping Act 1995 s 214(1), sums in respect of those benefits may with the approval of the Secretary of State be paid out of that Fund: s 214(2) (as so added). As to the Secretary of State see PARA 36.
3 Merchant Shipping Act 1995 s 214(1)(a) (renumbered: see note 2).
4 As to the meaning of 'general lighthouse authority' see PARA 1017.
5 Merchant Shipping Act 1995 s 214(1)(b) (renumbered: see note 2).
6 Merchant Shipping Act 1995 s 214(1) (renumbered: see note 2).

1043. Borrowing powers of general lighthouse authorities; limit on borrowing. A general lighthouse authority[1] may, with the consent of the Secretary of State[2] and the Treasury[3], borrow money for the purpose of defraying any expenses incurred or to be incurred by the authority in connection with the discharge of its functions under Part VIII[4] or IX[5] of the Merchant Shipping Act 1995[6].

A general lighthouse authority may, in connection with any such advance[7], mortgage any land or other property belonging to it[8].

Any sums payable by a general lighthouse authority under the terms of such an advance[9] by way of principal, interest or otherwise must be paid out of the General Lighthouse Fund[10].

The aggregate amount outstanding in respect of the principal of any sums so borrowed[11] must not at any time exceed £100 million[12]; but the Secretary of State may, by order, with the approval of the Treasury, increase or further increase that limit, but not by more than £33 million at a time[13].

1 As to the meaning of 'general lighthouse authority' see PARA 1017.
2 As to the Secretary of State see PARA 36.

3 As to the Treasury see CONSTITUTIONAL AND ADMINISTRATIVE LAW vol 20 (2014) PARAS 262–265.
4 Ie the Merchant Shipping Act 1995 Pt VIII (ss 193–223) (lighthouses): see s 215(1).
5 Ie the Merchant Shipping Act 1995 Pt IX (ss 224–255) (salvage and wreck) (see PARA 849 et seq): see s 215(1).
6 Merchant Shipping Act 1995 s 215(1). As to guarantees by the Secretary of State see PARA 1044.
7 Ie any advance to it under the Merchant Shipping Act 1995 s 215: see s 215(2).
8 Merchant Shipping Act 1995 s 215(2).
9 Ie an advance under the Merchant Shipping Act 1995 s 215: see s 215(3).
10 Merchant Shipping Act 1995 s 215(3). As to the General Lighthouse Fund see PARA 1039.
11 Ie borrowed under the Merchant Shipping Act 1995 s 215 (see the text and notes 1–10): see s 216(1).
12 Merchant Shipping Act 1995 s 216(1).
13 See the Merchant Shipping Act 1995 s 216(2), (3). At the date at which this volume states the law, no such order had been made and none has effect as if so made. As to the making of orders by the Secretary of State under the Merchant Shipping Act 1995 generally see PARA 39.

1044. Guarantees by the Secretary of State of sums borrowed by general lighthouse authority. The Secretary of State[1] with the consent of the Treasury[2] may guarantee, in such manner and on such conditions as he thinks fit, the repayment of the principal of, the payment of interest on, and the discharge of any other financial obligation in connection with, any sums borrowed[3] by a general lighthouse authority[4].

Immediately after such a guarantee is given, the Secretary of State must lay a statement of the guarantee before each House of Parliament; and, where any sum is issued for fulfilling a guarantee so given, the Secretary of State must, as soon as possible after the end of each financial year beginning with that in which the sum is issued and ending with that in which all liability in respect of the principal of the sum and in respect of interest thereon is finally discharged, lay before each House of Parliament a statement relating to that sum[5].

Any sums required by the Secretary of State for fulfilling any such guarantee must be paid out of money provided by Parliament[6].

If any sums are issued in fulfilment of any guarantee so given, there must be made to the Secretary of State out of the General Lighthouse Fund[7], at such times and in such manner as the Secretary of State may determine with the consent of the Treasury, payments of such amounts as the Secretary of State may so determine in or towards repayment of the sums so issued, and payments of interest on what is outstanding for the time being in respect of sums so issued at such rate as the Secretary of State may so determine[8]. The Secretary of State with the consent of the Treasury may vary or revoke any determination so made by him[9]. Any sums so received by the Secretary of State must be paid into the Consolidated Fund[10].

1 As to the Secretary of State see PARA 36.
2 As to the Treasury see CONSTITUTIONAL AND ADMINISTRATIVE LAW vol 20 (2014) PARAS 262–265.
3 Ie under the Merchant Shipping Act 1995 s 215 (see PARA 1043): see s 217(1).
4 Merchant Shipping Act 1995 s 217(1). As to the meaning of 'general lighthouse authority' see PARA 1017.
5 Merchant Shipping Act 1995 s 217(2).
6 Merchant Shipping Act 1995 s 217(3).
7 As to the General Lighthouse Fund see PARA 1039.
8 Merchant Shipping Act 1995 s 217(4).
9 Merchant Shipping Act 1995 s 217(5).
10 Merchant Shipping Act 1995 s 217(6). As to payments to be made into the Consolidated Fund under the Merchant Shipping Act 1995 see PARA 64. As to the Consolidated Fund generally see CONSTITUTIONAL AND ADMINISTRATIVE LAW vol 20 (2014) PARA 480 et seq.

1045. Accounts of general lighthouse authorities. Each of the general lighthouse authorities[1] must account to the Secretary of State[2] for the general light dues[3] and other sums received by or accruing to it by virtue of, or in connection with, the discharge of its functions under Parts VIII[4] or IX[5] of the Merchant Shipping Act 1995 and for its expenditure in respect of expenses paid out of the General Lighthouse Fund[6] in such form, at such times, and with such details, explanations and vouchers as the Secretary of State requires[7].

Each of the general lighthouse authorities must, when required by the Secretary of State, permit all accounting records kept by or under its respective direction to be inspected and examined by such persons as the Secretary of State appoints for the purpose[8].

1   As to the meaning of 'general lighthouse authority' see PARA 1017.
2   As to the Secretary of State see PARA 36. Accounts must also be sent to the Scottish Ministers: see the Merchant Shipping Act 1995 Sch 8 para 4A (added by the Scotland Act 2016 s 55).
3   As to the meaning of 'general light dues' see PARA 1033.
4   Ie the Merchant Shipping Act 1995 Pt VIII (ss 193–223) (lighthouses): see s 218(1).
5   Ie the Merchant Shipping Act 1995 Pt IX (ss 224–255) (salvage and wreck) (see PARA 849 et seq): see s 218(1).
6   As to the General Lighthouse Fund see PARA 1039.
7   Merchant Shipping Act 1995 s 218(1).
8   Merchant Shipping Act 1995 s 218(2).

(8) EXEMPTIONS FROM TAXES, RATES ETC AND HARBOUR DUES

1046. Exemptions from taxes, duties, rates etc. The following, that is to say:
(1)   all lighthouses[1], buoys and beacons[2];
(2)   all general light dues[3] and other rates, fees or payments accruing to or forming part of the General Lighthouse Fund[4]; and
(3)   all premises or property belonging to or occupied by any of the general lighthouse authorities[5],
which are used or applied for the purposes of any of the services for which those dues, rates, fees and payments are received are exempt from all public or local taxes, duties or rates[6].

All instruments used by or under the direction of any general lighthouse authority in carrying on those services are exempt from stamp duty[7]; and, for the purposes of stamp duty land tax, any land transaction entered into:
(a)   by or under the direction of any general lighthouse authority for the purposes of carrying on those services[8]; or
(b)   by or under the direction of the Secretary of State[9] for the purposes of carrying into effect the Merchant Shipping Act 1995 provisions[10] relating to lighthouses[11],
is exempt from charge[12].

All instruments used by or under the direction of the Secretary of State as mentioned in head (b) above are exempt from stamp duty[13]; and all instruments which are required by any of the Merchant Shipping Act 1995 provisions[14] relating to lighthouses to be in a form approved by the Secretary of State, if made in that form, are exempt from stamp duty[15].

1   As to the meaning of 'lighthouse' see PARA 1017 note 1.
2   Merchant Shipping Act 1995 s 221(1)(a). As to the meaning of 'buoys and beacons' see PARA 1017 note 2.
3   As to the meaning of 'general light dues' see PARA 1033.
4   Merchant Shipping Act 1995 s 221(1)(b). As to the General Lighthouse Fund see PARA 1039.
5   Merchant Shipping Act 1995 s 221(1)(c).

6   Merchant Shipping Act 1995 s 221(1). A hereditament is exempt from local non-domestic rating to the extent that it belongs to or is occupied by the Trinity House and consists of any of the following:
    (1)   a lighthouse (Local Government Finance Act 1988 Sch 5 para 12(1)(a));
    (2)   a buoy (Sch 5 para 12(1)(b));
    (3)   a beacon (Sch 5 para 12(1)(c));
    (4)   property within the same curtilage as, and occupied for the purposes of, a lighthouse (Sch 5 para 12(1)(d)).
    No other hereditament, or part of a hereditament, belonging to or occupied by the Trinity House is exempt, notwithstanding anything in the Merchant Shipping Act 1995 s 221(1): Local Government Finance Act 1988 Sch 5 para 12(2) (amended by the Merchant Shipping Act 1995 Sch 13 para 83). As to the Trinity House see PARA 1018. See also LOCAL GOVERNMENT FINANCE vol 70 (2012) PARA 104. As to the meaning of 'hereditament' see LOCAL GOVERNMENT FINANCE vol 70 (2012) PARA 82; and as to the meaning of 'exempt' for these purposes see the Local Government Finance Act 1988 Sch 5 para 21(1), (2); and LOCAL GOVERNMENT FINANCE vol 70 (2012) PARA 86.
7   Merchant Shipping Act 1995 s 221(2). Stamp duty is not chargeable on any proposal under the Merchant Shipping Act 1995 s 202, Sch 9 (repealed) (general transfer of lighthouses to harbour authorities): see s 221(3).
8   Merchant Shipping Act 1995 s 221(2A) (added by SI 2003/2867).
9   As to the Secretary of State see PARA 36; and as to the Secretary of State's power to give directions under the Merchant Shipping Act 1995 see PARA 39.
10 Ie the Merchant Shipping Act 1995 Pt VIII (ss 193–223) (lighthouses): see s 221(4).
11 Merchant Shipping Act 1995 s 221(4A) (s 221(4A)–(4C) added by SI 2003/2867).
12 See the Merchant Shipping Act 1995 s 221(2A) (as added: see note 8), s 221(4A) (as added: see note 11). Relief under s 221(2A) or under s 221(4A) must be claimed in a land transaction return or an amendment of such a return: s 221(4B) (as added: see note 11). For these purposes, 'land transaction' has the meaning given in the Finance Act 2003 s 43(1) (see STAMP TAXES vol 96 (2012) PARA 426); and 'land transaction return' has the meaning given by s 76(1) (see STAMP TAXES vol 96 (2012) PARA 477): see the Merchant Shipping Act 1995 s 221(4C) (as added: see note 11).
13 Merchant Shipping Act 1995 s 221(4).
14 Ie the Merchant Shipping Act 1995 Pt VIII: see s 221(5).
15 Merchant Shipping Act 1995 s 221(5).

1047. Harbour dues. All ships[1] belonging to or used by any of the general lighthouse authorities[2] or the Secretary of State[3] are entitled to enter, resort to and use any harbours[4], ports[5], docks or piers in the United Kingdom[6] without payment of tolls, dues or rates of any kind[7].

1   As to the meaning of 'ship' see PARA 229.
2   As to the meaning of 'general lighthouse authority' see PARA 1017.
3   As to the Secretary of State see PARA 36.
4   As to the meaning of 'harbour' see PARA 49 note 5.
5   As to the meaning of 'port' see PARA 46 note 12.
6   As to the meaning of 'United Kingdom' see PARA 16 note 3.
7   Merchant Shipping Act 1995 s 222.

(9) WRECKS

1048. Powers of lighthouse authorities in relation to wrecks. Where:
    (1)   any vessel[1] is sunk, stranded or abandoned in any fairway or on the seashore or on or near any rock, shoal or bank in the United Kingdom[2] or any of the adjacent seas or islands[3]; and
    (2)   there is no harbour authority[4] or conservancy authority[5] having power to raise, remove or destroy the vessel[6],
the general lighthouse authority[7] for the place in or near which the vessel is situated has, if in the authority's opinion the vessel is, or is likely to become, an

obstruction or danger to navigation or to lifeboats engaged in lifeboat service, the same powers in relation thereto as those conferred[8] on harbour and conservancy authorities in relation to wrecks[9].

Where a general lighthouse authority has incurred expenses in its exercise of these powers[10] in relation to any vessel, then[11]:

(a)   if the proceeds of any sale made[12] in connection with the exercise of those powers in relation to the vessel are insufficient to reimburse the authority for the full amount of those expenses, the authority may recover the amount of the deficiency from the relevant person[13]; or

(b)   if there is no such sale, the authority may recover the full amount of those expenses from the relevant person[14].

Any expenses so incurred which are not recovered by the authority either out of the proceeds of any such sale or in accordance with head (a) or head (b) above must be paid out of the General Lighthouse Fund[15].

If any question arises between a harbour authority or conservancy authority and a general lighthouse authority as to their respective powers[16] in relation to any place in or near an approach to a harbour or tidal water[17], that question must, on the application of either authority, be referred to the Secretary of State[18] for his decision[19]; and any such decision of the Secretary of State is final[20].

1   As to the meaning of 'vessel' see PARA 850 note 2.
2   As to the meaning of 'United Kingdom' see PARA 16 note 3.
3   Merchant Shipping Act 1995 s 253(1)(a).
4   As to the meaning of 'harbour authority' see PARA 69 note 4.
5   As to the meaning of 'conservancy authority' see PARA 72 note 2.
6   Merchant Shipping Act 1995 s 253(1)(b).
7   As to the meaning of 'general lighthouse authority' see PARA 1017.
8   Ie conferred by the Merchant Shipping Act 1995 s 252 (see PARA 939): see s 253(1).
9   Merchant Shipping Act 1995 s 253(1).
10   Ie the exercise of its powers under the Merchant Shipping Act 1995 s 253: see s 253(2).
11   Merchant Shipping Act 1995 s 253(2).
12   Ie under the Merchant Shipping Act 1995 s 252 (see PARA 939): see s 253(2)(a).
13   Merchant Shipping Act 1995 s 253(2)(a). For these purposes, 'relevant person', in relation to any vessel, means the owner of the vessel at the time of the sinking, stranding or abandonment of the vessel: s 253(4).
14   Merchant Shipping Act 1995 s 253(2)(b).
15   Merchant Shipping Act 1995 s 253(3). However, the provisions of s 213 (see PARA 1041) apply to those expenses as if they were expenses of the authority falling within s 213(1) other than establishment expenses: see s 253(3). As to the General Lighthouse Fund see PARA 1039.
16   Ie under the Merchant Shipping Act 1995 s 252 or under s 253: see s 254(1).
17   As to the meaning of 'tidal water' see PARA 923 note 13.
18   As to the Secretary of State see PARA 36.
19   Merchant Shipping Act 1995 s 254(1).
20   Merchant Shipping Act 1995 s 254(2). As to the respective powers of harbour authorities, conservancy authorities and a general lighthouse authority in relation to wrecks see also PARAS 939–940.

14. OFFENCES AND LEGAL PROCEEDINGS

(1) PROSECUTION OF OFFENCES GENERALLY

(i) Time Limits

1049. Time limit for summary offences. No person may be convicted of an offence under the Merchant Shipping Act 1995 in summary proceedings unless[1]:

(1)   the proceedings were commenced within six months beginning with the date on which the offence was committed[2]; or

(2)   in a case where the accused happens during that period to be out of the United Kingdom[3], the proceedings were commenced within two months after he first happens to arrive within the United Kingdom and before the expiration of three years beginning with the date on which the offence was committed[4].

However, nothing in this provision[5] applies in relation to any indictable offence[6]; nor does that provision[7] prevent a conviction for an offence in summary proceedings begun before the expiration of three years beginning with the date on which the offence was committed[8], and before:

(a)   the expiration of the period of six months beginning with the day when evidence which the Secretary of State[9] considers is sufficient to justify a prosecution for the offence came to his knowledge[10]; or

(b)   the expiration of two months beginning with the day when the accused was first present in the United Kingdom after the expiration of the period mentioned in head (a) above if throughout that period the accused was absent from the United Kingdom[11].

For these purposes:

(i)   a certificate of the Secretary of State stating that evidence came to his knowledge on a particular day is conclusive evidence of that fact[12]; and

(ii)   a document purporting to be a certificate of the Secretary of State and to be signed on his behalf is presumed to be such a certificate unless the contrary is proved[13].

1   Merchant Shipping Act 1995 s 274(1). Section 274(1) is subject to s 274(2), (3) (see the text and notes 5–11): see s 274(1).
2   Merchant Shipping Act 1995 s 274(1)(a). See note 1.
3   As to the meaning of 'United Kingdom' see PARA 16 note 3.
4   Merchant Shipping Act 1995 s 274(1)(b). See note 1.
5   Ie nothing in the Merchant Shipping Act 1995 s 274(1) (see the text and notes 1–4): see s 274(2).
6   Merchant Shipping Act 1995 s 274(2). As to the meaning of 'indictable offence' see STATUTES AND LEGISLATIVE PROCESS vol 96 (2012) PARA 1216.
7   Ie the Merchant Shipping Act 1995 s 274(1) (see the text and notes 1–4): see s 274(3).
8   Merchant Shipping Act 1995 s 274(3).
9   As to the Secretary of State see PARA 36.
10 Merchant Shipping Act 1995 s 274(3)(a).
11 Merchant Shipping Act 1995 s 274(3)(b).
12 Merchant Shipping Act 1995 s 274(4)(a).
13 Merchant Shipping Act 1995 s 274(4)(b).

1050. Time limit for summary orders. No order for the payment of money may be made under the Merchant Shipping Act 1995 in proceedings before a magistrates' court unless[1]:

(1)   the proceedings were commenced within six months beginning with the date on which the matter of complaint arose[2]; or

(2)　　in a case where both or either of the parties to the proceedings happen during that period to be out of the United Kingdom[3], the proceedings were commenced within six months after they both first happen to arrive, or to be at one time, within the United Kingdom[4].

1　Merchant Shipping Act 1995 s 275.
2　Merchant Shipping Act 1995 s 275(a).
3　As to the meaning of 'United Kingdom' see PARA 16 note 3.
4　Merchant Shipping Act 1995 s 275(b).

(ii) Bodies Corporate

1051. Offences by officers of bodies corporate. Where a body corporate is guilty of an offence under the Merchant Shipping Act 1995 or any instrument made under it, and that offence is proved to have been committed with the consent or connivance of, or to be attributable to any neglect on the part of, a director, manager, secretary or other similar officer of the body corporate or any person who was purporting to act in such a capacity, he as well as the body corporate is guilty of that offence and is liable to be proceeded against and punished accordingly[1].

Where the affairs of a body corporate are managed by its members, this provision[2] applies in relation to the acts and defaults of a member in connection with his functions of management as if he were a director of the body corporate[3].

1　Merchant Shipping Act 1995 s 277(1).
2　Ie the Merchant Shipping Act 1995 s 277(1) (see the text and note 1): see s 277(2).
3　Merchant Shipping Act 1995 s 277(2).

(iii) Jurisdiction

1052. Jurisdiction in relation to offences. For the purpose of conferring jurisdiction, any offence under the Merchant Shipping Act 1995 is deemed to have been committed in any place in the United Kingdom[1] where the offender may for the time being be[2].

For the same purpose, any matter of complaint under the Merchant Shipping Act 1995 is deemed to have arisen in any place in the United Kingdom where the person complained against may for the time being be[3].

The jurisdiction so conferred[4] is in addition to and not in derogation of any jurisdiction or power of a court under any other enactment[5].

1　As to the meaning of 'United Kingdom' see PARA 16 note 3.
2　Merchant Shipping Act 1995 s 279(1).
3　Merchant Shipping Act 1995 s 279(2).
4　Ie under the Merchant Shipping Act 1995 s 279(1), (2) (see the text and notes 1–3): see s 279(3).
5　Merchant Shipping Act 1995 s 279(3).

1053. Jurisdiction over ships lying off coasts. Where the area within which a court in any part of the United Kingdom[1] has jurisdiction is situated on the coast of any sea or abuts on or projects into any bay, channel, lake, river or other navigable water, the court has jurisdiction as respects offences under the Merchant Shipping Act 1995 over any vessel being on, or lying or passing off, that coast or being in or near that bay, channel, lake, river or navigable water and over all persons on board that vessel or for the time being belonging to it[2].

The jurisdiction so conferred[3] is in addition to and not in derogation of any jurisdiction or power of a court under the Magistrates' Courts Act 1980[4].

1　As to the meaning of 'United Kingdom' see PARA 16 note 3.
2　Merchant Shipping Act 1995 s 280(1). Section 280 applies in relation to other offences under the law of England and Wales as it applies in relation to offences under the Merchant Shipping Act

1995 or instruments under that Act: Magistrates' Courts Act 1980 s 3A (added by the Merchant Shipping Act 1995 Sch 13 para 55); Senior Courts Act 1981 s 46A(1) (added by the Merchant Shipping Act 1995 Sch 13 para 59(1), (4)). As to the meanings of 'England' and 'Wales' see PARA 16 note 2. See further CRIMINAL PROCEDURE vol 27 (2015) PARA 14.
3 Ie under the Merchant Shipping Act 1995 s 280(1) (see the text and notes 1–2): see s 280(2).
4 Merchant Shipping Act 1995 s 280(2).

1054. Jurisdiction in case of offences on board ship. Where any person is charged with having committed any offence under the Merchant Shipping Act 1995, then:

(1) if he is a British citizen[1] and is charged with having committed it on board any United Kingdom ship[2] on the high seas, in any foreign port[3] or harbour[4] or on board any foreign ship[5] to which he does not belong[6]; or

(2) if he is not a British citizen and is charged with having committed it on board any United Kingdom ship on the high seas[7],

and he is found within the jurisdiction of any court in any part of the United Kingdom which would have had jurisdiction in relation to the offence if it had been committed on board a United Kingdom ship within the limits of its ordinary jurisdiction to try the offence, that court has jurisdiction to try the offence as if it had been so committed[8].

1 As to the meaning of 'British citizen' see PARA 18 note 7.
2 As to the meaning of 'United Kingdom ship' see PARA 230. As to the meaning of 'ship' under the Merchant Shipping Act 1995 see PARA 229; and as to the meaning of 'United Kingdom' see PARA 16 note 3.
3 As to the meaning of 'port' see PARA 46 note 12.
4 As to the meaning of 'harbour' see PARA 49 note 5.
5 As to the meaning of 'foreign', in relation to a ship, see PARA 18 note 2.
6 Merchant Shipping Act 1995 s 281(a). See note 8.
7 Merchant Shipping Act 1995 s 281(b). See note 8.
8 Merchant Shipping Act 1995 s 281. However, nothing in s 281 is to be taken to limit the jurisdiction of any court in the United Kingdom to deal with an offence under s 103 (stowaways) (see PARA 1137) which has been committed in a country outside the United Kingdom by a person who is not a British citizen (s 103(2)); and the Aviation and Maritime Security Act 1990 s 14(1) (see PARA 1152) has effect without prejudice to the Merchant Shipping Act 1995 s 281 (Aviation and Maritime Security Act 1990 s 14(3) (amended by the Merchant Shipping Act 1995 Sch 13 para 88(1), (2))).
  The Merchant Shipping Act 1995 s 281 applies in relation to other offences under the law of England and Wales as it applies in relation to offences under the Merchant Shipping Act 1995 or instruments under that Act: Magistrates' Courts Act 1980 s 3A (added by the Merchant Shipping Act 1995 Sch 13 para 55); Senior Courts Act 1981 s 46A(1) (added by the Merchant Shipping Act 1995 Sch 13 para 59(1), (4)). As to the meanings of 'England' and 'Wales' see PARA 16 note 2. See further CRIMINAL PROCEDURE vol 27 (2015) PARA 14.

1055. Offences committed by British seamen. Any act[1] in relation to property or person done in or at any place, ashore or afloat, outside the United Kingdom[2] by any master[3] or seaman[4] who at the time is employed in a United Kingdom ship[5], which, if done in any part of the United Kingdom, would be an offence under the law of any part of the United Kingdom, is an offence under that law and is to be treated, for the purposes of jurisdiction and trial, as if it had been done within the jurisdiction of the Admiralty of England[6]; and this provision[7] also applies in relation to a person who had been so employed within the period of three months expiring with the time when the act was done[8].

1 The Merchant Shipping Act 1995 s 282(1), (2) applies to omissions as it applies to acts: s 282(3). The Merchant Shipping Act 1995 s 282 applies in relation to other offences under the law of England and Wales as it applies in relation to offences under the Merchant Shipping Act 1995 or instruments under that Act: Magistrates' Courts Act 1980 s 3A (added by the Merchant Shipping Act 1995 Sch 13 para 55); Senior Courts Act 1981 s 46A(1) (added by the Merchant Shipping Act 1995 Sch 13 para 59(1), (4)). As to the meanings of 'England' and 'Wales' see PARA 16 note 2. See further CRIMINAL PROCEDURE vol 27 (2015) PARA 14. The Aviation and Maritime Security Act

1990 s 14(1) (see PARA 1152) has effect without prejudice to the Merchant Shipping Act 1995 s 282: Aviation and Maritime Security Act 1990 s 14(3) (amended by the Merchant Shipping Act 1995 Sch 13 para 88(1), (2)).

2   As to the meaning of 'United Kingdom' see PARA 16 note 3.
3   As to the meaning of 'master' see PARA 444 note 1.
4   As to the meaning of 'seaman' see PARA 457 note 5.
5   As to the meaning of 'United Kingdom ship' see PARA 230. As to the meaning of 'ship' under the Merchant Shipping Act 1995 see PARA 229.
6   Merchant Shipping Act 1995 s 282(1). See note 1.
7   Ie the Merchant Shipping Act 1995 s 282(1) (see the text and notes 1–6): see s 282(2).
8   Merchant Shipping Act 1995 s 282(2). See note 1.

(iv) Return of Offenders

1056. Powers exercisable in relation to offenders outside the United Kingdom. The powers conferred on a British consular officer[1]:

(1)   to inquire into the case upon oath[2]; and

(2)   if the case so requires, to take any steps in his power for the purpose of placing the offender under the necessary restraint and sending him by United Kingdom ship[3] as soon as practicable in safe custody to the United Kingdom for proceedings to be taken against him[4],

are exercisable in the event of any complaint being made to such an officer[5]:

(a)   that any offence against property or persons has been committed at any place, ashore or afloat, outside the United Kingdom by any master[6] or seaman[7] who at the time when the offence was committed, or within three months before that time, was employed in a United Kingdom ship[8]; or

(b)   that any offence on the high seas has been committed by any master or seaman belonging to any United Kingdom ship[9].

The consular officer may order the master of any United Kingdom ship bound for the United Kingdom to receive and carry[10] the offender and the witnesses to the United Kingdom; and the officer must indorse upon the agreement of the ship such particulars with respect to them as the Secretary of State requires[11]. A consular officer must not, however, exercise the power so conferred[12] unless no more convenient means of transport is available or it is available only at disproportionate expense[13]; nor may any master of a ship be so required[14] to receive more than one offender for every 100 tons of his ship's registered tonnage, or more than one witness for every 50 tons of his ship's registered tonnage[15].

The master of any ship to whose charge an offender has been so committed[16] must, on his ship's arrival in the United Kingdom, give the offender into the custody of some police officer or constable[17].

If any master of a ship, when so required[18] to receive and carry any offender or witness in his ship either fails to do so or, in the case of an offender, fails to deliver him as required[19], he is liable, on summary conviction, to a fine[20].

The expense of imprisoning any such offender and of carrying him and witnesses to the United Kingdom otherwise than in the ship to which they respectively belong must be paid out of money provided by Parliament[21].

1   Merchant Shipping Act 1995 s 283(1). As to British consular officers see INTERNATIONAL RELATIONS LAW vol 61 (2010) PARA 30.
2   Merchant Shipping Act 1995 s 283(2)(a).
3   As to the meaning of 'United Kingdom ship' see PARA 230. As to the meaning of 'ship' under the Merchant Shipping Act 1995 see PARA 229; and as to the meaning of 'United Kingdom' see PARA 16 note 3.
4   Merchant Shipping Act 1995 s 283(2)(b).
5   Merchant Shipping Act 1995 s 283(1).

6 As to the meaning of 'master' see PARA 444 note 1.
7 As to the meaning of 'seaman' see PARA 457 note 5.
8 Merchant Shipping Act 1995 s 283(2)(a).
9 Merchant Shipping Act 1995 s 283(2)(b).
10 For these purposes, references to carrying a person in a ship include affording him subsistence during the voyage: Merchant Shipping Act 1995 s 283(9).
11 Merchant Shipping Act 1995 s 283(3). Section s 283(3) is subject to s 283(4), (5) (see the text and notes 12–15): see s 283(3). As to the Secretary of State see PARA 36.
12 Ie by the Merchant Shipping Act 1995 s 283(3) (see the text and notes 10–11): see s 283(4).
13 Merchant Shipping Act 1995 s 283(4).
14 Ie by the Merchant Shipping Act 1995 s 283(3) (see the text and notes 10–11): see s 283(5).
15 Merchant Shipping Act 1995 s 283(5).
16 Ie under the Merchant Shipping Act 1995 s 283(3) (see the text and notes 10–11): see s 283(6).
17 Merchant Shipping Act 1995 s 283(6).
18 Ie under the Merchant Shipping Act 1995 s 283(3) (see the text and notes 10–11): see s 283(7).
19 Ie as required by the Merchant Shipping Act 1995 s 283(6) (see the text and notes 16–17): see s 283(7).
20 Merchant Shipping Act 1995 s 283(7). As to the time limit for summary offences see PARA 1049; as to offences by officers of bodies corporate see PARA 1051; as to jurisdiction in relation to offences see PARA 1052; as to jurisdiction over ships lying off the coast see PARA 1053; as to jurisdiction in the case of offences on board ship see PARA 1054; as to offences committed by British seamen see PARA 1055; and as to proof etc of exemption see PARA 1061. As to the powers of magistrates' courts to issue fines on summary conviction see SENTENCING vol 92 (2015) PARA 176.
21 Merchant Shipping Act 1995 s 283(8).

(v) Special Evidential Provisions

1057. Depositions of persons abroad admissible. If the evidence of any person is required in the course of any legal proceeding before a judge or magistrate in relation to the subject matter of the proceeding and it is proved that that person cannot be found in the United Kingdom[1], any deposition that he may have previously made at a place outside the United Kingdom in relation to the same subject matter is admissible in evidence in those proceedings[2]. However, for a deposition to be so admissible in any proceedings, the deposition:

(1)   must have been taken on oath[3];
(2)   must have been taken before a justice or magistrate in any colony[4] or a British consular officer[5] in any other place[6];
(3)   must be authenticated by the signature of the justice, magistrate or officer taking it[7]; and
(4)   must, if the proceedings are criminal proceedings, have been taken in the presence of the accused[8];

and, in a case falling within head (4) above, the deposition must be certified by the justice, magistrate or officer taking it to have been taken in the presence of the accused[9].

No proof need be given of the signature or official character of the person appearing to have signed any such deposition[10]; and, in any criminal proceedings, a certificate stating that the deposition was taken in the presence of the accused is evidence of that fact, unless the contrary is proved[11].

These provisions[12] also apply to proceedings before any person authorised by law or consent of the parties to receive evidence[13]; but nothing in these provisions[14] affects the admissibility in evidence of depositions under any other enactment or the practice of any court[15].

1 As to the meaning of 'United Kingdom' see PARA 16 note 3.
2 Merchant Shipping Act 1995 s 286(1).
3 Merchant Shipping Act 1995 s 286(2)(a).

4 As to the meaning of 'colony' see STATUTES AND LEGISLATIVE PROCESS vol 96 (2012) PARA 1208.
5 As to British consular officers see INTERNATIONAL RELATIONS LAW vol 61 (2010) PARA 30.
6 Merchant Shipping Act 1995 s 286(2)(b).
7 Merchant Shipping Act 1995 s 286(2)(c).
8 Merchant Shipping Act 1995 s 286(2)(d).
9 Merchant Shipping Act 1995 s 286(2).
10 Merchant Shipping Act 1995 s 286(3).
11 Merchant Shipping Act 1995 s 286(3).
12 Ie the Merchant Shipping Act 1995 s 286: see s 286(4).
13 Merchant Shipping Act 1995 s 286(4).
14 Ie nothing in the Merchant Shipping Act 1995 s 286: see s 286(5).
15 Merchant Shipping Act 1995 s 286(5).

1058. Admissibility in evidence and inspection of certain documents. The following documents are admissible in evidence and, when in the custody of the Registrar General of Shipping and Seamen[1], must be open to public inspection[2]:

(1)   documents purporting to be submissions to or decisions by[3] superintendents[4] or proper officers[5] in disputes relating to the amount payable to a seaman[6] employed under a crew agreement[7];

(2)   the official log book[8] of any ship[9] and[10] any document purporting to be a copy of an entry therein and to be certified as a true copy by the master[11] of the ship[12];

(3)   crew agreements, lists of crews[13] and notices given[14] of additions to or changes in crew agreements and lists of crews[15];

(4)   returns or reports[16] of births and deaths in ships etc[17];

(5)   documents transmitted[18] to the Registrar General of Shipping and Seamen[19].

A certificate issued under the provisions relating to manning[20] is admissible in evidence[21].

1 As to the Registrar General of Shipping and Seamen see PARA 62.
2 Merchant Shipping Act 1995 s 287(1).
3 Ie under the Merchant Shipping Act 1995 s 33 (see PARA 486): see s 287(1)(a).
4 As to the meaning of 'superintendent' see PARA 61 note 1. As to the appointment of superintendents see PARA 61.
5 As to the meaning of 'proper officer' see PARA 48 note 4.
6 As to the meaning of 'seaman' see PARA 457 note 5.
7 Merchant Shipping Act 1995 s 287(1)(a). As to the meaning of 'crew agreement' see PARA 457. As from a day to be appointed by the Secretary of State by order under the Merchant Shipping Act 1995 Sch 14 para 6(1), s 287(1)(a) ceases to have effect: see Sch 14 para 6(1), (2). However, at the date at which this volume states the law, no such day had been appointed. As to the Secretary of State see PARA 36.
8 Ie kept under the Merchant Shipping Act 1995 s 77 (see PARA 551): see s 287(1)(b).
9 As to the meaning of 'ship' see PARA 229.
10 Ie without prejudice to the Merchant Shipping Act 1995 s 288(2) (see PARA 1059): see s 287(1)(b).
11 As to the meaning of 'master' see PARA 444 note 1.
12 Merchant Shipping Act 1995 s 287(1)(b).
13 Ie made under the Merchant Shipping Act 1995 s 78 (see PARA 553 et seq): see s 287(1)(c).
14 Ie under the Merchant Shipping Act 1995 Pt III (ss 24–84) (see PARA 423 et seq): see s 287(1)(c).
15 Merchant Shipping Act 1995 s 287(1)(c).
16 Ie under the Merchant Shipping Act 1995 s 108 (see PARA 644): see s 287(1)(d).
17 Merchant Shipping Act 1995 s 287(1)(d).
18 Ie under the Merchant Shipping Act 1995 s 298 (see PARA 41 note 7): see s 287(1)(e).
19 Merchant Shipping Act 1995 s 287(1)(e).
20 Ie under the Merchant Shipping Act 1995 s 47 (see PARA 503): see s 287(2).
21 Merchant Shipping Act 1995 s 287(2).

1059. Admissibility of documents in evidence. Where a document is, by the Merchant Shipping Act 1995, declared to be admissible in evidence[1], the document is, on its production from proper custody:

(1)   admissible in evidence in any court or before any person having by law or consent of parties authority to receive evidence[2]; and
(2)   subject to all just exceptions, evidence of the matters stated in the document[3].

A copy of, or extract from, any document so made admissible in evidence is also admissible in evidence and evidence of the matters stated in the document[4]. However, a copy of, or extract from, a document is not so admissible in evidence unless:

(a)   it is proved to be an examined copy or extract[5]; or
(b)   it purports to be signed and certified as a true copy or extract by the officer to whose custody the original document was entrusted[6];

and that officer must furnish the certified copy or extract to any person who applies for it at a reasonable time and pays such reasonable price as the Secretary of State determines[7].

A person is entitled, on payment of such reasonable price as the Secretary of State determines, to have a certified copy of any declaration or document a copy of which is made evidence by the Merchant Shipping Act 1995[8].

If any officer having duties of certification[9] in relation to any document intentionally certifies any document being a true copy or extract knowing that the copy or extract is not a true copy or extract, he is liable, on conviction on indictment, to imprisonment for a term not exceeding two years or a fine (or to both) or, on summary conviction, to imprisonment for a term not exceeding six months or a fine[10].

1   Unless made in the form approved by the Secretary of State, certain books, instruments etc are not admissible: see the Merchant Shipping Act 1995 s 300(4); and PARA 40.
2   Merchant Shipping Act 1995 s 288(1)(a).
3   Merchant Shipping Act 1995 s 288(1)(b).
4   Merchant Shipping Act 1995 s 288(2). For these purposes, in the application of s 288(2) to documents in the custody of the Registrar General of Shipping and Seaman, a copy is to be taken to be the copy of a document notwithstanding that it is taken from a copy or other reproduction of the original: s 289(3). As to the Registrar General of Shipping and Seamen see PARA 62.
5   Merchant Shipping Act 1995 s 288(3)(a).
6   Merchant Shipping Act 1995 s 288(3)(b).
7   Merchant Shipping Act 1995 s 288(3). As to the Secretary of State see PARA 36.
8   Merchant Shipping Act 1995 s 288(4).
9   Ie under the Merchant Shipping Act 1995 s 288(3) (see the text and notes 5–7): see s 288(5).
10 Merchant Shipping Act 1995 s 288(5). As to the time limit for summary offences see PARA 1049; as to offences by officers of bodies corporate see PARA 1051; as to jurisdiction in relation to offences see PARA 1052; as to jurisdiction over ships lying off the coast see PARA 1053; as to jurisdiction in the case of offences on board ship see PARA 1054; as to offences committed by British seamen see PARA 1055; and as to proof etc of exemption see PARA 1061. As to the powers of magistrates' courts to issue fines on summary conviction see SENTENCING vol 92 (2015) PARA 176.

1060. Inspection and admissibility in evidence of copies of certain documents. Where under any enactment a document is open to public inspection when in the custody of the Registrar General of Shipping and Seamen[1]:

(1)   there may be supplied for public inspection a copy or other reproduction of the document instead of the original[2]; but
(2)   the original must nevertheless be made available for public inspection if the copy or other reproduction is illegible[3].

Where the Registrar General of Shipping and Seamen destroys any document which has been sent to him under or by virtue of any enactment, and keeps a copy or other reproduction of that document, then:

(a)   any enactment providing for that document to be admissible in evidence or open to public inspection[4]; and

(b)   in the case of a document falling within heads (1) and (2) above, those provisions[5],

apply to the copy or other reproduction as if it were the original[6].

For these purposes, a copy is to be taken to be the copy of a document notwithstanding that it is taken from a copy or other reproduction of the original[7].

1   Merchant Shipping Act 1995 s 289(1). As to the Registrar General of Shipping and Seamen see PARA 62.
2   Merchant Shipping Act 1995 s 289(1)(a).
3   Merchant Shipping Act 1995 s 289(1)(b).
4   Merchant Shipping Act 1995 s 289(2)(a).
5   Merchant Shipping Act 1995 s 289(2)(b).
6   Merchant Shipping Act 1995 s 289(2).
7   Merchant Shipping Act 1995 s 289(3).

1061. Proof etc of exemptions. Where any exception, exemption, excuse or qualification applies in relation to an offence under the Merchant Shipping Act 1995, it may be proved by the accused but need not be specified or negatived in any information or complaint[1]. However, if any exception, exemption, excuse or qualification is so specified or negatived, it does not require to be proved by the informant or complainant[2].

These provisions[3] apply in relation to an offence whether or not the exception, exemption, excuse or qualification is contained in the statutory provision creating the offence[4].

1   Merchant Shipping Act 1995 s 290(1).
2   Merchant Shipping Act 1995 s 290(1).
3   Ie the Merchant Shipping Act 1995 s 290: see s 290(2).
4   Merchant Shipping Act 1995 s 290(2).

(2) SPECIFIC OFFENCES

(i) Offences relating to Registration of Ships

1062. Offences relating to British character of ship. If the master[1] or owner of a ship[2] which is not a British ship[3] does anything, or permits anything to be done, for the purpose of causing the ship to appear to be a British ship[4], the ship is[5] liable to forfeiture[6] and the master, the owner and any charterer are each guilty of an offence[7]. However, no such liability arises where the assumption of British nationality has been made for the purpose of escaping capture by an enemy or by a foreign[8] ship of war in the exercise of some belligerent right[9]; and where the registration of any ship has terminated by virtue of any provision of registration regulations[10], any marks prescribed by registration regulations displayed on the ship within the period of 14 days beginning with the date of termination of that registration are disregarded for the purposes of establishing such liability[11].

If the master or owner of a British ship does anything, or permits anything to be done, for the purpose of concealing the nationality of the ship[12], the ship is liable to forfeiture and the master, the owner and any charterer of the ship are each guilty of an offence[13].

Any person guilty of an offence relating to the British character of a ship[14] is liable, on conviction on indictment, to imprisonment for a term not exceeding two years or a fine (or to both) or, on summary conviction, to a fine[15].

These offences[16] apply to things done outside, as well as to things done within, the United Kingdom[17].

1 As to the meaning of 'master' for these purposes see PARA 444 note 1.
2 As to the meaning of 'ship' for these purposes see PARA 229.
3 As to the meaning of 'British ship' see PARA 230.
4 This provision applies in particular to acts or deliberate omissions as respects:
    (1)   the flying of a national flag (Merchant Shipping Act 1995 s 3(5)(a));
    (2)   the carrying or production of certificates of registration or other documents relating to the nationality of the ship (s 3(5)(b)); and
    (3)   the display of marks required by the law of any country (s 3(5)(c)).
    This is without prejudice to the generality of s 3(1): see s 3(5).
5 Ie subject to the Merchant Shipping Act 1995 s 3(2), (3) (see the text and notes 8–11): see s 3(1).
6 As to proceedings on forfeiture of a ship see PARA 235.
7 Merchant Shipping Act 1995 s 3(1).
8 As to the meaning of 'foreign', in relation to a ship, see PARA 18 note 2.
9 Merchant Shipping Act 1995 s 3(2).
10 As to the meaning of 'registration regulations' see PARA 247.
11 Merchant Shipping Act 1995 s 3(3).
12 This provision applies in particular to acts or deliberate omissions as respects:
    (1)   the flying of a national flag (Merchant Shipping Act 1995 s 3(5)(a));
    (2)   the carrying or production of certificates of registration or other documents relating to the nationality of the ship (s 3(5)(b)); and
    (3)   the display of marks required by the law of any country (s 3(5)(c)).
    This is without prejudice to the generality of s 3(4): see s 3(5).
13 Merchant Shipping Act 1995 s 3(4).
14 Ie under the Merchant Shipping Act 1995 s 3: see s 3(6).
15 Merchant Shipping Act 1995 s 3(6) (amended by SI 2015/664). As to the time limit for summary offences see PARA 1049; as to offences by officers of bodies corporate see PARA 1051; as to jurisdiction in relation to offences see PARA 1052; as to jurisdiction over ships lying off the coast see PARA 1053; as to jurisdiction in the case of offences committed on board ship see PARA 1054; as to offences committed by British seamen see PARA 1055; and as to proof etc of exemption see PARA 1061. As to the powers of magistrates' courts to issue fines on summary conviction see SENTENCING vol 92 (2015) PARA 176.
16 Ie the offences set out in the Merchant Shipping Act 1995 s 3: see s 3(7).
17 Merchant Shipping Act 1995 s 3(7). As to the meaning of 'United Kingdom' see PARA 16 note 3.

1063. Penalty for carrying improper colours. If any of the following colours[1], namely:
    (1)   any distinctive national colours except:
        (a)   the red ensign[2];
        (b)   the Union flag (commonly known as the Union Jack) with a white border[3]; or
        (c)   any colours duly authorised or confirmed for adoption by British ships[4] registered[5] in a relevant British possession[6];
    (2)   any colours usually worn by Her Majesty's ships or resembling those of Her Majesty[7]; or
    (3)   the pendant usually carried by Her Majesty's ships or any pendant resembling that pendant[8],
are hoisted on board any British ship without warrant from Her Majesty or from the Secretary of State[9], the master[10] of the ship, or the owner of the ship (if on board), and every other person hoisting them are guilty of an offence[11]; and each person so guilty is liable, on conviction on indictment, to a fine or, on summary conviction, to a fine[12].

If any colours are hoisted on board a ship in contravention[13] of the above prohibition[14], any of the following, namely:
    (i)   any commissioned naval[15] or military officer[16];
    (ii)   any officer of Revenue and Customs[17]; and
    (iii)   any British consular officer[18],

may board the ship and seize and take away the colours[19]; and any colours so seized are forfeited to Her Majesty[20].

1 For these purposes, 'colours' includes any pendant: Merchant Shipping Act 1995 s 4(5).
2 Merchant Shipping Act 1995 s 4(1)(a)(i).
3 Merchant Shipping Act 1995 s 4(1)(a)(ii).
4 As to the meaning of 'British ship' see PARA 230; and as to the meaning of 'ship' see PARA 229.
5 As to the meaning of 'registered' for these purposes see PARA 254 note 2.
6 Merchant Shipping Act 1995 s 4(1)(a)(iii). The text refers to any colours authorised or confirmed under s 2(3)(b) (see PARA 231): see s 4(1)(a)(iii). As to the meaning of 'relevant British possession' for these purposes see PARA 16 note 3.
7 Merchant Shipping Act 1995 s 4(1)(b).
8 Merchant Shipping Act 1995 s 4(1)(c).
9 As to the Secretary of State see PARA 36.
10 As to the meaning of 'master' for these purposes see PARA 444 note 1.
11 Merchant Shipping Act 1995 s 4(1).
12 Merchant Shipping Act 1995 s 4(2). As to the time limit for summary offences see PARA 1049; as to offences by officers of bodies corporate see PARA 1051; as to jurisdiction in relation to offences see PARA 1052; as to jurisdiction over ships lying off the coast see PARA 1053; as to jurisdiction in the case of offences on board ship see PARA 1054; as to offences committed by British seamen see PARA 1055; and as to proof etc of exemption see PARA 1061. As to the powers of magistrates' courts to issue fines on summary conviction see SENTENCING vol 92 (2015) PARA 176.
13 As to the meaning of 'contravention' see PARA 51 note 3.
14 Ie in contravention of the Merchant Shipping Act 1995 s 4(1) (see the text and notes 1–11): see s 4(3).
15 As to the meaning of 'commissioned naval officer' see PARA 47 note 12.
16 Merchant Shipping Act 1995 s 4(3)(a). As to the meaning of 'commissioned military officer' see PARA 235 note 4.
17 Merchant Shipping Act 1995 s 4(3)(b) (amended by virtue of the Commissioners for Revenue and Customs Act 2005 s 50(1), (2), (7)). As to the appointment of officers of Revenue and Customs see INCOME TAXATION vol 58 (2014) PARA 33.
18 Merchant Shipping Act 1995 s 4(3)(c). As to British consular officers see INTERNATIONAL RELATIONS LAW vol 61 (2010) PARA 30.
19 Merchant Shipping Act 1995 s 4(3).
20 Merchant Shipping Act 1995 s 4(4).

1064. Contravention of registration provisions. A person is liable, on summary conviction, to a fine[1] if he contravenes[2] the provision[3] that requires the owner of a ship that becomes registered under the Merchant Shipping Act 1995 at a time when it is already registered under the law of a country other than the United Kingdom[4] to take all reasonable steps to secure the termination of the ship's registration under the law of that country[5].

1 As to the time limit for summary offences see PARA 1049; as to offences by officers of bodies corporate see PARA 1051; as to jurisdiction in relation to offences see PARA 1052; as to jurisdiction over ships lying off the coast see PARA 1053; as to jurisdiction in the case of offences on board ship see PARA 1054; as to offences committed by British seamen see PARA 1055; and as to proof etc of exemption see PARA 1061. As to the powers of magistrates' courts to issue fines on summary conviction see SENTENCING vol 92 (2015) PARA 176.
2 As to the meaning of 'contravention' see PARA 51 note 3.
3 Ie the provision contained in the Merchant Shipping Act 1995 s 9(5) (see PARA 245): see s 9(7). Section 9(5) does not apply to a ship which becomes registered on a transfer of registration to the register from a relevant British possession: see s 9(6); and PARA 245. As to the meaning of 'register' and 'registered' for these purposes see PARA 254 note 2. As to the meaning of 'relevant British possession' for these purposes see PARA 16 note 3. As to the meaning of 'ship' see PARA 229.
4 As to the meaning of 'United Kingdom' see PARA 16 note 3.
5 Merchant Shipping Act 1995 s 9(7).

1065. Offences relating to a ship's British connection. Any person who, in relation to any matter relevant to the British connection[1] of a ship[2]:

(1)   makes to the registrar[3] a statement which he knows to be false or recklessly makes a statement which is false[4]; or

(2)   furnishes to the registrar information which is false[5],

is guilty of an offence[6].

If at any time there occurs, in relation to a registered[7] ship, any change affecting the British connection of the ship, the owner of the ship must, as soon as practicable after the change occurs, notify the registrar of that change; and, if he fails to do so, he is guilty of an offence[8].

Any person who intentionally alters, suppresses, conceals or destroys a document which contains information relating to the British connection of the ship and which he has been required to produce to the registrar in pursuance of registration regulations[9] is guilty of an offence[10].

A person guilty of any such offence[11] is liable, on conviction on indictment, to imprisonment for a term not exceeding two years or a fine (or to both) or, on summary conviction, to a fine[12].

1   As to the meaning of references to a ship's having a British connection see PARA 245 note 3.
2   As to the meaning of 'ship' see PARA 229.
3   As to the meaning of 'registrar' see PARA 254 note 11.
4   Merchant Shipping Act 1995 s 14(1)(a).
5   Merchant Shipping Act 1995 s 14(1)(b).
6   Merchant Shipping Act 1995 s 14(1).
7   As to the meaning of 'registered' for these purposes see PARA 254 note 2.
8   Merchant Shipping Act 1995 s 14(2).
9   As to the registration regulations see PARA 247.
10 Merchant Shipping Act 1995 s 14(3).
11 Ie any offence under the Merchant Shipping Act 1995 s 14 (see the text and notes 1–10): see s 14(4). Section 14 applies to things done outside, as well as to things done within, the United Kingdom: s 14(5). As to the meaning of 'United Kingdom' see PARA 17 note 3.
12 As to the time limit for summary offences see PARA 1049; as to offences by officers of bodies corporate see PARA 1051; as to jurisdiction in relation to offences see PARA 1052; as to jurisdiction over ships lying off the coast see PARA 1053; as to jurisdiction in the case of offences on board ship see PARA 1054; as to offences committed by British seamen see PARA 1055; and as to proof etc of exemption see PARA 1061. As to the powers of magistrates' courts to issue fines on summary conviction see SENTENCING vol 92 (2015) PARA 176.

1066. Offences in relation to fishing vessels not registered under the Merchant Shipping Act 1995. If a fishing vessel[1]:

(1)   which is either entitled to be registered under the Merchant Shipping Act 1995[2], or wholly owned by persons qualified to be owners of British ships[3]; but

(2)   which is registered neither under the Merchant Shipping Act 1995 in the part of the register[4] relating to fishing vessels nor under the law of any country outside the United Kingdom[5],

fishes for profit, the vessel is liable to forfeiture[6] and the skipper, the owner and the charterer of the vessel are each guilty of an offence[7]. This prohibition does not, however, apply to fishing vessels of such classes or descriptions or in such circumstances as may be specified in regulations made by the Secretary of State[8].

If the skipper or owner of a fishing vessel which is not registered in the United Kingdom does anything, or permits anything to be done, for the purpose of causing the vessel to appear to be a vessel registered in the United Kingdom, the vessel is liable to forfeiture and the skipper, the owner and any charterer of the vessel are each guilty of an offence[9]. Where, however, the registration of a fishing vessel has terminated by virtue of any provision of registration regulations, any marks prescribed by registration regulations displayed on the fishing vessel within the period of 14 days beginning with the date of termination of that registration are to be disregarded for the purposes of this offence[10].

Any person guilty of any such offence[11] is liable, on conviction on indictment, to imprisonment for a term not exceeding two years or a fine (or to both) or, on summary conviction, to a fine[12]. Proceedings for such an offence[13] may not be instituted in England and Wales[14] except by or with the consent of the Attorney General or the Secretary of State[15].

1 As to the meaning of 'fishing vessel' see PARA 230 note 9.
2 As to the meaning of 'registered' for these purposes see PARA 254 note 2.
3 Merchant Shipping Act 1995 s 15(1)(a). As to the meaning of 'British ship' see PARA 230; and as to the meaning of 'ship' see PARA 229.
4 As to the meaning of 'register' for these purposes see PARA 254 note 2.
5 Merchant Shipping Act 1995 s 15(1)(b). As to the meaning of 'United Kingdom' see PARA 16 note 3.
6 As to proceedings on forfeiture of a ship for these purposes see PARA 253.
7 Merchant Shipping Act 1995 s 15(1). Section 15 applies to things done outside, as well as to things done within, the United Kingdom: s 15(8).
    The Sea Fisheries Act 1968 ss 8, 9 (general powers of British sea-fishery officers and powers of sea-fishery officers to enforce conventions) (see FISHERIES AND AQUACULTURE vol 51 (2013) PARAS 276–278) is to apply in relation to any provision of the Merchant Shipping Act 1995 s 15 or of registration regulations in their application to fishing vessels or fishing vessels of any class or description as they apply in relation to any order mentioned in the Sea Fisheries Act 1968 s 8 and in relation to any convention mentioned in s 9 respectively; and ss 10–12, 14 (offences and supplemental provisions as to legal proceedings) apply accordingly: Merchant Shipping Act 1995 s 15(9). As to the meaning of 'registration regulations' see PARA 247.
8 Merchant Shipping Act 1995 s 15(2). As to the Secretary of State see PARA 36. At the date at which this volume states the law, no such regulations had been made under s 15(2) but, by virtue of the Interpretation Act 1978 s 17(2)(b), the Merchant Shipping (Registration of Ships) Regulations 1993, SI 1993/3138 (as to which see PARA 255 et seq) have effect as if so made. As to the Secretary of State's power to make regulations under the Merchant Shipping Act 1995 generally see PARA 39.
9 Merchant Shipping Act 1995 s 15(3). See note 7.
10 Merchant Shipping Act 1995 s 15(4). The text refers to marks being disregarded for the purposes of s 15(3) (see the text and note 9): see s 15(4).
11 Ie an offence under the Merchant Shipping Act 1995 s 15 (see the text and notes 1–10): see s 15(5).
12 Merchant Shipping Act 1995 s 15(5) (amended by SI 2015/664). As to the time limit for summary offences see PARA 1049; as to offences by officers of bodies corporate see PARA 1051; as to jurisdiction in relation to offences see PARA 1052; as to jurisdiction over ships lying off the coast see PARA 1053; as to jurisdiction in the case of offences on board ship see PARA 1054; as to offences committed by British seamen see PARA 1055; and as to proof etc of exemption see PARA 1061. As to the powers of magistrates' courts to issue fines on summary conviction see SENTENCING vol 92 (2015) PARA 176.
13 Ie an offence under the Merchant Shipping Act 1995 s 15 (see the text and notes 1–10): see s 15(6).
14 As to the meanings of 'England' and 'Wales' see PARA 16 note 2.
15 Merchant Shipping Act 1995 s 15(6) (amended by SI 2002/794). As to the Attorney General see CONSTITUTIONAL AND ADMINISTRATIVE LAW vol 20 (2014) PARA 273.

1067. Failure to supply details of engine power of fishing vessels on certain applications.

Where an application is made:

(1)   to register[1] certain fishing vessels (whether new or second hand)[2];
(2)   to record[3] a change in the length, breadth or engine power of a registered fishing vessel[4]; or
(3)   to register[5] a change of ownership of a registered fishing vessel (or share in such vessel)[6],

the applicant must submit details of the maximum continuous engine power[7] and, where an engine is permanently de-rated[8], the modification explanation[9]. Any owner[10] who contravenes the requirement to submit such details is guilty of an offence[11] and is liable, on summary conviction, to a fine[12].

1 Ie under the Merchant Shipping (Registration of Ships) Regulations 1993, SI 1993/3138, reg 28 (see PARA 275): see reg 29A(1)(a); and PARA 275. The text refers to fishing vessels other than those requiring simple registration: see reg 28(1); and PARA 275. As to the meaning of 'fishing vessel' for these purposes see PARA 255 note 7; and as to the meaning of 'simple registration' see PARA 256.
2 See the Merchant Shipping (Registration of Ships) Regulations 1993, SI 1993/3138, reg 29A(1)(a); and PARA 275.

3 Ie under the Merchant Shipping (Registration of Ships) Regulations 1993, SI 1993/3138, reg 51 (see PARA 314): see reg 29A(1)(b); and PARA 314.
4 See the Merchant Shipping (Registration of Ships) Regulations 1993, SI 1993/3138, reg 29A(1)(b); and PARA 314.
5 Ie under the Merchant Shipping (Registration of Ships) Regulations 1993, SI 1993/3138, reg 50 (see PARA 313): see reg 29A(1)(c); and PARA 313.
6 See the Merchant Shipping (Registration of Ships) Regulations 1993, SI 1993/3138, reg 29A(1)(c); and PARA 313.
7 See the Merchant Shipping (Registration of Ships) Regulations 1993, SI 1993/3138, reg 29A(2)(a); and PARAS 275, 313. As to the meaning of 'maximum continuous engine power' see PARA 275 note 14.
8 As to the meaning of 'permanently de-rated engine power' see PARA 275 note 15.
9 See the Merchant Shipping (Registration of Ships) Regulations 1993, SI 1993/3138, reg 29A(2)(b); and PARAS 275, 313. As to the meaning of 'modification explanation' see PARA 275 note 15.
10 As to the meaning of 'owner' for these purposes see PARA 255 note 13.
11 Merchant Shipping (Registration of Ships) Regulations 1993, SI 1993/3138, reg 29A(3) (reg 29A added by SI 1999/3206).
12 Merchant Shipping (Registration of Ships) Regulations 1993, SI 1993/3138, reg 114(7) (amended by SI 1999/3206). As to the powers of magistrates' courts to issue fines on summary conviction see SENTENCING vol 92 (2015) PARA 176.

1068. Failure to notify changes of ownership etc of ship. If at any time there occurs, in relation to a registered ship[1]:

(1) any change affecting the eligibility of the ship to be registered, not being a change which affects the qualification or eligibility of the owner[2] or the British connection of a ship[3]; or

(2) in respect of a fishing vessel[4], any change, not affecting that eligibility, in the percentage of the property in the ship beneficially owned[5] by qualified persons or companies[6],

the owner of the ship must, as soon as practicable after the change occurs, notify the registrar[7].

Any person who contravenes the requirement to notify the registrar of such changes as are mentioned in heads (1) and (2) above is guilty of an offence[8] and is liable, on summary conviction, to a fine[9].

Where there is any transfer or transmission of a registered ship or share in a registered ship[10], any person who fails to notify the registrar, to surrender the certificate of registry[11], or to make the applications that are required for such a transfer or transmission to be registered[12] is guilty of an offence[13] and is liable, on summary conviction, to a fine[14].

When there is a change either in the registered particulars of a ship (including a change in the tonnage of the ship) or in the name or address of an owner entered in the register[15] (not being a change of ownership)[16], any person who fails to make such an application as is required for the change to be recorded in the register[17] is guilty of an offence[18] and is liable, on summary conviction, to a fine[19].

If at any time there occurs, in relation to a bareboat charter ship[20], any change affecting the eligibility of the ship to be registered[21], the charterer of the ship must, as soon as practicable after the change occurs, notify the registrar[22]. Any person who contravenes this requirement[23] is guilty of an offence[24] and is liable, on summary conviction, to a fine[25].

1 As to the meaning of 'ship' for these purposes see PARA 255 note 4.
2 Ie as prescribed in the Merchant Shipping (Registration of Ships) Regulations 1993, SI 1993/3138, reg 7 (qualification) (see PARA 258) and reg 12 (eligibility) (see PARA 262): see reg 49(1)(a); and PARA 313. As to the meaning of 'owner' for these purposes see PARA 255 note 13.
3 See the Merchant Shipping (Registration of Ships) Regulations 1993, SI 1993/3138, reg 49(1)(a); and PARA 313. The text refers to changes affecting the British connection of a ship as prescribed in reg 8 (British connection and majority interest in the ship) (see PARA 259) and reg 14 (British connection and representative persons for fishing vessels) (see PARA 263): see reg 49(1)(a); and

PARA 313. As to the meaning of references under the Merchant Shipping Act 1995 to a ship's having a British connection see PARA 245 note 3.

4 As to the meaning of 'fishing vessel' for these purposes see PARA 255 note 7.
5 As to the meaning of 'beneficial ownership' for these purposes see PARA 262 note 15.
6 See the Merchant Shipping (Registration of Ships) Regulations 1993, SI 1993/3138, reg 49(1)(b); and PARA 313.
7 See the Merchant Shipping (Registration of Ships) Regulations 1993, SI 1993/3138, reg 49(1); and PARA 313. As to the meaning of 'registrar' see PARA 255 note 2.
8 Merchant Shipping (Registration of Ships) Regulations 1993, SI 1993/3138, reg 49(3).
9 Merchant Shipping (Registration of Ships) Regulations 1993, SI 1993/3138, reg 114(7) (amended by SI 1999/3206). As to the powers of magistrates' courts to issue fines on summary conviction see SENTENCING vol 92 (2015) PARA 176.
10 As to an application for the transfer of a registered ship (or shares therein) see the Merchant Shipping Act 1995 s 16(1), Sch 1 para 2; and PARA 306. As to an application for the transmission of a registered ship (or shares therein) see Sch 1 para 3; and PARA 306.
11 As to the meaning of 'certificate of registry' see PARA 255 note 17.
12 Ie as required by the Merchant Shipping (Registration of Ships) Regulations 1993, SI 1993/3138, reg 50(1), (2) or (3) (as to which see PARA 313): see reg 50(4) (added by SI 1999/3206).
13 Merchant Shipping (Registration of Ships) Regulations 1993, SI 1993/3138, reg 50(4) (as added: see note 12).
14 Merchant Shipping (Registration of Ships) Regulations 1993, SI 1993/3138, reg 114(9) (added by SI 1999/3206).
15 As to the meaning of 'register' see PARA 255 note 1.
16 See the Merchant Shipping (Registration of Ships) Regulations 1993, SI 1993/3138, reg 51; and PARA 314. The provisions of reg 51 apply to Pt X (regs 73–87) (see PARA 358 et seq) as if any reference in those provisions to the owner were a reference to the charterer: see reg 85; and PARA 366.
17 Ie as required by the Merchant Shipping (Registration of Ships) Regulations 1993, SI 1993/3138, reg 51(1) or (3) (as to which see PARA 314): see reg 51(5) (added by SI 1999/3206). See note 16.
18 Merchant Shipping (Registration of Ships) Regulations 1993, SI 1993/3138, reg 51(5) (as added: see note 17).
19 Merchant Shipping (Registration of Ships) Regulations 1993, SI 1993/3138, reg 114(9) (as added: see note 14).
20 As to the meaning of 'bareboat charter ship' see PARA 255 note 9.
21 As to the qualification and entitlement to register bareboat charter ships other than fishing vessels see PARA 358; and as to the qualification and entitlement to register a fishing vessel as a bareboat charter ship see PARA 359.
22 See the Merchant Shipping (Registration of Ships) Regulations 1993, SI 1993/3138, reg 84(1); and PARA 366.
23 Ie any person who contravenes the Merchant Shipping (Registration of Ships) Regulations 1993, SI 1993/3138, reg 84(1) (see the text and notes 20–22): see reg 84(3).
24 Merchant Shipping (Registration of Ships) Regulations 1993, SI 1993/3138, reg 84(3).
25 Merchant Shipping (Registration of Ships) Regulations 1993, SI 1993/3138, reg 114(7) (as amended: see note 9).

1069. Offence of obscuring registration markings. It is an offence on the part of the owner[1] or master of a registered ship[2] if any of the marks required[3] to be marked on a ship is effaced, altered, allowed to become illegible, covered or concealed[4]. Such an offence is punishable, on conviction on indictment, by a fine or, on summary conviction, by a fine[5]. It is, however, a defence for a person charged with such an offence to prove that he took all reasonable precautions and exercised all due diligence to avoid the commission of the offence or that the effacing, alteration, covering or concealing of the marking was for the purpose of escaping capture by an enemy[6].

1 As to the meaning of 'owner' for these purposes see PARA 255 note 13.
2 As to the meaning of 'ship' for these purposes see PARA 255 note 4.
3 Ie required by the Merchant Shipping (Registration of Ships) Regulations 1993, SI 1993/3138: see reg 114(2).
4 Merchant Shipping (Registration of Ships) Regulations 1993, SI 1993/3138, reg 114(2).

5   Merchant Shipping (Registration of Ships) Regulations 1993, SI 1993/3138, reg 114(8). As to the powers of magistrates' courts to issue fines on summary conviction see SENTENCING vol 92 (2015) PARA 176.
6   Merchant Shipping (Registration of Ships) Regulations 1993, SI 1993/3138, reg 114(3).

1070. Offences related to registration documents and the supply of information.
Any person who:

(1)   with an intent to deceive, uses or lends or allows to be used by another, a certificate of registry[1], whether in force or not[2]; or

(2)   in connection with the registration of a ship[3] knowingly or recklessly furnishes information which is false in a material particular[4]; or

(3)   intentionally alters, suppresses, conceals or destroys a document which he has been required[5] to produce to the registrar[6],

is guilty of an offence[7]. The offences under heads (1) to (3) above are punishable, on summary conviction, with a fine[8].

1   As to the meaning of 'certificate of registry' see PARA 255 note 17.
2   Merchant Shipping (Registration of Ships) Regulations 1993, SI 1993/3138, reg 114(1).
3   As to the meaning of 'ship' for these purposes see PARA 255 note 4.
4   Merchant Shipping (Registration of Ships) Regulations 1993, SI 1993/3138, reg 114(5).
5   Ie required by the Merchant Shipping (Registration of Ships) Regulations 1993, SI 1993/3138: see reg 114(8).
6   Merchant Shipping (Registration of Ships) Regulations 1993, SI 1993/3138, reg 114(6). As to the meaning of 'registrar' see PARA 255 note 2.
7   See the Merchant Shipping (Registration of Ships) Regulations 1993, SI 1993/3138, reg 114(1), (5), (6).
8   Merchant Shipping (Registration of Ships) Regulations 1993, SI 1993/3138, reg 114(7) (amended by SI 1999/3206). As to the powers of magistrates' courts to issue fines on summary conviction see SENTENCING vol 92 (2015) PARA 176.

1071. Refusal to surrender certificate of registry when required.
If any person refuses, without reasonable cause, to surrender the certificate of registry[1] when in his possession or under his control to the person entitled to its custody for the purposes of the lawful navigation of the ship[2], or to the registrar[3], or an officer of revenue and customs[4] or any other person entitled by law to demand such delivery, he is guilty of an offence[5] and is liable, on summary conviction, to a fine[6].

Any person who fails, without reasonable cause, to surrender a certificate of registry when required to do so by the provisions which govern the issue of duplicate certificates[7], or to return a certificate of registry when required to do so on the termination or expiry of a ship's registration[8], also commits an offence[9] and is liable, on summary conviction, to a fine[10].

1   As to the meaning of 'certificate of registry' see PARA 255 note 17.
2   As to the meaning of 'ship' for these purposes see PARA 255 note 4.
3   As to the meaning of 'registrar' see PARA 255 note 2.
4   As to the appointment of officers of Revenue and Customs see INCOME TAXATION vol 58 (2014) PARA 33 et seq.
5   Merchant Shipping (Registration of Ships) Regulations 1993, SI 1993/3138, reg 109(2) (amended by virtue of the Commissioners for Revenue and Customs Act 2005 s 50(1), (2), (7)); Merchant Shipping (Registration of Ships) Regulations 1993, SI 1993/3138, reg 114(4).
6   Merchant Shipping (Registration of Ships) Regulations 1993, SI 1993/3138, reg 114(7) (amended by SI 1999/3206). As to the powers of magistrates' courts to issue fines on summary conviction see SENTENCING vol 92 (2015) PARA 176.
7   Ie when required to do so by the Merchant Shipping (Registration of Ships) Regulations 1993, SI 1993/3138, reg 108 (see PARA 373): see reg 114(4).
8   Ie when required to do so by the Merchant Shipping (Registration of Ships) Regulations 1993, SI 1993/3138, reg 110 (see PARA 375): see reg 114(4).
9   Merchant Shipping (Registration of Ships) Regulations 1993, SI 1993/3138, reg 114(4).
10   Merchant Shipping (Registration of Ships) Regulations 1993, SI 1993/3138, reg 114(7) (as amended: see note 6).

1072. Contravention of provisions relating to the registration, certification, maintenance and operation of hovercraft. If any of the provisions governing the registration, certification, maintenance and operation of hovercraft[1] is contravened in relation to a hovercraft, the hovercraft's operator[2] and captain[3] (without prejudice to the liability of any other person for that contravention) are deemed[4] to have contravened that provision unless he proves that the contravention occurred without his consent or connivance and that he exercised all due diligence to prevent it[5]. If it is proved that an act or omission of any person which would otherwise have been a contravention by that person of any of those provisions was due to any cause not avoidable by the exercise of reasonable care by that person, the act or omission is deemed not to be a contravention by that person of that provision[6].

Varying penalties are imposed for contravention of the provisions relating to hovercraft[7].

1   Ie the provisions of the Hovercraft (General) Order 1972, SI 1972/674 (see PARA 387 et seq): see art 33(1). As to the meaning of 'hovercraft' under the Hovercraft Act 1968 see PARA 381. As to the hovercraft to which the Hovercraft (General) Order 1972, SI 1972/674, applies see PARA 387; and as to Crown application see PARA 388.

2   As to the meaning of 'operator' see PARA 388 note 2.

3   As to the meaning of 'captain' see PARA 388 note 6.

4   Ie for the purposes of the Hovercraft (General) Order 1972, SI 1972/674, art 33(3)–(5) (as to which see note 7): see art 33(1).

5   Hovercraft (General) Order 1972, SI 1972/674, art33(1).

6   Hovercraft (General) Order 1972, SI 1972/674, art33(2).

7   The penalties referred to in the text are:
     (1)   if any person contravenes any of the Hovercraft (General) Order 1972, SI 1972/674, art 4 (see PARA 390), art 6 (see PARA 394), art 21 (see PARA 406), art 23 (see PARA 407), art 24 (see PARA 409), and art 30 (see PARA 410), he is liable, on summary conviction, to a fine (art 33(4), Schedule Pt A (art 33(3)–(5) substituted by SI 1996/3173));
     (2)   if any person contravenes any of the Hovercraft (General) Order 1972, SI 1972/674, art 7 (see PARA 395), art 8 (see PARA 397), art 13 (see PARA 400), art 15 (see PARA 401), art 18 (see PARA 403), art 19 (see PARA 404), art 20 (see PARA 405), art 22 (see PARA 408), art 26 (see PARA 410), art 27 (see PARA 411) and art 28 (see PARA 413), he is liable, on summary conviction, to a fine (art 33(5), Schedule Pt B (art 33(5) as so substituted));
     (3)   if any person contravenes any provision of the Hovercraft (General) Order 1972, SI 1972/674, other than those referred to in heads (1), (2) above, he is liable, on summary conviction, to a fine (art 33(3) (as so substituted)).

   As to the powers of magistrates' courts to issue fines on summary conviction see SENTENCING vol 92 (2015) PARA 176. As to the time limit for summary offences see PARA 1049; as to offences by officers of bodies corporate see PARA 1051; and as to jurisdiction in relation to offences see PARA 1052 et seq.

(ii) Crew-related Offences

A.   OFFENCES COMMITTED IN RELATION TO CREW

1073. Offences relating to crew agreements. If a ship[1] goes to sea[2] or attempts to go to sea in contravention[3] of the requirements relating to crew agreements[4], the master[5] or the person employing the crew is liable, on summary conviction, to a fine[6]. The ship in question, if in the United Kingdom, may be detained[7].

A person who fails to comply with an obligation imposed on him by or under the provisions relating to the delivery of a crew agreement[8] is guilty of an offence[9] and liable, on summary conviction, to a fine[10].

Similarly, a master who fails to comply with an obligation imposed on him by or under the provisions relating either to the display of a crew agreement[11] or to the production to specified officers on demand of such an agreement (or of an exemption from the requirement to carry such an agreement)[12] is guilty of an offence[13] and liable, on summary conviction, to a fine[14].

A person or, as the case may be, a master who fails to comply with an obligation imposed on him to supply and produce copy documents related to the crew agreement on demand to a seaman[15] also is guilty of an offence[16] and liable, on summary conviction, to a fine[17].

1 As to the meaning of 'ship' under the Merchant Shipping Act 1995 see PARA 229.
2 For these purposes, references to going to sea include references to going to sea from any country outside the United Kingdom: Merchant Shipping Act 1995 s 84(2). As to the meaning of 'United Kingdom' see PARA 16 note 3.
3 As to the meaning of 'contravention' see PARA 51 note 3.
4 Ie in contravention of the requirements of the Merchant Shipping Act 1995 s 25 (as to which see PARA 457): see s 25(8). As to the meaning of 'crew agreement' see PARA 457.
5 As to the meaning of 'master' see PARA 444 note 1.
6 Merchant Shipping Act 1995 s 25(8). As to the time limit for summary offences see PARA 1049; as to offences by officers of bodies corporate see PARA 1051; as to jurisdiction in relation to offences see PARA 1052; as to jurisdiction over ships lying off the coast see PARA 1053; as to jurisdiction in the case of offences on board ship see PARA 1054; as to offences committed by British seamen see PARA 1055; and as to proof etc of exemption see PARA 1061. As to the powers of magistrates' courts to issue fines on summary conviction see SENTENCING vol 92 (2015) PARA 176.
7 Merchant Shipping Act 1995 s 25(8). As to enforcing the detention of a ship see PARA 1253.
8 Ie under the Merchant Shipping (Crew Agreements, Lists of Crew and Discharge of Seamen) Regulations 1991, SI 1991/2144, reg 6 (see PARA 460): see reg 10(1).
9 Merchant Shipping (Crew Agreements, Lists of Crew and Discharge of Seamen) Regulations 1991, SI 1991/2144, reg10(1).
10 Merchant Shipping (Crew Agreements, Lists of Crew and Discharge of Seamen) Regulations 1991, SI 1991/2144, reg10(3).
11 Ie under the Merchant Shipping (Crew Agreements, Lists of Crew and Discharge of Seamen) Regulations 1991, SI 1991/2144, reg 7 (see PARA 461): see reg 10(2).
12 Ie under the Merchant Shipping (Crew Agreements, Lists of Crew and Discharge of Seamen) Regulations 1991, SI 1991/2144, reg 9 (see PARA 463): see reg 10(1), (2).
13 Merchant Shipping (Crew Agreements, Lists of Crew and Discharge of Seamen) Regulations 1991, SI 1991/2144, reg10(2).
14 Merchant Shipping (Crew Agreements, Lists of Crew and Discharge of Seamen) Regulations 1991, SI 1991/2144, reg10(3).
15 Ie under the Merchant Shipping (Crew Agreements, Lists of Crew and Discharge of Seamen) Regulations 1991, SI 1991/2144, reg 8 (see PARA 462): see reg 10(1), (2).
16 Merchant Shipping (Crew Agreements, Lists of Crew and Discharge of Seamen) Regulations 1991, SI 1991/2144, reg10(1), (2).
17 Merchant Shipping (Crew Agreements, Lists of Crew and Discharge of Seamen) Regulations 1991, SI 1991/2144, reg10(3).

1074. Failure to observe proper procedure when a seaman is discharged.
Any person, including a master, who fails to comply with an obligation imposed on him:

(1)   by or under the provisions requiring him on a seaman's discharge (where the seaman is present) to record specified particulars:
    (a)   in the seaman's discharge book[1] (or to give him a certificate of discharge containing the like particulars)[2];
    (b)   by making an entry in the official log book[3]; or
    (c)   by making an entry in a crew agreement or in a list of crew[4]; or
(2)   by or under the provisions requiring the master (or one of the ship's officers authorised by him in that behalf) to give to the seaman on request a certificate (which must be separate from any other document) either as to the quality of his work or indicating whether he has fully discharged his obligations under his contract of employment[5],

is guilty of an offence[6] and liable, on summary conviction, to a fine[7].

A master who fails to comply with an obligation imposed on him:

(i)   by or under the provisions requiring him to ensure that the seaman is discharged in the presence of the master himself, or the seaman's employer or a person authorised in that behalf by the master or employer[8];

(ii)   by or under the provisions requiring him (or a person authorised in that behalf by the master), where a seaman is not present when he is discharged, to make the entries referred to in heads (1)(b) and (1)(c) above[9]; or

(iii)   by or under the provisions mentioned in head (2) above[10],

is guilty of an offence[11] and liable, on summary conviction, to a fine[12].

A seaman who fails to comply with an obligation imposed on him by or under the provisions requiring him to sign the entry in the crew agreement and list of crew referred to in head (1)(c) above[13] is guilty of an offence[14] and liable, on summary conviction, to a fine[15].

1   As to discharge books see PARA 565 et seq.
2   Ie an obligation imposed by or under the Merchant Shipping (Crew Agreements, Lists of Crew and Discharge of Seamen) Regulations 1991, SI 1991/2144, reg 25(1)(a) (see PARA 468): see reg 26(1)(a) (amended by SI 2014/614).
3   Ie an obligation imposed by or under the Merchant Shipping (Crew Agreements, Lists of Crew and Discharge of Seamen) Regulations 1991, SI 1991/2144, reg 25(1)(c)(i) (see PARA 468): see reg 26(1)(a) (as amended: see note 2). As to the official log book see PARA 551 et seq.
4   Ie an obligation imposed by or under the Merchant Shipping (Crew Agreements, Lists of Crew and Discharge of Seamen) Regulations 1991, SI 1991/2144, reg 25(1)(c)(ii) (see PARA 468): see reg 26(1)(b) (as amended: see note 2). As to crew agreements see PARA 457 et seq.
5   Ie an obligation imposed by or under the Merchant Shipping (Crew Agreements, Lists of Crew and Discharge of Seamen) Regulations 1991, SI 1991/2144, reg 25(4) (see PARA 468): see reg 26(1)(a) (as amended: see note 2).
6   Merchant Shipping (Crew Agreements, Lists of Crew and Discharge of Seamen) Regulations 1991, SI 1991/2144, reg26(1).
7   Merchant Shipping (Crew Agreements, Lists of Crew and Discharge of Seamen) Regulations 1991, SI 1991/2144, reg 26(4)(a). As to the powers of magistrates' courts to issue fines on summary conviction see SENTENCING vol 92 (2015) PARA 176.
8   Ie an obligation imposed by or under the Merchant Shipping (Crew Agreements, Lists of Crew and Discharge of Seamen) Regulations 1991, SI 1991/2144, reg 25(1)(b) (see PARA 468): see reg 26(2).
9   Ie an obligation imposed by or under the Merchant Shipping (Crew Agreements, Lists of Crew and Discharge of Seamen) Regulations 1991, SI 1991/2144, reg 25(2) (see PARA 462): see reg 26(2).
10 Ie an obligation imposed by or under the Merchant Shipping (Crew Agreements, Lists of Crew and Discharge of Seamen) Regulations 1991, SI 1991/2144, reg 25(4) (see PARA 468): see reg 26(2).
11 Merchant Shipping (Crew Agreements, Lists of Crew and Discharge of Seamen) Regulations 1991, SI 1991/2144, reg26(2).
12 Merchant Shipping (Crew Agreements, Lists of Crew and Discharge of Seamen) Regulations 1991, SI 1991/2144, reg26(4)(a).
13 Ie an obligation imposed by or under the Merchant Shipping (Crew Agreements, Lists of Crew and Discharge of Seamen) Regulations 1991, SI 1991/2144, reg 25(1)(d) (see PARA 468): see reg 26(3).
14 Merchant Shipping (Crew Agreements, Lists of Crew and Discharge of Seamen) Regulations 1991, SI 1991/2144, reg26(3).
15 Merchant Shipping (Crew Agreements, Lists of Crew and Discharge of Seamen) Regulations 1991, SI 1991/2144, reg26(4)(b).

1075. Failure to administer proper payment of seamen's wages. If a person fails without reasonable excuse to comply with the provisions which govern the accounting of a seaman's wages[1], he is liable, on summary conviction, to a fine[2].

If a person fails without reasonable excuse to comply with the provisions which govern the accounting of wages (and catch where wages are related to catch) in relation to a United Kingdom fishing vessel[3], he is liable, on summary conviction, to a fine[4].

1 Ie the Merchant Shipping Act 1995 s 31(1)–(5) (as to which see PARA 485): see s 31(6). As to the meaning of 'seaman' see PARA 457 note 5; and as to the meaning of 'wages' see PARA 464 note 6.
2 Merchant Shipping Act 1995 s 31(6). As to the time limit for summary offences see PARA 1049; as to offences by officers of bodies corporate see PARA 1051; as to jurisdiction in relation to offences see PARA 1052; as to jurisdiction over ships lying off the coast see PARA 1053; as to jurisdiction in the case of offences on board ship see PARA 1054; as to offences committed by British seamen see PARA 1055; and as to proof etc of exemption see PARA 1061. As to the powers of magistrates' courts to issue fines on summary conviction see SENTENCING vol 92 (2015) PARA 176.
3 Ie the Merchant Shipping Act 1995 s 112(1)–(4) (see PARA 489): see s 112(5). As to the meaning of 'fishing vessel' see PARA 230 note 9; and as to the meaning of 'United Kingdom fishing vessel' see PARA 230. As to the meaning of 'United Kingdom' see PARA 16 note 3. As to crew agreements relating to fishing vessels see PARA 457.
4 Merchant Shipping Act 1995 s 112(5).

1076. Failure to provide approved equipment in crew accommodation.
Any owner who fails to ensure the supply of approved equipment[1] as required by the regulations relating to crew accommodation[2] is guilty of an offence and liable, on summary conviction, to a fine[3]. However, it is a defence in any proceedings for such an offence to prove that the person so charged took all reasonable steps to ensure that the regulations were complied with[4].

Any ship that does not comply with the requirements for equipment in crew accommodation to be of an approved type[5] is liable to be detained[6].

1 Ie any owner who contravenes the Merchant Shipping (Crew Accommodation) Regulations 1997, SI 1997/1508, reg 36(1) (see PARA 490): see reg 38(1). As to the meaning of 'approved', in relation to an item of equipment, for these purposes see PARA 490 note 39.
2 Ie the Merchant Shipping (Crew Accommodation) Regulations 1997, SI 1997/1508: see PARA 490. As to exemptions see PARA 490.
3 Merchant Shipping (Crew Accommodation) Regulations 1997, SI 1997/1508, reg 38(1). As to the powers of magistrates' courts to issue fines on summary conviction see SENTENCING vol 92 (2015) PARA 176.
4 Merchant Shipping (Crew Accommodation) Regulations 1997, SI 1997/1508, reg 38(2).
5 Ie the requirements of the Merchant Shipping (Crew Accommodation) Regulations 1997, SI 1997/1508, Pt III (regs 36–39) (see PARA 490): see reg 39.
6 Merchant Shipping (Crew Accommodation) Regulations 1997, SI 1997/1508, reg 39. The Merchant Shipping Act 1995 s 284(1)–(6), (8) (enforcing detention of ships) (see PARA 1190) has effect in relation to the ship, subject to the modification that, for the words 'this Act' wherever they appear, there are to be substituted 'the Merchant Shipping (Crew Accommodation) Regulations 1997, SI 1997/1508, Pt III': see reg 39.

1077. Master's failure to deal with complaints about provisions or water.
If the master[1] fails without reasonable excuse to comply with the procedure governing complaints made to a superintendent[2] or proper officer[3] by seamen[4] employed in a United Kingdom ship[5] about provisions or water[6], he is liable, on summary conviction, to a fine[7]; and, if the master has been notified in writing by the person duly making an examination of the provisions or water[8] that any provisions or water are found to be unfit for use or not of the quality required by the safety regulations[9], then:

(1) if they are not replaced within a reasonable time, the master or owner is liable, on summary conviction, to a fine unless he proves that the failure to replace them was not due to his neglect or default[10]; or

(2) if the master without reasonable excuse permits them to be used, he is liable, on summary conviction, to a fine[11].

1 As to the meaning of 'master' see PARA 444 note 1.
2 As to the meaning of 'superintendent' see PARA 61 note 1. As to the appointment of superintendents see PARA 61.
3 As to the meaning of 'proper officer' see PARA 48 note 4.

4   As to the meaning of 'seaman' see PARA 457 note 5.
5   As to the meaning of 'ship' see PARA 229; and as to the meaning of 'United Kingdom ship' see PARA 230. As to the meaning of 'United Kingdom' see PARA 16 note 3.
6   Ie a failure to comply with the provisions of the Merchant Shipping Act 1995 s 44(2) (see PARA 500): see s 44(4).
7   Merchant Shipping Act 1995 s 44(4). As to the time limit for summary offences see PARA 1049; as to offences by officers of bodies corporate see PARA 1051; as to jurisdiction in relation to offences see PARA 1052; as to jurisdiction over ships lying off the coast see PARA 1053; as to jurisdiction in the case of offences on board ship see PARA 1054; as to offences committed by British seamen see PARA 1055; and as to proof etc of exemption see PARA 1061. As to the powers of magistrates' courts to issue fines on summary conviction see SENTENCING vol 92 (2015) PARA 176.
8   Ie under the Merchant Shipping Act 1995 s 44(3) (see PARA 500): see s 44(4).
9   Merchant Shipping Act 1995 s 44(4). As to the meaning of 'safety regulations' see PARA 602 note 1.
10 Merchant Shipping Act 1995 s 44(4)(a).
11 Merchant Shipping Act 1995 s 44(4)(b).

1078. Falsely obtaining documents issued in relation to manning. If a person makes a statement which he knows to be false or recklessly makes a statement which is false in a material particular for the purpose of obtaining for himself or another person a certificate or other document which may be issued under the provisions governing the manning of ships[1], he is liable, on summary conviction, to a fine[2].

If a person makes a statement which he knows to be false or recklessly makes a statement which is false in a material particular for the purpose of obtaining for himself or another person a British seaman's card[3], he is liable, on summary conviction, to a fine[4].

1   Ie the Merchant Shipping Act 1995 s 47 (see PARA 503): see s 47(5). As to the meaning of 'ship' see PARA 229.
2   Merchant Shipping Act 1995 s 47(5). As to the time limit for summary offences see PARA 1049; as to offences by officers of bodies corporate see PARA 1051; as to jurisdiction in relation to offences see PARA 1052; as to jurisdiction over ships lying off the coast see PARA 1053; as to jurisdiction in the case of offences on board ship see PARA 1054; as to offences committed by British seamen see PARA 1055; and as to proof etc of exemption see PARA 1061. As to the powers of magistrates' courts to issue fines on summary conviction see SENTENCING vol 92 (2015) PARA 176.
3   As to British seaman's cards see PARA 559 et seq.
4   Merchant Shipping Act 1995 s 79(4).

1079. Contravention of requirement to provide personal protective equipment. Any contravention by an employer of the provisions relating to personal protective equipment[1] that govern his duty to ensure:

(1)   that the personal protective equipment required to be used is provided, and that such personal protective equipment is suitable[2];

(2)   that an assessment is made to identify those circumstances where risk to the health and safety of individual workers at work cannot be avoided or reduced by other means, and to identify the characteristics required of personal protective equipment in order to provide protection to workers from that risk[3];

(3)   that personal protective equipment is provided to a worker for his individual use, that appropriate instructions for the proper use and maintenance of any such personal protective equipment is readily available to any worker required to use that equipment, and that that personal protective equipment is properly stored and maintained, and is regularly inspected and, where appropriate, checked that it is in satisfactory working order[4]; or

(4)   that workers are provided with adequate and appropriate information, training and instruction[5],

is an offence punishable, on summary conviction, by a fine[6].

Any contravention by an employer of his duty to ensure that personal protective equipment is used as instructed[7], or by a worker of his obligation to use such equipment which has been duly provided to him and to use it as instructed[8], is an offence punishable, on summary conviction, by a fine[9].

A relevant inspector[10] may inspect any United Kingdom ship[11] and if he is satisfied that there has been a failure to comply in relation to that ship[12] may detain the ship until the health and safety of all workers and other persons aboard ship is secured, but he must not in the exercise of these powers detain or delay the ship unreasonably[13]. Such an inspector may inspect and detain or exercise other measures in respect of any ship which is not a United Kingdom ship when the ship is in a United Kingdom port[14].

1 See generally the Merchant Shipping and Fishing Vessels (Personal Protective Equipment) Regulations 1999, SI 1999/2205; and PARA 632. As to the application of those regulations see PARA 632 note 2. As to the meaning of 'personal protective equipment' see PARA 632 note 1.
2 Ie any contravention of the Merchant Shipping and Fishing Vessels (Personal Protective Equipment) Regulations 1999, SI 1999/2205, reg 6 (see PARA 632): see reg 11(1).
3 Ie any contravention of the Merchant Shipping and Fishing Vessels (Personal Protective Equipment) Regulations 1999, SI 1999/2205, reg 7 (see PARA 632): see reg 11(1).
4 Ie any contravention of the Merchant Shipping and Fishing Vessels (Personal Protective Equipment) Regulations 1999, SI 1999/2205, reg 8 (see PARA 632): see reg 11(1).
5 Ie any contravention of the Merchant Shipping and Fishing Vessels (Personal Protective Equipment) Regulations 1999, SI 1999/2205, reg 9 (see PARA 632): see reg 11(1).
6 Merchant Shipping and Fishing Vessels (Personal Protective Equipment) Regulations 1999, SI 1999/2205, reg 11(1). As to offences by bodies corporate see reg 12. In any proceedings for an offence under any of the Merchant Shipping and Fishing Vessels (Personal Protective Equipment) Regulations 1999, SI 1999/2205, consisting of a failure to comply with a duty or requirement to do something so far as is reasonably practicable, it is for the defendant to prove that it was not reasonably practicable to do more than was in fact done to satisfy the duty or requirement: reg 13. As to the powers of magistrates' courts to issue fines on summary conviction see SENTENCING vol 92 (2015) PARA 176.
7 Ie any contravention of the Merchant Shipping and Fishing Vessels (Personal Protective Equipment) Regulations 1999, SI 1999/2205, reg 10(1) (see PARA 632): see reg 11(2).
8 Ie any contravention of the Merchant Shipping and Fishing Vessels (Personal Protective Equipment) Regulations 1999, SI 1999/2205, reg 10(2) (see PARA 632): see reg 11(2).
9 Merchant Shipping and Fishing Vessels (Personal Protective Equipment) Regulations 1999, SI 1999/2205, reg 11(2). See note 6.
10 Ie a person mentioned in the Merchant Shipping Act 1995 s 258(1)(a), (b) or (c) (powers to inspect ships and their equipment, etc) (see PARA 48): see the Merchant Shipping and Fishing Vessels (Personal Protective Equipment) Regulations 1999, SI 1999/2205, reg 2(2).
11 As to the meaning of 'United Kingdom ship' see PARA 632 note 2.
12 Ie a failure to comply with the requirements of the Merchant Shipping and Fishing Vessels (Personal Protective Equipment) Regulations 1999, SI 1999/2205 (see PARA 639): see reg 14.
13 Merchant Shipping and Fishing Vessels (Personal Protective Equipment) Regulations 1999, SI 1999/2205, reg 14. Where a ship is liable to be detained under the Merchant Shipping and Fishing Vessels (Personal Protective Equipment) Regulations 1999, SI 1999/2205, the Merchant Shipping Act 1995 s 284(1)–(5), (8) (enforcing detention of ships) (see PARA 1190) has effect in relation to the ship, subject to modifications: see the Merchant Shipping and Fishing Vessels (Personal Protective Equipment) Regulations 1999, SI 1999/2205, reg 16. The Merchant Shipping Act 1995 ss 96, 97 (arbitration and compensation in connection with detention notices) (see PARAS 1142, 1143) apply in relation to a detention notice or order under the Merchant Shipping and Fishing Vessels (Personal Protective Equipment) Regulations 1999, SI 1999/2205, as they apply in relation to a detention notice under the Merchant Shipping Act 1995 s 95(3) (power to detain dangerously unsafe ship) (see PARA 1141) but with modifications: see the Merchant Shipping and Fishing Vessels (Personal Protective Equipment) Regulations 1999, SI 1999/2205, reg 17. The provisions of reg 15 (see the text and note 14) and regs 16, 17 apply to ships other than United Kingdom ships which are in United Kingdom waters: see reg 3(2).
14 See the Merchant Shipping and Fishing Vessels (Personal Protective Equipment) Regulations 1999, SI 1999/2205, reg 15. See note 13.

1080. Contravention of provisions relating to the employment of young persons on ships. Any contravention of the provisions relating to the employment of young persons on ships[1] is an offence punishable, on summary conviction, by a fine[2].

Where a body corporate is guilty of an offence under any of those provisions[3] and that offence is proved to have been committed with the consent or connivance of (or to have been attributable to any neglect on the part of) any director, manager, secretary or other similar officer of the body corporate or a person who was purporting to act in any such capacity, he as well as the body corporate is guilty of that offence and is liable to be proceeded against and punished accordingly[4]. Where the affairs of a body corporate are managed by its members, this provision[5] applies in relation to the acts and defaults of a member in connection with his functions of management as if he were a director of the body corporate[6].

In any proceedings for any such offence[7] consisting of a failure to comply with a duty or requirement to do something so far as is reasonably practicable, it is for the defendant to prove that it was not reasonably practicable to do more than was in fact done to satisfy the duty or requirement[8].

1 Ie any contravention of the Merchant Shipping and Fishing Vessels (Health and Safety at Work) (Employment of Young Persons) Regulations 1998, SI 1998/2411 (as to which see PARA 450): see reg 10. As to the meaning of 'young person' in relation to employment on a sea-going United Kingdom ship see PARA 450 note 1.
2 Merchant Shipping and Fishing Vessels (Health and Safety at Work) (Employment of Young Persons) Regulations 1998, SI 1998/2411, reg 10. As to the powers of magistrates' courts to issue fines on summary conviction see SENTENCING vol 92 (2015) PARA 176.
3 Ie any of the Merchant Shipping and Fishing Vessels (Health and Safety at Work) (Employment of Young Persons) Regulations 1998, SI 1998/2411 (as to which see PARA 504): see reg 11(1).
4 Merchant Shipping and Fishing Vessels (Health and Safety at Work) (Employment of Young Persons) Regulations 1998, SI 1998/2411, reg 11(1).
5 Ie the Merchant Shipping and Fishing Vessels (Health and Safety at Work) (Employment of Young Persons) Regulations 1998, SI 1998/2411, reg 11(1) (see the text and notes 3–4): see reg 11(2).
6 Merchant Shipping and Fishing Vessels (Health and Safety at Work) (Employment of Young Persons) Regulations 1998, SI 1998/2411, reg 11(2).
7 Ie an offence under any of the Merchant Shipping and Fishing Vessels (Health and Safety at Work) (Employment of Young Persons) Regulations 1998, SI 1998/2411: see reg 12.
8 Merchant Shipping and Fishing Vessels (Health and Safety at Work) (Employment of Young Persons) Regulations 1998, SI 1998/2411, reg 12.

1081. Failure to produce certificates and other documents of qualification. Any person serving or engaged to serve in any ship[1] and holding any certificate or other document which is evidence that he is duly qualified[2] must on demand produce it to any superintendent[3], surveyor of ships[4] or proper officer[5] and, if he is not himself the master[6], to the master of the ship[7]. If without reasonable excuse a person fails to comply with this requirement[8], he is liable, on summary conviction, to a fine[9].

Any person serving or engaged to serve in a United Kingdom fishing vessel[10] and holding any certificate or other document which is evidence that he is duly qualified[11] must on demand produce it to any person who is a British sea-fishery officer for the purposes of the Sea Fisheries Acts[12]. If a person fails without reasonable excuse to produce on demand any such certificate or other document, he is liable, on summary conviction, to a fine[13].

1 Ie any ship to which the Merchant Shipping Act 1995 s 50 applies: see s 50(1); and PARA 503. As to the meaning of 'ship' see PARA 229.
2 Ie qualified for the purposes of the Merchant Shipping Act 1995 s 47 (see PARA 503): see s 50(1).
3 As to the meaning of 'superintendent' see PARA 61 note 1. As to the appointment of superintendents see PARA 61.

4 As to the meaning of 'surveyor of ships' see PARA 46 note 13. As to the appointment of surveyors see PARA 46.
5 As to the meaning of 'proper officer' see PARA 48 note 4.
6 As to the meaning of 'master' see PARA 444 note 1.
7 See the Merchant Shipping Act 1995 s 50(1); and PARA 503. As to the power to grant exemptions with respect to fishing vessels see PARA 423.
8 Ie fails to comply with the Merchant Shipping Act 1995 s 50(1) (see the text and notes 1–7): see s 50(2). As to the powers of inspectors appointed under s 256(6) (see PARA 46) to serve improvement notices or prohibition notices where s 50 and the provisions of any instrument of a legislative character having effect thereunder are being contravened, or where activities to which s 50 applies are carried on so as to involve serious personal injury or serious pollution, see PARA 51 et seq.
9 Merchant Shipping Act 1995 s 50(2). As to the time limit for summary offences see PARA 1049; as to offences by officers of bodies corporate see PARA 1051; as to jurisdiction in relation to offences see PARA 1052; as to jurisdiction over ships lying off the coast see PARA 1053; as to jurisdiction in the case of offences on board ship see PARA 1054; as to offences committed by British seamen see PARA 1055; and as to proof etc of exemption see PARA 1061. As to the powers of magistrates' courts to issue fines on summary conviction see SENTENCING vol 92 (2015) PARA 176.
10 As to the meaning of 'fishing vessel' see PARA 230 note 9; and as to the meaning of 'United Kingdom fishing vessel' see PARA 230. As to the meaning of 'United Kingdom' see PARA 16 note 3. As to crew agreements relating to fishing vessels see PARA 457.
11 Ie qualified for the purposes of the Merchant Shipping Act 1995 s 47 (see PARA 503): see s 116(1).
12 See the Merchant Shipping Act 1995 s 116(1);. As to who are British sea-fishery officers for the purposes of the Sea Fisheries Acts see FISHERIES AND AQUACULTURE vol 51 (2013) PARA 226.
13 Merchant Shipping Act 1995 s 116(2).

1082. Going to sea where crew's knowledge of English is insufficient.

Where, in the opinion of a superintendent[1] or proper officer[2], the crew of a ship[3] consists of or includes persons who may not understand orders given to them in the course of their duty because of their insufficient knowledge of English and the absence of adequate arrangements for transmitting the orders in a language of which they have sufficient knowledge[4], then:

(1)   if the superintendent or proper officer has informed the master[5] of that opinion, the ship must not go to sea[6]; and

(2)   if the ship is in the United Kingdom[7], it may be detained[8].

If a ship goes to sea or attempts to go to sea in contravention of these restrictions[9], the owner or master is liable, on summary conviction, to a fine[10].

1 As to the meaning of 'superintendent' see PARA 61 note 1. As to the appointment of superintendents see PARA 61.
2 As to the meaning of 'proper officer' see PARA 48 note 4.
3 Ie any ship to which the Merchant Shipping Act 1995 s 51 applies: see s 51(1); and PARA 506. As to the meaning of 'ship' see PARA 229. As to the application of s 51 see PARA 423.
4 See the Merchant Shipping Act 1995 s 51(1); and PARA 506. As to the powers of inspectors appointed under s 256(6) (see PARA 46) to serve improvement notices or prohibition notices where s 51 and the provisions of any instrument of a legislative character having effect thereunder are being contravened, or where activities to which s 51 applies are carried on so as to involve serious personal injury or serious pollution, see PARA 51 et seq.
5 As to the meaning of 'master' see PARA 444 note 1.
6 See the Merchant Shipping Act 1995 s 51(1)(a); and PARA 506. As to the meaning of references to 'going to sea' for these purposes see PARA 457 note 15.
7 As to the meaning of 'United Kingdom' see PARA 16 note 3.
8 Merchant Shipping Act 1995 s 51(1)(b); and PARA 506. As to enforcing the detention of a ship see PARA 1190.
9 Ie in contravention of the Merchant Shipping Act 1995 s 51(1) (see the text and notes 1–8): see s 51(2).
10 Merchant Shipping Act 1995 s 51(2). As to the time limit for summary offences see PARA 1049; as to offences by officers of bodies corporate see PARA 1051; as to jurisdiction in relation to offences see PARA 1052; as to jurisdiction over ships lying off the coast see PARA 1053; as to jurisdiction in the case of offences on board ship see PARA 1054; as to offences committed by

British seamen see PARA 1055; and as to proof etc of exemption see PARA 1061. As to the powers of magistrates' courts to issue fines on summary conviction see SENTENCING vol 92 (2015) PARA 176.

1083. Unqualified persons going to sea as qualified officers or seamen. If a person goes to sea[1] as a qualified[2] officer or seaman[3] of any description without being such a qualified officer or seaman[4], he is liable, on conviction on indictment, to a fine or, on summary conviction, to a fine[5].

1　As to the meaning of references to 'going to sea' for these purposes see PARA 457 note 15.
2　For these purposes, 'qualified' means qualified for the purposes of the Merchant Shipping Act 1995 s 47 (see PARA 503): s 52(2).
3　As to the meaning of 'seaman' see PARA 457 note 5.
4　As to the powers of inspectors appointed under the Merchant Shipping Act 1995 s 256(6) (see PARA 46) to serve improvement notices or prohibition notices where s 52 and the provisions of any instrument of a legislative character having effect thereunder are being contravened, or where activities to which s 52 applies are carried on so as to involve serious personal injury or serious pollution, see PARA 51 et seq.
5　Merchant Shipping Act 1995 s 52(1). As to the time limit for summary offences see PARA 1049; as to offences by officers of bodies corporate see PARA 1051; as to jurisdiction in relation to offences see PARA 1052; as to jurisdiction over ships lying off the coast see PARA 1053; as to jurisdiction in the case of offences on board ship see PARA 1054; as to offences committed by British seamen see PARA 1055; and as to proof etc of exemption see PARA 1061. As to the powers of magistrates' courts to issue fines on summary conviction see SENTENCING vol 92 (2015) PARA 176.

1084. Improperly obtaining special certificates of competence. If a person makes a statement which he knows to be false or recklessly makes a statement which is false in a material particular for the purpose of obtaining for himself or another person a document which may be issued under the provisions governing special certificates of competence[1], he is liable, on summary conviction, to a fine[2].

1　Ie issued under the Merchant Shipping Act 1995 s 54: see s 54(2). The text refers to the power of the Secretary of State to issue and record documents certifying the attainment of any standard of competence relating to ships or their operation, notwithstanding that the standard is not among those prescribed or otherwise specified under s 47(1)(b) (see PARA 503): see s 54(1). As to the meaning of 'ship' see PARA 229. As to the Secretary of State see PARA 36.
　　As to the powers of inspectors appointed under s 256(6) (see PARA 46) to serve improvement notices or prohibition notices where s 54 and the provisions of any instrument of a legislative character having effect thereunder are being contravened, or where activities to which s 54 applies are carried on so as to involve serious personal injury or serious pollution, see PARA 51 et seq.
2　Merchant Shipping Act 1995 s 54(2). As to the time limit for summary offences see PARA 1049; as to offences by officers of bodies corporate see PARA 1051; as to jurisdiction in relation to offences see PARA 1052; as to jurisdiction over ships lying off the coast see PARA 1053; as to jurisdiction in the case of offences on board ship see PARA 1054; as to offences committed by British seamen see PARA 1055; and as to proof etc of exemption see PARA 1061. As to the powers of magistrates' courts to issue fines on summary conviction see SENTENCING vol 92 (2015) PARA 176.

1085. Failure to deliver cancelled or suspended seaman's certificate. If a person fails to deliver a cancelled or suspended certificate as required following an inquiry into fitness or conduct[1], he is liable, on summary conviction, to a fine[2].

If a person fails to deliver a certificate as required[3] after it has been cancelled or suspended on account of the holder's unfitness to discharge his duties, or negligence in the discharge of his duties, so that he caused or contributed to an accident[4], he is liable, on summary conviction, to a fine[5].

1　Ie as required under the Merchant Shipping Act 1995 s 61 (see PARA 524), s 62 (see PARA 508) or s 63 (see PARA 530): see s 66.
2　Merchant Shipping Act 1995 s 66. As to the time limit for summary offences see PARA 1049; as to offences by officers of bodies corporate see PARA 1051; as to jurisdiction in relation to offences see PARA 1052; as to jurisdiction over ships lying off the coast see PARA 1053; as to jurisdiction in the case of offences on board ship see PARA 1054; as to offences committed by British seamen

see PARA 1055; and as to proof etc of exemption see PARA 1061. As to the powers of magistrates' courts to issue fines on summary conviction see SENTENCING vol 92 (2015) PARA 176.
3 Ie as required under the Merchant Shipping Act 1995 s 268(5) (see PARA 830): see s 268(6).
4 As to the meaning of 'accident' see PARA 830 note 1.
5 Merchant Shipping Act 1995 s 268(6).

1086. Improper destruction, mutilation or alteration of official log book.

If a person intentionally destroys or mutilates or renders illegible any entry in an official log book[1], he is liable, on summary conviction, to a fine[2].

1 As to the requirement to keep official log books see PARA 551 et seq.
2 Merchant Shipping Act 1995 s 77(6). As to the time limit for summary offences see PARA 1049; as to offences by officers of bodies corporate see PARA 1051; as to jurisdiction in relation to offences see PARA 1052; as to jurisdiction over ships lying off the coast see PARA 1053; as to jurisdiction in the case of offences on board ship see PARA 1054; as to offences committed by British seamen see PARA 1055; and as to proof etc of exemption see PARA 1061. As to the powers of magistrates' courts to issue fines on summary conviction see SENTENCING vol 92 (2015) PARA 176.

1087. Offences relating to copies of lists of crew.

A copy of every list of crew[1], including all changes in it notified to the owner, must be maintained by the owner of the ship[2] at an address in the United Kingdom[3]; and a person who fails to do so commits an offence and is liable, on summary conviction, to a fine[4].

The master must, as soon as practicable and in any event within three days of any change being made in the list of crew, notify the change to the owner of the ship[5]; and a master who fails to do so commits an offence and is liable, on summary conviction, to a fine[6].

When any person having in his possession the copy of a list of crew[7] has reason to believe that the ship to which it relates has been lost or abandoned, he must immediately deliver the copy of the list to a superintendent[8]. A person who fails to do so commits an offence and is liable, on summary conviction, to a fine[9].

A person having in his possession a copy of a list of crew[10] must produce it on demand to a superintendent[11]; and a person who fails to so comply commits an offence and is liable, on summary conviction, to a fine[12].

1 As to the requirement to keep a list of the crew see PARA 553.
2 As to the meaning of 'owner of the ship' for these purposes see PARA 555 note 2; and as to the meaning of 'ship' for these purposes see PARA 458 note 2.
3 See the Merchant Shipping (Crew Agreements, Lists of Crew and Discharge of Seamen) Regulations 1991, SI 1991/2144, reg15(1); and PARA 555. As to the meaning of 'United Kingdom' see PARA 16 note 3.
4 Merchant Shipping (Crew Agreements, Lists of Crew and Discharge of Seamen) Regulations 1991, SI 1991/2144, reg 22(2), (3). As to the powers of magistrates' courts to issue fines on summary conviction see SENTENCING vol 92 (2015) PARA 176.
5 See the Merchant Shipping (Crew Agreements, Lists of Crew and Discharge of Seamen) Regulations 1991, SI 1991/2144, reg15(2); and PARA 555.
6 Merchant Shipping (Crew Agreements, Lists of Crew and Discharge of Seamen) Regulations 1991, SI 1991/2144, reg22(1), (3).
7 Ie which is required to be maintained under the Merchant Shipping (Crew Agreements, Lists of Crew and Discharge of Seamen) Regulations 1991, SI 1991/2144, reg 15 (see the text and notes 1–3, 5): see reg 16.
8 See the Merchant Shipping (Crew Agreements, Lists of Crew and Discharge of Seamen) Regulations 1991, SI 1991/2144, reg16; and PARA 555.
9 Merchant Shipping (Crew Agreements, Lists of Crew and Discharge of Seamen) Regulations 1991, SI 1991/2144, reg22(2), (3).
10 Ie which is required to be maintained under the Merchant Shipping (Crew Agreements, Lists of Crew and Discharge of Seamen) Regulations 1991, SI 1991/2144, reg 15 (see the text and notes 1–3, 5): see reg 17; and PARA 555.
11 See the Merchant Shipping (Crew Agreements, Lists of Crew and Discharge of Seamen) Regulations 1991, SI 1991/2144, reg17; and PARA 555.
12 Merchant Shipping (Crew Agreements, Lists of Crew and Discharge of Seamen) Regulations 1991, SI 1991/2144, reg22(2), (3).

1088. Failure to deliver list of crew on demand to Registrar General. The owner[1] must, on demand, deliver to the Registrar General of Shipping and Seamen[2] within 28 days of such demand being made a list of the crew on board the ship at a date specified by the Registrar General of Shipping and Seamen[3]. A person who fails to comply with an obligation so imposed on him[4] commits an offence[5] and is liable, on summary conviction, to a fine[6].

1 As to the meaning of 'owner of the ship' for these purposes see PARA 555 note 2; and as to the meaning of 'ship' see PARA 458 note 2.
2 As to the Registrar General of Shipping and Seamen see PARA 62.
3 See the Merchant Shipping (Crew Agreements, Lists of Crew and Discharge of Seamen) Regulations 1991, SI 1991/2144, reg18; and PARA 556.
4 Ie by or under the Merchant Shipping (Crew Agreements, Lists of Crew and Discharge of Seamen) Regulations 1991, SI 1991/2144, reg 18 (see the text and notes 1–3): see reg 22(2).
5 Merchant Shipping (Crew Agreements, Lists of Crew and Discharge of Seamen) Regulations 1991, SI 1991/2144, reg22(2).
6 Merchant Shipping (Crew Agreements, Lists of Crew and Discharge of Seamen) Regulations 1991, SI 1991/2144, reg22(3).

1089. Failure to deliver expired or changed list of crew. The master must, within three days after a list of crew[1] has ceased to be in force (or, if it is not practicable within that period, as soon as practicable thereafter) deliver the list to a superintendent or proper officer for the place where the ship is when the list of crew ceases to be in force[2]. A master who fails to comply with an obligation so imposed on him[3] commits an offence[4] and is liable, on summary conviction, to a fine[5].

The shipowner must deliver a list of crew to the Registrar-General of Shipping and Seamen[6] within seven days of the expiry of each period of six months after the date on which it is made, for so long as it remains in force[7]. A person who fails to comply with an obligation so imposed on him commits an offence[8] and is liable, on summary conviction, to a fine[9].

1 Ie other than one relating to a ship of less than 25 gross tons or to a ship belonging to a general lighthouse authority: see the Merchant Shipping (Crew Agreements, Lists of Crew and Discharge of Seamen) Regulations 1991, SI 1991/2144, reg 20(1); and PARA 557. As to the meaning of 'ship' for these purposes see PARA 458 note 2; and as to the meaning of references to the gross tonnage of a ship see PARA 458 note 5. As to general lighthouse authorities see PARA 1017.
2 See the Merchant Shipping (Crew Agreements, Lists of Crew and Discharge of Seamen) Regulations 1991, SI 1991/2144, reg20(1); and PARA 557.
3 Ie by or under the Merchant Shipping (Crew Agreements, Lists of Crew and Discharge of Seamen) Regulations 1991, SI 1991/2144, reg 20(1) (see the text and notes 1–2): see reg 22(1).
4 Merchant Shipping (Crew Agreements, Lists of Crew and Discharge of Seamen) Regulations 1991, SI 1991/2144, reg22(1).
5 Merchant Shipping (Crew Agreements, Lists of Crew and Discharge of Seamen) Regulations 1991, SI 1991/2144, reg 22(3). As to the powers of magistrates' courts to issue fines on summary conviction see SENTENCING vol 92 (2015) PARA 176.
6 As to the Registrar General of Shipping and Seamen see PARA 62.
7 See the Merchant Shipping (Crew Agreements, Lists of Crew and Discharge of Seamen) Regulations 1991, SI 1991/2144, reg20(2); and PARA 557.
8 Merchant Shipping (Crew Agreements, Lists of Crew and Discharge of Seamen) Regulations 1991, SI 1991/2144, reg22(2).
9 Merchant Shipping (Crew Agreements, Lists of Crew and Discharge of Seamen) Regulations 1991, SI 1991/2144, reg22(3).

1090. Failure to produce lists of crew on demand to officials. A master must, on demand, produce to the Registrar General of Shipping and Seamen[1], a proper officer, a surveyor of ships in the course of any inspection of the ship[2] or an officer of revenue and customs[3] the list of crew required to be maintained in the ship[4].

A master who fails to comply with an obligation so imposed on him[5] commits an offence[6] and is liable on summary conviction to a fine[7].

1 As to the Registrar General of Shipping and Seamen see PARA 62.
2 Ie in pursuance of his functions under the Merchant Shipping Act 1995 s 256 (see PARA 46) or under s 258 (see PARA 48): see the Merchant Shipping (Crew Agreements, Lists of Crew and Discharge of Seamen) Regulations 1991, SI 1991/2144, reg 21; and PARA 558.
3 As to the appointment of officers of Revenue and Customs see INCOME TAXATION vol 58 (2014) PARA 33.
4 See the Merchant Shipping (Crew Agreements, Lists of Crew and Discharge of Seamen) Regulations 1991, SI 1991/2144, reg21; and PARA 558. As to the requirement to keep a list of the crew see PARA 553.
5 Ie by or under the Merchant Shipping (Crew Agreements, Lists of Crew and Discharge of Seamen) Regulations 1991, SI 1991/2144, reg 21 (see the text and notes 1–4): see reg 22(1).
6 Merchant Shipping (Crew Agreements, Lists of Crew and Discharge of Seamen) Regulations 1991, SI 1991/2144, reg22(1).
7 Merchant Shipping (Crew Agreements, Lists of Crew and Discharge of Seamen) Regulations 1991, SI 1991/2144, reg 22(3). As to the powers of magistrates' courts to issue fines on summary conviction see SENTENCING vol 92 (2015) PARA 176.

1091. Failure to produce British seaman's card on demand to officials. A person who fails to produce his British seaman's card[1] to the Registrar General of Shipping and Seamen[2] or a superintendent, a proper officer, his employer or the master of his ship, on demand (or within such period as the person requiring its production may allow)[3] commits an offence[4] and is liable, on summary conviction, to a fine[5]; but it is a defence for a person so charged to prove that he took all reasonable precautions to avoid the commission of the offence[6].

1 As to British seamen's cards see PARA 559 et seq.
2 As to the Registrar General of Shipping and Seamen see PARA 62.
3 Ie in pursuance of a requirement made under the Merchant Shipping (Seamen's Documents) Regulations 1987, SI 1987/408, reg 10 (see PARA 562): see reg 10(2).
4 Merchant Shipping (Seamen's Documents) Regulations 1987, SI 1987/408, reg 10(2).
5 Merchant Shipping (Seamen's Documents) Regulations 1987, SI 1987/408, reg 30(1). As to the powers of magistrates' courts to issue fines on summary conviction see SENTENCING vol 92 (2015) PARA 176.
6 Merchant Shipping (Seamen's Documents) Regulations 1987, SI 1987/408, reg 30(2).

1092. Failure to surrender British seaman's card when required. A person who fails to comply with the requirement[1] to surrender a British seaman's card[2] to the Registrar General of Shipping and Seamen[3] or to a superintendent[4] commits an offence[5] and is liable, on summary conviction, to a fine[6]; but it is a defence for a person so charged to prove that he took all reasonable precautions to avoid the commission of the offence[7].

1 Ie the requirements of the Merchant Shipping (Seamen's Documents) Regulations 1987, SI 1987/408, reg 11 (see PARA 563): see reg 11(2).
2 As to British seamen's cards see PARA 559 et seq.
3 As to the Registrar General of Shipping and Seamen see PARA 62.
4 Ie either forthwith, upon his ceasing to be a British seaman or upon the card being defaced, and on demand, after he has ceased to have the right of abode: see the Merchant Shipping (Seamen's Documents) Regulations 1987, SI 1987/408, reg 11(1); and PARA 563.
5 Merchant Shipping (Seamen's Documents) Regulations 1987, SI 1987/408, reg 11(2).
6 Merchant Shipping (Seamen's Documents) Regulations 1987, SI 1987/408, reg 30(1). As to the powers of magistrates' courts to issue fines on summary conviction see SENTENCING vol 92 (2015) PARA 176.
7 Merchant Shipping (Seamen's Documents) Regulations 1987, SI 1987/408, reg 30(2).

1093. Failure to deliver British seaman's card. Where any person comes into possession of a British seaman's card[1] of which he is not the holder[2] and that person fails to comply with the requirement to deliver that card to the Registrar General of Shipping and Seamen[3] or to a superintendent[4], that person commits an offence[5] and is liable, on summary conviction, to a fine[6]; but it is a defence for a person so charged to prove that he took all reasonable precautions to avoid the commission of the offence[7].

1 As to British seamen's cards see PARA 559 et seq.
2 As to the meaning of 'holder' see PARA 559 note 14.
3 As to the Registrar General of Shipping and Seamen see PARA 62.
4 Ie where any person fails to comply with the Merchant Shipping (Seamen's Documents) Regulations 1987, SI 1987/408, reg 12 (see PARA 564): see reg 12(2).
5 Merchant Shipping (Seamen's Documents) Regulations 1987, SI 1987/408, reg 12(2).
6 Merchant Shipping (Seamen's Documents) Regulations 1987, SI 1987/408, reg 30(1). As to the powers of magistrates' courts to issue fines on summary conviction see SENTENCING vol 92 (2015) PARA 176.
7 Merchant Shipping (Seamen's Documents) Regulations 1987, SI 1987/408, reg 30(2).

1094. Employment when disentitled to discharge book. As from a day to be appointed[1] a person who, in the United Kingdom[2] or elsewhere[3]:

(1)	obtains employment as a seaman[4] on board a United Kingdom ship[5] and does so when he is disentitled to a discharge book[6]; or

(2)	employs as such a seaman a person who he knows or has reason to suspect is so disentitled[7],

is liable, on conviction on indictment, to imprisonment for a term not exceeding two years or a fine (or to both) or, on summary conviction, to a fine[8].

1 The Merchant Shipping Act 1995 s 80(4) (see the text and notes 2–8) does not have effect until the Secretary of State by order appoints a day for s 80(4) to come into force: see Sch 14 para 5(1), (2); and PARA 15. At the date at which this volume states the law, no such day had been appointed. As to the Secretary of State see PARA 36.
2 As to the meaning of 'United Kingdom' see PARA 16 note 3.
3 Merchant Shipping Act 1995 s 80(4) (not yet in force). See note 1.
4 As to the meaning of 'seaman' see PARA 457 note 5.
5 As to the meaning of 'United Kingdom ship' see PARA 230. As to the meaning of 'ship' under the Merchant Shipping Act 1995 see PARA 229.
6 Merchant Shipping Act 1995 s 80(4)(a) (not yet in force). The text refers to disentitlement by virtue of regulations made under s 80(2)(a) (not yet in force) (see PARA 565): see s 80(4)(a) (not yet in force). See note 1.
7 Merchant Shipping Act 1995 s 80(4)(b) (not yet in force). See note 1.
8 Merchant Shipping Act 1995 s 80(4) (not yet in force). See note 1. As to the time limit for summary offences see PARA 1049; as to offences by officers of bodies corporate see PARA 1051; as to jurisdiction in relation to offences see PARA 1052; as to jurisdiction over ships lying off the coast see PARA 1053; as to jurisdiction in the case of offences on board ship see PARA 1054; as to offences committed by British seamen see PARA 1055; and as to proof etc of exemption see PARA 1061. As to the powers of magistrates' courts to issue fines on summary conviction see SENTENCING vol 92 (2015) PARA 176.

1095. Failure to make proper application for discharge book when required. Any person required[1] to apply for a discharge book[2] who fails to make an application for a discharge book in accordance with the statutory provisions[3] commits an offence[4] and is liable, on summary conviction, to a fine[5]; but it is a defence for a person so charged to prove that he took all reasonable precautions to avoid the commission of the offence[6].

1 Ie under the provisions of the Merchant Shipping (Seamen's Documents) Regulations 1987, SI 1987/408, reg 15(1) (see PARA 565): see reg 17(2).
2 As to applications for a discharge book see PARA 565.
3 Ie in accordance with the Merchant Shipping (Seamen's Documents) Regulations 1987, SI 1987/408 (see PARA 565): see reg 17(2).
4 Merchant Shipping (Seamen's Documents) Regulations 1987, SI 1987/408, reg 17(2).
5 Merchant Shipping (Seamen's Documents) Regulations 1987, SI 1987/408, reg 30(1). As to the powers of magistrates' courts to issue fines on summary conviction see SENTENCING vol 92 (2015) PARA 176.
6 Merchant Shipping (Seamen's Documents) Regulations 1987, SI 1987/408, reg 30(2).

1096. Failure to produce discharge book on demand. The holder[1] of a discharge book[2] who fails to produce it on demand when required to do so[3] commits an offence[4] and is liable, on summary conviction, to a fine[5]; but it is a defence for a person so charged to prove that he took all reasonable precautions to avoid the commission of the offence[6].

1 As to the meaning of 'holder' see PARA 559 note 14.
2 As to discharge books see PARA 565 et seq.
3 Ie in accordance with the Merchant Shipping (Seamen's Documents) Regulations 1987, SI 1987/408, reg 22 (see PARA 567): see reg 22(2).
4 Merchant Shipping (Seamen's Documents) Regulations 1987, SI 1987/408, reg 22(2).
5 Merchant Shipping (Seamen's Documents) Regulations 1987, SI 1987/408, reg 30(1). As to the powers of magistrates' courts to issue fines on summary conviction see SENTENCING vol 92 (2015) PARA 176.
6 Merchant Shipping (Seamen's Documents) Regulations 1987, SI 1987/408, reg 30(2).

1097. Failure to deliver discharge book. Where any person, having possession of a discharge book[1], is required[2] to deliver it to a superintendent or proper officer or to the Registrar General of Shipping and Seamen[3], and that person fails to comply with the requirement so to deliver that discharge book[4], that person commits an offence[5] and is liable, on summary conviction, to a fine[6]; but it is a defence for a person so charged to prove that he took all reasonable precautions to avoid the commission of the offence[7].

1 As to discharge books see PARA 565 et seq.
2 Ie because he becomes aware that the holder has died, has been discharged from any ship, or has been left behind in any country: see the Merchant Shipping (Seamen's Documents) Regulations 1987, SI 1987/408, reg 23(1); and PARA 568. As to the meaning of 'holder' see PARA 559 note 14.
3 As to the Registrar General of Shipping and Seamen see PARA 62.
4 Ie where any person fails to comply with requirements of the Merchant Shipping (Seamen's Documents) Regulations 1987, SI 1987/408, reg 23 (see PARA 568): see reg 23(2).
5 Merchant Shipping (Seamen's Documents) Regulations 1987, SI 1987/408, reg 23(2).
6 Merchant Shipping (Seamen's Documents) Regulations 1987, SI 1987/408, reg 30(1). As to the powers of magistrates' courts to issue fines on summary conviction see SENTENCING vol 92 (2015) PARA 176.
7 Merchant Shipping (Seamen's Documents) Regulations 1987, SI 1987/408, reg 30(2).

1098. Failure to notify errors in seamen's documents. Any person who fails to comply with the requirement[1] to inform the Registrar General of Shipping and Seamen[2] or a superintendent of any entry in a seaman's document[3] which appears to the holder[4] thereof not to be correct, commits an offence[5] and is liable, on summary conviction, to a fine[6]; but it is a defence for a person so charged to prove that he took all reasonable precautions to avoid the commission of the offence[7].

1 Ie any person who fails to comply with requirements of the Merchant Shipping (Seamen's Documents) Regulations 1987, SI 1987/408, reg 26 (see PARA 570): see reg 26(1); and PARA 570.
2 As to the Registrar General of Shipping and Seamen see PARA 62.
3 As to the meaning of 'seaman's document' for these purposes see PARA 570 note 2.
4 As to the meaning of 'holder' for these purposes see PARA 570 note 1.
5 Merchant Shipping (Seamen's Documents) Regulations 1987, SI 1987/408, reg 26(2).
6 Merchant Shipping (Seamen's Documents) Regulations 1987, SI 1987/408, reg 30(1). As to the powers of magistrates' courts to issue fines on summary conviction see SENTENCING vol 92 (2015) PARA 176.
7 Merchant Shipping (Seamen's Documents) Regulations 1987, SI 1987/408, reg 30(2).

1099. Failure to surrender seamen's documents when required. Any person who fails to comply with the requirement[1] to surrender a seaman's document[2] commits an offence[3] and is liable, on summary conviction, to a fine[4]; but it is a defence for a person so charged to prove that he took all reasonable precautions to avoid the commission of the offence[5].

1 Ie the requirements of the Merchant Shipping (Seamen's Documents) Regulations 1987, SI 1987/408, reg 27 (see PARA 571): see reg 27(3); and PARA 571.

2　As to the meaning of 'seaman's document' for these purposes see PARA 570 note 2.
3　Merchant Shipping (Seamen's Documents) Regulations 1987, SI 1987/408, reg 27(3).
4　Merchant Shipping (Seamen's Documents) Regulations 1987, SI 1987/408, reg 30(1). As to the powers of magistrates' courts to issue fines on summary conviction see SENTENCING vol 92 (2015) PARA 176.
5　Merchant Shipping (Seamen's Documents) Regulations 1987, SI 1987/408, reg 30(2).

1100. Making of improper marks or entries in seamen's documents. Any person, other than a person duly authorised and duly acting[1], who makes any mark or entry upon, or erases, cancels or alters any mark or entry made upon or otherwise defaces or destroys a seaman's document[2] commits an offence[3] and is liable, on summary conviction, to a fine[4]; but it is a defence for a person so charged to prove that he took all reasonable precautions to avoid the commission of the offence[5].

1　Ie a person authorised by the Merchant Shipping (Seamen's Documents) Regulations 1987, SI 1987/408, reg 5 (issue of British seamen's cards) (see PARA 560), reg 8 (validity of previously issued British seamen's cards) (see PARA 561), reg 18 (issue of discharge books) (see PARA 566), reg 20 (entries in discharge books) (see PARA 566) or reg 21 (correction of entries in discharge books) (see PARA 566), as the case may be, acting in accordance with the provisions of those regulations: see reg 28(1); and PARA 572.
2　Ie any person who contravenes the provisions of the Merchant Shipping (Seamen's Documents) Regulations 1987, SI 1987/408, reg 28 (see PARA 572): see reg 28(2); and PARA 572. As to the meaning of 'seaman's document' for these purposes see PARA 570 note 2.
3　Merchant Shipping (Seamen's Documents) Regulations 1987, SI 1987/408, reg 28(2).
4　Merchant Shipping (Seamen's Documents) Regulations 1987, SI 1987/408, reg 30(1). As to the powers of magistrates' courts to issue fines on summary conviction see SENTENCING vol 92 (2015) PARA 176.
5　Merchant Shipping (Seamen's Documents) Regulations 1987, SI 1987/408, reg 30(2).

1101. Master's failure to deliver documents where he ceases to be master during voyage. If a person ceases to be the master[1] of a United Kingdom ship[2] during a voyage of the ship, he must deliver to his successor the documents relating to the ship or its crew which are in his custody[3]; and if, without reasonable excuse, the master of such a ship fails to comply with this requirement[4], he is liable, on summary conviction, to a fine[5].

1　As to the meaning of 'master' see PARA 444 note 1.
2　As to the meaning of 'United Kingdom ship' see PARA 230. As to the meaning of 'ship' under the Merchant Shipping Act 1995 see PARA 229; and as to the meaning of 'United Kingdom' see PARA 16 note 3.
3　See the Merchant Shipping Act 1995 s 81(1); and PARA 447.
4　Ie if he fails to comply with the Merchant Shipping Act 1995 s 81(1) (see PARA 447): see s 81(2).
5　Merchant Shipping Act 1995 s 81(2). As to the time limit for summary offences see PARA 1049; as to offences by officers of bodies corporate see PARA 1051; as to jurisdiction in relation to offences see PARA 1052; as to jurisdiction over ships lying off the coast see PARA 1053; as to jurisdiction in the case of offences on board ship see PARA 1054; as to offences committed by British seamen see PARA 1055; and as to proof etc of exemption see PARA 1061. As to the powers of magistrates' courts to issue fines on summary conviction see SENTENCING vol 92 (2015) PARA 176.

B.　CONDUCT-RELATED OFFENCES COMMITTED BY CREW

(A)　General Conduct

1102. Conduct endangering ships, structures or individuals. If a master or seaman[1], while on board his ship or in its immediate vicinity[2]:

(1)　does any act which causes or is likely to cause:
　　(a)　the loss or destruction of or serious damage to his ship or its machinery, navigational equipment or safety equipment[3];
　　(b)　the loss or destruction of or serious damage to any other ship or any structure[4]; or

(c)   the death of or serious injury to any person[5]; or

(2)   omits to do anything required:

(a)   to preserve his ship or its machinery, navigational equipment or safety equipment from being lost, destroyed or seriously damaged[6];

(b)   to preserve any person on board his ship from death or serious injury[7]; or

(c)   to prevent his ship from causing the loss or destruction of or serious damage to any other ship or any structure or the death of or serious injury to any person not on board his ship[8],

and either of the specified conditions is satisfied with respect to that act or omission, he is guilty of an offence[9]. Those conditions are that the act or omission was deliberate or amounted to a breach or neglect of duty[10] or that the master or seaman in question was under the influence of drink or a drug at the time of the act or omission[11].

If a master or seaman[12]:

(i)   discharges any of his duties, or performs any other function in relation to the operation of his ship or its machinery or equipment, in such a manner as to cause, or to be likely to cause, any such loss, destruction, death or injury as is mentioned in head (1) above[13]; or

(ii)   fails to discharge any of his duties, or to perform any such function, properly to such an extent as to cause, or to be likely to cause, any of those things[14],

he is guilty of an offence[15].

A person guilty of any such offence[16] is liable, on conviction on indictment, to imprisonment for a term not exceeding two years or a fine (or to both) or, on summary conviction, to a fine[17]. In proceedings for such an offence[18], it is a defence to prove[19]:

(A)   in the case of an offence under head (1) or (2) above, where the act or omission alleged against the accused constituted a breach or neglect of duty, that the accused took all reasonable steps to discharge that duty[20];

(B)   in the case of an offence under head (1) or (2) above, that at the time of the act or omission alleged against the accused he was under the influence of a drug taken by him for medical purposes and either that he took it on medical advice or that he had no reason to believe that the drug might have the influence it had[21];

(C)   in the case of an offence under head (i) or (ii) above, that the accused took all reasonable precautions and exercised all due diligence to avoid committing the offence[22]; or

(D)   in the case of an offence under any of heads (1), (2), (i) or (ii) above, that he could have avoided committing the offence only by disobeying a lawful command, or that in all the circumstances the loss, destruction, damage, death or injury in question or, as the case may be, the likelihood of its being caused, either could not reasonably have been foreseen by the accused or could not reasonably have been avoided by him[23].

No proceedings for any such offence[24] may be instituted against any such person except by or with the consent of the Secretary of State[25] or the Director of Public Prosecutions[26].

1   The Merchant Shipping Act 1995 s 58 applies:

(1)   to the master of, or any seaman employed in, a United Kingdom ship (s 58(1)(a)); and

(2)   to the master of, or any seaman employed in, a ship which is registered under the law
       of any country outside the United Kingdom and is in a port in the United Kingdom or
       within United Kingdom waters while proceeding to or from any such port (s 58(1)(b)).
   In the application of s 58 to any person falling within s 58(1)(b) (see head (2) above), s 58(2)
(see the text and notes 2–9) and s 58(4) (see the text and notes 12–15) have effect as if s 58(2)(a)(i)
(see head (1)(a) in the text) and s 58(2)(b)(i) (see head (2)(a) in the text) were omitted: s 58(7). As
to the meanings of 'master' and 'seaman' see PARAS 444 note 1, 457 note 5. As to the meaning of
'port' see PARA 46 note 12. As to the meaning of 'United Kingdom waters' see PARA 48 note 10;
and as to the meaning of 'United Kingdom' see PARA 16 note 3. As to the meaning of 'United
Kingdom ship' see PARA 230; and as to the meaning of 'ship' see PARA 229. As to whether a jet-ski
is a 'ship' within the meaning of the Merchant Shipping Act 1995 s 58 see *R v Goodwin* [2005]
EWCA Crim 3184, [2006] 2 All ER (Comm) 281, [2006] 1 Lloyd's Rep 432; and see *R v Goodwin*
[2005] All ER (D) 286 (Dec), CA (regarding a reference to the House of Lords).
2   Merchant Shipping Act 1995 s 58(2).
3   Merchant Shipping Act 1995 s 58(2)(a)(i).
4   Merchant Shipping Act 1995 s 58(2)(a)(ii). For these purposes, 'structure' means any fixed or
    movable structure, of whatever description, other than a ship: s 58(8).
5   Merchant Shipping Act 1995 s 58(2)(a)(iii).
6   Merchant Shipping Act 1995 s 58(2)(b)(i).
7   Merchant Shipping Act 1995 s 58(2)(b)(ii).
8   Merchant Shipping Act 1995 s 58(2)(b)(iii).
9   Merchant Shipping Act 1995 s 58(2). This provision is subject to s 58(6) (see the text and notes
    18–23) and s 58(7) (see notes 1, 24–26): see s 58(2).
10 Merchant Shipping Act 1995 s 58(3)(a). For these purposes, 'breach or neglect of duty', except in
    relation to a master, includes any disobedience to a lawful command; and 'duty', in relation to a
    master or seaman, means any duty falling to be discharged by him in his capacity as such; and, in
    relation to a master, includes his duty with respect to the good management of his ship and his duty
    with respect to the safety of operation of his ship, its machinery and equipment: s 58(8).
11 Merchant Shipping Act 1995 s 58(3)(b). As to general provisions involving shipping and alcohol-
    or drugs-related offences see the Railways and Transport Safety Act 2003 Pt 4 (ss 78–91); and
    PARA 1105 et seq.
12 Ie being a person to whom the Merchant Shipping Act 1995 s 58 applies (see note 1): see s 58(4).
13 Merchant Shipping Act 1995 s 58(4)(a).
14 Merchant Shipping Act 1995 s 58(4)(b).
15 Merchant Shipping Act 1995 s 58(4). This provision is subject to s 58(6) (see the text and notes
    18–23) and s 58(7) (see notes 1, 24–26): see s 58(4).
16 Ie an offence under the Merchant Shipping Act 1995 s 58: see s 58(5).
17 Merchant Shipping Act 1995 s 58(5). As to the time limit for summary offences see PARA 1049;
    as to offences by officers of bodies corporate see PARA 1051; as to jurisdiction in relation to
    offences see PARA 1052; as to jurisdiction over ships lying off the coast see PARA 1053; as to
    jurisdiction in the case of offences on board ship see PARA 1054; as to offences committed by
    British seamen see PARA 1055; and as to proof etc of exemption see PARA 1061. As to the powers
    of magistrates' courts to issue fines on summary conviction see SENTENCING vol 92 (2015)
    PARA 176.
18 Ie an offence under the Merchant Shipping Act 1995 s 58: see s 58(6).
19 Merchant Shipping Act 1995 s 58(6).
20 Merchant Shipping Act 1995 s 58(6)(a).
21 Merchant Shipping Act 1995 s 58(6)(b).
22 Merchant Shipping Act 1995 s 58(6)(c).
23 Merchant Shipping Act 1995 s 58(6)(d).
24 Ie an offence under the Merchant Shipping Act 1995 s 58: see s 58(7).
25 As to the Secretary of State see PARA 36.
26 Merchant Shipping Act 1995 s 58(7). As to the Director of Public Prosecutions see CRIMINAL
    PROCEDURE vol 27 (2015) PARAS 25, 30 et seq.

1103.   Concerted disobedience and neglect of duty. If a seaman[1] employed in
a United Kingdom ship[2] combines with other seamen employed in that ship[3]:
   (1)   to disobey lawful commands which are required to be obeyed at a time
          while the ship is at sea[4];
   (2)   to neglect any duty which is required to be disregarded at such a time[5];
          or

(3)   to impede, at such a time, the progress of a voyage or the navigation of the ship[6],

he is liable, on conviction on indictment, to imprisonment for a term not exceeding two years or a fine (or to both) or, on summary conviction, to a fine[7].

However, neither head (1) nor head (2) above applies to fishing vessels[8] and persons serving in them[9].

1   As to the meaning of 'seaman' see PARA 457 note 5.
2   As to the meaning of 'United Kingdom ship' see PARA 230. As to the meaning of 'ship' see PARA 229; and as to the meaning of 'United Kingdom' see PARA 16 note 3.
3   Merchant Shipping Act 1995 s 59(1).
4   Merchant Shipping Act 1995 s 59(1)(a). For these purposes, a ship is treated as being at sea at any time when it is not securely moored in a safe berth: s 59(2).
5   Merchant Shipping Act 1995 s 59(1)(b).
6   Merchant Shipping Act 1995 s 59(1)(c).
7   Merchant Shipping Act 1995 s 59(1). As to the time limit for summary offences see PARA 1049; as to offences by officers of bodies corporate see PARA 1051; as to jurisdiction in relation to offences see PARA 1052; as to jurisdiction over ships lying off the coast see PARA 1053; as to jurisdiction in the case of offences on board ship see PARA 1054; as to offences committed by British seamen see PARA 1055; and as to proof etc of exemption see PARA 1061. As to the powers of magistrates' courts to issue fines on summary conviction see SENTENCING vol 92 (2015) PARA 176.
8   As to the meaning of 'fishing vessel' see PARA 230 note 9.
9   Merchant Shipping Act 1995 s 119(1).

1104. Offences related to wearing of the merchant navy uniform. Until a day to be appointed[1], if any person, not being entitled to wear the merchant navy uniform, wears that uniform or any part thereof, or any dress having the appearance or bearing any of the distinctive marks of that uniform, he is guilty of an offence[2]. A person guilty of such an offence is liable on summary conviction[3]:
(1)   except in a case falling within head (2) below, to a fine[4];
(2)   if he wears it in such a manner or under such circumstances as to be likely to bring contempt on the uniform, to a fine or to imprisonment for a term not exceeding one month[5].

If any person entitled to wear the merchant navy uniform when aboard a ship[6] in port[7] or on shore appears dressed partly in uniform and partly not in uniform under such circumstances as to be likely to bring contempt on the uniform, or, being entitled to wear the uniform appropriate to a particular rank or position, wears the uniform appropriate to some higher rank or position, he is liable, on summary conviction, to a fine[8].

1   The Merchant Shipping Act 1995 s 57 ceases to have effect on such day as the Secretary of State by order appoints: see Sch 14 para 6(1), (2). At the date at which this volume states the law, no such day had been appointed. As to the Secretary of State see PARA 36.
2   Merchant Shipping Act 1995 s 57(1). However, s 57(1) does not prevent any person from wearing any uniform or dress in the course or for the purposes of a stage play or representation, or a music-hall or circus performance if the uniform is not worn in such a manner or under such circumstances as to bring it into contempt: s 57(3). See note 1.
3   Merchant Shipping Act 1995 s 57(2). See note 1.
4   Merchant Shipping Act 1995 s 57(2)(a). See note 1. As to the time limit for summary offences see PARA 1049; as to offences by officers of bodies corporate see PARA 1051; as to jurisdiction in relation to offences see PARA 1052; as to jurisdiction over ships lying off the coast see PARA 1053; as to jurisdiction in the case of offences on board ship see PARA 1054; as to offences committed by British seamen see PARA 1055; and as to proof etc of exemption see PARA 1061. As to the powers of magistrates' courts to issue fines on summary conviction see SENTENCING vol 92 (2015) PARA 176.
    As from a day to be appointed under the Criminal Justice Act 2003 s 336(3), the Merchant Shipping Act 1995 s 57(2)(b) is repealed by the Criminal Justice Act 2003 s 332, Sch 37 Pt 9 and the reference in head (1) in the text to 'except in a case falling within head (2) [in the text]' is omitted: see the Merchant Shipping Act 1995 s 57(2)(a) (prospectively amended by the Criminal

Justice Act 2003 Sch 37 Pt 9), the Merchant Shipping Act 1995 s 57(2)(b) (prospectively repealed by the Criminal Justice Act 2003 Sch 37 Pt 9). However, at the date at which this volume states the law, no such day had been appointed.
5   Merchant Shipping Act 1995 s 57(2)(b). See notes 1, 4.
6   As to the meaning of 'ship' see PARA 229.
7   As to the meaning of 'port' see PARA 46 note 12.
8   Merchant Shipping Act 1995 s 57(4). See note 1.

(B)   Alcohol and Drugs Offences

1105.   Alcohol and drugs offences applying to professional shipping staff.
Any of the following persons[1]:
(1)   a professional master[2] of a ship[3];
(2)   a professional pilot of a ship[4]; and
(3)   a professional seaman in a ship while on duty[5],
commits an offence if his ability to carry out his duties is impaired because of drink or drugs[6]; and such a person[7] commits an offence if the proportion of alcohol in his breath, blood or urine exceeds the prescribed limit[8]. Where a person is charged with such an offence[9] in respect of the effect of a drug on his ability to carry out duties on a fishing vessel[10], it is a defence for him to show[11]:
(a)   that he took the drug for a medicinal purpose on, and in accordance with, medical advice[12]; or
(b)   that he took the drug for a medicinal purpose and had no reason to believe that it would impair his ability to carry out his duties[13].

A professional seaman[14] in a ship, at a time when:
(i)   he is not on duty[15]; but
(ii)   in the event of an emergency, he would or might be required by the nature or terms of his engagement or employment to take action to protect the safety of passengers[16],
commits an offence if his ability to take the action mentioned in head (ii) above is impaired because of drink or drugs[17]; and such a person[18] also commits an offence if the proportion of alcohol in his breath, blood or urine exceeds the prescribed limit[19]. Where a person is charged with such an offence[20] in respect of the effect of a drug on his ability to take action it is a defence for him to show[21]:
(A)   that he took the drug for a medicinal purpose on, and in accordance with, medical advice[22]; or
(B)   that he took the drug for a medicinal purpose and had no reason to believe that it would impair his ability to take the action[23].

A person guilty of any such offence[24] is liable, on conviction on indictment, to imprisonment for a term not exceeding two years, to a fine (or to both) or, on summary conviction, to a fine[25].

1   Ie persons to whom the Railways and Transport Safety Act 2003 s 78 applies (see heads (1) to (3) in the text): see s 78(1).
2   For the purposes of the Railways and Transport Safety Act 2003 s 78, a master, pilot or seaman is professional if (and only if) he acts as master, pilot or seaman in the course of a business or employment: s 78(4). As to the meanings of 'master' and 'seaman' see PARAS 444 note 1, 457 note 5; definitions applied by s 89(2)(d), (f). In Pt 4 (ss 78–91), 'pilot' has the meaning given by the Pilotage Act 1987 s 31(1) (see PARA 563): Railways and Transport Safety Act 2003 s 89(3).
3   Railways and Transport Safety Act 2003 s 78(1)(a). In Pt 4, 'ship' includes every description of vessel used in navigation; and a reference to the navigation of a vessel includes a reference to the control or direction, or participation in the control or direction, of the course of a vessel: s 89(1). Pt 4 has effect in relation to United Kingdom ships, foreign ships in United Kingdom waters, and un-registered ships in United Kingdom waters: ss 91(1), 121(d). As to the meaning of 'foreign', in relation to a ship, see PARA 18 note 2; definition applied by s 89(2)(b). As to the meaning of 'registered' for these purposes see PARA 254 note 2; definition applied by s 89(2)(e). As to the meaning of 'United Kingdom ship' see PARA 230; definition applied by s 89(2)(g). As to the

meaning of 'United Kingdom waters' see PARA 48 note 10; definition applied by s 89(2)(h). As to the meaning of 'United Kingdom' see PARA 16 note 3.

Pt 4 applies also to a person in the service of the Crown (s 90(2)) except any of Her Majesty's forces (within the meaning of the Armed Forces Act 2006: see ARMED FORCES) while acting in the course of his duties: Railways and Transport Safety Act 2003 s 90(1) (amended by the Armed Forces Act 2006 Sch 16 para 198). The Railways and Transport Safety Act 2003 Pt 4 does not apply to a member of a visiting force, within the meaning which that expression has in the Visiting Forces Act 1952 s 3 by virtue of s 12(1) (see ARMED FORCES), while acting in the course of his duties, or to a member of a civilian component of a visiting force, within that meaning, while acting in the course of his duties: Railways and Transport Safety Act 2003 s 90(4).

4 Railways and Transport Safety Act 2003 s 78(1)(b).

5 Railways and Transport Safety Act 2003 s 78(1)(c).

6 Railways and Transport Safety Act 2003 s 78(2). In Pt 4, 'drug' includes any intoxicant other than alcohol: s 89(5).

7 Ie a person to whom the Railways and Transport Safety Act 2003 s 78 applies (see heads (1) to (3) in the text): see s 78(3).

8 Railways and Transport Safety Act 2003 s 78(3). The prescribed limit of alcohol for the purposes of Pt 4 is:

    (1)   in the case of breath, 25 microgrammes of alcohol in 100 millilitres (s 81(1)(a) (s 81(1)(a)–(c) amended by SI 2015/1730) (made under the Railways and Transport Safety Act 2003 ss 81(2), 88(6)));

    (2)   in the case of blood, 50 milligrammes of alcohol in 100 millilitres (s 81(1)(b) (as so amended)); and

    (3)   in the case of urine, 67 milligrammes of alcohol in 100 millilitres (s 81(1)(c) (as so amended)).

9 Ie under the Railways and Transport Safety Act 2003 s 78: see s 78(5).

10 As to the meaning of 'fishing vessel' see PARA 230 note 9; definition applied by the Railways and Transport Safety Act 2003 s 89(2)(a).

11 Railways and Transport Safety Act 2003 s 78(5).

12 Railways and Transport Safety Act 2003 s 78(5)(a).

13 Railways and Transport Safety Act 2003 s 78(5)(b).

14 Ie to whom the Railways and Transport Safety Act 2003 s 79 applies (see heads (i), (ii) in the text): see s 79(1). For the purposes of s 79, a seaman is professional if (and only if) he acts as seaman in the course of a business or employment: s 79(4).

15 Railways and Transport Safety Act 2003 s 79(1)(a).

16 Railways and Transport Safety Act 2003 s 79(1)(b).

17 Railways and Transport Safety Act 2003 s 79(2).

18 Ie a person to whom the Railways and Transport Safety Act 2003 s 79 applies (see heads (i), (ii) in the text): see s 79(3).

19 Railways and Transport Safety Act 2003 s 79(3).

20 Ie an offence under the Railways and Transport Safety Act 2003 s 79: see s 79(5).

21 Railways and Transport Safety Act 2003 s 79(5).

22 Railways and Transport Safety Act 2003 s 79(5)(a).

23 Railways and Transport Safety Act 2003 s 79(5)(b).

24 Ie an offence under the Railways and Transport Safety Act 2003 Pt 4: see s 82.

25 Railways and Transport Safety Act 2003 s 82. As to the powers of magistrates' courts to issue fines on summary conviction see SENTENCING vol 92 (2015) PARA 176. In relation to an offence under Pt 4, the following provisions of the Road Traffic Act 1988 and of the Road Traffic Offenders Act 1988 (as the case may be) have effect, subject to specified modifications and to any other necessary modifications (see the Railways and Transport Safety Act 2003 s 83(1), (1A) (s 83(1) amended, s 83(1A) added, by the Deregulation Act 2015 Sch 11 para 14)), namely:

    (1)   the Road Traffic Act 1988 s 6 (power to administer preliminary tests) (see ROAD TRAFFIC vol 90 (2011) PARAS 736, 742);

    (2)   s 6A (preliminary breath test) (see ROAD TRAFFIC vol 90 (2011) PARA 737);

    (3)   s 6B (preliminary impairment test) (see ROAD TRAFFIC vol 90 (2011) PARA 738);

    (4)   s 6C (preliminary drug test) (see ROAD TRAFFIC vol 90 (2011) PARA 739);

    (5)   s 6D (arrest) (see ROAD TRAFFIC vol 90 (2011) PARA 740);

    (6)   s 6E (power of entry) (see ROAD TRAFFIC vol 90 (2011) PARA 741);

    (7)   s 7 (provision of specimens for analysis) (see ROAD TRAFFIC vol 90 (2011) PARAS 743, 745);

    (8)   s 7A (specimens of blood taken from persons incapable of consenting) (see ROAD TRAFFIC vol 90 (2011) PARA 744);

    (9)   s 8 (choice of specimens of breath) (see ROAD TRAFFIC vol 90 (2011) PARA 743);

    (10)   s 9 (protection for hospital patients) (see ROAD TRAFFIC vol 90 (2011) PARA 746);

(11)   s 10 (detention of persons affected by alcohol or a drug) (see ROAD TRAFFIC vol 90 (2011) PARA 747);

(12)   s 11 (interpretation of ss 4–10);

(13)   the Road Traffic Offenders Act 1988 s 15 (use of specimens) (see ROAD TRAFFIC vol 90 (2011) PARA 748);

(14)   s 16 (documentary evidence) (see ROAD TRAFFIC vol 90 (2011) PARA 748).

The Secretary of State may by regulations amend the Railways and Transport Safety Act 2003 s 83(1), Table: see s 83(2), (3).

1106. Alcohol and drugs offences applying to non-professional shipping staff.

As from a day to be appointed[1] a person[2] who:

(1)   is on board a ship[3] which is under way[4];

(2)   is exercising, or purporting or attempting to exercise, a function in connection with the navigation of the ship[5]; and

(3)   is not a person to whom the provisions relating to professional staff[6] applies[7],

commits an offence if his ability to exercise the function mentioned in head (2) above is impaired because of drink or drugs[8]; and such a person[9] also commits an offence if the proportion of alcohol in his breath, blood or urine exceeds the prescribed limit[10].

A person guilty of such an offence[11] is liable, on conviction on indictment, to imprisonment for a term not exceeding two years, to a fine (or to both) or, on summary conviction, to a fine[12].

1   The Railways and Transport Safety Act 2003 s 80 comes into force as from a day appointed under s 120(1). At the date at which this volume states the law, such a day had been appointed in relation to s 80(4), (5) (see note 10) only (ie 30 March 2004: see the Railways and Transport Safety Act 2003 (Commencement No 2) Order 2004, SI 2004/827, art 3(c)); but no such day had been appointed in relation to the Railways and Transport Safety Act 2003 s 80(1)–(3) (see the text and notes 2–10).

2   Ie a person to whom the Railways and Transport Safety Act 2003 s 80 applies (see heads (1) to (3) in the text): see s 80(1).

3   As to the meaning of 'ship' for these purposes, and as to the ships and persons to which the Railways and Transport Safety Act 2003 Pt 4 applies generally, see PARA 1105 note 3.

4   Railways and Transport Safety Act 2003 s 80(1)(a). See note 1.

5   Railways and Transport Safety Act 2003 s 80(1)(b). See note 1. As to the meaning of references to the navigation of a vessel see PARA 1105 note 3.

6   Ie the Railways and Transport Safety Act 2003 s 78 or s 79 (see PARA 1105): see s 80(1)(c).

7   Railways and Transport Safety Act 2003 s 80(1)(c). See note 1.

8   Railways and Transport Safety Act 2003 s 80(2). See note 1. As to the meaning of 'drug' for these purposes see PARA 1105 note 6.

9   Ie a person to whom the Railways and Transport Safety Act 2003 s 80 applies (see heads (1) to (3) in the text): see s 80(3).

10 Railways and Transport Safety Act 2003 s 80(3). See note 1. As to the prescribed limit of alcohol for the purposes of Pt 4 see PARA 1105 note 8.

    The Secretary of State may make regulations providing for s 80(3) not to apply in specified circumstances (s 80(4)); and regulations under s 80(4) may make provision by reference, in particular, to the power of a motor, to the size of a ship, or to location (s 80(5)). See note 1. As to the Secretary of State see PARA 36.

11 Ie an offence under the Railways and Transport Safety Act 2003 Pt 4: see s 82.

12 Railways and Transport Safety Act 2003 s 82. As to the powers of magistrates' courts to issue fines on summary conviction see SENTENCING vol 92 (2015) PARA 176. In relation to an offence under Pt 4, specified provisions of the Road Traffic Act 1988 and of the Road Traffic Offenders Act 1988 have effect, subject to specified modifications and to any other necessary modifications: see the Railways and Transport Safety Act 2003 s 83(1), Table; and PARA 1105 note 25.

1107. Powers of police and marine officials where alcohol and drugs offences are suspected.

A marine official[1] may detain a ship[2] if he reasonably suspects that a person who is or may be on board the ship either is committing an offence related to alcohol or drugs[3], or has committed such an offence[4]. This power of detention is conditional upon the marine official making a request (either before the detention or as soon as possible after its commencement) for a constable in uniform to attend, and it lapses when a constable in uniform has decided whether or not to exercise one of the powers available to him in such circumstances[5] and has informed the marine official of his decision[6].

A constable may arrest a person without a warrant if the constable reasonably suspects that the person (because his ability to exercise a function required of him is impaired due to drink or drugs) either is committing an offence[7], or has committed such an offence and is still under the influence of drink or drugs[8].

A constable in uniform may board a ship if he reasonably suspects that he may wish to exercise one of the powers available to him in relation to suspected alcohol or drugs offences[9] or exercise his right of arrest without a warrant in such circumstances[10] in respect of a person who is or may be on the ship[11]. A constable in uniform also may enter any place if he reasonably suspects that he may wish to exercise such a power[12] in respect of a person who is or may be in that place[13].

1 For these purposes, 'marine official' means:
    (1)   a harbour master (or an assistant of a harbour master) appointed by a harbour authority (Railways and Transport Safety Act 2003 s 84(3)(a));
    (2)   a person listed in the Merchant Shipping Act 1995 s 284(1)(a)–(d) (detention of ship) (see PARA 1190) (Railways and Transport Safety Act 2003 s 84(3)(b)); and
    (3)   a person falling within a class designated by order of the Secretary of State (s 84(3)(c)).
    In construing the Merchant Shipping Act 1995 s 284(1)(b) (detention by person authorised by Secretary of State) for the purpose of head (2) above, the reference to authorisation to exercise powers under s 284 is to be taken as a reference both to general authorisation to exercise powers under s 284, and to general or particular authorisation to exercise powers under the Railways and Transport Safety Act 2003 s 84: s 84(4). The power under head (3) above for the Secretary of State to designate a class of person includes a power for him to designate either himself, or one or more persons employed in his Department (s 88(2)) and an order under head (3) above is subject to annulment in pursuance of a resolution of either House of Parliament (s 88(5)). Orders under Pt 4 (ss 78–91) may make transitional, supplemental and incidental provision, make provision generally or for specified purposes only, and make different provision for different purposes (s 88(1)); and such orders must be made by statutory instrument (s 88(3)). As to the Secretary of State see PARA 36. As to the meaning of 'harbour authority' see PARA 69 note 4; definition applied by s 89(2)(c).
2 As to the meaning of 'ship' for these purposes, and as to the ships and persons to which the Railways and Transport Safety Act 2003 Pt 4 applies generally, see PARA 1105 note 3. However, s 84 does not have effect in relation to a ship which is being used for a purpose of Her Majesty's forces, or forms part of the Royal Fleet Auxiliary Service: s 90(3).
3 Ie under the Railways and Transport Safety Act 2003 s 78 or s 79 (see PARA 1105) or s 80 (see PARA 1106): see s 84(1). As to the meaning of 'drug' for these purposes see PARA 1105 note 6.
4 Railways and Transport Safety Act 2003 s 84(1).
5 Ie by virtue of the Railways and Transport Safety Act 2003 s 83 (see PARA 1105 note 25): see s 84(2).
6 Railways and Transport Safety Act 2003 s 84(2).
7 Ie an offence under the Railways and Transport Safety Act 2003 s 78(2) or s 79(2) (see PARA 1105) or s 80(2) (see PARA 1106): see s 85(1).
8 Railways and Transport Safety Act 2003 s 85(1). However, a person may not be arrested under s 85(1) while he is at a hospital as a patient: s 85(2). For this purpose, 'hospital' means an institution which provides medical or surgical treatment for in-patients or out-patients, and is not on a ship: s 85(3).
    An arrest under s 85 is treated as arrest for an offence for the purposes of the Police and Criminal Evidence Act 1984 Pt IV (ss 34–51) (detention) (see POLICE AND INVESTIGATORY POWERS vol 84A (2013) PARA 503 et seq): Railways and Transport Safety Act 2003 s 85(4).
9 Ie by virtue of the Railways and Transport Safety Act 2003 s 83 (see PARA 1105 note 25): see s 86(1).
10 Ie by virtue of the Railways and Transport Safety Act 2003 s 85 (see the text and notes 7–8): see s 86(1).
11 Railways and Transport Safety Act 2003 s 86(1). For the purposes of boarding a ship under s 86 a constable may use reasonable force and he may be accompanied by one or more persons: s 86(3).
12 Ie by virtue of the Railways and Transport Safety Act 2003 s 83 (see PARA 1105 note 25) or by virtue of s 85 (see the text and notes 7–8): see s 86(2).

13 Railways and Transport Safety Act 2003 s 86(2). For the purposes of entering a place under s 86 a constable may use reasonable force and he may be accompanied by one or more persons: s 86(3).

1108. Unauthorised liquor on board a United Kingdom fishing vessel. As from a day to be appointed[1] a person who, in the United Kingdom[2] or elsewhere[3]:

(1)   takes any unauthorised liquor[4] on board a United Kingdom fishing vessel[5];

(2)   has any unauthorised liquor in his possession on board such a vessel[6];

(3)   permits another person to take on board such a vessel, or to have in his possession on board such a vessel, any unauthorised liquor[7]; or

(4)   intentionally obstructs another person in the exercise of powers conferred on the other person[8] in relation to suspected offences under head (1) or head (2) above[9],

is guilty of an offence[10]. A person guilty of such an offence is liable, on conviction on indictment, to imprisonment for a term not exceeding two years or a fine (or to both) or, on summary conviction, to a fine[11].

It is a defence in proceedings for an offence under head (1) or head (2) above to prove:

(a)   that the accused believed that the liquor in question was not unauthorised liquor in relation to the vessel in question and that he had reasonable grounds for the belief[12]; or

(b)   that the accused did not know that the liquor in question was in his possession[13].

It is a defence in proceedings for an offence under head (3) above to prove that the accused believed that the liquor in question was not unauthorised liquor in relation to the vessel in question and that he had reasonable grounds for the belief[14].

If an authorised person[15] has reason to believe that an offence under head (1) or head (2) above has been committed by another person in connection with a fishing vessel, the authorised person[16]:

(i)   may go on board the vessel and search it and any property on it and may, if the other person is on board the vessel, search him there in an authorised manner[17]; and

(ii)   may take possession of any liquor which he finds on the vessel and has reason to believe is unauthorised liquor and may detain the liquor for the period needed to ensure that the liquor is available as evidence in proceedings for the offence[18].

1 The Merchant Shipping Act 1995 s 118 does not have effect until the Secretary of State by order appoints a day for s 118 to come into force: see Sch 14 para 5(1), (2); and PARA 15. At the date at which this volume states the law, no such order had been made. As to the Secretary of State see PARA 36.

2 As to the meaning of 'United Kingdom' see PARA 16 note 3.

3 Merchant Shipping Act 1995 s 118(1). See note 1.

4 For these purposes, 'unauthorised liquor' means, in relation to a vessel, liquor as to which permission to take it on board the vessel has been given neither by the master nor the owner of the vessel nor by a person authorised by the owner of the vessel to give such permission; and 'liquor' means spirits, wine, beer, cider, perry and any other fermented, distilled or spirituous liquor: Merchant Shipping Act 1995 s 118(6). Any reference in s 118(6) to the owner of a vessel is to be construed as excluding any member of the crew of the vessel and, subject thereto, as a reference to the person or all the persons who, in the certificate of registration of the vessel, is or are stated to be the registered owner or owners of the vessel: s 118(7). As to the meaning of 'master' see PARA 444 note 1. As to rights of ownership under the Merchant Shipping Act 1995 see PARA 237 et seq; and as to certificates of registration under the Merchant Shipping Act 1995 see PARA 298 et seq.

5 Merchant Shipping Act 1995 s 118(1)(a). See note 1. As to the meaning of 'fishing vessel' see PARA 230 note 9; and as to the meaning of 'United Kingdom fishing vessel' see PARA 230.

6 Merchant Shipping Act 1995 s 118(1)(b). See note 1.
7 Merchant Shipping Act 1995 s 118(1)(c). See note 1.
8 Ie by the Merchant Shipping Act 1995 s 118(5) (see the text and notes 15–18): see s 118(1)(d).
9 Merchant Shipping Act 1995 s 118(1)(d). See note 1.
10 Merchant Shipping Act 1995 s 118(1). See note 1.
11 Merchant Shipping Act 1995 s 118(2). See note 1. As to the time limit for summary offences see PARA 1049; as to offences by officers of bodies corporate see PARA 1051; as to jurisdiction in relation to offences see PARA 1052; as to jurisdiction over ships lying off the coast see PARA 1053; as to jurisdiction in the case of offences on board ship see PARA 1054; as to offences committed by British seamen see PARA 1055; and as to proof etc of exemption see PARA 1061. As to the powers of magistrates' courts to issue fines on summary conviction see SENTENCING vol 92 (2015) PARA 176.
12 Merchant Shipping Act 1995 s 118(3)(a). See note 1.
13 Merchant Shipping Act 1995 s 118(3)(b). See note 1.
14 Merchant Shipping Act 1995 s 118(4). See note 1.
15 For these purposes, 'authorised person', in relation to a vessel, means a superintendent, a proper officer, a person appointed in pursuance of the Merchant Shipping Act 1995 s 258(1)(c) (see PARA 48), the master of the vessel in question, the owner of the vessel in question, or any person instructed by the master or owner to prevent the commission of offences under s 118(1) (see the text and notes 1–10) in relation to the vessel: s 118(6). As to the meaning of 'superintendent' see PARA 61 note 1; and as to the appointment of superintendents see PARA 61. As to the meaning of 'proper officer' see PARA 48 note 4.
16 Merchant Shipping Act 1995 s 118(5). See note 1.
17 Merchant Shipping Act 1995 s 118(5)(a). For these purposes, 'authorised manner' means a manner authorised by regulations made by the Secretary of State: Merchant Shipping Act 1995 s 118(6). See note 1. At the date at which this volume states the law, no such regulations had been made and none have effect as if so made. As to the power of the Secretary of State to make subordinate legislation under the Merchant Shipping Act 1995 generally, and as to the Secretary of State's power to appoint committees for the purpose of advising him when considering the making or alteration of any regulations etc, see PARA 39.
18 Merchant Shipping Act 1995 s 118(5)(b). See note 1.

(iii) Safety Offences

A. OFFENCES UNDER GENERAL SAFETY PROVISIONS

1109. Contravention of safety requirements applicable to commercially operated vessels. Contravention of any of the provisions governing the safety requirements that are applicable to commercially operated vessels[1] is an offence by the owner and master of the vessel which renders both of them liable, on conviction on indictment, to imprisonment for a term not exceeding two years and a fine, or, on summary conviction, to a fine[2].

It is a good defence to such a charge to prove that the person charged took all reasonable steps to avoid the commission of the offence[3].

1 Ie contravention of any of the Merchant Shipping (Vessels in Commercial Use for Sport or Pleasure) Regulations 1998, SI 1998/2771 (see PARA 612 et seq): see reg 8(1). As to the vessels generally to which the Merchant Shipping (Vessels in Commercial Use for Sport or Pleasure) Regulations 1998, SI 1998/2771, apply see PARA 612.
2 Merchant Shipping (Vessels in Commercial Use for Sport or Pleasure) Regulations 1998, SI 1998/2771, reg 8(1). As to the powers of magistrates' courts to issue fines on summary conviction see SENTENCING vol 92 (2015) PARA 176.
3 Merchant Shipping (Vessels in Commercial Use for Sport or Pleasure) Regulations 1998, SI 1998/2771, reg 8(2).

1110. Contravention of safety requirements applicable to high speed craft. Any contravention of the Merchant Shipping (High Speed Craft) Regulations 2004[1] in respect of a high speed craft[2] is an offence by both the owner[3] and the master of that craft punishable, on summary conviction, by a fine[4] and, on conviction on indictment, by imprisonment for a term not exceeding two years or a fine (or both)[5].

Any contravention of the restrictions on the behaviour of persons on passenger craft[6] is an offence punishable, on summary conviction, by a fine[7].

It is a defence for a person charged under the Merchant Shipping (High Speed Craft) Regulations 2004[8] to show that he took all reasonable steps to ensure compliance with the Regulations[9].

1 Ie the Merchant Shipping (High Speed Craft) Regulations 2004, SI 2004/302 (see PARA 614 et seq), other than reg 9 (as to which see PARA 624): see reg 10(1).
2 As to the meaning of 'high speed craft' see PARA 617 note 2.
3 As to references in the Merchant Shipping (High Speed Craft) Regulations 2004, SI 2004/302, to the owner see PARA 617 note 21.
4 As to the powers of magistrates' courts to issue fines on summary conviction see SENTENCING vol 92 (2015) PARA 176.
5 Merchant Shipping (High Speed Craft) Regulations 2004, SI 2004/302, reg 10(1).
6 Ie the Merchant Shipping (High Speed Craft) Regulations 2004, SI 2004/302, reg 9 (as to which see PARA 624): see reg 10(2).
7 Merchant Shipping (High Speed Craft) Regulations 2004, SI 2004/302, reg 10(2).
8 Ie under the Merchant Shipping (High Speed Craft) Regulations 2004, SI 2004/302, other than reg 9(1) or (2): see reg 10(3) (amended by SI 2012/2636).
9 Merchant Shipping (High Speed Craft) Regulations 2004, SI 2004/302, reg 10(3).

1111. Contravention of fishing vessel construction rules. If:

(1) the fishing vessel construction rules[1] are contravened[2] with respect to any vessel[3]; or

(2) a vessel is exempted[4] from any requirement subject to a condition and the condition is not complied with[5],

the owner or master[6] of the vessel is liable, on conviction on indictment, to a fine or, on summary conviction, to a fine[7].

1 As to the meaning of 'fishing vessel construction rules' see PARA 607. As to the meaning of 'fishing vessel' see PARA 230 note 9.
2 As to the meaning of 'contravention' see PARA 51 note 3.
3 Merchant Shipping Act 1995 s 121(5)(a).
4 Ie under the Merchant Shipping Act 1995 s 121(2) (see PARA 607): see s 121(5)(b).
5 Merchant Shipping Act 1995 s 121(5)(b).
6 As to the meaning of 'master' see PARA 444 note 1.
7 Merchant Shipping Act 1995 s 121(5). As to the time limit for summary offences see PARA 1049; as to offences by officers of bodies corporate see PARA 1051; as to jurisdiction in relation to offences see PARA 1052; as to jurisdiction over ships lying off the coast see PARA 1053; as to jurisdiction in the case of offences on board ship see PARA 1054; as to offences committed by British seamen see PARA 1055; and as to proof etc of exemption see PARA 1061. As to the powers of magistrates' courts to issue fines on summary conviction see SENTENCING vol 92 (2015) PARA 176.

1112. Contravention of provisions governing control of fishing vessel certificates.

The Secretary of State[1] may require a fishing vessel certificate[2] which has expired or been cancelled, to be delivered up as he directs[3]. If the owner or skipper of the fishing vessel[4] fails without reasonable excuse to comply with such a requirement, he is liable, on summary conviction, to a fine[5].

The owner or skipper of a fishing vessel to whom a fishing vessel certificate is issued must forthwith, on the receipt of the certificate by him (or his agent), cause a copy of it to be put up in some conspicuous place on board the vessel, so as to be legible to all persons on board, and to be kept so put up and legible while the certificate remains in force and the vessel is in use[6]. If the owner or skipper of a fishing vessel fails without reasonable excuse to comply with that requirement, he is liable, on summary conviction, to a fine[7].

If any person intentionally makes, or assists in making, or procures to be made, a false or fraudulent fishing vessel certificate, he is liable, on conviction on indictment, to imprisonment for a term not exceeding two years or a fine (or to both) or, on summary conviction, to a fine or imprisonment for a term not exceeding six months (or to both)[8].

A fishing vessel certificate is admissible in evidence[9].

1   As to the Secretary of State see PARA 36.
2   As to the meaning of 'fishing vessel certificate' see PARA 609.
3   See the Merchant Shipping Act 1995 s 124(1): and PARA 609. As to the powers of inspectors appointed under s 256(6) (see PARA 46) to serve improvement notices or prohibition notices where s 124 and the provisions of any instrument of a legislative character having effect thereunder are being contravened, or where activities to which s 124 applies are carried on so as to involve serious personal injury or serious pollution, see PARA 51 et seq.
4   As to the meaning of 'fishing vessel' see PARA 230 note 9.
5   Merchant Shipping Act 1995 s 124(2). As to the time limit for summary offences see PARA 1049; as to offences by officers of bodies corporate see PARA 1051; as to jurisdiction in relation to offences see PARA 1052; as to jurisdiction over ships lying off the coast see PARA 1053; as to jurisdiction in the case of offences on board ship see PARA 1054; as to offences committed by British seamen see PARA 1055; and as to proof etc of exemption see PARA 1061. As to the powers of magistrates' courts to issue fines on summary conviction see SENTENCING vol 92 (2015) PARA 176.
6   See the Merchant Shipping Act 1995 s 124(3): and PARA 609.
7   Merchant Shipping Act 1995 s 124(4).
8   Merchant Shipping Act 1995 s 124(5).
9   Merchant Shipping Act 1995 s 124(7). As to admissibility of documents in evidence see PARA 1059.

1113. Contravention of prohibition on going to sea without appropriate certificate.

No fishing vessel[1] required to be surveyed under the fishing vessel survey rules[2] must go to sea unless there are in force fishing vessel certificates[3] showing that the vessel complies with such of the requirements of the fishing vessel construction and equipment provisions[4] as are applicable to the vessel[5]. If a fishing vessel goes to sea in contravention[6] of this prohibition, the owner or skipper of the vessel is liable, on conviction on indictment, to a fine or, on summary conviction, to a fine[7].

1   As to the meaning of 'fishing vessel' see PARA 230 note 9.
2   As to the meaning of 'fishing vessel survey rules' see PARA 608.
3   As to the meaning of 'fishing vessel certificate' see PARA 609.
4   As to the meaning of 'fishing vessel construction and equipment provisions' see PARA 608 note 2.
5   See the Merchant Shipping Act 1995 s 125(1); and PARA 610.
6   As to the meaning of 'contravention' see PARA 51 note 3. As to the powers of inspectors appointed under the Merchant Shipping Act 1995 s 256(6) (see PARA 46) to serve improvement notices or prohibition notices where s 125 and the provisions of any instrument of a legislative character having effect thereunder are being contravened, or where activities to which s 125 applies are carried on so as to involve serious personal injury or serious pollution, see PARA 51 et seq.
7   Merchant Shipping Act 1995 s 125(2). As to the time limit for summary offences see PARA 1049; as to offences by officers of bodies corporate see PARA 1051; as to jurisdiction in relation to offences see PARA 1052; as to jurisdiction over ships lying off the coast see PARA 1053; as to jurisdiction in the case of offences on board ship see PARA 1054; as to offences committed by British seamen see PARA 1055; and as to proof etc of exemption see PARA 1061. As to the powers of magistrates' courts to issue fines on summary conviction see SENTENCING vol 92 (2015) PARA 176.

1114. Failure to give notice of alterations when a fishing vessel certificate is in force.

If the notice that is required[1] when an alteration[2] is made to a fishing vessel[3] in respect of which a fishing vessel certificate[4] is in force, is not given as so required, the owner or skipper of the fishing vessel is liable, on summary conviction, to a fine[5].

1   Ie by the Merchant Shipping Act 1995 s 126(1) (see PARA 611): see s 126(2).
2   As to the meaning of 'alteration' for these purposes see PARA 611 note 4.
3   As to the meaning of 'fishing vessel' see PARA 230 note 9.
4   As to the meaning of 'fishing vessel certificate' see PARA 609.

5   Merchant Shipping Act 1995 s 126(2). As to the time limit for summary offences see PARA 1049; as to offences by officers of bodies corporate see PARA 1051; as to jurisdiction in relation to offences see PARA 1052; as to jurisdiction over ships lying off the coast see PARA 1053; as to jurisdiction in the case of offences on board ship see PARA 1054; as to offences committed by British seamen see PARA 1055; and as to proof etc of exemption see PARA 1061. As to the powers of magistrates' courts to issue fines on summary conviction see SENTENCING vol 92 (2015) PARA 176.

As to the powers of inspectors appointed under the Merchant Shipping Act 1995 s 256(6) (see PARA 46) to serve improvement notices or prohibition notices where s 126 and the provisions of any instrument of a legislative character having effect thereunder are being contravened, or where activities to which s 126 applies are carried on so as to involve serious personal injury or serious pollution, see PARA 51 et seq.

1115. Contravention of duties imposed by health and safety provisions. Contravention of the requirements imposed by the general health and safety at work provisions which apply to activities of workers on merchant shipping and fishing vessels[1], or by the related provisions governing manual handling operations[2] and safety signs and signals[3], is an offence[4].

1   Ie the Merchant Shipping and Fishing Vessels (Health and Safety at Work) Regulations 1997, SI 1997/2962: see PARA 626.
2   Ie the Merchant Shipping and Fishing Vessels (Manual Handling Operations) Regulations 1998, SI 1998/2857: see PARA 626.
3   Ie the Merchant Shipping and Fishing Vessels (Safety Signs and Signals) Regulations 2001, SI 2001/3444: see PARA 626.
4   See the Merchant Shipping and Fishing Vessels (Health and Safety at Work) Regulations 1997, SI 1997/2962, reg 24; the Merchant Shipping and Fishing Vessels (Manual Handling Operations) Regulations 1998, SI 1998/2857, reg 7; and the Merchant Shipping and Fishing Vessels (Safety Signs and Signals) Regulations 2001, SI 2001/3444, reg 7. As to related powers of inspection and detention see PARA 626. Provisions of the Merchant Shipping Act 1995 dealing with the enforcement of detention (ie s 284(1)–(5), (8) (see PARA 1190)) and with arbitration and compensation (ie ss 96, 97 (see PARAS 1142, 1143)) are applied with modifications: see PARA 626.

1116. Contravention of duties imposed by working time provisions. Any contravention of the requirements imposed by the provisions which govern the organisation of working time for seafarers[1], for sea-fishermen[2], or for workers on the inland waterways[3], is an offence[4].

1   Ie the Merchant Shipping (Hours of Work) Regulations 2002, SI 2002/2125: see PARA 511.
2   Ie the Fishing Vessels (Working Time: Sea-fishermen) Regulations 2004, SI 2004/1713: see PARAS 515, 516.
3   Ie the Merchant Shipping (Working Time: Inland Waterways) Regulations 2003, SI 2003/3049: see PARA 520 et seq.
4   See the Merchant Shipping (Hours of Work) Regulations 2002, SI 2002/2125, reg 20 (cited in PARA 511); the Fishing Vessels (Working Time: Sea-fishermen) Regulations 2004, SI 2004/1713, reg 18 (cited in PARA 515); and the Merchant Shipping (Working Time: Inland Waterways) Regulations 2003, SI 2003/3049, reg 17 (cited in PARA 520).

1117. Contravention of requirement to carry on board prescribed medical stores. Any contravention of the provisions which require every United Kingdom ship and government ship (other than a ship employed in inland navigation, a pleasure vessel used for non-commercial purposes and not manned by a professional crew, or a tug[1] operating in harbour areas)[2] to carry on board prescribed medical stores[3], is an offence[4].

1   As to the meaning of 'tug' see PARA 498 note 1.
2   As to the meaning of 'harbour area' see PARA 498 note 2.
3   Ie as required by the Merchant Shipping and Fishing Vessels (Medical Stores) Regulations 1995, SI 1995/1802: see PARA 498.
4   See the Merchant Shipping and Fishing Vessels (Medical Stores) Regulations 1995, SI 1995/1802, regs 12, 13; and PARA 498.

1118. Failure to comply with the International Safety Management ('ISM') Code for large vessels. Any contravention of the provisions which require compliance with the ISM Code[1] is an offence[2]. It is a defence for a person charged with such an offence to show that he took all reasonable precautions and exercised all due diligence to avoid the commission of the offence[3].

1 Ie any contravention of the provisions of the Merchant Shipping (International Safety Management (ISM) Code) Regulations 2014, SI 2014/1512 (see PARA 627).

2 See the Merchant Shipping (International Safety Management (ISM) Code) Regulations 2014, SI 2014/1512, reg 15.

3 See the Merchant Shipping (International Safety Management (ISM) Code) Regulations 2014, SI 2014/1512, reg 16.

1119. Failure to comply with the safety management code for domestic passenger ships. Any contravention of the provisions which require compliance with the Safety Management Code for Domestic Passenger Ships[1] is an offence[2]. It is a defence for a person charged with such an offence to show that he took all reasonable precautions and exercised all due diligence to avoid the commission of the offence[3].

1 Ie any contravention of the provisions of the Merchant Shipping (Domestic Passenger Ships) (Safety Management Code) Regulations 2001, SI 2001/3209: see PARA 627.

2 See the Merchant Shipping (Domestic Passenger Ships) (Safety Management Code) Regulations 2001, SI 2001/3209, reg 10.

3 See the Merchant Shipping (Domestic Passenger Ships) (Safety Management Code) Regulations 2001, SI 2001/3209, reg 10.

1120. Contravention of general safety of navigation requirements. Provision is made for offences and penalties to apply where various requirements relating to the safety of navigation[1] are contravened[2], and for the detention of a ship in any such case of non-compliance[3].

1 See the Merchant Shipping (Safety of Navigation) Regulations 2002, SI 2002/1473; and PARA 634. These regulations give effect to those provisions of the International Convention for the Safety of Life at Sea 1974 (London, 1 November 1974 to 1 July 1975; TS 46 (1980); Cmnd 7874), with Protocol (London, 1 June 1978 to 1 March 1979; TS 40 (1981); Cmnd 8277) (see PARA 7) which identify certain navigation safety services which should be provided by contracting governments: see PARA 634.

2 See the Merchant Shipping (Safety of Navigation) Regulations 2002, SI 2002/1473, reg 10, Sch 4 (amended by SI 2011/2978).

3 Ie in any case where a ship does not comply with the requirements of the Merchant Shipping (Safety of Navigation) Regulations 2002, SI 2002/1473, the ship is liable to be detained and the Merchant Shipping Act 1995 s 284(1)–(6), (8) (enforcing detention of ships) (see PARA 1190) has effect in relation to the ship, subject to modifications: see the Merchant Shipping (Safety of Navigation) Regulations 2002, SI 2002/1473, reg 11.

1121. Contravention of requirements relating to counting and recording passengers on board. If there is any breach of the provisions which require the counting and registration of persons[1] on board passenger ships[2], in respect of a passenger ship, the owner[3] is guilty of an offence punishable, on summary conviction, by a fine[4] and, on conviction on indictment, by imprisonment for a term not exceeding two years or a fine (or both)[5].

If there is any breach of the prohibition on such a ship leaving any landing point[6] in circumstances where:

(1)   the total number of persons on board has not been communicated to the master of the ship and the passenger registrar[7] or the owner has not properly recorded and communicated to the master of the ship any person's declared need for special care or assistance in emergency situations[8]; or

(2)   the total number of persons on board the ship exceeds the number of persons the ship is permitted to carry[9],

the master is guilty of an offence punishable, on summary conviction, by a fine and, on conviction on indictment, by imprisonment for a term not exceeding two years or a fine (or both)[10].

Any person who[11], either knowingly or recklessly makes any false statement liable or intended to lead to error in the determination of the total number of persons on board a passenger ship or in the collection of information so required[12], or any person who falsifies the information collected or transmitted to the passenger registrar, is guilty of an offence punishable, on summary conviction, to a fine or, on conviction on indictment, to imprisonment for a term not exceeding two years or a fine (or both)[13].

It is a good defence to such a charge[14] for the person charged to prove that he took all reasonable steps to avoid the commission of the offence[15]; and, without prejudice to this provision[16], it is a good defence to a charge of knowingly or recklessly making any false statement or of falsifying the information collected or transmitted to the passenger registrar[17], for a person providing information to the owner of a ship in respect of other persons not being members of his family, being information required by the owner[18], to prove that the information was collected by him in good faith[19].

1   As to the meaning of 'person' for these purposes see PARA 640 note 3.
2   Ie any breach of the requirements of the Merchant Shipping (Counting and Registration of Persons on Board Passenger Ships) Regulations 1999, SI 1999/1869 (see PARAS 640, 641): see reg 11(1). As to the meaning of 'passenger ship' for these purposes see PARA 640 note 1.
3   As to the meaning of references to the owner of a ship see PARA 640 note 1.
4   As to the powers of magistrates' courts to issue fines on summary conviction see SENTENCING vol 92 (2015) PARA 176.
5   Merchant Shipping (Counting and Registration of Persons on Board Passenger Ships) Regulations 1999, SI 1999/1869, reg 11(1).
6   As to the meaning of 'landing point' for these purposes see PARA 640 note 2.
7   As to the meaning of 'passenger registrar' for these purposes see PARA 640 note 19.
8   Ie if there is a breach of the requirements of the Merchant Shipping (Counting and Registration of Persons on Board Passenger Ships) Regulations 1999, SI 1999/1869, reg 5(6)(a) (see PARA 640): see reg 11(1).
9   Ie if there is a breach of the requirements of the Merchant Shipping (Counting and Registration of Persons on Board Passenger Ships) Regulations 1999, SI 1999/1869, reg 5(6)(b) (see PARA 640): see reg 11(1).
10 Merchant Shipping (Counting and Registration of Persons on Board Passenger Ships) Regulations 1999, SI 1999/1869, reg 11(1).
11 Ie any person who contravenes the Merchant Shipping (Counting and Registration of Persons on Board Passenger Ships) Regulations 1999, SI 1999/1869, reg 10 (see PARA 640): see reg 11(2).
12 Ie the information required by the Merchant Shipping (Counting and Registration of Persons on Board Passenger Ships) Regulations 1999, SI 1999/1869, reg 6(3) (see PARA 640): see reg 11(2).
13 Merchant Shipping (Counting and Registration of Persons on Board Passenger Ships) Regulations 1999, SI 1999/1869, reg 11(2).
14 Ie under the Merchant Shipping (Counting and Registration of Persons on Board Passenger Ships) Regulations 1999, SI 1999/1869: see reg 12(1).
15 Merchant Shipping (Counting and Registration of Persons on Board Passenger Ships) Regulations 1999, SI 1999/1869, reg 12(1).
16 Ie without prejudice to the Merchant Shipping (Counting and Registration of Persons on Board Passenger Ships) Regulations 1999, SI 1999/1869, reg 12(1): see reg 12(2).
17 Ie a charge under the Merchant Shipping (Counting and Registration of Persons on Board Passenger Ships) Regulations 1999, SI 1999/1869, reg 10: see reg 12(2).
18 Ie information required by the owner pursuant to the Merchant Shipping (Counting and Registration of Persons on Board Passenger Ships) Regulations 1999, SI 1999/1869: see reg 12(2).
19 Merchant Shipping (Counting and Registration of Persons on Board Passenger Ships) Regulations 1999, SI 1999/1869, reg 12(2).

1122. Failure to furnish, or falsifying, returns in respect of carriage of goods and passengers by sea. If any person required to furnish periodical or

other returns about cargo, passenger and vessel movement, certain particulars in relation to the transport of containers or ro-ro units, and information in relation to the vessel[1], fails to furnish those returns as required, or makes a return which he knows to be false or recklessly makes a false return, he is, unless he proves that he had reasonable excuse for the failure or false return, liable, on summary conviction, to a fine[2].

1 Ie any person required to furnish returns under the Statistical Returns (Carriage of Goods and Passengers by Sea) Regulations 1997, SI 1997/2330 (see PARA 42): see reg 4.
2 Statistical Returns (Carriage of Goods and Passengers by Sea) Regulations 1997, SI 1997/2330, reg 4. As to the powers of magistrates' courts to issue fines on summary conviction see SENTENCING vol 92 (2015) PARA 176.

1123. Failure to furnish, or falsifying, returns in respect of passengers on board ship. If:

(1)   the master[1] of a passenger ship[2] fails to make a return as required by the Secretary of State[3] giving the total number of any passengers carried, or makes a false return[4];

(2)   any passenger refuses to give any information required by the master of the ship for the purpose of the return so required, or, for that purpose, gives to the master information which he knows to be false or recklessly gives to him information which is false[5],

the master or, as the case may be, passenger is liable, on summary conviction, to a fine[6].

1 As to the meaning of 'master' see PARA 444 note 1.
2 Ie a ship, whether or not a United Kingdom ship, which carries any passenger to a place in the United Kingdom from any place out of the United Kingdom, or from any place in the United Kingdom to any place out of the United Kingdom: see the Merchant Shipping Act 1995 s 107(1). As to the meaning of 'ship' see PARA 229; and as to the meaning of 'United Kingdom ship' see PARA 230. As to the meaning of 'United Kingdom' see PARA 16 note 3.
3 Ie as required by the Merchant Shipping Act 1995 s 107 (see PARA 643): see s 107(3)(a). As to the Secretary of State see PARA 38.
4 Merchant Shipping Act 1995 s 107(3)(a).
5 Merchant Shipping Act 1995 s 107(3)(b).
6 Merchant Shipping Act 1995 s 107(3). As to the time limit for summary offences see PARA 1049; as to offences by officers of bodies corporate see PARA 1051; as to jurisdiction in relation to offences see PARA 1052; as to jurisdiction over ships lying off the coast see PARA 1053; as to jurisdiction in the case of offences on board ship see PARA 1054; as to offences committed by British seamen see PARA 1055; and as to proof etc of exemption see PARA 1061. As to the powers of magistrates' courts to issue fines on summary conviction see SENTENCING vol 92 (2015) PARA 176.

1124. Master's failure to make returns as to births and deaths occurring in his ship. The master of a ship who fails to comply with any of the requirements to make returns in relation to the following births and deaths occurring in his ship[1], namely:

(1)   where a child is born in a ship which is registered in the United Kingdom[2];

(2)   where a person dies in a ship registered in the United Kingdom or where any person employed in such a ship dies outside the United Kingdom[3];

(3)   where a citizen of the United Kingdom and Colonies[4] is born or dies in a ship not registered in the United Kingdom, and the ship thereafter calls at a port in the United Kingdom in the course of or at the end of the voyage during which the death occurs[5],

or if he fails to make the required returns in the manner prescribed[6], he is guilty of an offence[7] and liable, on summary conviction, to a fine[8].

1 Ie the master of a ship who fails to comply with the provisions of the Merchant Shipping (Returns of Births and Deaths) Regulations 1979, SI 1979/1577, reg 2 (see head (1) in the text), including reg 2 as extended to unregistered British ships by reg 12(1) (see PARA 644 note 1), reg 3 (see head

(2) in the text), including reg 3 as so extended, reg 4 (see head (3) in the text), or regs 5, 6 (see PARA 644), including regs 5, 6 as so extended: see reg 13(1).

2   See the Merchant Shipping (Returns of Births and Deaths) Regulations 1979, SI 1979/1577, reg 2 (see PARA 644), including reg 2 as extended to unregistered British ships by reg 12(1): see reg 13(1). As to the meaning of 'United Kingdom' see PARA 16 note 3.

3   See the Merchant Shipping (Returns of Births and Deaths) Regulations 1979, SI 1979/1577, reg 3 (see PARA 644), including reg 3 as extended to unregistered British ships by reg 12(1): see reg 13(1).

4   As to the meaning of 'colony' for the purposes of the British Nationality Act 1981 see BRITISH NATIONALITY vol 4 (2011) PARA 415.

5   See the Merchant Shipping (Returns of Births and Deaths) Regulations 1979, SI 1979/1577, reg 4 (see PARA 644): see reg 13(1).

6   Ie in the manner prescribed by the provisions of the Merchant Shipping (Returns of Births and Deaths) Regulations 1979, SI 1979/1577, reg 5, 6 (see PARA 644), including regs 5, 6 as extended to unregistered British ships by reg 12(1): see reg 13(1).

7   Merchant Shipping (Returns of Births and Deaths) Regulations 1979, SI 1979/1577, reg 13(1).

8   Merchant Shipping (Returns of Births and Deaths) Regulations 1979, SI 1979/1577, reg 13(2). As to the powers of magistrates' courts to issue fines on summary conviction see SENTENCING vol 92 (2015) PARA 176.

1125. Contravention of requirements relating to dangerous goods, marine pollutants etc.

Provision is made for offences and penalties to apply where various requirements relating to the handling, stowage and carriage of dangerous goods and marine pollutants by merchant shipping[1] are contravened[2], and for the detention of a ship in any such case of non-compliance[3].

Any contravention by the operator[4] or master of their duty to ensure that a ship carrying INF cargo[5] complies with the requirements of the INF Code[6] or of their duty to refuse such cargo for carriage in a ship which has not been issued with a Certificate of Fitness[7] is an offence for which each of them is liable[8], on summary conviction, to a fine[9] and on conviction on indictment, to imprisonment for a term not exceeding two years or a fine (or both)[10]. In any case where a ship does not comply with the requirements relating to the carriage of packaged irradiated nuclear fuel by sea[11], the ship is liable to be detained[12].

Offences and penalties apply also where various requirements relating to the reporting of dangerous goods[13] or harmful substances in packaged form[14] which are being carried by merchant shipping[15] are contravened[16], and for the detention of a ship in any such case of non-compliance[17].

1   See the Merchant Shipping (Dangerous Goods and Marine Pollutants) Regulations 1997, SI 1997/2367; and PARA 646. As to the meaning of 'dangerous goods' and 'marine pollutant' for these purposes see PARA 646 note 1.

2   See the Merchant Shipping (Dangerous Goods and Marine Pollutants) Regulations 1997, SI 1997/2367, reg 6 (general duties of operators and employers), reg 7 (general duties of employees aboard ship), reg 8 (misconduct endangering a United Kingdom ship or persons aboard), reg 10 (dangerous goods declaration or marine pollutants declaration), reg 11 (preparation of goods for transport), reg 12 (Container or Vehicle Packing Certificates), reg 14 (list, manifest or stowage plans), reg 15 (marking, labelling or placarding of packaged goods), reg 16 (stowage of packaged goods on board ship), regs 17, 18 (cargo securing documentation), reg 19 (duty of operator and master to ensure that all employees are familiar with the essential actions to be taken in an emergency involving such packaged goods as are carried on the ship), reg 20 (dangerous goods or marine pollutants handled or carried in bulk), reg 21 (documentation related to dangerous goods or marine pollutants handled or carried in bulk), reg 22 (spaces for carriage of packaged goods and dangerous goods in solid form in bulk); and PARA 646. As to penalties see reg 24 (amended by SI 2011/2616); and as to offences due to the fault of another person see the Merchant Shipping (Dangerous Goods and Marine Pollutants) Regulations 1997, SI 1997/2367, reg 25. In any proceedings for an offence under reg 6 consisting of a failure to comply with a duty or requirement to do something so far as is reasonably practicable, it is for the accused to prove that it was not reasonably practicable to do more than was in fact done to satisfy the duty or requirement: reg 9 (amended by SI 2004/2110).

3   See the Merchant Shipping (Dangerous Goods and Marine Pollutants) Regulations 1997, SI 1997/2367, reg 23. In any case where a ship does not comply with the requirements of the

Merchant Shipping (Dangerous Goods and Marine Pollutants) Regulations 1997, SI 1997/2367, the ship is liable to be detained and the Merchant Shipping Act 1995 s 284 (enforcing detention of ships) (see PARA 1190) has effect in relation to the ship, subject to modifications: see the Merchant Shipping (Dangerous Goods and Marine Pollutants) Regulations 1997, SI 1997/2367, reg 23.

4 As to the meaning of 'operator' for these purposes see PARA 647 note 3.

5 As to the meaning of 'INF cargo' for these purposes see PARA 647 note 1.

6 Ie where there is a breach of the Merchant Shipping (Carriage of Packaged Irradiated Nuclear Fuel etc) (INF Code) Regulations 2000, SI 2000/3216, reg 4(2) (see PARA 647): see reg 6(1). As to the meaning of 'Certificate of Fitness' for these purposes see PARA 647 note 6.

7 Ie where there is a breach of the Merchant Shipping (Carriage of Packaged Irradiated Nuclear Fuel etc) (INF Code) Regulations 2000, SI 2000/3216, reg 5 (see PARA 647): see reg 6(1).

8 Merchant Shipping (Carriage of Packaged Irradiated Nuclear Fuel etc) (INF Code) Regulations 2000, SI 2000/3216, reg 6(1). It is, however, a defence for a person so charged to show that he took all reasonable steps to avoid the commission of the offence (reg 6(3)); and where the commission by any person of such an offence is due to the act or default of some other person, that other person is guilty of the offence and a person may be charged with and convicted of the offence by virtue of this provision whether or not proceedings are taken against the first-mentioned person (reg 8).

9 As to the powers of magistrates' courts to issue fines on summary conviction see SENTENCING vol 92 (2015) PARA 176.

10 Merchant Shipping (Carriage of Packaged Irradiated Nuclear Fuel etc) (INF Code) Regulations 2000, SI 2000/3216, reg 6(2).

11 Ie where there is a failure to comply with the Merchant Shipping (Carriage of Packaged Irradiated Nuclear Fuel etc) (INF Code) Regulations 2000, SI 2000/3216 (see PARA 647): see reg 7.

12 See the Merchant Shipping (Carriage of Packaged Irradiated Nuclear Fuel etc) (INF Code) Regulations 2000, SI 2000/3216, reg 7. In any case where a ship does not comply with the requirements of the Merchant Shipping (Carriage of Packaged Irradiated Nuclear Fuel etc) (INF Code) Regulations 2000, SI 2000/3216, the Merchant Shipping Act 1995 s 284 (enforcing detention of ships) (see PARA 1190) has effect in relation to the ship, subject to modifications: see the Merchant Shipping (Carriage of Packaged Irradiated Nuclear Fuel etc) (INF Code) Regulations 2000, SI 2000/3216, reg 7.

13 As to the meaning of 'dangerous goods' for these purposes see PARA 648 note 3.

14 As to the meaning of 'harmful substances in packaged form' for these purposes see PARA 648 note 4.

15 See the Merchant Shipping (Reporting Requirements for Ships Carrying Dangerous or Polluting Goods) Regulations 1995, SI 1995/2498; and PARA 648.

16 See the Merchant Shipping (Reporting Requirements for Ships Carrying Dangerous or Polluting Goods) Regulations 1995, SI 1995/2498, reg 15 (amended by SI 1999/2121; SI 2001/1638; SI 2004/2110). It is a good defence to a charge under the Merchant Shipping (Reporting Requirements for Ships Carrying Dangerous or Polluting Goods) Regulations 1995, SI 1995/2498, reg 15 to prove that the person charged took all reasonable steps to avoid committing the offence (see reg 15(6)): and where such an offence is committed, or would have been committed except for the operation of reg 15(6), by any person due to the act or default of some other person, that other person is guilty of the offence, and a person may be charged with and convicted of the offence by virtue of this provision whether or not proceedings are taken against the first mentioned person (reg 16).

17 Any person duly authorised by the Secretary of State may inspect any ship to which the Merchant Shipping (Reporting Requirements for Ships Carrying Dangerous or Polluting Goods) Regulations 1995, SI 1995/2498, apply and, if he is satisfied that there is a failure to comply in relation to that ship with relation to the requirements of reg 5 (see PARA 648), he may detain the ship until such requirements are met: reg 17. Where a ship is liable to be detained under the Merchant Shipping (Dangerous Goods and Marine Pollutants) Regulations 1997, SI 1997/2367, the Merchant Shipping Act 1995 s 284 (enforcing detention of ships) (see PARA 1190) has effect in relation to the ship, subject to modifications: see the Merchant Shipping (Reporting Requirements for Ships Carrying Dangerous or Polluting Goods) Regulations 1995, SI 1995/2498, reg 18 (amended by SI 2004/2110). As to the Secretary of State see PARA 36.

1126. Contravention of requirements relating to cargoes in need of special precautions.

The following persons are guilty of an offence under the provisions which relate to the carriage of cargoes in need of special precautions[1]:

(1)   a shipper[2] or forwarder[3] who fails to provide appropriate cargo[4] information as required[5], or who furnishes cargo information which he knows to be false or who recklessly furnishes cargo information which is false[6];

(2)   an owner[7] or master who accepts for carriage, or takes or receives on board, any cargo for which appropriate cargo information[8] has not been furnished[9];

(3)   an owner or master who contravenes the requirements[10] to carry the appropriate documentation, including the International Grain Code[11];

(4)   an owner or master who contravenes the requirements[12] regarding the stowage and securing of cargo[13];

(5)   a shipper or forwarder who contravenes the requirements[14] relating to packaged goods which have been packed into or onto a cargo unit[15];

(6)   an owner of a ship which transports, or a master who accepts for carriage, a bulk cargo[16] which is liable to emit a toxic or flammable gas, or cause oxygen depletion in the cargo hold, without ensuring that the requirement[17] for oxygen analysis and gas detection equipment has been complied with[18];

(7)   an owner and master (individually) if the requirement[19] as to the safe use of pesticides in ships is not complied with[20];

(8)   an owner who contravenes the requirement[21] to ensure that the master is furnished with the required stability information[22];

(9)   a master who contravenes the conditions[23] for accepting for loading concentrates or other cargoes which may liquefy[24] or who contravenes the conditions[25] for accepting bulk cargo[26];

(10)   an owner who contravenes the duty[27] to ensure the ship is provided with a cargo loading manual[28];

(11)   a master who contravenes the provisions which require a plan for loading or unloading the ship to be agreed[29], or who fails to ensure that loading and unloading operations are conducted in accordance with the plan so agreed[30], or who fails to ensure that cargoes are loaded and trimmed as necessary[31], or who fails to ensure that corrective action is taken where, during loading or unloading, any of the ship's limits[32] are exceeded or are likely to become so[33], or who fails to ensure that the unloading method does not damage the ship's structure[34], or who fails to monitor cargo operations as required or fails to ensure that deviations from the plan agreed for loading or unloading are corrected[35];

(12)   a terminal representative[36] in the United Kingdom[37] who contravenes the provisions which require a plan for loading or unloading the ship to be agreed[38], or who fails to ensure that loading and unloading operations are conducted in accordance with the plan so agreed[39], or who fails to ensure that corrective action is taken where, during loading or unloading, any of the ship's limits[40] are exceeded or are likely to become so[41], or who fails to ensure that the unloading method does not damage the ship's structure[42];

(13)   an owner or master who fails to ensure that a ship loading grain[43] complies with the International Grain Code and has on board a document of authorisation as required by that Code[44], or who permits a ship loaded in contravention of the International Grain Code outside the United Kingdom to enter any port in the United Kingdom so laden[45];

(14)   a person who orders the commencement of the loading of grain into a ship in the United Kingdom without satisfying himself first as to the conditions which are so required[46].

A person guilty of an offence under any of heads (1) to (14) above is liable, on conviction on indictment, to imprisonment for a term not exceeding two years or a fine (or to both) or, on summary conviction, to a fine[47]. In any proceedings for such an offence, it is a defence for a person to prove that all reasonable steps had been taken by that person to ensure compliance with the provisions[48].

In any case where a ship does not comply with the provisions relating to the carriage of cargoes[49], the ship is liable to be detained[50].

1 Ie under the Merchant Shipping (Carriage of Cargoes) Regulations 1999, SI 1999/336 (see PARA 649 et seq).
2 As to the meaning of 'shipper' see PARA 649 note 1.
3 As to the meaning of 'forwarder' see PARA 649 note 9.
4 As to the meaning of 'cargo' for these purposes see PARA 649 note 1.
5 Ie as required by the Merchant Shipping (Carriage of Cargoes) Regulations 1999, SI 1999/336, reg 4 (see PARA 649): see reg 4(6).
6 Merchant Shipping (Carriage of Cargoes) Regulations 1999, SI 1999/336, reg 4(6).
7 As to references to the owner see PARA 649 note 3.
8 Ie as required by the Merchant Shipping (Carriage of Cargoes) Regulations 1999, SI 1999/336, reg 4: see reg 4(7).
9 Merchant Shipping (Carriage of Cargoes) Regulations 1999, SI 1999/336, reg 4(7).
10 Ie who contravenes the Merchant Shipping (Carriage of Cargoes) Regulations 1999, SI 1999/336, reg 5(1), (3) (see PARA 650): see reg 5(5).
11 Merchant Shipping (Carriage of Cargoes) Regulations 1999, SI 1999/336, reg 5(5). As to the meaning of 'International Grain Code' see PARA 650 note 6.
12 Ie an owner or master who contravenes the Merchant Shipping (Carriage of Cargoes) Regulations 1999, SI 1999/336, reg 6(1) (see PARA 651): see reg 6(3)(a).
13 Merchant Shipping (Carriage of Cargoes) Regulations 1999, SI 1999/336, reg 6(3)(a).
14 Ie the requirements of the Merchant Shipping (Carriage of Cargoes) Regulations 1999, SI 1999/336, reg 6(2) (see PARA 651): see reg 6(3)(b).
15 Merchant Shipping (Carriage of Cargoes) Regulations 1999, SI 1999/336, reg 6(3)(b). As to the meaning of 'cargo unit' for these purposes see PARA 649 note 2.
16 As to the meaning of 'bulk cargo' see PARA 649 note 2.
17 Ie the requirement of the Merchant Shipping (Carriage of Cargoes) Regulations 1999, SI 1999/336, reg 7(1) (see PARA 652): see reg 7(2).
18 Merchant Shipping (Carriage of Cargoes) Regulations 1999, SI 1999/336, reg 7(2).
19 Ie the requirements of the Merchant Shipping (Carriage of Cargoes) Regulations 1999, SI 1999/336, reg 8(1) (see PARA 653): see reg 8(2).
20 Merchant Shipping (Carriage of Cargoes) Regulations 1999, SI 1999/336, reg 8(2).
21 Ie the requirement of the Merchant Shipping (Carriage of Cargoes) Regulations 1999, SI 1999/336, reg 9(4) (see PARA 655): see reg 9(6).
22 Merchant Shipping (Carriage of Cargoes) Regulations 1999, SI 1999/336, reg 9(6). The text refers to the stability information required by reg 9(1) (see PARA 655): see reg 9(6).
23 Ie a master who contravenes the Merchant Shipping (Carriage of Cargoes) Regulations 1999, SI 1999/336, reg 9(2) (see PARA 655): see reg 9(7).
24 As to the meaning of 'cargoes which may liquefy' see PARA 649 note 2.
25 Ie a master who contravenes the Merchant Shipping (Carriage of Cargoes) Regulations 1999, SI 1999/336, reg 9(5) (see PARA 655): see reg 9(7).
26 Merchant Shipping (Carriage of Cargoes) Regulations 1999, SI 1999/336, reg 9(7).
27 Ie an owner who contravenes the Merchant Shipping (Carriage of Cargoes) Regulations 1999, SI 1999/336, reg 10(2) (see PARA 656): see reg 10(9)(a).
28 Merchant Shipping (Carriage of Cargoes) Regulations 1999, SI 1999/336, reg 10(9)(a).
29 Ie a master who contravenes the Merchant Shipping (Carriage of Cargoes) Regulations 1999, SI 1999/336, reg 10(3) (see PARA 656): see reg 10(9)(b).
30 Ie a master who contravenes the Merchant Shipping (Carriage of Cargoes) Regulations 1999, SI 1999/336, reg 10(6) (see PARA 656): see reg 10(9)(b).
31 Ie a master who contravenes the Merchant Shipping (Carriage of Cargoes) Regulations 1999, SI 1999/336, reg 10(4), (5) (see PARA 656): see reg 10(9)(b). As to the meaning of 'trimming' for these purposes see PARA 649 note 2.
32 Ie the limits of the ship referred to in the Merchant Shipping (Carriage of Cargoes) Regulations 1999, SI 1999/336, reg 10(2): see reg 10(7)(a); and PARA 656.
33 Ie a master who contravenes the Merchant Shipping (Carriage of Cargoes) Regulations 1999, SI 1999/336, reg 10(7)(b) (see PARA 656): see reg 10(9)(b).
34 Ie a master who contravenes the Merchant Shipping (Carriage of Cargoes) Regulations 1999, SI 1999/336, reg 10(7)(c) (see PARA 656): see reg 10(9)(b).

35 Merchant Shipping (Carriage of Cargoes) Regulations 1999, SI 1999/336, reg 10(9)(b). The text
    refers to a master who fails to monitor cargo operations as required by reg 10(8) or fails to ensure
    that deviations from the plan agreed for loading or unloading are corrected as required by reg
    10(8) (see PARA 656): see reg 10(9)(b).
36 As to the meaning of 'terminal representative' see PARA 656 note 14.
37 As to the meaning of 'United Kingdom' see PARA 16 note 3.
38 Ie a terminal representative in the United Kingdom who contravenes the Merchant Shipping
    (Carriage of Cargoes) Regulations 1999, SI 1999/336, reg 10(3) (see PARA 656): see reg 10(9)(c).
39 Ie a terminal representative in the United Kingdom who contravenes the Merchant Shipping
    (Carriage of Cargoes) Regulations 1999, SI 1999/336, reg 10(6) (see PARA 656): see reg 10(9)(c).
40 Ie the limits of the ship referred to in the Merchant Shipping (Carriage of Cargoes) Regulations
    1999, SI 1999/336, reg 10(2): see reg 10(7)(a); and PARA 656.
41 Ie a terminal representative in the United Kingdom who contravenes the Merchant Shipping
    (Carriage of Cargoes) Regulations 1999, SI 1999/336, reg 10(7)(b) (see PARA 656): see reg
    10(9)(c).
42 Merchant Shipping (Carriage of Cargoes) Regulations 1999, SI 1999/336, reg 10(9)(c). The text
    refers to a terminal representative in the United Kingdom who fails to ensure that the unloading
    method does not damage the ship's structure as required by reg 10(7)(c) (see PARA 656): see reg
    10(9)(c).
43 As to the meaning of 'grain' see PARA 650 note 2.
44 Ie an owner or master who contravenes the Merchant Shipping (Carriage of Cargoes) Regulations
    1999, SI 1999/336, reg 11(2) (see PARA 657): see reg 11(5).
45 Merchant Shipping (Carriage of Cargoes) Regulations 1999, SI 1999/336, reg 11(5). The text
    refers to an owner or master who permits a ship to enter any port in the United Kingdom in
    contravention of reg 11(3) (see PARA 657): see reg 11(5).
46 Merchant Shipping (Carriage of Cargoes) Regulations 1999, SI 1999/336, reg 11(6). The text
    refers to a person who contravenes reg 11(4) (see PARA 657): see reg 11(6).
47 Merchant Shipping (Carriage of Cargoes) Regulations 1999, SI 1999/336, reg 13(1). Where the
    commission by any person of an offence under the Merchant Shipping (Carriage of Cargoes)
    Regulations 1999, SI 1999/336, is due to the act or default of some other person, the other person
    is guilty of the offence; and a person may be charged with and convicted of the offence by virtue
    of this provision whether or not proceedings are taken against the first-mentioned person: reg 14.
    As to the powers of magistrates' courts to issue fines on summary conviction see SENTENCING vol
    92 (2015) PARA 176.
48 Merchant Shipping (Carriage of Cargoes) Regulations 1999, SI 1999/336, reg 13(2).
49 Ie with the provisions of the Merchant Shipping (Carriage of Cargoes) Regulations 1999, SI
    1999/336 (see PARA 649 et seq): see reg 12.
50 See the Merchant Shipping (Carriage of Cargoes) Regulations 1999, SI 1999/336, reg 12. Where
    a ship is liable to be detained under the Merchant Shipping (Carriage of Cargoes) Regulations
    1999, SI 1999/336, the Merchant Shipping Act 1995 s 284 (enforcing detention of ships) (see
    PARA 1190) has effect in relation to the ship, subject to modifications: see the Merchant Shipping
    (Carriage of Cargoes) Regulations 1999, SI 1999/336, reg 12.

**1127. Failure to comply with requirements prescribed for ships receiving
trans-shipped fish.** If, without reasonable excuse, the master[1] of a ship[2], in
respect of which a transhipment licence[3] is in force, causes or permits any
prohibition imposed by notice[4] to be contravened in respect of the ship, that
master is liable, on conviction on indictment, to imprisonment for a term not
exceeding two years or a fine (or to both) or, on summary conviction, to a fine[5].

   If there is any contravention of the requirement for such ships to have
compulsory insurance in place (or to have such other form of security which meets
those same requirements)[6], the owner, charterer and master are each guilty of an
offence punishable, on summary conviction, by a fine[7].

   Any contravention of the requirement to carry documentary evidence of such
insurance or other security[8] is an offence by any person required to produce such
evidence punishable, on summary conviction, by a fine[9].

   In any case where a ship does not comply with the requirements relating to
compulsory insurance for ships receiving trans-shipped fish[10], the ship is liable to
be detained[11].

1   As to the meaning of 'master' see PARA 444 note 1.

2 As to the meaning of 'ship' see PARA 229.

3 As to the meaning of 'transhipment licence' see PARA 658 note 4.

4 Ie imposed by a notice under the Merchant Shipping Act 1995 s 100G(2) (see PARA 670): see s 100G(5) (s 100G added by the Merchant Shipping and Maritime Security Act 1997 s 11; amended by SI 2015/664). The text refers to a notice served on the master of a ship under the Merchant Shipping Act 1995 s 100G(2) which specifies that his ship is contravening a requirement of regulations made by the Secretary of State under s 100F(2) (requirements to be met by ships in respect of which transhipment licences are in force) (see PARA 658) or under s 192A (compulsory insurance or security) (see PARA 1016): see s 100G(1), (2); and PARA 659.

5 Merchant Shipping Act 1995 s 100G(5) (as added and amended: see note 4). As to the time limit for summary offences see PARA 1049; as to offences by officers of bodies corporate see PARA 1051; as to jurisdiction in relation to offences see PARA 1052; as to jurisdiction over ships lying off the coast see PARA 1053; as to jurisdiction in the case of offences on board ship see PARA 1054; as to offences committed by British seamen see PARA 1055; and as to proof etc of exemption see PARA 1061. As to the powers of magistrates' courts to issue fines on summary conviction see SENTENCING vol 92 (2015) PARA 176.

6 Ie if there is any contravention of the Merchant Shipping (Compulsory Insurance: Ships Receiving Trans-shipped Fish) Regulations 1998, SI 1998/209, reg 4 (see PARA 1016): see reg 8(1) (amended by SI 2015/664).

7 Merchant Shipping (Compulsory Insurance: Ships Receiving Trans-shipped Fish) Regulations 1998, SI 1998/209, reg 8(1) (as amended: see note 6). It is a defence for a person charged with an offence under reg 8(1) to show that he took all reasonable precautions and exercised all due diligence to avoid the commission of the offence: reg 8(3).

8 Ie any contravention of the Merchant Shipping (Compulsory Insurance: Ships Receiving Trans-shipped Fish) Regulations 1998, SI 1998/209, reg 7 (see PARA 1016): see reg 8(2).

9 Merchant Shipping (Compulsory Insurance: Ships Receiving Trans-shipped Fish) Regulations 1998, SI 1998/209, reg 8(2). It is a defence for a person charged with an offence under reg 8(2) to show that he took all reasonable precautions and exercised all due diligence to avoid the commission of the offence: reg 8(3).

10 Ie the requirements of the Merchant Shipping (Compulsory Insurance: Ships Receiving Trans-shipped Fish) Regulations 1998, SI 1998/209 (see PARA 1016): see reg 9.

11 See the Merchant Shipping (Compulsory Insurance: Ships Receiving Trans-shipped Fish) Regulations 1998, SI 1998/209, reg 9. Where a ship is liable to be detained under the Merchant Shipping (Compulsory Insurance: Ships Receiving Trans-shipped Fish) Regulations 1998, SI 1998/209, the Merchant Shipping Act 1995 s 284 (enforcing detention of ships) (see PARA 1190) has effect in relation to the ship, subject to necessary modifications: see the Merchant Shipping (Compulsory Insurance: Ships Receiving Trans-shipped Fish) Regulations 1998, SI 1998/209, reg 9.

1128. Penalties relating to contravention of load line provisions. Where a ship proceeds, or attempts to proceed, to sea[1], without having been surveyed in accordance with the load lines rules[2], or marked with the appropriate marks[3], or without complying with the conditions of assignment applicable to it[4], or without the information as to the stability of the ship[5], or as to the loading and ballasting of any ship of more than 150 metres in length[6], that must be provided for the guidance of the ship's master[7], the owner and master of the ship are each guilty of an offence and liable, on summary conviction or conviction on indictment, to a fine[8].

Where a ship has been so loaded that the appropriate load line[9] on each side of the ship either:

(1)   is submerged[10]; or

(2)   would be submerged if the ship were in salt water and had no list[11],

that amounts to an offence by both the owner and master and is punishable[12], on summary conviction, by a fine including such additional fine, subject to specified limits[13], as the court thinks fit to impose, having regard to the extent to which the earning capacity of the ship was increased by reason of the contravention[14]; and, on conviction on indictment, by a fine[15]. If a ship which is so loaded[16] proceeds to sea[17], that is an offence by the master and by any other person who, having reason to believe that the ship is so loaded, sends or is party to sending the ship to sea, punishable[18], on summary conviction or conviction on indictment, by a fine[19].

Any contravention of the duty of the owner and master to keep the ship marked with the appropriate marks[20] is an offence by both the owner and the master punishable, on summary conviction, by a fine[21]; and any contravention by any person of the requirement not to conceal, remove, alter, deface or obliterate the marks without the authority of the Assigning Authority[22], is an offence punishable, on summary conviction, by a fine[23].

Any contravention of the requirement, subject to any exemption, not to proceed, or attempt to proceed, to sea unless the appropriate certificate[24] is in force in respect of the ship[25] is an offence by the master punishable, on summary conviction or conviction on indictment, by a fine[26].

Any contravention of the requirements relating to publication of the load line certificate or notification of draughts[27] is an offence by both the master and owner punishable, on summary conviction, by a fine[28].

Any ship which proceeds or attempts to proceed to sea without being duly surveyed and marked[29] may be detained until it has been so surveyed and marked[30]; any ship which does not comply with the conditions of assignment applicable to it is liable to be detained until it complies[31]; and any ship which is so loaded that the appropriate load line on each side of the ship either is submerged (or would be submerged if the ship were in salt water and had no list)[32] may[33] be detained until it ceases to be so loaded[34]. In any case where a ship is liable to be detained in this way, provision is made in relation to enforcement[35]; and provisions relating to compensation have effect[36].

1   Ie subject to any exemption conferred under the Merchant Shipping (Load Line) Regulations 1998, SI 1998/2241 (as to which see PARA 661): see reg 6(1); and PARA 662. As to the meaning of 'sea' see PARA 660 note 6.
2   Ie in contravention of the Merchant Shipping (Load Line) Regulations 1998, SI 1998/2241, reg 6(1)(a): see reg 35(1). As to the meaning of 'load line' see PARA 660 note 1. The text refers to a requirement for a ship to be surveyed in accordance with the Merchant Shipping (Load Line) Regulations 1998, SI 1998/2241: see reg 6(1)(a); and PARA 662. As to the surveys so required see PARA 664.
3   Ie in contravention of the Merchant Shipping (Load Line) Regulations 1998, SI 1998/2241, reg 6(1)(b): see reg 35(1). As to the meaning of 'appropriate marks' for these purposes see PARA 662 note 4.
4   Ie in contravention of the Merchant Shipping (Load Line) Regulations 1998, SI 1998/2241, reg 6(1)(c): see reg 35(1). As to the meaning of 'conditions of assignment' for these purposes see PARA 662 note 5. As to compliance with the applicable conditions of assignment of freeboards see PARA 663.
5   Ie the information required by the Merchant Shipping (Load Line) Regulations 1998, SI 1998/2241, reg 32 (as to which see PARA 671): see reg 6(1)(d); and PARA 662.
6   Ie the information required by the Merchant Shipping (Load Line) Regulations 1998, SI 1998/2241, reg 33 (as to which see PARA 671): see reg 6(1)(d).
7   Ie in contravention of the Merchant Shipping (Load Line) Regulations 1998, SI 1998/2241, reg 6(1)(d): see reg 35(1).
8   Merchant Shipping (Load Line) Regulations 1998, SI 1998/2241, reg 35(1). The ship may be liable to detention also: see the text and notes 29–30. As to the powers of magistrates' courts to issue fines on summary conviction see SENTENCING vol 92 (2015) PARA 176.
9   As to the meaning of 'appropriate load line' for these purposes see PARA 662 note 4.
10 Ie in contravention of the Merchant Shipping (Load Line) Regulations 1998, SI 1998/2241, reg 6(3)(a) (see PARA 662): see reg 35(2).
11 Ie in contravention of the Merchant Shipping (Load Line) Regulations 1998, SI 1998/2241, reg 6(3)(b) (see PARA 662): see reg 35(2).
12 Merchant Shipping (Load Line) Regulations 1998, SI 1998/2241, reg 35(2) (amended by SI 2000/1335). Where a person is charged with an offence under the Merchant Shipping (Load Line) Regulations 1998, SI 1998/2241, reg 35(2), it is a defence to prove that the contravention was due solely to deviation or delay and that the deviation or delay was caused solely by stress of weather or other circumstances which neither the master nor the owner nor the charterer (if any) could have prevented or forestalled: reg 35(5).

13 Any additional fine imposed under the Merchant Shipping (Load Line) Regulations 1998, SI 1998/2241, reg 35(2)(a) must not exceed £1,000 for each complete centimetre by which, in a case falling within reg 6(3)(a) (see head (1) in the text), the appropriate load line on each side of the ship was submerged, or, in a case falling within reg 6(3)(b) (see head (2) in the text), the appropriate load line on each side of the ship would have been submerged: reg 35(3).

14 Merchant Shipping (Load Line) Regulations 1998, SI 1998/2241, reg 35(2)(a).

15 Merchant Shipping (Load Line) Regulations 1998, SI 1998/2241, reg 35(2)(b). The ship may be liable to detention also: see the text and notes 32–34.

16 Ie which is loaded in contravention of the Merchant Shipping (Load Line) Regulations 1998, SI 1998/2241, reg 6(3): see reg 6(4); and PARA 662.

17 Ie in contravention of the Merchant Shipping (Load Line) Regulations 1998, SI 1998/2241, reg 6(4): see reg 35(4).

18 Ie without prejudice to any fine liable in respect of an offence under the Merchant Shipping (Load Line) Regulations 1998, SI 1998/2241, reg 35(2) (see the text and notes 9–15): see reg 35(4).

19 Merchant Shipping (Load Line) Regulations 1998, SI 1998/2241, reg 35(4).

20 Ie any contravention of the Merchant Shipping (Load Line) Regulations 1998, SI 1998/2241, reg 23(a) (see PARA 670): see reg 35(6)(a) (amended by SI 2000/1335).

21 Merchant Shipping (Load Line) Regulations 1998, SI 1998/2241, reg 35(6)(a) (as amended: see note 20). It is a defence for a person charged under reg 35(6) to show he had reasonable excuse for the contravention: reg 35(6)(c).

22 Ie any contravention of the Merchant Shipping (Load Line) Regulations 1998, SI 1998/2241, reg 23(b) (see PARA 670): see reg 35(6)(b) (amended by SI 2000/1335). As to the meaning of 'Assigning Authority' see PARA 663 note 1.

23 Merchant Shipping (Load Line) Regulations 1998, SI 1998/2241, reg 35(6)(b) (as amended: see note 22). As to defences for a person charged under reg 35(6) see note 21.

24 As to the meaning of 'appropriate certificate' for these purposes see PARA 664 note 6.

25 Ie any contravention of the Merchant Shipping (Load Line) Regulations 1998, SI 1998/2241, reg 9(4) (see PARA 665): see reg 35(7).

26 Merchant Shipping (Load Line) Regulations 1998, SI 1998/2241, reg 35(7).

27 Ie any contravention of the Merchant Shipping (Load Line) Regulations 1998, SI 1998/2241, reg 13 (see PARA 669): see reg 35(8).

28 Merchant Shipping (Load Line) Regulations 1998, SI 1998/2241, reg 35(8).

29 Ie in contravention of the Merchant Shipping (Load Line) Regulations 1998, SI 1998/2241, reg 6(1) (see PARA 662): see reg 37(1).

30 Merchant Shipping (Load Line) Regulations 1998, SI 1998/2241, reg 37(1). See also the text and notes 1–8.

31 Merchant Shipping (Load Line) Regulations 1998, SI 1998/2241, reg 37(2). See also the text and notes 1–8.

32 Ie in contravention of the Merchant Shipping (Load Line) Regulations 1998, SI 1998/2241, reg 6(3) (see PARA 662): see reg 37(3) (amended by SI 2000/1335).

33 Ie without prejudice to any proceedings under the Merchant Shipping (Load Line) Regulations 1998, SI 1998/2241, reg 35 (see the text and notes 16–19): see reg 37(3) (as amended: see note 32).

34 Merchant Shipping (Load Line) Regulations 1998, SI 1998/2241, reg 37(3) (as amended: see note 32).

35 In any case where a ship is liable to be detained under the Merchant Shipping (Load Line) Regulations 1998, SI 1998/2241, the Merchant Shipping Act 1995 s 284 (enforcing detention of ships) (see PARA 1190) has effect in relation to the ship, subject to modifications: see the Merchant Shipping (Load Line) Regulations 1998, SI 1998/2241, reg 37(4) (amended by SI 2000/1335).

36 The provisions of the Merchant Shipping Act 1995 ss 96, 97 (arbitration and compensation in connection with detention notices) (see PARAS 1142, 1143) apply in relation to a detention notice issued pursuant to the Merchant Shipping (Load Line) Regulations 1998, SI 1998/2241, reg 37, as they apply in relation to detention notices issued pursuant to the Merchant Shipping Act 1995 s 95(3) (power to detain dangerously unsafe ship) (see PARA 1141) but with modifications: see the Merchant Shipping (Load Line) Regulations 1998, SI 1998/2241, reg 37(5) (amended by SI 2000/1335).

1129. Offences and penalties in relation to load line certificates and surveys.

No person may:

(1)   intentionally alter a certificate referred to in the provisions relating to load lines[1];

(2)   falsely make a certificate referred to in those provisions[2];

(3)   in connection with any survey required by those provisions[3], knowingly or recklessly furnish false information[4];

(4)   with intent to deceive, use, lend, or allow to be used by another, a certificate referred to in those provisions[5]; or
(5)   fail to surrender, as directed by the Secretary of State[6], a certificate that the Secretary of State requires to be surrendered[7].

Contravention of any of heads (1) to (5) above is an offence punishable, on summary conviction, by a fine[8], or, on conviction on indictment, by imprisonment for a term not exceeding six months, or a fine (or both)[9].

1   Merchant Shipping (Load Line) Regulations 1998, SI 1998/2241, reg 36(1)(a). Head (1) in the text refers to a certificate referred to in the Merchant Shipping (Load Line) Regulations 1998, SI 1998/2241 (see PARA 660 et seq): see reg 36(1)(a).
2   Merchant Shipping (Load Line) Regulations 1998, SI 1998/2241, reg 36(1)(b).
3   As to the surveys so required see PARA 664.
4   Merchant Shipping (Load Line) Regulations 1998, SI 1998/2241, reg 36(1)(c).
5   Merchant Shipping (Load Line) Regulations 1998, SI 1998/2241, reg 36(1)(d).
6   As to the Secretary of State see PARA 36.
7   Merchant Shipping (Load Line) Regulations 1998, SI 1998/2241, reg 36(1)(e) (substituted by SI 2000/1335). Head (5) in the text refers to a certificate required to be surrendered under the Merchant Shipping (Load Line) Regulations 1998, SI 1998/2241, reg 11(6) (see PARA 668): see reg 36(1)(e) (as so substituted).
8   As to the powers of magistrates' courts to issue fines on summary conviction see SENTENCING vol 92 (2015) PARA 176.
9   Merchant Shipping (Load Line) Regulations 1998, SI 1998/2241, reg 36(2).

1130. Failure to observe controls imposed in relation to temporary exclusion zones. If a ship[1] enters or remains in a temporary exclusion zone[2] or a part of such a zone in contravention[3] of the restrictions in force[4], its owner and its master[5] are each guilty of an offence and liable, on conviction on indictment, to imprisonment for a term not exceeding two years or a fine (or both) or, on summary conviction, to a fine[6]. It is, however, a defence for a person charged with such an offence[7] to prove that the existence or area of the temporary exclusion zone was not, and would not on reasonable inquiry have become, known to the master[8].

1   As to the meaning of 'ship' see PARA 229.
2   As to the meaning of 'temporary exclusion zone' see PARA 673.
3   As to the meaning of 'contravention' see PARA 51 note 3.
4   Ie in contravention of the Merchant Shipping Act 1995 s 100B(1) (see PARA 674) or s 100B(3) (see PARA 674): see s 100B(6) (s 100B added by the Merchant Shipping and Maritime Security Act 1997 s 1; amended by SI 2015/664).
5   As to the meaning of 'master' see PARA 444 note 1.
6   Merchant Shipping Act 1995 s 100B(6) (as added and amended: see note 4). As to the time limit for summary offences see PARA 1049; as to offences by officers of bodies corporate see PARA 1051; as to jurisdiction in relation to offences see PARA 1052; as to jurisdiction over ships lying off the coast see PARA 1053; as to jurisdiction in the case of offences on board ship see PARA 1054; as to offences committed by British seamen see PARA 1055; and as to proof etc of exemption see PARA 1061. As to the powers of magistrates' courts to issue fines on summary conviction see SENTENCING vol 92 (2015) PARA 176.
7   Ie under the Merchant Shipping Act 1995 s 100B (see PARA 674): see s 100B(7) (as added: see note 4).
8   Merchant Shipping Act 1995 s 100B(7) (as added: see note 4).

1131. Interference with, or failure to comply with, safety directions or action taken in lieu. A person to whom a safety direction is given[1] must comply with the direction[2], and he commits an offence if he fails so to comply[3].
   If a person intentionally obstructs another person who is:
(1)   acting on behalf of the Secretary of State[4] in connection with the giving of a safety direction[5];
(2)   complying with such a direction[6]; or
(3)   taking action in lieu of such a direction[7],
that first-named person commits an offence[8].

A person guilty of either such offence[9] is liable, on summary conviction or conviction on indictment, to a fine[10].

However, proceedings for such an offence[11] may be brought only by or with the consent of the Attorney General[12], or by or with the authority of the Secretary of State[13].

1 Ie a person to whom a direction is given under the Merchant Shipping Act 1995 Sch 3A (see PARA 675): see Sch 3A para 5 (Sch 3A added by the Marine Safety Act 2003 s 1(1), (2), Sch 1).
2 See the Merchant Shipping Act 1995 Sch 3A para 5(a); and PARA 675.
3 Merchant Shipping Act 1995 Sch 3A para 6(1) (as added: see note 1). It is a defence for a person charged with an offence under Sch 3A para 6(1) to prove that he tried as hard as he could to comply with the relevant direction, or that he reasonably believed that compliance with the direction would involve a serious risk to human life: Sch 3A para 6(2) (as so added).
4 As to the Secretary of State see PARA 36.
5 Merchant Shipping Act 1995 Sch 3A para 7(a) (as added: see note 1). The text refers to the giving of a direction under Sch 3A (see PARA 686): see Sch 3A para 7(a) (as so added).
6 Merchant Shipping Act 1995 Sch 3A para 7(b) (as added: see note 1).
7 Merchant Shipping Act 1995 Sch 3A para 7(c) (as added: see note 1). Head (3) in the text refers to a person who is acting by virtue of Sch 3A para 4 (see PARA 676): see Sch 3A para 7(c) (as so added).
8 Merchant Shipping Act 1995 Sch 3A para 7 (as added: see note 1).
9 Ie under the Merchant Shipping Act 1995 Sch 3A para 6 (see the text and notes 1–3) or under Sch 3A para 7 (see the text and notes 4–8): see Sch 3A para 8 (as added: see note 1).
10 Merchant Shipping Act 1995 Sch 3A para 8 (as added (see note 1); amended by SI 2015/664). As to the time limit for summary offences see PARA 1049; as to offences by officers of bodies corporate see PARA 1051; as to jurisdiction in relation to offences see PARA 1052; as to jurisdiction over ships lying off the coast see PARA 1053; as to jurisdiction in the case of offences on board ship see PARA 1054; as to offences committed by British seamen see PARA 1055; and as to proof etc of exemption see PARA 1061. As to the powers of magistrates' courts to issue fines on summary conviction see SENTENCING vol 92 (2015) para 176.
11 Ie under the Merchant Shipping Act 1995 Sch 3A para 6 (see the text and notes 1–3) or under Sch 3A para 7 (see the text and notes 4–8): see Sch 3A para 9 (as added: see note 1).
12 As to the Attorney General see CONSTITUTIONAL AND ADMINISTRATIVE LAW vol 20 (2014) PARA 273.
13 Merchant Shipping Act 1995 Sch 3A para 9 (as added: see note 1).

1132. Failure to comply with requirements imposed in relation to ship and port facility security.

Any person who, without reasonable excuse, fails to comply with a requirement imposed on him[1] to furnish to a duly authorised officer[2] inspecting a ship or a port facility[3] such information as that officer may consider necessary for the purpose for which the inspection is carried out[4], or any person who, in furnishing any information so required makes a statement which he knows to be false in a material particular, or recklessly makes a statement which is false in a material particular[5], commits an offence[6], and is liable, on summary conviction, to a fine[7] or, on conviction on indictment, to a fine or to imprisonment for a term not exceeding two years[8].

A person who:

(1) intentionally obstructs a duly authorised officer acting in the exercise of a power duly conferred[9] upon him[10]; or

(2) falsely pretends to be a duly authorised officer[11],

commits an offence[12]. A person guilty of an offence under head (1) above is liable, on summary conviction, to a fine or, on conviction on indictment, to a fine or to imprisonment for a term not exceeding two years[13]. A person guilty of an offence under head (2) above is liable, on summary conviction, to a fine[14].

A person who, without reasonable excuse, fails to comply with a requirement of a detention notice[15], served in respect of a ship pursuant to control and compliance measures[16], commits an offence[17], and is liable, on summary conviction, to a fine or, on conviction on indictment, to a fine or to imprisonment for a term not exceeding two years[18].

Any person who, without reasonable excuse, fails to comply with an enforcement notice[19] served on him is guilty of an offence[20]; and is liable, on summary conviction, to a fine or, on conviction on indictment, to a fine[21].

1   Ie under the Ship and Port Facility (Security) Regulations 2004, SI 2004/1495, reg 6(2)(d) (as to which see PARA 685): see reg 6(5)(a).
2   As to the meaning of 'duly authorised officer' for these purposes see PARA 685 note 1.
3   Ie under the Ship and Port Facility (Security) Regulations 2004, SI 2004/1495, reg 7 (as to which see PARA 685).
4   Ship and Port Facility (Security) Regulations 2004, SI 2004/1495, reg 6(5)(a).
5   Ship and Port Facility (Security) Regulations 2004, SI 2004/1495, reg 6(5)(b).
6   Ship and Port Facility (Security) Regulations 2004, SI 2004/1495, reg 6(5).
7   As to the powers of magistrates' courts to issue fines on summary conviction see SENTENCING vol 92 (2015) PARA 176.
8   Ship and Port Facility (Security) Regulations 2004, SI 2004/1495, reg 6(6) (amended by SI 2005/1434).
9   Ie a power conferred by Parliament and Council Regulation (EC) 725/2004 (OJ L129, 29.04.2004, p 6) on enhancing ship and port facility security (as to which see PARA 684) or by the Ship and Port Facility (Security) Regulations 2004, SI 2004/1495 (as to which see PARA 684 et seq): see reg 12(1)(a).
10 Ship and Port Facility (Security) Regulations 2004, SI 2004/1495, reg 12(1)(a).
11 Ship and Port Facility (Security) Regulations 2004, SI 2004/1495, reg 12(1)(b).
12 Ship and Port Facility (Security) Regulations 2004, SI 2004/1495, reg 12(1).
13 Ship and Port Facility (Security) Regulations 2004, SI 2004/1495, reg 12(2) (amended by SI 2005/1434).
14 Ship and Port Facility (Security) Regulations 2004, SI 2004/1495, reg 12(3).
15 As to the meaning of 'detention notice' see PARA 688.
16 Ie pursuant to the control and compliance measures specified in the SOLAS Convention Ch XI-2 reg 9: see the Ship and Port Facility (Security) Regulations 2004, SI 2004/1495, reg 8(1); and PARA 688. As to the meaning of 'SOLAS Convention' see PARA 684 note 5.
17 Ship and Port Facility (Security) Regulations 2004, SI 2004/1495, reg 8(8).
18 Ship and Port Facility (Security) Regulations 2004, SI 2004/1495, reg 8(9) (amended by SI 2005/1434).
19 As to the meaning of 'enforcement notice' see PARA 689.
20 Ship and Port Facility (Security) Regulations 2004, SI 2004/1495, reg 15(1) (amended by SI 2005/1434).
21 Ship and Port Facility (Security) Regulations 2004, SI 2004/1495, reg 15(1) (as amended: see note 20). Where a person is convicted of an offence under reg 15(1) and if without reasonable excuse the failure in respect of which he was convicted is continued after the conviction, he is guilty of a further offence and liable, on summary conviction, to a fine not exceeding £100 for each day on which the failure continues: reg 15(2).

1133. Penalties for unauthorised presence in restricted areas of ship or port facility. A person must not:

(1)   go onto or into any part of a restricted area[1] of a ship except with the permission of the master[2] or the ship security officer[3] or a person acting on their behalf, and in accordance with any conditions subject to which that permission is for the time being granted[4]; or

(2)   remain in any part of such a restricted area after being requested to leave by the master or the ship security officer or a person acting on their behalf[5].

A person who contravenes either prohibition set out in heads (1) and (2) above without lawful authority or reasonable excuse is guilty of an offence and liable, on summary conviction, to a fine[6]. However, a person who contravenes head (1) above is not guilty of an offence unless it is proved that, at the material time, notices stating that the area concerned was a restricted area were posted so as to be readily seen and read by persons entering the area[7].

A constable[8] or the master or the ship security officer (or a person acting on behalf of the master or the ship security officer) may use such force as is reasonable in the circumstances to remove from a restricted area a person remaining in it in contravention of head (2) above[9].

A person must not:

(a)   go onto or into any part of a restricted area of a port facility except with the permission of the port facility security officer[10] or a person acting on his behalf, and in accordance with any conditions subject to which that permission is for the time being granted[11]; or

(b)   remain in any part of such a restricted area after being requested to leave by the port facility security officer or a person acting on his behalf[12].

A person who contravenes either prohibition set out in heads (a) and (b) above without lawful authority or reasonable excuse is guilty of an offence and liable, on summary conviction, to a fine[13]. However, a person who contravenes head (1) above is not guilty of an offence unless it is proved that, at the material time, notices stating that the area concerned was a restricted area were posted so as to be readily seen and read by persons entering the area[14].

A constable or the port facility security officer (or a person acting on behalf of the port facility security officer) may use such force as is reasonable in the circumstances to remove from a restricted area a person remaining in it in contravention of head (b) above[15].

1   For these purposes, 'restricted area' means an area in a ship or a port facility that is identified as such in a ship security plan or port facility security plan: Ship and Port Facility (Security) Regulations 2004, SI 2004/1495, reg 2(1). As to the regulations see PARA 684. As to the port facility security plan see PARA 685 note 2. As to the purpose of the Ship and Port Facility (Security) Regulations 2004, SI 2004/1495, see PARA 684.
2   As to the meaning of 'master' see PARA 685 note 2.
3   As to the meaning of 'ship security officer' see PARA 685 note 2.
4   Ship and Port Facility (Security) Regulations 2004, SI 2004/1495, reg 10(1)(a).
5   Ship and Port Facility (Security) Regulations 2004, SI 2004/1495, reg 10(1)(b).
6   Ship and Port Facility (Security) Regulations 2004, SI 2004/1495, reg 10(3) (amended by SI 2005/1434). As to the powers of magistrates' courts to issue fines on summary conviction see SENTENCING vol 92 (2015) PARA 176.
7   Ship and Port Facility (Security) Regulations 2004, SI 2004/1495, reg 10(3A) (added by SI 2005/1434).
8   For these purposes, 'constable' includes any person having the powers and privileges of a constable: Ship and Port Facility (Security) Regulations 2004, SI 2004/1495, reg 2(1).
9   Ship and Port Facility (Security) Regulations 2004, SI 2004/1495, reg 10(4).
10 As to the meaning of 'port facility security officer' see PARA 685 note 2.
11 Ship and Port Facility (Security) Regulations 2004, SI 2004/1495, reg 11(1)(a).
12 Ship and Port Facility (Security) Regulations 2004, SI 2004/1495, reg 11(1)(b).
13 Ship and Port Facility (Security) Regulations 2004, SI 2004/1495, reg 11(3) (amended by SI 2005/1434).
14 Ship and Port Facility (Security) Regulations 2004, SI 2004/1495, reg 11(3A) (added by SI 2005/1434).
15 Ship and Port Facility (Security) Regulations 2004, SI 2004/1495, reg 11(4).

1134. Contravention of provisions governing distress signals and prevention of collisions.

Where any of the provisions governing distress signals and the prevention of collisions[1] is contravened, the owner of the vessel, the master and any person for the time being responsible for the conduct of the vessel are each guilty of an offence[2] and liable, on conviction on indictment, to imprisonment for a term not exceeding two years and a fine, or on summary conviction by a fine[3]. It is a defence for any person so charged[4] to show that he took all reasonable precautions to avoid the commission of the offence[5].

In any case where a ship does not comply with the requirements of the provisions governing distress signals and the prevention of collisions[6], the ship[7] is liable to be detained[8].

1 Ie any of the Merchant Shipping (Distress Signals and Prevention of Collisions) Regulations 1996, SI 1996/75 (as to which see PARA 690 et seq): see reg 6(1) (amended by SI 2015/664).
2 Merchant Shipping (Distress Signals and Prevention of Collisions) Regulations 1996, SI 1996/75, reg 6(1) (as amended: see note 1).
3 Merchant Shipping (Distress Signals and Prevention of Collisions) Regulations 1996, SI 1996/75, reg 6(1) (as amended: see note 1). As to the powers of magistrates' courts to issue fines on summary conviction see SENTENCING vol 92 (2015) PARA 176.
4 Ie charged under the Merchant Shipping (Distress Signals and Prevention of Collisions) Regulations 1996, SI 1996/75: see reg 6(2).
5 Merchant Shipping (Distress Signals and Prevention of Collisions) Regulations 1996, SI 1996/75, reg 6(2).
6 Ie does not comply with the requirements of the Merchant Shipping (Distress Signals and Prevention of Collisions) Regulations 1996, SI 1996/75 (as to which see PARA 690 et seq): see reg 7.
7 As to the meaning of 'ships' see PARA 690 note 3.
8 Merchant Shipping (Distress Signals and Prevention of Collisions) Regulations 1996, SI 1996/75, reg 7. The Merchant Shipping Act 1995 s 284 (which relates to enforcing the detention of a ship) (see PARA 1190) has effect in relation to the ship, subject to modifications: see the Merchant Shipping (Distress Signals and Prevention of Collisions) Regulations 1996, SI 1996/75, reg 7.

1135. Master's failure to comply with his duties to assist ships etc in distress or persons in danger. If the master[1] of a ship[2] fails without reasonable excuse to comply with the duty imposed on him[3] to assist the other ship in a case of collision, he is liable[4]:

(1)   in the case of a failure to render to the other ship, its master, crew and passengers, if any, such assistance as may be practicable and necessary to save them from any danger caused by the collision, or to stay by the other ship until he has ascertained that it has no need of further assistance[5], on conviction on indictment, to imprisonment for a term not exceeding two years or a fine (or to both) or, on summary conviction, to imprisonment for a term not exceeding six months or a fine (or to both)[6];

(2)   in the case of a failure to give to the master of the other ship the name of his own ship and also the names of the ports[7] from which it comes and to which it is bound[8], on conviction on indictment or summary conviction, to a fine[9].

In either case mentioned in heads (1) and (2) above, if the master of the ship is a certified officer, an inquiry into his conduct may be held[10] and his certificate cancelled or suspended[11].

If the master of a ship fails to comply with the duty imposed on him[12] to assist an aircraft in distress, he is liable, on conviction on indictment, to imprisonment for a term not exceeding two years or a fine (or to both) or, on summary conviction, to imprisonment for a term not exceeding six months or a fine (or to both)[13].

The master of a vessel[14] who fails to comply with the duty imposed on him under the Salvage Convention[15] to render assistance to any person in danger of being lost at sea[16] commits an offence[17] and is liable, on conviction on indictment, to imprisonment for a term not exceeding two years or a fine, or to both[18], or, on summary conviction, to imprisonment for a term not exceeding six months or a fine, or to both[19].

1 As to the meaning of 'master' see PARA 444 note 1.
2 As to the meaning of 'ship' see PARA 229.

3 Ie by the provisions of the Merchant Shipping Act 1995 s 92 (see PARA 727): see s 92(4) (amended by SI 2015/664). As to the application of the Merchant Shipping Act 1995 s 92 see PARA 727 note 2.
4 Merchant Shipping Act 1995 s 92(4) (as amended: see note 3).
5 Ie in the case of failure to comply with the Merchant Shipping Act 1995 s 92(1)(a) (see PARA 727): see s 92(4)(a) (as amended: see note 3).
6 Merchant Shipping Act 1995 s 92(4)(a) (as amended: see note 3). As to the time limit for summary offences see PARA 1049; as to offences by officers of bodies corporate see PARA 1051; as to jurisdiction in relation to offences see PARA 1052; as to jurisdiction over ships lying off the coast see PARA 1053; as to jurisdiction in the case of offences on board ship see PARA 1054; as to offences committed by British seamen see PARA 1055; and as to proof etc of exemption see PARA 1061. As to the powers of magistrates' courts to issue fines on summary conviction see SENTENCING vol 92 (2015) PARA 176.
7 As to the meaning of 'port' see PARA 46 note 12.
8 Ie in the case of failure to comply with the Merchant Shipping Act 1995 s 92(1)(b) (see PARA 727): see s 92(4)(b).
9 Merchant Shipping Act 1995 s 92(4)(b).
10 As to inquiries into the conduct of an officer see PARA 524 et seq.
11 Merchant Shipping Act 1995 s 92(4).
12 Ie by the provisions of the Merchant Shipping Act 1995 s 93(1)–(5) (see PARA 448): see s 93(6). As to the application of the Merchant Shipping Act 1995 s 93 see PARA 448 note 1.
13 Merchant Shipping Act 1995 s 93(6).
14 As to the meaning of 'vessel' under the Convention see PARA 893 note 3.
15 Ie the International Convention on Salvage 1989 (London, 28 April 1989; Cm 1526): see PARA 851.
16 Ie the duty imposed on him by the International Convention on Salvage 1989 art 10(1) (see PARA 858): see the Merchant Shipping Act 1995 Sch 11 Pt II para 3(1).
17 Merchant Shipping Act 1995 Sch 11 Pt II para 3(1).
18 Merchant Shipping Act 1995 Sch 11 Pt II para 3(1)(b).
19 Merchant Shipping Act 1995 Sch 11 Pt II para 3(1)(a).

1136. Offences in connection with passenger ships.

A person commits an offence if, in relation to a ship[1] for which there is in force a Passenger Ship Safety Certificate or Passenger Certificate, as the case may be, issued under or recognised by safety regulations[2], he does any of the following things[3], that is to say:

(1)   if, being drunk or disorderly, he has been on that account refused admission to the ship by the owner or any person in his employment, and, after having the amount of his fare, if he has paid it, returned or tendered to him, nevertheless persists in attempting to enter the ship[4];

(2)   if, being drunk or disorderly on board the ship, he is requested by the owner or any person in his employment to leave the ship at any place in the United Kingdom[5] at which he can conveniently do so, and, after having the amount of his fare, if he has paid it, returned or tendered to him, does not comply with the request[6];

(3)   if, on board the ship, after warning by the master[7] or other officer thereof, he molests or continues to molest any passenger[8];

(4)   if, after having been refused admission to the ship by the owner or any person in his employment on account of the ship being full, and having had the amount of his fare, if he has paid it, returned or tendered to him, he nevertheless persists in attempting to enter the ship[9];

(5)   if, having gone on board the ship at any place, and being requested, on account of the ship being full, by the owner or any person in his employment to leave the ship before it has left that place, and having had the amount of his fare, if he has paid it, returned or tendered to him, he does not comply with that request[10];

(6)   if, on arriving in the ship at a point to which he has paid his fare, he knowingly and intentionally refuses or neglects to leave the ship[11]; and

(7)   if, on board the ship he fails, when requested by the master or other officer thereof, either to pay his fare or show such ticket or other receipt, if any, showing the payment of his fare, as is usually given to persons travelling by and paying their fare for the ship[12];

but his liability in respect of any such offence does not prejudice the recovery of any fare payable by him[13].

A person commits an offence if, on board any ship for which there is in force a Passenger Ship Safety Certificate or Passenger Certificate, as the case may be, issued under or recognised by safety regulations, he intentionally does or causes to be done anything in such a manner as to[14]:

(a)   obstruct or damage any part of the machinery or equipment of the ship[15]; or

(b)   obstruct, impede or molest the crew, or any of them, in the navigation or management of the ship, or otherwise in the execution of their duty on or about the ship[16].

The master or other officer of any ship for which there is in force a Passenger Ship Safety Certificate or Passenger Certificate, as the case may be, issued under or recognised by safety regulations, and all persons called by him to his assistance, may, without any warrant, detain any person who commits any such offence[17] and whose name and address are unknown to the master or officer, and deliver that person to a constable[18].

A person guilty of any such offence[19] is liable, on summary conviction, to a fine[20]; and if any person commits any such offence[21] and, on the application of the master of the ship, or any other person in the employment of the owner thereof, refuses to give his name and address, or gives a false name or address, that person is liable, on summary conviction, to a fine[22].

1   As to the meaning of 'ship' see PARA 229.
2   As to the meaning of 'safety regulations' see PARA 602 note 1.
3   See the Merchant Shipping Act 1995 s 101(1), (6).
4   Merchant Shipping Act 1995 s 101(1)(a).
5   As to the meaning of 'United Kingdom' see PARA 16 note 3.
6   Merchant Shipping Act 1995 s 101(1)(b).
7   As to the meaning of 'master' see PARA 444 note 1.
8   Merchant Shipping Act 1995 s 101(1)(c).
9   Merchant Shipping Act 1995 s 101(1)(d).
10   Merchant Shipping Act 1995 s 101(1)(e).
11   Merchant Shipping Act 1995 s 101(1)(f).
12   Merchant Shipping Act 1995 s 101(1)(g).
13   Merchant Shipping Act 1995 s 101(1).
14   Merchant Shipping Act 1995 s 101(2), (6).
15   Merchant Shipping Act 1995 s 101(2)(a).
16   Merchant Shipping Act 1995 s 101(2)(b).
17   Ie under the Merchant Shipping Act 1995 s 101(1), (2) (see the text and notes 1–16): see s 101(3), (6).
18   Merchant Shipping Act 1995 s 101(3), (6).
19   Ie under the Merchant Shipping Act 1995 s 101(1), (2) (see the text and notes 1–16): see s 101(4).
20   Merchant Shipping Act 1995 s 101(4). As to the time limit for summary offences see PARA 1049; as to offences by officers of bodies corporate see PARA 1051; as to jurisdiction in relation to offences see PARA 1052; as to jurisdiction over ships lying off the coast see PARA 1053; as to jurisdiction in the case of offences on board ship see PARA 1054; as to offences committed by British seamen see PARA 1055; and as to proof etc of exemption see PARA 1061. As to the powers of magistrates' courts to issue fines on summary conviction see SENTENCING vol 92 (2015) PARA 176.
21   Ie under the Merchant Shipping Act 1995 s 101(1), (2) (see the text and notes 1–16): see s 101(5).
22   Merchant Shipping Act 1995 s 101(5).

1137. Stowaways. If a person, without the consent of the master[1] or of any other person authorised to give it, goes to sea or attempts to go to sea in a United Kingdom ship[2], he is liable, on summary conviction, to a fine[3].

Nothing in the provisions relating to jurisdiction in cases of offences on board ship[4] is to be taken to limit the jurisdiction of any court in the United Kingdom to deal with such an offence[5] which has been committed in a country outside the United Kingdom by a person who is not a British citizen[6].

1   As to the meaning of 'master' see PARA 444 note 1.
2   As to the meaning of 'United Kingdom ship' see PARA 230; as to the meaning of 'ship' see PARA 229; and as to the meaning of 'United Kingdom' see PARA 16 note 3.
3   Merchant Shipping Act 1995 s 103(1). As to the time limit for summary offences see PARA 1049; as to offences by officers of bodies corporate see PARA 1051; as to jurisdiction in relation to offences see PARA 1052; as to jurisdiction over ships lying off the coast see PARA 1053; as to jurisdiction in the case of offences on board ship see PARA 1054; as to offences committed by British seamen see PARA 1055; and as to proof etc of exemption see PARA 1061. As to the powers of magistrates' courts to issue fines on summary conviction see SENTENCING vol 92 (2015) PARA 176.
4   Ie nothing in the Merchant Shipping Act 1995 s 281 (see PARA 1054): see s 103(2).
5   Ie under the Merchant Shipping Act 1995 s 103 (see the text and notes 1–3): see s 103(2).
6   Merchant Shipping Act 1995 s 103(2). As to the meaning of 'British citizen' see PARA 18 note 7.

1138. Unauthorised presence on board ship. Where a United Kingdom ship[1] or a ship registered in any other country is in a port[2] in the United Kingdom and a person who is neither in Her Majesty's service nor authorised by law to do so[3]:

(1)   goes on board the ship without the consent of the master[4] or of any other persons authorised to give it[5]; or

(2)   remains on board the ship after being requested to leave by the master, a constable, an officer authorised by the Secretary of State[6] or an officer of Revenue and Customs[7],

he is liable, on summary conviction, to a fine[8].

1   As to the meaning of 'United Kingdom ship' see PARA 230; as to the meaning of 'ship' see PARA 229; and as to the meaning of 'United Kingdom' see PARA 16 note 3.
2   As to the meaning of 'port' see PARA 46 note 12.
3   Merchant Shipping Act 1995 s 104.
4   As to the meaning of 'master' see PARA 444 note 1.
5   Merchant Shipping Act 1995 s 104(a).
6   As to the Secretary of State see PARA 36.
7   Merchant Shipping Act 1995 s 104(b) (amended by virtue of the Commissioners for Revenue and Customs Act 2005 s 50(1), (2), (7)). As to the appointment of officers of Revenue and Customs see INCOME TAXATION vol 58 (2014) PARA 33.
8   Merchant Shipping Act 1995 s 104. As to the time limit for summary offences see PARA 1049; as to offences by officers of bodies corporate see PARA 1051; as to jurisdiction in relation to offences see PARA 1052; as to jurisdiction over ships lying off the coast see PARA 1053; as to jurisdiction in the case of offences on board ship see PARA 1054; as to offences committed by British seamen see PARA 1055; and as to proof etc of exemption see PARA 1061. As to the powers of magistrates' courts to issue fines on summary conviction see SENTENCING vol 92 (2015) PARA 176.

1139. Unauthorised persons; offences relating to safety. Where a person goes to sea in a ship[1] without the consent of the master[2] or of any other person authorised to give it or is conveyed in a ship[3], the statutory provisions which govern offences relating to conduct endangering ships, structures or individuals[4] and which govern offences relating to concerted disobedience and neglect of duty[5] apply as if he were a seaman[6] employed in the ship[7].

1   As to the meaning of 'ship' see PARA 229. The Merchant Shipping Act 1995 s 106 does not apply to fishing vessels: s 106(3). As to the meaning of 'fishing vessel' see PARA 230 note 9. The act of going to sea involves a material alteration of position or location, by the act of moving or travelling or proceeding in a ship from one place to another, the other place being the sea: *R v Ayliffe* [2006] 1 Lloyd's Rep 86 (a person who joins a ship which is already at sea does not 'go to sea in a ship' within the meaning of the Merchant Shipping Act 1995 s 106).

2 As to the meaning of 'master' see PARA 444 note 1.
3 Ie in pursuance of the Merchant Shipping Act 1995 s 73(5)(b) (see PARA 548): see s 106(1).
4 Ie the Merchant Shipping Act 1995 s 58 (see PARA 1102): see s 106(1). See note 7.
5 Ie the Merchant Shipping Act 1995 s 59 (see PARA 1103): see s 106(1).
6 As to the meaning of 'seaman' see PARA 457 note 5.
7 Merchant Shipping Act 1995 s 106(1). However, s 106(1) has effect, in its application to s 58 (see note 4) so far as s 58 applies to ships which are not sea-going ships, with the omission of the words 'goes to sea in a ship' and with the insertion, after the words 'to give it', of the words 'is on board a ship while it is on a voyage or excursion': s 106(2). See note 1.

B. OFFENCES RELATING TO USE OF UNSAFE SHIPS ETC

1140. Meaning of 'dangerously unsafe ship'. A ship[1] in port[2] is[3] 'dangerously unsafe' if, having regard to the nature of the service for which it is intended, the ship is, by reason of the following matters[4], namely:

(1)   the condition, or the unsuitability for its purposes, of the ship or its machinery or equipment or any part of the ship or its machinery or equipment[5];
(2)   undermanning[6];
(3)   overloading or unsafe or improper loading[7];
(4)   any other matter relevant to the safety of the ship[8],

unfit to go to sea[9] without serious danger to human life[10].

A ship at sea is[11] 'dangerously unsafe' if, having regard to the nature of the service for which it is being used or is intended, the ship is, by reason of the matters mentioned in heads (1) to (4) above, either[12]:

(a)   unfit to remain at sea without serious danger to human life[13]; or
(b)   unfit to go on a voyage without serious danger to human life[14].

The matters referred to in heads (1) to (4) above are referred to, in relation to any ship, as 'the matters relevant to its safety'[15].

1 As to the meaning of 'ship' see PARA 229.
2 As to the meaning of 'port' see PARA 46 note 12.
3 Ie for the purposes of the Merchant Shipping Act 1995 s 95 (see PARA 1141), s 96 (see PARA 1142), s 97 (see PARA 1143) and s 98 (see PARA 1144): see s 94(1) (amended by the Merchant Shipping and Maritime Security Act 1997 Sch 1 para 1(1), (2)). See *Club Cruise Entertainment and Travelling Services Europe BV v Department for Transport, The Van Gogh* [2008] EWHC 2794 (Comm), [2009] 1 All ER (Comm) 955.
4 See the Merchant Shipping Act 1995 s 94(1) (as amended: see note 3).
5 Merchant Shipping Act 1995 s 94(2)(a).
6 Merchant Shipping Act 1995 s 94(2)(b). As to manning see PARA 502 et seq.
7 Merchant Shipping Act 1995 s 94(2)(c).
8 Merchant Shipping Act 1995 s 94(2)(d).
9 Any reference in the Merchant Shipping Act 1995 ss 95–98 (see also PARAS 1141–1144) to 'going to sea' is to be construed, in a case where the service for which the ship is intended consists of going on voyages or excursions that do not involve going to sea, as a reference to going on such a voyage or excursion: see s 94(3).
10 Merchant Shipping Act 1995 s 94(1) (as amended: see note 3).
11 Ie for the purposes of the Merchant Shipping Act 1995 s 95 (see PARA 1141), s 96 (see PARA 1142), s 97 (see PARA 1143) and s 98 (see PARA 1144): see s 94(1A) (added by the Merchant Shipping and Maritime Security Act 1997 Sch 1 para 1(1), (3)).
12 Merchant Shipping Act 1995 s 94(1A) (as added: see note 11).
13 Merchant Shipping Act 1995 s 94(1A)(a) (as added: see note 11).
14 Merchant Shipping Act 1995 s 94(1A)(b) (as added: see note 11).
15 Merchant Shipping Act 1995 s 94(2).

1141. Power to detain dangerously unsafe ship. Where a ship[1] which is:

(1)   in a port[2] in the United Kingdom[3]; or
(2)   at sea in United Kingdom waters[4],

appears to a relevant inspector[5] to be a dangerously unsafe ship[6], the ship may be detained[7]. The power of detention so conferred[8] is exercisable in relation to foreign ships[9] as well as United Kingdom ships[10], although the power of detention conferred by head (2) above is not exercisable in relation to a qualifying foreign ship[11] while the ship is exercising either the right of innocent passage[12], or the right of transit passage through straits used for international navigation[13].

The officer detaining the ship must serve on the master[14] of the ship a detention notice[15] which must:

(a)   state that the relevant inspector is of the opinion that the ship is a dangerously unsafe ship[16];

(b)   specify the matters which, in the relevant inspector's opinion, make the ship a dangerously unsafe ship[17]; and

(c)   require the ship to comply with the terms of the notice until it is released by a competent authority[18].

In the case of a ship which is not a British ship[19], the officer detaining the ship must cause a copy of the detention notice to be sent as soon as practicable to the nearest consular officer for the country to which the ship belongs[20].

1   As to the meaning of 'ship' see PARA 229.
2   As to the meaning of 'port' see PARA 46 note 12.
3   Merchant Shipping Act 1995 s 95(1)(a) (s 95(1) substituted by the Merchant Shipping and Maritime Security Act 1997 s 9, Sch 1 para 2(1), (2)). As to the meaning of 'United Kingdom' see PARA 16 note 3.
4   Merchant Shipping Act 1995 s 95(1)(b) (as substituted: see note 3). As to the meaning of 'United Kingdom waters' see PARA 48 note 11.
5   For these purposes, 'relevant inspector' means any person mentioned in the Merchant Shipping Act 1995 s 258(1)(a), (b) or (c) (see PARA 48): see s 95(5).
6   As to the meaning of 'dangerously unsafe ship' see PARA 1140.
7   Merchant Shipping Act 1995 s 95(1) (as substituted: see note 3). As to the detention of ships see PARA 1190.
8   Ie by the Merchant Shipping Act 1995 s 95(1) (see the text and notes 1–7): see s 95(2).
9   As to the meaning of 'foreign', in relation to a ship, see PARA 18 note 2.
10   Merchant Shipping Act 1995 s 95(2) (amended by the Merchant Shipping and Maritime Security Act 1997 Sch 1 para 2(1), (3)). As to the meaning of 'United Kingdom ship' see PARA 230.
11   As to the meaning of 'qualifying foreign ship' see PARA 18.
12   As to the meaning of 'right of innocent passage' see PARA 69 note 10. As to innocent passage generally see INTERNATIONAL RELATIONS LAW vol 61 (2010) PARA 133.
13   Merchant Shipping Act 1995 s 95(2A) (added by the Merchant Shipping and Maritime Security Act 1997 Sch 1 para 2(1), (3)). As to the meaning of 'right of transit passage' see PARA 69 note 11; and as to the meaning of 'straits used for international passage' see PARA 69 note 12. As to transit passage generally see INTERNATIONAL RELATIONS LAW vol 61 (2010) PARA 143.
14   As to the meaning of 'master' see PARA 444 note 1.
15   See the Merchant Shipping Act 1995 s 95(3). As to the service of documents under the Merchant Shipping Act 1995 see PARA 74.
16   Merchant Shipping Act 1995 s 95(3)(a).
17   Merchant Shipping Act 1995 s 95(3)(b).
18   Merchant Shipping Act 1995 s 95(3)(c) (amended by the Merchant Shipping and Maritime Security Act 1997 Sch 1 para 2(1), (4)). For these purposes, 'competent authority' means any officer mentioned in the Merchant Shipping Act 1995 s 284(1) (see PARA 1190): s 95(5).
19   As to the meaning of 'British ship' see PARA 230.
20   Merchant Shipping Act 1995 s 95(4). As to the meaning of 'consular officer' for these purposes see PARA 48 note 12.

1142. References of detention notices to arbitration.

Any question as to whether any of the matters specified in relation to a ship[1] in a detention notice[2] in connection with any opinion formed by the relevant inspector[3] constituted a valid basis for that opinion must be referred, if the master[4] or owner of the ship so requires by a notice given to the relevant inspector within 21 days from the service of the detention notice, to a single arbitrator appointed by agreement between the parties for that question to be decided by him[5].

A person is not qualified for appointment as an arbitrator for these purposes[6] unless he is[7]:

(1)   a person holding a certificate of competency as a master mariner or as a marine engineer officer class 1, or a person holding a certificate equivalent to any such certificate[8];

(2)   a naval architect[9];

(3)   a person who satisfies the judicial-appointment eligibility condition on a seven-year basis[10]; or

(4)   a person with special experience of shipping matters, of the fishing industry, or of activities carried on in ports[11].

Where a notice is so given by the master or owner of the ship[12], the giving of the notice does not suspend the operation of the detention notice unless, on the application of the person requiring the reference, the arbitrator so directs[13].

The arbitrator must have regard, in coming to his decision, to any other matters not specified in the detention notice which appear to him to be relevant to whether the ship was or was not a dangerously unsafe ship[14].

Where on such a reference[15] the arbitrator decides, as respects any matter to which the reference relates, that in all the circumstances the matter did not constitute a valid basis for the inspector's opinion, he must either cancel the detention notice or affirm it with such modifications as he may in the circumstances think fit; and in any other case the arbitrator must affirm the notice in its original form[16].

The arbitrator must include in his decision a finding whether there was or was not a valid basis for the detention of the ship as a dangerously unsafe ship[17].

1   As to the meaning of 'ship' see PARA 229.
2   Ie in pursuance of the Merchant Shipping Act 1995 s 95(3)(b) (see PARA 1141): see s 96(1).
3   For these purposes, 'relevant inspector' has the same meaning as in the Merchant Shipping Act 1995 s 95 (see PARA 1141 note 5): s 96(11).
4   As to the meaning of 'master' see PARA 444 note 1.
5   Merchant Shipping Act 1995 s 96(1). In connection with his functions under s 96, an arbitrator has the powers conferred on an inspector by s 259 (see PARA 49): s 96(8). The provisions of the Arbitration Act 1996 Pt I (ss 1–84) apply to every arbitration under an enactment (a 'statutory arbitration') (see s 94), subject to certain adaptions and exclusions (see ss 95–98); and see ARBITRATION vol 2 (2017) PARA 509 et seq. See *Club Cruise Entertainment and Travelling Services Europe BV v Department for Transport, The Van Gogh* [2008] EWHC 2794 (Comm), [2009] 1 All ER (Comm) 955.
6   Ie under the Merchant Shipping Act 1995 s 96: see s 96(6).
7   Merchant Shipping Act 1995 s 96(6).
8   Merchant Shipping Act 1995 s 96(6)(a).
9   Merchant Shipping Act 1995 s 96(6)(b).
10 Merchant Shipping Act 1995 s 96(6)(c), (7)(a) (s 96(7)(a) substituted by the Tribunals, Courts and Enforcement Act 2007 s 50, Sch 10 Pt 1 para 26(1), (2)).
11 Merchant Shipping Act 1995 s 96(6)(d). As to the meaning of 'port' see PARA 46 note 12.
12 Ie in accordance with the Merchant Shipping Act 1995 s 96(1) (see the text and notes 1–5): see s 96(2).
13 Merchant Shipping Act 1995 s 96(2).
14 Merchant Shipping Act 1995 s 96(3). As to the meaning of 'dangerously unsafe ship' see PARA 1140.
15 Ie under the Merchant Shipping Act 1995 s 96: see s 96(4).
16 Merchant Shipping Act 1995 s 96(4).
17 Merchant Shipping Act 1995 s 96(5).

1143. Compensation in connection with invalid detention of ship. If, on a reference[1] relating to a detention notice in relation to a ship[2]:

(1)   the arbitrator decides that any matter did not constitute a valid basis for the relevant inspector's[3] opinion[4]; and

(2)   it appears to him that there were no reasonable grounds for the inspector to form that opinion[5],

the arbitrator may award the owner of the ship such compensation in respect of any loss suffered by him in consequence of the detention of the ship as the arbitrator thinks fit[6].

Any compensation so awarded[7] is payable by the Secretary of State[8].

1 Ie under the Merchant Shipping Act 1995 s 96 (see PARA 1142): see s 97(1).
2 Merchant Shipping Act 1995 s 97(1). As to the meaning of 'ship' see PARA 229.
3 For these purposes, 'relevant inspector' has the same meaning as in the Merchant Shipping Act 1995 s 95 (see PARA 1141 note 5): s 97(4).
4 Merchant Shipping Act 1995 s 97(1)(a).
5 Merchant Shipping Act 1995 s 97(1)(b).
6 Merchant Shipping Act 1995 s 97(1).See *Club Cruise Entertainment and Travelling Services Europe BV v Department for Transport, The Van Gogh* [2008] EWHC 2794 (Comm), [2009] 1 All ER (Comm) 955 (arbitrator may award compensation even though no cause of action against Maritime and Coastguard Agency at common law).
7 Ie under the Merchant Shipping Act 1995 s 97: see s 97(2).
8 Merchant Shipping Act 1995 s 97(2). As to the Secretary of State see PARA 36.

1144. Owner and master liable in respect of dangerously unsafe ship. If a ship[1] which is in a port[2] in the United Kingdom[3], or which is a United Kingdom ship[4] and is in any other port, is dangerously unsafe[5], the master[6] and the owner of the ship are each guilty of an offence[7]. However, where, at the time when a ship is dangerously unsafe, any responsibilities of the owner with respect to the matters relevant to its safety[8] have been assumed, whether wholly or in part, by any person or persons other than the owner, and have been so assumed by that person or, as the case may be, by each of those persons either directly, under the terms of a charterparty or management agreement made with the owner[9], or indirectly, under the terms of a series of charterparties or management agreements, the reference to the owner for these purposes[10] is to be construed as a reference to that other person or, as the case may be, to each of those other persons[11].

A person guilty of such an offence[12] is liable, on conviction on indictment, to imprisonment for a term not exceeding two years or a fine (or to both) or, on summary conviction, to a fine[13].

It is, however, a defence in proceedings for such an offence[14] to prove that at the time of the alleged offence[15]:

(1)   arrangements had been made which were appropriate to ensure that, before the ship went to sea[16], it was made fit to do so without serious danger to human life by reason of the matters relevant to its safety which are specified in the charge[17]; or

(2)   it was reasonable for such arrangements not to have been made[18].

It is also a defence in proceedings for such an offence to prove:

(a)   that, under the terms of one or more charterparties or management agreements entered into by the accused, the relevant responsibilities, namely (where the accused is the owner) his responsibilities with respect to the matters relevant to the ship's safety, or (where any of the accused's responsibilities have been assumed by any person or persons other than the owner[19]) so much of those responsibilities as had been assumed by him[20], had at the time of the alleged offence been wholly assumed by some other person or persons party thereto[21]; and

(b)   that in all the circumstances of the case the accused had taken such steps as it was reasonable for him to take, and exercised such diligence as it was reasonable for him to exercise, to secure the proper discharge of the relevant responsibilities during the period during which they had been assumed by some other person or persons as mentioned in head (a) above[22].

In determining whether the accused had done so, regard is to be had in particular to the following matters[23], namely:

(i)   whether prior to the time of the alleged offence the accused was, or in all the circumstances of the case ought reasonably to have been, aware of any deficiency in the discharge of the relevant responsibilities[24]; and

(ii)   the extent to which the accused was or was not able, under the terms of any such charterparty or management agreement as is mentioned in head (a) above, either to terminate it or to intervene in the management of the ship, in the event of any such deficiency, and whether it was reasonable for the accused to place himself in that position[25].

No proceedings for such an offence[26] may be instituted in England and Wales[27] except by or with the consent of the Secretary of State[28] or the Director of Public Prosecutions[29].

1   As to the meaning of 'ship' see PARA 229.
2   As to the meaning of 'port' see PARA 46 note 12.
3   As to the meaning of 'United Kingdom' see PARA 16 note 3.
4   As to the meaning of 'United Kingdom ship' see PARA 230.
5   As to the meaning of 'dangerously unsafe ship' see PARA 1140.
6   As to the meaning of 'master' see PARA 444 note 1.
7   Merchant Shipping Act 1995 s 98(1). This provision is subject to s 98(4), (5) (see the text and notes 14–23): see s 98(1).
8   As to the meaning of 'the matters relevant to its safety' see PARA 1140.
9   For these purposes, references to responsibilities being assumed by a person under the terms of a charterparty or management agreement are references to their being so assumed by him whether or not he has entered into a further charterparty or management agreement providing for them to be assumed by some other person: Merchant Shipping Act 1995 s 98(9). 'Management agreement', in relation to a ship, means any agreement, other than a charterparty or a contract of employment, under which the ship is managed, either wholly or in part, by a person other than the owner, whether on behalf of the owner or on behalf of some other person: see s 98(8).
10 Ie in the Merchant Shipping Act 1995 s 98(1) (see the text and notes 1–7): see s 98(2).
11 Merchant Shipping Act 1995 s 98(2).
12 Ie under the Merchant Shipping Act 1995 s 98: see s 98(3).
13 Merchant Shipping Act 1995 s 98(3) (amended by SI 2015/664). As to the time limit for summary offences see PARA 1049; as to offences by officers of bodies corporate see PARA 1051; as to jurisdiction in relation to offences see PARA 1052; as to jurisdiction over ships lying off the coast see PARA 1053; as to jurisdiction in the case of offences on board ship see PARA 1054; as to offences committed by British seamen see PARA 1055; and as to proof etc of exemption see PARA 1061. As to the powers of magistrates' courts to issue fines on summary conviction see SENTENCING vol 92 (2015) PARA 176.
14 Ie under the Merchant Shipping Act 1995 s 98: see s 98(4).
15 Merchant Shipping Act 1995 s 98(4).
16 As to the meaning of 'going to sea' for these purposes see PARA 1140 note 9.
17 Merchant Shipping Act 1995 s 98(4)(a).
18 Merchant Shipping Act 1995 s 98(4)(b).
19 Ie where the accused is liable to proceedings under the Merchant Shipping Act 1995 s 98 by virtue of s 98(2) (see the text and notes 8–11): see s 98(5)(a).
20 Ie as mentioned in the Merchant Shipping Act 1995 s 98(2) (see the text and notes 8–11): see s 98(5)(a).
21 Merchant Shipping Act 1995 s 98(5)(a).
22 Merchant Shipping Act 1995 s 98(5)(b).
23 Merchant Shipping Act 1995 s 98(5).
24 Merchant Shipping Act 1995 s 98(6)(a). For these purposes, 'relevant responsibilities' must be construed in accordance with s 98(5) (see head (a) in the text): see s 98(8).
25 Merchant Shipping Act 1995 s 98(6)(b).
26 Ie under the Merchant Shipping Act 1995 s 98: see s 98(7).
27 As to the meanings of 'England' and 'Wales' see PARA 17 note 2.
28 As to the Secretary of State see PARA 38.
29 Merchant Shipping Act 1995 s 98(7). As to the Director of Public Prosecutions see CRIMINAL PROCEDURE vol 27 (2015) PARAS 25, 30 et seq.

1145. Use of unsafe lighters etc. If any person uses or causes or permits to be used in navigation any lighter, barge or like vessel when, because of:

(1)   the defective condition of its hull or equipment[1];

(2)   overloading or improper loading[2]; or

(3)   undermanning[3],

it is so unsafe that human life is thereby endangered, he is liable, on conviction on indictment, to a fine or, on summary conviction, to a fine[4].

Proceedings for such an offence[5] may not be instituted in England and Wales[6] except by or with the consent of the Secretary of State[7].

These provisions[8] do not affect the liability of the owners of any lighter, barge or like vessel in respect of loss of life or personal injury caused to any person carried in the vessel[9].

1   Merchant Shipping Act 1995 s 99(1)(a).
2   Merchant Shipping Act 1995 s 99(1)(b).
3   Merchant Shipping Act 1995 s 99(1)(c).
4   Merchant Shipping Act 1995 s 99(1). As to the time limit for summary offences see PARA 1049; as to offences by officers of bodies corporate see PARA 1051; as to jurisdiction in relation to offences see PARA 1052; as to jurisdiction over ships lying off the coast see PARA 1053; as to jurisdiction in the case of offences on board ship see PARA 1054; as to offences committed by British seamen see PARA 1055; and as to proof etc of exemption see PARA 1061. As to the powers of magistrates' courts to issue fines on summary conviction see SENTENCING vol 92 (2015) PARA 176.
        As to the powers of inspectors appointed under s 256(6) (see PARA 46) to serve improvement notices or prohibition notices where s 99 and the provisions of any instrument of a legislative character having effect thereunder are being contravened, or where activities to which s 99 applies are carried on so as to involve serious personal injury or serious pollution, see PARA 51 et seq.
5   Ie under the Merchant Shipping Act 1995 s 99: see s 99(2).
6   As to the meanings of 'England' and 'Wales' see PARA 16 note 2.
7   Merchant Shipping Act 1995 s 99(2). As to the Secretary of State see PARA 36.
8   Ie the Merchant Shipping Act 1995 s 99: see s 99(3).
9   Merchant Shipping Act 1995 s 99(3).

1146. Owner liable for unsafe operation of ship. It is the duty of the owner of:

(1)   any United Kingdom ship[1]; and

(2)   any ship which is registered under the law of any country outside the United Kingdom and is within United Kingdom waters[2] while proceeding to or from a port[3] in the United Kingdom (unless the ship would not be so proceeding but for weather conditions or any other unavoidable circumstances)[4],

to take all reasonable steps to secure that the ship is operated in a safe manner[5].

If the owner of a ship which falls within head (1) or head (2) above fails to discharge the duty so imposed on him[6], he is liable, on conviction on indictment, to imprisonment for a term not exceeding two years or a fine (or to both) or, on summary conviction, to a fine[7].

However, where any such ship:

(a)   is chartered by demise[8]; or

(b)   is managed, either wholly or in part, by a person other than the owner under the terms of a management agreement[9],

any reference to the owner of the ship for these purposes[10] must be construed as including a reference:

(i)   to the charterer under the charter by demise[11]; or

(ii)   to any such manager as is referred to in head (b) above[12]; or

(iii)   if the ship is both chartered and managed as mentioned above, to both the charterer and any such manager[13], and accordingly the reference[14] to the taking of all reasonable steps is to be construed, in relation to the owner, the charterer or any such manager, as a reference to the taking of all such steps as it is reasonable for him to take in the circumstances of the case[15].

No proceedings for such an offence[16] may be instituted in England and Wales[17] except by or with the consent of the Secretary of State[18] or the Director of Public Prosecutions[19].

1 See the Merchant Shipping Act 1995 s 100(1), (2)(a). As to the meaning of 'ship' see PARA 229; and as to the meaning of 'United Kingdom ship' see PARA 230. As to the meaning of 'United Kingdom' see PARA 16 note 3.
2 As to the meaning of 'United Kingdom waters' see PARA 48 note 11.
3 As to the meaning of 'port' see PARA 46 note 12.
4 See the Merchant Shipping Act 1995 s 100(1), (2)(b).
5 See the Merchant Shipping Act 1995 s 100(1).
6 Ie by the Merchant Shipping Act 1995 s 100(1) (see the text and notes 1–5): see s 100(3).
7 Merchant Shipping Act 1995 s 100(3) (amended by SI 2015/664). As to the time limit for summary offences see PARA 1049; as to offences by officers of bodies corporate see PARA 1051; as to jurisdiction in relation to offences see PARA 1052; as to jurisdiction over ships lying off the coast see PARA 1053; as to jurisdiction in the case of offences on board ship see PARA 1054; as to offences committed by British seamen see PARA 1055; and as to proof etc of exemption see PARA 1061. As to the powers of magistrates' courts to issue fines on summary conviction see SENTENCING vol 92 (2015) PARA 176.
8 Merchant Shipping Act 1995 s 100(4)(a).
9 Merchant Shipping Act 1995 s 100(4)(b). The agreement referred to in head (b) in the text is a management agreement within the meaning of s 98 (see PARA 1144 note 9): see s 100(4)(b).
10 Ie in the Merchant Shipping Act 1995 s 100(1), (3) (see the text and notes 1–7): see s 100(4).
11 Merchant Shipping Act 1995 s 100(4)(i).
12 Merchant Shipping Act 1995 s 100(4)(ii).
13 Merchant Shipping Act 1995 s 100(4)(iii).
14 Ie in the Merchant Shipping Act 1995 s 100(1) (see the text and notes 1–5): see s 100(4).
15 Merchant Shipping Act 1995 s 100(4).
16 Ie under the Merchant Shipping Act 1995 s 100: see s 100(5).
17 As to the meanings of 'England' and 'Wales' see PARA 16 note 2.
18 As to the Secretary of State see PARA 36.
19 Merchant Shipping Act 1995 s 100(5). As to the Director of Public Prosecutions see CRIMINAL PROCEDURE vol 27 (2015) PARAS 25, 30 et seq.

(iv) Offences against Maritime Security

A. SAFETY OF SHIPS AND FIXED PLATFORMS

1147. Hijacking of ships. A person who unlawfully, by the use of force or by threats of any kind, seizes a ship[1] or exercises control of it, commits the offence of hijacking a ship, whatever his nationality and whether the ship is in the United Kingdom[2] or elsewhere[3]. However, this offence[4] does not apply in relation to a warship or any other ship used as a naval auxiliary or in customs or police service unless[5]:

(1) the person seizing or exercising control of the ship is a United Kingdom national[6]; or

(2) his act is committed in the United Kingdom[7]; or

(3) the ship is used in the naval[8] or customs service of the United Kingdom or in the service of any police force in the United Kingdom[9].

A person guilty of the offence of hijacking a ship is liable, on conviction on indictment, to imprisonment for life[10].

1 For these purposes, 'ship' means any vessel (including hovercraft, submersible craft and other floating craft) other than one which permanently rests on, or is permanently attached to, the sea bed and has been withdrawn from navigation or laid up: Aviation and Maritime Security Act 1990 s 17(1).

2   As to the meaning of 'United Kingdom' see PARA 16 note 3. For these purposes, the territorial waters adjacent to any part of the United Kingdom are to be treated as included in that part of the United Kingdom: Aviation and Maritime Security Act 1990 s 17(2).
3   Aviation and Maritime Security Act 1990 s 9(1).
4   Ie the Aviation and Maritime Security Act 1990 s 9(1) (see the text and notes 1–3): see s 9(2).
5   Aviation and Maritime Security Act 1990 s 9(2).
6   Aviation and Maritime Security Act 1990 s 9(2)(a).
    For these purposes, 'United Kingdom national' means an individual who is (1) a British citizen (see BRITISH NATIONALITY vol 4 (2011) PARAS 406, 421–444), a British overseas territories citizen (see BRITISH NATIONALITY vol 4 (2011) PARAS 406, 445–458), a British National (Overseas) (see BRITISH NATIONALITY vol 4 (2011) PARAS 406, 465–467) or a British Overseas citizen (see BRITISH NATIONALITY vol 4 (2011) PARA 459 et seq); (2) a person who under the British Nationality Act 1981 is a British subject (see BRITISH NATIONALITY vol 4 (2011) PARAS 407, 469–470); or (3) a British protected person within the meaning of the 1981 Act (see BRITISH NATIONALITY vol 4 (2011) PARAS 408, 476–480): Aviation and Maritime Security Act 1990 s 17(1) (definition amended by virtue of the British Overseas Territories Act 2002 s 2(3)).
7   Aviation and Maritime Security Act 1990 s 9(2)(b).
8   For these purposes, 'naval service' includes military and air force service: Aviation and Maritime Security Act 1990 s 17(1).
9   Aviation and Maritime Security Act 1990 s 9(2)(c).
10 Aviation and Maritime Security Act 1990 s 9(3). As to prosecution of offences under Pt II (ss 9–17) see PARA 1154; as to ancillary offences see PARA 1152; and as to the master's power of delivery see PARA 1153.

1148.   Seizing or exercising control of fixed platforms. A person who unlawfully, by the use of force or by threats of any kind, seizes a fixed platform[1] or exercises control of it, commits an offence, whatever his nationality and whether the fixed platform is in the United Kingdom[2] or elsewhere[3].

A person guilty of such an offence is liable, on conviction on indictment, to imprisonment for life[4].

1   For these purposes 'fixed platform' means (by virtue of the Aviation and Maritime Security Act 1990 s 17(1)):
    (1)   any offshore installation, within the meaning of the Mineral Workings (Offshore Installations) Act 1971, which is not a ship; and
    (2)   any other artificial island, installation or structure which:
          (a)   permanently rests on, or is permanently attached to, the sea bed;
          (b)   is maintained for the purposes of the exploration or exploitation of resources or for other economic purposes; and
          (c)   is not connected with dry land by a permanent structure providing access at all times and for all purposes.
    In the Mineral Workings (Offshore Installations) Act 1971, unless the context otherwise requires, 'offshore installation' has the same meaning as in the Offshore Installations and Pipeline Works (Management and Administration) Regulations 1995, SI 1995/738, reg 3 (see ENERGY AND CLIMATE CHANGE vol 44 (2011) PARA 1078): see the Mineral Workings (Offshore Installations) Act 1971 s 12(1) (definition added by the Oil and Gas (Enterprise) Act 1982 s 37, Sch 3 para 11; and substituted by SI 1995/738). As to the meaning of 'ship' see PARA 1147 note 1.
2   As to the meaning of 'United Kingdom' see PARA 16 note 3; and as to the territorial extent of the United Kingdom for these purposes see PARA 1147 note 2.
3   Aviation and Maritime Security Act 1990 s 10(1).
4   Aviation and Maritime Security Act 1990 s 10(2). As to prosecution of offences under Pt II (ss 9–17) see PARA 1154; and as to ancillary offences see PARA 1152.

1149.   Destroying ships or fixed platforms or endangering their safety. A person commits an offence[1] if he unlawfully[2] and intentionally[3]:
    (1)   destroys a ship[4] or a fixed platform[5];
    (2)   damages a ship, its cargo or a fixed platform so as to endanger, or to be likely to endanger, the safe navigation of the ship or, as the case may be, the safety of the platform[6]; or
    (3)   commits on board a ship or on a fixed platform an act of violence[7] which is likely to endanger the safe navigation of the ship or, as the case may be, the safety of the platform[8].

A person commits an offence[9] if he unlawfully and intentionally places, or causes to be placed, on a ship or fixed platform any device or substance which[10]:

(a)   in the case of a ship, is likely to destroy the ship or is likely so to damage it or its cargo as to endanger its safe navigation[11]; or

(b)   in the case of a fixed platform, is likely to destroy the fixed platform or so to damage it as to endanger its safety[12];

but nothing in this provision[13] is to be construed as limiting the circumstances in which the commission of any act may constitute an offence under heads (1) to (3) above[14], or may constitute attempting or conspiring to commit, or aiding, abetting, counselling, procuring or inciting, or being art and part in, the commission of such an offence[15].

These offences[16] apply whether any such act that is required to be committed by them is committed in the United Kingdom or elsewhere and whatever the nationality of the person committing the act[17]; but those offences[18] do not apply in relation to any act committed in relation to a warship or any other ship used as a naval auxiliary or in customs or police service unless:

(i)   the person committing the act is a United Kingdom national[19]; or

(ii)   his act is committed in the United Kingdom[20]; or

(iii)   the ship is used in the naval[21] or customs service of the United Kingdom or in the service of any police force in the United Kingdom[22].

A person guilty of any such offence[23] is liable, on conviction on indictment, to imprisonment for life[24].

1   Ie subject to the Aviation and Maritime Security Act 1990 s 11(5) (see the text and notes 18–22): see s 11(1).

2   For these purposes 'unlawfully' means (by virtue of the Aviation and Maritime Security Act 1990 s 11(7)):

    (1)   in relation to the commission of an act in the United Kingdom, so as, apart from the Aviation and Maritime Security Act 1990, to constitute an offence under the law of the part of the United Kingdom in which the act is committed; and

    (2)   in relation to the commission of an act outside the United Kingdom, so that the commission of the act would, apart from the Aviation and Maritime Security Act 1990, have been an offence under the law of England and Wales if it had been committed in England and Wales.

    As to the meanings of 'England' and 'Wales' see PARA 16 note 2. As to the meaning of 'United Kingdom' see PARA 16 note 3; and as to the territorial extent of the United Kingdom for these purposes see PARA 1147 note 2.

3   Aviation and Maritime Security Act 1990 s 11(1).

4   As to the meaning of 'ship' see PARA 1147 note 1.

5   Aviation and Maritime Security Act 1990 s 11(1)(a). As to the meaning of 'fixed platform' see PARA 1148 note 1.

6   Aviation and Maritime Security Act 1990 s 11(1)(b).

7   For these purposes 'act of violence' means (by virtue of the Aviation and Maritime Security Act 1990 s 11(7)):

    (1)   any act done in the United Kingdom which constitutes the offence of murder, attempted murder, manslaughter, culpable homicide or assault (as to which see CRIMINAL LAW vol 25 (2016) PARA 97 et seq) or an offence under the Offences against the Person Act 1861 s 18 (shooting or attempting to shoot, or wounding, with intent to do grievous bodily harm, or to resist apprehension) (see CRIMINAL LAW vol 25 (2016) PARA 141), s 20 (inflicting bodily injury, with or without weapon) (see CRIMINAL LAW vol 25 (2016) PARA 140), s 21 (attempting to choke, etc, in order to commit or assist in the committing of any indictable offence) (see CRIMINAL LAW vol 25 (2016) PARA 143), s 22 (using chloroform, etc, to commit or assist in the committing of any indictable offence) (see CRIMINAL LAW vol 25 (2016) PARA 144), s 23 (maliciously administering poison, etc, so as to endanger life or inflict grievous bodily harm) (see CRIMINAL LAW vol 25 (2016) PARA 145), s 24 (maliciously administering poison, etc, with intent to injure, aggrieve, or annoy any other person) (see CRIMINAL LAW vol 25 (2016) PARA 145), s 28 (causing bodily injury by gunpowder) (see CRIMINAL LAW vol 25

(2016) PARA 147), s 29 (causing gunpowder to explode, or sending to any person an explosive substance, or throwing corrosive fluid on a person, with intent to do grievous bodily harm) (CRIMINAL LAW vol 25 (2016) PARA 148) or under the Explosive Substances Act 1883 s 2 (see CRIMINAL LAW vol 25 (2016) PARA 149); and
   (2)   any act done outside the United Kingdom which, if done in the United Kingdom, would constitute such an offence as is mentioned in head.
8   Aviation and Maritime Security Act 1990 s 11(1)(c).
9   Ie subject to the Aviation and Maritime Security Act 1990 s 11(5) (see the text and notes 18–22): see s 11(2).
10   Aviation and Maritime Security Act 1990 s 11(2).
11   Aviation and Maritime Security Act 1990 s 11(2)(a).
12   Aviation and Maritime Security Act 1990 s 11(2)(b).
13   Ie nothing in the Aviation and Maritime Security Act 1990 s 11(2): see s 11(3)(a).
14   Aviation and Maritime Security Act 1990 s 11(3)(a).
15   Aviation and Maritime Security Act 1990 s 11(3)(b). The reference in s 11(3)(b) to, or to conduct amounting to, the common law offence of inciting the commission of another offence (which is abolished under the Serious Crime Act 2007 s 94(1) by s 59), now has effect as a reference to, or to conduct amounting to, offences under the Serious Crime Act 2007 Pt 2 (ss 44–67): see Sch 6 Pt 1 para 18(a).
16   Ie the Aviation and Maritime Security Act 1990 s 11(1), (2) (see the text and notes 1–12): see s 11(4).
17   Aviation and Maritime Security Act 1990 s 11(4).
18   Ie the Aviation and Maritime Security Act 1990 s 11(1), (2) (see the text and notes 1–12): see s 11(5).
19   Aviation and Maritime Security Act 1990 s 11(5)(a). As to the meaning of 'United Kingdom national' see PARA 1147 note 6.
20   Aviation and Maritime Security Act 1990 s 11(5)(b).
21   As to the meaning of 'naval service' see PARA 1147 note 8.
22   Aviation and Maritime Security Act 1990 s 11(5)(c).
23   Ie under the Aviation and Maritime Security Act 1990 s 11: see s 11(6).
24   Aviation and Maritime Security Act 1990 s 11(6). As to prosecution of offences under Pt II (ss 9–17) see PARA 1154; as to ancillary offences see PARA 1152; and as to the master's power of delivery see PARA 1153.

1150. Other acts endangering or likely to endanger safe navigation. It is an offence[1] for any person unlawfully[2] and intentionally[3]:
   (1)   to destroy or damage any property used for the provision of maritime navigation facilities (including any land, building or ship[4] so used, and including any apparatus or equipment so used, whether it is on board a ship or elsewhere)[5]; or
   (2)   seriously to interfere with the operation of any such property[6],
where the destruction, damage or interference is likely to endanger the safe navigation of any ship[7].

It is also an offence[8] for any person intentionally to communicate any information which he knows to be false in a material particular, where the communication of the information endangers the safe navigation of any ship[9]; but it is a defence for a person charged with such an offence to prove that, when he communicated the information, he was lawfully employed to perform duties which consisted of or included the communication of information and that he communicated the information in good faith in performance of those duties[10].

These offences[11] apply whether any such act that is required to be committed by them is committed in the United Kingdom[12] or elsewhere and whatever the nationality of the person committing the act[13]; but, for the purposes of those offences[14], any danger, or likelihood of danger, to the safe navigation of a warship or any other ship used as a naval auxiliary or in customs or police service is to be disregarded unless:
   (a)   the person committing the act is a United Kingdom national[15]; or
   (b)   his act is committed in the United Kingdom[16]; or

(c)   the ship is used in the naval[17] or customs service of the United Kingdom or is in the service of any police force in the United Kingdom[18].

A person guilty of any such offence[19] is liable, on conviction on indictment, to imprisonment for life[20].

1 Ie subject to the Aviation and Maritime Security Act 1990 s 12(6) (see the text and notes 14–18): see s 12(1).
2 For these purposes, 'unlawfully' has the same meaning as in the Aviation and Maritime Security Act 1990 s 11 (see PARA 1149 note 2): s 12(8).
3 Aviation and Maritime Security Act 1990 s 12(1).
4 As to the meaning of 'ship' see PARA 1147 note 1.
5 Aviation and Maritime Security Act 1990 s 12(1)(a), (2).
6 Aviation and Maritime Security Act 1990 s 12(1)(b).
7 Aviation and Maritime Security Act 1990 s 12(1).
8 Ie subject to the Aviation and Maritime Security Act 1990 s 12(6) (see the text and notes 14–18): see s 12(3).
9 Aviation and Maritime Security Act 1990 s 12(3).
10 Aviation and Maritime Security Act 1990 s 12(4).
11 Ie the Aviation and Maritime Security Act 1990 s 12(1), (3) (see the text and notes 1–9): see s 12(5).
12 As to the meaning of 'United Kingdom' see PARA 16 note 3; and as to the territorial extent of the United Kingdom for these purposes see PARA 1147 note 2.
13 Aviation and Maritime Security Act 1990 s 12(5).
14 Ie for the purposes of the Aviation and Maritime Security Act 1990 s 12(1), (3) (see the text and notes 1–9): see s 12(6).
15 Aviation and Maritime Security Act 1990 s 12(6)(a). As to the meaning of 'United Kingdom national' see PARA 1147 note 6.
16 Aviation and Maritime Security Act 1990 s 12(6)(b).
17 As to the meaning of 'naval service' see PARA 1147 note 8.
18 Aviation and Maritime Security Act 1990 s 12(6)(c).
19 Ie under the Aviation and Maritime Security Act 1990 s 12: see s 12(7).
20 Aviation and Maritime Security Act 1990 s 12(7). As to prosecution of offences under Pt II (ss 9–17) see PARA 1154; as to ancillary offences see PARA 1152; and as to the master's power of delivery see PARA 1153.

1151. Offences involving threats. A person commits an offence if:
(1)   in order to compel any other person to do or abstain from doing any act, he threatens that he or some other person will do, in relation to any ship[1] or fixed platform[2], an act which is an offence by virtue of the provisions[3] relating to destroying or damaging ships or fixed platforms or committing on board a ship or fixed platform acts of violence[4] which are likely to endanger the safe navigation of the ship or, as the case may be, the safety of the platform[5]; and
(2)   the making of that threat is likely to endanger the safe navigation of the ship or, as the case may be, the safety of the fixed platform[6].

A person commits an offence[7] if:
(a)   in order to compel any other person to do or abstain from doing any act, he threatens that he or some other person will do an act which is an offence by virtue of the provisions[8] relating to destroying or damaging, or seriously interfering with the operation of, property used for the provision of maritime navigation facilities[9]; and
(b)   the making of that threat is likely to endanger the safe navigation of any ship[10].

These offences[11] apply whether any such act that is required to be committed by them is committed in the United Kingdom[12] or elsewhere and whatever the nationality of the person committing the act[13]; but, for the purposes of head (b) above, any danger, or likelihood of danger, to the safe navigation of a warship or any other ship used as a naval auxiliary or in customs or police service is to be disregarded unless[14]:

(i)   the person committing the act is a United Kingdom national[15]; or
(ii)   his act is committed in the United Kingdom[16]; or
(iii)   the ship is used in the naval[17] or customs service of the United Kingdom or is in the service of any police force in the United Kingdom[18].

A person guilty of any such offence[19] is liable, on conviction on indictment, to imprisonment for life[20].

1   As to the meaning of 'ship' see PARA 1147 note 1.
2   As to the meaning of 'fixed platform' see PARA 1148 note 1.
3   Ie by virtue of the Aviation and Maritime Security Act 1990 s 11(1) (see PARA 1149): see s 13(1)(a).
4   As to the meaning of 'act of violence' see PARA 1149 note 7.
5   Aviation and Maritime Security Act 1990 s 13(1)(a).
6   Aviation and Maritime Security Act 1990 s 13(1)(b).
7   Ie subject to the Aviation and Maritime Security Act 1990 s 13(4) (see the text and notes 14–18): see s 13(2).
8   Ie by virtue of the Aviation and Maritime Security Act 1990 s 12(1) (see PARA 1150): see s 13(2)(a).
9   Aviation and Maritime Security Act 1990 s 13(2)(a).
10 Aviation and Maritime Security Act 1990 s 13(2)(b).
11 Ie the Aviation and Maritime Security Act 1990 s 13(1), (2) (see the text and notes 1–10): see s 13(3).
12 As to the meaning of 'United Kingdom' see PARA 16 note 3; and as to the territorial extent of the United Kingdom for these purposes see PARA 1147 note 2.
13 Aviation and Maritime Security Act 1990 s 13(3).
14 Aviation and Maritime Security Act 1990 s 12(6), applied by s 13(4).
15 Aviation and Maritime Security Act 1990 s 12(6)(a), applied by s 13(4). As to the meaning of 'United Kingdom national' see PARA 1147 note 6.
16 Aviation and Maritime Security Act 1990 s 12(6)(b), applied by s 13(4).
17 As to the meaning of 'naval service' see PARA 1147 note 8.
18 Aviation and Maritime Security Act 1990 s 12(6)(c), applied by s 13(4).
19 Ie under the Aviation and Maritime Security Act 1990 s 13: see s 13(5).
20 Aviation and Maritime Security Act 1990 s 13(5). As to prosecution of offences under Pt II (ss 9–17) see PARA 1154; as to ancillary offences see PARA 1152; and as to the master's power of delivery see PARA 1153.

1152. Ancillary offences. Where a person, of whatever nationality, does outside the United Kingdom[1] any act which, if done in the United Kingdom, would constitute a specified violent offence[2], his act constitutes that offence if it is done in connection with an offence that is provided for in relation to the hijacking of ships[3], seizing or exercising control of fixed platforms[4], destroying ships or fixed platforms or endangering their safety[5] or committing other acts endangering or likely to endanger safe navigation[6] committed or attempted by him[7].

It is an offence for any person in the United Kingdom to induce or assist the commission outside the United Kingdom of any act which[8]:

(1)   would otherwise[9] be an offence under the provisions[10] relating to the hijacking of ships[11]; or
(2)   would otherwise[12] be an offence under the provisions[13] relating to destroying ships or fixed platforms or endangering their safety[14]; or
(3)   would otherwise[15] be an offence under the provisions[16] relating to committing other acts endangering or likely to endanger safe navigation[17]; or
(4)   would otherwise[18] be an offence under the provisions[19] relating to offences involving threats[20].

A person who commits an offence under any of heads (1) to (4) above is liable, on conviction on indictment, to imprisonment for life[21].

1   As to the meaning of 'United Kingdom' see PARA 16 note 3; and as to the territorial extent of the United Kingdom for these purposes see PARA 1147 note 2.

2   The offences so specified are murder, attempted murder, manslaughter, culpable homicide or assault (as to which see CRIMINAL LAW vol 25 (2016) PARA 97 et seq) or an offence under the Offences against the Person Act 1861 s 18 (shooting or attempting to shoot, or wounding, with intent to do grievous bodily harm, or to resist apprehension) (see CRIMINAL LAW vol 25 (2016) PARA 141), s 20 (inflicting bodily injury, with or without weapon) (see CRIMINAL LAW vol 25 (2016) PARA 140), s 21 (attempting to choke, etc, in order to commit or assist in the committing of any indictable offence) (see CRIMINAL LAW vol 25 (2016) PARA 143), s 22 (using chloroform, etc, to commit or assist in the committing of any indictable offence) (see CRIMINAL LAW vol 25 (2016) PARA 144), s 23 (maliciously administering poison, etc, so as to endanger life or inflict grievous bodily harm) (see CRIMINAL LAW vol 25 (2016) PARA 145), s 28 (causing bodily injury by gunpowder) (see CRIMINAL LAW vol 25 (2016) PARA 147), s 29 (causing gunpowder to explode, or sending to any person an explosive substance, or throwing corrosive fluid on a person, with intent to do grievous bodily harm) (see CRIMINAL LAW vol 25 (2016) PARA 148) or under the Explosive Substances Act 1883 s 2 (see CRIMINAL LAW vol 25 (2016) PARA 149): Aviation and Maritime Security Act 1990 s 14(2).

3   Ie the Aviation and Maritime Security Act 1990 s 9 (see PARA 1147): see s 14(1).
4   Ie the Aviation and Maritime Security Act 1990 s 10 (see PARA 1148): see s 14(1).
5   Ie the Aviation and Maritime Security Act 1990 s 11 (see PARA 1149): see s 14(1).
6   Ie the Aviation and Maritime Security Act 1990 s 12 (see PARA 1150): see s 14(1).
7   Aviation and Maritime Security Act 1990 s 14(1). Section 14(1) has effect without prejudice to the Merchant Shipping Act 1995 s 281 (offences committed on board ship) (see PARA 1054) or s 282 (offences committed by British seamen) (see PARA 1055) or the Petroleum Act 1998 s 10 (application of criminal law etc to offshore activities) (see ENERGY AND CLIMATE CHANGE vol 44 (2011) PARA 1079): Aviation and Maritime Security Act 1990 s 14(3) (amended by the Merchant Shipping Act 1995 Sch 13 para 88(1), (2); and the Petroleum Act 1998 Sch 4 para 29).

8   Aviation and Maritime Security Act 1990 s 14(4). Section 14(4) has effect without prejudice to the operation, in relation to any offence under s 9 (see PARA 1147), s 11 (see PARA 1149), s 12 (see PARA 1150), or s 13 (offences involving threats) (see PARA 1151), of the Accessories and Abettors Act 1861 s 8 (see CRIMINAL LAW vol 25 (2016) PARAS 51, 53): Aviation and Maritime Security Act 1990 s 14(6).

9   Ie but for the Aviation and Maritime Security Act 1990 s 9(2) (see PARA 1147): see s 14(4)(a).
10 Ie under the Aviation and Maritime Security Act 1990 s 9 (see PARA 1147): see s 14(4)(a).
11 Aviation and Maritime Security Act 1990 s 14(4)(a).
12 Ie but for the Aviation and Maritime Security Act 1990 s 11(5) (see PARA 1149): see s 14(4)(b).
13 Ie under the Aviation and Maritime Security Act 1990 s 11 (see PARA 1149): see s 14(4)(b).
14 Aviation and Maritime Security Act 1990 s 14(4)(b).
15 Ie but for the Aviation and Maritime Security Act 1990 s 12(6) (see PARA 1150): see s 14(4)(c).
16 Ie under the Aviation and Maritime Security Act 1990 s 12 (see PARA 1150): see s 14(4)(c).
17 Aviation and Maritime Security Act 1990 s 14(4)(c).
18 Ie but for the Aviation and Maritime Security Act 1990 s 13(4) (see PARA 1151): see s 14(4)(d).
19 Ie under the Aviation and Maritime Security Act 1990 s 13 (see PARA 1151): see s 14(4)(d).
20 Aviation and Maritime Security Act 1990 s 14(4)(d).
21 Aviation and Maritime Security Act 1990 s 14(5). As to prosecution of offences under Pt II (ss 9–17) see PARA 1154; and as to the master's power of delivery see PARA 1153.

1153.   Master's power of delivery. For the purposes of any proceedings before any court in the United Kingdom[1], if the master[2] of a ship[3], wherever that ship may be, and whatever the state, if any, in which it may be registered, has reasonable grounds to believe that any person on board the ship has[4]:

(1)   committed an offence under any of the provisions relating to hijacking of ships[5], destroying ships or fixed platforms or endangering their safety[6], committing other acts endangering or likely to endanger safe navigation[7] or under the provisions[8] that govern offences involving threats[9];

(2)   attempted to commit such an offence[10]; or

(3)   aided, abetted, counselled, procured or incited, or been art and part in, the commission of such an offence[11],

in relation to any ship other than a warship or other ship used as a naval auxiliary or in customs or police service, he may deliver that person to an appropriate officer[12] in the United Kingdom or any other Convention country[13].

Where the master of a ship intends so to deliver any person in the United Kingdom or any other Convention country, he must give notification to an appropriate officer in that country[14]:

(a)   of his intention to deliver that person to an appropriate officer in that country[15]; and

(b)   of his reasons for intending to do so[16];

and any such notification must be given[17]:

(i)   before the ship in question has entered the territorial sea of the country concerned[18]; or

(ii)   if in the circumstances it is not reasonably practicable to comply with head (i) above, as soon as reasonably practicable after the ship has entered that territorial sea[19].

Where the master of a ship so delivers any person to an appropriate officer in any country, he must[20]:

(A)   make to an appropriate officer in that country such oral or written statements relating to the alleged offence as that officer may reasonably require[21]; and

(B)   deliver to an appropriate officer in that country such other evidence relating to the alleged offence as is in the master's possession[22].

The master of a ship who without reasonable excuse fails to comply with either of these requirements as to delivery or notification[23] is guilty of an offence and liable, on summary conviction, to a fine[24]; but it is a defence for a master of a ship charged with the offence of failing to give notification to an appropriate officer[25] to show that he believed on reasonable grounds that the giving of the required notification would endanger the safety of the ship and, except where the country concerned is the United Kingdom, that either he notified some other competent authority in the country concerned within the required time[26], or he believed on reasonable grounds that the giving of notification to any competent authority in that country would endanger the safety of the ship[27].

1   Aviation and Maritime Security Act 1990 s 15(1). As to the meaning of 'United Kingdom' see PARA 16 note 3; and as to the territorial extent of the United Kingdom for these purposes see PARA 1147 note 2.

2   For these purposes, 'master' has the same meaning as in the Merchant Shipping Act 1995 (see PARA 444 note 1): see the Aviation and Maritime Security Act 1990 s 15(8) (definition amended by the Merchant Shipping Act 1995 Sch 13 para 88(1), (3)).

3   As to the meaning of 'ship' see PARA 1147 note 1.

4   Aviation and Maritime Security Act 1990 s 15(2).

5   Ie the Aviation and Maritime Security Act 1990 s 9 (see PARA 1147): see s 15(2)(a).

6   Ie under the Aviation and Maritime Security Act 1990 s 11 (see PARA 1149): see s 15(2)(a).

7   Ie under the Aviation and Maritime Security Act 1990 s 12 (see PARA 1150): see s 15(2)(a).

8   Ie under the Aviation and Maritime Security Act 1990 s 13 (see PARA 1151): see s 15(2)(a).

9   Aviation and Maritime Security Act 1990 s 15(2)(a).

10   Aviation and Maritime Security Act 1990 s 15(2)(b).

11   Aviation and Maritime Security Act 1990 s 15(2)(c). The reference in s 15(2)(c) to, or to conduct amounting to, the common law offence of inciting the commission of another offence (which is abolished under the Serious Crime Act 2007 s 94(1) by s 59), now has effect as a reference to, or to conduct amounting to, offences under the Serious Crime Act 2007 Pt 2 (ss 44–67): see Sch 6 Pt 1 para 18(b).

12   For these purposes, 'appropriate officer' means (by virtue of the Aviation and Maritime Security Act 1990 s 15(8)):

     (1)   in relation to the United Kingdom, a constable or immigration officer; and

     (2)   in relation to any other Convention country, an officer having functions corresponding to the functions in the United Kingdom either of a constable or of an immigration officer.

     For these purposes, 'Convention country' means a country in which the Convention for the Suppression of Unlawful Acts against the Safety of Maritime Navigation with Protocol for the Suppression of Unlawful Acts against the Safety of Fixed Platforms located on the Continental

Shelf (Rome, 10 March 1988; TS 64 (1995); Cm 2947) (as to which see INTERNATIONAL RELATIONS LAW), is for the time being in force; and Her Majesty may by Order in Council certify that any country specified in the Order is for the time being a Convention country and any such Order in Council for the time being in force is conclusive evidence that the country in question is for the time being a Convention country: see the Aviation and Maritime Security Act 1990 s 15(8). At the date at which this volume states the law, no such Order in Council had been made.

13 Aviation and Maritime Security Act 1990 s 15(2).
14 Aviation and Maritime Security Act 1990 s 15(3).
15 Aviation and Maritime Security Act 1990 s 15(3)(a).
16 Aviation and Maritime Security Act 1990 s 15(3)(b).
17 Aviation and Maritime Security Act 1990 s 15(4).
18 Aviation and Maritime Security Act 1990 s 15(4)(a). As to the extent of the territorial and non-territorial sea, the baselines used for delimitation, and associated rights see INTERNATIONAL RELATIONS LAW vol 61 (2010) PARA 121 et seq.
19 Aviation and Maritime Security Act 1990 s 15(4)(b).
20 Aviation and Maritime Security Act 1990 s 15(5).
21 Aviation and Maritime Security Act 1990 s 15(5)(a).
22 Aviation and Maritime Security Act 1990 s 15(5)(b).
23 Ie fails to comply with the Aviation and Maritime Security Act 1990 s 15(3) (see the text and notes 14–16) or s 15(5) (see the text and notes 20–22): see s 15(6).
24 Aviation and Maritime Security Act 1990 s 15(6). As to the powers of magistrates' courts to issue fines on summary conviction see SENTENCING vol 92 (2015) PARA 176. As to prosecution of offences under Pt II (ss 9–17) see PARA 1154.
25 Ie failing to comply with the Aviation and Maritime Security Act 1990 s 15(3) (see the text and notes 14–16): see s 15(7).
26 Ie the time required by the Aviation and Maritime Security Act 1990 s 15(4) (see the text and notes 17–19): see s 15(7).
27 Aviation and Maritime Security Act 1990 s 15(7).

1154. Prosecution of offences under Part II of the Aviation and Maritime Security Act 1990. Proceedings for an offence under any provision of Part II of the Aviation and Maritime Security Act 1990[1] may not be instituted in England and Wales[2] except by or with the consent of the Attorney General[3].

1 Ie under any provision of the Aviation and Maritime Security Act 1990 Pt II (ss 9–17) (see PARA 1147 et seq): see s 16(1)(a). As to offences by bodies corporate see s 50; and PORTS AND HARBOURS vol 85 (2012) PARA 137.
2 As to the meanings of 'England' and 'Wales' see PARA 16 note 2.
3 Aviation and Maritime Security Act 1990 s 16(1)(a). As to the Attorney General see CONSTITUTIONAL AND ADMINISTRATIVE LAW vol 20 (2014) PARA 273.

B.   PROTECTION OF SHIPS AGAINST ACTS OF VIOLENCE

1155. Statutory provisions relating to the protection of ships and harbour areas against acts of violence. The purposes to which Part III of the Aviation and Maritime Security Act 1990[1] applies are the protection against acts of violence[2]:

(1)   of ships[3], and of persons or property[4] on board ships[5]; and
(2)   of harbour areas[6], of such persons as are at any time present in any part of a harbour area and of any such property as forms part of a harbour area or is at any time, whether permanently or temporarily, in any part of a harbour area[7].

Specific provision is made under Part III of the Aviation and Maritime Security Act 1990 in relation to the following matters:

(a)   the power of the Secretary of State[8] to require information[9];
(b)   the designation of restricted zones of harbour areas[10];
(c)   the power to impose restrictions in relation to ships[11];
(d)   the power to require harbour authorities to promote searches in harbour areas[12];
(e)   the power to require other persons to promote searches[13];

(f)   the general power to direct measures to be taken for purposes to which Part III of the Aviation and Maritime Security Act 1990 applies[14];

(g)   supplemental provisions with respect to directions[15];

(h)   offences relating to the security of ships and harbour areas[16];

(i)   the power to apply Part III of the Aviation and Maritime Security Act 1990 to sea cargo agents[17];

(j)   the Secretary of State's power to impose a duty on specified persons to report certain occurrences[18];

(k)   general supplemental matters[19].

1   Ie the Aviation and Maritime Security Act 1990 Pt III (ss 18–46) (as to which generally see PORTS AND HARBOURS vol 85 (2012) PARA 113 et seq): see s 18(1).

2   Aviation and Maritime Security Act 1990 s 18(1). In Pt III, 'act of violence' means any act (whether actual or potential, and whether done or to be done in the United Kingdom or elsewhere) which either, being an act done in Great Britain constitutes, or, if done in Great Britain would constitute, the offence of murder, attempted murder, manslaughter, culpable homicide or assault (as to which see CRIMINAL LAW vol 25 (2016) PARA 97 et seq) or an offence under the Offences against the Person Act 1861 s 18 (shooting or attempting to shoot, or wounding, with intent to do grievous bodily harm, or to resist apprehension) (see CRIMINAL LAW vol 25 (2016) PARA 141), s 20 (inflicting bodily injury, with or without weapon) (see CRIMINAL LAW vol 25 (2016) PARA 140), s 21 (attempting to choke, etc, in order to commit or assist in the committing of any indictable offence) (see CRIMINAL LAW vol 25 (2016) PARA 143), s 22 (using chloroform, etc, to commit or assist in the committing of any indictable offence) (see CRIMINAL LAW vol 25 (2016) PARA 144), s 23 (maliciously administering poison, etc, so as to endanger life or inflict grievous bodily harm) (see CRIMINAL LAW vol 25 (2016) PARA 145), s 24 (maliciously administering poison, etc, with intent to injure, aggrieve, or annoy any other person) (see CRIMINAL LAW vol 25 (2016) PARA 145), s 28 (causing bodily injury by gunpowder) (see CRIMINAL LAW vol 25 (2016) PARA 147), s 29 (causing gunpowder to explode, or sending to any person an explosive substance, or throwing corrosive fluid on a person, with intent to do grievous bodily harm) (see CRIMINAL LAW vol 25 (2016) PARA 148) or under the Explosive Substances Act 1883 s 2 (see CRIMINAL LAW vol 25 (2016) PARA 149) or under the Criminal Damage Act 1971 s 1 (see CRIMINAL LAW vol 25 (2016) PARA 392): Aviation and Maritime Security Act 1990 ss 18(2), 46(1). As to the meanings of 'United Kingdom' and 'Great Britain' see PARA 16 note 3.

3   For these purposes, 'ship' includes hovercraft and every other description of vessel used in navigation: Aviation and Maritime Security Act 1990 s 46(1).

4   For these purposes, 'property' includes any land, buildings or works, any ship or vehicle and any baggage, cargo or other article of any description; and 'article' includes any substance, whether in solid or liquid form or in the form of a gas or vapour: Aviation and Maritime Security Act 1990 s 46(1).

5   Aviation and Maritime Security Act 1990 s 18(1)(a).

6   For these purposes, 'harbour area' means (by virtue of the Aviation and Maritime Security Act 1990 s 18(3) (substituted by the Merchant Shipping and Maritime Security Act 1997 s 25, Sch 4 paras 1, 2)):

     (1)   the aggregate of:

         (a)   any harbour in the United Kingdom in respect of which there is a harbour authority within the meaning of the Merchant Shipping Act 1995 (see PARA 69 note 4) (Aviation and Maritime Security Act 1990 s 18(3)(a)(i) (as so substituted)); and

         (b)   any land which is adjacent to such a harbour and which is either land occupied by the harbour authority or land in respect of which the harbour authority has functions of improvement, maintenance or management (s 18(3)(a)(ii) (as so substituted)); or

     (2)   any hoverport which does not form part of any area which falls within heads (1)(a), (b) above (s 18(3)(b) (as so substituted)).

     'Harbour' has the same meaning as in the Merchant Shipping Act 1995 (see PARA 49 note 5): Aviation and Maritime Security Act 1990 s 46(1) (definition substituted by the Merchant Shipping and Maritime Security Act 1997 Sch 4 para 11(2)(a)). 'Hoverport' has the same meaning as in the Hovercraft Act 1968 (see PARA 382 note 3): Aviation and Maritime Security Act 1990 s 46(1).

7   Aviation and Maritime Security Act 1990 s 18(1)(b).

8   As to the Secretary of State see PARA 36.

9   See the Aviation and Maritime Security Act 1990 s 19; and PORTS AND HARBOURS vol 85 (2012) PARA 114.

10 See the Aviation and Maritime Security Act 1990 s 20; and PORTS AND HARBOURS vol 85 (2012) PARA 115.
11 See the Aviation and Maritime Security Act 1990 s 21; and PORTS AND HARBOURS vol 85 (2012) PARA 117.
12 See the Aviation and Maritime Security Act 1990 s 22; and PORTS AND HARBOURS vol 85 (2012) PARA 118.
13 See the Aviation and Maritime Security Act 1990 s 23; and PORTS AND HARBOURS vol 85 (2012) PARA 119.
14 See the Aviation and Maritime Security Act 1990 s 24; and PORTS AND HARBOURS vol 85 (2012) PARA 120.
15 See the Aviation and Maritime Security Act 1990 ss 25–36A; and PORTS AND HARBOURS vol 85 (2012) PARA 121 et seq. Head (g) in the text includes references to: s 25 (matters which may be included in directions under ss 21–24) (see PORTS AND HARBOURS vol 85 (2012) PARA 121); s 26 (limitations on scope of directions under ss 21–24) (see PORTS AND HARBOURS vol 85 (2012) PARA 122); s 27 (general or urgent directions under ss 21–24) (see PORTS AND HARBOURS vol 85 (2012) PARA 124); s 28 (objections to certain directions under s 24) (see PORTS AND HARBOURS vol 85 (2012) PARA 125), ss 29–33 (enforcement notices) (see PORTS AND HARBOURS vol 85 (2012) PARAS 126–128), s 34 (operation of directions under Pt III in relation to rights and duties under other laws) (see PORTS AND HARBOURS vol 85 (2012) PARA 123), s 35 (detention of ships) (see PORTS AND HARBOURS vol 85 (2012) PARA 129), s 36 (inspection of ships and harbour areas) (see PORTS AND HARBOURS vol 85 (2012) PARA 130), and s 36A (maritime security services: approved providers) (see PORTS AND HARBOURS vol 85 (2012) PARA 132).
16 See the Aviation and Maritime Security Act 1990 ss 37–40; and PORTS AND HARBOURS vol 85 (2012) PARAS 115, 133 et seq. Head (h) in the text includes references to: s 37 (false statements relating to baggage, cargo etc) (see PORTS AND HARBOURS vol 85 (2012) PARA 133), s 38 (false statements in connection with identity documents) (see PORTS AND HARBOURS vol 85 (2012) PARA 134), s 39 (unauthorised presence in restricted zone) (see PORTS AND HARBOURS vol 85 (2012) PARA 115), and s 40 (offences relating to authorised persons) (see PORTS AND HARBOURS vol 85 (2012) PARA 135).
17 See the Aviation and Maritime Security Act 1990 s 41; and PORTS AND HARBOURS vol 85 (2012) PARA 116.
18 See the Aviation and Maritime Security Act 1990 s 42; and PORTS AND HARBOURS vol 85 (2012) PARA 136.
19 See the Aviation and Maritime Security Act 1990 ss 43–46; and PORTS AND HARBOURS vol 85 (2012) PARAS 131, 138 et seq. Head (k) in the text includes references to: s 43, Sch 2 (compensation in respect of certain measures taken under Pt III) (see PORTS AND HARBOURS vol 85 (2012) PARA 131), s 44 (annual report by Secretary of State as to notices and directions under Pt III) (see PORTS AND HARBOURS vol 85 (2012) PARA 138), s 45 (service of documents) (see PORTS AND HARBOURS vol 85 (2012) PARA 139), and s 46 (interpretation of Pt III).

C.   EXTENSION OF MARITIME SECURITY PROVISIONS

1156. Extension of Aviation and Maritime Security Act 1990 provisions.
Her Majesty may by Order in Council[1] make provision for extending any of the provisions of Part II[2] and Part III[3] of the Aviation and Maritime Security Act 1990[4], with such exceptions, adaptations or modifications as may be specified in the order, to any of the Channel Islands, the Isle of Man or any colony[5].

1   The power to make Orders in Council is exercisable by statutory instrument: see the Statutory Instruments Act 1946 s 1(1); and STATUTES AND LEGISLATIVE PROCESS vol 96 (2012) PARA 1045.
2   Ie the Aviation and Maritime Security Act 1990 Pt II (ss 9–17) (as to which see PARA 1147 et seq): see s 51(1).
3   Ie the Aviation and Maritime Security Act 1990 Pt III (ss 18–46) (as to which generally see PARA 1155): see s 51(1).
4   The power also extends to the Aviation and Maritime Security Act 1990 s 50 (offences by bodies corporate) (as to which see PORTS AND HARBOURS vol 85 (2012) PARA 137): see s 51(1). See the Aviation Security and Piracy (Overseas Territories) Order 2000, SI 2000/3059.
5   Aviation and Maritime Security Act 1990 s 51(1). In exercise of the power so conferred from a maritime perspective, Her Majesty has made the Maritime Security (Jersey) Order 2014, SI 2014/4265. As to the meaning of 'colony' see STATUTES AND LEGISLATIVE PROCESS vol 96 (2012) PARA 1208. See also COMMONWEALTH vol 13 (2017) PARA 603.

(v) Offences in respect of Salvage and Wreck

1157. Failure to obey directions of receiver where vessel in distress. In circumstances where the statutory provisions relating to vessels in distress[1] apply in relation to any vessel, the receiver[2] must, among other duties, give such directions to each person as he thinks fit for the preservation of the vessel and of the lives of the shipwrecked persons[3].

If any person intentionally disobeys the direction of the receiver, he is liable, on summary conviction, to a fine[4].

1   Ie where the Merchant Shipping Act 1995 s 232 applies by virtue of s 231 (see PARA 936): see s 232(1); and PARA 936. As to the meaning of 'vessel' see PARA 919 note 5.
2   As to the meaning of 'receiver' see PARA 887 note 4.
3   See the Merchant Shipping Act 1995 s 232(1), (2); and PARA 936. In giving such a direction, the receiver must not interfere between the master and crew of the vessel in reference to the management of the vessel unless he is requested to do so by the master: see s 232(3); and PARA 936. As to the meaning of 'shipwrecked persons' see PARA 936 note 6. As to the meaning of 'master' see PARA 444 note 1.
4   Merchant Shipping Act 1995 s 232(4). Section 232(4) is subject to s 232(3) (see note 3): see s 232(4). As to the time limit for summary offences see PARA 1049; as to offences by officers of bodies corporate see PARA 1051; as to jurisdiction in relation to offences see PARA 1052; as to jurisdiction over ships lying off the coast see PARA 1053; as to jurisdiction in the case of offences on board ship see PARA 1054; as to offences committed by British seamen see PARA 1055; and as to proof etc of exemption see PARA 1061. As to the powers of magistrates' courts to issue fines on summary conviction see SENTENCING vol 92 (2015) PARA 176.

1158. Failure to comply with requirements imposed by receiver in case of vessel in distress. In circumstances where the statutory provisions relating to vessels in distress[1] apply in relation to any vessel, the receiver[2] may, for the purpose of the preservation of shipwrecked persons[3] or of the vessel, cargo and equipment, require such persons as he thinks necessary to assist him, require the master[4] (or other person having the charge) of any vessel near at hand to give such assistance with his men, or vessel, as may be in his power and require the use of any vehicle that may be near at hand[5]. If any person refuses without reasonable excuse to comply with any requirement so made, he is liable, on summary conviction, to a fine[6].

1   Ie where the Merchant Shipping Act 1995 s 233 applies by virtue of s 231 (see PARA 936): see s 233(1); and PARA 936. As to the meaning of 'vessel' see PARA 919 note 5.
2   As to the meaning of 'receiver' see PARA 887 note 4.
3   As to the meaning of 'shipwrecked persons' see PARA 936 note 6.
4   As to the meaning of 'master' see PARA 444 note 1.
5   See the Merchant Shipping Act 1995 s 233(1); and PARA 936.
6   Merchant Shipping Act 1995 s 233(2). As to the time limit for summary offences see PARA 1049; as to offences by officers of bodies corporate see PARA 1051; as to jurisdiction in relation to offences see PARA 1052; as to jurisdiction over ships lying off the coast see PARA 1053; as to jurisdiction in the case of offences on board ship see PARA 1054; as to offences committed by British seamen see PARA 1055; and as to proof etc of exemption see PARA 1061. As to the powers of magistrates' courts to issue fines on summary conviction see SENTENCING vol 92 (2015) PARA 176.

1159. Obstruction of power to use adjoining land in case of vessel in distress. If the owner or occupier of any land:

(1)   impedes or hinders any person in the exercise of rights conferred[1] to use adjoining land in the case of a vessel in distress[2];
(2)   impedes or hinders the deposit on the land of any cargo or other article recovered from the vessel[3]; or
(3)   prevents or attempts to prevent any cargo or other article recovered from the vessel from remaining deposited on the land for a reasonable time until it can be removed to a safe place of public deposit[4],

he is liable, on summary conviction, to a fine[5].

1 Ie by the Merchant Shipping Act 1995 s 234(1) (see PARA 946), where s 234 applies in relation to a vessel by virtue of s 231 (see PARA 936): see s 234(1); and PARA 946. As to the meaning of 'vessel' see PARA 919 note 5.
2 Merchant Shipping Act 1995 s 234(7)(a).
3 Merchant Shipping Act 1995 s 234(7)(b).
4 Merchant Shipping Act 1995 s 234(7)(c).
5 Merchant Shipping Act 1995 s 234(7). As to the time limit for summary offences see PARA 1049; as to offences by officers of bodies corporate see PARA 1051; as to jurisdiction in relation to offences see PARA 1052; as to jurisdiction over ships lying off the coast see PARA 1053; as to jurisdiction in the case of offences on board ship see PARA 1054; as to offences committed by British seamen see PARA 1055; and as to proof etc of exemption see PARA 1061. As to the powers of magistrates' courts to issue fines on summary conviction see SENTENCING vol 92 (2015) PARA 176.

1160. Failure to comply with duty to notify receiver of wrecks. If any person who finds or takes possession of any wreck[1] in United Kingdom waters[2], or finds or takes possession of any wreck outside United Kingdom waters and brings it within those waters[3], fails without reasonable excuse to comply with the following duties[4], namely:

(1) if he is the owner of it, to give notice to the receiver[5] stating that he has found or taken possession of it and describing the marks by which it may be recognised[6];

(2) if he is not the owner of it, to give notice to the receiver that he has found or taken possession of it and, as directed by the receiver, either hold it to the receiver's order or deliver it to the receiver[7],

he is liable, on summary conviction, to a fine[8]; and, if he is not the owner of the wreck, he must also:

(a) forfeit any claim to salvage[9]; and

(b) be liable to pay twice the value of the wreck to its owner (if it is claimed) or (if it is unclaimed) to the person entitled to the wreck[10].

Any sum so payable to the owner of the wreck or to the persons entitled to the wreck may, in England and Wales[11], be recovered summarily as a civil debt[12].

1 As to the meaning of 'wreck' see PARA 923.
2 As to the meaning of 'United Kingdom waters' see PARA 48 note 11. As to the meaning of 'United Kingdom' see PARA 16 note 3.
3 See the Merchant Shipping Act 1995 s 236(1); and PARA 935.
4 Ie fails to comply with the Merchant Shipping Act 1995 s 236(1) (see PARA 935): see s 236(2). Section 236 is directed towards a criminal and improper detention by which it is sought to practise a fraud upon the Crown or the owner and not towards salvors who have restored the property to the owners: *The Zeta* (1875) LR 4 A & E 460, 3 Asp MLC 73. It does not apply to salvors who remain in possession for the safety of the vessel (*The Glynoeron* (1905) 21 TLR 648) or to a person who takes possession of a stranded vessel under the bona fide belief that it is his property by purchase or otherwise (*The Liffey* (1887) 58 LT 351, 6 Asp MLC 255).
5 As to the meaning of 'receiver' see PARA 887 note 4. As to the giving of notices under the Merchant Shipping Act 1995 see PARA 74.
6 See the Merchant Shipping Act 1995 s 236(1)(a); and PARA 935.
7 See the Merchant Shipping Act 1995 s 236(1)(b); and PARA 935.
8 Merchant Shipping Act 1995 s 236(2). As to the time limit for summary offences see PARA 1049; as to offences by officers of bodies corporate see PARA 1051; as to jurisdiction in relation to offences see PARA 1052; as to jurisdiction over ships lying off the coast see PARA 1053; as to jurisdiction in the case of offences on board ship see PARA 1054; as to offences committed by British seamen see PARA 1055; and as to proof etc of exemption see PARA 1061. As to the powers of magistrates' courts to issue fines on summary conviction see SENTENCING vol 92 (2015) PARA 176.
9 Merchant Shipping Act 1995 s 236(2)(a). As to the meaning of 'salvage' see PARA 849.
10 Merchant Shipping Act 1995 s 236(2)(b).
11 As to the meanings of 'England' and 'Wales' see PARA 16 note 2.
12 Merchant Shipping Act 1995 s 236(3).

1161. Failure to deliver to receiver cargo etc from vessel wrecked, stranded, or in distress. If any person, whether the owner or not:

(1)   instead of ensuring delivery to the receiver[1], conceals or keeps possession of any cargo or article washed on shore or otherwise lost or taken from a vessel[2] which is wrecked, stranded, or in distress at any place on or near the coasts[3] of the United Kingdom[4] or any tidal water[5] within United Kingdom waters[6]; or

(2)   refuses to deliver any such cargo or article to the receiver or to any person authorised by the receiver to require delivery[7],

he is liable, on summary conviction, to a fine[8].

The receiver or any person authorised by him may take any such cargo or article, if necessary by force, from any person who refuses to deliver it[9].

1   Ie instead of complying with the Merchant Shipping Act 1995 s 237(1) (see PARA 947). As to the meaning of 'receiver' see PARA 887 note 4.
2   As to the meaning of 'vessel' see PARA 919 note 5.
3   As to the meaning of 'on or near the coast' see *The Fulham* [1898] P 206 at 213, 8 Asp MLC 425 at 426, 427 (on appeal [1899] P 251, 8 Asp MLC 559, CA).
4   As to the meaning of 'United Kingdom' see PARA 16 note 3.
5   As to the meaning of 'tidal water' see PARA 923 note 13.
6   See the Merchant Shipping Act 1995 s 237(1), (2)(a); and PARA 947. As to the meaning of 'United Kingdom waters' see PARA 48 note 11.
7   See the Merchant Shipping Act 1995 s 237(1), (2)(b); and PARA 947.
8   Merchant Shipping Act 1995 s 237(2). As to the time limit for summary offences see PARA 1049; as to offences by officers of bodies corporate see PARA 1051; as to jurisdiction in relation to offences see PARA 1052; as to jurisdiction over ships lying off the coast see PARA 1053; as to jurisdiction in the case of offences on board ship see PARA 1054; as to offences committed by British seamen see PARA 1055; and as to proof etc of exemption see PARA 1061. As to the powers of magistrates' courts to issue fines on summary conviction see SENTENCING vol 92 (2015) PARA 176.
9   Merchant Shipping Act 1995 s 237(3).

1162. Taking wreck to foreign port. A person commits an offence if he takes into any foreign port[1] and sells:

(1)   any vessel[2] stranded, derelict or otherwise in distress found on or near the coasts[3] of the United Kingdom[4] or any tidal water[5] within United Kingdom waters[6];

(2)   any part of the cargo[7] or equipment of, or anything belonging to, such a vessel[8]; or

(3)   any wreck[9] found within those waters[10].

A person who is guilty of such an offence[11] is liable, on conviction on indictment, to imprisonment for a term not exceeding five years[12].

1   As to the meaning of 'port' see PARA 46 note 12.
2   As to the meaning of 'vessel' see PARA 919 note 5.
3   As to the meaning of 'on or near the coast' see *The Fulham* [1898] P 206 at 213, 8 Asp MLC 425 at 426, 427 (on appeal [1899] P 251, 8 Asp MLC 559, CA).
4   As to the meaning of 'United Kingdom' see PARA 16 note 3.
5   As to the meaning of 'tidal water' see PARA 923 note 13.
6   Merchant Shipping Act 1995 s 245(1)(a). As to the meaning of 'United Kingdom waters' see PARA 48 note 11.
7   As to the meaning of 'cargo' for salvage purposes see PARA 860.
8   Merchant Shipping Act 1995 s 245(1)(b).
9   As to the meaning of 'wreck' see PARA 923.
10   Merchant Shipping Act 1995 s 245(1)(c).
11   Ie an offence under the Merchant Shipping Act 1995 s 245 (see the text and notes 1–10): see s 245(2).
12   Merchant Shipping Act 1995 s 245(2). As to offences by officers of bodies corporate see PARA 1051; as to jurisdiction in relation to offences see PARA 1052; as to jurisdiction over ships lying off the coast see PARA 1053; as to jurisdiction in the case of offences on board ship see PARA 1054; as to offences committed by British seamen see PARA 1055; and as to proof etc of

exemption see PARA 1061. As to the powers of magistrates' courts to issue fines on summary conviction see SENTENCING vol 92 (2015) PARA 176.

1163. Interfering with wrecked vessel or wreck. A person commits an offence if, without the permission of the master[1], he boards or attempts to board any vessel[2] which is wrecked, stranded or in distress[3]; and the master of a vessel may forcibly repel any person committing or attempting to commit such an offence[4]. No such offence is, however, committed if the person is the receiver[5] or a person lawfully acting as the receiver or if he acts by command of the receiver or a person so acting[6]. A person who is guilty of such an offence is liable, on summary conviction, to a fine[7].

A person commits an offence if:

(1)   he impedes or hinders or attempts to impede or hinder the saving of[8]:

    (a)   any vessel stranded or in danger of being stranded, or otherwise in distress, on or near any coast or tidal water[9]; or

    (b)   any part of the cargo or equipment of any such vessel[10]; or

    (c)   any wreck[11];

(2)   he conceals any wreck[12];

(3)   he defaces or obliterates any mark on a vessel[13]; or

(4)   he wrongfully carries away or removes[14]:

    (a)   any part of any vessel stranded or in danger of being stranded, or otherwise in distress, on or near any coast or tidal water[15];

    (b)   any part of the cargo or equipment of any such vessel[16]; or

    (c)   any wreck[17].

A person who is guilty of such an offence is liable, on summary conviction, to a fine[18].

1   As to the meaning of 'master' see PARA 444 note 1.
2   As to the meaning of 'vessel' see PARA 919 note 5.
3   Merchant Shipping Act 1995 s 246(1).
4   Merchant Shipping Act 1995 s 246(4).
5   As to the meaning of 'receiver' see PARA 887 note 4.
6   Merchant Shipping Act 1995 s 246(2).
7   Merchant Shipping Act 1995 s 246(5)(a). As to the time limit for summary offences see PARA 1049; as to offences by officers of bodies corporate see PARA 1051; as to jurisdiction in relation to offences see PARA 1052; as to jurisdiction over ships lying off the coast see PARA 1053; as to jurisdiction in the case of offences on board ship see PARA 1054; as to offences committed by British seamen see PARA 1055; and as to proof etc of exemption see PARA 1061. As to the powers of magistrates' courts to issue fines on summary conviction see SENTENCING vol 92 (2015) PARA 176.
8   Merchant Shipping Act 1995 s 246(3)(a).
9   Merchant Shipping Act 1995 s 246(3)(a)(i). As to the meaning of 'tidal water' see PARA 987 note 6. As to the meaning of 'on or near the coast' see *The Fulham* [1898] P 206 at 213, 8 Asp MLC 425 at 426, 427 (on appeal [1899] P 251, 8 Asp MLC 559, CA).
10 Merchant Shipping Act 1995 s 246(3)(a)(ii).
11 Merchant Shipping Act 1995 s 246(3)(a)(iii). As to the meaning of 'wreck' see PARA 923.
12 Merchant Shipping Act 1995 s 246(3)(b).
13 Merchant Shipping Act 1995 s 246(3)(c).
14 Merchant Shipping Act 1995 s 246(3)(d).
15 Merchant Shipping Act 1995 s 246(3)(d)(i).
16 Merchant Shipping Act 1995 s 246(3)(d)(ii).
17 Merchant Shipping Act 1995 s 246(3)(d)(iii).
18 Merchant Shipping Act 1995 s 246(5)(b).

1164. Impeding a person endeavouring to save himself or another from shipwreck. Any person who unlawfully or maliciously prevents or impedes any person being on board or having quitted any ship or vessel in distress or wrecked, stranded or cast on shore in his endeavour to save his life or the life of any other person endeavouring to escape is guilty of an offence and liable, on conviction on indictment, to imprisonment for life or for any shorter term[1].

1 See the Offences against the Person Act 1861 s 17 (amended by the Statute Law Revision Act 1892; and the Statute Law Revision (No 2) Act 1893).

1165. Assaulting a magistrate etc on account of his preserving wreck. Any person who assaults, strikes or wounds any magistrate, officer or other person whatsoever lawfully authorised in the exercise of his duty in the preservation of any vessel in distress or of any vessel, goods or effects stranded or cast on shore or lying under water is guilty of an offence and liable, on conviction on indictment, to imprisonment for a term not exceeding seven years[1].

1 See the Offences against the Person Act 1861 s 37 (amended by the Statute Law Revision Act 1892).

1166. Contravention of provisions which protect sites of historic wrecks. A person commits an offence if, in a restricted area[1], he does any of the following things otherwise than under the authority of a licence granted by the Secretary of State (or by the Welsh Ministers, as the case may be)[2]:

(1) he tampers with, damages or removes any part of a vessel lying wrecked on or in the sea bed[3], or any object formerly contained in such a vessel[4]; or

(2) he carries out diving or salvage operations directed to the exploration of any wreck or to removing objects from it or from the sea bed, or uses equipment constructed or adapted for any purpose of diving or salvage operations[5]; or

(3) he deposits, so as to fall and lie abandoned on the sea bed, anything which, if it were to fall on the site of a wreck (whether it so falls or not), would wholly or partly obliterate the site or obstruct access to it or damage any part of the wreck[6];

and he commits an offence if he causes or permits any of those things to be done by others in a restricted area, otherwise than under the authority of such a licence[7].

A person also commits an offence if, without authority in writing granted by the Secretary of State[8], he enters a prohibited area[9], whether on the surface or under water[10].

A person guilty of any such offence[11] is liable, on conviction on indictment or on summary conviction, to a fine[12]; and proceedings for such an offence may be taken, and the offence may for all incidental purposes be treated as having been committed, at any place in the United Kingdom[13] where the offender is for the time being[14]. Nothing is, however, to be regarded as constituting such an offence where it is done by a person:

(a) in the course of any action taken by him for the sole purpose of dealing with an emergency of any description[15]; or

(b) in exercising, or seeing to the exercise of, functions conferred by or under an enactment, local or other, on him or a body for which he acts[16]; or

(c) out of necessity due to stress of weather or navigational hazards[17].

1 As to the meaning of 'restricted area' for these purposes see PARA 1133 note 1.
2 Protection of Wrecks Act 1973 s 1(3). This provision is subject to s 3(3) (see the text and notes 15–17): see s 1(3).
    A licence granted by the Secretary of State (or by the Welsh Ministers, as the case may be) for the purposes of s 1(3) must be in writing (s 1(5)); and:
    (1) the Secretary of State (or the Welsh Ministers, as the case may be) must, in respect of a restricted area, grant licences only to persons who appear to him (or to them, as the case may be) either (s 1(5)(a)):

(a)   to be competent and properly equipped to carry out salvage operations in a manner appropriate to the historical, archaeological or artistic importance of any wreck which may be lying in the area and of any objects contained or formerly contained in a wreck (s 1(5)(a)(i)); or

(b)   to have any other legitimate reason for doing in the area that which can only be done under the authority of a licence (s 1(5)(a)(ii));

(2)   a licence may be granted subject to conditions or restrictions, and may be varied or revoked by the Secretary of State (or by the Welsh Ministers, as the case may be) at any time after giving not less than one week's notice to the licensee (s 1(5)(b)); and

(3)   anything done contrary to any condition or restriction is to be treated for the purposes of s 1(3) as done otherwise than under the authority of the licence (s 1(5)(c)).

As to the Secretary of State see PARA 36. Functions of the Secretary of State under the Protection of Wrecks Act 1973, except s 2 (see the text and notes 8–10; and PARA 948), are transferred so as to be exercisable in relation to Wales by the Welsh Ministers: see the National Assembly for Wales (Transfer of Functions) Order 1999, SI 1999/672, Sch 1; and PARA 36. As to the meaning of 'Wales' see PARA 16 note 2.

Where a person is authorised by a licence granted by the Secretary of State (or by the Welsh Ministers, as the case may be) under the Protection of Wrecks Act 1973 s 1 to carry out diving or salvage operations, it is an offence for any other person to obstruct him, or cause or permit him to be obstructed, in doing anything which is authorised by the licence, subject however to s 3(3) (see the text and notes 15–17): s 1(6).

3   References to the 'sea bed' include any area submerged at high water of ordinary spring tides: Protection of Wrecks Act 1973 s 3(1).

4   Protection of Wrecks Act 1973 s 1(3)(a).

5   Protection of Wrecks Act 1973 s 1(3)(b).

6   Protection of Wrecks Act 1973 s 1(3)(c).

7   Protection of Wrecks Act 1973 s 1(3).

8   See note 2.

9   As to the meaning of 'prohibited area' for these purposes see PARA 948.

10 Protection of Wrecks Act 1973 s 2(3). This provision is subject to s 3(3) (see the text and notes 15–17): see s 2(3).

11 Ie under the Protection of Wrecks Act 1973 s 1 (see the text and notes 1–7) or under s 2 (see the text and notes 8–10): see s 3(4) (amended by the Magistrates' Courts Act 1980 s 32(2)).

12 Protection of Wrecks Act 1973 s 3(4) (as amended: see note 11). As to the powers of magistrates' courts to issue fines on summary conviction see SENTENCING vol 92 (2015) PARA 176.

13 As to the meaning of 'United Kingdom' see PARA 16 note 3.

14 Protection of Wrecks Act 1973 s 3(4) (as amended: see note 11).

15 Protection of Wrecks Act 1973 s 3(3)(a).

16 Protection of Wrecks Act 1973 s 3(3)(b).

17 Protection of Wrecks Act 1973 s 3(3)(c).

(vi) Offences Committed in Wartime

1167. Illegal activities in wartime. It is an offence:

(1)   for any person having British nationality without Her Majesty's licence to quit, or go on board any ship with a view of quitting, Her Majesty's dominions with intent to accept any commission or engagement in the naval service of any foreign state at war with any friendly state, that is, a foreign state which is at peace with Her Majesty[1];

(2)   for anyone, whether having British nationality or not, within Her Majesty's dominions to induce any other person to quit, or to go on board any ship with a view of quitting, Her Majesty's dominions with the like intent[2];

(3)   for the master or owner of any ship without Her Majesty's licence knowingly to take, or engage to take, or to have on board the ship within Her Majesty's dominions any illegally enlisted person[3];

(4) for any person without Her Majesty's licence to build, commission, equip or dispatch any ship to be employed in the military or naval service of any foreign state at war with a friendly state, or to build any vessel of war, adapt any ship for use as a vessel of war or dispatch or deliver any such ship from any part of Her Majesty's dominions[4];

(5) for any person within Her Majesty's dominions and without Her Majesty's licence to prepare or fit out any naval expedition to proceed against the dominions of any friendly state, or to engage in the preparation or fitting out or assisting in it, or to be employed in any capacity in that expedition[5].

1 See the Foreign Enlistment Act 1870 ss 4, 5; and ARMED CONFLICT AND EMERGENCY vol 3 (2011) PARA 12.
2 See the Foreign Enlistment Act 1870 ss 4, 5; and ARMED CONFLICT AND EMERGENCY vol 3 (2011) PARA 12.
3 See the Foreign Enlistment Act 1870 s 7; and ARMED CONFLICT AND EMERGENCY vol 3 (2011) PARA 12.
4 See the Foreign Enlistment Act 1870 ss 8, 10, 13; and ARMED CONFLICT AND EMERGENCY vol 3 (2011) PARA 13.
5 See the Foreign Enlistment Act 1870 ss 11–13; and ARMED CONFLICT AND EMERGENCY vol 3 (2011) PARA 14.

(vii) Pilotage Offences

1168. Pilots operating in areas without proper authorisation. If any person who is not an authorised pilot[1] for an area describes himself whilst he is in that area as being such a pilot or so holds himself out as to indicate or be reasonably understood to indicate that he is such a pilot[2], he is guilty of an offence and liable, on summary conviction, to a fine[3].

1 As to the meaning of 'authorised pilot' see PARA 574.
2 As to the authorisation of pilots by a competent harbour authority in or in any part of the area in relation to which its statutory duty to provide pilotage services is exercisable see PARA 577.
3 Pilotage Act 1987 s 3(8). As to the powers of magistrates' courts to issue fines on summary conviction see SENTENCING vol 92 (2015) PARA 176.

1169. Failure to meet requirements where compulsory pilotage in force. If any ship[1], which is being navigated[2] in an area and in circumstances in which pilotage[3] is compulsory for it by virtue of a pilotage direction[4], is not under pilotage as required[5] after an authorised pilot[6] has offered to take charge of the ship, the master[7] of the ship is guilty of an offence and liable, on summary conviction, to a fine[8].

The master of a ship commits an offence if the ship is navigated in an area in which a pilotage direction applies to it[9] and the competent harbour authority[10] which gave the direction has not been given pilotage notification[11]. A person guilty of this offence is liable on summary conviction to a fine[12].

1 As to the meaning of 'ship' see PARA 574 note 1.
2 As to the meaning of references to a ship navigating or being navigated see PARA 576 note 4.
3 As to the meaning of 'pilotage' see PARA 574.
4 As to the meaning of 'pilotage direction' see PARA 580.
5 Ie as required by the Pilotage Act 1987 s 15(1) (see PARA 588): see s 15(2).
6 As to the meaning of 'authorised pilot' see PARA 574. As to the rights of authorised pilots see PARA 590 et seq.
7 As to the meaning of 'master' see PARA 581 note 3.
8 Pilotage Act 1987 s 15(2). As to the powers of magistrates' courts to issue fines on summary conviction see SENTENCING vol 92 (2015) PARA 176.
9 Pilotage Act 1987 s 15(3)(a) (s 15(3) substituted, s 15(4), (5) added, by the Marine Navigation Act 2013 s 4).
10 As to the meaning of 'competent harbour authority' see PARA 575.

11 Pilotage Act 1987 s 15(3)(b) (as substituted: see note 9). 'Pilotage notification' is notification that the ship will be navigated in an area in which a pilotage direction will apply to it and that an authorised pilot is required to pilot the ship (s 15(4)(a) (as so added)) or that an authorised pilot is not required because the ship will be piloted by a specified person acting in accordance with a pilotage exemption certificate (s 15(4)(b) (as so added)).
12 Pilotage Act 1987 s 15(5) (as added: see note 9).

1170. Pilotage by unauthorised pilot. If:
(1)   the master[1] of any ship[2] navigates it[3] in any part of a harbour[4] under the pilotage[5] of an unauthorised person[6] without first notifying the competent harbour authority[7] that he proposes to do so, he is guilty of an offence[8];
(2)   an unauthorised person pilots a ship within a harbour knowing that an authorised pilot has offered to pilot it, he is guilty of an offence[9];
(3)   the master of a ship navigating within a harbour knowingly employs or continues to employ an unauthorised person to pilot the ship after an authorised pilot has offered to pilot it, he is guilty of an offence[10].

Any person who is guilty of an offence under any of heads (1), (2) or (3) above is liable, on summary conviction, to a fine[11].

1   As to the meaning of 'master' see PARA 581 note 3.
2   As to the meaning of 'ship' see PARA 574 note 1.
3   As to the meaning of references to a ship navigating or being navigated see PARA 576 note 4.
4   As to the meaning of 'harbour' see PARA 575.
5   As to the meaning of 'pilotage' see PARA 574.
6   For these purposes, a person is an unauthorised person if he is neither an authorised pilot nor the holder of a pilotage exemption certificate in respect of the ship and the area in question; and any person, other than the master or one of the crew of a ship, who is on the bridge of the ship or in any other position from which the ship is navigated, whether on board or elsewhere, is deemed to be piloting the ship unless he proves otherwise: Pilotage Act 1987 s 17(5). As to the meaning of 'authorised pilot' see PARA 574; and as to the meaning of 'pilotage exemption certificate' see PARA 581. As to the meaning of 'pilot' see PARA 574.
7   As to the meaning of 'competent harbour authority' see PARA 575.
8   Pilotage Act 1987 s 17(2). As to the application of s 17(2)–(4) see PARA 590 note 5.
9   Pilotage Act 1987 s 17(3). See also note 8. The offer by the licensed pilot must be made or communicated in relation to the particular movement of the vessel which is in question: *Montague v Babbs* [1972] 1 All ER 240, [1971] 1 WLR 176, [1972] 1 Lloyd's Rep 65, DC; *Babbs v Press* [1971] 3 All ER 654, [1971] 1 WLR 1739, [1971] 2 Lloyd's Rep 383, DC (pilot flag two miles down river not an offer). Where such an offer is made, the fact that the task of piloting is almost complete is no defence: *Smith v Cocking* [1959] 1 Lloyd's Rep 88, DC.
10   Pilotage Act 1987 s 17(4). See also note 8.
11   Pilotage Act 1987 s 17(6). As to the powers of magistrates' courts to issue fines on summary conviction see SENTENCING vol 92 (2015) PARA 176.

1171. Failure of master to supply sufficient information to enable pilot to carry out his duties. Any master[1] of a ship[2] who:
(1)   refuses to comply with a request made to him by a pilot[3] to declare the piloted ship's draught of water, length and beam, and to provide him with such other information relating to the ship or its cargo as the pilot specifies and is necessary to enable him to carry out his duties as the pilot of the ship[4]; or
(2)   makes a statement which is false in a material particular in answer to such a request as is mentioned in head (1) above, knowing it to be false or being reckless as to whether it is false, or fails without reasonable excuse to correct such a statement made by another person in answer to such a request, although himself knowing it to be false[5]; or
(3)   without reasonable excuse fails to bring to the notice of any person who pilots the ship any defects in, and any matter peculiar to, the ship and its machinery and equipment of which the master knows and which might materially affect the navigation of the ship[6],

is guilty of an offence[7], and liable, on summary conviction, to a fine[8].

1 As to the meaning of 'master' see PARA 581 note 3.
2 As to the meaning of 'ship' see PARA 574 note 1.
3 As to the meaning of 'pilot' see PARA 574.
4 Pilotage Act 1987 s 18(3)(a). The text refers to a request made to the master of a ship in pursuance of s 18(1) (see PARA 591): see s 18(3)(a).
5 Pilotage Act 1987 s 18(3)(b).
6 Pilotage Act 1987 s 18(3)(c). The text refers to any person who without reasonable excuse contravenes s 18(2) (see PARA 591): see s 18(3)(c).
7 Pilotage Act 1987 s 18(3).
8 Pilotage Act 1987 s 18(4). As to the powers of magistrates' courts to issue fines on summary conviction see SENTENCING vol 92 (2015) PARA 176.

1172. Taking authorised pilot out of his area. A master[1] of a ship[2] who, without reasonable excuse, contravenes the prohibition on taking an unauthorised pilot[3] without his consent beyond the point up to which he has been engaged to pilot the ship[4], is guilty of an offence and liable, on summary conviction, to a fine[5].

1 As to the meaning of 'master' see PARA 581 note 3.
2 As to the meaning of 'ship' see PARA 574 note 1.
3 As to the meaning of 'authorised pilot' see PARA 574.
4 Ie a person who contravenes the Pilotage Act 1987 s 19(1) (see PARA 592): see s 19(2).
5 Pilotage Act 1987 s 19(2). As to the powers of magistrates' courts to issue fines on summary conviction see SENTENCING vol 92 (2015) PARA 176.

1173. Failure to provide facilities for authorised pilot boarding or leaving ship. If the master[1] of any ship[2] without reasonable excuse contravenes the requirements to facilitate a pilot[3] boarding and subsequently leaving the ship in circumstances where the master is offered the services of an authorised pilot[4] (or if the master of a ship accepts the services of an authorised pilot in any other circumstances)[5], he is guilty of an offence and liable, on summary conviction, to a fine[6].

1 As to the meaning of 'master' see PARA 581 note 3.
2 As to the meaning of 'ship' see PARA 574 note 1.
3 As to the meaning of 'pilot' see PARA 574.
4 As to the meaning of 'authorised pilot' see PARA 574.
5 Ie if the master of any ship contravenes the Pilotage Act 1987 s 20(1) (see PARA 593): see s 20(2).
6 Pilotage Act 1987 s 20(2). As to the powers of magistrates' courts to issue fines on summary conviction see SENTENCING vol 92 (2015) PARA 176.

1174. Misconduct by pilot endangering ship or persons on board ship. If the pilot[1] of a ship[2]:

(1) does any act which causes or is likely to cause the loss or destruction of, or serious damage to, the ship or its machinery, navigational equipment or safety equipment, or the death of, or serious injury to, a person on board the ship[3]; or

(2) omits to do anything required to preserve the ship or its machinery, navigational equipment or safety equipment, from loss, destruction or serious damage, or to preserve any person on board the ship from death or serious injury[4],

and the act or omission is deliberate or amounts to a breach or neglect of duty or he is under the influence of drink or a drug at the time of the act or omission, he is guilty of an offence[5]; and he is liable, on conviction on indictment, to imprisonment for a term not exceeding two years or a fine (or to both) or, on summary conviction, to imprisonment for a term not exceeding six months or a fine[6].

1 As to the meaning of 'pilot' see PARA 574.
2 As to the meaning of 'ship' see PARA 574 note 1.

3   Pilotage Act 1987 s 21(1)(a).
4   Pilotage Act 1987 s 21(1)(b).
5   Pilotage Act 1987 s 21(1).
6   Pilotage Act 1987 s 21(2). As to the powers of magistrates' courts to issue fines on summary
     conviction see SENTENCING vol 92 (2015) PARA 176.

(viii) Obstruction of Enforcement Powers

1175. Interference with power to require production of ships' documents.
If any person, on being duly required[1] by an officer to produce a log book or any
document[2], fails without reasonable excuse to produce the log book or document,
he is liable, on summary conviction, to a fine[3].
   If any person, on being duly required[4] by any officer:

(1)   to produce a log book or document, refuses to allow the log book or
        document to be inspected or copied[5];
(2)   to muster the crew, impedes the muster[6]; or
(3)   to give any explanation, refuses or neglects to give the explanation or
        knowingly misleads or deceives the officer[7],

he is liable, on summary conviction, to a fine[8].

1   Ie duly required under the Merchant Shipping Act 1995 s 257 (see PARA 47): see s 257(3).
2   As to official log books see PARA 551 et seq.
3   Merchant Shipping Act 1995 s 257(3). As to the time limit for summary offences see PARA 1049;
     as to offences by officers of bodies corporate see PARA 1051; as to jurisdiction in relation to
     offences see PARA 1052; as to jurisdiction over ships lying off the coast see PARA 1053; as to
     jurisdiction in the case of offences on board ship see PARA 1054; as to offences committed by
     British seamen see PARA 1055; and as to proof etc of exemption see PARA 1061. As to the powers
     of magistrates' courts to issue fines on summary conviction see SENTENCING vol 92 (2015)
     PARA 176.
4   Ie duly required under the Merchant Shipping Act 1995 s 257 (see PARA 47): see s 257(4).
5   Merchant Shipping Act 1995 s 257(4)(a).
6   Merchant Shipping Act 1995 s 257(4)(b).
7   Merchant Shipping Act 1995 s 257(4)(c).
8   Merchant Shipping Act 1995 s 257(4).

1176. Interference with powers to inspect ships and their equipment etc.
If any person obstructs a person in the exercise of his powers to inspect ships and
their equipment etc[1], or fails to comply with a requirement made by a person
exercising his powers, he is liable, on summary conviction, to a fine[2].

1   Ie his powers under the Merchant Shipping Act 1995 s 258 (see PARA 48): see s 258(5).
2   Merchant Shipping Act 1995 s 258(5). As to the time limit for summary offences see PARA 1049;
     as to offences by officers of bodies corporate see PARA 1051; as to jurisdiction in relation to
     offences see PARA 1052; as to jurisdiction over ships lying off the coast see PARA 1053; as to
     jurisdiction in the case of offences on board ship see PARA 1054; as to offences committed by
     British seamen see PARA 1055; and as to proof etc of exemption see PARA 1061. As to the powers
     of magistrates' courts to issue fines on summary conviction see SENTENCING vol 92 (2015)
     PARA 176.

**1177. Interference with powers of inspectors in relation to premises and
ships.** A person who:
(1)   intentionally obstructs an inspector[1] in the exercise of any power
        available to him[2] in relation to premises and ships[3]; or
(2)   without reasonable excuse does not comply with a requirement duly
        imposed[4] or prevents another person from complying with such a
        requirement[5]; or
(3)   without prejudice to the generality of head (2) above, makes a statement
        or signs a declaration which he knows is false, or recklessly makes a
        statement or signs a declaration which is false, in purported compliance
        with a requirement duly made[6],

is liable, on conviction on indictment, to imprisonment for a term not exceeding two years or a fine (or to both) or, on summary conviction, to a fine[7].

1 As to the powers of inspectors for these purposes see PARA 49.
2 Ie under the Merchant Shipping Act 1995 s 259 (see PARA 49): see s 260(1)(a).
3 Merchant Shipping Act 1995 s 260(1)(a). As to the meaning of 'ship' see PARA 229.
4 Ie in pursuance of the Merchant Shipping Act 1995 s 259 (see PARA 49): see s 260(1)(b).
5 Merchant Shipping Act 1995 s 260(1)(b). See note 3.
6 Merchant Shipping Act 1995 s 260(1)(c). The text refers to a requirement made in pursuance of s 259(2)(i) (see PARA 49): see s 260(1)(c).
7 Merchant Shipping Act 1995 s 260(1). As to the time limit for summary offences see PARA 1049; as to offences by officers of bodies corporate see PARA 1051; as to jurisdiction in relation to offences see PARA 1052; as to jurisdiction over ships lying off the coast see PARA 1053; as to jurisdiction in the case of offences on board ship see PARA 1054; as to offences committed by British seamen see PARA 1055; and as to proof etc of exemption see PARA 1061. As to the powers of magistrates' courts to issue fines on summary conviction see SENTENCING vol 92 (2015) PARA 176.

1178. Contravention of a requirement imposed by prohibition notice and improvement notice. Any person who contravenes any requirement imposed by an improvement notice[1] is liable, on conviction on indictment, to a fine or, on summary conviction, to a fine[2].

Any person who contravenes any prohibition imposed by a prohibition notice[3] is liable, on conviction on indictment, to imprisonment for a term not exceeding two years or a fine (or to both) or, on summary conviction, to a fine[4].

It is a defence for a person charged with such an offence[5] to prove that he exercised all due diligence to avoid a contravention of the requirement or prohibition in question[6].

1 As to the meaning of 'improvement notice' see PARA 51. For these purposes, any reference to an improvement notice includes a reference to such a notice as modified under the Merchant Shipping Act 1995 s 264(3) (see PARA 54): s 266(4).
2 Merchant Shipping Act 1995 s 266(1). As to the time limit for summary offences see PARA 1049; as to offences by officers of bodies corporate see PARA 1051; as to jurisdiction in relation to offences see PARA 1052; as to jurisdiction over ships lying off the coast see PARA 1053; as to jurisdiction in the case of offences on board ship see PARA 1054; as to offences committed by British seamen see PARA 1055; and as to proof etc of exemption see PARA 1061. As to the powers of magistrates' courts to issue fines on summary conviction see SENTENCING vol 92 (2015) PARA 176.
3 As to the meaning of 'prohibition notice' see PARA 52. For these purposes, any reference to a prohibition notice includes a reference to such a notice as modified under the Merchant Shipping Act 1995 s 264(3) (see PARA 54): s 266(4).
4 Merchant Shipping Act 1995 s 266(2).
5 Ie an offence under the Merchant Shipping Act 1995 s 266: see s 266(3).
6 Merchant Shipping Act 1995 s 266(3).

1179. Failure to give required information or assistance to surveyor of ships. If the owner, master[1] or engineer of any ship[2] being surveyed by a surveyor of ships[3], on being required to give any information or assistance for the purpose of making returns to the Secretary of State[4], fails without reasonable excuse to give the information or assistance, he is liable, on summary conviction, to a fine[5].

1 As to the meaning of 'master' see PARA 444 note 1.
2 As to the meaning of 'ship' see PARA 229.
3 As to the meaning of 'surveyor of ships' see PARA 46 note 13.
4 Ie on being required under the Merchant Shipping Act 1995 s 299(5) to give any information or assistance for the purposes of returns under s 299(4) (see PARA 41): see s 299(6). As to the Secretary of State see PARA 36.
5 Merchant Shipping Act 1995 s 299(6). As to the time limit for summary offences see PARA 1049; as to offences by officers of bodies corporate see PARA 1051; as to jurisdiction in relation to offences see PARA 1052; as to jurisdiction over ships lying off the coast see PARA 1053; as to jurisdiction in the case of offences on board ship see PARA 1054; as to offences committed by

British seamen see PARA 1055; and as to proof etc of exemption see PARA 1061. As to the powers of magistrates' courts to issue fines on summary conviction see SENTENCING vol 92 (2015) PARA 176.

1180. Enforcement of orders regulating shipping services in the event of foreign action. If a person discloses any information which has been furnished or obtained by him under, or in connection with the execution of, the provisions relating to the regulation of shipping services in the event of foreign action[1], he is liable, unless the disclosure is made:

(1)	with the consent of the person from whom the information was obtained[2]; or

(2)	in connection with the execution of those provisions[3]; or

(3)	for the purposes of any legal proceedings arising out of the enforcement provisions[4] of or any report of such proceedings[5]; or

(4)	in pursuance of an EU obligation to an EU institution[6],

on summary conviction to a fine[7].

A person who:

(a)	refuses or intentionally neglects to furnish any information which he is required to furnish under the provisions relating to the relating to the regulation of shipping services in the event of foreign action[8]; or

(b)	in furnishing any such information makes any statement which he knows to be false in a material particular, or recklessly makes any statement which is false in a material particular[9],

is liable, on summary conviction, to a fine[10].

A person who intentionally contravenes or fails to comply with any provision of an order or direction made or given under the provisions relating to the regulation of shipping services in the event of foreign action[11], other than a provision requiring him to give any information, is liable, on conviction on indictment or on summary conviction, to a fine[12]. Where the order or direction requires anything to be done, or not to be done, by, to or on a ship[13], and the requirement is not complied with, the owner and master[14] of the ship are each to be regarded as intentionally failing to comply, without prejudice to the liability of anyone else[15].

A person is not guilty of an offence against any provision contained in or having effect under the provisions relating to the regulation of shipping services in the event of foreign action[16] by reason only of something done by that person wholly outside the territory of the United Kingdom[17] unless that person is a Commonwealth citizen under the British Nationality Act 1981[18] or a company incorporated under the law of any part of the United Kingdom[19].

1	Ie under the Shipping and Trading Interests (Protection) Act 1995 ss 1, 2 (see PARA 75): see s 3(4). As to the meaning of 'shipping services' for these purposes see PARA 75 note 6.

2	Shipping and Trading Interests (Protection) Act 1995 s 3(4)(a).

3	Shipping and Trading Interests (Protection) Act 1995 s 3(4)(b). The text refers to the execution of ss 1, 2: see s 3(4)(b).

4	Ie arising out of the Shipping and Trading Interests (Protection) Act 1995 s 3: see s 3(4)(c).

5	Shipping and Trading Interests (Protection) Act 1995 s 3(4)(c).

6	Shipping and Trading Interests (Protection) Act 1995 s 3(4)(d) (amended by SI 2011/1043).

7	Shipping and Trading Interests (Protection) Act 1995 s 3(4). In relation to the extension of disclosure powers under s 3(4) see the Anti-terrorism, Crime and Security Act 2001 s 17, Sch 4 Pt 1 para 36; and CRIMINAL LAW vol 26 (2016) PARA 443. The Merchant Shipping Act 1995 Pt XII (ss 274–291) (provision in relation to legal proceedings and related matters) (see PARA 1049 et seq) applies for the purposes of the Shipping and Trading Interests (Protection) Act 1995 as it applies for the purposes of the Merchant Shipping Act 1995: Shipping and Trading Interests (Protection) Act 1995 s 7(1). As to the time limit for summary offences see PARA 1049; as to offences by officers of bodies corporate see PARA 1051; as to jurisdiction in relation to offences see PARA 1052; as to jurisdiction over ships lying off the coast see PARA 1053; as to jurisdiction in the case of offences on board ship see PARA 1054; as to offences committed by British seamen see PARA 1055; and as to proof etc of exemption see PARA 1061. As to the powers of magistrates' courts to issue fines on summary conviction see SENTENCING vol 92 (2015) PARA 176.

8 Shipping and Trading Interests (Protection) Act 1995 s 3(5)(a). The text refers to a requirement to furnish any information under ss 1, 2 (see PARA 75): see s 3(4)(b).

9 Shipping and Trading Interests (Protection) Act 1995 s 3(5)(b).

10 Shipping and Trading Interests (Protection) Act 1995 s 3(5).

11 Ie an order or direction made or given pursuant to the Shipping and Trading Interests (Protection) Act 1995 ss 1, 2: see s 3(6).

12 Shipping and Trading Interests (Protection) Act 1995 s 3(6) (amended by SI 2015/664).

13 As to the meaning of 'ship' for these purposes see PARA 75 note 6.

14 For these purposes, 'master' has the same meaning as in the Merchant Shipping Act 1995 (see PARA 444 note 1): Shipping and Trading Interests (Protection) Act 1995 s 9(2).

15 Shipping and Trading Interests (Protection) Act 1995 s 3(6).

16 Ie under the Shipping and Trading Interests (Protection) Act 1995 ss 1, 2: see s 3(7).

17 As to the meaning of 'United Kingdom' see PARA 16 note 3.

18 As to who are Commonwealth citizens under the British Nationality Act 1981 see BRITISH NATIONALITY vol 4 (2011) PARA 409.

19 Shipping and Trading Interests (Protection) Act 1995 s 3(7).

1181. Enforcement of orders regulating coastal shipping services which are not British-based. Where:

(1)   any ship[1] is used in the course of the provision of any coastal shipping services which are not British-based[2]; or

(2)   anything is done on board a ship with a view to its being used to provide such services[3],

and where the provision of those services is prohibited[4] and is not sanctioned by any licence duly issued[5], the master[6] and the owner of the ship[7] are each guilty of an offence[8]. It is a defence in such proceedings:

(a)   against the master of a ship to prove that he did not know and had no reason to suspect that, in the circumstances of the case, the provision of the shipping services referred to in head (1) above or, as the case may be, head (2) above, was prohibited[9] or that he had reasonable grounds for believing that the provision of those services was sanctioned by a licence duly issued[10];

(b)   against a person other than the master of a ship to prove that, under the terms of one or more charterparties or management agreements entered into by the accused, the right to determine the purpose for which the ship in question was being used at the time of the alleged offence was wholly vested in some other person or persons party thereto, whether or not such other person or persons had entered into a further charterparty or management agreement providing for that right to be vested in some other person[11].

Any person who in connection with an application for a licence[12] or in purported compliance with the requirements of any notice served on him requiring the production or furnishing of documents or information[13] knowingly or recklessly furnishes information which is false in a material particular is guilty of an offence[14]. Any person who:

(i)   without reasonable excuse, the proof of which lies on him, fails to comply with the requirements of any such notice[15]; or

(ii)   intentionally alters, suppresses, conceals or destroys a document which he has been so required to produce[16],

is guilty of an offence[17].

Any person guilty of any such offence[18] is liable, on conviction on indictment, to imprisonment for a term not exceeding two years or a fine (or to both) or, on summary conviction, to a fine[19].

1 As to the meaning of 'ship' for these purposes see PARA 75 note 6.
2 Shipping and Trading Interests (Protection) Act 1995 s 6(1)(a). The text refers to the provision of any shipping services to which s 5 (see PARA 77) applies: see s 6(1)(a). As to the meaning of 'shipping services' for these purposes see PARA 75 note 6.
3 Shipping and Trading Interests (Protection) Act 1995 s 6(1)(b).
4 Ie by virtue of the Shipping and Trading Interests (Protection) Act 1995 s 5(1): see s 6(1).
5 Ie any licence issued by virtue of the Shipping and Trading Interests (Protection) Act 1995 s 5(3)(b): see s 6(1).
6 For these purposes, 'master' has the same meaning as in the Merchant Shipping Act 1995 (see PARA 444 note 1): Shipping and Trading Interests (Protection) Act 1995 s 9(2).
7 For these purposes, where the ship is chartered by demise or is managed (either wholly or in part) by a person other than the owner under the terms of a management agreement, the reference to the owner of the ship is to be construed as including a reference to the charterer under the charter by demise, to any such manager under the terms of a management agreement or (if the ship is both chartered and managed in this way), to both the charterer and any such manager: Shipping and Trading Interests (Protection) Act 1995 s 6(2). 'Management agreement', in relation to a ship, means any agreement, other than a charterparty or a contract of employment, under which the ship is managed, either wholly or in part, by a person other than the owner, whether on behalf of the owner or on behalf of some other person: s 6(9).
8 Shipping and Trading Interests (Protection) Act 1995 s 6(1). The provisions of s 6(1) apply to offences falling within s 6(1) wherever committed: s 6(8). Without prejudice to the Merchant Shipping Act 1995 s 291 (service of documents) (see PARA 74) in its application to the Shipping and Trading Interests (Protection) Act 1995, any document required or authorised by or under any enactment to be served for the purpose of the institution of, or otherwise in connection with proceedings for an offence under s 6(1) is treated, where it is to be served on a person who was, at the time of the alleged offence, either the owner of the ship in question or such a charterer by demise or manager of that ship as is mentioned in s 6(2) (see note 7), as duly served on that person if sent to him by post at his last-known address, whether of his residence or of a place where he carries on business, or left for him at that address, or if the document is served on the master of the ship in question: s 7(3).
9 Shipping and Trading Interests (Protection) Act 1995 s 6(6)(a). The text refers to shipping services prohibited by virtue of s 5(1): see s 6(6)(a).
10 Shipping and Trading Interests (Protection) Act 1995 s 6(6)(b). The text refers to a licence issued by virtue of s 5(3)(b): see s 6(6)(b).
11 Shipping and Trading Interests (Protection) Act 1995 s 6(7).
12 Ie a licence such as is mentioned in the Shipping and Trading Interests (Protection) Act 1995 s 5(3)(b): see s 6(3).
13 Ie any notice served on him by virtue of the Shipping and Trading Interests (Protection) Act 1995 s 5(3)(e) (see PARA 77): see s 6(3).
14 Shipping and Trading Interests (Protection) Act 1995 s 6(3). The provisions of s 6(3) apply to offences falling within s 6(3) wherever committed: s 6(8).
15 Shipping and Trading Interests (Protection) Act 1995 s 6(4)(a).
16 Shipping and Trading Interests (Protection) Act 1995 s 6(4)(b). The text refers to a document which the person has been required to produce in pursuance of s 5(3)(e): see s 6(4)(b).
17 Shipping and Trading Interests (Protection) Act 1995 s 6(4). The provisions of s 6(4) apply to offences falling within s 6(4) wherever committed: s 6(8).
18 Ie any offence under the Shipping and Trading Interests (Protection) Act 1995 s 6: see s 6(5).
19 Shipping and Trading Interests (Protection) Act 1995 s 6(5) (amended by SI 2015/664). The Merchant Shipping Act 1995 Pt XII (ss 274–291) (provision in relation to legal proceedings and related matters) (see PARA 1049 et seq) applies for the purposes of the Shipping and Trading Interests (Protection) Act 1995 as it applies for the purposes of the Merchant Shipping Act 1995: Shipping and Trading Interests (Protection) Act 1995 s 7(1). However, proceedings for any offence under s 6 may not be instituted except by or with the consent of the Attorney General or the Secretary of State: s 7(2). As to the Secretary of State see PARA 36. As to the Attorney General see CONSTITUTIONAL AND ADMINISTRATIVE LAW vol 20 (2014) PARA 273.

(ix) Improper Disclosures; Giving False Information

1182. Printing, selling etc of forms not prepared or approved by the Secretary of State. If any person prints, sells or uses any document purporting to be a form approved by the Secretary of State[1] knowing that the document is not the form approved for the time being or that the document has not been prepared or issued by the Secretary of State, that person is liable, on summary conviction, to a fine[2].

1   As to the Secretary of State see PARA 36; and as to his power to prepare and approve forms see PARA 40.
2   Merchant Shipping Act 1995 s 300(7). As to the time limit for summary offences see PARA 1049; as to offences by officers of bodies corporate see PARA 1051; as to jurisdiction in relation to offences see PARA 1052; as to jurisdiction over ships lying off the coast see PARA 1053; as to jurisdiction in the case of offences on board ship see PARA 1054; as to offences committed by British seamen see PARA 1055; and as to proof etc of exemption see PARA 1061. As to the powers of magistrates' courts to issue fines on summary conviction see SENTENCING vol 92 (2015) PARA 176.

(x) Damage to Lighthouses etc; False Lights

1183. Offences in connection with damage etc to lighthouses etc. A person who, without lawful authority:

(1)   intentionally or recklessly damages any lighthouse[1] or the lights exhibited in it, or any lightship, buoy or beacon[2];
(2)   removes, casts adrift or sinks any lightship, buoy or beacon[3]; or
(3)   conceals or obscures any lighthouse, buoy or beacon[4],

commits an offence[5]; and a person who, without reasonable cause, rides by, makes fast to, or runs foul of, any lightship, buoy or beacon commits an offence[6].

A person who is guilty of any such offence[7] is liable, in addition to being liable for the expenses of making good any damage so occasioned, on summary conviction, to a fine[8].

1   As to the meaning of 'lighthouse' see PARA 1017 note 1.
2   Merchant Shipping Act 1995 s 219(1)(a). As to the meaning of 'buoys and beacons' see PARA 1017 note 2.
3   Merchant Shipping Act 1995 s 219(1)(b).
4   Merchant Shipping Act 1995 s 219(1)(c).
5   Merchant Shipping Act 1995 s 219(1).
6   Merchant Shipping Act 1995 s 219(2).
7   Ie under the Merchant Shipping Act 1995 s 219 (see the text and notes 1–6): see s 219(3).
8   Merchant Shipping Act 1995 s 219(3). As to the time limit for summary offences see PARA 1049; as to offences by officers of bodies corporate see PARA 1051; as to jurisdiction in relation to offences see PARA 1052; as to jurisdiction over ships lying off the coast see PARA 1053; as to jurisdiction in the case of offences on board ship see PARA 1054; as to offences committed by British seamen see PARA 1055; and as to proof etc of exemption see PARA 1061. As to the powers of magistrates' courts to issue fines on summary conviction see SENTENCING vol 92 (2015) PARA 176.

1184. Offences in connection with prevention of false lights. Whenever any light is exhibited at such place or in such manner as to be liable to be mistaken for a light proceeding from a lighthouse[1], the general lighthouse authority[2] within whose area[3] the place is situated may serve a notice (a 'prevention notice') upon the owner of the place where the light is exhibited or upon the person having the charge of the light[4].

A prevention notice is a notice directing the person to whom it is addressed to take, within a reasonable time specified in the notice, effectual means for extinguishing or effectually screening the light and for preventing for the future any similar light[5].

A prevention notice may, in addition to any other mode of service authorised by the Merchant Shipping Act 1995[6], be served by affixing the notice in some conspicuous spot near to the light to which it relates[7].

If a person on whom a prevention notice is served fails, without reasonable excuse, to comply with the directions contained in the notice, he is liable, on summary conviction, to a fine[8].

If a person on whom a prevention notice is served neglects for a period of seven days to extinguish or effectually screen the light mentioned in the notice, the general lighthouse authority may enter the place where the light is and forthwith extinguish it, doing no unnecessary damage[9]. Where a general lighthouse authority incurs any expenses in exercising these powers[10], it may recover the expenses from the person on whom the prevention notice is served[11]. Any such expenses may, in England and Wales[12], be recovered summarily as a civil debt[13].

1   As to the meaning of 'lighthouse' see PARA 1017 note 1.
2   As to the meaning of 'general lighthouse authority' see PARA 1017.
3   As to the meaning of 'area' see PARA 1017 note 12.
4   Merchant Shipping Act 1995 s 220(1).
5   Merchant Shipping Act 1995 s 220(2).
6   As to the service of documents under the Merchant Shipping Act 1995 generally see PARA 74.
7   Merchant Shipping Act 1995 s 220(3).
8   Merchant Shipping Act 1995 s 220(4). As to the time limit for summary offences see PARA 1049; as to offences by officers of bodies corporate see PARA 1051; as to jurisdiction in relation to offences see PARA 1052; as to jurisdiction over ships lying off the coast see PARA 1053; as to jurisdiction in the case of offences on board ship see PARA 1054; as to offences committed by British seamen see PARA 1055; and as to proof etc of exemption see PARA 1061. As to the powers of magistrates' courts to issue fines on summary conviction see SENTENCING vol 92 (2015) PARA 176.
9   Merchant Shipping Act 1995 s 220(5).
10 Ie under the Merchant Shipping Act 1995 s 220(5) (see the text and note 9): see s 220(6).
11 Merchant Shipping Act 1995 s 220(6).
12 As to the meanings of 'England' and 'Wales' see PARA 16 note 2.
13 Merchant Shipping Act 1995 s 220(7).

(3) BARRATRY AND PIRACY

1185. Barratry. A master or a member of a crew who wilfully commits a wrongful act to the prejudice of the owner or, as the case may be, charterer is guilty of the offence of barratry[1].

1   See the Marine Insurance Act 1906 s 30(2), Sch 1 r 11; and INSURANCE vol 60 (2011) PARA 333. See also *Earle v Rowcroft* (1806) 8 East 126. The commission of a crime is not necessary to constitute barratry: *Compania Naviera Bachi v Henry Hosegood & Co Ltd* [1938] 2 All ER 189, 60 Ll L Rep 236.

1186. Piracy under the United Nations Convention on the Law of the Sea. For the avoidance of doubt, it is declared that, for the purposes of any proceedings before a court in the United Kingdom[1] in respect of piracy, the following provisions[2] are to be treated as part of the law of nations[3].

Piracy consists of any of the following acts:

(1)   any illegal acts of violence or detention, or any act of depredation, committed for private ends by the crew or the passengers of a private ship or a private aircraft, and directed[4]:

(a)   on the high seas[5], against another ship or aircraft, or against persons or property on board such ship or aircraft[6];

(b)   against a ship, aircraft, persons or property in a place outside the jurisdiction of any state[7];

(2)   any act of voluntary participation in the operation of a ship or of an aircraft with knowledge of facts making it a pirate ship or aircraft[8];

(3)   any act of inciting or of intentionally facilitating an act described in head (1) or head (2) above[9].

The acts of piracy, as so defined, committed by a warship, government ship or government aircraft whose crew has mutinied and taken control of the ship or aircraft are assimilated to acts committed by a private ship or aircraft[10].

1   As to the meaning of 'United Kingdom' see PARA 16 note 3.
2   Ie the provisions of the United Nations Convention on the Law of the Sea (Montego Bay, 10 December 1982 to 9 December 1984; TS 3 Misc 11 (1983); Cmnd 8941) arts 101–103 (see the text and notes 4–10) which are set out in the Merchant Shipping and Maritime Security Act 1997 s 26(1), Sch 5: see s 26(1). See also note 3.
3   Merchant Shipping and Maritime Security Act 1997 s 26(1). Her Majesty may by Order in Council direct that s 26(1)–(3), Sch 5 are to extend to the Isle of Man, any of the Channel Islands or any colony with such modifications, if any, as appear to Her to be appropriate: s 26(4). In exercise of the power so conferred, Her Majesty has made the Aviation Security and Piracy (Overseas Territories) Order 2000, SI 2000/3059. As to the meaning of 'colony' see STATUTES AND LEGISLATIVE PROCESS vol 96 (2012) PARA 1208. In connection with piracy generally see INTERNATIONAL RELATIONS LAW vol 61 (2010) PARA 155 et seq.
4   United Nations Convention on the Law of the Sea 1982 art 101(a).
5   For these purposes, the high seas are to be taken, in accordance with the United Nations Convention on the Law of the Sea 1982 art 58(2), to include all waters beyond the territorial sea of the United Kingdom or any other state: Merchant Shipping and Maritime Security Act 1997 s 26(2). As to the extent of the territorial sea (or waters) of the United Kingdom see INTERNATIONAL RELATIONS LAW vol 61 (2010) PARA 121 et seq.
6   United Nations Convention on the Law of the Sea 1982 art 101(a)(i). For these purposes, a ship or aircraft is considered a pirate ship or aircraft if it is intended by the persons in dominant control to be used for the purpose of committing one of the acts referred to in art 101 (see heads (1)–(3) in the text): art 103. The same applies if the ship or aircraft has been used to commit any such act, so long as it remains under the control of the persons guilty of that act: art 103.
7   United Nations Convention on the Law of the Sea 1982 art 101(a)(ii).
8   United Nations Convention on the Law of the Sea 1982 art 101(b).
9   United Nations Convention on the Law of the Sea 1982 art 101(c).
10 United Nations Convention on the Law of the Sea 1982 art 102.

(4) CIVIL LIABILITY OF SEAMEN FOR OFFENCES

1187. Seaman's liability for damages when absent without leave. Provision is made[1] with respect to the liability of a seaman[2] employed in a United Kingdom ship[3] to damages for being absent from his ship at a time when he is required under his contract of employment to be on board[4].

If he proves that his absence was due to an accident[5] or mistake or some other cause beyond his control and that he took all reasonable precautions to avoid being absent, his absence is not to be treated as a breach of contract[6]. Where, however, this does not apply, then, if no special damages are claimed, his liability is £10 and, if special damages are claimed, his liability is not more than £100[7].

1   Ie by the Merchant Shipping Act 1995 s 70(2), (3) (see the text and notes 5–7), whose application is determined by s 70(1): see s 70(1).
2   As to the meaning of 'seaman' see PARA 457 note 5.
3   As to the meaning of 'United Kingdom ship' see PARA 230. As to the meaning of 'ship' under the Merchant Shipping Act 1995 see PARA 229; and as to the meaning of 'United Kingdom' see PARA 16 note 3.
4   Merchant Shipping Act 1995 s 70(1). As to the contract of employment generally see EMPLOYMENT vol 39 (2014) PARA 1 et seq.
5   'Accident' in the popular and ordinary sense of the word denotes an unlooked-for mishap or an untoward event which is not expected or designed: *Fenton v J Thorley & Co Ltd* [1903] AC 443

at 448, HL, per Lord Macnaghten. See also *R v Morris* [1972] 1 All ER 384, [1972] 1 WLR 228, CA (an unintended occurrence which has an adverse physical effect).

6 Merchant Shipping Act 1995 s 70(2).
7 Merchant Shipping Act 1995 s 70(3). This does not apply in respect of an agreement to reimburse repatriation costs: s 70(5) (added by SI 2014/1614).

1188. Seaman's civil liability for acts of smuggling. If a seaman[1] employed in a United Kingdom ship[2] is found in civil proceedings before a court in the United Kingdom to have committed an act of smuggling, whether within or outside the United Kingdom, he is liable to make good any loss or expense that the act has caused to any other person[3].

1 As to the meaning of 'seaman' see PARA 457 note 5.
2 As to the meaning of 'United Kingdom ship' see PARA 230. As to the meaning of 'ship' under the Merchant Shipping Act 1995 see PARA 229; and as to the meaning of 'United Kingdom' see PARA 16 note 3.
3 Merchant Shipping Act 1995 s 71.

1189. Fines imposed under foreign immigration laws. Provision is made[1] where, at a time when a United Kingdom ship[2] is in the national or territorial waters of any country outside the United Kingdom, a seaman[3] employed in the ship is absent without leave and present in that country in contravention[4] of that country's laws[5].

If, by reason of the contravention, a penalty is incurred under those laws by the persons employing the seaman, the penalty is to be treated as attributable to his absence without leave and may be recovered[6] from him as special damages for breach of contract[7].

If, by reason of the contravention, a penalty is incurred under those laws by any other person, the amount thereof (or, if that amount exceeds £100, £100) may be recovered by him from the seaman[8].

1 Ie by the Merchant Shipping Act 1995 s 72(2), (3) (see the text and notes 6–8), whose application is determined by s 72(1): see s 72(1).
2 As to the meaning of 'United Kingdom ship' see PARA 230. As to the meaning of 'ship' under the Merchant Shipping Act 1995 see PARA 229; and as to the meaning of 'United Kingdom' see PARA 16 note 3.
3 As to the meaning of 'seaman' see PARA 457 note 5.
4 As to the meaning of 'contravention' see PARA 51 note 3.
5 Merchant Shipping Act 1995 s 72(1).
6 Ie subject to the Merchant Shipping Act 1995 s 70 (see PARA 1187): see s 72(2).
7 Merchant Shipping Act 1995 s 72(2).
8 Merchant Shipping Act 1995 s 72(3).

(5) DETENTION OF SHIPS

1190. Enforcing detention of ship under the Merchant Shipping Act 1995. Where, under the Merchant Shipping Act 1995, a ship[1] is to be or may be detained, any of the following officers may detain the ship[2]:
(1) any commissioned naval[3] or military[4] officer[5];
(2) any officer of a Minister of the Crown[6] who is authorised by the Secretary of State[7], either generally or in a particular case, to exercise powers[8] for the purposes of enforcing the detention of a ship[9];
(3) any officer of Revenue and Customs[10]; and
(4) any British consular officer[11].
A notice of detention may[12]:
(a) include a direction that the ship either must remain in a particular place[13], or must be moved to a particular anchorage or berth[14]; and

(b)   if it includes such a direction, specify circumstances relating to safety or the prevention of pollution in which the master may move his ship from that place, anchorage or berth[15].

If a ship, as respects which notice of detention has been served on the master[16], either:

(i)   proceeds to sea[17], otherwise than in accordance with such a notice, before it is released by a competent authority[18]; or

(ii)   fails to comply with a direction given under head (a) above[19],

the master of the ship is guilty of an offence[20] and liable, on conviction on indictment or on summary conviction, to a fine[21]. The owner of a ship, and any person who sends to sea a ship, as respects which an offence is committed under head (i) or head (ii) above, is also guilty, if party or privy to the offence, of an offence and liable accordingly[22].

Where a ship proceeding to sea in contravention[23] of head (i) above, or failing to comply with a direction given under head (a) above, carries away without his consent any of the following who is on board the ship in the execution of his duty[24], namely:

(A)   any officer authorised[25] to detain the ship[26]; or

(B)   any surveyor of ships[27],

the owner and master of the ship are each liable to pay all expenses of and incidental to the officer or surveyor being so carried away[28], and are guilty of an offence[29] and liable, on conviction on indictment, to a fine, or, on summary conviction, to a fine not exceeding the statutory maximum[30].

Where, under the Merchant Shipping Act 1995, a ship is to be detained, an officer of Revenue and Customs must, and where under that Act a ship may be detained an officer of Revenue and Customs may, refuse to clear the ship outwards or grant a transire[31] to the ship[32]; and, where any provision of the Merchant Shipping Act 1995 provides that a ship may be detained until any document is produced to the proper officer of Revenue and Customs, the officer able to grant a clearance or transire of the ship is, unless the context otherwise requires, that officer[33].

1   As to the meaning of 'ship' see PARA 229.
2   Merchant Shipping Act 1995 s 284(1). See also the Aviation and Maritime Security Act 1990 s 35 (detention of ships) (cited in PORTS AND HARBOURS vol 85 (2012) PARA 129); the Animal Welfare Act 2006 s 55(3) (power to stop and detain vessels, aircraft and hovercraft) (cited in ANIMALS vol 2 (2017) PARA 145); the Merchant Shipping (Prevention of Oil Pollution) Regulations 1996, SI 1996/2154 (cited in ENVIRONMENTAL QUALITY AND PUBLIC HEALTH vol 45 (2010) PARA 365 et seq); and the Merchant Shipping and Fishing Vessels (Port Waste Reception Facilities) Regulations 2003, SI 2003/1809 (cited in ENVIRONMENTAL QUALITY AND PUBLIC HEALTH vol 45 (2010) PARAS 421–424).
3   As to the meaning of 'commissioned naval officer' see PARA 47 note 12.
4   As to the meaning of 'commissioned military officer' see PARA 235 note 4.
5   Merchant Shipping Act 1995 s 284(1)(a).
6   As to the meaning of 'Minister of the Crown' see PARA 72 note 6.
7   As to the Secretary of State see PARA 36.
8   Ie under the Merchant Shipping Act 1995 s 284: see s 284(1)(b) (substituted by the Merchant Shipping and Maritime Security Act 1997 s 9, Sch 1 para 5(1), (2)).
9   Merchant Shipping Act 1995 s 284(1)(b) (as substituted: see note 8).
10   Merchant Shipping Act 1995 s 284(1)(c) (amended by virtue of the Commissioners for Revenue and Customs Act 2005 s 50(1), (2), (7)). As to the appointment of officers of Revenue and Customs see INCOME TAXATION vol 58 (2014) PARA 33.
11   Merchant Shipping Act 1995 s 284(1)(d). As to British consular officers see INTERNATIONAL RELATIONS LAW vol 61 (2010) PARA 30.
12   Merchant Shipping Act 1995 s 284(1A) (added by the Merchant Shipping and Maritime Security Act 1997 Sch 1 para 5(1), (3)).

13 Merchant Shipping Act 1995 s 284(1A)(a)(i) (as added: see note 12).
14 Merchant Shipping Act 1995 s 284(1A)(a)(ii) (as added: see note 12).
15 Merchant Shipping Act 1995 s 284(1A)(b) (as added: see note 12).
16 As to the meaning of 'master' see PARA 444 note 1.
17 For these purposes, any reference to proceeding to sea includes a reference to going on a voyage or excursion that does not involve going to sea; and references to sending or taking to sea are to be construed accordingly: Merchant Shipping Act 1995 s 284(8).
18 Merchant Shipping Act 1995 s 284(2) (substituted by the Merchant Shipping and Maritime Security Act 1997 Sch 1 para 5(1), (4)).
19 Merchant Shipping Act 1995 s 284(2A) (s 284(2A), (2B) added by the Merchant Shipping and Maritime Security Act 1997 Sch 1 para 5(1), (4)).
20 Merchant Shipping Act 1995 s 284(2), (2A) (s 284(2) as substituted (see note 18), s 284(2A) as added (see note 19)).
21 Merchant Shipping Act 1995 s 284(2B) (as added (see note 19); amended by SI 2015/664). As to the time limit for summary offences see PARA 1049; as to offences by officers of bodies corporate see PARA 1051; as to jurisdiction in relation to offences see PARA 1052; as to jurisdiction over ships lying off the coast see PARA 1053; as to jurisdiction in the case of offences on board ship see PARA 1054; as to offences committed by British seamen see PARA 1055; and as to proof etc of exemption see PARA 1061. As to the powers of magistrates' courts to issue fines on summary conviction see SENTENCING vol 92 (2015) PARA 176.
22 Merchant Shipping Act 1995 s 284(3) (amended by the Merchant Shipping and Maritime Security Act 1997 Sch 1 para 5(1), (5)).
23 As to the meaning of 'contravention' see PARA 51 note 3.
24 Merchant Shipping Act 1995 s 284(4) (amended by the Merchant Shipping and Maritime Security Act 1997 Sch 1 para 5(1), (6)).
25 Ie under the Merchant Shipping Act 1995 s 284(1) (see the text and notes 1–11): see s 284(4)(a).
26 Merchant Shipping Act 1995 s 284(4)(a).
27 Merchant Shipping Act 1995 s 284(4)(b). As to the meaning of 'surveyor of ships' see PARA 46 note 13. As to the appointment of surveyors see PARA 46.
28 Merchant Shipping Act 1995 s 284(4)(i) (amended by the Merchant Shipping and Maritime Security Act 1997 Sch 1 para 5(1), (6)).
29 Merchant Shipping Act 1995 s 284(4)(a)(ii).
30 Merchant Shipping Act 1995 s 284(5).
31 A transire is a warrant from the custom-house to let goods pass: see CUSTOMS AND EXCISE vol 31 (2012) PARA 1061.
32 Merchant Shipping Act 1995 s 284(6) (amended by virtue of the Commissioners for Revenue and Customs Act 2005 s 50(1), (2), (7)).
33 Merchant Shipping Act 1995 s 284(7) (amended by virtue of the Commissioners for Revenue and Customs Act 2005 s 50(1), (2), (7)).

1191. Sums ordered to be paid leviable by distress on the ship.

Where any court has power to make an order directing payment to be made of any seaman's wages[1], fines or other sums of money, then, if the person directed to pay is the master[2] or owner of the ship[3] and the money directed to be paid is not paid in accordance with the order, the court which made the order may direct the amount remaining unpaid to be levied by distress of the ship and its equipment[4]. The remedy so made available[5] is in addition to any other powers for compelling the payment of money ordered to be paid[6].

1 As to the meaning of 'seaman' see PARA 457 note 5; and as to the meaning of 'wages' see PARA 464 note 6.
2 As to the meaning of 'master' see PARA 444 note 1.
3 As to the meaning of 'ship' see PARA 229.
4 Merchant Shipping Act 1995 s 285(1).
5 Ie by the Merchant Shipping Act 1995 s 285: see s 285(2).
6 Merchant Shipping Act 1995 s 285(2).

INDEX

Shipping and Maritime Law

ADMIRALTY AND COMMERCIAL
　REGISTRY
　meaning 142
ADMIRALTY APPEAL
　additional evidence, receiving of 220
　Admiralty Registrar, reference to 221
　costs of 222
　Divisional Court, appeals to—
　　further appeal 226
　　inquiries, in relation to 224
　　power to hear 223
　　procedure 225
　　rehearings, in relation to 224, 227
　　statutory marine investigations, in
　　　relation to 224
　general law, application of 218
　pilotage appeals 228
　principles governing hearing 220
ADMIRALTY COURT
　assignment of business to 91
　claim in personam. *See* CLAIM IN
　　PERSONAM (OTHER CLAIM)
　claim in rem. *See* CLAIM IN REM
ADMIRALTY JURISDICTION
　assignment of business to Admiralty
　　Court 91
　bottomry, claims arising from 134
　cargo claims 111
　carriage claims 111, 156
　Cinque Ports, courts of 210
　claims in personam, origin of 84
　claims in rem, origin of 83
　co-ownership—
　　dealings with shares, restraint
　　　on 108
　　extent of jurisdiction 106
　　minority of co-owners, sale at
　　　instance of 107
　collision claims 180
　Colonial Courts of Admiralty, of 217
　common law courts, conflict with 80
　county courts 209

ADMIRALTY
　JURISDICTION—*continued*
　damage done to or by ships, as
　　to 110, 810
　droits of Admiralty 139
　foreign aspects of 86
　forfeiture, condemnation and
　　restoration of ship or goods—
　　dangerous goods 138
　　extent of jurisdiction 135
　　Foreign Enlistment Act, cases
　　　under 138
　　Merchant Shipping Act, under 136,
　　　137
　former local courts, of 214
　general average act, as to 133
　Guernsey, courts of 216
　hovercraft—
　　generally 383
　　Hovercraft Act, under 87
　　Isle of Man, courts of 216
　　Jersey, courts of 216
　　limitation claims 194
　　loss of life or personal injury, claims
　　　as to 112
　　maritime law: meaning 82
　　mortgage or charge, claims in
　　　respect of 109
　　oil pollution, claims as to 88, 155
　　origin of 80
　　outline of 79
　　pilotage, as to 125
　　possession or ownership of ship, as
　　　to—
　　　extent of jurisdiction 104
　　　register, rectification of 105
　　prize court, as 89
　　recovery of wages, proceedings as
　　　to 478
　　restrictions on 90
　　salvage. *See* SALVAGE (MARITIME)
　　Senior Courts Act, under 85

ADMIRALTY
　JURISDICTION—*continued*
　hovercraft—*continued*
　　statutory jurisdiction, advent of 81
　　supplies, repairs and dock charges,
　　　as to 126
　　towage, as to 125
　　Vice-Admirals of coast, courts
　　　of 215
　　wages and disbursements, as to—
　　　agent, disbursements by 132
　　　charterer, disbursements by 132
　　　extent of 127
　　　foreign ships 128
　　　shipper, disbursements by 132
　　　time limit for proceedings 129
　wages and disbursements, as to—
　　sums recoverable—
　　　master's disbursements, as 131
　　　wages, as 130
ADMIRALTY PROCEEDINGS
　assessors 205
　execution of judgment 208
　payment of money found due 207
　procedure—
　　offers to settle 203
　　outline of 157
　　trial 204
　rehearing 206
　stay of—
　　arbitration agreement, under 102,
　　　103
　　foreign jurisdiction clause,
　　　under 102
　　forum non conveniens, on grounds
　　　of 100
　　lis alibi pendens, on grounds of 101
　writ of control, execution of judgment
　　by 208
ADMIRALTY REGISTRAR
　meaning 140
　Admiralty and Commercial
　　Registry 142
　applications in claims, role in 45
　general jurisdiction of 141
　reference to—
　　meaning 143
　　appeals—
　　　order on 150
　　　powers on 149
　　case management conference 145
　　collision claims 143

ADMIRALTY REGISTRAR—*continued*
　reference to—*continued*
　　costs 148
　　decision 147
　　evidence 146
　　filing of claim or defence 144
　　hearing 147
　　interim matters 146
ANIMAL
　sea, importation by 27
BAREBOAT CHARTER SHIP
　changes, notification of 366
　identifying number, allocation of 362
　inspection of 363
　marking of 363
　names of 361
　port numbers 362
　port of choice 362
　registration—
　　application for 360
　　British charterers, chartered-in
　　　by 357
　　closure by registrar 368
　　entitlement to—
　　　fishing vessels 359
　　　ships other than fishing
　　　　vessels 358
　　entry of 364
　　foreign registries, notification
　　　of 367
　　period of 365
　　qualification for—
　　　fishing vessels 359
　　　ships other than fishing
　　　　vessels 358
　　renewal of 365
BOTTOMRY
　claims arising from 134
　maritime liens for 972, 980
　master's authority to make
　　contract 435
BRITISH SEAMAN'S CARD
　alterations in 572
　application for 559
　applications relating to 573
　delivery of, requirement as to 564
　issue of 560
　notification of errors in 570
　offence as to. *See* OFFENCE
　　(MARITIME)
　production of, requirement as to 562
　surrender of 563, 571

References are to paragraph numbers; superior figures refer to notes

BRITISH SEAMAN'S CARD—*continued*
  validity of 561
CARGO (CARRIAGE BY SEA)
  bulk cargo other than grain—
    conditions required before
      loading 655
    loading, unloading and stowage
      of 656
  dangerous goods. *See* DANGEROUS
    GOODS
  documentation, required 650
  grain, compliance with international
    code as to 657
  information to be provided 649
  securing, duties regarding 651
  special precautions, cargo requiring—
    documentation, required 650
    equivalents and exemptions, power
      to provide 654
    information to be provided 649
    oxygen analysis and gas detection
      equipment, requirement
      for 652
    pesticides, safe use of 653
    securing and stowing, duties
      regarding 651
  stowage, duties regarding 651, 656
CINQUE PORTS
  Court of Admiralty of—
    appeal from 213
    jurisdiction 210
  jurisdiction—
    appeal from courts, as to 213
    courts, of 210
    Salvage Commissioners, of 211
  Salvage Commissioners—
    appeal from award of 212
    duties of 211
    jurisdiction of 211
CLAIM IN PERSONAM (OTHER
    CLAIM)
  Civil Jurisdiction and Judgments Act—
    cases governed by 96, 98
    stay of proceedings under 99
  claim form—
    acknowledgment of service of 187
    service of 187
    service out of jurisdiction 188
  collision, arising from 810
  Commercial Court practice,
    proceeding in accordance
    with 186
  generally 93
  judgment in default 193

CLAIM IN PERSONAM (OTHER
    CLAIM)—*continued*
  jurisdictional issues—
    Civil Jurisdiction and Judgments
      Act, effect of 96, 99
    conflicts of jurisdiction 95
    generally 94
    origin of admiralty jurisdiction 84
  nature of 92
  particulars of claim etc 189
  salvor, rights in personam of 914
CLAIM IN REM
  admiralty jurisdiction, origin of 83
  appeals, security for costs of 219
  appraisement and sale of ship by
    court 178
  arrest—
    caution against—
      effect of 167
      entry of 166
    warrant—
      application for 161
      custody of arrested property 164
      execution of 162
      issue of 161
      service, mode of effecting 163
      undertakings made by solicitor,
        forgoing of service
        where 165
  arrested property, dealings with—
    custody of property 164
    release—
      caution against 174
      obtaining 175
      payment out, where 174
      security previously given,
        where 176
    removal of property 173
    security given to prevent arrest 172
    statement of value and
      appraisal 177
  Civil Jurisdiction and Judgments Act—
    cases governed by 96, 97
    stay of proceedings under 99
  claim form—
    acknowledgment of service—
      generally 168
      late acknowledgment 170
      persons able to acknowledge 169
    issue and form of 158
    service of 160
  collision, arising from 810
  Crown, against 179
  judgment in default 190

References are to paragraph numbers; superior figures refer to notes

CLAIM IN REM—*continued*
limitation period 151
nature of 92
notice of arrest entered, judgment
    against party where 191
particulars of claim etc 189
procedure, outline of 157
right to sue of owners of ship or
    cargo 159
salvor, rights in rem of 913
security for release of property—
    means of providing 171
    order, application for 172
ship or property subject of 93
COASTGUARD
meaning 58
COLLISION
meaning 690
accident investigation. *See* MARINE
    ACCIDENT
admiralty jurisdiction as to claims 180
application of regulations 690
assistance, duty as to rendering 727
damages, measure of—
    burden of proof 795
    detention of ship—
      expenses of 802, 803
      profits lost due to 802, 804
    dry-docking, dues for 801
    foreign state, recoverable by 806
    general average expenses 807
    general principles 793
    indemnity, nature of 794
    interest 809
    loss after collision, for 798
    market value, valuation in absence
      of 797
    public authority, recoverable by 806
    repairs, cost of 800
    total loss, in case of 796
    use of another vessel, cost of 805
    vessel damaged but not lost,
      where 799
duties after 727
good seamanship, rules of. *See* GOOD
    SEAMANSHIP, RULES OF
inevitable accident, defence of—
    burden of proof 788
    circumstances where applicable 789
International Regulations for
    Preventing Collisions at Sea—
    application of 690
    breach of duty, onus of proof as
      to 694
    construction of 692

COLLISION—*continued*
International Regulations for
    Preventing Collisions at
    Sea—*continued*
infringement of 694
lights and shapes—
    anchored vessels, required by 720
    application of rules 710
    draught, lights required by vessels
      constrained by 718
    fishing vessels underway, required
      by 716
    pilot vessels, required by 719
    power-driven vessels underway,
      lights required by 712
    sailing vessels underway, required
      by 715
    seaplanes, required by 721
    vessels aground, required by 720
    vessels being towed or pushed,
      required by 714
    vessels not under command,
      required by 717
    vessels restricted in ability to
      manoeuvre, required by 717
    vessels towing and pushing,
      required by 713
    vessels under oars 715
    visibility of lights 711
    wing-in-ground aircraft, required
      by 721
responsibility under 693
scope of 691
signals—
    attention, to attract 725
    distress signals 726
    equipment for 722
    manoeuvring and warning 723
    restricted visibility, in 724
steering and sailing rules—
    action to avoid collision 698
    narrow channel rule 699, 700
    proper look-out, maintaining 695
    risk of collision, determining 697
    safe speed 696
    traffic separation schemes 701
vessels proceeding in restricted
    visibility, conduct of 709
vessels within sight of each other,
    conduct of—
    crossing rule 705
    give-way vessel, action by 706

References are to paragraph numbers; superior figures refer to notes

COLLISION—*continued*
International Regulations for
  Preventing Collisions at
  Sea—*continued*
  vessels within sight of each other,
    conduct of—*continued*
    head-on situation 704
    overtaking rules 703
    responsibilities between
      vessels 708
    sailing vessels 702
    stand-on vessel, action by 707
liability for—
  chartered ship 782
  master, liability of 781
  national ships 786
  orders of dock or harbour master,
    vessel acting under 785
  owner, vicarious liability of 780
  personal liability 779
  tug and tow, collision between 783
  tug or tow colliding with third
    vessel 784
  wreck, collision with 787
limitation of time for proceedings 812
log book, required entry in 728
maritime lien 811
negligence causing damage—
  both parties at fault, liability
    where—
    antecedent and subsequent
      negligence 770
    one or more negligent acts 768
    principles 767
    simultaneous negligence 769
  burden of proof 757
  care and skill—
    meaning 761
    afloat and ashore 764
  cause of action, as 756
  collateral negligence as
    immaterial 763
  construction, in 759
  division of loss in proportion to
    fault—
    cargo owners and others, rights
      of 776
    limitation of liability 773
    loss of life or personal injuries,
      liability for 777, 778
    more than two ships in fault 774
    right of contribution 778
    rule as to 771

COLLISION—*continued*
negligence causing damage—*continued*
  division of loss in proportion to
    fault—*continued*
    shipowners, working out
      between 772
    third innocent vessel, position
      of 775
  equipment, in 759
  manning, in 759
  navigation, in 760
  other than to ship 765
  proof—
    burden of 757
    rules as to 758
  reasonable care: meaning 761
  reasonable skill: meaning 761
  sudden difficulty, degree of skill
    required in 762
persons entitled to recover—
  cargo or other property in ship,
    owners of 791
  personal injuries or death, in case
    of 792
  shipowners 790
salvage—
  assistance after collision 813
  damage received during 814
COLLISION CLAIM
acknowledgment of service 181
assessors 205
claim form 181
judgment in default 192
particulars of claim etc 189
statement of case—
  contents of 183
  filing of 182
  power of court to dispense
    with 184
stay of proceedings 185
CONSOLIDATED FUND
payment into—
  fees paid into 63
  Hovercraft Act, sums payable
    under 384
  mandatory payments 64
CONVENTION ON LIMITATION OF
  LIABILITY FOR MARITIME
  CLAIMS
application of provisions 992, 1007
counterclaims under 997
limitation fund—
  constitution of—
    generally 1003
    governing law 1006

References are to paragraph numbers; superior figures refer to notes

CONVENTION ON LIMITATION OF
LIABILITY FOR MARITIME
CLAIMS—*continued*
limitation fund—*continued*
constitution of—*continued*
other actions, as bar to 1005
distribution of—
governing law 1006
proportionate distribution 1004
limitation of liability without
constitution of 1002
limits of liability under—
aggregation of claims 1001
general limits 998
passenger claims 999
unit of account 1000
reservations under 1008
right of limitation under—
claims subject to 994
conduct barring limitation 996
counterclaims 997
excepted claims 995
persons entitled to 993
CONVOY
war, in time of 5
CREW AGREEMENT
carrying of copy of agreement in
ships 459
copy documents, supply and
production on demand of 462,
463
delivery of 460
display of agreement on ship 461
exemptions from general provision
for 458
general provision for 457
officers, production of documents on
demand of 463
DANGEROUS GOODS
carriage—
sea, by—
generally 645
handling 646
marine pollutants 646
merchant shipping, by 646
packages, irradiated nuclear
fuel 647
reporting requirements 648
stowage 646
DEATH
hovercraft, on. *See* HOVERCRAFT
on board ship—
joint and several liability 1011

DEATH—*continued*
on board ship—*continued*
limitation period for claims 152,
1013
persons entitled to recover 792
regulations 28, 644
right of contribution 1012
FISHING VESSEL
construction rules for 607
survey rules—
meaning 608
certificates confirming compliance
with 609
going to sea without certificate,
prohibition against 610
notice of alterations, requirements
as to 611
GOOD SEAMANSHIP, RULES OF
carrying and dropping anchor, as
to 733
Collision Regulations, relationship
with 730
coming to anchor, as to 734
dangerous vessels 745
dumb barges 746
foul berth, as to 734
launching of vessel, as to 731
officers and watch on look-out 739
rivers and narrow waters, navigation
in—
bend, waiting at 748
crossing or turning 751
dock or harbour master, obeying
orders of 755
dredging up stern first 749
fairway—
aground in 753
anchoring in 752
incoming vessel to wait for
outgoing 754
smelling the ground 750
tide and current, preparation
for 747
warping 750
sailing vessels 744
scope of 729
special weather conditions, as to 732
speed 740
standing close and speaking 741
steering gear 737
tug and tow—
duties between vessels 742
manoeuvring for other vessels 743
tug assistance 738

References are to paragraph numbers; superior figures refer to notes

GOOD SEAMANSHIP, RULES
  OF—*continued*
  vessel at anchor—
    keeping clear of 736
    precautions 735
  vessel moored alongside, precautions
    where 735
HARBOUR AUTHORITY
  limitation of liability 1014
  local lighthouse authority, powers
    as 1030
  wreck, powers as to—
    removal of wreck 939, 945
    sale of wreck 957
HEALTH AND SAFETY AT WORK
  safety management codes 627
  shipping activities, general duties as
    to 626
HIGH-SPEED CRAFT
  application of provisions 617
  approvals, power to grant 619
  behaviour of persons on 624
  codes 620
  equivalent provision outside
    regulations 618
  offences 625
  permit, operation in accordance
    with 623
  persons with reduced mobility, safety
    requirements for 621
  power to detain 625
  wash, risk assessment as to 622
HOVERCRAFT
  meaning 381
  Admiralty jurisdiction—
    generally 383
    Hovercraft Act, under 87
  birth and death—
    foreign and Commonwealth
      hovercraft, requirements
      for 422
    missing persons, rectification of
      entries as to 421
    record retention 419
    rectification of entries 421
    returns of—
      Registrar General, transmission
        to 420
      Secretary of State, transmission
        to 418
  captain—
    application of provisions 402
    duties of—
      generally 405

HOVERCRAFT—*continued*
  captain—*continued*
    duties of—*continued*
      operational records, as to
        keeping 406
    duty to obey 411
  casualties, notification of 409
  certification—
    application of provisions 396
    documents to be carried 407
    international standards, certificate of
      compliance with 399
    revocation of certificate 401, 414
    safety certificate—
      issue of 398
      requirement for 397
    suspension of 401
    variation of certificate 401
  civil liability, general provisions as
    to 386
  death in. *See* birth and death *above*
  directions, enforcement of 415
  enactments applied to 384
  exemptions from provisions 416
  fees relating to 417
  financial provisions 385
  hoverport, right of access to 412
  jurisdiction 383
  maintenance—
    application of provisions 396
    inspection 400
    requirement for 400
  medical equipment, requirement to
    carry 408
  Merchant Shipping Acts, under 21
  missing persons, rectification of entries
    as to 421
  offence, as to registration,
    certification, maintenance and
    operation of 1072
  operating permits 403
  operator—
    application of provisions 402
    duties of—
      generally 404
      operational records, as to
        keeping 406
  Orders in Council, power to
    make 382
  owner, duties of 404
  power to prevent use of 401, 413
  registration—
    application for 392
    changes in particulars, notification
      of 393

References are to paragraph numbers; superior figures refer to notes

HOVERCRAFT—*continued*
  registration—*continued*
    Crown application 388
    extra-territorial effect of
      provisions 389
    general provisions, application
      of 387
    marks 394
    nationality marks 394
    necessity for 390
    outside UK 395
    procedure for 391
  safety—
    captain, duty to obey 411
    persons and property, of 410
IMPROVEMENT NOTICE
  contents and effect of 53
  generally 50
  offence, contravention as 1178
  references of notices to arbitration 54
JOINT AND SEVERAL LIABILITY
  on board ship, for loss of life or
    personal injuries 1011
LIFE SALVAGE
  nature of 120
  statutory jurisdiction as to 121
LIGHTHOUSE AUTHORITY
  Commissioners of Irish Lights 1020
  Commissioners of Northern
    Lighthouses 1019
  exemptions—
    harbour dues 1047
    taxes, duties, rates etc 1046
  general—
    meaning 1017
    accounts 1045
    borrowing—
      guarantees 1044
      limit on 1043
      powers 1043
    commercial activities, agreements as
      to 1026
    control of local lighthouse
      authorities 1028
    disclosure of information to 1029
    general function of 1023
    general powers 1025
    inspection of lighthouses, duty as
      to 1027
    joint discharge of functions 1024
  General Lighthouse Fund—
    estimates or accounts of expenses,
      reporting duty as to 1041
    expenses and receipts 1039
    pension rights of employees 1042

LIGHTHOUSE
  AUTHORITY—*continued*
  General Lighthouse Fund—*continued*
    Secretary of State, role of 1040,
      1041
  harbour authorities, powers of 1030
  light dues—
    general—
      distress on ship for 1036
      information to determine, power
        to require 1034
      levy of 1033
      receipt for 1037
      recovery of 1035
    local, levy of 1038
  list of authorities 56
  local—
    meaning 1017
    control by general lighthouse
      authorities 1028
    harbour authorities as 1030
    light dues leviable by 1038
  Secretary of State—
    General Lighthouse Fund, role
      in 1040, 1041
    powers of inspection of 1022
    returns and information to 1021
  transfers between—
    individual transfers 1031
    surrender of local lighthouses 1032
  Trinity House: meaning 1018
  wrecks, powers relating to 939, 945,
    1048
LIMITATION OF LIABILITY
  (ADMIRALTY)
  acknowledgment of service of claim
    form 197
  apportionment rules as to damage or
    loss 1010
  claim form 197
  commencement of proceedings 196
  conservancy authority 1014
  Crown, application of provisions
    to 1015
  decree—
    effect of granting 199
    general—
      obtaining 198
      proceedings to set aside 200
    restricted decree, obtaining 198
  general exclusions 1009
  harbour authority 1014
  jurisdiction 194
  limitation fund—
    distribution of 201

References are to paragraph numbers; superior figures refer to notes

LIMITATION OF LIABILITY

(ADMIRALTY)—*continued*

limitation fund—*continued*

repayment to claimant 202

Merchant Shipping Act, under 195

service of claim form 197

LIMITATION PERIOD

maritime lien 1013

owners or ship, claim against—

damage, loss personal injury or
death, for 152, 1013

extension of period 153

LINER CONFERENCE

Code of Conduct 78

LIST OF CREW

copies, duty with regard to 555

delivery—

crew, to 557

Registrar General, on demand
to 556

duty to maintain 553

particulars to be specified 554

production on demand to officials 558

LOAD LINE

application of provisions 660

certificates—

appropriate, issue of 665

cancellation of 668

ceasing to be valid 668

duration of 667

extension of 667

non-UK ship, following survey
of 666

publication of 669

surrender of 668

certificates and surveys, offences as
to 1129

contravention of provisions, penalties
for 1128

draughts, notification of 669

equivalents, power to allow 672

exemption from rules 661

freeboards, assignment of 663

general compliance with rules 662

marks, specification of 670

master, information provided to 671

specification of 670

stability, loading and ballasting,
information as to 671

surveys—

annual survey 664

initial survey 664

non-UK ship, of 666

renewal survey 664

LOG BOOK

ship's official—

collision, accident etc, required
entry following 728

destruction, mutilation or alteration
of 1086

entries in 552, 728

form of 551

MARINE ACCIDENT

meaning 816

deaths—

inquiries into 846

joint and several liability for 1011

reports of 846, 848

right of contribution 1012

transmission of particulars 848

duty to notify 823

evidence, preservation of 827

injuries, inquiries into 847

inquiries—

deaths of crew members and others,
into 846

injuries, into 847

inspectors, appointment of 815

investigation—

accident: meaning 816

application of provisions 821

co-operation with other states 826

conduct of 825

inspectors, appointment of 815

marine casualty: meaning 817

marine incident: meaning 820

objective of 822

report of safety investigation 828

safety investigation: meaning 824

serious marine casualty:
meaning 819

very serious marine casualty:
meaning 818

wreck commissioner, formal
investigation by. *See* WRECK
COMMISSIONER

log book, required entry in 728

marine casualty: meaning 817

marine incident: meaning 820

personal injury—

joint and several liability 1011

right of contribution 1012

preliminary assessment 824

recommendations to prevent future
accidents 829

reports—

deaths, of 846, 848

duty as to 823

particulars of deaths 848

MARINE ACCIDENT—*continued*
　reports—*continued*
　　safety investigation report 828
　　safety investigation: meaning 824
　　serious marine casualty: meaning 819
　　very serious marine casualty:
　　　meaning 818
　　wreck commissioner, formal
　　　investigation by. *See* WRECK
　　　COMMISSIONER
MARINE INSURANCE
　scope of 32
　Wrecks Convention, requirements
　　under. *See* WRECKS
　　CONVENTION (INSURANCE
　　PROVISIONS)
MARITIME AND COASTGUARD
　AGENCY
　safety policy, responsibility for 57
MARITIME LAW
　meaning 2
　Admiralty Court, applied by 1
　English jurisdiction, extended scope
　　of 3
　EU legislation 14
　international conventions and
　　organisations—
　　Comité Maritime International 13
　　International Maritime
　　　Organisation 12
　　International Sea-Bed Authority 11
　　International Tribunal for the Law
　　　of the Sea 10
　　list of 7
　　United Nations Conference on the
　　　Law of the Sea 8
　　United Nations Convention on the
　　　Law of the Sea 9
　Merchant Shipping Acts. *See*
　　MERCHANT SHIPPING ACTS
　Secretary of State, role of. *See*
　　SHIPPING (SECRETARY OF
　　STATE)
　UK legislation—
　　births and deaths on ship,
　　　regulations as to 28
　　importation of animals 27
　　public health precautions 26
　　reports of craft movement for
　　　customs control 24
MARITIME LIEN
　bottomry, for 972, 980
　collision, arising from 811
　damage done by ship, for 967, 977
　disbursements, for 971, 981

MARITIME LIEN—*continued*
　enforcement of—
　　generally 987
　　possessory liens 990
　　statutory liens 989
　　time limitation for 1013
　English law, recognised by 966
　extent of 964
　extinction of 991
　liabilities, for 971
　limitation period for enforcement
　　of 1013
　master's remuneration, as to 433, 981
　nature of 964
　possessory lien—
　　enforcement of 990
　　generally 974
　　ranking 984
　property to which attached 968
　ranking—
　　bottomry, lien for 980
　　damage, lien for 977
　　determination, method for 986
　　general priority—
　　　liens 975
　　　maritime liens 976
　　lex fori, effect of 986
　　master's lien for wages and
　　　disbursements 981
　　possessory lien 984
　　salvage, lien for 979
　　seafarer's wages, lien for 982
　　several actions for damage, lien
　　　for 978
　　solicitor's lien for costs 985
　　supply of goods etc, lien for 983
　respondentia bond, for 972
　salvage, for 915, 969, 979
　seaman's wages, for 970, 982
　statutory lien—
　　enforcement of 989
　　generally 973
　　transfer of 988
MARITIME SECURITY
　Aviation and Maritime Security Act—
　　extension of 1156
　　prosecution under 1154
　　protection of ships and harbour
　　　areas against violence 1155
MARITIME SERVICES
　charges—
　　amount of 71
　　Consolidated Fund, payments
　　　into 64

References are to paragraph numbers; superior figures refer to notes

MARITIME SERVICES—*continued*
  charges—*continued*
    expenses charged on money
        provided by Parliament 65
    General Lighthouse Fund, charges
        as to expenses payable out
        of 68
    persons paying 70
    power to regulate fees 63
    ships subject to 69
  funding—
    collection and recovery 73
    generally 66
    information, power to require and
        disclose 72
    maritime functions: meaning 67
    maritime matters, charges as to 67
MASTER OF SHIP
  account of wages, duty as to 485
  aircraft in distress, duty to assist 446
  applicable provisions 423
  appointment of 425
  arrest, power of 445
  authority—
    arrest, power of 445
    cargo—
      jettison of 436, 437
      rights of owner 443
      sale of 442, 443
      transhipment of 436
    contract, to make—
      bottomry, of 435
      general instances 431
      necessaries, for 432
    drunken passengers, power to
        exclude 444
    hypothecation of ship and freight,
        as to 435
    owner's agent, as—
      extent of 428
      generally 427
    sale of ship—
      disputing 441
      foreign judgment for 440
      necessity: meaning 439
      powers as to 438
  ceasing to be master during voyage—
    change of master during
        voyage 426
    duty to deliver documents 447
    removal, due to 425
  change of master during voyage 426
  contract of service 424

MASTER OF SHIP—*continued*
  drunken passengers, power to
      exclude 444
  exoneration of 430
  food and water, duty as to provision
      of 492
  liability of—
    generally 429
    third persons, to 434
  lien 433
  nationality requirements for masters of
      strategic ships 507
  remedies for remuneration,
      disbursements and liabilities 480
  removal of 425
  right of indemnity 433
  ship's protest by 430
  wrongful dismissal, compensation
      on 472
MERCANTILE MARINE
    SUPERINTENDENT
  meaning 61
MERCHANT SHIP
  meaning 229
  British ship: meaning 230
  flag, flying of—
    duty to show flag 232
    ensigns 234
    entitlement to fly 231
  forfeiture of ship, proceedings on 235,
      253
  liabilities—
    bills of lading 242
    part owners, as between 244
    private law provisions 252
    wages 243
  mortgage. *See* MORTGAGE
  mortgagee. *See* MORTGAGEE
  ownership—
    acquisition, methods of 236
    forfeiture of ship, proceedings
        on 235, 253
    liabilities—
      bills of lading 242
      part owners, as between 244
      private law provisions 252
      wages 243
    rights of—
      control of ship 240
      court order for sale of ship 241
      managing owner: meaning 238
      profits, distribution of 239
      registered owner, powers of 237
  register of British ships—
    central register 254

References are to paragraph numbers; superior figures refer to notes

MERCHANT SHIP—*continued*
register of British ships—*continued*
  fishing vessels 256
  parts of 255
  trusts, no entry for 257
registered—
  changes in registration,
    re-measurement of tonnage
    on 380
  mortgage. *See* MORTGAGE
  mortgagee. *See* MORTGAGEE
  ownership, notification of changes
    in 313
  registered particulars, change in 314
  transfer of—
    application for 306, 307
    bill of sale, by 306–309
    eligibility, declaration of 311
    evidence of title 307, 310
    refusal of registration 312
  transmission—
    eligibility, declaration of 311
    evidence of title 310
    refusal of registration 312
registration—
  application for—
    applicant 270
    bodies corporate, by 273
    declaration of intent 274
    evidence to support 275
    form of 269
    managing owner, appointment
      of 271
    supplementary requirements 272,
      273
  basic provisions 245
  British possessions, in 246
  carving and marking—
    cancellation of carving and
      marking note 288
    cessation of registration, removal
      on 378
    fishing vessels 284
    general requirements 281
    inspection of marks 286
    means of marking 282
    measurement, verification of 287
    pleasure vessels 283
    ship's draught, marking of 285
    verification of 287
  certificate of registry—
    bareboat charter ship, details as
      to 301

MERCHANT SHIP—*continued*
registration—*continued*
  certificate of registry—*continued*
    custody of 374
    details in 299–301
    duplicate certificates 373
    fishing vessel, details as to 300
    issue of 298
    production of, dispensing
      with 376
    sea fisheries legislation, status of
      Part II certificate under 377
    status of 302, 377
    termination or expiry of
      registration, surrender
      upon 375
  completion of 289
  declaration or evidence, dispensing
    with 371
  disclosure of information 251
  documents—
    registrar, to be retained by 297
    translation of 369
    witnessing of 370
  entitlement to registration 245
  fees payable to registrar 379
  fishing vessels 256
  name of ship—
    approval of 278
    change of 315
    proposed 277
  official number, allocation of 279
  owners' particulars, entry of—
    bodies corporate 291
    charters of fishing vessels 292
    individuals 290
    representative persons 292
  Part I, on—
    bareboat charter ships, particulars
      of 295
    British connection 259
    fishing vessels 261
    government ships 260
    majority interest in ship 259
    owner, persons qualified to
      be 258
    particulars of ships 293
  Part II, on—
    bareboat charter ships, particulars
      of 295
    British connection 263
    dispensations 264
    eligibility 262

References are to paragraph numbers; superior figures refer to notes

MERCHANT SHIP—*continued*
  registration—*continued*
    Part II, on—*continued*
      exemptions 266
      fishing vessels, particulars of 294
      fishing vessels, representative
        persons for 263
      inspectors, appointment of 265
      sea fisheries legislation, status of
        certificate under 377
    period of 296
    port of choice—
      generally 280
      transfer of 316
    power to make 247
    private law provisions 252
    provisional—
      application for 337, 338
      certification of 339
      fishing vessels, for 340
      ship outside British Islands,
        for 337
    refusal of 289
    renewal—
      application for 305
      notice of 304
      time limit for 304
    small ship. *See* SMALL SHIP
    supplementary information required
      by registrar 372
    survey and measurement of
      ship 276
    temporary registration
      documents 303
    termination of—
      mortgage, effect on 336
      removal from register on 317
    transfer—
      relevant British possession,
        from 342
      relevant British possession,
        to 341
      within register 343
  representative persons—
    appointment of 267
    fishing vessels 263
    service on 268
  ship: meaning 229
  tonnage regulations—
    ascertainment of tonnage 249
    changes in registration,
      re-measurement on 380
    foreign ships, adoption of
      regulations by 250

MERCHANT SHIP—*continued*
  tonnage regulations—*continued*
    general regulations 248
    UK fishing vessel: meaning 230
    UK ship: meaning 230
MERCHANT SHIPPING
  certification 604
  safety—
    mandatory surveys 606
    passenger ships on domestic
      voyages 605
    ro-ro ferry 606
    survey and certification 604
  survey 604
MERCHANT SHIPPING ACTS
  detention of ship under 21, 1190
  fishing vessels, application to 23
  forfeiture, condemnation and
    restoration of ship or goods
    under 136, 137
  government ships, application to 19
  health and safety under 626
  hovercraft, application to 21
  limitation of liability under 195
  non-UK ships, application to 17
  principal legislation 15
  qualifying foreign ship: meaning 18
  Secretary of State's role and powers
    under. *See* SHIPPING (SECRETARY
    OF STATE, ROLE AND POWERS
    OF)
  service of documents under 74
  ships chartered by demise to
    Crown 20
  structures, application to 22
  territorial extent of 16
  wrecks under 926
MORTGAGE
  registered ship, of—
    discharge of mortgage 335, 336
    form of mortgage 319
    general requirements 318
    notices by intending
      mortgagees 322
    priority notices 322
    priority of registered mortgages 321
    registration of mortgage 320
    transfer of mortgage 323, 326
    transmission of mortgage—
      evidence of 325
      general requirements 326
      operation of law, by 324
MORTGAGEE
  out of possession, injunction at suit of
    charterer against 329

MORTGAGEE—*continued*
  registered mortgagee—
    power of sale 333
    protection of 328
  rights of—
    assignee of freight 334
    contractual rights 331
    freight, to 332, 334
    possession, to 330
    power of sale 333
    rules of law governing 327

NAVIGATION
  closing of openings in hulls 637
  collision, negligence as causing 760
  good seamanship, rules of. *See* GOOD
    SEAMANSHIP, RULES OF
  offences as to—
    endangering or likely to endanger,
      acts 1150
    requirements, contravention
      of 1120
  radio installations, requirements as
    to 636
  radio signals as to dangers to 635
  SOLAS Convention 634

OFFENCE (MARITIME)
  alcohol and drugs—
    fishing vessel, unauthorised liquor
      on 1108
    non-professional shipping staff,
      offences applying to 1106
    police and marine officials, powers
      of 1107
    professional shipping staff, offences
      applying to 1105
  ancillary offences 1152
  Aviation and Maritime Security Act,
    prosecution under 1154
  barratry 1185
  British seaman's card—
    failure to deliver 1093
    failure to surrender 1092
    officials, failure to produce to 1091
  civil liability of seafarers for—
    absent without leave, damages
      where 1187
    foreign immigration laws, fines
      under 1189
    smuggling 1188
  coastal shipping services, as to orders
    regulating 1180
  conduct-related—
    alcohol and drugs. *See* alcohol and
      drugs *above*
    disobedience, concerted 1103

OFFENCE (MARITIME)—*continued*
  conduct-related—*continued*
    merchant navy uniform, relating to
      wearing of 1104
    neglect of duty 1103
    ships, structures or individuals,
      endangering 1102
  crew list—
    copies of, relating to 1087
    expired or changed list, failure to
      deliver 1089
    officials, failure to produce on
      demand to 1090
    Registrar General, failure to deliver
      to 556, 1088
  crew-related—
    complaints about provisions or
      food, failure to deal with 1077
    crew accommodation, failure as
      to 1076
    crew agreements, as to 1073
    crew list. *See* crew list *above*
    discharge of seafarer, failure as to
      procedure for 1074
    English, crew's insufficient
      knowledge of 1082
    equipment, failure as to provision
      of 1076, 1079
    personal protective equipment,
      failure as to provision of 1079
    unqualified persons going to sea as
      qualified 1083
    wages of seafarer, failure as to
      payment of 1075
    young persons, contravention of
      provisions as to employment
      of 1080
  dangerously unsafe ship—
    meaning 1140
    compensation for invalid
      detention 1143
    owner and master, liability as
      to 1144
    power to detain 1141
    references of detention notices to
      arbitration 1142
  destroying or endangering ships or
    fixed platforms 1149
  discharge book—
    application for, failure to
      make 1095
    deliver, failure to 1097
    employment when disentitled
      to 1094
    produce, failure to 1096

References are to paragraph numbers; superior figures refer to notes

OFFENCE (MARITIME)—*continued*
documents—
  British seaman's card. *See* British
    seaman's card *above*
  cancelled or suspended seafarer's
    certificate, failure to
    deliver 1085
  certificates, failure to produce 1081
  certificates of competence,
    improperly obtaining 1084
  discharge book. *See* discharge book
    above
  errors in document, failure to
    notify 1098
  failure to produce 1078
  falsely obtaining documents as to
    manning 1078
  improper marks in, making 1100
  master's failure to deliver 1101
  official log book, destruction,
    mutilation or alteration
    of 1086
  other documents of qualification,
    failure to produce 1081
  surrender, failure to 1099
employment when disentitled to
  discharge book 1094
English, as to crew's insufficient
  knowledge of 1082
evidence—
  depositions of persons abroad,
    admissibility of 1057
  documents—
    admissibility of 1058–1060
    copies, admissibility of 1060
    inspection of 1058, 1060
  expired or changed crew list, failure to
    deliver 1089
false lights, as to prevention of 1184
fixed platforms—
  destroying or endangering 1149
  seizing or exercising control
    of 1148
foreign action, as to orders regulating
  shipping services in event of 1180
forms not approved by Secretary of
  State, printing, selling etc of 1182
hijacking 1147
hovercraft, as to registration,
  certification, maintenance and
  operation of 1072
improvement notice, contravention of
  requirement imposed by 1178
inspection of ships and equipment,
  interference with 1176

OFFENCE (MARITIME)—*continued*
jurisdiction—
  British seafarers, as to offences
    by 1055
  on board ship, as to offences 1054
  ships lying off coast, over 1053
  UK, deemed to have been
    committed in 1052
lighthouses, damage to 1183
load lines—
  certificates and surveys, offences as
    to 1129
  contravention of provisions,
    penalties for 1128
manning, falsely obtaining documents
  as to 1078
master—
  complaints about provisions or
    food, failure to deal with 1077
  dangerously unsafe ship, liability as
    to 1144
  failure to deliver documents on
    ceasing to be 1101
  persons in danger, failure in duty as
    to 1135
  power of delivery 1153
  ships in distress, failure in duty as
    to 1135
navigation—
  endangering or likely to endanger,
    acts 1150
  requirements, contravention
    of 1120
offenders outside UK, powers
  over 1056
officers of bodies corporate, by 1051
official log book, destruction,
  mutilation or alteration of 1086
owner, liability of—
  dangerously unsafe ship, as to 1144
  unsafe operation of ship, as to 1146
passenger ships, in connection
  with 1136
pilotage offences. *See* PILOTAGE
piracy 1186
power to require production of
  documents, interference
  with 1175
powers of inspectors, interference
  with 1177
prohibition notice, contravention of
  requirement imposed by 1178
proof etc of exemptions 1061
receiver of wreck—
  cargo etc from vessel, failure of
    person to deliver 1161

References are to paragraph numbers; superior figures refer to notes

OFFENCE (MARITIME)—*continued*
  receiver of wreck—*continued*
    duty to notify receiver, failure as
      to 1160
    vessel in distress—
      directions, failure to comply
        with 1157
      requirements, failure to comply
        with 1158
  registration of ships, as to—
    British character of ship, as to 1062
    British connection of ship, as
      to 1065
    certificate of registry, refusal to
      surrender 1071
    changes of ownership etc, failure to
      notify 1068
    contravention of provisions 1064
    documents and supply of
      information, as to 1070
    fishing vessels—
      details of engine power, failure to
        provide 1067
      not registered under Merchant
        Shipping Act 1066
    hovercraft 1072
    improper colours, carrying 1063
    obscuring markings as offence 1069
  return of offenders 1056
  safety, as to—
    births and deaths on ship, master's
      failure to make returns as
      to 1124
    cargoes in need of special
      precautions, contravention of
      requirements as to 1126
    commercially operated vessels,
      contravention of requirements
      for 1109
    counting and recording passengers,
      contravention of requirements
      as to 1121
    dangerous goods, marine pollutants
      etc, contravention of
      requirements as to 1125
    distress signals, contravention of
      provisions as to 1134
    fishing vessels—
      alterations, failure to give notice
        of 1114
      appropriate certificate,
        contravention of prohibition
        as to going to sea
        without 1113

OFFENCE (MARITIME)—*continued*
  safety, as to—*continued*
    fishing vessels—*continued*
      certificates, contravention of
        provisions governing 1112
      construction rules, contravention
        of 1111
    health and safety provisions,
      contravention of duties imposed
      by 1115
    high speed craft, contravention of
      requirements for 1110
    interference with or failure to
      comply with safety
      directions 1131
    International Safety Management
      Code, failure to comply
      with 1118
    load line provisions. *See* load lines
      above
    navigation requirements,
      contravention of 1120
    persons in danger, failure in duty as
      to 1135
    prescribed medical stores,
      contravention of requirement to
      carry 1117
    prevention of collisions,
      contravention of provisions as
      to 1134
    restricted areas of ship or port,
      penalties for unauthorised
      presence in 1133
    returns as to carriage of goods and
      passengers, failure to furnish or
      falsification of 1122
    returns as to passengers on board,
      failure to furnish or falsification
      of 1123
    safety management code for
      domestic passenger ships,
      failure to comply with 1119
    ship and port facility security,
      failure to comply with
      requirements as to 1132
    ships in distress, failure in duty as
      to 1135
    temporary exclusion zones, failure
      to observe controls as to 1130
    trans-shipped fish, failure to comply
      with requirements as to 1127
    unauthorised persons on ship 1139
    working time provisions,
      contravention of duties imposed
      by 1116

OFFENCE (MARITIME)—*continued*
  shipping services—
    coastal shipping services, as to
      orders regulating 1181
    foreign action, as to orders
      regulating shipping services in
      event of 1180
  stowaways 1137
  summary offence, time limit for 1049
  summary order, time limit for 1050
  surveyor of ships, failure to give
    information or assistance to 1179
  threats, offences involving 1151
  unauthorised persons on ship 1139
  unauthorised presence on ship 1138
  unqualified persons going to sea as
    qualified 1083
  unsafe lighters etc, use of 1145
  unsafe operation of ship, as to 1146
  vessel in distress—
    adjoining land, obstruction of
      power to use 1159
    receiver—
      directions, failure to comply
        with 1157
      requirements, failure to comply
        with 1158
  wartime, illegal acts during 1167
  wreck—
    cargo etc from vessel, failure of
      person to deliver 1161
    duty to notify receiver, failure as
      to 1160
    foreign port, taking to 1162
    historic wrecks—
      contravention of provisions
        protecting site of 1166
      Titanic. *See* TITANIC
    impeding persons trying to save
      themselves or others 1164
    interference with 1163
    magistrate preserving wreck,
      assaulting 1165
PERSONAL INJURY
  on board ship—
    joint and several liability 1011
    right of contribution 1012
PILOTAGE
  appeals 228
  charges 583
  competent harbour authority—
    meaning 575
    agents, use of 584
    joint arrangements—
      directions 585

PILOTAGE—*continued*
  competent harbour
    authority—*continued*
    joint arrangements—*continued*
      dispute resolution 586
      information 585
      provision for 584
    statement of accounts, duty to
      provide 587
  compulsory—
    directions 580
    discrimination, prevention of 582
    exemption certificates 581
    failure to meet requirements where
      in force 1169
    liability for ships under 589
    requirements where in force 588
  deep sea—
    certificates 595
    North Sea and English Channel,
      in 596
  harbour: meaning 575
  offences—
    authorised pilot—
      facilities for boarding or leaving
        ship, failure to provide 1173
      taking pilot out of area 1172
    compulsory pilotage in force, failure
      to meet requirements
      where 1169
    failure of master to supply
      information 1171
    misconduct by pilot endangering
      ship or persons on board 1174
    proper authorisation, pilot operating
      without 1168
    unauthorised pilot, pilotage
      by 1170
  pilot—
    meaning 574
    authorised—
      meaning 574
      area, not to be taken out of
        his 592
      employment of 578
      generally 577
      liability, limitation of 594
      right to supersede unauthorised
        pilot 590
    boarding or leaving ship, facilities
      for 593
    draught of ship, power to require
      declaration of 591
  pilot boats 579

References are to paragraph numbers; superior figures refer to notes

PILOTAGE—*continued*
services, provision of 576
PIRACY
cooperation required as to 33
offence, as maritime 1186
PLEASURE VESSEL
provisions for 612
safety—
code of practice—
equivalent provisions outside
regulations and code 615
large vessels 613
small vessels 614
equivalent provisions outside
regulations and code 615
general regulations 35
offences 616
power to detain 616
provisions for 612
PORT STATE CONTROL
anomalies, duty to report 682
complaints 683
detention—
deficiencies, in case of 680
prohibition against entering UK
ports if repairs needed 681
EU ports, shipping using—
application of provisions 678
detention—
deficiencies, in case of 680
inspection—
meaning 679
deficiencies, rectification and
detention in case of 680
prohibition against entering UK ports
if repairs needed 681
PROHIBITION NOTICE
contents and effect of 53
generally 52
invalid notice, compensation for 55
offence, contravention as 1178
references of notices to arbitration 54
RECEIVER OF WRECK
appointment of 929
claims of owners to wrecks in
possession of 949
duty to notify receiver, failure as
to 1160
notification of wreck, duties and
powers on 936
ownership of items, investigations as
to 60
power of entry 940
sale of wreck, powers as to 956

RECEIVER OF WRECK—*continued*
salvage powers of—
apportionment of reward 902
receiver of wreck, powers of 919
sale of detained property, as to 920
valuation of property, as to 887
taking possession of wreck, duty to
give notice on 937
unclaimed—
Crown's right to 950
disposal after one year of 952
notice to persons entitled to 951
RECREATIONAL CRAFT
safety regulations as to 35
REGISTRAR GENERAL OF SHIPPING
AND SEAMEN
meaning 62
appointment and removal of 62
crew list, failure as to delivery of 556,
1088
registration of merchant ship—
documents to be retained 297
fees payable to registrar 379
supplementary information required
by registrar 372
SAFETY
recreational craft, safety regulations as
to 35
terrorism, prevention of 34
SALVAGE (MARITIME)
meaning 849
arbitral awards—
publication of 922
reward, as to 918
claims—
aircraft, in respect of 114
jurisdiction, extent of 113
limitation period 154
contract—
application of Salvage
Convention 853
Lloyd's Open Form: meaning 853
Crown—
claims against 854
rights of 854
humanitarian cargoes, prohibition
against seizure of 921
jurisdiction 113, 852
life. *See* LIFE SALVAGE
Lloyd's Open Form: meaning 853
operations—
meaning 850
co-operation, obligations as to 859
duty to render assistance 858
master, duties of 856

SALVAGE (MARITIME)—*continued*
  operations—*continued*
    owner, duties of 856
    pollution, rights of coastal states to
      protect against 857
    port of destination, whether salvage
      ending at 889
    salvor, duties of 856
  persons, salvage of 864
  property, of—
    Crown, application of law to 118
    remuneration—
      apportionment of 119
      persons liable to pay 116
      services entitled to 115
    salvor, damage caused by 117
  receiver of wreck, powers of—
    apportionment of reward, as to 902
    detention of property, as to 919
    sale of detained property, as to 920
    valuation of property, as to 887
  reward—
    agreement as to amount—
      generally 883
      persons bound by 885
      setting aside 884
    apportionment—
      agreements for 904
      associates, share of 907
      court, by 903
      crew's share 906
      criteria under Salvage
        Convention 901
      independent salvors 909
      intervention by other salvors,
        effect of 911
      master's share 906
      misconduct of salvors, effect
        of 912
      officers' share 906
      other services, share of 908
      owners, to 905
      passengers, share of 907
      receiver, by 902
      Royal Navy officers and sailors,
        share of 908
      separate sets of salvors,
        between 910–912
    arbitral proceedings as to 918
    coastguards, for 872
    common law, at 866
    common law principles, application
      of 886

SALVAGE (MARITIME)—*continued*
  reward—*continued*
    conditions for—
      evidence of danger 862, 891
      property subject of salvage
        service 860
      requisite danger 861
      useful result 863
    contribution—
      cargo owner and shipowner,
        between 875
      liability for 874
      life salvage, for 877
      proportionate shares 876
    court, amount fixed by—
      appeal, grounds of 900
      assessment by 881
      care, skill and knowledge of
        salvors, requirement to
        show 893
      common law principles 886
      duration of services, element
        of 898
      evidence of danger as
        consideration 891
      losses or expenses of salvor as
        factor 899
      misconduct by salvors, effect
        of 894
      negligence of salvors, effect
        of 895
      port of destination, whether
        salvage ending at 889
      risk to salving property as
        consideration 897
      valuation of property by receiver,
        consideration of 887
      value of property salved as
        consideration 892
      value of salving property as
        consideration 896
      value of ship, cargo and freight,
        consideration of 888
    crew of salved vessel, for 869
    derelict, as to 890
    disqualifications 865
    finality of award 882
    fixing, criteria for 878
    foyboatmen, for 872
    interim payment 917
    lifeboat crews, for 873
    limitation of actions as to 918
    passengers, for 870

References are to paragraph numbers; superior figures refer to notes

SALVAGE (MARITIME)—*continued*
　reward—*continued*
　　personal services, requirement
　　　of 867
　　persons, salvage of 864
　　pilots, for 869
　　public officers, for 872
　　recovery of—
　　　maritime lien 915
　　　rights in personam 914
　　　rights in rem 913
　　　security, duty to provide 916
　　rights in personam 914
　　rights in rem 913
　　Salvage Convention principles 878
　　security, duty to provide 916
　　ship's agent, for 870
　　special compensation 879, 880
　　tugs under towage contract, for 871
　　voluntariness criterion 868
　Salvage Convention 851, 852
　salvage operation: meaning 850
　service. *See* SALVAGE SERVICE
　　(MARITIME)
　state-owned cargoes, prohibition
　　against seizure of 921
　wreck and derelict, of—
　　aircraft 124
　　nature of 122
　　scope of provision 123
　　vessels wrecked, stranded or in
　　　distress 123
SALVAGE SERVICE (MARITIME)
　port of destination, whether ending
　　at 889
　rendering of 855
　scope of 855
SALVOR (MARITIME)
　duties of 856
　maritime lien 915
　rights in rem of 913
SEAFARER
　meaning 423
　British seaman's card. *See* BRITISH
　　SEAMAN'S CARD
　burial of 547
　certification—
　　application of provisions 502
　　cancellation of certificate 509
　　disqualification of holder 508
　　mandatory standards of
　　　competence 503
　　suspension of certificate 509
　codes of conduct 539

SEAFARER—*continued*
　compensation payments—
　　insurance against 544
　　lost ship, where 545
　competence, mandatory standards
　　of 503
　cremation of 547
　crew accommodation—
　　inspections of 491
　　records as to 491
　　requirements 490
　crew agreement. *See* CREW
　　AGREEMENT
　discharge—
　　payment of wages on 484
　　procedure 468
　　ship ceasing to be registered in UK,
　　　on 469
　discharge book—
　　alterations in 572
　　application for 565
　　applications relating to 573
　　content of 566
　　defacement of 569
　　delivery of, requirement as to 568
　　destruction of 569
　　filling up of 569
　　form of 566
　　issue of 566
　　loss of 569
　　notification of errors in 570
　　production of, requirement as
　　　to 567
　　surrender of 571
　employment agreement—
　　content of 451
　　documentation 454
　　general requirements 452
　　provision of agreement to seafarer
　　　as requirement 454
　　understanding of agreement by
　　　seafarer, requirement as to 453
　English, requirements as to crew's
　　knowledge of 506
　fitness or conduct, inquiries into—
　　appeal 537
　　court, appointment of 532
　　decision 535
　　holding of 533
　　notice of 531
　　power to hold 530
　　procedure 534
　　rehearing—
　　　power to order 537
　　　procedure 538

References are to paragraph numbers; superior figures refer to notes

WRECK COMMISSIONER
  formal investigation by—
    addresses to commissioner 839
    adjournment of 840
    appeal of cancellation or suspension
      of certificate 844
    assessors, role of 831
    Attorney General, remittance of case
      to 832
    conduct of 838
    costs of 843
    direction for 831
    evidence—
      admission of 834
    holding of 836
    meeting preliminary to
      commencement of 835
    notice of 833
    opening statements 837
    parties to 833
    provision for 830
    rehearings—
      generally 844
      procedure for 845
    reports of 842
    result of 841
    written statements 837

WRECK COMMISSIONER—*continued*
  generally 59
WRECKS CONVENTION
  claims for costs 954
  co-operation and consultation between
    states 941
  Convention area: meaning 927
  geographical application of 927
  hazard: meaning 925
  insurance provisions—
    compulsory insurance 930
    contravention of provisions, effect
      of 933
    registered ships, duty of state party
      as to 931
    wreck removal insurance
      certificates 932
  locating wreck, duty as to 938
  maritime casualty: meaning 923
  marking of wreck, duty as to 938
  matters excluded from scope of 928
  registered owner, liability of 953
  removal: meaning 942
  scope of 926, 928
  wreck: meaning 923

References are to paragraph numbers; superior figures refer to notes